C000229593

STREET ATLAS

Kent

First published 2005 by

Philip's, a division of
Octopus Publishing Group Ltd
2-4 Heron Quays, London E14 4JP

First edition 2005
First impression 2005

ISBN-10   0-540-08750-5 (spiral)
ISBN-13   978-0-540-08750-1 (spiral)

© Philip's 2005

Ordnance Survey®

This product includes mapping data licensed
from Ordnance Survey® with the permission of
the Controller of Her Majesty's Stationery Office.
© Crown copyright 2005. All rights reserved.
Licence number 100011710.

Printed and bound in Spain
by Cayfosa-Quebecor

Contents

III	**Key to map symbols**
IV	**Key to map pages**
VI	**Route planning**
X	**Administrative and Postcode boundaries**
1	**Street maps** at 3½ inches to 1 mile
381	**Index** of towns and villages
384	**Index** of streets, hospitals, industrial estates, railway stations, schools, shopping centres, universities and places of interest

Digital Data

The exceptionally high-quality mapping found in this atlas is available as digital data in TIFF format, which is easily convertible to other bitmapped (raster) image formats.

The index is also available in digital form as a standard database table. It contains all the details found in the printed index together with the National Grid reference for the map square in which each entry is named.

For further information and to discuss your requirements, please contact Philip's on 020 7644 6932 or james.mann@philips-maps.co.uk

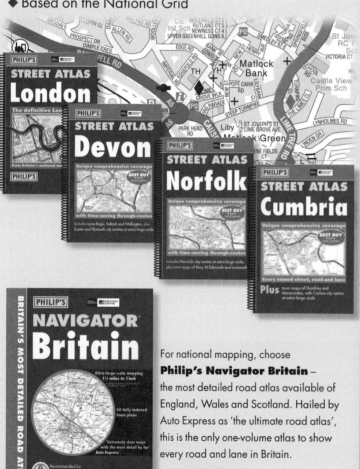

Key to map symbols

III

	Motorway with junction number (22a)
	Primary route – dual/single carriageway
	A road – dual/single carriageway
	B road – dual/single carriageway
	Minor road – dual/single carriageway
	Other minor road – dual/single carriageway
	Road under construction
	Tunnel, covered road
	Rural track, private road or narrow road in urban area
	Gate or obstruction to traffic (restrictions may not apply at all times or to all vehicles)
	Path, bridleway, byway open to all traffic, road used as a public path
	Pedestrianised area
DY7	Postcode boundaries
	County and unitary authority boundaries
	Railway, tunnel, railway under construction
	Tramway, tramway under construction
	Miniature railway
	Railway station Walsall
	Private railway station
	Docklands Light Railway station
	Tram stop, tram stop under construction
	Bus, coach station

	Ambulance station
	Coastguard station
	Fire station
	Police station
+	Accident and Emergency entrance to hospital
H	Hospital
+	Place of worship
i	Information Centre (open all year)
	Shopping Centre
P P&R	Parking, Park and Ride
PO	Post Office
	Camping site
	Caravan site
	Golf course
	Picnic site
Prim Sch	Important buildings, schools, colleges, universities and hospitals
	Built up area
	Woods
River Medway	Water name
	River, weir, stream
	Canal, lock, tunnel
	Water
	Tidal water
Church	Non-Roman antiquity
ROMAN FORT	Roman antiquity
87 24	Adjoining page indicators and overlap bands

Abbr.	Full	Abbr.	Full	Abbr.	Full
Acad	Academy	Inst	Institute	Recn Gd	Recreation Ground
Allot Gdns	Allotments	Ct	Law Court		
Cemy	Cemetery	L Ctr	Leisure Centre	Resr	Reservoir
C Ctr	Civic Centre	LC	Level Crossing	Ret Pk	Retail Park
CH	Club House	Liby	Library	Sch	School
Coll	College	Mkt	Market	Sh Ctr	Shopping Centre
Crem	Crematorium	Meml	Memorial	TH	Town Hall/House
Ent	Enterprise	Mon	Monument	Trad Est	Trading Estate
Ex H	Exhibition Hall	Mus	Museum	Univ	University
Ind Est	Industrial Estate	Obsy	Observatory	W Twr	Water Tower
IRB Sta	Inshore Rescue Boat Station	Pal	Royal Palace	Wks	Works
		PH	Public House	YH	Youth Hostel

■ The small numbers around the edges of the maps identify the 1 kilometre National Grid lines

■ The dark grey border on the inside edge of some pages indicates that the mapping does not continue onto the adjacent page

The scale of the maps on the pages numbered in blue is 5.52 cm to 1 km • 3½ inches to 1 mile • 1: 18103

0	¼	½	¾	1 mile
0	250 m 500 m	750 m 1 kilometre		

London STREET ATLAS

Essex STREET ATLAS

South Essex STREET ATLAS

Surrey STREET ATLAS

West Sussex STREET ATLAS

East Sussex STREET ATLAS

Rochford
Rayleigh
Romford
Laindon Basildon
Hackney
Barking
Dagenham
Southend-on-Sea
Corringham
Canvey Island
Greenwich
London City
Beckton
Stanford le Hope
South Ockendon
Aveley
Chadwell St Mary
Lewisham
Woolwich
Abbey Wood
Erith
Allhallows-on-Sea

	5	6 7	8 9	10	

Welling
Slade Green
West Thurrock
Grays Tilbury
East Tilbury
Cliffe
Allhallows
Grain

11 12 13 14 15 16 17 18 19 20 21 22 23 24 25 26 27
Eltham Falconwood Dartford Swanscombe Northfleet Church Street High Halstow Fenn Street

New Eltham Old Bexley Bean Gravesend Hoo St Werburgh Kingsnorth
29 30 31 32 33 34 35 36 37 38 39 40 41 42 43 44 45
Grove Park Sidcup Hawley Darenth Southfleet Shorne Higham St Mary's Island
Chislehurst West Beckenham

Bromley Chislehurst Swanley South Darenth Longfield New Barn Cobham Rochester Gillingham Grange 66 67
52 53 54 55 56 57 58 59 60 61 62 63 64 65 Upchurch 68
Petts Wood Orpington Farningham Hartley Sole Street Chatham Luton Lower Halstow Iwade

Keston Chelsfield Eynsford New Ash Green Meopham Halling Wayfield Rainham Newington
85 86 87 88 89 90 91 92 93 94 95 96 97 98 99 100 101
Green Street Green Well Hill West Kingsdown Culverstone Green Upper Halling Walderslade Bredhurst Hartlip Borden

Downe Halstead Shoreham Fairseat Birling Snodland Kit's Coty Stockbury 134
118 119 120 121 122 123 124 125 126 127 128 129 130 131 132 133 Bredgar
Biggin Hill Cudham Knockholt Kemsing Wrotham Addington Ditton Sandling Boxley Detling Bicknor

Tatsfield Dunton Green Seal Borough Green West Malling East Malling Bearsted Wormshill
150 151 152 153 154 155 158 159 160 161 162 163 164 165
Westerham Brasted Stone Street Ightham Platt Tovil Maidstone Hollingbourne 166
Sevenoaks Kent Street

Limpsfield Plaxtol Mereworth Teston East Farleigh Leeds Harrietsham
183 184 185 186 187 188 189 190 191 192 193 194 195 196 197 198 199
Oxted Crockham Hill Ide Hill Sevenoaks Weald Shipbourne Hadlow Yalding Boughton Monchelsea Langley Heath Lenham

Langhurst Four Elms Hildenborough Golden Green East Peckham Hunton Sutton Valence Grafty Green
216 217 218 219 220 221 222 223 224 225 226 227 228 229 232
Edenbridge Chiddingstone Causeway Leigh Tonbridge Beltring Chainhurst Cross-at-Hand Ulcombe 230 231 Egerton

Marsh Green Hever Chiddingstone Tudeley Paddock Wood Marden Headcorn Swift's Green
249 250 251 252 253 254 255 256 257 258 259 260 261 262 263 264
Lingfield Markbeech Penshurst Bidborough Southborough Staplehurst Sinkhurst Green Smarden

Cowden Fordcombe Speldhurst Pembury Petteridge Horsmonden Winchet Hill Frittenden
281 282 283 284 285 286 287 288 289 290 291 292 293 294 295 296
Holtye Ashurst Royal Tunbridge Wells Brandfold Camden Hill Biddenden Standen

Groombridge Bells Yew Green Lamberhurst Goudhurst Sissinghurst High Halden
311 312 313 314 315 316 317 318 319 320 321 322 323 324
Withyham Eridge Green Frant Little Bayham Hook Green Kilndown Hartley Cranbrook East End St Michaels

Cousley Wood 338 339 Gill's Green Benenden Tenterden
336 337 340 341 342 343 344 345
Wadhurst Flimwell Hawkhurst Rolvenden Rolvenden Layne
Crowborough Ticehurst

The Moor Sandhurst Potman's Heath
354 355 356 357 358 359
Hurst Green Newenden Wittersham

367
Peasmarsh

Haywards Heath
Uckfield Heathfield
Mayfield
Winchelsea
Battle
Lewes
Hailsham
Hastings
Bexhill

Shoeburyness

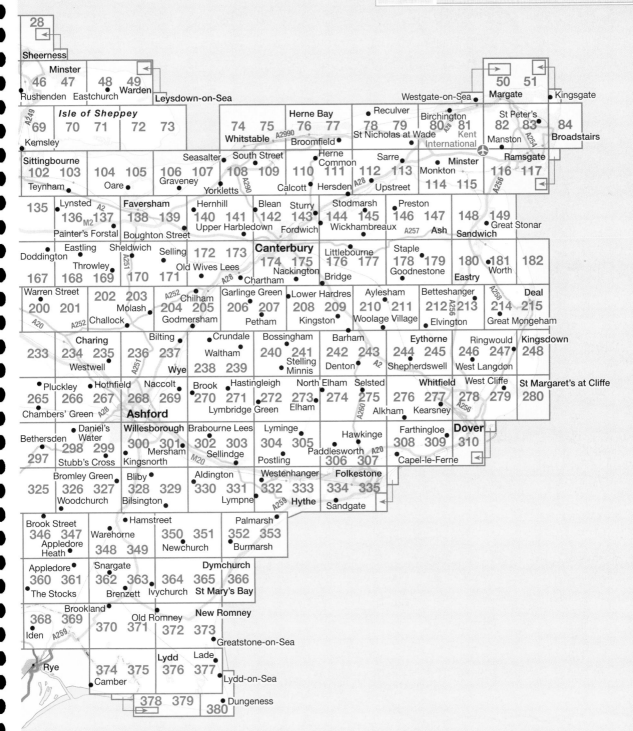

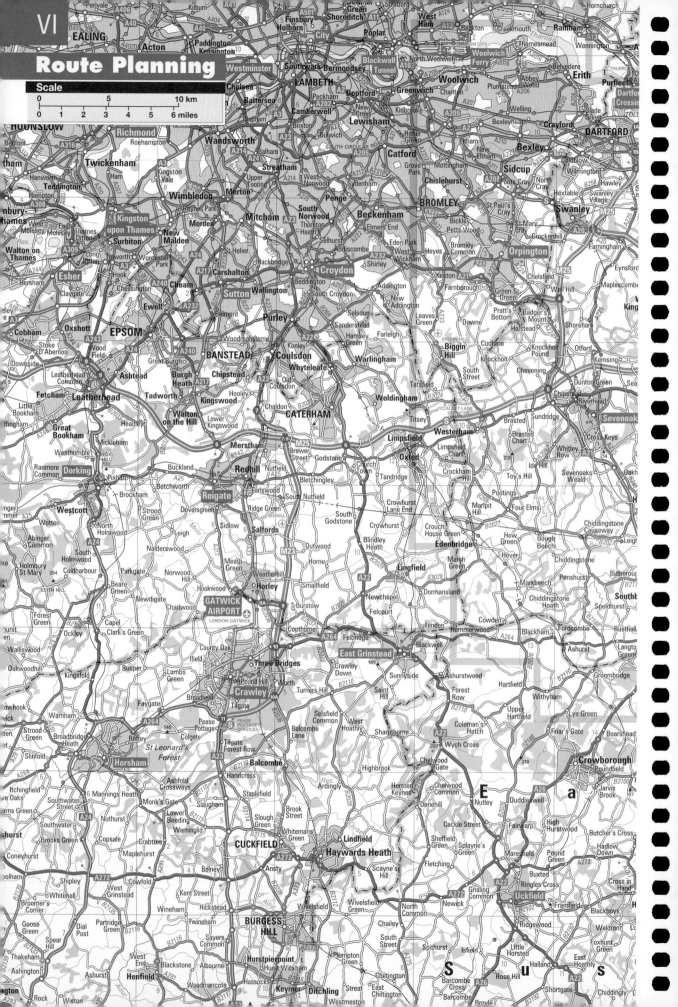

Route Planning

Scale

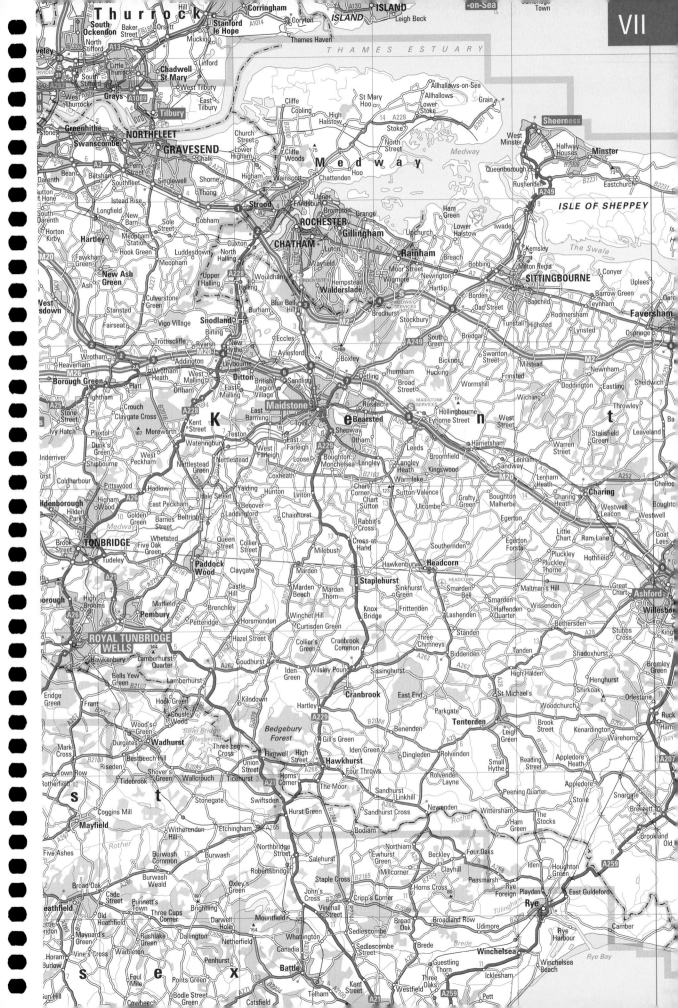

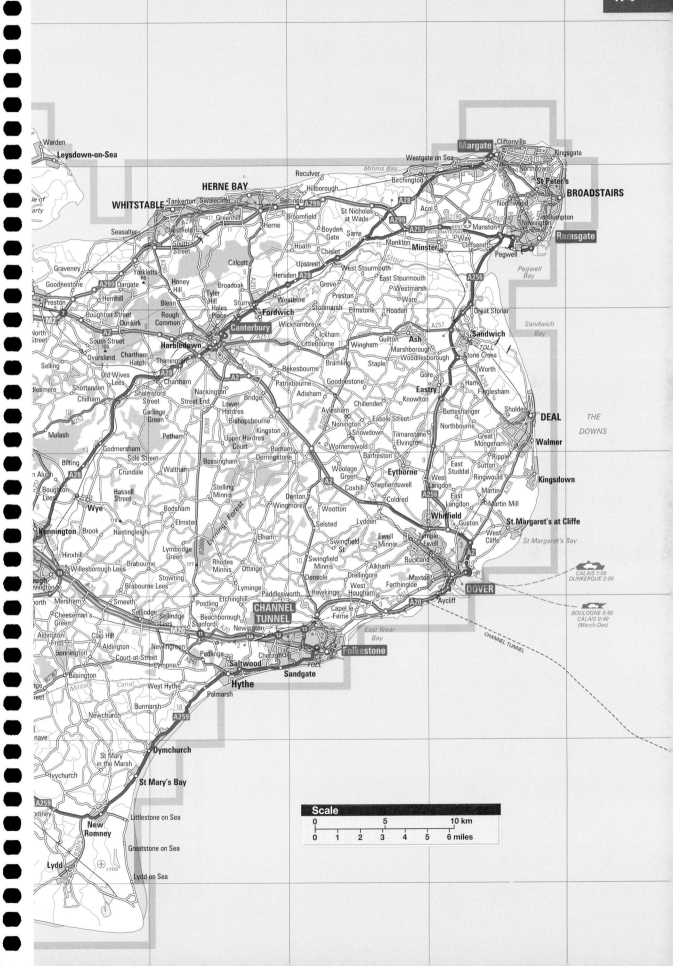

Scale

0	5	10 km
0 1 2 3 4 5		6 miles

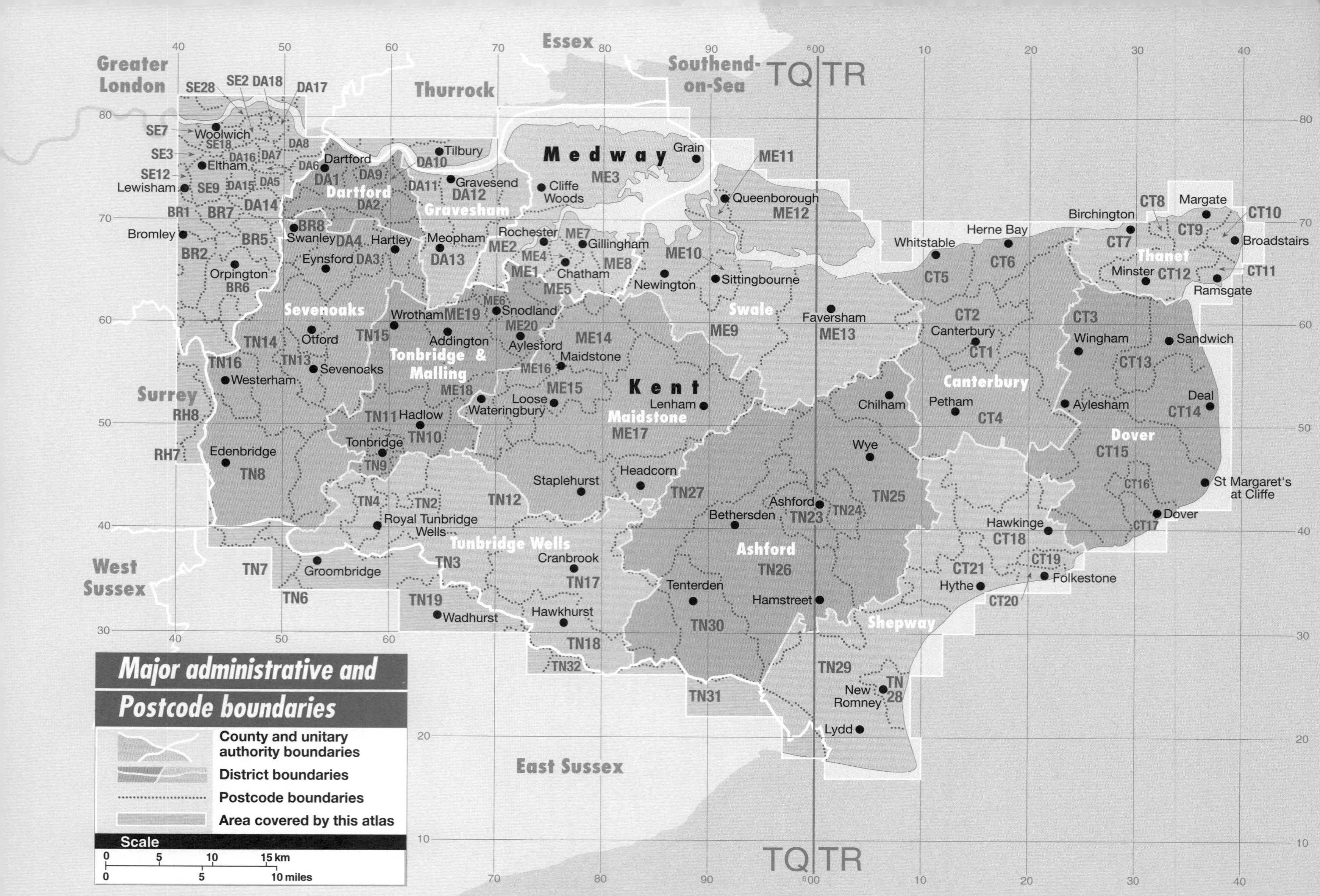

Major administrative and
Postcode boundaries
County and unitary authority boundaries
District boundaries
Postcode boundaries
Area covered by this atlas
Scale
0 5 10 15 km
0 5 10 miles
TQ TR
Greater London
Essex
Thurrock
Southend-on-Sea
Surrey
West Sussex
East Sussex
Kent
Medway
Dartford
Gravesham
Sevenoaks
Tonbridge & Malling
Maidstone
Tunbridge Wells
Swale
Canterbury
Thanet
Dover
Ashford
Shepway
Woolwich
Eltham
Lewisham
Bromley
Orpington
Dartford
Tilbury
Gravesend
Swanley
Hartley
Meopham
Eynsford
Otford
Sevenoaks
Westerham
Edenbridge
Wrotham
Addington
Tonbridge
Hadlow
Royal Tunbridge Wells
Groombridge
Wadhurst
Cliffe Woods
Grain
Rochester
Chatham
Gillingham
Snodland
Aylesford
Maidstone
Loose
Wateringbury
Staplehurst
Cranbrook
Hawkhurst
Headcorn
Lenham
Newington
Sittingbourne
Queenborough
Faversham
Whitstable
Herne Bay
Canterbury
Petham
Chilham
Wye
Ashford
Bethersden
Tenterden
Hamstreet
New Romney
Lydd
Hythe
Folkestone
Hawkinge
Dover
St Margaret's at Cliffe
Deal
Aylesham
Wingham
Sandwich
Birchington
Minster
Margate
Broadstairs
Ramsgate
SE28 SE2 DA18 DA17 SE7 SE18 SE3 DA16 DA7 DA8 DA6 SE12 SE9 DA15 DA5 DA1 DA9 DA10 BR1 BR7 DA14 DA2 DA11 DA12 BR8 BR5 BR2 BR6 DA4 DA3 DA13
ME1 ME2 ME3 ME4 ME5 ME6 ME7 ME8 ME9 ME10 ME11 ME12 ME13 ME14 ME15 ME16 ME17 ME18 ME19 ME20
TN2 TN3 TN4 TN6 TN7 TN8 TN9 TN10 TN11 TN12 TN13 TN14 TN15 TN16 TN17 TN18 TN19 TN23 TN24 TN25 TN26 TN27 TN28 TN29 TN30 TN31 TN32
RH7 RH8
CT1 CT2 CT3 CT4 CT5 CT6 CT7 CT8 CT9 CT10 CT11 CT12 CT13 CT14 CT15 CT16 CT17 CT18 CT19 CT20 CT21

London STREET ATLAS

A8
1 ODEON CT
2 EDWARD CT
3 AVENONS RD
4 NEWHAVEN LA
5 RAVENSCROFT CL
6 DOUGLAS RD

7 BOTHWELL CL
8 FERRIER POINT
9 HARVEY POINT
10 WOOD POINT
11 McDOWALL CL
12 TRINITY ST
13 VINCENT ST

14 PATTINSON POINT
15 CLINCH CT
D8
1 PARTRIDGE CL
2 VANBRUGH CL
3 PARTRIDGE SQ
4 ST MICHAELS CL

5 LONG MARK RD
E8
1 ORCHID CL
2 BELLFLOWER CL
3 PARTRIDGE SQ
4 LARKSPUR CL

5 LOBELIA CL
6 STONECHAT CL
7 BEDDALLS FARM CT
8 WINTERGREEN CL
9 GARNET WLK
10 MAVIS WLK
11 BEACONS CL

12 ABBESS CL
13 DENNY CL
14 SELBY CL
15 CHETWOOD WLK
16 ELMLEY CL
F7
1 BOWERS WLK

2 BARTON CL
3 CLAYTON CL
4 DIXON CL
5 GAUTREY SQ
6 WAKERLEY CL
7 CANTERBURY CL
8 GOOSE SQ

F7
9 COVENTRY CL
10 BUTTERFIELD SQ
11 WINCHESTER CL
F8
1 FLEETWOOD CL
2 LYMINGTON CL

3 HOLYHEAD CL
4 BONDFIELD RD
5 TULIP CL
6 AMBROSE CL
7 SAGE CL
8 LINDWOOD CL

A1
1 TUNNEL AVE
2 DENHAM ST
3 CHEVENING RD
4 LAYFIELD HO
5 WESTERDALE RD
6 MAYSTON MEWS
7 HUMBER RD
B1
1 PHIPPS HO

2 HARTWELL ..
3 REYNOLAH GDNS
4 NICHOLAS STACEY HO
5 FRANK BURTON CL
6 EASTCOMBE AVE
C1
1 RANSOM RD
2 LINTON CL
3 CEDAR PL
4 BUDD HO

5 VALIANT CL
6 CHAFFEY HO
7 WELLESLEY CL
8 GOLLOGLY TERR
9 OUTTS HO
E2
1 HARDEN CT
2 ALBION ST
3 VIKING HO
4 FREDERIC HO

5 PARISH WHARF
6 McINTYRE CT
7 GLENALVON WAY
8 ELSINORE HO
9 LOLLAND HO
10 DENMARK HO
11 RANCE HO
12 PEEL YATES HO
13 ROSEBANK WLK
14 PARADISE PL

E2
15 WOODVILLE ST
F2
1 BOWLING GREEN ROW
2 EUSTACE PL
3 SARA TURNBULL HO
4 RED BARRACKS RD
5 CAMBRIDGE BARRACKS RD
6 LEN CLIFTON HO

F2
7 CAMBRIDGE HO
8 HARDING HO
9 RUTLAND HO
10 MILNE HO
11 RENDLEBURY HO
12 MULGRAVE HO
13 TOWNSEND HO
14 MURRAY HO

16 CHATHAM HO
17 BIDDULPH HO
18 CAREW HO
19 ELEANOR WLK

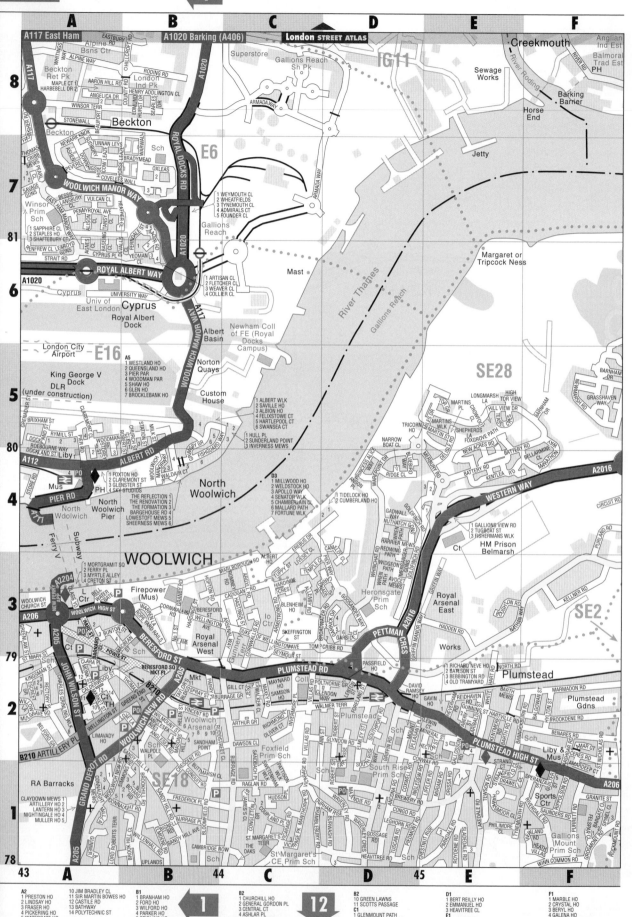

B5	B6				3

B5
1 ROWNTREE PATH
2 MACAULAY WAY
3 MANNING CT
4 CHADWICK CT
5 SIMON CT

B6
1 BEVERIDGE CT
2 HAMMOND WAY
3 LEONARD ROBBINS PATH
4 LANSBURY CT
5 RAYMOND POSTGATE CT
6 WEBB CT

7 CURTIS WAY
8 LYTTON STRACHEY PATH
9 KEYNES CT
10 MARSHALL PATH
11 CROSS CT
12 OCTAVIA WAY
13 PASSFIELD PATH

14 MILL CT
15 BESANT CT

C5
1 KINGSLEY CT
2 WILBERFORCE CT
3 SHAFTESBURY CT
4 HAZLITT CT

5 RICARDO PATH
6 NASSAU PATH
7 MALTHUS PATH
8 BRIGHT CT
9 COBDEN CT

4 ▶   **3**

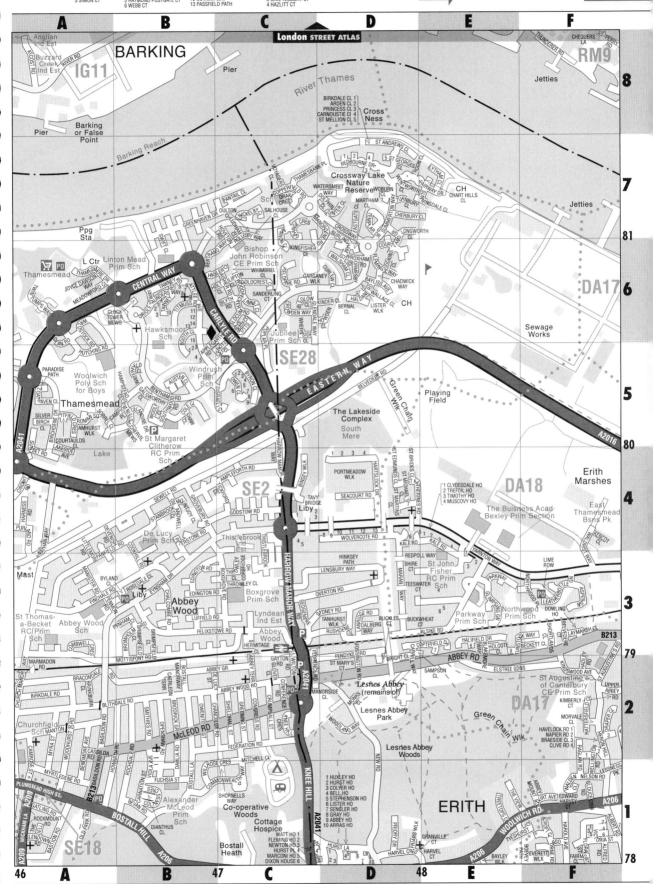

C4
1 BINSEY WLK
2 TILEHURST POINT
3 BLEWBURY HO
4 CORALLINE WLK
5 EVANLODE HO

D4
1 OAKENHOLT HO
2 TREWSBURY HO
3 PENTON HO
4 OSNEY HO
5 JACOB HO
6 MASHAM HO
7 ST HELENS RD

D4
8 CLEWER HO
9 MAPLIN HO
10 WYFOLD HO
11 HIBERNIA POINT
12 DUXFORD HO
13 RADLEY HO

E3
1 HARLEQUIN HO
2 DEXTER HO
3 ARGALI HO
4 MANGOLD WAY
5 LUCERNE CT
6 HOLSTEIN WAY
7 ABBOTSWOOD CL
8 PLYMPTON CL
9 BENEDICT CL

F1
1 SHAKESPEARE HO
2 TENNYSON HO
3 DICKENS HO
4 LANSBURY HO
5 SCOTT HO
6 SHAW HO
7 THE CHESTNUTS

13   4 ▶

London STREET ATLAS

A13 Dagenham, London

RAINHAM

RM9

RM13

DA18

DA17

DA8

Belvedere

ERITH

Lessness
Heath

A1
1 STEVANNE CT
2 TOLCAIRN CT
3 CHALFONT CT
4 ALONSO HO
5 ARIEL CT
6 MIRANDA HO
7 PROSPERO HO
8 SMARDEN CL
9 BERKHAMPSTEAD RD

10 CAMDEN CT
11 THE CHESTNUTS
12 LESSNESS RD
13 HARTFORD WLK
14 WINCHESTER CT
15 BRAMLEY CT
16 RIVERVIEW CT
17 RUSSET CT
18 THE LAURELS

A2
1 BRUSHWOOD LODGE
2 STICKLAND RD
3 BLETCHINGTON CT
4 VENMEAD CT
5 MITRE CT
6 CHAPELSITE CT

A3
1 CRESSINGHAM CT
2 TELFORD HO
3 KELVIN HO
4 JENNER HO
5 MARY MACARTHUR HO
6 LENNOX HO
7 KEIR HARDY HO
8 MONARCH RD
9 ELIZABETH GARRETT ANDERSON HO

A3
10 WILLIAM SMITH HO
11 BADEN POWELL HO
12 BOYLE HO
13 BAIRD HO
14 MARY SLESSOR HO

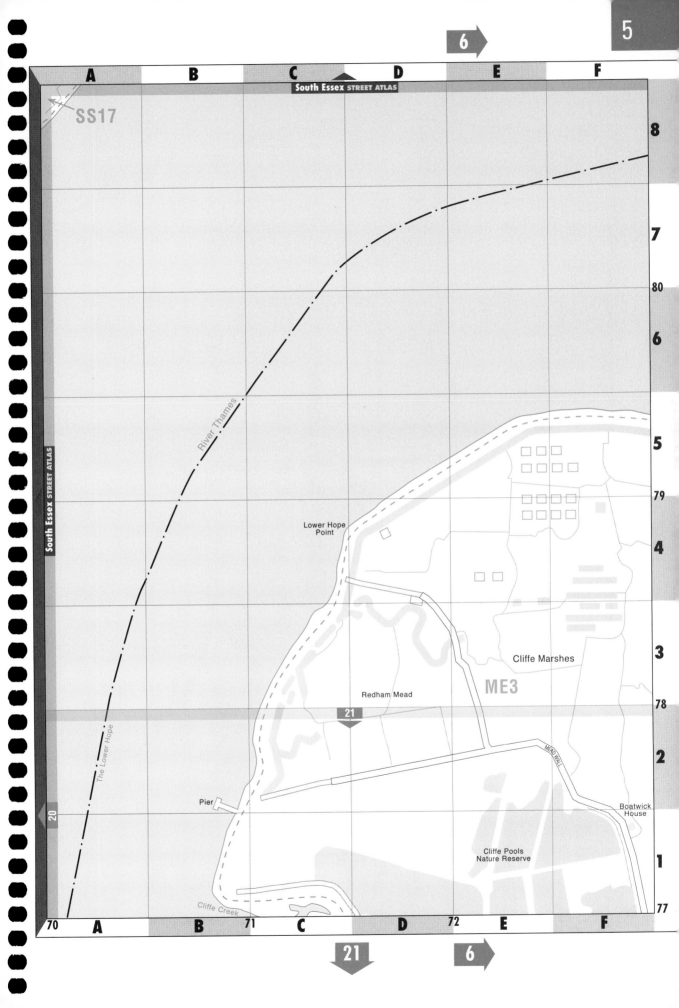

SS17

River Thames

The Lower Hope

Lower Hope Point

Redham Mead

Cliffe Marshes

ME3

Pier

MEAD WALL

Boatwick House

Cliffe Pools Nature Reserve

Cliffe Creek

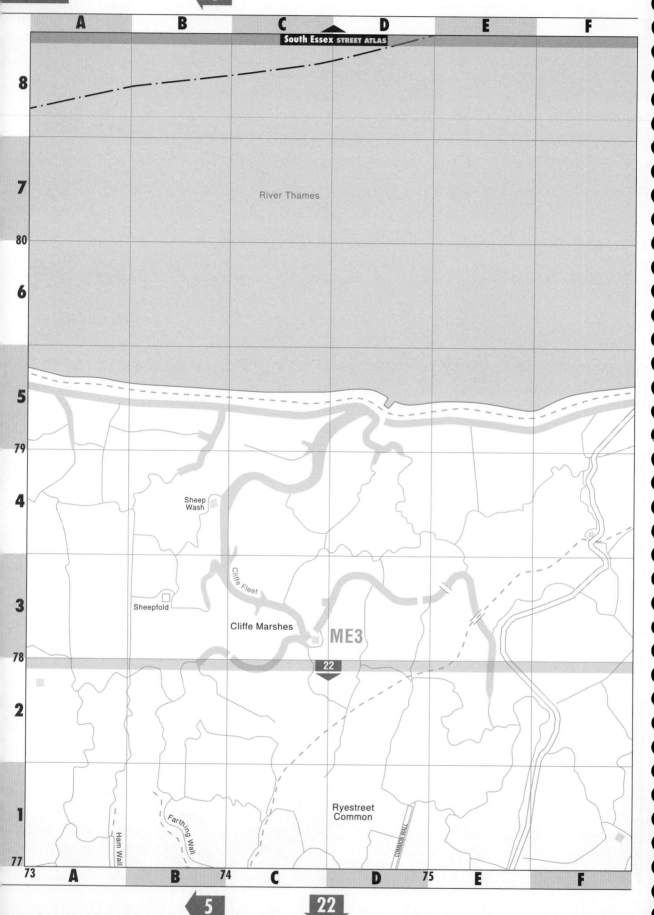

South Essex STREET ATLAS

River Thames

Sheep
Wash

Cliffe Fleet

Sheepfold

Cliffe Marshes

ME3

22

Ryestreet
Common

COMMON WALL

Ham Wall

Farthing Wall

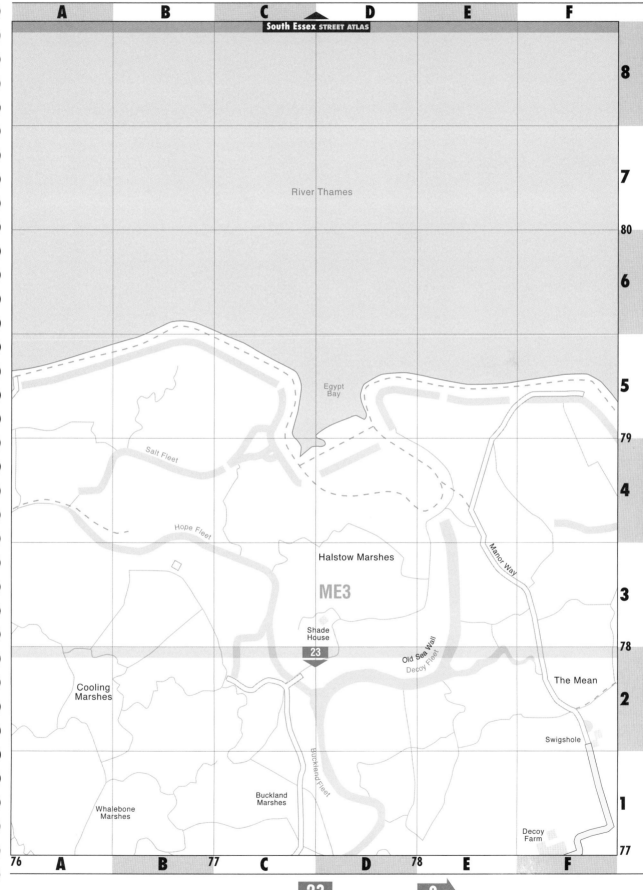

South Essex STREET ATLAS

A B C D E F

8

River Thames

7

80

6

Egypt
Bay

5

79

Salt Fleet

4

Hope Fleet

Halstow Marshes

Manor Way

ME3

3

Shade
House

78

23

Old Sea Wall
Decoy Fleet

The Mean

Cooling
Marshes

2

Swigshole

Buckland
Fleet

Buckland
Marshes

1

Whalebone
Marshes

Decoy
Farm

77

76 A B 77 C D 78 E F

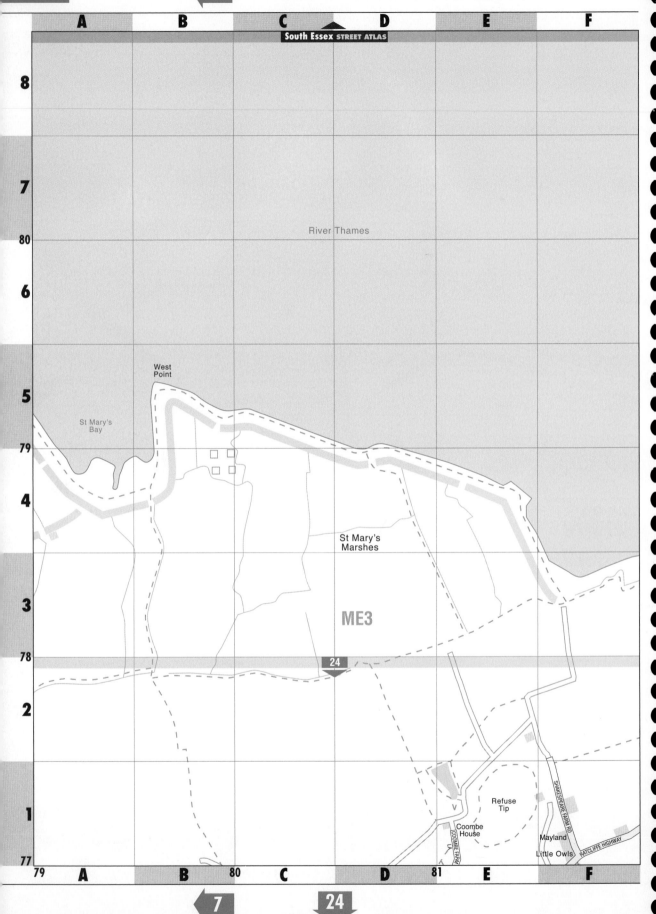

A   B   C   D   E   F

South Essex STREET ATLAS

8

7

80

6

River Thames

5

West
Point

St Mary's
Bay

79

4

St Mary's
Marshes

3

ME3

78

24

2

Refuse
Tip

1

SHAKESPEARE FARM RD

Coombe
House

COOMBE FARM
LA

Mayland

Little Owls

RATCLIFFE HIGHWAY

77

79   A   B   80   C   D   81   E   F

South Essex STREET ATLAS

River Thames

Dagnam Saltings

Holiday Park

Slough Fort

ALLHALLOWS-ON-SEA EST

THE BRIMP

Avery House

British Pilot (Hotel)

Allhallows-on-Sea

QUEENSWAY

AVERY WAY

PO

AVERY CL

AVERY CT

CH

KINGSMEAD PK

ME3

25

Allhallows Prim Sch

HOMEWARDS RD

PARKER'S CNR

AVERY WAY

ST LUKE'S WAY

ST GEORGE'S WLK

ST ANDREW'S WLK

ST DAVID'S RD

BINNEY RD

Dagnam Farm

Wr Twr & Beacon

Windhill Green

Rose & Crown (PH)

Allhallows

Allhallows Marshes

Two Rivers

Baytree Farm

BEATTY COTTS

STOKE RD

Allhallows

Binney Farm

RATCLIFFE HIGHWAY

Brick House Farm

The Chimneys

82 83 84

25 10

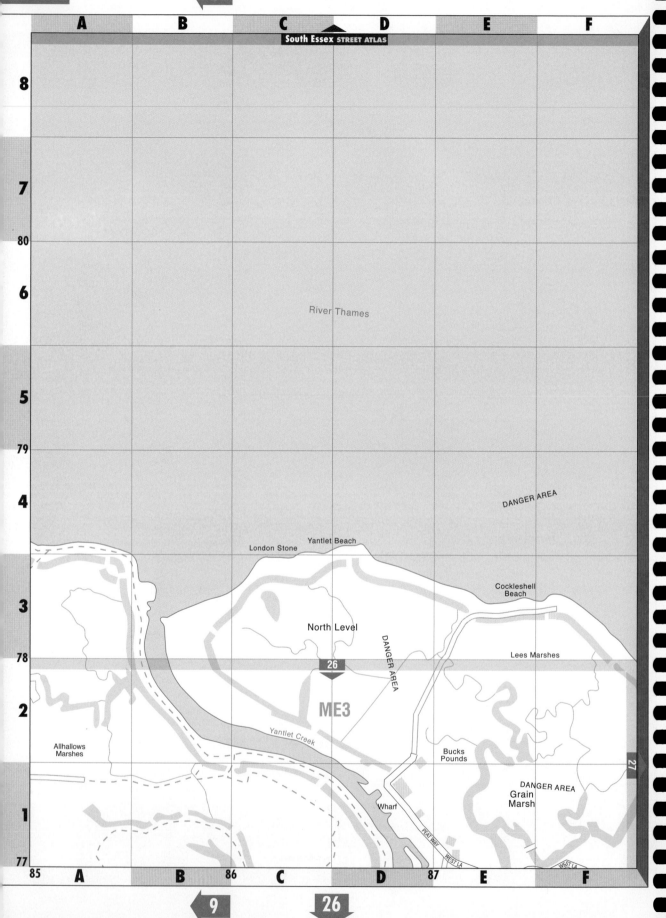

South Essex STREET ATLAS

River Thames

DANGER AREA

Yantlet Beach

London Stone

Cockleshell
Beach

North Level

DANGER AREA

Lees Marshes

26

ME3

Yantlet Creek

Allhallows
Marshes

Bucks
Pounds

DANGER AREA
Grain
Marsh

Wharf

PEAT WAY

WEST LA

WEST LA

27

A7
1 MANDEVILLE CL
2 MARY LAWRENSON PL
3 WENTWORTH HO
4 BRADBURY CT
5 DUNSTABLE CT

A8
1 COLERAINE RD
2 HARDY RD
3 INGLESIDE GR
4 NETHERCOMBE RD

B8
1 CAPELLA HO
2 DUNCAN HO
3 COLLINGTON HO
4 JACKSON HO
5 TURNER HO

C8
1 WARREN WLK
2 THE WARREN
3 WILSON HO
4 PRIORY HO
5 MAR HO
6 LANGHORNE HO

7 GAMES HO
8 ERSKINE HO
9 DUCIE HO
10 DOWNE HO
11 BAYEUX HO
12 FELMA HO
13 MATTHEWS HO

14 NORRIS HO
15 KELLY HO
16 BRAMHOPE HO
17 EAST MASCALLS
18 BIRCH TREE HO
19 CHERRY TREE CT
20 ELM TREE CT

C8
21 CEDAR CT
22 LEILA PARNELL PL
23 MASCALLS CT

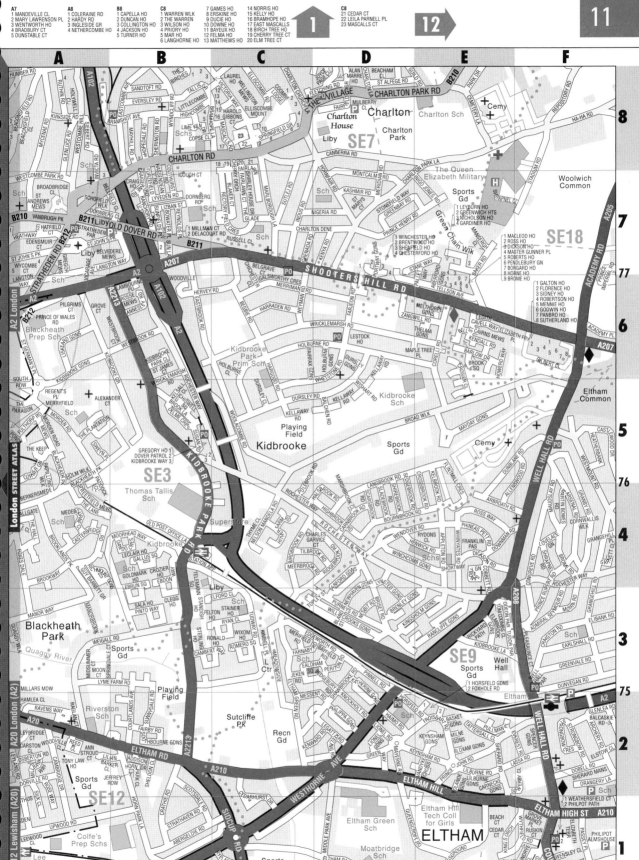

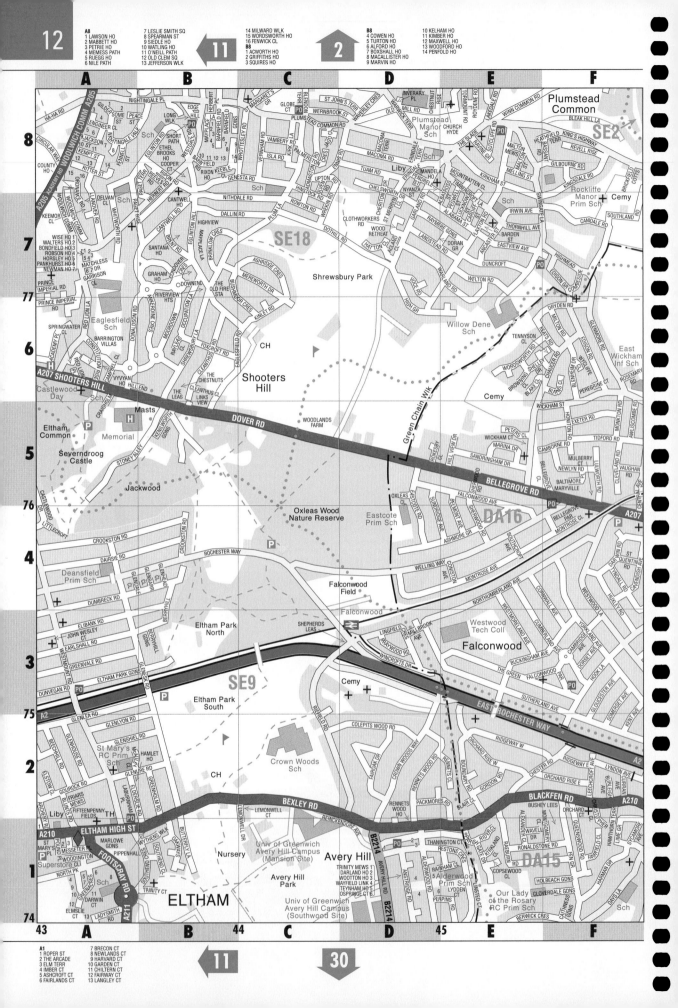

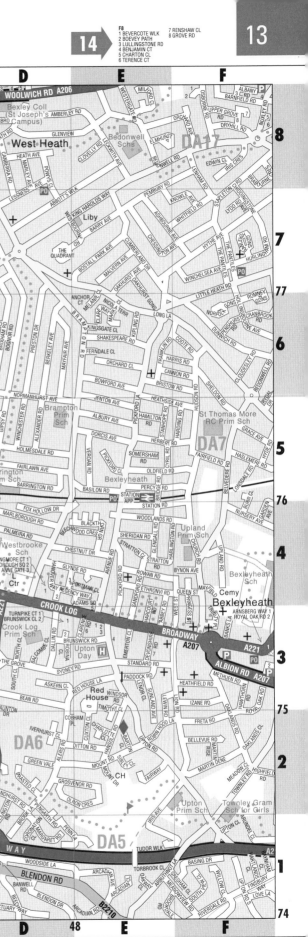

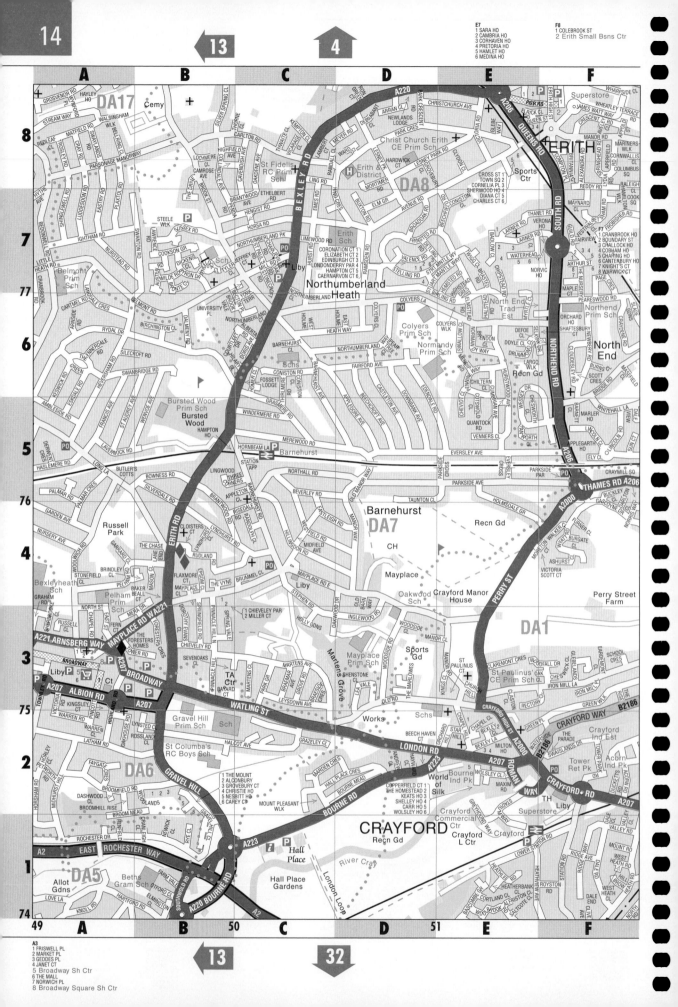

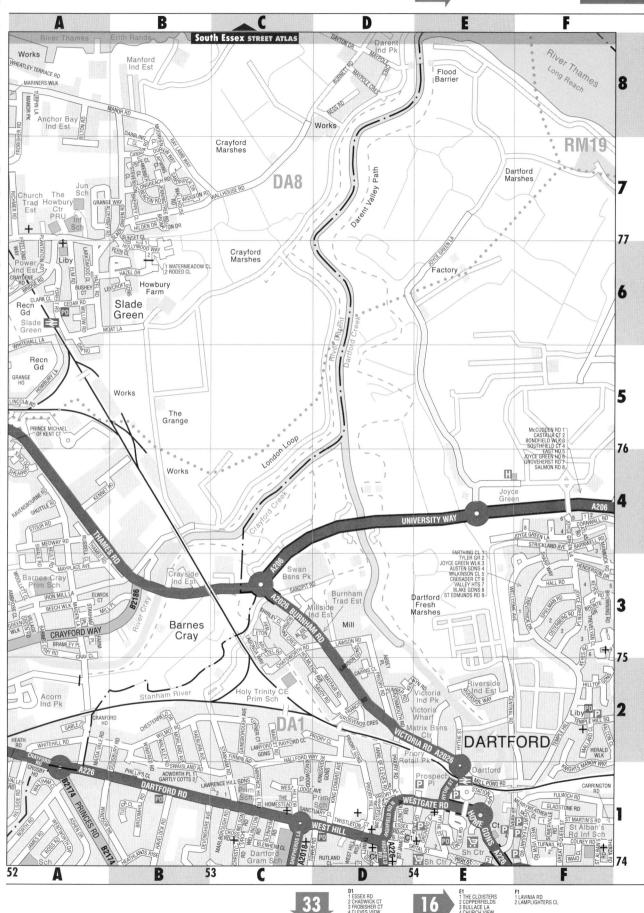

South Essex STREET ATLAS

D1
1 ESSEX RD
2 CHADWICK CT
3 FROBISHER CT
4 CLEVES VIEW
5 PRIORY CT
6 WESTGATE HO

E1
1 THE CLOISTERS
2 COPPERFIELDS
3 BULLACE LA
4 CHURCH VIEW

F1
1 LAVINIA RD
2 LAMPLIGHTERS CL

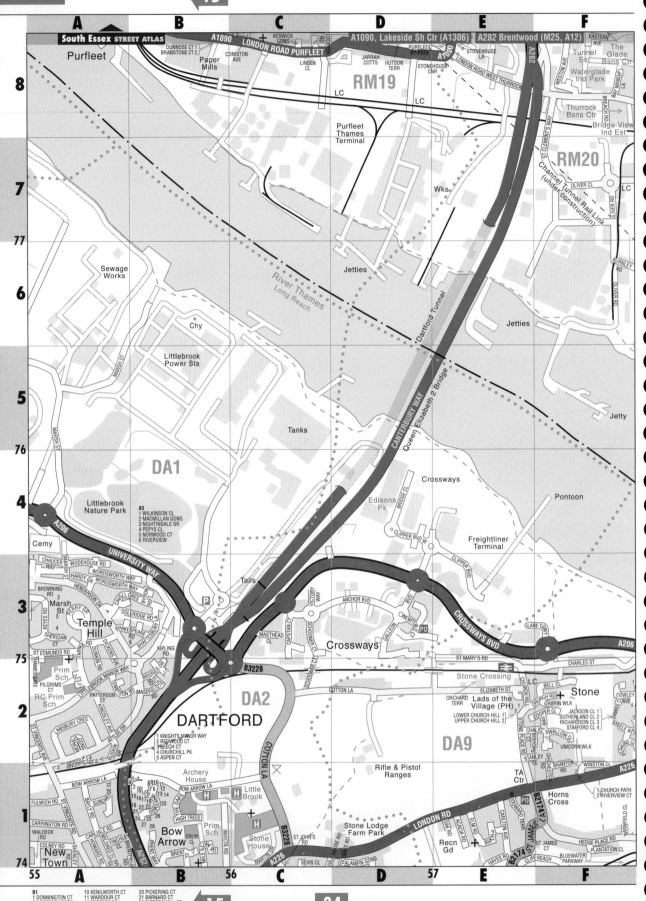

South Essex STREET ATLAS

Purfleet

RM19

RM20

Channel Tunnel Rail Link (under construction)

River Thames
Long Reach

Jetties

Dartford Tunnel

Jetties

Jetty

Sewage
Works

Chy

Littlebrook
Power Sta

Tanks

DA1

Queen Elizabeth 2 Bridge

CANTERBURY WAY

Crossways

Littlebrook
Nature Park

Edisons
Pk

Pontoon

A3
1 WILKINSON CL
2 MACMILLAN GDNS
3 NIGHTINGALE GR
4 PEPYS CL
5 NORWOOD CT
6 RIVERVIEW

Freightliner
Terminal

Cemy

UNIVERSITY WAY

A206

Tolls

Temple
Hill

Marsh
St

Crossways

CROSSWAYS BVD

A206

Stone Crossing

Crossways

DA2

DARTFORD

B3228

Stone

Lads of the
Village (PH)

DA9

1 KNIGHTS MANOR WAY
2 REDWOOD CT
3 BEECH CT
4 CHURCHILL PK
5 ASPEN CT

COTTON LA

Rifle & Pistol
Ranges

TA
Ctr

Horns
Cross

Archery
House

Little
Brook

1 CHURCH PATH
2 RIVERVIEW CL

B2174

Bow
Arrow

Stone
House

Stone Lodge
Farm Park

LONDON RD

Recn
Gd

Bluewater
Parkway

New Town

B1
1 DONNINGTON CT
2 HARDWICK CRES
3 DENNY CT
4 BEESTON CT
5 BROUGHAM CT
6 GRANGE CRES
7 ORFORD CT
8 ALNWICK CT
9 BRAMBER CT
10 KENILWORTH CT
11 WARDOUR CT
12 BERWICK CT
13 CONISBOROUGH CT
14 STOKESAY CT
15 PEVERIL CT
16 DUNSTER CT
17 CALSHOT CT
18 LYDFORD CT
19 LONGTOWN CT
20 PICKERING CT
21 BARNARD CT
22 TATTERSHALL CT
23 CARISBROOKE CT
24 BOWES CT
25 NORHAM CT
26 MIDDLEHAM CT
27 PRUDHOE CT
28 BRIDGE CT

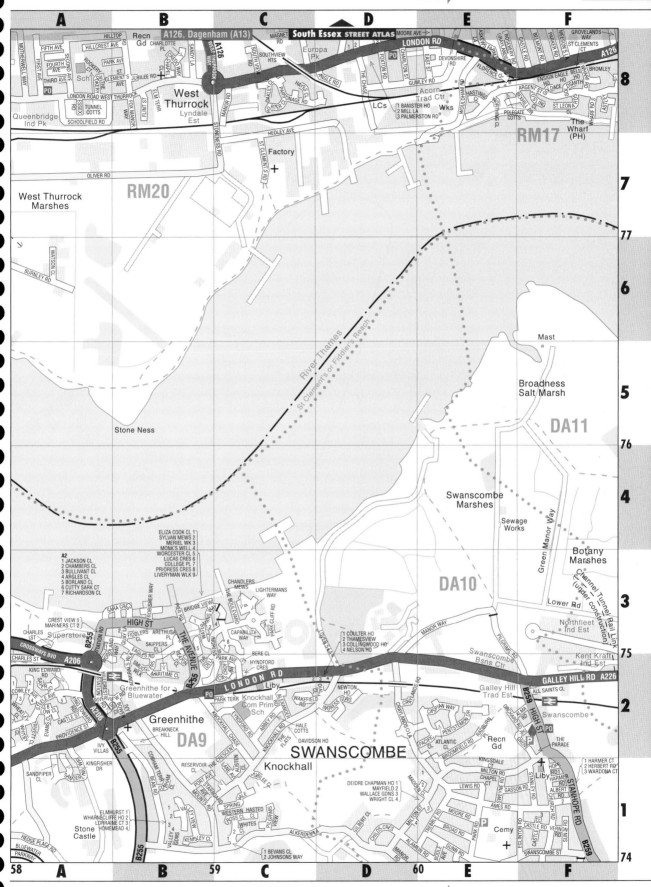

A126, Dagenham (A13)

LONDON RD

RM17

The Wharf
(PH)

West
Thurrock

Lyndale
Est

RM20

West Thurrock
Marshes

Stone Ness

River Thames

St Clement's or Fiddler's Reach

Broadness
Salt Marsh

DA11

Mast

Swanscombe
Marshes

Sewage
Works

Botany
Marshes

DA10

Green Manor Way

Channel Tunnel Rail Link
(under construction)

Lower Rd

Northfleet
Ind Est

Kent Kraft
Ind Est

ELIZA COOK CL 1
SYLVAN MEWS 2
MERIEL WLK 3
MONK'S WELL 4
WORCESTER CL 5
LUCAS CRES 6
COLLEGE PL 7
PRIORESS CRES 8
LIVERYMAN WLK 9

A2
1 JACKSON CL
2 CHAMBERS CL
3 BULLIVANT CL
4 ARGLES CL
5 BORLAND CL
6 CUTTY SARK CT
7 RICHARDSON CL

CHANDLERS
MEWS

LIGHTERMANS
WAY

CREST VIEW 1
MARINERS CT 2

HIGH ST

Superstore

CROSSWAYS BLVD   A206

B255

Swanscombe
Bsns Ctr

GALLEY HILL RD   A226

Galley Hill
Trad Est

King Edward
Rd

Greenhithe for
Bluewater

LONDON RD

Liby

Knockhall
Com Prim
Sch

1 COULTER HO
2 THAMESVIEW
3 COLLINGWOOD HO
4 NELSON HO

Swanscombe

HIGH ST   B259

The Parade

Greenhithe

DA9

SWANSCOMBE

Knockhall

Liby
1 HARMER CT
2 HERBERT RD
3 WARDONA CT

Stone
Castle

DEIDRE CHAPMAN HO 1
MAYFIELD 2
WALLACE GDNS 3
WRIGHT CL 4

Cemy

1 BEVANS CL
2 JOHNSONS WAY

1 ELMHURST 1
2 WHARNECLIFFE HO 2
3 LORRAINE CT 3
4 HOMEMEAD 4

B255   B259

A8
1 EASTERN WAY
2 HIGH ST
3 JETTY WLK
B8
1 DARNLEY RD
2 CLARENCE CT

3 WYVERN HO
4 SEJANT HO
5 LIONEL OXLEY HO
6 ARTHUR TOFT HO
7 GEORGE CROOKS HO
8 GREENWOOD HO
9 BUTLER HO

B8
10 DAVALL HO
C8
1 RICHMOND RD
2 SALISBURY RD
3 HARWOOD CT
4 KENT RD

5 KENSINGTON CT
6 WHITEHALL LA
7 BLOCKHOUSE RD
8 CEMENT BLOCK
COTTS
9 WOOD ST
10 TRASA CT

C8
11 ARTHUR CT
12 DOUG SIDDONS CT
13 PERCY ST
14 HENRY ST
15 ST THOMAS'S PL

D8
1 CRESCENT CT
2 KEMPLEY CT
3 RECTORY CT
4 RECTORY RD
5 TYRRELLS HALL CL
6 CAMPION CT

D8
7 MULLEIN CT
8 SORREL CT
9 SUNDEW CT
10 SYRINGA CT
11 SCILLA CT
12 CLOVER CT

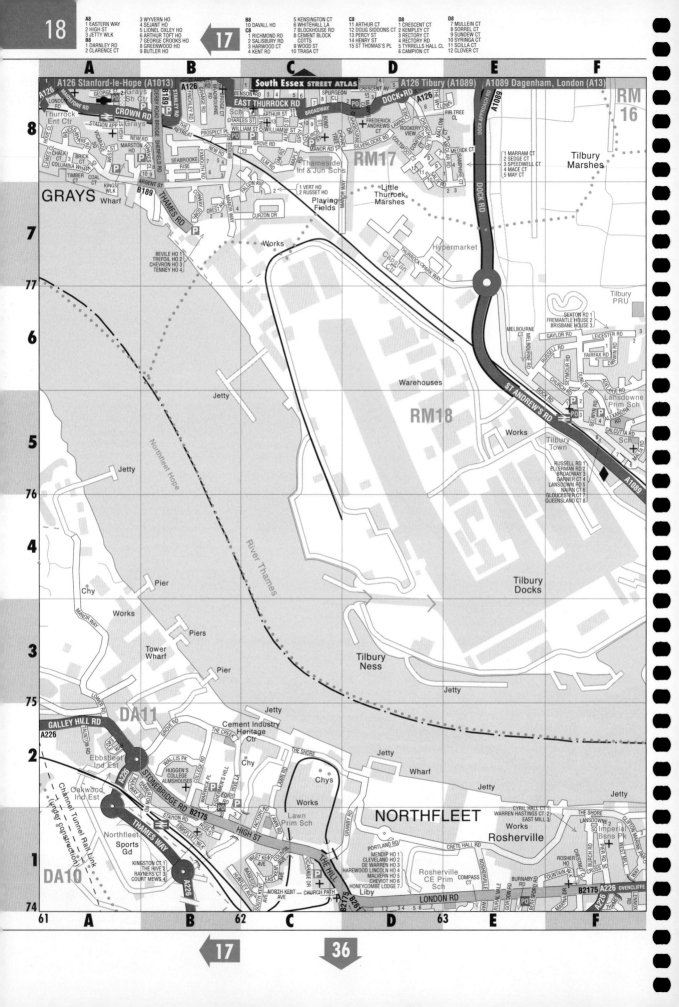

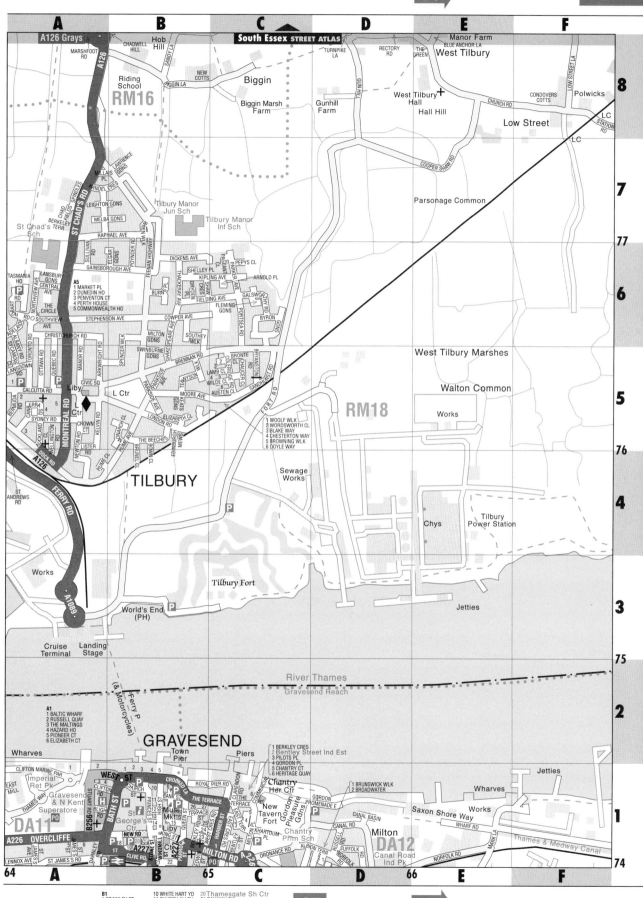

South Essex STREET ATLAS

A126 Grays

MARSHFOOT RD
CHADWELL HILL
Hob Hill
SANDY LA
Manor Farm
BLUE ANCHOR LA
West Tilbury
LOW STREET LA
Polwicks

Riding School
RM16
NEW COTTS
PIGGIN LA
Biggin
TURNPIKE LA
RECTORY RD
THE GREEN
West Tilbury

8

Biggin Marsh Farm
Gunhill Farm
GUN HILL
West Tilbury Hall
CHURCH RD
CONDOVERS COTTS
Low Street
LC
LC STATION RD

St Chad's Sch
TASMANIA HO
MILLAIS PL
SPINDLES
LAWRENCE GDNS
ST CHAD'S RD
LEIGHTON GDNS
HANDEL CRES
Tilbury Manor Jun Sch
Tilbury Manor Inf Sch
COOPER SHAW RD
Parsonage Common
LC

7

77

CHAD HILL
BERKELEY TERR
SOUTHVIEW AVE
RAPHAEL AVE
MELBA GDNS
POYNDER RD
KESTIN RD
FENNAN HIGHWAY
DICKENS AVE
SHELLEY PL
PEPYS CL
PAGEANT RD
PARKER AVE
ARNOLD PL
6

TASMANIA HO
LANSBURY GDNS
NORTHVIEW AVE
CENTRAL AVE
A5
1 MARKET PL
2 DUNEDIN HO
3 PENVENTON CT
4 PERTH HOUSE
5 COMMONWEALTH HO
SULLIVAN RD
ELGAR GDNS
GAINSBOROUGH AVE
THACKERAY RD
KIPLING AVE
DRYDEN RD
SHAW CRES
FIELDING ST
GALSWORTHY RD

THE CIRCLE
SOUTHVIEW AVE
CHRISTCHURCH RD
STEPHENSON AVE
COWPER AVE
FLEMING GDNS
SOUTHEY WLK
PORTSEA RD
BYRON

6

STUART RD
TORONTO RD
OTTAWA RD
QUEBEC RD
MANOR RD
ARKWRIGHT RD
MILTON GDNS
SHAKESPEARE RD
SWINBURNE GDNS
SPENCER WLK

LANSDOWN RD
CALCUTTA RD
Liby
PARKSIDE AVE
BRENNAN RD
TENNYSON
LAMB CL
COLERIDGE RD
WILDE CL
BRAYNSTON RD
CHAUCER CL
SANDHURST RD
West Tilbury Marshes

5

BERMUDA RD
CANBERRA RD
SYDNEY RD
AUCKLAND CL
WELLINGTON
MONTREAL RD
NEWTON RD
LISTER RD
HUME CL
BRUNEL CL
THE BEECHES
BROWN CL
EDINBURGH MEWS
LONDON RD
ELIZABETH CL
MOORE AVE
SIMS
AUSTEN CL
FORT RD
RM18
Walton Common
Works

A126
DOCK RD
FERRY RD
KELVIN RD
CROWN RD
JONACH RD
GARRICK AVE
THE BEECHES
L Ctr
Civic Sq
LONDON RD
1 WOOLF WLK
2 WORDSWORTH CL
3 BLAKE WAY
4 CHESTERTON WAY
5 BROWNING WLK
6 DOYLE WAY

76

ST ANDREWS RD
TILBURY
Sewage Works

4

Works
Tilbury Fort
Chys
Tilbury Power Station

A1089
World's End (PH)
Jetties

3

Cruise Terminal
Landing Stage
75

River Thames
Gravesend Reach

2

A1
1 BALTIC WHARF
2 RUSSELL QUAY
3 THE MALTINGS
4 HAZARD HO
5 PIONEER CT
6 ELIZABETH CT

Wharves
GRAVESEND
Town Pier
Piers
1 BERKLEY CRES
2 BENTLEY STREET IND EST
3 PILOTS PL
4 GORDON PL
5 CHANTRY CT
6 HERITAGE QUAY

Chantry Her Ctr
1 BRUNSWICK WLK
2 BROADWATER
Jetties

CLIFTON MARINE PAR
EAST MILL
Imperial Ret Pk
Gravesend & N Kent Superstore
WEST ST
CHURCH ST
ROYAL PIER RD
CROOKED LA
THE TERRACE
New Tavern Fort
Gordon Pleasure Gdns
GORDON PROMENADE E
Saxon Shore Way
Works
Wharves

1

DA11
THAMES WAY
CLIFTON RD
STUART RD
BATH ST
B256
H
St George's Ctr
BANK ST
PRINCES ST
Mkt
Mus
Liby
HARMER ST
CLARENCE
COMMERCIAL
THE TERRACE
EAST TERR
Chantry Prim Sch
CANAL BASIN
CANAL RD
Milton
DA12
MARK LA

A226 OVERCLIFFE
LENNOX AVE
ST JAMES'S RD
NEW RD
WINDMILL ST
CLIVE RD
DARNLEY RD
MILTON RD
A226
KING ST
ORDNANCE RD
ALBION TERR
KHARTOUM
SUFFOLK RD
NORFOLK RD
Canal Road Ind Pk
Thames & Medway Canal

74

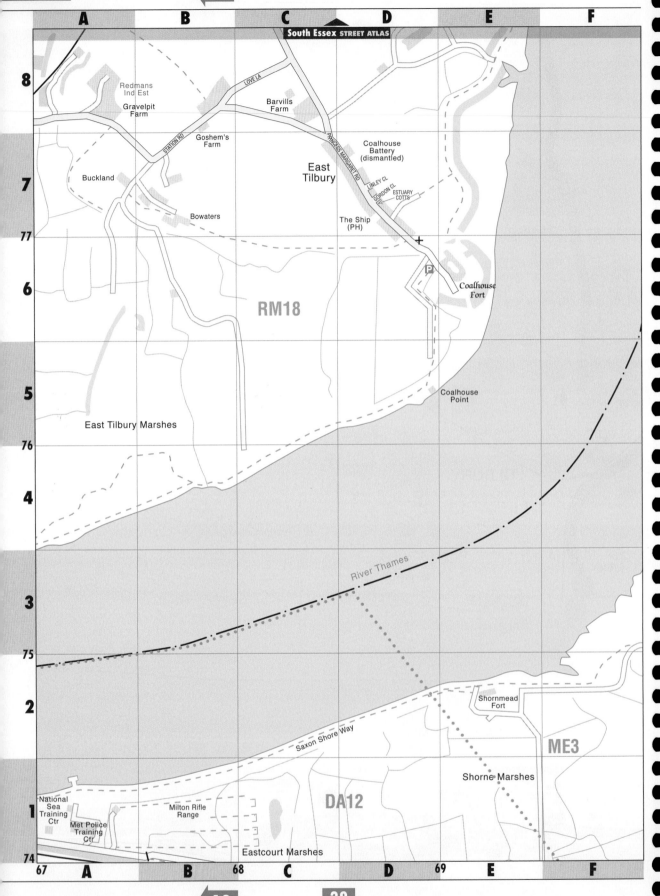

South Essex STREET ATLAS

RM18

Coalhouse
Battery
(dismantled)

East
Tilbury

Coalhouse
Fort

Coalhouse
Point

Redmans
Ind Est

Gravelpit
Farm

Goshem's
Farm

Barvills
Farm

Buckland

Bowaters

LOVE LA

STATION RD

PRINCESS MARGARET RD

LINLEY CL

GORDON CL

ESTUARY
COTTS

The Ship
(PH)

East Tilbury Marshes

River Thames

Saxon Shore Way

Shornmead
Fort

ME3

Shorne Marshes

DA12

National
Sea
Training
Ctr

Met Police
Training
Ctr

Milton Rifle
Range

Eastcourt Marshes

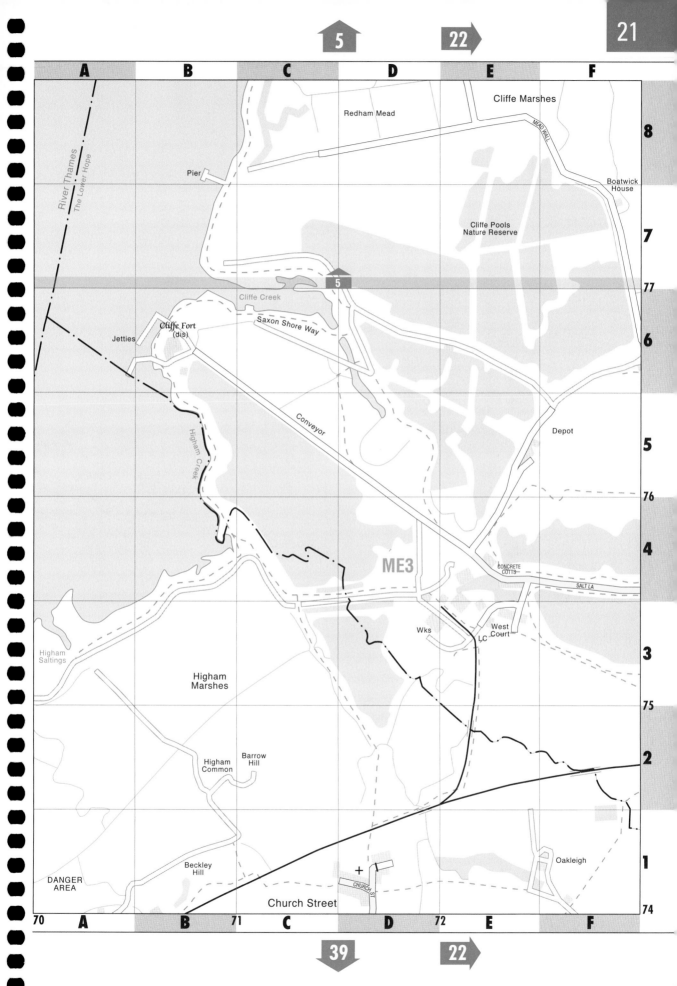

5
22

| A | B | C | D | E | F |

Cliffe Marshes

Redham Mead

MEAD WALL

Boatwick House

8

Pier

Cliffe Pools Nature Reserve

7

77

Cliffe Creek

5

River Thames

The Lower Hope

Saxon Shore Way

6

Cliffe Fort (dis)

Jetties

Higham Creek

Conveyor

Depot

5

76

ME3

4

CONCRETE COTTS

SALT LA

Wks

West Court

LC

3

Higham Saltings

Higham Marshes

75

Barrow Hill

Higham Common

2

DANGER AREA

Beckley Hill

Oakleigh

1

CHURCH ST

Church Street

74

| 70 | A | | B | 71 | C | | D | 72 | E | | F |

39
22

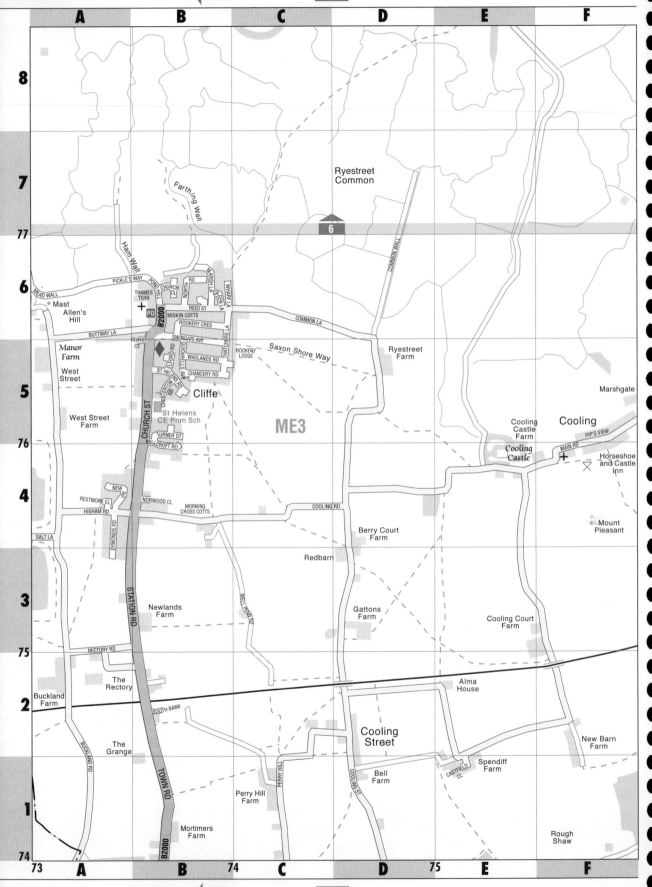

8

7

77

6

5

76

4

3

75

2

1

74

Ryestreet
Common

6

Farthing Wall

Ham Wall

MEAD WALL

PICKLE'S WAY

Mast
Allen's
Hill

THAMES
TERR

PO

B2000

MISKIN COTTS

ROOKERY CRES

BUTTWAY LA

CLIFFE
CT

SWINGATE AVE

WADLANDS RD

CHANCERY RD

West
Street

Manor
Farm

West Street
Farm

St HELENS AVE

CHESTERTON RD

St Helens
CE Prim Sch

Cliffe

TURNER ST

MILLCROFT RD

CHURCH ST

NEW
RD

RESTMORE CL

HIGHAM RD

SYMONDS RD

NORWOOD CL

MORNING
CROSS COTTS

SALT LA

STATION RD

Newlands
Farm

RECTORY RD

The
Rectory

Buckland
Farm

BUCKLAND RD

The
Grange

SOUTH BANK

TOWN RD

B2000

Mortimers
Farm

POND HILL

CHURCH CL

MARSH LA

RD

GEN LA

REED ST

WHARF LA

St SUPPLY STH

ROOKERY
LODGE

COMMON LA

Saxon Shore Way

Ryestreet
Farm

COMMON WALL

ME3

Marshgate

Cooling
Castle
Farm

Cooling

PIP'S VIEW

Cooling
Castle

MAIN RD

Horseshoe
and Castle
Inn

COOLING RD

Berry Court
Farm

Redbarn

Gattons
Farm

Mount
Pleasant

Cooling Court
Farm

WELL PINT RD

Alma
House

Cooling
Street

New Barn
Farm

PERRY HILL

Perry Hill
Farm

COOLING ST

Bell
Farm

CASTFIELD
CL

Spendiff
Farm

Rough
Shaw

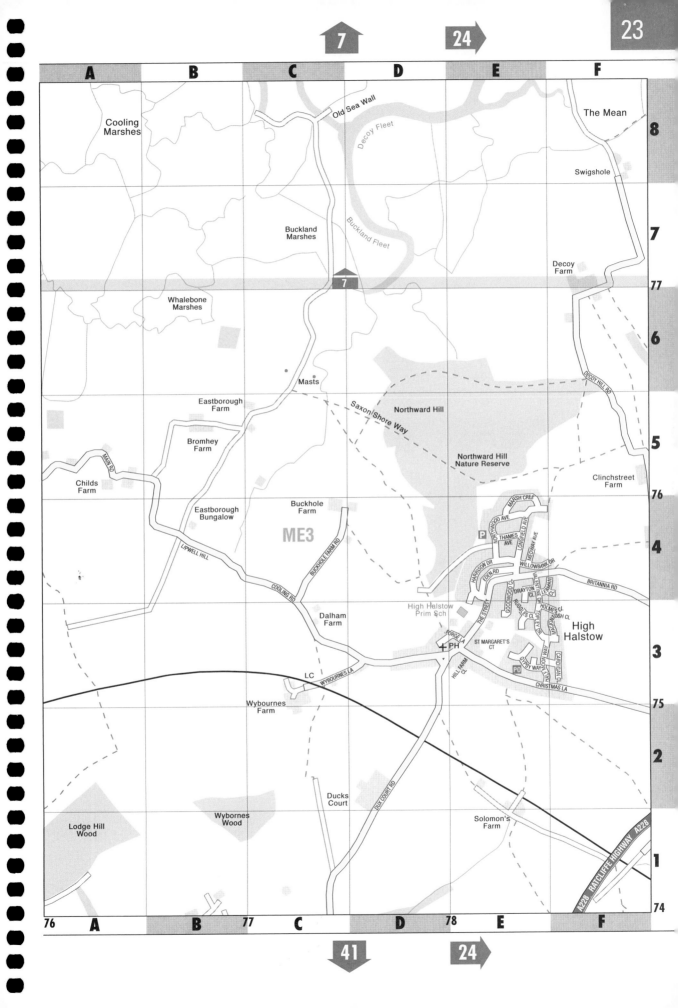

A B C D E F

8

7

77
8

6

Ramsgreen

Refuse Tip

Coombe House

Mayland

Little Owls

SHAKESPEARE FARM RD

COOMBE FARM LA

ROSE COTTS

Noreland Cottage

Moat Farm

MOAT FARM RD

St Mary Hoo

HALL RD

Ross Farm

HOOPERS LA

5

Newlands Farm

RATCLIFFE HIGHWAY

ME3

ST MARY'S

76

Bell Wood

NEWLANDS FARM RD

4

Walnut Tree Farm

CLINCH ST

Saxon Shore Way

Fenn Bell Inn (PH)

Malmaynes Hall Farm

Fenn Street

BELLWOOD CT

Turkey Hall Farm

MALMAYNES HALL RD

A228

JACKSON'S CNR

FENN ST

BRITANNIA RD

Fenn Farm

3

SHARNAL ST

Fisher's Wood

New Barn Farm

75

CHRISTMAS LA

PARBROOK RD

Parbrook House

RATCLIFFE HIGHWAY

2

Tudor Farm

A228

SHARNAL ST

ROPER'S GREEN LA

Sharnal Street

Cold Arbour

STOKE RD

North Street Farm

1

North Street

74
79 A B 80 C D 81 E F

Tunbridge Hill

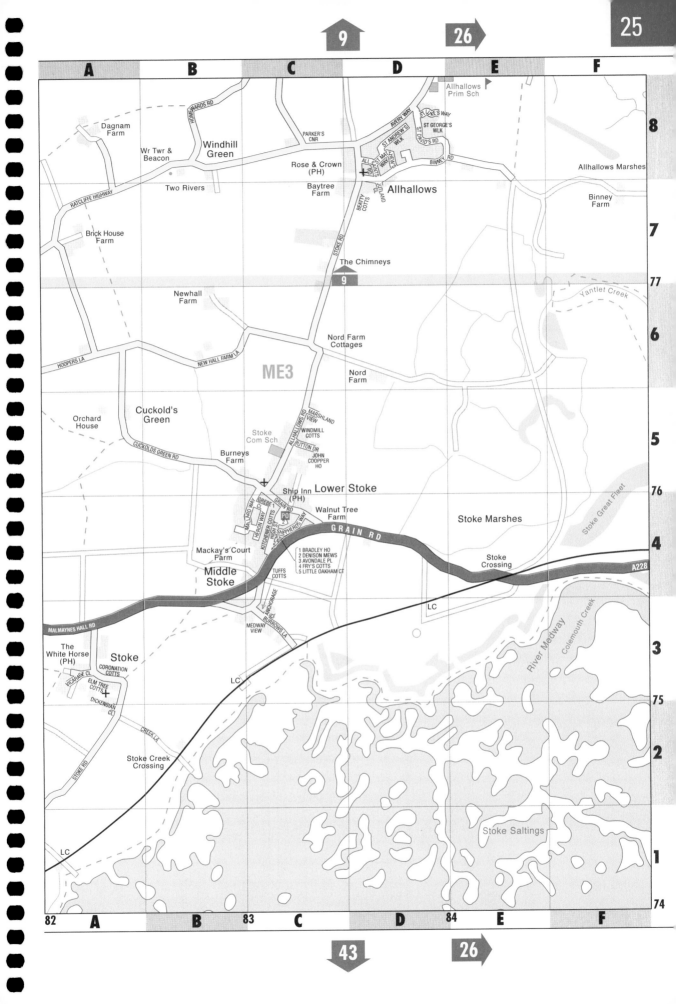

25
10

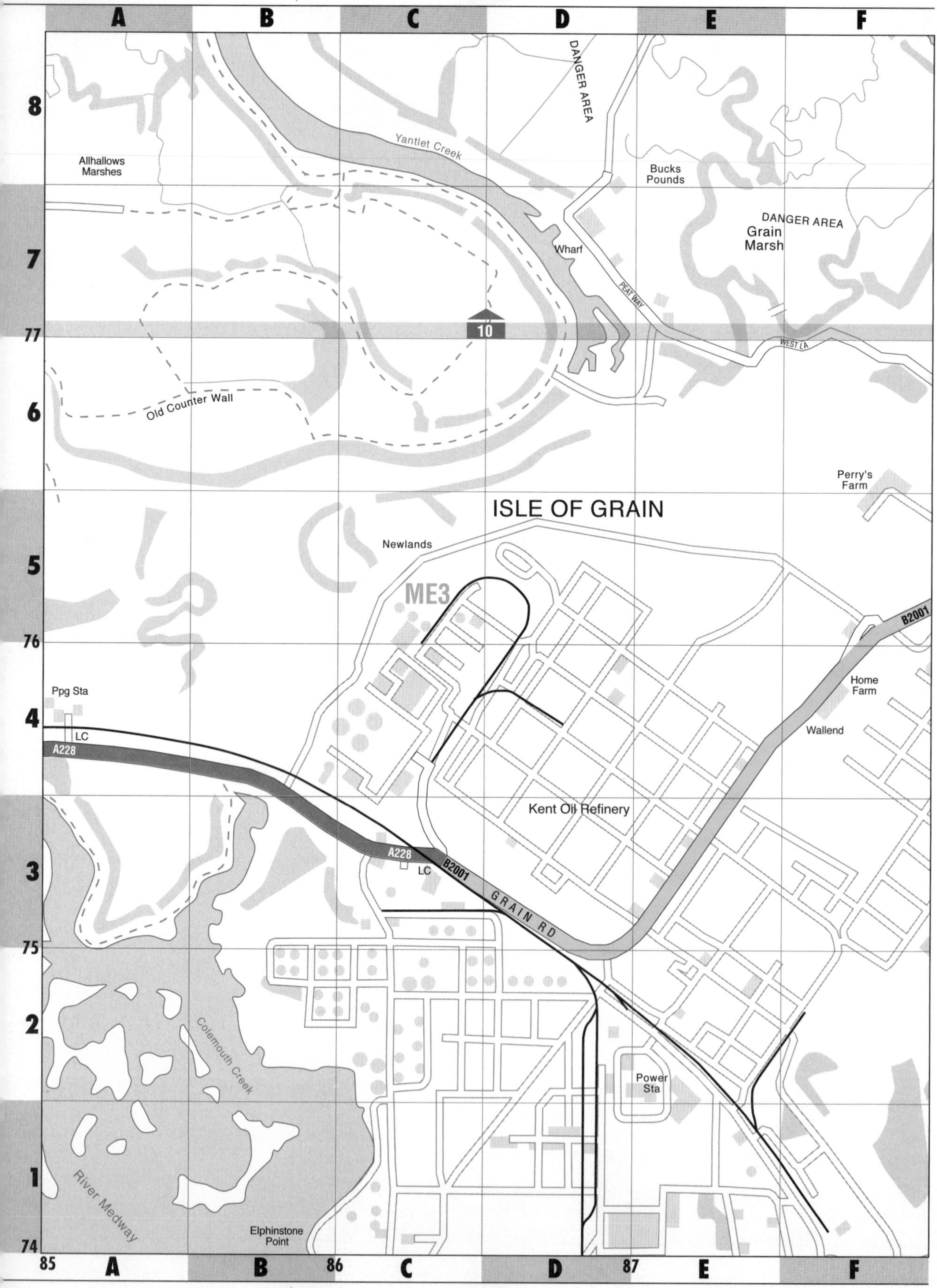

A B C D E F

8

Allhallows
Marshes

Yantlet Creek

DANGER AREA

Bucks
Pounds

DANGER AREA
Grain
Marsh

7

Wharf

PEAT WAY

WEST LA

77

10

6

Old Counter Wall

Perry's
Farm

ISLE OF GRAIN

Newlands

5

ME3

B2001

76

Home
Farm

Ppg Sta

Wallend

4

LC

A228

Kent Oil Refinery

A228

3

LC

B2001

GRAIN RD

75

Colemouth Creek

2

Power
Sta

1

River Medway

Elphinstone
Point

74

85 A 86 B C 86 D 87 E F

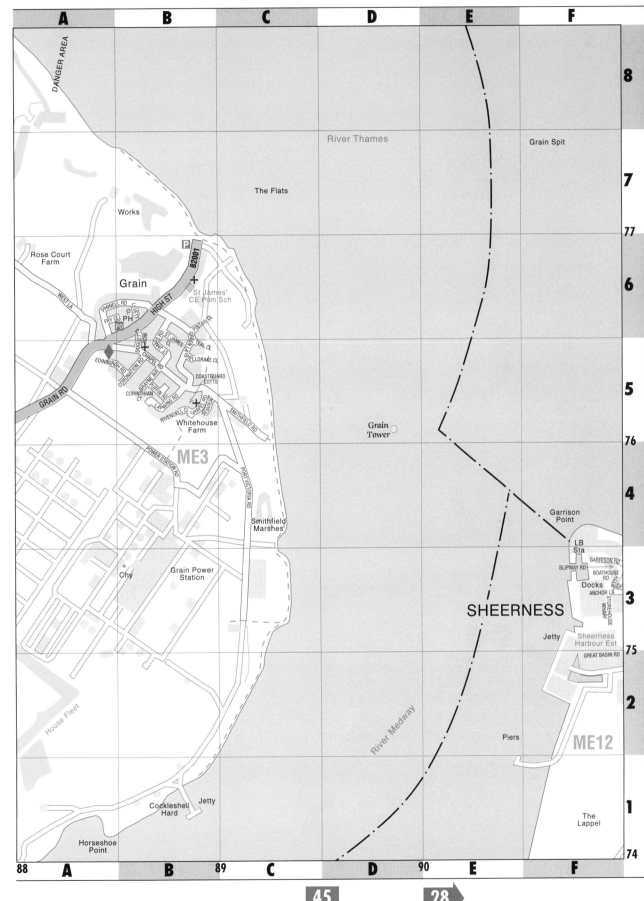

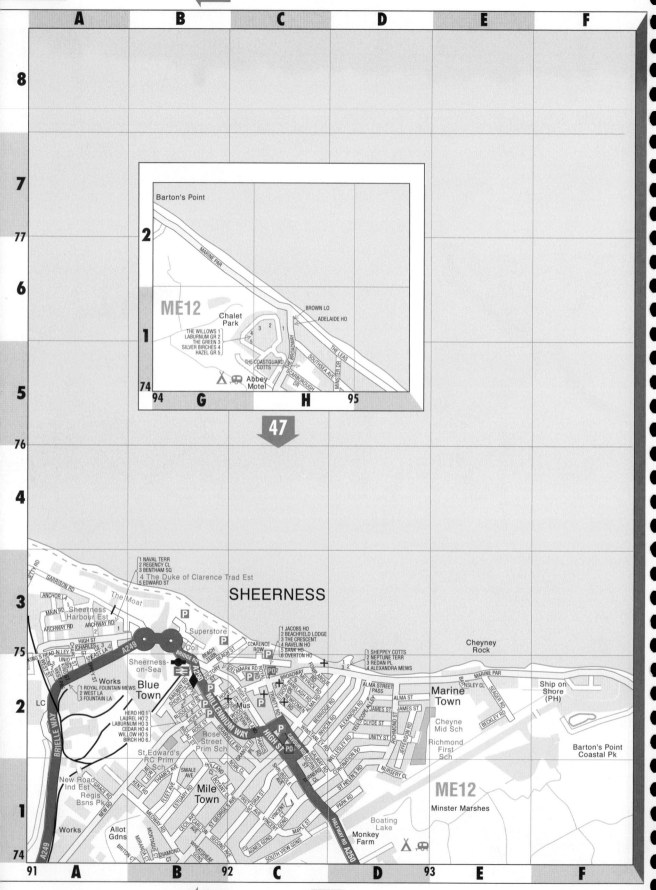

27

A B C D E F

8

7

77

6

2

ME12

Chalet Park

BROWN LO
ADELAIDE HO

1

THE WILLOWS 1
LABURNUM GR 2
THE GREEN 3
SILVER BIRCHES 4
HAZEL GR 5

3 2 1
4
5

THE COASTGUARD COTTS

THE BROADWAY

SOUTHSEA AVE

SCARBROUGH DR

MINSTER DR

THE LEAS

74

Abbey Motel

94 G H 95

Barton's Point

MARINE PAR

47

5

76

4

3

1 NAVAL TERR
2 REGENCY CL
3 BENTHAM SQ
4 The Duke of Clarence Trad Est
5 EDWARD ST

SHEERNESS

NETTY RD

GARRISON RD

The Moat

ANCHOR LA

MAIN RD

Sheerness Harbour Est

ARCHWAY RD

ARCHWAY RD

Superstore

1 JACOBS HO
2 BEACHFIELD LODGE
3 THE CRESCENT
4 RAVELIN HO
5 BANK HO
6 OVERTON HO

Cheyney Rock

Coll

75

KING'S HEAD ALLEY

CHARLES

HIGH ST

EAST LA

UNIO

BRIDGE RD

BEACH ST

BEACH TERR

CLARENCE ROW

DELAMARK RD

1 SHEPPEY COTTS
2 NEPTUNE TERR
3 REDAN PL
4 ALEXANDRA MEWS

1 2 3 4

Marine Par

Ship on Shore (PH)

Sheerness-on-Sea

VICTORY

BROADWAY

MEYRICK RD

FONTAINE

ALMA STREET PASS

BANSLEY CL

SEAGER RD

BECKLEY RD

Barton's Point Coastal Pk

2

LC

Works

1 ROYAL FOUNTAIN MEWS
2 WEST LA
3 FOUNTAIN LA

Blue Town

RAILWAY RD

SHORT ST

RUSSELL ST

HOPE ST

MILLENNIUM WAY

WELAGH RD

BERCHMEN

TRINITY RD

INVICTA RD

ALEXANDRA RD

JAMES ST

ALMA ST

CLYDE ST

UNITY ST

RICHMOND ST

JEFFERSON RD

Marine Town

Cheyne Mid Sch

Richmond First Sch

1

BRIELLE WAY

A249

HERO HO 1
LAUREL HO 2
LABURNUM HO 3
CEDAR HO 4
WILLOW HO 5
BIRCH HO 6

Rose Street Prim Sch

GRANVILLE RD

GRANVILLE

HIGH ST

CAMDEN RD

GALWAY RD

WINSTANLEY RD

CORONATION RD

WELLESLEY RD

ST HELEN'S RD

NURSERY CL

ME12

Minster Marshes

St.Edward's RC Prim Sch

New Road Ind Est

Regis Bsns Pk

NEW RD

GRACE RD

Works

Allot Gdns

MONTAGUE CT

MIRANDA CT

DIAMOND CT

BRITON RD

MEDWAY RD

KENT RD

FLEET AVE

THAMES AVE

ESTUARY RD

Swale AVE

HOLLAND RD

HOPE CL

BOART CL

WREATHSHEAF

CECH AVE

CLARTON AVE

AGNES GDNS

FIRST AVE

ST GEORGE'S AVE

SECOND AVE

VICTORIA AVE

VINCENT GDNS

VINCENT CT

SOUTH VIEW GDNS

MAPLE ST

Mile Town

SHERBURN CL

PARK RD

HALFWAY RD

A250

Boating Lake

Monkey Farm

91 A B 92 C D 93 E F

27

46

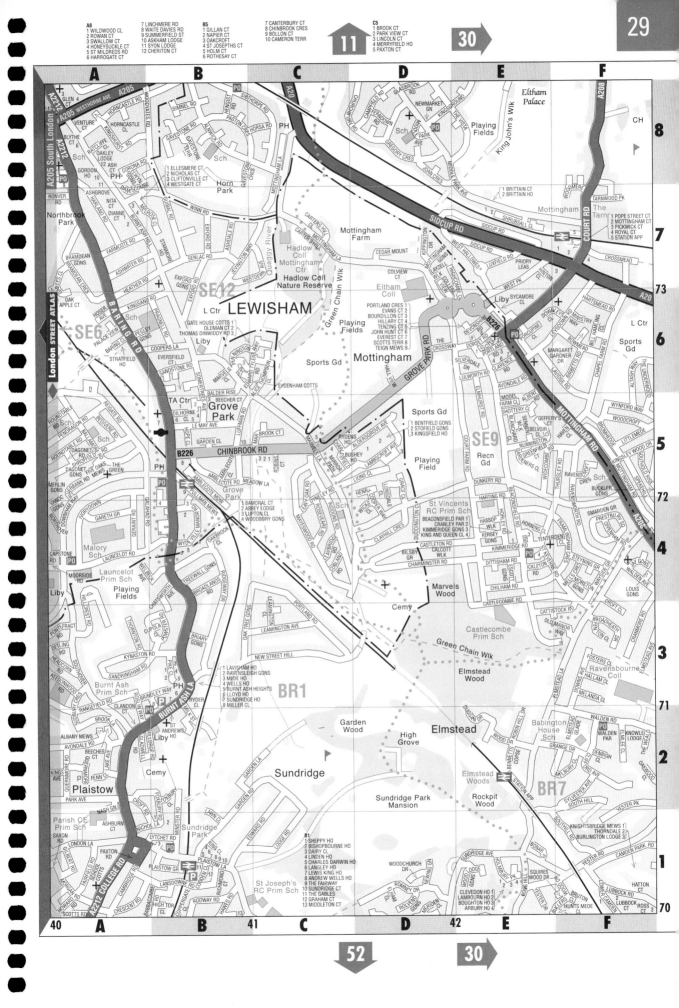

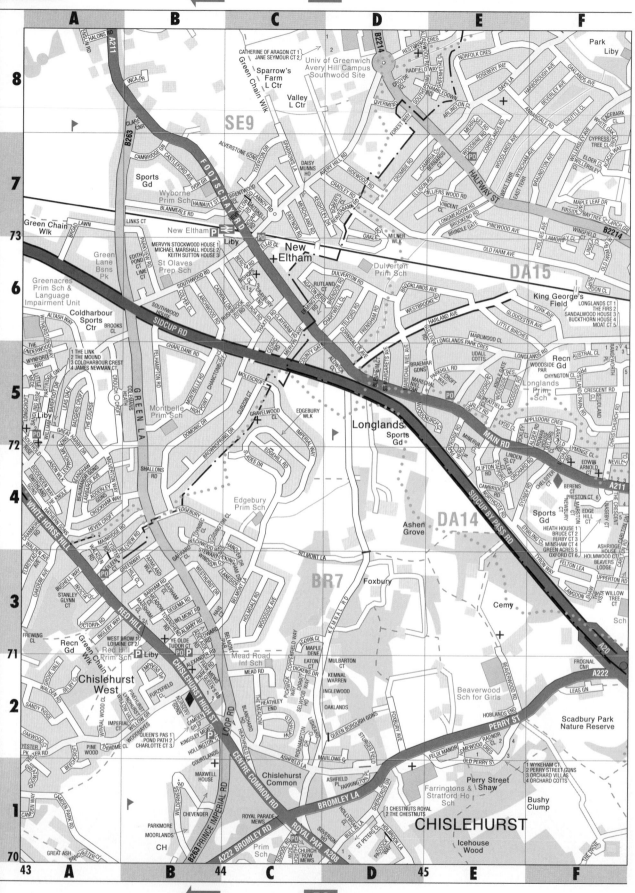

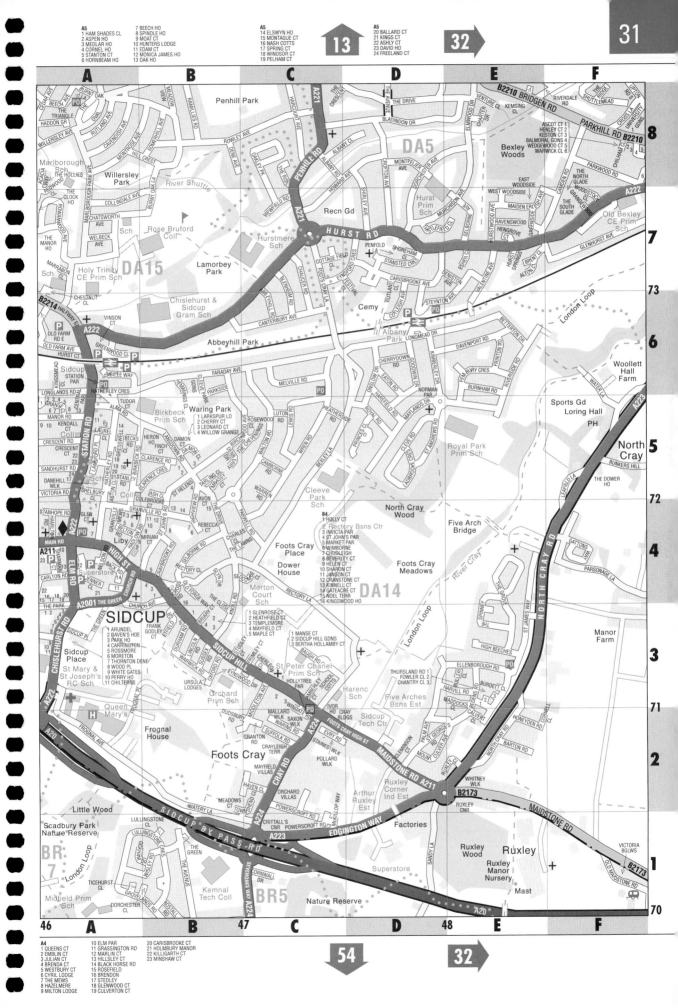

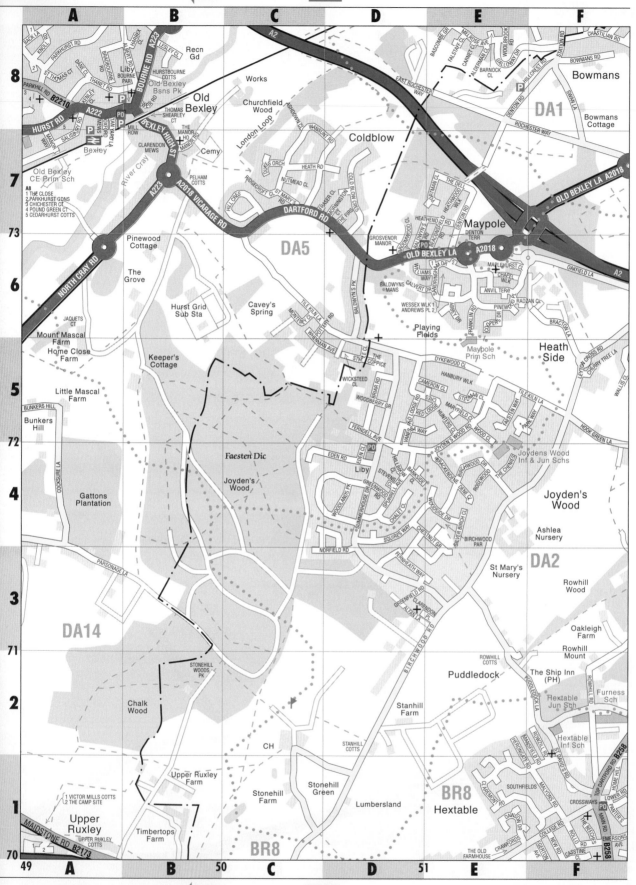

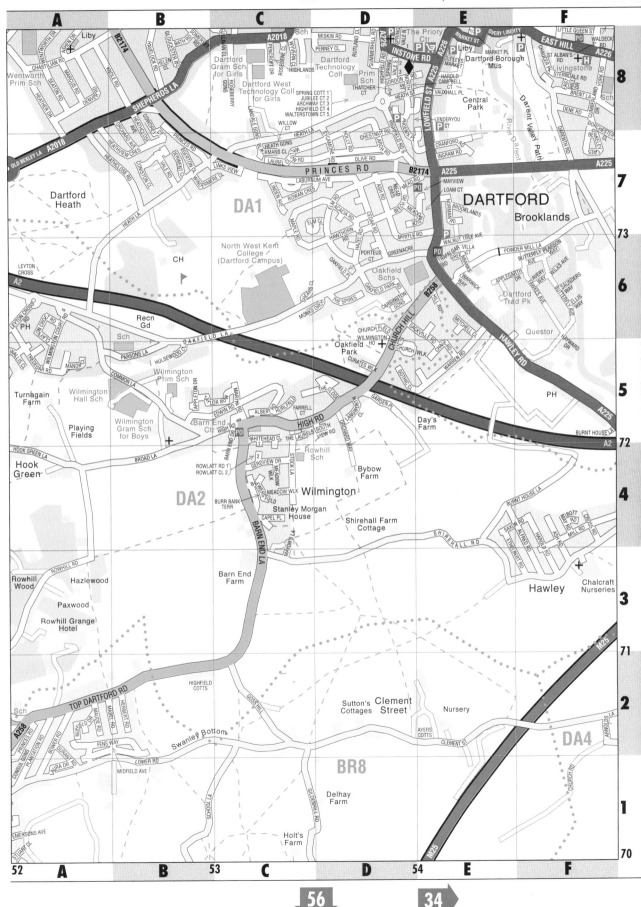

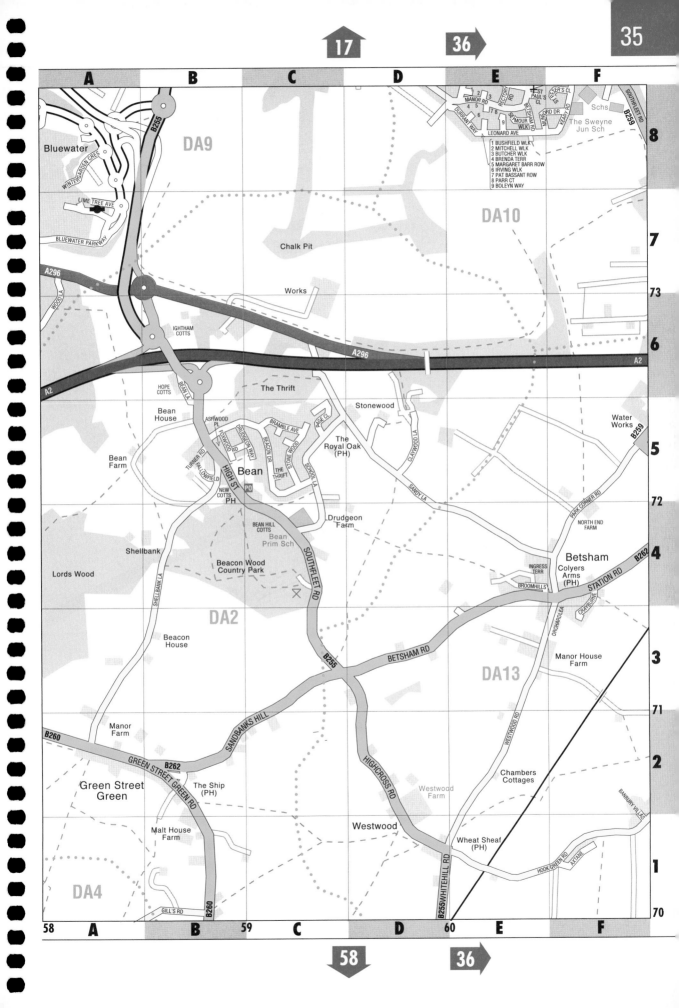

E5
1 EVEREST CL
2 SWALLOWFIELDS
3 DOWDING WLK
4 GREENDALE WLK
5 LANGDALE WLK
6 ROBYNS CROFT

E8
1 COMPASS CT
2 LIGHTERMAN'S MEWS
3 GALLEON MEWS
4 CAPSTAN MEWS
5 MARINERS WAY

F7
1 May Avenue Est
2 HUNTSMAN HO
3 BRADBERY CT
4 BOUNDARY HO
5 ALFRED HO
6 WYCLIFFE HO

7 THANET HO
8 SOUTHFLEET RD
F8
1 CREMORNE RD
2 BYCLIFFE MEWS
3 BYCLIFFE TERR
4 PELHAM TERR

DA10

NORTHFLEET

Sewage Works

Channel Tunnel Rail Link (under construction)

Spring Head Nursery

Brookvale Workshops

Springhead Ent Pk

Cemy

Wombwell Park

Northfleet Tech Coll

St Joseph's RC Prim Sch

Hartfield Pl

St Margaret's Rd 1
Stanley Rd 2

Cygnet L Ctr

Liby

DA11

New House

Sports Gd

Northfleet Sch for Girls

Superstore

Pepper Hill

Prim Sch

WATLING ST

Hazells

Mast

Scadbury Manor

Northfleet Green

Southfleet

Sedley's CE Prim Sch

Redstreet

Friary Court

DEAN & CHAPTER COTTS

Madam Wood

DA13

Banbury Villas

WEAVER'S ORCH

Hook Place Cotts

Hook Green

THOMAS COTTS

Brakefield House

DA3

Perry Street

Ashmore Gdns
Rowmarsh Cl 2
Foxberry Wlk 3

Nightingale Cl 1
Brightlands 2
Mallow Cl 3

Superstore

BURGHFIELD RD

FAIRVIEW   THE DROVE WAY   BRAMLEY CL

THE KNOLE   HADLOW WAY   THE DROVE WAY

LITTLECROFT   FLOWERHILL WAY   HILL CL   UPPER AVE   ISTEAD RISE

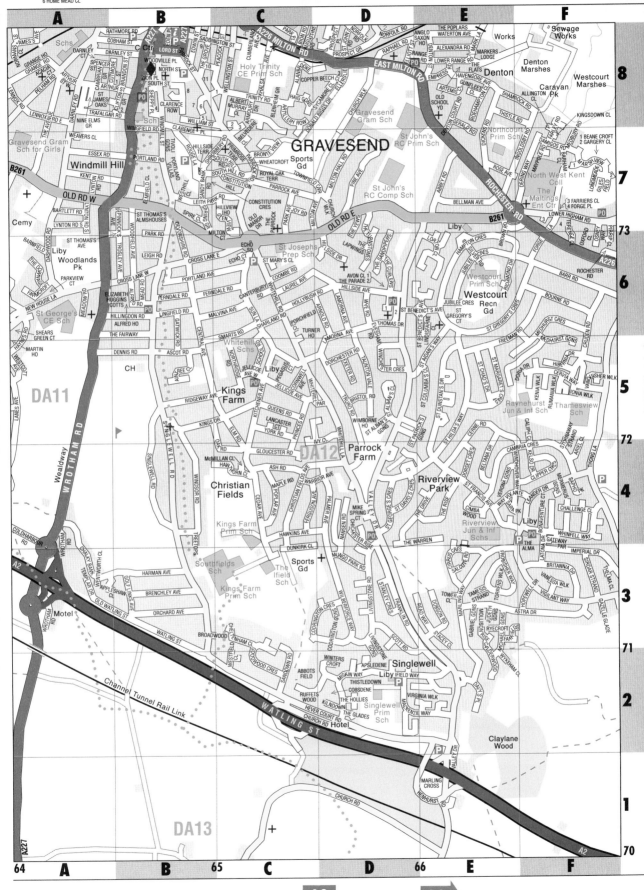

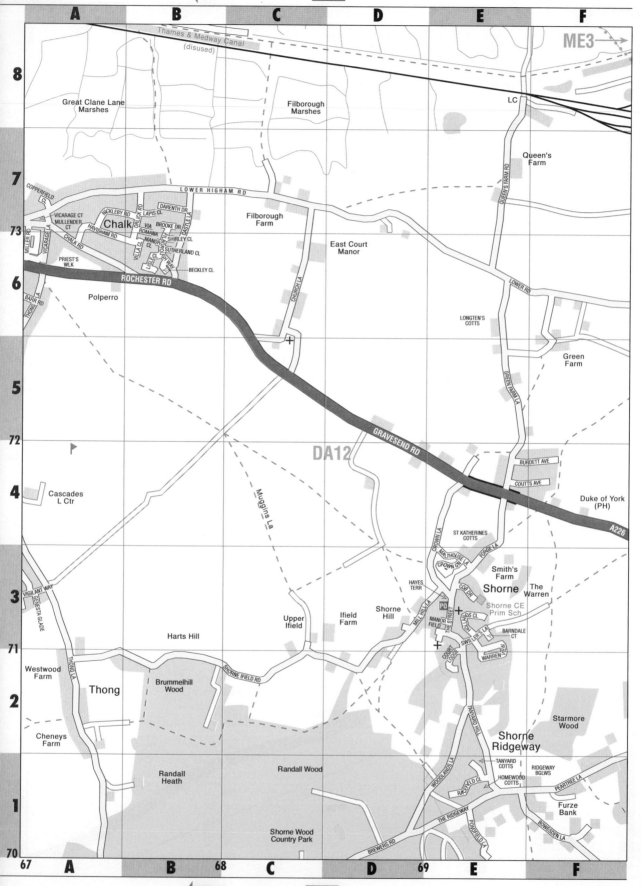

37
20

ME3 →

Thames & Medway Canal (disused)

Great Clane Lane Marshes

Filborough Marshes

LC

Queen's Farm

QUEEN'S FARM RD

COPPERFIELD CL

LOWER HIGHAM RD

VICARAGE CT

MULLENDER CT

ACKLEBY RD

DARENTH DR

ORLICK RD

LAPIS CL

Chalk

BROOKE DR

CASTLE LA

Filborough Farm

East Court Manor

VICARAGE LA

HAVISHAM RD

VILLA CL

MANOR

VIA ROMANA

SHIRLEY CL

MILLER RD

CHALK RD

LISLE CL

SUTHERLAND CL

LONGTON'S WAY

PRIEST'S WLK

BECKLEY CL

CHURCH LA

LOWER RD

ROCHESTER RD

BARR RD

THONG LA

Polperro

LONGTEN'S COTTS

GREEN FARM LA

Green Farm

GRAVESEND RD

DA12

BURDETT AVE

COUTTS AVE

Cascades L Ctr

Muggins La

Duke of York (PH)

A226

CROWN LA

St KATHERINES COTTS

MALTHOUSE LA

FORGE LA

Smith's Farm

The Warren

CROWN GN

Shorne

VIGILANT WAY

HAYES TERR

C89 DR

GENESTA GLADE

PO

Shorne CE Prim Sch

Upper Ifield

Ifield Farm

Shorne Hill

MILL HILL LA

THE STREET

HOLLANDS CL

SWILLER LA

BARNDALE CT

Harts Hill

MANOR FIELD

WARREN VIEW

THONG LA

SHORNE IFIELD RD

COURT LODGE

Westwood Farm

Thong

Brummelhill Wood

Starmore Wood

TANYARD HILL

Shorne Ridgeway

Cheneys Farm

TANYARD COTTS

RIDGEWAY BGLWS

WOODLANDS LA

HOMEWOOD COTTS

PEARTREE LA

Randall Heath

Randall Wood

RAVENSFIELD CL

Furze Bank

BOMESDEN LA

THE RIDGEWAY

POMFRET LA

Shorne Wood Country Park

BREWERS RD

37
61

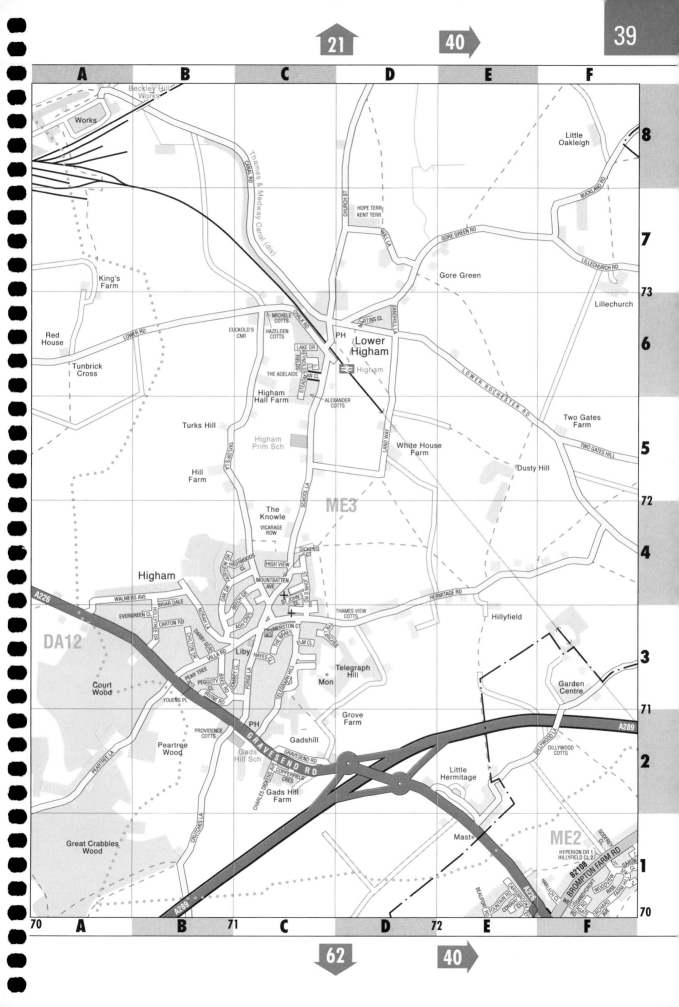

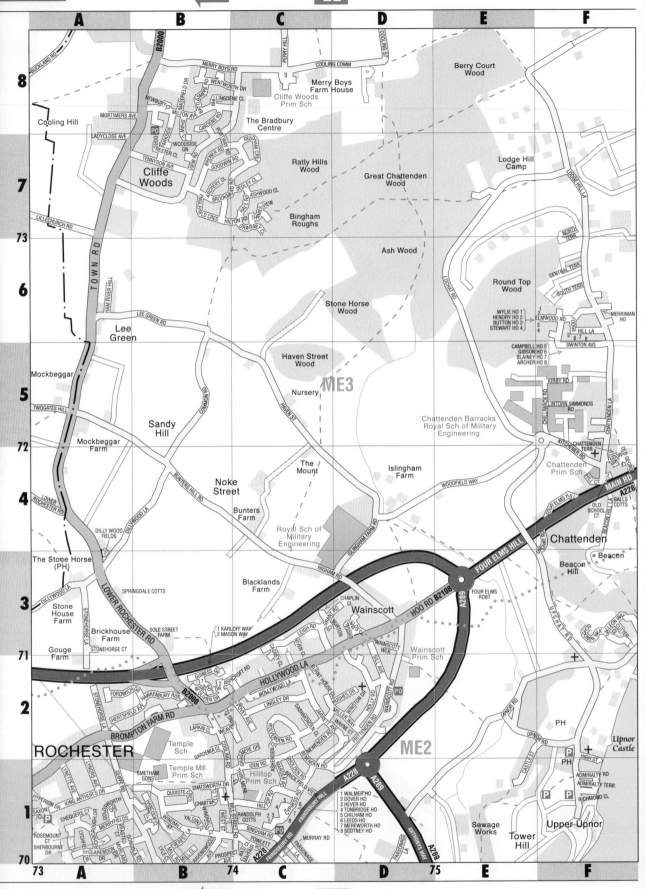

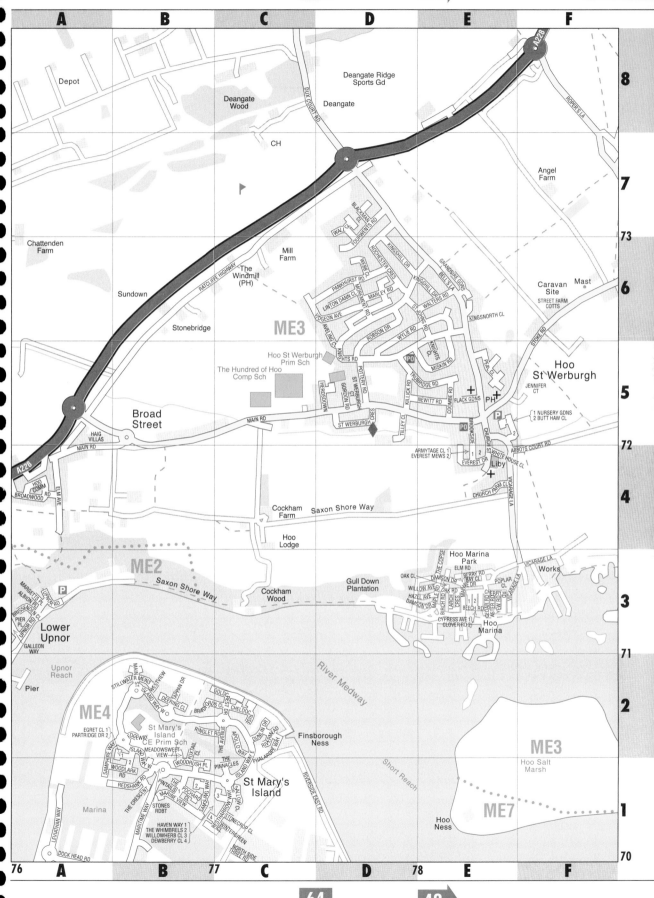

41
24

A B C D E F

White Hall
Farm House

Roper's
Farm

Saxon Shore Way

ROPER'S GREEN LA

8

Beluncle
Farm

BELUNCLE
VILLAS

STOKE RD

ROPER'S LA

7

STOKE RD

BETA RD

JETTY RD

GAMMA RD

ALPHA CT

MAIN RD

Kingsnorth
Ind Est

73

STURDEE
COTTS

JACOB'S LA

ESHCOL RD

Works

6

ME3

Kingsnorth

5

Abbots
Court

Saxon Shore Way

Power
Station

72

Mast

Sewage
Works

Jetty

4

Hoo Flats

3

Long Reach

River Medway

71

Middle Creek

Darnet Ness

Bishop Saltings

2

Darnet
Fort

ME3

Pinup Reach

Damhead Creek

ME3

South Yantlet Creek

ME7

Hoo Fort

1

ME7

Folly Point

Nor Marsh

70

Gillingham Reach

79 A B 80 C D 81 E F

41
65

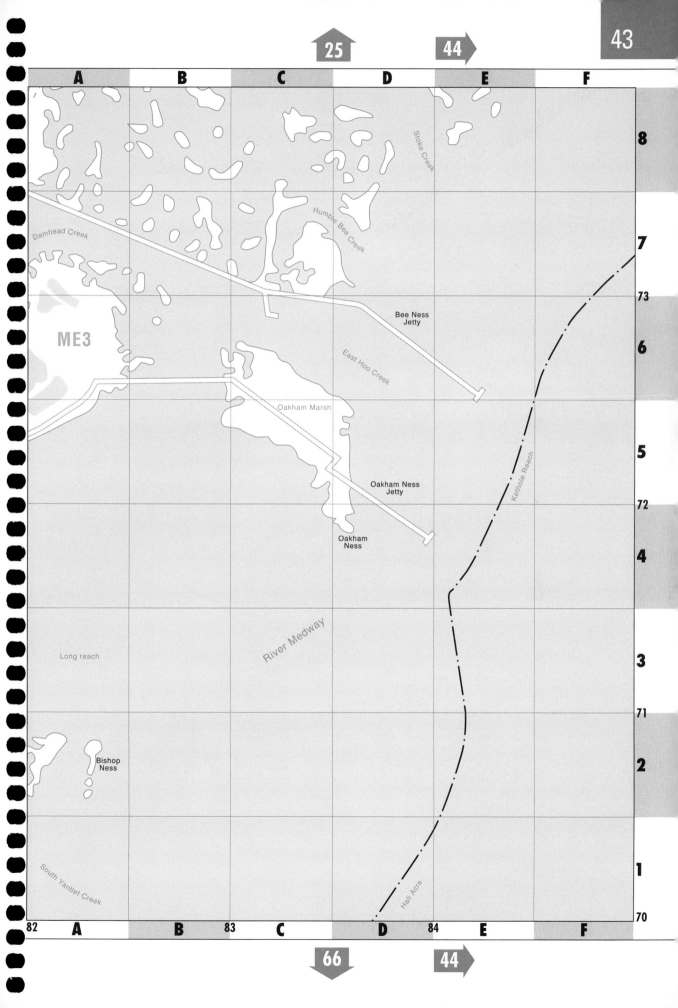

A   B   C   D   E   F

8

Stoke Creek

Humble Bee Creek

7

73

Damhead Creek

Bee Ness
Jetty

6

East Hoo Creek

ME3

Oakham Marsh

Kethole Reach

5

Oakham Ness
Jetty

72

Oakham
Ness

4

River Medway

Long reach

3

71

Bishop
Ness

2

South Yantlet Creek

1

Hall Acre

70

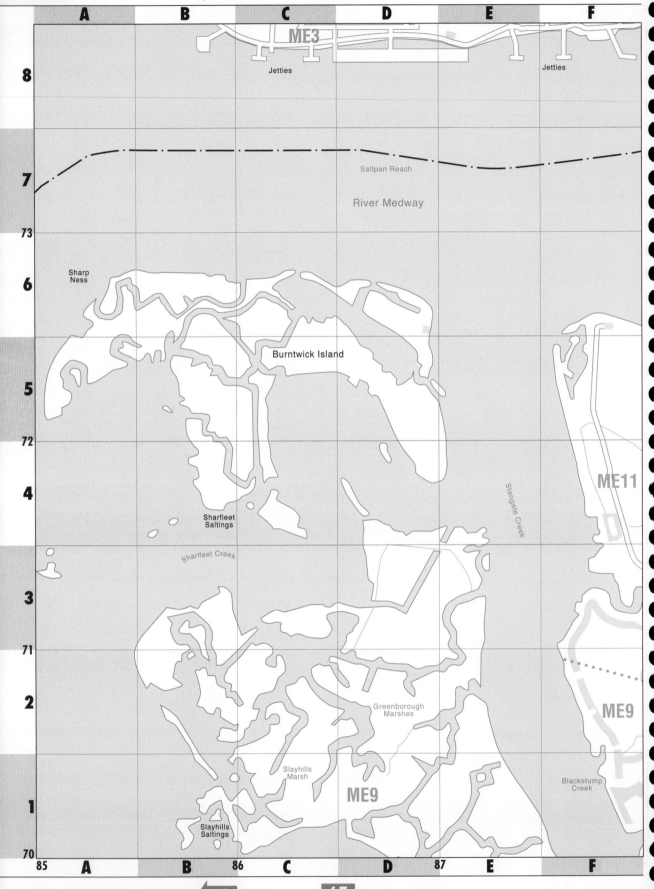

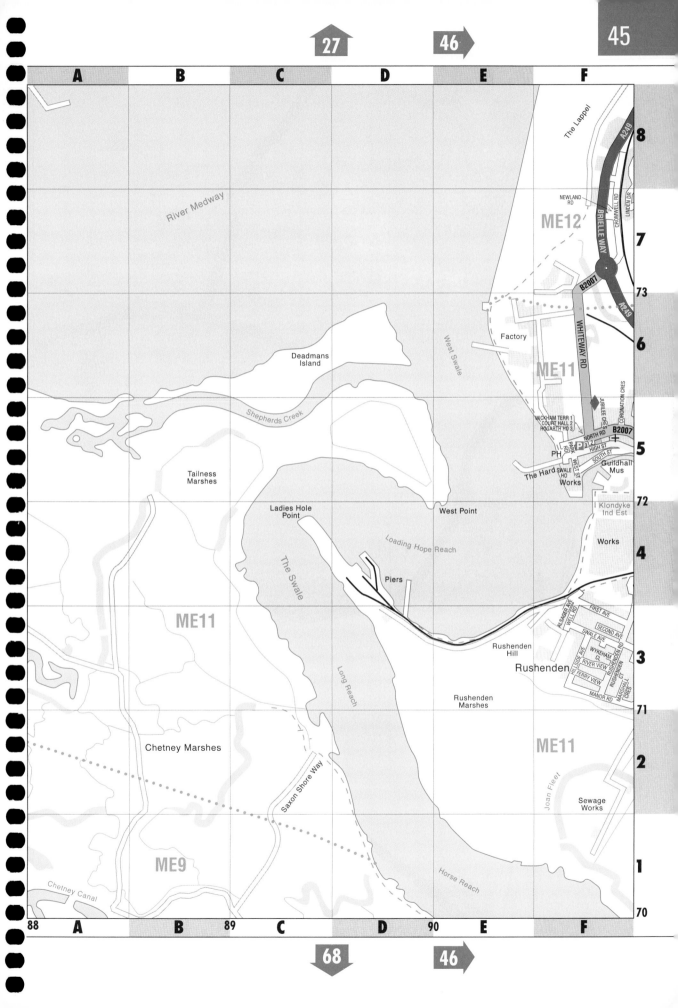

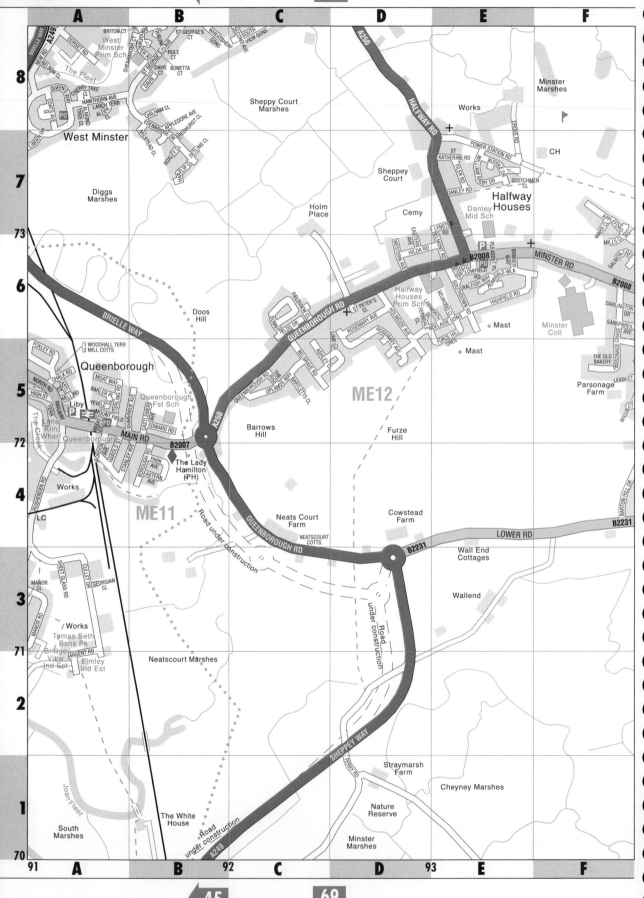

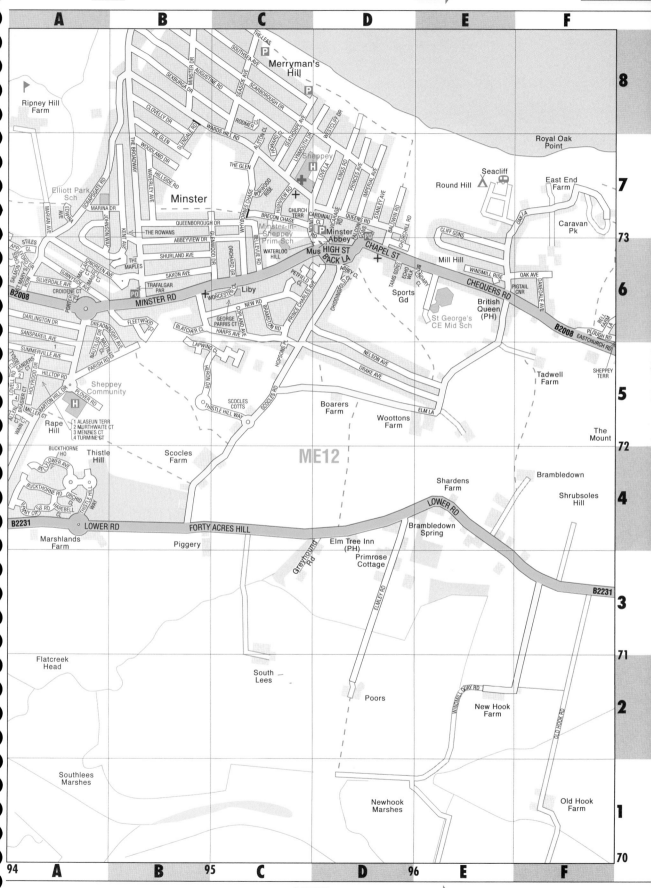

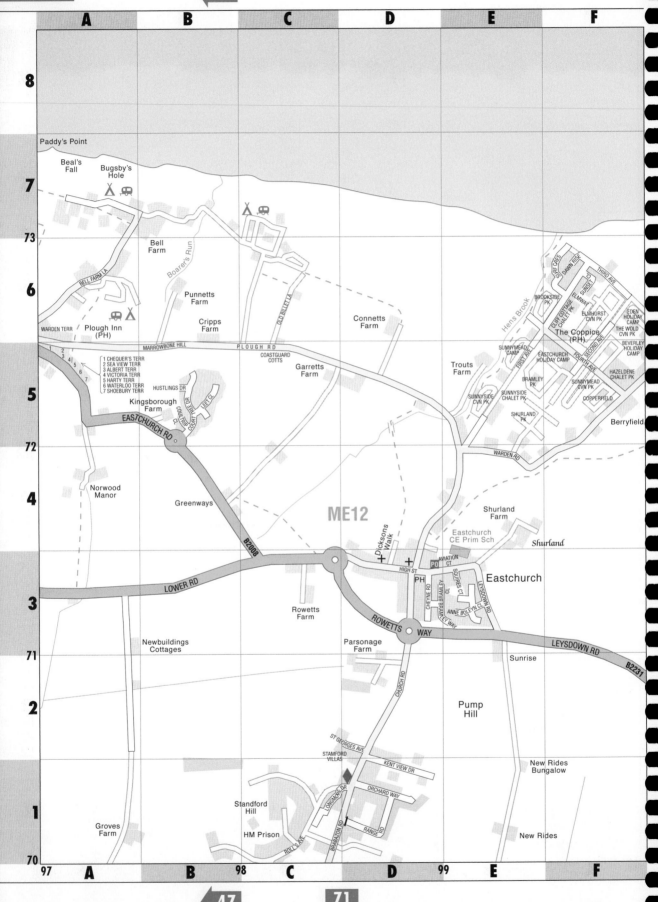

47

A B C D E F

8

7

Paddy's Point

Beal's
Fall
Bugsby's
Hole

73

Bell
Farm

Boarer's Run

6

BELL FARM LA

Punnetts
Farm

OLD BILLET LA

Connetts
Farm

Hens Brook

SURF CRES
DAWN RISE
THIRD AVE

BROOKSIDE PK
CLIFF COTTAGE CHALET PK
ELMWAY
SUNSET
ELMHURST CVN PK
EDEN HOLIDAY CAMP
THE WOLD CVN PK

WARDEN TERR
Plough Inn
(PH)

Cripps
Farm

MARROWBONE HILL
PLOUGH RD

COASTGUARD COTTS

Garretts
Farm

Trouts
Farm

EASTCHURCH HOLIDAY CAMP
SECOND AVE
FIRST AVE
FOURTH AVE

BEVERLEY HOLIDAY CAMP
HAZELDENE CHALET PK

5

1 CHEQUER'S TERR
2 SEA VIEW TERR
3 ALBERT TERR
4 VICTORIA TERR
5 HARTY TERR
6 WATERLOO TERR
7 SHOEBURY TERR

HUSTLINGS DR

COULTRIP CL
COURT TREE DR
FET CL

Kingsborough
Farm

SUNNYMEAD CAMP

BRAMLEY PK

SUNNYSIDE CVN PK

SUNNYSIDE CHALET PK

SUNNYMEAD CVN PK

COPPERFIELD

The Coppice
(PH)

72

EASTCHURCH RD

Norwood
Manor

SHURLAND PK

WARDEN RD

Berryfield

4

Greenways

B2008

ME12

Shurland
Farm

Shurland

3

LOWER RD

Rowetts
Farm

Dicksons Walk
HIGH ST
PO
AVIATION CT
PH
CHEYNE RD
SQUIRES CT
BRAMLEY CL
ANNE BOLEYN CL
SHURLEY WAY
LEYSDOWN RD

Eastchurch CE Prim Sch

Eastchurch

ROWETTS WAY
LEYSDOWN RD
B2231

71

Newbuildings
Cottages

Parsonage
Farm

CHURCH RD

Sunrise

2

Pump
Hill

New Rides
Bungalow

ST GEORGES AVE
STAMFORD VILLAS
KENT VIEW DR
ORCHARD WAY
LONGMORE DR
BRABAZON RD
RANGE RD
ROLL'S AVE

1

Standford
Hill

Groves
Farm

HM Prison

New Rides

70

97 A 98 B C 99 D E F

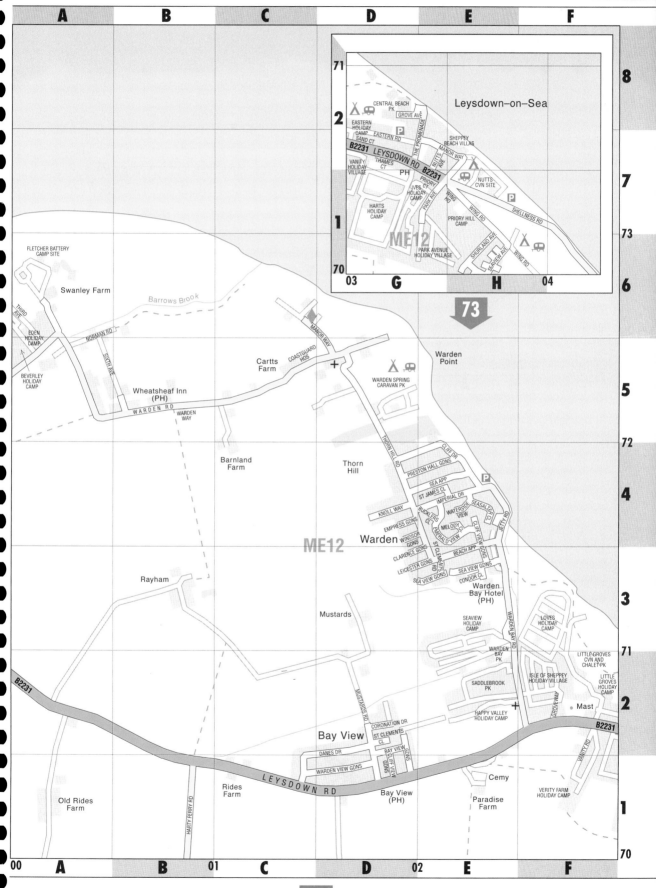

Leysdown-on-Sea inset map:

71
CENTRAL BEACH PK
GROVE AVE
Leysdown-on-Sea
2
EASTERN HOLIDAY CAMP
SAND CT
EASTERN RD
P
SHEPPEY BEACH VILLAS
B2231 LEYSDOWN RD
MANOR WAY
B2231
VANITY HOLIDAY VILLAGE
THAMES CT
PH
PRIORY
NUTTS AVE
WING HO
NUTTS CVN SITE
P
SHELLNESS RD
7
IVES HOLIDAY CAMP
PARK AVE
1
HARTS HOLIDAY CAMP
ME12
PRIORY HILL CAMP
73
WING RD
PARK AVENUE HOLIDAY VILLAGE
SHURLAND AVE
SEAVIEW AVE
WING RD
70
03
G
H
04
6

73

FLETCHER BATTERY CAMP SITE
Swanley Farm
Barrows Brook
THIRD AVE
NORMAN RD
SIXTH AVE
EDEN HOLIDAY CAMP
BEVERLEY HOLIDAY CAMP
Wheatsheaf Inn (PH)
WARDEN RD
WARDEN WAY
Cartts Farm
MANOR WAY
COASTGUARD HOS
Warden Point
Warden Spring Caravan Pk
5
Barnland Farm
Thorn Hill
THORN HILL RD
CLIF DR
PRESTON HALL GDNS
P
72
SEA APP
ST JAMES CL
IMPERIAL DR
SEASALTER
KNOLL WAY
BUCKLERS CL
WATERSIDE VIEW
CLIF VIEW GDNS
JETTY RD
4
EMPRESS GDNS
EMERALD VIEW
MELODY
Warden
WINDSOR GDNS
CLARENCE GDNS
ST CLEMENTS RD
BEACH APP
ME12
LEICESTER GDNS
SEA VIEW GDNS
SEA VIEW GDNS
CONDOR CL
Warden Bay Hotel (PH)
3
Rayham
Mustards
SEAVIEW HOLIDAY CAMP
WARDEN BAY RD
LOVES HOLIDAY CAMP
LITTLE GROVES CVN AND CHALET PK
71
WARDEN BAY PK
ISLE OF SHEPPEY HOLIDAY VILLAGE
LITTLE GROVES HOLIDAY CAMP
B2231
MUSTARDS RD
SADDLEBROOK PK
HAPPY VALLEY HOLIDAY CAMP
GROVEWAY
Mast
B2231
2
CORONATION DR
Bay View
ST CLEMENTS CL
DANES DR
BAY VIEW GDNS
CLIF VIEW GDNS
WARDEN VIEW GDNS
Cemy
VANITY RD
VERITY FARM HOLIDAY CAMP
Old Rides Farm
HARTY FERRY RD
Rides Farm
LEYSDOWN RD
Bay View (PH)
Paradise Farm
1
70
00
A
B
01
C
D
02
E
F

72

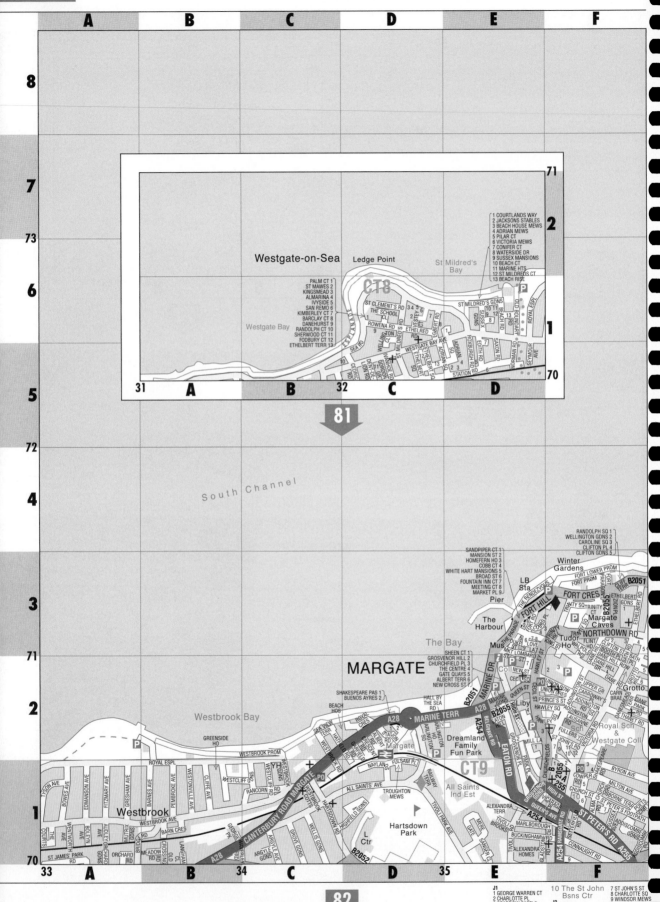

Westgate-on-Sea

CT8

Westgate Bay

Ledge Point

St Mildred's Bay

Palm Ct 1
St Mawes 2
Kingsmead 3
Almarina 4
Ivyside 5
San Remo 6
Kimberley Ct 7
Barclay 8
Danehurst 9
Randolph Ct 10
Sherwood Ct 11
Fodbury Ct 12
Ethelbert Terr 13

1 COURTLANDS WAY
2 JACKSONS STABLES
3 BEACH HOUSE MEWS
4 ADRIAN MEWS
5 PILAR CT
6 VICTORIA MEWS
7 CONIFER CT
8 WATERSIDE DR
9 SUSSEX MANSIONS
10 BEACH CT
11 MARINE HTS
12 ST MILDREDS CT
13 BEACH RISE

ST MILDRED'S GDNS

81

South Channel

SANDPIPER CT 1
MANSION ST 2
HOMEFERN HO 3
COBB CT 4
WHITE HART MANSIONS 5
BROAD ST 6
FOUNTAIN INN CT 7
MEETING CT 8
MARKET PL 9

RANDOLPH SQ 1
WELLINGTON GDNS 2
CAROLINE SQ 3
CLIFTON PL 4
CLIFTON GDNS 5

Winter Gardens

FORT CRES

Margate Caves

NORTHDOWN RD

The Bay

MARGATE

SHEEN CT 1
GROSVENOR HILL 2
CHURCHFIELD PL 3
THE CENTRE 4
GATE QUAYS 5
ALBERT TERR 6
NEW CROSS ST 7

Pier

The Harbour

SHAKESPEARE PAS 1
BUENOS AYRES 2

Westbrook Bay

BEACH HO

MARINE TERR

Dreamland Family Fun Park

CT9

Royal Sch & Westgate Coll

GREENSIDE HO

WESTBROOK PROM

Margate

Westbrook

Hartsdown Park

CANTERBURY ROAD MARGATE

All Saints Ind Est

82

J1
1 GEORGE WARREN CT
2 CHARLOTTE PL
3 SPARROW CASTLE
4 MILTON SQ
5 ARNOLD RD
6 OXFORD ST
7 HOMESTEAD CL
8 VICARAGE CRES
9 CONNAUGHT GDNS

10 The St John Bsns Ctr
J2
1 PUMP LA
2 COLLEGE SQ
3 COLLEGE WLK
4 ANCHOR HILL
5 GROTTO RD
6 GROTTO GDNS

7 ST JOHN'S ST
8 CHARLOTTE SQ
9 WINDSOR MEWS
10 PRINCES CRES
11 LAUSANNE TER
12 VENTNOR LA

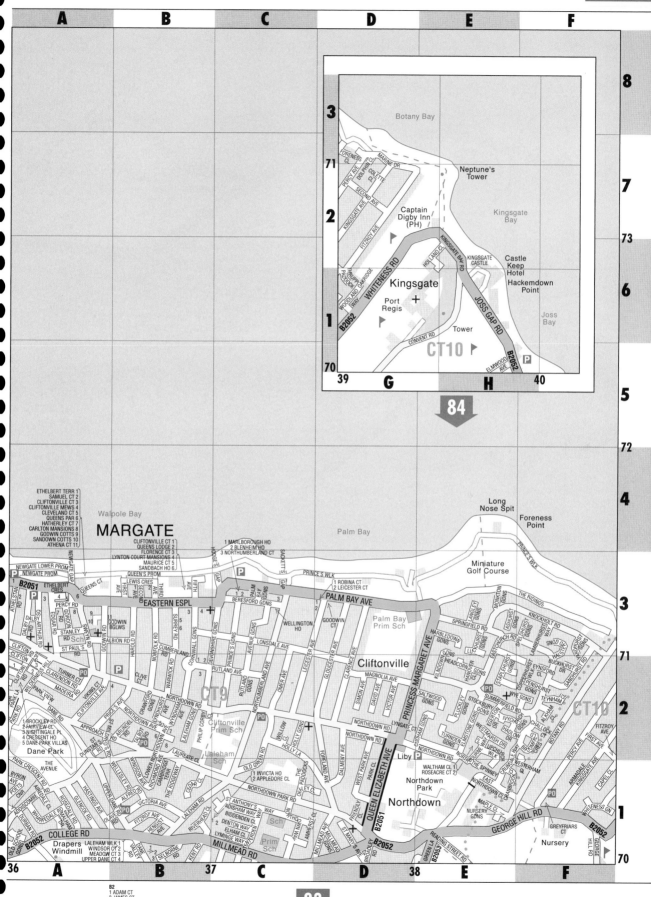

Inset map (top right)

Botany Bay

Neptune's Tower

Kingsgate Bay

Captain Digby Inn (PH)

Kingsgate Castle

Castle Keep Hotel

Hackemdown Point

Kingsgate

Port Regis

Joss Bay

Tower

CT10

MARINE DR
FORENESS CL
PERCY AVE
DOLPHIN CL
COLETTE
SECOND AVE
KINGSGATE AVE
FITZROY AVE
THIRD
PADDOCK
WOODLAND WAY
OAKRIDGE
WHITENESS RD
HOLLAND CL
KINGSGATE BAY RD
JOSS GAP RD
CONVENT RD
ELMWOOD AVE
B2052
B2052

3
71
2
1
70
39
G
H
40

→ 84

Main map

MARGATE

Walpole Bay

Palm Bay

Long Nose Spit

Foreness Point

Miniature Golf Course

Cliftonville

CT9

CT10

Dane Park

Northdown

Northdown Park

Drapers Windmill

ETHELBERT TERR 1
SAMUEL CT 2
CLIFTONVILLE CT 3
CLIFTONVILLE MEWS 4
CLEVELAND CT 5
QUEENS PAR 6
HATHERLEY CT 7
CARLTON MANSIONS 8
GODWIN COTTS 9
SANDOWN COTTS 10
ATHENA CT 11

CLIFTONVILLE CT 1
QUEENS LODGE 2
FLORENCE CT 3
LYNTON COURT MANSIONS
MAURICE CT 5
SANDBACH HO 6

1 MARLBOROUGH HO
2 BLENHEIM HO
3 NORTHUMBERLAND CT

1 ROBINA CT
2 LEICESTER CT

1 BROCKLEY RD
2 FAIRVIEW CL
3 NIGHTINGALE PL
4 CRESCENT HO
5 DANE PARK VILLAS

1 INVICTA HO
2 APPLEDORE CL

WALTHAM CL 1
ROSEACRE CT 2

Newgate Prom
Newgate Lower Prom
Queen's Prom
Queens Ct
Eastern Espl
Prince's Wlk
Palm Bay Ave
Prince's Wlk

B2051
B2052
B2052
B2051
B2053

College Rd
Millmead Rd
George Hill Rd

Palm Bay Prim Sch
Cliftonville Prim Sch
Laleham Sch
Prim Sch
St Anthony's Sch
Liby
Nursery
Northdown Park Rd

NEWGATE GAP
HODGE'S GAP
SACKETT'S GAP
ATHELSTAN RD
DALBY SQ
ARTHUR RD
EDGAR RD
STANLEY RD
ST PAUL'S
GORDON RD
SURREY RD
ALBION RD
CLIFTON GDNS
CLIFTON PL
TURNER CT
CLARENDON RD
MADEIRA RD
PARK VIEW
VIKING CT
CLIFTONVILLE AVE
DANE RD
BYRON AVE
POETS CNR
ADDISCOMBE RD
ARKLEY RD
ARUNDEL RD
ST DUNSTAN'S CT
PRICE'S AVE
CRAWFORD GDNS
APPROACH RD
LOWER NORTHDOWN AVE
NORTHDOWN AVE
LALEHAM RD
NORFOLK RD
WARWICK RD
HAROLD RD
CUMBERLAND RD
CORNWALL RD
DEVONSHIRE GDNS
PRINCE'S GDNS
RUTLAND AVE
RUTLAND GDNS
NORTHUMBERLAND AVE
AVENUE GDNS
LONSDALE AVE
BERESFORD GDNS
WELLINGTON HO
GOODWIN CT
LEICESTER AVE
GLOUCESTER AVE
CLARENCE AVE
MAGNOLIA AVE
SIMON AVE
DAVID AVE
VICTOR AVE
SALTWOOD GDNS
PRINCESS MARGARET AVE
HARBLEDOWN GDNS
KILNDOWN GDNS
HEADCORN GDNS
PICKLEY GDNS
STOCKBURY GDNS
KEYSTONE GDNS
SUMMERFIELD RD
SPRINGFIELD RD
LANGLEY GDNS
ASHURST
KNOCKHOLT RD
MONKTON GDNS
THE RIDINGS
EASTCHURCH RD
STAPLEHURST GDNS
EYNSFORD RD
PENSHURST GDNS
LUTON
BUCKHURST DR
SANDHURST RD
SNO GO
WYE GDNS
IVYCARS
TEYNHAM
CHALLOCK
FITZROY AVE
FIRST AVE
PERCY AVE
ARMADALE AVE
KINGSGATE AVE
CAPEL CL
WHITENESS GN
GREYFRIARS CT
GEORGE HILL RD
Nursery
B2052

PARK CRESCENT RD
THE AVENUE
PARK RD
DURBAN RD
BRISTOL RD
OLD CROSSING RD
WILDERNESS HILL
ROSEDALE RD
GLENCOE RD
HASTINGS AVE
WELLESLEY RD
WINDSOR AVE
UPPER DANE RD
ALFRED RD
FITZROY AVE
VICTORIA AVE
CAMBRIDGE TERR
THE RIDGEWAY
CEDAR CL
THE PADDOCKS
RIVERHEAD CL
LAUREATE CL
HOLLY LA
HOLLY GDNS
OLD GREEN RD
CEELEY RD
FORELAND AVE
DALMENY AVE
WEST PARK AVE
PARK AVE
FRINDLY
QUEEN ELIZABETH AVE
B2051
LYNGATE CL
NORTHDOWN RD
NORTHDOWN WAY
NORTHDOWN RD
HADDON
WESTMARSH DR
CASTLE GDNS
CUNDALL CL
THE SPINNEY
WESTERHAM RD
EAST NORTHDOWN CL
NORTH FORELAND WLK
MAPLE CL
NURSERY GDNS
GREEN LA
READING STREET RD
ADISHAM WAY
BIDDENDEN CL
DENTON WAY
ELHAM CL
LYMINGE WAY
ST MARY'S AVE
AYLESHAM
AMHERST CL
MILLMEAD AVE
BROADLEY

B2052

B2
1 ADAM CT
2 JAMES CT
3 RUTLAND HO
4 WESTMOUNT HO
5 HIGHFIELD CT
6 REBECCA CT
7 RICHARD CT
8 LEONA CT

B8
1 HANSOM TERR
2 DAINTON CL
3 ST TIMOTHY'S MEWS
4 NORTH CT
5 PALACE CT
6 SUMMERFIELD
7 ANDRINGHAM LODGE
8 PARK PLACE
9 KENDALL LODGE
10 WINSTON CT
11 VOGUE CT
12 THE LAURELS

29

C5
1 SHERIDAN LODGE
2 LANGLEY GDNS
3 GAINSBOROUGH CT
4 GERRARD HO

C7
1 RUXLEY CT
2 WESTLAND LODGE
3 EASTLAND CT
4 DAIRSIE CT
5 NORTHLANDS
6 BEECHFIELD COTTS
7 THE OASIS
8 CROMARTY CT
9 STANTON CT
10 SILVERSTONE CT
11 SOUTH VIEW CT

E6
1 WINDSOR CT
2 BICKLEY CT
3 BANSTEAD CT
4 NEWTON CT
5 HOLMDENE CT
6 CHELSEA CT

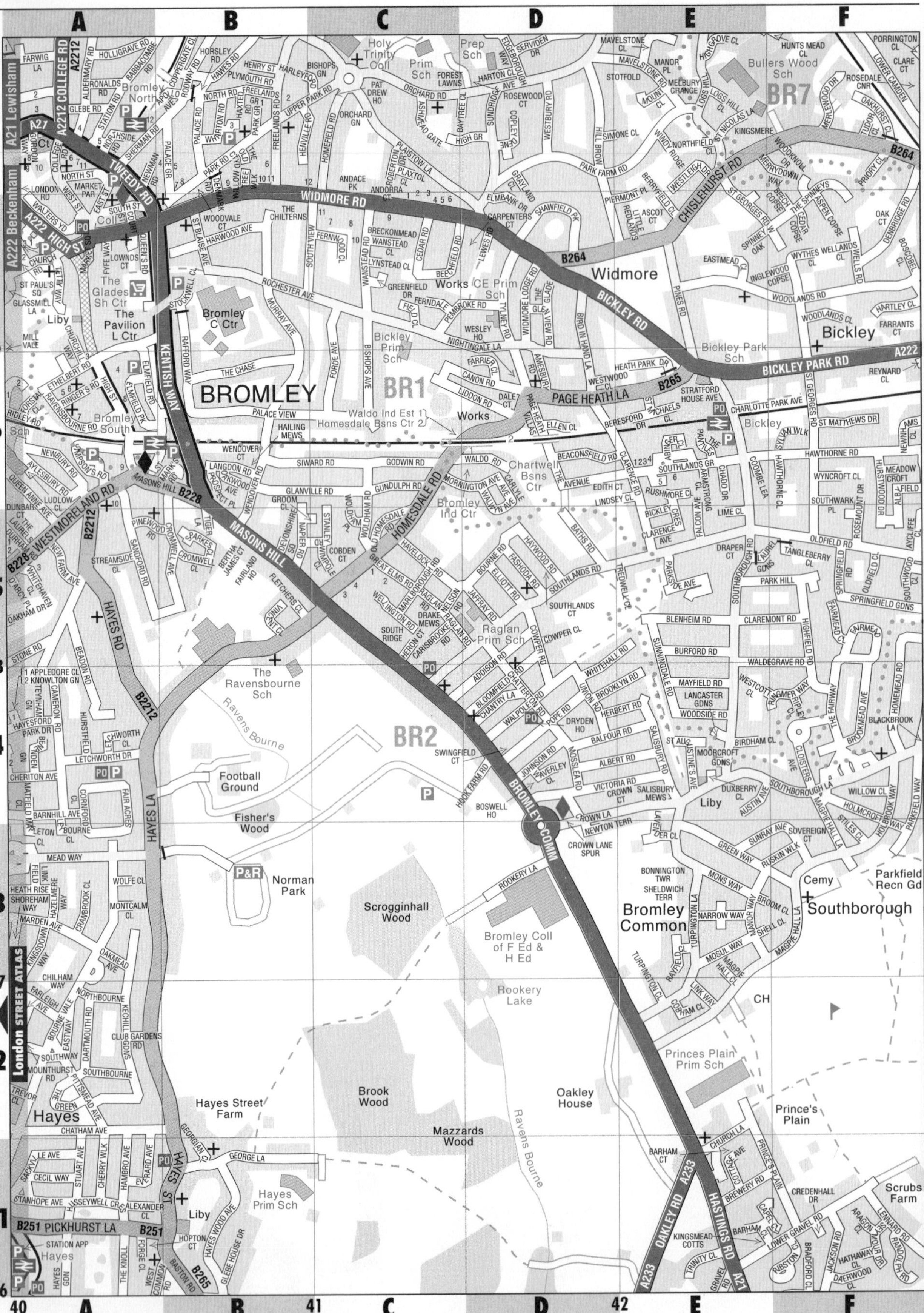

A5
1 MONTAGUE TERR
2 TAVISTOCK RD
3 CHATSWORTH HO
A6
1 MARINA CL
2 CHEVENEY WLK
3 BROMLEY MANOR MANS
4 THE MALL
5 RINGER'S CT
6 SIMPSONS PL
7 NUTFIELD CT
8 COACH HOUSE MEWS
9 WESTMORELAND PL
10 HANOVER CT

A7
1 HARMONY WAY
2 EDISON RD
3 ST JAMES CT
A8
1 MOORELAND RD
2 HAMMELTON RD
3 BROOMLEIGH
4 FLORENCE RD
5 MITCHELL WAY
6 BAGSHAW HO
7 HARRINGTON HO
8 SHEPPARDS COLL
9 BROMLEY COLL
10 COLLEGE GN
11 NEWMAN CT
12 NORTHPOINT

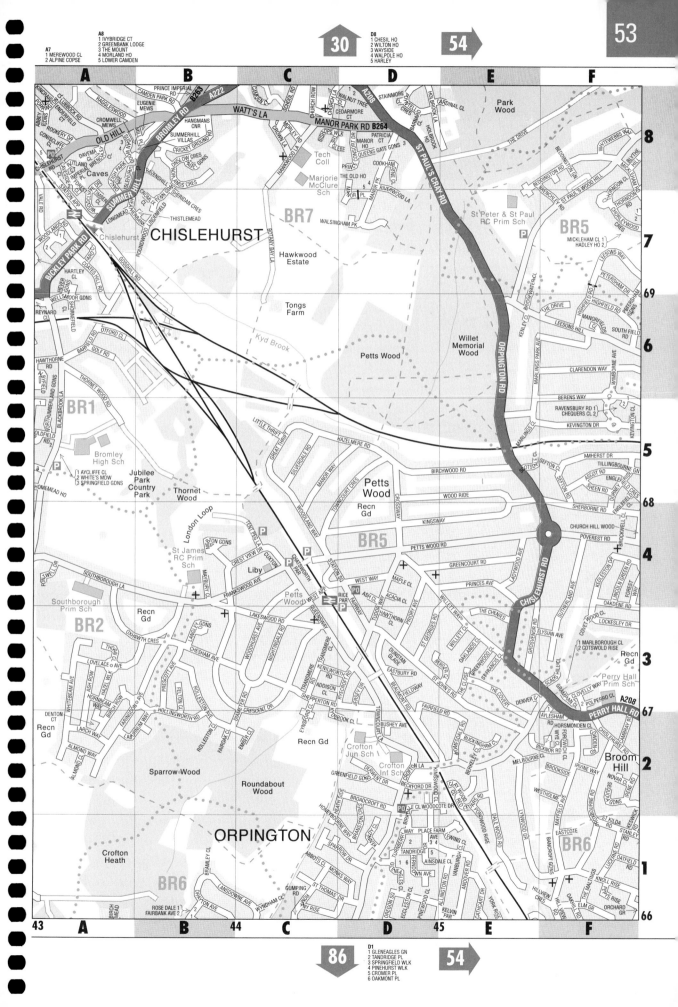

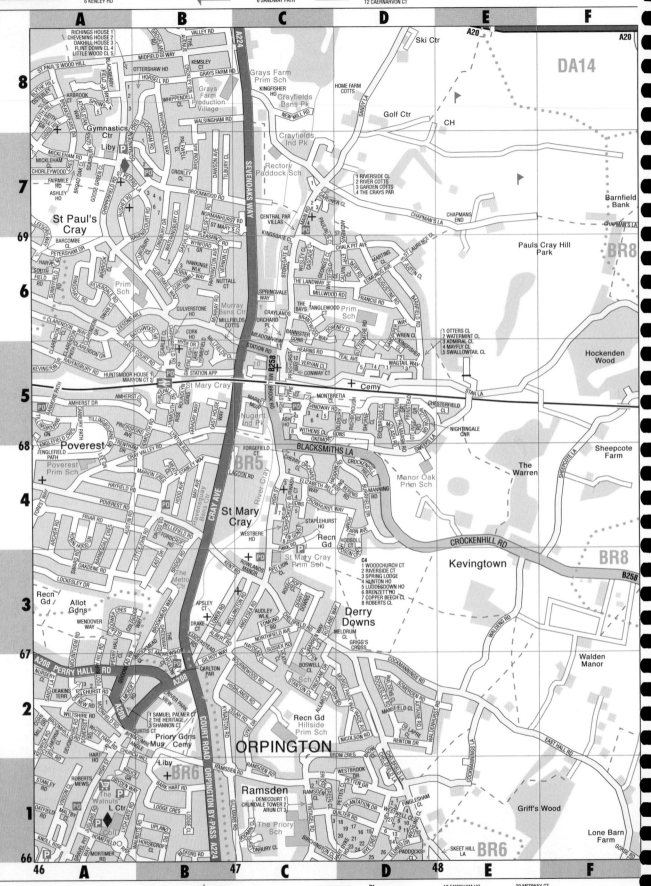

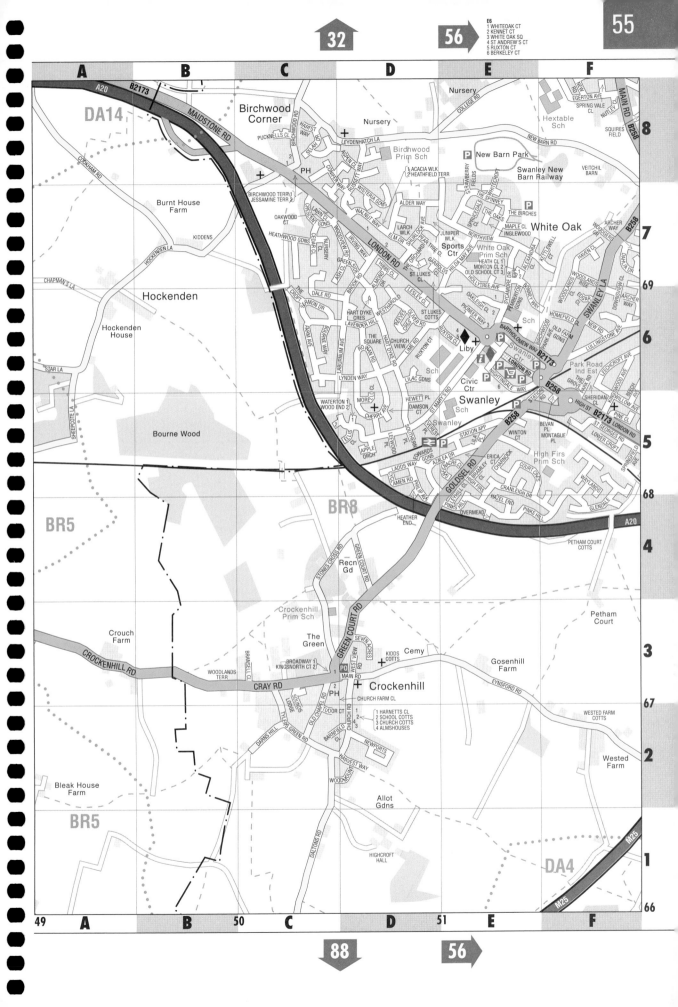

55
33

A B C D E F

8

MILLBRO
VICTORIA HILL RD
SQUIRES FIELD
B258
MAIN RD
St Paul's CE Prim Sch
HOGS ORCH
SCHOOL LA
HOTHAM CL
ANTHONYS LA
THE STAPLES
The Red Lion (PH)
ELM COTTS
Highlands Farm
HIGHLANDS HILL
SWANLEY VILLAGE RD
WOOD ST
SHIP LA
GILDENHILL RD
CHURCH RD
SHIP LA
Homefield Farm

Swanley Village
PARK LA
M25

7

SWANLEY LA
B258
FIVE WENTS
ARCHER WAY
Ram's Wood

69

LEECHCROFT AVE
BEECH AVE
BIRCHEN LA
Canada Heights
Downsview Prim Sch
THE ANNEX

6

HILLSIDE CT
WEST VIEW RD
HOLLY HILL
WILLOW AVE
ISOURVIEW CL
ROS
ABBOTTS CL
MANSE WAY
Parkwood Hall Sch
L Ctr
BUTTON ST
Farningham Wood (Nature Reserve)
P
P
CALFSTOCK LA

5

B2173
HIGH CROFT COTTS
SALISBURY AVE
MANSBURY WAY
MEAD
LONDON RD
BREWERS CL
PO
MANSE PAR
ROBINA CT
Broom Hill
BR8
DA4

68

MAYS CT
A20
M20
MARK WAY
WESTED
B2173
3
1
RADARD TERR
Hill Farm
FARNINGHAM HILL RD
The Folly

4

Moreton Ind Est
Pedham Place Est
A20
Teardrop Ctr
LONDON RD
OLD DARTFORD RD
M20

3

WESTED LA
LONDON RD
ELIZABETH PL
RABLUS PL
MAIN RD
DARTFORD RD
PO
P
A225
A20
HORTON WAY
COUNTY HILL
SOUTH HILL

67

Little Wested House
The Mill House
HIGH ST
Farningham
EYNSFORD RD
Fort Farningham (dis)
SPAREPENNY LA
SPAREPENNY LA
Darent Valley Path
OLIVER CRES
River Darent
A225
TILL
VALLEY VIEW TERR

2

Mast
CROCKENHILL LA

1

Eynsford Hill
Eynsford Hill
MILL HOUSE CL
OLD MILL CL
MILL LA
PRIORY LA
EYNSFORD RD
A225

66

52 A B 53 C D 54 E F

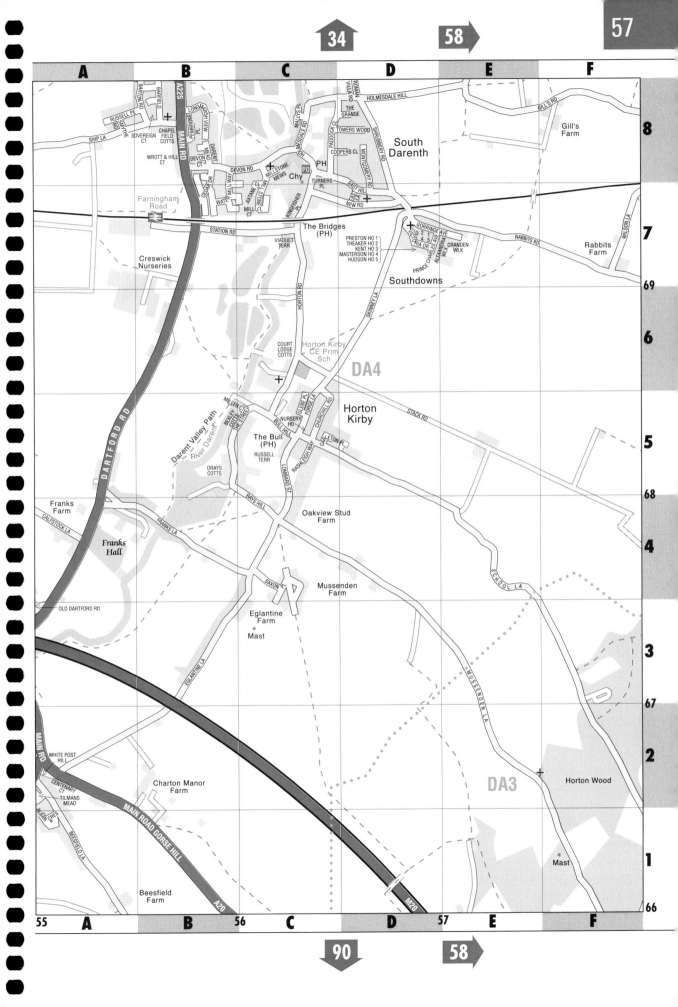

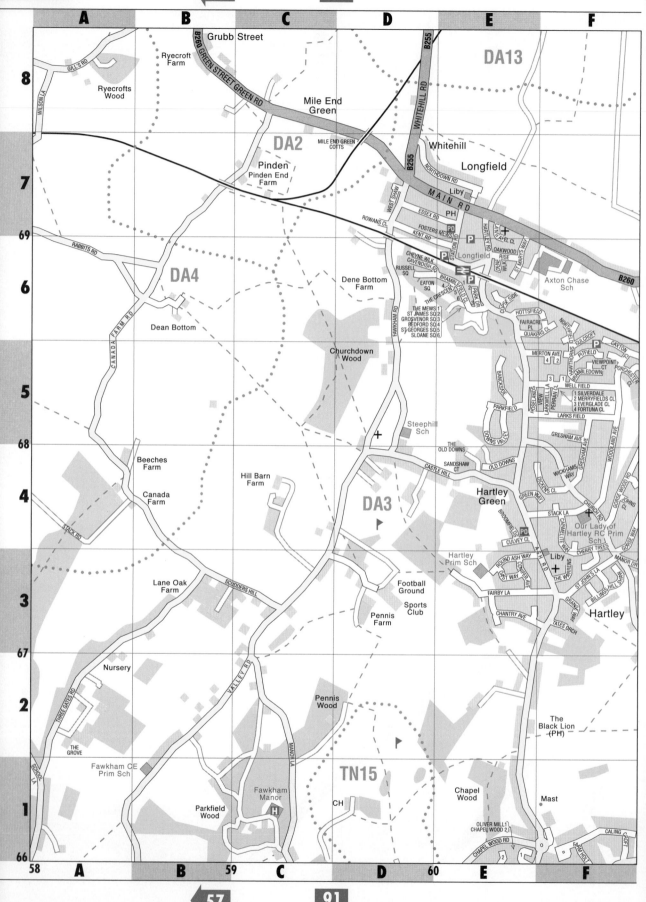

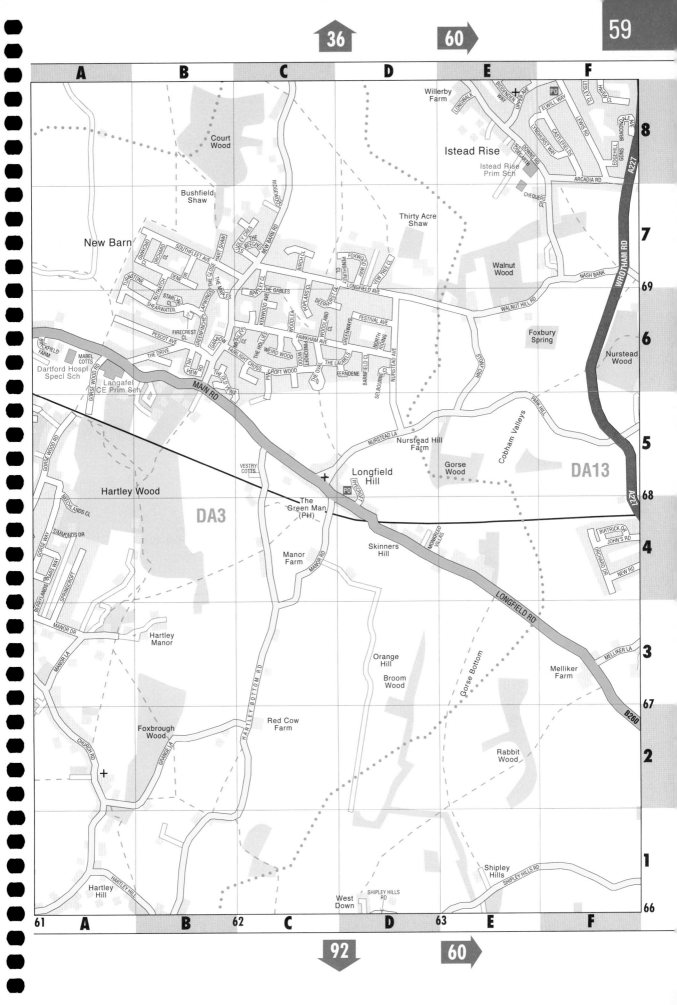

59
37

A B C D E F

A2

WROTHAM RD
A227

8

Huntondown Wood

Ifield Court

New Cottages

CHURCH RD

Henhurst

HENHURST HILL

HENHURST RD

Henhurst Dale

Winstead Hill

7

Dabbs Place Farm

Jeskyns Court

69

NASH ST

Nash Street

Cozendon Wood

Tollingtrough Green

Dabbs Place

JESKYNS RD

DA12

Owletts

BATTLE ST

SCOTLAND LA

6

Nurstead Court

The Park

Mill Hill

Wealdway

COPT HALL RD

ROUND ST

Jeskyns Farm

Cobham

Battle Street

CARSERS CT

THE STREET

P

NURSTEAD CHURCH LA

Round Street

Cobham College

5

WHITE POST LA

Lordscroft Shaw

THE BEECHES

SHAW

Sweep's Hole

+

68

Meopham

STATION RD

Sole Street

SALLOWS

MANOR RD

Danes Place

Gold Street

GOLD ST

4

JOHN'S RD
NEW RD
A227

HOOK GREEN CT

P

PO

EDMUND CL
NURSERY RD
FAIRVIEW GDNS

Meopham Station

ARBORFIELD

Blundells Shaw

Sole Street

MANOR CT

SCRATTON
FIELDS
SOLE ST
GREENLANDS

MAY PL

PO

The Railway Inn (PH)

The Cock Inn (PH)

HENLEY ST

Henley Street

HAY'S MEAD

3

PINE RISE

Hook Green

THE MEDLARS
THE TIPPINS

P

WROTHAM RD

THE RUSHETS

WALNUT TREE WAY

DENESWAY

POPLAR WLK

TRADESCANT DR

MULBERRY CL

NORWOOD LA

ASHWAY

LILAC PL

DORMERS DR

DA13

Camer Farm

CAMER RD

CAMER GDNS

CAMER ST

Camer

Reynold's Farm

67

MELLIKER LA

CAMDEN RD
CHINNERY CT

HUNTINGFIELD RD
STRAND
CARTERS HILL

+

P

GREEN LA

GREEN LANE

P

Camer Park Country Park

2

LONGFIELD RD
B260

Helen Allison Sch

Meopham Com Prim Sch

SCHOOL CL
CLIFE
PADDOCK

CAMER PARK RD

Henley Wood

Henley Down

1

+

Meopham Court

Bramble Hall Farm

Oakenden

OAKENDEN RD

DEAN RD

Luddesdown

+

66

SHIPLEY MILLS RD

THE OLD VICARAGE

A227

PO

THE STREET

FOXENDOWN LA

BRIMSTONE HILL

Luddesdown Court

64 A B 65 C D 66 E F

A B C D E F

8

Inn On
The Lake
(Hotel)

Puckle Hill

Brewers
Wood

Boysden
Shaw

BOWESDEN LA

Scalers
Hill House

THONG LA

SCOTLAND LA

Park
Pale

WATLING ST

A2

The Mount

West Park

Peggy Taylor's
Hill

7

Ashenbank
Wood

HALFPENCE LA

69

DA12

Cobham Hall
Sch

CH

Cobham
Hall

6

The Avenue

Cobham Park

Deer Park

PH

Cobham
Prim Sch

THE STREET

LAWRENCE DR

NEW COLLEGE
OF COBHAM

LODGE LA

Lodge
Farm

Mausoleum

William's
Hill

Norwood Grove

5

Cobhambury
Farm

Winterham
Hill

Lodge Wood

Nor Wood

68

BATT'S RD

COBHAMBURY RD

4

Shoulder of Mutton
Shaw

ME2

Lower
Bush

BUSH RD

Bush Farm
House

3

Cobhambury
Wood

WARREN RD

Warren
House

UPPER BUSH RD

67

HENLEY ST

DA13

LUDDESDOWN RD

PIGDEAN RD

Bowman's
Hill

Red
Wood

Upper
Bush

2

Golden
Lion
(PH)

Brookers
Farm

Cutter
Ridge

BUCKLAND RD

Lower
Luddesdown

Longbottom
Wood

North Downs Way

Rectory

CUTTER RIDGE RD

Little Red
Wood

Stonereed
Shaw

North
Wood

Dean
Farm

1

Court
Lodge

Bush
Valley

66

67 A B 68 C D 69 E F

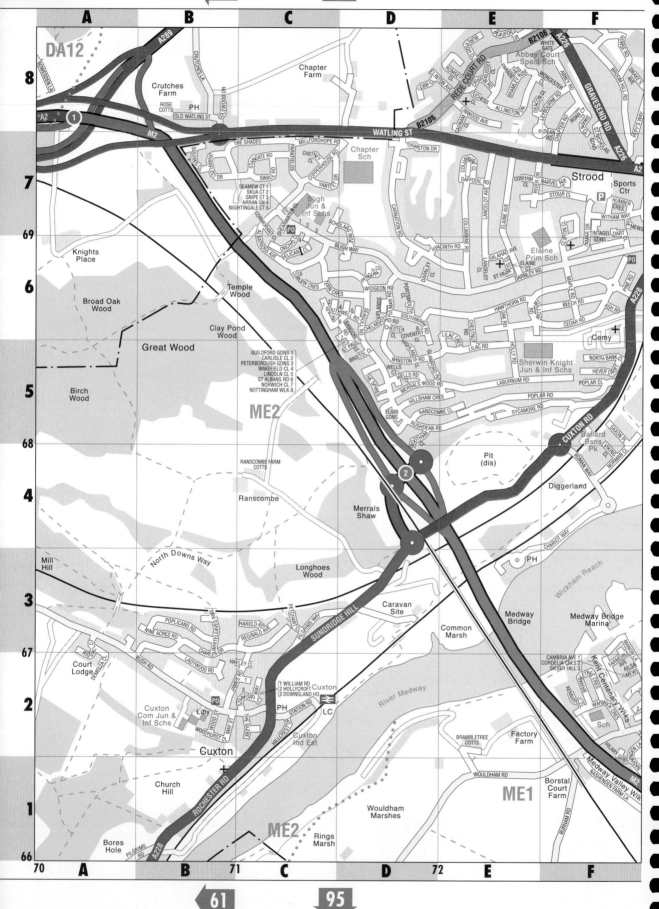

39

A   B   C   D   E   F

DA12

8

Crutches
Farm

ROSE
COTTS

PH

Chapter
Farm

CRUTCHES LA

GLEWOOD DR

OLD WATLING ST

A289

A2

M2

Chapter
Sch

THE SHADES

STANGATE RD

SWARTH RD

SQUIRES GT

SMARR FLY DR

PARKFIELDS

MILLFORDHOPE RD

COPPERHOUSE RD

YANTLET DR

CHETNEY
CL

WATLING ST   B2108

THURSTON DR

Abbey Court
Specl Sch

WHITE
GATE

B2108   A226

GRAVESEND RD

BEAUFORT

BIRCH RD

CLINTON AVE

ROMSEY
CL

COBB CL

LINTON AVE

PARADE
THE

BRAMBLE RISE

DUCHESS
CL

CADLAM
CL

ALLINGTON
AVE

LINWOOD AVE

WORCESTER
CL

ABBEY RD

ROARI CL

LE BOURNE RD

DEACON
CL

CHESTER RD

ST NICHOLAS
GDNS

DEAN
RD

CHAPTER RD

Strood

Sports
Ctr

A226

A2

7

SEAMEW CT 1
SKUA CT 2
SNIPE CT 3
ARRAN GN 4
NIGHTINGALE CT 5

SHEARWATER CL

Bligh
Jun &
Inf Schs

CORMORANT CL

ORCHID CL

SCHOLARS RISE

CARNATION RD

DAFFODIL RD

COLUMBINE CL

HYACINTH RD

COBHAM
CL

RIVER DR

STOUR CL

HARVEL AVE

HUMBER
CRES

WITHAM WAY

MEWS

TINTAGEL
GDNS

DART
CL

PO

P

69

ALBATROSS AVE

PELICAN CL

BLIGH WAY

PENGUIN CL

WIDGEON RD

PORTSMOUTH RD

DARNLEY
CL

LANCELOT AVE

ELAINE AVE

COLUMBINE RD

GALAHAD AVE

LANCELOT
RD

ST FRAN
CL

ELAINE
CL

DARNLEY RD

Elaine
Prim Sch

MAPLE RD

PINE RD

A228

PO

6

Knights
Place

Broad Oak
Wood

Temple
Wood

Clay Pond
Wood

CURLEW CRES

TERN CRES

SOUTHWELL RD

CHELMSFORD RD

BANGOR RD

ST PAUL'S

SOUTHWARK RD

FULMAR RD

CHESTER
CL

COVENTRY RD

HIGHLANDS

LILAC CRES

HAWTHORN RD

CHESTNUT RD

CEDAR RD

BEECH RD

HOLLY RD

ASH RD

LILAC RD

Cemy

5

Birch
Wood

Great Wood

ME2

GUILDFORD GDNS 1
CARLISLE CL 2
PETERBOROUGH GDNS 3
WAKEFIELD CL 4
LINCOLN CL 5
ST ALBANS RD 6
NORWICH CL 7
NOTTINGHAM WLK 8

BRISTOL CL

THE SPIRES

WINSTON RD

WELLS
CL

WELLS RD

MERRALS WOOD RD

HILLSHAW CRES

LABURNUM RD

POPLAR RD

SYCAMORE RD

Sherwin Knight
Jun & Inf Schs

NORTH BANK

HEVER CRES

POPLAR CL

68

RANSCOMBE FARM
COTTS

ELGIN
GDNS

RUSHDEAN RD

RANSCOMBE CL

BOTHAM

CUXTON RD

Ballard
Bsns
Pk

SAXON PL

VIKING CL

ROMAN WAY

NORMAN CL

4

Ranscombe

②

Pit
(dis)

Diggerland

CHARIOT WAY

3

Mill
Hill

North Downs Way

Longhoes
Wood

Merrals
Shaw

Caravan
Site

SUNDRIDGE HILL

Common
Marsh

Medway
Bridge

PH

Medway Bridge
Marina

Wickham Reach

67

Court
Lodge

RIGS CL

DEMELZA CL

BUSH RD

POPLICANS RD

NINE ACRES RD

CHARLES DR

WHITELEAVES RISE

PETCHART CL

PILGRIMS WAY

HAROLD RD

REGINALD AVE

LADYWOOD RD

JAMES RD

HAYLEY CL

STANFORD

1 WILLIAM RD
2 HOLLYCROFT
3 DOWNSLAND HO

Cuxton

CAMBRIA AVE 1
CORDELIA CRES 2
SILVER HILL 3

Kent Cenenary Wks

MANOR LA

FARMDALE
AVE

AILSA
MEWS

LETTR
CRES

WARWICK CRES

KENDAL RD

HILARY GRDS

Sch

2

Cuxton
Com Jun &
Inf Schs

Liby

PO

MAY ST

WOOD ST

THE GLEBE

WOODHURST CL

STATION RD

HILL CRES

PH

LC

River Medway

Cuxton
Ind Est

BRAMBLETREE
COTTS

Factory
Farm

Borstal
Court
Farm

ME1

BURHAM RD

NASHENDEN FARM LA

Medway Valley Wlk

M2

1

Cuxton

Church
Hill

ROCHESTER RD

A228

Bores
Hole

PILGRIMS RD

Wouldham
Marshes

WOULDHAM RD

Rings
Marsh

ME2

66

A7
1 WYATT HO
2 HILLSIDE CT
3 WARBLERS CL

B7
1 NEWARK CT
2 AVELING CT
3 FRIARY PREC
4 GROVE CT

B8
1 ALEXANDER CT
2 EPPE CL
3 FLORENCE ST
4 ARCHWAY CT
5 SANDRA CT
6 ST MICHAEL'S CT

C8
1 BILL STREET RD
2 MAYFAIR
3 CHRISTIAN CT
4 PEMBERTON SQ
5 EVELYN HO

D4
1 ROSEMARY CT
2 YEWTREE HO
3 HUXLEY CT
4 NEW COVENANT PL
5 FIVE BELLS LA
6 ROBIN CT

40   64

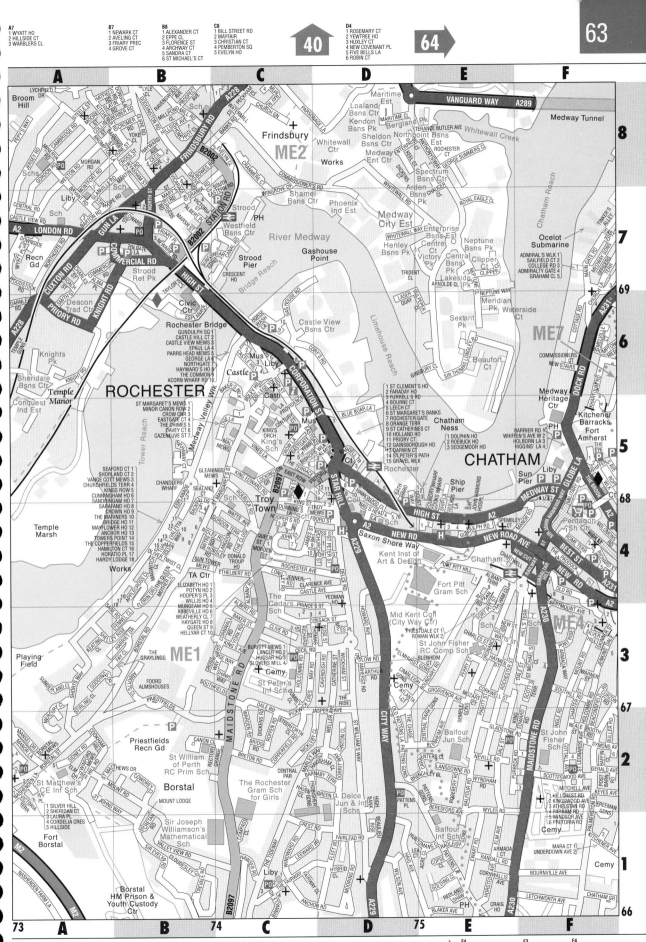

73   74   96   64   75

C1
1 BAKENHAM HO
2 LEAKE HO
3 TRANSOM HO
4 SPINNAKER CT

E4
1 BINGLEY RD
2 ST BARTHOLOMEW'S TERR
3 HOSPITAL LA
4 ST BARTHOLOMEW'S LA
5 MEDWAY HEIGHTS
6 HAMOND HILL
7 CRESSEY RD
8 LUMSDEN TERR
9 ORDNANCE TERR

F3
1 ORCHARD VILLAS
2 CLAREMONT WAY
3 MOUNT VIEW CT
4 SILVER HILL GDNS
5 CORONATION FLATS
6 RIVER VIEW CL
7 SAUNDERS ST

F4
1 CAMBRIDGE TERR
2 MEETING HOUSE LA
3 CLOVER ST
4 MILLWOOD CT
5 JAMES ST
6 COPPERFIELD HO
7 SPRINGFIELD TERR
8 BERKELEY MOUNT
9 LANSDOWNE CT

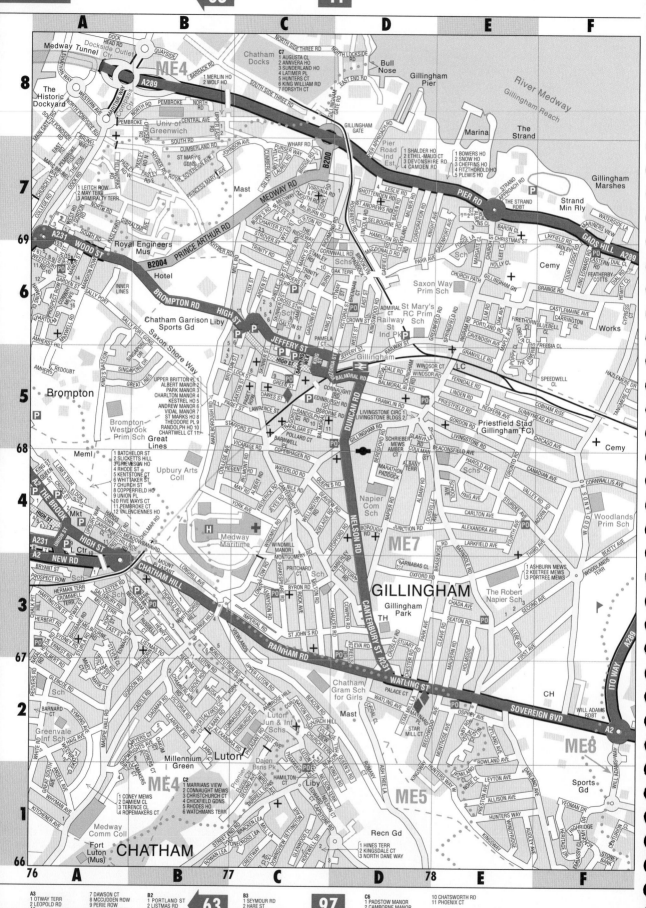

A3
1 OTWAY TERR
2 LEOPOLD RD

A6
1 VICTORY MANOR
2 TEMERAIRE MANOR
3 BARFLEUR MANOR
4 MIDDLE ST
5 CAMPERDOWN MANOR
6 RIVER ST

7 DAWSON CT
8 MCCUDDEN ROW
9 PERIE ROW
10 PLEASANT ROW
11 LENDRIM CT
12 MELVILLE CT
13 FLAXMANS CT
14 MANOR HO
15 ESMONDE HO
16 CONWAY HALL

B2
1 PORTLAND ST
2 LISTMAS CT
3 BRIGHT RD
4 COBDEN RD
5 SAILMAKERS CT
6 EVORG HO
7 CAULKERS HO
8 THE ENDEAVOUR FOYER

B3
1 SEYMOUR RD
2 HARE ST
3 SHORT ST
4 PICCADILLY APARTMENTS
5 WEALDEN CT
6 OCELOT CT
7 LEONARD RD
8 CONSTITUTION HILL

C6
1 PADSTOW MANOR
2 CAMBORNE MANOR
3 REDRUTH MANOR
4 PENRYN MANOR
5 AUSTELL MANOR
6 TINTAGEL MANOR
7 GRAND CT
8 DEANE CT
9 WILL ADAMS CT

10 CHATSWORTH RD
11 PHOENIX CT

C2
1 MARRIANS VIEW
2 CONNAUGHT MEWS
3 CHRISTCHURCH CT
4 CHICKFIELD GDNS
5 RHODES HO
6 WATCHMANS TERR

C7
1 AUGUSTA CL
2 ANNVERA HO
3 SUNDERLAND HO
4 LATIMER PL
5 HUNTERS CT
6 KING WILLIAM RD
7 FORSYTH CT

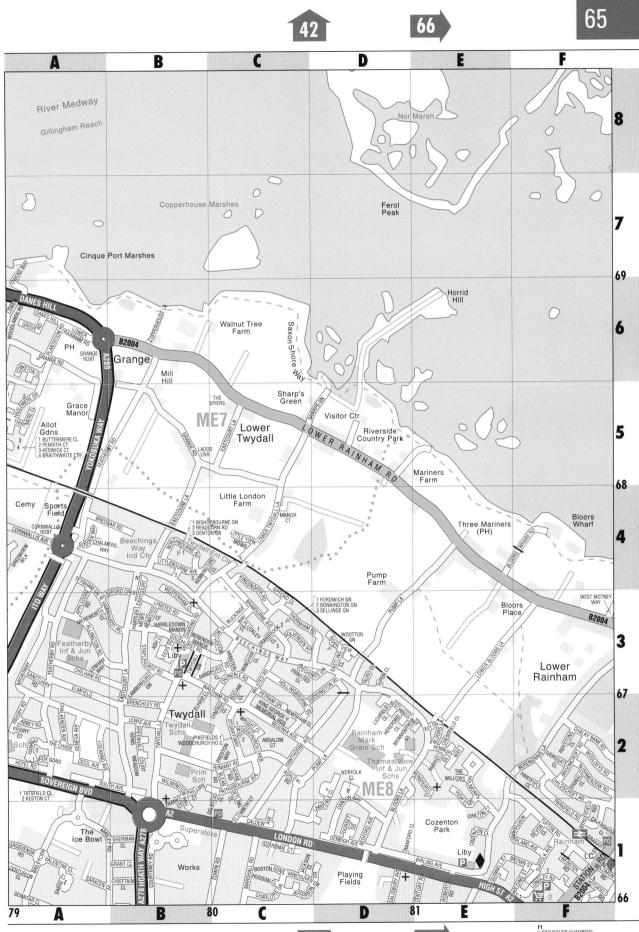

A B C D E F

8
7
69
6
5
68
4
3
67
2
1
66

River Medway
Gillingham Reach

Nor Marsh

Copperhouse Marshes

Ferol Peak

Cinque Port Marshes

Horrid Hill

DANES HILL
B2004
Grange
Walnut Tree Farm
Saxon Shore Way
PH
GRANGE RDBT
Mill Hill
THE SPIERS
Sharp's Green
Grace Manor
ME7
Lower Twydall
Sharps Gn
Visitor Ctr
Riverside Country Park
Allot Gdns
1 BUTTERMERE CL
2 PENRITH CT
3 KESWICK CT
4 BRAITHWAITE CT
LADDS CNR
LOWER RAINHAM RD
Mariners Farm

Cemy
Sports Field
CORNWALLIS RDBT
Little London Farm
1 BISHOPBOURNE GN
2 HEADGORN RD
3 DENTON GN
MANOR CT
LITTLE YORK MDWS
Three Mariners (PH)
Bloors Wharf
BLOORS WHARF RD

Beechings Way Ind Ctr
Twydall Ent Ctr
LITTLEBOURNE AVE
Pump Farm
Bloors Place
WEST MOTNEY WAY
B2004

Featherby Inf & Jun Schs
KINGSNORTH GN
1 FORDWICH GN
2 BONNINGTON GN
3 SELLINGE GN
WOOTTON GN
RIVER VIEW
Lower Rainham
LOWER BLOORS LA
Liby
P
PO
Twydall
BEECHINGS WAY
67
Twydall Schs
PIKEFIELDS 1
WOODCHURCH HO 2
KING GEORGE V MEMORIAL HOS
Rainham Mark Gram Sch
Prim Sch
Thames View Inf & Jun Schs
ME8
1 TATSFIELD CL
2 KESTON CT
The Ice Bowl
SOVEREIGN BVD
A2
Superstore
LONDON RD
Norfolk CL
Cozenton Park
Liby
P
Rainham
Works
HIGH ST A2
Playing Fields
B2004
LC

F1
1 CREVEQUER CHAMBERS
2 Rainham Sh Ctr
3 GRESHAM CL
4 HARRISON CT
5 MAPLINS CL
6 SIGNAL CT
7 SUFFOLK CT

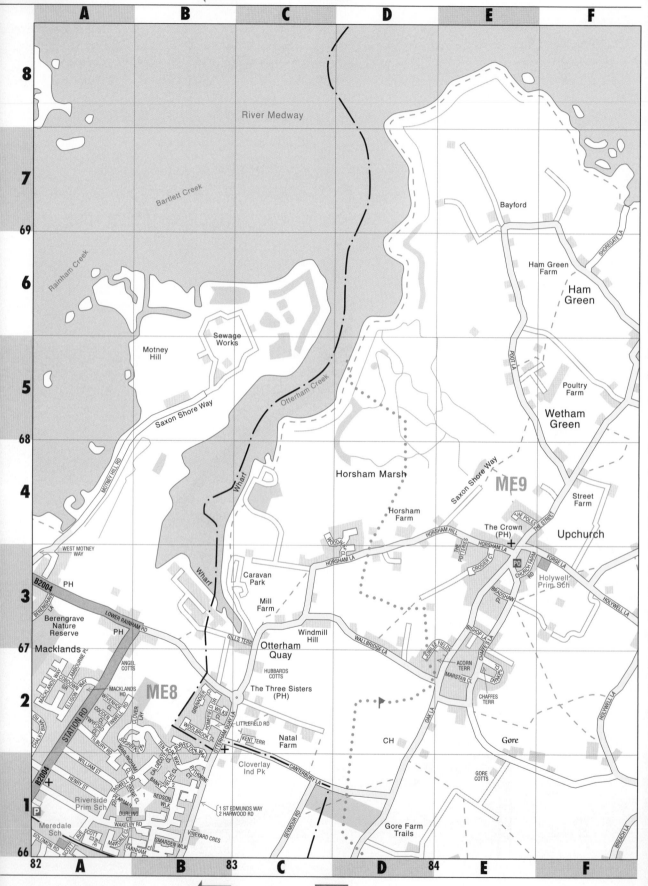

A B C D E F

8

River Medway

7

Bartlett Creek

69

Rainham Creek

6

Ham Green
Farm

Bayford

Ham
Green

Motney
Hill

Sewage
Works

Poultry
Farm

Wetham
Green

5

Otterham Creek

Saxon Shore Way

68

Horsham Marsh

Saxon Shore Way

ME9

4

Horsham
Farm

Street
Farm

Wharf

THE POLES

THE STREET

The Crown
(PH)

Upchurch

West Motney
Way

Caravan
Park

WOODRUFF CL

HORSHAM LA

HORSHAM HILL

THE POTTERIES

CROSIER CT

HORSHAM LA

PO

CHURCH FARM RD

FORGE LA

Holywell
Prim. Sch

HOLYWELL LA

3

B2004

PH

LOWER RAINHAM RD

Mill
Farm

Windmill
Hill

WALLBRIDGE LA

BRADSHAW CL

BISHOP LA

CHAFFES LA

HOLYWELL LA

BERENGRAVE LA

Berengrave
Nature
Reserve

PH

GILLS TERR

Otterham
Quay

JUBILEE FIELDS

67

Macklands

ANGEL
COTTS

HUBBARDS
COTTS

ACORN
TERR

10 DYKES

MARSTAN CL

2

MACKLANDS WAY

COBDOWN WAY

LAMBOURNE PL

ELLSON GR

WIVENHOE RD

FINNELL RD

CLOVER LA

MACKLANDS
HO

GREENACRE

HOMEFIELD

WILKS

OTTERHAM QUAY LA

ME8

The Three Sisters
(PH)

CHAFFES
TERR

Gore

STATION RD

GOODEN GL

WYFORD

TILBURY RD

WOOLBROOK CL

LITTLEFIELD RD

KENT TERR

Natal
Farm

CH

OAK LA

GORE
COTTS

CHALKY BK RD

WILLIAM ST

HENRY ST

WARLINGHAM RD

SKOREKE LA

TASWELL RD

CALDECOTT CL

BANKY FIELDS

B. THORNE CT

BURSTOCK WAY

TEN ACRE WAY

Cloverlay
Ind Pk

CANTERBURY LA

SEYMOUR RD

Gore Farm
Trails

1

B2004

P

Riverside
Prim Sch

Meredale
Sch

SOLOMON RD

SCOTT AVE

SCOTT CL

PEARMAN
CL

DURLING
CT

WAKELEY RD

BEDSON
WLK

FARNHAM

SMARDEN WLK

VINEYARD CRES

1 ST EDMUNDS WAY
2 HARWOOD RD

66

A B C D E F

8
7
69
6
5
68
4
3
67
2
1
66

Millfordhope Creek

Greenborough Marshes

Slaughterhouse Point

Stangate Creek

The Shade

Millfordhope Marsh

Twinney Creek

Barksore Marshes

River Medway

Halstow Creek

Funton Creek

Callows House

Twinney Wharf

Twinney Acre

Funton Brickworks

FROG FARM COTTS

Funton

Frog Farm

Saxon Shore Way

Great Barksore Farm

Saxon Shore Way

Sewage Works

GREENWAYS

CHURCH PATH

Stray Farm

Little Barksore

Tiptree Hill

BELL COTTS

PO

PH

THE CRESCENT

WESTMOR

VICARAGE COTTS

Lower Halstow

BASSER HILL

Holywell

Green Farm

BURNTNICK DR

SCHOOL LA

CUMBERLAND DR

VICARAGE LA

ME9

Tiptree

SEA VIEW COTTS

Elm Farm

WESTFIELD COTTS

Lower Halstow Prim Sch

Callum Hill

STICKFAST LA

BREACH LA

The Laurels

WARDWELL LA

Boxted Farm

BOXTED LA

HIGH OAK HILL

BELMONT AVE

Hawes Wood

Great Norwood

← 67
↑ 45

A | B | C | D | E | F

8

Chetney Hill

The Shade

Horse Reach

Ferry Marshes

7

Furton Reach

Saxon Shore Way

Saxon Shore Way

69

River Medway

Chetney Cottages

Marshbank

Old Ferry Rd

Ridham Fleet

A249

6

Bedlams Bottom

Raspberry Hill

Willow Cottages

Willow Bank Ind Est

RASPBERRY HILL LA

SHEPPEY WAY

5

Raspberry Hill Park

Saxon Shore Way

68

Saxon Shore Way

SANDERLING WAY

Iwade Com Prim Sch

Wool-Pack Inn

THE STREET

CHURCH MEWS

4

ME9

ELM TREE AVE

STANGATE DR

MALLARD

MEADOW

EVERGREEN CL

FANS LA

UPPER FANS LA

SHERRCK CRES

SEW NO

CHETNEY CL

WICK

LINKWAY

SPRINGVALE

PO

WOODPECKER DR

TURNSTONE CL

SCHOOL LA

Iwade

MEADOW RISE

SHE

ERSTONE

FERRY RD

HELEN THOMPSON CL

KINGFISHER CL

3

Moat Farm Cottages

Culnell's Cottages

COLESHALL COTTS

MANSFIELD DR

COLSON DR

MINSTER

ALLE WAY

Coleshall Farm

TEA WAY

PINTAIL CT

Orchard Farm

Coleshall

67

2

Culnells

FEATHERBED LA

B2005

GROVEHURST RD

LC

ME10

Road under construction

Corbiere

SHEPPEY WAY

Great Grovehurst Farm

1 OSTEND CT
2 BRUGES CT
3 MELLOR ROW

The Kemsley Arms (PH)

1

STICKFAST LA

Cambray Farm

Pheasants Farm

Kemsley

PO

DANES MEADOW CL

MONS CT

FLANDERS CL

RIDHAM AVE

COLDHARBOUR LA

LIEGE CL

CASTLE ROUGH

GLOVER CL

PASSONAGE LA

Cambray Cottages

LAYFIELD COTTS

WOODSDALE COTTS

A249

Kemsley

SANDSTONE DR

B2005

BRAMBLEFIELD LA

COLEMAN DR

CREATION WAY

66

88 | A | B | 89 | C | D | 90 | E | F

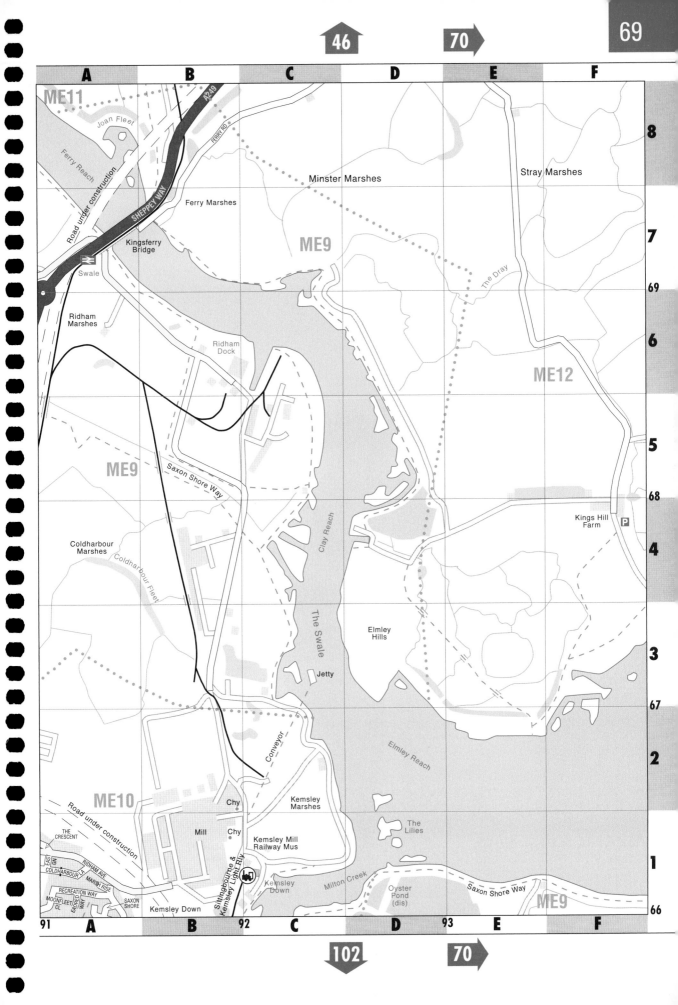

ME11

Joan Fleet

Ferry Reach

Road under construction

SHEPPEY WAY

A249

FERRY RD

Ferry Marshes

Minster Marshes

Stray Marshes

ME9

Kingsferry Bridge

The Dray

Swale

Ridham Marshes

Ridham Dock

ME12

ME9

Saxon Shore Way

Coldharbour Marshes

Coldharbour Fleet

Clay Reach

Kings Hill Farm

Elmley Hills

The Swale

Jetty

Elmley Reach

Conveyor

ME10

Road under construction

THE CRESCENT

RIDHAM AVE

MARSH RISE

COLDHARBOUR LA

RECREATION WAY

MOONFLEET WAY

EADING WAY

SAXON SHORE

EAST GIN

CL

Mill

Chy

Chy

Kemsley Marshes

Kemsley Mill Railway Mus

Kemsley Down

Sittingbourne & Kemsley Light Rly

The Lilies

Milton Creek

Oyster Pond (dis)

Saxon Shore Way

ME9

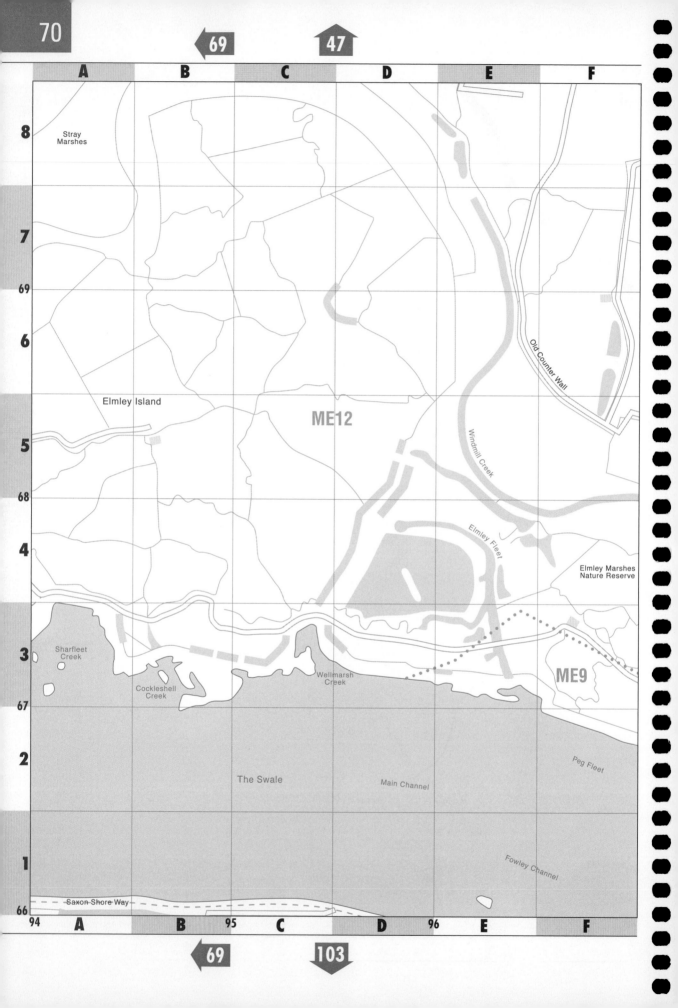

A B C D E F

8

7

69

6

Stray
Marshes

Elmley Island

ME12

Old Counter Wall

Windmill Creek

5

68

Elmley Fleet

4

Elmley Marshes
Nature Reserve

Sharfleet
Creek

3

67

Cockleshell
Creek

Wellmarsh
Creek

ME9

2

The Swale

Main Channel

Peg Fleet

1

66

Saxon Shore Way

Fowley Channel

94 A B 95 C D 96 E F

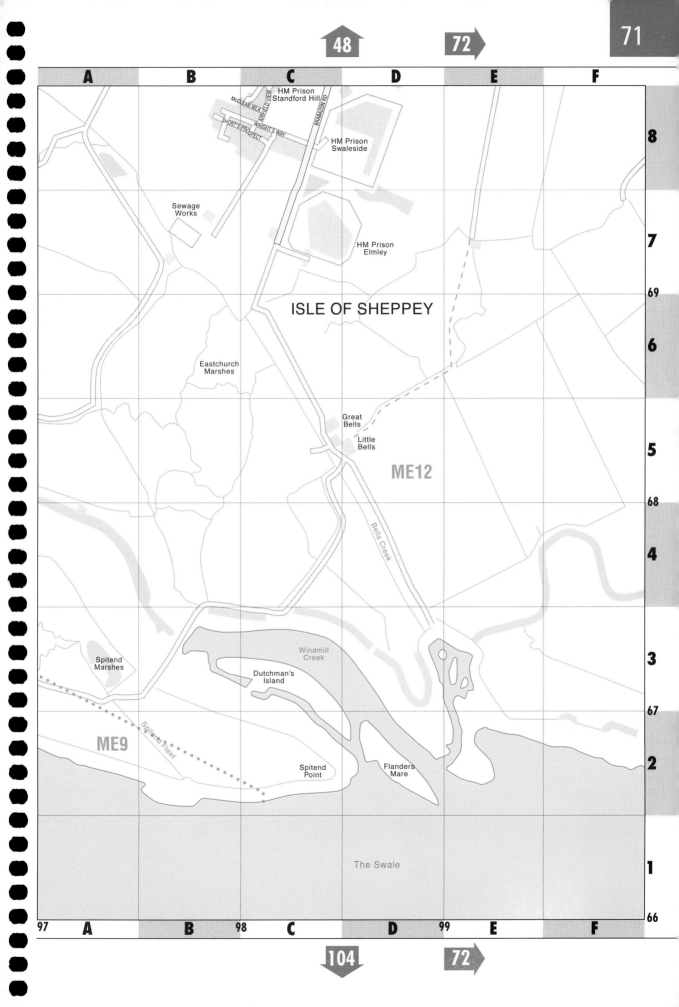

71
49

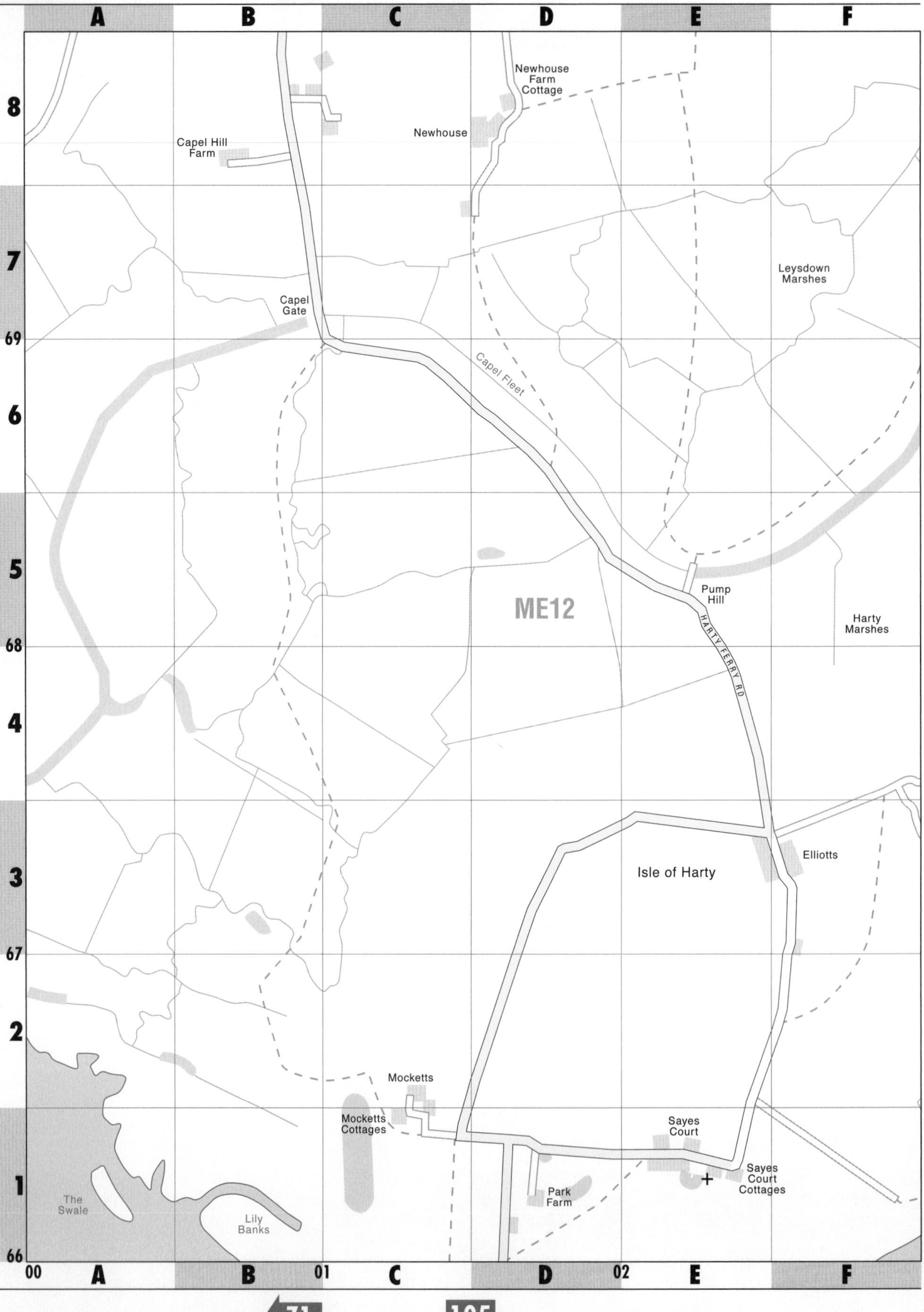

| | A | B | C | D | E | F |

8

7

69

6

5

68

4

3

67

2

1

66

Capel Hill
Farm

Newhouse
Farm
Cottage

Newhouse

Leysdown
Marshes

Capel
Gate

Capel Fleet

ME12

Pump
Hill

Harty
Marshes

HARTY FERRY RD

Isle of Harty

Elliotts

Mocketts

Mocketts
Cottages

Sayes
Court

Sayes
Court
Cottages

Park
Farm

The
Swale

Lily
Banks

00 | A | B | 01 | C | D | 02 | E | F

71
105

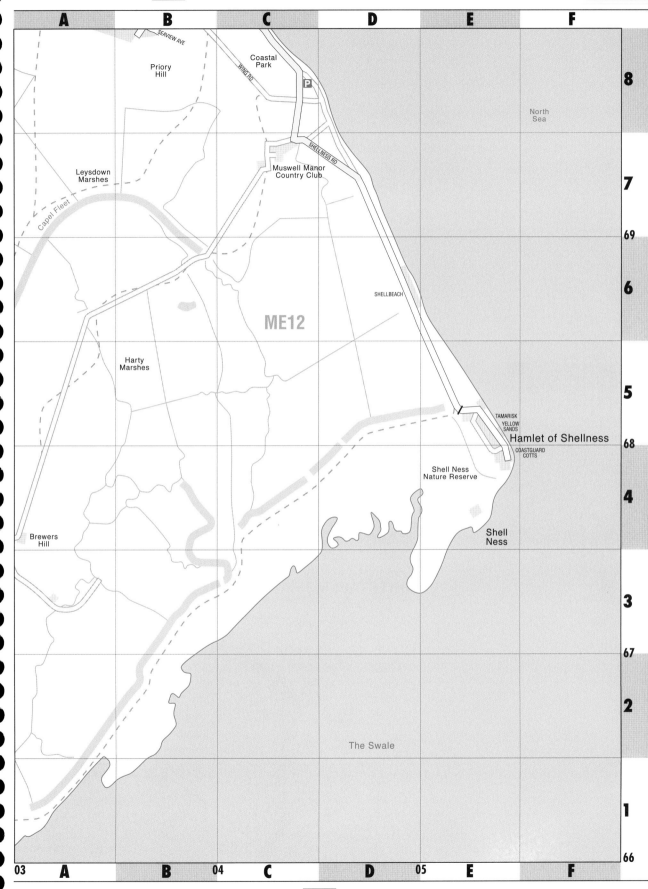

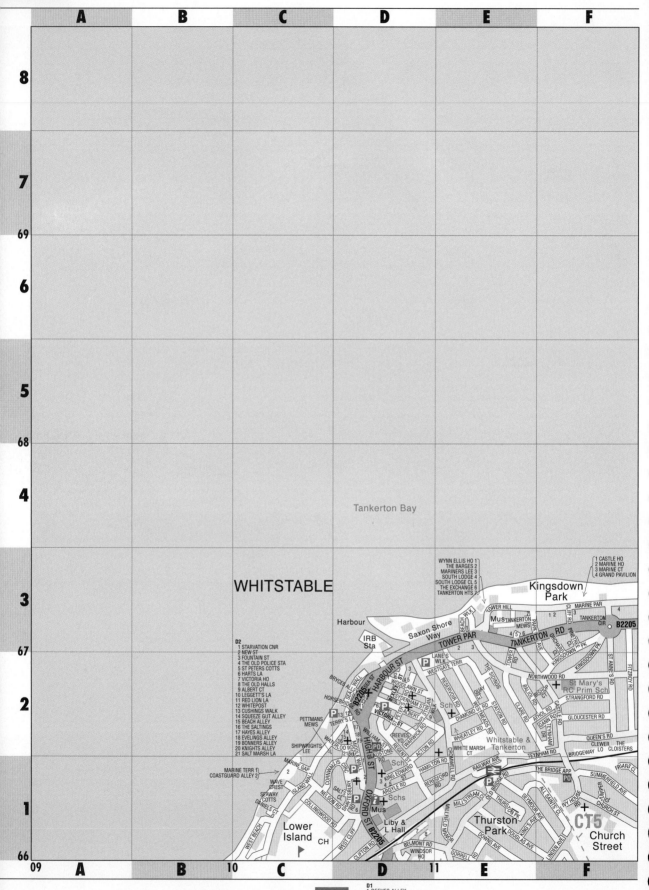

WHITSTABLE

Tankerton Bay

D2
1 STARVATION CNR
2 NEW ST
3 FOUNTAIN ST
4 THE OLD POLICE STA
5 ST PETERS COTTS
6 HARTS LA
7 VICTORIA HO
8 THE OLD HALLS
9 ALBERT CT
10 LEGGETT'S LA
11 RED LION LA
12 WHITEPOST
13 CUSHINGS WALK
14 SQUEEZE GUT ALLEY
15 BEACH ALLEY
16 THE SALTINGS
17 HAYES ALLEY
18 EVELINGS ALLEY
19 BONNERS ALLEY
20 KNIGHTS ALLEY
21 SALT MARSH LA

D1
1 REEVES ALLEY
2 KEMP ALLEY
3 SKINNER'S ALLEY
4 OYSTER MEWS
5 OXFORD CL
6 OXFORD MANS
7 THE OLD COAL YD
8 BELMONT YD

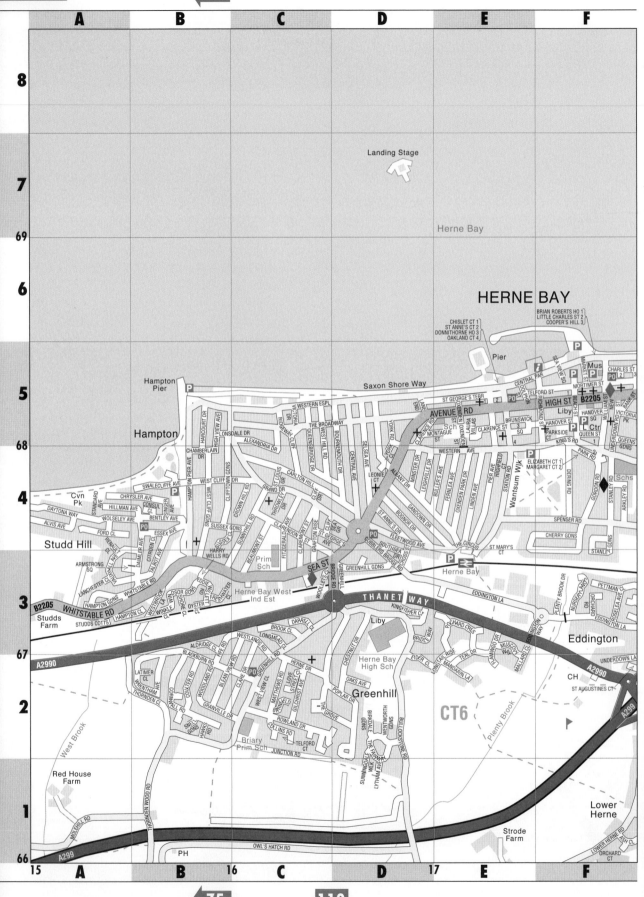

75

A B C D E F

8

7

69

6

HERNE BAY

5

68

4

Studd Hill

67

3

2

CT6

1

66

15 A B 16 C D 17 E F

Landing Stage

Herne Bay

CHISLET CT 1
ST ANNE'S CT 2
DONNITHORNE HO 3
OAKLAND CT 4

BRIAN ROBERTS HO 1
LITTLE CHARLES ST 2
COOPER'S HILL 3

Pier

Hampton Pier

Hampton

Saxon Shore Way

AVENUE RD

HIGH ST

B2205

Liby

Western Espl

Victoria

Ridgeway Cliff

West Hill Rd

Queensbridge Dr

Bournemouth Dr

Central Ave

ST GEORGE'S TERR

CENTRAL PDN

Telford St

RICHMOND ST

Charles St

PO

Mus

Market St

Mortimer St

William St

Victoria Pk

Harcourt Dr

High View Ave

Lonsdale Dr

Alexandria Dr

Selsea Ave

York Rd

Clarence St

Montague St

Brunswick Sq

Hanover St

Hanover St

King's Rd

Queen St

L Ctr

Parkside

Underdown Rd

Queens Gdns

Chamberlain Dr

Swalecliffe Ave

West Cliff Gdns

Clifftown Gdns

Crown Hill

Grand Dr

Carlton Hill

Cliff Dr

Minster Dr

Leighville Dr

Sandown Dr

Western Ave

Pier Ave

Highfield

Station Rd

Wantsum Wlk

Elizabeth Ct 1
Margaret Ct 2

Park Rd

Dering Rd

Gordon Rd

Stanley Rd

Arkley Rd

Schs

Cvn Pk

Chrysler Ave

Hillman Ave

Wolseley Ave

Consul Cl

Bentley Ave

Essex Ave

PO

Sussex Gdns

Sunnyhill Rd

Clarendon St

Fitzgerald

Claremont St

Grafton Rise

Cliff Ave

St George's

Albany Dr

St Anne's Dr

Fleetwood Ave

Bognor Dr

Oxenden Park Dr

Fernlea Ave

Linden Ave

Southsea Dr

Cobblers Bridge Rd

The Circus

St Mary's Ct

Cherry Gdns

Spenser Rd

Stanley

Daytona Way

Alvis Ave

Ford Cl

Renault Cl

Citroen Cl

Damler Ave

Talbot Ave

Whitstable Rd

Beaumont St

Prim Sch

Harry Wells Rd

Eddie

Windsor Gdns

Freshwater Cl

Oyster Cl

SEA ST

Bridge Rd

Greenhill Gdns

Woollets Cl

Herne Bay West Ind Est

THANET WAY

Herne Bay

Eddington La

Plenty Brook Dr

Nursery La

Orchard

Eddington

Orchard

Rosella Ave

Pettman Cl

UNDERDOWN LA

A2990

CH

ST AUGUSTINES CT

A299

Lower Herne

Armstrong Sq

Lanchester Cl

Hampton Gdns

B2205 WHITSTABLE RD

Studds Farm

STUDDS COTTS

Hampton Cl

Winkle Cl

Westbrook

Aldridge Cl

Kingfisher Ct

Bridle Way

Orchard Cres

Teal Dr

Mandarin La

Mallard Cl

Longmead

Darrel Cl

Brook Cl

Westlands

Fife Rd

Blackburn Rd

Greenhill Rd

Herne Dr

Chestnut Dr

Eider Cl

Curlew Rise

Lammoor Dr

Muscovy Way

Eddington Way

Red House Farm

Molehill Rd

Thornden Wood Rd

Latimer Cl

Wrentham Ave

Thornden Cl

Cornwall Ave

Coxater Rd

Woodland Rd

Blean Dr

Clare Dr

PO

West View Rd

Matthews Rd

Lloyd St

Greenfield Ave

Gilchrist Rd

Herne Bay High Sch

Oaks Ave

Poplar Dr

Liby

Greenhill

Snell Gdns

Hawks Rd

Granville Dr

Rowland Dr

Collins Rd

The Grove

Telford Ct

Junction Rd

Birngale Gdns

Sunningdale Gdns

Lytham Gdns

Bullockstone Rd

Briary Prim Sch

West Brook

Strode Farm

OWL'S HATCH RD

PH

LOWER HERNE RD

ORCHARD CT

A2990

A299

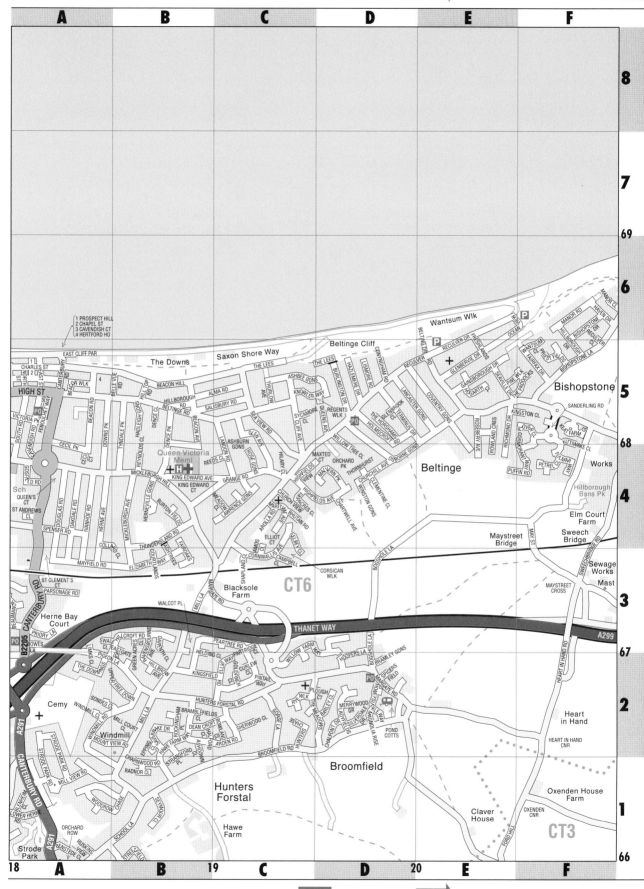

77

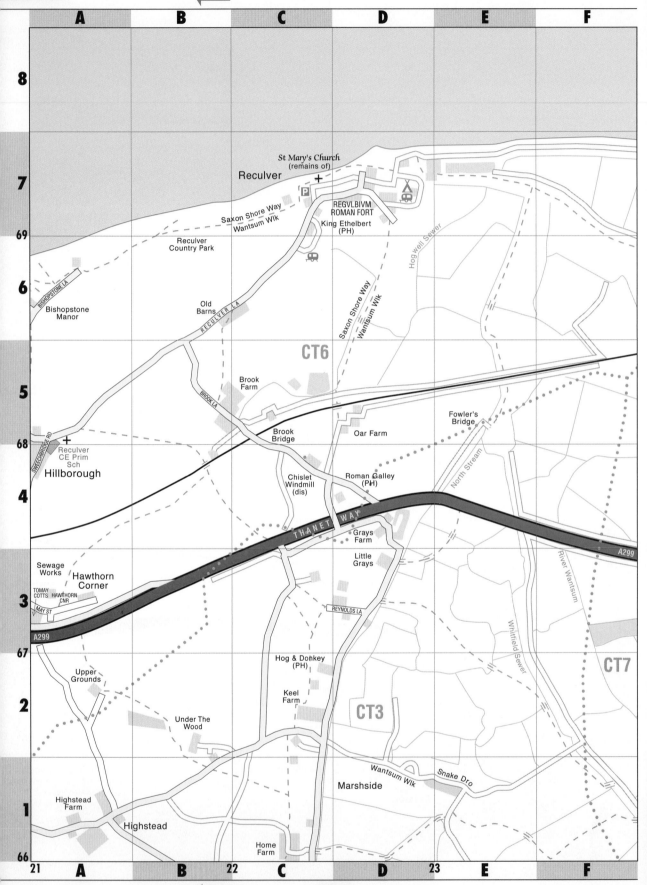

77
112

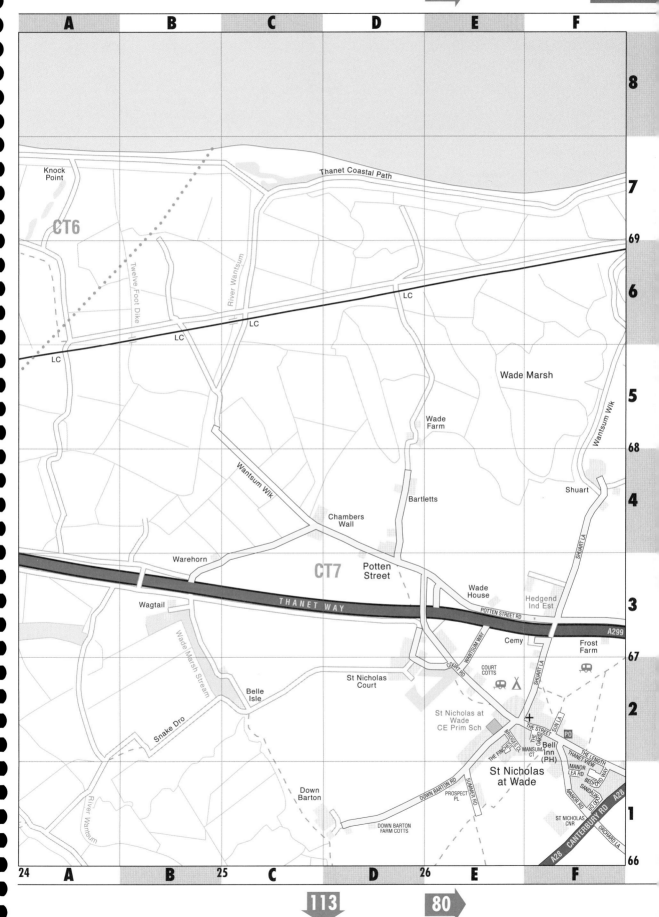

79

F8
1 DALLINGER RD
2 CARMEL CT
3 SANDPIPER CT
4 GAINSBORO RD
5 LYELL CT
6 HOMEBIRCH HO

7 BERESFORD CT

A B C D E F

LARKESCLIFF CT 1
SEA VIEW HTS 2
APRIL RISE 3
BAY VIEW HTS 4
McKINLAY CT 5
RINGSLOE CT 6
SHORE CL 7
FERNDOWN 8
FORELAND CT 9
HAZEL CT 10
COASTGUARD COTTS 11

Minnis Bay

Groynes

Wantsum Wlk
Thanet Coastal Path

Plumpudding Island

LC
LC
LC

THE PARADE
WALKER
HENGIST RD
QUEEN'S AVE
KING'S AVE
CANUTE RD
VIKING CL
DARYNGTON AVE
DANE RD
HORSA RD
OLD FARM RD
INGOLDSBY RD
P

ALFRED RD
ARTHUR RD
EGGERT RD
PRINCES CL

HAROLD RD
HEREWARD RD
SEA VIEW AVE
GRENHAM BAY AVE
RECULVER AVE
ST MILDRED'S AVE
GALLIWEY AVE
CONWAY RD
DUNN DR
MINNIS RD
GORE END
GRENVILLE GDNS
GREEN RD
GRENHAM RD
NELSON CT
WATLING CRES
MILES WAY

CLIFF RD
PROMENADE
WILD AIR
PARK
ALBION RD
BERESFORD GDNS
ROSSITER RD
SPENCER RD
BEELEY RD
HERSCHELL RD
DALLINGER RD
LYELL RD
BEACH AVE
RHS
HS

Birchington-On-Sea
Mus
PO

Gore End Farm

Birchington

BIERCE CT 1
BIERCE CT COTTS 2
ROSSETTI CT 3
UPPER MALTINGS PL 4
THE MALTHOUSES 5
SANDLE'S RD 6

GORDON SQ
RUTLAND GDNS
KENT GDNS
SURREY GDNS
CLAIRE CT
PROSPECT RD
LINCOLN GDNS
HEREFORD GDNS
DIXON GDNS
WINDSOR GDNS
ESSEX GDNS
LANCASTER GDNS
MANOR

A28

MILL LA
MILL ROW
ESSEX VIEW RD
ROSE GDNS
KING EDWARD RD
NOTTINGHAM RD
WOOD RD
BRADLEY AVE
PO

FLINT COTTS 1
RANSOME WAY 2

Brooksend Stream

Wade Marsh

Resrs

CT7

Great Brooksend Farm

Upper Hale Court

Brooks End

College Farm

CRISPE RD

CANTERBURY ROAD BIRCHINGTON

Hale

Nether Hale Farm

NETHERHALE FARM RD

Coney Close

Monkton Road Farm

SEAMARK RD

POTTEN STREET RD
A299 THANET WAY
CANTERBURY RD
A28

ST NICHOLAS RDBT

PLUMSTONE RD

CT12

ORCHARD LA
A299

27 A B 28 C D 29 E F

8 7 69 6 5 68 4 3 67 2 1 66

79 114

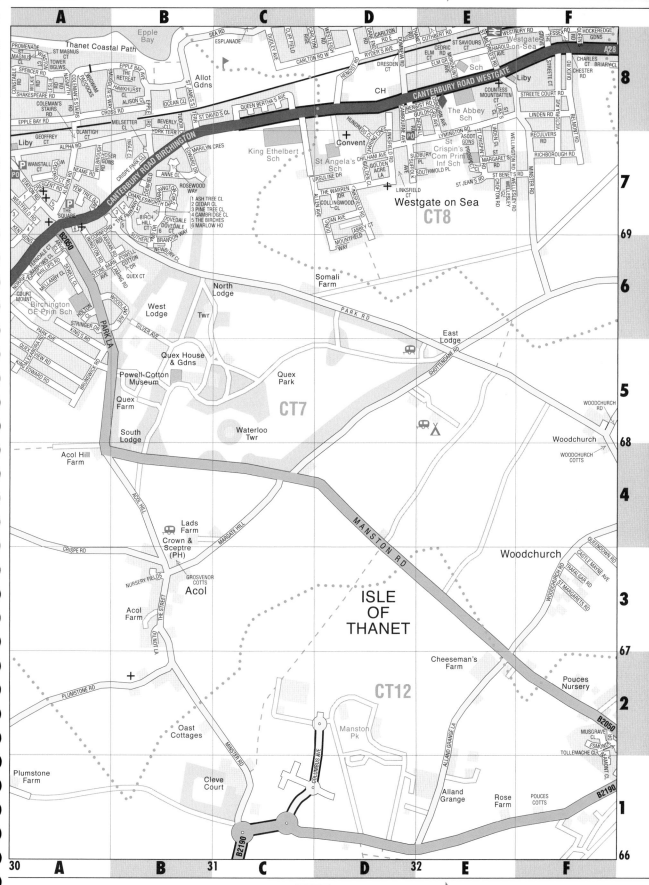

A7
1 EASTFIELD RD
2 PADDOCK RD
3 SHEPPEY CL
4 ROMNEY CL
5 TAPLIN CT
6 WALNUT TREE CL

Thanet Coastal Path

Epple Bay

Westgate-on-Sea

CANTERBURY ROAD WESTGATE

CANTERBURY ROAD BIRCHINGTON

King Ethelbert Sch

Convent

St Angela's Sch

The Abbey Sch

St Crispin's Com Prim Inf Sch

Westgate on Sea

CT8

Birchington CE Prim Sch

West Lodge

North Lodge

Somali Farm

PARK RD

East Lodge

Quex House & Gdns

Powell-Cotton Museum

Quex Farm

Quex Park

CT7

South Lodge

Waterloo Twr

Woodchurch

WOODCHURCH RD

WOODCHURCH COTTS

Acol Hill Farm

MANSTON RD

Lads Farm

Crown & Sceptre (PH)

MARGATE HILL

Woodchurch

Nursery Fields

GROSVENOR COTTS

Acol

Acol Farm

THE STREET

ISLE OF THANET

Cheeseman's Farm

Pouces Nursery

CT12

B2050

Plumstone Farm

Oast Cottages

Manston Pk

MINSTER RD

COLUMBUS AVE

ALLAND GRANGE LA

Alland Grange

Rose Farm

POUCES COTTS

Cleve Court

B2190

B2190

1 ASH TREE CL
2 CEDAR CL
3 PINE TREE CL
4 CAMBRIDGE CL
5 THE BIRCHES
6 MARLOW HO

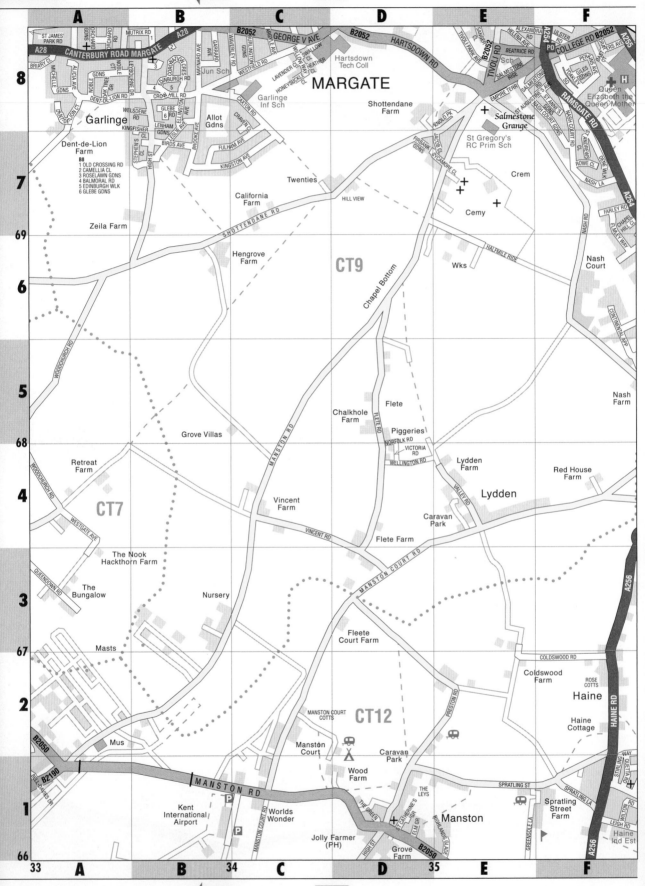

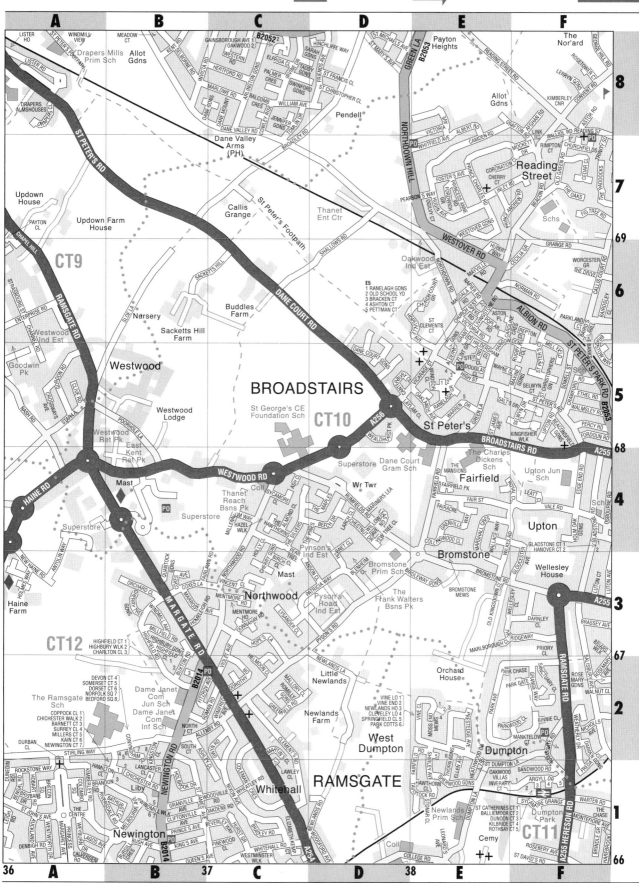

North Foreland

CH

8 Kingsate Coll

CONVENT RD
ELMWOOD AVE
B2052
NORTH FORELAND HILL
Hunton House
CRESCENT RD

READING ST
ELMWOOD RD
Elmwood Farm
NORTHCLIFFE GDNS
CALLIS COURT RD
Mast
Stella Maris Convent
ST STEPHEN'S MANOR
BROADMEAD MANOR 1
VILLIERS HO 2
YARDLEY HO 3
GLENAVON HO 4
FORELAND PARK HO 5
STONE HO 6
STONE HOUSE MEWS 7
NORTH FORELAND RD
NORTH FORELAND AVE
CLIFF PROM
NALDERA
NORTH ANNE'S RD
ST CUBY
MARCROFT

7

69
JULIE CL
DORCAS GDNS
LANTHORNE RD
NEWMANS
The Foreland Sch
BISHOP'S AVE
FRANCIS
LAKING
J CL
CLIFF RD
FORELAND HTS
ELIZABETH CT
PLACE GDNS
THANET

6
RHODES GDNS
RADLEY CL
TINA GDNS
CATHERINE WAY
STANLEY RD
HILLER CL
CORNWALLIS GDNS
SEA VIEW RD
KING'S AVE
QUEEN'S AVE
CASTLE AVE
WAINWRIGHT CT
PARK RD
Stone Bay Sch

KENDAL RISE
LINDENTHORPE RD
HARBLEDOWN GDNS
LAURISTON MOUNT
MAGDALEN
LYNDHURST RD
KNIGHT'S AVE
STONE RD
BEDFORD CT
EASTERN ESP
WINGS CL
CHEVIOT CL
Thanet Coastal Path
East Cliff
1 THANET CL
2 FORGE COTTS
3 STAINES PL

5
MASON'S RISE
BRADSTOW WAY
CUMBERLAND AVE
CARLTON AVE
CROW HILL
DELMANEY CL
STONE GDNS
CT
DICKENS RD
CT

WILLOW CT
ROWAN CT
CT10
LLOYD RD
Broadstairs
LAWN RD
CAERNARVON GDNS
NELSON CT
RECTORY RD
SHUTTLE RD
COPPERFIELD CT
FORT COTTS
FORT RD
BROADSTAIRS

B4
1 CHURCH RD
2 CHURCH SQ
3 UNION SQ
4 ELDON PL
5 ST MARY'S RD
6 SEAVIEW COTTS
7 PROSPECT PL
8 CROFT'S PL
9 SERENE PL
10 RAGLAN PL
11 DUNDONALD RD
12 SERENE CT
13 CHARLOTTE ST
14 TROTWOOD PL
15 BUCKINGHAM RD
16 CHANDOS SQ
17 CHANDOS RD
18 YORK AVE
19 JUBILEE CT
20 WROTHAM AVE
21 ASHTON MEWS

68
Liby
Mus
The BROADWAY
HIGH ST
A255
YH
PO
Sch
STANLEY
PIERREMONT
CINDER PATH
CRAMPTON
GROSVENOR
ST GEORGE'S
MILL
PIERREMONT AVE
KING EDWARD AVE
BELVEDERE RD
PROSPECT RD
THANET RD
QUEEN'S RD
JOHN ST
ALBION ST
ALEXANDRA RD
HARBOUR ST
DICKENS WLK
VICTORIA PAR
Mus
Bleak House
Slipway
Pier
Viking Bay
A4
1 CLARENDON MEWS
2 SOMERSET CT
3 MANOR RD
4 KENT HO
5 JO-ANN'S CT

4
CHAUCER RD
THE VALE
TERR
NASH
PO
YORK ST
OSCAR RD
WROTHAM RD
GRANVILLE RD
B2052
PO
15
16
17
21

67
ROSEMARY AVE
SWINBURNE AVE
HOWARD RD
RAMSGATE RD
A255
WEST CLIFF RD
W ARROW CL
SEAPOINT RD
ST DAVIDS CL
PALMERSTON AVE
Louisa Bay
1 GRANVILLE AVE
2 WEST CLIFF CT
3 WEST CLIFF AVE
4 QUEENS GDNS
5 GRAND MANS
6 CHARLESTON CT
7 SEAVIEW CT
8 THE LANCASTER
9 VIKING CT
10 BRAESIDE

3
Thanet Coll
1 UPPER APPROACH RD
2 APPROACH RD
3 WOODBERRY FLATS
The Hereson Sch
Bradstow Sch
MERIVALE HTS
LEYBOURN RD
WESTERN ESPL
South Cliff
Dumpton Point

2
DUMPTON PARK DR
DUMPTON GAP RD
MINSTER RD
HURST WAY
ELHAM WAY
STAPLEHURST AVE
WALDRON RD
Gap House Sch
Dumpton Bay

DETLING AVE
COLBRAN
BROUGHTON AVE
SEACROFT RD
CLIFFSIDE DR
SOUTH CLIFF PAR

1
Holy Trinity CE Prim Sch
OCEAN'S VIEW
SEA RD
CT11

66

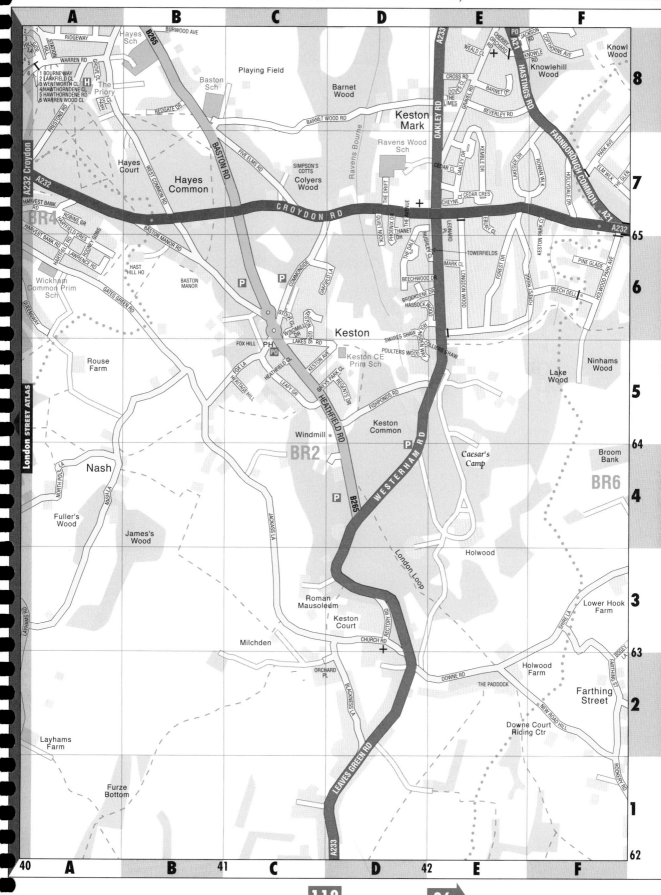

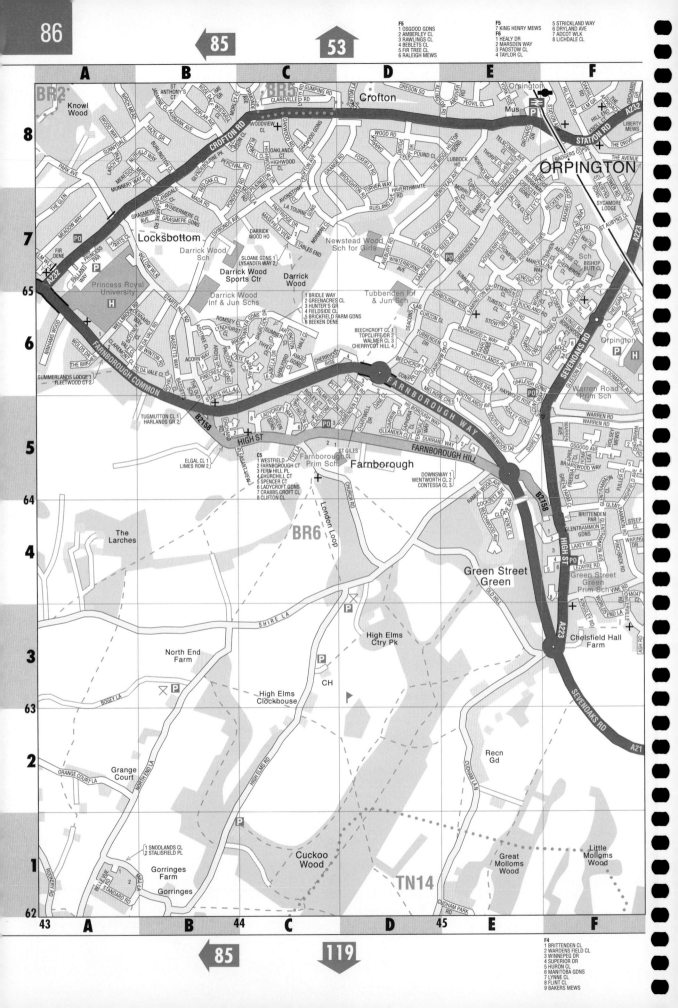

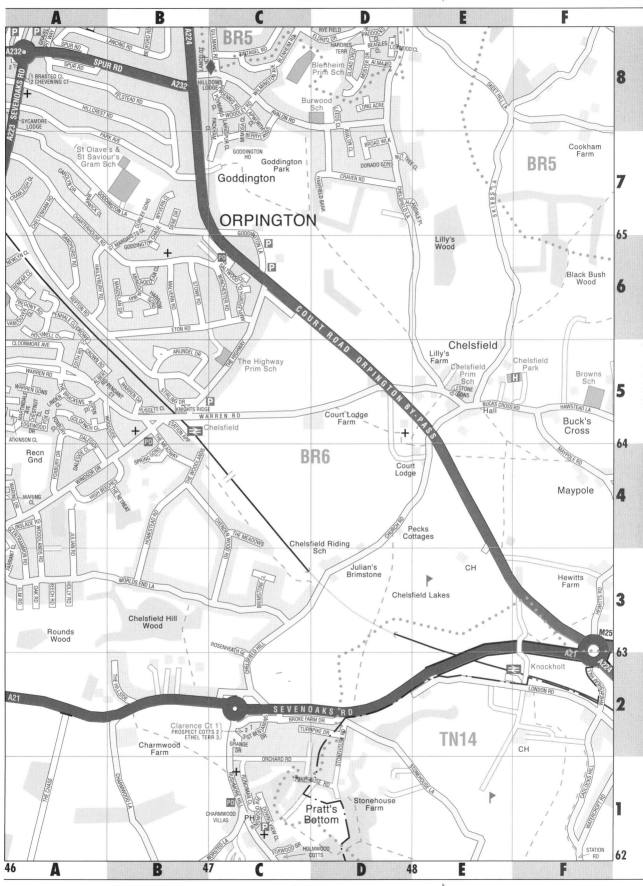

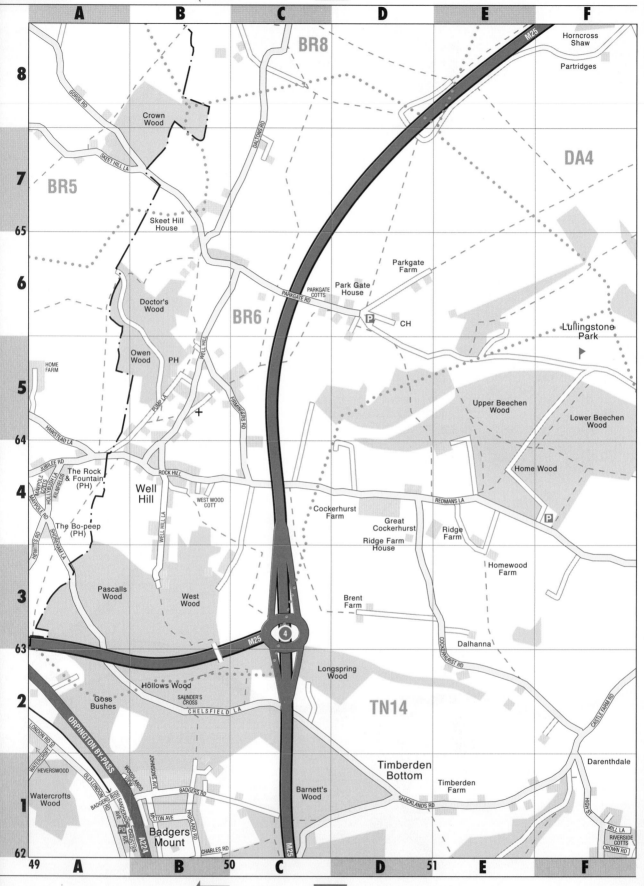

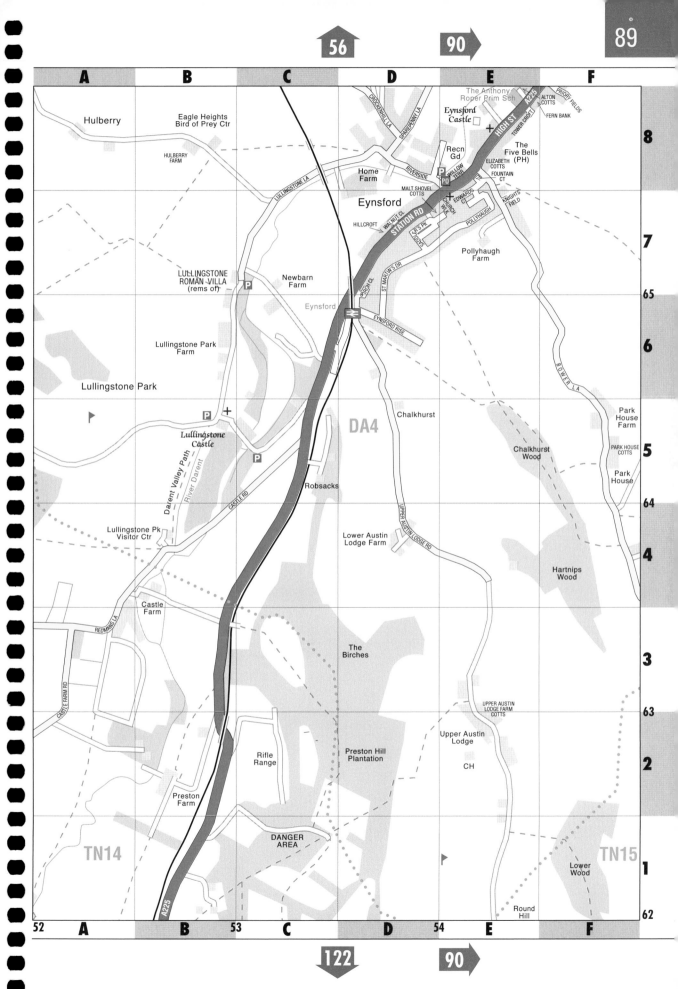

56
90

A B C D E F

8
7
65
6
5
64
4
3
63
2
1
62

Hulberry

Eagle Heights
Bird of Prey Ctr

HULBERRY
FARM

The Anthony
Roper Prim Sch

Eynsford
Castle

HIGH ST
A225

TOWER CROFT

PRIORY FIELDS

ALTON COTTS

FERN BANK

Recn
Gd

P
PO
WILLOW TERR

The Five Bells
(PH)

ELIZABETH
COTTS

FOUNTAIN
CT

Riverside

Home
Farm

MALT SHOVEL
COTTS

EDWARDS
CT

KNIGHTS
FIELD

Eynsford

HILLCROFT

STATION RD

WALNUT CL

CHURCH
WK

POLLYHAUGH

CR'S PK

LULLINGSTONE LA

CROCKENHILL LA

SPAREPENNY LA

LULLINGSTONE
ROMAN VILLA
(rems of)

P

Newbarn
Farm

St MARTIN'S DR

BIRCH CL

Eynsford

EYNSFORD RISE

Pollyhaugh
Farm

Lullingstone Park
Farm

Chalkhurst

DA4

Chalkhurst
Wood

BOWER LA

Park
House
Farm

PARK HOUSE
COTTS

Park
House

Lullingstone Park

P

Lullingstone
Castle

Darent Valley Path

River Darent

CASTLE RD

Robsacks

UPPER AUSTIN LODGE RD

Lower Austin
Lodge Farm

Hartnips
Wood

Lullingstone Pk
Visitor Ctr

Castle
Farm

REDMANS LA

CASTLE FARM RD

The
Birches

UPPER AUSTIN
LODGE FARM
COTTS

Upper Austin
Lodge

CH

Rifle
Range

Preston Hill
Plantation

Preston
Farm

A225

DANGER
AREA

TN14

Lower
Wood

TN15

Round
Hill

52 A B 53 C D 54 E F

90

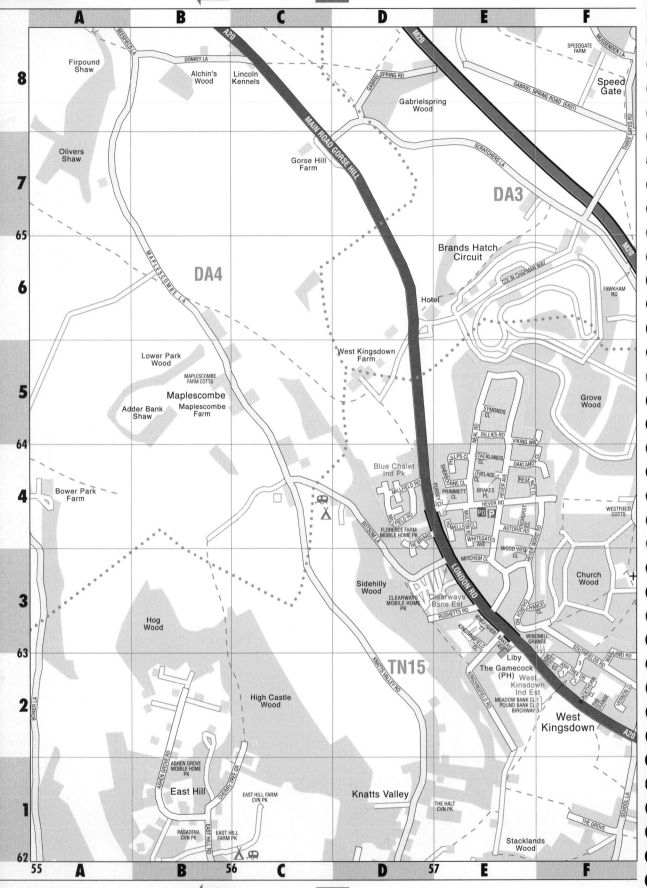

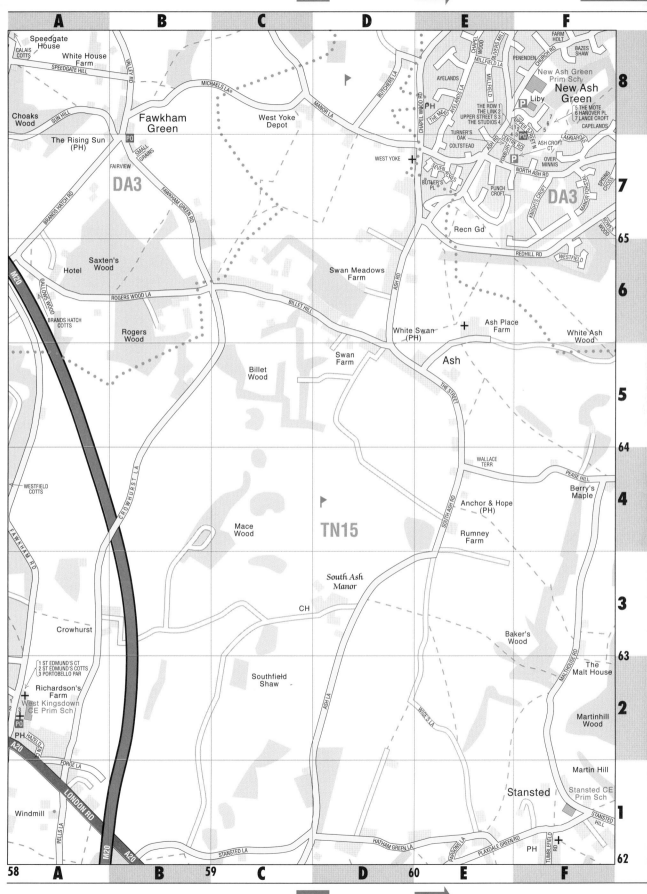

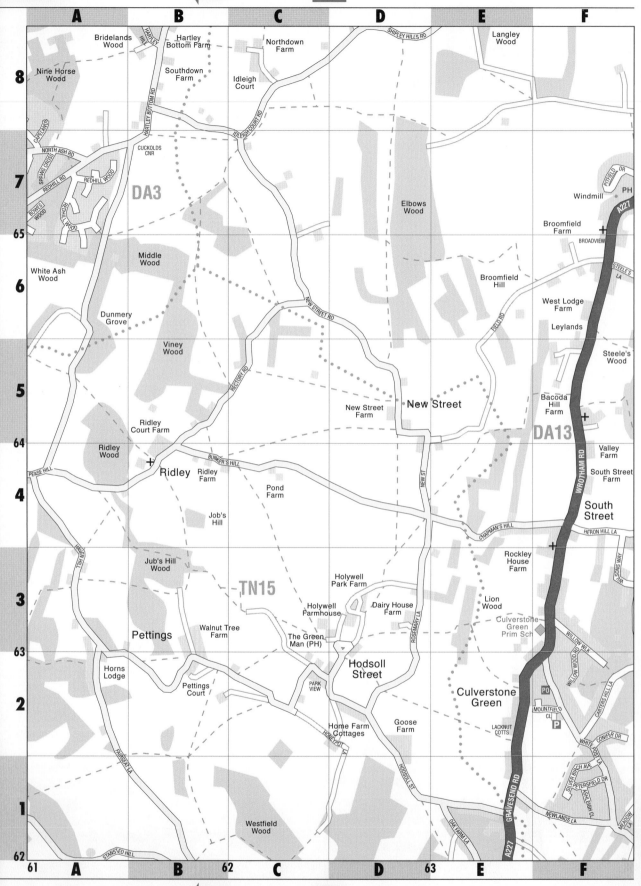

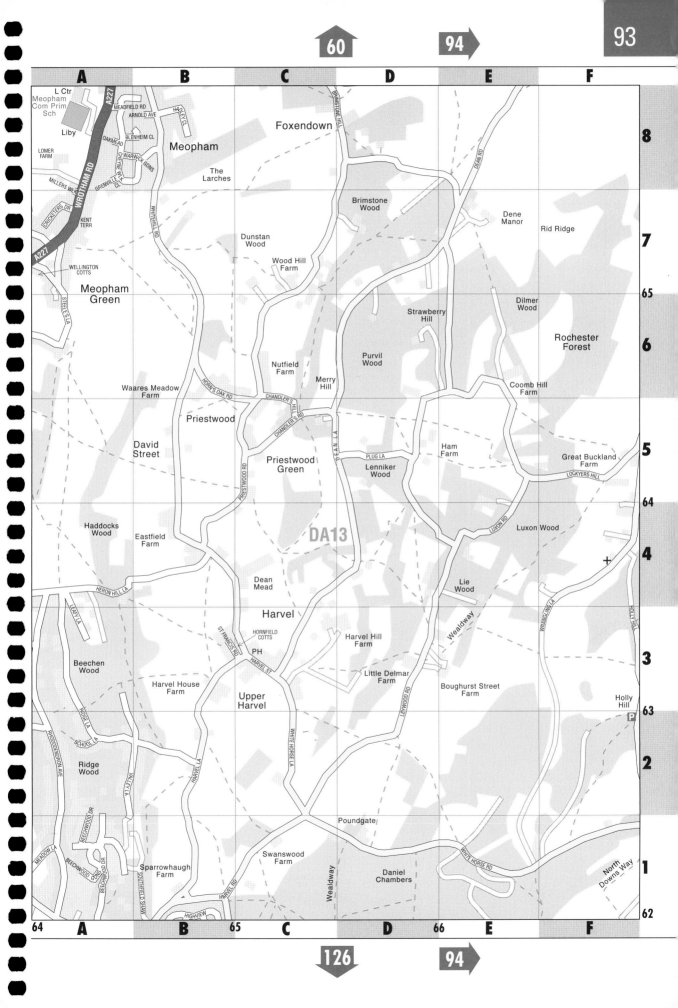

A   B   C   D   E   F

8

Bowling Alley

Bushy Wood

Halling Wood

Hatch Hill

Home Bavins

The Warren

7

Wealdway

Wingate Wood

Gag Plantation

Longbottom Bank

65

Rochester Forest

Chalk Pit

6

Canon Wood

Pastead Wood

Horseholders Wood

North Downs Way

Scrub Wood

Court Farm

DA13

Pilgrims Rest (PH)

VICARAGE RD

ME2

PRIMROSE RD

REDFERN HO

HANES DENE

5

Ten Acre Wood

GROVE RD

BRADLEY RD

TURKS HALL PL

THE STREET

Upper Halling

WOODBINE COTTS

64

Greatpark Wood

CHAPEL LA

South Hill

CHAPEL HOS

BROWNDENS RD

Dean Hill

P

CHILLINGTON CL

MEADOW CL

4

Lad's Hill

Clements Farm

MEADOW CRES

BARN MDW

Mount Ephraim

Holly Hill House

Hanginghill Wood

3

HOLLY HILL

Lad's Farm

PILGRIMS WAY

Home Farm

63

LADDS LA

2

P

Crookhorn Wood

Crookhorn Bungalow

ME6

HOLLY HILL

Holly Hill Lodge

P

BIRLING HILL

Whitedyke Rd

1

ME19

Cemy

Paddlesworth Farm

Mark Farm

CEMETERY RD

Woodlands Farm

LEE RD

PADDLESWORTH RD

TOWNSEND RD

62

67   A   B   68   C   D   69   E   F

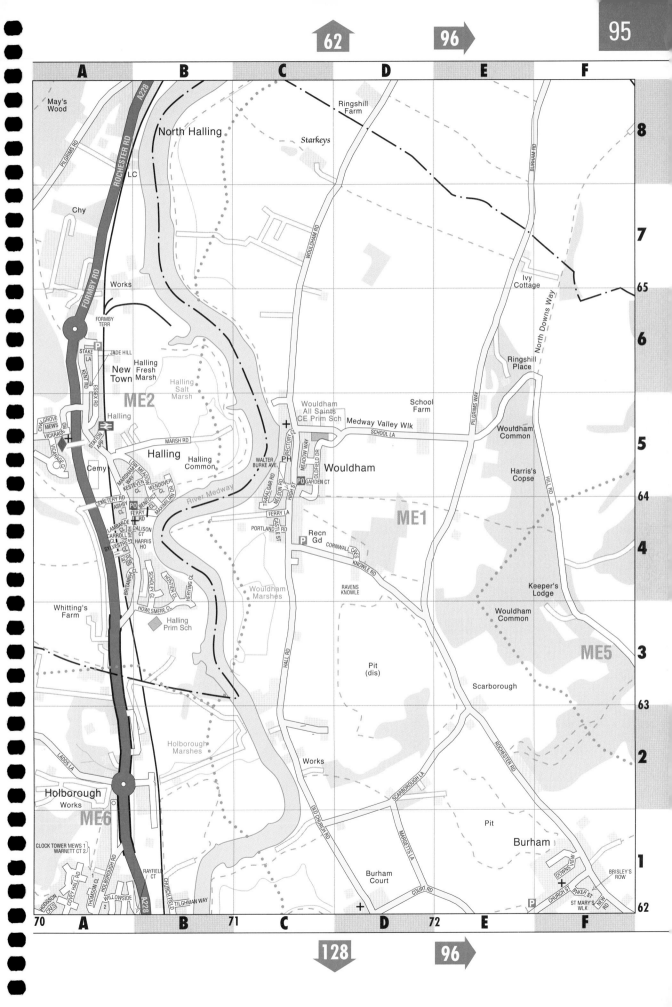

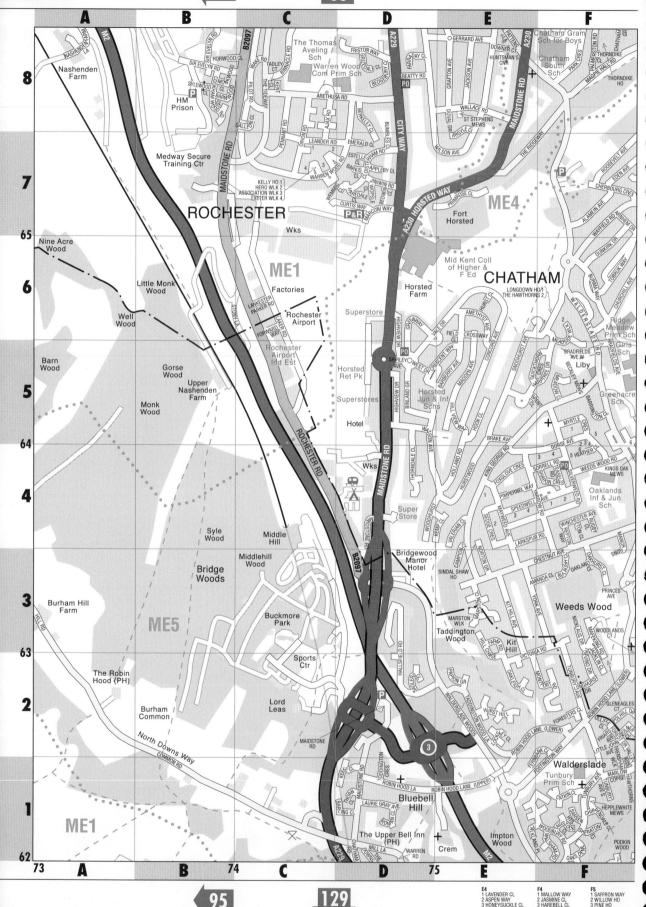

E4
1 LAVENDER CL
2 ASPEN WAY
3 HONEYSUCKLE CL
4 GENTIAN CL

F4
1 MALLOW WAY
2 JASMINE CL
3 HAREBELL CL
4 ROSEMARY CL
5 LINDEN HO
6 OAK HO

F5
1 SAFFRON WAY
2 WILLOW HO
3 PINE HO
4 ROWAN HO
5 HAWTHORN HO
6 BLEAKWOOD RD

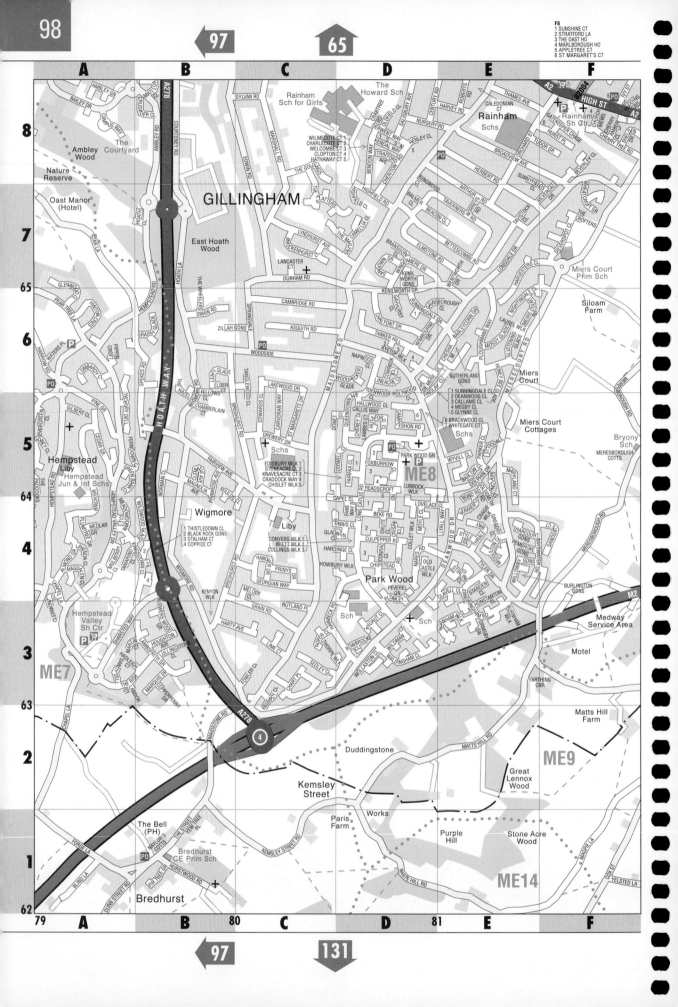

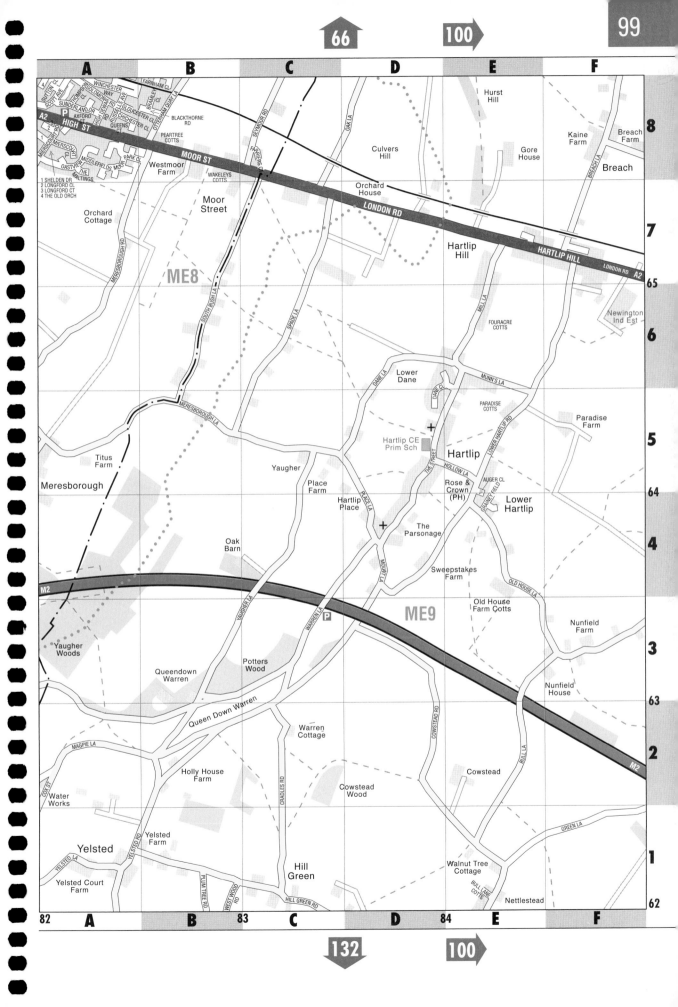

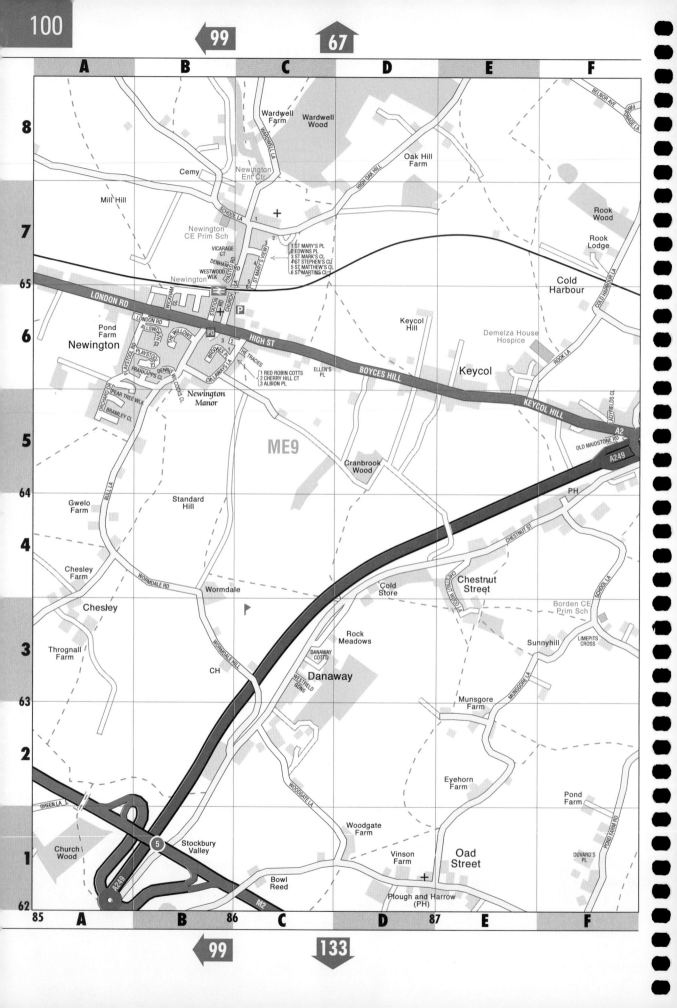

99
67

A B C D E F

8

Wardwell Farm

Wardwell Wood

Oak Hill Farm

Rook Wood

Mill Hill

Cemy

Newington Ent Ctr

WARDWELL LA

HIGH OAK HILL

Rook Lodge

7

Newington CE Prim Sch

VICARAGE CT

DENHAM WLK

WESTWOOD WLK

Newington

SCHOOL LA

HASTED RD

ST MARY'S VIEW

1 ST MARY'S PL
2 EDWINS PL
3 ST MARK'S CL
4 ST STEPHEN'S CL
5 ST MATTHEW'S CL
6 ST MARTINS CL

Cold Harbour

COLD HARBOUR LA

65

LONDON RD

WICKHAM CL

STATION RD

CHURCH LA

P

Keycol Hill

Demelza House Hospice

ROOK LA

6

Pond Farm

Newington

LONDON RD

ALLSWORTH CL

THE WILLOWS

PLAYSTOLE RD

FRANKAPPS CL

DENLY CL

WILCOCKS CL

PO

BROOKES CL

CALLAWAYS LA

THE TRACIES

1
2
3

1 RED ROBIN COTTS
2 CHERRY HILL CT
3 ALBION PL

ELLEN'S PL

HIGH ST

BOYCES HILL

Keycol

KEYCOL HILL

LADYFIELDS CL

5

ORCHARD DR

PEAR TREE WLK

BRAMLEY CL

Newington Manor

ME9

Cranbrook Wood

A2

Old Maidstone RD

A249

64

Gwelo Farm

BULL LA

Standard Hill

PH

CHESTNUT ST

SCHOOL LA

4

Chesley Farm

WORMDALE RD

Wormdale

Cold Store

SHRUB WOOD LA

Chestnut Street

Borden CE Prim Sch

Chesley

WORMDALE HILL

Rock Meadows

Sunnyhill

LIMEPITS CROSS

MUNSGORE LA

3

Thrognall Farm

CH

DANAWAY COTTS

WESTFIELD GDNS

Danaway

Munsgore Farm

63

2

GREEN LA

WOODGATE LA

Eyehorn Farm

Pond Farm

POND FARM RD

1

Church Wood

A249

5

Stockbury Valley

Woodgate Farm

Vinson Farm

Oad Street

DUVARD'S PL

62

Bowl Reed

M2

Plough and Harrow (PH)

85 A 86 B C D 87 E F

99
133

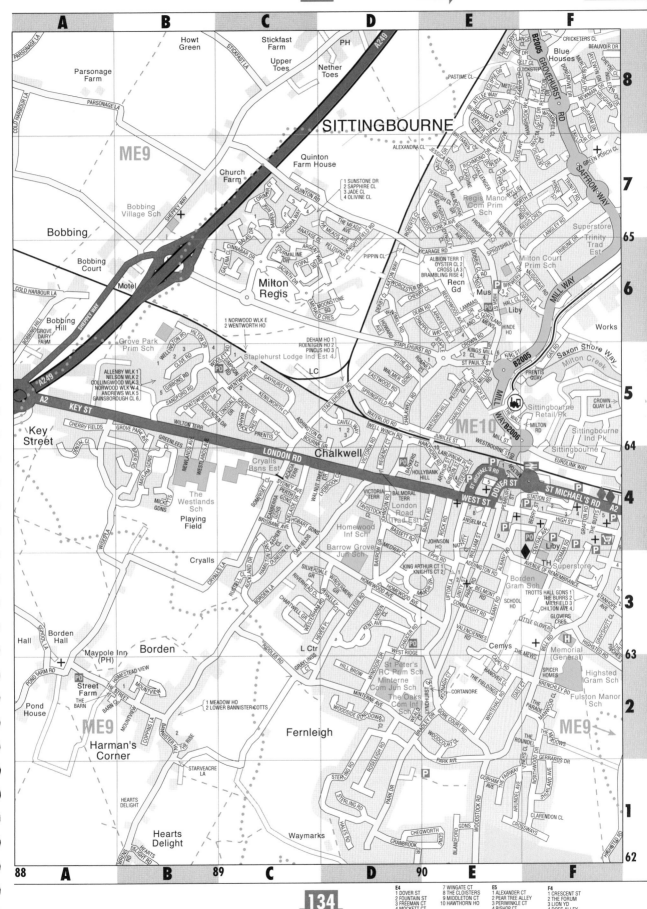

SITTINGBOURNE

ME9

Parsonage Farm

Bobbing

Bobbing Court

Bobbing Hill

Grove Dairy Farm

Motel

Key Street

Borden Hall

Hall

Maypole Inn (PH)

Street Farm

Pond House

ME9

Harman's Corner

Hearts Delight

Howt Green

Stickfast Farm

Upper Toes

Nether Toes

Church Farm

Bobbing Village Sch

Grove Park Prim Sch

Milton Regis

Quinton Farm House

1 SUNSTONE DR
2 SAPPHIRE CL
3 JADE CL
4 OLIVINE CL

1 NORWOOD WLK E
2 WENTWORTH HO

DEHAM HO 1
ROENTGEN CL 2
PINCUS HO 3
Staplehurst Lodge Ind Est 4

ALLENBY WLK 1
NELSON WLK 2
COLLINGWOOD WLK 3
NORWOOD WLK W 4
ANDREWS WLK 5
GAINSBOROUGH CL 6

The Westlands Sch

Playing Field

Cryalls

Cryalls Bsns Est

London Road Trad Est

Homewood Inf Sch

Barrow Grove Jun Sch

Borden

Fernleigh

St Peter's RC Prim Sch

Minterne Com Jun Sch

The Oaks Com Inf Sch

1 MEADOW HO
2 LOWER BANNISTER COTTS

Hearts Delight

Waymarks

Regis Manor Com Prim Sch

ALBION TERR 1
OYSTER CL 2
CROSS LA 3
BRAMBLING RISE 4

Recn Gd

Mus

Milton Court Prim Sch

Superstore

Trinity Trad Est

Works

Saxon Shore Way

Milton Creek

Prentis Quay

ME10

Sittingbourne Retail Pk

Sittingbourne Ind Pk

Sittingbourne

CROWN QUAY LA

Eurolink Way

Chalkwell

KING ARTHUR CT 1
KNIGHTS CT 2

Borden Gram Sch

Memorial (General)

Highsted Gram Sch

Fulston Manor Sch

ME9

TROTTS HALL GDNS 1
THE BURRS 2
MITCHFIELD 3
CHILTON CT 4

Spicer Homes

Blue Houses

B2005

GROVEHURST RD

SAFFRON WAY

MILL WAY

E4
1 DOVER ST
2 FOUNTAIN ST
3 FREEMAN ST
4 MOCKETT CT
5 CHURCH ST
6 PEMBURY CT

7 WINGATE CT
8 THE CLOISTERS
9 MIDDLETON CT
10 HAWTHORN HO

E5
1 ALEXANDER CT
2 PEAR TREE ALLEY
3 PERIWINKLE CT
4 BISHOP CT
5 TANNERY CT
6 RIGDEN'S CT
7 GILES-YOUNG CT

F4
1 CRESCENT ST
2 THE FORUM
3 LION YD
4 DOES ALLEY
5 ST MICHAEL'S CL
6 RIVERBOURNE CT

101 69

| | A | B | C | D | E | F |

8 Castle Rough · Saxon Shore · Beauvoir Dr · Colfe Way · Newman Dr · Walsby Dr · Kemsley Marshes · Nature Reserve · Little Murston

7 Church Marshes Country Park · Milton Creek · Works · Tonge Corner Farm · Tonge Corner · Saxon Shore Way · Sittingbourne & Kemsley Light Rly · Road under construction

65 Trinity Trad Est · Milton Regis · Sewage Works · Telegraph Hill · Wilford Court · Blacketts Rd

6 Brickmakers Ind Est · Castleacres Ind Pk · Castle Road Bsns Prec · Anchor Bsns Pk · D2 Trad Est · Church Road Bsns Ctr · Stadium Way · Central Park · Mere Court

5 Works · ME10 · Eaves Ct · Eurolink Bsns Pk · Dolphin Rd · Murston · Castle Road Tech Ctr · East Hall · West Tonge Farm · Swale Heritage Trail · St Giles Houses

64 Dolphin Yard Sailing Barge Mus · West Lane Trad Est · Dolphin Pk · Murston Jun Sch · Murston Inf Sch · Allot Gdns · Churchill Ho · ME9 · Bunces Farm · 1 FIELDER CL · 2 HUTCHINGS CL · 3 HEARNE CL · 4 BRACKEN CT · 5 THE CEDARS

4 Bayford Court · The Smeed-Dean Ctr · Eurolink Way · St Georges Bsns Pk · Swan Cl · Tonge Rd · All Saints Rd · Lomas Rd · Tonge Mill · ST MICHAEL'S RD · Wheatcroft · Peel Dr · Scraps Hill

3 CANTERBURY RD · EAST ST · Snipeshill · Stones Farm · Fox & Goose (PH) · FOX HILL · Bapchild · THE STREET · Hempstead Farm · Canterbury Road Prim Sch · Lansdowne Prim Sch · 1 OAKTREE HO · 2 BIRCH HO · 3 ASHTREE HO · 4 WILLOW HO

63 Sports Ctr · Bapchild & Tonge CE Sch · Bapchild Court · LONDON RD · A2 · Radfield

2 Sittingbourne Com Coll · The Old Vicarage · Morris Court · Heywood Cottages

1 Ashgores House · Little Dully Cottages

62 New Cottages

| 91 | A | 92 | B | C | 92 | D | 93 | E | F |

101 135

A4: 1 GOSHAWK HO · 2 MERLIN HO · 3 FALCON HO · 4 KESTREL CT · 5 CROWN QUAY LA · 6 RONALDS CT · 7 PLAZA CT · 8 Centre 2000 · 9 THE TURRETS

B4: 1 JARRETT'S CT · 2 HOMEVIEW TERR · 3 HOMEVIEW · 4 SMEED CL · 5 PRICES CL · 6 HARKNESS CT · 7 DICKSON CT · 8 POULSEN CT · 9 THOMAS CT

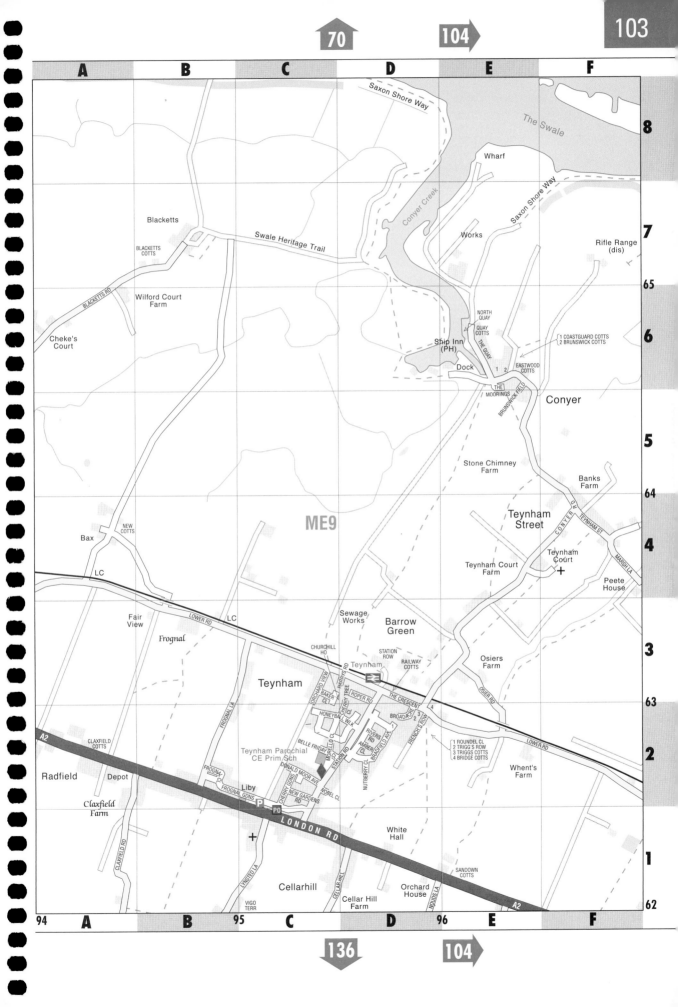

A B C D E F

8

Saxon Shore Way

The Swale

Wharf

Conver Creek

Blacketts

Swale Heritage Trail

Works

7

BLACKETTS COTTS

Saxon Shore Way

Rifle Range (dis)

BLACKETTS RD

Wilford Court Farm

65

NORTH QUAY

66

Cheke's Court

Ship Inn (PH)

QUAY COTTS

THE QUAY

1 COASTGUARD COTTS
2 BRUNSWICK COTTS

Dock

1 2

EASTWOOD COTTS

THE MOORINGS

BRUNSWICK FIELD

Conyer

5

Stone Chimney Farm

Banks Farm

64

ME9

Teynham Street

CONYER RD

TEYNHAM ST

Bax

NEW COTTS

Teynham Court Farm

Teynham Court

MARSH LA

4

LC

Peete House

Fair View

LOWER RD

LC

Sewage Works

Barrow Green

Osiers Farm

OSIER RD

Frognal

CHURCHILL HO

STATION ROW

RAILWAY COTTS

3

Teynham

Teynham

63

FROGNAL LA

ORCHARD VIEW

BAKER CL

MARK RD

CHERRY TREE CL

ROPER RD

THE CRESCENT

BROADOAK RD

FRENCH'S ROW

HONEYBALL WLK

1 ROUNDEL CL
2 TRIGG'S ROW
3 TRIGGS COTTS
4 BRIDGE COTTS

1 3 2 4

A2

CLAXFIELD COTTS

BELLE FRIDAY LA

Teynham Parochial CE Prim Sch

MIRABELLE CL

STATION RD

RIVERS RD

AMBER CL

NUTBERRY CL

BRADFIELD AVE

Whent's Farm

2

Radfield

Depot

FROGNAL

FROGNAL GDNS

DONALD MOOR AVE

CHERRY GDNS

NEW GARDENS RD

ROBEL CL

Liby

P

PO

White Hall

Claxfield Farm

LONDON RD

1

Cellarhill

CLAXFIELD RD

LYNSTED LA

CELLAR HILL

CELLAR HILL

Orchard House

INGLIS LA

SANDOWN COTTS

VIGO TERR

Cellar Hill Farm

A2

62

103
71

A **B** **C** **D** **E** **F**

8
Fowley
Island

The Swale

South Deep

Saxon Shore Way

7
Rifle Range
(dis)

Luddenham Gut

65

Teynham Level

6

Little
Uplees

UPLEES
COTTS

Howletts

5
ME9

ME13

64

Luddenham
Marshes

Poplar
Hall

4
MARSH LA

3
Luddenham
Court

CHERRY TREE
DR

63
BROOK
COTTS

Elverton

Hawks & Beetles
Farm

Swale Heritage Trail

2
Deerton
Street

The Old
Farmhouse

Wildmarsh

Nash's
Farm

Lower
Newlands

The
Old Rectory

Luddenham
Sch

Mockbeggar

1
THE ELMS

LOWER RD

Mockbeggar
Farm

LC

Stone
Farm

Bysing
Wood

BYSING WOOD
COTTS

BYSING WOOD RD

62
97 **A** **B** 98 **C** **D** 99 **E** **F**

103
137

72
106

A   B   C   D   E   F

The Ferry Inn (PH)

HARTY FERRY RD

ME12

8

Uplees Marshes

The Swale

7

65

Visitor Ctr

P

6

Gate House Bungalow

Oare Marshes Nature Reserve

Saxon Shore Way

HARTY FERRY COTTS

ME13

5

Nagden Marshes

64

Broomfield Farm

UPLEES RD

Court Lodge

Norman's Hill

Faversham Creek

4

+ Pheasant Farm

CHURCH RD

Shipwright's Arms (PH)

Hollowshore

Oare Creek

Ham Marshes

3

Wharf

Works

RUSSELL CL

Oare

PD

PH

HARRISON TERR

COLEGATES CL

MOUNT PLEASANT

COLEGATES RD

TILE STREET

63

Ham Farm

2

COLEGATES RD

Piggery

B2045

JOHN HALL CL

Works

Gravel Works

HAM RD

SEAGAR RD

Windmill (dis)

WINDMILL LA

Gate House

FAVERSHAM
The Brents

Saxon Shore Way

Sewage Works

1

Works

WESTERN LINK

MAITLAND CT

WYBORN CT

WELL WAY

SHERWOOD CL

ORE RD

PRIORY PL

FINCH CL

COSTALL RD

LARKSFIELD RD

SPRINGHEAD RD

BROOK RD

Brents Ind Est

North Quay

South Quay

Shipyard Area

UPPER BRENTS

WATERSIDE CL

Wharf

Faversham Creek

Works

ABBEY FIELDS

62

BYSING WOOD RD

B2045

WILDISH RD

BYSING WOOD RD

JOHNSON CT

CHURCHILL CL

IVORY CL

Davington Prim Sch

00   A   B   01   C   D   02   E   F

138
106

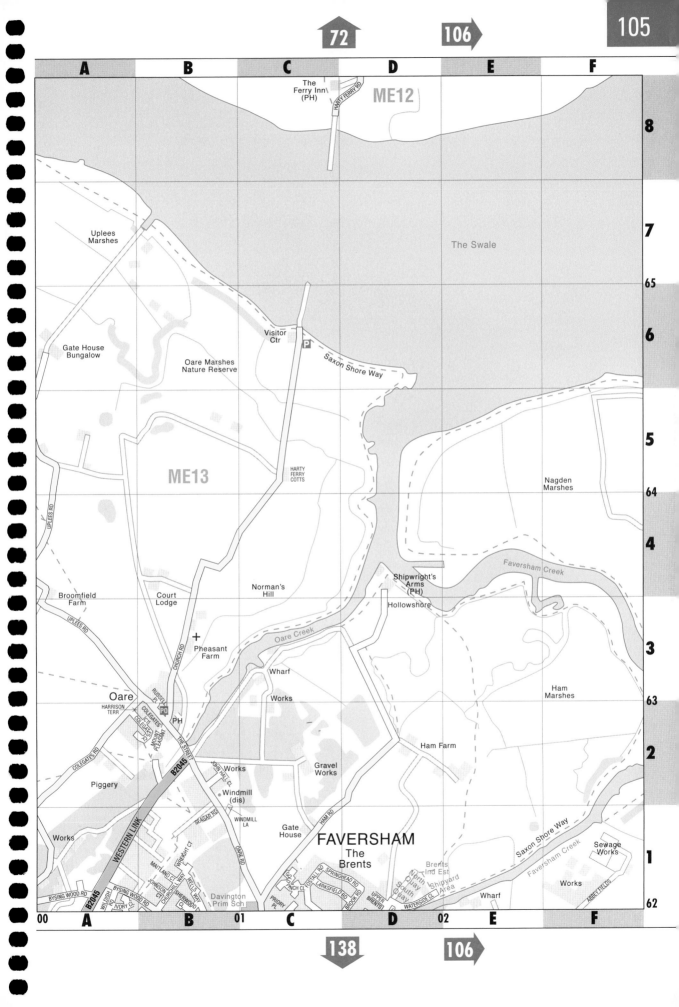

A B C D E F

8

The
Swale

Whitstable
Bay

7

65

Groynes

Saxon Shore Way

6

South Swale
Nature Reserve

CT5

Cleve
Marshes

5

Cleve
Hill

64

Crown
Cottages

4

Graveney
Marshes

ME13

Graveney
Hill

FAVERSHAM RD

Saxon Shore Way

3

Nagden

Nagden
Cottages

Warm
House

Coney
Banks

Denley Hill
Farm

SEASALTER RD

63

Brook
Bridge

Broom
Street

MONKSHILL RD

2

Sandbanks
Cottages

SANDBANKS RD

The Old
Vicarage

ALL SAINTS VIEW

+
Graveney

Graveney
Crossing

Sandbanks
Farm

Sandbanks

Murtons
Farm

MURTON
PL

1

JINSOM CL

Plantation
House

GOOSEFIELDS

P.O.

HEAD HILL RD

Graveney
Prim Sch

62

FOUR HORSESHOES
PK

PH

Culmers

03 A B 04 C D 05 E F

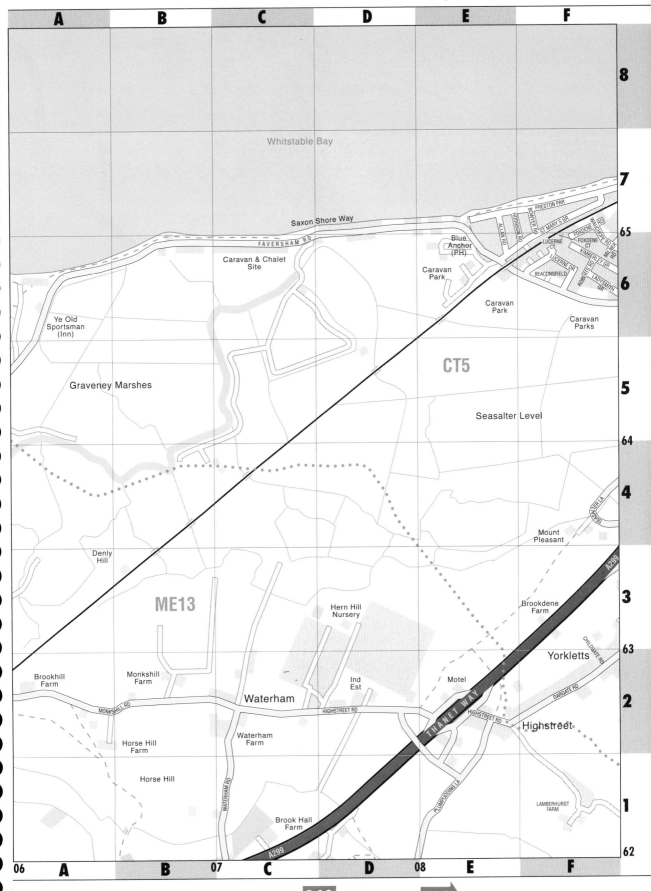

Whitstable Bay

Saxon Shore Way

FAVERSHAM RD

Caravan & Chalet
Site

Blue
Anchor
(PH)

Caravan
Park

PRESTON PAR

HODGSON RD

BOWYER RD

ALLAN RD

ST MARY'S GR

LUCERNE
CT

FOXDENE
CT

FOXDENE
GR

WALMORE RD

KIMBERLEY GR

LUCERNE DR

BEACONSFIELD

ROBERTS RD

LADYSMITH
GR

Caravan
Park

Caravan
Parks

Ye Old
Sportsman
(Inn)

CT5

Graveney Marshes

Seasalter Level

SEASALTER LA

Mount
Pleasant

Denly
Hill

ME13

Hern Hill
Nursery

Brookdene
Farm

A299

CHILDGATE RD

Yorkletts

Brookhill
Farm

Monkshill
Farm

Ind
Est

Motel

THANET WAY

DARGATE RD

Waterham

MONKSHILL RD

HIGHSTREET RD

HIGHSTREET RD

Highstreet

Horse Hill
Farm

Waterham
Farm

WATERHAM RD

PLUMPUDDING LA

LAMBERHURST
FARM

Horse Hill

Brook Hall
Farm

A299

107 74

A B C D E F

WHITSTABLE

Seasalter

8

Saxon Shore Way
Saxon Shore Way
Seasalter Beach

CLIFTON GDNS
WEST CLIFF
CLIFTON
PORTLAND
CANTERBURY RD
B2205
GLEBE WAY
SUFFOLK
SUFFOLK
SWAN FIELD
HARWICH ST
ST JAMES GDNS
KENT ST
VALE RD
HILLVIEW RD
MILLSTREAM COTTS
GODFREY RD
CRANLEIGH CT
CRANLEIGH GDNS
Cemy
DOWNS AVE
INVICTA RD
Sports Ctr
The Com Coll Whitstable

The Larches
JAFFA CT 1
MARINERS CT 2
NORFOLK ST 3
WHITBOURNE CT 4
ALEXANDRA RD
TOLLGATE

BLACKSTABLE
MAUGHAM CT
GORDON RD
GREEN LA
SYDNEY
NORMAN RD
KINGSLEY RD
WALMER
GOSSELIN ST
SEESHILL CL
ST MARK'S RD
ST LUKE'S RD
MILLSTROOD RD
BELLEVUE RD
CLIFFORD RD
FIRBANKS
A2990
SPIRE AVE

JOY LA
Joy Lane Schs
VULCAN CL
DOVE CL
GRANVILLE
PIERPOINT
GROSVENOR RD
DUNCAN CL
HILLTOP
Duncan Down
ST ANDREW'S CL
ST GEORGE'S CL
ST PATRICK'S CL
ST VINCENT'S CL
DOGGEREL ACRE
DEBO RD
GOLDEN HILL
REGENCY CL
Mill Strood Farm
Superstore
Eversleigh Rise
Joseph Wilson Ind Est

7

Seasalter Beach
ADMIRALTY WLK
CUNDISHALL CL
GENESTA AVE
METEOR AVE
MEDINA AVE
SHAMROCK AVE
SUNRAY AVE
COLUMBIA AVE
VALENTINE AVE
BRITANNIA AVE
CYPRESS CL
KINGFISHER CL
HAWK CL
OSPREY CL
WINDMILL CT
Windmill Hotel
CLOVELLY RD
BORSTAL HILL
BORSTAL AVE

Preston Par
FAIRWAY
CRES
PRESTON PAR
GEORGE'S AVE
ST ALPHEGE CL
SOMERSET CL
CORYLUS CL
DR
FIELD VIEW
SCEPTRE WAY
AIRVIEW RD
SHEARWATER AVE
GRIMTHORPE AVE

65

ASHLEY DR
MILNER RD
EDEN RD
FLORENCE AVE
HAZLEMERE RD
SHAMROCK AVE
DORSET
SANDPIPER CL
SWALLOW CL
MEADOW WLK
SPRING LA
THE HEIGHTS
MARTINDOWN RD
WILDS RD
SUNSET
SHERWOOD DR
WARREN
SHERWOOD CL
South View Farm
Benacre Wood
Mast

6

FREEMAN'S CL
HERITAGE CL
CHANCTONBURY CHASE
GRANGE CL
MACDONALD PAR
CORDINGHAM RD
PORTLIGHT PL
NIGHTINGALE WLK
CAROLINE CL
JAY CRES
MAJOR CL
FAVOURITE RD
JAYNE WLK
TRILBY WAY
SANDY END
PARTY FERRY VIEW
SAND END
LAMB'S WLK
LONG REACH CL
THE BRIARS
SOUTH VIEW RD
B2205
BENACRE RD
Benacre Wood

Seasalter Cross
APPLEGARTH PK
CHURCH LA
ROWAN TREE PK
TRAVEWINDS
HERON
SPEEDWELL CL
EMELINA WAY
WRYAK HILL
LEYSDOWN VIEW 1
WARDEN POINT WAY 2
POLLARD PL 3
COLUMBINE CL 4
Motel
BLUEFIELD MEWS
PH
THANET WAY
Montpelier Ave
A290

5

Caravan Parks
SEASALTER LA
A2990
HARRIETS CNR
LADYSMITH RD
The Oaks
WILLOW RD
ROYAL AVE
WELLINGTON ST
MARLBOROUGH RD
CLAPHAM HILL
Clapham Hill
Hillside Bungalow
CT5
Seeshill Farm
Bogshole Farm

64

PILGRIMS LA
Seasalter Dairy Farm
WYRAK HILL
Lincey
Burgess Farm

4

Sunset Farm
Elmcroft
BOGSHOLE LA
Court Lees Farm

FOX'S CROSS
PYE ALLEY LA
Holme Lodge Farm

3

Fox's Cross Bottom
DARGATE RD
GLEN WLK
PEAN COURT RD
April Cottage
Court Lees Manor

BARN CL
FORD WLK
COOMBE WLK
FOX'S CROSS HILL
FOX'S CROSS RD
CARLTON RD
PEAN HILL

63

Ellenden Farm
Oakapple Cottage
Marley Wood

2

Coombe Wood
Ellenden Wood
CT2
Works
Hempshall Wood

1

ME13
Tong Wood
Dockers Field Farm
A290
HONEY HILL

62

09 A B 10 C D 11 E F

A299
CT5
Bogshole Farm

107 141

A   B   C   D   E   F

8

A299
OWLS RD
HOUSE RD
Prospect Farm
West End
Knowel Hill
Ruckinge Farm
THORNDEN WOOD RD
Bleanbottom Shaw

Round Wood

Plenty Brook
Bullockstone Farm
Bullockstone
LOWER HERNE RD
Home Farm

BULLOCKSTONE RD
A291
CURTIS WOOD RD
SWALLOW CT
FALCON CL
DOVE CL
ANEMONE WAY
ASPEN RD
Grove Farm
First & Last (PH)
NIGHTINGALE RD

7

65

West Brook
Warren Farm

Herne Common
CANTERBURY RD
Nursery
BUSHEYFIELDS RD

6

Banker's Wood
CT6
BRAGGS LA

Bleangate
Hoath Wood

Knockhimdown Hill

5

Cripps Wood
West Blean Wood
NEW ROAD COTTS

64

Wildwood Wealden Forest Park
Saw Mill
West Blean House
Boarded House Farm
HICKS FORSTAL RD

4

NEW RD

3

Blaxland Farm
Belce Wood
Farthings Wood
Woodlands Farm

Greenacres
CT2
Punch Tavern (PH)
CT3

Cole Wood

63

2

Brambles Farm
Calcott
HERNE BAY RD
Cadehill Wood

Little Mayton
MAYTON LA
Vale Farm
BARN ST LA
Nursery
Nursery

1

Aspley Lodge
A291
CT2

62

15   A   B   16   C   D   17   E   F

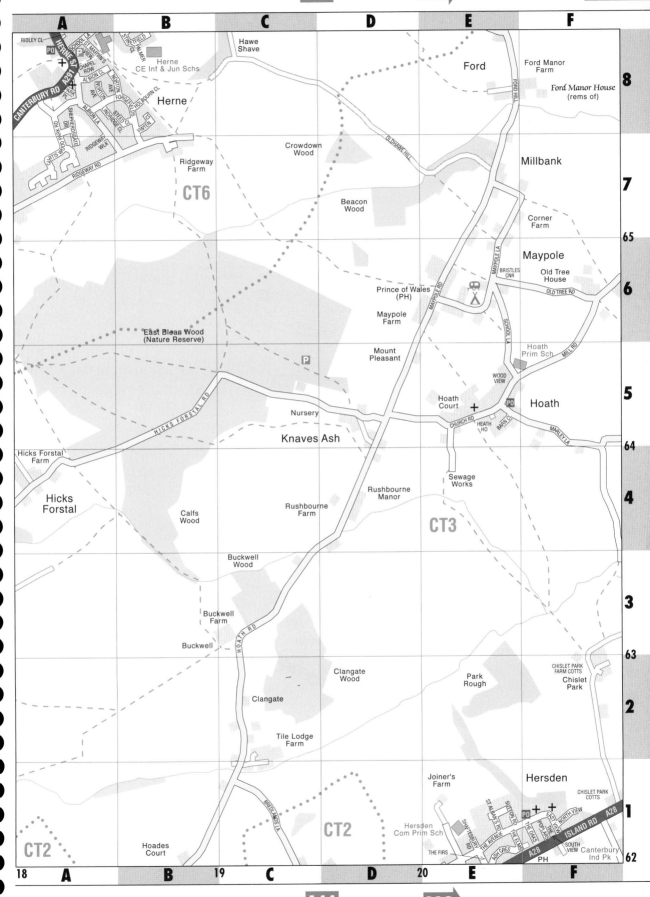

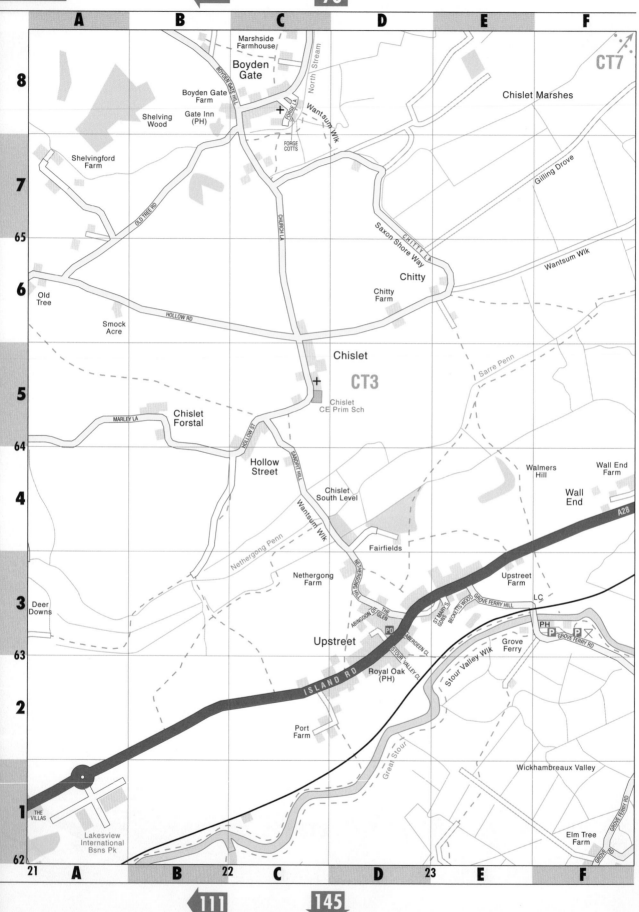

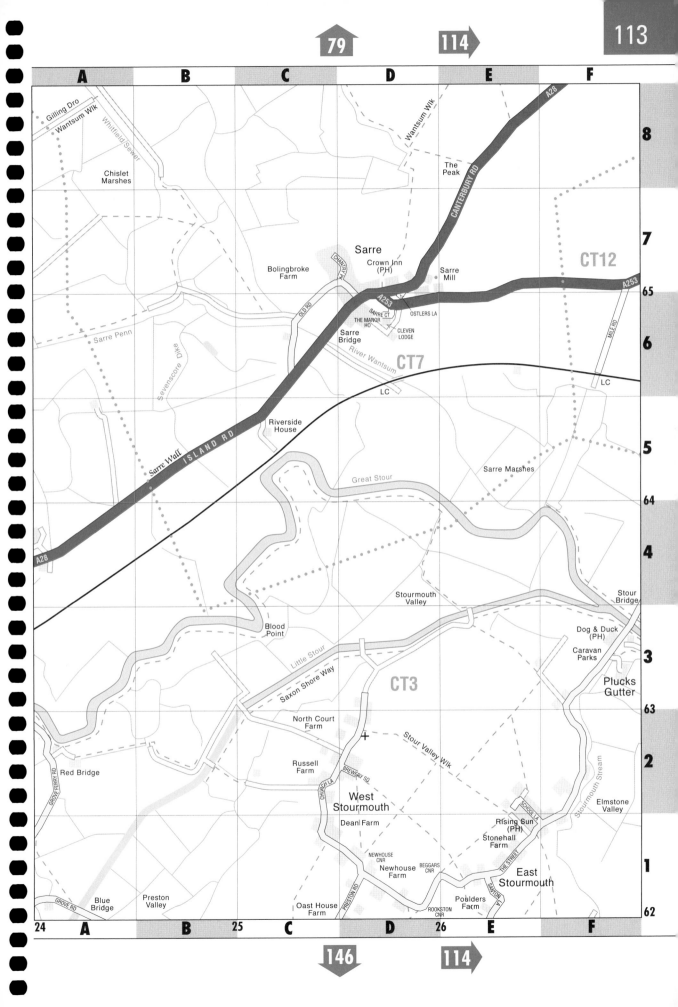

A   B   C   D   E   F

8
7
65
6
5
64
4
63
3
2
1
62

CT12
CT7
CT3

Gilling Dro
Wantsum Wlk
Whitfield Sewer
Chislet Marshes
Sarre Penn
Sevenscore Dike
Bolingbroke Farm
CHANTRY PK
OLD RD
Sarre
Crown Inn (PH)
Wantsum Wlk
The Peak
CANTERBURY RD
A28
Sarre Mill
A253
SARRE CT
THE MANOR HO
OSTLERS LA
CLEVEN LODGE
Sarre Bridge
River Wantsum
A253
MILE RD
LC
LC
Riverside House
ISLAND RD
Sarre Wall
Great Stour
Sarre Marshes
A28
Stourmouth Valley
Stour Bridge
Blood Point
Little Stour
Saxon Shore Way
Dog & Duck (PH)
Caravan Parks
Plucks Gutter
North Court Farm
Stour Valley Wlk
Russell Farm
CHURCH LA
BREWERY SQ
West Stourmouth
Deanl Farm
Stourmouth Stream
SCHOOL LA
Elmstone Valley
Rising Sun (PH)
Stonehall Farm
THE STREET
GROVE FERRY RD
Red Bridge
Preston Valley
NEWHOUSE CNR
Newhouse Farm
BEGGARS CNR
East Stourmouth
PRESTON RD
SAFFON LA
Poulders Farm
GROVE RD
Blue Bridge
Oast House Farm
ROOKSTON CNR

24   A   B   25   C   D   26   E   F

A   B   C   D   E   F

CT7

ORCHARD LA

A299

SEAMARK RD

Nature Reserve

MONKTON RDBT

A299

A253

8

Chipman's Way

MILLERS LA

PARSONAGE OAST

Monkton

PARSONAGE FIELDS

VICARAGE GDN

COLLARDS CL

WILLETTS HILL

Monkton CE Prim Sch

7

Monkton Court Farm

Monkton MANOR

GORE STREET FARM COTTS

THE DROVE

SEAMARK CL

MONKTON ST

Walters Hall Farm

HOO FARM

Hoo

65

PH

MONKTON RD

Hoo Corner Farm

THE FOXHUNTER PK

THE ORCHARD

CENTRAL PK

SHERRIFFS COURT LA

6

LONG MDW

MEADOW VIEW

Caravan Park

Sherriffs Court

CT12

LC

LC

LC

5

Monkton Marshes

Coxon's Hill

64

Eastern Monkton Stream

Minster Stream

4

Western Monkton Stream

Docker Hill

Minster Marshes

Abbot's Wall

Abbot's Wall

3

River Stour

63

Saxon Shore Way

2

CT3

Corner Dro

Goldstone Dro

1

Westmarsh Dro

Ash Level

62

27 A   B 28 C   D 29 E   F

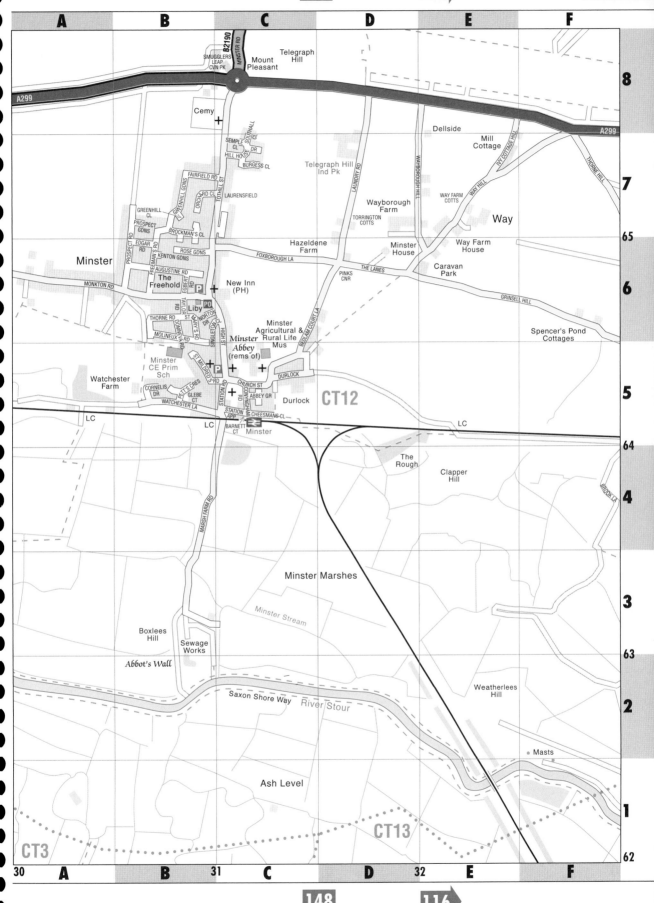

A B C D E F

8

7

65

6

5

64

4

3

63

2

1

62

A B C D E F

MINSTER RD

B2190

SMUGGLERS LEAP CVN PK

Mount Pleasant

Telegraph Hill

A299

Cemy

Dellside

Mill Cottage

IVY COTTAGE HILL

THORNE HILL

A299

SEMPLE CL

SOUTHALL CL

HILL HO

BURGESS CL

HILL ST

FAIRFIELD RD

SD DR

Telegraph Hill Ind Pk

LAUNDRY RD

WAYBOROUGH HILL

WAY HILL

WAY FARM COTTS

Way

GREENHILL CL

GREENHILL GDNS

ORCHARD CL

TOTHILL ST

Laurensfield

Wayborough Farm

Way Farm House

PROSPECT GDNS

EDGAR RD

FREEMAN SD

BROCKMAN'S CL

ROSE GDNS

KENTON GDNS

TORRINGTON COTTS

Minster House

Minster

AUGUSTINE RD

Foxborough LA

Hazeldene Farm

THE LANES

Caravan Park

MONKTON RD

The Freehold

EGBERT RD

P

New Inn (PH)

PINKS CNR

GRINSELL HILL

TAYLOR RD

Liby

PO

NORTON DR

Spencer's Pond Cottages

THORNE RD

ST MARY'S RD

DOMNEVA RD

MOLINEUX RD

SINGLETON CL

ST HIGH

Minster Abbey (rems of)

Minster Agricultural & Rural Life Mus

BEDLAM COURT LA

Minster CE Prim Sch

ST MILDRED'S RD

P

Watchester Farm

CORNELIS DR

PETT'S CRES

GLEBE CT

STATION RD

STATION RD

WINDMILL RD

CHURCH ST

DURLOCK

CT12

WATCHESTER LA

STATION APP

ABBEY GR

Durlock

LC

LC

BARNETT CT

CHEESMANS CL

Minster

LC

The Rough

Clapper Hill

BROOK LA

MARSH FARM RD

Minster Marshes

Minster Stream

Boxlees Hill

Sewage Works

Weatherlees Hill

Abbot's Wall

Saxon Shore Way

River Stour

Masts

Ash Level

CT13

CT3

30 31 32

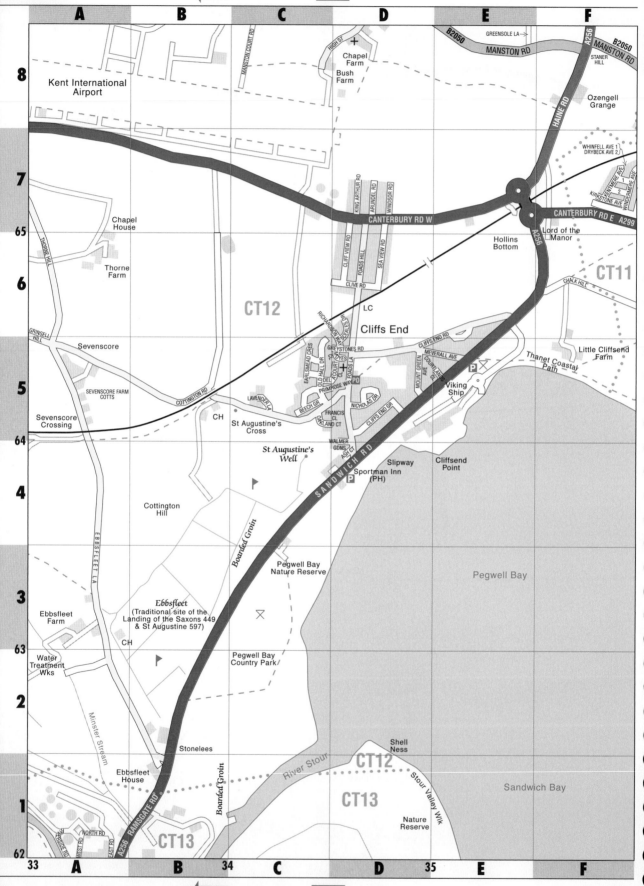

A **B** **C** **D** **E** **F**

Kent International
Airport

GREENSOLE LA →

MANSTON RD

B2050

B2050

MANSTON RD

STANER HILL

HAINE RD

A256

Ozengell
Grange

WHINFELL AVE 1
DRYBECK AVE 2

KIRKSTONE AVE

WINDERMERE AVE

High St

Chapel
Farm
Bush
Farm

King Arthur Rd
Arundel Rd
Windsor Rd

CANTERBURY RD W

CANTERBURY RD E A299

Hollins
Bottom

Lord of the
Manor

CT11

Chapel
House

THORNE HILL

Thorne
Farm

Cliff View Rd
Foads Hill
Sea View Rd

Clive Rd

CT12

LC

Chalk Hill

Little Cliffsend
Farm

GRINSELL HILL

Sevenscore

Richardson Way
Foads La

Sceales Dr

Cliffs End

Cliffs End Rd

Greystones Rd
EARLSMEAD CRES
OLD HALL DR

YES

Meverall Ave

Mount Green

Court Rd

Thanet Coastal
Path

SEVENSCORE FARM COTTS

COTTINGTON RD

LAVENDER LA

BEECH GR

DEL

PRIMROSE WAY

FRANCIS CL
OAKLAND CT

NICHOLAS DR

Cliffs End Gr

P

Viking
Ship

Sevenscore
Crossing

CH

St Augustine's
Cross

WALMER GDNS
ASH CT

SANDWICH RD

Sportman Inn
(PH)

Slipway

Cliffsend
Point

*St Augustine's
Well*

EBBSFLEET LA

Cottington
Hill

Boarded Groin

Pegwell Bay
Nature Reserve

Pegwell Bay

Ebbsfleet
(Traditional site of the
Landing of the Saxons 449
& St Augustine 597)

Ebbsfleet
Farm

CH

Pegwell Bay
Country Park

Water
Treatment
Wks

Minster Stream

Stonelees

RAMSGATE RD

Boarded Groin

Ebbsfleet
House

River Stour

Shell
Ness

CT12

Stour Valley Wlk

Sandwich Bay

CT13

Nature
Reserve

PENSIDE RD
WEST RD
NORTH RD
EAST RD

A256

CT13

33 **A** **B** 34 **C** **D** 35 **E** **F**

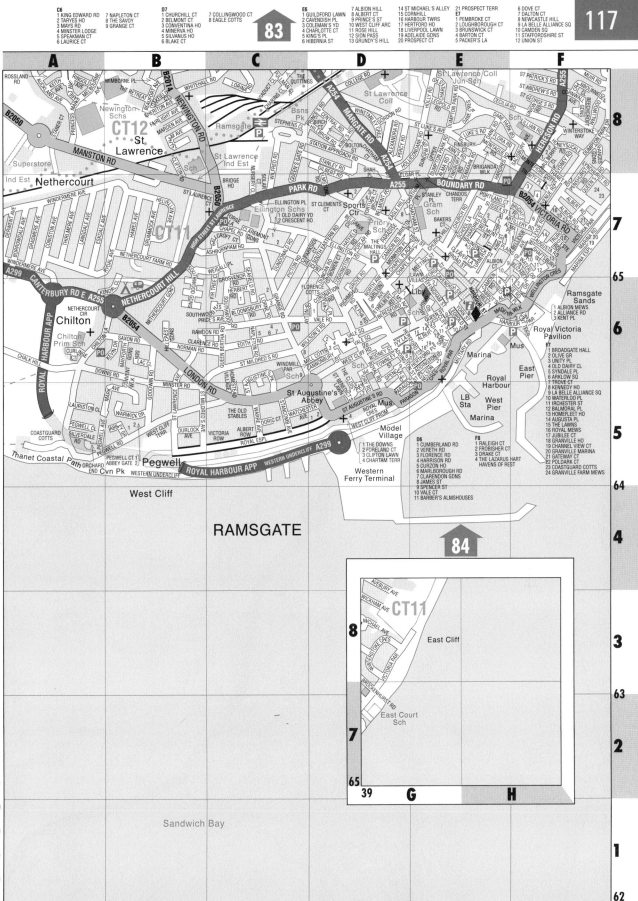

C6
1 KING EDWARD RD
2 TARYES HO
3 MAYS RD
4 MINSTER LODGE
5 SPEAKMAN CT
6 LAURICE CT

7 NAPLETON CT
8 THE SAVOY
9 GRANGE CT

D7
1 CHURCHILL CT
2 BELMONT CT
3 CONVENTINA HO
4 MINERVA HO
5 SILVANUS HO
6 BLAKE CT

7 COLLINGWOOD CT
8 EAGLE COTTS

E6
1 GUILDFORD LAWN
2 CAVENDISH PL
3 COLEMAN'S YD
4 CHARLOTTE CT
5 KING'S PL
6 HIBERNIA ST

7 ALBION HILL
8 ALBERT CT
9 PRINCE'S ST
10 WEST CLIFF ARC
11 ROSE HILL
12 SION PASS
13 GRUNDY'S HILL

14 ST MICHAEL'S ALLEY
15 CORNHILL
16 HARBOUR TWRS
17 HERTFORD HO
18 LIVERPOOL LAWN
19 ADELAIDE GDNS
20 PROSPECT CT

21 PROSPECT TERR
E7
1 PEMBROKE CT
2 LOUGHBOROUGH CT
3 BRUNSWICK CT
4 BARTON CT
5 PACKER'S LA

6 DOVE CT
7 DALTON CT
8 NEWCASTLE HILL
9 LA BELLE ALLIANCE SQ
10 CAMDEN SQ
11 STAFFORDSHIRE ST
12 UNION ST

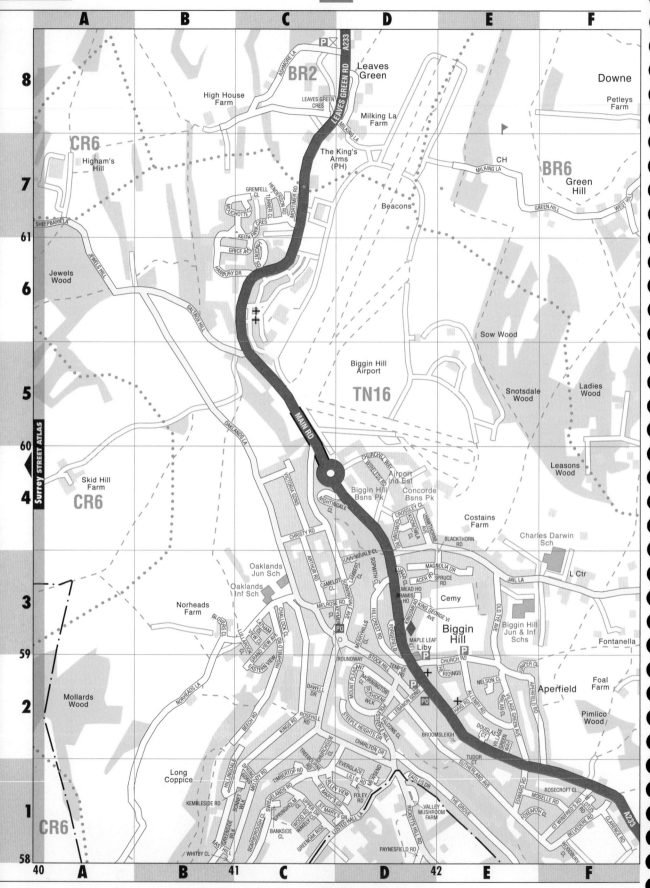

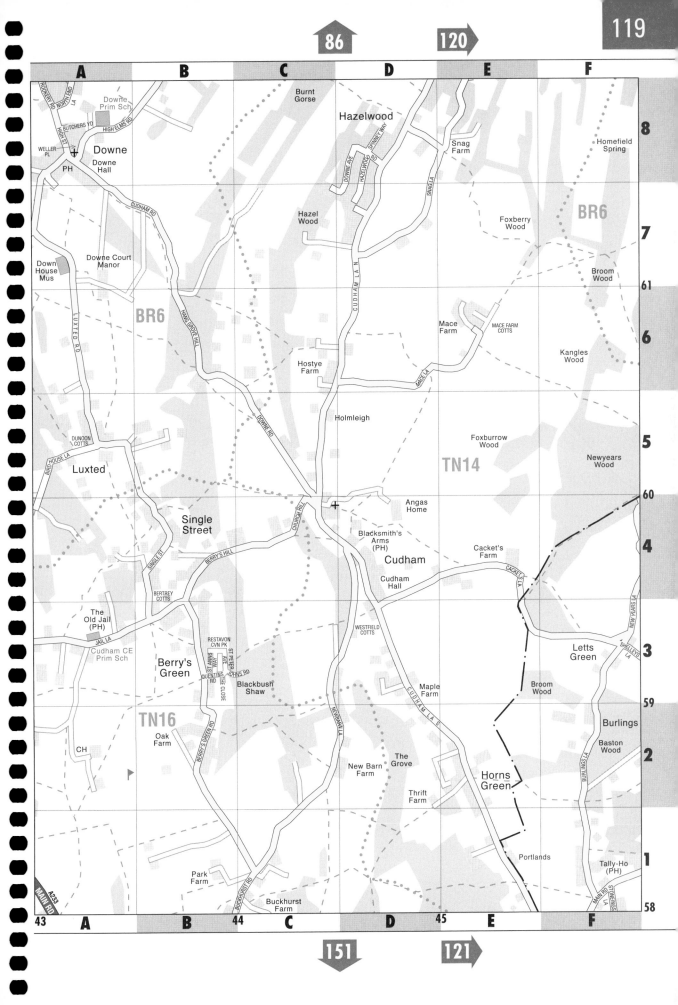

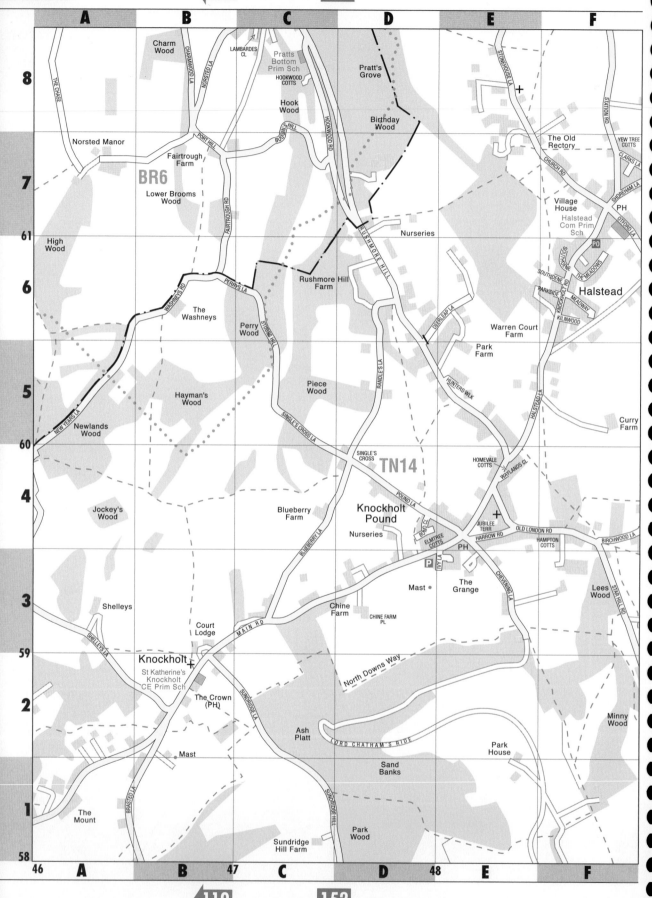

A   B   C   D   E   F

8

Charm
Wood

LAMBARDES
CL

Pratts
Bottom
Prim Sch

HOOKWOOD
COTTS

Pratt's
Grove

Hook
Wood

Birthday
Wood

STONEHOUSE LA

The Old
Rectory

YEW TREE
COTTS

CLARK'S LA

Norsted Manor

CHARMWOOD LA

NORSTED LA

7

Fairtrough
Farm

PORT HILL

BR6

Lower Brooms
Wood

HOOKWOOD RD

BUGDEN'S HILL

CHURCH RD

Village
House

SHOREHAM LA

PH

OTFORD LA

61

FAIRTROUGH RD

RUSHMORE HILL

Nurseries

Halstead Com Prim Sch

SOUTHDENE RD

PO

THE MEADOWS

High
Wood

PERRY'S LA

Rushmore Hill
Farm

PARKSIDE

KNOCKHOLT RD

MEADWAY

Halstead

6

WASHNEYS RD

The
Washneys

Perry
Wood

STUBBS HILL

DEERLEAP LA

Warren Court
Farm

KILNWOOD

Piece
Wood

Park
Farm

HUNTERS WLK

HALSTEAD LA

5

Hayman's
Wood

NEW YEARS LA

Newlands
Wood

SINGLE'S CROSS LA

RANDLE'S LA

Curry
Farm

60

Single's
Cross

TN14

HOMEVALE
COTTS

WAYLANDS CL

4

Jockey's
Wood

Blueberry
Farm

POUND LA

Knockholt
Pound

POND CL

JUBILEE
TERR

Old London Rd

HARROW RD

HAMPTON
COTTS

BIRCHWOOD LA

Nurseries

ELMTREE
COTTS

PH

STAR HILL RD

Lees
Wood

3

Shelleys

Court
Lodge

MAIN RD

Chine
Farm

CHINE FARM
PL

Mast

P

IVY LA

The
Grange

CHEVENING LA

SHELLEYS LA

59

Knockholt

St Katherine's
Knockholt
CE Prim Sch

2

The Crown
(PH)

SUNDRIDGE LA

Ash
Platt

LORD CHATHAM'S RIDE

North Downs Way

Park
House

Minny
Wood

Mast

BRASTED LA

Sand
Banks

1

The
Mount

SUNDRIDGE HILL

Park
Wood

58

Sundridge
Hill Farm

46   A   47   B   C   47   D   48   E   F

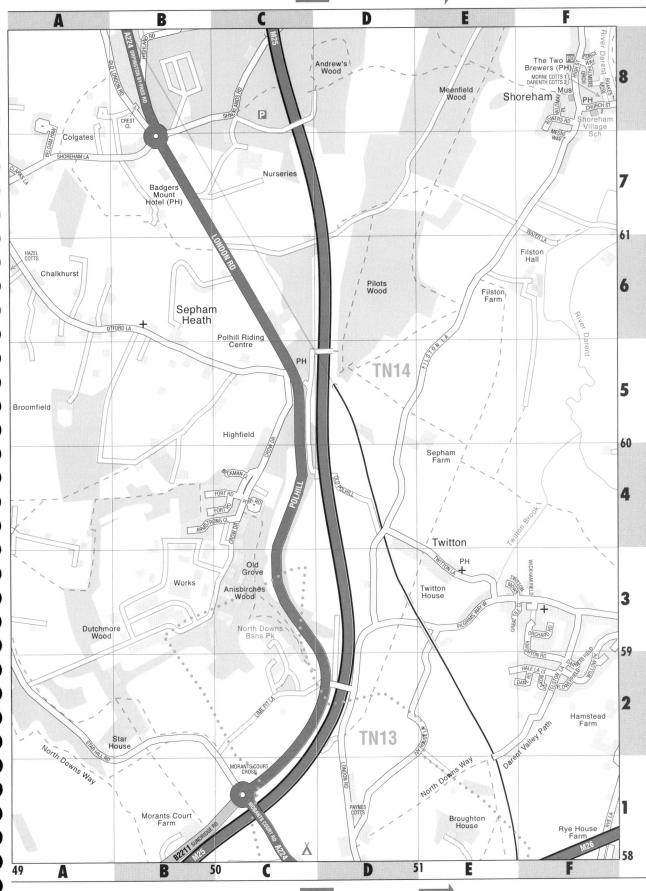

← 121
89

A B C D E F

DA4

8

Dunstall Priory

Chapel Alley Cotts
CHURCH COTTS
CHURCH ST
DARENT WAY

Austin Spring

Romney Street Farm

PH

Shoreham

SHOREHAM HO

STATION RD

Dunstall Woods

CH

7

River Darent

SHOREHAM RD

White Hill

FACKENDEN LA

Dunstall Farm

Rose Cottage Farm

MAGPIE BOTTOM

61

Home Farm

Whitehill Farm

Doctor's Wood

Eastdown

6

Warren Farm

Highfield

Sevenacre Stubs

Darent Valley Path

Mast

Greenhill Wood

Paine's Farm

Great Wood

TN15

5

SHOREHAM RD

The Mount

60

Lower Barn

GREENHILL RD

Birchin Cross Rd

ROWDOW LA

SHOREHAM LA

TN14

HILLYDEAL RD

Hillydeal Wood

4

North Downs Way

Otford Mount

Otford Court (St Michael's Sch)

Rowdow Wood

COOMBE RD

Shore Hill

The Horns (PH)

Park Farm

Russell House Sch

LEONARD AVE

P

Liby
HIGH ST

STATION RD

Otford

Pilgrims Way E

ST MICHAELS DR

Kemsing Down Nature Reserve

3

Otford

PILGRIMS WAY W

Otford Prim Sch

COLETS ORCH

STATION APP

P

Bishop's Palace (remains of)

TUDOR DR

TUDOR CRES

BEECHY LEES RD

PILGRIMS WAY

CHALKWAYS

THE CHASE

HIGHFIELD RD

HILLSIDE RD

SHOREHILL CT

COPPERFIELDS ORCH

WARHAM RD

SHINECROFT

River Darent

PICKMOSS LA

WELL RD

SIDLEY GDNS

EVELYN RD

PARK HILL RD

NORTHDOWN RD

BARN FIELD

COLLET RD

COPPERFIELDS WLK

COPPERFIELDS CL

59

WILLOW PK

BROUGHTON RD

THE CHARNE

BUBBLESTONE RD

THE OLD WLK

THE BUTTS

PO

KNOLE WOOD

DYNES RD

BROOKFIELD

GREYSTONES CL

WEST END

Liby

RYE LA

RYECROFT RD

OTFORD RD

SEVENOAKS RD

THE PARADE
BARCLAY FIELD 2

NORMAN CL

NIGHTINGALE RD

EDGAR RD

OXENHILL RD

MONTIORT RD

SPRING HEAD RD

Kemsing

2

Oxenhill Shaw

CLEVES RD

STYLE DR

CHILDSBRIDGE LA

CHILDSBRIDGE WAY

M26

1

A225

OLD OTFORD RD

Ladds House

Childsbridge House

M26

58

52 A 53 B C 54 D E F

← 121
154

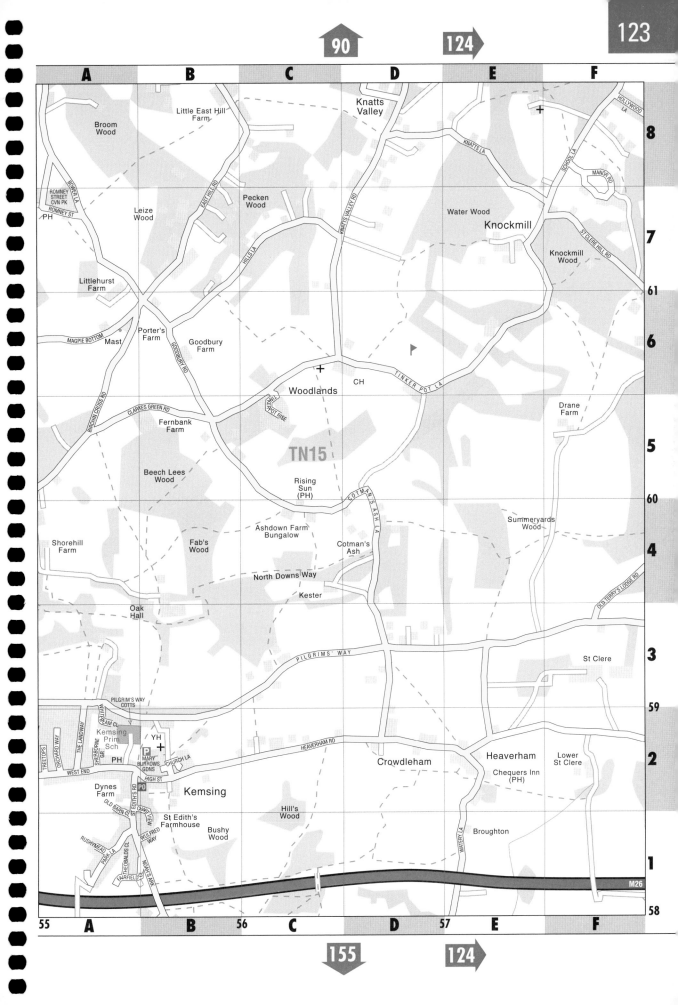

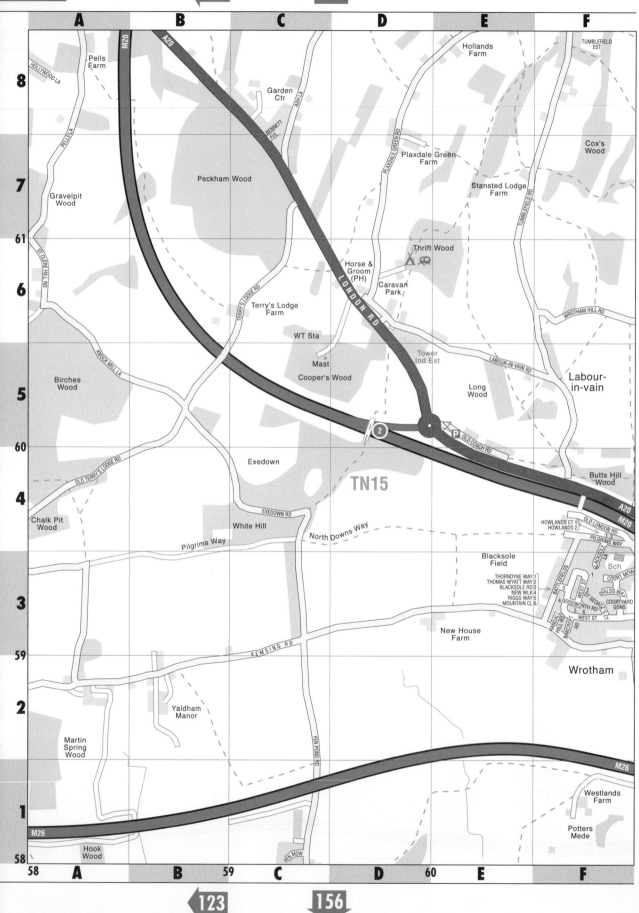

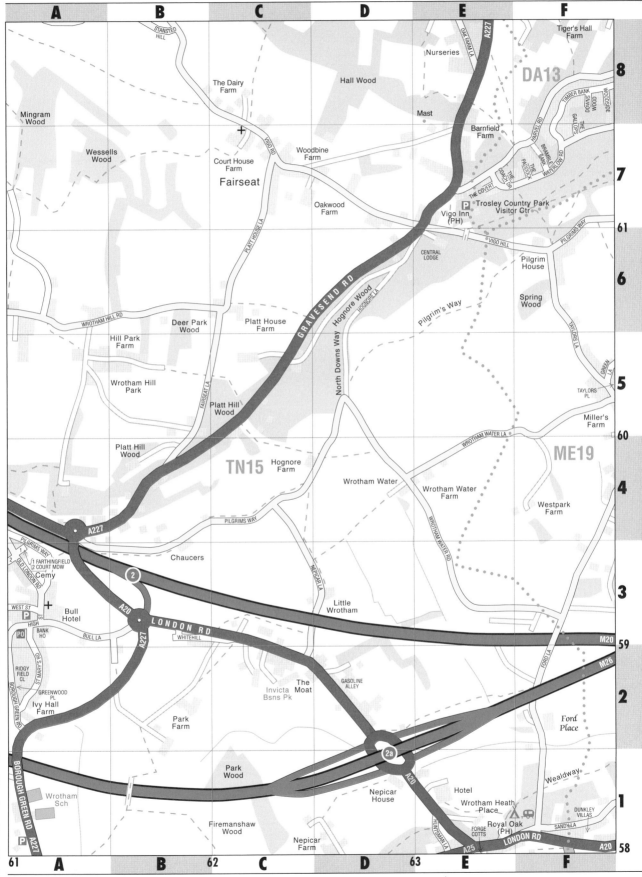

A B C D E F

STANSTED HILL

The Dairy Farm

Nurseries

Hall Wood

DA13

Mingram Wood

Wessells Wood

Court House Farm

Fairseat

Woodbine Farm

Mast

Barnfield Farm

TIMBER BANK

WOODSIDE

THE GALLOPS

Oakwood Farm

THE COVERT

THE PADDOCK

BRAMBLE BANK

WATERLOW CL

Trosley Country Park Visitor Ctr

Vigo Inn (PH)

VIGO HILL

PILGRIMS WAY

CENTRAL LODGE

Pilgrim House

GRAVESEND RD

Hognore Wood

HOGNORE LA

Pilgrim's Way

Spring Wood

Wrotham Hill Rd

Deer Park Wood

Platt House Farm

North Downs Way

TAYLORS LA

GREEN LA

Hill Park Farm

FAIRSEAT LA

PLATT HOUSE LA

Wrotham Hill Park

Platt Hill Wood

TAYLORS PL

Miller's Farm

WROTHAM WATER LA

Platt Hill Wood

TN15

Hognore Farm

ME19

Wrotham Water

Wrotham Water Farm

Westpark Farm

A227

Chaucers

PILGRIMS WAY

WROTHAM WATER RD

2

PILGRIMS WAY

1 FARTHINGFIELD 2 COURT MDW

Cemy

A20

LONDON RD

NEPICAR LA

Little Wrotham

WEST ST

Bull Hotel

A227

WHITEHILL

M20

HIGH ST

BANK HO

BULL LA

PO

RIDGY FIELD CL

GREENWOOD PL

ST MARY'S RD

Invicta Bsns Pk

The Moat

GASOLINE ALLEY

M26

FORD LA

Ivy Hall Farm

OLD LONDON RD

BOROUGH GREEN RD

Park Farm

2a

Ford Place

Park Wood

A20

Wealdway

Nepicar House

Hotel

Wrotham Heath Place

DUNKLEY VILLAS

Wrotham Sch

Firemanshaw Wood

Nepicar Farm

HUNTSMAN LA

FORGE COTTS

Royal Oak (PH)

A25

SANDY LA

LONDON RD

A20

P A227

8

7

61

6

5

60

4

3

59

2

1

58

61

62

63

125
93

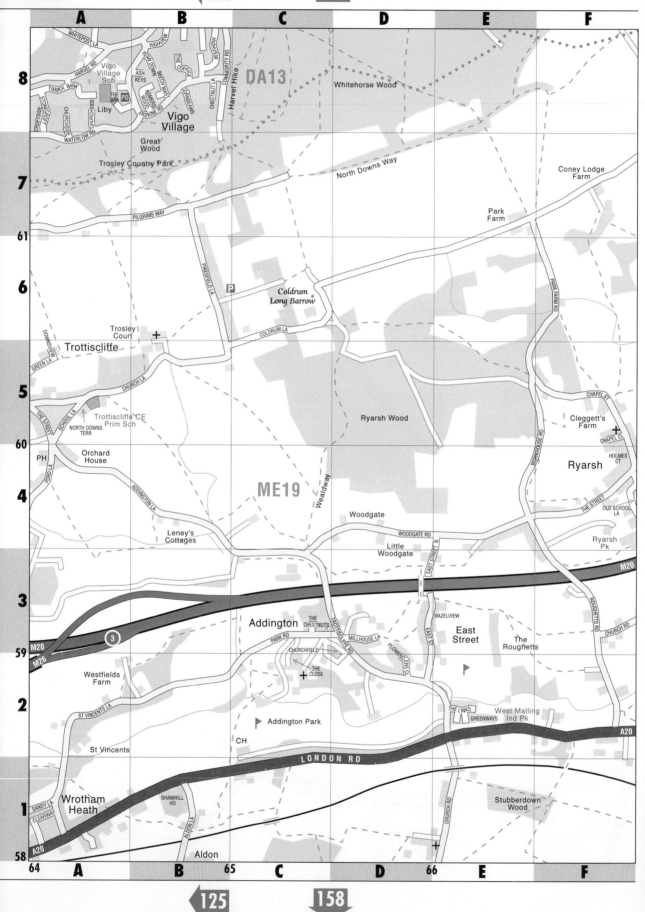

125
158

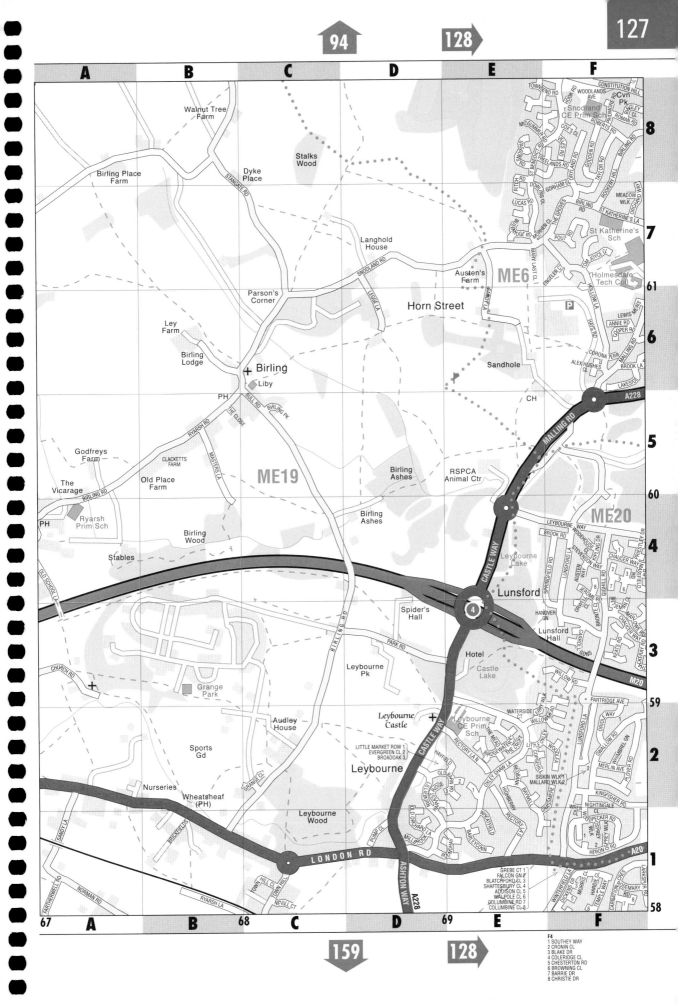

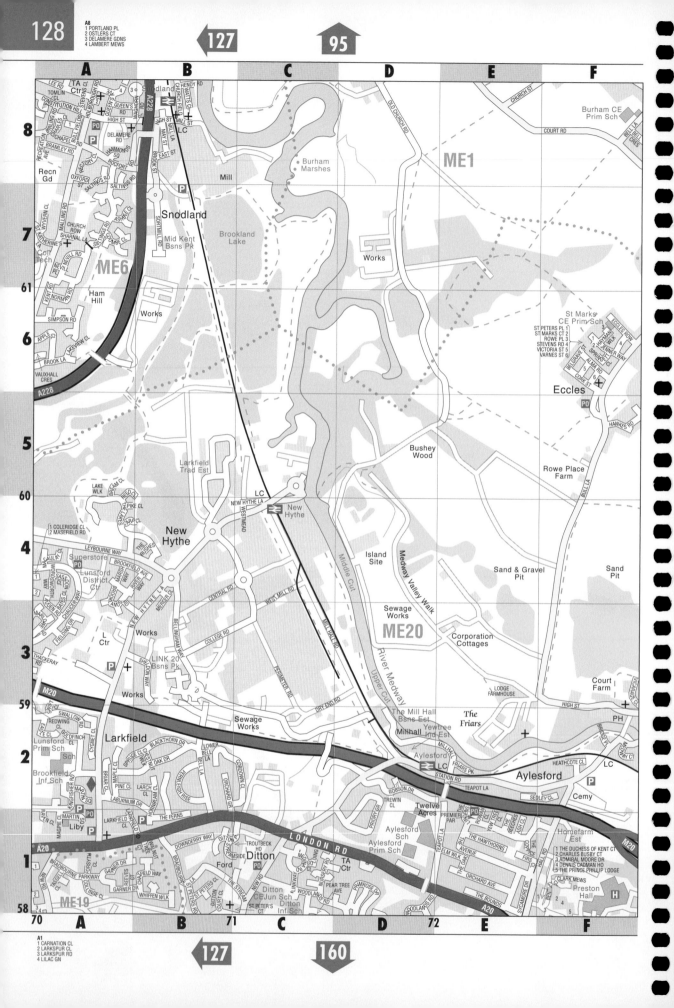

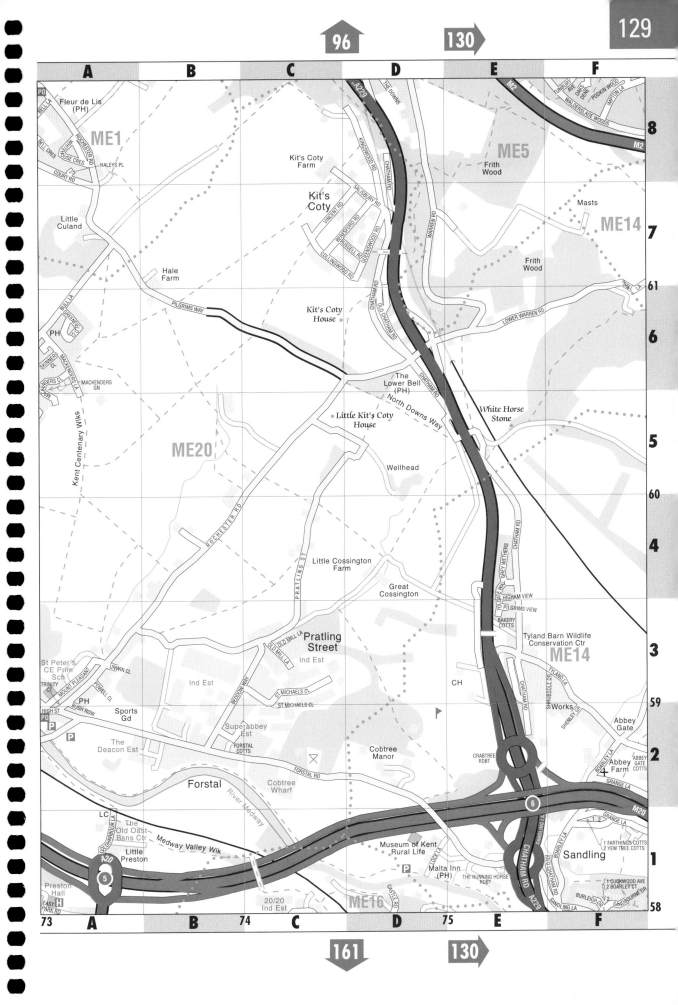

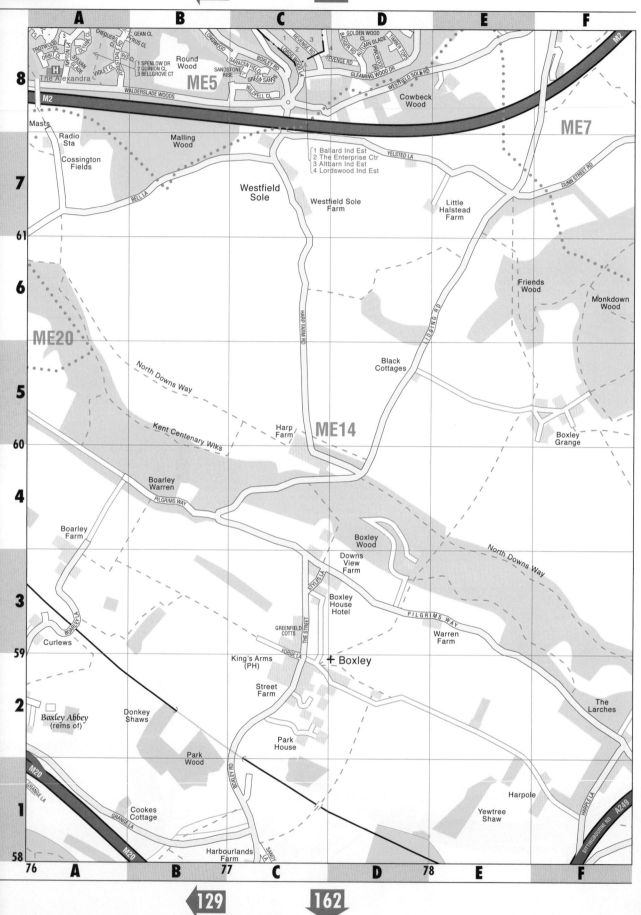

129
97
129
162

1 Ballard Ind Est
2 The Enterprise Ctr
3 Altbarn Ind Est
4 Lordswood Ind Est

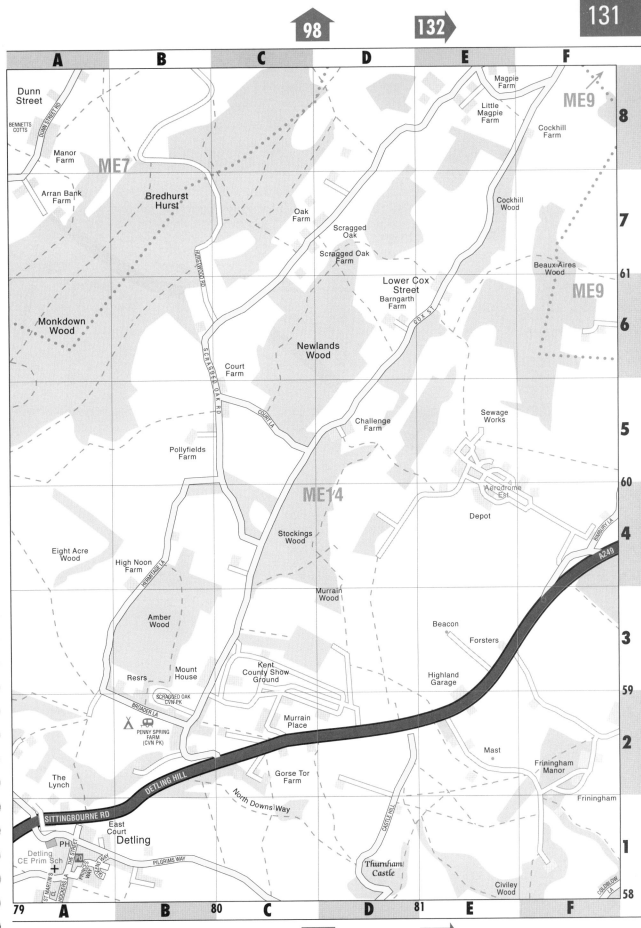

A   B   C   D   E   F

Dunn Street
BENNETTS COTTS
Manor Farm
ME7
Arran Bank Farm
Bredhurst Hurst
HURSTWOOD RD
Oak Farm
Scragged Oak
Scragged Oak Farm
Magpie Farm
ME9
Little Magpie Farm
Cockhill Farm
Cockhill Wood
Beaux Aires Wood
ME9

Monkdown Wood
SCRAGGED OAK RD
Court Farm
Newlands Wood
Lower Cox Street
Barngarth Farm
COX ST

Pollyfields Farm
COURT LA
Challenge Farm
ME14
Sewage Works
Aerodrome Est
Depot

Eight Acre Wood
HERMITAGE LA
High Noon Farm
Stockings Wood
Murrain Wood
Beacon
Forsters
BINBURY LA
A249
Highland Garage

Amber Wood
Resrs
Mount House
Kent County Show Ground
Murrain Place
Mast
Friningham Manor
Friningham

BROADER LA
SCRAGGED OAK CVN PK
PENNY SPRING FARM (CVN PK)
Murrain Place
Gorse Tor Farm
DETLING HILL
North Downs Way
CASTLE HILL

The Lynch
SITTINGBOURNE RD
East Court
Detling
Detling CE Prim Sch
PH
PO
ST MARTIN'S CL
HOCKERS LA
PRINCES WAY
THE STREET
THE STREET
PILGRIMS WAY
Thurnham Castle
Civiley Wood
COLDBLOW LA

8
7
61
6
5
60
4
59
3
2
1
58

A   B   C   D   E   F

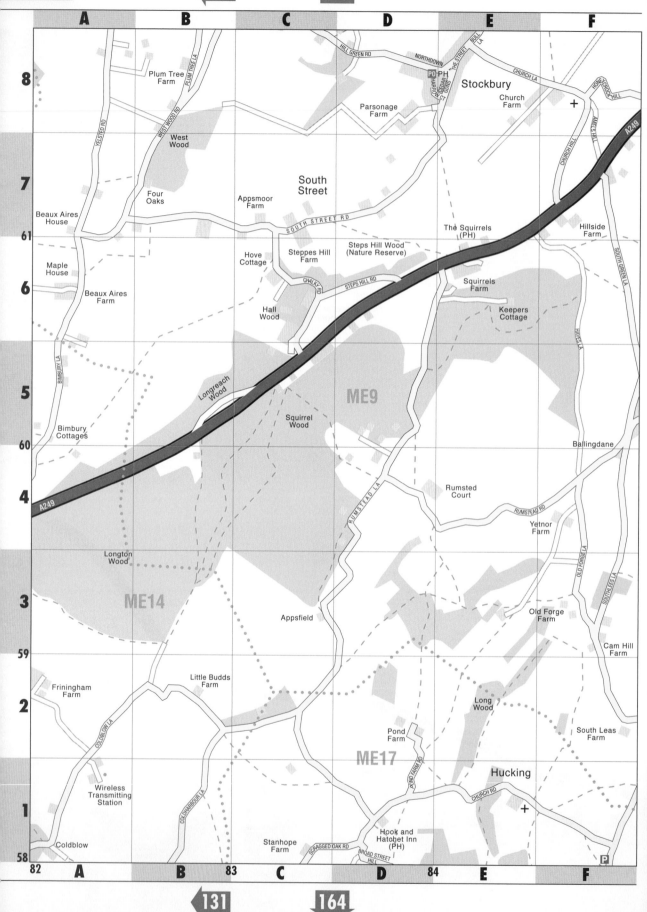

131
99

A B C D E F

8

Plum Tree Farm

YELSTED RD
WEST WOOD RD
PLUM TREE LA

West Wood

Stockbury

HILL GREEN RD
NORTHDOWN
THE STREET
BULL LA
CHURCH LA
PO PH
HARROW CT

Church Farm

HONEYCROCK HILL
AMES HILL
CHURCH HILL
A249

7

South Street

Four Oaks

Appsmoor Farm

Beaux Aires House

The Squirrels (PH)

Hillside Farm

61

SOUTH STREET RD

Maple House

Hove Cottage

Steppes Hill Farm

Steps Hill Wood (Nature Reserve)

Squirrels Farm

SOUTH GREEN LA

6

Beaux Aires Farm

CHALKY RD
STEPS HILL RD

Keepers Cottage

Hall Wood

BIMBURY LA

HATES LA

5

Longreach Wood

Squirrel Wood

ME9

Bimbury Cottages

Ballingdane

60

Rumsted Court

RUMSTEAD RD

A249

4

RUMSTEAD LA

Yetnor Farm

Longton Wood

OLD FORGE LA

SOUTH LEES LA

3

ME14

Appsfield

Old Forge Farm

Cam Hill Farm

59

Friningham Farm

Little Budds Farm

Long Wood

2

COLDBLOW LA
COLDHARBOUR LA

Pond Farm

ME17

South Leas Farm

Hucking

CHURCH RD

1

Wireless Transmitting Station

POND FARM RD

Coldblow

Stanhope Farm

SCRAGGED OAK RD
BROAD STREET HILL

Hook and Hatchet Inn (PH)

P

58

82 A B 83 C D 84 E F

131
164

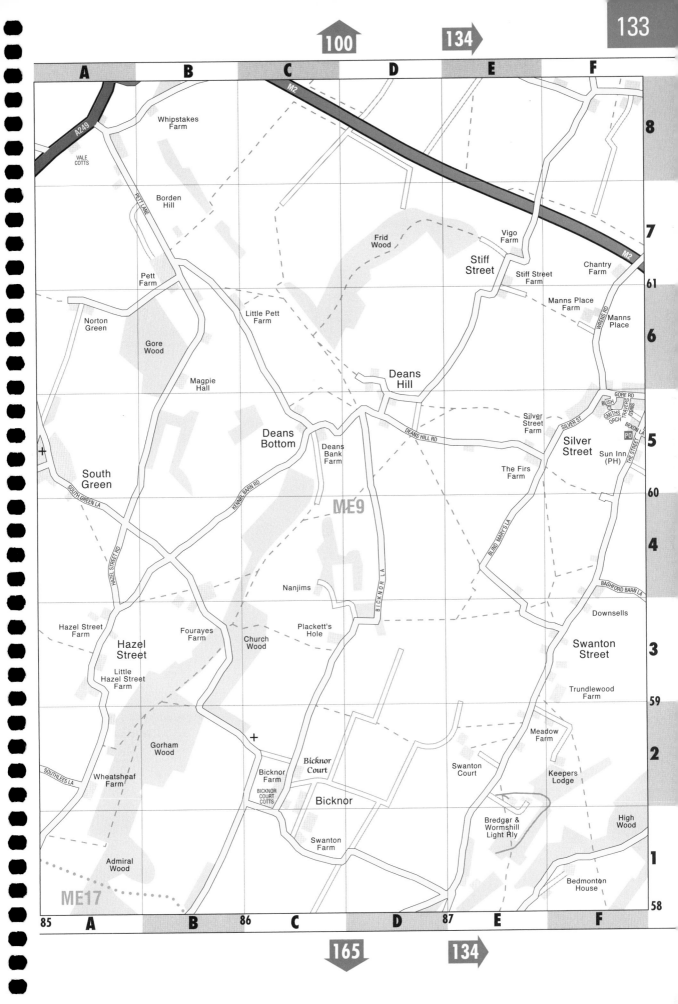

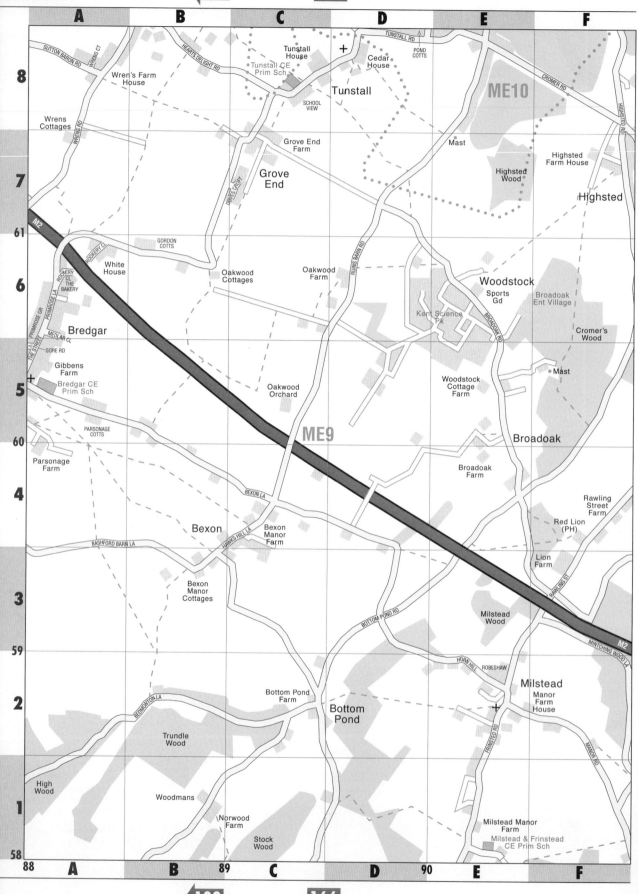

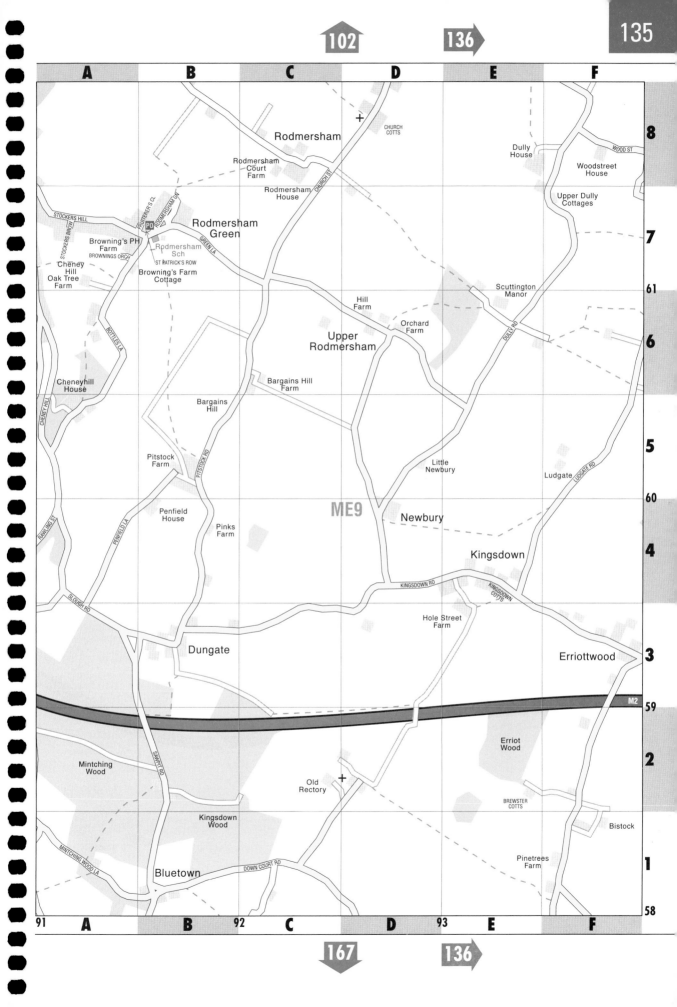

A   B   C   D   E   F

8

Rodmersham

CHURCH COTTS

Dully House

Woodstreet House

WOOD ST

Rodmersham Court Farm

Rodmersham House

Upper Dully Cottages

7

STOCKERS HILL

STOCKERS BROW

TRUMPER'S CL

RODMERSHAM GRN

PO

Rodmersham Green

Browning's PH Farm
BROWNINGS ORCH

Rodmersham Sch

ST PATRICK'S ROW

Browning's Farm Cottage

GREEN LA

CHURCH ST

Scuttington Manor

61

Cheney Hill Oak Tree Farm

Hill Farm

Orchard Farm

DULLY RD

6

BOTTLES LA

Cheneyhill House

Upper Rodmersham

CHENEY HILL

Bargains Hill Farm

Bargains Hill

5

Pitstock Farm

PITSTOCK RD

Little Newbury

Ludgate

LUDGATE RD

RAWLINS ST

ME9

60

PENFIELD LA

Penfield House

Pinks Farm

Newbury

4

Kingsdown

KINGSDOWN COTTS

SLOUGH RD

KINGSDOWN RD

Hole Street Farm

Dungate

Erriottwood

3

M2

59

SAWPIT RD

Mintching Wood

Erriot Wood

2

Old Rectory

BREWSTER COTTS

Kingsdown Wood

Bistock

MINTCHING WOOD LA

Pinetrees Farm

1

Bluetown

DOWN COURT RD

58

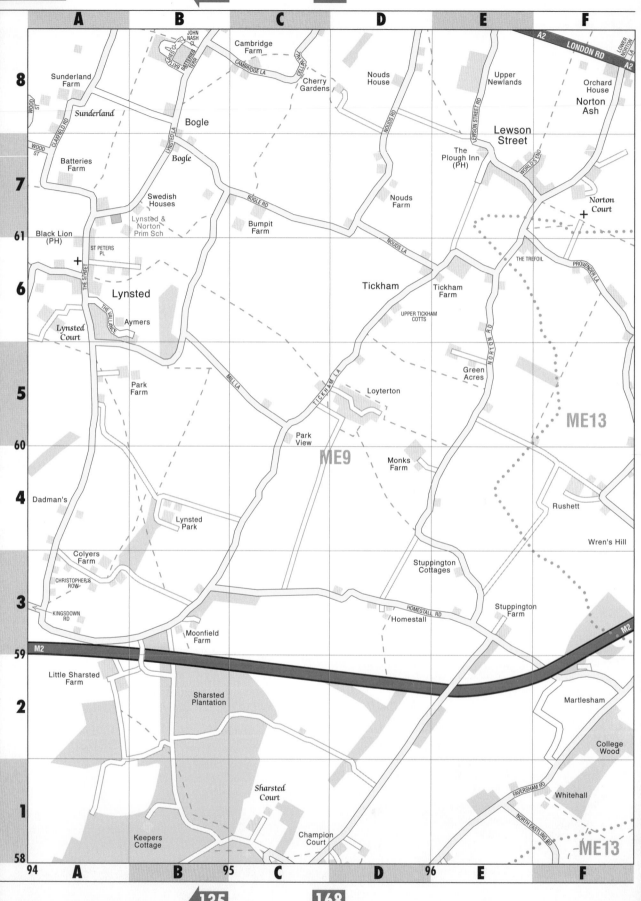

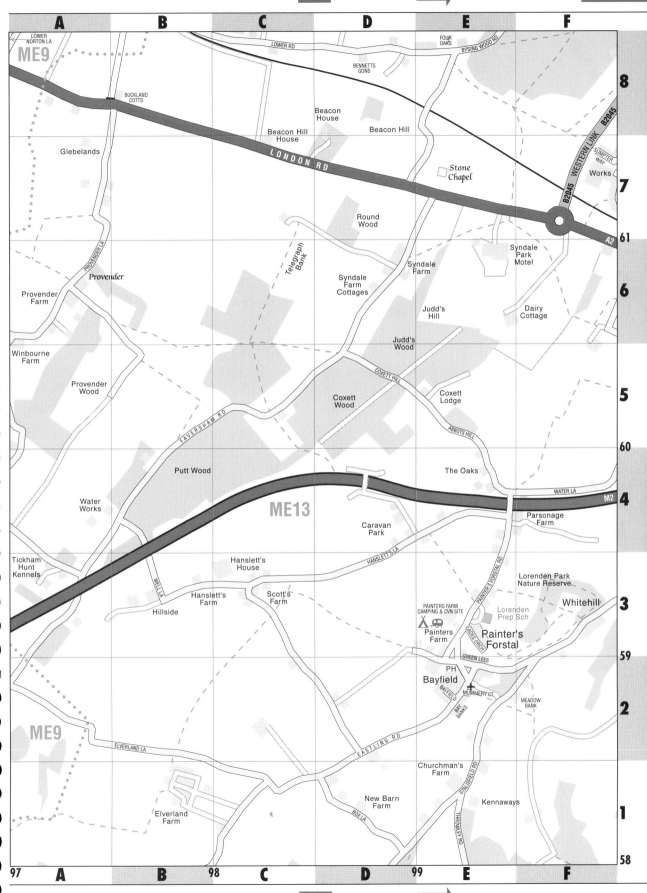

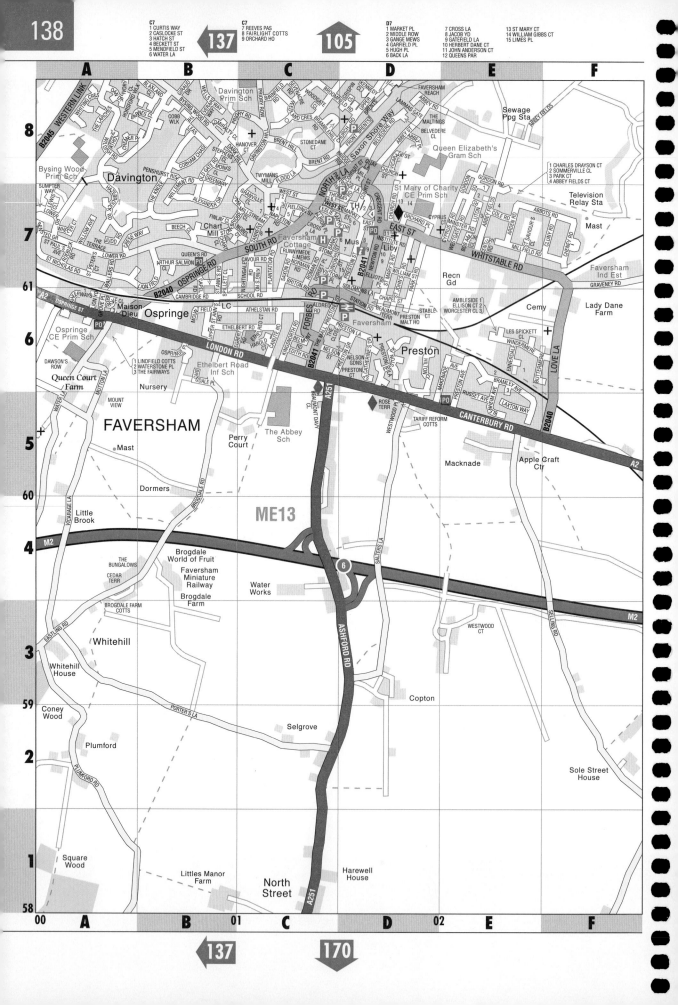

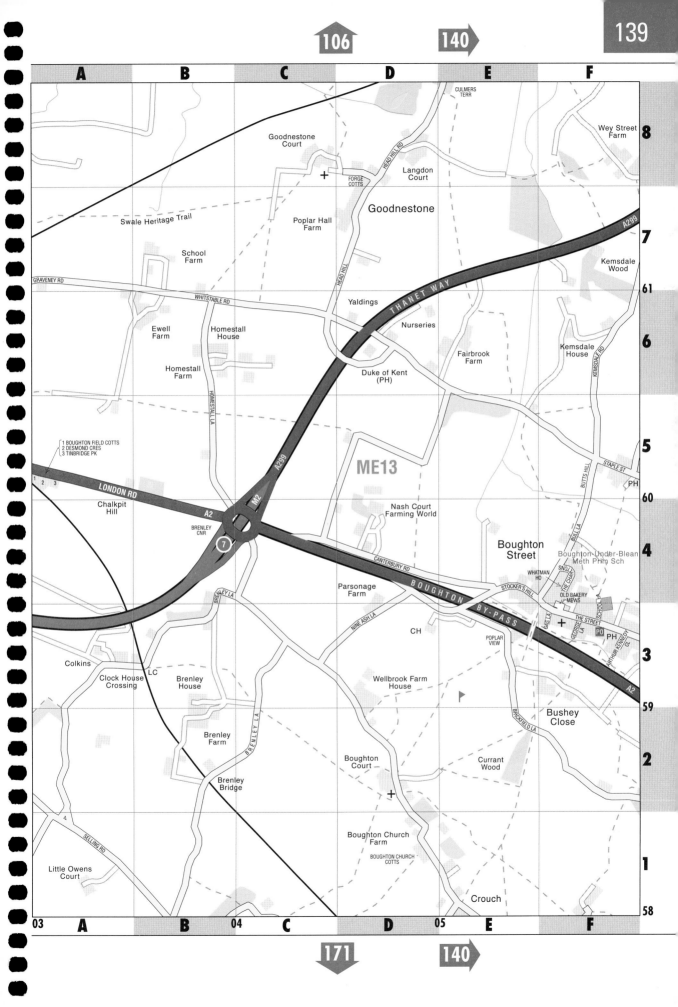

A B C D E F

CULMERS TERR

Wey Street Farm

8

Goodnestone Court

Langdon Court

HEAD HILL RD

FORGE COTTS

Goodnestone

A299

7

Swale Heritage Trail

Poplar Hall Farm

School Farm

HEAD HILL

THANET WAY

Kemsdale Wood

61

GRAVENEY RD

WHITSTABLE RD

Yaldings

Nurseries

6

Ewell Farm

Homestall House

Fairbrook Farm

Kemsdale House

KEMSDALE RD

Homestall Farm

HOMESTALL LA

Duke of Kent (PH)

1 BOUGHTON FIELD COTTS
2 DESMOND CRES
3 TINBRIDGE PK

ME13

BUTTS HILL

STAPLE ST

PH

5

1 2 3

A299

LONDON RD

M2

Nash Court Farming World

60

A2

Chalkpit Hill

BRENLEY CNR

7

Boughton Street

BULL LA

Boughton-Under-Blean Meth Prim Sch

4

CANTERBURY RD

BOUGHTON BY-PASS

WHATMAN HO

STOCKER'S HILL

SNOUT

THE CHART

THE STREET

SCHOOL LA

Parsonage Farm

Old Bakery Mews

GAS LA

GEORGE LA

PO

PH

A2

Colkins

Clock House Crossing

LC

Brenley House

BRENLEY LA

NINE ASH LA

CH

POPLAR VIEW

ARTHUR KENNEDY CL

3

Wellbrook Farm House

59

Brenley Farm

BRENLEY LA

Bushey Close

BRICKFIELD LA

Boughton Court

Currant Wood

2

Brenley Bridge

SELLING RD

Boughton Church Farm

1

Little Owens Court

BOUGHTON CHURCH COTTS

Crouch

58

03 A B 04 C D 05 E F

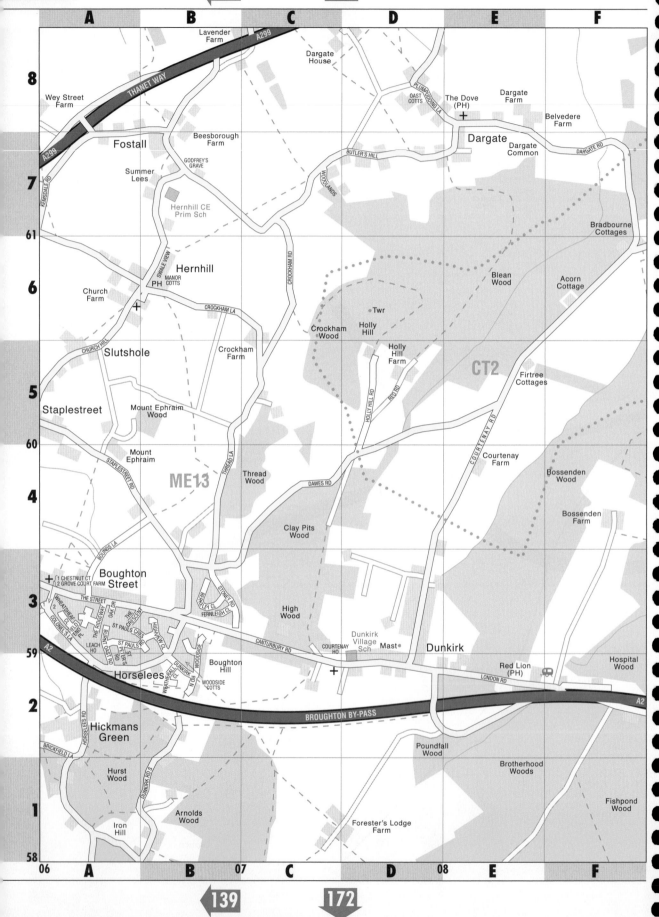

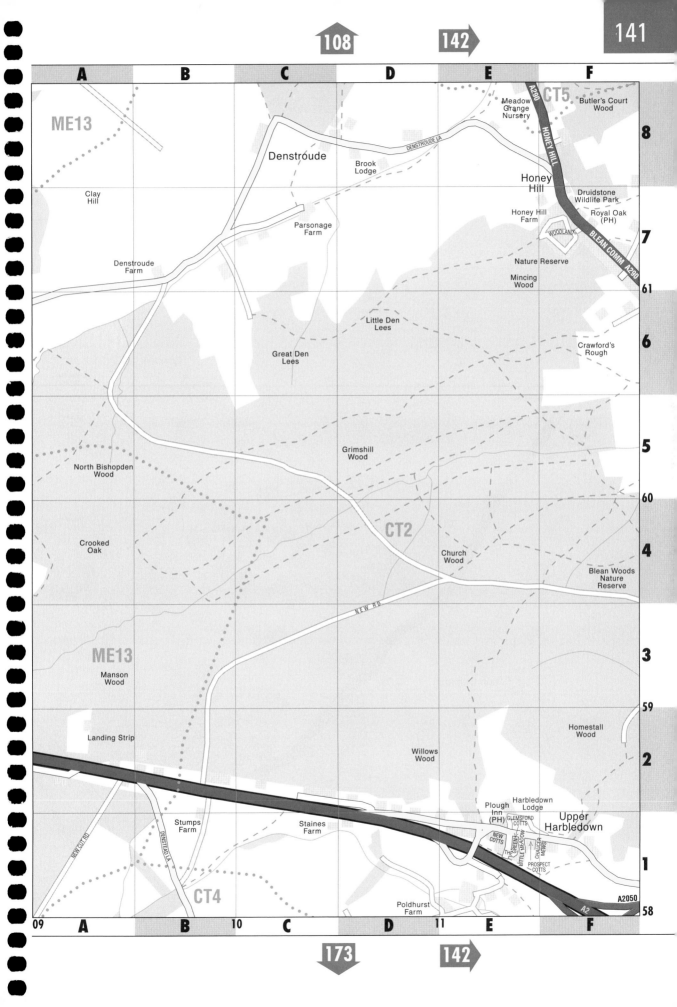

A B C D E F

ME13

8

Denstroude

Clay
Hill

Brook
Lodge

Meadow
Grange
Nursery

CT5

Butler's Court
Wood

Honey
Hill

Druidstone
Wildlife Park

Royal Oak
(PH)

7

Parsonage
Farm

Honey Hill
Farm

WOODLANDS

Denstroude
Farm

Nature Reserve

Mincing
Wood

61

Little Den
Lees

6

Great Den
Lees

Crawford's
Rough

Grimshill
Wood

5

North Bishopden
Wood

60

CT2

Crooked
Oak

Church
Wood

4

Blean Woods
Nature
Reserve

NEW RD

ME13

3

Manson
Wood

59

Landing Strip

Homestall
Wood

Willows
Wood

2

Harbledown
Lodge

Plough
Inn
(PH)

GLEMSFORD
COTTS

Upper
Harbledown

Stumps
Farm

THE
GREEN

LITTLE MEADOW

CHAUCER
MEWS

NEW
COTTS

Staines
Farm

PROSPECT
COTTS

1

CT4

Poldhurst
Farm

A2050

A2

58

09 A 10 B C 10 C D 11 E F

DENSTROUDE LA

HONEY HILL

A290

BLEAN COMM A290

NEW CUT RD

DENSTEAD LA

141 109

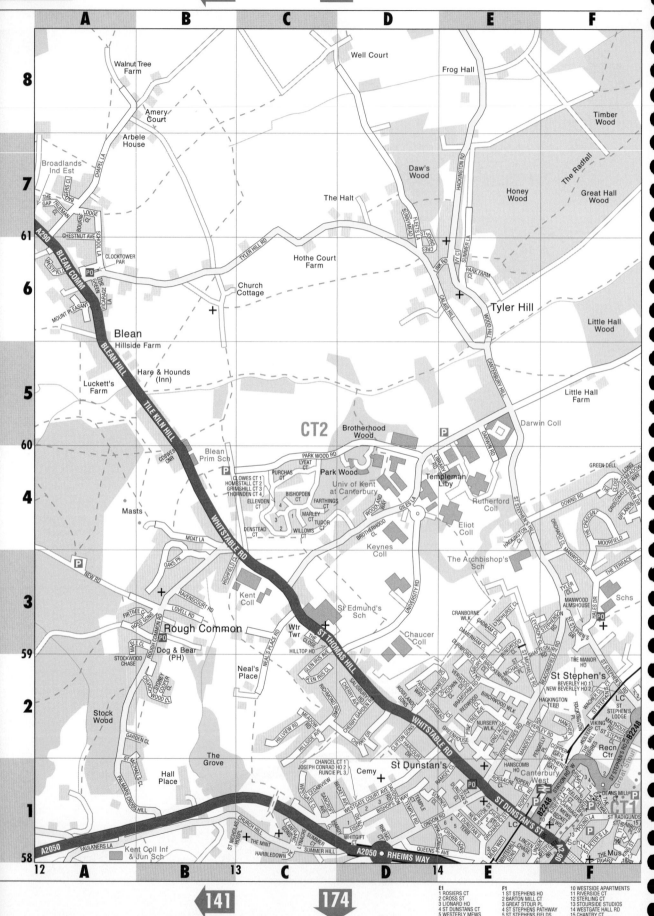

141 174

E1
1 ROSIERS CT
2 CROSS ST
3 LIONARD HO
4 ST DUNSTANS CT
5 WESTERLY MEWS
6 CRANMER HO
7 THE MALTINGS
8 WESTGATE CT

F1
1 ST STEPHENS HO
2 BARTON MILL CT
3 GREAT STOUR PL
4 ST STEPHENS PATHWAY
5 ST STEPHENS FIELDS
6 GAMMONS YD
7 THE MERCHANT STORE
8 KIRBY'S HEIGHTS
9 TEMPLAR CT

10 WESTSIDE APARTMENTS
11 RIVERSIDE CT
12 STERLING CT
13 STOURSIDE STUDIOS
14 WESTGATE HALL RD
15 CHANTRY CT
16 BLACKFRIARS ST
17 ST ALPHEGE LA
18 THE CLOISTERS

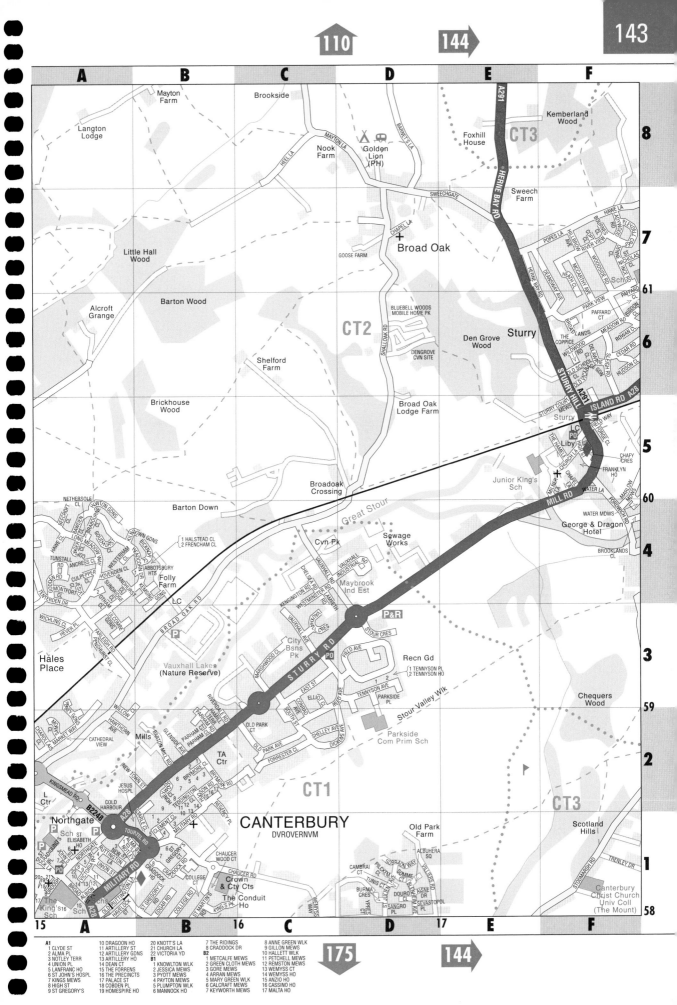

A B C D E F

8 7 61 6 5 60 4 3 59 2 1 58

15 A 16 C 17 E F

Mayton Farm
Brookside
Kemberland Wood
CT3
Foxhill House
Langton Lodge
HEEL LA
Nook Farm
MAYTON LA
Golden Lion (PH)
BARNETS LA
SWEECHGATE
Sweech Farm
HERNE BAY RD
A291
Little Hall Wood
CHAPEL LA
Broad Oak
GOOSE FARM
HAWE LA
POPES LA
RIVER VIEW
PLEYDELL CRS
Sch
Barton Wood
CT2
BLUEBELL WOODS Mobile Home Pk
Den Grove Wood
Sturry
Alcroft Grange
SHALLOAK RD
DENGROVE CVN SITE
THE COPPICE
WILDWOOD
ROWAN CL
CEDAR RD
HUDSON CL
Shelford Farm
STURRY HILL
A291
Brickhouse Wood
Broad Oak Lodge Farm
ISLAND RD A28
Sturry
PO
LC
Liby
CHAFY CRES
FRANKLYN CL
Broadoak Crossing
Junior King's Sch
WATER LA
MARLOW
Barton Down
Great Stour
MILL RD
WATER MDWS
George & Dragon Hotel
BROOKLANDS CL
NETHERSOLE CL
1 HALSTEAD CL
2 FRENCHAM CL
Cvn Pk
Sewage Works
VAUXHALL RD
TUNSTALL RD
ABBOTSBURY HTS
Folly Farm
LC
Maybrook Ind Est
BROAD OAK RD
P
Hales Place
Vauxhall Lakes (Nature Reserve)
CHELSEA RD
KENSINGTON RD
WESTMINSTER RD
VAUXHALL AVE
STURRY RD
P&R
STOUR CRES
Recn Gd
1 TENNYSON PL
2 TENNYSON HO
City Bsns Pk
PO
FIELD AVE
TENNYSON AVE
PARKSIDE PL
Stour Valley Wlk
Chequers Wood
EAST ST
ELLIOT
MARSHWOOD CL
OLD PARK CT
RIVERDALE RD
PARHAM CL
Mills
OLD PARK AVE
SHELLEY AVE
Parkside Com Prim Sch
HAWTHORN AVE
WILLOW
TA Ctr
BARTON MILL RD
FORRESTER CL
CT1
CATHEDRAL VIEW
KINGSMEAD RD
NEW TOWN ST
JESUS HOSPL
COLD HARBOUR
Old Park Farm
Scotland Hills
L Ctr
B2248
Northgate
A28
MILITARY RD
TOURTEL RD
CANTERBURY
DVROVERNVM
ALBUHERA SQ
SOBRAON WAY
WOMME
VILLIERS HO
TRENLEY DR
P
Sch
ST ELISABETH HO
PO
STORMARSH RD
CHAUCER WOOD CT
CHAUCER RD
CAMBRAI CT
TUNIS CT
DOURO CT
SANGRO PL
Canterbury Christ Church Univ Coll (The Mount)
The King's Sch
Crown & Cty Cts
The Conduit Ho
BURMA CRES
YPRES CT
WELYS WAY

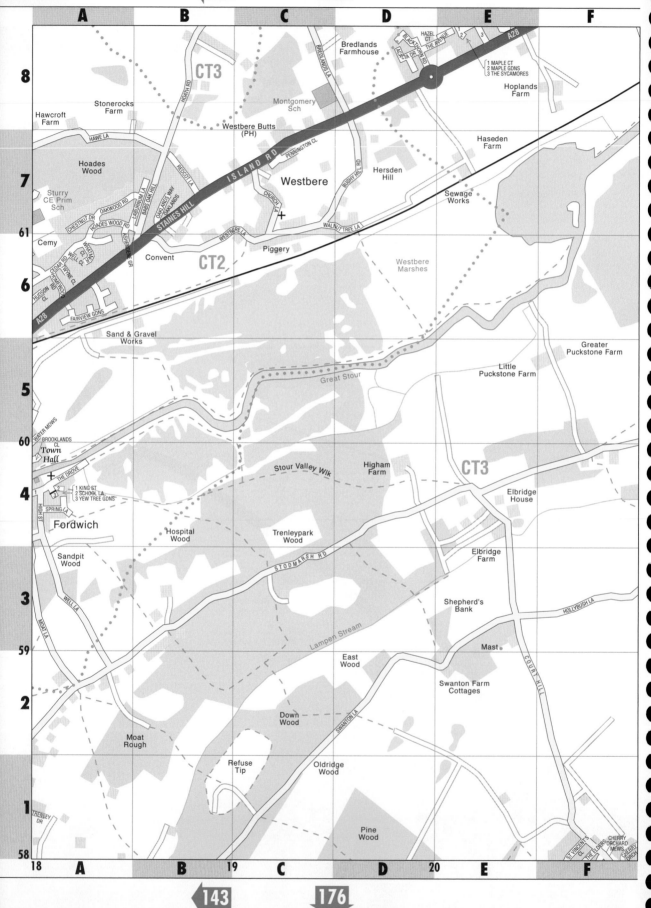

A B C D E F

8

CT3

Bredlands
Farmhouse

HAZEL
CT

A28

BLACKTHORN RD

THE AVENUE

ACACIA DR

1 MAPLE CT
2 MAPLE GDNS
3 THE SYCAMORES

Stonerocks
Farm

Montgomery
Sch

Hoplands
Farm

HOATH RD

BREDLANDS LA

Hawcroft
Farm

Westbere Butts
(PH)

Haseden
Farm

HAWE LA

ISLAND RD

7

Hoades
Wood

REDGOT LA

PENNINGTON CL

Westbere

Hersden
Hill

BUSHY HILL RD

Sewage
Works

Sturry
CE Prim
Sch

OAKLANDS WAY

LABURNUM LA

BABS OAK HILL

OAKLANDS

STAINES HILL

CHURCH LA

CHESTNUT DR

OAKWOOD RD

HOADES WOOD RD

WELL CL

WHITSEY

61

Cemy

WESTBERE LA

WALNUT TREE LA

CEDAR RD

BYRNE CL

THOMSON RD

HUDSON CL

Convent

CT2

Piggery

Westbere
Marshes

A28

FAIRVIEW GDNS

6

ASHENDENE GR

Sand & Gravel
Works

Greater
Puckstone Farm

Great Stour

Little
Puckstone Farm

5

WATER MDWS

60

BROOKLANDS
CL

Town
Hall

Stour Valley Wlk

Higham
Farm

CT3

Elbridge
House

THE DROVE

1 KING ST
2 SCHOOL LA
3 YEW TREE GDNS

SPRING LA

HIGH ST

4

Fordwich

Hospital
Wood

Trenleypark
Wood

Elbridge
Farm

WELL LA

Sandpit
Wood

STODMARSH RD

Shepherd's
Bank

HOLLYBUSH LA

MOAT LA

3

Lampen Stream

Mast

COURT HILL

59

East
Wood

Swanton Farm
Cottages

2

Moat
Rough

Down
Wood

SWANTON LA

Refuse
Tip

Oldridge
Wood

TRENLEY
DR

1

Pine
Wood

ST VINCENT'S
CL

THE ELDERS

CHERRY
ORCHARD
MEWS

CHERRY
ORCHARD

58

18 A B 19 C D 20 E F

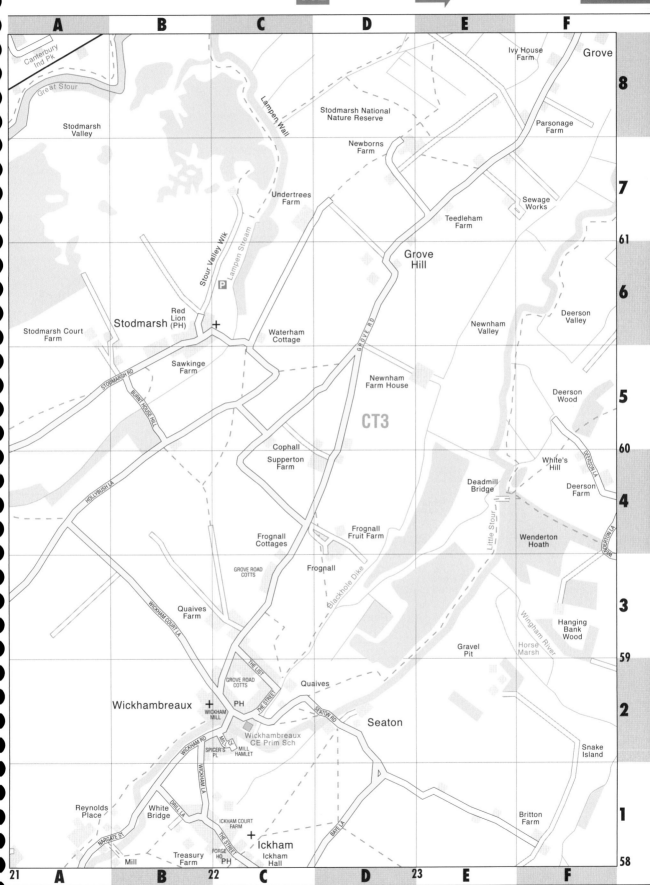

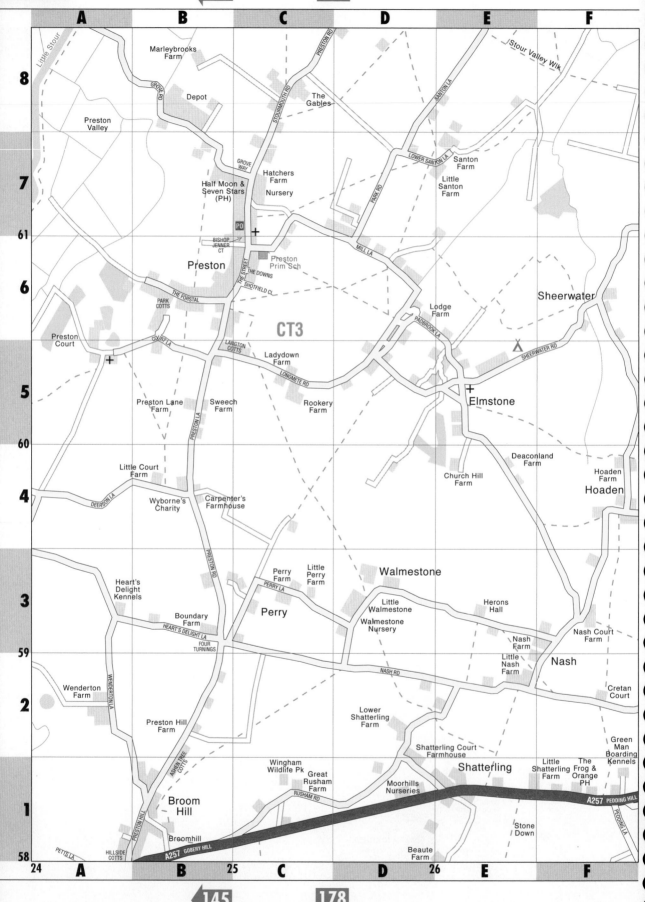

145
113
145
178

A **B** **C** **D** **E** **F**

Little Stour

Marleybrooks Farm

Depot

GROVE RD

Preston Valley

Stour Valley Wlk

The Gables

STOURMOUTH RD

PRESTON RD

SANTON LA

LOWER SANTON LA

Santon Farm

Little Santon Farm

GROVE WAY

Hatchers Farm

Nursery

Half Moon & Seven Stars (PH)

PARK RD

PO

BISHOP JENNER CT

Preston

THE STREET

THE DOWNS

Preston Prim Sch

MILL LA

SHOTFIELD CL

THE FORSTAL

PARK COTTS

Lodge Farm

Sheerwater

PADBROOK LA

CT3

COURT LA

LANGTON COTTS

Ladydown Farm

LONGMETE RD

SHEERWATER RD

Preston Court

Elmstone

Preston Lane Farm

Sweech Farm

Rookery Farm

PRESTON LA

Little Court Farm

Deaconland Farm

Church Hill Farm

Hoaden Farm

Hoaden

DEERSON LA

Wyborne's Charity

Carpenter's Farmhouse

PRESTON RD

Walmestone

Perry Farm

Little Perry Farm

Herons Hall

Nash Court Farm

Heart's Delight Kennels

PERRY LA

Perry

Little Walmestone

Walmestone Nursery

Nash Farm

Boundary Farm

HEART'S DELIGHT LA

FOUR TURNINGS

Little Nash Farm

Nash

Wenderton Farm

NASH RD

Cretan Court

WENDERTON LA

Preston Hill Farm

Lower Shatterling Farm

ASHEN TREE COTTS

Shatterling Court Farmhouse

Green Man Boarding Kennels

Wingham Wildlife Pk

Great Rusham Farm

Shatterling

Little Shatterling Farm

The Frog & Orange PH

PRESTON HILL

Broom Hill

RUSHAM RD

Moorhills Nurseries

A257 PEDDING HILL

Broomhill

HILLSIDE COTTS

A257 GOBERY HILL

Stone Down

Beaute Farm

PEDDING LA

PETT'S LA

A **B** **C** **D** **E** **F**

8 7 61 6 5 60 4 3 59 2 1 58

24 25 26

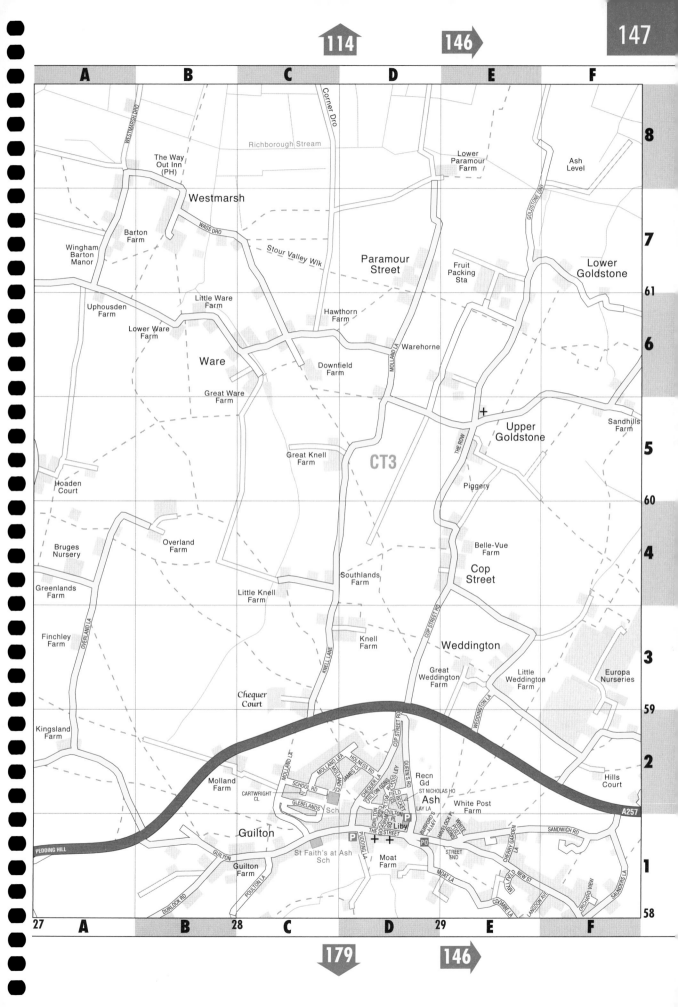

147
115

A B C D E F

8

Ash Level

White House

7

Richborough Stream

61

Guston Farm

Bride Farm

WHITEHOUSE DRO

Sparrow Castle

6

Richborough Farm

RUBERY DRO

Fleet Farm

Castle Farm

Richborough Castle
ROMAN FORT
(remains of)

CT3

CT13

CASTLE COTTS

5

Cooper Street Farmhouse

Swallows Brook Farm

Mus

60

Stour Valley Wlk

Roman Amphitheatre

Sewage Works

COOPER STREET DRO

Cooper Street

River Stour

A256

4

Goshall Valley

Goshall Stream

Brookestreet Farmyard

The Monks Wall

3

Little East Street Farm

LC

RICHBOROUGH RD

Saxon Shore Way

59

East Street

North Poulders Stream

East Street Farm

Nature Reserve

2

North Poulders

White Mill & Folk Mus

Ind Est

WANTSUME LEES

Goss Hall

GOSS HALL LA

A257

THE CAUSEWAY

ASH RD

MILL CL

LC

A257 SANDWICH RD

P

P

STRAND ST

Each End

South Poulders

Sandwich Inf Sch

THE BUTTS

PARADISE ROW

COTTAGE ROW

DELF ST

MILLBERRY
1 2 3 4
5 6
7 8
9 10
11

1

Each End House

A256

The Butts

Sandwich Town Mus

12

MOAT SOLE

CATTLE MKT

Each Manor Farm

Mary-le-bone Hill

WOODNESBOROUGH RD

ST THOMAS'S HOSP

LC

P

15

58

30 A 31 B C 32 D E F

F1
1 GUESTLING MILL CT
2 CREIGHTON FLATS
3 CHURCH ST
4 VICARAGE LA
5 GUILDCOUNT LA
6 HARNET ST
7 WANTSUM MEWS
8 STOUR CT
9 LOOP COURT MEWS
10 THE OLD COACHWORKS
11 TANNERY LA
12 ST JOHN'S COTTS
13 WATTS YD
14 WHITEFRIARS WAY
15 WHITEFRIARS MDW

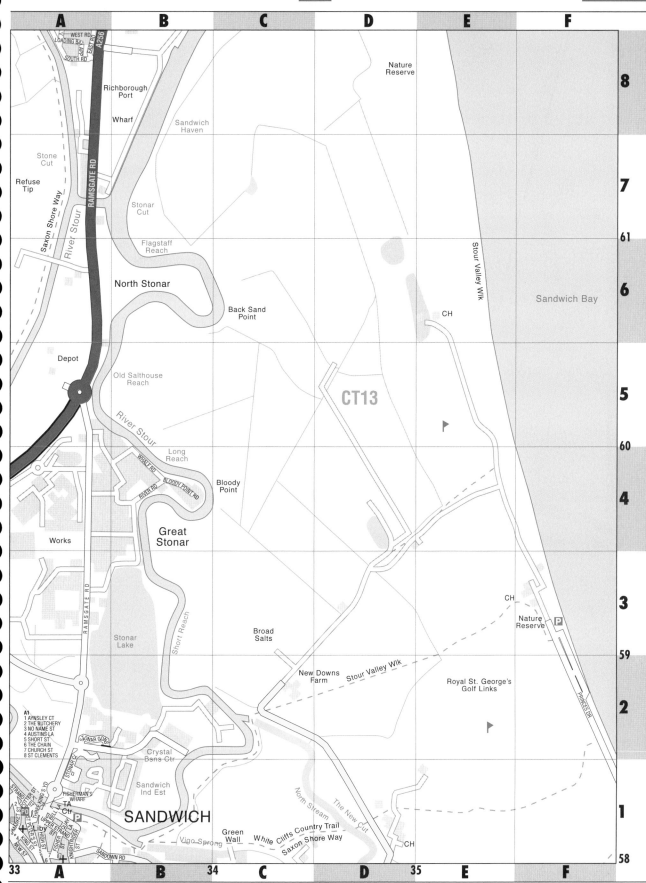

118

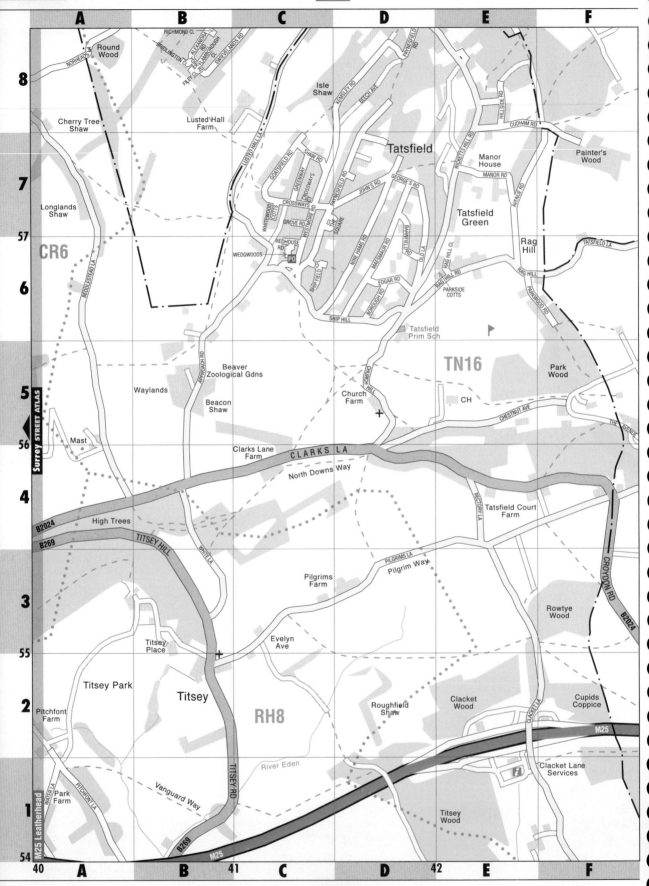

183

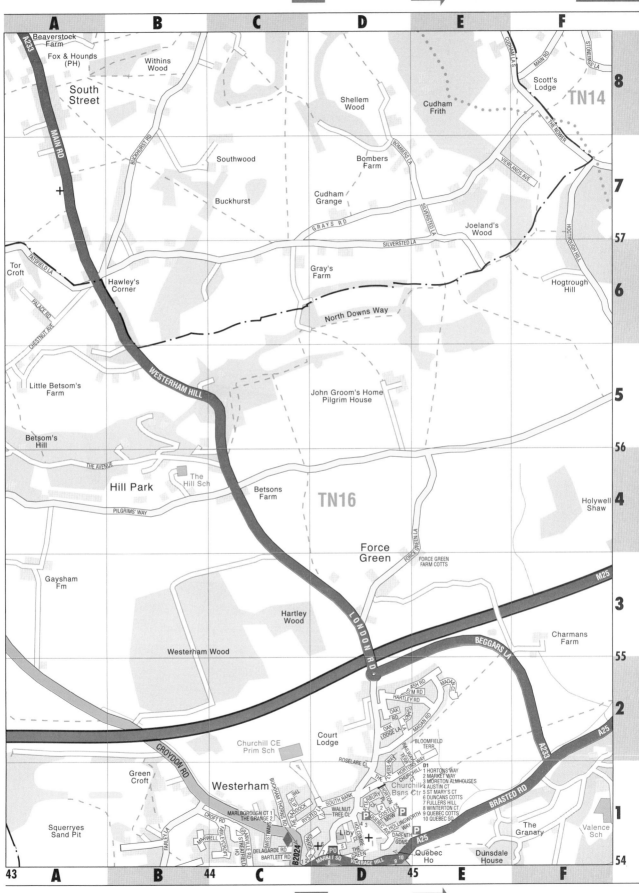

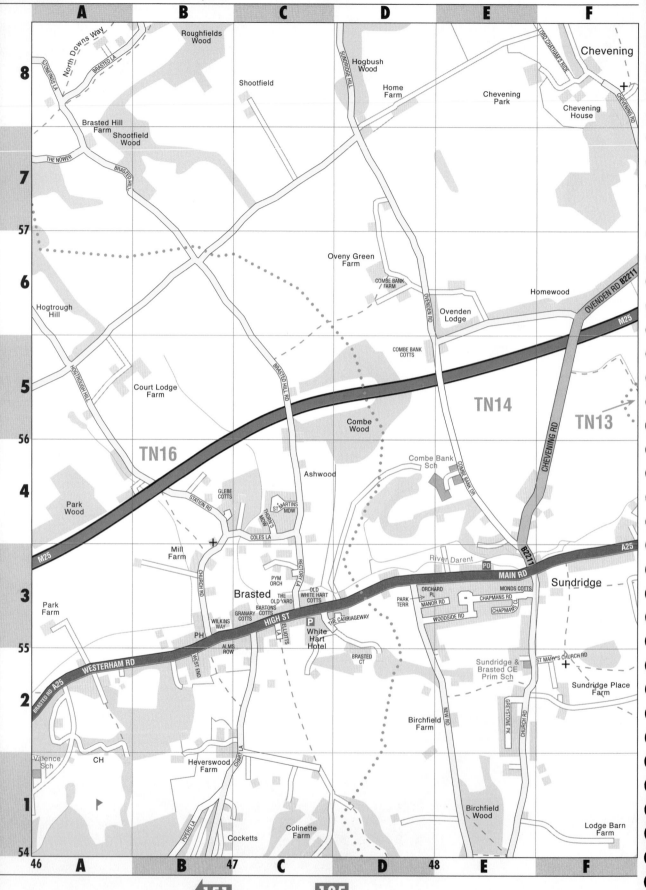

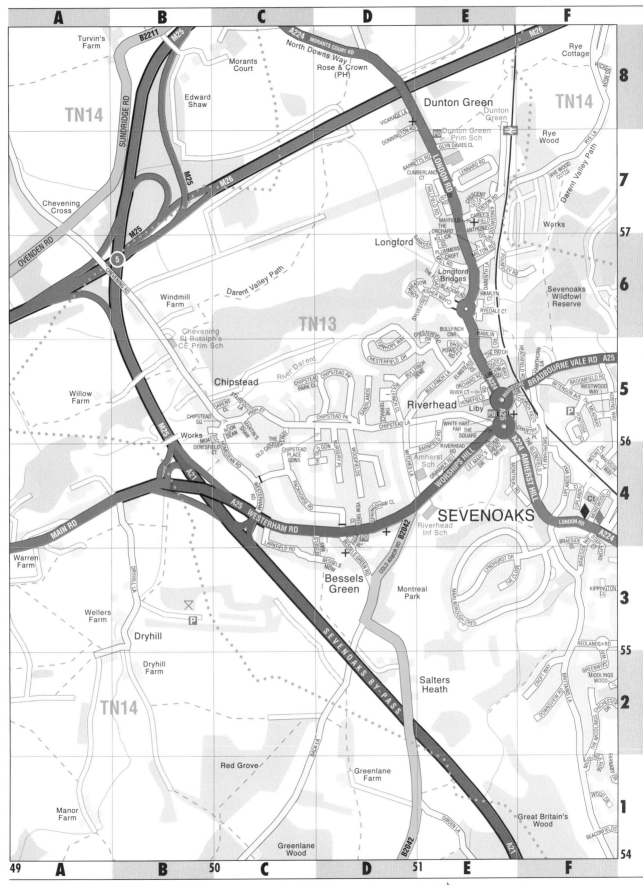

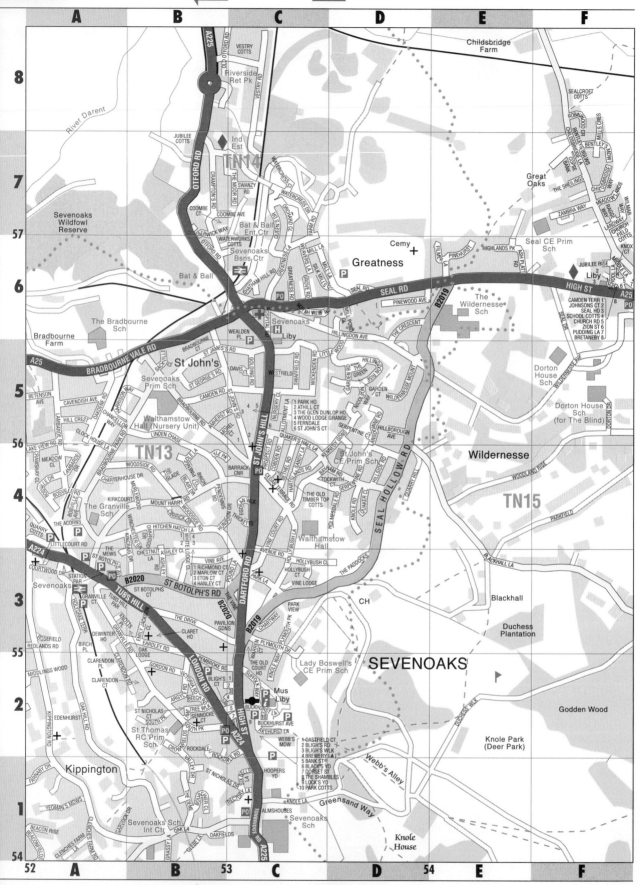

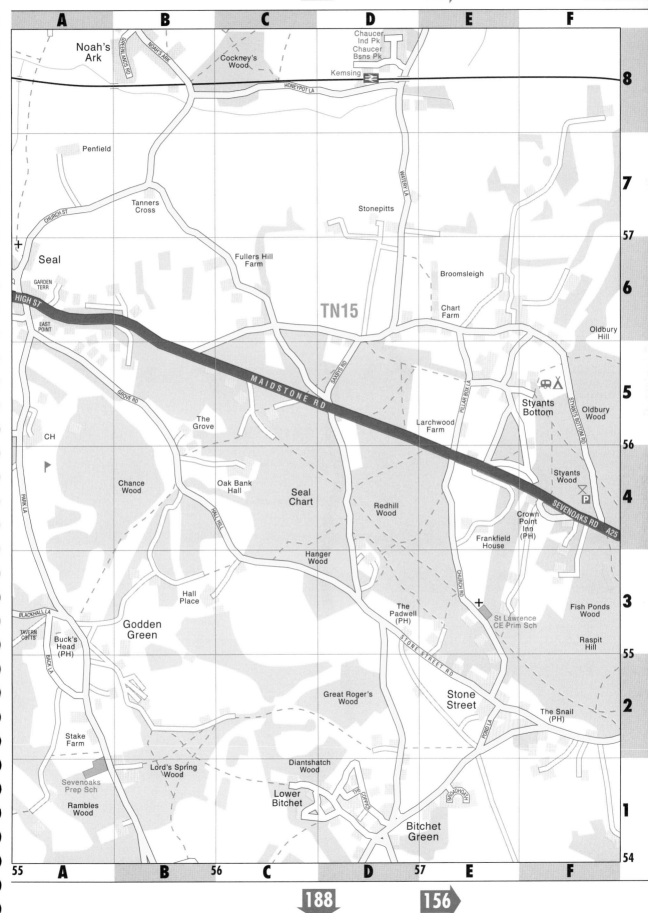

155
124

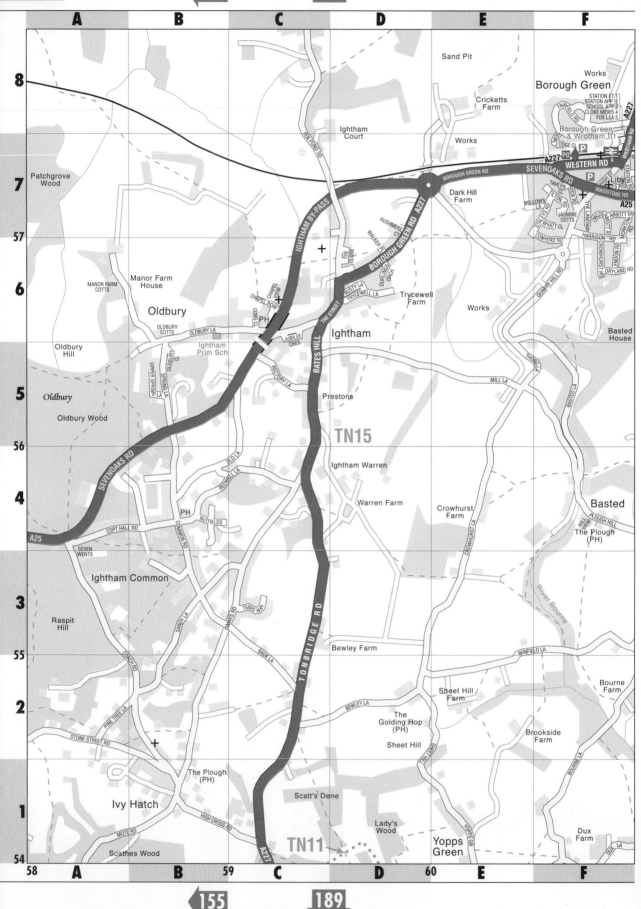

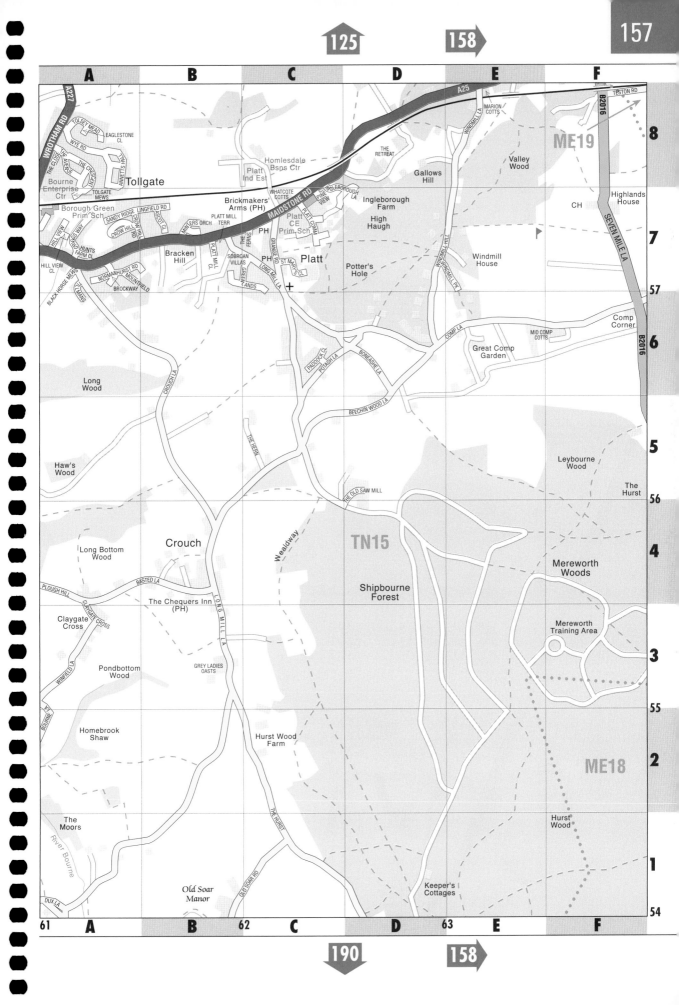

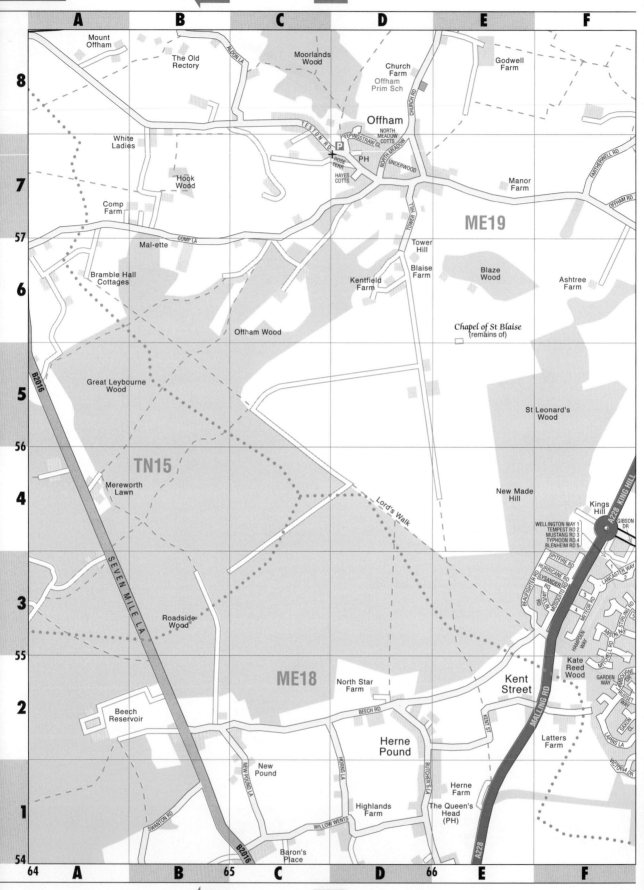

Mount Offham

The Old Rectory

Moorlands Wood

Church Farm
Offham Prim Sch

Godwell Farm

ALDON LA

Offham

White Ladies

TESTON RD

PEPINGSTRAW CL

NORTH MEADOW COTTS

P
ROSE TERR
PH
HAYES COTTS

NORTH MEADOW

UNDERWOOD

Manor Farm

FARTHERWELL RD

Hook Wood

CHURCH RD

ME19

OFFHAM RD

Comp Farm

COMP LA

Mal-ette

TOWER HILL

Tower Hill

Blaise Farm

Blaze Wood

Ashtree Farm

Bramble Hall Cottages

Kentfield Farm

Offham Wood

Chapel of St Blaise (remains of)

Great Leybourne Wood

St Leonard's Wood

B2016

TN15

Mereworth Lawn

Lord's Walk

New Made Hill

Kings Hill

A228 KING HILL

GIBSON DR

WELLINGTON WAY 1
TEMPEST RD 2
MUSTANG RD 3
TYPHOON RD 4
BLENHEIM RD 5

SPITFIRE RD

HURRICANE RD

BEAUFIGHTER RD

LYSANDER RD

JAVELIN RD

MOSQUITO RD

METEOR RD

LANCASTER WAY

HAMPDEN WAY

MITCHELL RD

ANSON AVE

STIRLING RD

Roadside Wood

SEVEN MILE LA

ME18

North Star Farm

Kent Street

Kate Reed Wood

GARDEN WAY

CAMBOURNE DR

RUSSET WAY

LASLINS LA

SAXON CL

Beech Reservoir

BEECH RD

Herne Pound

KENT ST

MALLING RD

Latters Farm

VICTORIA DR

NEW POUND LA

New Pound

HORNS LA

Highlands Farm

BUTCHER S LA

Herne Farm

The Queen's Head (PH)

SWANTON RD

WILLOW WENTS

B2016

Baron's Place

A228

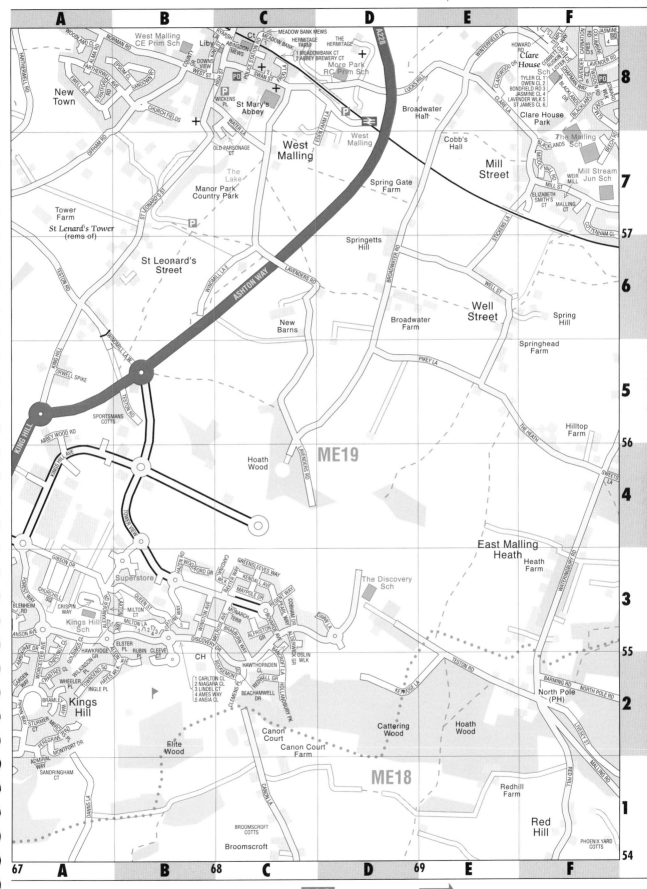

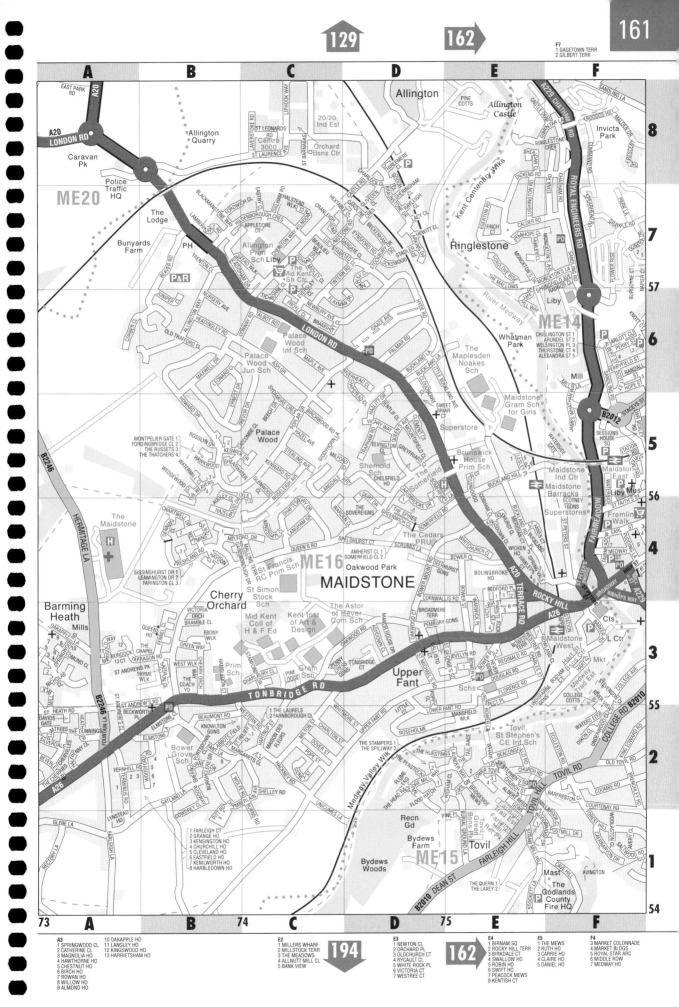

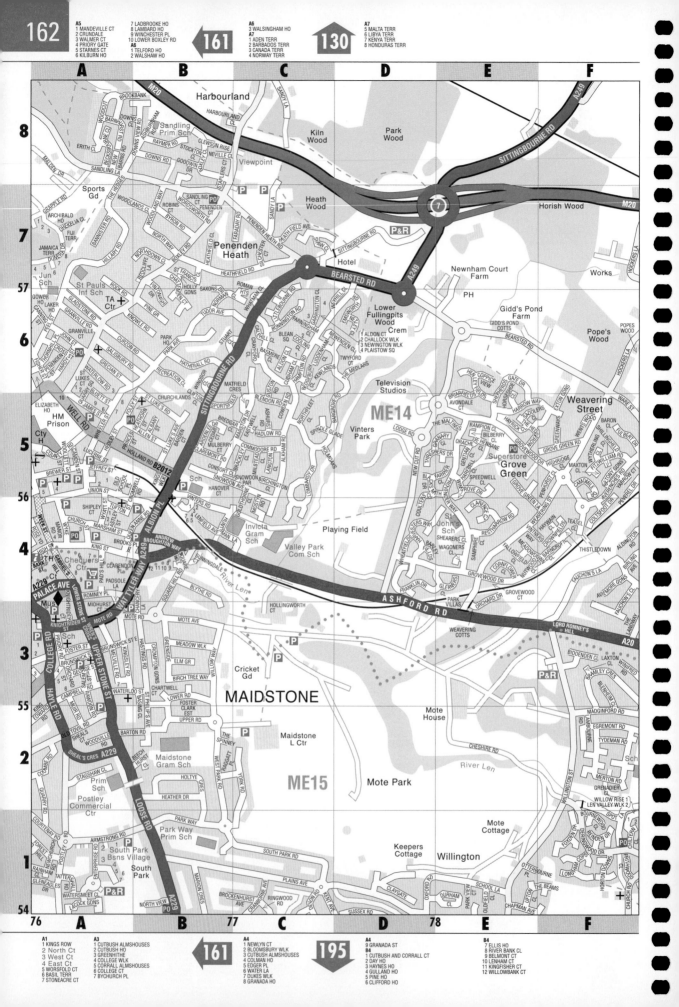

162

A5
1 MANDEVILLE CT
2 CRUNDALE
3 WALMER CT
4 PRIORY GATE
5 STARNES CT
6 KILBURN HO

7 LADBROOKE HO
8 LAMBARD HO
9 WINCHESTER PL
10 LOWER BOXLEY RD

A6
1 TELFORD HO
2 WALSHAW HO

← **161**

A6
3 WALSINGHAM HO
A7
1 ADEN TERR
2 BARBADOS TERR
3 CANADA TERR
4 NORWAY TERR

130

A7
5 MALTA TERR
6 LIBYA TERR
7 KENYA TERR
8 HONDURAS TERR

A1
1 KINGS ROW
2 NORTH CT
3 WEST CT
4 EAST CT
5 WORSFOLD CT
6 BASIL TERR
7 STONEACRE CT

A3
1 CUTBUSH ALMSHOUSES
2 CUTBUSH HO
3 GREENHITHE
4 COLLEGE WLK
5 CORRALL ALMSHOUSES
6 COLLEGE CT
7 BYCHURCH PL

← **161**

A4
1 NEWLYN CT
2 BLOOMSBURY WLK
3 CUTBUSH ALMSHOUSES
4 COLMAN HO
5 EDGER PL
6 WATER LA
7 DUKES WLK
8 GRANADA HO

195

A4
9 GRANADA ST
B4
1 CUTBUSH AND CORRALL CT
2 DAY HO
3 HAYNES HO
4 GULLAND HO
5 PINE HO
6 CLIFFORD HO

B4
7 ELLIS HO
8 RIVER BANK CL
9 BELMONT CT
10 LENHAM CT
11 KINGFISHER CT
12 WILLOWBANK CT

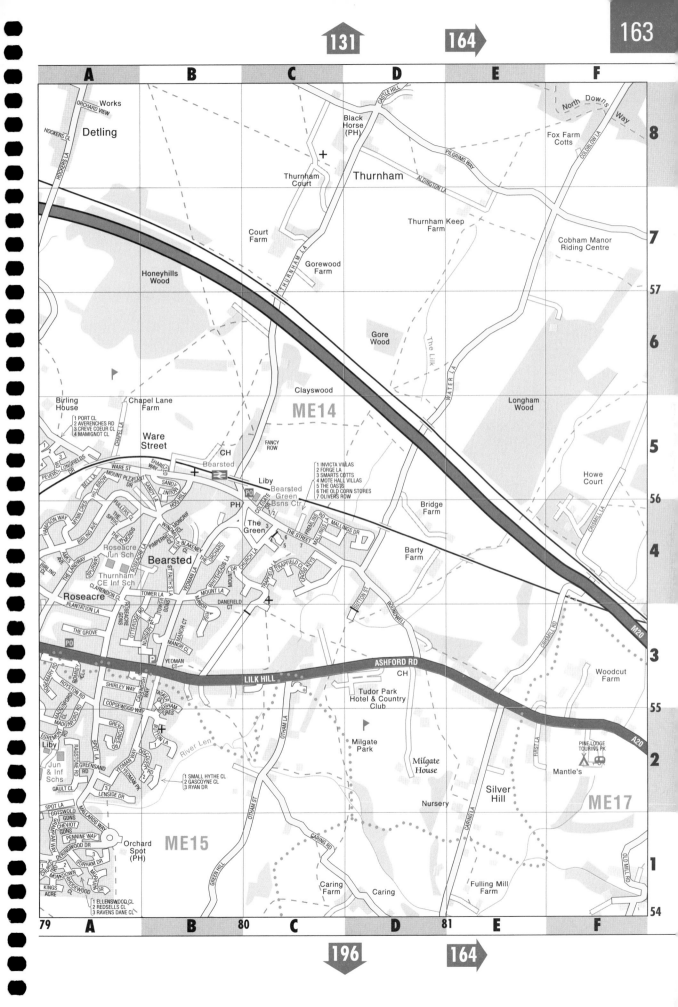

163 132

A B C D E F

8

Coldharbour
Cat's Mount
North Downs Way
COLDHARBOUR LA
SCRAGGED OAK RD
Eastfield Farm
Little Scragged Oak Farm
Scragged Oak
Hucking Hill House
Smokes Wood
Admiral House

7

Whitehall
BROAD STREET HILL
London Wood
Bolton's Wood
Chitt's Wood

57

WHITEHALL RD
ME14
Broad Street Farm
Broad Street
PILGRIMS WAY

6

Ripple

5

ME17
North Downs Way
Allington Farm
Little Allington

56

4

Snarkhurst Wood
Newlands Wood
Strickets Garden
HOLLINGBOURNE HILL

3

M20
Maidstone Service Area
Hollingbourne
Little Snagbrook
BANK COTTS
Manor House
UPPER ST
CHURCH GN
PH
PILGRIMS WAY

55

Hollingbourne
Hollingbourne Prim Sch

2

White Heath
A20
MUSKET LA
Eyhorne Farm
MUSKET LA
ATHELSTAN GN
THE PAVINGS
Eyhorne Street
BOURNESIDE TERR
EYHORNE ST
HASTERS
TILE FIELDS
CLAYGATE
Godfrey House
PROS MEAD
CULPEPER CL
HADLEY GDNS
Oak Meadow Farm
GREENWAY COURT RD
PH PO
Eyhorne Green

1

Old Mill Farm
OLD MILL RD
ASHFORD RD
The Great Danes Hotel
B2163 PENFOLD HILL
Oakfield
ASHFORD RD
A20
M20
Coombe Wood
HOSPITAL RD
HARPSWOOD
Target Cottage

54

River Len

82 A B 83 C D 84 E F

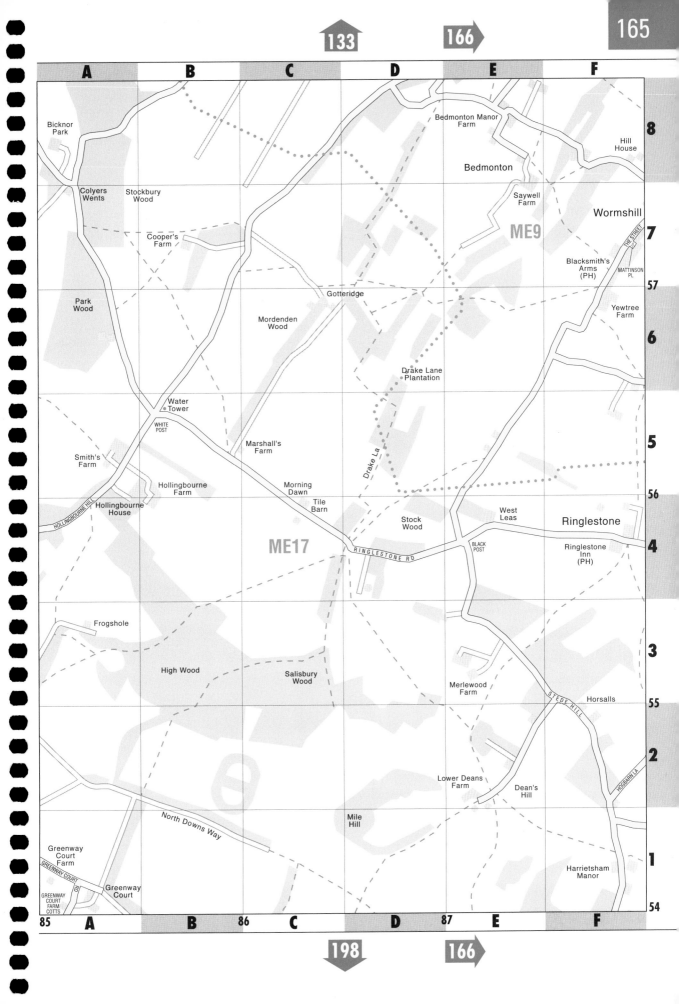

133
166

A   B   C   D   E   F

8

Bicknor
Park

Bedmonton Manor
Farm

Hill
House

Colyers
Wents

Stockbury
Wood

Bedmonton

Saywell
Farm

Wormshill

ME9

7

Cooper's
Farm

Blacksmith's
Arms
(PH)

THE STREET

MATTINSON
PL

57

Gotteridge

Park
Wood

Mordenden
Wood

Yewtree
Farm

6

Drake Lane
Plantation

Water
Tower

WHITE
POST

Marshall's
Farm

Drake La

5

Smith's
Farm

56

Hollingbourne
Farm

Morning
Dawn

Tile
Barn

Stock
Wood

West
Leas

Ringlestone

HOLLINGBOURNE HILL

Hollingbourne
House

ME17

RINGLESTONE RD

BLACK
POST

Ringlestone
Inn
(PH)

4

Frogshole

3

High Wood

Salisbury
Wood

Merlewood
Farm

STEDE HILL

Horsalls

55

2

HOGBARN LA

Lower Deans
Farm

Dean's
Hill

North Downs Way

Mile
Hill

1

Greenway
Court
Farm

GREENWAY COURT RD

Greenway
Court

Harrietsham
Manor

GREENWAY
COURT
FARM
COTTS

54

85   A   B   86   C   D   87   E   F

198
166

165
134

A B C D E F

8

Hogshaw
Wood

Manor
Farm

BOTTOM POND RD

FAIRVIEW
COTTS

+ Frinsted

Torry Hill
Park

THE STREET

+

DIX'S FIELD

Copes
Farm

7

Wormshill

Kippen

Torry
Hill

57

New Purchase
Farm

Park
Farm

Timbold
Hill

COALPIT LA

6

Oorlair

ME9

Yoke's
Court

Sweet's
Wood

Park Farm

OAST
COTTS

5

Lord's
Hill

Madam's
Court

Ashdown
Hill

56

RINGLESTONE RD

4

Minnels
Farm

Lenniker
Farm

Wrinsted
Court

Ashdown

ASHDOWN RD

Lord's
Wood

The
Dell

3

HOGBARN LA

Plummers
Farm

Butts
Bank

ME17

55

Hogbarn

2

Stedehill
Wood

Broomy Lees
Wood

Greenways

West Street
Farm

1

WEST ST

West
Street

Flint Barn
Farm

Newage
Farm

FAVERSHAM RD

54

FLINT LA

88 A B 89 C D 90 E F

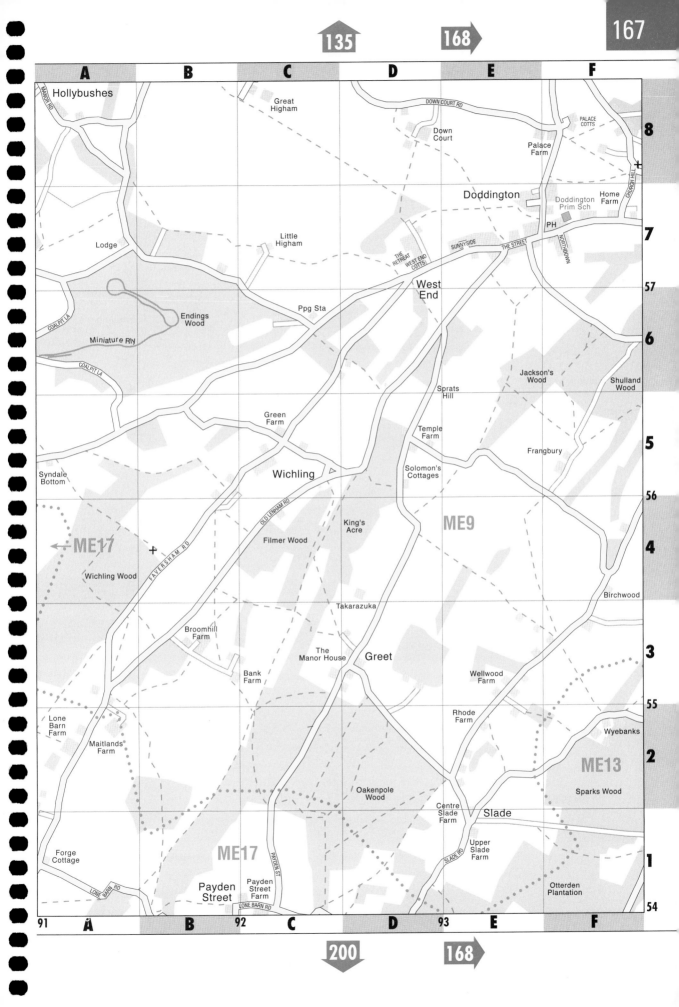

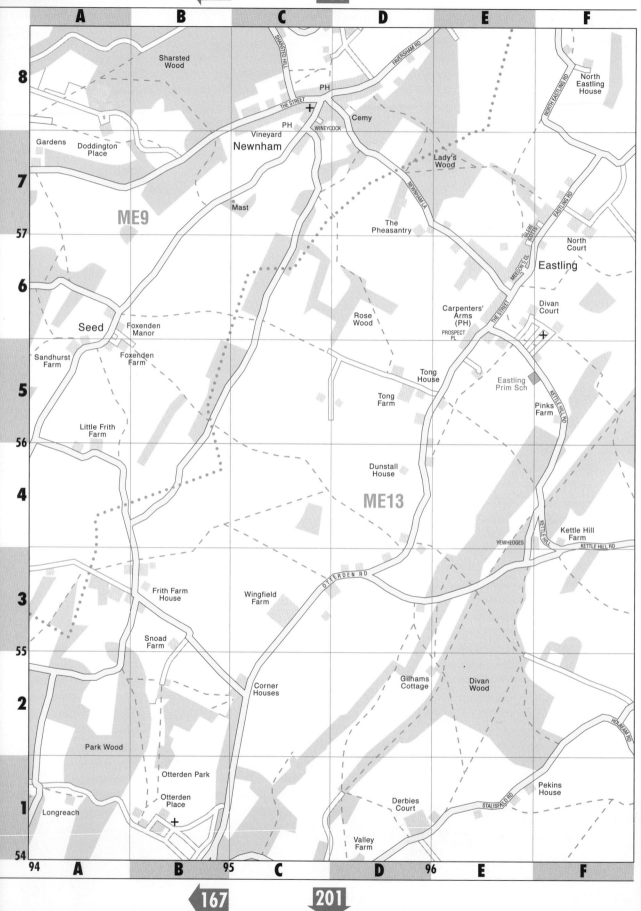

A B C D E F

8

Sharsted
Wood

North
Eastling
House

FAVERSHAM RD

SHARSTED HILL

PH

THE STREET

Cemy

PH

WINEYCOCK

Gardens

Doddington
Place

Vineyard

Newnham

Lady's
Wood

NEWNHAM LA

NORTH EASTLING RD

7

ME9

Mast

The
Pheasantry

EASTLING RD

57

North
Court

GLEBE
COTTS

Eastling

6

Seed

Foxenden
Manor

Rose
Wood

Carpenters'
Arms
(PH)

PROSPECT
PL

Divan
Court

THE STREET

Sandhurst
Farm

Foxenden
Farm

Tong
House

Eastling
Prim Sch

KETTLE HILL RD

5

Little Frith
Farm

Tong
Farm

Pinks
Farm

56

Dunstall
House

ME13

4

Kettle Hill
Farm

KETTLE HILL

YEWHEDGES

KETTLE HILL RD

3

Frith Farm
House

Wingfield
Farm

OTTERDEN RD

55

Snoad
Farm

2

Corner
Houses

Gilhams
Cottage

Divan
Wood

HOLBEAM RD

Park Wood

Otterden Park

Pekins
House

1

Otterden
Place

Derbies
Court

STALISFELD RD

Longreach

Valley
Farm

54

94 A B 95 C D 96 E F

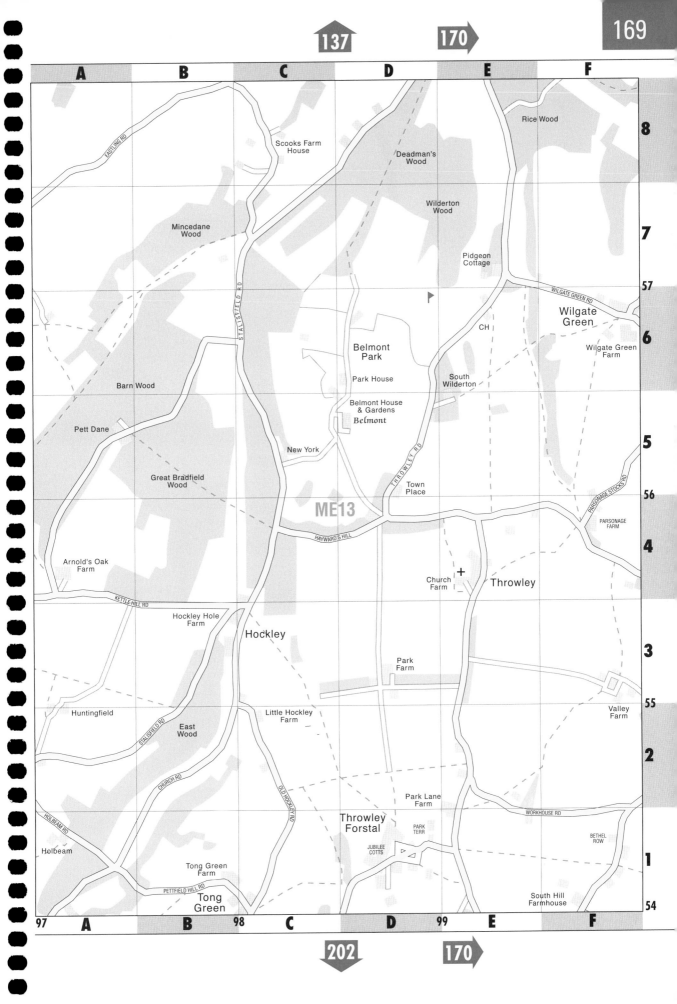

169
138

A B C D E F

8

7

57

6

56

5

4

3

55

2

1

54

Badgin Wood

PLUMFORD RD

OAST COTTS

North Street

A251

OWENS COURT COTTS

Owens Court

Saffery Farm

Gosmere

GOSMERE FARM BARNS

NEWHOUSE LA

NEWHOUSE FARM COTTS

Newhouse Farm

WINDING HILL

Throwley House

Sheldwich

OLD BADGINS RD

THE STOCKS

Church Plantation

Winding Hill Wood

Cobrahamsole Farm

Sheldwich Prim Sch

AMOS CL

LEES COURT RD

HUNTERS WAY

REST HARROW

NURSERY LA

MORGAN

KIRBY'S GDN

CARRIAGE HO

Sheldwich Lees

ASHFORD RD

Lees Court

Lords Farm

Lees Court Park

ME13

Little Lords

LORDS COTTS

BAGSHILL RD

Poultry Farm

Stocking Wood

MILLEN'S ROW

DAYTON RD

LEAVELAND COTTS

Badlesmere Court

FISHER STREET RD

Black Shaw

Leaveland Court

Woods Court

Leaveland Wood

Badlesmere Park Wood

Holly Grove

Workhouse Wood

Tenant Wood

Badlesmere

Stringmans Farm

Leaveland

A251

00 A B 01 C D 02 E F

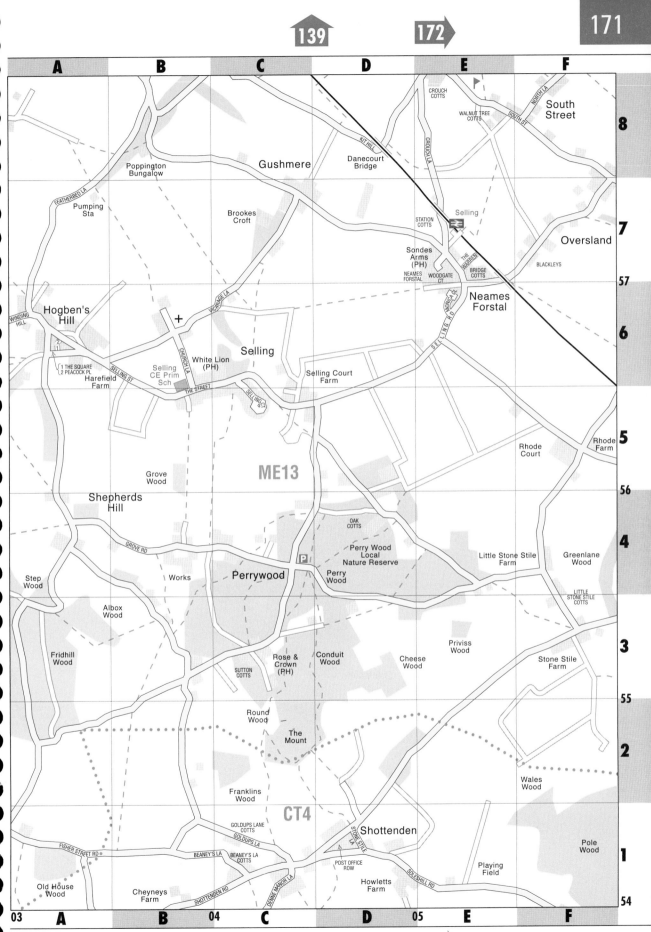

A B C D E F

8 7 57 6 5 56 4 3 55 2 1 54

South Street

CROUCH COTTS

WALNUT TREE COTTS

NORTH LA

SOUTH ST

Gushmere

KIT HILL

Danecourt Bridge

CHURCH LA

Poppington Bungalow

FEATHERBED LA

Pumping Sta

Brookes Croft

VICARAGE LA

Selling

STATION COTTS

Sondes Arms (PH)

NEAMES FORSTAL

WOODGATE CT

THE WARREN

BRIDGE COTTS

Oversland

BLACKLEYS

Neames Forstal

SELLING RD

MONICA LA

Hogben's Hill

WINDING HILL

1 THE SQUARE
2 PEACOCK PL

Harefield Farm

SELLING ST

Selling CE Prim Sch

White Lion (PH)

THE STREET

SELLING ST

Selling

Selling Court Farm

Rhode Court

Rhode Farm

ME13

Grove Wood

Shepherds Hill

GROVE RD

OAK COTTS

Perry Wood Local Nature Reserve

Perry Wood

Little Stone Stile Farm

Greenlane Wood

LITTLE STONE STILE COTTS

Works

Perrywood

Step Wood

Albox Wood

Priviss Wood

Fridhill Wood

SUTTON COTTS

Rose & Crown (PH)

Conduit Wood

Cheese Wood

Stone Stile Farm

Round Wood

The Mount

Wales Wood

Franklins Wood

CT4

GOLDUPS LANE COTTS

GOLDUPS LA

STONE STILE LA

Shottenden

Pole Wood

FISHER STREET RD

BEANEY'S LA

BEANEY'S LA COTTS

SHOTTENDEN RD

DENNE MANOR LA

POST OFFICE ROW

SOLESHILL RD

Playing Field

Howletts Farm

Old House Wood

Cheyneys Farm

03 04 05

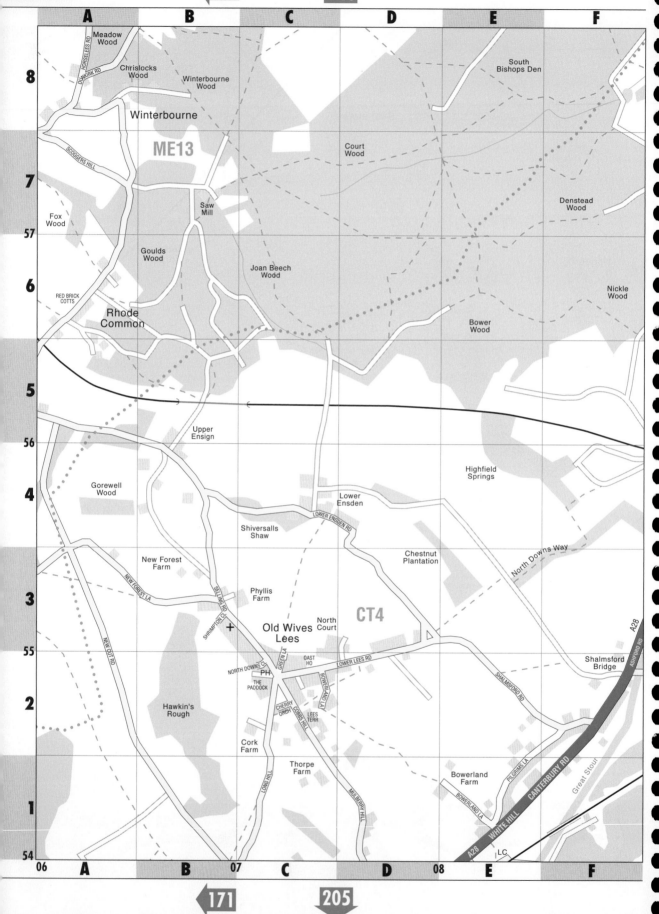

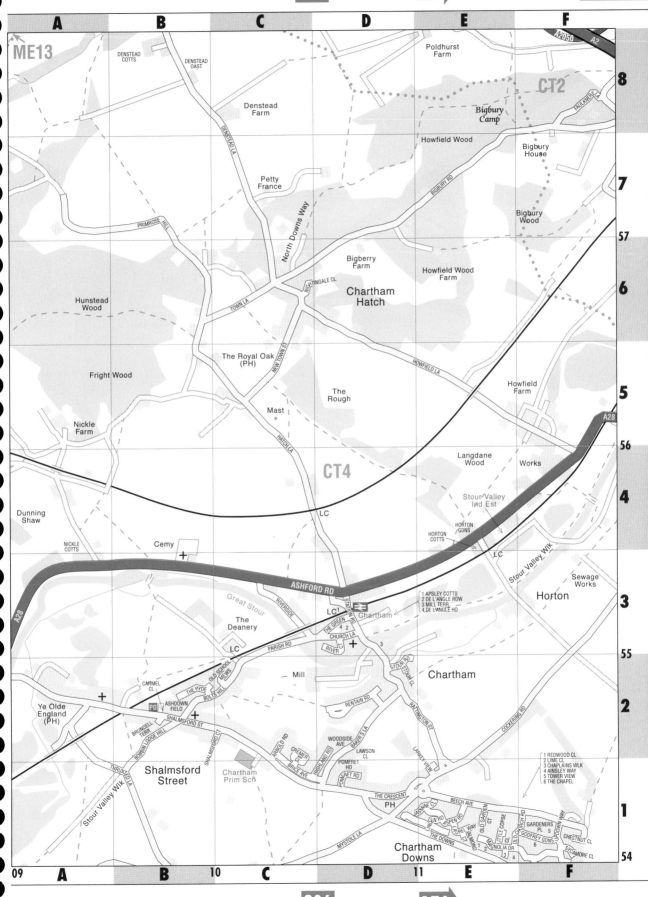

173 142

F7
1 DANE JOHN MEWS
2 WORTHGATE PL
3 DANE JOHN CT
4 WINCHEAP GN
5 CAREY HO
6 RUNCIE HO

7 COGGAN HO
8 RAMSEY HO
9 GREENFIELD COTTS
10 ELGAR BRETTS CT
F8
1 TOWER WAY
2 ALL SAINTS LA

F8
3 TURNAGAIN LA
4 GUILDHALL ST
5 MERCERY LA
6 WHITE HORSE LA
7 STOUR CT
8 GREY FRIARS COTTS

F8
9 STOURVILLE
10 TEMPLE MEWS
11 MARLOWE ARC
12 GRAVEL WLK
13 MARLOWE CT
14 WILLOUGHBY CT

15 LULLINGSTONE CT
16 ROSEMARY LA
17 ST MARY'S CT
18 THE PRECINCTS
19 HERITAGE CT

CANTERBURY
DVROVERNVM

Harbledown
Golden Hill
North Downs Way
Gorse Meadow Farm
MILL LA
SHIPMAN AVE
MILLER AVE
PRIORESS
SQUIRE AVE
CITY VIEW
WIFE OF BATH HILL
KNIGHT AVE
Recn Gd
The Canterbury High Sch
Beauherne Com Sch
Bingley's Island
WHITEHALL BRIDGE RD 1
WESTGATE GARDEN FLATS 2
ST MILDREDS CT 3
A2050 RHEIMS WAY
WHITEHALL RD
A290
ST PETER'S PL
St Peters
Mus Sch
Mus
Mus

CT2
CT1
Castle
PIN HILL
A28
Canterbury East
Martyr's Field
MILLERS YD 1
GROVE TERR 2
CANON APPLETON CT 3
SEYMOUR PL 4
RHEIMS WAY A290
INVICTA
MOAT HO

MERCHANTS WAY
FRANKLYN RD
MANCIPLE CL
PRIEST AVE
BAKERS
PARDONER CL
Stour Valley Wlk
LC

Tonford Manor Farm
Tonford Manor
Great Stour
Thanington CT Farm
Recn Gd
GRAYS WAY
Tonford La
HASSALL REACH
BRAMLEY AVE
MILLENIUM TERR
STRANGER'S CL
ALFRED CL
ALFRED RD
WINDSOR RD
ASHENDEN CL
ATHELSTAN RD
MANOR
INGOLDSBY RD
THE CLOSE
THANINGTON RD
Wincheap Ind Est
Riverside Ret Pk
P&R
Hope Villas
BARNES CT
MAIDEN LA
WOODVILLE
HOMERSHAM
Wincheap Foundation Prim Sch
1 PRIORY OF ST JACOB
2 FORGE HO
HOWLAND MEWS
Hop Garden Way
CAMBRIDGE WAY
CHINEHAM WAY
Nunnery Fields
Schs
COXTON RD
MAYNARD RD
SIMMONDS RD
NEW ST
VALLEY RD
NORFOLK RD
NEATON RD
SCOTT AVE
HOLLOW LA

Thanington
WARREN LO
ASHFORD RD
Milton Manor
Cockering Farm
COCKERING RD
Milton Manor Farm
P

CT4
Larkeyvalley Wood
New House Farm
NEW HOUSE LA
STUPPINGTON LA
STUPPINGTON COURT FARM
MERTON LA
IFFIN LA
Merton Farm
Iffin Farm
Upper Horton Farm
Hand Wood
A2

173 207

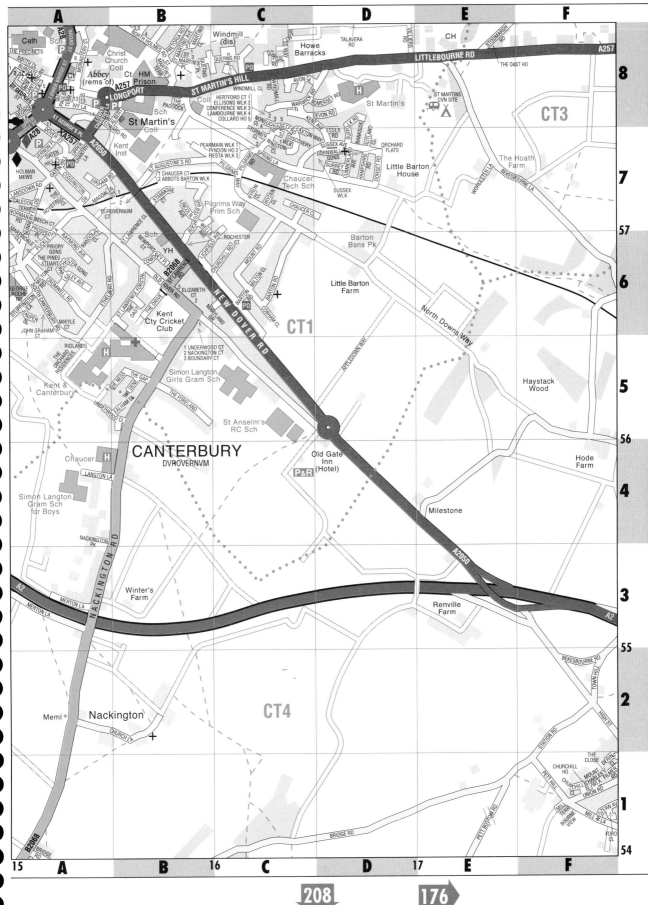

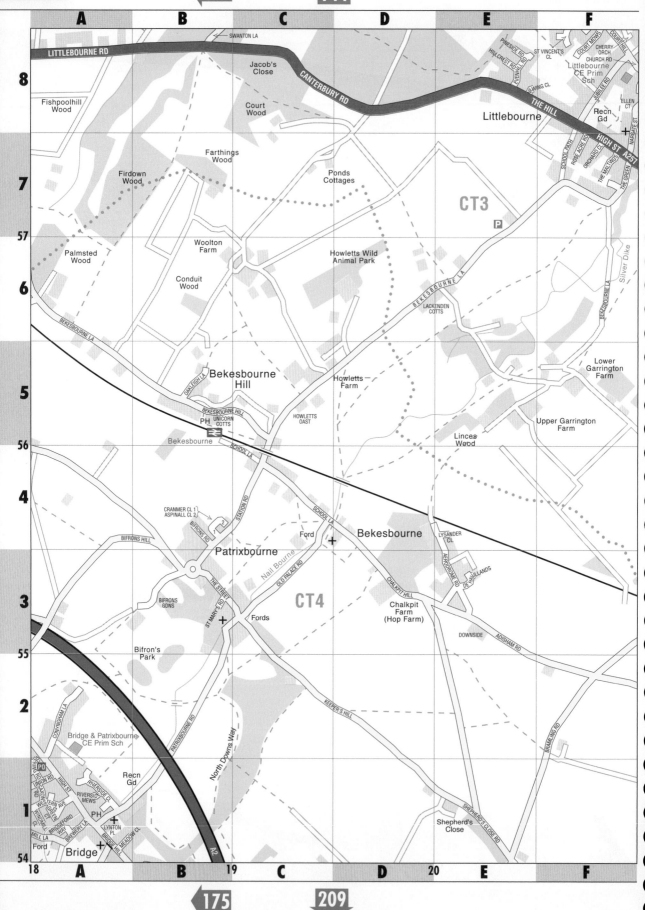

175
144

LITTLEBOURNE RD

SWANTON LA

Jacob's Close

CANTERBURY RD

Fishpoolhill Wood

Court Wood

PINESIDE RD
St VINCENT'S CL
HILL CREST RD
AVENVILL RD
CHERRY ORCH
COURT MDWS
COURT HILL
CHURCH RD
Littlebourne CE Prim Sch
NEWING CL
JUBILEE RD
ELLEN CT

THE HILL
Littlebourne
Recn Gd

Farthings Wood

Firdown Wood

Ponds Cottages

CT3

P

SCHOOL PATH
ROSE ACRE RD
ORCHARD CL
THE MALTINGS
THE GREEN
HIGH ST A257
MARGATE ST

Palmsted Wood

Woolton Farm

Howletts Wild Animal Park

BEKESBOURNE LA

Silver Dike

Conduit Wood

BEKESBOURNE LA

LACKENDEN COTTS

BEKESBOURNE LA

Lower Garrington Farm

OAKLEIGH LA

Bekesbourne Hill

Howletts Farm

Upper Garrington Farm

BEKESBOURNE HILL
PH
UNICORN COTTS
Bekesbourne

HOWLETTS OAST

Linces Wood

SCHOOL LA

SCHOOL LA

CRANMER CL 1
ASPINALL CL 2

BIFRONS HILL

STATION RD
BIFRONS RD

Ford

Bekesbourne

LYSANDER CL

AERODROME RD
DE VILLANDS

Patrixbourne

Nail Bourne

OLD PALACE RD

CT4

CHALKPIT HILL

Chalkpit Farm (Hop Farm)

BIFRONS GDNS

THE STREET

ST MARY'S RD

Fords

Downside

ADISHAM RD

Bifron's Park

PATRIXBOURNE RD

KEEPER'S HILL

North Downs Way

BRAMLING RD

Bridge & Patrixbourne CE Prim Sch

CONYNGHAM LA

Recn Gd

Riverside Mews
RIVERSIDE CL

A2

SHEPHERD'S CLOSE RD

Shepherd's Close

CHINA RD
PO
UNION ST
HIGH ST
SAXON RD
WESTERN AVE
WINDMILL
BRIDGEFORD WAY
BRIDGE HILL
BREWERY LA
LYNTON PL
BRIDGE MEADOW CL
PH
MILL LA
Ford
Bridge

175
209

A B C D E F

8 7 57 6 5 56 4 55 3 2 1 54

18 19 20

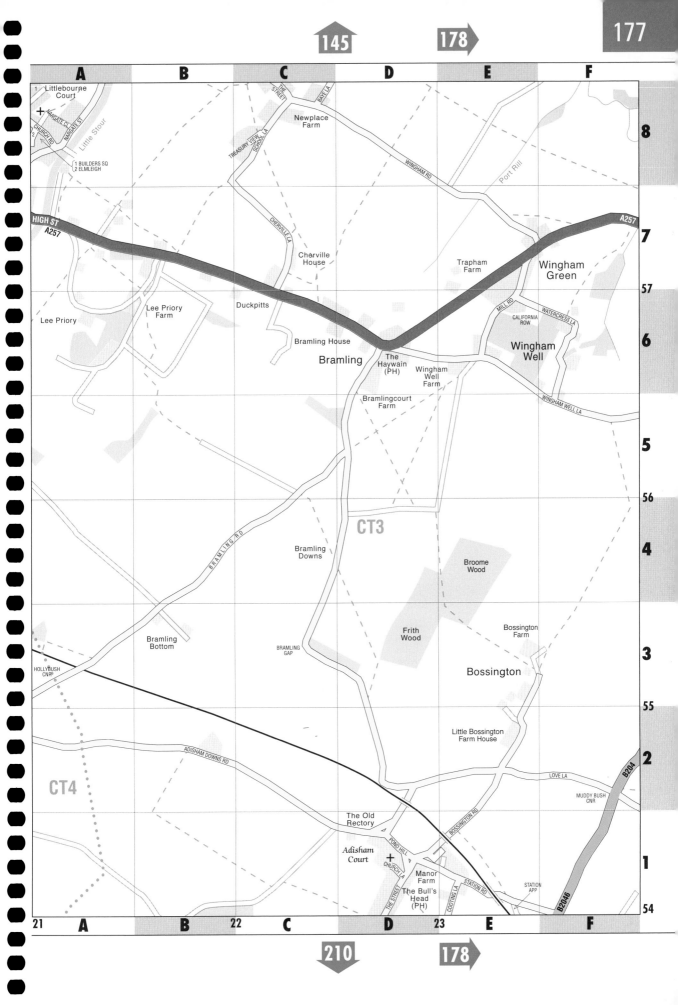

A B C D E F

8

7

57

6

5

56

4

55

2

1

54

HIGH ST
A257
A257

1 Littlebourne Court
MARGATE ST
CHURCH RD
Little Stour
1 BUILDERS SQ
2 ELMLEIGH

THE STREET
TREASURY VIEW
SCHOOL LA
BAYE LA
Newplace Farm
WINGHAM RD
Port Rill

CHERVILLE LA
Charville House

Lee Priory Farm
Lee Priory
Duckpitts
Bramling House
Bramling
The Haywain (PH)
Wingham Well Farm
Bramlingcourt Farm

Trapham Farm
Wingham Green
MILL RD
CALIFORNIA ROW
WATERCRESS LA
Wingham Well
WINGHAM WELL LA

CT3

BRAMLING RD
Bramling Downs
Broome Wood
Bossington Farm

Bramling Bottom
HOLLYBUSH CNR
BRAMLING GAP
Frith Wood
Bossington

Little Bossington Farm House

CT4
ADISHAM DOWNS RD
LOVE LA
MUDDY BUSH CNR
B204

The Old Rectory
BOSSINGTON RD
STATION RD

Adisham Court
CHURCH LA
POND HILL
Manor Farm
The Bull's Head (PH)
THE STREET
COOTING LA
STATION APP
B2046

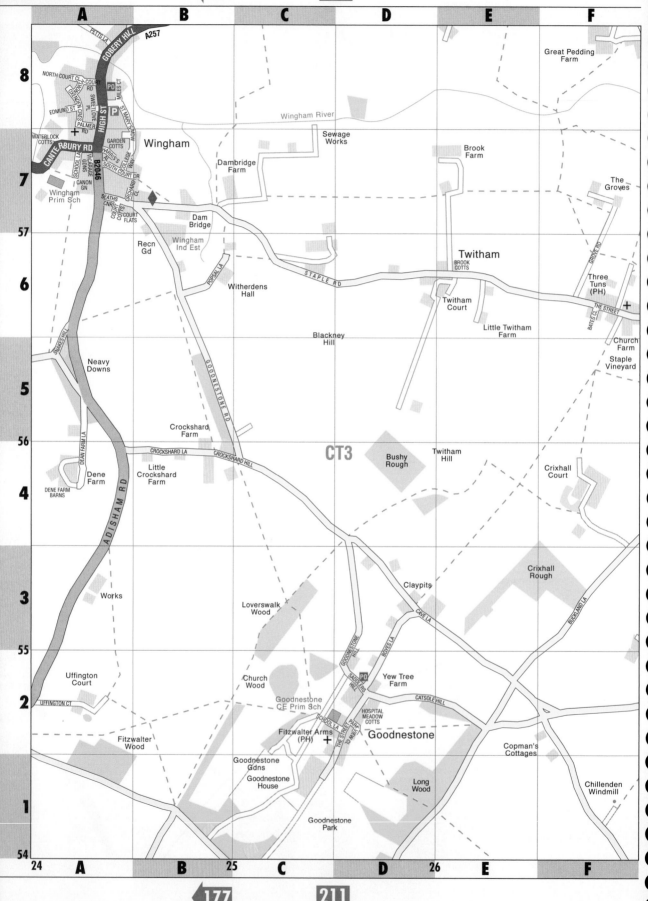

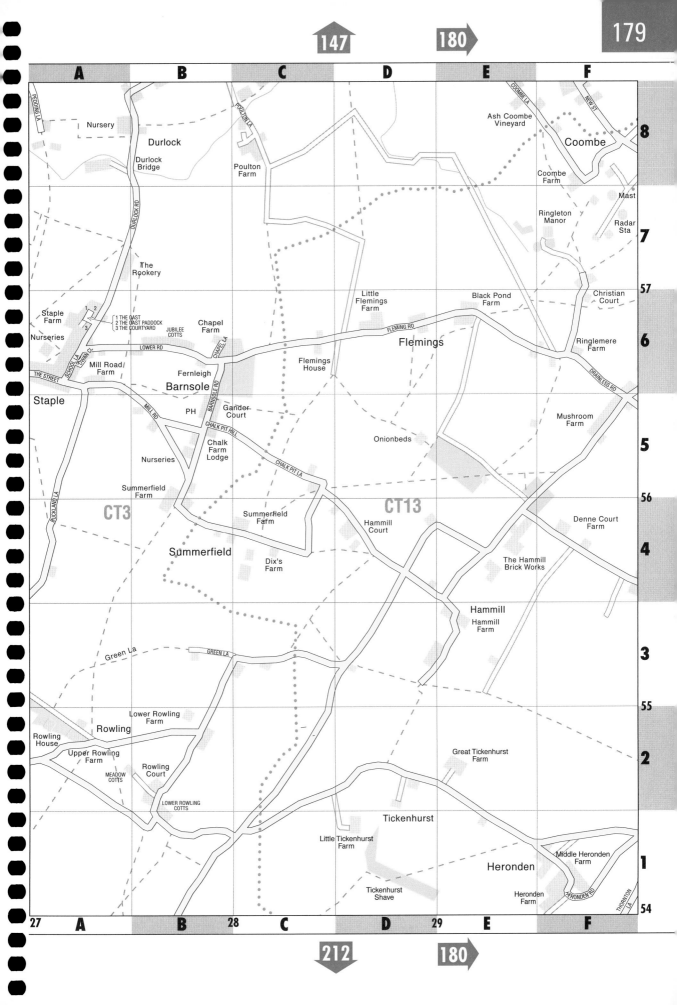

A · B · C · D · E · F

8
7
57
6
5
56
4
3
55
2
1
54

CT3

Marshborough Farm

Chestnut Farm

Marshborough

Vine Farm

Parsonage Farm

Mast

MARSHBOROUGH RD

Great Poulders Farm

Little Poulders Farm

POULDERS RD

POULDERS GDNS

WOODNESBOROUGH RD

PLAYING FIELDS

CLAREMONT TERR

SANDWICH RD

Stone Cross

Black La

Sandwich Jun Sch

SANDWICH

ROPE WALK MEWS

Cemy

ALEXANDER C.

HOWE FUR RD

JUBILEE RD

WRIGHT ROSSA

CLAIRE PL

HOROWICH PL

HASTINGS PL

NEW ROMNEY PL

SANDWOOD RD

LABURNUM AVE

BURCH AVE

ST BARTS RD

HAZELWOOD MDW

THE OLD VICARAGE

PO

THE STREET

PH

MELVILLE LEA

WOODLAND WAY

PARK TERR

Nurseries

Grove Manor

OAK HILL

FIR TREE HILL

CHURCH FARM WAY

ST MARY'S CL

HIGH ST

FOXBOROUGH

THE AIREYS

Church Street

CHURCH ST

Churchgate Farm

Woodnesborough

THE BUNGALOWS

Beacon Lane Farm

BEACON LA

FOXBOROUGH HILL

Hill Cross Farm

CT13

Highborough Hill

Nursery

DRAINLESS RD

Drove Farm

POISON CROSS

Statenborough

Nursery

Nursery

Statenborough Farm

JOHN'S GN

Beller's Bush

Nursery

Nursery

Nursery

A258

THE CRESC

DOVER RD

L Ctr

Sandwich Tech Sch

Felderland Farm

FELDERLAND C.

FELDERLAND LA

BOWES VILLAS

Bowes Farm

Felderland

DEAL RD

A258

DEAL RD LA

COTON RD

Mill House

Reedbrook Wood

Nurseries

Sewage Works

White Cliffs Country Trail

North Stream

CT14

Great Selson Farm

Selson

Little Selson Farm

Wells Farm

LOWER GORE LA

ORCHARD RD

PEAR DR

WOODNESBOROUGH LA

HILL DR

LITTLE WALTON

Walton House

Gore

GORE TERR

GORE RD

BELMONT TERR

BOYSTON PL

THE PARADE

Eastry

GORE LA

UPPER GORE LA

GORE CL

COTS LEA

MILL GN

QUARRY GDNS

MAYMILLS COTTS

Eastry CE Prim Sch

Works

WRIGHTS WAY

SWAYNES WAY

EASTRY MEWS

THE GREVILLE CROSS HOMES

PO

P

ST MARY'S CL.

HIGH ST

THE CHURCH YARD

Eastry Court

Vicarage

LONG LA

Farthingate

Hay Farm

Ham Manor

Ham

HAY LA

HERONDEN VIEW

BOTELER COTTS

ALE GN RD

MILL BANK COTTS

LISS RD

WHITE WOOD RD

MILL LA

Eastry Mill

Great Oaks Small Sch

HOLLY CL

PH

Brook House

The Lynch

BROOK ST

Blazing Donkey (PH)

HAY HILL

Cherry Trees Farm

Finglesham Grange

West Street

HAM FARM COTTS

West Street Farm

THORNTON LA

HERONDEN RD

Works

LOWER ST

DOVER RD

Buttsole Pond

EASTRY PK

Buttsole

A256

A256

A256

SANDWICH RD

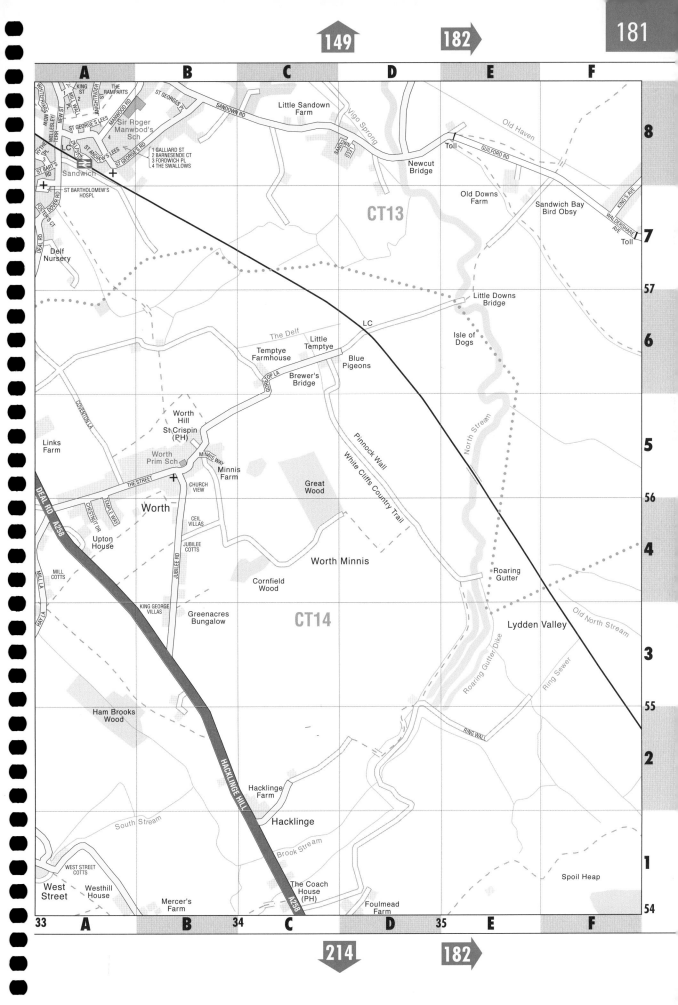

Sandwich Bay

Royal
St George's
Golf Links

KING'S AVE

COASTGUARD
COTTS

NORTH RD

PRINCES DR

Sandwich Bay
Estate

3

WHITEHALL

WALDERSHARE AVE

FAIRWAY 1
THE SANCTUARY 2
GUILFORD HO 3
THE DUNES 4

SHAWOON AVE

2   1

4

CAMBRIDGE AVE

DICKSON'S
CNR

CT13

Lyddcourt
Stile

Lydden

Mary Bax's
Stone

White Cliffs Country Trail

Saxon Shore Way

Chequers
(PH)

GREENACRES

Old North Stream

CT14

Tenants
Hills

Walnut Tree
Farm

SANDHILLS
CVN PK

REDHOUSE WALL

REDHOUSE
FARM

CH

GOLF RD

Sandown Castle
(remains of)

1 CASTLE WLK
2 CANUTE WLK

CANUTE RD

SANDOWN RD

THE MARINA

Penfield Sewer

Spoil
Heap

GOLF CT 1
LINKS CT 2
WALCHEREN CL 3

ETHELBERT RD

GODWYN
RD

A   36   B   37   C   D   38   E   F

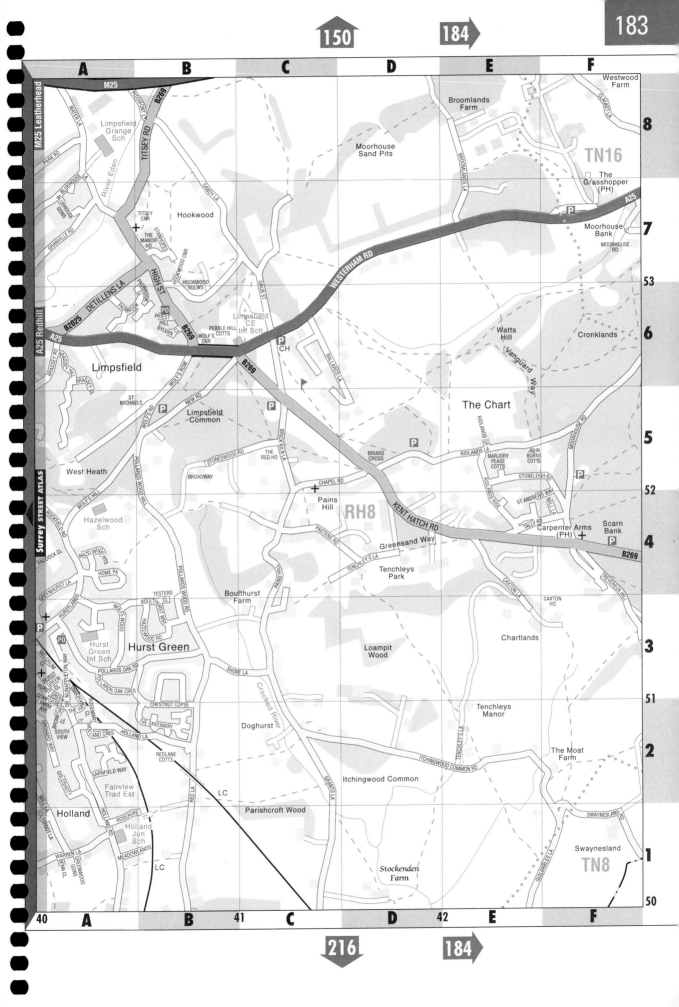

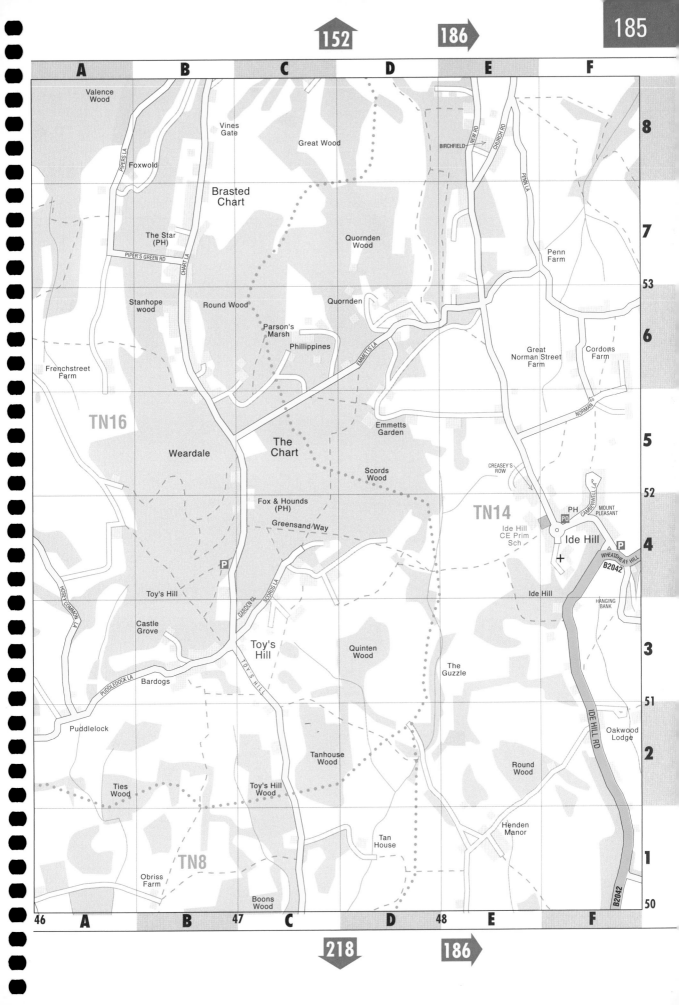

185 153

A B C D E F

8

Willow Wood

Hawks Wood

BACK LA

Greenlane Wood

Whitley

Mildridge Wood

Dibden

DIBDEN LA

New Beacon Sch

TN13

SEVENOAKS BY-PASS

A21

7

Mill Bank Wood

OAK LA

53

Brook Place

Whitley Row

Whitley Forest

TN13

6

The Woodman (PH)

Apps Hollow

Roundabout Wood

Dust Wood

CHAPEL WLK

Hyde's Forest

Pitfield Wood

GRACIOUS LANE END

WHITE HOUSE LA

5

NIGHTINGALE LA

THE PANTYLES

Goathurst Common

York's Hill

Sheephill Wood

RYCROFT LA

WHITE HOUSE RD

52

Everlands

Bayley's Hill

4

P

Stubbs Wood

Brockhill Wood

Hanging Bank

TN14

Greensand Way

Yorkshill Farm

BAILEY'S HILL

WICKHURST RD

3

Boarhill

Harbour Hook

Hatchlands Farm

Wickhurst Manor

51

2

Bowzell Farm

BOWZELL RD

1

Bowzell Wood

Old House Farm

50

Scollops Farm

49 A B 50 C D 51 E F

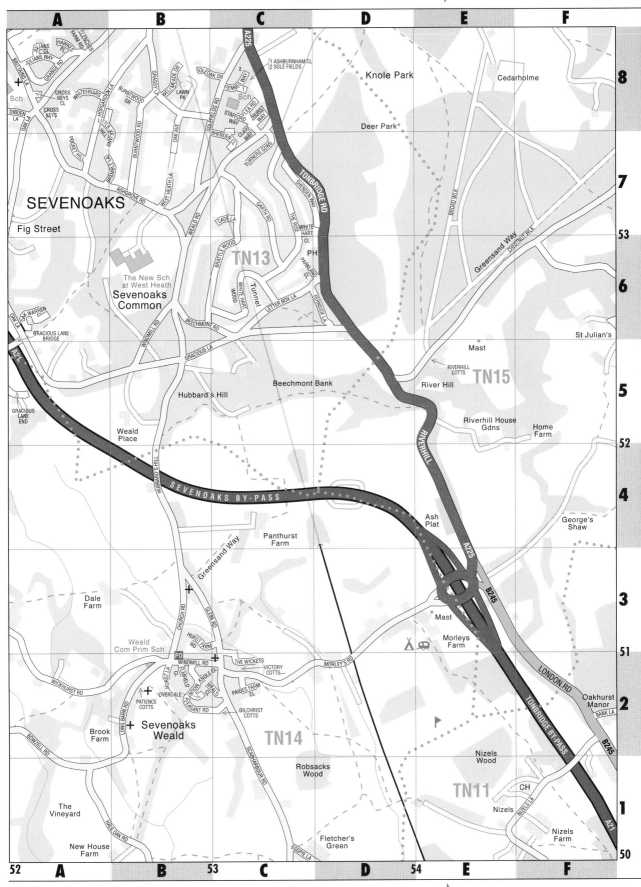

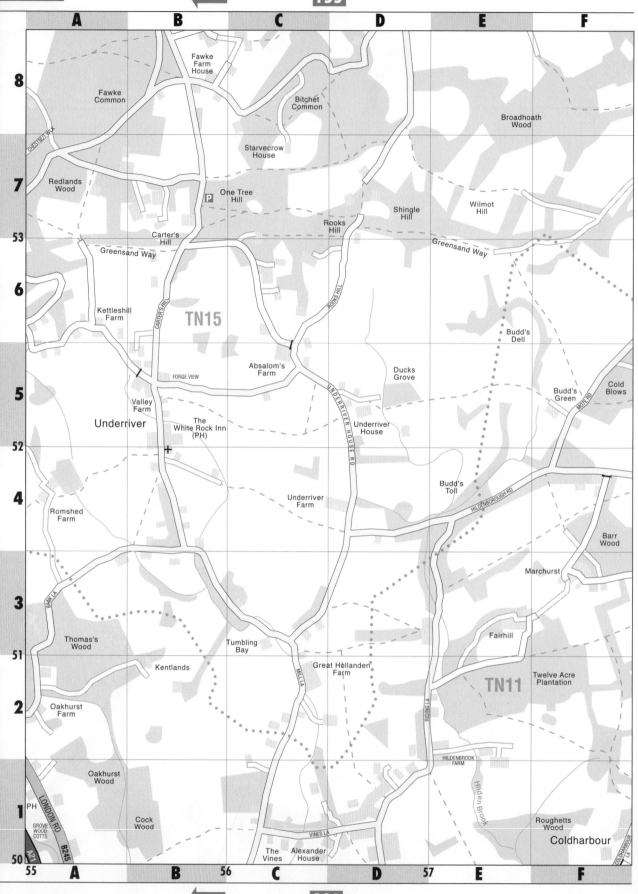

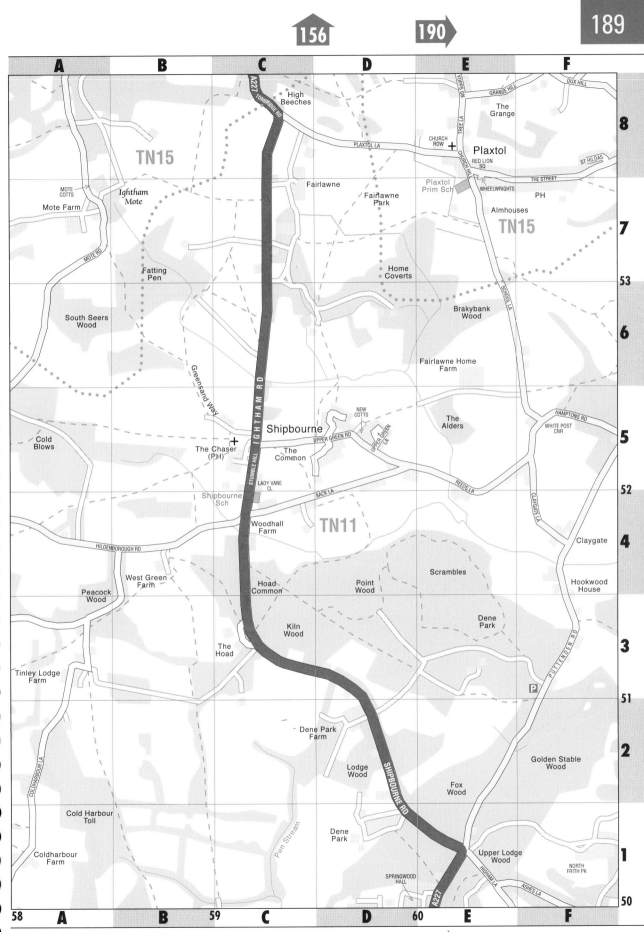

189 157

A B C D E F

8

Dux Hill
SHRUBSHALL MDW
BOURNE VALE
THE STREET
HYDERS FORGE
COUNCIL HOS
Plaxtol Spoute
BROOK LA
Broadfield Farm
Quarry Wood
SPINNERS WENTS
SWANTON RD

TN15

7
Allen's Farm
Upper Farm
Rats Castle
Wealdway
PECKHAM HURST RD
Crooked Chimneys
Peckham Hurst

53
Mills
Roughway
ROUGHWAY LA
Gover Hill
GOVER VIEW
ME18

BARTON COTTS
6
Dunk's Green
Greensand Way
Stickland's Wood
Gover Hill
Adams Well
FORGE LA

The Kentish Rifleman (PH)
DUNK'S GREEN RD
The Artichoke Inn (PH)

5
Puttenden Manor Farm
Fish Farm
Hamptons
PARK RD
PILLAR BOX LA
Oxen Hoath

52
HAMPTONS RD
Hamptons Park
OXENHOATH RD
TN11
Vines Farm
MATTHEWS LA

4
River Bourne
Four Wents
Oxenhoath Mill Farm
Oxen Hoath Park
Park Farm

3
Clearhedges Wood
Frith Wood
Mount Pleasant
Cricketers Cottage Farm
Pear Tree Farm

51
CARPENTERS LA
The Common
COMMON RD
A26

2
Stallion's Green
HIGH HOUSE LA
STEERS PL
PALMERS BROOK
LONEWOOD WAY
MAIDSTONE RD

Yewtree Wood
Hadlow
CEMETERY LA
The Harrow (PH)
Cemy

1
North Frith Farm
Hope
MILL VIEW
THE FREEBELD
HOPE AVE
MARSHALL GDNS
TWYFORD RD
GREAT ELMS
SPAR CL
CHESFIELD CL

50
WATER SLIPPE
SCHOOL LA
BROOKFIELDS
SMITHERS CL
A26

61 **A** 62 **B** **C** 63 **D** **E** **F**

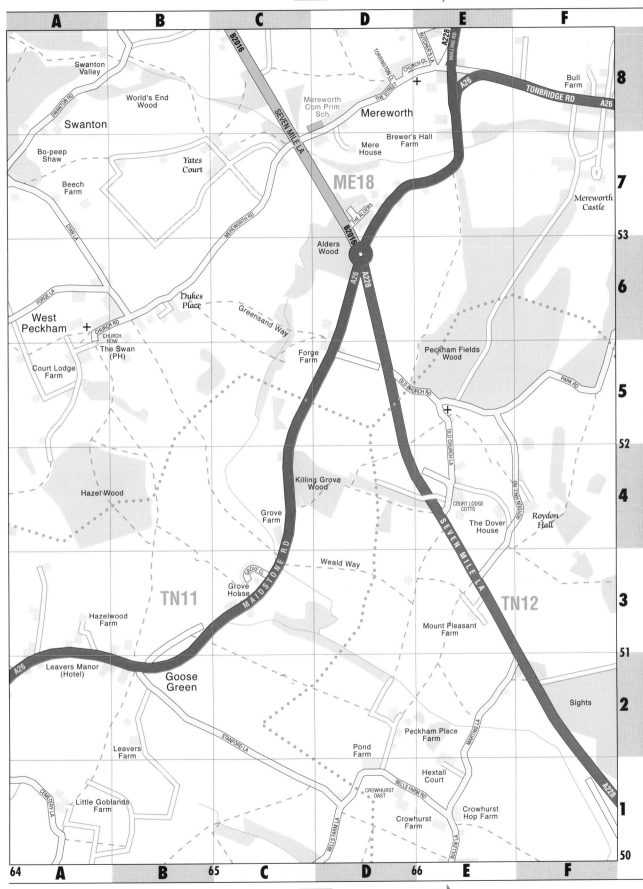

191
159

A B C D E F

8

Hermitage Farm

PAVILION LA

DANNS LA

Fuller's Corner

CANON LA

TONBRIDGE RD

VINE CT

RED HILL

Cemy

Manor Farm

OLD RD

RED HOUSE GDNS

MILL LA

UPPER MILL

LODGE CL

LOVE LA

ALLINGTON GDNS

BOORMAN'S MEWS

THE ORPINES

PO

P

Hotel

A26

7

PIZIEN WELL RD

Pizien Well

Wateringbury

HANBURY CL

CRESC MDW

OLD RD

B2015

BOW RD

HILL SIDE CT

COBBS CL

THE BRICKS

FIELDS LA

BOW TERR

WARDEN MILL CL

RIVERS CL

LEA RD

Sewage Works

53

East Woods

PARK RD

NETTLESTEAD LA

SILVER BIRCH WLK

PHOENIX COTTS

WATERSIDE MEWS

PHOENIX DR

Wateringbury CE Prim Sch

THE RETREAT CVN PK

ORCHARD CRES

GLENLEIGH RD

HENRYS CL

PH

Wateringbury

6

Rock Farm

Nettlestead

BRYANT CL

KING'S COTTS

BISHOPS CL

SCHOOL VILLAS

LC

Bow Bridge

Waregrave's Wood

GIBBS HILL

ROCK FARM OASTHOUSE

BOW HILL

ME18

ME15

5

Birchetts Wood

Nettlestead Court Farm

NETTLESTEAD CT

Nettlestead Place

Bowhill Farm

52

HUNT ST

SMALL PROFITS

4

Bow Hill House

Diamond Place Farm

MAIDSTONE RD

Medway Valley Wlk

River Medway

Kenward House

Hillside Cotts

TN12

Moat Wood

Green Farm

3

Greensand Way

Kenward Farm

KENWARD RD

51

Milbay's Wood

FORGE COTTS

WELLS COTTS

Court Lodge Farm

WARDE'S

THE NOOK

MEDWAY AVE

2

Hale Park Wood

Nettlestead Green

PH

WALNUT CL

YALDING HILL

Beech Wood

Hook Wood

STANIN RD

STAKELY PK

Hampstead Marina

Marina

Yalding

HOPGARDEN OAST

OAST CT

B2162

ORCHARD COTTS

Yalding

LC

HAMPSTEAD LA

Works

Cvn Pk

B2162

River Beult

PH

HIGH ST

B2010

BORTON CL

ELVEYS COTTS

1

A228

B2015

ACOTT FIELDS

Liby

50

67 A B 68 C D 69 E F

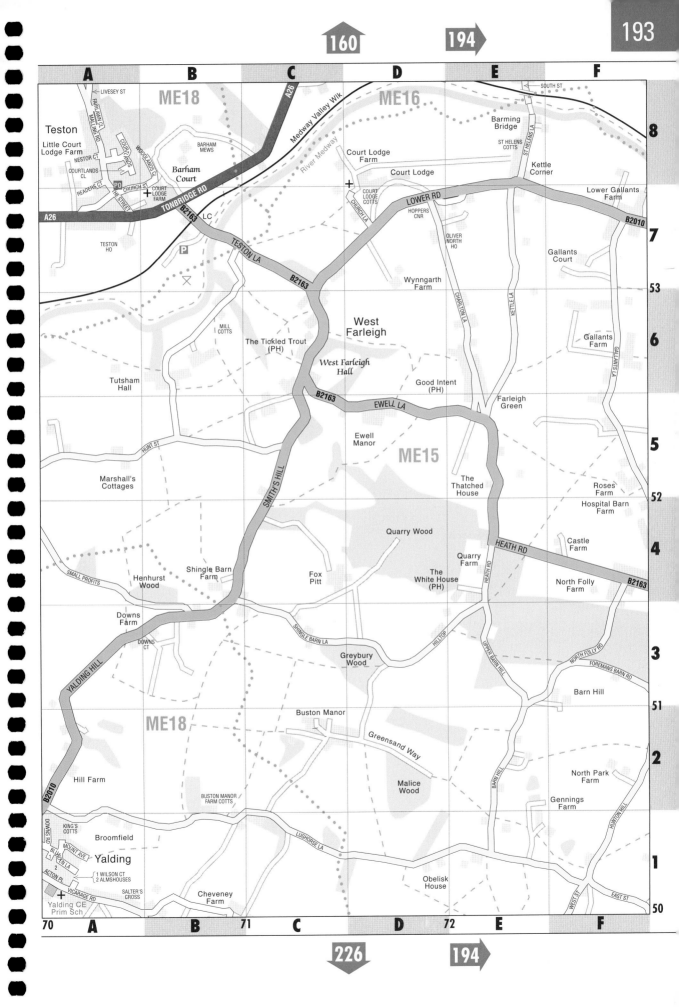

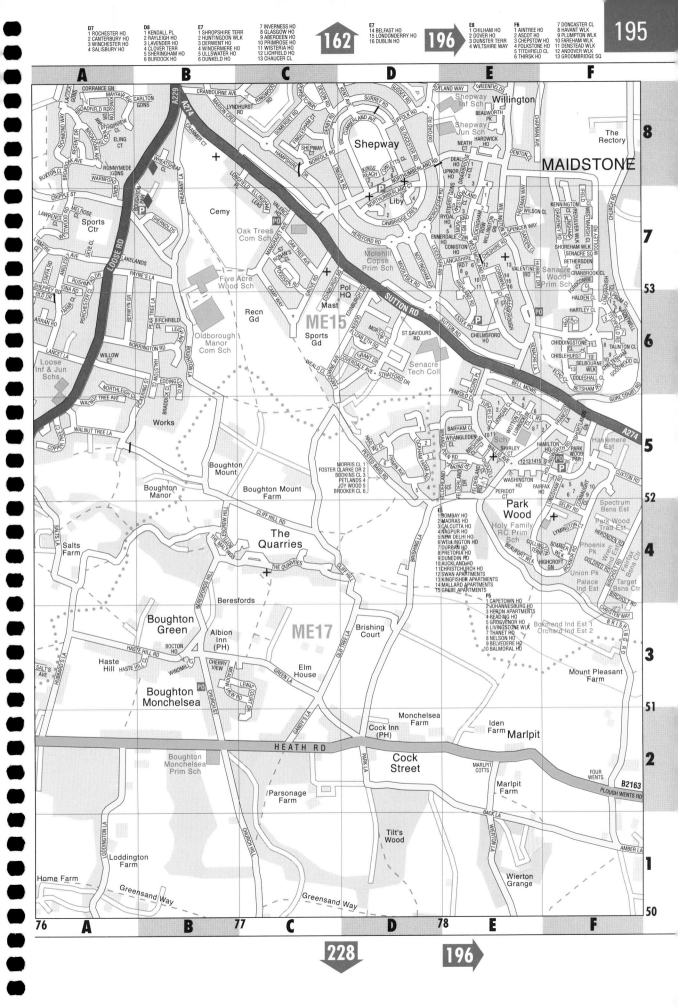

D7
1 ROCHESTER HO
2 CANTERBURY HO
3 WINCHESTER HO
4 SALISBURY HO

D8
1 KENDALL PL
2 RAYLEIGH HO
3 LAVENDER HO
4 CLOVER TERR
5 SHERINGHAM HO
6 BURDOCK HO

E7
1 SHROPSHIRE TERR
2 HUNTINGDON WLK
3 DERWENT HO
4 WINDERMERE HO
5 ULLSWATER HO
6 DUNKELD HO

7 INVERNESS HO
8 GLASGOW HO
9 ABERDEEN HO
10 PRIMROSE HO
11 WISTERIA HO
12 LICHFIELD HO
13 CHAUCER CL

E7
14 BELFAST HO
15 LONDONDERRY HO
16 DUBLIN HO

E8
1 CHILHAM HO
2 DOVER HO
3 DUNSTER TERR
4 WILTSHIRE WAY

F6
1 AINTREE HO
2 ASCOT HO
3 CHEPSTOW CL
4 FOLKSTONE HO
5 TITCHFIELD CL
6 THIRSK HO

7 DONCASTER CL
8 HAVANT WLK
9 PLUMPTON WLK
10 FAREHAM WLK
11 DENSTEAD WLK
12 ANDOVER WLK
13 GROOMBRIDGE SQ

162   196

228   196

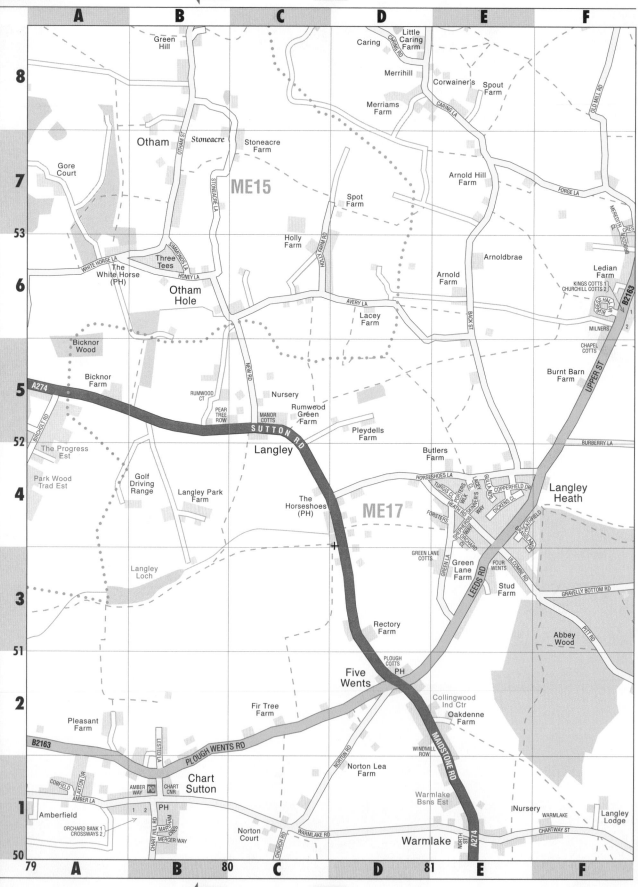

A   B   C   D   E   F

8

7

53

6

5

52

4

3

51

2

1

50

79   A   80   B   C   D   81   E   F

Green Hill
Otham
Stoneacre
Stoneacre Farm
Caring
Little Caring Farm
Merrihill
Corwainer's
Spout Farm
Merriams Farm
CARING LA
CARING RD
ME15
Gore Court
Arnold Hill Farm
FORGE LA
MEREDITH CL
CRES
PETERFIELD
Spot Farm
Holly Farm
HOLLY FARM RD
STONEACRE LA
OTHAM ST
SIMMONDS LA
Arnoldbrae
Ledian Farm
KINGS COTTS 1
CHURCHILL COTTS 2
B2163
Three Tees
The White Horse (PH)
WHITE HORSE LA
HONEY LA
Otham Hole
AVERY LA
Lacey Farm
Arnold Farm
BACK ST
MILNERS
Bicknor Wood
NEW RD
CHAPEL COTTS
UPPER ST
Burnt Barn Farm
Bicknor Farm
A274
RUMWOOD CT
Nursery
Rumwood Green Farm
BURBERRY LA
BICKNOR RD
PEAR TREE ROW
MANOR COTTS
Pleydells Farm
SUTTON RD
Langley
Butlers Farm
HORSESHOES LA
Copperfield Dr
Langley Heath
The Progress Est
Park Wood Trad Est
Golf Driving Range
Langley Park Farm
The Horseshoes (PH)
ME17
TURGIS CL
PORTERS WLK
SKINNER'S GUILLA RD
HEATH RD
DICKENS CL
FORSTERS
SHEPHERDS WAY
ST ORCHARD CL
HEATHFIELD
EAST LA
Langley Loch
Green Lane Cotts
GREEN LA
Green Lane Farm
LEEDS RD
ULCOMBE RD
Stud Farm
FOUR WENTS
GRAVELLY BOTTOM RD
PITT RD
Rectory Farm
Abbey Wood
Five Wents
PLOUGH COTTS PH
Fir Tree Farm
Collingwood Ind Ctr
Oakdenne Farm
Pleasant Farm
B2163
PLOUGH WENTS RD
LESTED LA
NORTON RD
Norton Lea Farm
WINDMILL ROW
MAIDSTONE RD
Warmlake Bsns Est
Nursery
WARMLAKE
Langley Lodge
COBFIELD
LAXTON DR
AMBER LA
AMBER WAY
PO
CHART CNR
PH
Chart Sutton
Amberfield
ORCHARD BANK 1
CROSSWAYS 2
CHART HILL RD
MAYSHAM
MERCER WAY
Norton Court
CHURCH RD
WARMLAKE RD
Warmlake
A274
NORTH ST
CHARTWAY ST

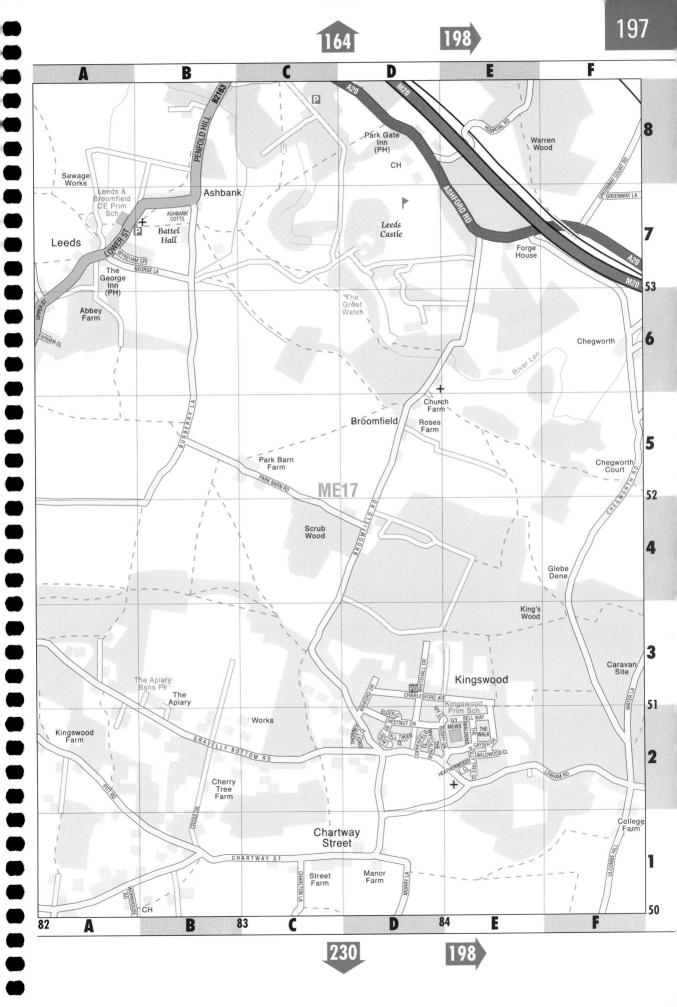

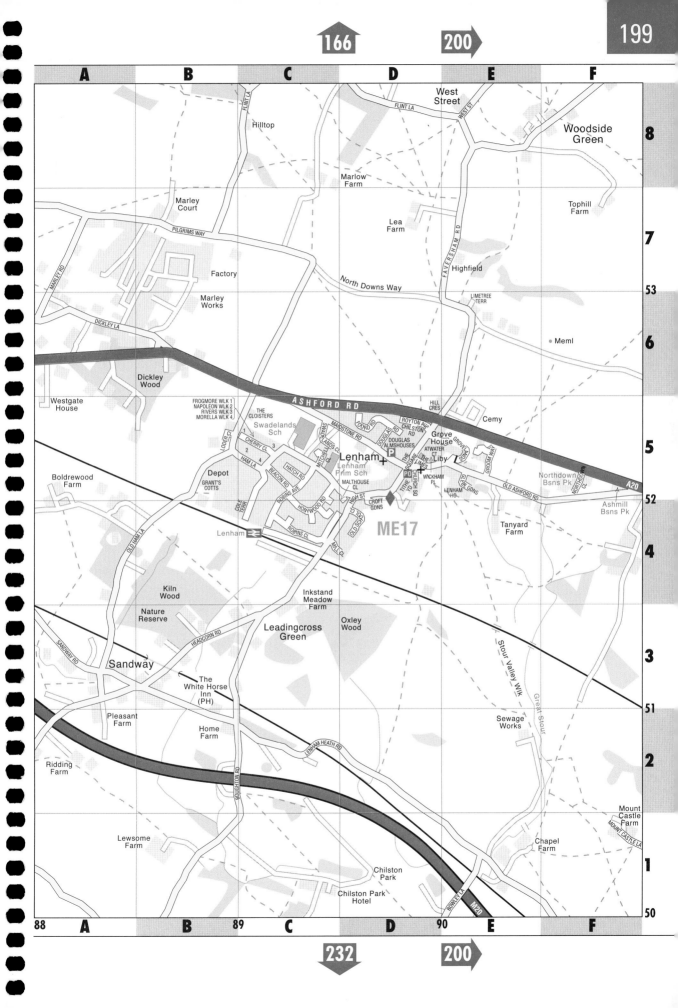

199 167

A B C D E F

ME9

8

Lone Barn Rd

Payden Street

Bunker's Hill

Panden St

Slade Rd

Hurst Farm

Hurstwood Rd

Warren Lodge Farm

ME13

7

Birch Wood

Warren Street

Stubblefield House

Bunce Court Rd

Bunce Court

53

Warren St

Blue House Farm

Little Pivington Farm

Wr Twr

The Harrow Inn (PH)

6

Middleton Farm

Great Pivington Farm

Oak Farm

Cold Harbour Rd

Cold Harbour

Hubbards Hill

Glebe Farm

Waterditch Farm

Waterditch La

Westbury Farm

5

Rayners Hill

Rayner Hill Cotts

Highbourne Pk

Pilgrims' Way

North Downs Way

ME17

Fair View

52

A20

4

ASHFORD RD

New Shelve Farm

Cobham Farm

Wheatgratten Farm

3

Old Shelve

Country Ways

Old Shelve Farm

51

Acton Farm

2

TN27

Maidstone Rd

Forstal Cotts

Sand Pit

Shepherd's Farm

Yew Tree Pk

Mount Castle La

The Forstal

Lenham Forstal

Bolton Farm

Hart Hill

A20

1

The Forstal

Bull Hill

Lenham Heath

Lenham Forstal Rd

Crabtree La

Rose La

Heathfield Bglws

Charing Heath Rd

50

91 **A** 92 **B** **C** 93 **D** **E** **F**

199 233

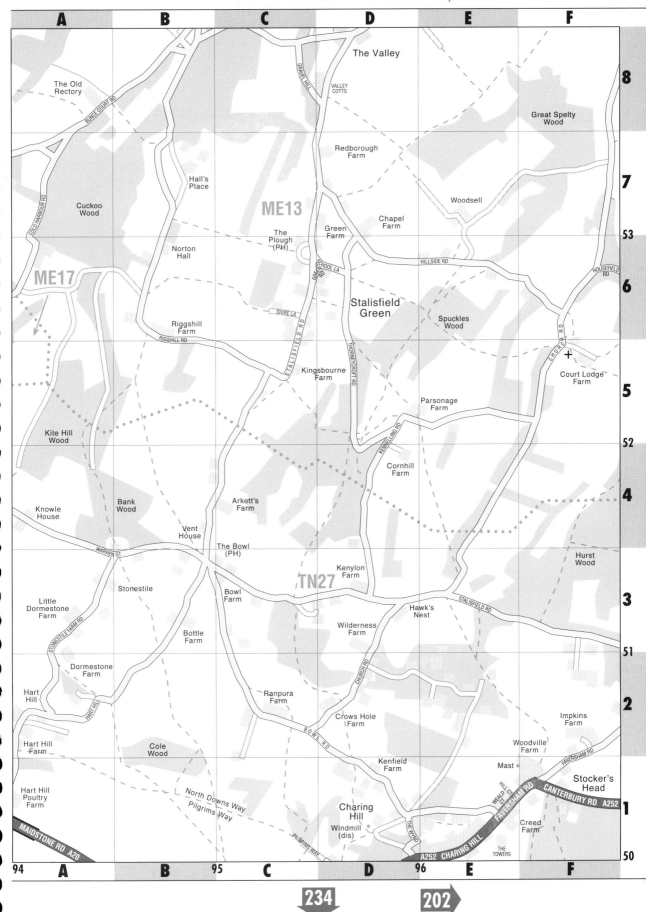

A   B   C   D   E   F

8

The Old
Rectory

Great Spelty
Wood

The Valley

VALLEY
COTTS

Redborough
Farm

7

Hall's
Place

Woodsell

BUNCE COURT RD

53

ME13

Cuckoo
Wood

Chapel
Farm

Green
Farm

The Plough
(PH)

HILLSIDE RD

HOUSEFIELD RD

COLD HARBOUR RD

Norton
Hall

ME17

SCHOOL LA

GREEN RD

6

Stalisfield
Green

Spuckles
Wood

SHIRE LA

Riggshill
Farm

STALISFIELD RD

CHURCH RD

RIGGSHILL RD

Kingsbourne
Farm

THORNEYCROFT RD

Court Lodge
Farm

5

Parsonage
Farm

Kite Hill
Wood

KENNELLING RD

52

Bank
Wood

Arkett's
Farm

Cornhill
Farm

4

Knowle
House

Vent
House

Hurst
Wood

WARREN ST

The Bowl
(PH)

TN27

Kenylon
Farm

STALISFIELD RD

3

Little
Dormestone
Farm

Stonestile

Bowl
Farm

Hawk's
Nest

STONESTILE FARM RD

Wilderness
Farm

CHURCH RD

51

Bottle
Farm

Dormestone
Farm

Impkins
Farm

2

Hart
Hill

HART HILL

Ranpura
Farm

Crows Hole
Farm

Woodville
Farm

FAVERSHAM RD

Hart Hill
Farm

Cole
Wood

BOWL RD

Kenfield
Farm

Mast

Stocker's
Head

HILL ST

WEALD CT

FAVERSHAM RD

CANTERBURY RD   A252

Hart Hill
Poultry
Farm

North Downs Way
Pilgrims Way

Charing
Hill

Windmill
(dis)

THE WIND

Creed
Farm

1

MAIDSTONE RD   A20

PILGRIMS WAY

A252   CHARING HILL

THE
TOWERS

50

94   A   95   B   C   96   D   E   F

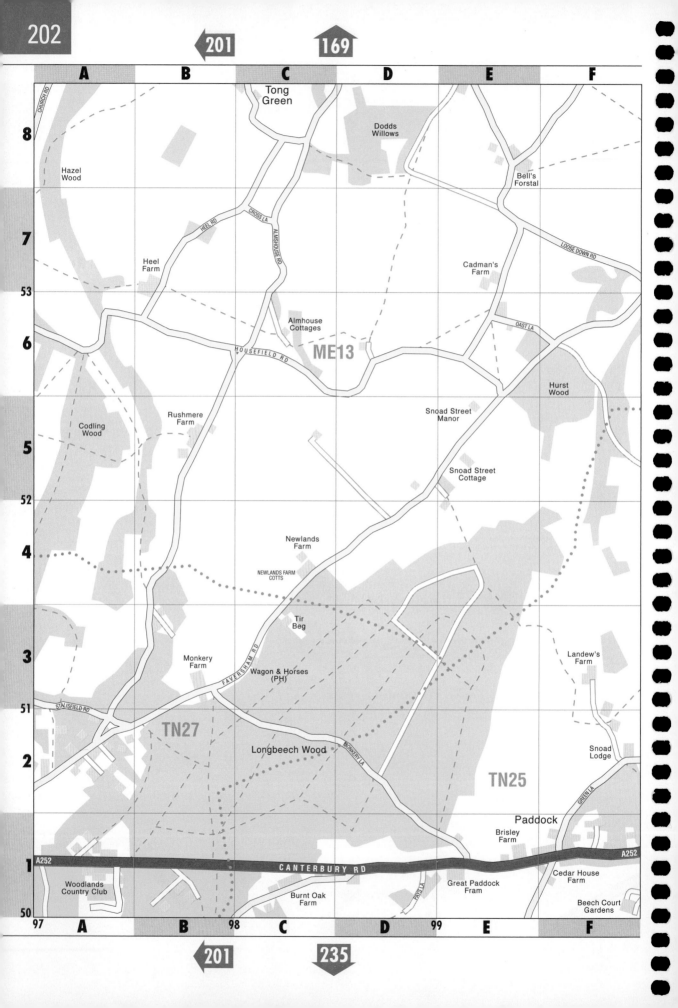

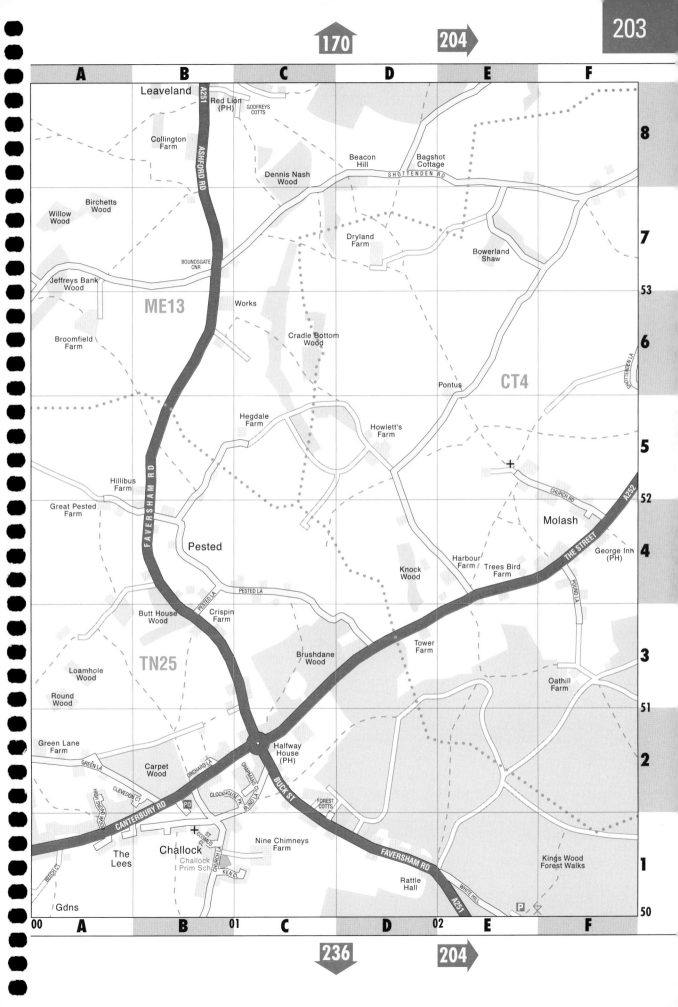

A   B   C   D   E   F

8
7
53
6
5
52
4
3
51
2
1
50

Leaveland

Red Lion (PH)
GODFREYS COTTS

Collington Farm

Dennis Nash Wood

Beacon Hill
Bagshot Cottage

SHOTTENDEN RD

Birchetts Wood

Willow Wood

Dryland Farm

Bowerland Shaw

Jeffreys Bank Wood

BOUNDSGATE CNR

ME13

Works

Cradle Bottom Wood

CT4

Pontus

SHOTTENDEN LA

Broomfield Farm

ASHFORD RD

A251

Hegdale Farm

Howlett's Farm

Hillibus Farm

FAVERSHAM RD

Great Pested Farm

Pested

Molash

CHURCH RD

A252

THE STREET

George Inn (PH)

Harbour Farm
Trees Bird Farm

Knock Wood

PESTED LA
PESTED LA

Butt House Wood

Crispin Farm

POUND LA

TN25

Brushdane Wood

Tower Farm

Oathill Farm

Loamhole Wood

Round Wood

Green Lane Farm

GREEN LA

Carpet Wood

ORCHARD LA

Halfway House (PH)

CHAPLAINS CL
POND LA

BUCK ST

CLEVEDON CT

CLOCKHOUSE PK

FOREST COTTS

HIGH SNOAD WOOD

PO

CANTERBURY RD

Challock
Challock I Prim Sch

COSMUS CT
CHURCH LA
KILN CL

Nine Chimneys Farm

FAVERSHAM RD

Kings Wood Forest Walks

The Lees

BEECH CT

Rattle Hall

WHITE HILL

A251

P

Gdns

00   A   B   01   C   D   02   E   F

203
171

A B C D E F

8

Chequers
Farm

Little Hurst
Wood

Great Hurst
Wood

Harts
Farm

SHOTTENDEN RD

DENNE MANOR LA

Dolfinch
Wood

Maggrllyden

7

Denne Manor
Farm

Danecourt
Shaw

Pigeonhouse
Wood

Little
Bower

SHOTTENDEN LA

Wytherling
Court

Dane
Court

A252

53

Great Bower

CT4

Old Park Shaw

Dane
Street

6

Park Wood

Young Manor
Farm

Flemings

Ridge
Wood

SHOTTENDEN LA

A252

5

Stanners Wood

Cutlers

Cutlers
Wood

Cutlers

52

Coppins Farm

4

North Downs Way

Godmersham
Park

3

51

King's Wood

2

North Downs Way

Godmersham
Downs

1

TN25

50

03 A B 04 C D 05 E F

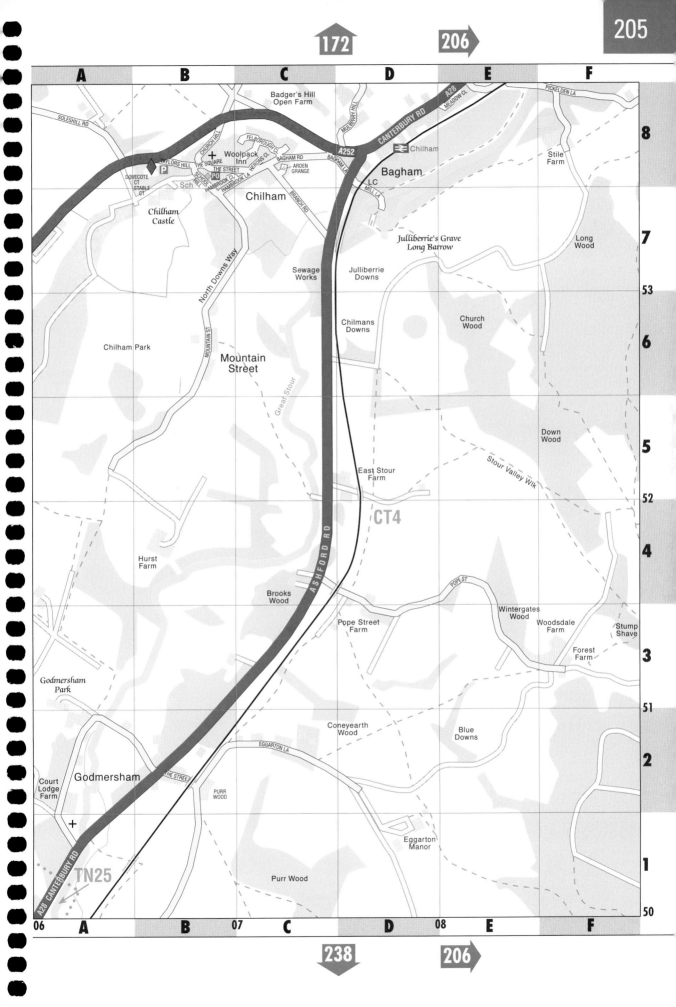

205
173

	A	B	C	D	E	F

8

PICKELDEN LA
MYSTOLE LA
Stour Valley Wlk
MYSTOLE LA
Underdown
MYSTOLE HO
Mystole Park
Thruxted
THE DOWNS
AINSLEY WAY
CANDLERS WAY
WINDMILL
Perry Hill Shaw

7

Perry Court Rudolf Steiner Sch
Perry Court Farm

53

Upper Mystole Park Farm
Sappington Court
GARLINGE GREEN RD
Walk Wood
Kenfield Hall
KENFIELD RD

6

Kenfield Hall Farm
Garlinge Green

5

52

Denge Wood
CT4

4

PENNY POT LA

Upper Thruxted Farm

3

Capel Farm
CAPEL RD
Saw Mill

51

Thruxted Mill
Mounts Wood
Buckholt Wood

2

Forest Wlks
P

1

Eggringe Wood
Dunstan's Wood
WALTHAM RD

Barton Wood
Buckholt Barn

50

09	A		B	10	C		D	11	E		F

205
239

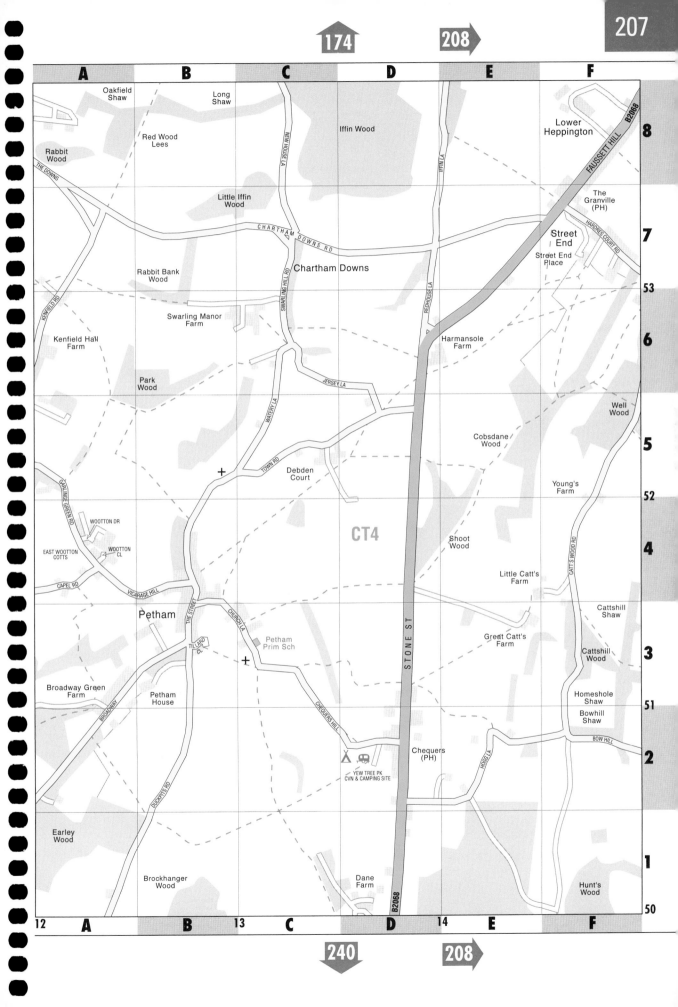

207
175

A B C D E F

8

B2068
WHITE HILL
BRIDGE RD

Whitehill
Wood

Middle
Pett
Farm

7

North Court
Farm

Little
Pett
Farm

Warren
Wood

Redhill
Wood

The
Shave

53

BUTTS CT

Lower
Hardres

SCHOOL LA

Little
Eaton
Farm

Lenhall
Farm

6

BUTTS
MDW
PH

Stockfield
Wood

Avenue
Wood

5

Pett
Bottom

PETT BOTTOM RD

The
Duck
(PH)

CT4

52

Cook's
Farm

TAPLEYS HILL

4

HARDRES COURT RD

PILOTS FARM RD

Pilot's
Wood

Broxhall
Wood

Broxhall
Farm

Gorsley
Wood

CROWS CAMP RD

3

BROXHALL RD

St Andrew's
Wood

Equestrian
Centre

Langham
Park
Farm

WOODGATE

51

Bursted
Manor

PHEASANTS HALL RD

2

BOW HILL

Hardres
Court
Farm

BURSTED HILL

Bursted
Wood

Park
Rough

Upper
Hardres
Court

Reed
Farm

1

The
Manor
House

50

15 A B 16 C D 17 E F

Westwood
Farm

Marley
Wood

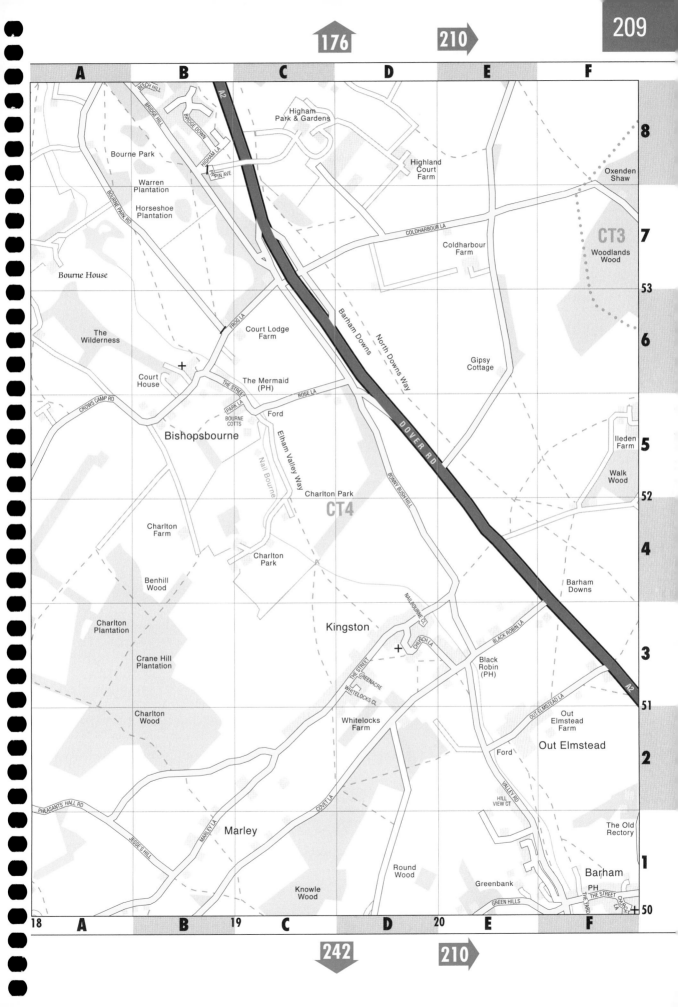

209
177

A B C D E F

CT4

Twelve Acre Shaw

Adisham CE Prim Sch

PO

Adisham

Bloodden

Adisham ⇆ Station App

B2046

Ratling Court

WOODLANDS RD

DONKEY LA

THE STREET

COOTING LA

8

Woodlands Manor

Oxenden Wood

Cooting Farm

7

53

Pitt Wood

Woodlands Wood

CT3

6

1 ULLSWATER GDNS
2 ENNERDALE GDNS

TENNYSON GDNS

COLERIDGE GDNS

THIRLMERE GDNS

BUTTERMERE GDNS

WORDSWORTH GDNS

CORNWALLIS AVE

GRASMERE RD

KINGS RD

BURGESS RD

RATLING RD

DORMAN AVE N

DERWENT WAY

WINDERMERE GDNS

Aylesham Prim Sch

WOODLAND AVE

NEWMAN RD

VALE VIEW RD

ATTLEE AVE

CRIPPS CL

MARKET

SNOWDOWN

PO

Liby

Aylesham

QUEENS RD

HYDE PL

CLARENDON RD

SPINNEY LA

DORMAN AVE S

BRIARS VIEW

EASTRY CT

BOULEVARD COURRIERES

HAWTHORN CL

HILL CRES

ASH

SYCAMORE

ELM RD

OAKSIDE

BEVAN

MMW

AVE

RD

COOTING RD

COX CL

WLK

Well Wood

Cooting Downs

5

52

Ileden Wood

4

Aylesham Wood

Aylesham Ind Est

COVERT RD

SPINNEY LA

CT4

CT15

Ackholt Wood

3

Barham Downs

Upper Digges Farm

AYLESHAM CNR

Willow Wood

A2

51

DOVER RD

ADISHAM RD

North Downs Way

POND LA

Well Wood

Nethersole Farm

Chalk Wood

RECTORY LA

Cemy

2

DOVER RD

B2046

A2

Westmore Ho

Woodpeckers Country Hotel

Aylesham Farm

CHURCH LA

THE STREET

Womenswold

Snow Down

1

GRAVEL CASTLE RD

A260

OLD DOVER RD

Woolage Village

THE GREEN

NETHERSOLE RD

THE PLACE

FORSTAL RD

FIRS RD

50

21 A B 22 C D 23 E F

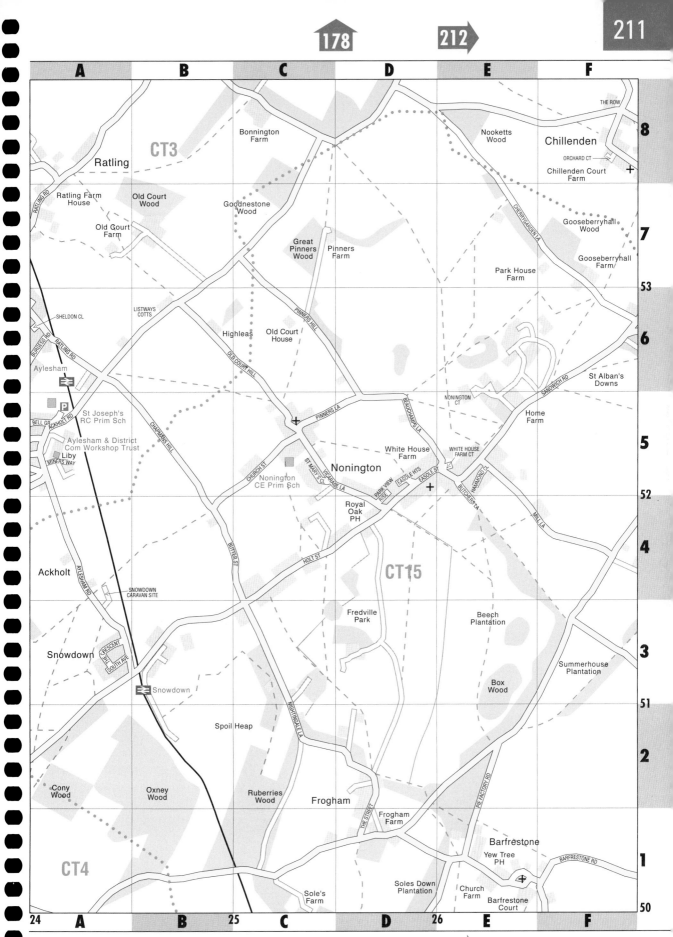

178
212
244
212

A B C D E F

8 7 53 6 5 52 4 3 51 2 1 50

24 25 26

THE ROW

Chillenden

CT3

Ratling

Bonnington Farm

Nooketts Wood

ORCHARD CT

Chillenden Court Farm

Ratling Farm House

Old Court Wood

Goodnestone Wood

Gooseberryhall Wood

CHERRYGARDEN LA

Old Court Farm

Great Pinners Wood

Pinners Farm

Park House Farm

Gooseberryhall Farm

RATLING RD

SHELDON CL

LISTWAYS COTTS

PINNERS HILL

St Alban's Downs

BURGESS RD

RATLING RD

Highleas

Old Court House

Old Court House

OLD COURT HILL

SANDWICH RD

NONINGTON CT

Aylesham

Home Farm

BELL GR

ACKHOLT RD

P

St Joseph's RC Prim Sch

CHAPMANS HILL

Aylesham & District Com Workshop Trust

Liby

MINERS WAY

CHURCH ST

ST MARY'S CL

Nonington CE Prim Sch

VICARAGE LA

PINNERS LA

Nonington

White House Farm

BEAUCHAMPS LA

EASOLE HTS

PARK VIEW RISE

EASOLE ST

WHITE HOUSE FARM CT

HAMMOND CL

BUTCHERS LA

MILL LA

Royal Oak PH

Ackholt

AYLESHAM RD

BUTTER ST

HOLT ST

CT15

Fredville Park

Beech Plantation

Summerhouse Plantation

Snowdown

SNOWDOWN CARAVAN SITE

CRESCENT THE

SOUTH AVE

Snowdown

Box Wood

NIGHTINGALE LA

Spoil Heap

PIE FACTORY RD

Cony Wood

Oxney Wood

Ruberries Wood

Frogham

THE STREET

Frogham Farm

Barfrestone

Yew Tree PH

BARFRESTONE RD

CT4

Sole's Farm

Soles Down Plantation

Church Farm

Barfrestone Court

211   179

A B C D E F

8

YEW TREE FARM

CT13

Griffin's Head (PH)

SHORT ST

War Meml

Home Wood

7

The Warren

Home Farm

CT3

Knowlton

Knowlton Court

Black La

THORNTON LA

CUCKOLDS CNR

Knowlton Park

SANDWICH RD

53

The Grove

Manorial Earthworks

Shingleton Wood

6

Dover Lodge Cottages

Shingleton Farm

Venson Farm

St Alban's Downs

Round Wood

Shingleton Cottages

CT14

Thorntonhill Cottages

5

Kelk Hill

Thornton Farm

Kittington Cottages

52

Brown Pudding Plantation

Thornton Wood

Garden Wood

4

The Downs

DANE CT

SCHOOL RD

Kittington Farm

PIKE RD

3

Beeches Farm

51

Craythorne Firs

CT15

2

Spoil Heap

POPLAR DR

ROMAN WAY

CYPRESS GR

ASH GR

BEECH DR

CHERRY GR

SWEETBRIAR LA

OAK GR

Burgess Hill

Works

BARVILLE RD

CHAUCER RD

ST JOHNS

FAIRVIEW RD

LARCH RD

MILNER RD

PO

ADELINE RD

MILNER

TERRACE RD

Elvington

1

Sports Gd

FELMTON LA

MILL YARD WAY

WIGMORE LA

SANDWICH RD

BARFRESTONE RD

50

27 A B 28 C D 29 E F

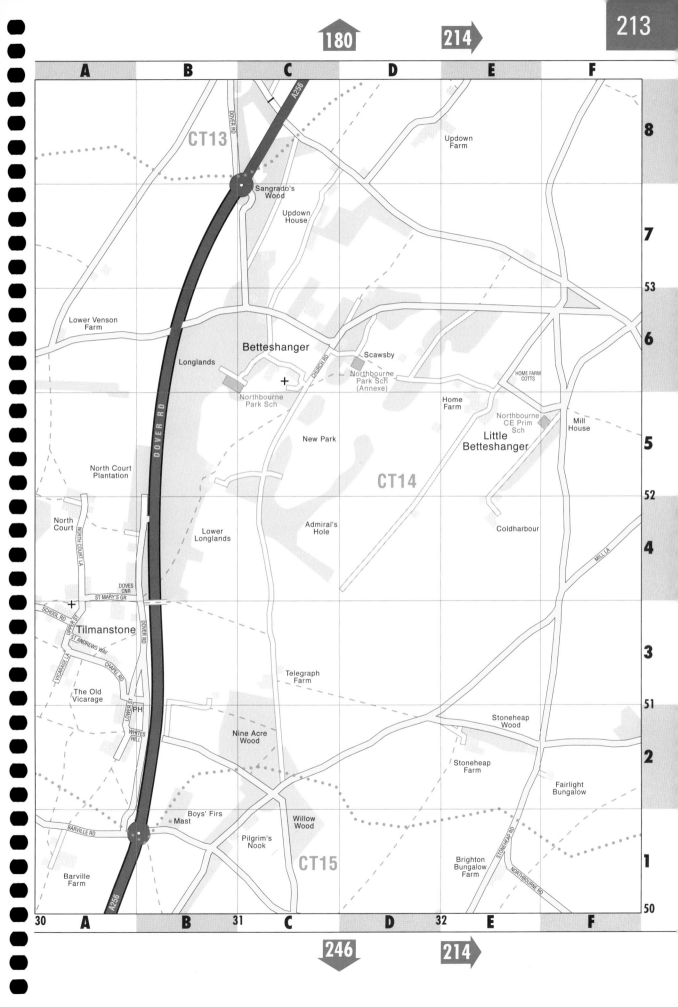

180
214
246
214

A   B   C   D   E   F

8
7
53
6
5
52
4
3
51
2
1
50

CT13

DOVER RD
A256

Sangrado's Wood

Updown Farm

Updown House

Lower Venson Farm

Betteshanger
Longlands
CHURCH RD

Scawsby
Northbourne Park Sch (Annexe)

HOME FARM COTTS

Northbourne Park Sch

New Park

Home Farm

Northbourne CE Prim Sch

Little Betteshanger

Mill House

CT14

North Court Plantation

North Court

NORTH COURT LA
DOVES CNR
ST MARY'S GR

Lower Longlands

Admiral's Hole

Coldharbour

MILL LA

SCHOOL RD

Tilmanstone
UPPER ST
ST ANDREWS WAY
VICARAGE LA
CHAPEL RD

DOVER RD

LOWER ST

The Old Vicarage
PH
WHITES HILL

Telegraph Farm

Stoneheap Wood

Nine Acre Wood

Willow Wood

Stoneheap Farm

Fairlight Bungalow

BARVILLE RD

Boys' Firs
Mast

Pilgrim's Nook

CT15

Brighton Bungalow Farm

STONEHEAP RD
NORTHBOURNE RD

Barville Farm

A256

30   31   32

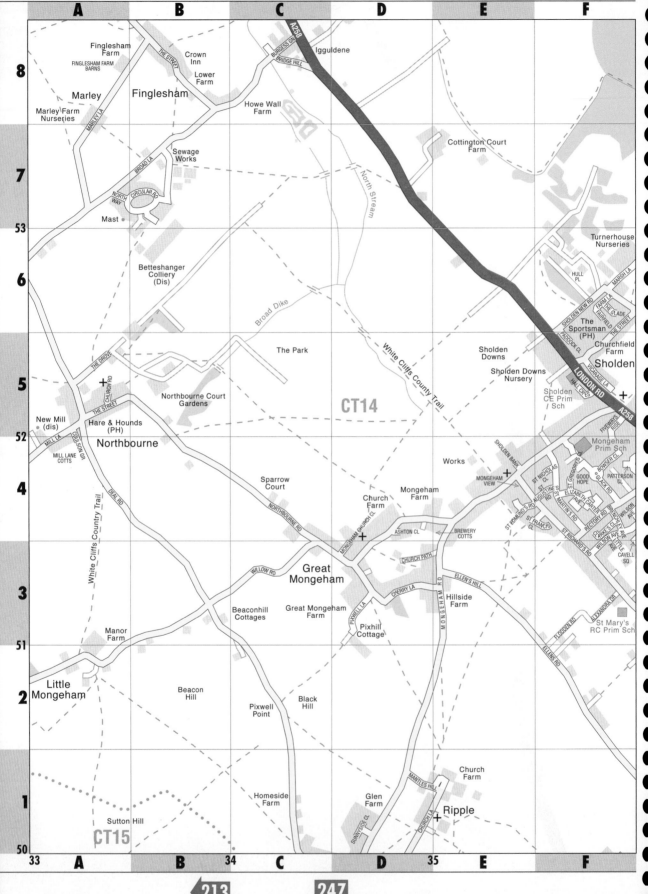

A   B   C   D   E   F

8

Finglesham
Farm
FINGLESHAM FARM
BARNS
Crown
Inn
Lower
Farm
Igguldene
Marley
Finglesham
Howe Wall
Farm
Cottington Court
Farm
Marley Farm
Nurseries
MARLEY LA
THE STREET

7
Sewage
Works
BROAD LA
NORTH
WAY
CIRCULAR RD
North Stream
Turnerhouse
Nurseries
53
Mast
HULL
PL
6
Betteshanger
Colliery
(Dis)
Broad Dike
The Park
White Cliffs County Trail
Sholden
Downs
SHOLDEN NEW RD
FARM LA
THE GLADE
FAIRFIELD
THE STREET
The
Sportsman
(PH)
Churchfield
Farm
Sholden
MARSH LA
PADDOCK CL
5
THE DROVE
CHURCH RD
CT14
Sholden Downs
Nursery
Sholden
CE Prim
Sch
LONDON RD
A258
HALL CRES
VICARAGE LA
New Mill
(dis)
THE STREET
Northbourne Court
Gardens
FIVEWAYS
RISE
52
Hare & Hounds
(PH)
MILL LA
COULSON GR
Northbourne
Works
Mongeham
Prim Sch
BOWSER CL
PATTERSON
CL
MILL LANE
COTTS
DEAL RD
Sparrow
Court
Mongeham
Farm
MONGEHAM VIEW
ST NICHOLAS
CL
GOOD
HOPE
4
NORTHBOURNE RD
Church
Farm
ST AUGUSTINE'S
ST EDMUND'S RD
ST MARTIN'S RD
ELIZABETH CARTER
BLACK RD
RECTORY RD
ST RICHARD'S RD
WILSON AVE
WILSON AVE
White Cliffs Country Trail
Ashton Cl
Brewery
Cotts
ST GREGORY'S
CL
ST FRANCIS
CL
CAVELL
SQ
MONGEHAM CHURCH RD
3
WILLOW RD
Great
Mongeham
Church Path
ELLEN'S HILL
Hillside
Farm
St Mary's
RC Prim Sch
ALEXANDRA DR
Beaconhill
Cottages
Great Mongeham
Farm
CHERRY LA
PIXWELL LA
MONGEHAM RD
FLODDEN RD
51
Manor
Farm
Pixhill
Cottage
ELLEN'S RD
2
Little
Mongeham
Beacon
Hill
Pixwell
Point
Black
Hill
1
Homeside
Farm
Glen
Farm
MANTLES HILL
Church
Farm
Ripple
Sutton Hill
SUNNYSIDE CL
CHURCH LA
CT15
50
33   A   B   34   C   D   35   E   F

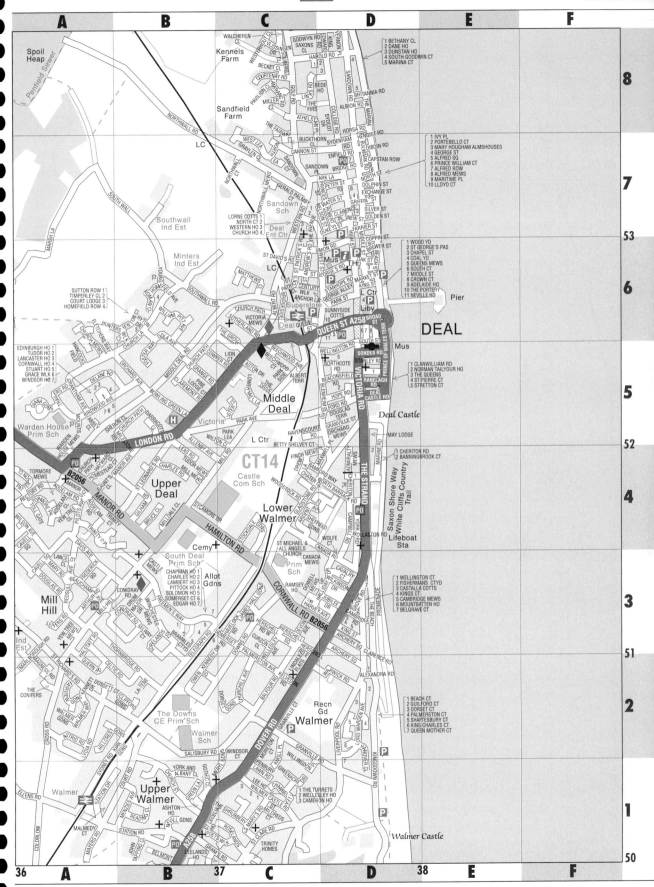

DEAL

CT14

Middle Deal

Upper Deal

Lower Walmer

Mill Hill

Walmer

Upper Walmer

1 BETHANY CL
2 DANE HO
3 DUNSTAN HO
4 SOUTH GOODWIN CT
5 MARINA CT

1 IVY PL
2 PORTEBELLO CT
3 MARY HOUGHAM ALMSHOUSES
4 GEORGE ST
5 ALFRED SQ
6 PRINCE WILLIAM CT
7 ALFRED ROW
8 ALFRED MEWS
9 MARITIME PL
10 LLOYD CT

1 WOOD YD
2 ST GEORGE'S PAS
3 CHAPEL ST
4 COAL YD
5 QUEENS MEWS
6 SOUTH CT
7 MIDDLE ST
8 CROWN CT
9 ADELAIDE RD
10 THE PORTERY
11 NEVILLE HO

1 CLANWILLIAM RD
2 NORMAN TAILYOUR HO
3 THE QUEENS
4 ST PIERRE CT
5 STRETTON CT

1 CHERITON RD
2 BANNINGBROOK CT

1 WELLINGTON CT
2 FISHERMANS CTYD
3 CASTALLA COTTS
4 KINGS CT
5 CAMBRIDGE MEWS
6 MOUNTBATTEN HO
7 BELGRAVE CT

1 BEACH CT
2 GUILFORD CT
3 DORSET CT
4 PALMERSTON CT
5 SHAFTESBURY CT
6 KING CHARLES CT
7 QUEEN MOTHER CT

EDINBURGH HO 1
TUDOR HO 2
LANCASTER HO 3
CORNWALL HO 4
STUART HO 5
GRACE WLK 6
WINDSOR HO 7

SUTTON ROW 1
TIMPERLEY CL 2
COURT LODGE LA 3
HOMEFIELD ROW 4

LORNE COTTS 1
NORTH CT 2
WESTERN HO 3
CHURCH HO 4

CHAPMAN HO 1
CHARLES HO 2
LAMBERT HO 3
PITTOCK HO 4
SOLOMON HO 5
SOMERSET CT 6
EDGAR HO 7

1 THE TURRETS
2 WELLESLEY HO
3 CAMERON HO

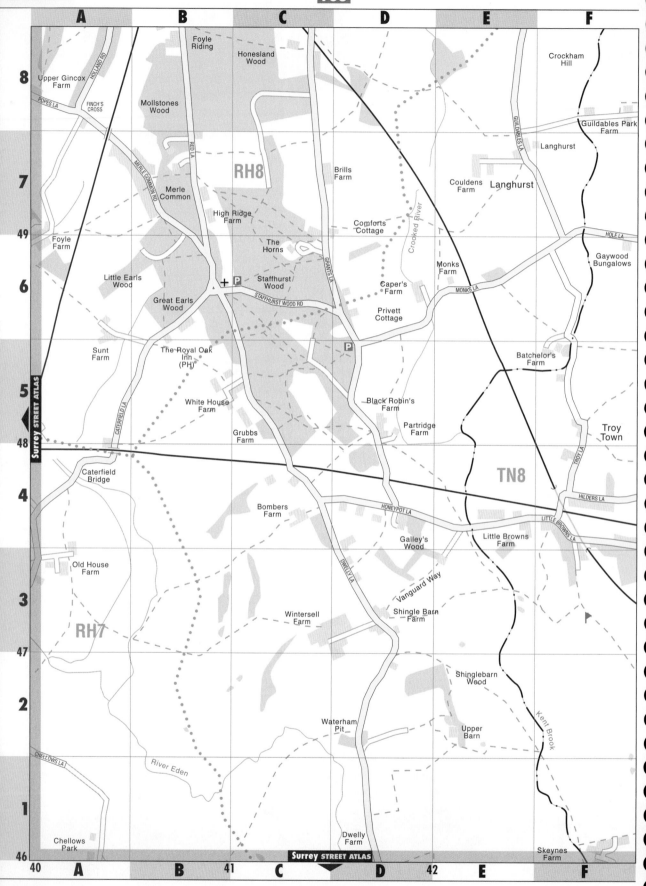

Upper Gincox Farm

POPES LA

FINCH'S CROSS

HOLLAND RD

Foyle Riding

Honesland Wood

Crockham Hill

Mollstones Wood

RED LA

MERLE COMMON RD

Merle Common

RH8

Brills Farm

GUILDABLES LA

Guildables Park Farm

Langhurst

High Ridge Farm

Couldens Farm

Langhurst

Foyle Farm

The Horns

Comforts Cottage

Crooked River

HOLE LA

Little Earls Wood

Staffhurst Wood

GRANTS LA

Caper's Farm

Monks Farm

MONKS LA

Gaywood Bungalows

Great Earls Wood

STAFFHURST WOOD RD

Privett Cottage

Batchelor's Farm

Sunt Farm

The Royal Oak Inn (PH)

CATERFIELD LA

White House Farm

Black Robin's Farm

Troy Town

Grubbs Farm

Partridge Farm

TN8

TROY LA

Caterfield Bridge

HONEYPOT LA

HILDERS LA

LITTLE BROWNS LA

Bombers Farm

Galley's Wood

Little Browns Farm

Old House Farm

DWELLY LA

Vanguard Way

Shingle Barn Farm

RH7

Wintersell Farm

Shinglebarn Wood

Waterham Pit

Upper Barn

Kent Brook

CHELLOWS LA

River Eden

Chellows Park

Dwelly Farm

Skeynes Farm

Surrey STREET ATLAS

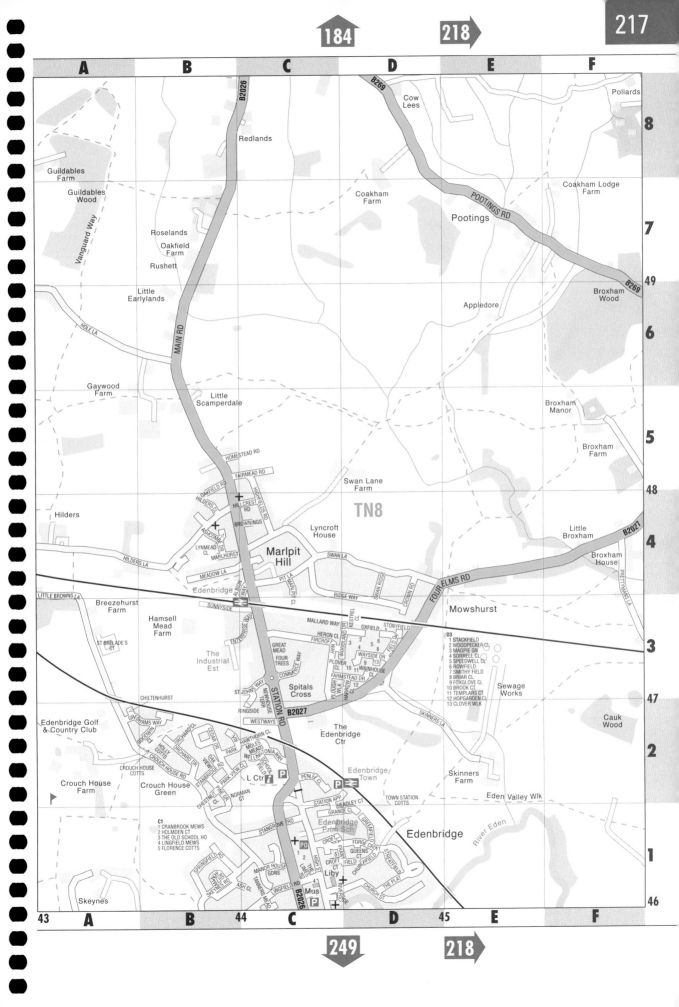

217
185

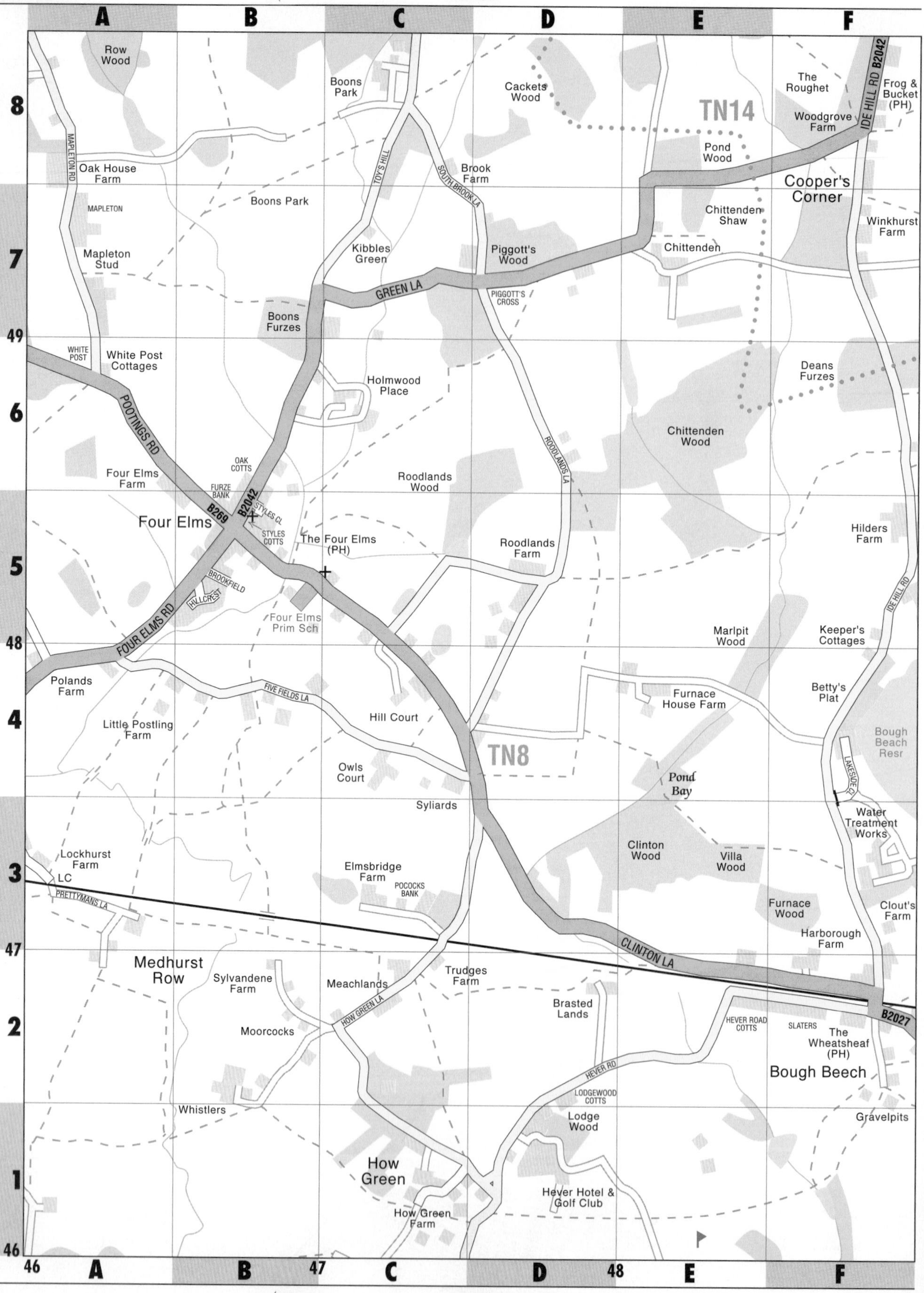
A
B
C
D
E
F
8
7
49
6
5
48
4
3
47
2
1
46
46
47
48
Row Wood
Boons Park
Cackets Wood
The Roughet
Frog & Bucket (PH)
TN14
Woodgrove Farm
IDE HILL RD B2042
MAPLETON RD
Oak House Farm
TOY'S HILL
SOUTH BROOK LA
Brook Farm
Pond Wood
Cooper's Corner
Boons Park
MAPLETON
Chittenden Shaw
Winkhurst Farm
Mapleton Stud
Kibbles Green
Piggott's Wood
Chittenden
GREEN LA
PIGGOTT'S CROSS
Boons Furzes
WHITE POST
White Post Cottages
Holmwood Place
Deans Furzes
POOTINGS RD
Chittenden Wood
ROODLANDS LA
OAK COTTS
Four Elms Farm
Roodlands Wood
FURZE BANK
B2042
B269
Four Elms
STYLES CL
STYLES COTTS
The Four Elms (PH)
Hilders Farm
Roodlands Farm
BROOKFIELD
HILLCREST
FOUR ELMS RD
Four Elms Prim Sch
Marlpit Wood
Keeper's Cottages
IDE HILL RD
Polands Farm
FIVE FIELDS LA
Furnace House Farm
Betty's Plat
Little Postling Farm
Hill Court
TN8
Bough Beach Resr
Owls Court
Pond Bay
LAKESIDE CL
Syliards
Water Treatment Works
Lockhurst Farm
Clinton Wood
Villa Wood
LC
Elmsbridge Farm
POCOCKS BANK
PRETTYMANS LA
Furnace Wood
Clout's Farm
Harborough Farm
CLINTON LA
Medhurst Row
Sylvandene Farm
Meachlands
Trudges Farm
Brasted Lands
B2027
HOW GREEN LA
HEVER ROAD COTTS
SLATERS
The Wheatsheaf (PH)
Moorcocks
HEVER RD
Bough Beech
LODGEWOOD COTTS
Whistlers
Lodge Wood
Gravelpits
How Green
Hever Hotel & Golf Club
How Green Farm

217
250

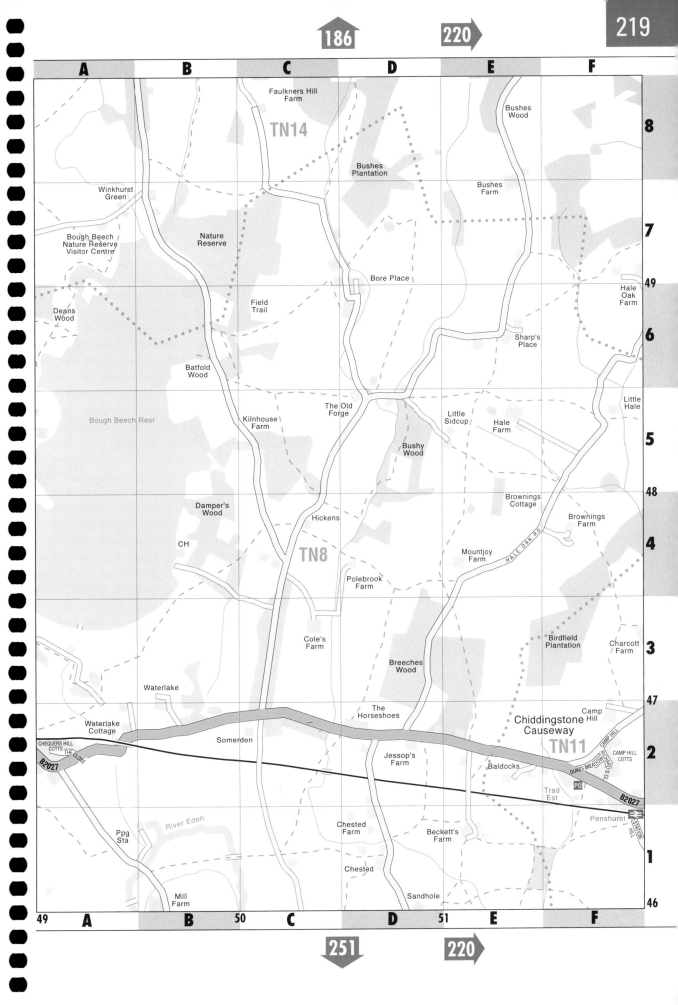

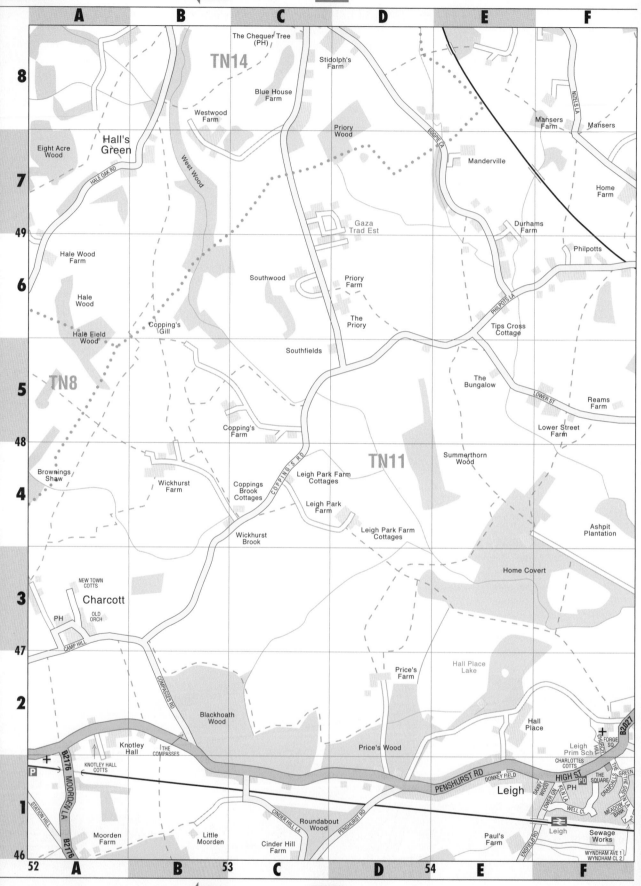

A B C D E F

8

TN14

The Chequer Tree (PH)

Stidolph's Farm

Blue House Farm

Westwood Farm

Priory Wood

EGRPIE LA

NIZELS LA

Mansers Farm

Mansers

Eight Acre Wood

Hall's Green

WEST WOOD

HALE OAK RD

Manderville

Home Farm

7

49

Gaza Trad Est

Durhams Farm

Philpotts

Hale Wood Farm

Southwood

Priory Farm

PHILPOTTS LA

Tips Cross Cottage

6

Hale Wood

Copping's Gill

The Priory

TN8

Southfields

The Bungalow

LOWER ST

Reams Farm

5

Hale Field Wood

Copping's Farm

Lower Street Farm

48

Brownings Shaw

Coppings Brook Cottages

Leigh Park Farm Cottages

COPPING'S RD

Summerthorn Wood

Wickhurst Farm

Leigh Park Farm

TN11

4

Wickhurst Brook

Leigh Park Farm Cottages

Ashpit Plantation

Home Covert

3

NEW TOWN COTTS

Charcott

OLD ORCH

PH

CAMP HILL

Price's Farm

Hall Place Lake

47

COMPASSES RD

2

Blackhoath Wood

Hall Place

B2027

Knotley Hall

THE COMPASSES

Price's Wood

Leigh Prim Sch

THE FORGE SQ

CHURCH HILL

B2176

KNOTLEY HALL COTTS

PENSHURST RD

Donkey Field

CHARLOTTES COTTS

HIGH ST

PO

THE SQUARE

CRADDALLS

THE GREEN

Leigh

MOORDEN LA

SABO'S WOOD

LOWER GRN

KILN LA

PH

WELL CL

MEADOW BANK

1

STATION HILL

Moorden Farm

CINDER HILL LA

Roundabout Wood

PENSHURST RD

Leigh

Sewage Works

B2176

Little Moorden

Cinder Hill Farm

Paul's Farm

ERSFELD RD

WYNDHAM AVE 1
WYNDHAM CL 2

46

52 A B 53 C D 54 E F

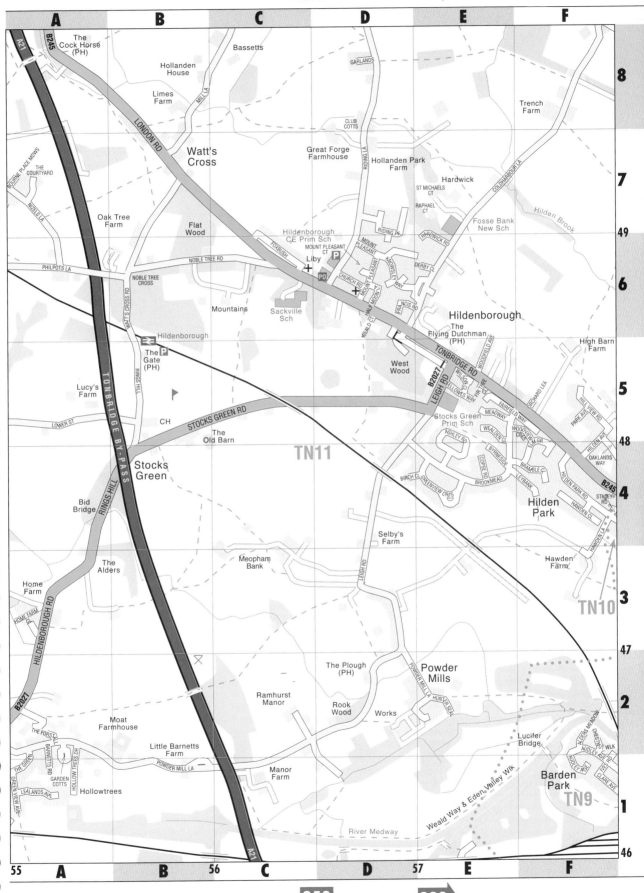

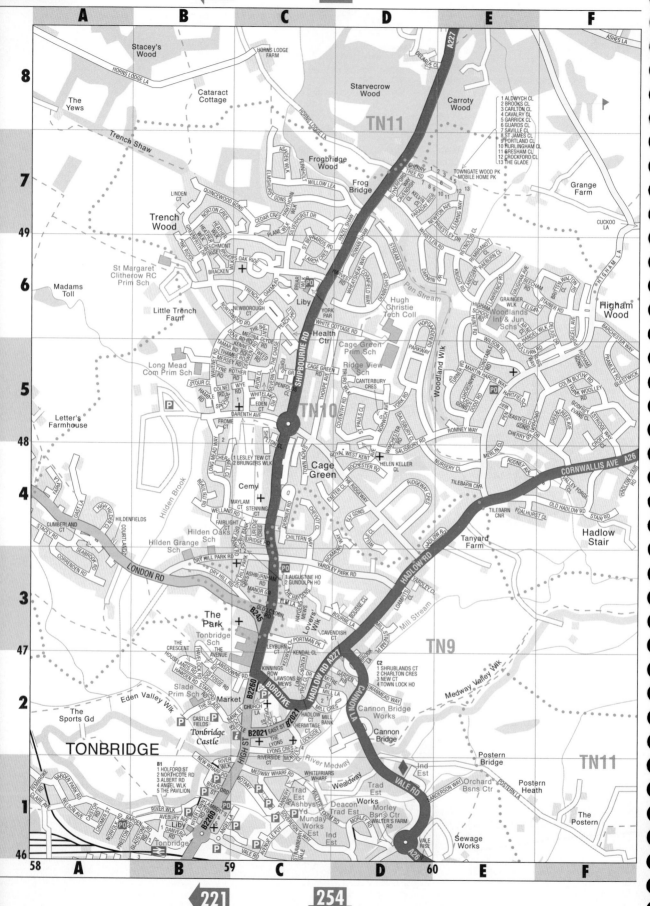

190
224

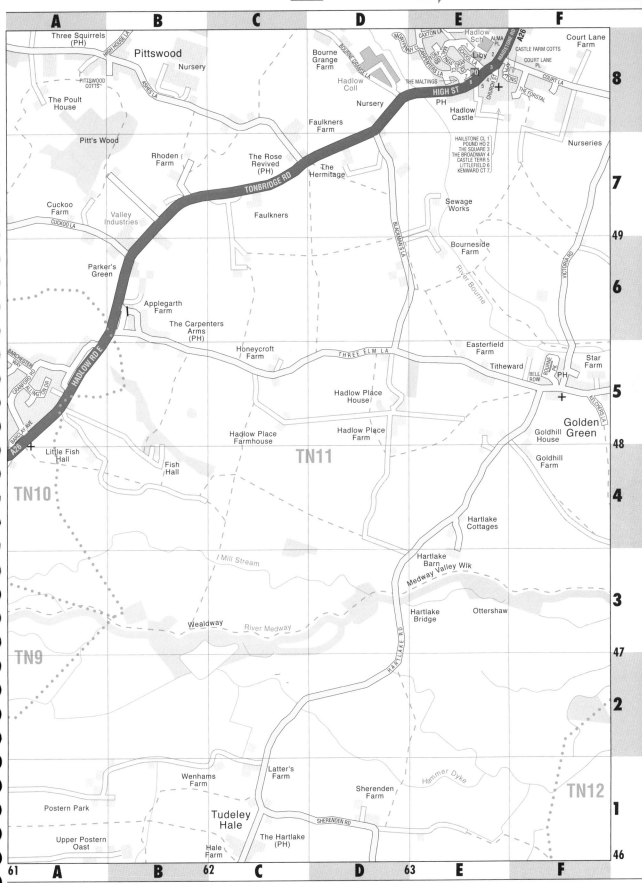

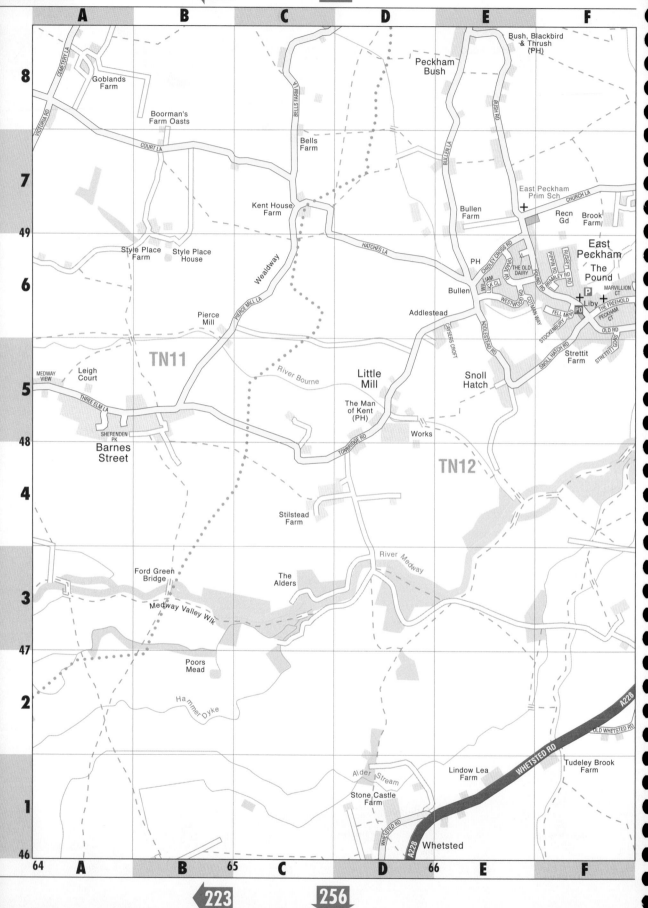

A B C D E F

8

7

49

6

TN11

5

48

4

3

47

2

1

46

64 A B 65 C D 66 E F

Goblands Farm

CEMETERY LA

VICTORIA RD

Boorman's Farm Oasts

COURT LA

Bells Farm

BELLS FARM LT

Kent House Farm

Style Place Farm

Style Place House

Wealdway

Pierce Mill

PIERCE MILL LA

Leigh Court

MEDWAY VIEW

THREE ELM LA

SHERENDEN PK

Barnes Street

River Bourne

Little Mill

The Man of Kent (PH)

TONBRIDGE RD

Works

Stilstead Farm

Ford Green Bridge

Medway Valley Wlk

The Alders

River Medway

Poors Mead

Hammer Dyke

Alder Stream

Stone Castle Farm

WHETSTED RD

A228

Whetsted

Lindow Lea Farm

WHETSTED RD

A228

OLD WHETSTED RD

Tudeley Brook Farm

TN12

Peckham Bush

Bush, Blackbird & Thrush (PH)

BUSH RD

BULLEN LA

East Peckham Prim Sch

Bullen Farm

PH

Bullen

Addlestead

CHIDLEY CROSS RD

DUKE RD

THE OLD DAIRY

WESTWOOD

COTMAN WAY

ADDLESTEAD RD

CARSERS CROFT

Snoll Hatch

SNOLL HATCH RD

STOCKENBURY

CHURCH LA

Recn Gd

Brook Farm

East Peckham

The Pound

PIPPIN RD

RUSSET RD

BRAMLEY RD

POUND RD

MARVILLION CT

Liby

PO

P

THE FREEHOLD

PECKHAM CT

OLD RD

FELL MEAD

Strettit Farm

STRETTIT CLOSE

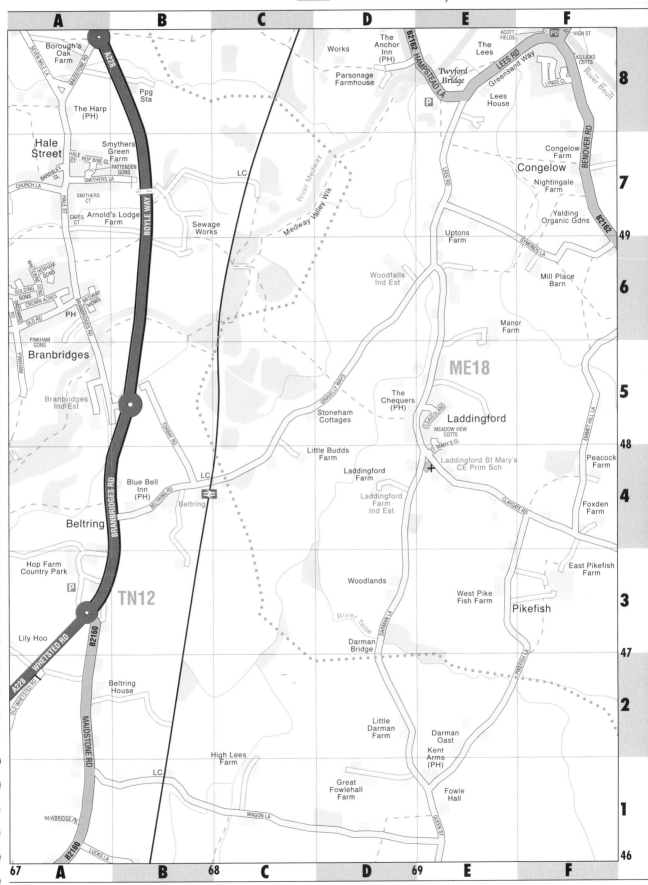

192
226
257
226

Borough's Oak Farm

Ppg Sta

The Harp (PH)

Hale Street

Smythers Green Farm

HALE CT
HOP BINE CL
PATTENDEN GDNS
SMITHERS LA

SEVEN MILE LA
MAIDSTONE RD
A228

Works

Parsonage Farmhouse

The Anchor Inn (PH)

HAMPSTEAD LA
B2162

Twyford Bridge

The Lees

ACOTT FIELDS

LEES RD

Greensand Way

PO
HIGH ST

KILLICKS COTTS

Lees House

LYNGS CL

River Beult

Congelow Farm

Congelow

BENOVER RD
B2162

Nightingale Farm

LC

BOYLE WAY

CHURCH LA
BARDSLEY CL
HALE ST
CATES CT

SMITHERS CT

Arnold's Lodge Farm

Sewage Works

River Medway

Medway Valley Wlk

LEES RD

Uptons Farm

SYMONDS LA

Yalding Organic Gdns

Mill Place Barn

WHITEBINE GDNS
HENHAM GDNS
GOLDING GDNS
CROWN ACRES
ORCHARD
OLD RD
PINKHAM GDNS
MEDWAY MDWS
BRANBRIDGES RD
PH
PINKHAM

Branbridges

Woodfalls Ind Est

Manor Farm

ME18

Branbridges Ind Est

TORBAY RD

Blue Bell Inn (PH)

BRANBRIDGES RD

LC

Beltring

Beltring

BELTRING RD

Stoneham Cottages

GRAVELLY WAYS

The Chequers (PH)

Little Budds Farm

Laddingford Farm

CLEAVESLAND
MEADOW VIEW COTTS
ST MARY'S CL

Laddingford

Laddingford St Mary's CE Prim Sch

Peacock Farm

EMMET HILL LA

Beltring

Hop Farm Country Park
P

Laddingford Farm Ind Est

CLAYGATE RD

Foxden Farm

TN12

Lily Hoo

WHETSTED RD
A228
OLD WHETSTED RD
B2160

Woodlands

River Teise

DARMAN LA

West Pike Fish Farm

East Pikefish Farm

Pikefish

PIKEFISH LA

Beltring House

MAIDSTONE RD
B2160

Darman Bridge

Little Darman Farm

Darman Oast

Kent Arms (PH)

High Lees Farm

LC

Great Fowlehall Farm

Fowle Hall

QUEEN ST

NEWBRIDGE PK

WAGON LA

LUCKS LA

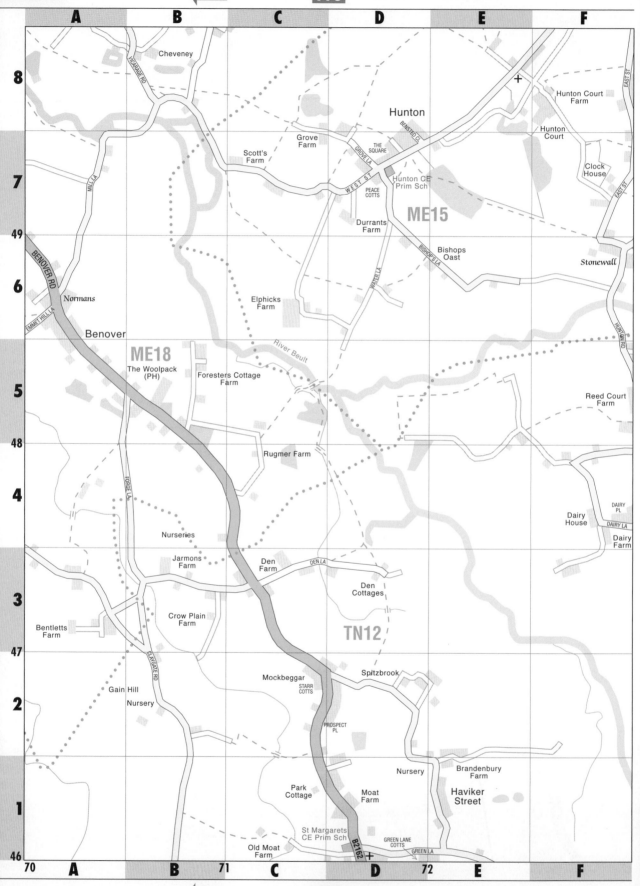

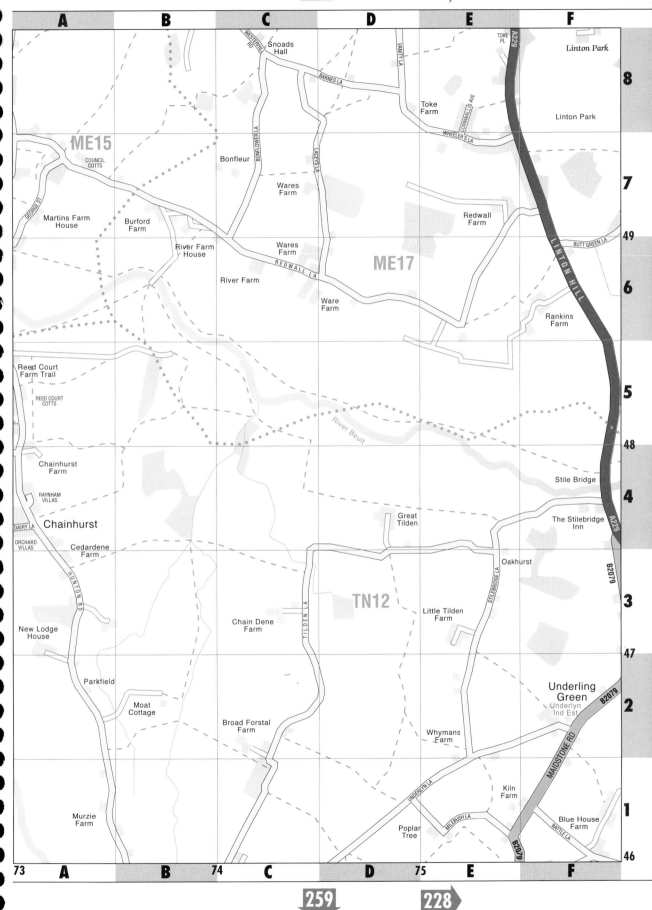

A B C D E F

8

Snoads Hall
WESTERHILL RD
BARNES LA
VANITY LA
TOKE PL
A229
Linton Park

Toke Farm
CORNWALLIS AVE
WHEELER'S LA
Linton Park

ME15
Council Cotts
Bonfleur
BONFLOWER LA
LACEY'S LA
Wares Farm
Redwall Farm
7

49

George St
Martins Farm House
Burford Farm
River Farm House
Wares Farm
REDWALL LA
ME17
LINTON HILL
BUTT GREEN LA

River Farm
Ware Farm
Rankins Farm
6

Reed Court Farm Trail
REED COURT COTTS
5

River Beult
48

Chainhurst Farm
RAYNHAM VILLAS
Stile Bridge
4

DAIRY LA
Chainhurst
ORCHARD VILLAS
Cedardene Farm
Great Tilden
The Stilebridge Inn
A229
B2079

HUNTON RD
TN12
Oakhurst
STILEBRIDGE LA
Little Tilden Farm
3

New Lodge House
Chain Dene Farm
TILDEN LA
47

Parkfield
Underling Green
Underlyn Ind Est
B2079
2

Moat Cottage
Broad Forstal Farm
Whymans Farm
MAIDSTONE RD

Murzie Farm
UNDERLYN LA
MILEBUSH LA
Kiln Farm
Blue House Farm
BATTLE LA
1

Poplar Tree
B2079
46

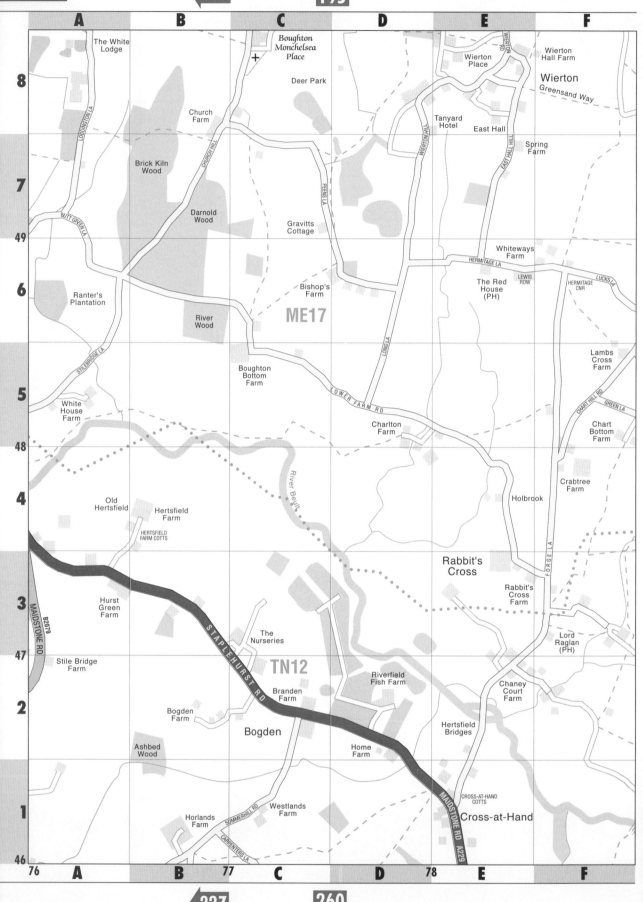

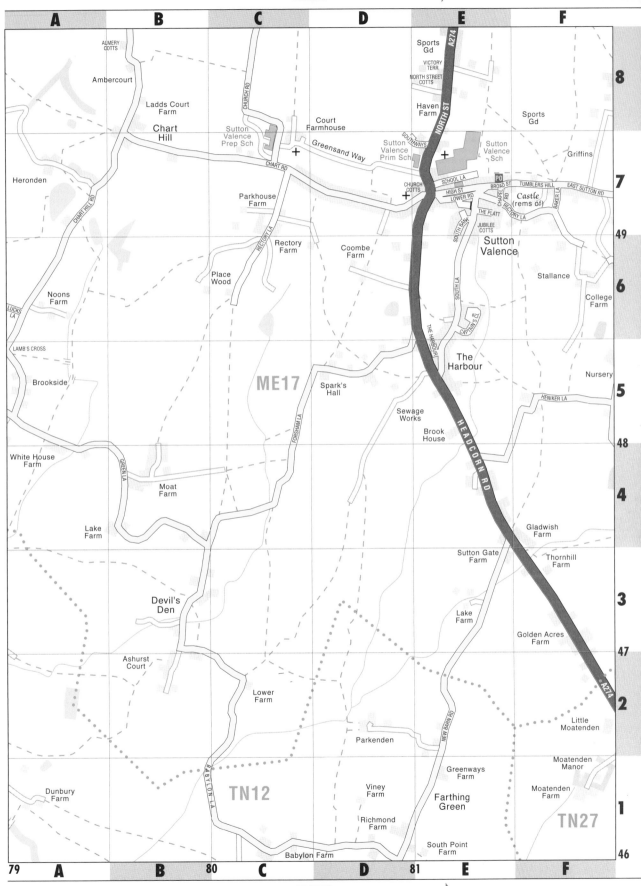

8
7
49
6
5
48
4
3
47
2
1
46

Almery Cotts

Ambercourt

Ladds Court Farm

Chart Hill

CHURCH RD

Court Farmhouse

Sutton Valence Prep Sch

Greensand Way

Sports Gd

VICTORY TERR

NORTH STREET COTTS

Haven Farm

NORTH ST

A274

SOUTHWAYS

Sutton Valence Prim Sch

Sutton Valence Sch

Sports Gd

Griffins

CHART RD

Heronden

CHART HILL RD

Parkhouse Farm

RECTORY LA

Rectory Farm

Coombe Farm

CHURCH COTTS

SCHOOL LA

Broad St

PO

Tumblers Hill

EAST SUTTON RD

BAKER LA

HIGH ST

LOWER RD

CHAPEL

RECTORY LA

THE PLATT

Castle (rems of)

Sutton Valence

SOUTH BANK

JUBILEE COTTS

Place Wood

Noons Farm

LUCKS LA

SOUTH LA

Stallance

College Farm

ME17

LAMB'S CROSS

Brookside

Spark's Hall

THE HARBOUR

CAPTAIN'S CL

The Harbour

Nursery

HENIKER LA

Sewage Works

Brook House

White House Farm

GREEN LA

Moat Farm

Lake Farm

HEADCORN RD

Gladwish Farm

Thornhill Farm

Sutton Gate Farm

Devil's Den

Ashurst Court

FORSHAM LA

Lower Farm

Lake Farm

Golden Acres Farm

A274

Little Moatenden

Moatenden Manor

BABYLON LA

TN12

NEW BARN RD

Parkenden

Viney Farm

Richmond Farm

Greenways Farm

Farthing Green

Moatenden Farm

TN27

Dunbury Farm

Babylon Farm

South Point Farm

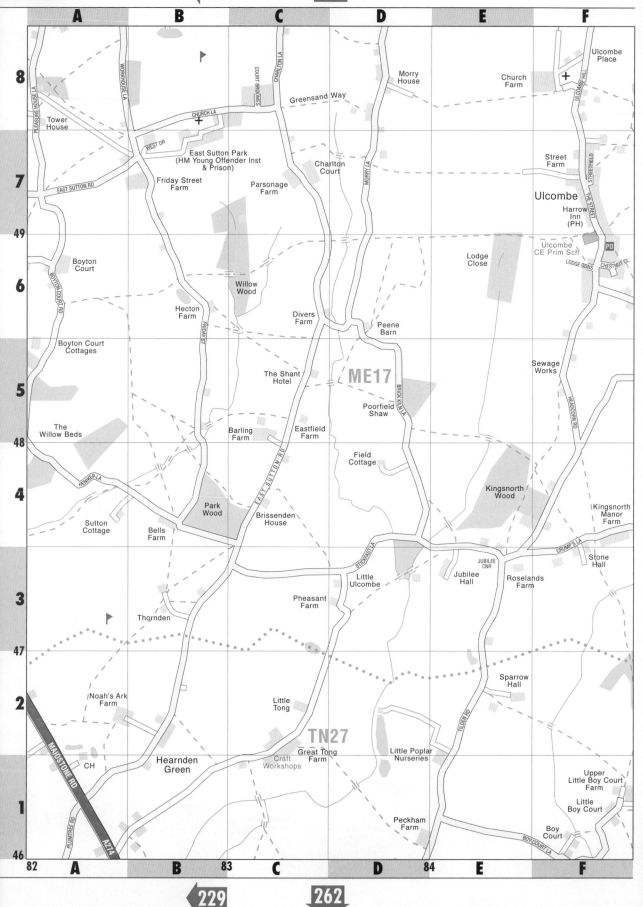

A B C D E F

8

Tower
House

PLEASURE HOUSE LA

WORKHOUSE LA

WEST DR

CHURCH LA

COURT BROOMES

CHARLTON LA

Greensand Way

Morry
House

Church
Farm

Ulcombe
Place

ULCOMBE HILL

7

EAST SUTTON RD

Friday Street
Farm

East Sutton Park
(HM Young Offender Inst
& Prison)

Parsonage
Farm

Charlton
Court

MORRY LA

Street
Farm

STREETFIELD

THE STREET

Ulcombe

Harrow
Inn
(PH)

49

Boyton
Court

BOYTON COURT RD

Willow
Wood

Lodge
Close

Ulcombe
CE Prim Sch

LODGE GDNS

CHESTNUT CL

PO

6

Hecton
Farm

FRIDAY ST

Divers
Farm

Peene
Barn

Sewage
Works

HEADCORN RD

Boyton Court
Cottages

The Shant
Hotel

ME17

Poorfield
Shaw

BRICK KILN LA

5

The
Willow Beds

Barling
Farm

Eastfield
Farm

Field
Cottage

Kingsnorth
Wood

48

HENIKER LA

EAST SUTTON RD

Park
Wood

Brissenden
House

STICKFAST LA

Kingsnorth
Manor
Farm

4

Sutton
Cottage

Bells
Farm

Little
Ulcombe

Jubilee
Hall

JUBILEE
CNR

Roselands
Farm

CRUMP'S LA

Stone
Hall

3

Thornden

Pheasant
Farm

47

Sparrow
Hall

TILDEN RD

2

MAIDSTONE RD

Noah's Ark
Farm

Little
Tong

TN27

Little Poplar
Nurseries

Upper
Little Boy Court
Farm

1

PLUMTREE RD

A274

CH

Hearnden
Green

Great Tong
Farm

Craft
Workshops

Peckham
Farm

BOY COURT LA

Boy
Court

Little
Boy Court

46

82 A 83 B C 83 D E 84 F

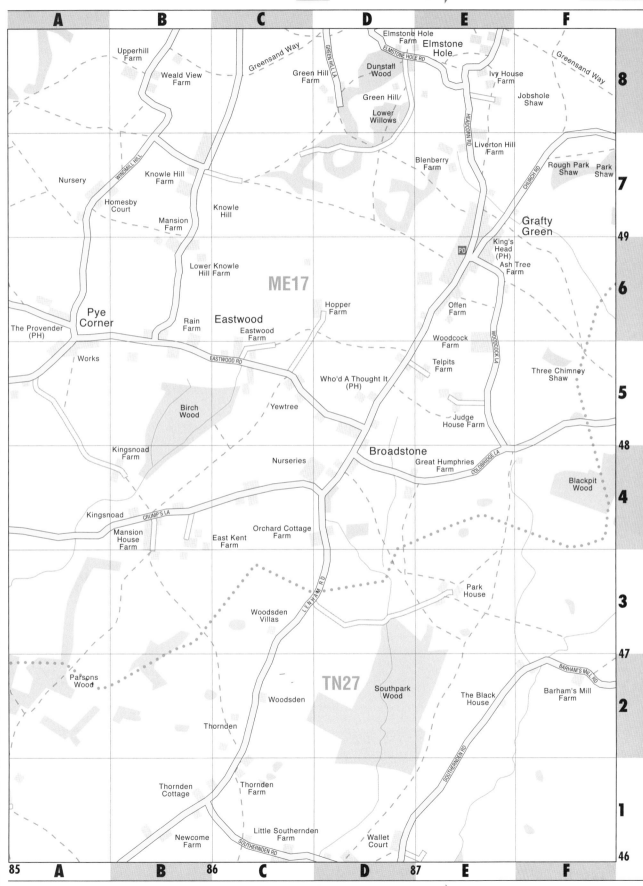

A B C D E F

8
7
49
6
5
48
4
3
47
2
1
46

Upperhill Farm
Weald View Farm
Greensand Way
Green Hill La
Green Hill Farm
Elmstone Hole Farm
Elmstone Hole
Elmstone Hole Rd
Dunstall Wood
Ivy House Farm
Greensand Way
Jobshole Shaw

Green Hill
Lower Willows

Nursery
Windmill Hill
Knowle Hill Farm
Blenberry Farm
Liverton Hill Farm
Church Rd
Rough Park Shaw
Park Shaw

Homesby Court
Knowle Hill
Mansion Farm
Headcorn Rd
Grafty Green

Lower Knowle Hill Farm
ME17
King's Head (PH)
Ash Tree Farm
PO

Hopper Farm
Offen Farm

The Provender (PH)
Pye Corner
Rain Farm
Eastwood
Eastwood Farm
Woodcock Farm
Woodcock La
Three Chimney Shaw

Works
Eastwood Rd
Who'd A Thought It (PH)
Telpits Farm

Birch Wood
Yewtree
Judge House Farm

Kingsnoad Farm
Nurseries
Broadstone
Great Humphries Farm
Coldbridge La
Blackpit Wood

Kingsnoad
Crump's La
East Kent Farm
Orchard Cottage Farm

Mansion House Farm
Lenham Rd
Park House

Woodsden Villas

Parsons Wood
TN27
Southpark Wood
Barham's Mill Rd
The Black House
Barham's Mill Farm

Woodsden
Southernden Rd

Thornden

Thornden Cottage
Thornden Farm

Newcome Farm
Southernden Rd
Little Southernden Farm
Wallet Court

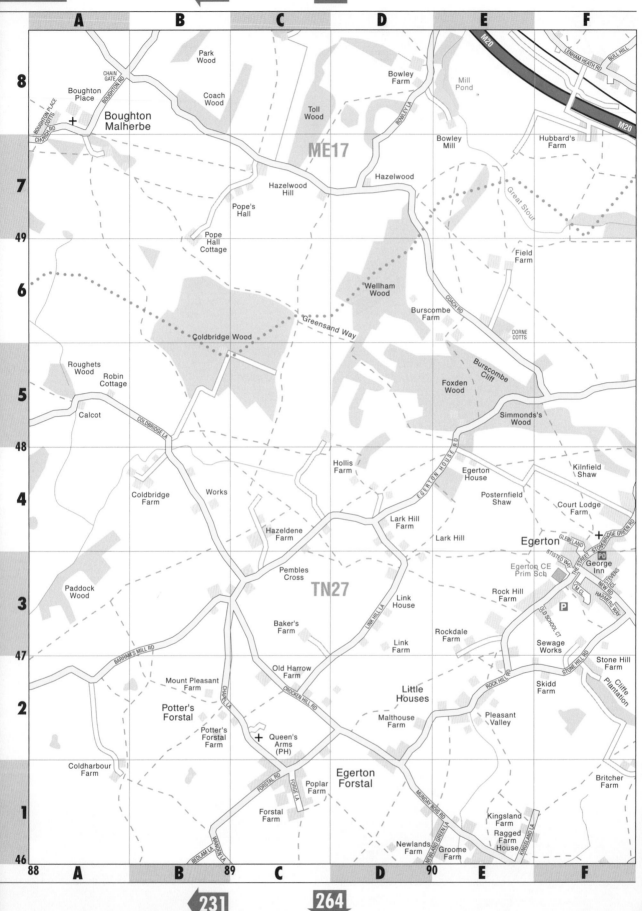

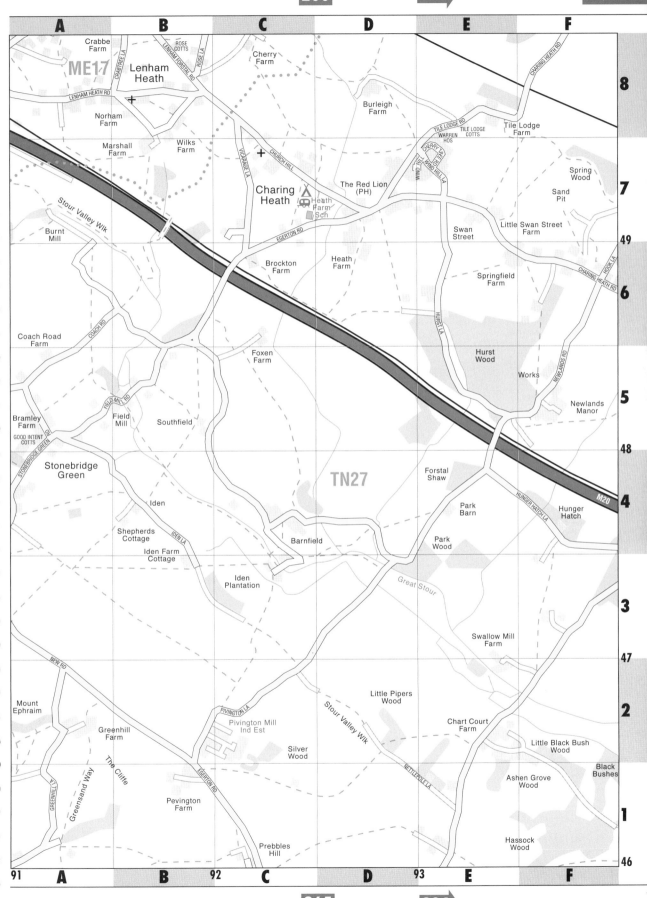

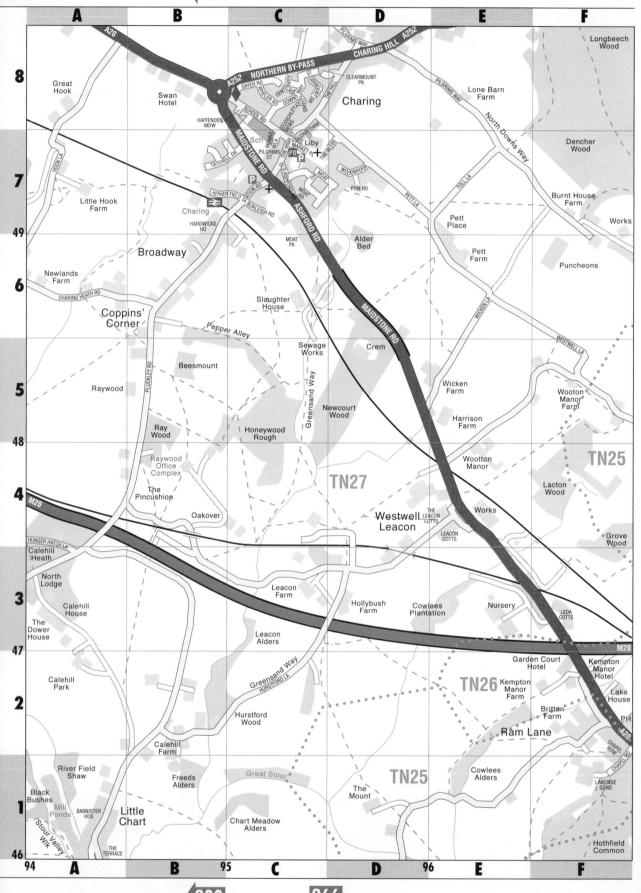

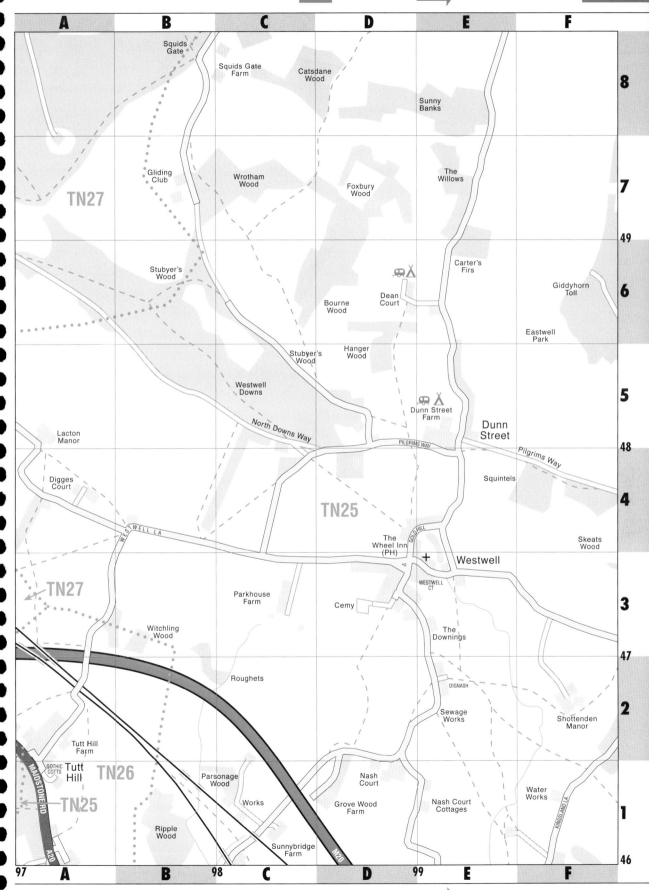

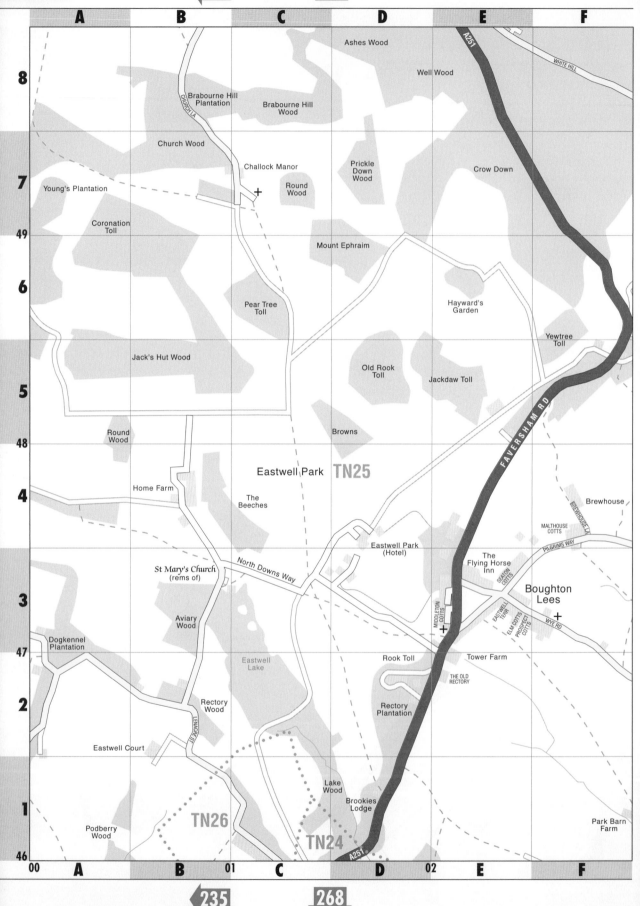

235
203

Ashes Wood

Well Wood

WHITE HILL

Brabourne Hill
Plantation

Brabourne Hill
Wood

Crow Down

Church Wood

Challock Manor

Prickle
Down
Wood

Young's Plantation

Round
Wood

Mount Ephraim

Coronation
Toll

Hayward's
Garden

Pear Tree
Toll

Yewtree
Toll

Jack's Hut Wood

Old Rook
Toll

Jackdaw Toll

FAVERSHAM RD

Round
Wood

Browns

Eastwell Park   **TN25**

The
Beeches

Home Farm

Eastwell Park
(Hotel)

Brewhouse

MALTHOUSE
COTTS

BREWHOUSE LA

PILGRIMS WAY

The
Flying Horse
Inn

St Mary's Church
(rems of)

North Downs Way

Boughton
Lees

SEATON COTTS

MIDDLETON COTTS

EASTWELL TERR

ELM COTTS

PROSPECT COTTS

WYE RD

Aviary
Wood

Dogkennel
Plantation

Eastwell
Lake

Rook Toll

Tower Farm

THE OLD
RECTORY

Rectory
Wood

LENACRE ST

Rectory
Plantation

Eastwell Court

Lake
Wood

TN26

Park Barn
Farm

Podberry
Wood

Brookies
Lodge

TN24

A251

235
268

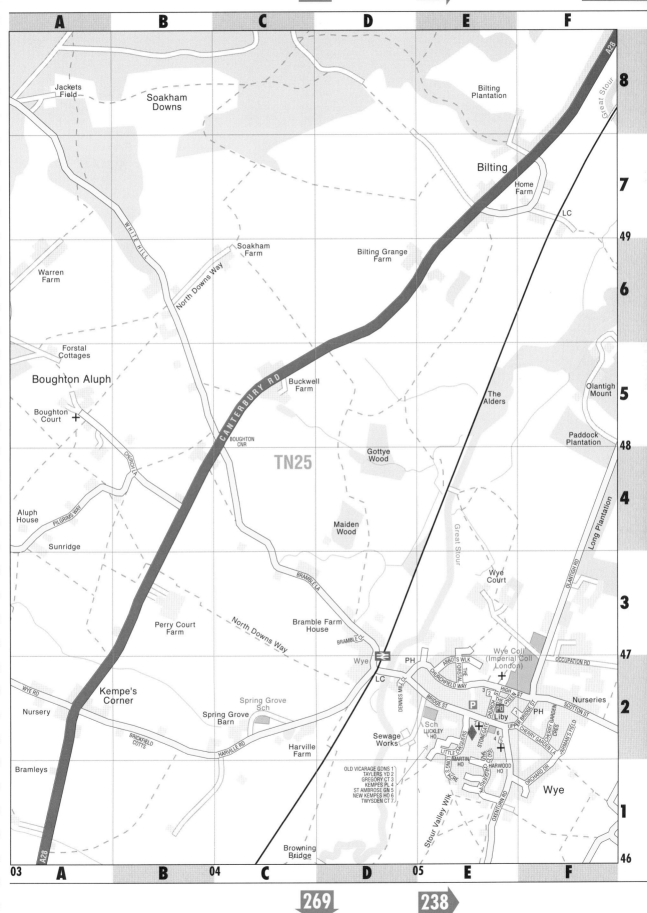

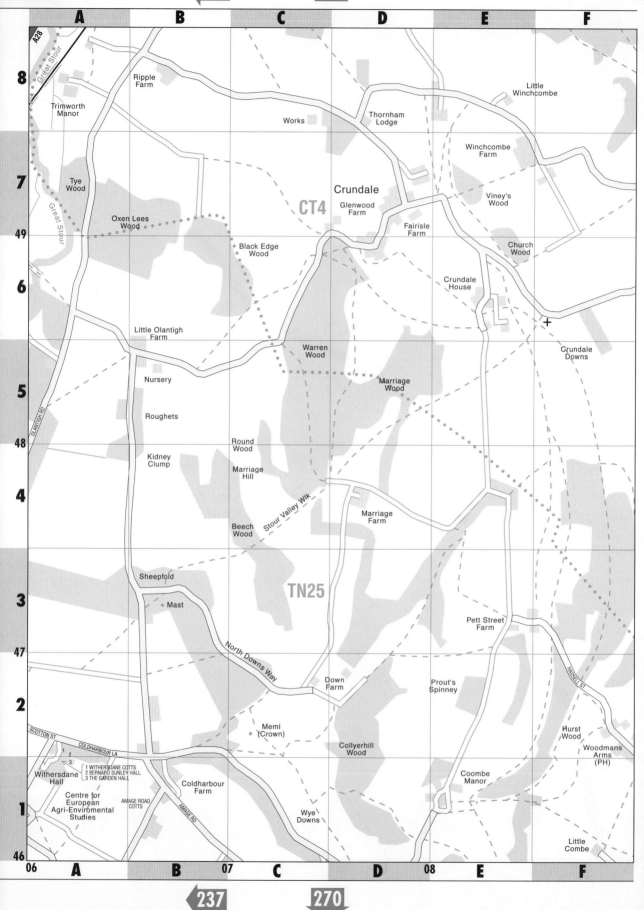

8
7
49
6
5
48
4
3
47
2
1
46

A28
Great Stour
Great Stour
Trimworth Manor
Ripple Farm
Tye Wood
Oxen Lees Wood
Black Edge Wood
Works
Thornham Lodge
Little Winchcombe
Winchcombe Farm
Crundale
CT4
Glenwood Farm
Viney's Wood
Fairisle Farm
Church Wood
Crundale House
Crundale Downs
Little Olantigh Farm
Warren Wood
Marriage Wood
Olantigh Rd
Nursery
Roughets
Kidney Clump
Round Wood
Marriage Hill
Stour Valley Wlk
Marriage Farm
Beech Wood
Sheepfold
Mast
TN25
Pett Street Farm
Hassell St
North Downs Way
Down Farm
Prout's Spinney
Scotton St
Coldharbour La
Meml (Crown)
Collyerhill Wood
Hurst Wood
Woodmans Arms (PH)
Withersdane Hall
1 WITHERSDANE COTTS
2 BERNARD SUNLEY HALL
3 THE GARDEN HALL
Coldharbour Farm
Amage Road Cotts
Amage Rd
Coombe Manor
Centre for European Agri-Enviromental Studies
Wye Downs
Little Combe

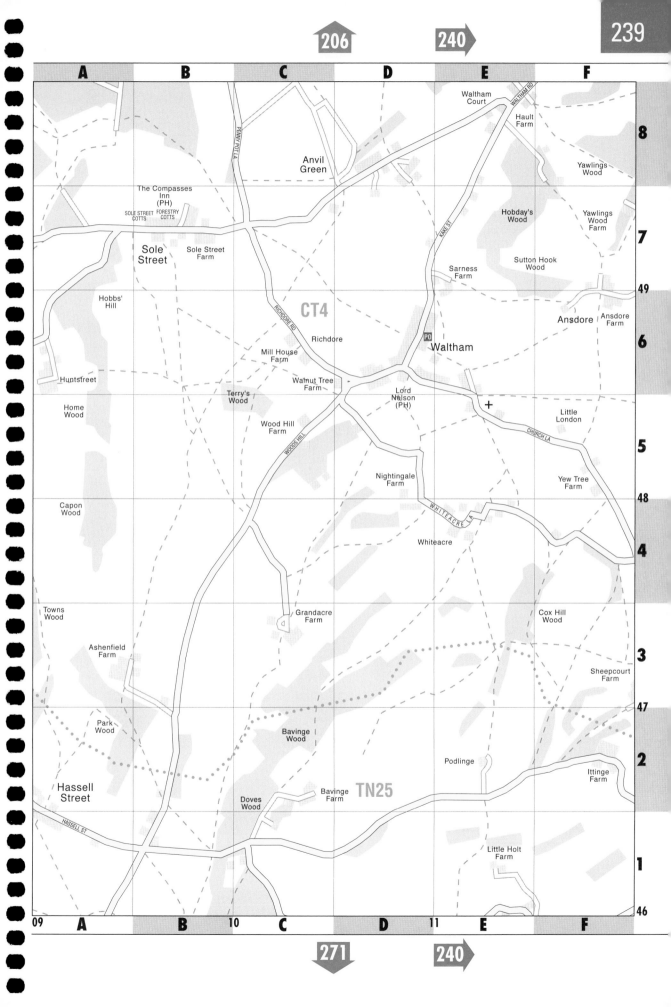

206 240

Waltham Court
Waltham Rd
Hault Farm
Yawlings Wood
8

Anvil Green
Lake St
Hobday's Wood
Yawlings Wood Farm
7

The Compasses Inn (PH)
Sole Street Cotts
Forestry Cotts
Sole Street
Sole Street Farm
Sarness Farm
49
Ansdore
Ansdore Farm

Hobbs' Hill
CT4
Richdore Rd
Richdore
PO
Waltham
6

Huntstreet
Mill House Farm
Walnut Tree Farm
Lord Nelson (PH)
Little London

Home Wood
Terry's Wood
Wood Hill Farm
Woods Hill
Church La
5

Capon Wood
Nightingale Farm
Yew Tree Farm
48

Whiteacre La
Whiteacre
4

Towns Wood
Grandacre Farm
Cox Hill Wood
3
Sheepcourt Farm

Ashenfield Farm
47

Park Wood
Bavinge Wood
Podlinge
Ittinge Farm
2

Hassell Street
TN25
Doves Wood
Bavinge Farm
Hassell St

Little Holt Farm
1

46
09 A B 10 C D 11 E F

271 240

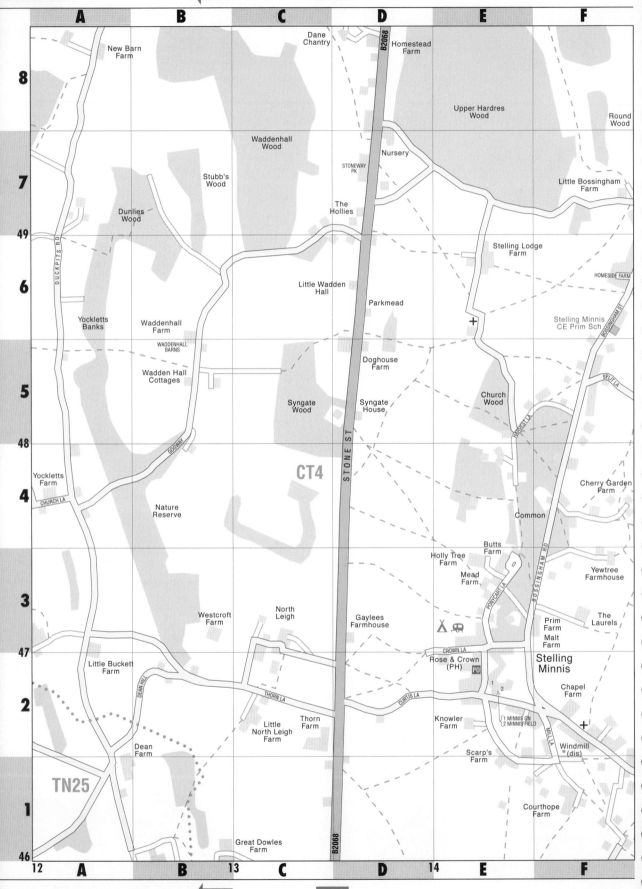

A   B   C   D   E   F

8

7

49

6

5

48

4

3

47

2

1

46

New Barn
Farm

Dane
Chantry

B2068

Homestead
Farm

Upper Hardres
Wood

Round
Wood

Waddenhall
Wood

Nursery

Little Bossingham
Farm

STONEWAY
PK

Stubb's
Wood

The
Hollies

Dunlies
Wood

Stelling Lodge
Farm

HOMESIDE FARM

DUCKPITS RD

Little Wadden
Hall

Parkmead

Stelling Minnis
CE Prim Sch

BOSSINGHAM ST

Yockletts
Banks

Waddenhall
Farm

WADDENHALL
BARNS

Doghouse
Farm

Church
Wood

SPLIT LA

Wadden Hall
Cottages

Syngate
Wood

Syngate
House

HARVEST LA

CT4

STONE ST

Cherry Garden
Farm

Yockletts
Farm

CHURCH LA

Nature
Reserve

Common

Butts
Farm

BOSSINGHAM RD

Yewtree
Farmhouse

Holly Tree
Farm

Mead
Farm

PONYCART LA

Prim
Farm

The
Laurels

North
Leigh

Westcroft
Farm

Gaylees
Farmhouse

Malt
Farm

Stelling
Minnis

Little Buckett
Farm

CROWN LA

Rose & Crown
(PH)

PO

Chapel
Farm

DEAN HILL

THORN LA

Thorn
Farm

CURTIS LA

1
2

Knowler
Farm

1 MINNIS GN
2 MINNIS FIELD

Windmill
(dis)

MILL LA

Little
North Leigh
Farm

Dean
Farm

Scarp's
Farm

TN25

Great Dowles
Farm

B2068

Courthope
Farm

12   A   13   B   C   D   14   E   F

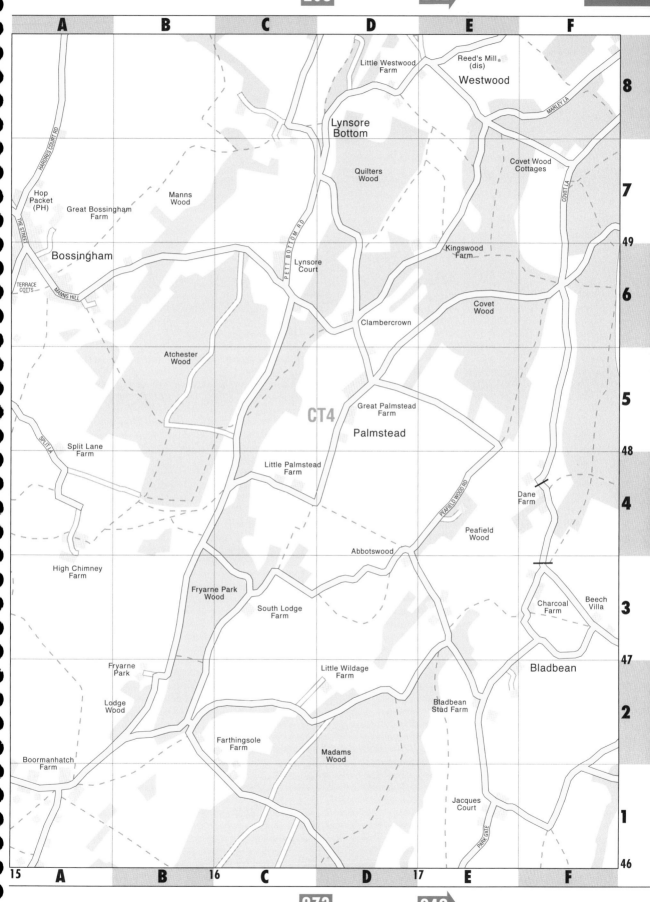

A B C D E F

8

Little Westwood
Farm

Reed's Mill
(dis)

Westwood

Lynsore
Bottom

Quilters
Wood

Covet Wood
Cottages

7

Hop
Packet
(PH)

Manns
Wood

Great Bossingham
Farm

49

HARDRES COURT RD

THE STREET

Kingswood
Farm

MARLEY LA

COVET LA

Bossingham

Lynsore
Court

PETT BOTTOM RD

6

Covet
Wood

TERRACE
COTTS

MANNS HILL

Clambercrown

Atchester
Wood

5

CT4

Great Palmstead
Farm

Split Lane
Farm

Palmstead

SPLIT LA

48

Little Palmstead
Farm

Dane
Farm

4

PEAFIELD WOOD RD

Peafield
Wood

High Chimney
Farm

Abbotswood

Fryarne Park
Wood

Charcoal
Farm

Beech
Villa

3

South Lodge
Farm

47

Fryarne
Park

Little Wildage
Farm

Bladbean

Lodge
Wood

Bladbean
Stud Farm

2

Boormanhatch
Farm

Farthingsole
Farm

Madams
Wood

Jacques
Court

1

PARK GATE

15 A B 16 C D 17 E F

46

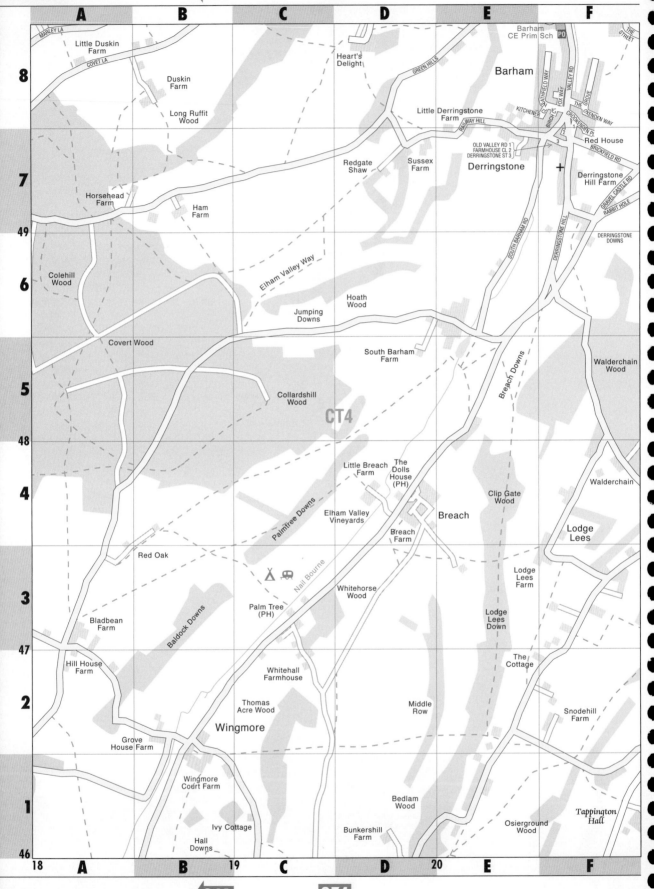

241 209

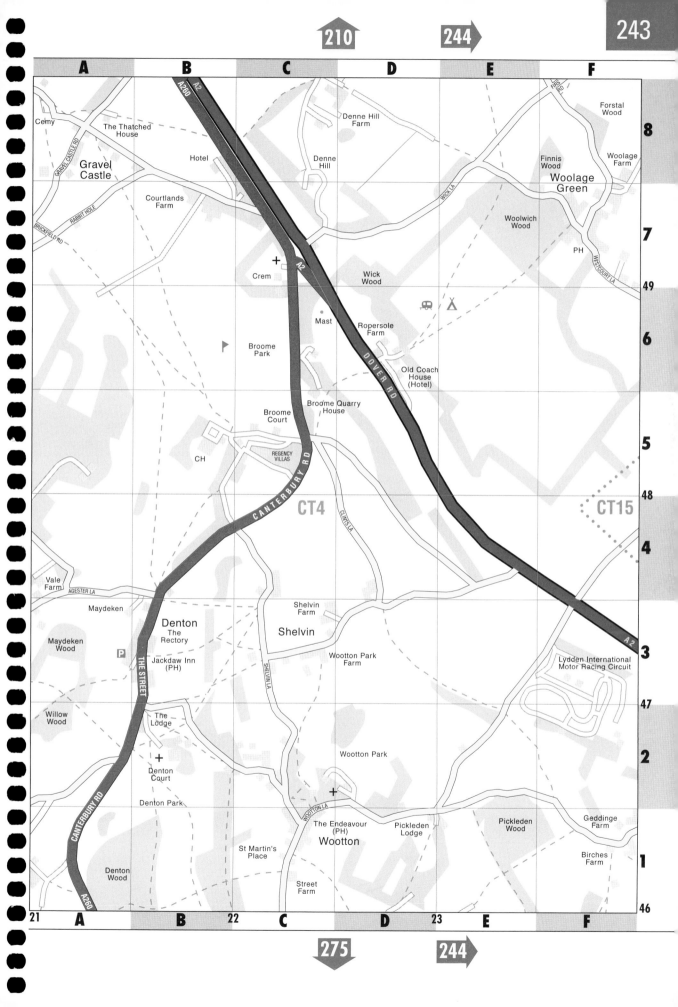

243
211

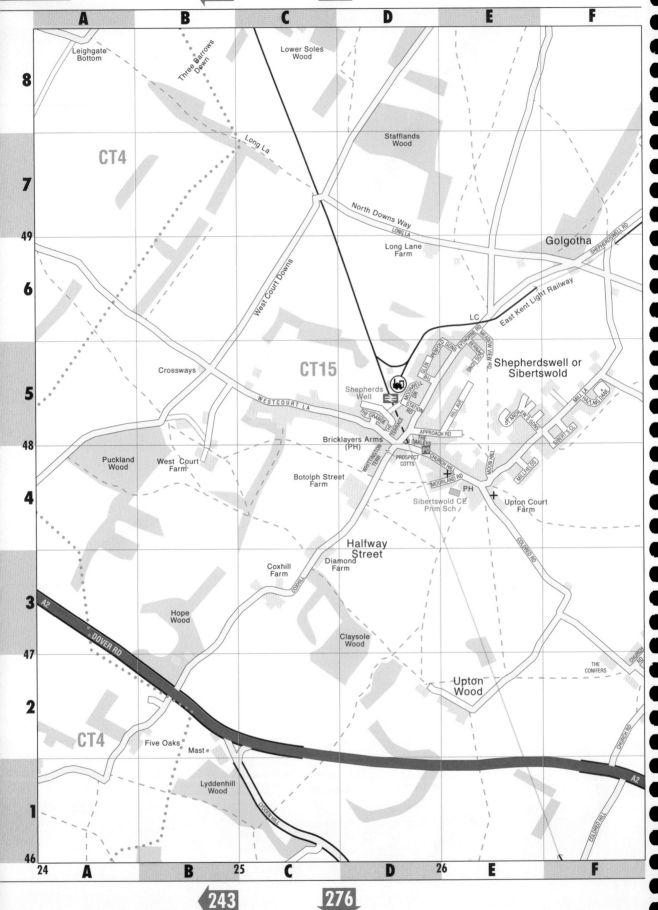

A B C D E F

8

CT4

7

49

6

Leighgate Bottom

Three Barrows Down

Long La

Lower Soles Wood

Stafflands Wood

North Downs Way
LONG LA

Long Lane Farm

Golgotha

SHEPHERDSWELL RD

East Kent Light Railway

LC

West Court Downs

Crossways

CT15

Shepherds Well

WESTCOURT LA

Shepherdswell or Sibertswold

THE GLEN
PERIVOLI GDNS
EYTHORNE RD
BERNARD GDNS
MEADOW VIEW RD

MOORWELL DR
STATION RD
HILL AVE
MILL LA
HAZLING DANE

ST ANDREW'S GDNS
SIBERT'S CL.

5

48

4

THE GRANGE
THE TERRACE
APPROACH RD

Bricklayers Arms (PH)

WHITTINGTON TERR
THE OAKLEYS
PROSPECT COTTS
PO
CHURCH HILL
MOON HILL
MILLFIELDS

Puckland Wood

West Court Farm

Botolph Street Farm

MOORLAND RD
PH
Sibertswold CE Prim Sch

Upton Court Farm

Halfway Street

Coxhill Farm

Diamond Farm

COXHILL

COLDRED RD

3

A2

47

DOVER RD

Hope Wood

Claysole Wood

Upton Wood

THE CONIFERS

CHURCH RD

2

CT4

Five Oaks

Mast

Lyddenhill Wood

LYDDENHILL

A2

COLDRED HILL

CHURCH RD

1

46

24 A B 25 C D 26 E F

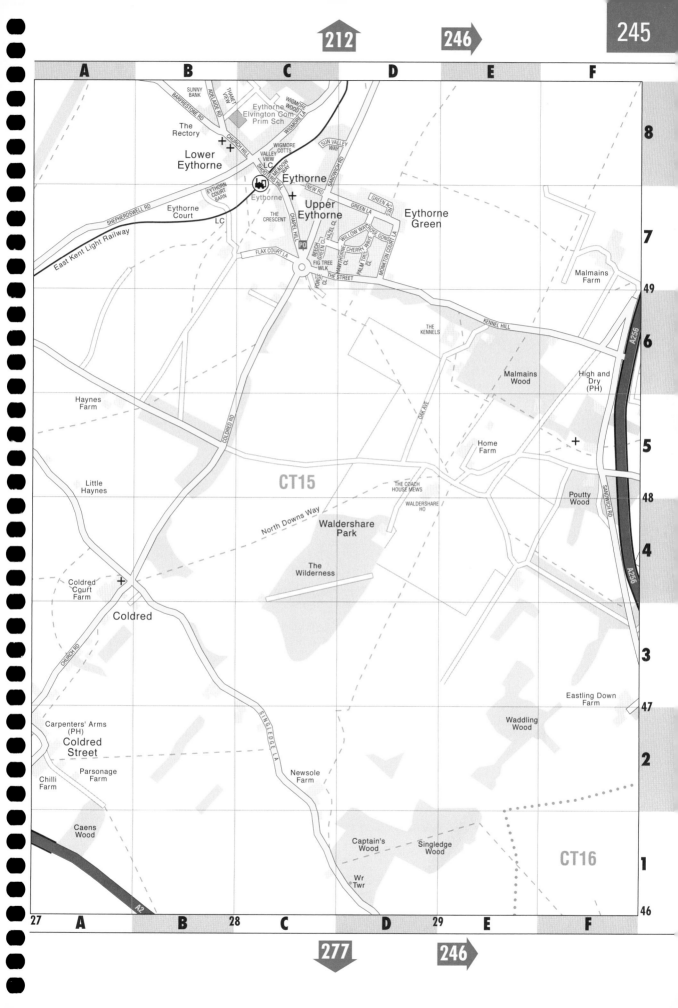

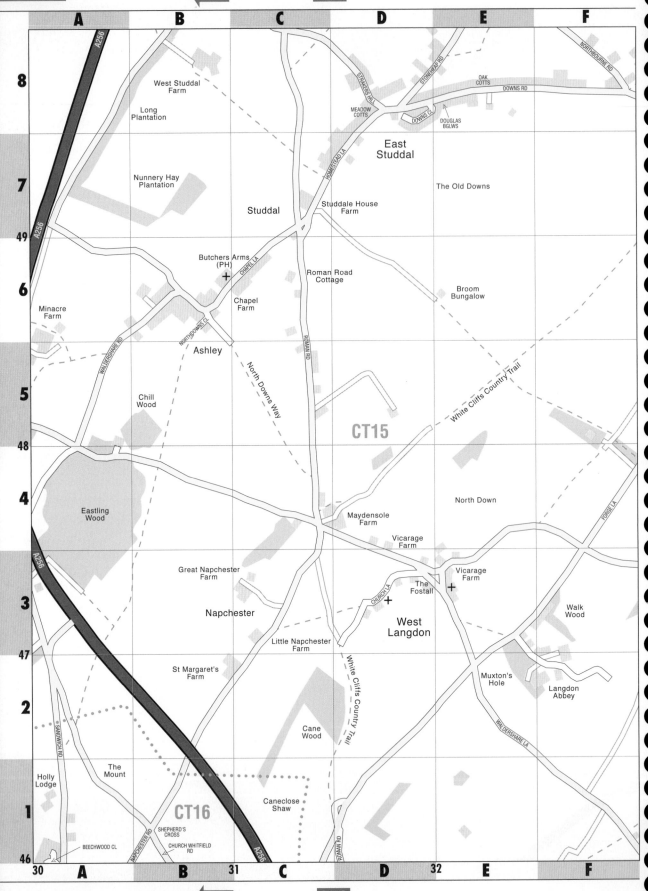

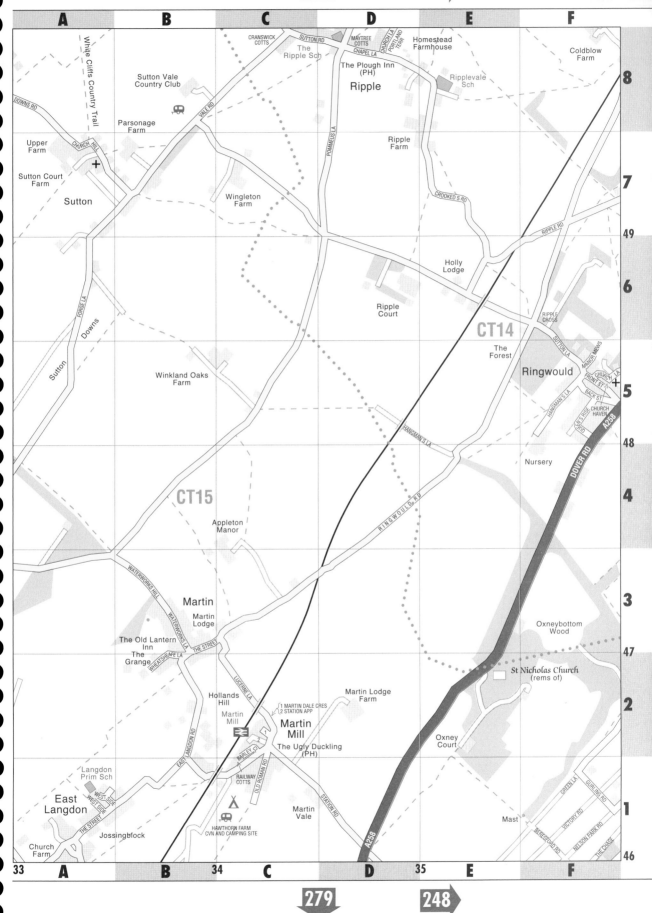

247
215

A   **B**   **C**   **D**   **E**   **F**

Cold Blow Crossing

ST MARGARETS DR 1
WHITE ACRE DR 2
KINGSLAND GDNS 3
DOWNLANDS 4
THE MALTINGS 5

BLAKE CL

GRAM'S RD

BADGERS RISE

Hawkshill RD

Hawkshill House

8

Hawksdown

Rays Bottom

Hawks Hill

Hawkshill Down

7

RIPPLE RD

Windmill (dis)

Claytons Hill

Hawkshill Activity Ctr

KINGSDOWN RD

CECIL RD

WELLINGTON PAR

49

DOVER RD

Knights Bottom

GLEN RD

CLAREMONT CL

CLAREMONT RD

COURTLANDS

BOUNDARY RD

6

Knights Hill

OSBORNE RD

CARLTON RD

EDWARD RD

BALMORAL RD

SEA RD

CLIM DOWN

KING'S C

CHURCH CLIFF

JARVIST PL

CLIFFE RD

WELLINGTON PAR

Ripple Down House

Kingsdown and Ringwould CE Prim Sch

ST MONICA'S RD

ST MONICAS RD

MOUNT PLEASANT

NORTH RD

SOUTH RD

PH

A258

CHURCH LA

RINGWOULD RD

CHALK HILL RD

THE RISE

ST JAMES RD

ALEXANDRA RD

PO

UPPER ST

Saxon Shore Way

UNDERCLIFFE RD

5

Chalk Hill

Kingsdown

Kingsdown Park Holiday Village

48

Great Coombe

Woodhill Farm

CT14

Oldstairs Bay

Wood Hill

VICTORIA RD

THE AVENUE

HILLCREST RD

KINGSDOWN HILL

COASTGUARD COTTS

OLDSTAIRS RD

CH

4

The Lynch

Barrows Hill

QUEENSDOWN RD

BAYVIEW RD

NORTHCOTE RD

The Swamp

Old Parker's Cap

Hill Farm

East Bottom Farm

Morningside

White Cliffs Country Trail

THE LEAS

3

VICTORIA RD

Kelf Farm

OLDSTAIRS RD

GRANVILLE RD

Otty Bottom

East Bottom

47

Free Down

GREEN LA

East Hill

Hope Point

2

ST MARGARETS RD

1

NELSON PARK RD

East Valley Farm

CT15

BOYNE RD

COLLINGWOOD RD

NORMAN RD

FLEET RD

Old Bottom Free Down

Barrow Mount

46

36   **A**   **B**   **37**   **C**   **D**   **38**   **E**   **F**

247
280

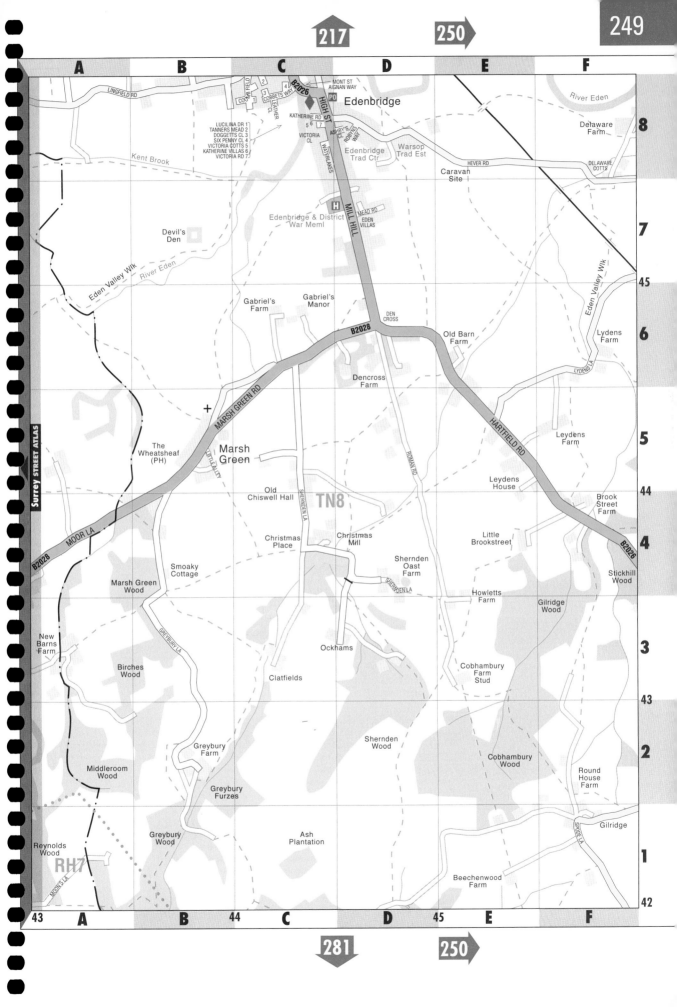

249
218

A B C D E F

8
7
45
6
5
44
4
43
2
1
42

46 A B 47 C D 48 E F

Swansnest Island
River Eden
Polebrook Farm
Two Bridges Island
Sixteen Acre Island
Hever Bridge
Hever Castle
Brocas Farm
HEVER RD
LYDENS LA
Brocas Cottages
Park Wood
P
PH
Eden Valley Wlk
Hever CE Prim Sch
Hever
Newhouse Farm
Hever Grange
Tangle Wood
Hever
The Red House
Lockskinners Farm
PARSON'S CROFT
Hever Warren
The Greyhound (PH)
Dyehurst Bridge
Meechlands Farm
Pigdown
Fell House
HARTFIELD RD
UCKFIELD LA
PIGDOWN LA
TN8
Newtown
Dogpits
Park Pl
Stick Hill
Greenland Farm
Wilderness Farm
Newtye Hurst
Heathen Street
Wychwood Fruit Farm
Markbeech Wood
St Andrew's Convent Eden Hall
Buck Hurst
Buckhurst Farm
Bramsell's Farm
Markbeech
HARTFIELD RD
The Queen's Arms (PH)
Kentish Horse (PH)
Mallett's Barn
Cowden Pound
SPODE LA
Falconhurst
Horseshoe Green
Lord's Land Wood
COW LA
Bilton's Gill
B2026
Horseshoe Green Farm
BLOWERS HILL
Lambert Cottage Wood
Edells

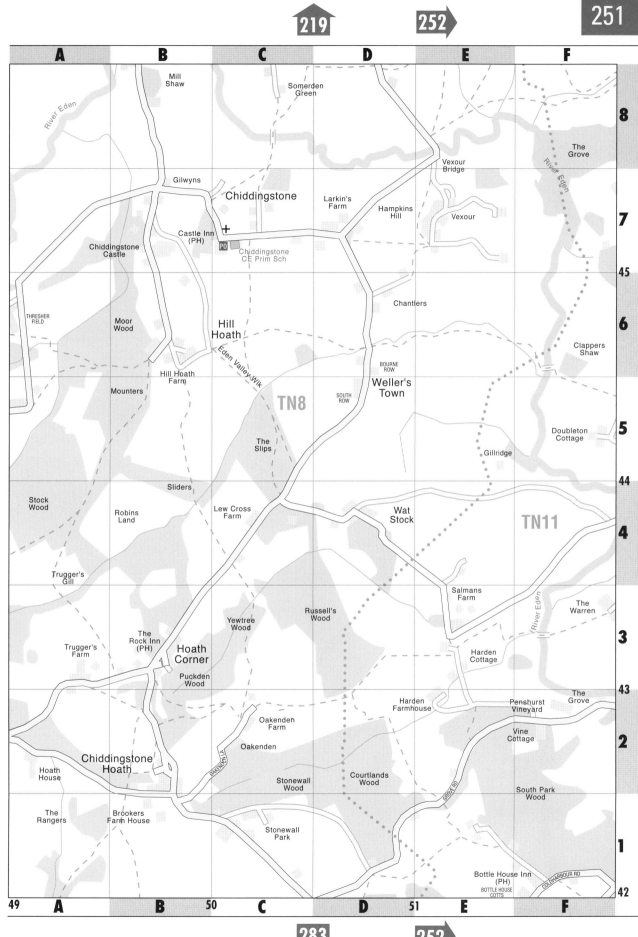

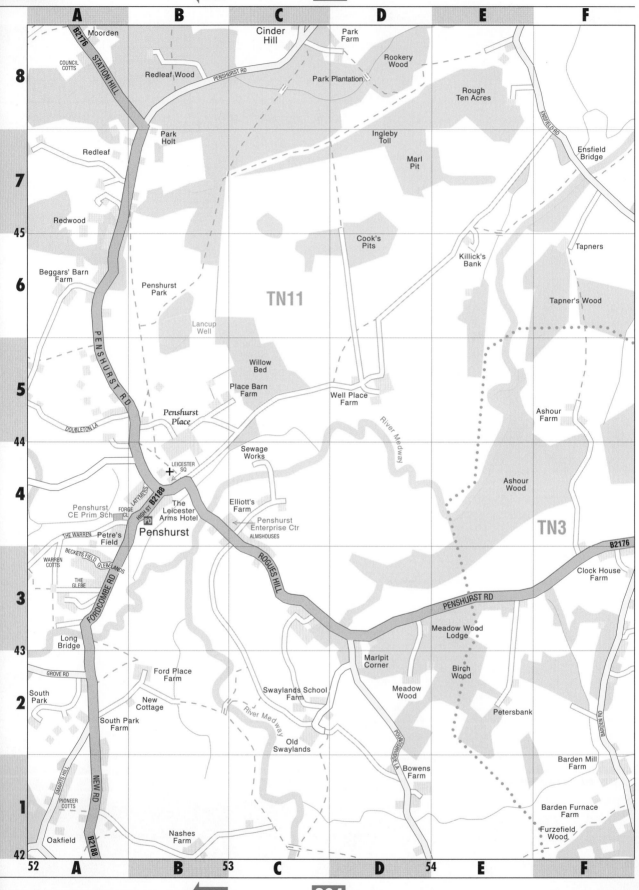

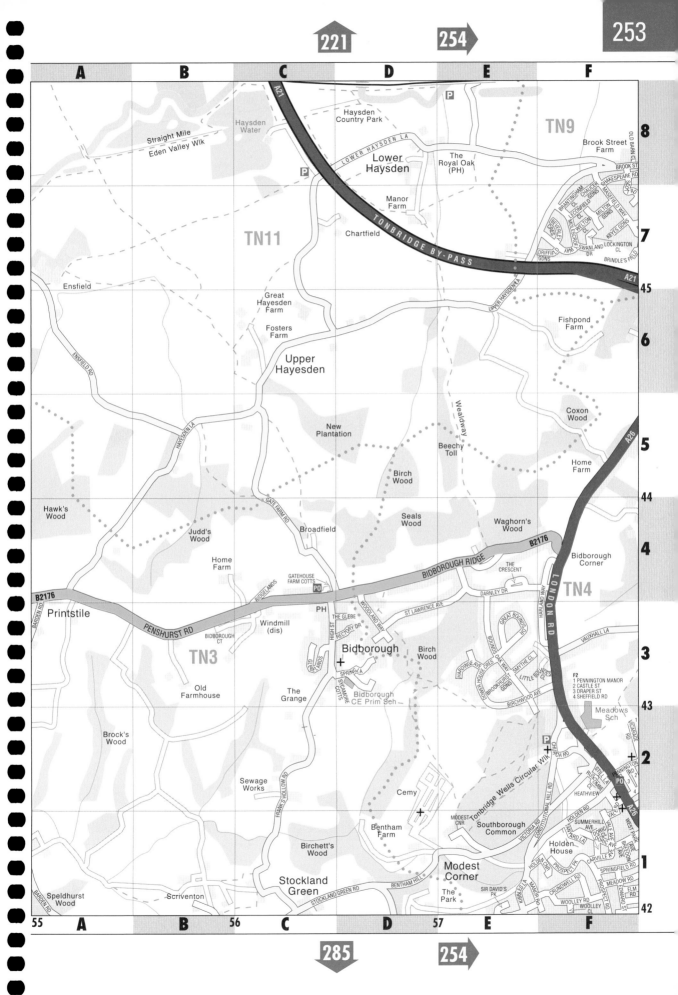

	A	B	C	D	E	F	

A21

TN9

Straight Mile
Eden Valley Wlk

Haysden
Water

Haysden
Country Park

P

Brook Street
Farm

OLD BARN CL

BROOK ST

8

LOWER HAYSDEN LA

Lower
Haysden

The
Royal Oak
(PH)

BRATTINGHAM CL
LECOMFIELD GDNS
BEVERLEY GDNS
MOLESCROFT
WELTON
APK
CHAUCER CL
MILTON GDNS
SWANLAND DR
CHAUCER WAY
MASEFIELD WAY
KEYES GDNS
SHAKESPEARE RD
SEC'Y RD
LOCKINGTON CL

7

TN11

P

Chartfield

TONBRIDGE BY-PASS

Manor
Farm

DRIFFIELD GDNS
BRINDLE'S FIELD

A21

Ensfield

Great
Hayesden
Farm

UPPER HAYSDEN LA

45

Fosters
Farm

Fishpond
Farm

6

ENSFIELD RD

Upper
Hayesden

Wealdway

Coxon
Wood

A26

5

HAYESDEN LA

New
Plantation

Beechy
Toll

Home
Farm

Hawk's
Wood

GATE FARM RD

Birch
Wood

44

Judd's
Wood

Broadfield

Seals
Wood

Waghorn's
Wood

B2176

Bidborough
Corner

4

BIDBOROUGH RIDGE

THE
CRESCENT

Home
Farm

RIDGELANDS

GATEHOUSE
FARM COTTS

PO

DARNLEY DR

LONDON RD

TN4

B2176

BARDEN RD

Printstile

PENSHURST RD

PH

THE GLEBE

ST LAWRENCE AVE

VAUXHALL LA

Windmill
(dis)

BIDBOROUGH
CT

HIGH ST
RECTORY DR

WOODLAND WAY

HARDINGE AVE
GREAT BOUNDS DR
BOUNDS OAK WAY
DENTON HOUSE CRES
BROOKHURST GDNS
LITTLE BOUNDS
SMYTHE CL

3

TN3

Old
Farmhouse

The
Grange

C19
ORCLANDS

SPRING LA
SYCAMORE
COTTS

Bidborough
CE Prim Sch

Birch
Wood

BIRCHWOOD AVE

F2
1 PENNINGTON MANOR
2 CASTLE ST
3 DRAPER ST
4 SHEFFIELD RD

VICARAGE RD

Meadows
Sch

43

Brock's
Wood

Sewage
Works

FRANKS HOLLOW RD

Cemy

P

CHURCH RD

PENNINGTON RD
STILL LA
RUSCOMBE

PO

HEATHVIEW
HOLDEN RD
SUMMERHILL AVE
VALE RD
DORIC AVE
DORIC CL

A26
WEST PARK RD

2

MODEST
CNR

Southborough
Common

Tonbridge Wells Circular Wlk

Speldhurst
Wood

Scriventon

Birchett's
Wood

Bentham
Farm

Stockland
Green

STOCKLAND GREEN RD

BENTHAM HILL

Modest
Corner

The
Park

SIR DAVID'S
PK

KIBBLES LA
MANOR RD

VICTORIA RD
CONSTITUTIONAL HILL RD

HOLDEN CNR
PROSPECT PK
VALE AVE
YARD LA

Holden
House

HOLDEN RD
CRUNDWELL RD
WOOLLEY RD
WOOLLEY RD

SPRINGFIELD RD
MEADOW RD
PROSPECT RD
ELM RD
BREEDON AVE
EDWARD ST
CARVILLE AVE

1

42

B8
1 ST AUGUSTINE HO
2 BECKET CT
3 QUARRY HILL PAR
4 THE LOWRY
5 BICKLEY RD
6 MONKS WLK
7 DEANS CT
8 MARY MAGDALENE HO
9 MERRYFIELD CT
10 TONBRIDGE CHAMBERS
11 ST GEORGES MEWS
12 GARDYNE MEWS
13 WHITE OAK CL
14 ALMSHOUSES
15 SKINNER'S TERR

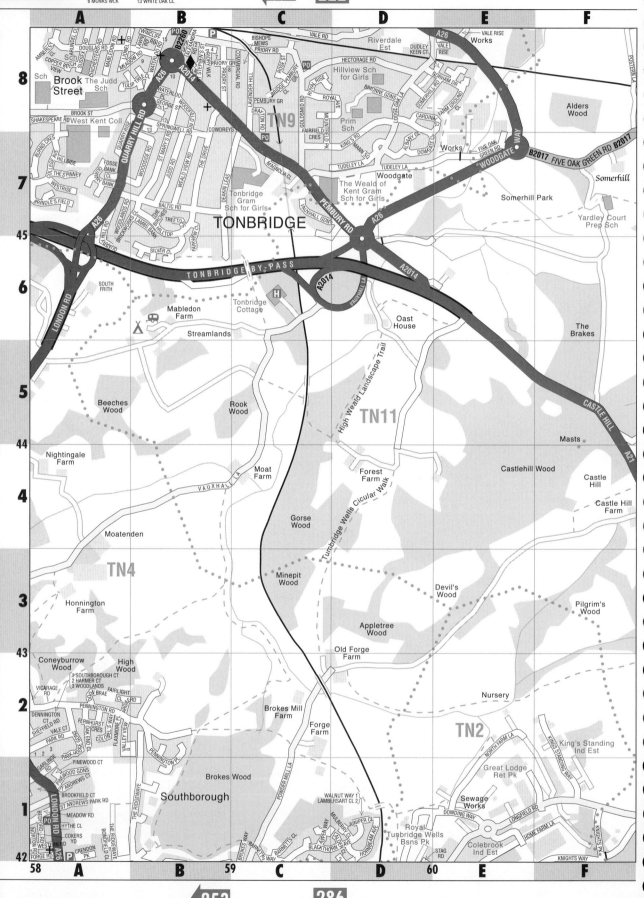

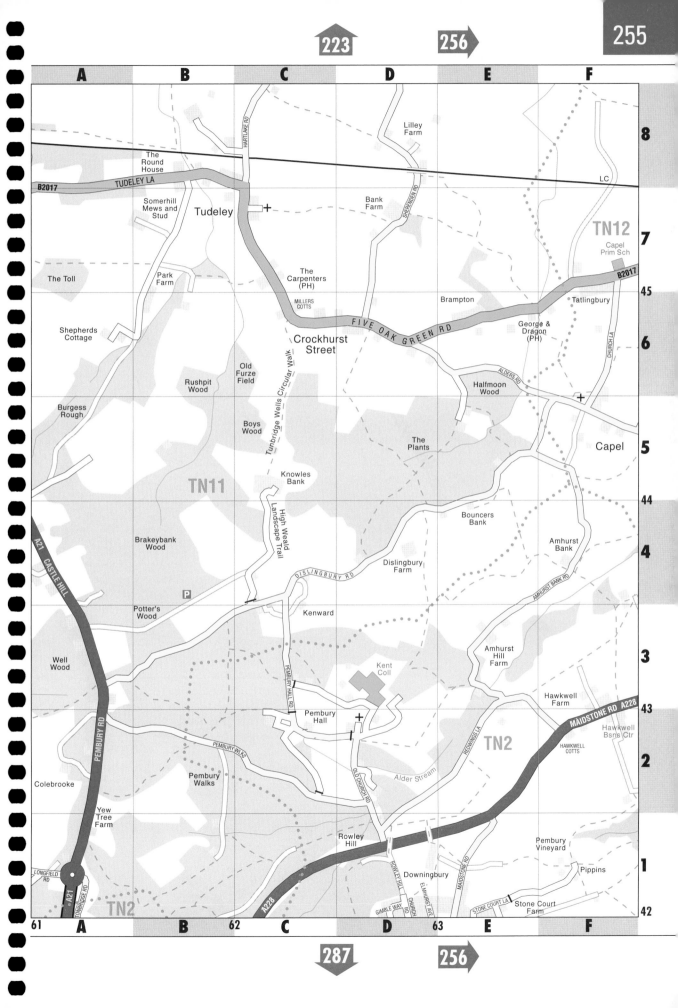

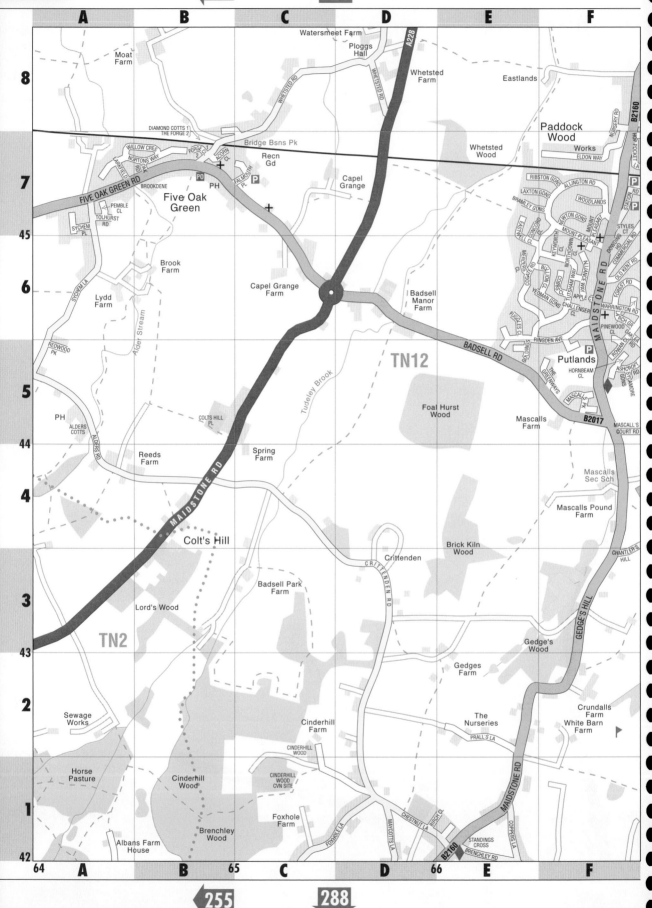

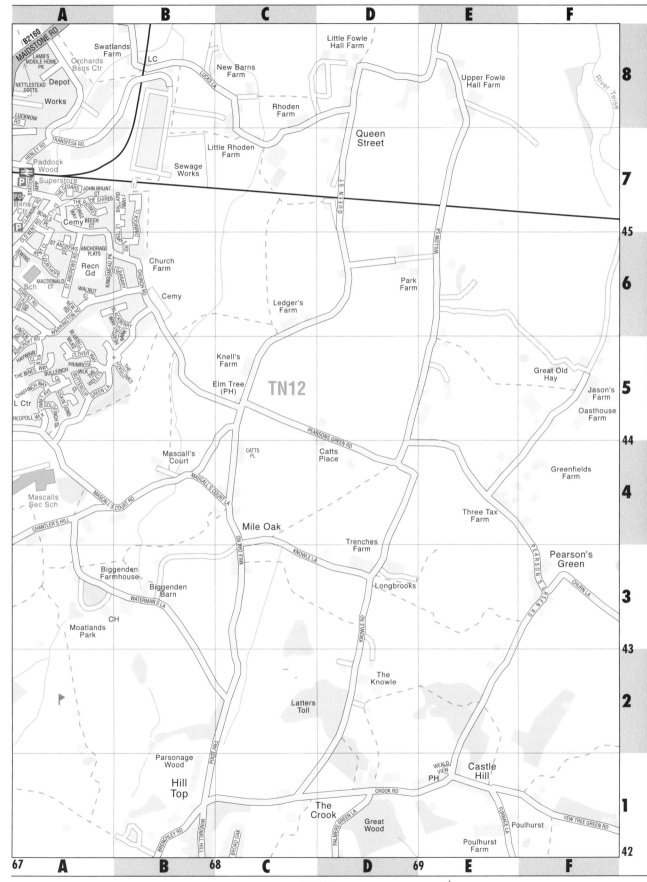

225
258
289
258

257
226

A B C D E F

8

Moors Farm

Little Brook Farm

GREEN LA

BROOK COTTS

Church Farm

Collier Street

PETTITS ROW

ST MARGARETS VILLAS

Duke of Wellington (PH)

Brook Farm

7

Spenny Farm

SPENNY LA

KINGS LA

Martin's Farm

Chequer Tree Farm

Longend Farm

45

6

Priestland

Bockingfold

White Hart (PH)

Longend Farm

Claygate

5

LITTLE SHEEPHURST COTTS

Little Sheephurst Farm

Little Cheveney Farm

44

SHEEPHURST LA

Gafford's Bridge

Summerlands Farm

Great Sheephurst Farm

4

TN12

Lesser Teise

GAFFORD'S BRIDGE COTTS

River Teise

3

August Pitts Farm

Bassett's Farm

MAIDSTONE RD

Bennetts Farm

Old Mill Bridge

Churn Farm

43

CHURN LA

2

Orchard House Farm

Baybrooks Cottages

Poplars Farm

Garage

1

Morris Wood

Castlemaine Farm

Rams Hill

B2162

MILL LA

42

YEW TREE GREEN RD

Yewtree Green

70 A B 71 C D 72 E F

257
290

B2162

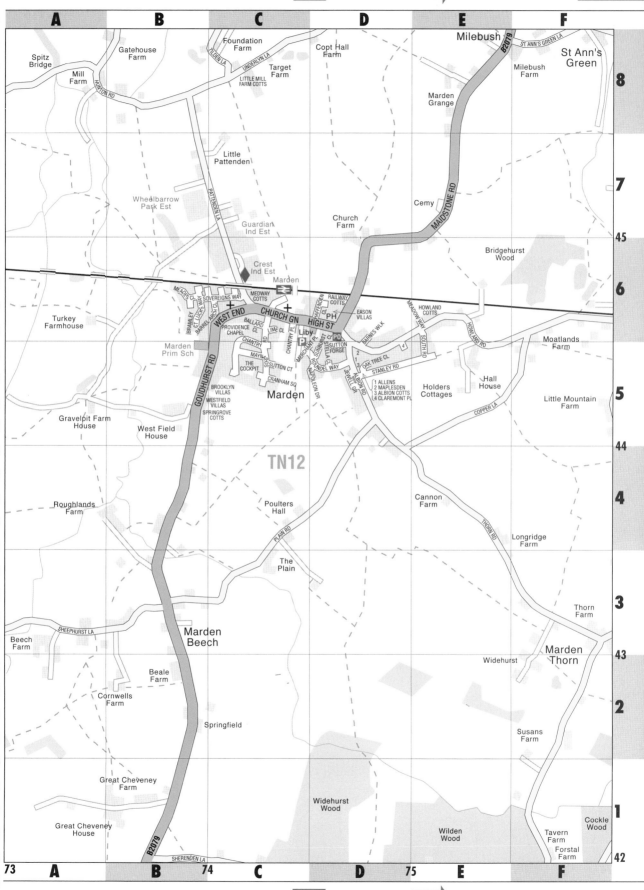

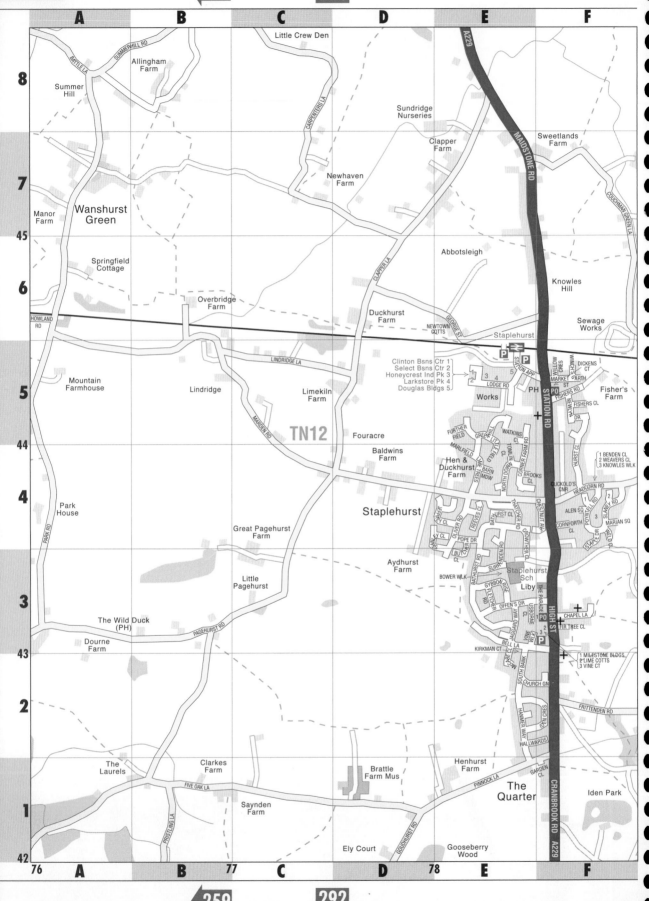

A B C D E F

8

7

45

6

HOWLAND RD

5

44

4

3

43

2

1

42

76 A B 77 C D 78 E F

Little Crew Den

Summerhill Rd

Battle La

Allingham Farm

Summer Hill

Cappers La

Sundridge Nurseries

Clapper Farm

Sweetlands Farm

Coughman Green La

Maidstone Rd

A229

Newhaven Farm

Manor Farm

Wanshurst Green

Springfield Cottage

Overbridge Farm

Clapper La

Abbotsleigh

Knowles Hill

Duckhurst Farm

Newtown Cotts

George St

Staplehurst

Sewage Works

Lindridge La

Clinton Bsns Ctr 1
Select Bsns Ctr 2
Honeycrest Ind Pk 3
Larkstore Pk 4
Douglas Bldgs 5

Dickens Ct

Mountain Farmhouse

Lindridge

Limekiln Farm

Marden Rd

Station App

William Crts

Market Pth

Station Rd

Lodge Rd

Fisher's Farm

PH

Works

Fishers Rd

Fishers Cl

TN12

Fouracre

Baldwins Farm

Further Field

Green Hill

Watkins Cl

Corner Farm Rd

Hurst Cl

1 Benden Cl
2 Weavers Cl
3 Knowles Wlk

Park House

Park Rd

Hen & Duckhurst Farm

Marlfield

Lime Barn

Little Fld Rd

Tomlin

North Down

Thatcher Rd

Brooks Cl

Chestnut Av

Cuckold's Cnr

Headcorn Rd

Alen Sq

Pownall Rd

Slaney Rd

Marian Sq

Great Pagehurst Farm

Kerry Cl

Oliver Rd

Reeves Cl

Bathurst Cl

Cowther Cl

Cornforth Cl

Staple Dr

Staplehurst

Little Pagehurst

Ainley Cl

Pope Dr

Butc

Bathurst Rd

Aydhurst Farm

Surrenden Rd

Staplehurst Sch

Liby

The Wild Duck (PH)

Pagehurst Rd

Bower Wlk

Fletcher

Offen's Dr

Gybbon Rise

Usborne

The Parade

High St

Chapel La

Fir Tree Cl

Dourne Farm

Kirkman Ct

Bell La

Haggard Av

Vine Wlk

1
2
3

1 Milestone Bldgs
2 Lime Cotts
3 Vine Ct

South Bank

Church Gn

Frittenden Rd

The Laurels

Clarkes Farm

Pristling La

Five Oak La

Saynden Farm

Brattle Farm Mus

Henhurst Farm

Pinnock La

Hanmer Way

Hallwards

Cranbrook Rd

A229

Garden Cl

The Quarter

Iden Park

Ely Court

Goudhurst Rd

Gooseberry Wood

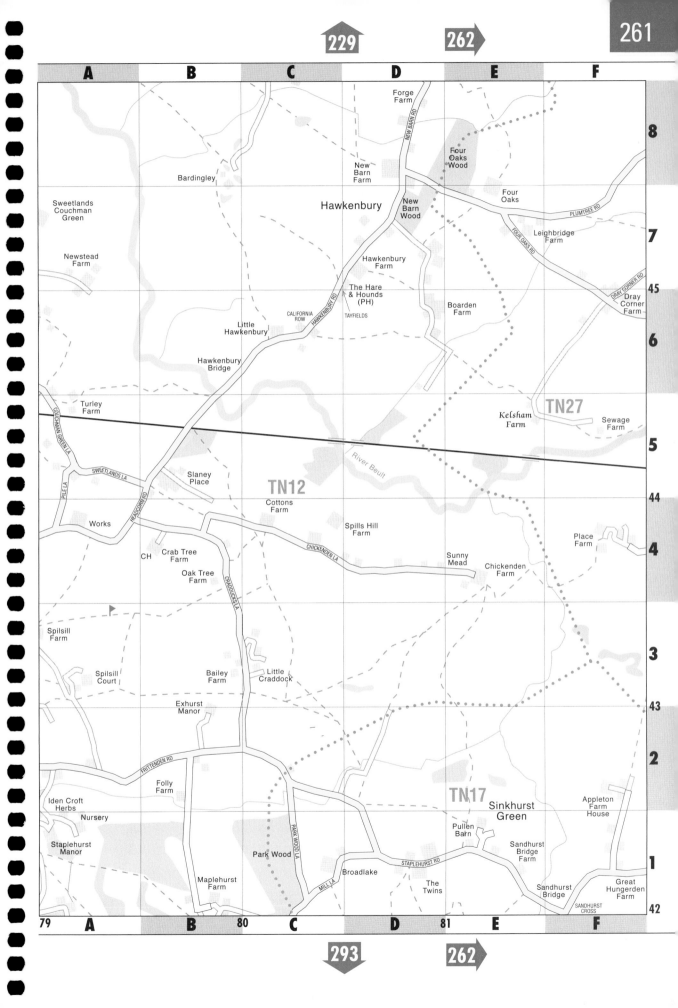

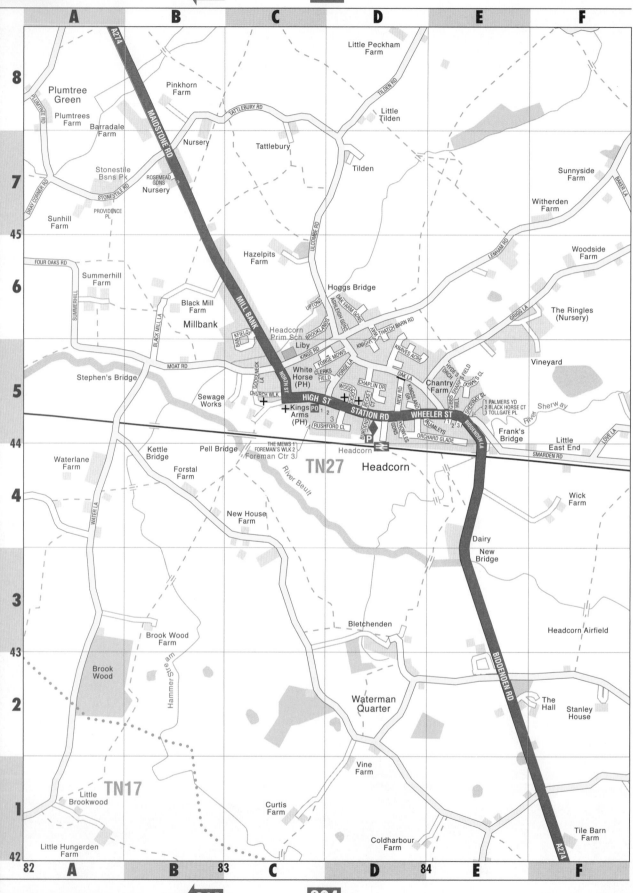

261
230

A   B   C   D   E   F

8

Little Peckham
Farm

Plumtree
Green

Pinkhorn
Farm

Little
Tilden

PLUMTREE RD

Plumtrees
Farm

Barradale
Farm

Nursery

MAIDSTONE RD

A274

TATTLEBURY RD

Tattlebury

TILDEN RD

Tilden

Sunnyside
Farm

7

Stonestile
Bsns Pk

ROSEMEAD
GDNS

Nursery

Witherden
Farm

BAKER LA

DRAY CORNER RD

STONESTILE RD

PROVIDENCE
PL

45

Sunhill
Farm

Hazelpits
Farm

LENHAM RD

FOUR OAKS RD

Woodside
Farm

6

Summerhill
Farm

MILL BANK

Hoggs Bridge

The Ringles
(Nursery)

SUMMERHILL

Black Mill
Farm

UPTONS

OAK FARM GDNS

ASHLEIGH GDNS

THATCH BARN RD

GRIGG LA

BLACK MILL LA

Millbank

Headcorn
Prim Sch

BROOKLANDS

KNIGHT

Vineyard

MOAT RD

Liby

KINGS RD

FORGE MDWS

KNAVES ACRE

HYDE'S FIELD

5

GOOSENECK LA

CLERKS
FIELD

FORGE LA

OAK LA

HILL SHARP DOWN'S CL

Stephen's Bridge

NORTH ST

CHURCH WLK

White
Horse
(PH)

WOOD
KNOLL

BECKET CT

CHAPLIN DR

NEW RD

KINGSLAND
GR

Chantry
Farm

GIBBS

SHARP

SECKINKY CL

1 PALMERS YD
2 BLACK HORSE CT
3 TOLLGATE PL

River   Sherway

Sewage
Works

Kings
Arms
(PH)

PO

HIGH ST

1
2
3

STATION RD

WHEELER ST

KNOWLES

BIDDENDEN LA

Frank's
Bridge

44

RUSHFORD CL

BIRDENS

CRAMLEYS

ORCHARD GLADE

Little
East End

Waterlane
Farm

Kettle
Bridge

Pell Bridge

THE MEWS 1
FOREMAN'S WLK 2
Foreman Ctr 3

KNOWLES
GDNS

Headcorn

SMARDEN RD

LOVE LA

WATER LA

Forstal
Farm

River Beult

TN27

Headcorn

Wick
Farm

4

New House
Farm

Dairy
New
Bridge

3

Brook Wood
Farm

HammerStream

Bletchenden

Headcorn Airfield

43

Brook
Wood

Waterman
Quarter

BIDDENDEN RD

The
Hall

Stanley
House

2

TN17

Vine
Farm

1

Little
Brookwood

Curtis
Farm

Coldharbour
Farm

A274

Tile Barn
Farm

Little Hungerden
Farm

42

82   A   B   83   C   D   84   E   F

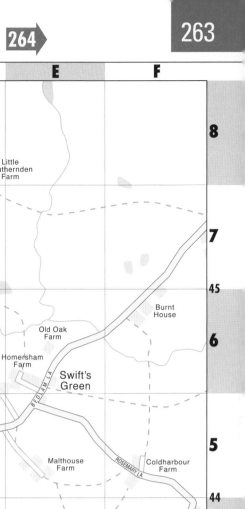

	A	B	C	D	E	F

Southernden

Springfield Farm

Southernden Farm

8

LENHAM RD

Barling Green Farm

Little Southernden Farm

SOUTHERNDEN RD

Gloversbridge Farm

Glover's Bridge

7

Little Grigg Farm

GRIGG LA

45

BAKER LA

Grigg Oasts

Burnt House

Grigg Farm

River Sherway

SHERWAY RD

Old Oak Farm

6

Sherway Bridge

Homersham Farm

Swift's Green

Hieland Glen

Little Swift's Green Farm

BEDLAM LA

Homestall Farm

Luckhurst Farm

Little Luckhurst

LOVE LA

Malthouse Farm

ROSEMARY LA

Coldharbour Farm

5

Manor Farm

Suncrest

TN27

44

Abbotts Skreen Farm

East End

SMARDEN RD

Roland House

LC

High Cross Wood

Hegg Hill Farm

4

Marley Farm

MARLEY LA

Watch House

Hegg Hill

Munk's Farm

HEADCORN RD

Westover Farm

3

Vane Farm

Bell Farm

The Roundabout

43

Smarden Bell

The Bell (PH)

Church Farm

Ash Farm

MILL LA

2

Lashenden Air Warfare Mus

Hadman's Place

Oxley Farm

WATER LA

ASHENDEN

THE OAKS

THE ACORNS

Shenley Farm

River Beult

BELL LA

Haylands Farm

White House

Hadman's Bridge

Sewage Works

PH

Ebenezer Farm

Braid Farm

Town Bridge

1

West Hoy Farm

BURNTHOUSE LA

CAGE LA

Snughorn Farm

42

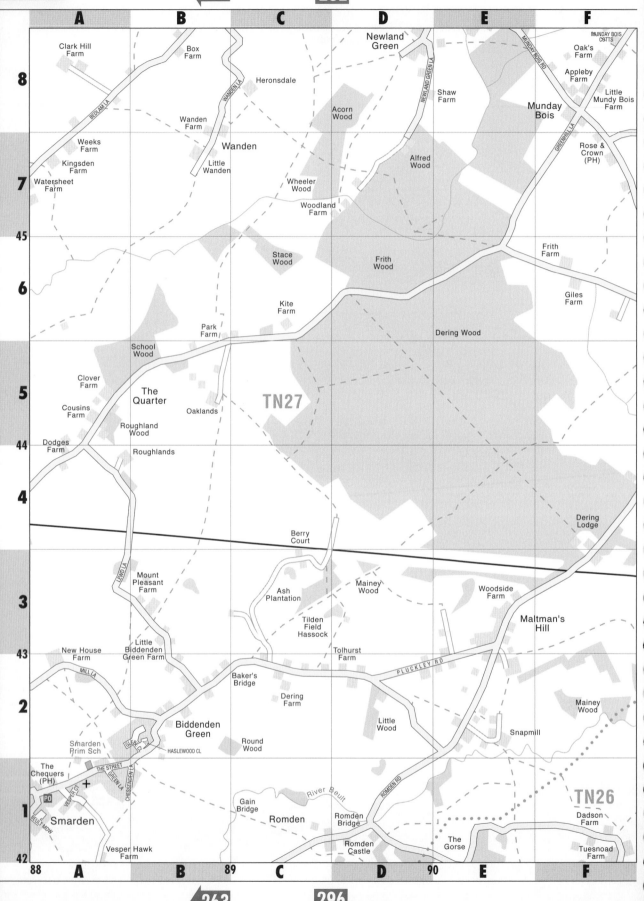

	A	B	C	D	E	F

8 Clark Hill Farm · Box Farm · Heronsdale · Newland Green · Shaw Farm · Oak's Farm · Appleby · Munday Bois · Little Mundy Bois Farm · MUNDAY BOIS COTTS

WANDEN LA · BEDLAM LA · Wanden Farm · Acorn Wood · NEWLAND GREEN LA · MUNDAY BOIS RD

7 Weeks Farm · Kingsden Farm · Watersheet Farm · Little Wanden · Wanden · Wheeler Wood · Alfred Wood · Rose & Crown (PH) · GREENHILL LA

45 Woodland Farm · Frith Farm

6 Stace Wood · Frith Wood · Giles Farm

Kite Farm · Dering Wood

Park Farm · School Wood

5 Clover Farm · The Quarter · Oaklands · **TN27**

Cousins Farm · Roughland Wood

44 Dodges Farm · Roughlands

4 Dering Lodge

Berry Court

3 Mount Pleasant Farm · Ash Plantation · Mainey Wood · Woodside Farm · Maltman's Hill · LEWD LA

Tilden Field Hassock

43 New House Farm · Little Biddenden Green Farm · Tolhurst Farm · PLUCKLEY RD · MILL LA

Baker's Bridge

2 Biddenden Green · Dering Farm · Little Wood · Snapmill · Mainey Wood

Round Wood

Smarden Prim Sch · HASLEWOOD CL

1 The Chequers (PH) · THE STREET · GREEN LA · CHESSENDEN LA · VESPER CT · Gain Bridge · Romden · River Beult · ROMDEN RD · Romden Bridge · The Gorse · **TN26** · Dadson Farm

PO · Smarden · BEULT MDW

42 Vesper Hawk Farm · Romden Castle · Tuesnoad Farm

88	A	B	89	C	D	90	E	F

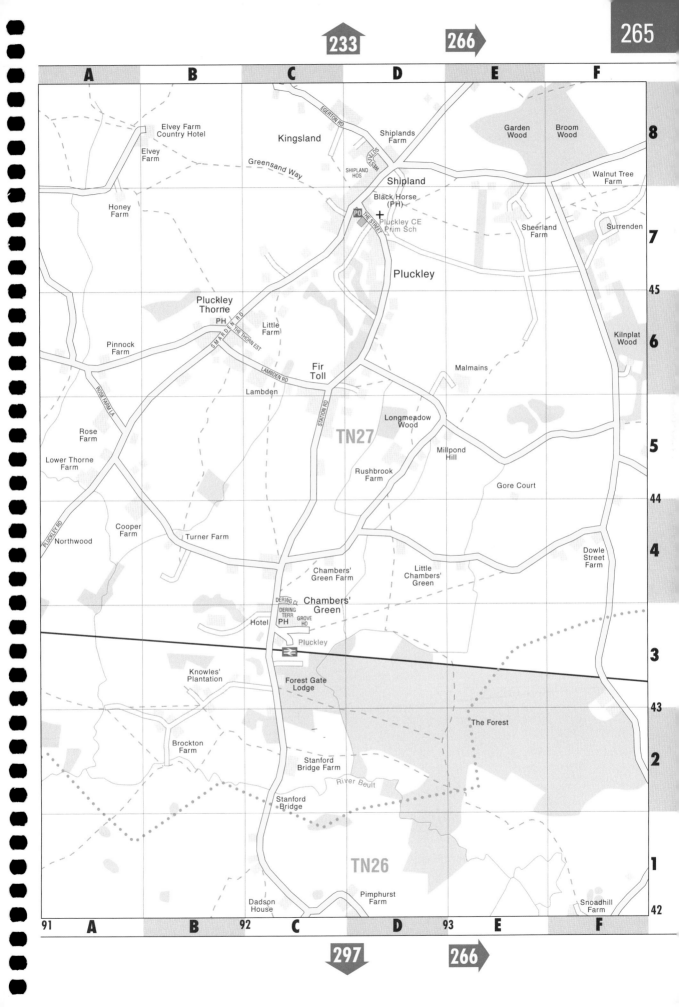

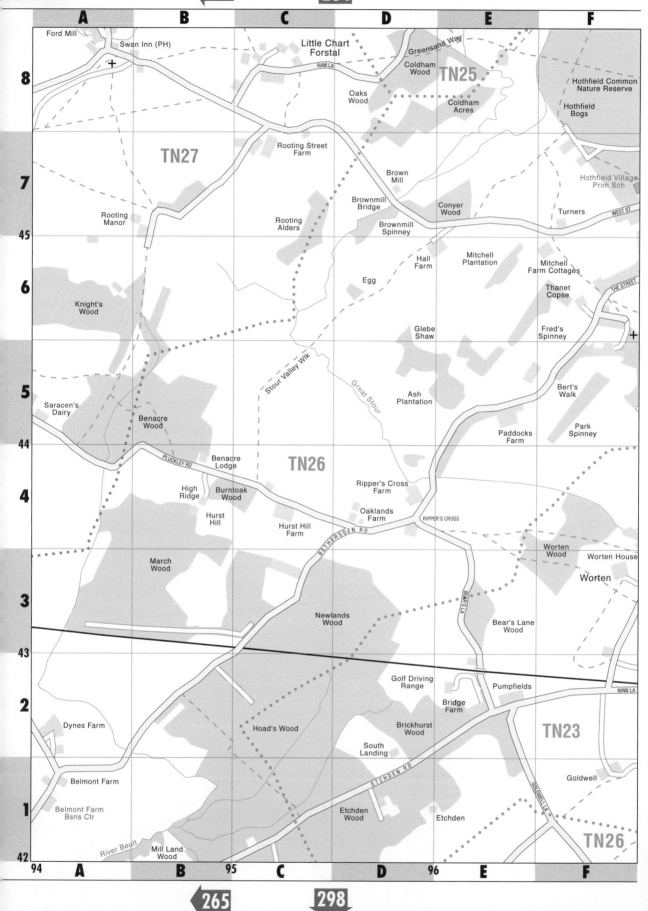

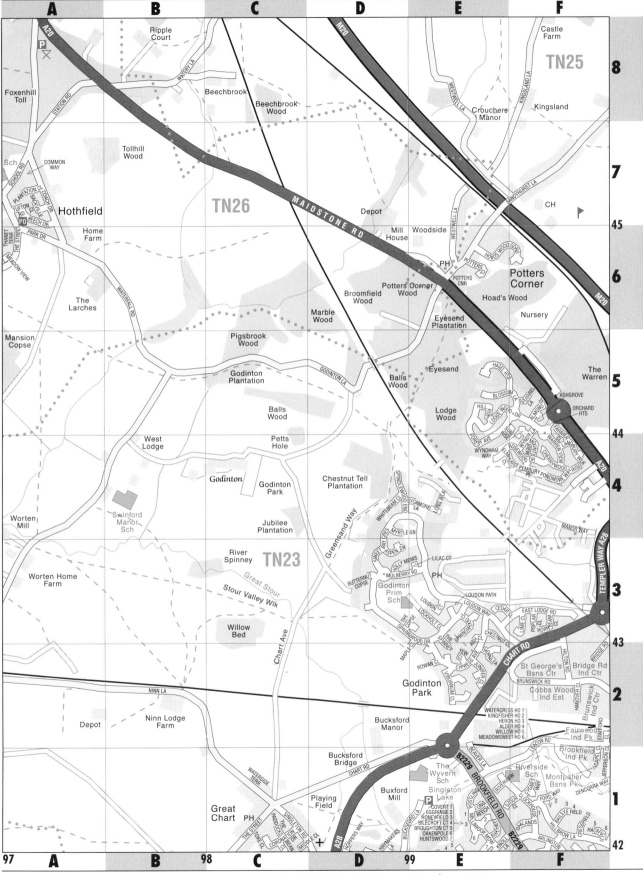

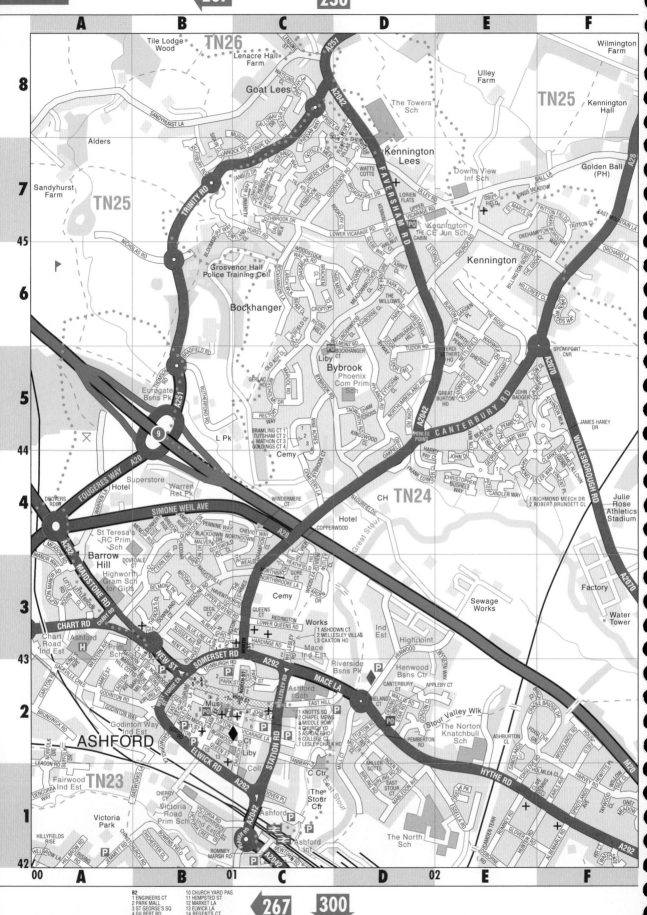

B2
1 ENGINEERS CT
2 PARK MALL
3 ST GEORGE'S SQ
4 GILBERT RD
5 NEW RENTS
6 CASTLE ST
7 KINGS PAR
8 COUNTY SQ
9 TUFTON WLK

10 CHURCH YARD PAS
11 HEMPSTED ST
12 MARKET LA
13 ELWICK LA
14 REGENTS CT
B3
1 BARROW HILL TERR
2 BARROW HILL PL
3 GRAVEL WLK
4 WOLSELEY PL

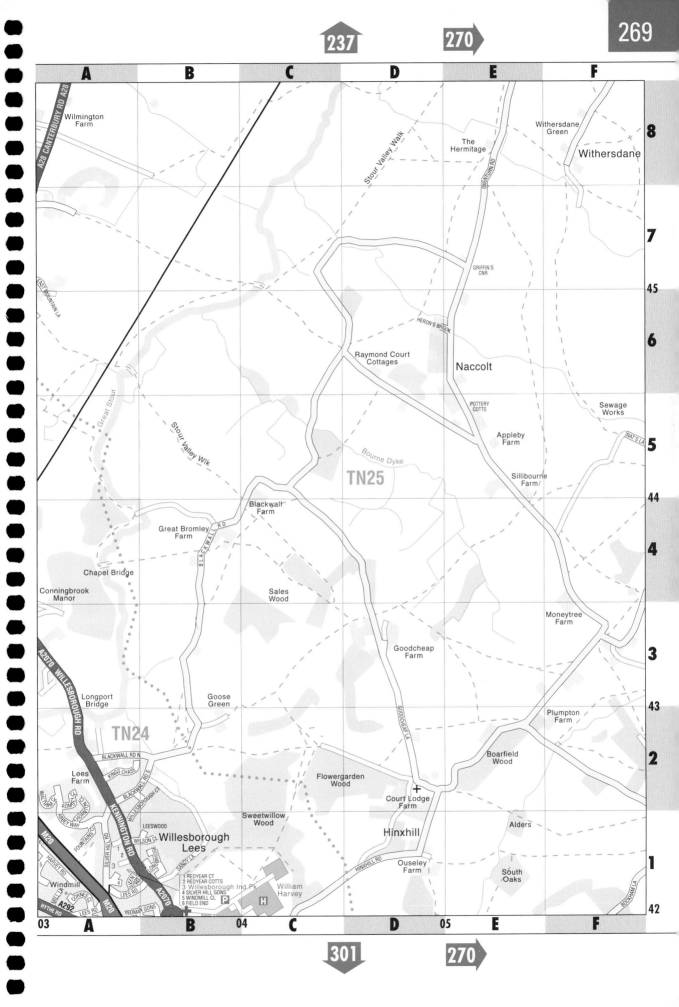

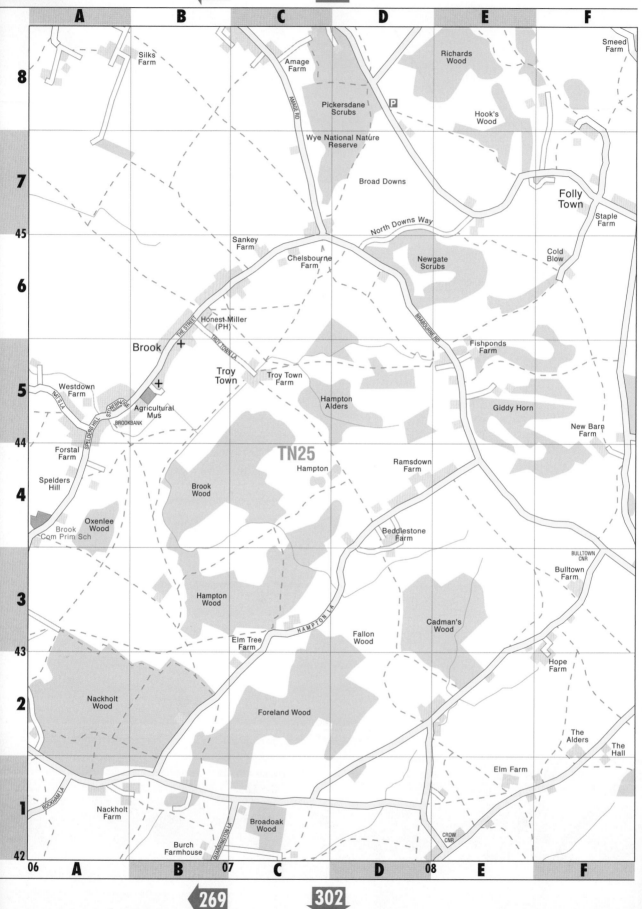

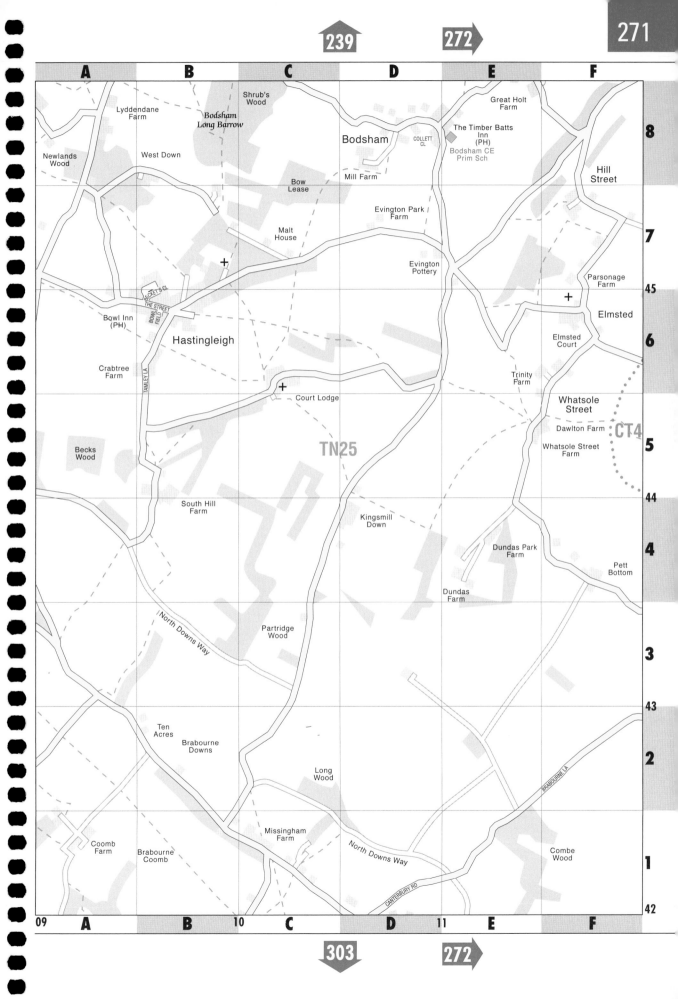

239

272

A   B   C   D   E   F

8

Lyddendane
Farm

Shrub's
Wood

Bodsham
Long Barrow

Bodsham

Great Holt
Farm

The Timber Batts
Inn
(PH)

COLLETT
CL

Newlands
Wood

West Down

Bodsham CE
Prim Sch

Hill
Street

Bow
Lease

Mill Farm

7

Evington Park
Farm

Malt
House

Evington
Pottery

Parsonage
Farm

45

BECKET'S CL

THE STREET

Bowl Inn
(PH)

BOWL
FIELD

Elmsted

Hastingleigh

Elmsted
Court

6

Crabtree
Farm

TAMLEY LA

Trinity
Farm

Court Lodge

Whatsole
Street

Dawlton Farm

CT4

Becks
Wood

Whatsole Street
Farm

TN25

5

44

South Hill
Farm

Kingsmill
Down

Dundas Park
Farm

4

Pett
Bottom

Dundas
Farm

North Downs Way

Partridge
Wood

3

43

Ten
Acres

Brabourne
Downs

Long
Wood

2

BRABOURNE LA

Coomb
Farm

Brabourne
Coomb

Missingham
Farm

North Downs Way

Combe
Wood

1

CANTERBURY RD

42

303

272

271
240

A B C D E F

8

TN25

Spong
Farm

Spong Wood

Stoneacre
Farm

Wheelbarrow
Town

7

Edards
Wood

Misling
Farm

Lower Courthope
Farm

Stone
Hall

Eastleigh
Court

Eastleigh
Wood

SANDGATES

45

MISLING LA

George Inn
(PH)

6

Upper
Maxted Street
Farm

Maxted
Street

Stone
Farm

Park Wood

Park
House

Little Pett Bottom
Place

Sixmile

Elmfield

Oakridge

5

Homelands
Farm

Yew Tree
Farm

Dinas Bran

CT4

44

Nature
Trail

4

Woodstock
Farm

Lymbridge
Green

Mockbeggar

Stowting
Common

West Wood

Cavalry
Farm

3

Highfields
Farm

TN25

Stowting
Rough

43

BRABOURNE LA

Park
Farm

Mariners

Little Rhode
Farm

2

GREEN LA

STOWTING HILL

Swinyard's
Hill

CT18

Tumulus
Farm

1

Mercer's
Farm

Sibton Wood

42

Cage
Farm

12 A B 13 C D 14 E F

B2068

STONE ST

271
304

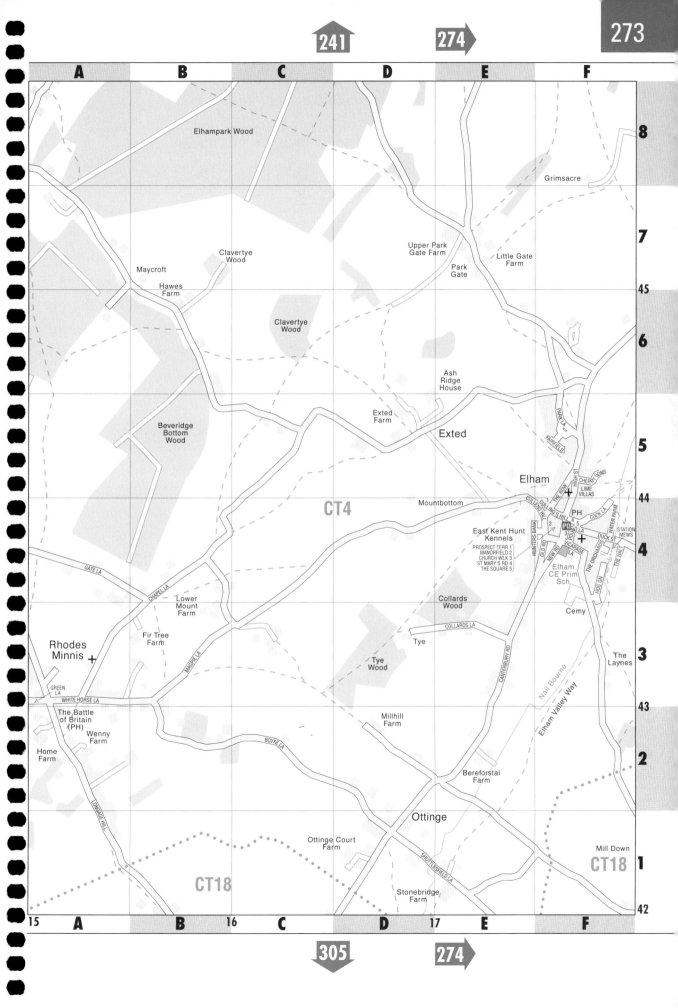

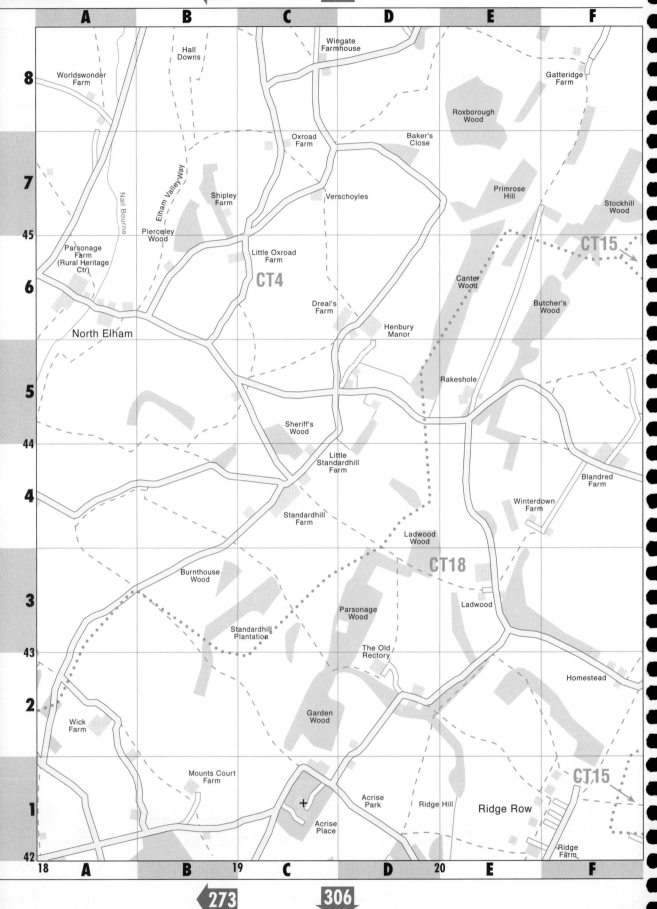

273
242

A | B | C | D | E | F

8

Worldswonder
Farm

Hall
Downs

Wingate
Farmhouse

Gatteridge
Farm

Roxborough
Wood

7

Oxroad
Farm

Baker's
Close

Primrose
Hill

Stockhill
Wood

Shipley
Farm

Verschoyles

Nail Bourne

Elham Valley Way

45

Pierceley
Wood

Little Oxroad
Farm

CT15

Parsonage
Farm
(Rural Heritage
Ctr)

CT4

Canter
Wood

Butcher's
Wood

6

Dreal's
Farm

Henbury
Manor

North Elham

Rakeshole

5

Sheriff's
Wood

44

Little
Standardhill
Farm

Blandred
Farm

4

Standardhill
Farm

Winterdown
Farm

Ladwood
Wood

CT18

Burnthouse
Wood

Parsonage
Wood

Ladwood

3

Standardhill
Plantation

The Old
Rectory

43

Homestead

2

Wick
Farm

Garden
Wood

Mounts Court
Farm

CT15

Acrise
Park

Ridge Hill

Ridge Row

1

Acrise
Place

Ridge
Farm

42

273
306

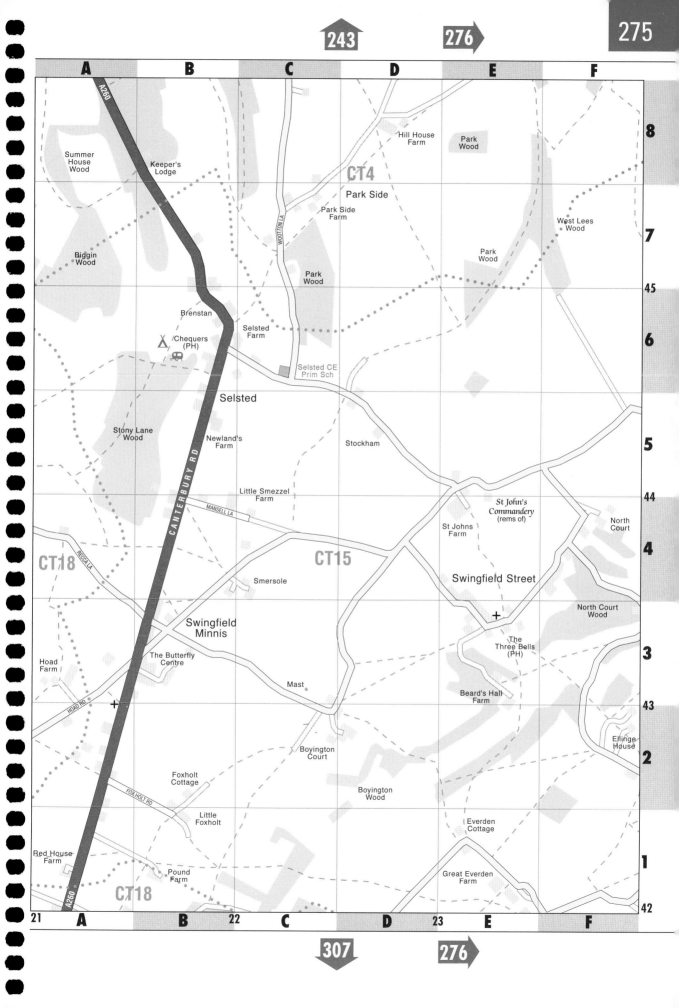

275
244

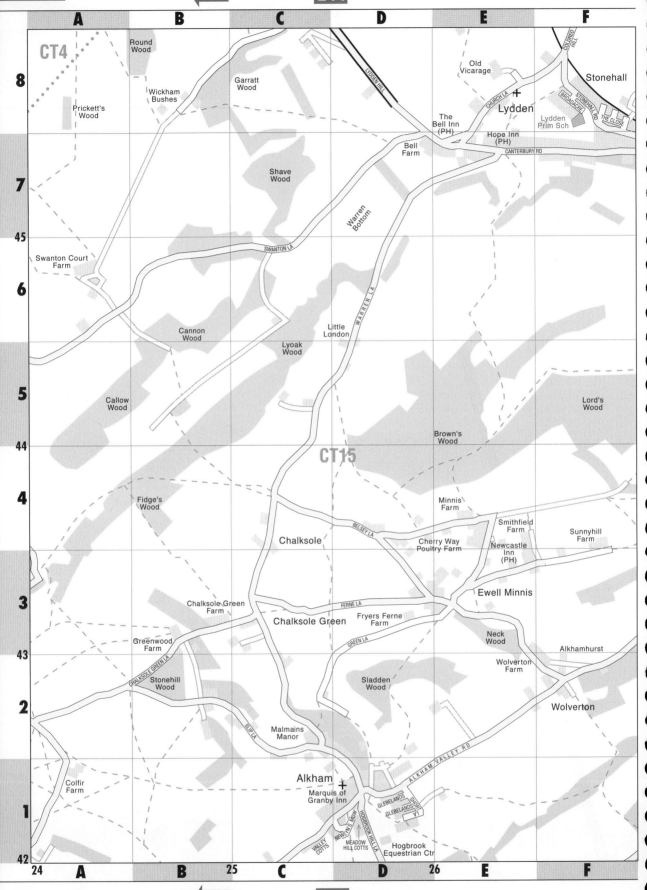

CT4

8

Round Wood

Prickett's Wood

Wickham Bushes

Garratt Wood

Old Vicarage

CHURCH LA

Lydden

The Bell Inn (PH)

Hope Inn (PH)

COLDRED HILL

Stonehall

BROADACRE

STONEHALL RD

Lydden Prim Sch

THE CLOSE

Bell Farm

CANTERBURY RD

LYDDEN HILL

7

Shave Wood

Warren Bottom

45

Swanton Court Farm

SWANTON LA

6

Cannon Wood

Little London

WARREN LA

Lyoak Wood

5

Callow Wood

Lord's Wood

44

Brown's Wood

CT15

4

Fidge's Wood

Minnis Farm

Smithfield Farm

Sunnyhill Farm

Chalksole

BELSEY LA

Cherry Way Poultry Farm

Newcastle Inn (PH)

3

Chalksole Green Farm

Chalksole Green

FERNE LA

Fryers Ferne Farm

Ewell Minnis

Neck Wood

Alkhamhurst

Greenwood Farm

GREEN LA

Wolverton Farm

43

CHALKSOLE GREEN LA

Stonehill Wood

Sladden Wood

2

SLIP LA

Malmains Manor

ALKHAM VALLEY RD

Wolverton

Colfir Farm

Alkham

Marquis of Granby Inn

GLEBELANDS

GLEBELANDS

SHORT LA

1

HOGBROOK HILL LA

NEW LYN MDW

VALLEY COTTS

MEADOW HILL COTTS

Hogbrook Equestrian Ctr

42

24 A   B   **25**   C   D   **26**   E   F

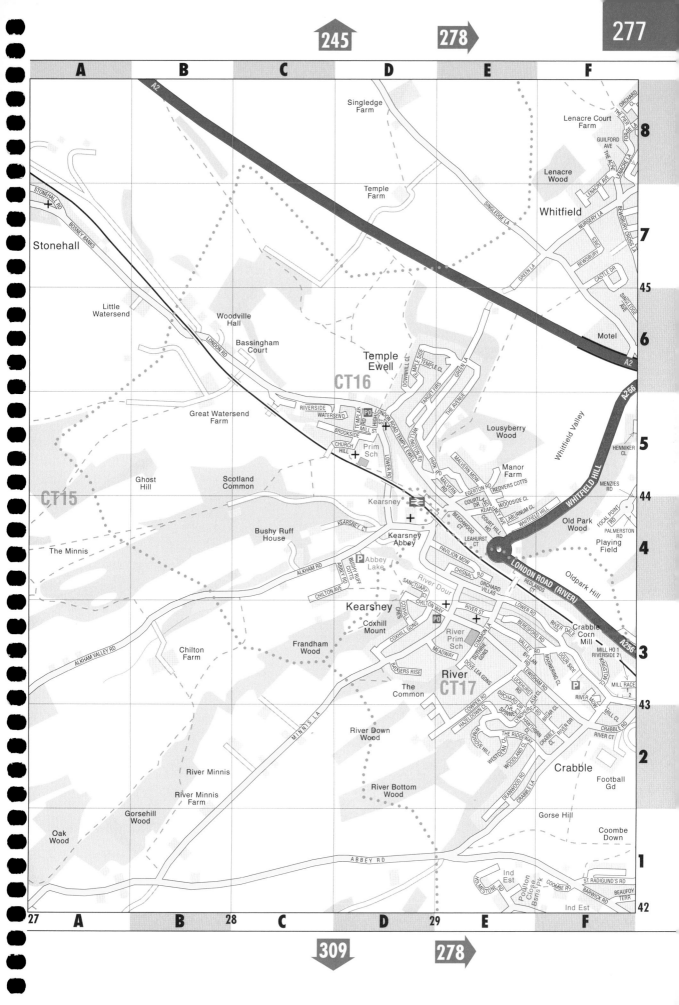

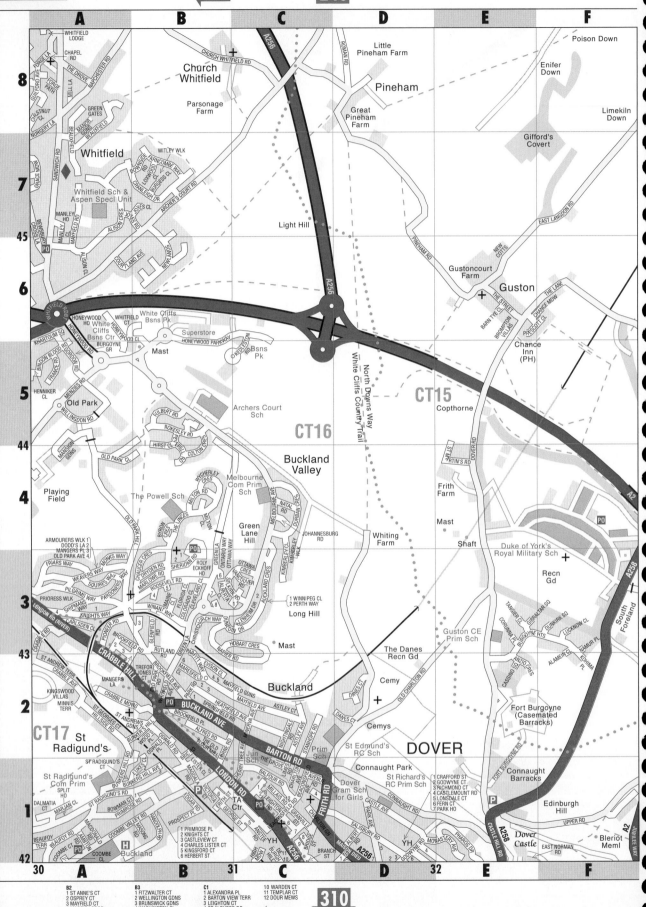

B2
1 ST ANNE'S CT
2 OSPREY CT
3 MAYFIELD CT
4 MAGPIE LODGE
5 CHAFFINCH LODGE
6 HERON LODGE

B3
1 FITZWALTER CT
2 WELLINGTON GDNS
3 BRUNSWICK GDNS
4 WASHINGTON CL
5 BOSTON CL
6 TORONTO CL
7 HUDSON CL
8 MONTREAL CL

C1
1 ALEXANDRA PL
2 BARTON VIEW TERR
3 LEIGHTON CT
4 ST ALPHEGE RD
5 SHOOTER'S HILL
6 BARTHOLOMEW ST
7 CHURCHILL ST
8 PAUL'S PL
9 MATTHEW'S PL

10 WARDEN CT
11 TEMPLAR CT
12 DOUR MEWS

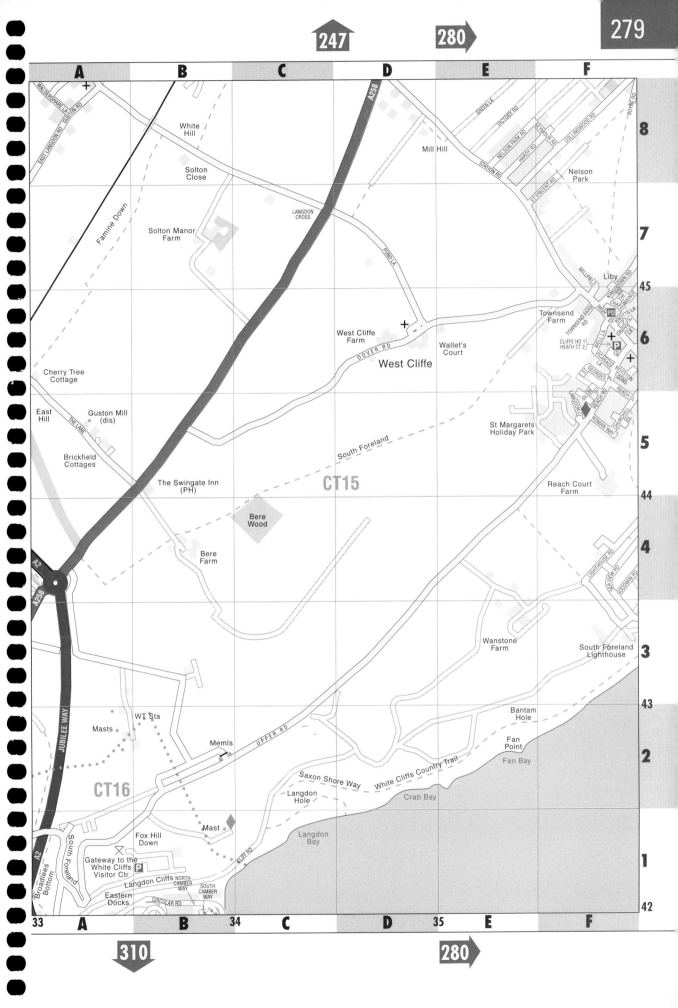

279
248

CT14

St Margaret's
Free Down

Hog's
Bush

Bockhill
Farm

The
Cut

Free Down

CT15

Dover Patrol
Meml

Leathercoat
Point

Bockell
Hill

St Margaret's
at Cliffe

1 BOLONIA
2 THE KNOLL

Coney Burrow
Point

St Margaret's-at-Cliffe
Prim Sch

The Leas

Saxon Shore Way

White Cliffs Country Trail

Portal House
Sch

BAY
COTTS

THE
GRANVILLE

Bay
Hill

The
Coastguard
(PH)

Bay Hill

The Bay
Mus

St Margaret's
Bay

The
Pines
Gardens

Ness
Point

The
Windmill

South
Foreland

The
Parlour

NORWAY DRO
KINGSDOWN RD
THE FREEDOWN
THE RISE
THE DROVEWAY
NORMAN RD
CAVENDISH RD
SALISBURY RD
VICTORIA AVE
GRANVILLE RD
CONVENT CL
KENILWORTH CL
DROVEWAY GDNS
DOWNSIDE
SEA ST
CHAPEL LA
REACH MDW
FORELAND CT
BAY HILL
HOTEL RD
BAY HILL CL
BEACH RD
LIGHTHOUSE RD
SEA VIEW RD
GODWIN RD
ST MARGARET'S RD
FORELAND RD
BEACH RD
THE CRESCENT
THE FRONT

36 A B 37 C D 38 E F

42
1
2
43
3
4
44
5
45
6
7
8

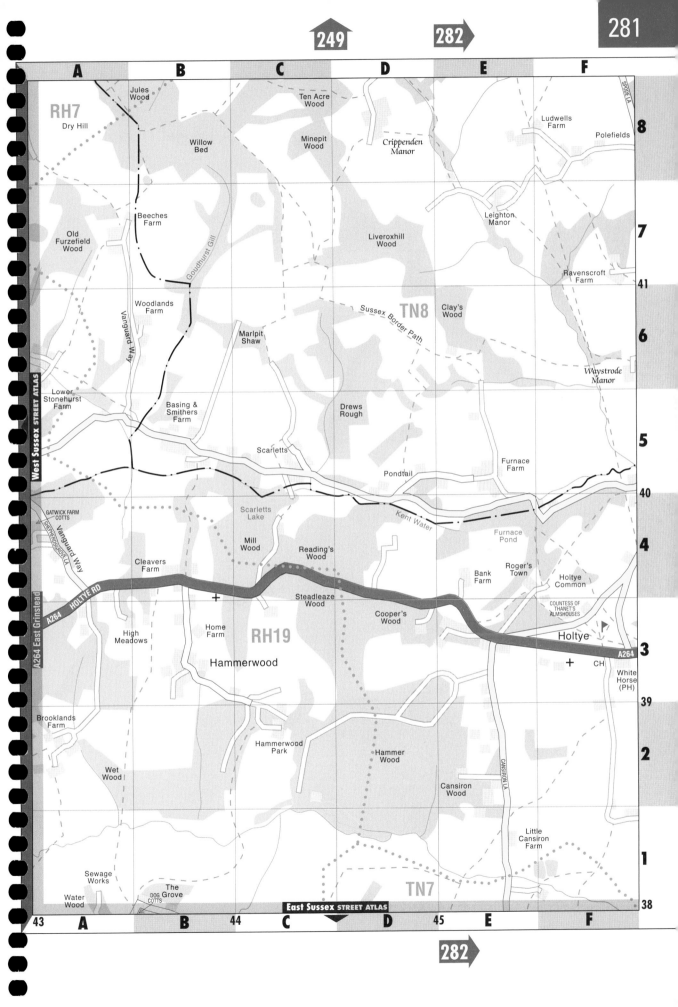

281
250

8

7

41

6

5

40

4

3

39

2

1

38

A B C D E F

B2026

Claydene

Pyle Gate Farm

Cowden

Mount Noddy

Rickwoods Farm

Wickens

RAILWAY COTTS

BLOWERS HILL

Saxbys Mead

Jones's Wood

THE PADDOCKS

COWDEN CROSS

Saxbys

MOAT LA

Sandfields Farm

Glover's Hawes

SPODE LA

Uphill Farm

Butterwell Bridge

Southlands

HARTFIELD RD

Moat Farm

TN8

Cowden

PRIOR'S WAY

CHESTNUT PL

NORTH ST

THE SQUARE

CHANTLERS MEAD

HIGH ST

CHURCH ST

Kentwater Cottages

Sussex Border Path

Kent Water

Holywych House

PH

COWDEN MEWS

Sewage Works

Kitford Bridge

Sussex House Farm

Holywych Farm

Holtye House

Heathersome's Wood

Langley Farm

Peter's Wood

Hethe House

Great Wood

TN3

Sussex Oak (PH)

Cullinghurst Farm

Cullinghurst Wood

Mast

A264

B2026

GOODTREES LA

Broomland Wood

Scragg's Farm

EDENBRIDGE RD

Tye Farm

TN7

BEECH GREEN LA

Chantlers Farm

Lower Brockshill Farm

Coomb Wood

Beech Green Park

Puckstye Farm

B2026

46 A B 47 C D 48 E F

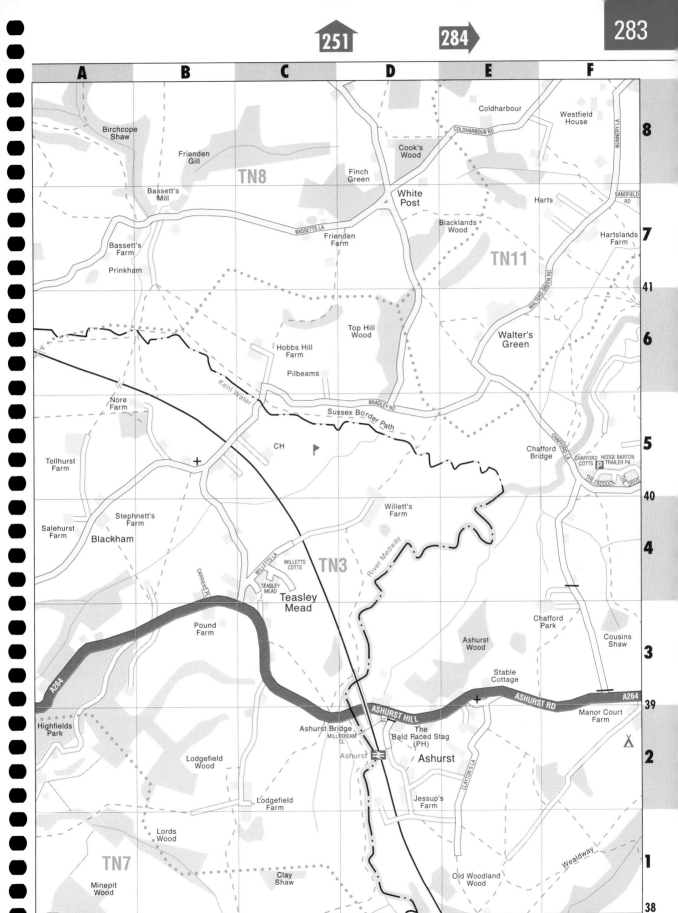

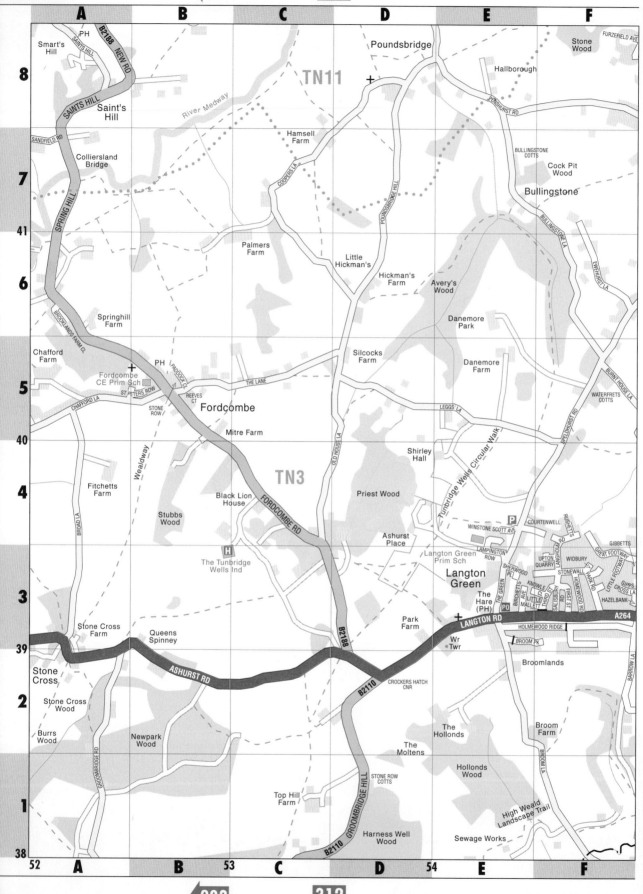

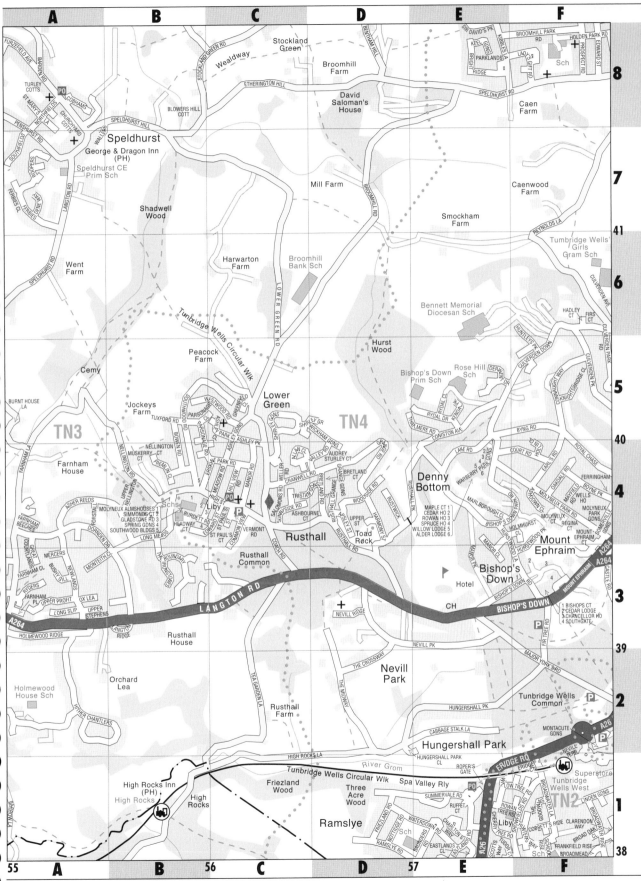

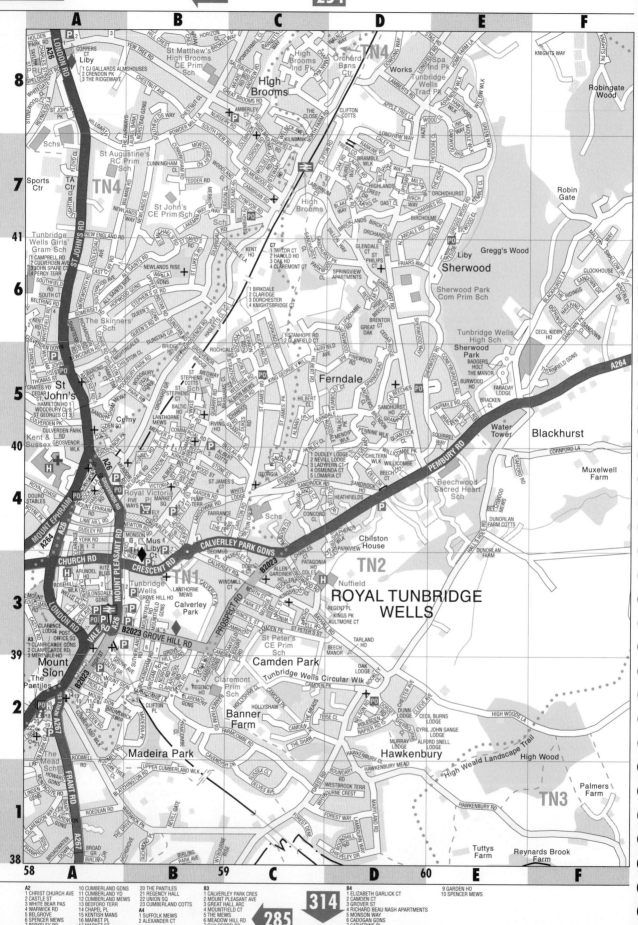

285 254

TN4

Knights Way

Robingate Wood

High Brooms

Robin Gate

Tunbridge Wells Trad Pk

Sherwood

Gregg's Wood

Sherwood Park Com Prim Sch

Tunbridge Wells High Sch

Sherwood Park

Blackhurst

Water Tower

Muxelwell Farm

Ferndale

PEMBURY RD

Beechwood Sacred Heart Sch

TN2

ROYAL TUNBRIDGE WELLS

Nuffield

Chilston House

Calverley Park

TN1

Tunbridge Wells

Camden Park

Tunbridge Wells Circular Wlk

Hawkenbury

High Wood

Mount Sion

The Pantiles

Madeira Park

Banner Farm

Claremont Prim Sch

High Weald Landscape Trail

TN3

Palmers Farm

Tuttys Farm

Reynards Brook Farm

314 285

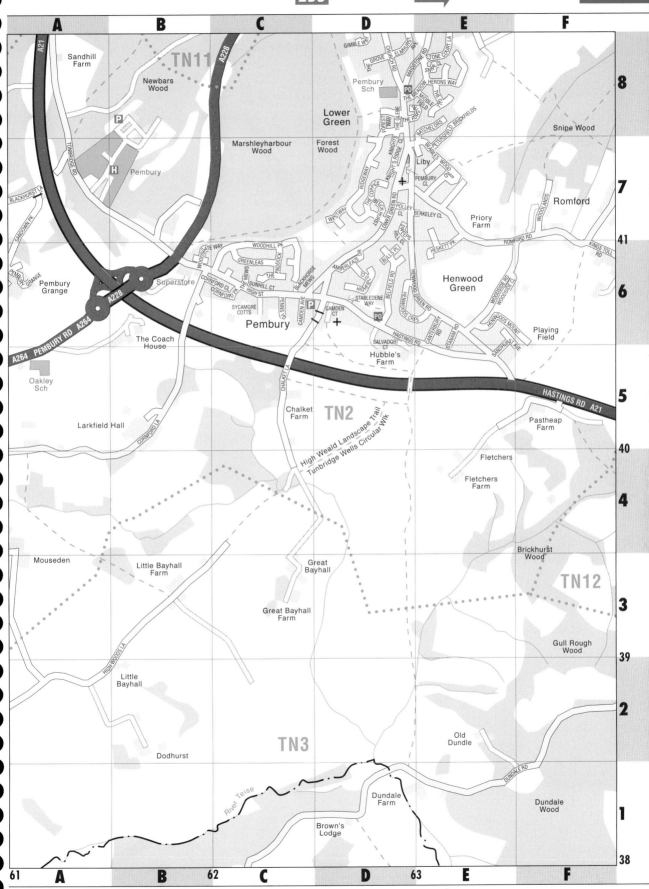

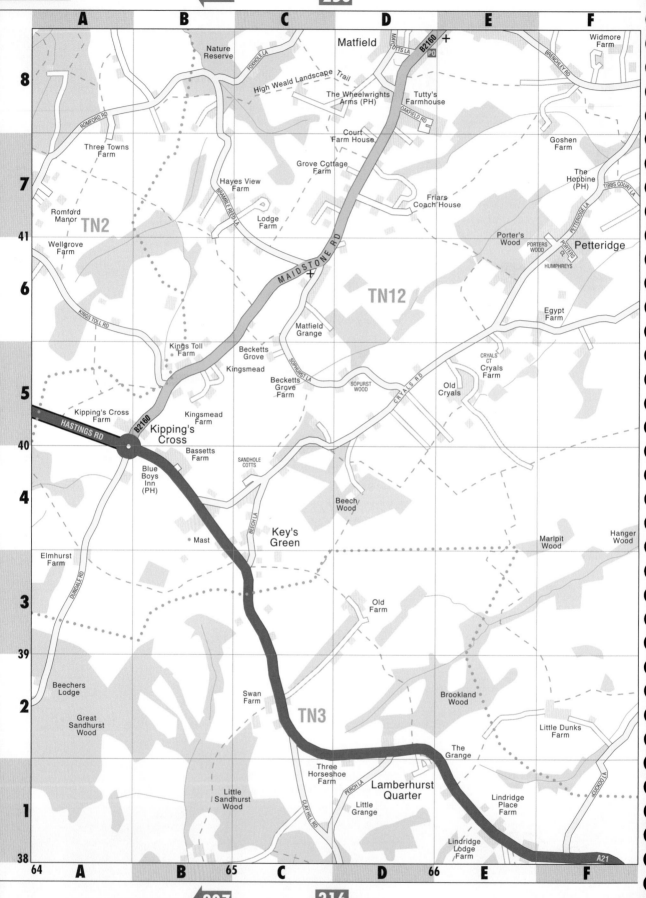

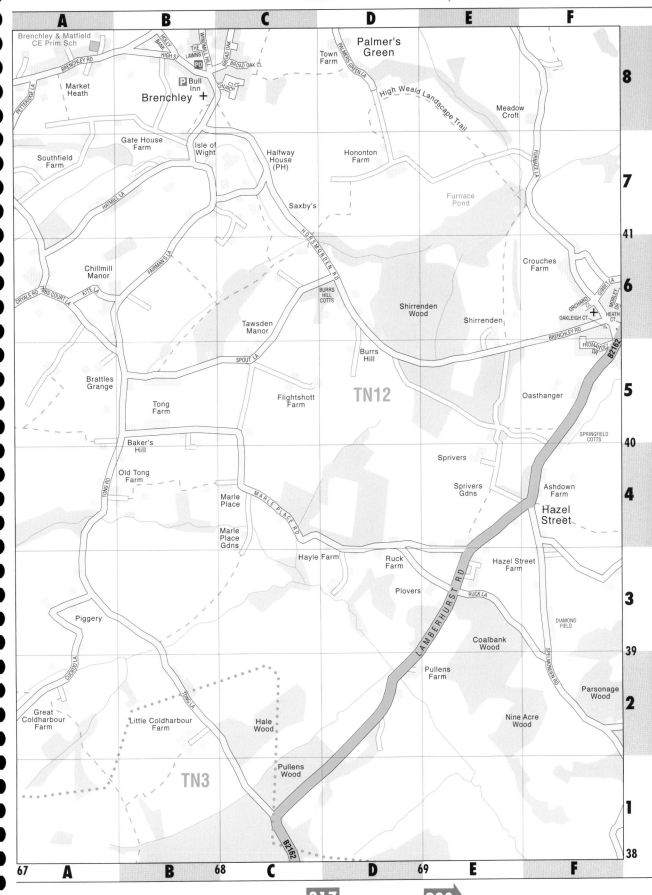

289
258

A B C D E F

8

Swigs Hole Farm

The Corner

Cocketts

Northiam Farm

Mount Easy Farmhouse

Smalls Farm

B2162

Haymans Hill Farm

Jackson's Wood

School House Farm

SCHOOL HOUSE LA

Lesser Teise

CHURCH MEADOW

MAIDSTONE RD

7

Stiles Farm

HAYMANS HILL

Lampkyns

Ash Farm

41

GIBBET LA
KIRKINS CL
GUNLANDS
BRIDGE COTTS

Grovehurst Farm

Liby

Horsmonden Prim Sch

GREEN RD
BACK LA
ORCHARD CRES
ORCHARD WAY
OAST VIEW

6

1 HEATH TERR
2 THE MANWARINGS
3 TABOR CT
4 MORLEY DR
5 KINGS CT
6 HOATH MDW

TN12

Grovehurst Farm House

Sewage Works

Harper's Farm

PO
GUN LA
ANGLEY CT

Bassetts Farm

NEW BASSETTS COTTS

GROVEHURST LA

B2079

5

Horsmonden

Works

GOUDHURST RD
STATION COTTS
LAMBERT'S PL

Spring Farm

Capel Cross

Hook Wood

River Teise

Finchurst Farm

40

Broad Ford Farm

Stone Bridge

TN17

Lewes Heath

4

Broad Ford

Gore Court

GORE LA

Etchinghill Farm

Shear Farm

Swan Farm

SWAN LA

Nevergood Farm

Share Farm

Grove Place

Brandfold

3

Evergood

Little Brandfold

39

BRICKKILN LA

Brickkiln Cottages

Brandfold Farm

Rectory Park

Lidwells

B2084

2

RECTORY RD
PARK RD

Park Farm

SMALL BRIDGE RD

Smallbridge

SMALL BRIDGE COTTS

High Weald Landscape Trail

Trottenden

The Oaks

LIDWELLS LA

NORTH RD

LOVERS LA

The Grange

Trowswell

SPELMONDEN RD

Lordship Wood

1

Church Farm

BLIND LA

B2079

Hammond's Farm

CHEQUER'S COTTS 1
BERESFORD RD 2
TATTLEBURY LA
B2084

38

70 A 71 B C 72 D E F

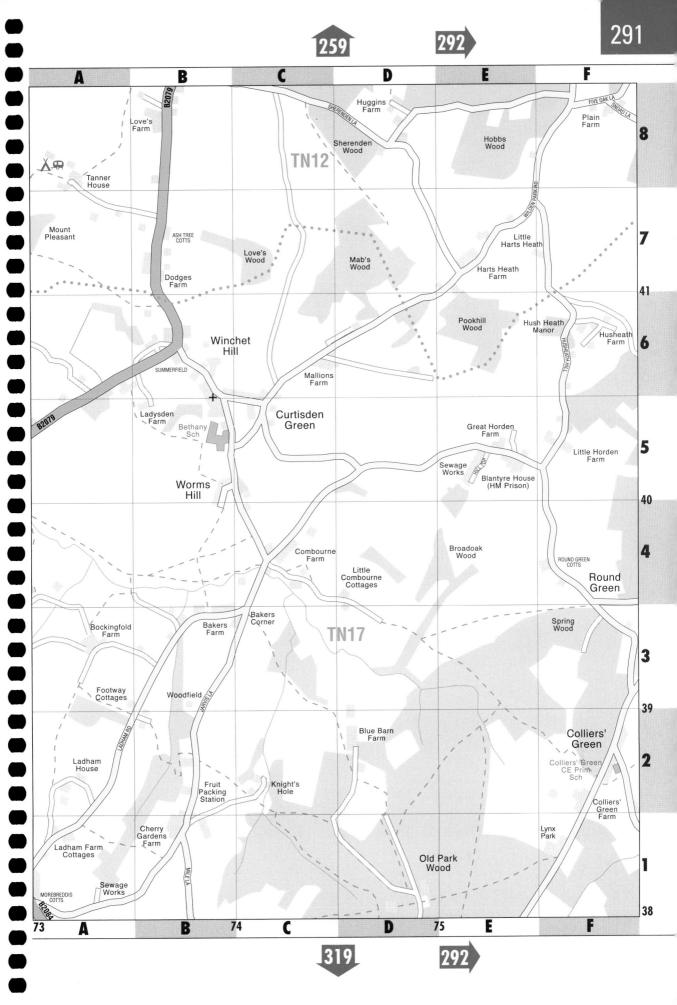

291
260

A B C D E F

8

Tank Wood
SNOAD LA
PRISTLING LA
Monk's Farm
Chapmans Farm Oast
Convent
Chittenden Farm
A229
Iden Grange
Bletchingley Farm
Iden Bridge

Snoad Wood
Birch Wood
Lovehurst Manor
Bromley Barn

7

TN12
Rabbits Farm
CRANBROOK RD

41

Mathurst Farm
Castle Bank
Earthworks
Knox Bridge

6

Strackna Wood
GOUDHURST RD
Knoxbridge Inn (PH)
A229

Playfoot Wood
Bowling Alley Wood
Bede House

5

Bounds End Farm
Paley Farm
Tolehurst Farm

40

MILLERS THUMB
Hartridge Manor Farm

4

Foxridge Wood
Folly Hill Farm
Hartridge Manor Cottages
Saunders' Wood

3

Little Dale
Snow Hill
TN17
Pond Wood
Brewers Wood
Saunders Farm

39

Hocker Edge
Sissinghurst Park
Camden Hill

2

Hazelden Farm
Hilly Wood
Roxburgh Lodge
Camden Hill Farm
CONVALESCENT LA
A229

Clayhill Farm
FRIEZLEY LA
Hawkridge Farmhouse

1

Dunley Wood
Harewood
Friezley

38
76 A B 77 C D 78 E F

291
320

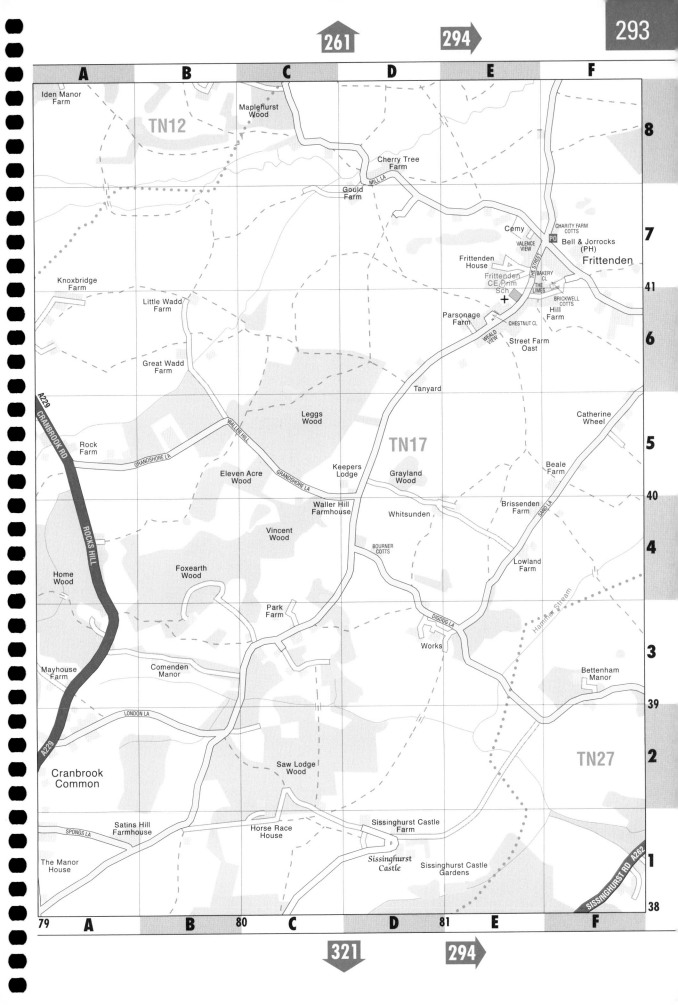

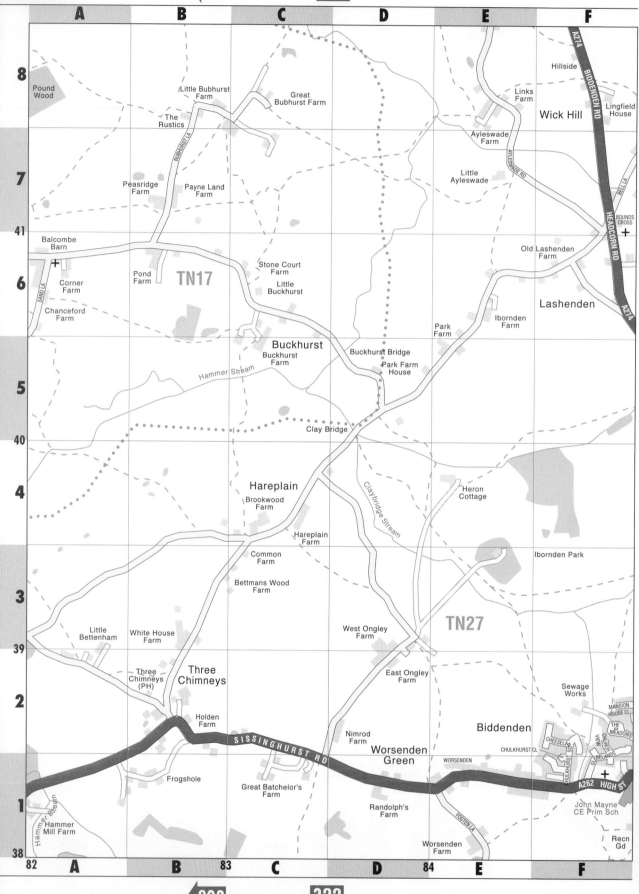

A B C D E F

323 296

Barnden Farm
Snughorne House
Burnthouse La
Cage La
Walford House
Biddenden Rd
Bethersden Rd

Hill View
Oak Acre
Bell La
Obeden Farm
Snughorne La
Grigsby Farm
Thorn Farm
Bardleden Farm
8

Stanlash
Limes Farmhouse
Lime Kiln Farm
Tilden Farm
7

Monk's Hill
Priory Farm
Smarden Bsns Est
Tylden
Gilham Land Farm
41

Monks Hill Farm
Roberts Farm
Gilham Farm

Lashenden Farm
Standen Wood
S Marden Rd
Vane Court Farm
Deadman's Wood
Kelsham
6

Cackle Hill
CH
Vane Court
Standen
Weeks La
Great Omenden Farm
Great Omenden Cottages
5

Ponds Farm
Standen
Forstal Farm
40

Newcastle Farm
Little Omenden Farm
4

Headcorn Rd
A274
Apsley
Gorse Farm
Pook La

Curteis' Corner
Cot La
Omenden Barn
Wagstaff
3

River Hall
39

North St
Elmstone
Gallops
2

Mansion House Cl
Sweet Meadow Farm

Shuttle Cl
Cloth Hall
Gdns Teasels
Guy House
High Halden Rd

PO
High St
A262
Whitfield Farm
Stede Quarter
High Halden Rd
1

P
John Mayne CE Prim Sch
Tenterden Rd A262
Washenden Manor
Podkin Farm
TN26
38

TN27

85 A B 86 C D 87 E F 38

295
264

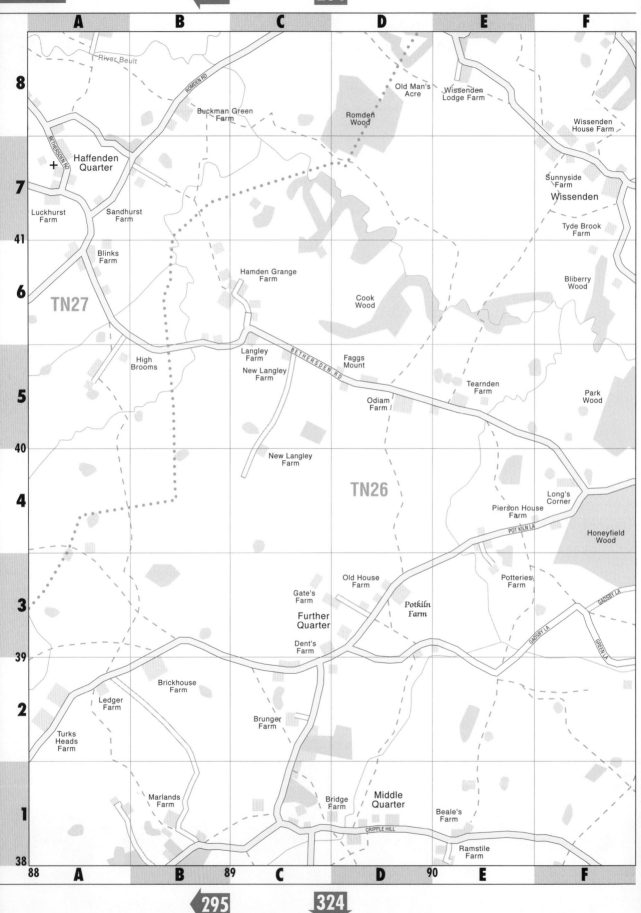

295
324

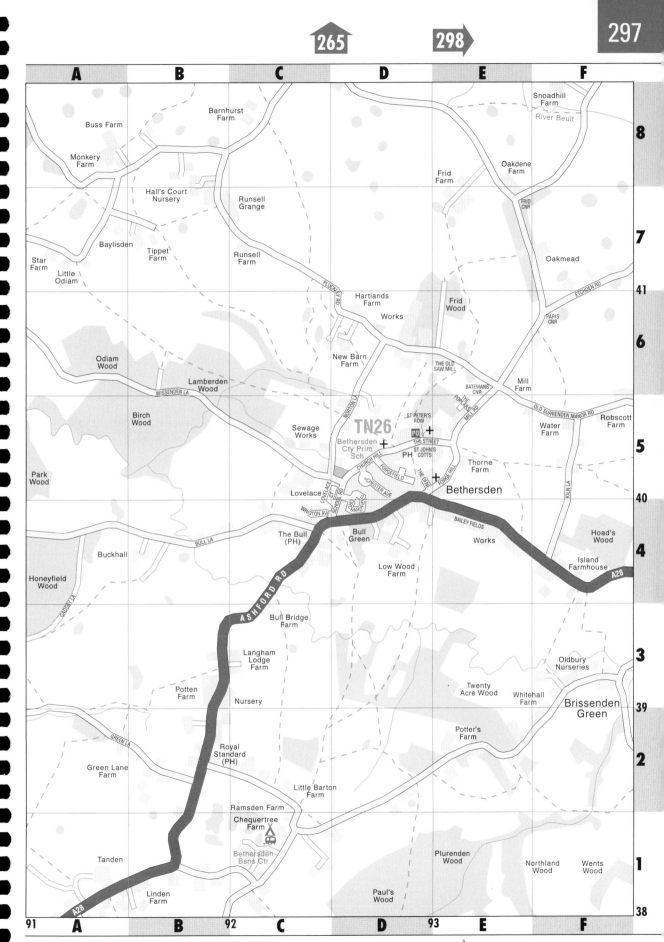

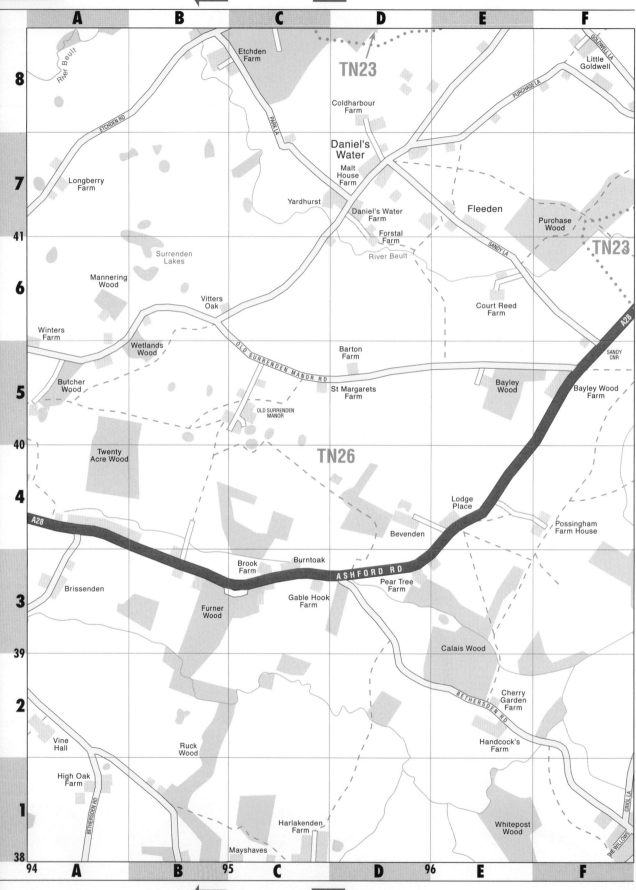

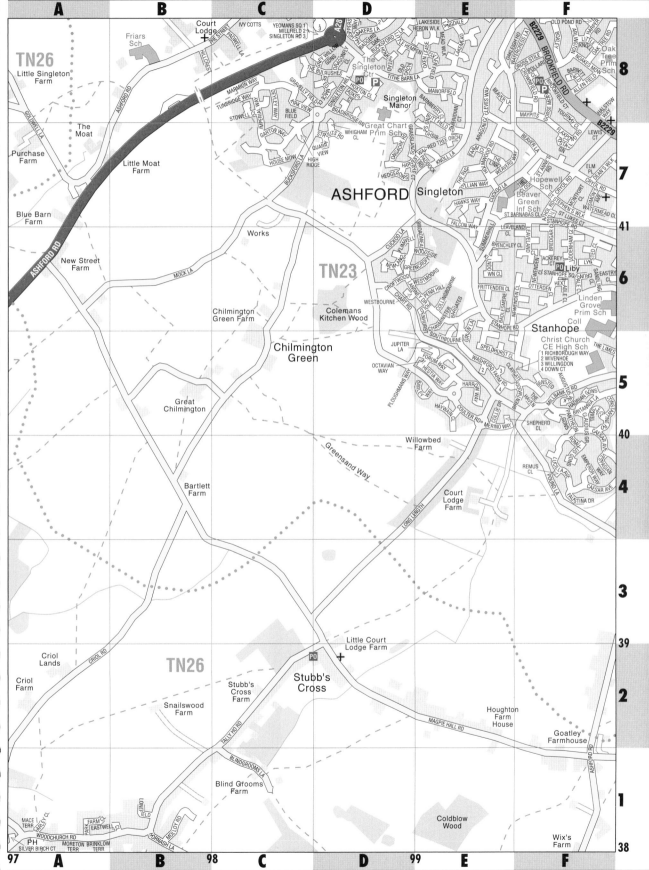

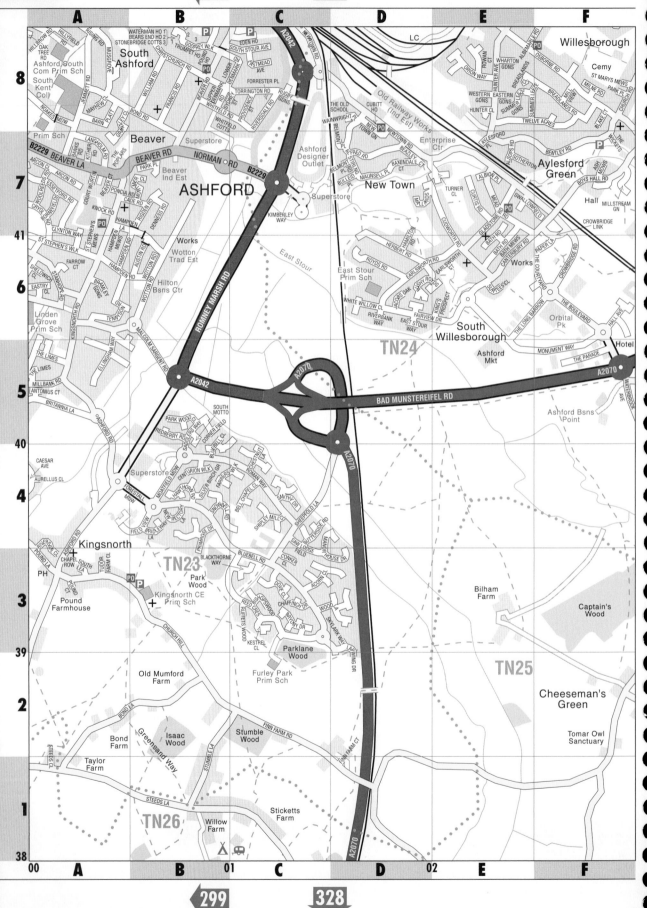

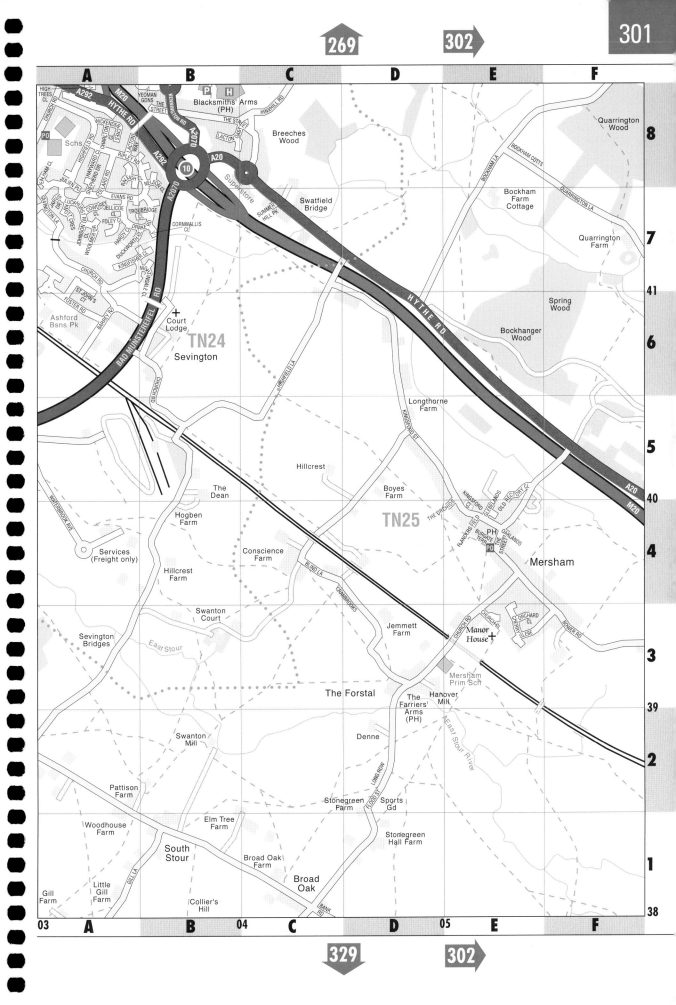

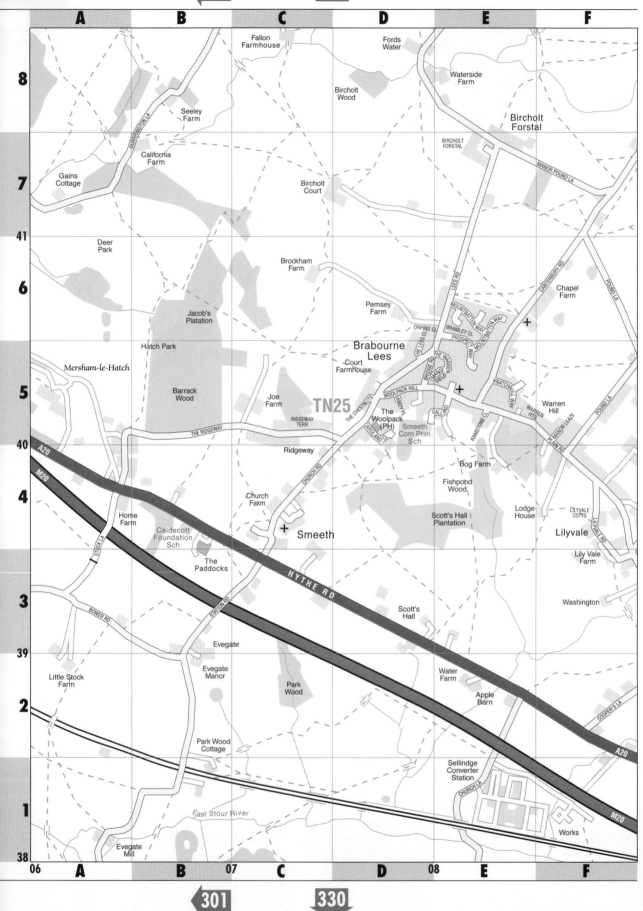

301

270

A B C D E F

8

7

41

6

5

40

4

39

2

1

38

06 A B 07 C D 08 E F

Fallon
Farmhouse

Fords
Water

Waterside
Farm

Bircholt
Wood

Bircholt
Forstal

BIRCHOLT
FORSTAL

MANOR POUND LA

Seeley
Farm

QUARRINGTON LA

California
Farm

Gains
Cottage

Bircholt
Court

LEES RD

Chapel
Farm

CANTERBURY RD

POUND LA

Deer
Park

Brockham
Farm

Pemsey
Farm

MOUNTBATTEN WAY

ORPINS CL

THE LEES CL

BRAMLEY CL

PROSPECT WAY

MOUNTBATTEN WAY

Jacob's
Platation

Brabourne
Lees

THE WARREN

BRIDGE RD

Hatch Park

Court
Farmhouse

Mersham-le-Hatch

LIMOUSE FIELD

KNATCHBULL WAY

WARREN HTS

Chapel
Farm

Barrack
Wood

Joe
Farm

WOOLPACK HILL

Warren
Hill

Warren
Hill

RAMSTONE CL

MANOR LEAZE

POUND LA

PLAIN RD

TN25

The
Woolpack
(PH)

CALL RD

THE RIDGEWAY

RIDGEWAY
TERR

THE CHESTNUTS

SANDY PL

CAROLAND CL

Smeeth
Com Prim
Sch

Ridgeway

CHURCH RD

Bog Farm

Fishpond
Wood

LILYVALE
COTTS

A20

M20

Home
Farm

Church
Farm

Smeeth

Scott's Hall
Plantation

Lodge
House

Lilyvale

LILYVALE RD

Caldecott
Foundation
Sch

STOCK LA

The
Paddocks

HYTHE RD

Lily Vale
Farm

STATION RD

BOWER RD

Evegate

Scott's
Hall

Washington

Little Stock
Farm

Evegate
Manor

Park
Wood

Water
Farm

Apple
Barn

COOPER'S LA

A20

Park Wood
Cottage

Sellindge
Converter
Station

CHURCH LA

M20

East Stour River

Works

Evegate
Mill

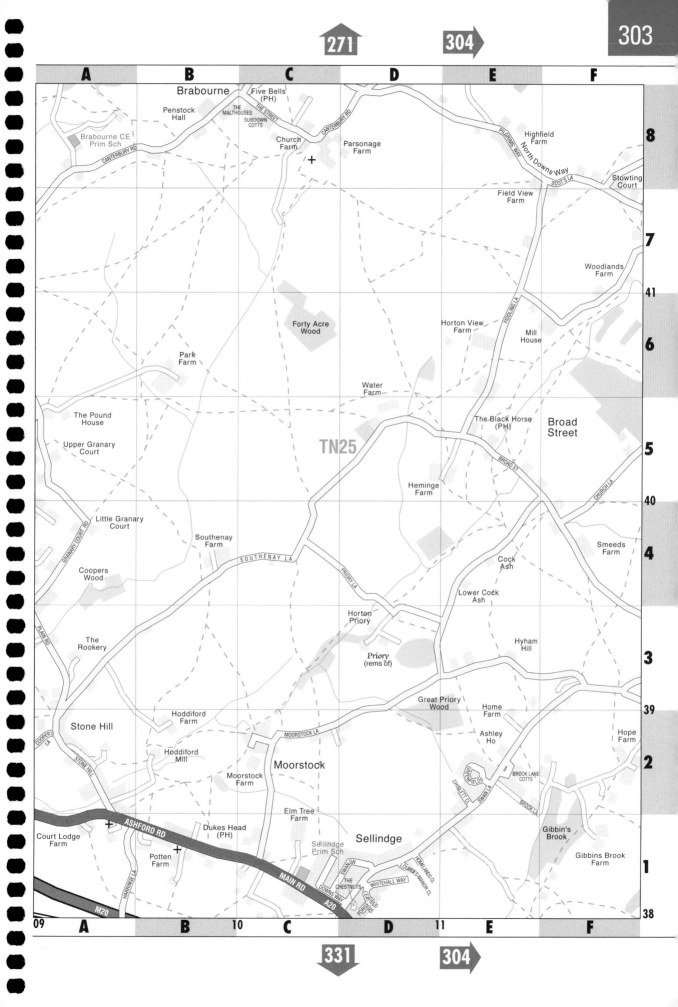

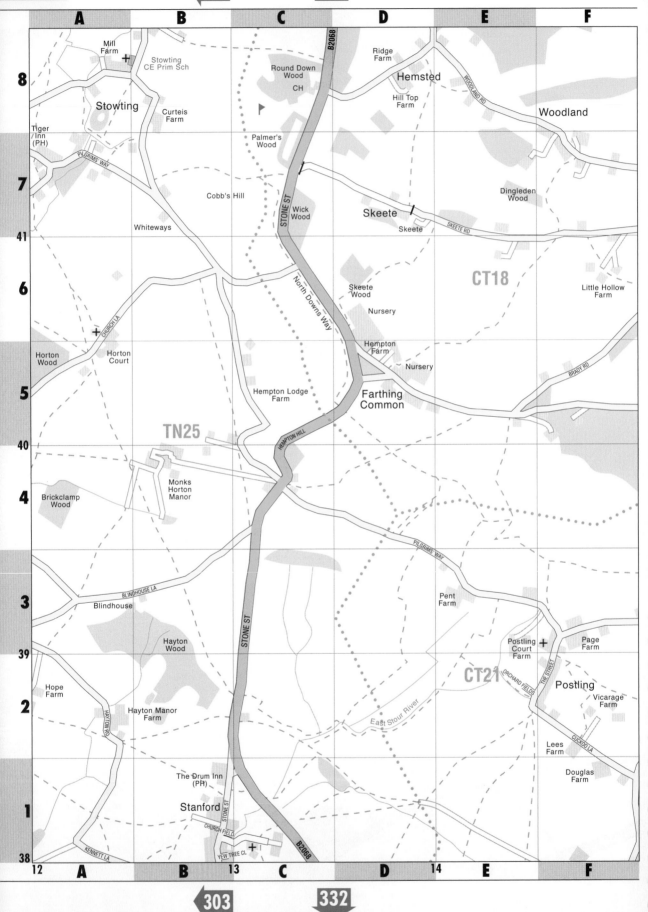

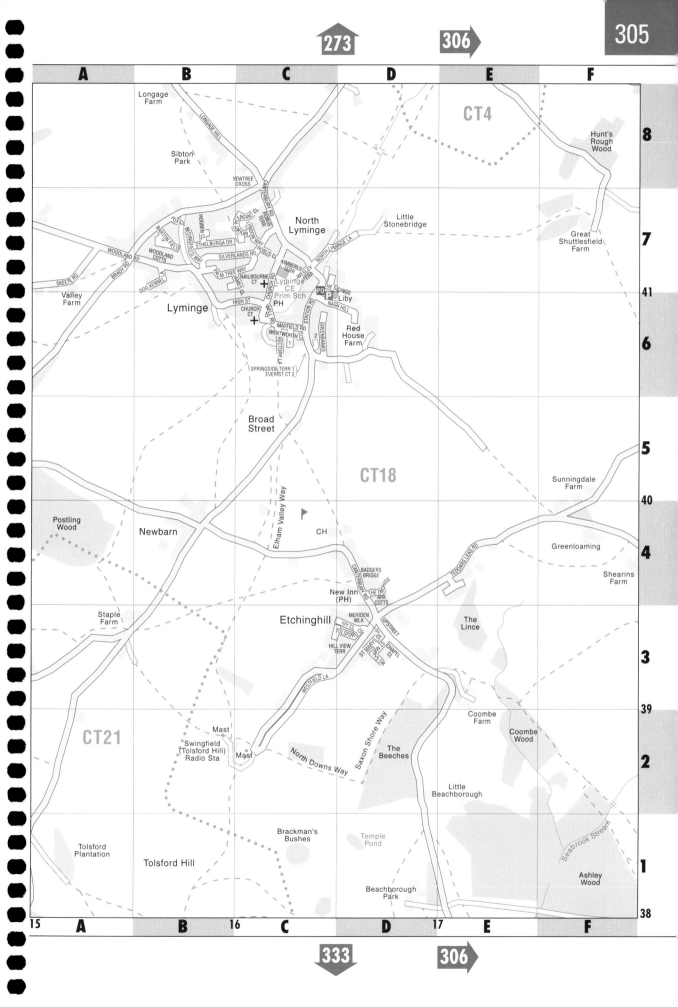

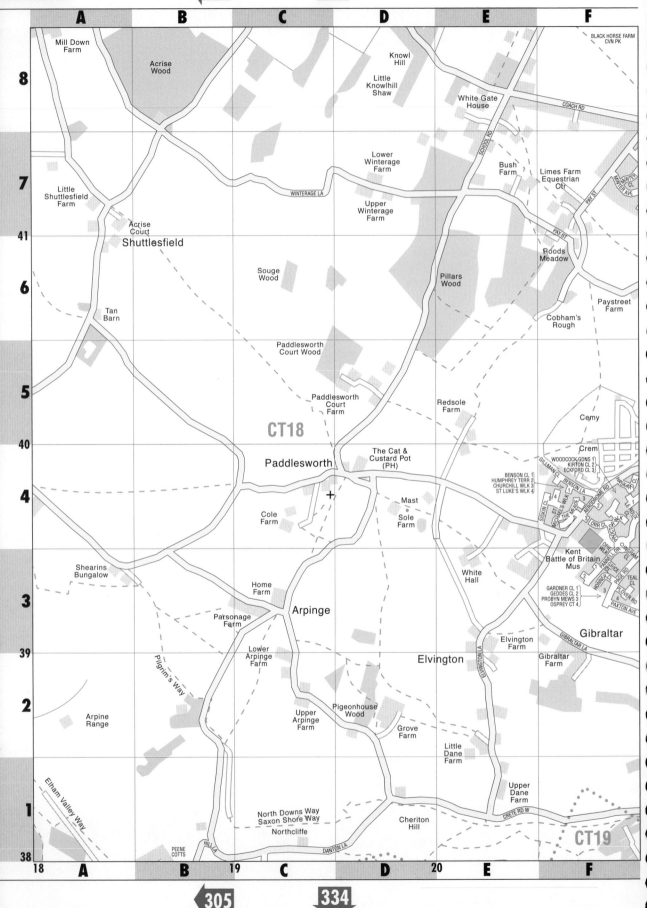

305
274

A   **B**   **C**   **D**   **E**   **F**

BLACK HORSE FARM
CVN PK

Mill Down
Farm

Acrise
Wood

Knowl
Hill

Little
Knowlhill
Shaw

White Gate
House

COACH RD

8

Little
Shuttlefield
Farm

Lower
Winterage
Farm

Bush
Farm

Limes Farm
Equestrian
Ctr

SCHOOL RD

PAY ST

WINTER CL

WINTER AVE

7

WINTERAGE LA

Upper
Winterage
Farm

PAY ST

Acrise
Court

41

Shuttlesfield

Souge
Wood

Pillars
Wood

Roods
Meadow

6

Tan
Barn

Paddlesworth
Court Wood

Cobham's
Rough

Paystreet
Farm

Paddlesworth
Court
Farm

Redsole
Farm

Cemy

5

Crem

40

CT18

Paddlesworth

The Cat &
Custard Pot
(PH)

WOODCOCK GDNS 1
KIRTON CL 2
ECKFORD CL 3

GILLMAN CL

BENSON LA

4

Cole
Farm

Mast

Sole
Farm

BENSON CL 1
HUMPHREY TERR 2
CHURCHILL WLK 3
ST LUKE'S WLK 4

SISKIN CL

ST MICHAEL'S WLK

AERODROME RD

THE MEADE

LE ROUX

Kent
Battle of Britain
Mus

Shearins
Bungalow

Home
Farm

White
Hall

LORR CL

PANFIELD DR

PAGE RD

TEAL CL

PLOVER RD

GARDNER CL 1
GEDDES CL 2
PROBYN MEWS 3
OSPREY CT 4

WYNNE CL

PARTRIDGE RD

INGRAM CL

3

Parsonage
Farm

Arpinge

Elvington
Farm

PAXTON AVE

Gibraltar

GIBRALTAR LA

39

Lower
Arpinge
Farm

Elvington

Gibraltar
Farm

Pilgrim's Way

ELVINGTON LA

2

Arpine
Range

Upper
Arpinge
Farm

Pigeonhouse
Wood

Grove
Farm

Little
Dane
Farm

Upper
Dane
Farm

1

Elham Valley Way

North Downs Way
Saxon Shore Way
Northcliffe

Cheriton
Hill

CRETE RD W

CT19

HILL LA

PEENE
COTTS

DANTON LA

38

18   **A**   **B**   **19**   **C**   **D**   **20**   **E**   **F**

305
334

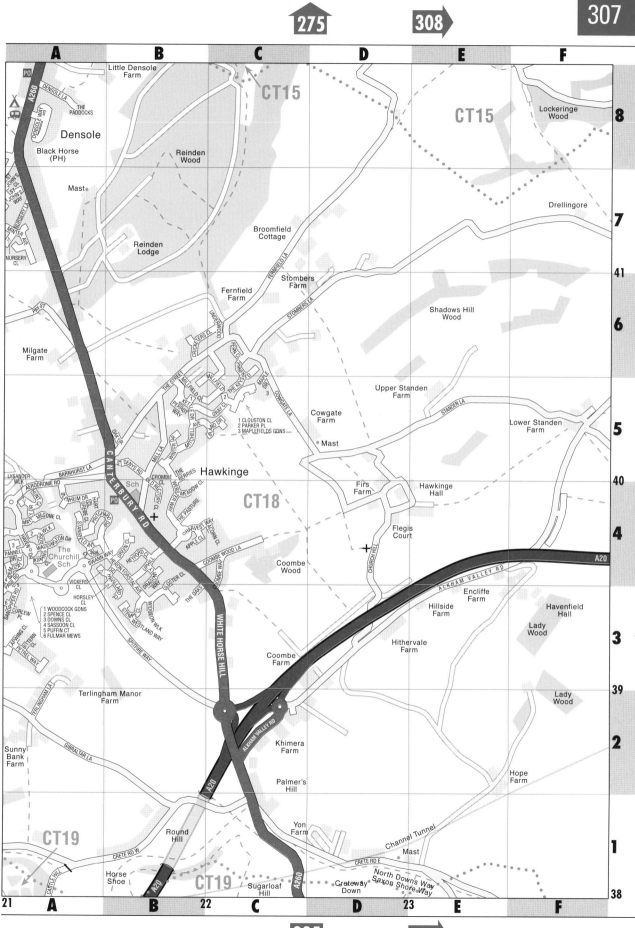

307
276

A B C D E F

8

Mount Ararat

Moorlands

Upton Farm House

South Alkham

Uplands Farm

HOGBROOK HILL LA

Lonebarn Farm

Poulton Farm

7

Drellingore Cottage

ALKHAM VALLEY RD

Ppg Sta

MEGGETT LA

Meggett Farm

Copt Hill Farm

Drellingore

41

Bramble Hill Cottage

CT15

Le Ferns Farm

6

5

Tumble Tye Farm

Capel Church Farm

BROADSOLE LA

YOUNG'S PL

LOWSLIP HILL

PATHFIELD COTTS

LADY GARN RD

THE STREET

Mill La

Chequers Inn (PH)

40

Hockley Sole

FORGE FIELD

QUEEN'S LEA

West Hougham

White Hill

CROOK'S COURT LA

GRAVEL LA

Capel Farm

SATMORE LA

Chalk Pit Wood

4

A20

Hurst Farm

HURST LA

Hollingbury Farm

SATMAR LA

Capel House Farm

Channel Tunnel

SATMORE LA

Great Satmar Farm

Dawkinge Wood

Swinge Hill

CT18

CAPEL ST

Satmar

3

A20

B2011

PO

GREEN LA

Capel-le-Ferne Prim Sch

WINEHOUSE LA

Abbot's Land Farm

The Royal Oak (PH)

39

Great Cauldham Farm

CAULDHAM LA

ELIZABETH DR

LANCASTER AVE

Masts

2

Mast

BEATRICE RD

ALEXANDRA RD

HELENA RD

AVONDALE RD

NEW DOVER RD

Capel Court Pk

Capel-le-Ferne

VICTORIA RD

CLARENCE RD

ALBERT RD

ALBANY RD

OLD DOVER RD

SEA VIEW CL

CAPEL ST

North Downs Way

Saxon Shore Way

Eagle's Nest East Cliff and Warren Country Park

REECE ADAMS HO

1

The Battle of Britain Meml

B2011

Steady Hole

The Warren

38
24 A B 25 C D 26 E F

335
307

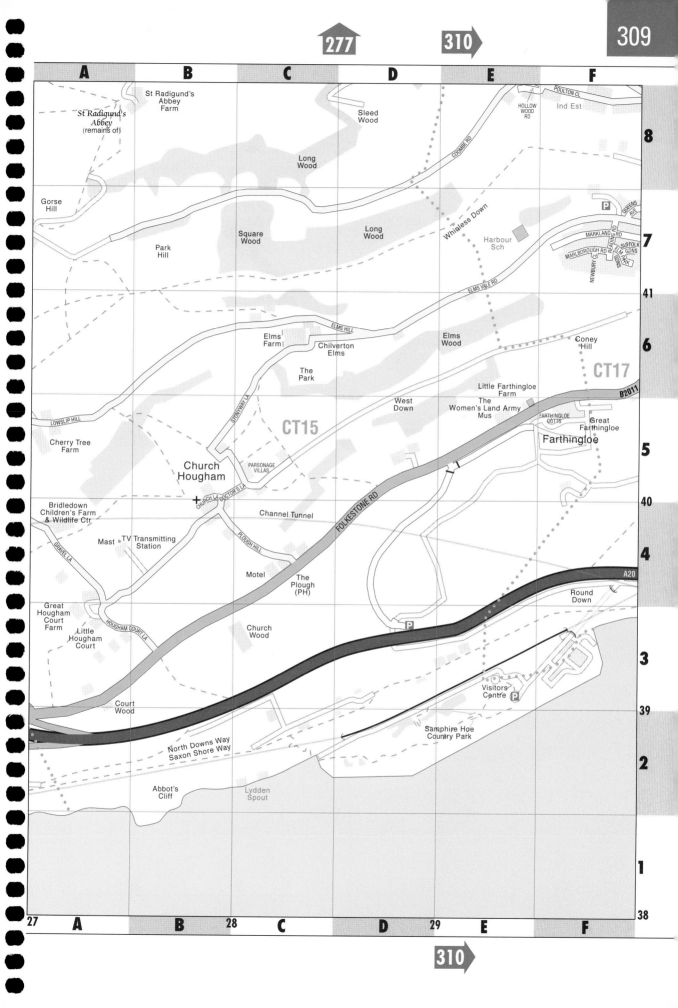

310

A B C D E F

8

St Radigund's
Abbey Farm

St Radigund's
Abbey
(remains of)

Sleed
Wood

HOLLOW
WOOD
RD

POULTON CL

Ind Est

Long
Wood

COOMBE RD

P

QUEENS AVE

Gorse
Hill

7

Park
Hill

Square
Wood

Long
Wood

Whinless Down

Harbour
Sch

MARKLAND RD

READING RD

SUFFOLK

ELM GDNS

MARLBOROUGH RD

NEWBURY CL

ELM GDNS PARK

ELMS VALE RD

41

6

Elms
Farm

ELMS HILL

Chilverton
Elms

Elms
Wood

Coney
Hill

The
Park

CT17

B2011

STONYWAY LA

West
Down

Little Farthingloe
Farm

LOWSLIP HILL

CT15

The
Women's Land Army
Mus

FARTHINGLOE
COTTS

Great
Farthingloe

Farthingloe

5

Cherry Tree
Farm

Church
Hougham

PARSONAGE
VILLAS

+

CHURCH LA

DOCTOR'S LA

40

Bridledown
Children's Farm
& Wildlife Ctr

Channel Tunnel

FOLKESTONE RD

Mast

TV Transmitting
Station

PLOUGH HILL

4

A20

GRAVEL LA

Motel

The
Plough
(PH)

Round
Down

Great
Hougham
Court Farm

HOUGHAM COURT LA

Church
Wood

P

Little
Hougham
Court

3

Visitors
Centre

P

Court
Wood

39

North Downs Way
Saxon Shore Way

Samphire Hoe
Country Park

2

Abbot's
Cliff

Lydden
Spout

1

27 A B 28 C D 29 E F 38

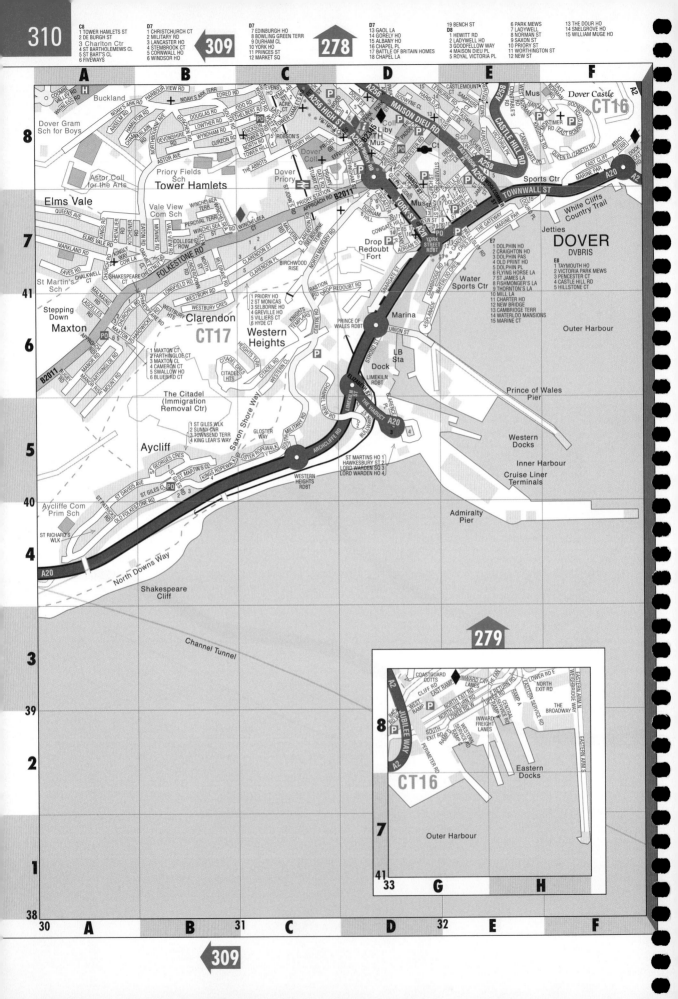

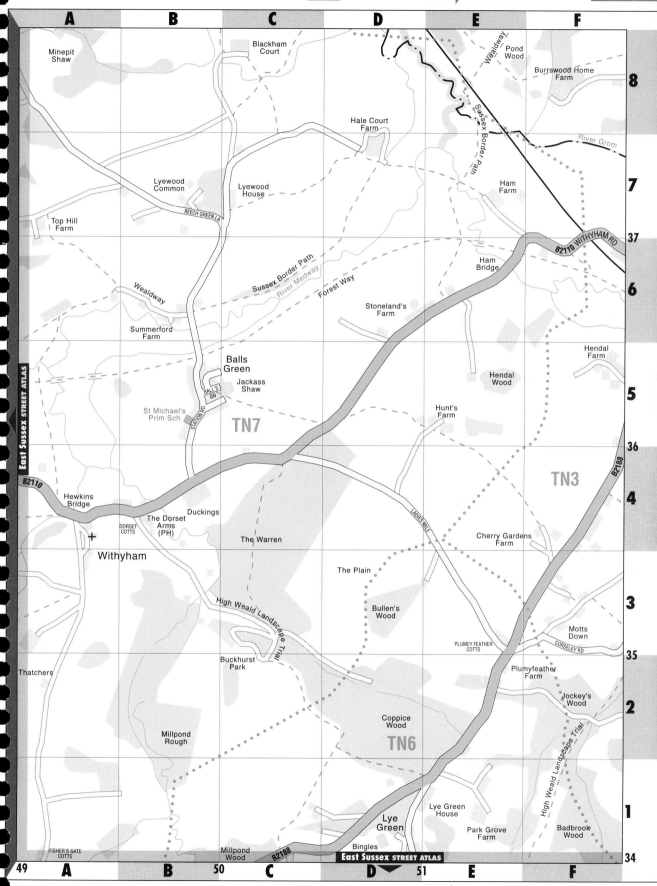

East Sussex STREET ATLAS

A B C D E F

8

Beech
Wood

GROOMBRIDGE RD

BIRD IN HAND ST

GROOMBRIDGE HILL B2110

PH
THE
WALKS

Burrswood

Florence
Farm

River Grom

Groombridge
Place Gardens

Tunbridge Wells Ciclular Walk

Pokehill

Groombridge
Place

YEW TREE
COTTS

Southern
Sewage Works

Spa Valley Rly

Groombridge

PH

JASMINE COTTS 1
THE CRESCENT 2
THE HOMESTEAD 3
SENLAC PL 4
FERDINAND TERR 5
SOMERSET VILLAS 6
PROVIDENCE COTTS 7

BURRSWOOD
VILLAS

PO

South
Farm

7

Tithe
Barn

WITHYHAM RD

OAKLAND
VILLAS

ORCHARD RISE

OAKLANDS RD

MEADOW RD

SPRINGFIELD RD

NEWTON WLL GWS

STATION RD

CROMICK

Groombridge

Lealands
Farm

BROADWATER FOREST LA

Broadwater
Bridge

37

B2110

B2188

FLORANCE LA

BROAD OAK

WALLIS
FIELD

LYNWOOD
THE CLOSE

LEALANDS CL

Groombridge
St Thomas' CE
Prim Sch

Little
Quarry
Farm

Birchden
Farm

6

THE RIDGE

Hendal
Bridge

Forest Way

BIRCHDEN
COTTS

Aytton's
Wood

Birchden

ERIDGE RD

The
Warren

Alksford
Farm

Cemy

CORSELEY RD

High Weald Landscape Trail

Park
Corner

5

Sherlock's
Wood

TN3

36

Mottsmill Stream

Harrison's Rocks

Bridgers

4

Sherlock's
Farm

Glen
Andred

Birchden
Wood

Pinstraw
Farm

Birchett's
Wood

Old
Birchden
Farm

Forge
Farm

3

Mott's
Mill

Leyswood

LC

FORGE RD

Cobbarn
House

Cobbarn

THE FORSTAL

A26

Rocks
Wood

Hamsell
Wood
Farm

35

THE OLD
RIDING
SCHOOL

Ligg's
Wood

2

Bullfinches

Mott's
Farm

Hamsell
Bridge

Square
Shaw

Penns in
the Rocks

Sussex Border Path

Holden
Wood

P

Eridge

PH

Hamsell
Shaw

1

Marchant
Wood

Renby
Farm

Hamsell
Farm

A26

Big
Wigsell

Little
Wigsell

Hollybridge
Wood

34

TN6

A26 Uckfield

52 A B 53 C D 54 E F

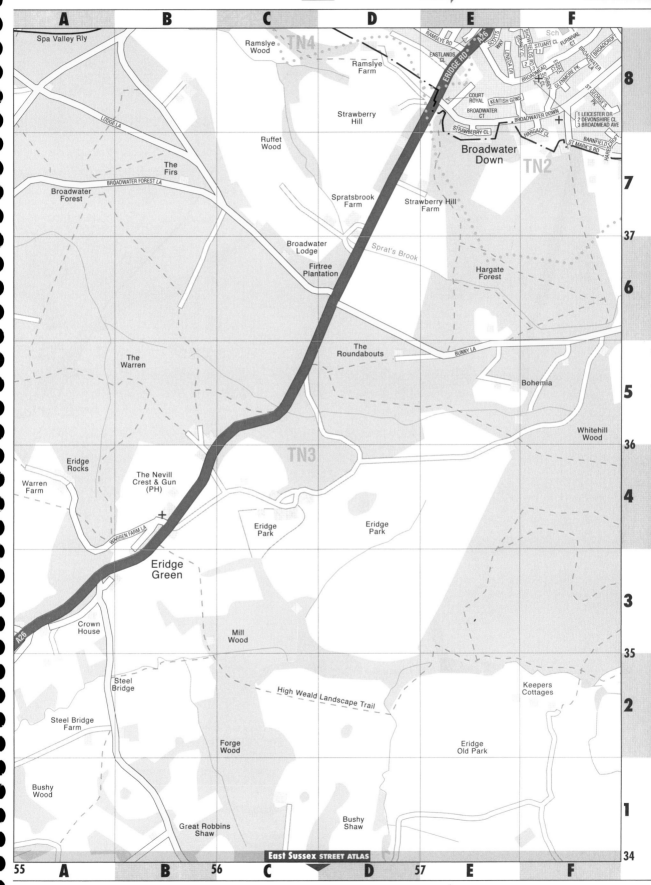

A B C D E F

8

7

37

6

5

36

4

3

35

2

1

34

Spa Valley Rly

Ramslye Wood

TN4

Ramslye Farm

RAMSLYE RD

EASTLANDS CL

SCOTS WAY

SNOWFIELDS RD

ERIDGE RD

A26

STUART CL

STANLEY CL

LENEDA DR

FURNIVAL CT

BROADMEAD

BROADCROFT

BROADWATER

Sch

Strawberry Hill

COURT ROYAL

BROADWATER CT

KENTISH GDNS

GLENMORE PK

ST GEORGE'S

BROADWATER DOWN

HARGATE CL

ST GEORGE'S PK

1 LEICESTER DR
2 DEVONSHIRE CL
3 BROADMEAD AVE

BARNFIELD RD

HARES CROFT

ST MARK'S RD

Ruffet Wood

LODGE LA

The Firs

BROADWATER FOREST LA

Broadwater Forest

Sprat's Brook

Spratsbrook Farm

Broadwater Lodge

Firtree Plantation

Strawberry Hill Farm

Broadwater Down

TN2

Hargate Forest

The Warren

The Roundabouts

BUNNY LA

Bohemia

Whitehill Wood

TN3

Eridge Rocks

Warren Farm

The Nevill Crest & Gun (PH)

WARREN FARM LA

Eridge Green

Crown House

Eridge Park

Eridge Park

Mill Wood

High Weald Landscape Trail

Keepers Cottages

Steel Bridge

Steel Bridge Farm

Forge Wood

Eridge Old Park

Bushy Wood

Great Robbins Shaw

Bushy Shaw

A26

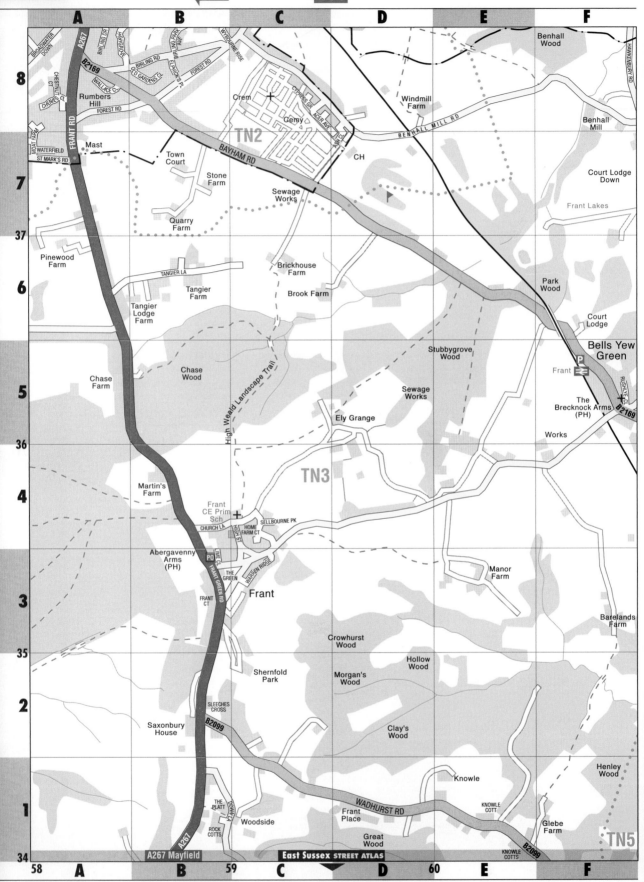

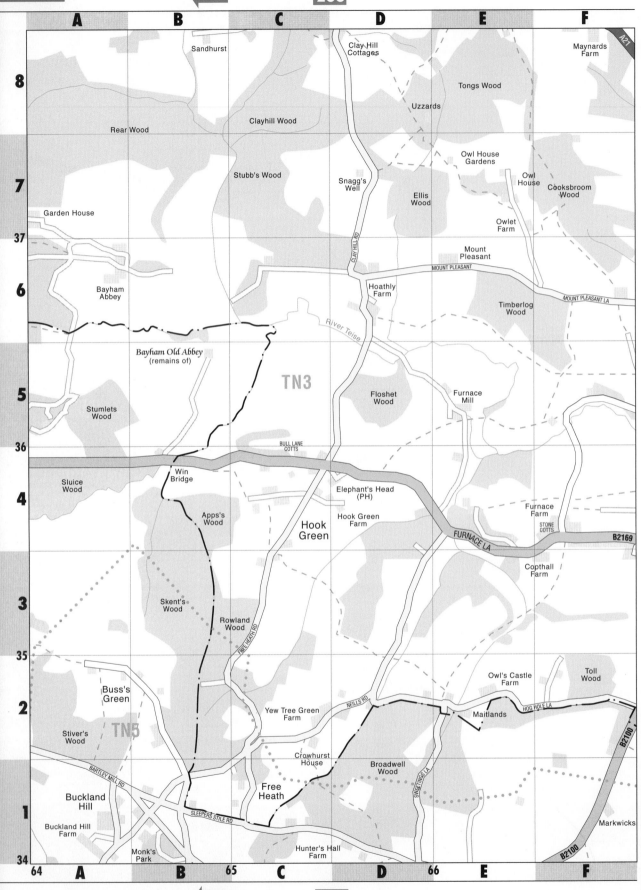

315
288

A B C D E F

A21

Sandhurst

Clay Hill Cottages

Maynards Farm

8

Tongs Wood

Uzzards

Clayhill Wood

Rear Wood

Stubb's Wood

Owl House Gardens

7

Snagg's Well

Ellis Wood

Owl House

Cooksbroom Wood

Garden House

Owlet Farm

37

Mount Pleasant

MOUNT PLEASANT

6

Bayham Abbey

Hoathly Farm

MOUNT PLEASANT LA

Timberlog Wood

River Teise

Bayham Old Abbey (remains of)

TN3

5

Stumlets Wood

Floshet Wood

Furnace Mill

36

BULL LANE COTTS

Win Bridge

Elephant's Head (PH)

Furnace Farm

4

Sluice Wood

Apps's Wood

Hook Green Farm

Hook Green

STONE COTTS

B2169

Copthall Farm

3

Skent's Wood

Rowland Wood

FREE HEATH RD

35

Owl's Castle Farm

Toll Wood

Buss's Green

2

TN5

Yew Tree Green Farm

NEILLS RD

Maitlands

HOG HOLE LA

Stiver's Wood

B2100

Crowhurst House

Broadwell Wood

SWEETINGS LA

Buckland Hill

BARTLEY MILL RD

Free Heath

1

Buckland Hill Farm

SLEEPERS STILE RD

Markwicks

34

Monk's Park

Hunter's Hall Farm

B2100

64 A B 65 C D 66 E F

315
337

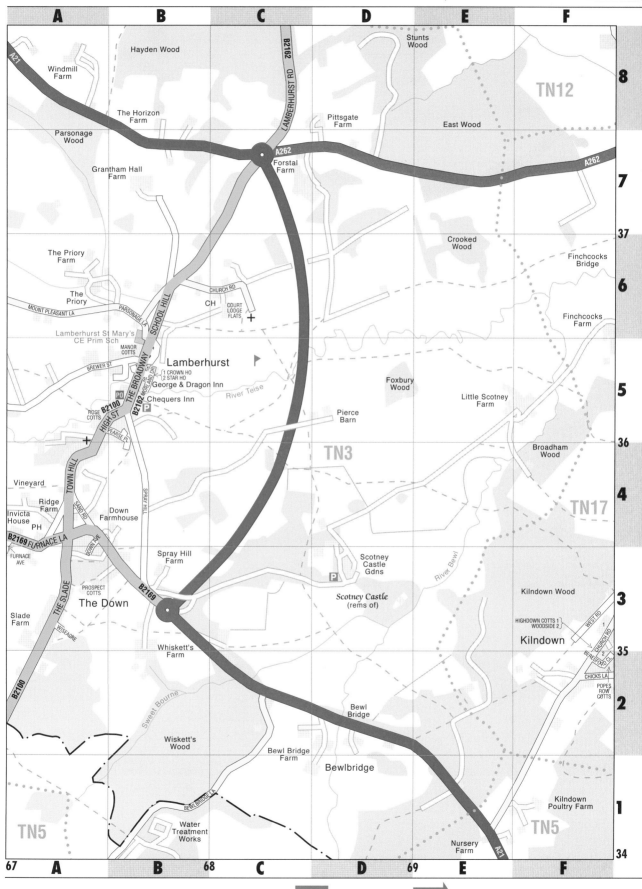

289
318
338
318

A B C D E F

8 7 37 6 5 36 4 3 35 2 1 34

TN12

Stunts Wood

Hayden Wood

Windmill Farm

A21

The Horizon Farm

Parsonage Wood

Pittsgate Farm

East Wood

LAMBERHURST RD

B2162

Grantham Hall Farm

A262

Forstal Farm

A262

Crooked Wood

Finchcocks Bridge

The Priory Farm

MOUNT PLEASANT LA

The Priory

PARSONAGE LA

SCHOOL HILL

CHURCH RD

CH

COURT LODGE FLATS

Finchcocks Farm

Lamberhurst St Mary's CE Prim Sch

MANOR COTTS

BREWER ST

Lamberhurst

THE BROADWAY

MORTLAND DRI

1 CROWN HO
2 STAR HO

George & Dragon Inn

PO

Chequers Inn

B2162

River Teise

Foxbury Wood

Little Scotney Farm

ROSE COTTS

B2100

HIGH ST

P

PEARSE PL

Pierce Barn

TN3

Broadham Wood

Vineyard

TOWN HILL

SAND RD

SPRAY HILL

Ridge Farm

Down Farmhouse

TN17

Invicta House

PH

DOWN AVE

Spray Hill Farm

B2169 FURNACE LA

FURNACE AVE

THE SLADE

PROSPECT COTTS

WISEACRE

B2169

Scotney Castle Gdns

P

River Bewl

Kilndown Wood

Slade Farm

The Down

Scotney Castle (rems of)

HIGHDOWN COTTS 1
WOODSIDE 2

WEST RD

Kilndown

CHURCH RD

B2100

Whiskett's Farm

BERESFORD CL

CHICKS LA

POPES ROW COTTS

Sweet Bourne

Bewl Bridge

Bewlbridge

Wiskett's Wood

Bewl Bridge Farm

BEWL BRIDGE LA

Water Treatment Works

Kilndown Poultry Farm

TN5

TN5

Nursery Farm

A21

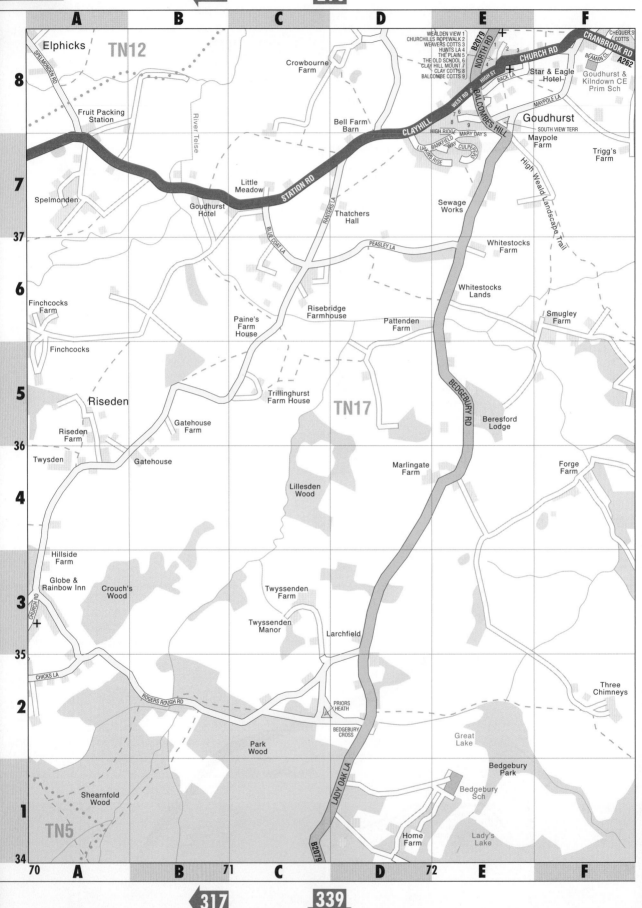

317
290

Elphicks

TN12

Crowbourne
Farm

WEALDEN VIEW 1
CHURCHILLS ROPEWALK 2
WEAVERS COTTS 3
HUNTS LA 4
THE PLAIN 5
THE OLD SCHOOL 6
CLAY HILL MOUNT 7
CLAY COTTS 8
BALCOMBE COTTS 9

B2079

NORTH RD

CHURCH RD

CRANBROOK RD

A262

CHEQUER'S
COTTS

BEAMAN CL

Star & Eagle
Hotel

Goudhurst &
Kilndown CE
Prim Sch

Fruit Packing
Station

WEST RD

HIGH ST

BACK LA

1
2
3
4

Goudhurst

SOUTH VIEW TERR

Maypole
Farm

Trigg's
Farm

River Teise

Bell Farm
Barn

CLAYHILL

BALCOMBES HILL

5

6

7
8
9

HIGH RIDGE

BANKFIELD

WAY

CULPEPERS

MARY DAY'S

LURKINS RISE

MAYPOLE LA

Spelmonden

Little
Meadow

STATION RD

Goudhurst
Hotel

Thatchers
Hall

RANTERS LA

BLUE COAT LA

Sewage
Works

Whitestocks
Farm

High Weald Landscape Trail

37

PEASLEY LA

Finchcocks
Farm

Paine's
Farm
House

Risebridge
Farmhouse

Pattenden
Farm

Whitestocks
Lands

Smugley
Farm

Finchcocks

Riseden

Trillinghurst
Farm House

TN17

BEDGEBURY RD

Beresford
Lodge

Gatehouse
Farm

Riseden
Farm

36

Twysden

Gatehouse

Lillesden
Wood

Marlingate
Farm

Forge
Farm

Hillside
Farm

Globe &
Rainbow Inn

Crouch's
Wood

CHURCH RD

Twyssenden
Farm

Three
Chimneys

CHICKS LA

35

Twyssenden
Manor

Larchfield

ROGERS ROUGH RD

PRIORS
HEATH

Bedgebury
Cross

Great
Lake

Park
Wood

LADY OAK LA

Bedgebury
Park

Bedgebury
Sch

Shearnfold
Wood

TN5

Home
Farm

Lady's
Lake

B2079

317
339

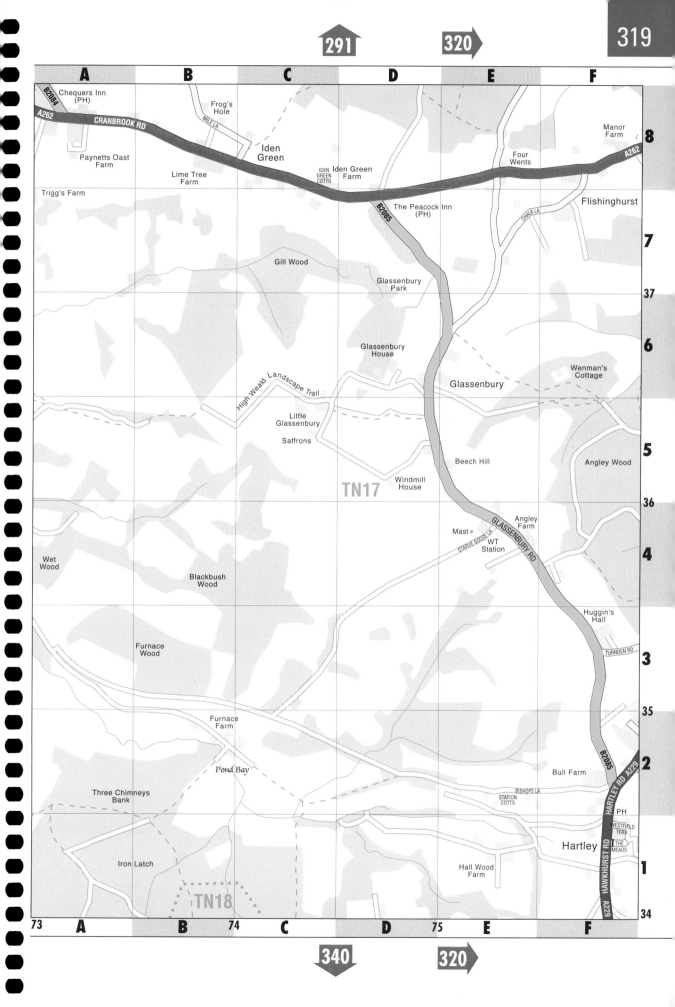

A B C D E F

8

Chequers Inn (PH)
B2084
A262
CRANBROOK RD
Paynetts Oast Farm
Frog's Hole
MILE LA
Iden Green
Lime Tree Farm
IDEN GREEN COTTS
Iden Green Farm
Trigg's Farm
B2085
The Peacock Inn (PH)
Manor Farm
A262
Four Wents
CHALK LA
Flishinghurst

7

Gill Wood
Glassenbury Park

37

6

Glassenbury House
Glassenbury
Wenman's Cottage

High Weald Landscape Trail
Little Glassenbury
Saffrons
Angley Wood

5

Beech Hill
Windmill House
TN17

36

Mast
Angley Farm
WT Station
STARVE GOOSE LA
GLASSENBURY RD

4

Wet Wood
Blackbush Wood
Huggin's Hall
TURNDEN RD

3

Furnace Wood
Furnace Farm

35

B2085
Bull Farm
HARTLEY RD A229

2

Pond Bay
BISHOPS LA
STATION COTTS
PH
WESTFIELD TERR
THE MEADS
Hartley
Three Chimneys Bank

1

Iron Latch
Hall Wood Farm
HAWKHURST RD
A229
TN18

34

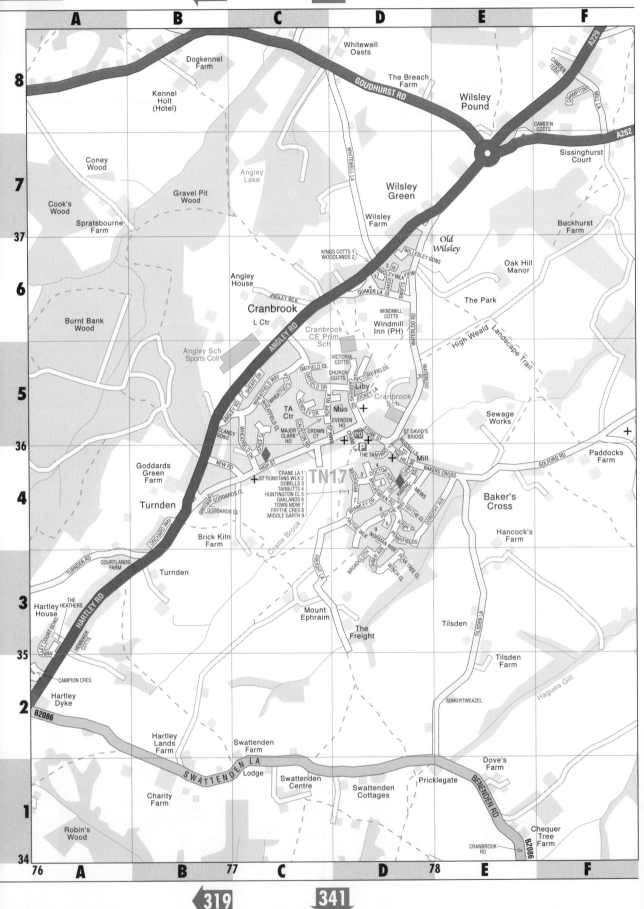

319
292

A B C D E F

8

Dogkennel Farm

Whitewell Oasts

The Breach Farm

GOUDHURST RD

Wilsley Pound

CAMDEN TERR

A229

CRAMPTONS

MILL LA

CAMDEN COTTS

A262

Kennel Holt (Hotel)

7

Coney Wood

Gravel Pit Wood

Angley Lake

WHITEWELL LA

Wilsley Green

Sissinghurst Court

Cook's Wood

Spratsbourne Farm

Wilsley Farm

Buckhurst Farm

37

KINGS COTTS 1
WOODLANDS 2

Old Wilsley

WILLESLEY GDNS

ANGLEY WLK

THE VIEW

SWIFTS

QUAKER LA

QUAKER LA

Oak Hill Manor

6

Angley House

ANGLEY WLK

Cranbrook

L Ctr

Cranbrook CE Prim Sch

WINDMILL COTTS

Windmill Inn (PH)

WATERLOO RD

The Park

Burnt Bank Wood

Angley Sch Sports Coll

ANGLEY RD

VICTORIA COTTS

RECTORY FIELDS

High Weald Landscape Trail

OATFIELD CL

CHURCH COTTS

CARRIERS RD

Liby

WATERLOO RD

5

SHEAFE DR

WHEATFIELD WAY

WHEATFIELD

OATFIELD DR

ROPE WLK

HENDLY DR

Mus

JOCKEY LA

Cranbrook Sch

Sewage Works

TA Ctr

BANK S

EVENDEN HO

STONE ST

ST DAVID'S BRIDGE

36

CLANCY GDNS

WHEATFIELD DR

CAUSTON RD

MAJOR CLARK HO

CROWN CT

CRANE LA

RUSSELL'S RD

THE HILL

Mill

PO
P
The Tanyard

GOLFORD RD

Paddocks Farm

Goddards Green Farm

NEW RD

JOCKEY LA

HIGH ST

CRANE LA 1
ST DUNSTANS WLK 2
DOBELLS 3
TARBUTTS 4
HUNTINGTON CL 5
OAKLANDS 6
TOWN MDW 7
FRYTHE CRES 8
MIDDLE GARTH 9.

TN17

DOCTOR
BUSK DR

BAKERS CROSS

MEWS

RAMMELL

4

Turnden

GREENS

GODDARDS CL

GODDARDS CL

Brick Kiln Farm

Crane Brook

BRAMLEY DR

BRICKENDEN RD

FRYTHE WY

FRYTHE CL

DOROTHY AVE

Baker's Cross

Hancock's Farm

KIRBY CL

PENNYFIELDS

3

ORCHARD WAY

TURNDEN RD

COURTLANDS FARM

Turnden

FREIGHT LA

FRYTHE WLK

NORMAN RISE

BAKER AVE

WINCH CL

PEAR TREE CL

Tilsden

TILSDEN LA

HARTLEY RD

THE HEATHERS

Hartley House

HENNIKER COTTS

Mount Ephraim

The Freight

BROADCLOTH

Tilsden Farm

35

HARTLEY COURT GDNS

CAMPION CRES

Hartley Dyke

SINKERTWEAZEL

Hagues Gill

2

B2086

Hartley Lands Farm

Swattenden Farm

SWATTENDEN LA

Lodge

Swattenden Centre

Swattenden Cottages

Pricklegate

Dove's Farm

BENENDEN RD

B2086

1

Charity Farm

Robin's Wood

CRANBROOK RD

Chequer Tree Farm

34

76 A 77 B C 77 D 78 E F

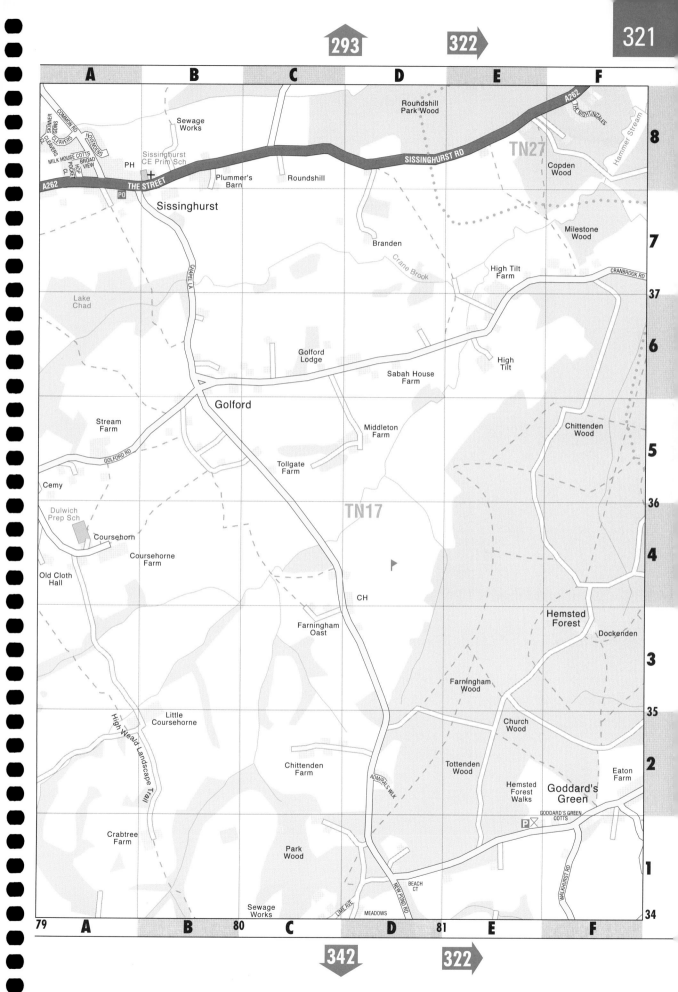

A   B   C   D   E   F

Roundshill Park Wood

A262

THE NIGHTINGALES

Hammer Stream

TN27

Copden Wood

SISSINGHURST RD

8

COMMON RD

SKINNER CLEAVERS CL

SNEBS CLEAVERS CL

HOP POCKET

MILK HOUSE COTTS

BROAD VIEW

PH

Sewage Works

Sissinghurst CE Prim Sch

Plummer's Barn

Roundshill

Branden

Milestone Wood

7

A262

THE STREET

PO

Sissinghurst

CHAPEL LA

Crane Brook

High Tilt Farm

CRANBROOK RD

37

Lake Chad

Golford Lodge

Sabah House Farm

High Tilt

6

Stream Farm

Golford

GOLFORD RD

Middleton Farm

Chittenden Wood

5

Cemy

Tollgate Farm

TN17

36

Dulwich Prep Sch

Coursehorn

4

Old Cloth Hall

Coursehorne Farm

CH

Hemsted Forest

Dockenden

3

Farningham Oast

Farningham Wood

Little Coursehorne

Church Wood

35

High Weald Landscape Trail

Chittenden Farm

ADMIRALS WLK

Tottenden Wood

Hemsted Forest Walks

Eaton Farm

Goddard's Green

2

Crabtree Farm

Park Wood

NEW POND RD

GODDARD'S GREEN COTTS

P

WALKHURST RD

1

Sewage Works

LIME AVE

MEADOWS

BEACH CT

34

321
294

321
343

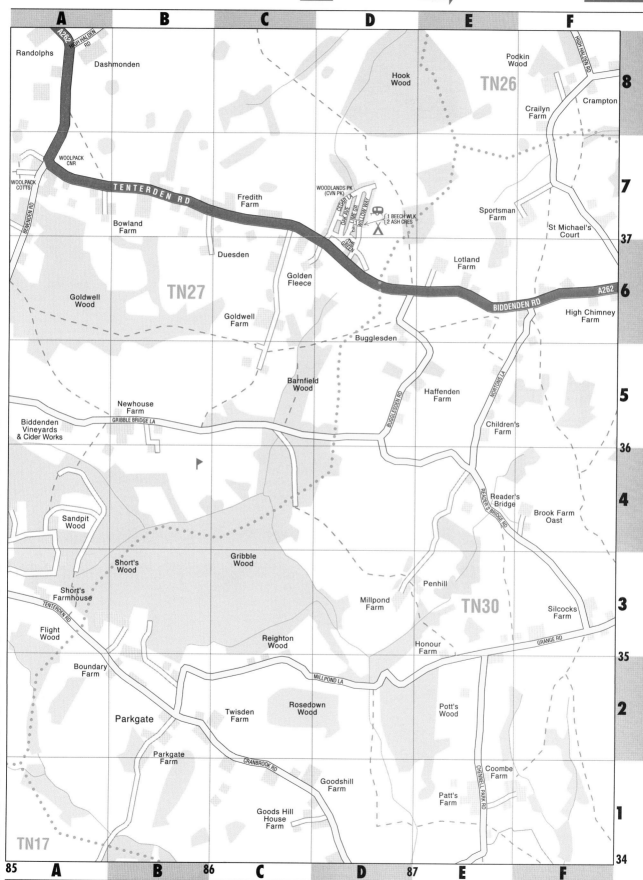

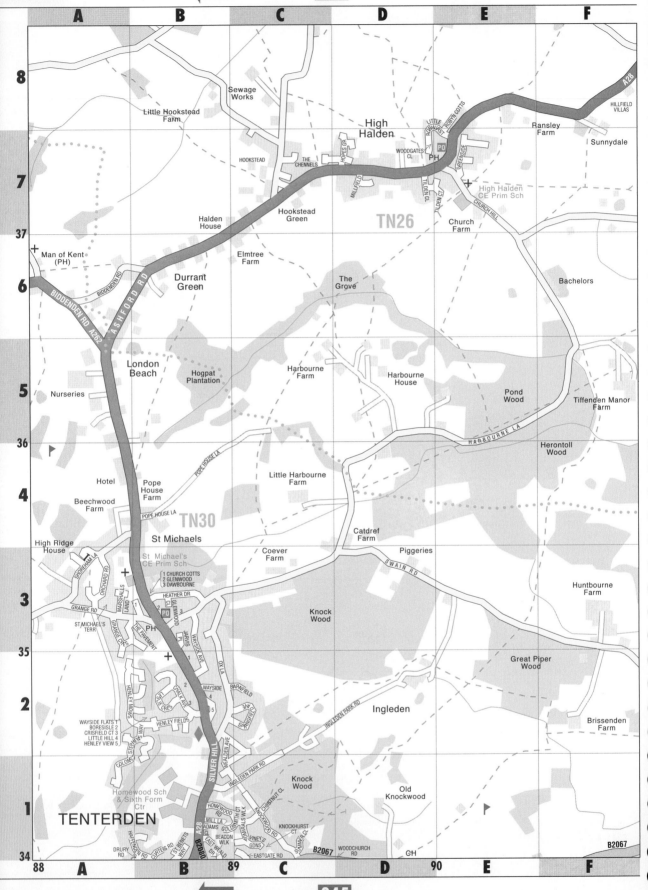

A   B   C   D   E   F

8

7

37

6

5

36

4

3

35

2

1

34

88   A   B   89   C   D   90   E   F

Sewage Works

Little Hookstead Farm

HOOKSTEAD

THE CHENNELS

High Halden

LITTLE ROBHURST
ROBYN COTTS
WOODGATES CL
PH
PO
GREENSIDE

HOPES GR

MILLFIELD

TILDEN CL

TILDEN CT

High Halden CE Prim Sch

Church Hill

HILLFIELD VILLAS

Ransley Farm

Sunnydale

Hookstead Green

Halden House

TN26

Church Farm

Elmtree Farm

Man of Kent (PH)

BIDDENDEN RD A262

BIDDENDEN RD

ASHFORD RD

Durrant Green

The Grove

Bachelors

London Beach

Hogpat Plantation

Harbourne Farm

Harbourne House

Pond Wood

Tiffenden Manor Farm

Nurseries

HARBOURNE LA

Herontoll Wood

Hotel

POPE HOUSE LA

Little Harbourne Farm

Beechwood Farm

Pope House Farm

POPE HOUSE LA

TN30

St Michaels

High Ridge House

St Michael's CE Prim Sch

1 CHURCH COTTS
2 GLENWOOD
3 DAWBOURNE

Catdref Farm

Coever Farm

Piggeries

SWAIN RD

Huntbourne Farm

SHOREHAM LA

ORCHARD RD

MARSHALLS LAND

HEATHER DR

GLENWOOD CL

PO

GRANGE RD

ST MICHAEL'S TERR

GRANGE CRES

THE PAVEMENT

PH

JARVIS PL

WAYSIDE AVE

Knock Wood

Great Piper Wood

WAYSIDE FLATS 1
BORESISLE 2
CRISFIELD CT 3
LITTLE HILL 4
HENLEY VIEW 5

HENLEY MDW

THE CRES

CHALK AVE

OXLEY LA

WAYSIDE

BARFIELD

Ingleden

Brissenden Farm

CALONG

STEPHENS WAY

HENLEY FIELDS

SILVER HILL

VFEALDEN AVE

INGLEDEN PARK RD

INGLEDEN PARK RD

Homewood Sch & Sixth Form Ctr

TENTERDEN

HOMEWOOD RD

MILL LA

ADAMS

HIGH ST

B2080

CURTEIS RD

ST BENETS WAY

EAST WEALD

DRURY RD

EASTGATE RD

GOLDSMITH CT

BEACON WLK

VINEY'S GDNS

STONNER CL

B2067

Knock Wood

CHESTNUT CL

KNOCKWOOD RD

Old Knockwood

WOODCHURCH RD

KNOCKHURST CT

CH

B2067

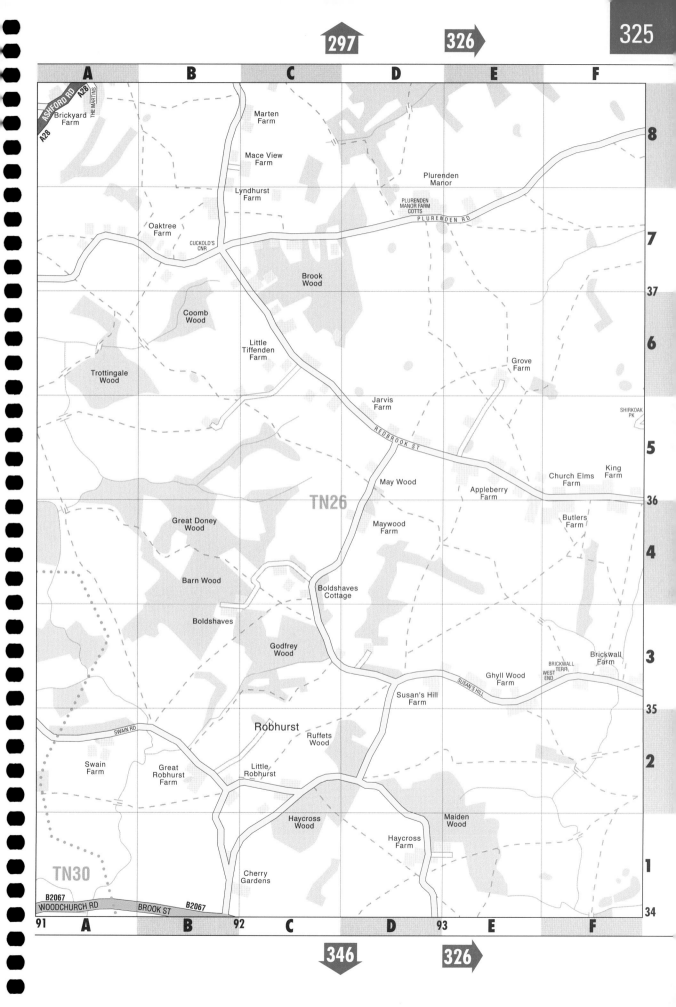

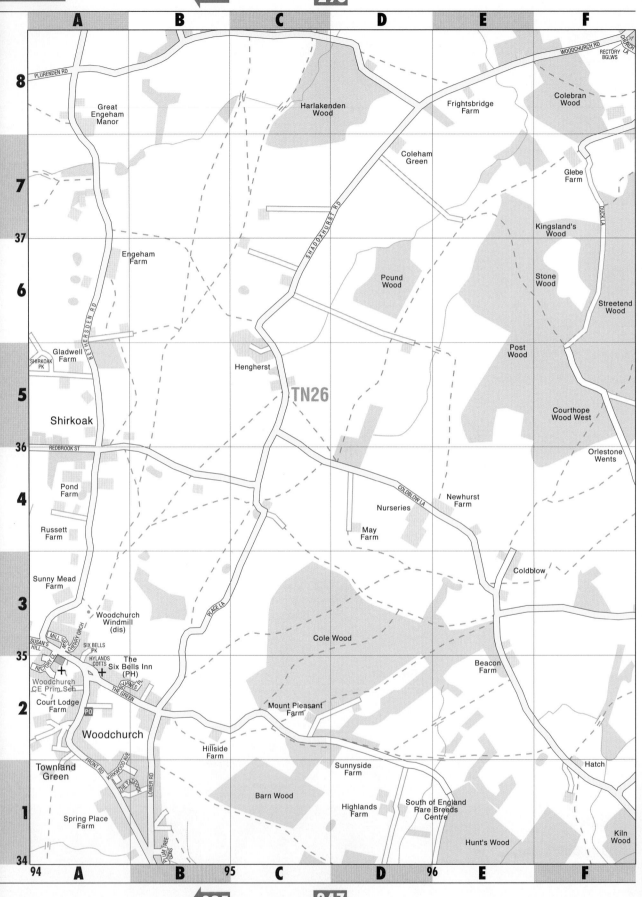

A | B | C | D | E | F

8
PLURENDEN RD
Great Engeham Manor
Harlakenden Wood
Frightsbridge Farm
Colebran Wood
WOODCHURCH RD
RECTORY BGLWS
CHURCH LA

Coleham Green

7
Engeham Farm
Glebe Farm
Kingsland's Wood
DUCK LA

37

6
SHADOXHURST RD
Pound Wood
Stone Wood
Streetend Wood

Gladwell Farm
SHIRKOAK PK
BETHERSDEN RD
Hengherst
Post Wood

5
Shirkoak
TN26
Courthope Wood West

36
REDBROOK ST
Orlestone Wents

4
Pond Farm
COLDBLOW LA
Nurseries
Newhurst Farm

Russett Farm
May Farm

Coldblow

3
Sunny Mead Farm
Woodchurch Windmill (dis)
PLACE LA
Cole Wood

MILL VW
SUSAN'S HILL
CHERRY ORCH
SIX BELLS PK
Beacon Farm

35
RECTORY LA
HYLANDS COTTS
The Six Bells Inn (PH)
LYDNES
Woodchurch CE Prim Sch

2
Court Lodge Farm
PO
THE GREEN
Mount Pleasant Farm
Hatch

Woodchurch
Hillside Farm
Sunnyside Farm

1
Townland Green
FRONT RD
KIRKWOOD AVE
THE EAGLE
LOWER RD
Barn Wood
Highlands Farm
South of England Rare Breeds Centre
Kiln Wood

Spring Place Farm
PLUM TREE GDNS
Hunt's Wood

34
94 | A | B | 95 | C | D | 96 | E | F

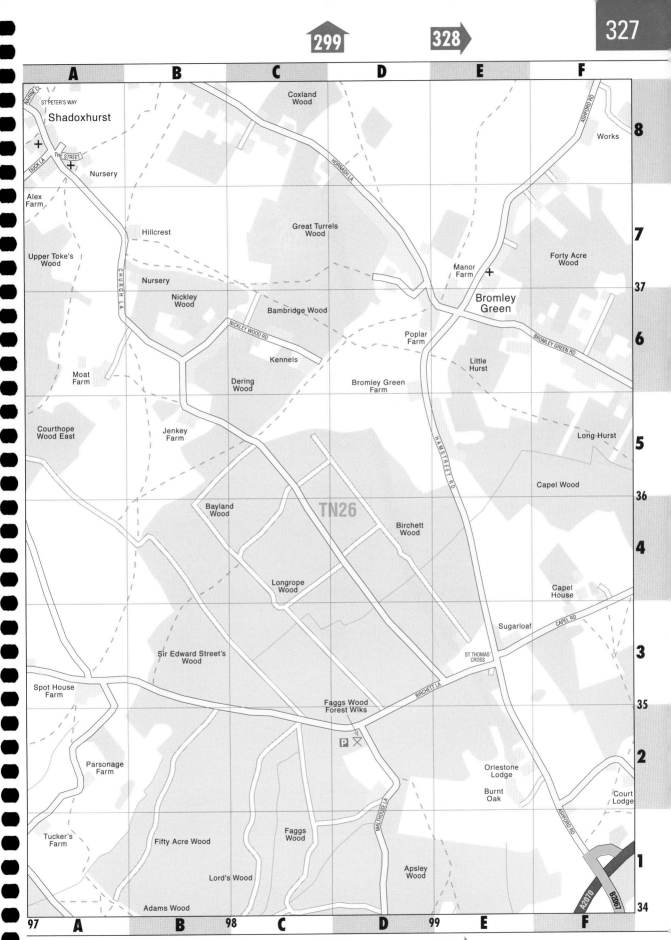

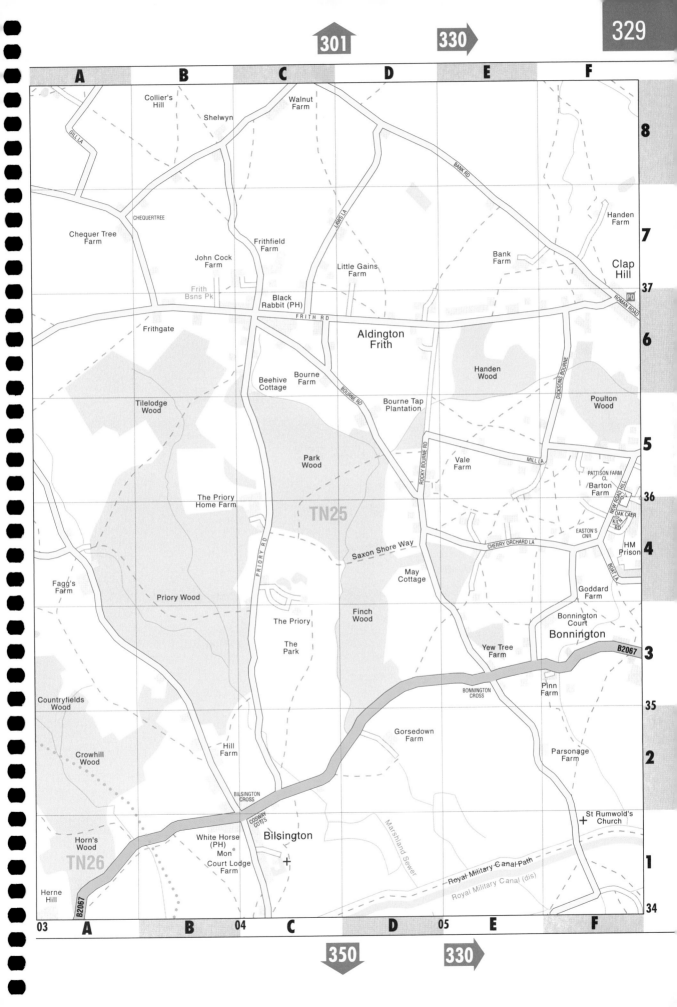

329
302

A B C D E F

8

Woodleas Farm
Backhouse Wood
Bested Hill
Partridge Plantation
Partridge Farm

7

Symnells
Little Goldwell Farm
The Paddock
Round Wood

Stonestreet Green
CALLEYWELL LA
GOLDWELL LA
Hogben Farm
Hungry Down

37

Goldwell Farm
CHURCH LA

Aldington
LONGSFIELD
QUARRY WOOD
GOLDWELL CL
BAGSTONE HOLLOW
CHURCH VIEW
Lower Park Farm

6

MOUNT PLEASANT
EARLSFIELD
WALNUT RIDGE
GOLDWELL HOS
Burch's Rough

The Walnut Tree Inn
ALDINGTON CNR
GOLDWELL HOS
Middle Park Farm
FORGE HILL
Aldington Prim Sch

5

Cobb's Hall
TN25
Court Lodge Farm

Blackthorn Wood

36

Pattison's Farm
Ruffin's Hill

4

Stockshill Wood
Saxon Shore Way
Postling Green
CT21
Upper Park Farm
B2067

BOAT LA
South Hurst
St John's Wood
Copperhurst

Wybourn Farm
Wood of Pan
KNOLL HILL
Bolden Wood
Dunk's Rough
Fostums Land
Honeypot Farm

3

White's Wood
Knoll Wood
Aldington Knoll
Curtis Wood

Golden Hurst

35

Knoll Farm

2

Goldenhurst Farm
Falconhurst
Marwood Farm
Honeypot Cottage
GIGGER'S GREEN RD
Royal Military Canal Path

1

Royal Military Canal (dis)
ROYAL MILITARY RD
Hoorne's Sewer
CT21

34

Marshland Sewer
Gigger's Green Bridge
Hurst Poultry Farm

06 A B 07 C D 08 E F

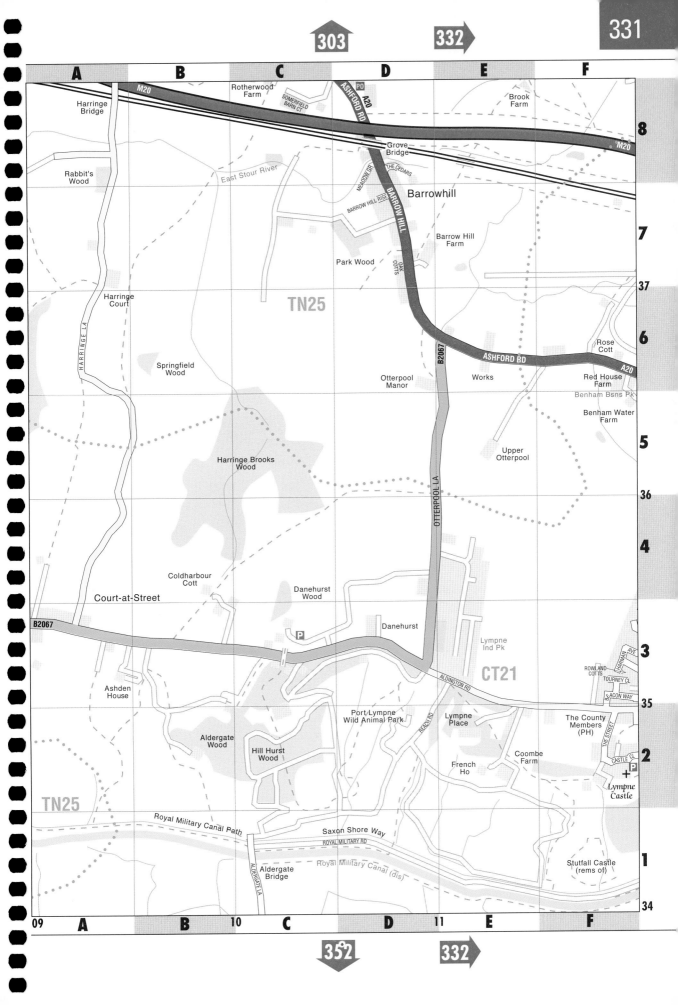

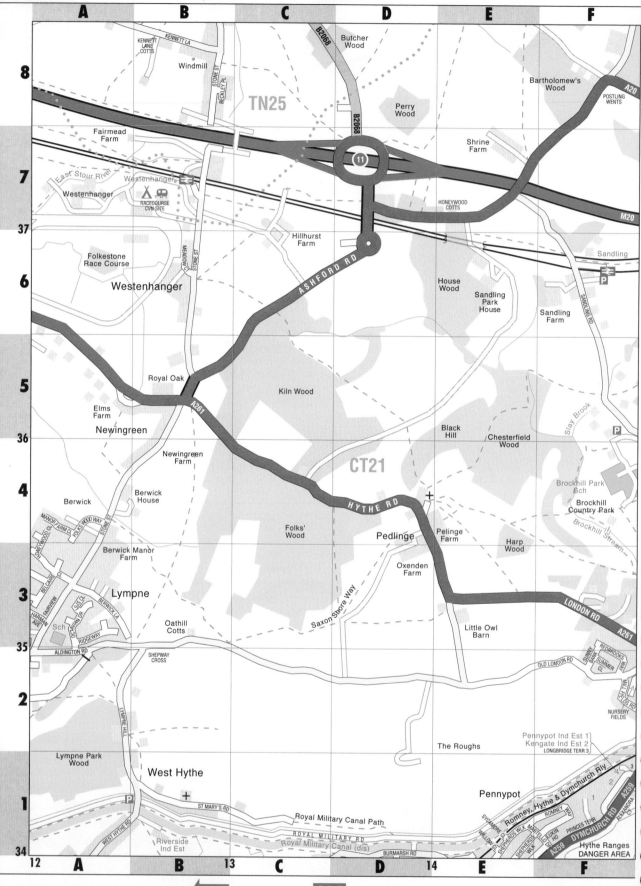

331

304

A B C D E F

8

7

37

6

5

36

4

3

35

2

1

34

12 A B 13 C D 14 E F

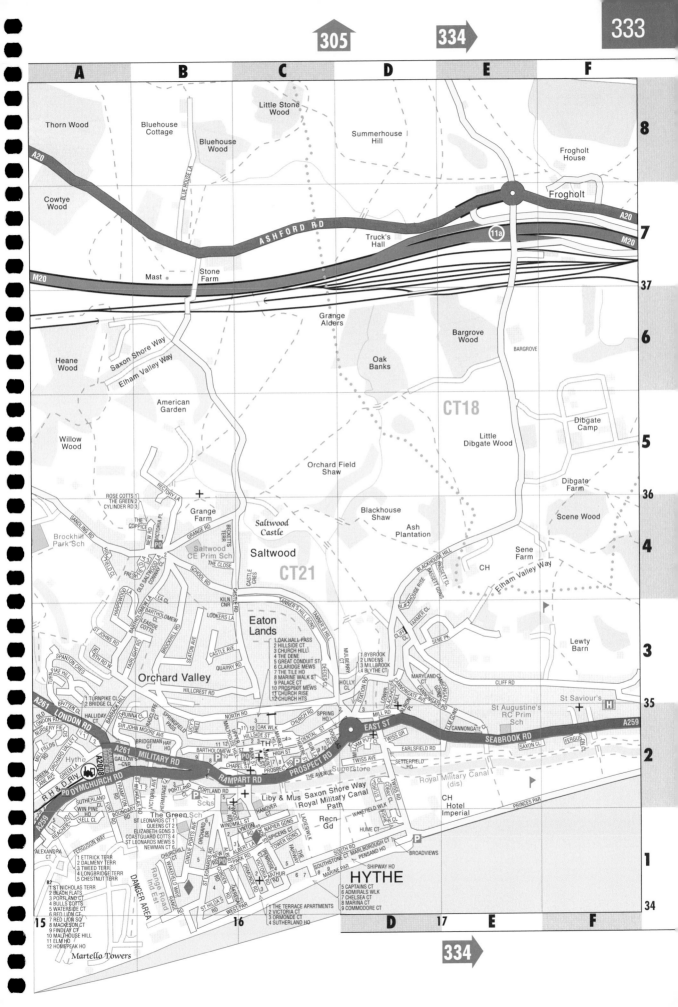

A | **B** | **C** | **D** | **E** | **F**

8

Thorn Wood

Little Stone Wood

Bluehouse Cottage

Summerhouse Hill

Bluehouse Wood

Frogholt House

A20

Cowtye Wood

Frogholt

A20

M20

7

11a

ASHFORD RD

Truck's Hall

M20

Mast

Stone Farm

37

Grange Alders

6

Bargrove Wood

Heane Wood

BARGROVE

Saxon Shore Way

Elham Valley Way

Oak Banks

CT18

American Garden

Little Dibgate Wood

Dibgate Camp

Willow Wood

5

Orchard Field Shaw

Dibgate Farm

36

ROSE COTTS 1
THE GREEN 2
CYLINDER RD 3

Scene Wood

Grange Farm

THE COPPICE

RECTORY LA

Saltwood Castle

Blackhouse Shaw

Sene Wood

Brockhill Park Sch

Saltwood CE Prim Sch

Saltwood

Ash Plantation

CH

Sene Farm

4

THE CLOSE

CT21

Elham Valley Way

CASTLE CRES

Eaton Lands

CH

KILN CNR

1 OAK HALL PASS
2 HILLSIDE CT
3 CHURCH HILL
4 THE DENE
5 GREAT CONDUIT ST
6 CLARIDGE MEWS
7 THE TILE HO
8 MANOR WALK ST
9 PALACE CT
10 PROSPECT MEWS
11 CHURCH RISE
12 CHURCH HTS

1 BYBROOK
2 LINDENS
3 MILLBROOK
4 BLYTHE CT

Lewty Barn

3

Orchard Valley

CLIFF RD

HILLCREST RD

MARYLAND CT

St Saviour's

35

NORTH RD

EAST ST

St Augustine's RC Prim Sch

A259

LONDON RD

A261

MILITARY RD

SEABROOK RD

PROSPECT RD

2

RAMPART RD

Royal Military Canal (dis)

R H & D Rly

DYMCHURCH RD

Hythe

A2008

The Avenue
Superstore

A261

Liby & Mus

Saxon Shore Way
Royal Military Canal Path

CH Hotel Imperial

PRINCES PAR

A259

The Green Sch

Recn Gd

1 ST LEONARDS CT 1
QUEENS CT 2
ELIZABETH GDNS 3
COASTGUARD COTTS 4
ST LEONARDS MEWS 5
NEWMAN CT 6

Broadviews

Alexandra Ct

1

Ferguson Way

1 ETTRICK TERR
2 DALMENY TERR
3 TWEED TERR
4 LONGBRIDGE TERR
5 CHESTNUT TERR

HYTHE

DANGER AREA

B2
1 ST NICHOLAS TERR
2 BEACH FLATS
3 PORTLAND CT
4 BULLS COTTS
5 WATERSIDE CT
6 RED LION CT
7 RED LION SQ
8 MACKESON CT
9 FINDLAY CT
10 MALTHOUSE HILL
11 ELM HO
12 HOMEPEAK HO

1 THE TERRACE APARTMENTS
2 VICTORIA CT
3 ORMONDE CT
4 SUTHERLAND HO

5 CAPTAINS CT
6 ADMIRALS WLK
7 CHELSEA CT
8 MARINA CT
9 COMMODORE CT

34

15 | 16 | 17 | **D** | **E** | **F**

Martello Towers

← 333

↑ 306

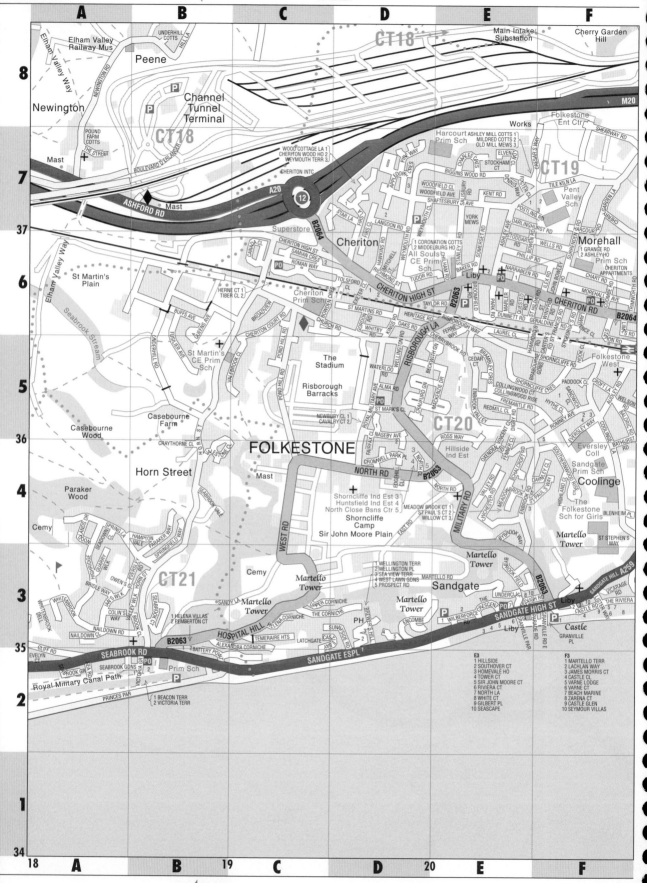

F5
1 WALMER WAY
2 CHURCHILL HO
3 SPENCER HO
4 WINSTON HO
5 TURNER CT

E3
1 HILLSIDE
2 SOUTHOVER CT
3 HOMEVALE HO
4 TOWER CT
5 SIR JOHN MOORE CT
6 RIVIERA CT
7 NORTH LA
8 WHITE CT
9 GILBERT PL
10 SEASCAPE

F3
1 MARTELLO TERR
2 LACHLAN WAY
3 JAMES MORRIS CT
4 CASTLE CL
5 VARNE LODGE
6 VARNE CT
7 BEACH MARINE
8 ZARENA CT
9 CASTLE GLEN
10 SEYMOUR VILLAS

← 333

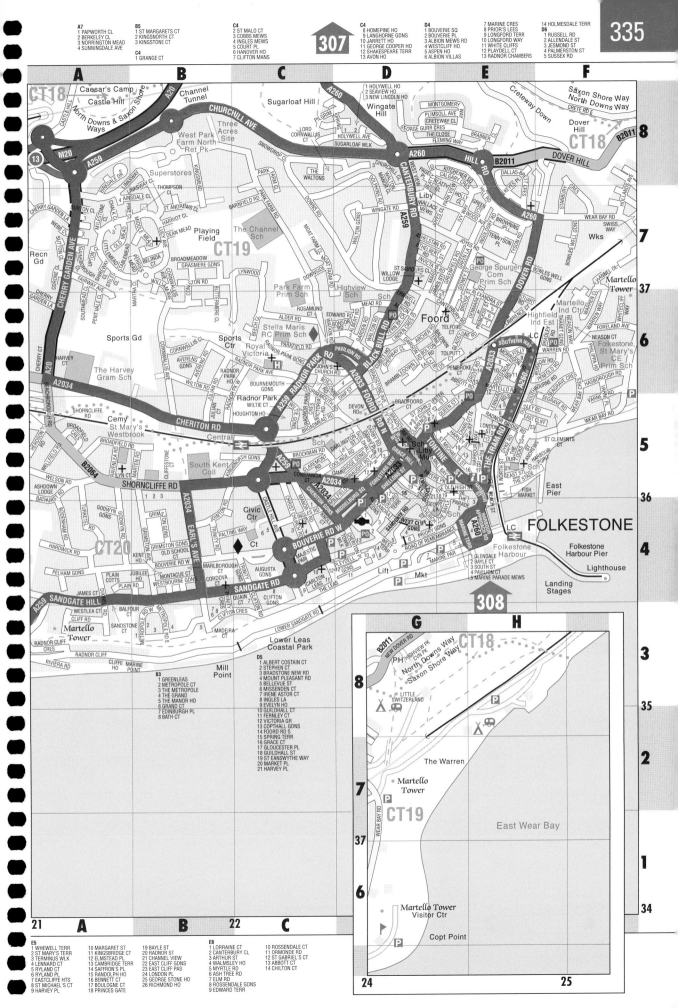

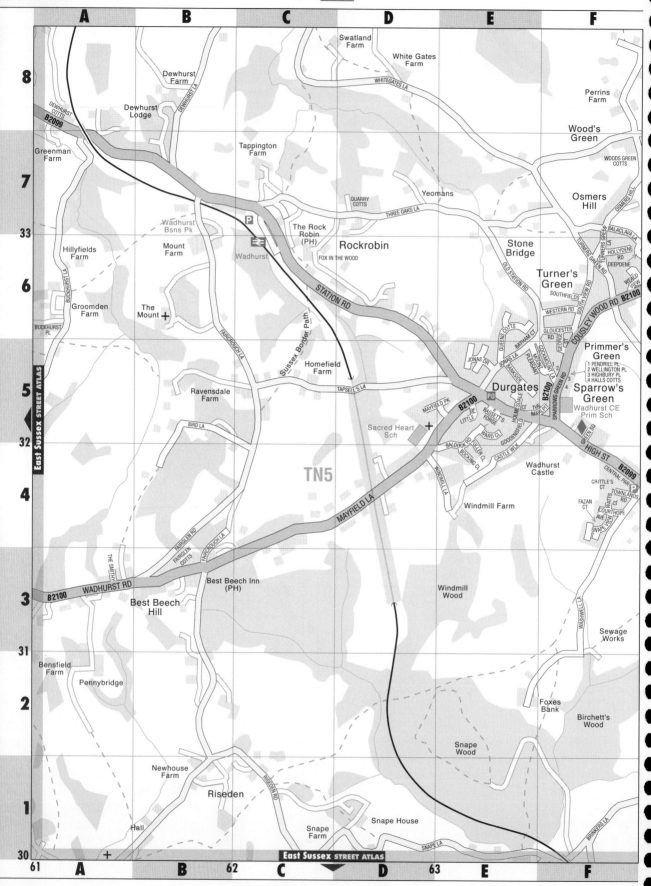

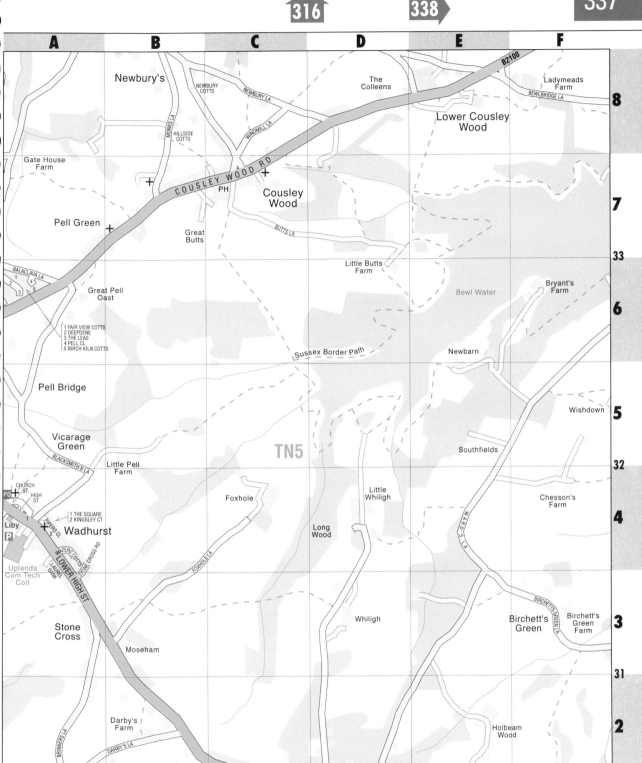

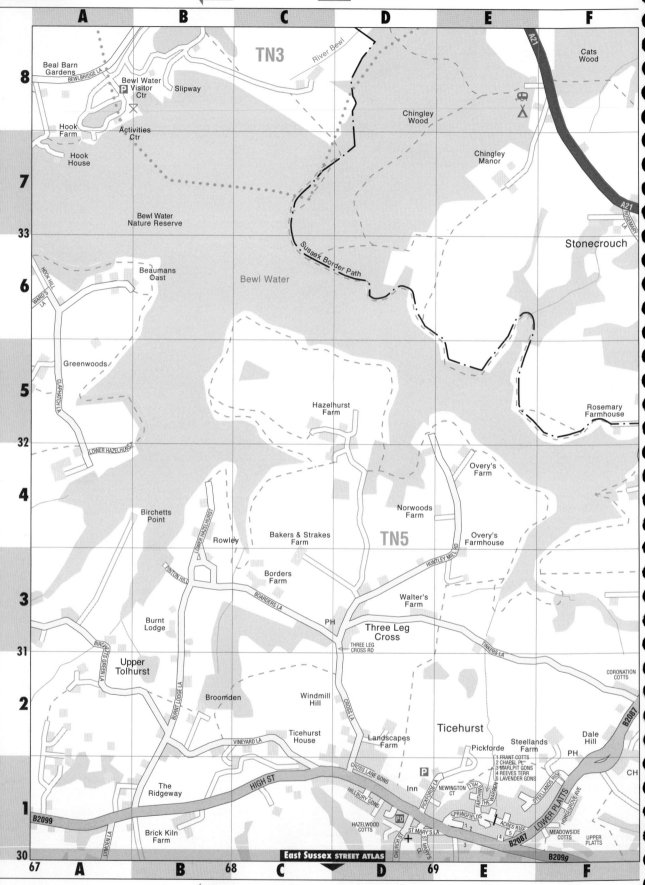

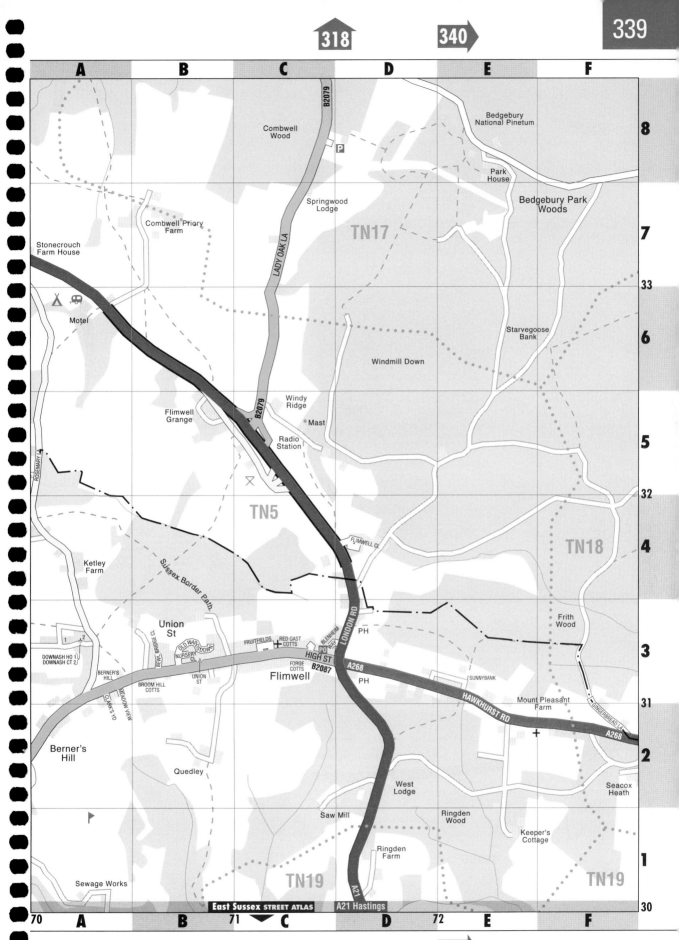

339
319

A B C D E F

8

Brick Kiln Cottages
Sugarloaf Hill
Hedgingford Wood
WHITELIMES

TN17

Louisa Lodge
Foresters Cottage
TN17
Tubslake

Frith Wood
PARK LA
Badger's Oak Farm

7

Osborne's Farm

HAWKHURST RD
A229

33

Rose's Farm

Louisa Lake
Trenley Farm
Yewtree Farm

6

Frith Farm
POTTER'S LA

Limes Grove Farm

Tanyard Farm
STATION COTTS
LIMES GR

5

Gill's Green

TN18
Gill's Green Farm

32

Siseley Farm
WELLINGTON COTTS

Soper's Lane Farm
SOPER'S LA
Trewint Farm
Wellington Arms (PH)
HEARTENOAK RD

CRANBROOK RD

4

SLIP MILL RD

Little Pix Hall Farm
Slip Mill
SYDNEY TERR 1
CASTLE TERR 2
SANDROOK VILLAS 3

3

Springfield Ind Est
A229

LIGHTFOOT GN
Lightfoot Green

31

Elm Hill Farm
CH

Hawkhurst Cottage
Philpott's Cross
High Street
OAKFIELD
P

2

A268
H
HIGH ST
Marlborough House Sch
WESTERN RD
A268

Elm Hill House
IDDENDEN COTTS
FAIRVIEW

Seacox Poultry Farm
LORENDEN PK
COPTHALL AVE
A229

NORTH HILL RD

F2
1 EDEN CT
2 DAINTONS COTTS
3 OAK TERR
4 NORMAN VILLAS
5 ARMITAGE PL
6 SCHOOL TERR
7 WESTERN AVE
8 HIGHGATE CT
9 NORTHGROVE RD
10 CRANE HOUSE GDNS
11 CRANE HO
12 POST OFFICE RD

Delmonden Manor
DELMONDEN RD
Hurstwood Cottage

1

TN19
Sussex Border Path
Cockshot
HIGHGATE HILL
A229

Hensill House
TALBOT RD

30

73 A B 74 C D 75 E F

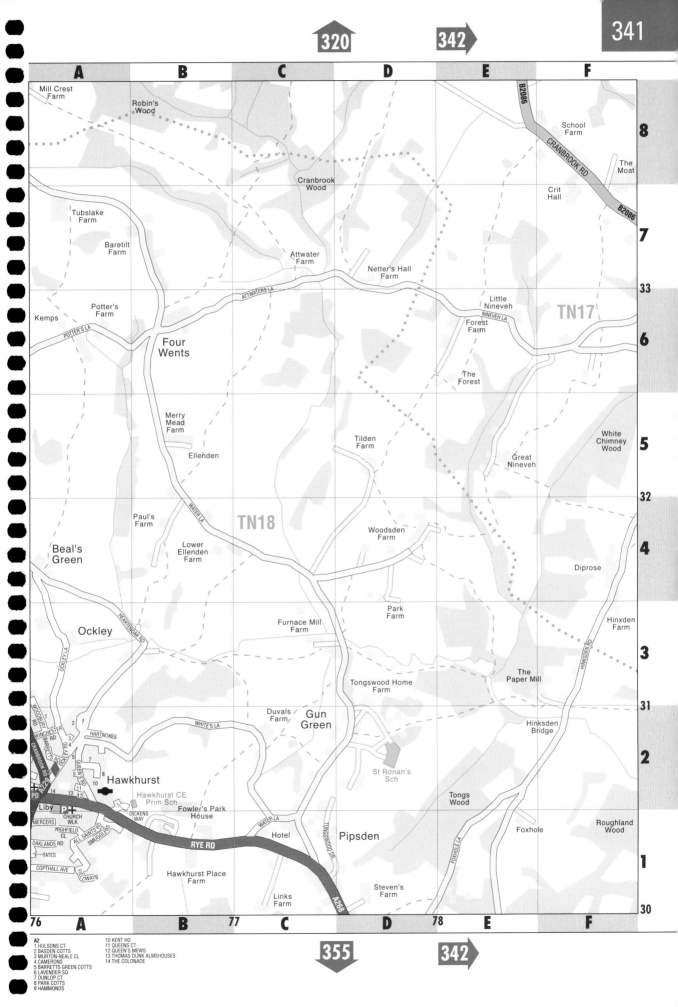

320 342

A B C D E F

8 School Farm
The Moat
Crit Hall
7
33
TN17
6
5 White Chimney Wood
32
4 Diprose
Hinxden Farm
3
31
2
1
30

76 A B 77 C D 78 E F

Mill Crest Farm
Robin's Wood
Cranbrook Wood
CRANBROOK RD
B2086
Tubslake Farm
Baretilt Farm
Attwater Farm
Netter's Hall Farm
Little Nineveh
NINEVEH LA
Kemps
Potter's Farm
ATTWATERS LA
POTTER'S LA
Four Wents
Forest Farm
The Forest
Great Nineveh
Merry Mead Farm
Ellenden
Tilden Farm
WATER LA
Paul's Farm
Lower Ellenden Farm
TN18
Woodsden Farm
Beal's Green
Park Farm
HEARTENOAK RD
Ockley
Furnace Mill Farm
HINKSDEN RD
The Paper Mill
Tongswood Home Farm
Hinksden Bridge
WHITE'S LA
Duvals Farm
Gun Green
WOODBURY RD
WINCHESTER RD
BARRETT'S RD
OCKLEY LA
CRANBROOK RD
QUEEN'S RD
HARTNOKES
Hawkhurst
Hawkhurst CE Prim Sch
St Ronan's Sch
Tongs Wood
Foxhole
Roughland Wood
PO
Liby
P
MERCERS
HIGHFIELD CL
OAKLANDS RD
CHURCH WLK
ALL SAINTS RD
SMUGGLERS
TATES
DICKENS WAY
Fowler's Park House
Pipsden
FOXHOLE LA
TONGSWOOD DR
COPTHALL AVE
FIELDWAYS
Hotel
WATER LA
Hawkhurst Place Farm
RYE RD
A268
Links Farm
Steven's Farm

A2
1 HULSONS CT
2 BASDEN COTTS
3 MURTON-NEALE CL
4 CAMERONS
5 BARRETTS GREEN COTTS
6 LAVENDER SQ
7 DUNLOP CT
8 PARK COTTS
9 HAMMONDS
10 KENT HO
11 QUEENS CT
12 QUEEN'S MEWS
13 THOMAS DUNK ALMSHOUSES
14 THE COLONADE

A B C D E F

8

7

33

6

5

32

4

31

3

2

1

30

New House
Coggers
Benenden Sch
Walkhurst Farm
Apple Pie Farm
Mount's Farm House
New Pond
Sewage Works
LIME AVE
MOUNTS HILL
B2086
CRANBROOK RD
FINCHER'S LA
BABB'S LA
NINEVEH LA
Babbes Farm
WALKHURST RD
WALKHURST COTTS
HORTONS CL
PO
THE STREET
1 CHERRYFIELDS
2 BARRACK ROW
FEOFFE COTTS
FUGGLES CT
KINGSFORD COTTS
PH
HARMSWORTH CT
ROTHERMERE CT
LEYBOURNE DELL
1 CHURCHILL HO
2 KENNEDY HO
The Green
ORCHARD CT
Collingwood Grange
Benenden CE Prim Sch
Benenden
PULLINGTON COTTS
BENENDEN RD
B2086
Pullington Farm
Scullsgate House
NEW POND RD
High Weald Landscape Trail
HUXSDEN RD
Iden Green Farm
Stream Farm
OLD WEAVERS COTTS
Ramsden Farm
RAMSDEN LA
TN17
Frame Farm
32
Sarnden
COLDHARBOUR RD
CLAREMONT PL
CHAPEL LA
Royal Oak (PH)
OAKFIELD COTTS
Sewage Works
Broom Hill
Yewtree Farm
Iden Green
Moor Wood
Reed Wood
VYVYAN COTTS
MEDWAY COTTS
WOODCOCK LA
Nurseries
Depot
The Woodcock (PH)
Standen Wood
Dingleden
MILL ST
Eaglesden
STANDEN ST
Trafford Farm
DINGLEDEN LA
Campion House
Wandle Mill
Mount Wood
SPONDEN LA
Standen Street
Old Standen
Springhill Farm
Cattsford
HOPEHOUSE LA
SANDHURST LA
TN18
Bankside Farm

79 A 80 B C 80 D 81 E F

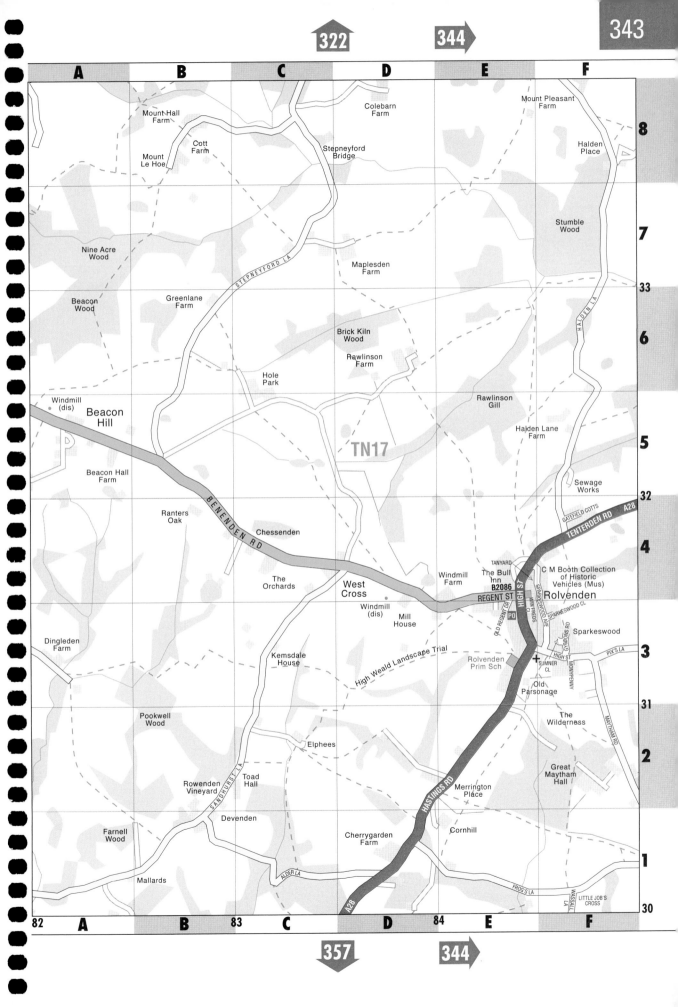

343
323

A B C D E F

8

Chennell Park

Little Halden
Place

GOODS
HILL

New Barn
Farm

LC

7

Ruffets

Cemy

WEST CROSS

HURST CL.
LAWN CL

WESTWELL
HO

A28
B2082

33

Ashbourne
Mill

ROLVENDEN RD

CASTWEAZLE

WESTFIELD HOUSE 1
PARKSIDE CT 2
OLD TANNERY CL 3

PLUMMER LA

6

LC

Rolvenden

West
View

H

Heronden
Hall

Old
Halden

Cold
Harbour

Plummer
Farm

TN30

5

Osborn
Farm

Folly Farm

ROLVENDEN HILL

PUDDINGCAKE LA

Sewage
Works

Plummer
Wood

32

A28

TENTERDEN RD

Strood

TN17

Puddingcake
Farmhouse

Kent & East Sussex Rly

4

Sparkes Gill

Winton
Farm

High Weald Landscape Trail

Heronden

3

PIX'S LA

MOUNTS LA

Lower
Woolwich

Newmill Channel

Gazedown
Wood

Morghew
Farm

31

Upper
Woolwich

Crayfish
Lagoons

2

Kingsgate

Winser
Farm

1

MAYTHAM RD

OAKFIELD

FROG'S LA

FRENSHAM RD

PH

WINSER LA

THORNDEN RD

Frensham
Manor

Rolvenden
Layne

Friezingham
Farm

MAYTHAM
BGLWS

30

85 A B 86 C D 87 E F

343
358

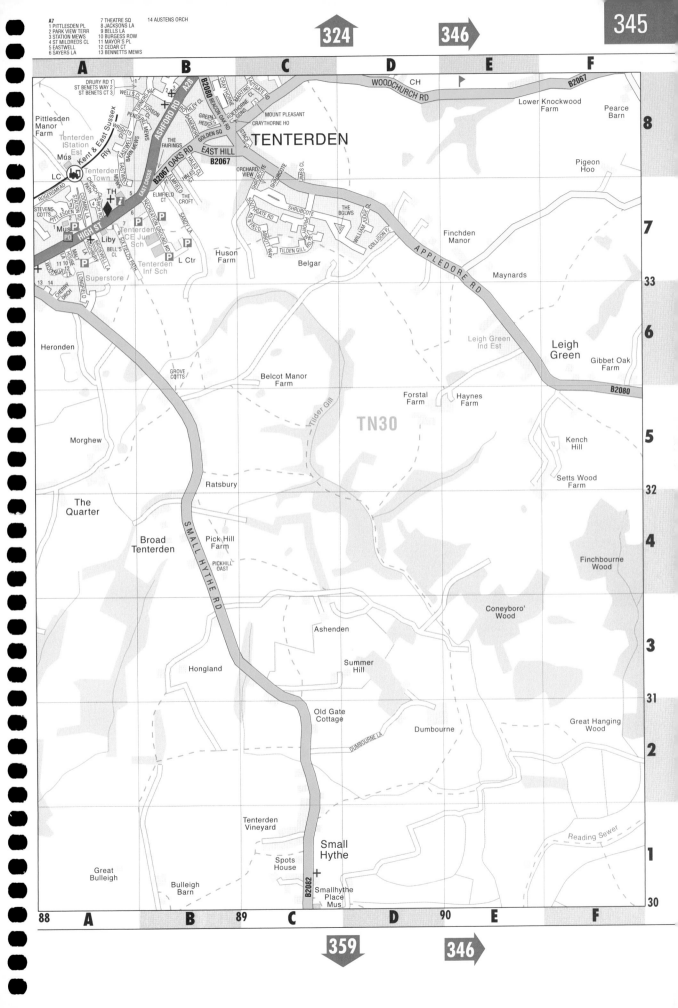

345
325

	A	B	C	D	E	F

8

The Dandy

Bourne Farm

B2067

Cott Farm

Bower Farm

Diamond House

Berridge Farm

Oakhurst Farm

Ditton Farm

Orange Farm

B R O O K   S T

Brook Street

B2067

Malt House Farm

7

33

Glover Farm

6

Highbank Farm

MOOR LA

B2080

Nurseries

Frenchay Wood

Shirley Farm

TN26

5

Shirley Moor

Tenterden Sewer

32

Frenchay Farm

New Bridge

Fleet Petty Sewer

4

APPLEDORE RD

TN30

Finchbourne Wood

3

Barrack Farm

The Century Farm

31

Little Ramsden

2

Reading Street

Willow Farm

READING ST

Nurseries

Chapel Bank Farm

Reading Sewer

TENTERDEN RD

1

Rother Levels

Redhill Bridge

Red Hill

30

Barrowsland Farm

B2080

91	A	B	92	C	D	93	E	F

345
360

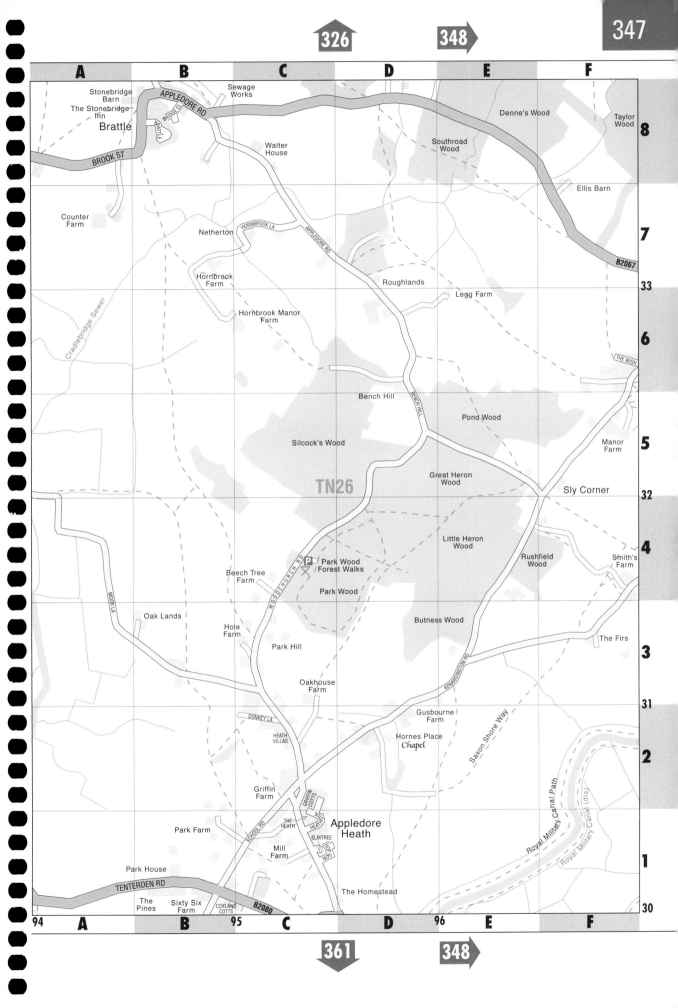

347 327

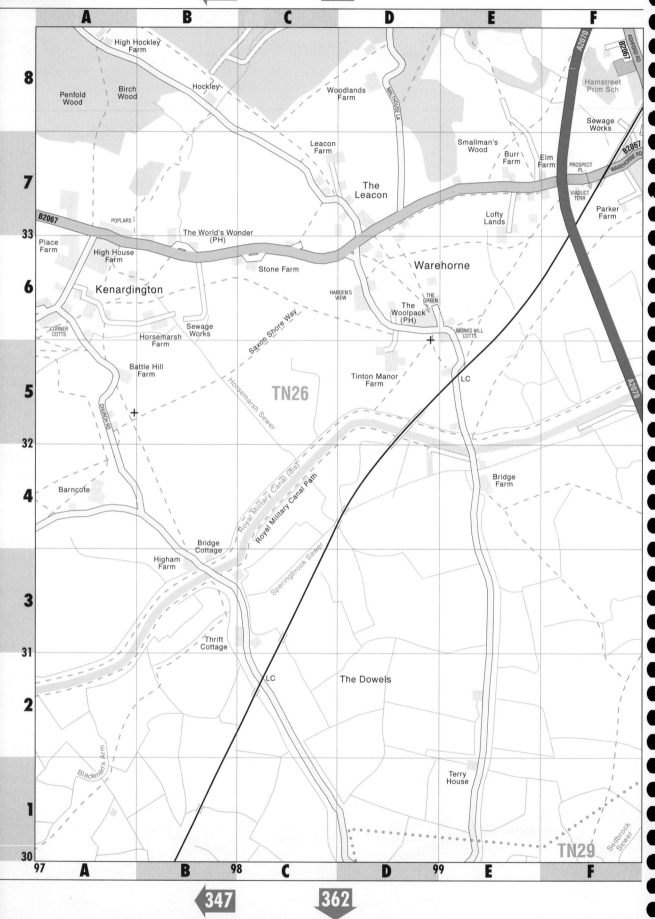

347 362

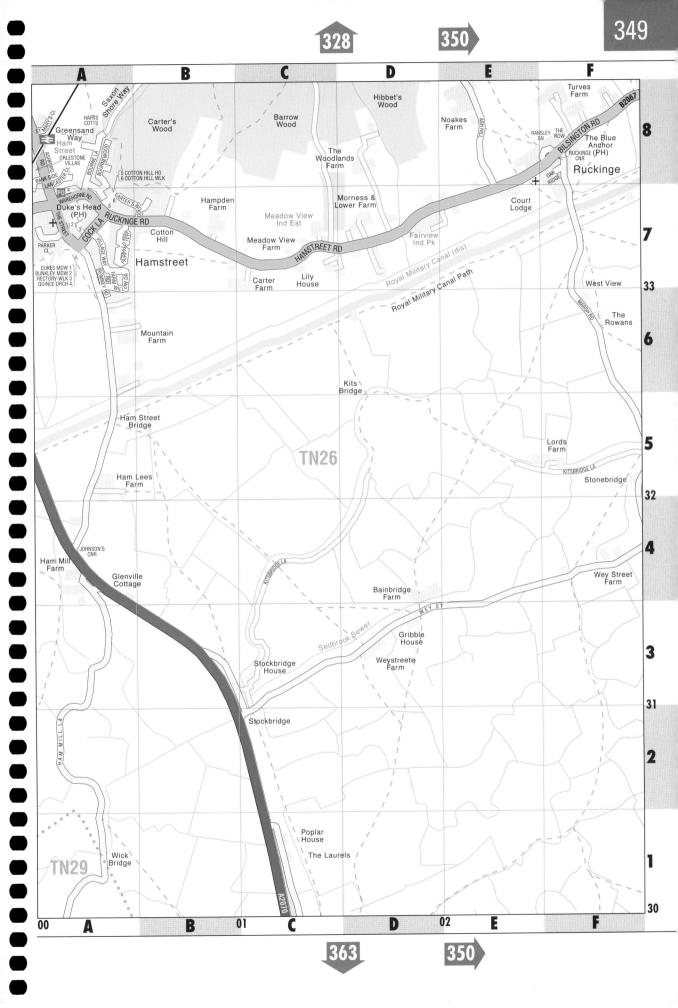

349
329

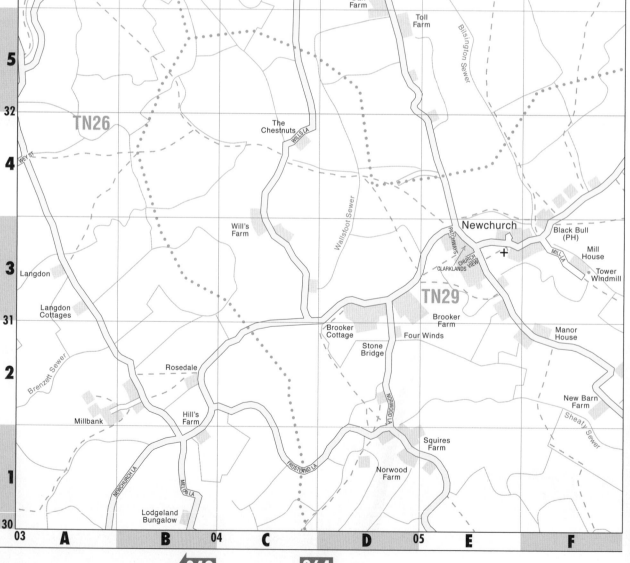

349
364

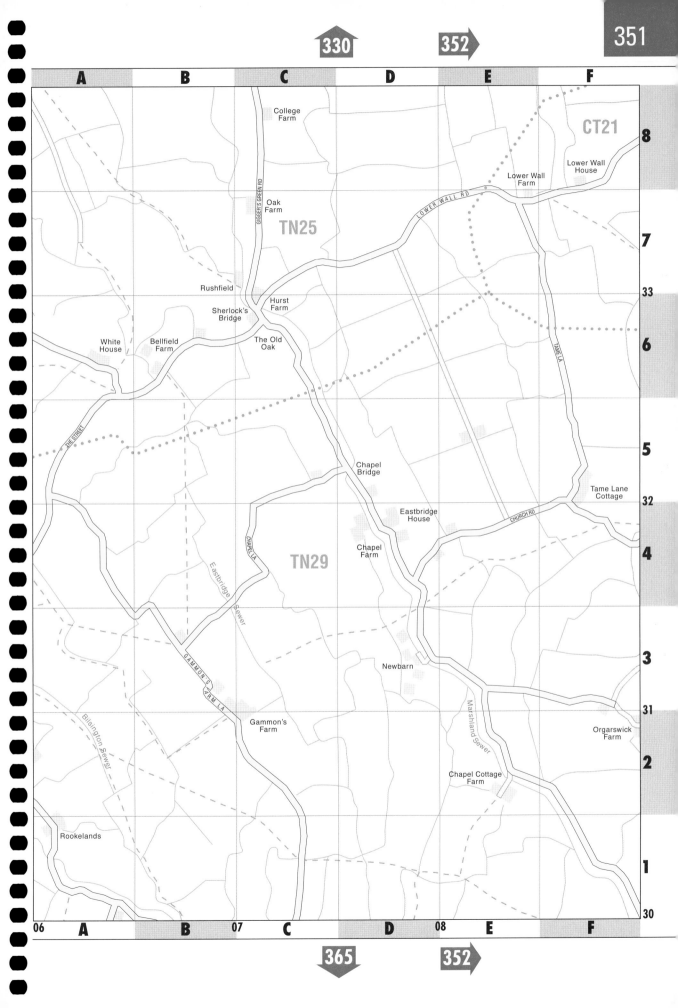

351
331

A B C D E F

8

Tontine Farm

ALDERGATE LA

Willop Sewer (Selby Arm)

SELBY FIELD CVN PK

Selby Farm

LOWER WALL RD

7

Hoorne's Sewer

CT21

33

Lone Barn

DALEACRES CVN PK

6

Abbott's Court

Willop Sewer

Abbott's Court Cottages

The Little Piece

DONKEY ST

Eaton Farm

SHEAR WAY

Lathe Barn

5

Donkey Street

Hoorne's Sewer

Hoorne's Sewer

32

+
PH

Burmarsh

PAINE'SFIELD CL

Dymchurch Sewage Disposal Works

Forty Acre Farm

CHURCH RD

THE GREEN

THORNDIKE RD

Baronet Bridge

4

TN29

Orchard CVN PK

3

Hazelhurst

BURMARSH RD

Haguelands Farm

Romney, Hythe & Dymchurch Rly

MARINE AVE

WILLOP WAY

Willop Basin

WILLOP RD

A259

31

Orgarswick Farm

2

Hoorne's Sewer

LC

GREEN MEWS

QUEENSWAY

KINGSWAY

CROSSWAYS CL

LOWER SANDS

LOWER SANDS

TOWER EST

AVE RD

+

1

KIPPI GDNS

TUDOR AVE

VENTURE CL

PEAR TREE CL

SEA WALL

HYTHE RD

Martello Tower

30

LC

WRAIGHTSFIELD AVE

A259

THE OVAL

09 A B 10 C D 11 E F

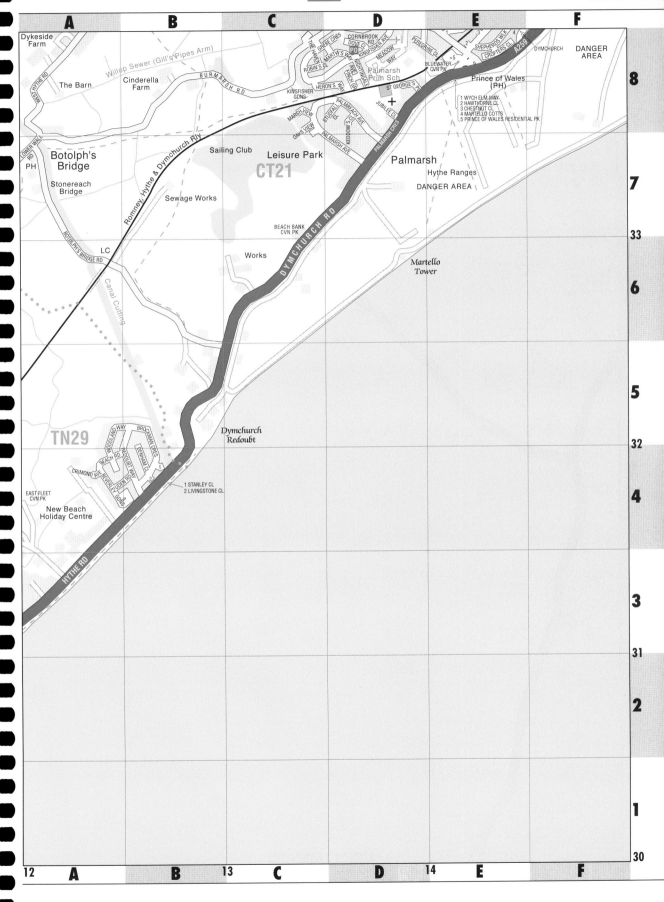

A B C D E F

8

7

33

6

5

32

4

3

31

2

1

30

12 A B 13 C D 14 E F

Dykeside Farm
The Barn
Cinderella Farm
Willop Sewer (Gill's Pipes Arm)
BURMARSH RD
WEST HYTHE RD
LOWER WALL RD
Botolph's Bridge
PH
Stonereach Bridge
Romney, Hythe & Dymchurch Rly
Sailing Club
Leisure Park
CT21
Sewage Works
BOTOLPH'S BRIDGE RD
LC
Canal Cutting
BEACH BANK CVN PK
Works
DYMCHURCH RD
THE HAVEN
GREBE CRES
CORNBROOK RD
MEADOW WAY
DOVE CL
KINGFISHER AVE
PEREGRINE CL
SHEPHERDS WLK
CROFTERS CL
A259
DYMCHURCH
DANGER AREA
ROBIN'S CL
MARTIN'S WAY
NIGHTINGALE
FINCH CL
PIKE'S
Palmarsh Prim Sch
BLUEWATER CVN PK
Prince of Wales (PH)
KINGFISHER GDNS
HERON'S WAY
ST GEORGE'S
ST UDFALL CL
PALMBEACH AVE
PADDOCK'S CL
JUBILEE CL
PALMARSH CRES
PALMARSH AVE
MARSH VIEW
OAKS VIEW
1 WYCH ELM WAY
2 HAWTHORNE CL
3 CHESTNUT CL
4 MARTELLO COTTS
5 PRINCE OF WALES RESIDENTIAL PK
Palmarsh
Hythe Ranges
DANGER AREA
Martello Tower
TN29
WOODLAND WAY
BROCKMAN CRES
BEACH RD
REDOUBT WAY
DENHAM CL
CRIMOND AVE
BEVERLEY GDNS
UDDEN RD
EAST FLEET CVN PK
New Beach Holiday Centre
Dymchurch Redoubt
1 STANLEY CL
2 LIVINGSTONE CL
HYTHE RD

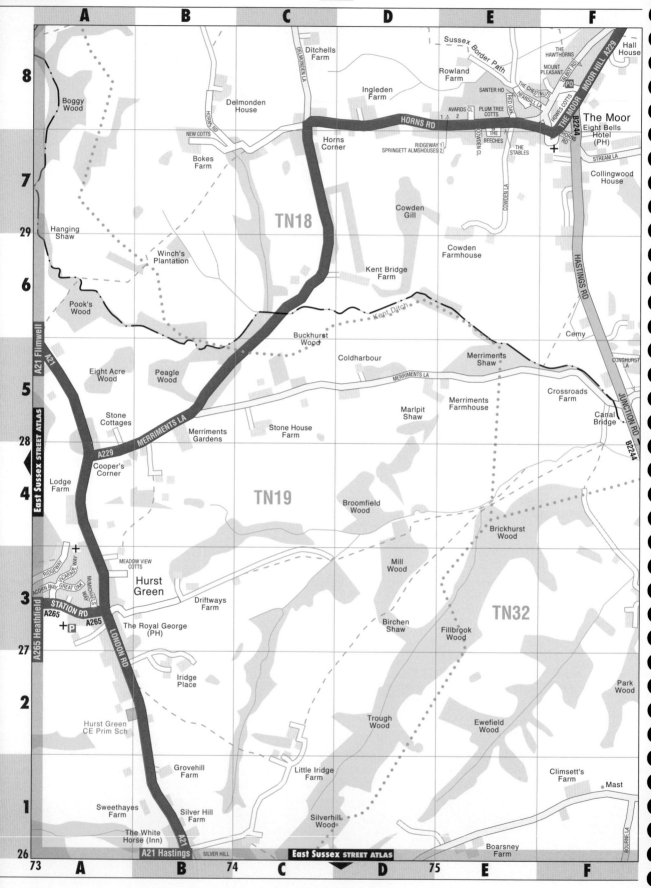

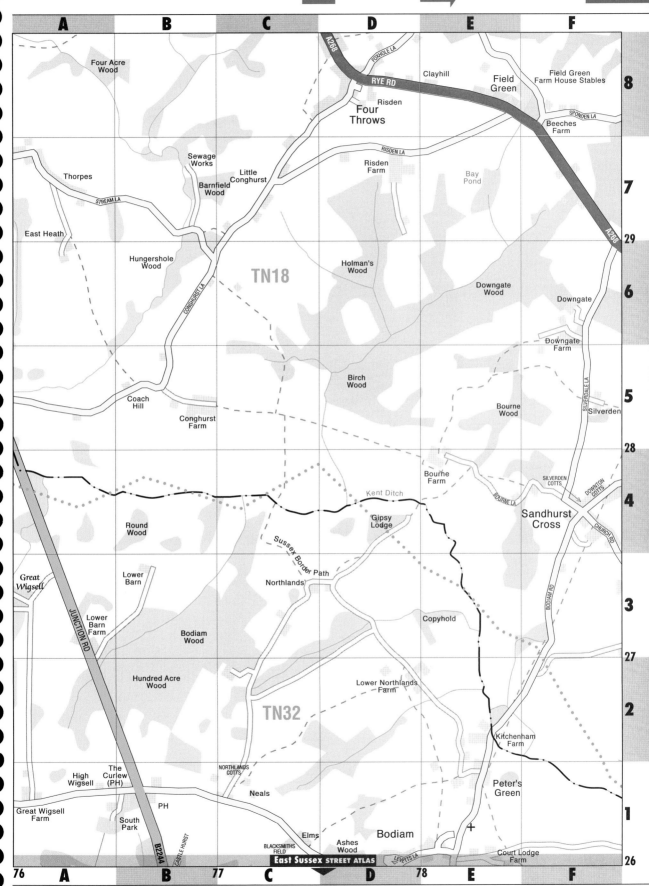

Four Acre Wood

RYE RD

A268

FOXHOLE LA

Clayhill

Field Green

Field Green Farm House Stables

8

Risden

Four Throws

RISDEN LA

SPONDEN LA

Beeches Farm

Thorpes

STREAM LA

Sewage Works

Little Conghurst

Barnfield Wood

Risden Farm

Bay Pond

7

East Heath

Hungershole Wood

CONGHURST LA

TN18

Holman's Wood

Downgate Wood

29

Downgate

6

Downgate Farm

Coach Hill

Conghurst Farm

Birch Wood

Bourne Wood

SILVERDALE LA

Silverden

5

Round Wood

Kent Ditch

Bourne Farm

BOURNE LA

SILVERDEN COTTS

DOWNTON COTTS

28

Gipsy Lodge

Sandhurst Cross

CHURCH RD

4

Great Wigsell

JUNCTION RD

Lower Barn

Sussex Border Path

Northlands

Copyhold

BODIAM RD

3

Lower Barn Farm

Bodiam Wood

Lower Northlands Farm

27

Hundred Acre Wood

TN32

Kitchenham Farm

2

High Wigsell

The Curlew (PH)

NORTHLANDS COTTS

Neals

Peter's Green

Great Wigsell Farm

PH

Elms

Bodiam

1

South Park

B2244

CASTLE HURST

BLACKSMITHS FIELD

Ashes Wood

LEVETTS LA

Court Lodge Farm

26

355
342

A **B** **C** **D** **E** **F**

8

TN17

Standen
Street

STANDEN ST

SPONDEN LA

Sponden
House

Hope
House

Sponden
Farmhouse

SPONDEN LA

HOPEHOUSE LA

7

Alderden
Manor

Reynolds
Farm

Orchard
Farm

Lords
Wood

Hopemill
Bridge

29

A268

MEGRIMS HILL

Sewage
Works

6

Puxtye

Malthouse
Farm

ANGEL
TERR BROOKFIELD

Sandhurst

CROUCH LA

Hoad's
Farm

ANGEL
ROW

QUEEN ST

THE ROPE WLK

Sandhurst
Prim Sch

Sandhurst
Vineyards

STONE PIT LA

STREAM PIT LA

POUNDFIELD RD

PH

PO

LOMAS LA

Lomas

OLD ORCHARD

BACK RD

Sandhurst
Farm

Scurms
Farm

LINKDEN
COTTS

5

BODIAM RD

OAKS PSTAL

BURNT HOUSE

RINGLE
GN

PH

Brickhouse
Farmhouse

Burnt Farm
House

Boxhurst
Farm

Linkhill

Hollowdene

28

TWYSDEN
COTTS

Castlegate
Farm

TN18

4

SANDHURST CL

1
2

Glassocks

1 BETHERINDEN COTTS
2 FORGEFIELD COTTS

Burnt House
Farm

Boxhurst

ETHNAM LA

CHURCH RD

Barnfield
Shaw

Little
Boxhurst

Ethnam Farm
Bungalow

3

Twisden
Plantation

Cledge
Wood

MARSH QUARTER LA

Old Sandhurst
Place

Ethnam

27

Old Place
Farm

Great
Ethnam Farm

2

Marsh Quarter
Farm

River Rother

1

TN32

Kent Ditch

Kent & East Sussex Rly

TN31

Dyneshill
Wood

26

79 **A** **B** 80 **C** **D** 81 **E** **F**

355

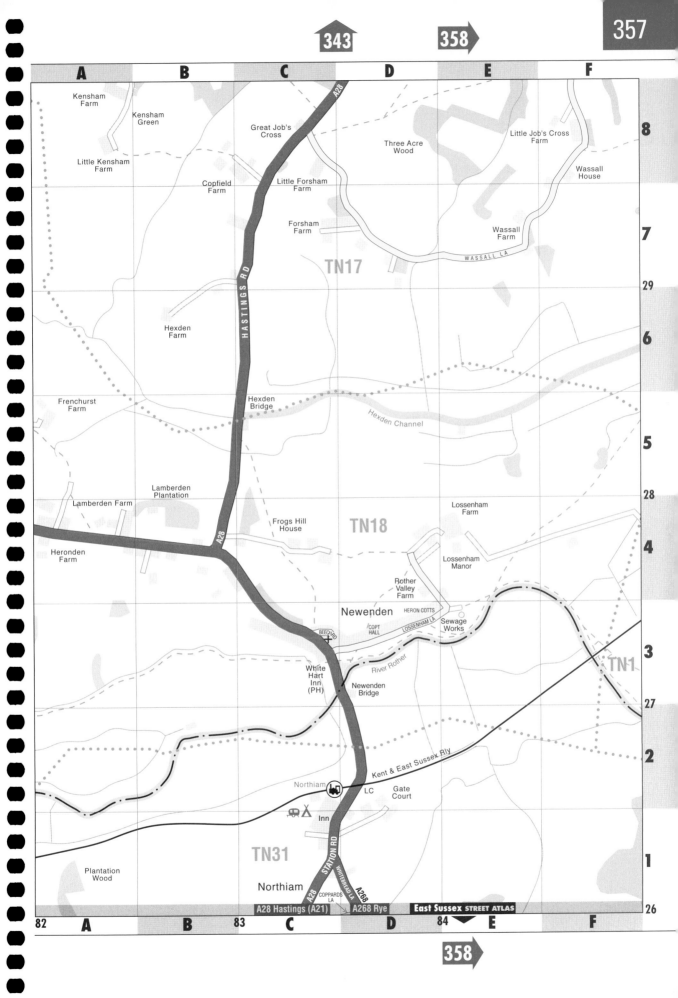

A B C D E F

8

Kensham Farm

Kensham Green

Great Job's Cross

Three Acre Wood

Little Job's Cross Farm

Little Kensham Farm

Copfield Farm

Little Forsham Farm

Wassall House

Forsham Farm

Wassall Farm

7

WASSALL LA

TN17

29

Hexden Farm

6

Frenchurst Farm

Hexden Bridge

Hexden Channel

5

Lamberden Plantation

28

Lamberden Farm

Frogs Hill House

Lossenham Farm

TN18

Heronden Farm

4

Lossenham Manor

Rother Valley Farm

Newenden

HERON COTTS

Sewage Works

/COPT HALL

LOSSENHAM LA

TN1

BEECH RD

River Rother

3

White Hart Inn (PH)

Newenden Bridge

27

Kent & East Sussex Rly

2

Northiam

LC

Gate Court

Inn

1

TN31

STATION RD

WHITEBREAD LA

Plantation Wood

Northiam

COPPARDS LA

A28

A268

82 A 83 B C 84 D E F

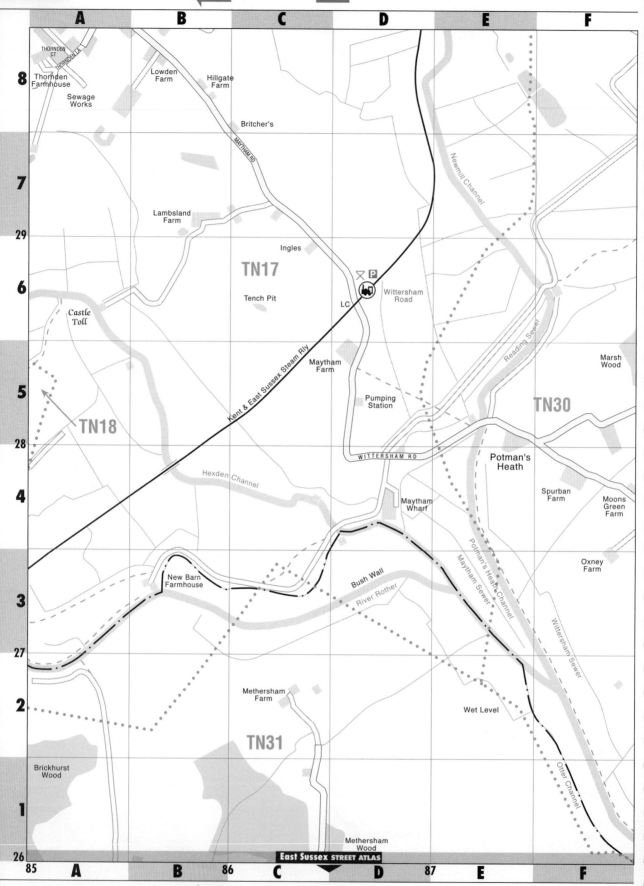

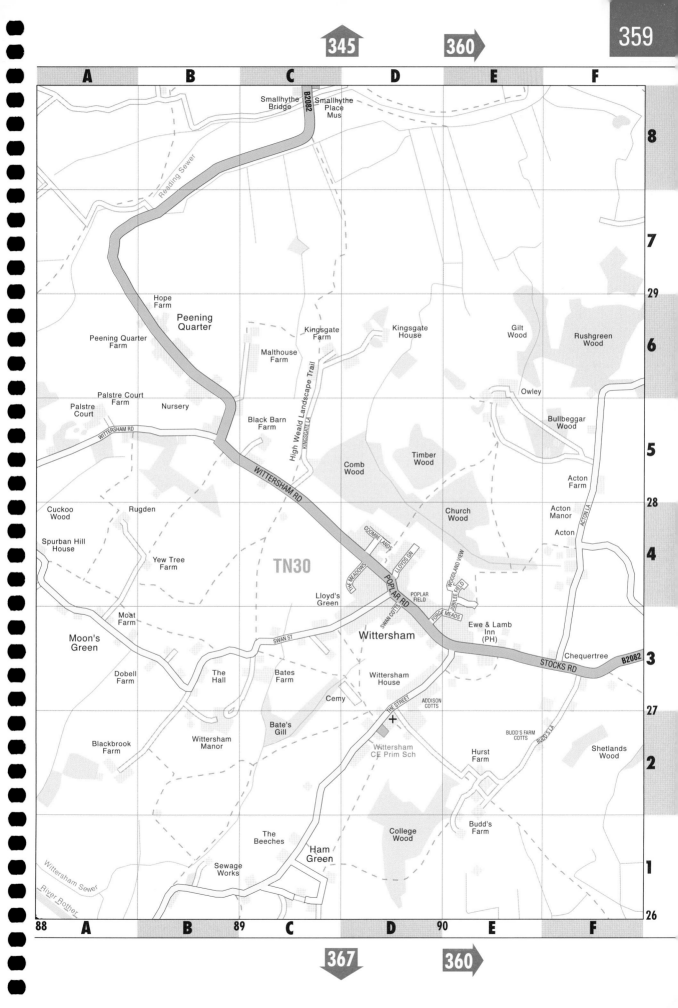

359 346

A B C D E F

TN26

8

High House Farm

Hayes Farm

Ramsden Farm

Chapel Bank

Reading Sewer

7

29

Stone Corner Farm

EBONY COTTS

STONE CNR

HOGPOUND CNR

Whole Farm

6

ACTON LA

Saxon Shore Way

Little Odiam Farm

LOWER RD

Luckhurst

5

Stemp's Wood

Rosehill Farmhouse

ROSE HILL

Odiam Farm

Stone Farm

28

TN30

Stone in Oxney

The Crown (PH)

THE STREET

4

Isle of Oxney

Curteis Wood

Twelve Acre Wood

Luckhurst Wood

STONE GN

Green Acres

Maynes Farm

Catt Farm

CATT'S HILL

The Stocks

Wr Twr

Lord's Wood

Scrub's Wood

Huggit's Farm

3

STOCKS RD

Four Acre Wood

WITTERSHAM RD

QUARRY COTTS

WATTLE CNR

TOP RD

CHURCH HILL

Windmill (dis)

Stocks Farm

Holman's Farm

WADDLE CNR

Prospect House

27

Oxenden

Little Prawls Farm

KNOCK HILL

2

Rook Wood

Tighe Farm

RYE RD

Tophill Farm

Great Prawls Farm

Saxon Shore Way

Underhill Farmhouse

Cliff Farm

1

Rother Levels

Stone Cliff

26

91 A B 92 C D 93 E F

B2082

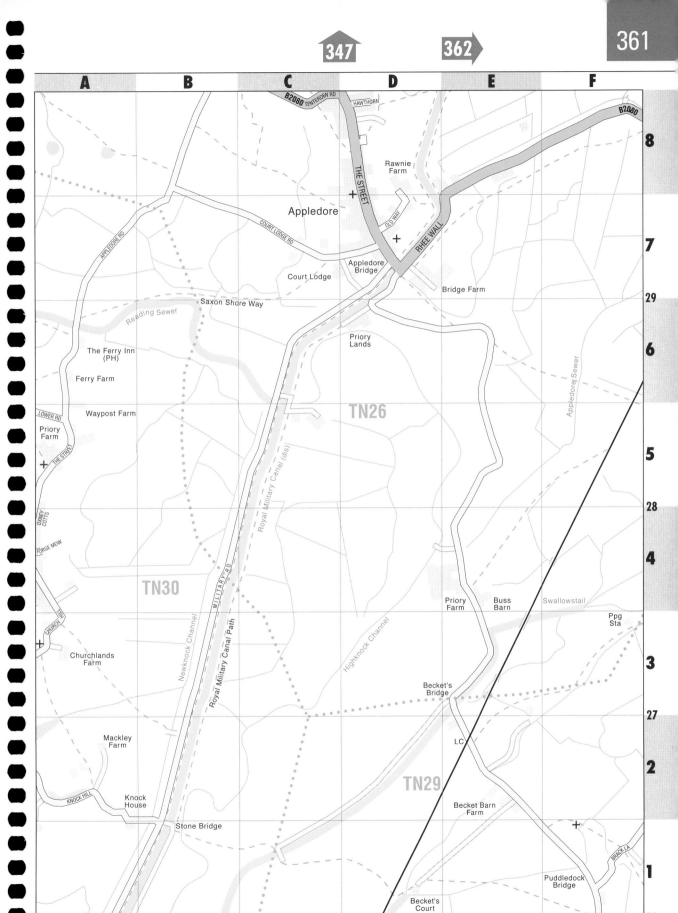

A   B   C   D   E   F

8

7

29

6

5

28

4

3

27

2

1

26

B2080 TENTERDEN RD

HAWTHORN

THE STREET

RHEE WALL

B2080

Rawnie
Farm

Appledore

Old Way

Appledore
Bridge

Court Lodge

Bridge Farm

APPLEDORE RD

COURT LODGE RD

Saxon Shore Way

Reading Sewer

Priory
Lands

The Ferry Inn
(PH)

Ferry Farm

TN26

Appledore Sewer

LOWER RD

Waypost Farm

Priory
Farm

THE STREET

Royal Military Canal (dis)

OXNEY
COTTS

FORGE MDW

TN30

Newknock Channel

MILITARY RD

Royal Military Canal Path

Highknock Channel

Priory
Farm

Buss
Barn

Swallowstail

Ppg
Sta

CHURCH LN

Churchlands
Farm

Becket's
Bridge

LC

Mackley
Farm

TN29

KNOCK HILL

Knock
House

Stone Bridge

Becket Barn
Farm

Puddledock
Bridge

BRACK LA

Becket's
Court

94   A   B   95   C   D   96   E   F

← 361
↑ 348

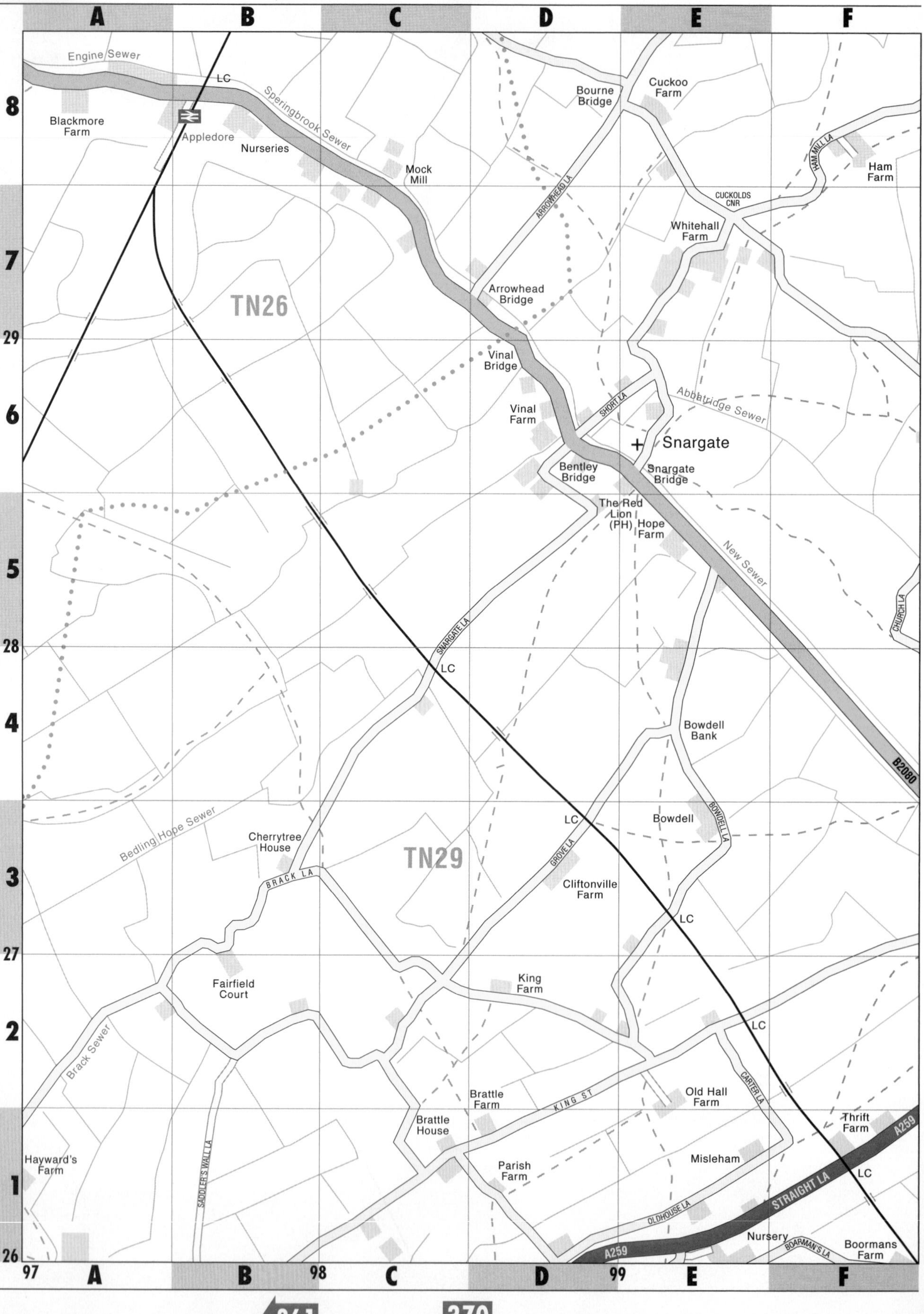

A B C D E F

8
Engine Sewer
LC
Blackmore Farm
Appledore
Nurseries
Springbrook Sewer
Mock Mill
Bourne Bridge
Cuckoo Farm
HAM MILL LA
Ham Farm

7
TN26
ARROWHEAD LA
CUCKOLDS CNR
Whitehall Farm

29
Arrowhead Bridge

6
Vinal Bridge
SHORT LA
Abbatridge Sewer
Vinal Farm
✚ Snargate
Bentley Bridge
Snargate Bridge
The Red Lion (PH)
Hope Farm
New Sewer

5
Snargate LA
LC

28

4
Bedling Hope Sewer
Bowdell Bank
Bowdell
BOWDELL LA
B2080

3
Cherrytree House
BRACK LA
TN29
LC
Bowdell
GROVE LA
Cliftonville Farm
LC

27
Fairfield Court
King Farm
LC

2
Brack Sewer
Brattle Farm
KING ST
Old Hall Farm
CARTER LA
LC
Thrift Farm
A259

1
Hayward's Farm
SADDLER'S WALL LA
Brattle House
Parish Farm
OLDHOUSE LA
Misleham
STRAIGHT LA
LC
Nursery
BOARMAN'S LA
Boormans Farm

26
A259

97 A 98 B C 98 D 99 E F

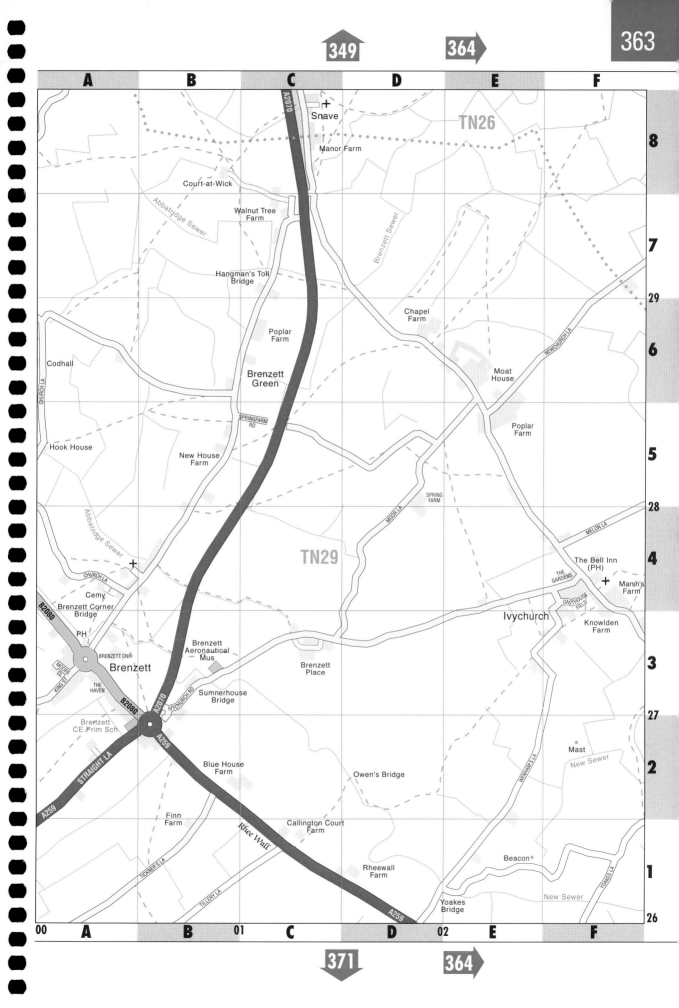

349
364
371
364

TN26

TN29

Snave

Manor Farm

Court-at-Wick

Abbatridge Sewer

Walnut Tree Farm

Brenzett Sewer

Hangman's Toll Bridge

Chapel Farm

Poplar Farm

Codhall

Brenzett Green

NEWCHURCH LA

Moat House

CHURCH LA

SPRINGFARM RD

Poplar Farm

Hook House

New House Farm

SPRING FARM

MOOR LA

Abbatridge Sewer

MELON LA

The Bell Inn (PH)

THE GARDENS

Marsh's Farm

CHURCH LA

Cemy

OASTHOUSE FIELD

Ivychurch

Brenzett Corner Bridge

Knowlden Farm

B2080

PH

Brenzett Aeronautical Mus

MOORE CL

Brenzett CNR

KING ST

Brenzett

THE HAVEN

B2080

A2070

IVYCHURCH RD

Sumnerhouse Bridge

Brenzett Place

Brenzett CE Prim Sch

A259

WENHAM'S LA

Mast

New Sewer

STRAIGHT LA

Blue House Farm

Owen's Bridge

A259

Finn Farm

Rhee Wall

Callington Court Farm

Beacon

TICKNER'S LA

TILLERY LA

Rheewall Farm

YOAKES LA

New Sewer

A259

Yoakes Bridge

8
7
29
6
5
28
4
3
27
2
1
26

A   B   01   C   D   02   E   F
00

363
350

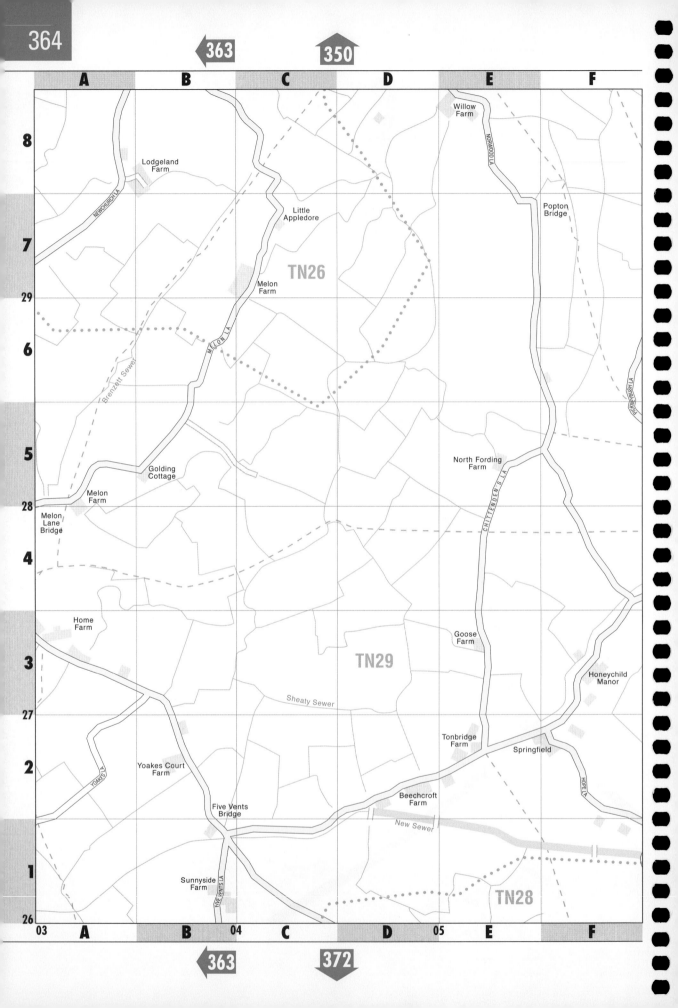

363
372

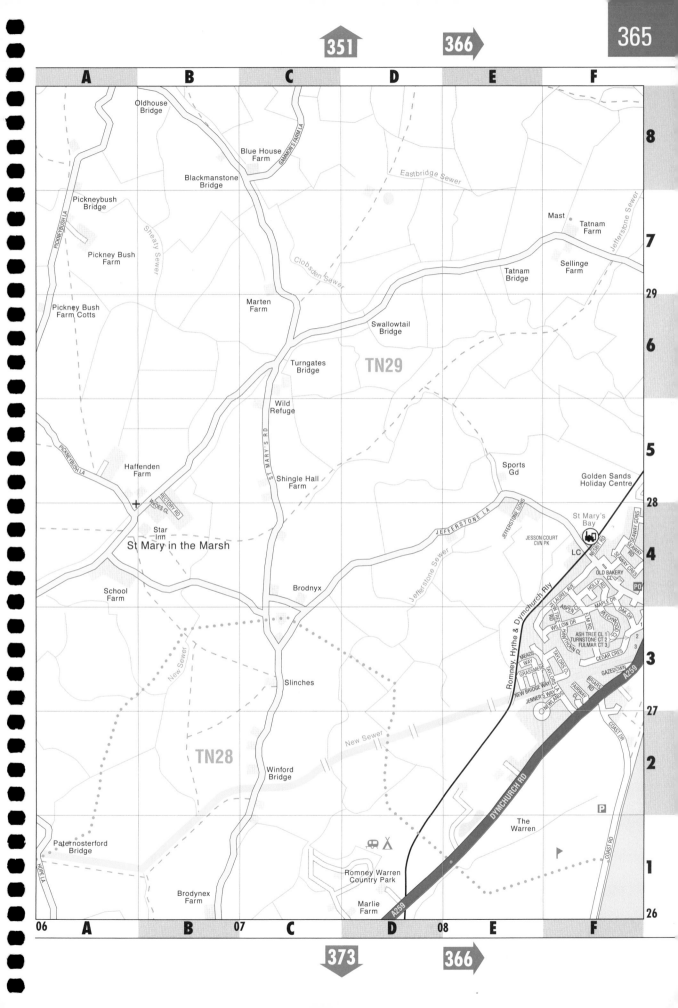

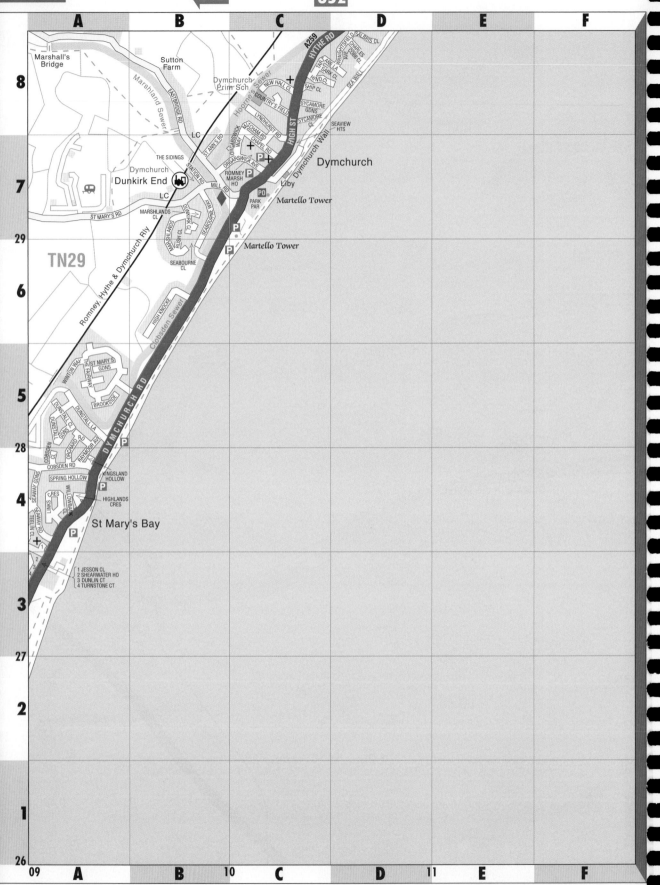

A B C D E F

8

Marshall's Bridge

Sutton Farm

Marshland Sewer

EASTBRIDGE RD

Dymchurch Prim Sch

Hoorne Sewer

A259

HYTHE RD

NEW HALL CL

COUNTRY'S FIELD

ORGARSWICK WAY

LYNDHURST RD

CHAPEL RD

MATCHAM RD

SARK CL

HIND CL

SHIP CL

SYCAMORE GDNS

SYCAMORE

SEAVIEW HTS

SEA WALL

SALBRIS CL

CHARLES

COBB CL

WHITFIELD

AVE

LA

AMB

AIR

HIGH ST

Dymchurch Wall

Dymchurch

LC

ST ANN'S RD

THE SIDINGS

STATION RD

Dymchurch
Dunkirk End

7

LC

ST MARY'S RD

MILL RD

MARSHLANDS CL

MARSH CL

DUNKIRK CL

THORNDYKE WAY

ROMNEY MARSH HO

P

P

PO

PARK PAR

Liby

Martello Tower

29

SEABOURNE CL

P

P

Martello Tower

TN29

Romney, Hythe & Dymchurch Rly

HIGH KNOCKE

Cobsden Sewer

6

DYMCHURCH RD

WINTON WAY

THE FAIRWAY

ST MARY'S GDNS

BROOKSIDE

5

DUNSTALL CL

DUNSTALL LA

DUNSTALL GDNS

ORCHARD CL

MAYNOP AVE

COBSDEN CL

28

COBSDEN RD

P

Spring Hollow

Kingsland Hollow

P

SEAWAY RD

SINKS

CRES

WILLOWBANK

HIGHLANDS CRES

4

SEAWAY GDNS

TEELIN CL

St Mary's Bay

P

1 JESSON CL
2 SHEARWATER HO
3 DUNLIN CT
4 TURNSTONE CT

3

27

2

1

26

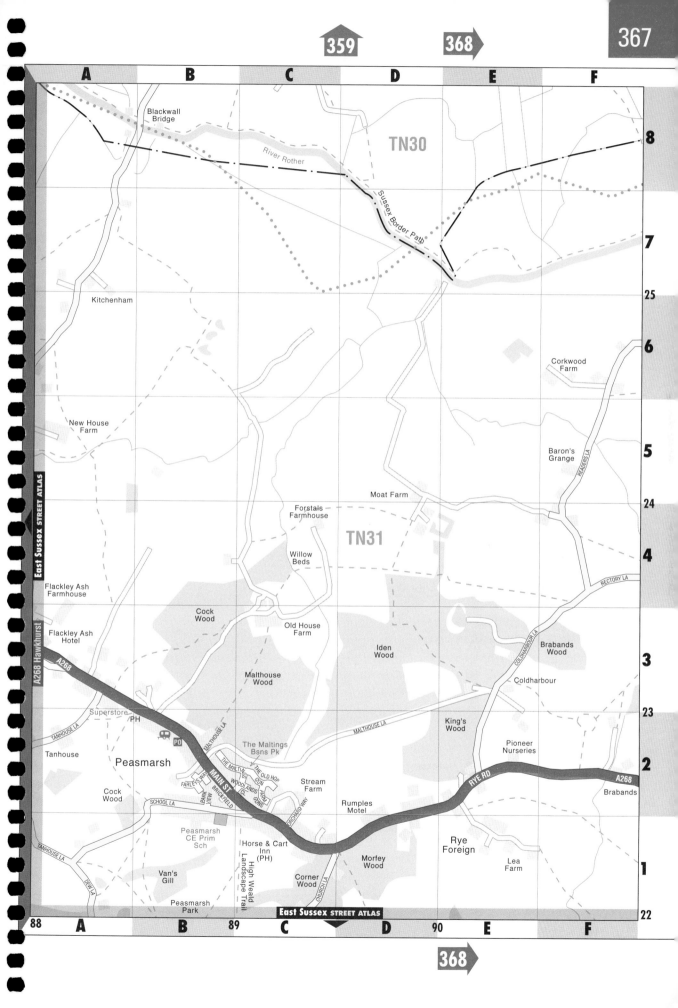

A   B   C   D   E   F

Blackwall Bridge

River Rother

TN30

8

Sussex Border Path

7

25

Kitchenham

6

Corkwood Farm

New House Farm

Baron's Grange

5

READERS LA

Moat Farm

24

Forstals Farmhouse

TN31

4

RECTORY LA

Willow Beds

Flackley Ash Farmhouse

Cock Wood

Old House Farm

Iden Wood

COLDHARBOUR LA

Brabands Wood

Flackley Ash Hotel

Coldharbour

3

A268 Hawkhurst

A268

Malthouse Wood

23

Superstore

PH

MALTHOUSE LA

King's Wood

Pioneer Nurseries

TANHOUSE LA

PO

The Maltings Bsns Pk

MALTHOUSE LA

Tanhouse

Peasmarsh

THE MALTINGS

THE OLD HOP

GUN GDNS

RYE RD

A268

2

Brabands

Cock Wood

MAIN ST

FARLEYS WAY

BARN VIEW

BRICKFIELD

WOODLANDS CL

ORCHARD WAY

Stream Farm

SCHOOL LA

Rumples Motel

Peasmarsh CE Prim Sch

Horse & Cart Inn (PH)

High Weald Landscape Trail

Morfey Wood

Rye Foreign

Lea Farm

1

TANHOUSE LA

Van's Gill

Corner Wood

CHURCH LA

DEW LA

Peasmarsh Park

East Sussex STREET ATLAS

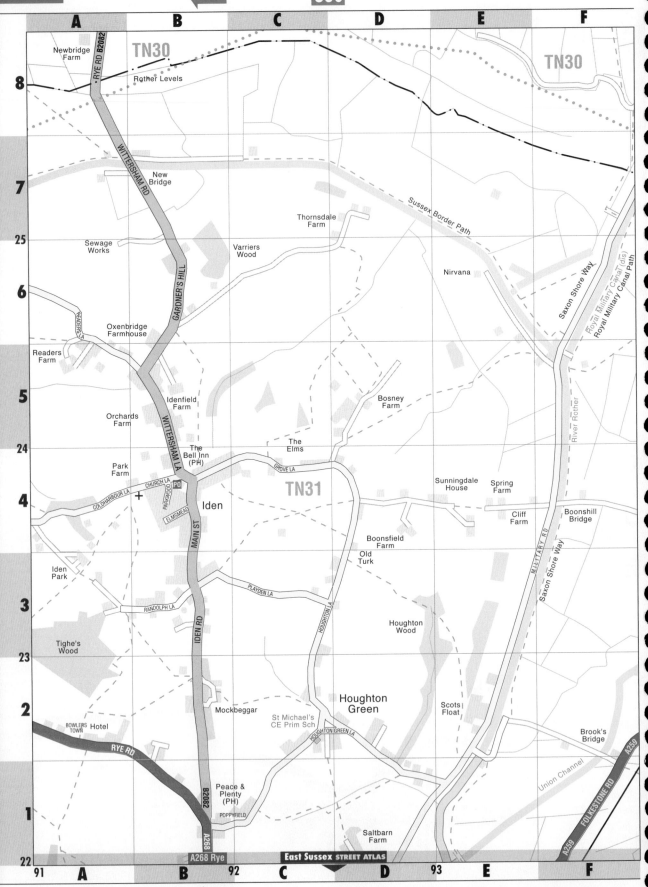

TN30

Newbridge Farm

RYE RD B2082

Rother Levels

TN30

WITTERSHAM RD

New Bridge

Sewage Works

Thornsdale Farm

Sussex Border Path

GARDNER'S HILL

Varriers Wood

Nirvana

Saxon Shore Way

Royal Military Canal (dis)
Royal Military Canal Path

Oxenbridge Farmhouse

READERS LA

Readers Farm

Orchards Farm

Idenfield Farm

WITTERSHAM LA

Bosney Farm

River Rother

The Bell Inn (PH)

The Elms

GROVE LA

Sunningdale House

Spring Farm

Park Farm

COLDHARBOUR LA

CHURCH LA

PARKWOOD

PO

TN31

Cliff Farm

Boonshill Bridge

ELMSMEAD

Iden

Boonsfield Farm

Iden Park

MAIN ST

Old Turk

MILITARY RD

PLAYDEN LA

Houghton Wood

Saxon Shore Way

RANDOLPH LA

IDEN RD

HOUGHTON LA

Tighe's Wood

Houghton Green

Scots Float

BOWLERS TOWN

Hotel

Mockbeggar

RYE RD

St Michael's CE Prim Sch

HOUGHTON GREEN LA

Brook's Bridge

A259

Union Channel

FOLKESTONE RD

B2082

Peace & Plenty (PH)

POPPYFIELD

Saltbarn Farm

East Sussex STREET ATLAS

A259

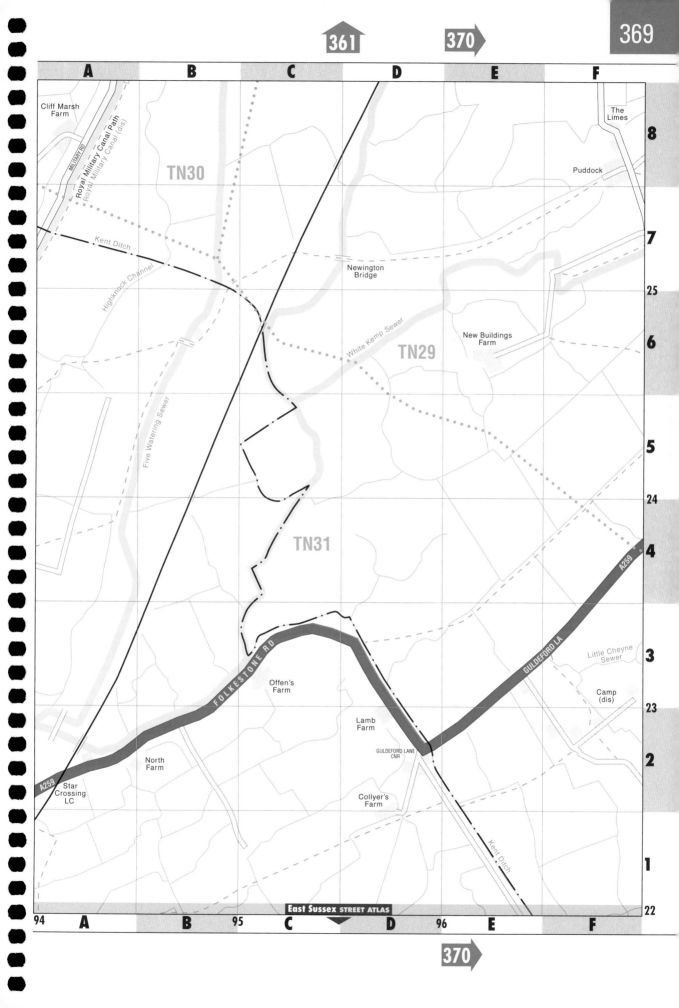

A B C D E F

8

7

25

6

5

24

4

3

23

2

1

22

Cliff Marsh
Farm

MILITARY RD

Royal Military Canal Path
Royal Military Canal (dis)

TN30

Kent Ditch

Highknock Channel

Five Watering Sewer

Newington
Bridge

White Kemp Sewer

TN29

New Buildings
Farm

Puddock

The
Limes

TN31

A259

GULDEFORD LA

Little Cheyne
Sewer

Camp
(dis)

FOLKESTONE RD

Offen's
Farm

Lamb
Farm

North
Farm

GULDEFORD LANE
CNR

Collyer's
Farm

A259

Star
Crossing
LC

Kent Ditch

94 A B 95 C D 96 E F

369
362

A   B   C   D   E   F

Old Farm

SADDLER'S WALL LA

KING ST

WEST PL

SALTER'S LA

Salter's Bridge

SALTHOUSE CL

RYE RD

A259

WHITEHALL

ROSEMARY CNR

HIGH ST

STRAIGHT LA

BOARMAN'S LA

BOARMAN'S LA

Pod Corner

PH

Brookland CE Prim Sch

Malthouse Sewer

8

Poplar Hall

EAST VIEW

Brookland

Dean Court

Harvey Farm

Hamilton Farm

CLUBB'S LA

TILLERY LA

7

Sconce Bridge

25

HOOK LA

Hook House

TN29

6

Depot

Flats Bridge

Philippine Village Craft Ctr

Woolpack Bridge

The Woolpack Inn (PH)

HOOK WALL

Blue House Farm

5

Whitehouse Farm

White Kemp Sewer

Hogstye Bridge

24

Ashentree Bridge

4

GUILDEFORD LA

Walland Marsh

Old Cheyne Court

3

23

2

TN31

1

22

97   A   98   B   C   98   D   99   E   F

369
374

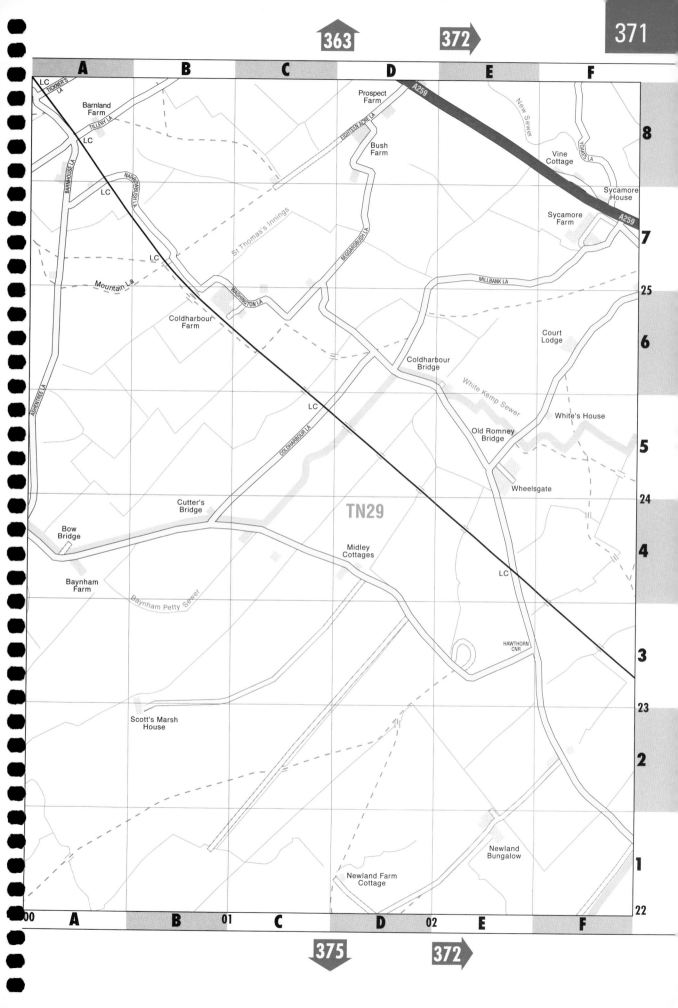

363
372

A   B   C   D   E   F

8
7
25
6
5
24
4
3
23
2
1
22

LC
Tickner's La
Barnland Farm
Tillery La
LC
Barnhouse La
Narrowbush La
LC
Prospect Farm
A259
Eighteen Acre La
Bush Farm
New Sewer
Vine Cottage
Yoakes La
Sycamore House
A259
Sycamore Farm
St Thomas's Innings
LC
Mountain La
Beggarsbush La
Millbank La
Washington La
Coldharbour Farm
Court Lodge
Ashentree La
Coldharbour Bridge
White Kemp Sewer
White's House
LC
Coldharbour La
Old Romney Bridge
Wheelsgate
Cutter's Bridge
TN29
Bow Bridge
Midley Cottages
LC
Baynham Farm
Baynham Petty Sewer
Hawthorn Cnr
Scott's Marsh House
Newland Bungalow
Newland Farm Cottage

00 A   B 01 C   D 02 E   F

375
372

371 364

A B C D E F

8

Hope Farm

Chapel Land Farm

TN28

The Homestead

FIVE VENTS LA

The Manor House

7

Stone Bridge

DOWLE CL

Old Romney

Wallingham Sewer

THE LIMES
ST CATHERINES

25

Rose & Crown (PH)

ELM FIELDS

LYDD RD

SPITALFIELD LA
PRIORY CL

SPITALFIELD TERR

HAMMOND'S CNR

A259

6

Plumtree Farm

Isles Bridge

B2075

Kemps Hill Farm

KINGSMARSH LA

5

Caldecot Petty Sewer

Romney Farm

24

BELL CNR

Kemps Hill Petty Sewer

TN29

Kemp's Hill

SWAMP RD

4

Mast

Kingsmarsh Lane Bridge

Swan Farm

ROMNEY RD

Dengemarsh Sewer

White Kemp Sewer

3

Castilore Farm

23

Swamp Road Bridge

Caldicott Farm

Belgar Farm

CALDECOT LA

Swamp Crossing Farm

2

Swamp Crossing LC

Footway Farm

CH

Horsebones Bridge

Westbrook Farm

Birds Kitchen

Gravel Pits

1

DEYNES LA

Horses Bones Farm

Caldecot Crossing LC

Forty Acre Farm

B2075

22

371 376

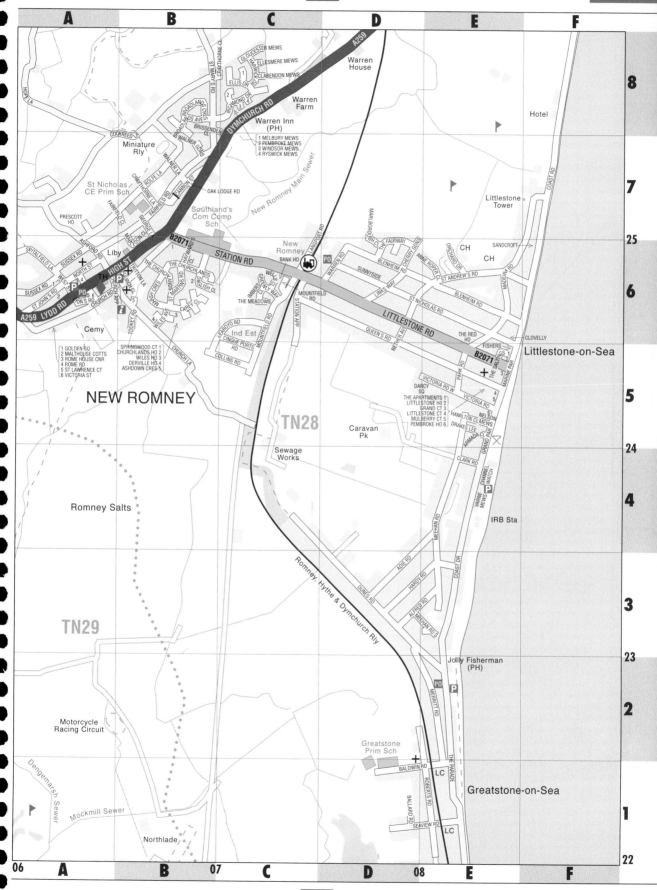

NEW ROMNEY

TN28

TN29

Romney Salts

Motorcycle
Racing Circuit

Dengemarsh Sewer

Mockmill Sewer

Northlade

Miniature
Rly

St Nicholas
CE Prim Sch

Prescott
Ho

SPITALFIELD LA

SUSSEX RD

SUSSEX RD

ST JOHN'S RD

A259 LYDD RD

Cemy

1 GOLDEN SQ
2 MALTHOUSE COTTS
3 ROME HOUSE CNR
4 ROME RD
5 ST LAWRENCE CT
6 VICTORIA ST

SPRINGWOOD CT 1
CHURCHLANDS HO 2
WILES HO 3
DERVILLE HO 4
ASHDOWN CRES 5

HIGH ST

Liby

DYMCHURCH RD

B2071   STATION RD

GLOUCESTER MEWS
ELLESMERE MEWS
CLARENDON MEWS

Warren
House

Warren
Farm

Warren Inn
(PH)

1 MELBURY MEWS
2 PEMBROKE MEWS
3 WINDSOR MEWS
4 RYSWICK MEWS

Southland's
Com Comp
Sch

OAK LODGE RD

New Romney Main Sewer

New
Romney

BANK HO

PO

THE MEADOWS

Ind Est

CINQUE PORTS
RD

COLLINS RD

STATION APP

MOUNTFIELD
RD

Sewage
Works

Romney, Hythe & Dymchurch Rly

Caravan
Pk

DUNES RD

QUEEN'S RD

LITTLESTONE RD   B2071

THE FAIRWAY

MARLBOROUGH CL

BLENHEIM RD

SUNNYSIDE

LINKS WAY

ST NICHOLAS RD

ST ANDREW'S RD

BLENHEIM RD

ANNE ROPER CL

ORCHARD DR

MADEIRA RD

CH

CH

SANDCROFT

Hotel

Littlestone
Tower

COAST RD

Littlestone-on-Sea

Clovelly

FISHERS

THE RED
HO

THE SALTINGS

MARINE PAR

VICTORIA RD W

DARCY
SQ

VICTORIA RD

THE APARTMENTS 1
LITTLESTONE HO 2
GRAND CT 3
LITTLESTONE CT 4
MULBERRY CT 5
PEMBROKE HO 6

NELSON

DRAKES LEE

ARMADA CL

GRAND PAR

HAMILTON CL

PARK RD

CLARK RD

MEEHAN RD

IRB Sta

CHANNEL
WATCH

VARNE
MEWS

ADIE RD

HARDY RD

ALFRED RD

MEEHAN RD S

COAST DR

Jolly Fisherman
(PH)

PO

MERRITT RD

Greatstone
Prim Sch

BALDWIN RD

ROBERTS RD

THE PARADE

LC

BALLARD RD

SEAVIEW RD

LC

Greatstone-on-Sea

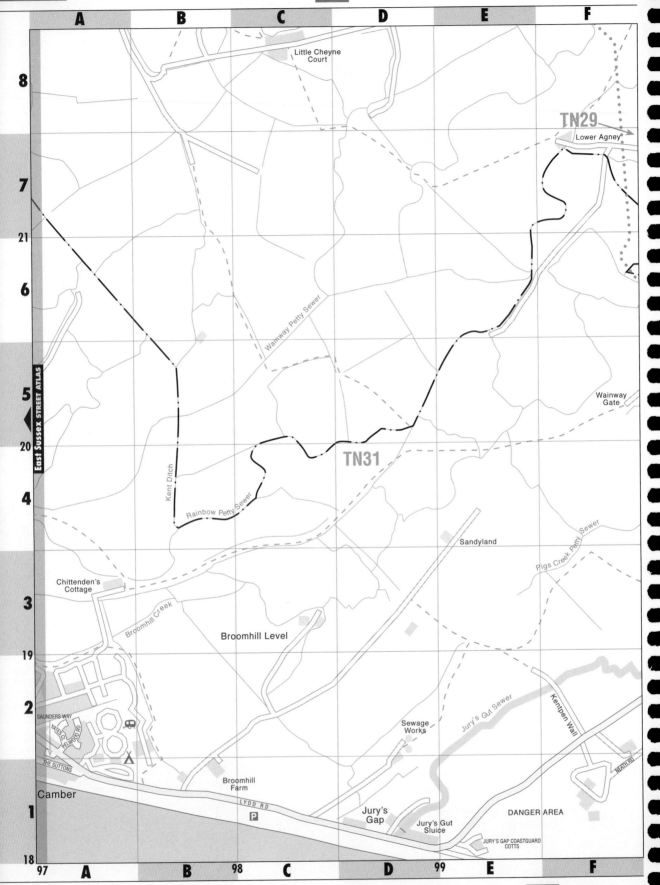

370

A   B   C   D   E   F

Little Cheyne
Court

TN29

Lower Agney

Wainway Petty Sewer

Wainway
Gate

TN31

Kent Ditch

Rainbow Petty Sewer

Pigs Creek Petty Sewer

Sandyland

Chittenden's
Cottage

Broomhill Creek

Broomhill Level

Jury's Gut Sewer

Kentpen Wall

Saunders Way

VALE CL

PELWOOD RD

THE SUTTONS

Camber

Sewage
Works

NEATH RD

LYDD RD

P

Broomhill
Farm

Jury's
Gap

Jury's Gut
Sluice

DANGER AREA

JURY'S GAP COASTGUARD
COTTS

97   A   B   98   C   D   99   E   F

378

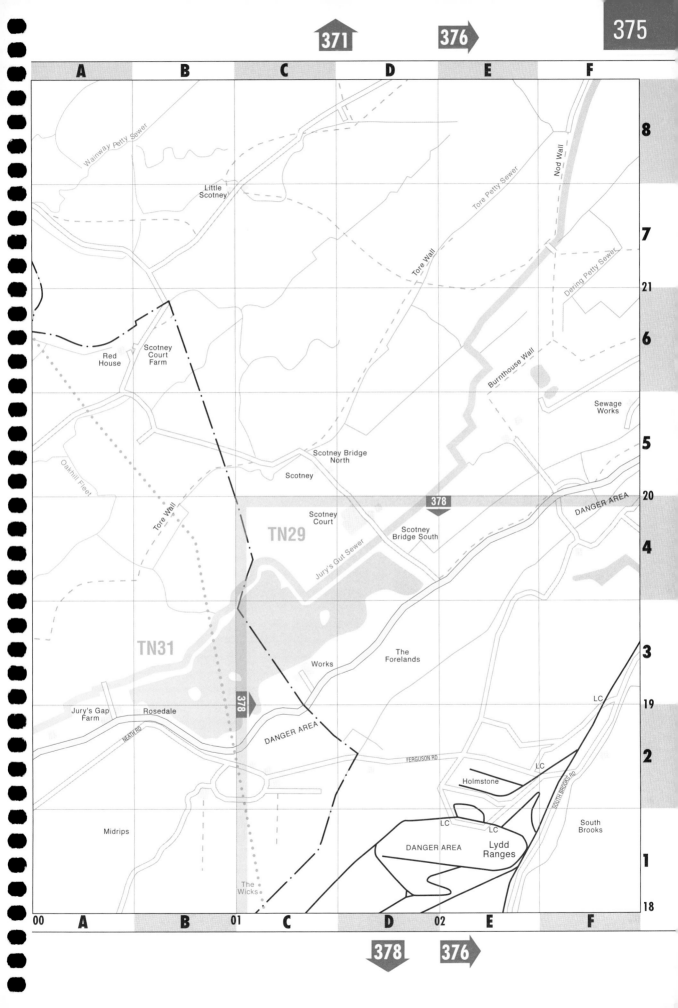

A   B   C   D   E   F

8

7

21

6

Wainway Petty Sewer

Little
Scotney

Nod Wall

Tore Petty Sewer

Tore Wall

Dering Petty Sewer

Red
House

Scotney
Court
Farm

Burnthouse Wall

Sewage
Works

Oakhill Fleet

Tore Wall

5

Scotney Bridge
North

Scotney

20

378

DANGER AREA

4

Scotney
Court

Scotney
Bridge South

TN29

Jury's Gut Sewer

3

The
Forelands

LC

Works

19

378

2

Jury's Gap
Farm

Rosedale

DANGER AREA

FERGUSON RD

LC

TN31

NEATH RD

Holmstone

LC

SOUTH BROOKS RD

South
Brooks

Midrips

LC

LC

1

DANGER AREA

Lydd
Ranges

The
Wicks

18

A B C D E F

8

Westbroke
Cottages

Westbroke
House

Whitehall
Farm

Walland
Marsh

BRIDGE
HOME PK

Jack's
Court

The
Glebe

7

Samuel Mews

STATION RD

Cemy

Ind
Est

21

Church Rd

Gravel
Pits

6

COPPERFIELDS

TH

HIGH ST

Mus

PO

Lydd
Prim
Sch

Liby

Green Hop
Farm

1 CHAPEL ROW
2 CORONATION SQ
3 OAK BGLWS
4 THE PRIORY
5 GRISBROOK RD
6 GRISBROOK FARM CL

Denge Marsh

Tourney
Hall

B2075

LYDD

Pigwell

THE GREEN
GREEN WAY
TOURNEY RD

WHITING
HO

TN29

Cockles
Bridge

5

Lydd Camp

WOLSELEY
TERR

GORDON
TERR

CULVER'S LA

Dungeness Rd

20

378 379

DANGER AREA

Works

Dengemarsh Sewer

4

West
Ripe

LC LC

LC

LC

Twr

SOUTH BROOKS RD

LC

3

LC

Lydd
Watersports
Centre

19

The
Quob

2

INVICTA RD

Hart's
Farm

Dengemarsh
Farm

1

LC

DANGER AREA

Brickwall
Farmhouse

Piper's
Pen

18

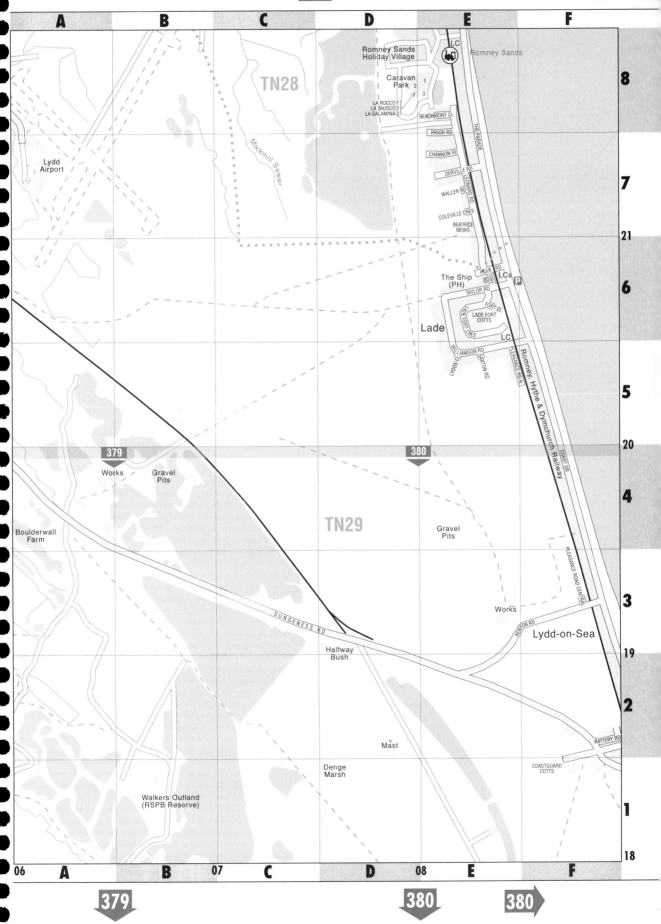

A B C D E F

8

7

21

6

5

20

4

3

19

2

1

18

TN28

Romney Sands
Holiday Village

LC

Romney Sands

Caravan
Park

LA ROCCO 1
LA TAUSCO 2
LA GALAMINA 3

BEACHMONT CL

PRIOR RD

CHANNON RD

DERVILLE RD

WALLER RD

LEONARD RD

COLEVILLE CRES

BEATRICE
MEWS

HULE RD
TOBY RD

THE PARADE

The Ship
(PH)

LCs

P

TAYLOR RD

FORT CL

LADE FORT
COTTS

Lade

THE FORT CRES

LC

WILLIAMSON RD

LYDOS CL

SAXTON RD

PLEASANCE RD N

Romney, Hythe & Dymchurch Railway

COAST DR

Lydd
Airport

Mockmill Sewer

379

Works

Gravel
Pits

TN29

Gravel
Pits

380

Boulderwall
Farm

Works

PLEASANCE ROAD CENTRAL

DUNGENESS RD

Halfway
Bush

KERTON RD

Lydd-on-Sea

Mast

Denge
Marsh

Walkers Outland
(RSPB Reserve)

BATTERY RD

COASTGUARD
COTTS

06 A B 07 C D 08 E F

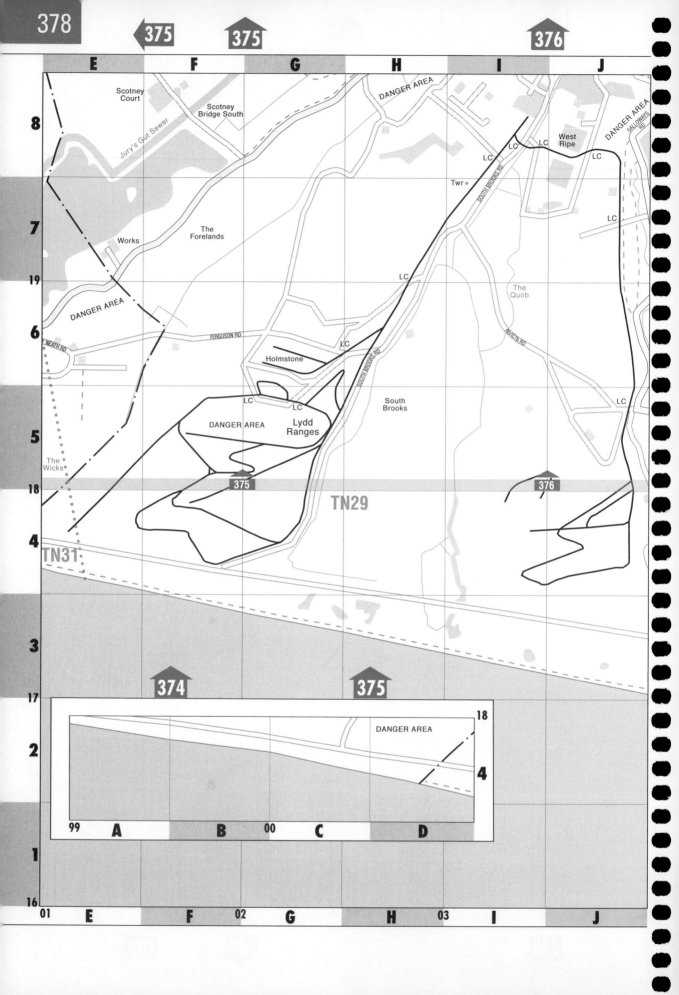

375
375
376

E   F   G   H   I   J

8

Scotney
Court

Scotney
Bridge South

DANGER AREA

West
Ripe

DANGER AREA

GALLOWAYS RD

Jury's Gut Sewer

LC   LC   LC

Twr ●

SOUTH BROOKS RD

LC

7

The Forelands

Works

LC

19

The
Quob

DANGER AREA

6

NEATH RD

FERGUSON RD

LC

INVICTA RD

Holmstone

LC

LC

South
Brooks

LC

5

The
Wicks

LC   LC

DANGER AREA

Lydd
Ranges

18

375

376

TN29

4

TN31

3

17

374   375

18

DANGER AREA

2

4

99   A   B   00   C   D

1

16

01   E   02   F   G   H   03   I   J

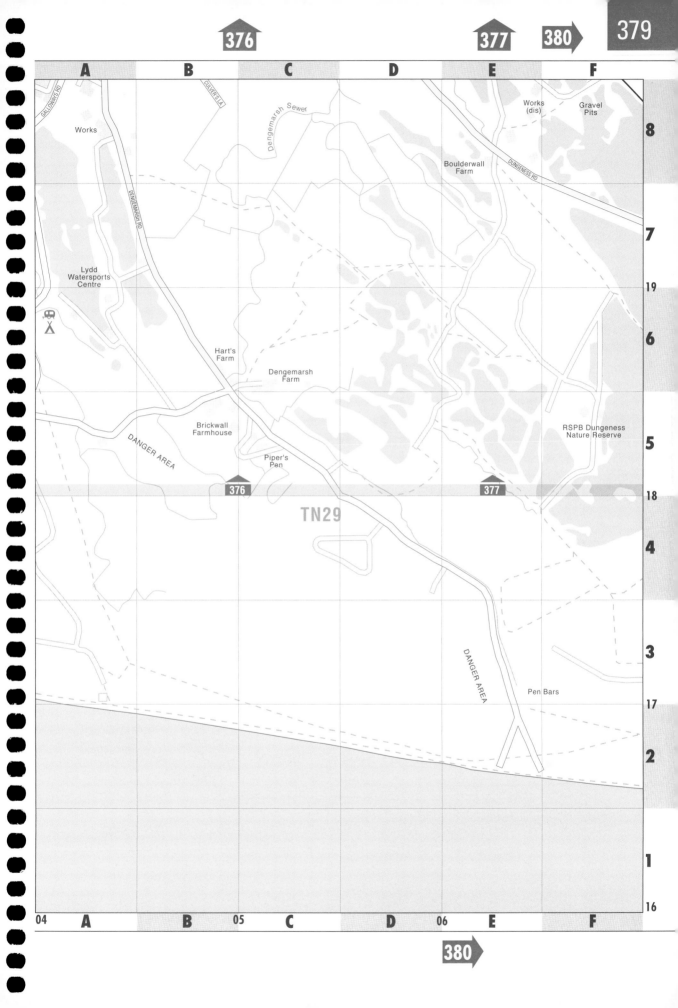

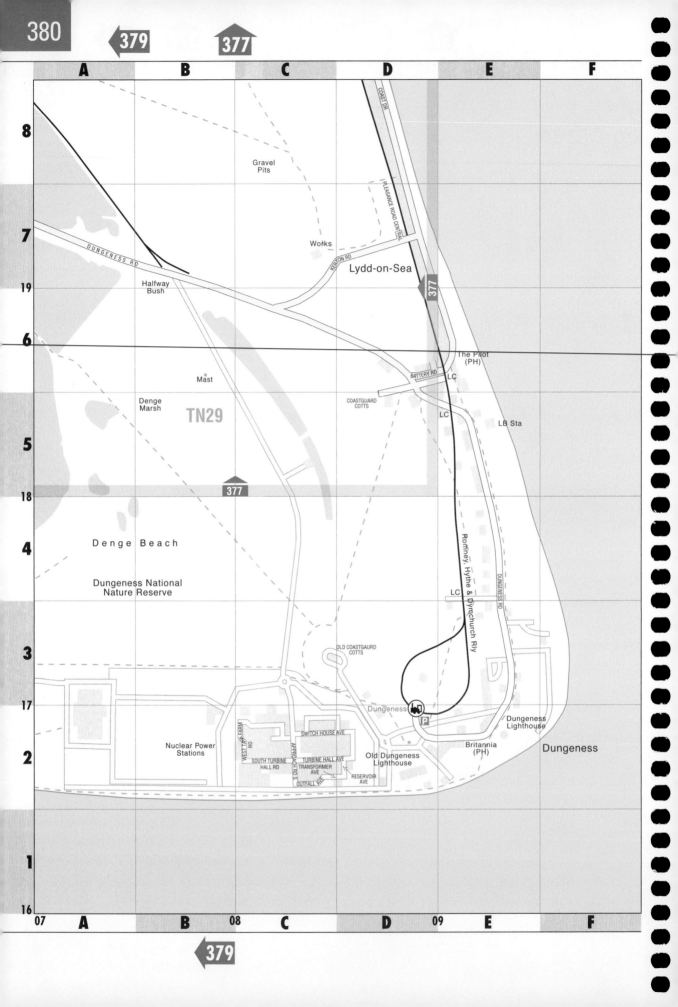

A   B   C   D   E   F

8

Gravel
Pits

COAST DR

7

Dungeness Rd

Works

Halfway
Bush

KERTON RD

PLEASANCE ROAD CENTRAL

Lydd-on-Sea

377

19

6

The Pilot
(PH)

Mast

BATTERY RD

LC

Denge
Marsh

TN29

COASTGUARD
COTTS

LC

LB Sta

5

377

18

4

Denge Beach

Dungeness National
Nature Reserve

Romney, Hythe & Dymchurch Rly

DUNGENESS RD

LC

3

OLD COASTGAURD
COTTS

17

Dungeness

P

Dungeness
Lighthouse

WEST TANK FARM RD

APPROACH RD S

2

Nuclear Power
Stations

SWITCH HOUSE AVE

SOUTH TURBINE
HALL RD

TURBINE HALL AVE

TRANSFORMER
AVE

OUTFALL AVE

RESERVOIR
AVE

Old Dungeness
Lighthouse

Britannia
(PH)

Dungeness

1

16

07   A   B   08   C   D   09   E   F

Church Rd [6] Beckenham BR2..........**53** C6

Place name	**Location number**	**Locality, town or village**	**Postcode district**	**Page and grid square**
May be abbreviated on the map	Present when a number indicates the place's position in a crowded area of mapping	Shown when more than one place has the same name	District for the indexed place	Page number and grid reference for the standard mapping

Public and commercial buildings are highlighted in magenta   **Places of interest** are highlighted in blue with a star★

Abbreviations used in the index

Acad	Academy	Comm	Common	Gd	Ground	L	Leisure	Prom	Prom
App	Approach	Cott	Cottage	Gdn	Garden	La	Lane	Rd	Road
Arc	Arcade	Cres	Crescent	Gn	Green	Liby	Library	Recn	Recreation
Ave	Avenue	Cswy	Causeway	Gr	Grove	Mdw	Meadow	Ret	Retail
Bglw	Bungalow	Ct	Court	H	Hall	Meml	Memorial	Sh	Shopping
Bldg	Building	Ctr	Centre	Ho	House	Mkt	Market	Sq	Square
Bsns, Bus	Business	Ctry	Country	Hospl	Hospital	Mus	Museum	St	Street
Bvd	Boulevard	Cty	County	HQ	Headquarters	Orch	Orchard	Sta	Station
Cath	Cathedral	Dr	Drive	Hts	Heights	Pal	Palace	Terr	Terrace
Cir	Circus	Dro	Drove	Ind	Industrial	Par	Parade	TH	Town Hall
Cl	Close	Ed	Education	Inst	Institute	Pas	Passage	Univ	University
Cnr	Corner	Emb	Embankment	Int	International	Pk	Park	Wk, Wlk	Walk
Coll	College	Est	Estate	Intc	Interchange	Pl	Place	Wr	Water
Com	Community	Ex	Exhibition	Junc	Junction	Prec	Precinct	Yd	Yard

Index of localities, towns and villages

A

Abbey Wood 3 B3
Ackholt...............211 A4
Acol................81 B3
Addington 126 C3
Adisham...............210 D8
Aldington.............330 A6
Aldington Frith 329 D6
Aldon 126 B1
Alkham...............276 C1
Allhallows...............9 C1
Allhallows-on-Sea.......9 D3
Allington 161 B8
Ansdore 239 F6
Anvil Green...........239 C8
Aperfield 118 F2
Appledore 361 C7
Appledore Heath.......347 C1
Arpinge...............306 C3
Ash New Ash Green.....91 E5
Ash Sandwich.........147 D2
Ashbank...............197 B7
Ashford...............268 A2
Ashley...............246 B5
Ashurst...............283 D2
Avery Hill.............12 C1
Aycliff...............310 B5
Aylesford.............128 E2
Aylesford Green.......300 F7
Aylesham.............210 F5

B

Badgers Mount 88 B1
Badlesmere.............170 C1
Bagham 205 D8
Baker's Cross 320 E4
Balls Green...........311 C5
Banner Farm 286 C2
Bapchild...............102 E3
Barden Park...........221 F1
Barfrestone...........211 E1
Barham...............209 F1
Barking 3 B8
Barming Heath 161 A3

Barnehurst 14 D4
Barnes Cray 15 B3
Barnes Street...........224 A4
Barnsole 179 B6
Barrow Green...........103 D3
Barrowhill 331 D7
Barrow Hill 268 A3
Basted 156 F4
Bay View 49 D2
Beacon Hill 343 A4
Beal's Green...........341 A4
Bean 35 C5
Bearsted 163 B4
Beaver 300 B7
Beckton 2 A8
Bedmonton 165 E8
Bekesbourne 176 D4
Bekesbourne Hill 176 B5
Bells Yew Green 314 F5
Beltinge...............77 E4
Beltring 225 A4
Belvedere 4 B2
Benenden 342 E6
Benover 226 A6
Berry's Green.........119 B3
Bessels Green 153 D3
Best Beech Hill 336 B3
Bethersden 297 E5
Betsham...............35 F4
Betteshanger 213 C6
Bewlbridge 317 D1
Bexley 13 C3
Bexleyheath 13 F4
Bexon 134 B4
Bickley...............52 F7
Bicknor...............133 C2
Bidborough...........253 D3
Biddenden.............294 E2
Biddenden Green 264 B2
Biggin Hill...........118 E3
Bilsington 329 C1
Bilting 237 E7
Birchden 312 D5
Birchett's Green 337 F3
Birchington...........80 E7
Bircholt Forstal 302 E8
Birchwood Corner 55 C8
Birling 127 C6

Bishopsbourne.........209 B5
Bishop's Down..........285 E3
Bishopstone 77 F5
Bitchet Green.........155 D1
Blackfen...............13 A1
Blackheath Park 11 A3
Blackhurst...........286 F5
Bladbean 241 F2
Blean 142 A6
Bliby 328 F8
Blooden 210 E8
Bluetown...............135 B1
Blue Town...............28 B2
Bluewater 35 A8
Bobbing 101 A7
Bockhanger 268 C6
Bodiam 355 D1
Bodsham 271 D8
Bogle 136 B8
Bonnington 329 F3
Borden 101 B3
Borough Green 156 F8
Borstal 63 B2
Bossingham 241 A6
Bossington 177 E3
Botolph's Bridge 353 A7
Bottom Pond 134 D2
Bough Beech 218 F2
Boughton Aluph 237 A5
Boughton Green 195 B3
Boughton Lees.........236 E3
Boughton Malherbe ...232 A8
Boughton Monchelsea 195 B3
Boughton Street 140 A3
Bow Arrow 16 B1
Bowmans...............32 F8
Boxley...............130 D2
Boyden Gate 112 C8
Brabourne...........303 B8
Brabourne Lees.......302 D5
Bramling 177 C6
Branbridges 225 A5
Brandfold 290 F3
Brasted...............152 C3
Brasted Chart.........185 B7
Brattle 347 A8
Breach 99 F8

Bredgar 134 A6
Bredhurst.............98 B1
Brenchley 289 B8
Brenzett...............363 A3
Brenzett Green 363 C6
Bridge...............176 A1
Broad Ford 290 C4
Broadoak...............134 E5
Broad Oak Ashford 301 C1
Broad Oak Sturry 143 D7
Broadstairs 84 C5
Broadstone 231 D4
Broad Street
  Hoo St Werburgh 41 B5
Broad Street Lyminge.. 305 C5
Broad Street Maidstone. 164 B6
Broad Street Sellindge. 303 F5
Broad Tenterden 345 B4
Broadwater Down.......313 E7
Broadway.............234 B6
Bromley...............52 B6
Bromley Common........52 E3
Bromley Green.........327 E6
Brompton 64 A5
Bromstone 83 E3
Brook 270 B5
Brookland 370 D8
Brooklands...........33 F7
Brooks End............80 E4
Brook Street Tenterden 346 E8
Brook Street Tonbridge 254 A8
Broomfield Herne Bay . 77 D1
Broomfield Kingswood . 197 D5
Broom Hill Ash 146 B1
Broom Hill Orpington ...53 F2
Broom Street 106 D2
Buckhurst 294 C5
Buckland 278 C2
Buckland Valley 278 C4
Buck's Cross...........87 F5
Bullingstone 284 F7
Bullockstone 110 D8
Burham...............95 E1
Burmarsh 352 C5
Buttsole 180 B1
Bybrook 268 D5

C

Cage Green 222 C4
Camber 374 A1
Camden Hill 292 F2
Camden Park 286 C2
Canning Town...........1 B8
Canterbury 174 C7
Capel...............255 F5
Capel Cross...........290 C5
Capel-le-Ferne 308 B2
Capstone...............97 E7
Castle Hill 257 E1
Cellarhill 103 C1
Chainhurst 227 A4
Chalk...............38 A7
Chalksole...............276 C4
Chalkwell.............101 D4
Challock.............203 B1
Chambers' Green 265 C4
Channel Tunnel
  Terminal 334 B8
Charcott...............220 A3
Charing 234 D8
Charing Heath 233 C6
Charing Hill 201 D1
Charlton...............11 D8
Chartham.............173 E2
Chartham Downs 173 D1
Chartham Hatch 173 D6
Chart Hill 229 B8
Chart Sutton 196 B1
Chartway Street 197 C1
Chatham...............63 E5
Chattenden...........40 F4
Cheeseman's Green....300 F2
Chelsfield...............87 E5
Cheriton...............334 D6
Cherry Orchard 161 B4
Chesley...............100 A3
Chestfield 75 E1
Chestnut Street 100 E4
Chevening.............152 F8
Chiddingstone 251 C7
Chiddingstone
  Causeway 219 F2
Chiddingstone Hoath.. 251 A2

Chilham 205 C7
Chillenden...........211 F8
Chilmington Green.....299 C5
Chipstead 153 C5
Chislehurst.............53 B7
Chislehurst West...... 30 A2
Chislet...............112 D5
Chislet Forstal 112 B5
Christian Fields.......37 C4
Church Hougham 309 B5
Church Street
  Higham.............21 C1
Church Street
  Whitstable...........74 F1
Church Whitfield......278 B8
Clapham Hill...........108 D5
Clap Hill 329 F7
Clarendon 310 B6
Claygate.............258 D6
Clement Street 33 D2
Cliffe...............22 B5
Cliffe Woods...........40 B7
Cliffs End.............116 D6
Cliftonville 51 D2
Cobbarn 312 F3
Cobham...............60 F6
Cockshot 340 F1
Cock Street...........195 D2
Coldblow 32 D7
Coldharbour 188 F1
Cold Harbour
  Lenham.............200 F6
Cold Harbour
  Sittingbourne....... 100 F7
Coldred 245 A3
Coldred Street.........245 A2
Colliers' Green.......291 F2
Collier Street 258 C8
Colt's Hill 256 B4
Congelow 225 F2
Conyer 103 F5
Cooling...............22 F5
Coolinge 334 F4
Cooling Street 22 D2
Coombe 179 F8
Cooper's Corner 218 F8
Cooper Street 148 B4
Coppins' Corner 234 A6

Cop Street 147 E4
Cousley Wood 337 C7
Cowden 282 A6
Cowden Pound 250 B2
Coxheath 194 C2
Crabble 277 F2
Cranbrook 320 C6
Cranbrook Common . . . 293 A2
Crayford 14 D1
Creekmouth 2 F8
Crockenhill 55 D3
Crockham Hill 184 C2
Crockhurst Street 255 C6
Crofton 86 D8
Cross-at-Hand 228 E1
Crossways 16 D3
Crouch 157 B4
Crowdleham 123 D2
Crundale 238 D7
Cudham 119 D4
Culmers 106 E1
Culverstone Green 92 E2
Curteis' Corner 295 A3
Curtisden Green 291 C5
Custom House 1 C7
Cuxton 62 B2
Cyprus 2 B6

D

Danaway 100 C3
Dane Street 204 F6
Daniel's Water 298 D7
Darenth 34 B4
Dargate 140 E7
Darland 97 E8
Dartford 15 E2
David Street 93 B5
Davington 138 A8
Deal 215 E6
Deans Bottom 133 C5
Deans Hill 133 D6
Dean Street 194 D7
Deerton Street 104 A2
Denny Bottom 285 E4
Densole 307 A8
Denstroude 141 C8
Denton Folkestone 243 B3
Denton Gravesend 37 E8
Derringstone 242 E7
Derry Downs 54 D3
Detling 131 B1
Devil's Den 229 B3
Ditton 128 C1
Doddington 167 E7
Donkey Street 352 D5
Dover 310 F7
Downe 119 A8
Dryhill 153 B3
Dumpton 83 E2
Dungate 135 B3
Dungeness 380 F2
Dunkirk 140 D3
Dunkirk End 366 B7
Dunk's Green 190 A6
Dunn Street Gillingham . 131 A8
Dunn Street Westwell . . 235 E5
Dunton Green 153 E8
Durgates 336 E5
Durlock 179 B8
Durrant Green 324 B6
Dymchurch 366 C7

E

Each End 148 B1
East Barming 160 F1
Eastchurch 48 E3
East End Benenden . . . 322 C3
East End Headcorn . . . 263 B4
East Farleigh 194 B7
East Hill 90 B1
East Langdon 247 A1
Eastling 168 F6
East Malling 160 A7
East Malling Heath . . . 159 E4
East Peckham 224 F6
Eastry 180 A2
East Stourmouth 113 E1
East Street Addington . 126 E3
East Street Sandwich . . 148 A2
East Studdal 246 D7
East Tilbury 20 C7
East Wickham 13 A7
Eastwood 231 C6
Eaton Lands 333 C3
Eccles 128 F6
Eddington 76 F3
Edenbridge 217 D1
Egerton 232 F4
Egerton Forstal 232 D1
Elham 273 F5
Elmstead 29 D2
Elmsted 271 F6
Elmstone 146 E5
Elmstone Hole 231 E8
Elms Vale 310 A7
Elphicks 318 A8
Eltham 11 E1
Elvington Eythorne . . . 212 C1
Elvington Hawkinge . . . 306 E2
Eridge Green 313 B3
Erith 4 C1
Erriottwood 135 F3
Etchinghill 305 C3
Ewell Minnis 276 E3
Exted 273 E5
Eyhorne Street 164 C2
Eynsford 89 D7
Eythorne 245 C8
Eythorne Green 245 D7

F

Fairbourne Heath 198 B1
Fairfield 83 E4
Fairseat 125 C7
Falconwood 12 E3
Farnborough 86 D5
Farningham 56 F2
Farthing Common 304 D5
Farthing Green 229 E1
Farthingloe 309 F5
Farthing Street 85 F2
Faversham 138 A5
Fawkham Green 91 B8
Felderland 180 F4
Fenn Street 24 B4
Ferndale 286 D5
Fernleigh 101 C2
Field Green 355 E8
Fig Street 187 A7
Finglesham 214 B8
Fir Toll 265 C6
Fishinghurst 319 F7
Five Oak Green 256 B7
Five Wents 196 D2
Fleet-Downs 34 D7
Flemings 179 D6
Flimwell 339 C3
Folkestone 335 F4
Folly Town 270 F7
Foord 335 D2
Foots Cray 31 B2
Force Green 151 D4
Ford 111 E8
Fordcombe 284 B5
Fordwich 144 A4
Forstal 129 B2
Fostall 140 A7
Fosten Green 322 D6
Four Elms 218 A5
Four Throws 355 D8
Four Wents 341 B6
Foxendown 93 C8
Frant 314 C3
French Street 184 F6
Frindsbury 63 C8
Frinsted 166 C7
Frittenden 293 F7
Frogham 211 C2
Froghole 184 D3
Frogholt 333 F7
Further Quarter 296 C3

G

Garlinge 82 A8
Garlinge Green 206 E5
Gibraltar 306 F3
Gillingham 64 D3
Gill's Green 340 F5
Glassenbury 319 E6
Goathurst Common . . . 186 B5
Goat Lees 268 C8
Goddard's Green 321 F2
Godden Green 155 B3
Goddington 87 C7
Godington Park 267 E2
Godmersham 205 A2
Golden Green 223 F5
Gold Street 60 E4
Golford 321 B5
Golgotha 244 F6
Goodnestone
   Faversham 139 D7
Goodnestone
   Wingham 178 D2
Goose Green
   Biddenden 322 E8
Goose Green Hadlow . . 191 B2
Gore 180 B3
Goudhurst 318 F8
Grafty Green 231 F7
Grain 27 B6
Grange 65 B6
Gravel Castle 243 A8
Graveney 106 E2
Gravesend 19 B2
Grays 18 A7
Great Chart 267 C1
Great Mongeham 214 C3
Greatness 154 D6
Great Stonar 149 B4
Greatstone-on-Sea . . . 373 E1
Greenhill 76 D2
Greenhithe 17 B2
Green Street Green
   Hartley 35 A2
Green Street Green
   Orpington 86 E4
Greenwich 1 A3
Greet 167 D3
Groombridge 312 C7
Grove 145 F8
Grove End 134 C7
Grove Green 162 E5
Grove Hill 145 D6
Grove Park 29 B5
Grubb Street 58 B8
Guilton 147 C1
Gun Green 341 C2
Gushmere 171 C8
Guston 278 E6

H

Hacklinge 181 C1
Hadlow 190 E1
Hadlow Stair 222 F4
Haffenden Quarter 296 A7
Haine 82 F2

Hale Birchington 80 B4
Hale Chatham 97 D8
Hales Place 143 A3
Hale Street 225 A3
Halfway Houses 46 E7
Halfway Street 244 D4
Halling 95 B5
Hall's Green 220 A7
Halstead 120 F6
Ham 180 F2
Ham Green Upchurch . . 66 F6
Ham Green Wittersham . 359 C1
Hamlet of Shellness 73 E5
Hammerwood 281 B3
Hammill 76 B5
Hampton 76 B5
Hamstreet 349 B2
Harbledown 174 B8
Harbourland 162 B5
Hareplain 294 C4
Harman's Corner 101 A2
Harrietsham 198 D5
Hartley Cranbrook 319 F1
Hartley New Barn 58 F3
Hartley Green 58 E4
Hartlip 99 E5
Harvel 93 C3
Hassell Street 239 A2
Hastingleigh 271 B6
Haviker Street 226 E1
Hawkenbury
   Royal Tunbridge Wells 286 D2
Hawkenbury
   Headcorn 261 D7
Hawkhurst 341 A4
Hawkinge 307 C5
Hawksdown 248 B8
Hawley 33 F3
Hawthorn Corner 78 A3
Hayes 52 A2
Hazel Street Bredgar . . 133 A3
Hazel Street
   Horsmonden 289 F4
Hazelwood 119 D8
Headcorn 262 D4
Hearnden Green 230 B1
Hearts Delight 101 B1
Heath Side 32 F5
Heaverham 123 C2
Hempstead 98 A5
Hemsted 304 D8
Henhurst 60 E8
Henley Street 60 F3
Henwood Green 287 E6
Herne 111 B8
Herne Bay 76 E6
Herne Common 110 F6
Herne Pound 158 D2
Hernhill 140 B6
Heronden 179 F1
Hersden 111 F1
Hever 250 D6
Hextable 32 E1
Hickmans Green 140 A2
Hicks Forstal 111 A4
Higham 39 B4
Higham Wood 222 F6
High Brooms 286 D5
High Halden 324 D7
High Halstow 23 F3
Highstead 78 A1
Highsted 134 F7
Highstreet 107 F2
High Street 340 D2
Hildenborough 221 E6
Hilden Park 221 F4
Hillborough 78 A4
Hill Green 99 C1
Hill Hoath 251 C6
Hill Park 151 B4
Hill Street 271 F8
Hill Top 257 B1
Hinxhill 269 D1
Hoaden 146 F4
Hoath 111 F5
Hoath Corner 251 B3
Hockenden 55 B6
Hocker Edge 292 D2
Hockley 169 C3
Hodsoll Street 92 D3
Hogben's Hill 171 A6
Holborough 95 A2
Holland 183 A1
Hollingbourne 164 E2
Hollow Street 112 C4
Hollybushes 167 A8
Holtye 281 F3
Hone Sundridge 152 F3
Honey Hill 141 E8
Hoo 114 F6
Hook Green
   Lamberhurst 316 C4
Hook Green
   Meopham Station . . . 60 A3
Hook Green Northfleet . . 36 A2
Horns Green 119 E2
Horn Street Folkestone 334 B4
Horn Street Snodland . 127 D6
Horselees 140 A2
Horseshoe Green 250 E1
Horsmonden 290 A5
Horton 173 F3
Horton Kirby 57 D5
Hothfield 267 A7
Houghton Green 368 D2
How Green 218 C1
Hucking 132 E1
Hungershall Park 285 E2
Hunters Forstal 77 C1
Hunton 226 F3
Hurst Green Hawkhurst 354 B3
Hurst Green Oxted . . . 183 B3
Hythe 333 D1

I

Ickham 145 C1
Ide Hill 185 F4
Iden 368 B4
Iden Green Goudhurst . 319 C8
Iden Green Hawkhurst . 342 D4
Ightham 156 D6
Igtham Common 156 A3
Istead Rise 59 E8
Ivychurch 363 E3
Ivy Hatch 156 A1
Iwade 68 D4

J

Joyden's Wood 32 F4
Jury's Gap 374 D1

K

Kearsney 277 D3
Kemsing 123 B2
Kemsley 68 C1
Kemsley Street 98 C2
Kenardington 348 A6
Kennington 268 C6
Kennington Lees 268 D7
Kent Hatch 184 B3
Kent Street 158 E2
Keston 85 D6
Keston Mark 85 D8
Kevingtown 54 E3
Keycol 100 E6
Key's Green 288 C4
Key Street 101 A5
Kidbrooke 11 C5
Kilndown 317 F3
Kingsdown Deal 248 D5
Kingsdown Lynsted . . . 135 E4
Kingsdown Park 74 F3
Kings Farm 37 C5
Kingsgate 51 G1
Kings Hill 159 A2
Kingsland 265 C8
Kingsnorth Ashford . . . 300 A4
Kingsnorth
   Hoo St Werburgh . . . 42 D5
Kingston 209 D3
Kingswood 197 E3
Kipping's Cross 288 B5
Kippington 154 A1
Kit's Coty 129 C7
Knatts Valley 123 D8
Knaves Ash 111 C5
Knockhall 17 C1
Knockholt 120 B2
Knockholt Pound 120 C1
Knockmill 123 E7
Knowlton 212 C7
Knox Bridge 292 F6

L

Labour-in-vain 124 F5
Laddingford 225 E5
Lade 377 E6
Lamberhurst 317 B5
Lamberhurst Quarter . . 288 D1
Lane End 34 D3
Langhurst 216 E7
Langley 196 C4
Langley Heath 196 F4
Langton Green 284 E3
Larkfield 128 A2
Lashenden 294 F6
Leadingcross Green . . . 199 C3
Leaveland 203 B8
Leaves Green 118 D8
Leeds 197 A7
Leigh 220 F1
Leigh Green 345 F6
Lenham 199 D5
Lenham Forstal 200 B1
Lenham Heath 233 B8
Lessness Heath 4 B1
Letts Green 119 F3
Lewisham 29 C6
Lewson Street 136 E7
Leybourne 127 D2
Leysdown-on-Sea 49 H2
Lidsing 97 F1
Lilyvale 302 F4
Limpsfield 183 A6
Linkhill 356 E4
Linton 194 F1
Little Bayham 315 F4
Little Betteshanger . . . 213 E5
Littlebourne 176 E8
Little Chart 234 A1
Little Chart Forstal 266 C3
Little Houses 232 D2
Little Mill 224 D5
Little Mongeham 214 A2
Littlestone-on-Sea 373 F5
Liverton Street 198 F1
Locksbottom 86 B7
Lodge Lees 242 F4
London Beach 324 B5
Longfield 58 C7
Longfield Hill 59 D5
Longford 153 D6
Longlands 30 D5
Loose 194 F4
Loose Hill 194 F5
Lords Wood 97 C3
Lower Bitchet 155 C1
Lower Bush 61 F3
Lower Cousley Wood . . 337 E8

Lower Cox Street 131 D6
Lower Eythorne 245 B8
Lower Goldstone 147 F7
Lower Green Pembury . 287 D8
Lower Green Rusthall . . 285 C5
Lower Halstow 67 C3
Lower Hardres 208 A6
Lower Hartlip 99 E4
Lower Haysden 253 D8
Lower Heppington 207 F8
Lower Herne 76 F1
Lower Higham 39 D6
Lower Island 74 C1
Lower Luddesdown 61 A2
Lower Newlands 104 A2
Lower Rainham 65 F3
Lower Stoke 25 C5
Lower Twydall 65 C5
Lower Upnor 41 A3
Lower Walmer 215 C4
Low Street 19 E8
Luddesdown 60 F1
Lunsford 127 E4
Luton 64 B2
Luxted 119 A5
Lydd 376 D6
Lydd Camp 376 B5
Lydden 276 E8
Lydd-on-Sea 380 D7
Lye Green 311 D1
Lymbridge Green 272 B4
Lyminge 305 B6
Lympne 332 A3
Lynsore Bottom 241 D8
Lynsted 136 A6

M

Macklands 66 A2
Madeira Park 286 B2
Maidstone 162 C3
Maltman's Hill 264 E3
Manston 82 C1
Maplescombe 90 B5
Marden 259 C5
Marden Beech 259 B3
Marden Thorn 259 F3
Margate 50 H2
Marine Town 28 E2
Markbeech 250 D2
Marley Barham 209 B1
Marley Deal 214 A8
Marlpit 195 E2
Marlpit Hill 217 C4
Marshborough 180 B7
Marsh Green 249 B5
Marshside 78 D1
Martin 247 B3
Martin Mill 247 C2
Martyr's Field 174 F7
Matfield 288 D8
Maxted Street 272 B6
Maxton 310 A6
Maypole Dartford 32 E7
Maypole Herne Bay . . . 111 F6
Maypole Orpington 87 F4
Medhurst Row 218 A2
Meopham 93 B8
Meopham Green 93 A2
Meopham Station 60 B4
Meresborough 99 A5
Mereworth 191 D8
Merryman's Hill 47 C8
Mersham 301 E4
Middle Deal 215 D5
Middle Quarter 296 D1
Middle Stoke 25 B4
Milebush 259 E8
Mile Oak 257 C4
Mile Town 28 E1
Millbank Headcorn 262 B6
Millbank Herne Bay . . . 111 F7
Mill Hill 215 A3
Mill Street 159 E7
Millstead 134 E2
Milton 19 E1
Milton Regis 101 C6
Minster Sheppey 47 B7
Minster Thanet 115 A6
Mockbeggar 104 B1
Modest Corner 253 E1
Molash 203 F4
Monkton 114 D7
Moon's Green 359 A3
Moorstock 303 C2
Moor Street 99 B7
Morehall 334 F6
Mottingham 29 D6
Mott's Hill 312 A3
Mountain Street 205 B6
Mount Ephraim 285 F4
Mount Sion 286 A2
Mowshurst 217 E3
Munday Bois 264 F8
Murston 102 B5

N

Naccolt 269 E6
Nackington 175 A2
Napchester 246 C3
Nash Ashford 146 F2
Nash Keston 85 A4
Nash Street 60 A7
Neames Forstal 171 C6
Nethercourt 117 A7
Nettlestead 192 D6
Nettlestead Green 192 B2
New Ash Green 91 B8
Newbarn 305 B4

New Barn 59 A7
Newbury 135 D4
Newbury's 337 B8
New Charlton 1 C2
Newchurch 350 E3
New Eltham 30 C1
Newenden 357 D3
Newham 1 A6
New House 36 F6
New Hythe 128 B4
Newingreen 332 A5
Newington Folkestone . 334 A8
Newington Ramsgate . . 83 B1
Newington Sittingbourne 100 A6
Newland Green 264 D8
Newnham 168 C7
New Romney 373 A5
New Street 92 D5
Newtown 250 D4
New Town Ashford 300 D7
New Town Dartford 16 A1
New Town Halling 95 A6
New Town West Malling 159 A8
Noah's Ark 155 A8
Noke Street 40 B4
Nonington 211 D5
Northbourne 214 A4
North Cray 31 F5
Northdown 51 D1
North Elham 274 A6
North End 14 F6
Northfleet 18 D1
Northfleet Green 36 C3
Northgate 143 B2
North Halling 95 B8
Northiam 357 C1
North Lyminge 305 C7
North Stonar 149 B6
North Street Faversham 138 C1
North Street
   Hoo St Werburgh . . . 24 E1
Northumberland Heath . 14 C7
Northwood 83 C3
North Woolwich 2 B4

O

Oad Street 100 E1
Oare 105 A3
Ockley 341 A3
Offham 158 D8
Old Bexley 32 B8
Oldbury 156 B6
Old Romney 372 B7
Old Wives Lees 172 C3
Orchard Valley 333 B3
Orpington 54 C2
Osmers Hill 336 F7
Ospringe 138 B6
Otford 122 A3
Otham 196 B7
Otham Hole 196 B6
Otterham Quay 66 C3
Ottinge 273 D1
Out Elmstead 209 F2
Overland 171 F7

P

Paddlesworth 306 C4
Paddock 202 E1
Paddock Wood 256 F6
Painter's Forstal 137 E3
Palmarsh 353 D7
Palmer's Green 289 D8
Palmstead 241 D5
Paramour Street 147 D7
Parkgate 323 B2
Park Wood Gillingham . . 98 D4
Park Wood Maidstone . 195 E4
Parrock Farm 37 D4
Patrixbourne 176 B3
Payden Street 167 B1
Pearson's Green 257 F3
Peasmarsh 367 A2
Peckham Bush 224 E8
Pedlinge 332 D4
Peene 334 B8
Peening Quarter 359 B6
Pegwell 117 B5
Pell Bridge 337 A5
Pell Green 337 A7
Pembury 287 C6
Penenden Heath 162 B7
Pennypot 332 E1
Penshurst 252 B4
Pepper Hill 36 C5
Perry 146 C3
Perry Street 36 F8
Perrywood 171 C4
Pested 203 B4
Petham 207 B3
Pett Bottom 208 B5
Petteridge 288 F6
Pettings 92 B3
Petts Wood 53 D5
Pikefish 225 F3
Pinden 58 C7
Pineham 278 D8
Pipsden 341 D1
Pittswood 223 B8
Plaistow 29 A2
Platt 157 C7
Platt's Heath 198 E1
Plaxtol 189 E8
Plaxtol Spoute 190 A8
Pluckley 265 D7
Pluckley Thorne 265 B6
Plucks Gutter 113 F3
Plumstead 2 E2
Plumtree Green 262 A8

Pootings 217 E7
Postling 304 F2
Potman's Heath. 358 E4
Potten Street 79 D3
Potters Corner 267 F6
Potter's Forstal 232 B2
Poundsbridge. 284 D8
Poverest. 54 A4
Powder Mills 221 E2
Pratling Street. 129 C3
Pratt's Bottom 87 D1
Preston Ash 146 B6
Preston Faversham 138 D6
Priestwood. 93 B5
Priestwood Green. . . . 93 C5
Primmer's Green 336 F5
Princes Park. 97 B6
Printstile 253 A3
Puddledock. 32 E2
Purfleet 16 A8
Putlands. 256 F5
Pye Corner 231 A6

Q

Queenborough. 46 A5
Queen Street 257 D7

R

Rabbit's Cross 228 E3
Radfall 109 C5
Radfield 103 A2
Rainham Essex 4 F8
Rainham Kent 65 E8
Ram Lane 234 E2
Ramsden 54 C1
Ramsgate 117 C4
Ramslye 285 D1
Ratling 211 A8
Reading Street
   Broadstairs 83 F7
Reading Street
   Tenterden 346 C2
Reculver. 78 C7
Red Hill 159 F1
Red Street. 36 B2
Rhode Common 172 A6
Rhodes Minnis. 273 A3
Ridge Row 274 E1
Ridley 92 B4
Ringlestone Harrietsham 165 F4
Ringlestone Maidstone . 161 E7
Ringwould 247 F5
Ripple 247 D8
Riseden Durgates 336 B1
Riseden Kilndown 318 A5
River 277 E3
Riverhead 153 E5
Riverview Park 37 E4
Robhurst 325 C2
Rochester 63 B6
Rockrobin 336 D6
Rodmersham 135 C8
Rodmersham Green . . 135 B7
Rolvenden 343 F4
Rolvenden Layne. 344 B1
Romden 264 C1
Romford 287 F7
Roseacre 163 A4
Rosherville 18 E1
Rough Common 142 B3
Round Green 291 F4
Round Street 60 D5
Rowling 179 A2
Rowling Street. 328 E6
Royal Tunbridge Wells. 286 D3
Ruckinge. 349 F8
Rushenden 45 C4
Rusthall 285 C4
Ruxley. 31 E1

Ryarsh 126 F4
Rye Foreign 367 E1

S

St Ann's Green 259 F8
St Dunstan's 142 D1
St John's
   Royal Tunbridge Wells . . . 286 A5
St John's Sevenoaks . . . 154 B5
St Lawrence 117 B8
St Leonard's Street . . . 159 B6
St Margarets. 34 D1
St Margaret's at Cliffe 280 A6
St Martin's 175 B8
St Mary Cray. 54 B4
St Mary Hoo 24 D6
St Mary in the Marsh. . 365 B4
St Mary's Bay 366 A4
St Mary's Island 41 C1
St Michaels. 324 B4
St Nicholas at Wade . . .79 E1
St Paul's Cray 54 A7
St Peter's 83 E5
St Radigund's. 278 A2
Saint's Hill 284 A8
St Stephen's 142 F2
Saltwood 333 C4
Sandgate 334 E3
Sandhurst 356 C6
Sandhurst Cross 355 F4
Sandling. 129 F1
Sandway 199 A3
Sandwich. 149 B1
Sarre 113 D7
Satmar 308 D3
Seal 155 A6
Seasalter 108 A7
Seaton 145 D2
Seed 168 A6
Sellindge 303 D1
Selling 171 C6
Selson 180 A3
Selsted 275 B5
Sepham Heath 121 B6
Sevenoaks. 154 D2
Sevenoaks Weald 187 B2
Sevington 301 B6
Shadoxhurst 327 A8
Shalmsford Street 173 B1
Shatterling 146 E1
Sheerness 28 C3
Sheerwater 146 F6
Sheldwich 170 C6
Sheldwich Lees 170 C5
Shelvin 243 C3
Shepherds Hill 171 A4
Shepherdswell or
   Sibertswold 244 E5
Shepway 195 D8
Sherwood 286 E6
Shipbourne 189 C5
Shipland 265 D8
Shirkoak. 326 A5
Sholden 214 B4
Shooters Hill 12 C6
Shoreham 121 F8
Shorne 38 E3
Shorne Ridgeway 38 E2
Shottenden 171 D1
Shover's Green 337 C1
Shuttlesfield 306 A6
Sibertswold or
   Shepherdswell 244 E5
Sidcup 31 A3
Silver Street 133 F5
Silvertown. 1 C4
Single Street 119 B4
Singleton 299 E7
Singlewell 37 D2
Sinkhurst Green 261 E2
Sissinghurst 321 B7

Sittingbourne. 101 D8
Sixmile 272 D5
Skeete 304 D7
Slade. 167 E1
Slade Green 15 B6
Slutshole 140 A5
Sly Corner 347 F5
Small Hythe 345 C1
Smarden 264 A1
Smarden Bell 263 D2
Smeeth. 302 C4
Snargate 362 E6
Snipeshill 102 D3
Snodland 128 B7
Snoll Hatch. 224 E5
Snowdown 211 A3
Sole Street Gravesend . . 60 C4
Sole Street Wye 239 B7
South Alkham 308 B8
South Ashford 300 A8
Southborough Bromley . . 52 F3
Southborough
   Royal Tunbridge Wells . 254 B1
South Darenth 57 D8
Southdowns 57 D7
South Green 133 A5
South Stour 301 B1
South Street Biggin Hill 151 A8
South Street Meopham . .92 F4
South Street Selling . . . 171 F8
South Street Stockbury . 132 C7
South Street Whitstable. 109 A7
South Tankerton 75 A1
South Willesborough. . 300 E6
Sparrow's Green 336 F5
Speed Gate. 90 F8
Speldhurst. 285 B7
Stalisfield Green 201 D6
Standen 295 B5
Standen Street. 342 D1
Stanford 304 B1
Stanhope 299 F6
Stansted 91 F1
Staple 179 A5
Staplehurst 260 D4
Staplestreet 140 A5
Statenborough. 180 C4
Stede Quarter 295 E1
Stelling Minnis 240 F2
Stiff Street 133 E7
Stocker's Head 201 F1
Stockland Green 253 C1
Stocks Green 221 B4
Stodmarsh 145 B6
Stoke. 25 A3
Stone 16 F2
Stone Bridge 336 E6
Stonebridge Green. . . . 233 A4
Stone Cross
   Aldington Frith 328 E6
Stone Cross
   Langton Green 284 A2
Stone Cross Sandwich . 180 E7
Stone Cross Wadhurst . 337 A3
Stonecrouch 338 F6
Stonehall. 276 F7
Stone Hill 303 A2
Stone in Oxney 360 F4
Stone Street 155 E2
Stonestreet Green 330 A7
Stowting 304 A8
Stowting Common . . . 272 A4
Street End 207 F7
Strood Rochester 62 F7
Strood Tenterden 344 B5
Stubb's Cross 299 C2
Studdal. 246 C7
Studd Hill 76 A4
Sturry 143 E6

Styants Bottom 155 F5
Summerfield. 179 B4
Sundridge 29 C2
Sutton 247 A7
Sutton at Hone 34 A1
Sutton Valence 229 E6
Swalecliffe 75 E3
Swanley. 55 E5
Swanley Village 56 B7
Swanscombe 17 D2
Swanton. 191 A8
Swift's Green 263 E6
Swingfield Minnis 275 B3
Swingfield Street 275 E4

T

Tankerton 75 A3
Tatsfield 150 D7
Teasley Mead 283 C4
Temple Ewell 277 D6
Temple Hill 16 A3
Tenterden 345 C8
Teston 193 A8
Teynham 103 C3
Teynham Street 103 E4
Thamesmead 3 A5
Thanington 174 B6
The Brents 105 D1
The Chart Limpsfield . . . 183 E5
The Chart Toys Hill 185 C5
The Crook 257 D1
The Down 317 A3
The Forstal 301 D3
The Harbour 229 E5
The Leacon 348 D7
The Lees 203 A1
The Moor 354 F8
The Quarries 195 C4
The Quarter Headcorn . 264 B5
The Quarter
   Staplehurst 260 E1
The Quarter Tenterden. 345 A4
The Stocks 360 A3
The Valley 201 D8
Thong 38 A2
Three Chimneys 294 B2
Three Legged Cross . . . 338 D3
Throwley 169 E4
Throwley Forstal 169 D1
Thurnham 163 D8
Thurston Park 74 E1
Ticehurst 338 E2
Tickenhurst 179 D1
Tickham 136 D6
Tilbury 19 B4
Tilmanstone 213 A3
Timberden Bottom . . . 88 D1
Titsey 150 B2
Tollgate 157 A8
Tonbridge 222 A2
Tonge Corner 102 F7
Tong Green 169 B1
Tovil 161 E1
Tower Hamlets 310 B8
Townland Green 326 A1
Toy's Hill 185 C3
Trench Wood 222 B7
Trottiscliffe 126 A5
Troy Town Brook 270 B5
Troy Town Edenbridge. . 216 F5
Tudeley 255 B7
Tudeley Hale. 223 C1
Tunstall 134 D8
Turnden 320 B4
Turner's Green 336 F6
Tutt Hill 235 A1
Twitham 178 E6
Twitton 121 E4
Twydall. 65 B2
Tylden 295 E7
Tyler Hill 142 E6

West Langdon 246 D3
West Malling 159 C7
Westmarsh 147 B7
West Minster 46 A7
West Peckham 191 A6
West Stourmouth 113 D2
West Street Eastry 180 F1
West Street Lenham . . 166 E1
West Thurrock 17 B8
West Tilbury 19 E8
Westwell 235 E3
Westwell Leacon 234 D4
Westwood Barham . . . 241 E8
Westwood Broadstairs . .83 B5
Westwood Hartley. . . . 35 D1
Wetham Green. 66 F5
Whatsole Street 271 F5
Wheelbarrow Town. . . 272 F8
Whetsted 224 E1
Whitehall 83 C1
Whitehill 58 D7
White Oak 55 F7
White Post 283 D7
Whitfield 278 A7
Whitstable. 74 C3
Wichling 167 C5
Wickhambreaux. 145 B2
Wick Hill 294 F8
Widmore 52 E7
Wierton 228 F8
Wigmore 98 B4
Wilgate Green 169 F6
Willesborough. 300 F8
Willesborough Lees . . 269 B1
Willington 162 E1
Wilmington 33 C4
Wilsley Green 320 D7
Wilsley Pound 320 E8
Winchet Hill 291 B6
Windmill Hill 37 A7
Wingham 178 B7
Wingham Green 177 F7
Wingham Well 177 E6
Wingmore 242 B2
Winterbourne. 172 A8
Wissenden 296 F7
Witherden. 269 F8
Withyham 311 A3
Wittersham 359 D3
Wolverton 276 F2
Wombwell Park 36 D6
Womenswold 210 D2
Woodchurch Margate . .81 F3
Woodchurch Tenterden. 304 F8
Woodland 123 C6
Woodlands 180 C6
Woodnesborough 180 C6
Wood's Green 336 F8
Woodside Green 199 F8
Woodstock 134 E6
Woolage Green 243 F8
Woolage Village. 210 F1
Woolwich 2 B3
Wooton. 243 C1
Wormshill 166 A7
Worms Hill 291 B5
Worsenden Green 294 D2
Worten 266 F3
Worth 181 B4
Wouldham 95 D5
Wrotham 124 F2
Wrotham Heath 126 A1
Wye 237 F1

U

Ulcombe 230 F7
Underdown 206 B8
Underling Green 227 F2
Underriver. 188 A5
Union Street 339 B3
Upchurch. 66 F4
Upper Bush 61 F2
Upper Deal 215 B4
Upper Eythorne 245 C7
Upper Fant 161 D3
Upper Goldstone 147 E5
Upper Halling. 94 E5
Upper Harbledown . . . 141 F1
Upper Harvel 93 C3
Upper Hayesden 253 C6
Upper Rodmersham. . . 135 C6
Upper Ruxley 32 A1
Upper Tolhurst 338 A2
Upper Upnor 40 F1
Upper Walmer 215 B1
Upstreet. 112 D3
Upton 83 F4
Upton Wood 244 E2

V

Vicarage Green 337 A5
Vigo Village 126 B8

W

Wadhurst. 337 A4
Wainscott 40 D3
Walderslade 96 F1
Walderslade Bottom . . 97 A2
Wallcrouch 337 F1
Walmer. 215 C2
Walmestone 146 D3
Walter's Green 283 E6
Waltham 239 E6
Wanden 264 B7
Wanshurst Green 260 A7
Warden. 49 D4
Warehorne 348 D6
Ware Street 163 B5
Warmlake 196 D1
Warren Street 200 D7
Waterham 107 C2
Wateringbury 192 D7
Waterman Quarter . . . 262 D2
Watts's Cross 221 B7
Way 115 E7
Wayfield 97 A8
Weardale 185 B5
Weavering Street 162 F5
Weddington 147 E3
Weed's Wood 96 F3
Weller's Town 251 D5
Well Hill 88 B4
Welling 13 B4
Well Street 159 E6
Westbere. 144 C7
Westbrook. 50 E1
West Cliffe 279 D6
Westcourt 37 E6
West Cross 343 D4
West Dumpton 83 D2
West End Doddington . 167 D7
West End Herne Bay . . 110 B8
Westenhanger 332 B6
Westerham 151 C1
Western Heights 310 C6
West Farleigh 193 D6
Westgate-on-Sea 50 B2
West Heath 13 D8
West Hougham 308 F5
West Hythe 332 B1
West Kingsdown 90 F2

Y

Yalding 192 F1
Yelsted 99 A1
Yewtree Green 258 B1
Yopps Green 156 E1
Yorkletts 107 F2

20/20 Ind Est ME16 ... 161 C8

A

Aaron Hill Rd E6 ....2 A8
Abbess Cl 12 E1 ....1 E8
Abbeville Ho ME1 ... 63 C4
Abbey Brewery Ct
  ME19 ....159 C8
Abbey Cl Deal CT14 .... 215 A5
  Minster (Sheppey) ME12 .. 47 C6
Abbey Court Specl Sch
  ME2 ....62 E8
Abbey Cres DA17 ....4 A2
Abbey Ct
  Westgate-on-S CT8 .... 81 D7
  Whitstable CT5 ....75 A3
Abbey Dr DA2 ....32 E6
Abbey Fields Cl ME13 .. 138 E7
Abbey Fields ME13 .... 138 E7
Abbey Gate Cotts
  ME14 ....129 F2
Abbey Gate CT11 .... 117 B5
Abbey Gdns
  Canterbury CT2 ...... 143 A2
  Chislehurst BR7 ..... 53 A8
Abbey Gr
  Minster (Thanet) CT12 .. 115 C5
  Ramsgate CT11 ..... 117 B5
  Woolwich SE2 ....3 B2
Abbeyhill Rd DA15 .... 31 C6
Abbey Ho SE2 ....3 D1
Abbey Life Ct E13 ....1 B8
Abbey Lodge SE12 .....29 B4
Abbey Mount DA17 .....3 F1
Abbey Pl Dartford DA1 .. 15 D2
  Faversham ME13 ..... 138 D8
Abbey Rd
  Bexley DA6,DA7 ...... 13 E3
  Erith DA8 ....3 E3
  Faversham ME13 ..... 138 D8
  Gillingham ME8 ...... 65 A2
  Gravesend DA12 ..... 37 E7
  Kearsney CT16 ...... 277 D1
  River CT16,CT17 .... 277 D1
  Rochester ME2 ....62 F8
  Swanscombe DA9 .... 17 C2
Abbey Sch The
  Faversham ME13 ..... 138 C5
  Westgate-on-S CT8 ... 81 E8
Abbey St ME13 ...... 138 D8
Abbey Ter SE2 ....3 C2
Abbeyview Dr ME12 ...47 B6
Abbey Way TN24 .... 269 A1
Abbey Wood Golden
  Jubilee Cvn site SE2 ...3 C1
Abbey Wood Rd
  Kings Hill ME19 ..... 159 A8
  Woolwich SE2 ....3 C2
Abbey Wood Sch SE2 .. 3 A3
Abbey Wood Sta SE2 ...3 A2
Abbots Barton Wlk
  CT1 ....175 B7
Abbotsbury Hts CT2 .. 143 B4
Abbots Cl BR5 ....53 C1
Abbots Court Rd ME3 .. 41 F4
Abbots Field
  Gravesend DA12 ..... 37 C2
  Maidstone ME16 .... 161 B2
Abbots Hill ME13 .... 137 E5
Abbot's Hill CT11 .... 117 E6
Abbots Pl CT1 ...... 142 F1
Abbots Rd ME13 .... 138 F7
Abbots The CT17 .... 310 C8
Abbots Wlk TN25 .... 237 E2
Abbotswood Cl 13 DA17 ..3 B3
Abbott Cl 13 CT20 .. 335 E6
Abbott Rd
  Borough Green TN15 .. 156 F7
  Folkestone CT20 .... 335 E6
Abbotts Cl
  Rochester ME1 ....63 B3
  Swanley BR8 ....56 A5
  Woolwich SE28 ....3 C6
Abbott's Wlk DA1 .... 13 D7
Abbott Way TN30 .... 345 C2
Aberdeen Cl CT13 .... 112 D3
Aberdeen Ho 9 ME15 . 195 E7
Aberford Gdns SE18 ....11 E6
Abergeldie Rd SE12 ....11 B1
Abery St SE18 ....2 E2
Abigail Cres ME5 ...... 97 A1
Abingdon Gr CT3 .... 112 C3
Abingdon Mews ME9 . 159 C8
Abingdon Rd ME16 .. 160 F2
Abingdon Way BR6 ....87 B6
Abinger Cl BR1 ....52 E6
Abinger Dr ME5 ...... 97 C2
Absalom Ct ME8 ...... 65 C2
Acacia Cl BR5 .... 53 D4
Acacia Ct DA11 ...... 37 A8
Acacia Dr CT3 ...... 144 D8
Acacia Rd
  Dartford DA1 .... 33 D7
  Stone DA9 ....16 E1
Acacia Terr ME10 .... 101 C4
Acacia Way DA15 .... 30 F7
Acacia Wlk BR8 ...... 55 D7
Academy Dr ME7 ......64 F1
Academy Pl SE18 .... 12 A6
Academy Rd SE18 .... 11 F7
Acer Ave TN2 ...... 314 C8
Acer Rd TN16 ...... 118 D3
Achilles Rd ME5 ...... 97 C2
Ackerey Ct TN23 .... 299 F6
Ackholt Rd CT3 ..... 211 A5
Acland Ct SE18 ...... 12 D7
Acol Hill CT7 ....81 B4
Acorn Cl Chislehurst BR7 . 30 C3

Acorn Cl continued
  Five Oak Green TN12 .. 256 B7
  Hawkinge CT18 ..... 307 C4
  Kingsnorth TN23 .... 300 C3
Acorn Gr ME20 ...... 160 D8
Acorn Pl ME15 ..... 195 E6
Acorn Rd Crayford DA1 ..14 F2
  Gillingham ME7 ......64 F4
Acorns The
  Sevenoaks TN13 .... 154 A4
  Smarden TN27 ..... 263 F1
Acorn St CT12 ...... 28 C1
Acorn Terr ME7 ...... 66 E2
Acorn Trad Ctr RM20 ...17 E8
Acorn Way
  Hurst Green TN19 .... 354 A3
  Orpington BR6 ....86 B6
Acorn Wharf Rd ME1 .. 63 C6
Acott Fields ME18 .. 225 F8
Acre Cl ME1 ....63 E1
Acre Ct CT17 ...... 310 C8
Acre Gr ME2 ....95 A4
Acres Rise TN5 .... 338 E1
Acre The CT16 ..... 277 F8
Acton La CT30 ..... 359 F4
Acton Pl ME18 ..... 193 A1
Acton Rd CT5 .... 74 D2
Acworth Ho 1 SE18 .. 12 B8
Acworth Pl DA1 ..... 15 C1
Adam Cl ME7 ...... 194 D3
Adam Ct 1 CT9 ......51 B2
Adams Cl TN30 .... 324 B1
Adamson Rd E16 ......1 A7
Adams Sq DA6 ....13 C4
Ada Rd CT1 .... 174 D6
Adbert Dr ME15 .... 194 B4
Adcot Wlk 7 BR6 ....86 F6
Addelam Cl CT14 ... 215 A4
Addelam Rd CT14 ... 215 A4
Adderley Gdns SE9 .. 30 A4
Addington La ME19 .. 126 B4
Addington Pl CT11 .. 117 C6
Addington Rd
  Margate CT9 ....50 J2
  Sittingbourne ME10 .. 101 C3
Addington Sq CT9 ....50 J2
Addington St
  Margate CT9 ....50 J2
  Ramsgate CT11 .... 117 D6
Addiscombe Gdns CT9 ..50 J1
Addiscombe Rd CT9 .. 51 A1
Addison Cl
  Orpington BR5 ...... 53 C3
  West Malling ME19 .. 127 F1
Addison Cotts TN30 .. 359 D3
Addison Dr SE12 .....11 B2
Addison Rd BR2 ...... 52 D4
Addlestead Rd TN12 . 224 E6
Adelaide Dr ME10 ... 101 C4
Adelaide Gdns
  Halfway Houses ME12 .. 46 E6
  19 Ramsgate CT11 .. 117 E6
Adelaide Ho
  Deal CT14 .... 215 D6
  Sheerness ME12 ..... 28 H1
Adelaide Pl CT1 .... 174 F8
Adelaide Rd
  Chislehurst BR7 ..... 30 B3
  Elvington CT15 ..... 212 B1
  Gillingham ME7 ..... 64 C4
  Tilbury RM18 ...... 18 F5
Adelaide The ME3 .. 39 C6
Aden Terr 1 ME14 .. 162 A7
Adie Rd TN28 ..... 373 D3
Adisham CE Prim Sch
  CT3 ....210 D8
Adisham Downs Rd
  CT3,CT4 ....177 B2
Adisham Dr ME16 ... 161 B7
Adisham Gn ME10 ... 101 F8
Adisham Rd
  Bekesbourne CT4 ... 176 B3
  Wingham CT3 ...... 178 A4
  Womenswold CT4,CT3 .. 210 C2
Adisham Sta CT3 ... 210 E8
Adisham Way CT9 ... 51 C1
Admaston Rd SE18 .. 12 C8
Admers Wood DA13 . 126 B8
Admiral Cl BR5 ...... 54 D5
Admiral Ct ME4 ...... 64 D6
Admiral Moore Dr
  ME20 ....128 F1
Admirals Ct E6 ....2 B7
Admiral Seymour Rd
  SE9 ....11 F3
Admiral's Wlk ME4 ...63 F7
Admirals Wlk
  Chatham ME5 ....97 B3
  Goddard's Green TN17 .. 321 D2
  Halfway Houses ME12 .. 46 E6
  Hythe CT21 .... 333 C1
  Swanscombe DA9 .... 17 B2
  Tenterden TN30 .... 324 C1
Admiralty Cl ME13 .. 138 B8
Admiralty Mews CT14 . 215 D4
Admiralty Rd ME2 .. 40 F1
Admiralty Terr
  1 Chatham ME7 ...... 64 A7
  Rochester ME2 ...... 40 F1
Admiralty Wlk CT5 .. 108 A7
Admiral Way ME19 .. 159 A1
Adrian Mews CT8 ... 50 D1
Adrian Sq CT8 ..... 50 D1
Adrian St CT17 .... 310 D7
Aerodrome Est ME14 . 131 E4
Aerodrome Rd
  Bekesbourne CT4 .... 176 E3
  Hawkinge CT18 .... 307 A4
Afghan Rd
  Broadstairs CT10 .... 83 F8
  Chatham ME4 ....63 E4
Agate La E16 ....1 D7

Agaton Rd SE9 .... 30 C6
Agester La CT4 .... 243 A4
Agnes Cl E6 ....2 A7
Agricultural Mus Brook
  The ★ TN25 ..... 270 B5
Ailsa Mews ME1 ...... 62 F2
Ainsdale Cl
  Folkestone CT19 .... 335 B7
  Orpington BR6 ...... 53 D1
Ainsley Way CT4 .... 206 F8
Aintree Cl DA12 ...... 37 B5
Aintree Ho 1 ME15 . 195 F6
Aintree Rd ME5 ...... 97 C3
Airedale Cl
  Dartford DA2 .... 34 C7
  Margate CT9 .... 51 A1
Aireys The CT13 .... 180 B6
Airfield View ME12 .. 71 C8
Airport Ind Est TN16 . 118 D4
Airport Rdbt E16 .... 1 D5
Aisher Rd SE28 ......3 C6
Aisher Way TN13 .... 153 E6
Aisne Dr CT1 ..... 143 D1
Ajax Rd ME1 ...... 96 C8
Akehurst La TN13 ... 154 C2
Alabama St SE18 .... 12 E7
Alamein Cl CT15 .... 278 F3
Alamein Gdns DA2 .. 34 D8
Alamein Rd DA10 ... 17 D1
Alanbrooke DA12 .... 37 C8
Alan Cl DA1 .... 15 C3
Alan Marre Ho SE7 .. 11 D8
Alanthus Cl SE12 .... 11 A1
Alaseun Terr ME12 .. 47 A5
Alban Cres DA4 ..... 57 A1
Albany Cl Sidcup DA5 . 31 D8
  Tonbridge TN9 ..... 254 D7
Albany Dr CT6 ...... 76 D4
Albany Hill TN2 .... 286 C5
Albany Ho 15 CT17 .. 310 D7
Albany Mews BR1 ... 29 A2
  Royal Tunbridge Wells
  TN4 ....254 D1
Albany Park Sta DA14 . 31 D6
Albany Pl CT17 .... 310 D7
Albany Rd Bexley DA17 . 13 F8
  Capel-le-F CT18 .... 308 C1
  Chatham ME4 .... 64 B2
  Chislehurst BR7 ..... 30 B3
  Gillingham ME7 ..... 64 D4
  Rochester ME1 ...... 63 C4
  Sidcup DA14 ...... 31 C8
  Tilbury RM18 ...... 19 A6
Albany St ME14 .... 162 B5
Albany Terr
  Chatham ME4 ...... 63 E4
  Gillingham ME7 ..... 64 D4
Albatross Ave ME2 .. 62 C6
Albatross Cl E6 ....1 F8
Albatross St SE18 .. 12 E7
Albemarle Rd
  Ashford TN24 ...... 268 F1
  Chatham ME5 .... 97 C2
Alberta Cl CT16 .... 278 B3
Alberta Rd DA8 ..... 14 C6
Albert Costain Ct 1
  CT20 ....335 D5
Albert Cotts TN1 ... 286 B4
Albert Ct
  8 Ramsgate CT12 .. 117 E6
  9 Whitstable CT5 ... 74 D2
Albert Ho SE28 ....2 C3
Albert La CT21 ..... 333 C1
Albert Manor ME7 ... 64 A7
Albert Murray Cl DA12 . 37 C8
Albert Pl ME2 .... 63 C4
Albert Rd Ashford TN24 . 268 B3
  Broadstairs CT10 .... 83 E8
  Bromley,Bromley Common
  BR2 ....52 B5
  Bromley,Mottingham SE9 .. 29 C5
  Canterbury CT1 .... 175 B8
  Capel-le-F CT18 .... 308 C2
  Chatham ME4 ...... 64 A3
  Dartford DA2 ...... 33 C5
  Deal CT14 .... 215 C6
  Dover CT16 .... 278 D1
  Erith DA17 ....3 F1
  Folkestone CT19 .... 335 D6
  Gillingham ME7 ..... 64 C4
  Hythe CT21 .... 333 B1
  Margate CT9 ...... 50 H2
  Newham E16 ...... 1 B5
  Orpington BR5 .... 54 B3
  Orpington,Green Street Green
  BR6 ....87 A5
  Ramsgate CT11 .... 117 F7
  Rochester ME1 ..... 63 C3
  Sidcup DA5 ......32 B8
  Swanscombe DA10 .. 17 F1
  3 Tonbridge TN9 .. 222 B1
Albert Reed Gdns
  ME15 ....161 E2
Albert Row CT11 ... 117 C5
Albert St
  Maidstone ME14 .... 161 F6
  Ramsgate CT11 .... 117 C6
  Royal Tunbridge Wells
  TN1 ....286 B4
  Whitstable CT5 ..... 74 D2
Albert Terr Deal CT14 . 215 C5
  Margate CT9 .... 50 I2
  Minster (Sheppey) ME12 . 48 A5
Albert Wlk E16 ...... 2 B4
Albion Cl CT6 ..... 111 A8
Albion Cotts TN12 . 259 D5
Albion Ct
  Ramsgate CT11 .... 117 C6
  2 Woolwich SE18 ...1 E2
Albion Hill ME7 .... 117 C6
Albion Ho E16 ....2 B5
Albion La CT6 ..... 111 A8
Albion Mews ME7 .. 117 F6

Albion Mews Rd 3
  CT20 ....335 D4
Albion Mews TN1 ... 286 C5
Albion Pl Ashford TN24 . 300 E7
  Canterbury CT1 .... 143 A1
  Chattenden ME2 ..... 41 A3
  Faversham ME13 ... 138 C7
  Hythe CT21 .... 333 D2
  Maidstone ME14 .... 162 B4
  Newington ME9 .... 100 B6
  Ramsgate CT11 .... 117 E6
Albion Rd Bexley DA6 .. 14 A3
  Birchington CT7 ..... 81 A7
  Broadstairs CT10 .... 83 F6
  Chatham ME5 ....97 B2
  Deal CT14 .... 215 D8
  Eastry CT13 ...... 180 A2
  Folkestone CT19 .... 335 D6
  Gravesend DA12 .... 37 C8
  Marden TN12 ..... 259 D5
  Margate CT9 .... 51 B3
  Ramsgate CT11 .... 117 F7
  Royal Tunbridge Wells
  TN1 ....286 C5
Albion St CT10 .... 84 B4
Albion Terr
  Gravesend DA12 .... 19 D1
  Sittingbourne ME10 . 101 E6
Albion Villas 6 CT20 . 335 D4
Albion Way TN1 .... 217 C4
Albright Ind Est RM13 . 4 F8
Albuhera Sq CT1 ... 143 D1
Albury Ave DA7 ..... 13 C5
Albury Cl ME5 ..... 97 D2
Albyfield BR1 ....52 F6
Alchins Cotts ME17 . 194 E2
Alconbury DA6 ..... 14 A2
Aldeburgh Pl SE10 ...1 A2
Aldeburgh St SE10 ...1 A1
Alder Cl
  Royal Tunbridge Wells
  TN4 ....254 D1
  West Minst ME12 ... 46 A8
Aldergate La CT21 .. 331 C5
Alder Ho TN23 .... 267 F1
Alder La TN17 ..... 343 C1
Alder Lodge TN4 ... 285 E4
Alderman Cl DA1 ... 32 E8
Aldermary Rd BR1 .. 52 A8
Alderney Gdns CT10 . 83 E5
Alderney Rd DA8 .... 15 A7
Alderney Way TN24 . 268 C7
Alder Rd
  Folkestone CT19 .... 335 C6
  Sidcup DA14 ...... 30 F5
Alders Cotts TN12 .. 256 A5
Aldersgrove Ave SE9 . 29 D5
Aldershot Rd ME5 ... 97 A7
Alders Meadow TN9 . 221 F2
Alders Rd TN11,TN12 . 255 E6
Alders The ME13 ... 191 D7
Alder Way BR8 ..... 55 D7
Alderwick Gr ME15 . 159 C3
Alderwood Prim Sch
  SE9 ....12 E1
Alderwood Rd SE9 . 12 D1
Aldington Cl ME5 .... 97 B5
Aldington Cnr TN25 . 330 A6
Aldington La ME14 . 163 D8
Aldington Prim Sch
  TN25 ....330 A5
Aldington Rd
  Greenwich SE18 .... 1 D3
  Lympne CT21 ...... 331 E3
  Maidstone ME14 .... 162 F4
Aldon Cl ME14 ..... 162 C6
Aldon Ct ME14 ..... 162 C6
Aldon La ME19 ..... 158 C8
Aldred Rd ME13 .... 138 C6
Aldridge Cl CT6 ..... 76 B3
Aldwick Rd SE9 ..... 30 D5
Aldwych Cl TN10 ... 222 D7
Alec Pemble Cl TN24 . 268 E5
Alefe Way ME9 ..... 68 D3
Alen Sq TN12 ...... 260 F4
Alers Rd DA6 .... 13 D2
Alestan Beck Rd E16 . 1 D7
Alexander Cl Hayes BR2 . 52 A1
  Sandwich CT13 .... 180 F8
  Sidcup DA15 ...... 12 E1
Alexander Cotts ME2 . 39 C6
Alexander Ct
  Greenwich SE3 ..... 11 B5
  1 Rochester ME2 ... 63 B8
  2 Royal Tunbridge Wells
  TN1 ....286 A4
Alexander Dr ME18 . 159 A3
Alexander McLeod Prim
  Sch SE2 ....3 B1
Alexander Rd
  Bexley DA7 .... 13 D5
  Chislehurst BR7 ..... 30 B3
  Swanscombe DA9 .... 17 C2
Alexandra Ave ME7 .. 64 E4
Alexandra Corniche
  CT20,CT21 ....334 C3
Alexandra Ct CT21 .. 333 A1
Alexandra Dr CT14 . 214 F3
Alexandra Gdns CT20 . 335 D4
Alexandra Glen ME5 . 97 A1
Alexandra Homes CT9 . 50 I1
Alexandra Hospl The
  ME5 ....161 C1
Alexandra Mews ME12 . 28 C2
Alexandra Rd
  Biggin Hill TN16 .... 150 B8
  Birchington CT7 .... 81 A5

Alexandra Rd continued
  Broadstairs CT10 .....84 B4
  Capel-le-F CT18 .... 308 C2
  Chatham ME4 ....64 B2
  Deal CT14 .... 215 D2
  Erith DA8 ....14 F8
  Gravesend DA12 .... 37 E8
  Kingsdown CT14 ... 248 C5
  Margate CT9 ....82 E8
  Ramsgate CT11 .... 117 D8
  Sheerness ME12 .... 28 D2
  Tilbury RM18 ...... 18 F5
  Tonbridge TN9 .... 254 B8
  Whitstable CT5 .... 108 C8
Alexandra St
  Folkestone CT19 .... 335 D6
  Maidstone ME14 .... 161 F6
  Newham E16 ......1 A8
Alexandra Terr CT9 .. 50 I1
Alexandra Wlk DA4 .. 57 E7
Alexandria Dr CT6 .. 76 C5
Alex Hughes Cl ME6 . 127 F6
Alfan La DA2 ...... 32 D3
Alford Ho 6 SE18 ... 12 B8
Alford Rd DA8 ....4 C1
Alford Snell Lodge
  TN2 ....286 D2
Alfred Cl
  Canterbury CT1 .... 174 C6
  Chatham ME4 ....64 B2
  Deal CT14 .... 215 D8
  Erith DA8 ....14 F8
  Gravesend DA11 .... 37 B6
  Greatstone-on-Sea
  TN28 ....373 D3
  Hawley DA2 .... 33 F4
  Margate CT9 ....51 B1
Alfred Row CT14 ... 215 D7
Alfred Sq CT14 .... 215 D7
Alfred St RM17 ..... 18 C8
Alfriston Cl DA1 .... 14 E1
Alfriston Gr ME19 .. 159 C3
Alice Thompson Cl
  SE12 ....29 C6
Alicia Ave CT9 ..... 82 A8
Alicia Ho DA16 ..... 13 B6
Alison Cl Birchington CT7 . 81 B8
  Newham E6 ....2 A7
Alison Cres CT16 ... 278 A7
Alkerden La DA9,DA10 . 17 C1
Alkham Rd
  Maidstone ME14 .... 162 C5
  Temple Ewell CT15,
  CT16 ....277 C4
Alkham Tower 9 BR5 . 54 C5
Alkham Valley Rd
  Alkham CT15 ...... 276 E1
  Hawkinge CT18,CT15 . 307 E4
Allan Cl TN4 ...... 285 C4
Allandale Pl BR6 .... 87 D7
Allandale Rd TN2 .. 286 D7
Allan Rd CT5 ...... 107 E6
Allard Cl BR5 ...... 54 C2
Allen Ave CT8 ..... 81 D7
Allenby Ave CT14 .. 215 B5
Allenby Rd
  Biggin Hill TN16 .... 118 E2
  Ramsgate CT12 .... 83 C2
  Woolwich SE28 ......2 C3
Allenby Wlk ME10 .. 101 B5
Allen Cl ME5 ...... 97 C6
Allen Ct ME12 ..... 47 A5
Allendale Cl DA2 ... 34 D7
Allendale St 2 CT19 . 335 D6
Allen Field TN23 .. 299 F8
Allen Gardiner Ho
  TN2 ....286 B2
Allens La TN15,TN11 . 190 A7
Allens St ME12 .... 259 D5
Allen St ME14 ..... 162 B5
Allenswood Rd SE9 . 11 F5
Allhallows-on-Sea Est
  ME3 ....9 E4
Allhallows Prim Sch
  ME3 ....9 D2
Allhallows Rd
  Lower Stoke ME3 ... 25 C5
  Newham E6 ....1 E7
Alliance Rd Newham E13 . 1 C8
  Woolwich SE18 ..... 13 A7
Alliance Way TN12 . 256 F6
Allington Cl DA12 ... 37 F7
Allington Dr
  Rochester ME2 ...... 62 E8
  Tonbridge TN10 ... 223 A5
Allington Gdns ME18 . 192 E7
Allington Prim Sch
  ME16 ....161 C2
Allington Rd
  Gillingham ME8 .... 65 A3
  Orpington BR6 .... 53 E1
  Paddock Wood TN12 . 256 F7
Allington Way ME16 . 161 B6
Allison Ave ME7 ....64 E1
Allnutt Mill Cl 4
  ME15 ....161 E2
Allotment La CT4 ... 154 C5
All Saints' Ave CT9 . 50 H1
All Saints' CE Prim Sch
  ME4 ....64 A3

ME15 ....162 A3
All Saints Cl DA10 ....17 F2
All Saints' Cl CT5 .... 74 F1
All Saints Ind Est CT9 . 50 I1
All Saints La 2 CT1 . 174 F8
All Saints Rd
  Allhallows ME3 ......9 D2
  Hawkhurst TN18 ... 341 A1
All Saints' Rd DA11 . 36 F7
All Saints Rd
  Royal Tunbridge Wells
  TN4 ....286 B6
  Sittingbourne ME10 . 102 C4
All Saints Rise TN4 . 286 A6
All Saints View ME13 . 106 E2
All Souls' CE Prim Sch
  CT19 ....334 E6
Allsworth Cl ME9 ... 100 B6
Alma Pl
  2 Canterbury CT1 .. 143 A1
  Hadlow TN11 ..... 223 E8
  Ramsgate CT11 .... 117 E7
  Rochester ME2 ..... 63 A7
Alma Rd Eccles ME20 . 128 F6
  Folkestone CT20 .... 334 D5
  Herne Bay CT6 ..... 77 C5
  Margate CT9 ....50 J1
  Orpington BR5 .... 87 D8
  Ramsgate CT11 .... 117 E8
  Sheerness ME12 .... 28 C2
  Sidcup DA14 ...... 31 A5
  Swanscombe DA10 .. 17 F2
  West Malling ME19 . 159 A8
Almarina CT8 ..... 50 C1
Alma St CT1 ...... 143 A1
Alma Street Pas ME12 . 28 C2
Alma St ME12 ..... 28 D2
Alma The CT2 ...... 37 F4
Almery Cotts ME17 . 229 B8
Almond Cl
  Ashford TN23 .... 267 F5
  Broadstairs CT10 ....83 C4
  Bromley BR2 ...... 53 A2
  Whitstable CT5 ..... 75 D1
Almond Ct CT4 .... 173 E1
Almond Dr BR8 ..... 55 D7
Almond Gr ME7 .... 98 A4
Almond Ho 9 ME16 . 161 A3
Almond Rd DA2 .... 34 C8
Almonds The ME14 . 163 A4
Almond Tree Cl ME12 . 46 A8
Almond Way BR2 ... 53 A2
Almon Pl ME1 ..... 63 D5
Almshouse Rd ME13 . 202 F2
Almshouses
  8 Canterbury CT1 .. 175 A8
  Crockenhill BR8 .... 55 D2
  Penshurst TN11 ... 252 C4
  Sevenoaks TN13 ... 154 C1
  14 Tonbridge TN9 .. 254 B8
  Yalding ME18 ..... 193 A1
Alms Row ME16 ... 152 B3
Alnwick Ct 8 DA2 ... 16 B1
Alnwick Rd Eltham SE12 . 29 B8
  Newham E6 ....1 C7
Alonso Ho 4 DA17 ...4 A1
Alpha Cl ME3 ..... 42 D7
Alpha Rd
  Birchington CT7 .... 81 A7
  Ramsgate CT11 .... 117 D6
Alpine Bsns Ctr E6 .... 2 A8
Alpine Copse 2 BR1 . 53 A7
Alpine Way E6 ......2 A8
Alsager Ave ME11 .. 45 F3
Alsike Rd DA18 ......3 E3
Alsops Rd TN24 .... 300 C1
Alston Cl ME12 .... 47 C7
Altash Way SE9 ..... 30 A6
Altbarn Ind Est ME5 . 130 C8
Alton Ave ME19 .... 159 A3
Alton Cl DA5 ....31 E7
Alton Cotts DA4 .... 89 E8
Alverstone Gdns SE9 . 30 C7
Alvis Ave CT6 ...... 76 A4
Alwold Cres SE12 .. 11 C1
Amage Rd TN25 ... 270 C8
Amage Road Cotts
  TN25 ....238 B1
Amanda Cl ME5 ..... 96 F3
Amar Ct SE18 ...... 2 F1
Amardeep Ct E6 ..... 2 F1
Ambassador Gdns E6 . 1 F8
Amber Cl ME7 ..... 103 D2
Amber Ct ME7 ..... 64 D5
Amber La ME17 ... 196 A1
Amberleaze Dr TN2 . 287 D6
Amberley Cl
  2 Orpington BR6 ...86 F5
  Tonbridge TN9 .... 254 A8
Amberley Ct
  Royal Tunbridge Wells
  TN4 ....286 C1
  Sidcup DA14 ...... 31 C3
Amberley Rd SE2 ... 13 D8
Amber Rise ME10 .. 101 C2
Amber Way ME17 .. 196 B1
Amblecote Cl SE12 .. 29 B5
Amblecote Mdw SE12 . 29 B5
Amblecote Rd SE12 . 29 B5
Ambleside ME13 ... 138 E6
Ambleside Rd DA7 .. 14 A5
Ambleside ME10 .. 102 C3
Ambley Gn ME8 ..... 98 A8
Ambley Rd ME8 .....98 B8
Ambley Wood Nature
  Reserve ★ ME7,ME8 . 98 A8
Ambrook Rd DA17 ...4 A3
Ambrose Cl
  Crayford DA1 ..... 15 A3
  6 Newham E6 ....1 F8
  Orpington BR6 .....86 F7
Ambrose Hill ME5 .. 64 C2

Amels Hill ME9 . . . 132 F8
Ames Ave ME14 . . . 163 A4
Amesbury Rd BR1 . . . 52 D6
Ames Rd DA10 . . . 17 E1
Ames Way ME18 . . . 159 B3
Amethyst Ave ME5 . . . 96 E6
Amherst Cl
Maidstone ME16 . . . 161 D4
Margate CT9 . . . 51 C1
Orpington BR5 . . . 54 A5
Amherst Dr BR5 . . . 54 A5
Amherst Hill
Chatham ME7 . . . 64 A6
Sevenoaks TN13 . . . 153 F4
Amherst Prim Sch
TN13 . . . 153 E4
Amherst Rd
Rochester ME1 . . . 63 D3
Royal Tunbridge Wells
TN4 . . . 286 A5
Sevenoaks TN13 . . . 154 B5
Amherst Redoubt ME4 . . . 64 A5
Amhurst Bank Rd TN2,
TN11,TN12 . . . 255 F4
Amhurst Wlk SE28 . . . 3 A5
Amies Ho ME15 . . . 194 F3
Amos Cl Herne Bay CT6 . . 77 C3
Sheldwich ME13 . . . 170 C5
Ampleforth Cl BR6 . . . 87 C6
Ampleforth Rd SE2 . . . 3 C4
Amsbury Rd ME15,
ME17 . . . 194 B2
Amshurst Villas ME15 . . 194 A4
Anatase Cl ME10 . . . 101 C7
Ancaster St SE18 . . . 12 E7
Anchorage Cl ME3 . . . 25 C3
Anchorage Flats
TN12 . . . 257 A6
Anchorage Point Ind Est
SE7 . . . 1 C3
Anchor Bay Ind Est
DA8 . . . 15 A8
Anchor Bsns Pk ME10 . . 102 B6
Anchor Bvd DA2 . . . 16 D3
Anchor Ct DA7 . . . 13 E6
Anchor Hill 4 CT9 . . . 50 J2
Anchor Ho E16 . . . 1 C7
Anchor & Hope La SE7 . . 1 C2
Anchor Ho ME1 . . . 63 B4
Anchor La Deal CT14 . . 215 C6
Sheerness ME12 . . . 27 F3
Sheerness ME12 . . . 28 A3
Anchor Rd ME1 . . . 63 C1
Ancona Rd SE18 . . . 2 D1
Ancress Cl CT2 . . . 143 A4
Andace Pk BR1 . . . 52 C8
Anderson Way DA17 . . . 4 B4
Andorra Ct BR1 . . . 52 C8
Andover Ave E16 . . . 1 D7
Andover Rd BR6 . . . 53 E1
Andover Wlk 12 ME15 . . 195 F6
Andrew Broughton Way
ME14 . . . 162 B4
Andrew Cl DA1 . . . 14 D2
Andrewes Gdns E6 . . . 1 E7
Andrew Manor ME7 . . . 64 C6
Andrew Rd TN4 . . . 286 C8
Andrews Cl
Orpington BR5 . . . 54 D6
Royal Tunbridge Wells
TN2 . . . 286 D5
Andrews Pl DA2 . . . 32 E6
Andrews Wlk ME10 . . . 101 B5
Andrew Wells Ho 8
BR1 . . . 29 B1
Andringham Lodge 7
BR1 . . . 52 B8
Andwell Cl SE2 . . . 3 B4
Anemone Way CT6 . . . 110 E7
Anerley Cl ME16 . . . 161 D7
Angel Cotts ME8 . . . 66 A2
Angelica Dr E6 . . . 2 A8
Angel La TN9 . . . 222 B1
Angel Row TN18 . . . 356 B5
Angel Terr TN18 . . . 356 B6
Angel Wlk 4 TN9 . . . 222 B1
Angerstein Bsns Pk
SE10 . . . 1 A2
Angle Rd RM20 . . . 17 D8
Anglesea Ave SE18 . . . 2 B2
Anglesea Pl 19 DA11 . . . 19 B1
Anglesea Rd
Orpington BR5 . . . 54 C3
Woolwich SE18 . . . 2 B2
Anglesey Ave ME15 . . . 195 A7
Anglesey Cl ME5 . . . 97 B7
Angley Ct TN12 . . . 290 A5
Angley Rd TN17 . . . 320 C6
Angley Sch Sports Coll
TN17 . . . 320 C5
Angley Wlk
Cranbrook TN17 . . . 320 C6
Cranbrook TN17 . . . 320 D6
Anglia Ctr The RM13 . . . 4 E8
Anglian Ind Est IG11 . . . 3 A8
Anglo Saxon Ho DA12 . . 37 E8
Angus Dr TN24 . . . 268 C7
Ankerdine Cres SE18 . . . 12 B6
Annandale Rd DA15 . . . 30 F8
Anna Pk CT7 . . . 80 F8
Anne Boleyn Cl ME12 . . . 48 E3
Anne Cl CT7 . . . 81 B7
Anne Green Wlk 8
CT1 . . . 143 B2
Anne of Cleves Rd DA1 . . 15 D1
Anne Roper Cl TN28 . . 373 E6
Annesley Rd SE3 . . . 11 B6
Anne's Rd CT10 . . . 84 C7
Annetts Hall TN15 . . . 157 A8
Annex The BR8 . . . 56 B6
Annie Rd ME6 . . . 127 F6
Ann's Rd CT11 . . . 117 E8
Ann Stroud Ct SE12 . . . 11 A2
Ann St SE18 . . . 2 D2
Annvera Ho 2 ME7 . . . 64 C7
Ansell Ave ME4 . . . 64 A1
Anselm Cl ME10 . . . 101 E4
Anselm Rd CT17 . . . 310 A8
Ansia Cl ME18 . . . 159 B3
Anson Ave ME18,ME19 . . 158 F3
Anson Cl
Broadstairs CT10 . . . 83 D3
Chatham ME5 . . . 97 C6
Anson Pl SE28 . . . 2 D4
Anstee Rd CT17 . . . 278 C1
Anstridge Rd SE9 . . . 12 D1
Antelope Rd SE18 . . . 1 F3
Anthony Cl TN13 . . . 153 E7
Anthony Cres CT5 . . . 108 B6
Anthony Rd DA16 . . . 13 A6
Anthony Roper Prim Sch
The DA4 . . . 89 E8
Anthonys La BR8 . . . 56 A8
Anthonys Way ME2 . . . 63 E8
Antolin Way CT10,CT12 . . 83 A3
Antonius Ct TN23 . . . 300 A5
Anvil Cl CT7 . . . 81 A6
Anvil Terr DA2 . . . 32 E6
Anzio Cres CT15 . . . 278 E2
Anzio Ho 15 CT1 . . . 143 B2
Apartments The TN28 . . 373 E5
Aperfield Rd
Biggin Hill TN16 . . . 118 E2
Erith DA8 . . . 14 F8
Apiary Bsns Pk The
ME17 . . . 197 B3
Apollo Ave BR1 . . . 52 B8
Apollo Ho ME5 . . . 97 A6
Apollo Way
St Mary's Island ME4 . . . 41 C2
3 Woolwich SE28 . . . 2 D3
Appleby Cl ME1 . . . 96 D7
Appleby Ct TN24 . . . 268 D2
Appleby Rd E16 . . . 1 A7
Apple Cl
Hawkinge CT18 . . . 307 B4
Snodland ME6 . . . 128 A6
Apple Craft Ctr★
ME13 . . . 138 E5
Applecross Cl ME1 . . . 63 B4
Apple Ct TN12 . . . 256 F6
Appledore Ave
Bexley DA7 . . . 14 D5
West Minst ME12 . . . 46 B8
Appledore Cl
Hayes BR2 . . . 52 A4
Margate CT9 . . . 51 C1
Appledore Cres
Folkestone CT19 . . . 334 D7
Sidcup DA14 . . . 30 F5
Appledore Ct ME16 . . . 161 C7
Appledore Rd
Appledore TN26,TN30 . . 361 A7
Brattle TN26 . . . 347 C7
Gillingham ME8 . . . 65 A3
Tenterden TN30 . . . 345 E7
Appledore Sta TN26 . . . 362 B8
Appledown Way CT1 . . 175 D5
Appleford Dr ME12 . . . 46 F7
Applegarth Dr DA1 . . . 33 F6
Applegarth Ho DA8 . . . 14 F5
Applegarth Pk CT5 . . . 108 A6
Applegarth Rd SE28 . . . 3 C6
Apple Orch BR8 . . . 55 D5
Appleshaw Cl DA11 . . . 37 A3
Appleton Cl DA7 . . . 14 C5
Appleton Dr DA2 . . . 33 B5
Appleton Rd SE9 . . . 11 E4
Appletons TN11 . . . 223 E8
Apple Tree Cl ME16 . . . 160 F2
Appletree Ct 5 ME8 . . . 98 F8
Apple Tree La TN2 . . . 286 D8
Appold St DA8 . . . 14 F8
Approach Rd
Broadstairs CT10 . . . 84 A4
Dover CT17 . . . 310 A6
Margate CT9 . . . 51 A2
Approach Rd S TN29 . . 380 C2
Approach Rd
Shepherdswell CT15 . . . 244 D5
Tatsfield CR6,TN16 . . . 150 B5
Approach The BR6 . . . 86 F8
April Cl BR6 . . . 86 F5
April Rise
Birchington CT7 . . . 80 D8
Whitstable CT5 . . . 108 B7
Apsledene DA12 . . . 37 D2
Apsley Cotts CT4 . . . 173 D3
Apsley Ct BR5 . . . 54 B3
Apsley St Ashford TN23 . . 268 B2
Rusthall TN4 . . . 285 D4
Aragon Cl
Ashford TN23 . . . 299 E7
Orpington BR2 . . . 52 F1
Arborfield DA13 . . . 60 A4
Arbroath Rd SE9 . . . 11 E4
Arbrook Cl BR5 . . . 54 A6
Arbrook Ct BR5 . . . 54 A8
Arbury Ho BR1 . . . 29 E1
Arbuthnot La DA5 . . . 13 E1
Arcade The 2 SE9 . . . 12 A1
Arcadian Ave DA5 . . . 13 E1
Arcadian Cl DA5 . . . 13 E1
Arcadian Rd DA5 . . . 13 E1
Arcadia Rd DA13 . . . 59 F8
Archbishop's Sch The
CT2 . . . 142 E3
Archcliffe Rd CT17 . . . 310 C5
Archer Ho ME3 . . . 40 F6
Archer Rd Chatham ME5 . . 97 B6
Folkestone CT19 . . . 335 D6
Orpington BR5 . . . 54 A4
Archer's Court Rd
CT15,CT16 . . . 278 B7
Archers Court Sch
CT16 . . . 278 B5
Archer Way BR8 . . . 56 A7
Archery Cl ME3 . . . 40 B7
Archery House Hospl
DA2 . . . 16 B1
Archery Rd SE9 . . . 11 F2
Archery Sq CT14 . . . 215 D3
Archibald Ho ME14 . . . 162 A7
Archway Ct
Dartford DA1 . . . 33 D8
4 Rochester ME2 . . . 63 B8
Archway Rd
Ramsgate CT11 . . . 117 E6
Sheerness ME12 . . . 28 A3
Arcon Ct TN23 . . . 300 A7
Arcon Rd TN23 . . . 300 A7
Arden Bsns Pk ME2 . . . 63 E7
Arden Cl SE28 . . . 3 D7
Arden Dr TN24 . . . 268 C3
Arden Grange CT4 . . . 205 C8
Arden Gr BR6 . . . 86 B6
Arden Jun Sch ME7 . . . 64 D6
Ardenlee Dr ME14 . . . 162 B5
Arden Rd
Faversham ME13 . . . 138 E7
Herne Bay CT6 . . . 77 C2
Arden St ME7 . . . 64 C6
Ardent Ave CT14 . . . 215 C4
Arethusa Pl DA9 . . . 17 B3
Arethusa Rd ME1 . . . 96 C8
Argali Ho 3 DA18 . . . 3 E3
Argent Rd ME11 . . . 46 A2
Argent St RM17 . . . 18 B7
Argent Way ME10 . . . 101 C6
Argles Cl 4 DA9 . . . 17 A2
Argyle Ave CT9 . . . 50 G1
Argyle Cl ME1 . . . 96 E8
Argyle Gdns CT9 . . . 50 G1
Argyle Rd Newham E16 . . . 1 B7
Royal Tunbridge Wells
TN4 . . . 254 A2
Sevenoaks TN13 . . . 154 B2
Whitstable CT5 . . . 74 D1
Argyll Dr CT11 . . . 83 F1
Argyll Rd SE18 . . . 2 C3
Ariel Cl DA12 . . . 37 F4
Ariel Ct 5 DA17 . . . 4 A1
Ark Cotts CT18 . . . 305 D4
Ark La CT14 . . . 215 D7
Arkley Rd CT6 . . . 76 F4
Arklow Sq 6 CT11 . . . 117 F7
Arkwright Rd RM18 . . . 19 A5
Arlington TN23 . . . 299 F8
Arlington Cl DA15 . . . 30 E8
Arlington Gdns CT9 . . . 83 C8
Arlington Ho CT9 . . . 50 H2
Arlington Sq CT9 . . . 50 H2
Arlott Cl ME14 . . . 161 F6
Armada Cl TN28 . . . 373 E5
Armada Ct ME4 . . . 63 E1
Armadale CT10 . . . 51 F1
Armada Way
Chatham ME4 . . . 63 F3
Newham E6 . . . 2 C7
Armitage Pl 5 TN18 . . 340 F2
Armourers Wlk CT16 . . 278 A3
Armoury Dr DA12 . . . 37 C8
Armstrong Cl
Badgers Mount TN14 . . . 121 B4
Bromley BR1 . . . 52 E6
Newham E6 . . . 1 F7
Armstrong Rd
Maidstone ME15 . . . 162 A1
Woolwich SE18 . . . 2 C3
Armstrong Sq CT6 . . . 76 A3
Armytage Cl ME3 . . . 41 E4
Arne Cl TN10 . . . 222 E6
Arne Gr BR6 . . . 86 F7
Arnhem Dr ME5 . . . 96 F7
Arnold Ave DA13 . . . 93 B8
Arnolde Cl ME2 . . . 63 E7
Arnold Pl RM18 . . . 19 C6
Arnold Rd
Chartham CT4 . . . 173 C2
Gravesend DA12 . . . 37 D6
5 Margate CT9 . . . 50 J1
Arnolds La DA4 . . . 34 A2
Arnott Cl SE28 . . . 3 C5
Arnsberg Way DA6,DA7 . . 14 A3
Arnside Rd DA7 . . . 14 A6
Arolla Rd CT6 . . . 77 C4
Arran Cl DA8 . . . 14 D8
Arrandene Ho 3 BR5 . . 54 B7
Arran Gn ME2 . . . 62 C6
Arran Mews 4 CT1 . . . 143 B2
Arran Rd ME15 . . . 195 A6
Arras Ho Bexley SE2 . . . 13 D8
Erith SE2 . . . 3 D1
Arrowhead La TN26,
TN29 . . . 362 D7
Arsenal Rd SE9 . . . 11 F4
Arsenal Way SE18 . . . 2 C3
Artemis Cl DA12 . . . 37 E8
Arthur Ct 11 RM17 . . . 18 C8
Arthur Gr SE18 . . . 2 C2
Arthur Kennedy Cl
ME13 . . . 139 F3
Arthur Rd
Biggin Hill TN16 . . . 118 C3
Birchington CT7 . . . 80 D8
Deal CT14 . . . 215 A3
Gillingham ME8 . . . 98 E7
Hythe CT21 . . . 333 C1
Margate CT9 . . . 51 A3
Rochester ME1 . . . 63 D3
Arthur Ruxley Est DA14 . . 31 D2
Arthur St W DA11 . . . 37 A8
Arthur Salmon Cl
ME13 . . . 138 B7
Arthur St Erith DA8 . . . 14 F7
3 Folkestone CT19 . . . 335 E6
Gravesend DA11 . . . 37 A8
Grays RM17 . . . 18 C8
Sittingbourne ME10 . . . 101 E4
Arthur Toft Ho 6
RM17 . . . 18 B8
Artillery Gdns 12 CT1 . . 143 A1
Artillery Ho
13 Canterbury CT1 . . . 143 A1
Woolwich SE18 . . . 2 A1
Artillery Pl SE18 . . . 2 A2
Artillery Rd CT11 . . . 117 F7
Artillery Row DA12 . . . 37 C8
Artillery St 11 CT1 . . . 143 A1
Artington Cl BR6 . . . 86 C6
Artisan Cl E6 . . . 2 B6
Arun Ct BR5 . . . 54 C1
Arundel Ave ME10 . . . 101 E1
Arundel Cl Bexley DA5 . . . 13 F1
Chatham ME5 . . . 97 D1
Tonbridge TN9 . . . 254 A8
Arundel Ct 2 DA6 . . . 13 E3
Arundel Dr BR6 . . . 87 B5
Arundel Ho TN1 . . . 286 A3
Arundel Rd
Cliffs End CT12 . . . 116 D7
Dartford DA1 . . . 15 C3
Margate CT9 . . . 51 B2
Royal Tunbridge Wells
TN1 . . . 286 B2
Arundel DA14 . . . 31 A3
Arundel St ME14 . . . 161 F6
Ascot Cl
Borough Green TN15 . . . 157 B7
Chatham ME5 . . . 97 C2
Ascot Ct Bromley BR1 . . . 52 E7
Sidcup DA5 . . . 31 F8
Ascot Gdns CT8 . . . 81 E7
Ascot Ho 2 ME15 . . . 195 F6
Ascot Rd
Gravesend DA12 . . . 37 B5
Orpington BR5 . . . 53 F5
Ashbank Cotts ME17 . . . 197 B7
Ashbee Cl ME6 . . . 128 A7
Ashbee Gdns CT6 . . . 77 C5
Ashborne Cl TN24 . . . 268 D6
Ashbourne Ave DA7 . . . 13 E7
Ashbourne Ct TN4 . . . 285 D4
Ashbourne Rise BR6 . . . 86 E6
Ashburn Ct BR1 . . . 29 A1
Ashburn Gdns CT6 . . . 77 C5
Ashburnham Cl TN13 . . 187 C8
Ashburnham Rd
Erith DA17 . . . 4 C2
Maidstone ME14 . . . 162 B8
Ramsgate CT11 . . . 117 C7
Tonbridge TN10 . . . 222 C3
Ashburn Mews ME7 . . . 64 E3
Ashburton Cl TN24 . . . 268 E2
Ashburton Rd E16 . . . 1 A7
Ashby Cl ME2 . . . 95 A4
Ashby's Cl TN8 . . . 249 D8
Ashbys Yd TN9 . . . 222 C1
Ash Cl Ashford TN23 . . . 267 E3
Aylesford ME20 . . . 128 E1
Broadstairs CT10 . . . 83 C4
Chatham ME5 . . . 64 C1
Crabble CT17 . . . 277 E3
Edenbridge TN8 . . . 217 B1
Gillingham ME8 . . . 65 B3
Herne Bay CT6 . . . 76 F1
Orpington BR5 . . . 53 D4
Royal Tunbridge Wells
TN2 . . . 314 D7
Sidcup DA14 . . . 31 B5
Swanley BR8 . . . 55 D7
Ashcombe Dr TN8 . . . 217 B4
Ash Cres
Biddenden TN27 . . . 323 D7
Hersden CT3 . . . 111 E1
Higham ME3 . . . 39 C3
Ashcroft Ave DA15 . . . 13 A1
Ashcroft Cres DA15 . . . 13 A1
Ashcroft Ct
Dartford DA1 . . . 34 A8
5 Eltham SE9 . . . 12 A1
Ash Croft Ct DA3 . . . 91 F7
Ashcroft Rd
Paddock Wood TN12 . . . 257 A5
Rochester ME2 . . . 40 B2
Ash Ct Cliffs End CT12 . . 116 D4
Lewisham SE12 . . . 29 A8
Ashdale Ho TN23 . . . 268 C2
Ashdale Rd SE12 . . . 29 B7
Ashden Wlk TN10 . . . 222 C7
Ashdown Cl
Coldblow DA5 . . . 32 C8
Herne Bay CT6 . . . 77 B2
Maidstone ME16 . . . 161 D3
Royal Tunbridge Wells
TN4 . . . 285 F4
Ashdown Cres TN28 . . . 373 B6
Ashdown Ct TN24 . . . 268 C3
Ashdown Field CT4 . . . 173 B2
Ashdown Lodge CT20 . . 335 A5
Ashdown Rd ME17,
ME9 . . . 166 F3
Ashenden Cl
Canterbury CT1 . . . 174 C5
Rochester ME2 . . . 40 C2
Ashendene Gr CT2 . . . 144 A6
Ashenden TN27 . . . 263 F2
Ashenden Wlk TN2 . . . 286 E8
Ashen Dr DA1 . . . 15 A1
Ashen Grove Mobile Home
Pk TN15 . . . 90 B1
Ashen Grove Rd TN15 . . . 90 B1
Ashen E6 . . . 2 A7
Ashen Tree Cotts CT3 . . 146 B1
Ashen Tree La CT16 . . . 310 E8
Ashentree La TN29 . . . 371 A5
Asher Reeds TN3 . . . 285 A4
Ashes La Plaxtol TN11 . . 189 F1
Tonbridge TN11 . . . 223 B8
Ashfield La BR7 . . . 30 C1
Ashfield Pl BR7 . . . 30 D1
Ashford Borough Mus★
TN23 . . . 268 B2
Ashford Bsns Pk
TN24 . . . 301 A6
Ashford Bsns Point
TN24 . . . 300 F5
Ashford Designer Outlet
TN24 . . . 300 C7
Ashford Dr ME17 . . . 197 D3
Ashford Hospl TN23 . . 268 A3
Ashford Int Sta TN24 . . 268 C1
Ashford Rd
Ashford TN23 . . . 299 B8
Bethersden TN26,TN23 . . 297 C4
Charing TN27 . . . 234 C7
Chartham CT4,CT1 . . . 173 C3
Folkestone CT18,CT19 . . 334 B7
Godmersham CT4 . . . 205 C4
Hamstreet TN26 . . . 327 F1
Harrietsham ME17 . . . 198 C6
Kingsnorth TN23,TN26 . . 300 A4
Maidstone,Grove Green
ME14 . . . 162 D4
Maidstone ME14 . . . 163 D3
New Romney TN28 . . . 373 A6
Sellindge TN25 . . . 303 B1
Sheldwich ME13 . . . 170 C4
Tenterden,High Halden
TN26,TN30 . . . 324 A6
Tenterden TN30 . . . 345 B8
Westenhanger CT21,
TN25,CT18 . . . 332 C6
Ashford Sch TN23 . . . 268 C2
Ashford South Com Prim
Sch TN23 . . . 300 A8
Ashford Sta TN24 . . . 268 C1
Ash Gr Elvington CT15 . . 212 B2
Lydd TN29 . . . 376 D7
Maidstone ME16 . . . 161 C6
Ashgrove Ashford TN23 . . 267 F5
Lewisham SE12 . . . 29 A7
Ashgrove Rd TN13 . . . 187 B7
Ash Ho BR5 . . . 54 C5
Ashington Cl ME10 . . . 101 C5
Ash Keys DA13 . . . 126 B8
Ashlar Pl 4 SE18 . . . 2 B2
Ash La TN15 . . . 91 D2
Ashleigh Cl DA13 . . . 92 F1
Ashleigh Commercial Est
SE18 . . . 1 D3
Ashleigh Gdns TN27 . . 262 D6
Ashley Ave CT19 . . . 334 E6
Ashley Cl
Halfway Houses ME12 . . . 46 C5
Ramsgate CT12 . . . 83 B2
Sevenoaks TN13 . . . 154 B3
Ashley Dr CT5 . . . 108 A7
Ashley Gdns
Orpington BR6 . . . 86 E5
Rusthall TN4 . . . 285 C5
Ashley Ho
Folkestone CT19 . . . 334 E6
Orpington BR5 . . . 54 A7
Ashley Mill Cotts
CT19 . . . 334 E7
Ashley Park Cl TN4 . . . 285 C5
Ashley Pk TN4 . . . 285 C5
Ashley Rd
Gillingham ME8 . . . 65 C2
Sevenoaks TN13 . . . 154 B3
Tonbridge TN11 . . . 221 E5
Ashly Ct 22 DA14 . . . 31 A5
Ash Mdws TN24 . . . 300 F7
Ashmead Cl ME5 . . . 97 C3
Ashmead Gate BR1 . . . 52 C8
Ashmill Bsns Pk ME17 . . 199 F6
Ashmore Gdns DA11 . . . 36 D5
Ashmore Gr DA16 . . . 12 E4
Ashmore La BR2 . . . 118 C8
Ash Platt Rd TN15 . . . 154 E6
Ash Rd Aylesham CT3 . . 210 E5
Dartford DA1 . . . 33 D7
Gravesend DA12 . . . 37 C4
Hartley DA3 . . . 58 F3
Hawley DA2 . . . 33 F4
New Ash Green DA3,
TN15 . . . 91 E7
Orpington BR6 . . . 86 F3
Rochester ME2 . . . 62 F6
Sandwich CT13 . . . 148 E2
Westerham TN16 . . . 151 E2
Ashridge Cres SE18 . . . 12 C7
Ashridge House DA14 . . . 30 F4
Ash Row BR2 . . . 53 A3
Ashtead Dr ME9 . . . 102 D2
Ashton Cl CT14 . . . 214 D4
Ashton Ct 4 CT10 . . . 83 E5
Ashton Ho CT14 . . . 215 B1
Ashton Mews 21 CT10 . . 84 B4
Ashton Way ME19 . . . 159 C6
Ash Tree Cl CT7 . . . 81 B7
Ashtree Cl BR6 . . . 86 B6
Ash Tree Cl
St Mary's Bay TN29 . . . 365 F3
West Kingsdown TN15 . . . 90 F2
Ash Tree Cotts TN12 . . . 291 B7
Ash Tree Dr TN15 . . . 90 F2
Ashtree Ho ME10 . . . 102 B3
Ash Tree La ME5 . . . 64 D1
Ash Tree Rd 6 CT19 . . 335 E6
Ashtrees CT6 . . . 77 B3
Ashurst Ave CT5 . . . 108 C6
Ashurst Cl DA1 . . . 14 F4
Ashurst Gdns CT9 . . . 51 E3
Ashurst Hill TN3 . . . 283 D2
Ashurst Rd
Maidstone ME14 . . . 162 C5
Stone Cross TN3 . . . 284 B2
Ashurst Sta TN3 . . . 283 D2
Ashwater Rd SE12 . . . 29 A7
Ashwell Cl 9 E6 . . . 1 E7
Ashwood Cl ME3 . . . 40 C7
Ashwood Pl DA2 . . . 35 B5
Askern Cl DA6 . . . 13 D3
Askes Ct TN23 . . . 299 D8
Askews Farm La RM17,
RM20 . . . 17 E8
Askham Lodge 10 SE12 . . 29 A8
Aspdin Rd DA11 . . . 36 E5
Aspen Cl Orpington BR6 . . 87 A5
St Mary's Bay TN29 . . . 365 F3
Swanley BR8 . . . 55 D8
Aspen Copse BR1 . . . 52 F7
Aspen Ct DA1 . . . 16 A2
Aspen Dr TN23 . . . 267 D3
Aspen Gn DA18 . . . 3 F3
Aspen Ho
5 Folkestone CT20 . . . 335 D4
2 Sidcup DA15 . . . 31 A5
Aspen Rd
Chartham CT4 . . . 173 E1
Herne CT6 . . . 110 E7
Aspen Way
2 Chatham ME5 . . . 96 E4
Royal Tunbridge Wells
TN4 . . . 254 C1
Aspian Dr ME17 . . . 194 D3
Aspinall Cl CT4 . . . 176 B4
Asquith Rd ME8 . . . 98 C6
Association Wlk ME1 . . . 96 C7
Aster Rd ME3 . . . 41 E3
Astley Ave CT16 . . . 278 C2
Astley Ct CT16 . . . 278 C2
Astley RM17 . . . 17 F8
Astley St ME14 . . . 162 A4
Aston Cl Chatham ME5 . . 97 A2
Sidcup DA14 . . . 31 A5
Aston Pl CT10 . . . 83 E6
Astor Ave CT17 . . . 310 B8
Astor Coll for the Arts
CT17 . . . 310 A8
Astor Ct E16 . . . 1 C7
Astor Dr CT14 . . . 215 C5
Astor of Hever Com Sch
The ME16 . . . 161 C3
Astor Rd
Broadstairs CT10 . . . 83 F8
West Kingsdown TN15 . . . 90 E4
Astra Dr DA12 . . . 37 F3
Astrid Rd CT14 . . . 215 A2
Atcost Rd IG11 . . . 3 A8
Athelstan Gn ME17 . . . 164 C2
Athelstan Pl CT14 . . . 215 C8
Athelstan Rd
Canterbury CT1 . . . 174 C5
Chatham ME4 . . . 63 F2
Faversham ME13 . . . 138 C6
Folkestone CT19 . . . 335 D7
Margate CT9 . . . 51 A3
Athelstan Way BR5 . . . 54 A8
Athena Ct CT9 . . . 51 A3
Athill Ct TN13 . . . 154 C5
Athol Pl ME13 . . . 138 A8
Athol Rd Ashford TN23 . . 299 F7
Erith DA8 . . . 4 C1
Whitstable CT5 . . . 74 F2
Athol Terr CT16 . . . 310 F8
Atkinson Cl BR6 . . . 87 A5
Atkinson Rd E16 . . . 1 C8
Atkinson Wlk TN24 . . . 268 F5
Atlanta Ct ME4 . . . 63 D3
Atlantic Cl DA10 . . . 17 E2
Atlas Gdns SE7 . . . 1 C2
Atlas Rd DA1 . . . 15 F4
Atterbury Cl TN16 . . . 151 D1
Attlee Ave CT3 . . . 210 E5
Attlee Dr DA1 . . . 16 A2
Attlee Rd SE28 . . . 3 B6
Attlee Way ME10 . . . 101 E8
Attwaters La TN18 . . . 341 C6
Atwater Ct ME17 . . . 199 D5
Aubretia Wlk ME10 . . . 102 A3
Auckland Ave CT12 . . . 117 A8
Auckland Cl RM18 . . . 19 A5
Auckland Cres CT16 . . . 278 C3
Auckland Dr ME10 . . . 101 C3
Auckland Ho 10 ME15 . . 195 E5
Auckland Rd TN1 . . . 286 C5
Auden Rd ME20 . . . 128 A3
Audley Ave
Gillingham ME7 . . . 64 E1
Margate CT9 . . . 50 E1
Tonbridge TN9 . . . 221 F2
Audley Cl ME16 . . . 161 B5
Audley Dr E16 . . . 1 B5
Audley Rd CT20 . . . 334 F5
Audley Rise TN9 . . . 221 F1
Audley Wlk BR5 . . . 54 C3
Audre Lorde Ho E16 . . . 1 B8
Audrey Sturley Ct
TN4 . . . 285 D4
Auger Cl ME9 . . . 99 E5
Augusta Cl 1 ME7 . . . 64 C7
Augusta Gdns CT20 . . . 335 C4
Augusta Pl 14 CT11 . . . 117 F7
Augusta Rd CT11 . . . 117 F7
Augustine Ho TN10 . . . 222 C3
Augustine Rd
Gravesend DA12 . . . 37 C8
Minster (Sheppey) ME12 . . 47 B8
Minster (Thanet) CT12 . . 115 B6
Orpington BR5 . . . 54 D6
Augustus Wlk TN23 . . . 299 F5
Aultmore Ct TN2 . . . 286 D3
Aurellus Cl TN23 . . . 300 A4
Austell Manor 5 ME7 . . . 64 C6
Austen Cl
Swanscombe DA9 . . . 17 C1
Tilbury RM18 . . . 19 C5
Woolwich SE28 . . . 3 B5
Austen Gdns DA1 . . . 15 F3
Austen Rd DA8 . . . 14 B7
Austens Orch 14 TN30 . . 345 A7

Austen Way ME20 ..... 127 F4
Austin Ave Bromley BR2 .. 52 E4
Herne Bay CT6 .... 75 F4
Austin Cl Gillingham ME5 .. 64 E2
Sittingbourne ME10 ..... 102 A8
Austin Ct 4 TN16 ..... 151 D1
Austin Rd
Ashford TN23 .... 300 B6
Northfleet DA11 .... 36 F7
Orpington BR5 .... 54 A4
Austins La 4 CT13 .... 149 A1
Austral Cl DA15 .... 30 F5
Autumn Glade ME5 .... 130 D8
Avalon Cl BR6 .... 87 D7
Avalon Rd BR5,BR6 ..... 87 C8
Avard Gdns BR6 .... 86 C6
Avards Cl TN18 .... 354 E8
Avebury Ave
Ramsgate CT11 .... 117 G8
Tonbridge TN9 .... 222 B1
Avebury Rd BR6 .... 86 D7
Aveley Cl DA8 .... 14 F8
Aveling Cl ME3 .... 41 D6
Aveling Ct 2 ME2 .... 63 B7
Avenons Rd 3 E16 .... 1 A8
Avent Wlk ME9 .... 102 B2
Avenue Gdns CT9 .... 51 C3
Avenue Le Puy TN9 ... 222 C1
Avenue of Remembrance
ME10 .... 101 F3
Avenue Rd
Bexley DA7,DA6 .... 13 E4
Dover CT16 .... 278 C1
Erith DA8 .... 14 D7
Herne Bay CT6 .... 76 E5
Ramsgate CT11 .... 117 F7
Sevenoaks TN13 .... 154 C3
Tatsfield TN16 .... 150 E7
Avenue The
Aylesford ME20 .... 128 E1
Biggin Hill TN16 ...... 150 F5
Borough Green TN15 ... 157 A8
Bromley BR1 .... 52 D6
Deal CT14 .... 215 C7
Gravesend DA11 .... 37 A8
Hersden CT3 .... 111 E1
Hill Park TN16 .... 151 A4
Hythe CT21 .... 333 C2
Kingsdown CT14 .... 248 D4
Margate CT9 .... 51 A1
Orpington BR6 .... 86 F8
Orpington,Keston Mark
BR2 .... 85 D7
Orpington,St Paul's Cray
BR5 .... 31 B1
St Margaret's at Cliffe
CT15 .... 279 F6
St Mary's Island ME4 .... 41 C2
Sidcup DA5 .... 31 D8
Swanscombe DA9 .... 17 B2
Temple Ewell CT16 ..... 277 E5
Tonbridge TN9 .... 222 B2
Averenches Rd ME14 .. 162 F5
Avereng Gdns CT19 ... 335 B6
Avereng Rd CT19 ...... 335 B6
Avery Cl
Allhallows-on-S ME3 .... 9 E3
Maidstone ME15 .... 161 F1
Avery Ct ME3 .... 9 E3
Avery Hill Rd SE9 ...... 30 D7
Avery La ME15, ME17 .. 196 D6
Avery Way Allhallows ME3 .. 9 D2
Dartford DA1 .... 33 F6
Aviation Ct ME12 .... 48 E3
Aviemore Gdns ME14 .. 162 F4
Avington Cl ME15 ..... 161 F1
Avocet Mews SE28 .... 2 D3
Avocet Wlk ME5 .... 97 D2
Avon Cl Canterbury CT1 . 175 C8
Gravesend DA12 .... 37 D6
Tonbridge TN10 .... 222 C5
Avon Ct DA14 .... 31 B5
Avondale Cl CT5 ...... 109 A8
Avondale Ct ME14 ..... 162 E5
Avondale Pl ME3 .... 25 C4
Avondale Rd
Bexley DA16 .... 13 C5
Bromley,Mottingham SE9 .. 29 E6
Bromley,Plaistow BR1 .... 29 A2
Capel-le-F CT18 ...... 308 C2
Gillingham ME7 .... 64 D5
Avon Ho 13 CT20 ..... 335 C4
Avonmouth Rd DA1 .... 15 D2
Avonstowe Cl BR6 ...... 86 C7
Avon St TN1 .... 286 C5
Awliscombe Rd DA16 .... 12 F5
Axford Ct ME8 .... 99 A8
Axminster Cres DA16 ... 13 C6
Axtaine Rd BR5 .... 54 D2
Axtane DA13 .... 35 F1
Axtane Cl DA4 .... 57 C8
Axton Chase Sch DA3 ... 58 F6
Aycliffe Cl BR1 .... 52 F5
Aycliffe Com Prim Sch
CT17 .... 310 A4
Ayelands La DA3 .... 91 E8
Ayelands DA3 .... 91 E8
Ayers Cotts BR8 .... 33 E2
Aylesbury Rd
Ashford TN25 .... 268 B7
Bromley BR2 .... 52 A6
Aylesford Cres ME8 ..... 65 B4
Aylesford Pl TN24 ..... 300 E7
Aylesford Prim Sch
ME20 .... 128 D1
Aylesford Sch ME20 ... 128 D1
Aylesford Sta ME20 ... 128 D2
Aylesham Cnr CT3 .... 210 D3
Aylesham & District Com
Workshop Trust CT3 .. 211 A5
Aylesham Ind Est CT3 . 210 E4
Aylesham Prim Sch
CT3 .... 210 E5
Aylesham Rd
Aylesham CT15,CT3 .... 211 A4
Orpington BR6 .... 53 F2
Aylesham Sta CT3 ..... 211 A6
Ayleswade Rd TN27 ... 294 E7
Aylewyn Gn ME10 ..... 101 F8
Aynscombe Angle BR6 . 54 A2
Aynsley Ct 1 CT13 .... 149 A1
Ayrshire Cl TN24 ...... 268 C7
Ayton Rd CT11 .... 117 C6
Azalea Dr BR8 .... 55 E5

B

Babbacombe Rd BR1 .... 29 B1
Babb's La TN17 .... 342 A6
Babington House Sch
BR7 .... 29 F2
Babs Oak Hill CT2 ..... 144 B7
Babylon La ME17,TN12 . 229 B1
Backfields ME1 .... 63 B4
Back La
6 Faversham ME13 .... 138 D7
Godden Green TN15 .... 155 A2
Goudhurst TN17 .... 318 E8
Horsmonden TN12 ..... 290 A6
Ightham TN15 .... 156 C2
Maidstone ME17 .... 195 E1
Minster (Sheppey) ME12 . 47 D6
Sevenoaks TN13,TN14 .. 153 C1
Shipbourne TN11 ...... 189 D4
Sidcup DA5 .... 32 A8
Back Rd
Sandhurst TN18 .... 356 B5
Sidcup DA14 .... 31 A4
Back Rd W CT16 ...... 310 G8
Back St Leeds ME17 ... 196 E6
Ringwould CT14 .... 247 F5
Baddlesmere Rd CT5 ... 75 A2
Baden Powell Ho 11
DA17 .... 4 A3
Baden Powell Rd
TN13 .... 153 E5
Baden Rd ME7 .... 64 D7
Bader Cres ME5 .... 97 A7
Bader Wlk DA11 .... 36 F5
Badger's Hill Open Farm★
CT4 .... 205 C8
Badger Rd ME5 .... 97 C1
Badgers Bridge CT18 .. 305 D4
Badgers Cl CT2 .... 142 A7
Badgers Copse BR6 ..... 86 F8
Badgers Croft SE9 ...... 30 A5
Badgers Holt TN2 ..... 286 E5
Badgers Oak TN23 .... 299 D8
Badgers Rd TN14 .... 88 B1
Badgers Rise
Badgers Mount TN14 .... 88 A1
Deal CT14 .... 248 C8
Kearsney CT17 .... 277 D3
Badlesmere Cl TN23 ... 299 E6
Badlow Cl DA8 .... 14 E7
Badminton Mews E16 .... 1 A5
Bad Munstereifel Rd
TN23,TN24 .... 300 D5
Badsell Park Farm
TN12 .... 256 C3
Badsell Rd TN12 ...... 256 E5
Baffin Cl ME4 .... 63 F2
Bagham La CT4 .... 205 D8
Bagham Rd CT4 .... 205 C8
Bagshaw Ho 6 BR1 .... 52 A8
Bagshill Rd ME13 ..... 170 A3
Bailey Dr ME7 .... 65 A1
Bailey Fields TN26 ... 297 E4
Baileys Field TN23 ... 267 F1
Baird Ho 13 DA17 .... 4 A3
Baird's Hill CT10 .... 83 F6
Bairdsley Cl CT10 ...... 83 F6
Bakenham Ho 1 ME1 ... 63 C1
Baker Beall Ct DA7 .... 14 B4
Baker Cl ME9 .... 103 C2
Baker Hill Cl DA11 ..... 36 F4
Baker La
Headcorn TN27 .... 262 F7
Sutton Valence ME17 ... 229 F7
Baker Rd
Folkestone CT19 ...... 334 E6
Woolwich SE18 .... 11 E7
Bakers Ave TN15 .... 90 E3
Bakers Cl CT2 .... 174 C7
Bakers Cross TN17 ... 320 E4
Bakers Ct CT11 .... 117 E7
Baker's La CT4 .... 173 D2
Bakers Mews 9 BR6 .... 86 F4
Baker St Burham ME1 ... 95 F1
Rochester ME1 .... 63 C3
Baker's Wlk ME1 .... 63 C6
Bakery Cl TN17 .... 293 E7
Bakery Cotts ME14 .... 129 E3
Bakery The ME9 .... 134 A6
Balaclava La TN5 ..... 337 A6
Balas Dr ME10 .... 101 C7
Balcaskie Rd SE9 .... 11 F2
Balchen Rd SE3 .... 11 D5
Balcomb Cres CT9 ...... 83 C8
Balcombe Cl DA6 .... 13 D3
Balcombe Cotts TN17 . 318 E8
Balcombes Hill TN17 .. 318 E8
Balder Rise SE12 .... 29 B6
Baldock Rd TN5 .... 336 E4
Baldric Rd CT20 ...... 334 F5
Baldwin Rd
Greatstone-on-Sea
TN28 .... 373 D1
Minster (Sheppey) ME12 . 47 D7
Baldwin Terr CT19 .... 335 D6
Baldwyns Mans DA2 .... 32 D6
Baldwyn's Pk DA5 ...... 32 D6
Baldwyn's Rd DA5 ...... 32 D6
Balfour Ct CT20 ...... 335 B3
Balfour Inf Sch ME1 .... 63 E1
Balfour Jun Sch ME4 ... 63 E2
Balfour Rd Bromley BR2 . 52 D4
Chatham ME4 .... 63 E2
Deal CT14 .... 215 C2
Dover CT16 .... 278 C1
Balgowan St SE18 .... 2 F2
Baliol Rd CT5 .... 74 E2
Ballamore Rd BR1 ...... 29 A5
Ballard Bsns Pk ME2 .... 62 F5
Ballard Cl TN12 ...... 259 C6
Ballard Ct 20 DA14 ..... 31 A5
Ballard Ind Est ME5 ... 130 C8
Ballard Rd TN28 ...... 373 D1
Ballards La RH8 ...... 183 C6
Ballard Way TN12 .... 257 B7
Ballens Rd ME5 .... 97 C3
Balliemoor Ct CT11 ..... 83 F1
Balliol Rd Bexley DA16 ... 13 B5
Broadstairs CT10 .... 83 F8
Ball La TN24 .... 268 F7
Balls Cotts ME3 .... 40 F4
Ball's Gn TN7 .... 311 B5
Balmer Cl ME8 .... 98 D7
Balmoral Ct SE12 .... 29 B4
Balmoral Gdns DA5 ..... 31 F8
Balmoral Ho 10 ME15 .. 195 F5
Balmoral Pl 12 CT11 .. 117 F7
Balmoral Rd
Gillingham ME7 .... 64 D5
Kingsdown CT14 ...... 248 C6
4 Margate CT9 .... 82 B8
Sutton at H DA4 .... 34 B1
Balmoral Terr ME10 ... 101 D4
Balmoral Trad Est E6 ..... 2 F8
Baltic Ho TN1 .... 286 B5
Baltic Rd TN9 .... 254 B7
Baltic Wharf 1 DA11 ... 19 A1
Baltimore Pl DA16 ...... 12 F5
Bamford Way CT14 .... 215 C4
Banbury Villas DA13 .... 35 F1
Banchory Rd SE3 .... 11 B7
Bankside DA3 .... 58 E5
Bancroft Gdns BR6 ..... 53 F1
Bancroft La ME18 ..... 159 C2
Bancroft Rd TN15 .... 124 F3
Bangor Rd ME2 .... 62 D6
Banister Ho RM20 ...... 17 D8
Bank Cotts ME17 ..... 164 E3
Bankfields TN27 ..... 262 C5
Bankfield Way TN17 ... 318 E7
Bank Ho
New Romney TN28 ..... 373 C6
Sheerness ME12 .... 28 C2
Bank Hos DA2 .... 34 A3
Bank Ho TN15 .... 125 A3
Bank La TN11,TN15 ... 188 A3
Bank Rd TN25 .... 329 E8
Bankside
Canterbury CT1 .... 175 D7
Chatham ME5 .... 97 B8
Bankside Cl
Biggin Hill TN16 ...... 118 C1
Joyden's Wood DA5 ..... 32 D4
Bankside TN5 .... 336 E5
Bank Side TN26 ...... 349 A8
Bankside
Northfleet DA11 .... 18 C1
Sevenoaks TN13 .... 153 E6
Banks La DA6 .... 13 F3
Banks Rd Ashford TN23 . 300 A7
Rochester ME2 .... 63 C8
Bank St Ashford TN23 .. 268 B2
Chatham ME4 .... 64 B3
Cranbrook TN17 ...... 320 C5
Faversham ME13 ...... 138 C7
Gravesend DA12 .... 19 B1
Banks The CT10 .... 83 F6
Bank St Herne Bay CT6 ... 76 F5
Hythe CT21 .... 333 C2
Maidstone ME14 ...... 162 A4
Sevenoaks TN13 ...... 154 C2
Tonbridge TN9 .... 222 C2
Bank View 5 ME15 .... 161 E2
Banky Fields Cl ME8 .... 66 B1
Banky Mdw ME16 ..... 160 F3
Banner Farm Rd TN2 .. 286 B2
Banner Way ME12 ...... 46 E6
Banningbrook Ct
CT14 .... 215 D4
Banning St ME2 .... 63 B8
Bannister Gdns BR5 .... 54 C6
Bannister Hill ME9 ... 101 B2
Bannister Hos TN26 ... 234 A1
Bannister Rd ME14 ... 162 A7
Bannockburn Prim Sch
SE18 .... 2 F2
Bannockburn Rd SE18 .... 2 F2
Banstead Ct 3 BR1 ..... 52 E6
Banwell Rd DA5 .... 13 D1
Bapchild Pl 8 BR5 ..... 54 C5
Bapchild & Tonge CE Prim
Sch ME9 .... 102 D3
Barbados Terr 2
ME14 .... 162 A7
Barber's Almshouses 11
CT11 .... 117 D6
Barberry Ave ME5 ...... 96 E5
Barcham Ct ME15 ..... 194 F5
Barchester Way TN10 . 222 F6
Barclay Ave TN10 .... 223 A5
Barclay Ct CT8 .... 50 C1
Barclay Field TN15 ... 122 E2
Barcombe Cl BR5 .... 54 A6
Bardell Terr ME1 .... 63 D5
Barden Ct ME14 ...... 162 B5
Barden Park Rd TN9 .. 222 A1
Barden Rd
Penshurst TN3 .... 252 F2
Speldhurst TN3 .... 285 A8
Tonbridge TN9 .... 222 B1
Barden St SE18 .... 12 E7
Bardsley Cl TN12 ..... 225 A7
Barfield Rd BR1,BR7 ... 53 A6
Barfield DA4 .... 57 B8
Barfleur Manor 3 ME7 . 64 A6
Barfreston Cl ME15 ... 161 F2
Barfrestone Rd CT15 .. 212 A1
Bargate Cl SE18 .... 2 F1
Bargates TN23 .... 299 E6
Bargehouse Rd E16 ...... 2 B4
Barges The CT5 .... 74 E3
Bargrove CT18 .... 333 E6
Bargrove Rd ME14 .... 162 C5
Barham CE Prim Sch
CT4 .... 242 F8
Barham Cl
Chislehurst BR7 .... 30 B3
Gravesend DA12 .... 37 F7
Maidstone ME15 ...... 195 E5
Orpington BR2 .... 52 E1
Barham Ct BR2 .... 52 E1
Barham Mews ME18 ... 193 B8
Barham Rd
Chislehurst BR7 .... 30 B3
Dartford DA1 .... 34 A8
Barham's Mill Rd
TN27 .... 232 B3
Baring Cl SE12 .... 29 A6
Baring Prim Sch SE12 .. 29 A8
Baring Rd SE12 .... 29 A6
Barker Rd ME16 ...... 161 F3
Barkers Ct ME10 ...... 101 D4
Bark Hart Rd BR6 ...... 54 B1
Barkis Cl ME1 .... 96 D7
Barler Pl ME11 .... 46 A5
Barley Cl Herne Bay CT6 . 77 D2
Martin Mill CT15 ...... 247 C2
Barleycorn Dr ME8 ..... 98 E6
Barleycorn ME19 ..... 127 E1
Barley Fields ME14 ... 162 D4
Barleymow Cl ME5 ..... 97 C7
Barley Way TN23 ..... 299 E5
Barling Cl ME5 .... 96 D1
Barlow Cl ME8 .... 98 E5
Barlow Dr SE18 .... 11 E6
Barlow Way RH13 .... 4 E8
Barlow Way S RM13 ...... 4 E7
Barming Prim Sch
ME16 .... 160 F2
Barming Rd ME18 .... 159 F2
Barming Sta ME16 .... 160 F6
Barnaby Terr ME1 ...... 63 D2
Barnard Cl
Chislehurst BR7 .... 53 D8
Woolwich SE18 .... 2 A3
Barnard Ct
Chatham ME4 .... 64 A2
21 Dartford DA2 .... 16 B1
Barnberry Cl TN23 .... 299 E8
Barn Cl Borden ME9 ... 101 A2
Hoath CT3 .... 111 E5
Yorkletts CT5 .... 108 A3
Barn Cres CT9 .... 50 F1
Barncroft Cl ME14 .... 162 F4
Barncroft Dr ME7 ...... 97 F4
Barndale Ct DA12 ...... 38 E3
Barned Ct ME16 ...... 160 F2
Barnehurst Ave DA7,
DA8 .... 14 C6
Barnehurst Cl DA8 .... 14 C6
Barnehurst Inf Sch
DA8 .... 14 C6
Barnehurst Jun Sch
DA8 .... 14 C6
Barnehurst Rd DA7 .... 14 C5
Barnehurst Sta DA7 ... 14 C5
Barn End Ctr DA2 ...... 33 C5
Barn End Dr DA2 .... 33 C5
Barn End La DA2 .... 33 C4
Barnes Ave CT9 .... 50 F1
Barnes Cl ME13 ...... 138 B8
Barnes Cray Prim Sch
DA1 .... 15 A3
Barnes Cray Rd DA1 ... 15 A3
Barnes Ct
Canterbury CT1 ...... 174 D6
Newham E16 .... 1 C8
Barnesdale Cres BR5 ... 54 A4
Barnesende Ct CT13 .. 181 A8
Barnes La ME17 ...... 227 D8
Barnes Wlk TN12 .... 259 D6
Barnet Dr BR2 .... 85 E8
Barnet's La CT2 ..... 143 D8
Barnett Cl DA8 .... 14 F5
Barnett Ct
Minster (Thanet) CT12 .. 115 C5
Ramsgate CT12 .... 83 B1
Barnett Field TN23 ... 299 F8
Barnetts Cl TN4 ..... 254 C1
Barnetts Rd TN11 .... 221 A2
Barnetts Way TN4 .... 286 C8
Barnet Wood Rd BR2 ... 85 C8
Barney Cl SE7 .... 1 C1
Barnfield ME5 .... 97 A8
Barnfield Cl
Crockenhill BR8 .... 55 C2
New Barn DA3 .... 59 D6
Stone DA9 .... 16 F1
Barnfield Cres TN15 .. 122 E2
Barnfield Gdns SE18 ... 12 B8
Barnfield
Gravesend DA11 .... 37 A6
Herne Bay CT6 .... 76 C2
Barnfield Rd
Bexley DA17 .... 13 F8
Faversham ME13 ..... 138 C8
Folkestone CT19 ..... 335 C7
Orpington BR5 .... 54 D6
Sevenoaks TN13 ...... 153 E4
Tatsfield TN16 .... 150 D6
Woolwich SE18 .... 12 B8
Barnfield
Royal Tunbridge Wells
TN2 .... 313 F7
Tenterden TN30 ...... 324 C2
Barnfield Way RH8 ... 183 A2
Barnham Dr SE28 .... 2 F5
Barnhill Ave BR2 ...... 52 A4
Barn Hill ME15 ...... 193 E2
Barnhouse La TN29 .. 371 A8
Barnhurst La CT18 ... 307 A5
Barnhurst Rd ME14 ... 162 A8
Barn Mdw
Staplehurst TN12 ..... 260 E4
Upper Halling ME2 ..... 94 E4
Barnock Cl DA1 .... 32 E8
Barn Platt TN23 ..... 300 A8
Barnsley Cl ME12 ...... 28 E2
Barnsole Inf Sch ME7 .. 64 E4
Barnsole Jun Sch ME7 .. 64 E4
Barnsole Rd
Gillingham ME7 .... 64 E3
Staple CT3 .... 179 B5
Barn The ME9 .... 101 A2
Barn Tye Cl CT15 .... 278 E6
Barnwell Pl ME7 ...... 64 C5
Barnwell Rd DA1 ...... 15 F4
Barnwood Cl ME1 ...... 96 B8
Baron Cl Gillingham ME7 .. 64 E7
Maidstone ME14 ..... 162 F5
Barons Ct TN4 .... 286 A5
Barrack Cnr TN13 ... 154 C4
Barrack Hill CT21 .... 333 A2
Barrack Rd ME4 .... 64 B8
Barrack Row
Benenden TN17 ...... 342 D6
17 Gravesend DA11 ..... 19 B1
Barrel Arch Cl TN12 .. 259 C6
Barretts Green Cotts 5
TN18 .... 341 A2
Barretts Rd
Hawkhurst TN18 ..... 341 A2
Sevenoaks TN13 ..... 153 E7
Barrey Rd TN24 ..... 301 A6
Barrie Dr 7 ME20 ... 127 F4
Barrier Point Rd E16 .... 1 C5
Barrier Rd ME4 .... 63 F5
Barrington Cl ME5 ..... 96 F5
Barrington Cres CT7 ... 81 B7
Barrington Prim Sch
DA7 .... 13 D5
Barrington Rd DA7 .... 13 D5
Barrington Villas SE18 .. 12 A6
Barrowfields ME5 ..... 97 D1
Barrow Grove Jun Sch
ME10 .... 101 D3
Barrow Gr ME10 ..... 101 D3
Barrow Hill
Ashford TN23 .... 268 B2
Barrowhill TN25 ..... 331 D7
Barrow Hill Cotts
TN23 .... 268 A2
Barrow Hill Pl 2
TN23 .... 268 B3
Barrow Hill Rise
TN25 .... 331 D7
Barrow Hill Terr 1
TN23 .... 268 B3
Barrow La TN3 ...... 284 F2
Barrows Cl CT7 .... 81 A6
Barr Rd DA12 .... 37 F6
Barry Ave DA7 .... 13 E7
Barry Cl BR6 .... 86 E7
Barry Rd E6 .... 1 E7
Barth Mews SE18 .... 2 E2
Bartholomew Cl CT21 . 333 B3
Bartholomew La CT21 . 333 B3
Bartholomew St
6 Dover CT16 .... 278 C1
Hythe CT21 .... 333 B2
Bartholomew Way BR8 .. 55 E6
Barth Rd SE18 .... 2 E2
Bartlett Cl ME5 .... 97 C1
Bartlett Dr CT5 .... 75 A1
Bartlett Rd
Gravesend DA11 .... 37 A7
Westerham TN16 ..... 151 C1
Bartletts Cl ME12 ..... 46 C5
Bartley Mill La TN3 .. 315 E4
Bartley Mill Rd TN3 .. 315 F3
Barton Bsns Pk CT1 .. 175 D6
Barton Cl Bexley DA6 ... 13 E2
2 Newham E6 .... 1 F7
Barton Cotts TN11 ... 190 A6
Barton Court Gram Sch
CT1 .... 175 B8
Barton Ct 4 CT11 .... 117 E7
Barton Field CT18 ... 305 B7
Barton Hill Dr ME12 ... 47 A5
Barton Jun Sch CT16 .. 278 C2
Barton Mill Ct 2 CT2 . 142 F1
Barton Mill Rd CT1 ... 143 B2
Barton Rd
Canterbury CT1 ..... 175 C6
Dover CT16 .... 278 C2
Maidstone ME15 ..... 162 A2
Rochester ME2 .... 63 A7
Sidcup DA14 .... 31 E2
Sutton at H DA4 ...... 57 B8
Bartons Cotts TN16 .. 152 C3
Barton's Point Coastal Pk★
ME12 .... 28 F2
Barton View Terr 2
CT17 .... 278 C1
Barville Rd CT15 .... 212 E2
Barwick Rd CT17 .... 277 F1
Bascombe Gr DA1 ..... 14 E1
Basden Cotts 2 TN18 . 341 A2
Baseing Cl E6 .... 2 A6
Bashford Barn La
Bredgar ME9 .... 134 A4
Silver Street ME9 ... 133 F4
Basi Cl ME2 .... 40 C1
Basildon Rd SE2 .... 3 A1
Basilon Rd DA7 .... 13 E5
Basil Terr 6 ME15 ... 162 A1
Basing Cl ME15 ..... 162 B3
Basing Dr DA5 .... 13 F1
Baskerville TN24 .... 268 B3
Basket Gdns SE9 ...... 11 E2
Basmere Cl ME14 .... 162 C6
Bassant Rd SE18 ...... 12 F8
Basser Hill ME9 .... 67 E3
Bassett Cl CT21 ..... 333 E4
Bassett Gdns CT21 ... 333 D4
Bassett Rd ME10 .... 101 D4
Bassetts Cl BR6 ...... 86 B6
Bassett's Forge TN5 .. 336 E5
Bassetts La TN8,TN11 .. 283 C7
Bassetts Way BR6 ..... 86 B6
Basted La Basted TN15 . 156 F5
Crouch TN15 .... 157 B4
Bastion Rd Dover CT17 . 310 C6
Woolwich SE2 .... 3 A1
Baston Manor BR2 .... 85 B6
Baston Manor Rd BR2,
BR4 .... 85 B6
Baston Rd BR2 .... 85 B7
Baston Sch BR2 .... 85 B8
Bat & Ball Ent Ctr
TN14 .... 154 C7
Bat & Ball Sta TN14 .. 154 C6
Batchelors TN2 ..... 287 E8
Batchelor St ME4 ..... 64 A4
Batchwood Gn BR5 .... 54 B6
Bateman Cnr TN26 ... 297 E6
Bates Cl
New Hythe ME20 .... 128 A3
Staple CT3 .... 178 F6
Bates Hill TN15 .... 156 C5
Bateson St SE18 .... 2 E2
Bath Ct 8 CT20 ..... 335 B3
Bath Hard ME1 .... 63 D5
Bath Mews TN24 .... 300 E6
Bath Pl CT9 .... 50 J2
Bath Rd Ashford TN24 .. 300 E6
Dartford DA1 .... 33 B8
Margate CT9 .... 50 J2
Baths Rd BR2 .... 52 D5
Bath St DA11 .... 19 B1
Bathurst Cl
Ramsgate CT12 .... 83 B1
Staplehurst TN12 ... 260 E4
Bathurst Rd
Folkestone CT20 .... 335 A5
Staplehurst TN12 ... 260 E3
Bathway 13 SE18 .... 2 A2
Batten Cl E6 .... 1 F7
Batteries Cl ME9 .... 136 B8
Batteries Terr ME9 .. 136 B8
Battery Point CT21 .. 334 B2
Battery Rd
Lydd-on-S TN29 ..... 380 D6
Woolwich SE28 .... 2 E4
Battlefields TN15 ... 124 F3
Battle La TN12 ..... 260 A8
Battle of Britain Homes 17
CT17 .... 310 D7
Battle of Britain Meml
The★ CT18 .... 308 A1
Battle Rd DA8,DA17 ..... 4 C2
Battlesmere Rd ME3 .. 40 B8
Battle St DA12 .... 60 F6
Batt's Rd DA12 .... 61 A4
Baugh Rd DA14 .... 31 C3
Bawden Cl CT2 ..... 143 A4
Baxendale Ct TN24 .. 300 D7
Baxter Rd E16 .... 1 C7
Baxter Way ME18 ... 159 C3
Bayard Ct DA6 .... 14 B3
Bay Banks ME13 ..... 137 E2
Bay Cl ME3 .... 41 E3
Bay Cotts CT15 ..... 280 C6
Baye La CT3 .... 145 D1
Bayeux Ho 11 SE7 ..... 11 C8
Bayfield ME13 ...... 137 E2
Bayfield Rd SE9 .... 11 D3
Bayford Rd ME10 ... 102 A4
Bayhall Rd TN2 ..... 286 C3
Bayham Ct TN5 ..... 336 E6
Bayham Old Abbey★
TN3 .... 316 B5
Bayham Rd
Bells Yew Green TN3 .. 315 B4
Royal Tunbridge Wells
TN2,TN3 .... 314 C7
Sevenoaks TN13 ... 154 D4
Bay Hill Cl CT15 ... 280 A5
Bay Hill CT15 ...... 280 B6
Bayle Ct CT20 ..... 335 E4
Bayle St 19 CT20 .... 335 E5
Bayle The CT20 .... 335 E4
Bayley's Hill TN14 .. 186 E3
Bayley Wlk SE2 .... 3 E1
Bayliss Ave SE28 .... 3 D6
Bayly Rd DA1 .... 16 A1
Bay Manor La RM20 .... 16 F8
Bay Mus The★ CT15 .. 280 B5
Bayne Cl E6 .... 1 F7
Baynham Cl DA5 ...... 13 F1
Bays The BR5 .... 54 C6
Bayswater Dr ME8 .... 98 E4
Bay The DA13 ...... 126 A8
Baytree Cl Bromley BR1 . 52 D8
Sidcup DA15 .... 30 F7
Bay View Gdns ME12 .. 49 D2
Bay View Hts CT7 ..... 80 D8
Bay View Rd CT10 .... 84 A2
Bayview Rd
Kingsdown CT14 .... 248 C4
Whitstable CT5 ..... 108 D7
Baywell ME19 ...... 127 E2
Bazes Shaw DA3 ...... 91 F8
Beach Alley 15 CT5 ... 74 D2
Beacham Cl SE7 .... 11 D8
Beachamwell Dr
ME18 .... 159 C2

Beach App ME12 .... 49 E3
Beach Ave CT7 .... 80 F8
Beach Bank Cvn Pk
  CT21 .... 353 C7
Beachborough Rd
  CT19,CT20 .... 335 A5
Beach Ct Deal CT14 ... 215 D2
  Eltham SE9 .... 11 E1
  Goddard's Green TN17 . 321 D1
  Westgate-on-S CT8 .... 50 D1
Beachfield Lodge
  ME12 .... 28 C2
Beach Flats 2 CT21 ... 333 E2
Beach Hos CT9 .... 50 G2
Beach House Mews
  CT8 .... 50 D1
Beach Marine 7 CT20 . 334 F3
Beachmont Cl TN28 ... 377 E8
Beach Rd
  Dymchurch TN29 ...... 353 A4
  St Margaret's at Cliffe
  CT15 .... 280 B5
  Westgate-on-S CT8 .... 50 D1
Beach Rise CT8 .... 50 D1
Beach St Deal CT14 ... 215 D6
  Folkestone CT20 ...... 335 E4
  Herne Bay CT6 .... 76 F5
  Sheerness ME12 .... 28 B2
Beach Terr ME12 .... 28 B2
Beach The CT14 .... 215 D3
Beach Wlk CT5 .... 74 E3
Beacon Ave CT6 .... 77 B8
Beacon Cl ME8 .... 98 D7
Beacon Dr DA2 .... 35 C5
Beaconfields TN13 .... 154 A1
Beacon Hill
  Gillingham ME5 .... 64 D2
  Herne Bay CT6 .... 77 B5
Beacon Hill La ME3 .... 40 F4
Beacon La CT13 .... 180 A6
Beacon Oak Rd TN30 . 345 B8
Beacon Rd
  Broadstairs CT10 ..... 83 F7
  Chatham ME5 .... 64 C2
  Erith DA8 .... 15 B7
  Herne Bay CT6 .... 77 A5
  Lenham ME17 .... 199 C5
Beacon Rise TN13 ..... 154 A1
Beacons Cl 11 E6 ...... 1 E8
Beaconsfield Ave
  Dover CT16 .... 278 C1
  Gillingham ME7 .... 64 E5
Beaconsfield Cl SE3 ... 11 A8
Beaconsfield Gdns
  CT10 .... 83 F5
Beaconsfield Par SE9 .. 29 E4
Beaconsfield Rd
  Bromley,Mottingham SE9 . 29 E4
  Bromley,Widmore BR1 .. 52 D6
  Canterbury CT2 .... 142 F2
  Chatham ME4 .... 63 D3
  Deal CT14 .... 215 D5
  Dover CT16 .... 278 C1
  Greenwich SE3 .... 11 A8
  Maidstone ME15 ...... 161 E2
  Maypole DA5 .... 32 E6
  Sittingbourne ME10 ... 102 C4
Beaconsfield CT5 ..... 107 F6
Beacons The ME17 .... 194 C4
Beacon Terr CT21 .... 334 B2
Beacon Way CT21 .... 331 F3
Beacon Wlk
  Herne Bay CT6 .... 77 A5
  Tenterden TN30 ...... 324 B1
Beacon Wood Cty Pk★
  DA2 .... 35 B4
Beadon Rd BR2 .... 52 A4
Beagles Cl BR5 .... 87 D8
Beagles Wood Rd
  TN2 .... 287 E7
Beal Cl DA16 .... 119 A6
Beaman Cl TN17 ...... 318 F6
Beamish Rd BR5 ...... 54 C2
Beamont Cl CT12 ..... 81 F2
Beams The ME15 ..... 162 F1
Bean Cl TN23 .... 267 C1
Beane Croft DA12 .... 37 F7
Beaney's La Cotts
  CT4 .... 171 C1
Beaney's La CT4 ..... 171 C1
Bean Hill Cotts DA2 .. 35 C4
Bean La DA2 .... 35 B6
Bean Prim Sch DA2 ... 35 C4
Bean Rd Bexley DA16 . 13 D3
  Swanscombe DA9 ..... 17 B1
Beanshaw SE9 .... 30 A4
Bears End Ho TN23 ... 300 B8
Bear's La TN23,TN26 . 266 E3
Bearsted CT ME8 ..... 65 B3
Bearsted Green Bsns Ctr
  ME14 .... 163 C4
Bearsted Rd ME14 .... 162 E6
Bearsted Sta ME14 ... 163 B5
Beaton Cl DA9 .... 17 B2
Beatrice Gdns DA11 .. 36 E6
Beatrice Hills Cl TN24 268 E5
Beatrice Mews TN28 . 377 E7
Beatrice Rd
  Capel-le-F CT18 ..... 308 C2
  Margate CT9 .... 82 E8
Beatty Ave ME7 ...... 64 F4
Beatty Cl CT19 ...... 335 E8
Beatty Cotts ME3 .... 9 D1
Beatty Rd
  Folkestone CT19 ..... 335 D8
  Rochester ME1 .... 96 D8
Beauchamp Ave CT14 . 215 A3
Beauchamp Cl TN24 .. 268 E5
Beauchamps La CT15 . 211 D5
Beaufighter Rd ME19 . 158 E3
Beaufort Ave CT16 ... 117 B8
Beaufort Ct ME2 ..... 63 E6
Beaufort E6 .... 2 A8

Beaufort Rd ME2 ..... 62 E8
Beaufort Wlk ME15 ... 195 E4
Beaufoy Rd CT17 ..... 278 A1
Beaufoy Terr CT17 ... 277 F1
Beauherne Com Sch
  CT2 .... 174 D8
Beaulieu Ave E16 ..... 1 B5
Beaulieu Rd TN10 .... 222 B4
Beaulieu Rise ME1 ... 63 D1
Beaulieu Wlk ME16 ... 161 C7
Beaumanor Gdns SE9 . 30 A4
Beaumanor CT6 ...... 77 A3
Beaumont Davy Cl
  ME13 .... 138 C5
Beaumont Dr DA11 ... 36 F8
Beaumont Rd
  Maidstone ME16 ..... 161 B2
  Orpington BR5 .... 53 D3
Beaumont St CT6 .... 76 C4
Beauvoir Dr ME10 .... 102 A8
Beauworth Pk ME15 . 195 E8
Beauxfield CT16 ..... 278 A7
Beaverbank Rd SE9 .. 30 D7
Beaver Ct TN23 ..... 300 A7
Beaver Green Inf Sch
  TN23 .... 299 E7
Beaver Ind Est TN23 . 300 B7
Beaver La
  Ashford,Beaver TN23 .. 300 A7
  Ashford,Singleton TN23 . 299 F7
  Ashford TN23 .... 267 E1
Beaver Rd
  Ashford TN23 .... 300 B8
  Maidstone ME16 ..... 161 B7
Beavers Lodge DA14 . 30 A1
Beaverwood Rd BR7 . 30 E2
Beaverwood Sch for Girls
  BR7 .... 30 D2
Beaver Zoological Gdns★
  TN16 .... 150 B5
Beazley Ct TN24 ..... 300 D7
Bebbington Rd SE28 .. 2 E2
Beblets Cl 4 BR6 .... 86 F5
Beckenham Dr ME16 . 161 D7
Becket Ave CT2 ...... 142 D1
Becket Cl Ash CT3 ... 147 D2
  Deal CT14 .... 215 C8
  Whitstable CT5 .... 75 B1
Becket Ct
  Headcorn TN27 ...... 262 D5
  2 Edenbridge TN9 ... 254 B8
Becket Mews CT2 .... 142 F1
Becket's Cl TN25 .... 271 B6
Beckets Field TN11 ... 252 A3
Beckett Cl DA17 ..... 3 E4
Becketts CI BR6 ..... 86 F7
Beckett St 4 ME13 .. 138 C7
Becketts Wood CT3 .. 112 E3
Beckford Dr BR5 ..... 53 D2
Beckley Cl DA12 ..... 38 B6
Beckley Hill Works
  ME2 .... 39 B8
Beckley Mews ME5 ... 96 F5
Beckley Pl TN25 ..... 332 B8
Beckley Rd ME12 .... 28 E2
Beckman Ct ME14 ... 121 C4
Becksbourne Cl ME14 162 A8
Becks Rd DA14 ...... 31 A5
Beckton Park Sta E6 .. 1 F6
Beckton Rd E16 ..... 1 A8
Beckton Ret Pk E6 ... 2 A8
Beckton Sta E6 ...... 2 A8
Beckwith Gn CT20 ... 334 E5
Beckworth Pl ME16 . 161 B2
Becton Pl DA8 .... 14 C6
Bedale Wlk DA2 ..... 34 B7
Beddalls Farm Ct 6 . 1 E8
Beddington Gn BR5 .. 53 F8
Beddington Rd BR5 .. 53 F8
Beddlestead La CR6 . 150 A6
Beddow Way ME20 .. 129 B3
Bede Ho CT14 .... 215 D8
Bedens Rd DA14 .... 31 E3
Bedford Ave ME8 ... 65 D1
Bedford Ct CT10 ..... 84 B6
Bedford Pl ME16 .... 161 E4
Bedford Rd
  Dartford DA1 .... 34 A8
  Northfleet DA11 ..... 36 F6
  Orpington BR6 .... 54 B1
  Royal Tunbridge Wells
  TN4 .... 254 A1
  Sidcup DA15 .... 30 C5
Bedford Sq
  Longfield DA3 .... 58 A8
  Ramsgate CT12 ...... 83 B2
Bedford Terr 13 TN1 . 286 A2
Bedford Way CT7 .... 79 F1
Bedgebury Cl
  Maidstone ME14 .... 162 C6
  Rochester ME1 ...... 96 D8
Bedgebury Cross
  TN17 .... 318 D2
Bedgebury National
  Pinetum★ TN17 .... 339 E8
Bedgebury Rd
  Goudhurst TN17 ..... 318 E5
  Bedgebury Sch TN17 . 318 E1
Bedingfield Way CT18 305 B7
Bedivere Rd BR1 .... 29 A5
Bedlam Court La
  CT12 .... 115 C6
Bedlam La
  Egerton Forstal TN27 . 264 A8
  Swift's Green TN27 .. 263 E6
Bedmonton La ME9 .. 134 B2
Bedonwell Inf Sch
  DA17 .... 13 E8
Bedonwell Jun Sch
  DA17 .... 13 E8

Bedonwell Rd
  Bexley,Bexleyheath DA7 . 13 F6
  Bexley,West Heath DA7,
  DA1 .... 13 E8
Bedson Wlk ME8 .... 66 B1
Bedwell Rd DA17 ..... 4 A1
Bedwin Cl ME1 ...... 96 D7
Beeby Rd E16 .... 1 B8
Beecham Rd TN10 ... 222 B6
Beech Ave
  Chartham CT4 ...... 173 E1
  Sidcup DA15 .... 31 A8
  Swanley BR8 .... 55 F5
  Tatsfield TN16 ..... 150 D8
Beech Cl
  Faversham ME13 .... 138 B7
  Folkestone CT19 .... 335 C6
Beech Copse BR1 .... 52 F7
Beech Court Gdns★
  TN25 .... 202 F1
Beechcote DA7 ..... 14 D5
Beechcroft BR7 ...... 30 A1
Beechcroft Cl BR6 ... 86 D6
Beechcroft Gdns CT11 117 E8
Beechcroft Rd BR6 .. 86 D6
Beechcroft CT5 ...... 75 D1
Beech Ct
  Canterbury CT1 ..... 175 A7
  Dartford DA1 .... 16 A1
  Paddock Wood TN12 . 257 A7
  Royal Tunbridge Wells
  TN2 .... 286 D4
Beech Dell BR2,BR4 . 85 F6
Beech Dr
  Broadstairs CT10 .... 83 D4
  Elvington CT15 ..... 212 B2
  Hothfield TN26 ..... 267 A7
  Maidstone ME16 .... 161 C6
Beechen Bank Rd ME5 97 A1
Beechenlea La BR8 .. 56 B6
Beecher Ct SE12 .... 29 B5
Beeches Ct BR1 .... 29 A2
Beeches The
  Aylesford ME20 .... 128 E1
  Chatham ME5 ...... 97 A4
  Hextable BR8 .... 32 F1
  Lydd TN29 .... 376 D7
  New Barn DA3 ..... 59 C7
  Royal Tunbridge Wells
  TN2 .... 286 D5
  Sole Street DA13 ... 60 D5
  The Moor TN18 .... 354 E7
  Tilbury RM18 ...... 19 B5
Beechfield Cotts 6
  BR1 .... 52 C7
Beechfield Rd
  Bromley BR1 .... 52 C7
  Erith DA8 .... 14 E7
Beech Gr Cl DA17 ... 116 C5
Beech Green Cl CT15 . 245 C7
Beech Green La
  Cowden TN7 .... 282 F1
  Withyham TN7 ...... 311 B7
Beech Haven Ct DA1 . 14 D2
Beech Hill CT4 ..... 209 B8
Beechhill Rd SE9 .... 12 A2
Beech Ho 7 DA15 ... 31 A5
Beech Hurst CT15 ... 162 B2
Beech Hurst TN2 .... 287 D7
Beeching Rd ME5 .... 97 B3
Beechings Gn ME8 .. 65 C3
Beechings Way ME8 . 65 C3
Beechings Way Ind Ctr
  ME8 .... 65 B4
Beechin Wood La
  TN15 .... 157 D5
Beech La TN12 ..... 288 C4
Beechlands Cl DA3 .. 59 A4
Beech Manor CT2 .. 286 D3
Beech Mast DA13 .. 126 B8
Beechmont Rd TN13 . 187 B6
Beechmont Rise TN10 222 B6
Beechmore Dr ME5 . 97 A2
Beecholme Dr TN24 . 268 C5
Beech Rd
  Biggin Hill TN16 ... 118 C2
  Dartford DA1 .... 33 D7
  East Malling ME19 .. 159 F7
  Herne Pound ME18 . 158 D2
  Hoo St Werburgh ME3 . 41 E3
  Newenden TN18 ... 357 C3
  Orpington BR6 ...... 87 A3
  Rochester ME2 ..... 62 F6
  Sevenoaks TN13 ... 154 B2
Beech St TN1 ...... 286 B4
Beechway
  Meopham Station DA13 . 60 B2
  Sidcup DA5 .... 13 D1
Beech Wlk
  Biddenden TN27 ... 323 D7
  Crayford DA1 ...... 15 A3
Beechwood Ave
  Deal CT14 .... 215 C5
  Gillingham ME5 ..... 64 D2
  Orpington BR6 ..... 86 E4
  Sittingbourne ME10 . 101 E6
Beechwood Cl
  St Mary's Bay TN29 . 365 F3
  Whitfield CT16 ..... 246 A1
Beechwood Cres DA7 . 13 E4
Beechwood Ct
  Deal CT14 .... 215 C5
  Temple Ewell CT16 . 277 E4
Beechwood Dr
  Culverstone Green DA13 . 93 A1
  Orpington BR2 ..... 85 D6
Beechwood Gdns DA13 93 A1
Beechwood Mews
  TN2 .... 286 E4
Beechwood Rd ME16 160 F3
Beechwood Rise BR7 . 30 B4

Beechwood Sacred Heart
  Sch TN2 .... 286 E4
Beechy Lees Rd TN14 . 122 E3
Beeken Dene BR6 ... 86 C6
Beer Cart La CT1 .... 174 F8
Beeston Ct 4 DA1 ... 16 B8
Begbie Rd SE3 ...... 11 C6
Beggarsbush La TN29 371 D7
Beggars Cnr CT3 ... 113 D1
Beggars La TN16 ... 151 E3
Begonia Ave ME8 ... 65 C2
Beke Rd ME8 .... 98 D4
Bekesbourne Hill CT4 . 176 B5
Bekesbourne La
  Bekesbourne CT3,CT4 . 176 E6
  Canterbury CT3 ..... 175 F7
  Littlebourne CT3 ... 176 F6
Bekesbourne Rd CT4 . 175 F2
  Bekesbourne Sta CT4 . 176 B5
Bekesbourne Tower 12
  BR5 .... 54 D1
Belcaire Cl CT21 ... 332 A3
Beldam Haw TN14 .. 121 A8
Belfast Ho 14 ME15 .. 195 E7
Belfield Rd TN2 .... 287 D6
Belford Gr SE18 ..... 2 A1
Belgrave Cl
  5 Orpington BR5 .. 54 C5
  Ramsgate CT11 .... 117 D7
Belgrave Ct Deal CT14 . 215 D3
  Greenwich SE7 ..... 11 C7
Belgrave Rd
  Dover CT17 .... 310 B7
  Halfway Houses ME12 . 46 C5
  Margate CT9 .... 50 I2
  Royal Tunbridge Wells
  TN1 .... 286 B4
Belgrave St ME20 .. 128 E8
Belgrove 5 TN1 ..... 286 A2
Belinda Ct CT19 .... 335 B7
Bellarmine Cl SE28 .. 2 F4
Bell Chapel Cl TN23 . 300 C4
Bell Cl DA9 .... 16 F2
Bell Cnr ME9 .... 372 A4
Bell Cotts ME9 ..... 67 B3
Bell Cres ME1 ...... 128 F8
Bell-Davies Dr CT12 . 82 A1
Bellefield Rd BR5 ... 54 B4
Belle Friday Cl ME9 . 103 C2
Bellegrove Cl DA16 . 12 F5
Bellegrove Par DA16 . 12 F4
Bellegrove Rd DA16 . 12 E5
Bellevue Ave CT11 .. 117 F7
Bellevue Rd DA6 ... 13 F2
Belle Vue Rd
  Farthing Street BR6 . 86 A1
  Herne Bay CT6 .... 77 B5
Bellevue Rd
  Minster (Sheppey) ME12 . 47 C6
  Ramsgate CT11 .... 117 F7
  Whitstable CT5 .... 108 F8
Bellevue St 5 CT20 . 335 D5
Bell Farm Gdns ME16 . 160 F2
Bell Farm La ME12 .. 48 A6
Bellfield CI SE3 .... 11 B7
Bellflower Ave ME12 . 47 A4
Bellflower Cl 2 E6 .. 1 E8
Bell Gdns BR5 ..... 54 C4
Bell Gr CT3 .... 211 A5
Bellgrove St ME5 .. 130 A8
Bell Ho Erith SE2 ... 3 D1
  Grays RM17 .... 17 F8
Bellingham Way
  ME20 .... 128 B3
Bell La Burham ME1 . 128 F8
  Chatham ME14 .... 130 B7
  Larkfield ME20 ..... 128 B2
  Maidstone ME14 ... 163 A5
  Newham E16 .... 1 A5
  Sandwich CT13 .... 149 A1
  Standen TN27 ..... 295 B8
  Staplehurst TN12 .. 260 E3
Bellman Ave CT12 .. 37 C7
Bellows La TN15 ... 156 F7
Bell Rd
  Maidstone ME15 ... 195 E5
  Sittingbourne ME10 . 101 F3
Bellring Cl DA17 .... 14 A8
Bell Row TN11 ..... 223 F5
Bell's Cl TN30 ..... 345 A7
Bells Farm La TN11 . 224 C8
Bells Farm Rd TN11,
  TN12 .... 191 D1
Bell Sh Ctr ME10 ... 101 F4
Bell's La ME1 ...... 41 E6
Bells La 9 TN30 ... 345 A7
Bell St SE18 .... 11 E6
Bell Water Gate SE18 . 2 A3
Bell Way ME17 .... 197 E2
Bellwood Ct ME3 ... 24 C3
Bell Wood Prim Sch
  ME15 .... 195 E5
Belmont Ave DA16 . 12 E4
Belmont Cl ME16 ... 160 F2
Belmont Ct
  9 Maidstone ME15 . 162 B4
  2 Ramsgate CT11 . 117 D7
Belmont CT14 ...... 215 B1
Belmont Farm Bsns Ctr
  TN26 .... 266 A1
Belmont House & Gdns★
  ME13 .... 169 D5
Belmont La BR7 .... 30 C3
Belmont Par BR7 ... 30 C3
Belmont Pl TN16 ... 118 A8
Belmont Prim Sch DA8 . 14 A7
Belmont Rd
  Ashford TN24 ..... 268 D6
  Broadstairs CT10 ... 84 A4
  Chislehurst BR7 ... 30 B3

Belmont Rd continued
  Erith DA8 .... 14 B6
  Faversham ME13 ... 138 C6
  Gillingham ME7 .... 64 C4
  Grays RM17 .... 17 F8
  Halfway Houses ME12 . 46 B4
  Ramsgate CT11 .... 117 D7
  Sittingbourne ME10 . 101 E3
  Westgate-on-S CT8 . 81 F8
  Whitstable CT5 .... 74 D1
Belmont St CT11 ... 117 E7
Belmont Terr CT13 . 180 B3
Belmont Yd 8 CT5 . 74 D1
Belmore Pk TN24 ... 268 B3
Belnor Ave
  Cold Harbour ME9 . 100 F8
  Lower Halstow ME9 . 67 F1
Belsey La CT15 ..... 276 D4
Belson Rd SE18 ..... 1 F2
Beltana Dr DA12 ... 37 E4
Belting Dr CT6 ..... 77 E5
Beltinge Rd CT6 ... 77 B5
Belton Cl CT5 ..... 108 E8
Belton Rd DA14 ... 31 A4
Beltring Rd
  Beltring TN12,ME18 . 225 B4
  Royal Tunbridge Wells
  TN1 .... 286 A6
Beltring Sta TN12 .. 225 B4
Beltwood Rd DA17 . 4 C8
Beluncle Villas ME3 . 42 C7
Belvedere Cl
  Faversham ME13 .. 138 D8
  Gravesend DA12 ... 37 C7
Belvedere Ct DA17 . 3 F3
Belvedere Ho 9
  ME15 .... 195 F5
Belvedere Ind Est DA17 . 4 D5
Belvedere Inf Sch DA17 . 4 B3
Belvedere Jun Sch DA17 . 4 B3
Belvedere Link Bsns Pk
  DA17 .... 4 C3
Belvedere Mews SE3 . 11 B7
Belvedere Rd
  Bexley DA7 .... 13 F5
  Biggin Hill TN16 ... 118 F1
  Broadstairs CT10 ... 84 B4
  Erith SE28 .... 3 D5
  Faversham ME13 .. 138 D8
  Belvedere Sta DA17 . 4 B3
Belvoir Cl SE9 ..... 29 E5
Benacre Rd CT5 ... 108 D6
Benares Rd SE18 ... 2 F2
Bench Hill TN26 ... 347 D5
Bench St CT16 ..... 310 D7
Benden Cl TN12 ... 260 F4
Bendmore Ave SE2 . 3 A2
Bendon Way ME8 . 98 D8
Benedict Cl 9 Erith DA17 . 3 E5
  Halling ME2 ...... 95 B4
  Orpington BR6 .... 86 E7
Benenden CE Prim Sch
  TN17 .... 342 D6
Benenden Gn BR2 .. 52 A4
Benenden Hospl
  TN17 .... 322 C3
Benenden Manor ME8 . 65 B3
Benenden Rd
  Benenden TN17 ... 343 B4
  Cranbrook TN17 ... 320 E1
  Fosten Green TN27 . 322 F5
  Rochester ME2 ... 40 C1
  Benenden Sch TN17 . 342 C8
Bengal Rd CT12 ... 83 A1
Benhall Mill Rd TN2,
  TN3 .... 314 D8
Benham Bsns Pk
  CT21 .... 331 F5
Benjamin Ct 4 DA17 . 13 F8
Benn Cl RH8 ...... 183 A1
Bennells Ave CT5 ... 75 B3
Bennett Cl DA16 ... 13 A5
Bennett Ct 16 CT20 . 335 E7
Bennett Ho 11 ME14 . 36 F5
Bennett Memorial Diocesan
  Sch TN4 .... 285 D4
Bennetts Ave CT11 . 124 C7
Bennetts Copse BR7 . 29 E2
Bennetts Cotts ME7 . 131 A8
Bennetts Gdns ME13 . 137 D8
Bennetts Mews 13
  TN30 .... 345 A7
Bennett Way DA2 .. 34 D3
Benn Ho SE7 ...... 1 C1
Benover Rd ME18 .. 225 F7
Benson Cl CT18 ... 306 F4
Benson Ct CT18 ... 306 F4
Benson Rd RM17 .. 18 D8
Bensted TN23 ..... 299 F5
Bensted Cl ME15 .. 226 D7
Bensted Cl CT6 ... 77 A1
Bensted Gr ME13 .. 138 A7
Bentham Hill TN3,TN4 . 253 D1
Bentham Rd SE28 ... 3 B5
Bentham Sq ME12 .. 28 A3
Ben Tillet Ct E16 ... 1 F5
Bentley Ave CT6 ... 76 B4
Bentley Cl
  Aylesford ME20 ... 128 E1
  Chatham ME5 ..... 97 D2
  New Barn DA3 .... 59 C7
Bentley Rd TN24 ... 300 F4
Bentleys Bglws TN15 . 154 F7
Bentley's Mdw TN15 . 154 F7
Bentley St DA12 ... 19 C1
Bentley Street Ind Est
  DA12 .... 19 C1
Bentlif Cl ME16 ... 161 D5
Berber Rd ME1 .... 63 D8
Bercta Rd SE9 .... 30 C6
Bere Cl DA9 ...... 17 C2
Berengrave La ME8 . 65 F2

Berengrave Nature
  Reserve★ ME8 .... 66 A3
Berens Ct DA14 .... 30 F4
Berens Rd BR5 ..... 54 C4
Berens Way BR5 ... 53 F6
Beresford Ave ME1 . 63 E2
Beresford Ct TN17 . 317 F2
Beresford Ct 7 CT7 . 80 F8
Beresford Dr BR1 .. 52 E6
Beresford Gap CT7 . 80 F8
Beresford Gdns CT9 . 51 C3
Beresford Rd
  Gillingham ME7 ... 64 D4
  Goudhurst TN17 ... 290 F1
  Kit's Coty ME20 ... 129 D7
  Northfleet DA11 ... 36 E8
  Ramsgate CT11 ... 117 D6
  River CT17 .... 277 E3
  St Margaret's at Cliffe
  CT15 .... 247 F1
  Whitstable CT5 .... 74 D1
Beresfords Hill ME17 . 195 B4
Beresford Square Market
  PI SE18 .... 2 B2
Beresford St SE18 .. 2 B3
Berger Cl BR5 ..... 53 E3
Bergland Pk ME2 .. 63 D8
Bering Wlk E16 .... 1 D7
Berkeley Ave CT6 .. 13 C6
Berkeley Cl
  Boughton Street ME13 . 140 B3
  2 Folkestone CT19 . 335 A7
  Orpington BR5 .... 53 E2
  Pembury TN2 ..... 287 F2
  Rochester ME1 .... 96 D8
Berkeley Cres DA1 . 33 F7
Berkeley Ct
  Sittingbourne ME10 . 101 D3
  6 Swanley BR8 .... 55 E4
Berkeley Mount 8
  ME4 .... 63 F4
Berkeley Rd
  Birchington CT7 ... 80 F8
  7 Royal Tunbridge Wells
  TN1 .... 286 A2
Berkeley Terr RM18 . 19 A7
Berkhampstead Rd 9
  DA17 .... 4 A1
Berkley Cres DA12 . 19 C1
Berkley Rd DA12 ... 19 B1
Berkshire Cl ME5 .. 97 C8
Bermuda Rd RM18 . 19 A5
Bernal Cl SE28 .... 3 D6
Bernard Ashley Dr SE7 . 1 B1
Bernards Ct DA15 . 30 E7
Bernards Gdns CT15 . 244 E5
Bernard St 24 DA12 . 19 B1
Bernard Sunley Hall
  TN25 .... 238 A2
Berner's Hill TN5 .. 339 A3
Bernersmede SE3 . 11 A4
Berridge Rd ME12 . 28 C2
Berries The CT18 .. 307 B5
Berryfield Cl BR1 .. 52 F7
Berryhill SE9 ...... 12 B3
Berryhill Gdns SE9 . 12 B3
Berrylands Hartley DA3 . 59 A3
  Orpington BR6 .... 87 C7
Berry Rd ME3 ..... 41 E3
Berry's Green Rd
  TN16 .... 119 B2
Berry's Hill TN16 . 119 B4
Berry St SE18 ..... 11 E6
Bertha Hollamby Ct
  DA14 .... 31 C3
Bertha James Ct BR2 . 52 B5
Bertrand Way SE28 . 3 C6
Bert Reilly Ho 1 SE18 . 2 D1
Bertrey Cotts TN15 . 119 B3
Berwick Cres CT15 . 12 E1
Berwick Ct 12 DA2 . 16 B1
Berwick La CT21 ... 332 A3
Berwick Rd Bexley DA16 . 13 B6
  Newham E16 ...... 1 C7
Berwick Way TN14 . 154 B7
Berwyn Gr ME15 ... 195 A6
Beryl Ave E6 .... 1 E8
Beryl Ho 3 SE18 .. 2 F1
Besant Ct 15 SE28 . 3 B6
Bessels Green Rd
  TN13 .... 153 D3
Bessels Meadow
  TN13 .... 153 D3
Bessels Way TN13 . 153 D4
Bessie Lansbury Cl E6 . 2 A7
Best La CT1 .... 174 F8
Best St ME4 .... 63 F4
Beta Rd ME3 ..... 42 D7
Betenson Ave TN13 . 153 F5
Bethany Cl CT14 ... 215 C8
Bethany Sch TN17 . 291 B5
Bethel Rd Bexley DA16 . 13 C4
  Sevenoaks TN13 .. 154 C4
Bethel Row ME13 .. 169 F1
Betherinden Cotts
  TN18 .... 356 A4
Bethersden Bsns Ctr
  TN26 .... 297 C1
Bethersden Ct TN26 . 195 F7
Bethersden Cty Prim Sch
  TN26 .... 297 D5
Bethersden Rd
  Hothfield TN26 .... 266 D4
  Shadoxhurst TN26 . 298 E2
  Smarden TN27,TN26 . 296 C5
  Woodchurch TN26 . 326 A6
Beths Grm Sch ME15 . 14 B1
Betjeman Cl ME20 . 127 D3
Betony Gdns ME14 . 162 F5

Betsham Rd
Betsham DA13 ... 35 D3
Erith DA8 ... 14 F7
Maidstone ME15 ... 195 F6
Swanscombe DA10 ... 35 E8
Betterton Dr DA14 ... 31 E6
Bettescombe Rd ME8 ... 98 E7
Betts Rd E16 ... 1 B6
Betty Shelvey Ct CT14 ... 215 D4
Beulah Rd TN1 ... 286 C4
Beult Mdw TN27 ... 264 A1
Beult Rd DA1 ... 15 A3
Bevan Pl BR8 ... 55 F5
Bevan Rd SE2 ... 3 B1
Bevans Cl DA9 ... 17 C1
Bevan Way CT3 ... 210 E5
Bevercote Wlk 1 DA17 ... 13 F8
Beveridge Ct 1 SE28 ... 3 B6
Beverley Ave DA15 ... 30 F8
Beverley Cl ME8 ... 98 F8
Beverley Cres TN9 ... 253 F7
Beverley Ct 8 DA14 ... 31 B4
Beverley Gdns TN29 ... 353 A4
Beverley Ho CT2 ... 142 F2
Beverley Holiday Camp
ME12 ... 49 A5
Beverley Rd Bexley DA7 ... 14 C5
Canterbury CT2 ... 142 E2
Maidstone ME16 ... 160 F2
Orpington BR2 ... 85 E8
Beverley Way CT12 ... 83 C1
Beverly Cl CT7 ... 81 B8
Bevile Ho RM17 ... 18 B7
Bevis Cl DA2 ... 34 C8
Bewl Bridge Cl TN5 ... 339 B3
Bewlbridge La
Lamberhurst TN3,TN5 ... 317 B1
Lower Cousley Wood
TN5 ... 337 F8
Bewley La TN15 ... 156 D2
Bewl Water Nature
Reserve★ TN5 ... 338 B7
Bewl Water Visitor Ctr★
TN3 ... 338 B8
Bewsbury Cres CT16 ... 277 F7
Bewsbury Cross La
CT16 ... 277 F7
Bexhill Dr RM17 ... 17 F8
Bexley Cl DA1 ... 14 E2
Bexley Coll Erith DA17 ... 4 B1
Erith DA17 ... 4 C2
Bexley Coll (St Joseph's
Campus) SE2 ... 13 D8
Bexley Cotts DA4 ... 57 C5
Bexley Gram Sch DA16 ... 13 B3
Bexleyheath Sch DA6 ... 13 F4
Bexleyheath Sta DA7 ... 13 E5
Bexley High St DA5 ... 32 B7
Bexley La Crayford DA1 ... 14 E2
Sidcup DA14 ... 31 C5
Bexley Rd Eltham SE9 ... 12 C2
4 Erith DA8 ... 4 E1
Erith DA8 ... 4 F1
Erith,Northumberland Heath
DA8 ... 14 C8
Bexley Sta DA5 ... 32 A7
Bexley St CT5 ... 74 D2
Bexon La Bredgar ME9 ... 134 C4
Silver Street ME9 ... 133 F5
Bhutan Rd CT6 ... 77 C4
Bickley Cres BR1 ... 52 E5
Bickley Ct 2 BR1 ... 52 E6
Bickley Park Rd BR1 ... 52 F6
Bickley Park Sch BR1 ... 52 E6
Bickley Prim Sch BR1 ... 52 C7
Bickley Rd Bromley BR1 ... 52 E7
5 Tonbridge TN9 ... 254 B8
Bickley Sta BR1 ... 52 E6
Bickmore Way TN9 ... 222 D3
Bicknor Cl CT2 ... 143 B4
Bicknor Court Cotts
ME9 ... 133 C2
Bicknor La ME9 ... 133 D3
Bicknor Rd
Maidstone ME15 ... 195 F4
Orpington BR6 ... 53 F2
Bidborough CE Prim Sch
TN3 ... 253 D3
Bidborough Ct TN3 ... 253 B3
Bidborough Ridge
TN4 ... 253 E4
Biddenden Cl
Maidstone ME15 ... 162 F3
Margate CT9 ... 51 C1
Biddenden La TN27 ... 262 E5
Biddenden Rd
Headcorn TN27 ... 262 E2
Tenterden TN26,TN26 ... 324 A6
Tenterden TN30 ... 323 E6
Tylden TN27 ... 295 F8
Biddenden Vineyards &
Cider Works★ TN27 ... 323 A5
Biddenden Way
Eltham SE9 ... 30 A4
Istead Rise DA13 ... 36 E1
Biddulph Ho 17 SE18 ... 1 F2
Bideford Rd DA16 ... 13 B7
Bierce Ct CT7 ... 80 F7
Bierce Ct Cotts CT7 ... 80 F7
Bifrons Gdns CT4 ... 176 B3
Bifrons Hill CT4 ... 176 B4
Bifrons Rd CT4 ... 176 B4
Bigbury Rd CT2,CT4 ... 173 F7
Biggin Hill Airport
TN16 ... 118 D5
Biggin Hill Bsns Pk
TN16 ... 118 D4
Biggin Hill Jun & Inf Schs
TN16 ... 118 E3
Biggin La RM16 ... 19 B8
Biggin St CT16 ... 310 D8
Biggins Wood Rd
CT19 ... 334 E7
Bigglestone Link 11
CT1 ... 175 A8
Bignell Rd SE18 ... 2 B1
Bilberry Cl ME14 ... 162 E5
Billet Hill TN15 ... 91 C6
Bill Hamling Cl SE9 ... 29 F6
Billings DA3 ... 58 F3
Billington Gdns TN24 ... 268 E6
Bill Street Rd ME2 ... 40 C1
Bilsby Gr SE9 ... 29 D4
Bilsington Cl ME5 ... 97 B5
Bilsington Cross
TN25 ... 329 C2
Bilton Rd DA8 ... 15 A8
Bimbury La ME14,ME9 ... 132 A5
Bindon Blood Rd
CT16 ... 278 A5
Bines The TN12 ... 257 A5
Bingham Point 5 SE18 ... 2 B2
Bingham Rd ME2 ... 40 C1
Bingley Cl ME6 ... 127 F8
Bingley Rd Newham E16 ... 1 C7
1 Rochester ME1 ... 63 E4
Binland Gr ME5 ... 96 D5
Binnacle Rd ME1 ... 96 C8
Binney Rd ME3 ... 9 D2
Binnie Cl CT10 ... 83 F2
Binsey Wlk 1 SE2 ... 3 C4
Birbetts Rd SE9 ... 29 F6
Birch Cl Ashford TN24 ... 268 F2
Broadstairs CT10 ... 83 C3
Eynsford DA4 ... 89 D7
Matfield TN12 ... 256 D1
New Barn DA3 ... 59 C7
Royal Tunbridge Wells
TN2 ... 286 D7
Sevenoaks TN13 ... 154 B4
Tonbridge TN11 ... 221 D4
Birch Cres ME20 ... 160 D8
Birch Ct Barham CT4 ... 242 F8
Ramsgate CT11 ... 117 D8
Birchden Cotts TN3 ... 312 C6
Birchdene Dr SE28 ... 3 A5
Birch Dr ME5 ... 97 D1
Birches The
Birchington CT7 ... 81 B7
Greenwich SE7 ... 11 B8
Orpington BR6 ... 86 A6
Swanley BR8 ... 55 E7
Tonbridge TN9 ... 254 B7
Birchett TN23 ... 267 E1
Birchett La TN26 ... 327 D3
Birchetts Ave TN3 ... 284 E3
Birchetts Green La
TN5 ... 338 A2
Birchfield Cl ME15 ... 195 B6
Birchfield TN14 ... 185 E8
Birchfields ME5 ... 97 A3
Birch Gr Bexley DA16 ... 13 A3
Gillingham ME7 ... 98 A4
Birch Hill Ct CT7 ... 81 B7
Birch Ho
6 Maidstone ME16 ... 161 A3
Sheerness ME12 ... 28 B2
Sittingbourne ME10 ... 102 B3
Birchin Cross Rd
TN15 ... 123 A5
Birchington CE Prim Sch
CT7 ... 81 A6
Birchington Cl
Bexley DA7 ... 14 B6
Maidstone ME14 ... 162 C5
Orpington BR5 ... 54 C1
Birchington-On-Sea Sta
CT7 ... 80 F7
Birch Kiln Cotts TN5 ... 337 A6
Birch Mead BR6 ... 86 A8
Bircholme TN2 ... 286 D7
Bircholt Forstal TN25 ... 302 E7
Bircholt Rd ME15 ... 195 F4
Birch Pl
Sevenoaks TN13 ... 154 A3
Stone DA9 ... 16 E1
Birch Rd
Hoo St Werburgh ME3 ... 41 E3
Paddock Wood TN12 ... 257 A6
Whitstable CT5 ... 109 A8
Birch Row BR2 ... 53 A3
Birch Tree Ho 18 SE7 ... 11 C8
Birch Tree Way ME15 ... 162 B3
Birch Way TN2 ... 286 D7
Birchway TN15 ... 90 F2
Birchwood Ave
Bidborough TN4 ... 253 E3
Sidcup DA14 ... 31 C5
Birchwood Dr DA2 ... 32 E4
Birchwood La TN14 ... 120 F4
Birchwood Par DA2 ... 32 E4
Birchwood Park Ave
BR8 ... 55 F6
Birchwood Prim Sch
BR8 ... 55 D8
Birchwood Rd
Joyden's Wood DA2,BR8 ... 32 D3
Maidstone ME16 ... 161 C5
Orpington BR5 ... 53 E5
Birchwood Rise CT17 ... 310 C7
Birchwood Terr BR8 ... 55 C8
Birchwood Wlk CT2 ... 142 E2
Birdbrook Rd SE3 ... 11 C4
Birdham Cl BR1 ... 52 E4
Bird House La BR6 ... 119 A5
Bird in Hand La BR1 ... 52 D7
Bird in Hand St TN3 ... 312 B8
Bird La TN5 ... 336 B5
Birds Ave CT9 ... 82 B7
Birdwood Ave CT14 ... 215 A5
Birkbeck Prim Sch
DA14 ... 31 B5
Birkbeck Rd DA14 ... 31 A5
Birkdale Cl Erith SE28 ... 3 D7
Orpington BR6 ... 53 D2
Whitstable CT5 ... 109 D8
Birkdale Ct 3 ME16 ... 161 E4
Birkdale Dr CT19 ... 335 A8
Birkdale Gdns CT6 ... 76 D2
Birkdale Rd SE2 ... 3 A2
Birkdale TN1 ... 286 B6
Birken Rd TN2 ... 286 D6
Birkhall Cl ME5 ... 97 A5
Birling Ave
Gillingham ME8 ... 65 E1
Maidstone ME14 ... 163 A4
Birling Cl ME14 ... 163 A4
Birling Dr TN2 ... 286 A1
Birling Hill DA13,ME19,
ME6 ... 94 B1
Birling Park Ave TN2 ... 314 B8
Birling Pk ME19 ... 127 C5
Birling Rd
Ashford TN24 ... 268 D1
Bexley DA8 ... 14 E6
Leybourne ME19 ... 127 C3
Royal Tunbridge Wells
TN2 ... 314 B8
Ryarsh ME19 ... 127 A5
Snodland ME6 ... 127 F7
Birnam Sq 1 ME16 ... 161 E4
Birtrick Dr DA13 ... 59 F4
Bishopbourne Gn ME8 ... 65 B4
Bishop Butt Cl BR6 ... 86 F7
Bishop Ct
4 Sittingbourne ME10 ... 101 E5
Whitstable CT5 ... 74 F2
Bishopden Ct CT2 ... 142 C4
Bishop Jenner Ct CT3 ... 146 C6
Bishop John Robinson CE
Prim Sch SE28 ... 3 C6
Bishop La ME9 ... 66 E3
Bishop's Ave CT10 ... 84 B6
Bishops Ave BR1 ... 52 C6
Bishopsbourne Ho 2
BR1 ... 29 B1
Bishops Cl Eltham SE9 ... 30 C6
Nettlestead ME18 ... 192 D6
Bishops Ct
Royal Tunbridge Wells
TN4 ... 285 F3
Stone DA9 ... 16 E2
Bishops Ctyd 14 CT1 ... 175 A8
Bishop's Down Park Rd
TN4 ... 285 F4
Bishop's Down Prim Sch
TN4 ... 285 E5
Bishop's Down Rd
TN4 ... 285 F3
Bishop's Down TN4 ... 285 F3
Bishops Gn
Ashford TN23 ... 299 E7
Bromley BR1 ... 52 C8
Bishops La TN17 ... 319 E2
Bishop's La ME15 ... 226 D6
Bishops Mews TN9 ... 254 C8
Bishops Oak Ride
TN10 ... 222 C6
Bishopstone Dr CT6 ... 77 F6
Bishopstone La CT6 ... 77 F5
Bishops Way
Canterbury CT2 ... 142 D1
Maidstone ME15 ... 161 F4
Bishops Wlk
Chislehurst BR7 ... 53 C8
Rochester ME1 ... 63 C5
Bishopswood TN23 ... 300 C3
Bittern Cl CT18 ... 307 A3
Blackberry Field BR5 ... 54 A8
Blackberry Way
Paddock Wood TN12 ... 257 B6
Whitstable CT5 ... 109 B8
Blackbrook La BR1,BR2 ... 53 A5
Black Bull Rd CT19 ... 335 D6
Blackburn Rd CT6 ... 76 B2
Blackdale Farm Cotts
DA1 ... 34 B6
Blackdown Dr TN24 ... 268 B4
Black Eagle Cl TN16 ... 184 C8
Blacketts Cotts ME9 ... 103 B7
Blacketts Rd ME9 ... 103 A6
Blackfen Par DA16 ... 13 A1
Blackfen Rd DA15 ... 13 B1
Blackfen Sch for Girls
DA15 ... 13 B1
Blackfriars St 16 CT1 ... 142 F1
Black Griffin La CT1 ... 174 F8
Blackhall La TN15 ... 154 E3
Blackheath Bluecoat CE
Sec Sch SE3 ... 11 B7
Blackheath High Sch
GPDST (Jun Dept)
SE3 ... 11 A5
Blackheath High Sch
SE3 ... 11 A7
Blackheath Pk SE3 ... 11 A5
Blackheath Prep Sch
SE3 ... 11 A6
Black Horse Ct TN27 ... 262 E5
Black Horse Farm Cvn Pk
CT18 ... 306 F8
Black Horse Mews
TN15 ... 157 A7
Blackhorse Mews
TN2 ... 287 C6
Black Horse Rd 14
DA14 ... 31 A4
Blackhouse Hill CT18,
CT21 ... 333 D4
Blackhouse Rise
CT21 ... 333 D3
Blackhurst La TN2 ... 286 F6
Blacklands Dr ME19 ... 159 F8
Blacklands
East Malling ME19 ... 159 F7
East Malling ME19 ... 159 F8
Blackleys ME13 ... 171 F7
Blackman Cl ME3 ... 41 D7
Blackmans Cl DA1 ... 33 C7
Blackman's La TN11 ... 223 D6
Blackmanstone Way
ME16 ... 161 B7
Blackmead TN13 ... 153 E6
Black Mill La TN27 ... 262 B6
Blackness La BR2 ... 85 D2
Black Post ME17 ... 165 E4
Black Robin La CT4 ... 209 E3
Black Rock Gdns ME7 ... 98 B4
Blacksmith Dr ME14 ... 162 D5
Blacksmiths Field
TN32 ... 355 C1
Blacksmiths La BR5 ... 54 C4
Blacksmith's La TN5 ... 337 A5
Blacksole La TN15 ... 124 F3
Blacksole Rd TN15 ... 124 F3
Blackstable Ct CT5 ... 108 D8
Black's Yd TN13 ... 154 C2
Blackthorn Ave
Chatham ME5 ... 97 A3
Royal Tunbridge Wells
TN4 ... 254 C1
Blackthorn Cl TN15 ... 90 F2
Blackthorn Dr ME20 ... 128 B2
Blackthorne Rd ME8 ... 99 B8
Blackthorne Way
TN23 ... 300 C3
Blackthorn Gr DA7 ... 13 E4
Blackthorn Rd
Biggin Hill TN16 ... 118 E3
Hersden CT3 ... 144 D8
Blackwall Rd TN24,
TN25 ... 269 B4
Blackwall Rd N TN24 ... 269 A2
Blackwall Rd S TN24 ... 269 A2
Blackwater Cl RM13 ... 4 E8
Bladindon Dr DA5 ... 31 D8
Blainey Ho ME3 ... 40 F6
Blair Cl DA15 ... 12 E2
Blair Dr TN13 ... 154 B4
Blake Cl Bexley DA16 ... 12 E6
Deal CT14 ... 248 C8
Blake Ct Ashford TN24 ... 300 F8
6 Ramsgate CT11 ... 117 D7
Blake Dr 3 ME20 ... 127 F4
Blake Gdns DA1 ... 15 F3
Blakemore Way DA17 ... 3 E3
Blakeney Cl ME14 ... 163 B4
Blaker Ave ME1 ... 63 E1
Blaker Ct SE7 ... 11 C7
Blake Way
Royal Tunbridge Wells
TN2 ... 286 D7
Tilbury RM18 ... 19 C5
Blanchard Cl SE9 ... 29 E5
Blanchard Ho BR7 ... 30 C2
Bland Dr CT18 ... 307 C5
Blandford Gdns ME10 ... 101 E1
Bland St SE9 ... 11 D3
Blanmerle Rd SE9 ... 30 B7
Blann Cl SE9 ... 11 D1
Blatcher Cl ME12 ... 47 B6
Blatchford Cl ME19 ... 127 F1
Blatchington Rd TN1 ... 286 B1
Blaxland Cl ME13 ... 138 B8
Bleak Hill La SE18 ... 12 F8
Bleak Ho★ CT10 ... 84 B4
Bleak Rd TN29 ... 376 C6
Bleakwood Rd 6 ME5 ... 96 F5
Blean Comm CT2 ... 142 A6
Blean Hill CT2 ... 142 A5
Blean Prim Sch CT2 ... 142 B4
Blean Rd ME8 ... 65 C2
Blean Sq ME14 ... 162 C6
Blean View Rd CT6 ... 76 B2
Blean Woods Nature
Reserve★ CT2 ... 141 F4
Bledlow Cl SE28 ... 3 C6
Blendon Dr DA5 ... 13 D1
Blendon Rd
Maidstone ME14 ... 162 C5
Sidcup DA5 ... 13 D1
Blendon Terr SE18 ... 12 C8
Blenheim Ave
Canterbury CT1 ... 143 D1
Chatham ME4 ... 63 E2
Faversham ME13 ... 138 E5
Blenheim Cl
Broadstairs CT10 ... 83 D3
Dartford DA1 ... 15 C1
Herne Bay CT6 ... 77 A1
Maidstone ME15 ... 162 F3
Meopham DA13 ... 93 B8
Blenheim Ct
Chatham ME4 ... 63 E3
Sidcup DA15 ... 30 D5
Blenheim Dr
Bexley DA16 ... 12 F6
Dover CT16 ... 278 C3
Hawkinge CT18 ... 307 A4
Blenheim Gr DA12 ... 37 C8
Blenheim Ho
Margate CT9 ... 51 C3
Woolwich SE18 ... 2 C3
Blenheim Pl CT20 ... 334 F4
Blenheim Prim Sch
BR6 ... 87 C8
Blenheim Rd
Bromley BR1 ... 52 E5
Dartford DA1 ... 15 C1
Deal CT14 ... 215 D5
Littlestone-on-Sea TN28 ... 373 D6
Orpington BR5,BR6 ... 87 C8
Sidcup DA15 ... 31 C7
Sittingbourne ME10 ... 102 B2
Blenheim Way TN5 ... 339 C3
Bleriot Meml★ CT16 ... 278 F1
Bletchington Ct 3 DA17 ... 4 A2
Blewbury Ho 3 SE2 ... 3 C4
Bliby Bsns Ctr TN25 ... 328 F7
Bliby Cnr TN25 ... 328 F8
Bligh Inf Sch ME2 ... 62 C7
Bligh Jun Sch ME2 ... 62 C7
Bligh Rd DA11 ... 19 A1
Bligh's Ct TN13 ... 154 B2
Bligh's Rd TN13 ... 154 B2
Bligh's Wlk TN13 ... 154 C2
Bligh Way ME2 ... 62 D6
Blindgrooms La TN26 ... 299 C1
Blindhouse La TN25 ... 304 B3
Blind La Bredhurst ME7 ... 98 A1
Challock TN25 ... 203 C2
Gillingham ME7 ... 97 F1
Goudhurst TN17 ... 290 E1
Mersham TN25 ... 301 C4
Blind Mary's La ME9 ... 133 E4
Bliss Way TN10 ... 222 E5
Blithdale Rd SE2 ... 3 A2
Blockhouse Rd 7
RM17 ... 18 C8
Blockmakers Ct ME4 ... 64 B1
Bloody Point Rd CT13 ... 149 B4
Bloomfield Rd
Bromley BR2 ... 52 D4
Woolwich SE18 ... 2 B1
Bloomfield Terr TN16 ... 151 E2
Bloomsbury Rd CT11 ... 117 C6
Bloomsbury Way
TN24 ... 268 B7
Bloomsbury Wlk 2
ME15 ... 162 A4
Bloors La ME8 ... 65 D1
Bloors Wharf Rd ME7 ... 65 F4
Blossom La TN25 ... 267 E5
Blowers Hil Cott TN3 ... 285 B8
Blowers Hill TN8 ... 282 D8
Blowers Wood Gr ME7 ... 98 B3
Bloxam Gdns SE9 ... 11 E2
Blue Anchor La RM18 ... 19 E8
Bluebell Cl
Gillingham ME7 ... 64 F6
Kingsnorth TN23 ... 300 B4
Orpington BR6 ... 86 C8
Bluebell Rd TN23 ... 300 C3
Bluebell Wlks TN12 ... 257 A5
**Bluebell Woods Mobile
Home Pk** CT2 ... 143 D6
Blueberry La TN14 ... 120 C4
Bluebird Ct CT17 ... 310 A6
Bluebird Way SE28 ... 2 D4
Blue Boar La ME1 ... 63 D5
Blue Chalet Ind Pk
TN15 ... 90 D4
Blue Coat La TN17 ... 318 C6
Blue Field TN23 ... 299 C8
Bluefield Mews CT5 ... 108 C6
Bluehouse Gdns RH8 ... 183 A8
Blue House La CT21 ... 333 B8
Bluehouse La RH8 ... 183 A8
Blue Line La TN24 ... 268 B3
Bluett St ME14 ... 162 A5
Bluewater Cvn Pk
CT21 ... 353 E8
Bluewater Parkway
DA9 ... 34 E8
Bluewater DA9 ... 34 F8
Blunden La ME18 ... 193 A1
Blunts Rd SE9 ... 12 A2
Blythe Cl ME10 ... 102 C5
Blythe Ct Hythe CT21 ... 333 D2
Lewisham SE12 ... 29 A8
Blythe Hill BR5 ... 54 A8
Blythe Rd ME15 ... 162 B4
Blyth Ho 5 DA8 ... 4 E1
Blyth Rd SE28 ... 3 C6
Boakes Mdw TN14 ... 121 F8
Boarders La TN5 ... 338 C3
Boarley Ct ME14 ... 129 F1
Boarley La ME14 ... 129 F2
Boarman's La TN29 ... 370 E8
Boathouse Rd ME12 ... 27 F3
Boat La TN25 ... 330 A4
Bob Amor Cl ME13 ... 138 E7
Bobbing Hill ME9 ... 101 A6
Bobbing Village Sch
ME9 ... 101 B7
Bobbin Lodge Hill
CT4 ... 173 B2
Bockham Cotts TN25 ... 301 E8
Bockham La
Ashford TN25 ... 270 A1
Mersham TN25 ... 301 E8
Bockhanger Ct TN24 ... 268 D5
Bockhanger La TN24 ... 268 C6
Bocking Cl TN5 ... 336 E4
Bockingford La ME15 ... 194 F8
Bocton Ho ME17 ... 195 B3
Bodenham Rd CT20 ... 335 A4
Bodiam Cl ME8 ... 65 C3
Bodiam Ct ME16 ... 161 F3
Bodiam Rd TN18,TN32 ... 355 F3
Bodkins Cl ME17 ... 195 D5
Bodle Ave DA10 ... 17 E1
Bodmin Cl BR5 ... 54 C1
Bodsham CE Prim Sch
TN25 ... 271 E8
Bodsham Cres ME15 ... 163 B3
Boevey Path
2 Bexley DA17 ... 13 F8
Erith DA17 ... 3 F1
Bogarde Dr ME2 ... 40 B2
Bogey La BR6 ... 86 A3
Bogle Rd ME9 ... 136 C7
Bognor Dr CT6 ... 76 D4
Bognor Rd DA16 ... 13 D6
Bogshole La
Herne Bay CT6 ... 77 D3
Whitstable CT5 ... 108 E4
Boley Hill ME1 ... 63 C6
Boleyn Ave CT9 ... 50 E1
Boleyn Ct 9 CT1 ... 175 A8
Boleyn Rd TN15 ... 122 E2
Boleyn Way DA10 ... 35 E8
Bolingbroke Ho ME16 ... 161 E3
Bollon Ct 9 SE12 ... 29 B5
Bolner Cl ME5 ... 96 F2
Bolonia CT15 ... 280 A6
Bolton Rd CT19 ... 335 D6
Bolton St CT11 ... 117 D8
Bolts Hill CT4 ... 173 C2
Bombay Ho 1 ME15 ... 195 E5
Bombers La TN16 ... 151 D7
Bonar Pl BR7 ... 29 E1
Bonaventure Ct DA12 ... 37 F4
Bonchester Cl BR7 ... 30 A1
Bond Cl TN14 ... 120 D4
Bondfield Cl TN4 ... 254 A1
Bondfield Ho SE18 ... 12 A7
Bondfield Rd
East Malling ME19 ... 159 F8
4 Newham E6 ... 1 F8
Bondfield Wlk DA1 ... 15 F4
Bond La TN23 ... 300 A2
Bond Rd Ashford TN23 ... 300 B8
Gillingham ME8 ... 98 E5
Bond St RM17 ... 18 C8
Boneashe La TN15 ... 157 D6
Boneta Rd SE18 ... 1 F3
Bonetta Ct ME12 ... 46 B8
Bonflower La ME17 ... 227 C7
Bonham Dr ME10 ... 102 B5
Bonners Alley 19 CT5 ... 74 D2
Bonney Way BR8 ... 55 E6
Bonnington Cross
TN25 ... 329 E3
Bonnington Gn ME8 ... 65 C3
Bonnington Rd ME14 ... 162 C6
Bonnington Twr BR2 ... 52 E3
Bonny Bush Hill CT4 ... 209 D5
Bonsor Rd CT19 ... 335 D6
Boorman's Mews
ME18 ... 192 E7
Bootham Cl ME2 ... 62 D5
Booth Cl SE28 ... 3 B6
Booth Pl CT9 ... 50 J3
Booth Rd ME4 ... 63 F2
Borden CE Prim Sch
ME9 ... 100 F3
Borden Gram Sch
ME10 ... 101 F3
Borden La ME10,ME9 ... 101 C3
Bordyke TN9 ... 222 C2
Boreham Ave E16 ... 1 A7
Boresisle TN30 ... 324 B2
Borgard Ho SE18 ... 11 E6
Borgard Rd SE18 ... 1 F2
Borkwood Ct BR6 ... 86 F6
Borkwood Pk BR6 ... 86 F6
Borkwood Way BR6 ... 86 E6
Borland Cl 5 DA9 ... 17 A2
Bornefields TN23 ... 300 A7
Borough CT1 ... 143 A1
Borough Green Prim Sch
TN15 ... 157 A7
Borough Green Rd
Borough Green TN15 ... 156 E7
Ightham TN15 ... 156 D6
Wrotham TN15 ... 125 A1
Borough Green & Wrotham
Sta TN15 ... 156 F7
Borough Rd
Gillingham ME7 ... 64 D4
Queenborough ME11 ... 46 B4
Tatsfield TN16 ... 150 D6
Borrowdale Ave CT11 ... 117 A7
Borstal Ave CT5 ... 108 D6
Borstal Hill CT5 ... 108 D7
Borstal HM Prison & Youth
Custody Ctr ME1 ... 63 B1
Borstal Manor Com Sch
ME1 ... 62 F2
Borstal Mews ME1 ... 63 A2
Borstal Rd ME1 ... 63 B3
Borstal St ME1 ... 63 A2
Borton Cl ME18 ... 192 F1
Boscobel Cl BR1 ... 52 F7
Boscombe Rd CT19 ... 335 C6
Bosney Banks CT15 ... 277 A7
Bossingham Rd CT4 ... 240 F3
Bossingham St CT4 ... 240 F6
Bossington Rd CT3 ... 177 E1
Bostall Hill SE2 ... 3 B1
Bostall La SE2 ... 3 B1
Bostall Manorway SE2 ... 3 B2
Bostall Park Ave DA7 ... 13 E7
Bostall Rd BR5 ... 31 B1
Boston Cl 5 CT16 ... 278 B3
Boston Gdns ME8 ... 65 C1
Boston Rd ME5 ... 97 C2
Bosville Ave TN13 ... 154 A4
Bosville Dr TN13 ... 154 A4
Bosville Rd TN13 ... 154 A4
Boswell Cl BR5 ... 54 C3
Boswell Ho BR2 ... 52 D4
Bosworth Ho 3 DA8 ... 4 E1
Botany Bay La BR7 ... 53 C7
Botany Cl ME12 ... 28 B1
Botany Rd CT10 ... 51 F2
Botany TN9 ... 222 C1
Boteler Cotts CT13 ... 180 A2
Botha Rd E13 ... 1 C8
Bothwell Cl 7 E16 ... 1 A8
Botolph's Bridge Rd
CT21 ... 353 A6
Botsom La TN15 ... 90 D4
Bottle House Cotts
TN11 ... 251 F1
Bottlescrew Hill ME17 ... 195 B4
Bottles La ME9 ... 135 A6
Bottom Pond Rd ME9 ... 134 D3
Bott Rd DA2 ... 33 F4
Boucher Dr DA11 ... 36 F4
Bough Beech Nature
Reserve Visitor Ctr★
TN14 ... 219 A7
Boughton Ave CT10 ... 84 A2

Boughton Church Cotts ME13 139 D1
Boughton Cl ME8 65 B3
Boughton Cnr TN25 237 C5
Boughton Field Cotts ME13 139 A5
Boughton Hill ME13 140 C3
Boughton Ho BR1 29 E1
Boughton La ME15 195 B6
Boughton Monchelsea Prim Sch ME17 195 B2
Boughton Par ME15 195 A7
Boughton Place Cotts ME17 232 A8
Boughton Rd
Sandway ME17 199 B2
Woolwich SE28 2 E3
Boughton-Under-Blean Meth Prim Sch ME13 139 F3
Boulevard Courrieres CT3 210 E5
Boulevard D'erlanger CT18 334 B7
Boulevard The
Ashford TN24 300 F6
Swanscombe DA9 17 C3
Boulogne Ct 17 CT20 335 E5
Boulthurst Way RH8 183 B3
Boultwood Rd E6 1 F7
Boundary Chase CT5 109 B8
Boundary Cl ME12 47 E6
Boundary Ct CT1 175 B6
Boundary Ho 4 DA11 36 F7
Boundary Rd
Chatham ME4 63 E3
Deal CT14 248 D6
Hythe CT21 333 A2
Ramsgate CT11 117 E7
Royal Tunbridge Wells TN2 286 D1
Sidcup DA15 12 E2
Boundary St 2 DA8 14 F7
Boundary The
Canterbury CT1 174 D7
Langton Green TN3 285 B3
Bounds Cross TN27 294 F7
Boundsgate Cnr ME13 203 B7
Bounds La ME13 140 A3
Bounds Oak Way TN4 253 E3
Bounds The ME20 128 E1
Bourchier Cl TN13 154 B1
Bourdillon Ct SE9 29 E6
Bournbrook Rd SE3, SE9 11 D4
Bourne Cl TN9 222 D3
Bourne Cotts CT4 209 C5
Bourne Ct ME1 63 D5
Bourne Ent Ctr TN15 157 A7
Bourne Grange La TN11 223 D8
Bourne Gr ME10 101 C5
Bourne Ind Pk DA1 14 E2
Bourne La
Cranbrook TN32 354 F1
Hamstreet TN26 349 A8
Plaxtol TN15 156 F1
Sandhurst Cross TN18 355 E4
Tonbridge TN9 222 D3
Bourne Lodge Cl CT2 142 A7
Bourne Mead DA5 14 D2
Bournemouth Dr CT6 76 D4
Bournemouth Gdns CT19 335 C6
Bournemouth Rd CT19 335 C5
Bourne Park Rd CT4 209 A7
Bourne Par DA5 32 B8
Bourne Pk TN11 223 F5
Bourne Place Mdws TN11 221 A7
Bourner Cotts TN17 293 D4
Bourne Rd
Aldington Frith TN25 329 D5
Bexley DA1,DA5 14 D2
Bromley BR2 52 D5
Gravesend DA12 37 F6
Sidcup DA5 32 B8
Bourne Row TN8 251 D6
Bournes Cl CT2 143 F7
Bourneside Terr ME17 164 D2
Bournes Pl TN26 326 A2
Bourne Vale Hayes BR2 52 A2
Plaxtol Spoute TN15 190 A8
Bourne View CT4 175 F1
Bourne Way Hayes BR2 85 A8
Swanley BR8 55 C6
Bournewood Cl ME15 162 F1
Bournewood TN26 349 A8
Bournewood Rd
Orpington BR5 54 C2
Woolwich SE18,SE2 13 A7
Bournville Ave ME4 63 F1
Bouverie Pl 2 CT20 335 D4
Bouverie Rd W CT20 335 C4
Bouverie Sq 1 CT20 335 D4
Bovarde Ave ME19 159 C3
Bow Arrow La
Dartford DA2 16 A1
Dartford DA2 16 B1
Bowater Pl SE3 11 B7
Bowater Rd SE18 1 D3
Bowdell La TN29 362 E3
Bowden Cres CT20 334 C6
Bowen Ct CT11 117 D7
Bowen Rd
Folkestone CT19 334 E6
Rusthall TN4 285 B4
Bowens Field TN23 268 B1
Bower Cl ME16 161 E4
Bower Gn ME5 97 C1
Bower Grove Sch ME16 161 B2
Bower La Eynsford DA4 89 F6
Maidstone ME16 161 E3
Bowerland La
Chilham CT4 172 E1
Old Wives Lees CT4 172 C2
Bower Mount Rd ME16 161 D4
Bower Pl ME16 161 E3
Bower Rd Hextable BR8 33 A2
Smeeth TN25 302 A3
Bowers Ave DA11 36 F4
Bowers Ho ME7 64 E7
Bowers Rd TN14 121 F8
Bower St ME16 161 E4
Bowers Wlk 1 E6 1 F7
Bower Terr ME16 161 E3
Bower Wlk TN12 260 E3
Bowes Ave CT9 50 E1
Bowes Cl DA15 13 B1
Bowes Ct 24 DA2 16 B1
Bowesden La DA12 38 F1
Bowes La CT6 77 A3
Bowes Rd ME2 63 B8
Bowes Villas CT14 180 E4
Bowes Wood DA3 91 F7
Bowford Ave DA7 13 E6
Bow Hill
Lower Hardres CT4 207 F2
Wateringbury ME18 192 D5
Bowland Cl CT6 77 C2
Bowlers Town TN31 368 A2
Bowles Well Gdns CT19 335 F7
Bowley La ME17 232 D8
Bowl Field TN25 271 B6
Bowling Green La CT14 215 B5
Bowling Green Row 1 SE18 1 F2
Bowling Green Terr 8 CT17 310 D7
Bowling St CT13 148 F1
Bowl Rd TN27 201 D2
Bowls Pl TN12 257 A7
Bowman Ave E16 1 A6
Bowman Cl ME5 97 C5
Bowman Ct CT17 278 A1
Bowmans Rd DA1 32 F8
Bowmead SE9 29 F6
Bown Cl RM18 19 B5
Bowness Rd DA7 14 B5
Bow Rd ME18 192 E7
Bowser Cl CT14 214 F4
Bow Terr ME18 192 E7
Bowyer Cl E6 1 F8
Bowyer Rd CT5 107 F7
Bowzell Rd TN14 187 A2
Boxgrove Prim Sch SE2 3 C3
Boxgrove Rd SE2 3 C3
Box La ME13 137 D1
Boxley TN23 299 F8
Boxley Cl
Maidstone ME14 162 B8
West Minst ME12 46 B7
Boxley Rd Chatham ME5 97 B2
Maidstone ME14 162 B7
Boxley St E16 1 B5
Boxmend Ind Est ME15 195 F3
Boxshall Ho 7 SE18 12 B8
Boxted La ME9 67 A1
Box Tree Wlk 26 BR5 54 D1
Boyard Rd SE18 2 B1
Boyces Hill ME9 100 D6
Boy Court La TN27 230 F1
Boyden Gate Hill CT3 112 B8
Boyes La CT3 178 D3
Boyke La CT4 273 C2
Boyle Ho 12 DA17 4 A3
Boyle Way TN12 225 B7
Boyne Pk TN4 285 F4
Boyne Rd CT15 248 A1
Boys Hall Rd TN24 300 F7
Boystown Pl CT13 180 C3
Boyton Court Rd ME17 230 A6
Brabazon Rd ME12 48 C1
Brabner Cl CT19 335 E8
Brabourne Ave ME8 65 C3
Brabourne CE Prim Sch TN25 303 A8
Brabourne Cl CT2 143 A4
Brabourne Cres DA7 13 F8
Brabourne Gdns CT20 334 E5
Brabourne La TN25 271 F2
Brabourne Rd TN25 270 D6
Bracken Cl
Ashford TN24 268 C6
Newham E6 1 F8
Royal Tunbridge Wells TN2 286 E5
Bracken Ct
3 Broadstairs CT10 83 E5
Sittingbourne ME10 102 C5
Brackendene DA2,DA5 32 E4
Bracken Hill ME5 97 A1
Bracken Lea ME5 64 C1
Bracken Rd TN2 286 E5
Brackens The BR6 87 A5
Bracken Wlk TN10 222 B6
Brack La TN29 362 B3
Brackley Cl ME14 162 C5
Brackwood Cl ME8 98 D5
Bracondale Ave DA13 59 F8
Bracondale Rd SE2 3 A2
Bracton La DA2 32 F6
Bradbery Ct 3 DA11 36 F7
Bradbourne Ct TN13 154 B6
Bradbourne La ME20 128 B1
Bradbourne Park Rd TN13 154 A4
Bradbourne Parkway ME19 128 A1
Bradbourne Rd
Grays RM17 18 B8
Sevenoaks TN13 154 B5
Sidcup DA5 32 A8
Bradbourne Sch The TN13 154 A6
Bradbourne Vale Rd TN13,TN14 154 A5
Bradbridge Gn TN23 299 D8
Bradbury Ct 4 SE3 11 A7
Braddick Cl ME15 195 B6
Bradenham Ave DA16 13 A3
Bradfield Ave ME9 103 D2
Bradfield Rd
Ashford TN24 268 B5
Newham E16 1 B4
Bradfields Ave ME5 96 F5
Bradfields Ave W ME5 96 F5
Bradfields Sch ME5 97 A6
Bradfoord Ct CT20 335 D5
Bradford Cl BR2 52 F1
Bradfords Cl ME4 41 B2
Bradford St TN9 222 B1
Bradley Dr ME10 101 E2
Bradley House ME3 25 C4
Bradley Rd
Ashurst TN3 283 D5
Folkestone CT19 335 F6
Ramsgate CT12 83 C1
Upper Halling ME2 94 E5
Bradley Stone Rd E6 1 F8
Bradshaw Cl ME9 66 E3
Bradstone Ave CT19 335 D6
Bradstone New Rd 3 CT20 335 D5
Bradstone Rd CT20 335 D5
Bradstow Sch CT10 84 A3
Bradstow Way CT10 84 A5
Bradymead E6 2 B7
Brady Rd CT18 305 A7
Braeburn Way ME19 159 C3
Braemar Ave DA7 14 C3
Braemar Gdns DA15 30 D5
Braeside Ave TN13 153 F3
Braeside CT10 84 B3
Braeside Cl TN13 153 F4
Braeside Cres DA7 14 C3
Braes The ME3 39 C3
Braesyde Cl DA17 3 F2
Braggs La CT6 110 E6
Braithwaite Ct ME7 65 A5
Brake Ave ME5 96 E5
Brakefield Rd DA13 36 B1
Brakes Pl TN15 90 E4
Bramber Ct 9 DA2 16 B1
Bramble Ave DA2 35 C5
Bramble Bank DA13 125 F7
Bramblebury Rd SE18 2 C1
Bramble Cl
Maidstone ME16 161 B3
Tonbridge TN11 221 F4
Wye TN25 237 D3
Bramble Croft DA8 4 C2
Brambledown
Chatham ME5 97 B8
Folkestone CT19 335 D6
Hartley DA3 58 F5
Bramblefield Cl DA3 58 E6
Bramblefield La ME10, ME9 68 E1
Bramblefields Cl CT6 77 B2
Bramblehill Rd ME13 138 C8
Bramble La
Sevenoaks TN13 187 B7
Wye TN25 237 C3
Bramble Reed La TN12 288 B7
Brambles Ctyd CT14 215 B3
Brambletree Cotts ME1 62 E2
Brambletree Cres ME1 62 F2
Bramble Wlk TN2 286 D7
Brambley Cres CT20 334 E5
Brambling Rise ME10 101 E6
Bramdean Cres SE12 29 A7
Bramdean Gdns SE12 29 A7
Bramhope Ho 16 SE7 11 C8
Bramhope La SE7 11 B8
Bramis Ho TN16 118 D3
Bramley Ave
Canterbury CT1 174 C6
Faversham ME13 138 E6
Bramley Cl
Brabourne Lees TN25 302 E6
Eastchurch ME12 48 D3
Gillingham ME8 99 B8
Istead Rise DA13 36 F1
Newington ME9 100 A5
Orpington BR6 53 B1
Swanley BR8 55 E5
Bramley Cres ME15 162 F3
Bramley Ct Bexley DA16 13 B6
15 Erith DA17 4 A1
Marden TN12 259 B6
Bramley Dr TN17 320 D4
Bramley Gdns
Ashford TN23 300 A6
Coxheath ME17 194 C3
Herne Bay CT6 77 D2
Paddock Wood TN12 256 E7
Bramley Pk ME12 48 E5
Bramley Pl DA1 15 A3
Bramley Rd
East Peckham TN12 224 F6
Snodland ME6 128 A8
Bramley Rise ME2 62 E8
Bramleys TN27 262 D5
Bramley Way
Eastchurch ME12 48 D3
Kings Hill ME19 159 A2
Bramling Gap CT3 177 C3
Bramling Rd CT3,CT4 177 B4
Brampton Prim Sch DA7 13 D5
Brampton Rd DA7 13 E6
Bramshaw Rd CT2 142 E2
Bramshot Ave SE3,SE7 11 B8
Bramshott Cl ME16 161 C6
Bramston Rd ME12 47 C6
Branbridges Ind Est TN12 225 A5
Branbridges Rd TN12 225 B4
Branchley Mews TN27 234 C8
Branch Rd CT4 205 C7
Branch St CT16 278 C1
Brandon Rd
Dartford DA1 34 A8
Ramsgate CT12 83 A1
Brandon St DA11 37 B8
Brandon Way CT7 81 B6
Brandreth Rd E6 1 F7
Brands Hatch Circuit★ DA3 90 E6
Brands Hatch Cotts DA3 91 A6
Brands Hatch Rd DA3 91 A7
Branham Ho 1 SE18 2 B1
Bransell Cl BR8 55 C3
Bransgore Cl ME8 98 D7
Branston Cres BR5 53 D1
Branstone Ct RM19 16 B8
Brantingham Cl TN9 253 F7
Branton Rd DA9 16 F1
Brantwood Ave DA8 14 C7
Brantwood Rd DA7 14 B4
Brantwood Way BR5 54 C6
Brasenose Rd ME7 64 E4
Brasier Ct ME12 47 A5
Brassey Ave CT10 83 F3
Brassey Cl RH8 183 A6
Brassey Dr ME20 160 D8
Brassey Hill RH8 183 A6
Brassey Rd RH8 183 A6
Brasted Cl Bexley DA6 13 D2
Orpington BR6 87 A8
Brasted Ct
Brasted TN16 152 D2
Rochester ME2 40 A1
Brasted Hill TN14 152 A7
Brasted Hill Rd TN16 152 C5
Brasted La TN14 120 A1
Brasted Rd Erith DA8 14 E7
Westerham TN16 151 E1
Brattle Farm Mus★ TN12 260 D1
Brattle TN26 347 B8
Brattle Wood TN13 187 C6
Braundton Ave DA15 30 F7
Braunstone Dr ME16 161 D7
Bray Gdns ME15 194 F5
Bray Pas E16 1 A6
Braywood Rd SE9 12 D3
Breach La
Lower Halstow ME9 67 A2
Newington ME9 99 F8
Breach Rd RM20 16 F8
Breadlands Cl TN24 300 E8
Breadlands Rd TN24 300 F8
Breakneck Hill DA9 17 B2
Breakspears Dr BR5 54 A8
Bream Cl ME20 128 A5
Breaside Prep Sch BR1 52 D8
Breckonmead BR1 52 C7
Brecon Chase ME12 47 C7
Brecon Ct 7 SE9 12 A1
Brecon Rise TN24 268 B4
Brecon Sq CT12 83 A1
Bredgar CE Prim Sch ME9 134 A5
Bredgar Cl
Ashford TN23 299 F6
Maidstone ME14 162 C5
Bredgar Ho 1 BR5 54 D1
Bredgar Rd ME8 65 B4
Bredgar & Wormshill Light Rly★ ME9 133 E1
Bredhurst CE Prim Sch ME7 98 B1
Bredhurst Cl ME12 46 B7
Bredhurst Rd ME8 98 B4
Bredlands La CT3,CT2 111 C1
Breedon Ave TN4 253 F1
Bremner Cl BR8 56 A5
Brenchley Ave
Deal CT14 214 F4
Gravesend DA11 37 B3
Brenchley Cl
Ashford TN23 299 E6
Chislehurst BR7 53 A8
Rochester ME1 63 D2
Brenchley & Matfield CE Prim Sch TN12 289 A8
Brenchley Rd
Gillingham ME8 65 B2
Horsmonden TN12 289 F6
Maidstone ME15 161 F2
Matfield TN12 288 F8
St Paul's Cray BR5 53 F7
Sittingbourne ME10 101 F2
Brenda Ct 4 DA14 31 A4
Brenda Terr DA10 35 E8
Brendon Ave ME5 97 A3
Brendon Cl Bexley DA8 14 E6
Royal Tunbridge Wells TN2 286 D5
Brendon Dr TN24 268 B3
Brendon Rd SE9 30 D6
Brendon 16 DA14 31 A4
Brenley Cnr ME13 139 B4
Brenley Gdns SE9 11 D3
Brenley La ME13 139 C2
Brennan Ct ME7 64 D6
Brennan Rd RM18 19 B5
Brent Cl Chatham ME5 96 E5
Dartford DA2 16 B1
Brent Cl *continued*
Sidcup DA5 31 E7
Brentfield Rd DA1 34 B8
Brent Hill ME13 138 C8
Brent La DA1 34 A7
Brentlands Dr DA1 34 A7
Brentor Ct TN2 286 D6
Brent Prim Sch The DA2 34 C8
Brent Rd
Faversham ME13 138 C8
Newham E16 1 A8
Woolwich SE18 12 B7
Brents Ind Est ME13 105 D1
Brent The Dartford DA1 34 B8
Tonbridge TN10 222 C6
Brent Way DA2 16 B1
Brentwood TN23 299 F5
Brentwood Cl SE9 30 C7
Brentwood Ho SE18 11 D7
Brenzett Aeronautical Mus★ TN29 363 B3
Brenzett CE Prim Sch TN29 363 A2
Brenzett Cl ME5 97 B5
Brenzett Cnr TN29 363 A3
Brenzett Ho 6 BR5 54 C4
Bretaneby TN15 154 F6
Bretland Ct TN4 285 D4
Bretland Rd TN4 285 D4
Breton Rd ME1 63 C2
Brett Wlk ME8 98 D4
Brewer Rd ME3 40 B7
Brewers Field DA2 33 C4
Brewer's Hill CT20 334 D3
Brewers Rd DA12 61 C8
Brewer St Deal CT14 215 D6
Lamberhurst TN3 317 A5
Maidstone ME14 162 A5
Brewery Cotts CT14 214 E4
Brewery La Bridge CT4 176 A1
Sevenoaks TN13 154 C2
Brewery Rd
Orpington BR2 52 E1
Sittingbourne ME10 101 E6
Woolwich SE18 2 D1
Brewery Sq CT3 113 D2
Brewhouse La TN25 236 F4
Brewhouse Rd SE18 1 F2
Brewhouse Yd 15 DA12 19 B1
Brewster Cotts ME9 135 E2
Brian Cres TN4 286 B8
Brian Roberts Ho CT6 76 F5
Briar Cl Ashford TN24 268 C6
Aylesham CT3 210 F5
Crabble CT17 277 F2
Larkfield ME20 128 A2
8 Marlpit Hill TN8 217 D3
Briar Dale ME3 39 B4
Briar Fields ME14 162 E5
Briar Rd DA5 32 D5
Briars Cross RH8 183 D5
Briars Rd TN29 365 F3
Briars The
West Kingsdown TN15 90 D4
Whitstable CT5 108 C6
Briars Way DA3 59 A4
Briars Wlk CT10 83 F3
Briarswood Way BR6 86 F5
Briar Wlk TN10 222 C6
Briary Cl CT9 82 A8
Briary Ct DA14 31 B3
Briary Gdns BR1 29 B3
Briary Prim Sch CT6 76 C2
Brice Ave CT4 173 C1
Brice Rd ME3 39 B3
Brick Ct RM17 18 A8
Brickenden Rd TN17 320 D4
Brickfield Cotts
Bexley SE18 12 F8
Wye TN25 237 B2
Brickfield Farm Gdns BR6 86 C6
Brickfield Farm DA3 59 A6
Brickfield La ME13 139 E2
Brickfield TN31 367 B2
Brickfield Rd CT4 242 F7
Brickfields
Pembury TN2 287 E8
West Malling ME19 127 B1
Brick Field View ME2 40 C1
Brick Kiln La
Horsmonden TN12 290 B2
Limpsfield RH8 183 C5
Ulcombe ME17 230 D5
Brickmakers Ind Est ME10 102 B6
Brickwall Terr TN26 325 F3
Brickwell Cotts TN17 293 F6
Brickworks Cl TN9 254 B7
Bridewell La TN30 345 A7
Bridewell Pk CT5 75 A1
Bridge App The CT5 74 F1
Bridge Bsns Pk TN12 256 C7
Bridge Cl Dartford DA2 16 D4
Hythe CT21 333 A2
Tonbridge TN9 254 C8
Woodchurch TN26 347 B8
Bridge Cotts
Horsmonden TN12 290 A6
Selling ME13 171 E7
Teynham ME9 103 D2
Bridge Ct
28 Dartford DA2 16 B1
Grays RM17 18 B8
Bridge Down CT4 209 B8
Bridgefield Ct CT5 75 B3
Bridgefield Rd CT5 75 B3
Bridgeford Way CT4 176 A1
Bridge Hill Bridge CT4 209 B8
Finglesham CT14 214 C8
Bridge Home Pk TN29 376 D8
Bridge Ho
Ramsgate CT11 117 C7
Rochester ME1 63 B4
Royal Tunbridge Wells TN4 286 B5
Bridgeland Rd E16 1 A6
Bridgeman Ct CT21 333 B2
Bridge Mill Way ME15 161 D2
Bridgen Rd DA5 31 E8
Bridge & Patrixbourne CE Prim Sch CT4 176 A2
Bridge Pl ME20 128 F2
Bridge Rd
Ashford TN23 267 F2
Bexley DA7 13 E5
Brabourne Lees TN25 302 D5
Bridge CT4 175 D1
Deal CT14 215 D7
Erith DA8 14 F6
Faversham ME13 138 D8
Gillingham ME7 64 C7
Grays RM17 18 B8
Bridge Rd Ind Ctr TN23 267 F2
Bridge Rd Margate CT9 50 E1
Orpington BR5 54 B3
Rochester ME1 63 C2
Sheerness ME12 28 B2
Bridges Cl CT7 79 E2
Bridges Dr DA1 16 B2
Bridgeside CT14 215 C6
Bridgeside Mews ME15 161 E2
Bridge St Dover CT16 278 C1
Folkestone CT19 335 E6
Maidstone ME15 194 F5
Wye TN25 237 E2
Bridge View Ind Est
Rushenden ME11 46 A2
West Thurrock RM20 16 F8
Bridge View DA9 17 B3
Bridgewater Cl BR7 53 E6
Bridgewater Pl ME19 127 E2
Bridgewater Rd ME12 46 B8
Bridgeway CT5 74 F2
Bridledown Children's Farm & Wildlife Ctr★ CT15 309 A4
Bridleway Gdns CT10 83 E3
Bridle Way
Herne Bay CT6 76 D3
Hythe CT21 334 A3
Bridleway La TN23 300 B4
Bridle Way BR6 86 E6
Bridlington Cl TN16 150 B8
Brielle Way
Queenborough ME11, ME12 46 A6
Sheerness ME12 28 A2
Brier Cl ME5 97 C8
Brier Rd ME10 101 B4
Briganda Wlk CT11 117 E8
Bright Cl DA17 3 D2
Bright Ct 8 SE28 3 C5
Brightlands DA11 36 E4
Brightlingsea Rd CT13 180 F8
Bright Rd 3 ME4 64 B2
Bright Ridge TN4 285 E8
Bright's Pl CT11 117 F7
Brigstock Rd DA17 4 B2
Brimpsfield Cl SE2 3 B3
Brimp The ME3 9 D3
Brimstone Cl BR6 87 C3
Brimstone Hill DA13 93 D8
Brindle Gate DA15 30 E7
Brindle Gr CT11 83 F1
Brindle's Field TN9 254 A7
Brindle Way ME5 97 C1
Brindley Cl DA7 14 B4
Brindley Way BR1 29 A3
Brinkburn Cl SE2 3 A2
Brinkers La TN5 337 A2
Brinklow Cres SE18 12 B7
Brinklow Terr TN26 299 A1
Brionne Gdns TN9 254 D8
Brisbane Ave ME10 101 C4
Brisbane Dr CT12 83 A1
Brisbane Ho RM18 18 F6
Brisbane Rd ME4 64 A3
Briset Rd SE9 11 D3
Brishing Cl ME15 195 E5
Brishing La ME17 195 D4
Brishing Rd ME15, ME17 195 F3
Brisley La TN26 328 D6
Brisley's Row ME1 95 F1
Brissenden Cl
Chattenden ME2 41 A3
New Romney TN28 373 B8
Bristles Cnr CT3 111 E6
Bristol Cl ME2 62 D5
Bristol Pl CT11 117 D7
Bristol Rd
Canterbury CT1 174 F6
Gravesend DA12 37 D5
Bristow Rd DA7 13 E6
Britannia Ave CT5 108 B7
Britannia Bsns Pk ME20 160 E7
Britannia Cl Erith DA8 14 F8
Halling ME2 95 A4
Sittingbourne ME10 101 E7
Britannia Dr DA12 37 F3
Britannia Gate E16 1 A5
Britannia La TN23 299 F5
Britannia Rd
Deal CT14 215 D8
Fenn Street ME3 24 A3

Britannia Village Prim Sch
E16 . . . . .1 B5
Briton Ct ME12 . . . . .46 B8
Briton Rd ME13 . . . . . . 138 C7
Brittain Ct SE9 . . . . .29 E7
Brittain Ho SE9 . . . . .29 E7
Brittains La TN13 . . . . . 153 F2
Britten Cl Hythe CT21 . . .333 A3
Tonbridge TN10 . . . . . . 222 F6
Brittenden ■ BR6 . . . . . .86 F4
Brittenden Par BR6 . . . . .86 F4
Britton St ME7 . . . . .64 B5
Brixham Rd DA16 . . . . . 13 D6
Brixham St E16 . . . . .2 A5
Broadacre
Lydden CT15 . . . . 276 F8
Teynham ME9 . . . . . . 103 D2
Broadbridge Cl SE3 . . . 11 A7
Broadcloth TN17 . . . . . . 320 D3
Broadcroft BR5 . . . . . . 53 D2
Broadcroft TN2 . . . . . . 313 F8
Broad Ditch Rd DA13 . . 36 D1
Broader La ME14 . . . . . 131 B2
Broadfield Cres CT20 . . 335 A5
Broadfield Rd
Folkestone CT20 . . . . 335 A5
Loose ME15 . . . . 195 A8
Broadgate Hall ■
CT11 . . . . 117 F7
Broadgate Rd E16 . . . . .1 D7
Broad Gr TN2 . . . . 286 A1
Broadheath Dr BR7 . . . .29 F3
Broadhoath TN15 . . . . . 155 E1
Broadhurst Dr TN24 . . . 268 D7
Broad La Dartford DA2 . .30 A4
Finglesham CT14 . . . . 214 B7
Fordcombe TN3 . . . . . 300 E2
Broadlands Ave TN28 . . 373 B8
Broadlands Cres
TN28 . . . . 373 B8
Broadlands Dr ME5 . . . .97 B4
Broadlands Ind Est
CT2 . . . . 142 A7
Broadlands Rd BR1 . . . .29 B4
Broadlands CT2 . . . . . 143 F6
Broad Lawn SE9 . . . . . 30 A7
Broadley Ave CT7 . . . . .80 F5
Broadley Rd CT10,CT9 . .83 C7
Broadmead TN23 . . . . . 299 E6
Broadmead Ave TN3 . . 313 F8
Broadmead Manor
CT10 . . . . .84 B7
Broadmeadow CT19 . . . 335 B7
Broadmead Rd TN19 . . . 335 C8
Broadmead TN2 . . . . . 313 F8
Broadmere Terr
ME16 . . . . 161 D3
Broadoak Ave ME15 . . . 195 A8
Broad Oak TN12 . . . . . 289 C8
Broad Oak Cl
Brenchley TN12 . . . . . 289 C8
Orpington BR5 . . . . . 54 A7
Royal Tunbridge Wells
TN2 . . . . 285 F1
Broadoak Cl DA4 . . . . . 34 A2
Broadoak Ent Village
ME9 . . . . 134 F6
Broad Oak TN3 . . . . . . 312 C6
Broadoak ME19 . . . . . . 127 E2
Broad Oak Rd CT2 . . . . 143 E8
Sittingbourne ME9 . . . 134 E6
Broad Rd DA10 . . . . . . .17 E1
Broadsole La CT15 . . . . 308 E5
Broadstairs Rd CT10 . . .83 E5
Broadstairs Sta CT10 . . 84 A4
Broad St
Canterbury CT1 . . . . . 143 A1
Deal CT14 . . . . 215 D6
Margate CT9 . . . . .50 I3
Ramsgate CT11 . . . . . 117 E7
Broad Street Hill
ME17 . . . . 164 D7
Broad St
Sellindge TN25 . . . . . 303 E5
Sheerness ME12 . . . . . .28 B2
Sutton Valence ME17 . . 229 E7
Broadview Ave ME8 . . . .98 E8
Broadview
Folkestone CT20 . . . . 334 C6
Meopham DA13 . . . . . . .92 F6
Broadviews CT21 . . . . . 333 D1
Broad View TN17 . . . . . 321 A8
Broadwater Ct TN2 . . . 313 E8
Broadwater Down Prim Sch
TN2 . . . . 285 F1
Broadwater Down
TN2 . . . . 313 F8
Broadwater Forest La
TN3 . . . . 313 B7
Broadwater Gdns BR6 . .86 C6
Broadwater Ho DA12 . . 19 D1
Broadwater La
Royal Tunbridge Wells
TN2 . . . . 313 F8
Royal Tunbridge Wells
TN2,TN4 . . . . 285 F1
Broadwater Rd
East Malling ME19 . . . 159 D6
Woolwich SE28 . . . . . 1 D2
Broadwater Rise TN2 . . 285 F1
Broadway Bexley DA6 . . 13 F3
Bexley DA6 . . . . 14 A3
Crockenhill BR8 . . . . . 55 C3
Gillingham ME8 . . . . . 65 A3
Grays RM17 . . . . 18 C8
Limpsfield RH8 . . . . . 183 B5
Maidstone ME14 . . . . 161 F4
Petham CT4 . . . . 207 A2

Broadway Sh Ctr ■
DA6 . . . . 14 A3
Broadway ME12 . . . . . 28 C2
Broadway Square Sh Ctr
DA6 . . . . 14 A3
Broadway The
Broadstairs CT10 . . . . 84 A4
Dover CT16 . . . . 310 H8
Hadlow TN11 . . . . . . 223 E8
Herne Bay CT6 . . . . . 76 C5
Lamberhurst TN3 . . . . 317 B5
Minster (Sheppey) ME12 . .47 B7
Broadway RM18 . . . . . .18 F5
Broad Wlk
Eltham SE3,SE9 . . . . . .11 E5
Orpington BR6 . . . . . 87 D7
Sevenoaks TN15 . . . . 187 E7
Broadwood DA11 . . . . .37 B3
Broadwood Rd ME3 . . . 41 A4
Brockbank Cl ME5 . . . . 97 A1
Brockdene Dr BR2 . . . . 85 D6
Brockenhurst Ave
ME15 . . . . 162 C1
Brockenhurst Cl
Canterbury CT2 . . . . . 142 E2
Gillingham ME8 . . . . . 98 C7
Brockenhurst Rd
CT11 . . . . 117 G8
Brockhill Ctry Pk★
CT21 . . . . 332 F4
Brockhill Park Sch
CT21 . . . . 332 F4
Brockhill Rd CT21 . . . . 333 B3
Brocklebank Ho ■ E16 . .2 A5
Brocklebank Rd ■
SE7 . . . . .1 B2
Brocklebank Rd Ind Est
SE7 . . . . .1 B2
Brockley Rd CT19 . . . . 51 A2
Brockman Cres TN29 . . 353 B4
Brockman Rd CT20 . . . 335 C5
Brock Rd E13 . . . . .1 B8
Brockway TN15 . . . . . . 157 A7
Brockwell Cl BR5 . . . . . 53 F4
Brodrick Gr SE2 . . . . . 3 B2
Brogdale Farm Cotts
ME13 . . . . 138 A3
Brogdale Farm★
ME13 . . . . 138 B4
Brogdale Pl ME13 . . . . 138 B6
Brogdale World of Fruit★
ME13 . . . . 138 B4
Brogden Cres ME17 . . . 196 F7
Broke Farm Dr BR6 . . . 87 C2
Brokes Way TN4 . . . . . 286 B8
Brome Ho SE18 . . . . . .11 E6
Brome Rd SE9 . . . . . . .11 F4
Bromford Cl RH8 . . . . . 183 A2
Bromhedge SE9 . . . . . .29 F5
Bromholm Rd SE2 . . . . 3 B3
Bromley Cl ME5 . . . . . . 97 B4
Bromley Coll ■ BR1 . . . 52 A8
Bromley Coll of F Ed & H
Ed (Old Town Hall)
BR1 . . . . 52 A7
Bromley Coll of F Ed & H
Ed (Rookery Lane
Campus) BR2 . . . . . . 52 D3
Bromley Comm BR2 . . . 52 D3
Bromley RM17 . . . . . . 17 F8
Bromley Green Rd
TN26 . . . . 328 A5
Bromley High Sch BR1 . 53 A5
Bromley Ind Ctr BR1 . . 52 D6
Bromley La BR7 . . . . . . 30 D1
Bromley Manor Mans ■
BR2 . . . . 52 A6
Bromley Mus★ BR6 . . .54 B2
Bromley North Sta BR1 . 52 A8
Bromley Rd BR7 . . . . . . 53 B8
Bromley South Sta
BR1 . . . . 52 A6
Bromley Valley Gymnastics
Ctr BR5 . . . . 54 A7
Brompton Dr DA8 . . . . .15 B7
Brompton Farm Rd
ME2 . . . . 40 A2
Brompton Hill ME4 . . . .63 F6
Brompton La ME2 . . . . 63 A8
Brompton Rd ME7 . . . . 64 B6
Brompton Villas CT15 . . 278 E6
Brompton-Westbrook Sch
ME7 . . . . 64 A5
Bromstone Mews CT10 . .83 E3
Bromstone Prim Sch
CT10 . . . . 83 D3
Bromstone Rd CT10 . . .83 E3
Bronington Cl ME5 . . . . 97 A5
Bronte Cl Erith DA8 . . . .14 B7
Lunsford ME20 . . . . . 127 F3
Tilbury RM18 . . . . . . 19 C5
Bronte Gr DA1 . . . . . . .15 F3
Bronte Sch DA11 . . . . . 37 A8
Bronte View DA12 . . . . 37 C7
Bronze Age Way DA8,
DA17 . . . . .4 C3
Brookbank Brook TN25 . 270 A5
Maidstone ME14 . . . . 162 A8
Brook Cl Herne Bay CT6 . 76 C3
Hythe CT21 . . . . 334 B3
Brook Com Prim Sch
TN25 . . . . 270 A4
Brook Cotts
Collier Street TN12 . . . 258 F8
East Farleigh ME15 . . . 194 C7
Staple CT3 . . . . 178 E6
Teynham ME9 . . . . . . 104 A3
Brook Ct
■ Lewisham SE12 . . . 29 C5
10 Marlpit Hill TN8 . . 217 D3
Brookdale Rd DA5 . . . .13 E1
Brookdene TN12 . . . . . 256 B7

Brookdene Rd SE18 . . . .2 F2
Brooke Ave CT9 . . . . . .82 B7
Brooke Dr DA12 . . . . . .38 B7
Brookend Rd DA15 . . . .30 E7
Brooker Cl ME17 . . . . . 195 D5
Brooke Rd TN24 . . . . . 268 B3
Brookes Pl ME9 . . . . . 100 B6
Brookfield Ave
Dover CT16 . . . . 278 B2
New Hythe ME20 . . . . 128 A4
Brookfield Ct
Ashford TN23 . . . . . . 299 F8
Royal Tunbridge Wells
TN4 . . . . 254 A1
Brookfield TN8 . . . . . . 218 B5
Brookfield Ind Pk
TN23 . . . . 267 F1
Brookfield Inf Sch
ME20 . . . . 128 A2
Brookfield Jun Sch
ME20 . . . . 128 A2
Brookfield TN5 . . . . . . 174 C8
Brookfield Pl CT16 . . . . 278 B2
Brookfield Rd
Ashford TN23 . . . . . . 299 F8
Dover CT16 . . . . 278 A3
Brookfield TN18 . . . . . 356 B5
Brook Hill SE18 . . . . . . 2 B1
■ Lunsford ME20 . . . 127 F4
Brookhurst Gdns TN4 . . 253 E3
Brook La Bexley DA5 . . . 13 D2
Bromley BR1 . . . . 29 A2
Cliffs End CT12 . . . . . 115 F4
Brook La Cotts TN25 . . 303 E2
Brook La SE3 . . . . .11 B5
Brookland CE Prim Sch
TN29 . . . . 370 D8
Brooklands Ave DA15 . . 30 D6
Brooklands Cl CT2 . . . . 143 F4
Brooklands DA1 . . . . . .33 E7
Brooklands Farm Cl
TN3 . . . . 284 A6
Brooklands TN27 . . . . . 262 C6
Brooklands Pk SE3 . . . .11 A4
Brooklands Prim Sch
SE3 . . . . .11 A4
Brooklands Rd ME20 . . 128 A4
Brooklands TN23 . . . . . 280 D7
Brook La
Plaxtol Spoute TN15 . . 190 A8
Reculver CT6 . . . . . . .78 B5
Sellindge TN25 . . . . . 303 E2
Snodland ME6 . . . . . . 128 A6
Tonbridge TN9 . . . . . 222 D2
Brooklyn Paddock
ME7 . . . . 64 D6
Brooklyn Rd BR2 . . . . . 52 B8
Brooklyn Villas TN12 . . 259 C5
Brookmead Ave BR1 . . .52 F4
Brookmead Cl BR5 . . . . 54 B3
Brookmead Oak ME3 . . 40 B7
Brookmead TN11 . . . . . 221 E6
Brookmead Way BR5 . . 54 B3
Brook Pk DA1 . . . . 34 A6
Brook Rd
Faversham ME13 . . . . 105 D1
Lunsford ME20 . . . . . 127 F4
Northfleet DA11 . . . . .36 E7
Royal Tunbridge Wells
TN2 . . . . 286 D7
Swanley BR8 . . . . 55 D7
Whitstable CT5 . . . . . .75 B4
Brooks Cl Eltham SE9 . . 30 A6
Staplehurst TN12 . . . . 260 E4
Tonbridge TN10 . . . . . 222 E7
Brookside
Cranbrook TN17 . . . . . 320 D4
Hoo St Werburgh ME3 . .41 E5
Orpington BR6 . . . . . 86 D8
Brookside Pk ME12 . . . .48 F6
Brookside Rd DA13 . . . .36 F1
Brookside
St Mary's Bay TN29 . . . 366 A5
Temple Ewell CT16 . . . 277 D5
Brooks Pl ME14 . . . . . . 162 A4
Brook The ME4 . . . . . . 64 A4
Brook Vale DA8 . . . . . .14 B6
Brooks Way TN29 . . . . 376 C5
Brookway SE3 . . . . 11 A4
Broom Ave BR5 . . . . . . 54 B7
Broom Cl BR2 . . . . 52 E3
Broomcroft Rd ME8 . . . .65 F2
Broomfield Cres CT5 . . .51 F2
Broomfield Gate CT5 . . 109 D5
Broomfield Ho ■ BR5 . . 54 B7
Broomfield Rd
Bexley DA6 . . . . 14 A2
Faversham ME13 . . . . 138 C8
Folkestone CT19 . . . . 334 E6
Herne Bay CT6 . . . . . 77 C2
Kingswood ME17 . . . . 197 D4
Sevenoaks TN13 . . . . 153 F5
Swanscombe DA10 . . .17 C2
Broomfields SE3 . . . . . .58 E4
Broomhill Bank Sch
TN3 . . . . 285 C6
Broom Hill Cotts TN5 . . 339 B3
Broomhill Park Rd
TN4 . . . . 285 F8
Broomhill Rd
Dartford DA1 . . . . . . .15 B1
Orpington BR6 . . . . . 54 A7
Broom Hill Rd ME2 . . . .62 F8
Broomhill Rd TN3 . . . . 285 D7

Broomhill Rise DA6 . . . 14 A2
Broomhills DA13 . . . . . 35 E4
Broom La TN3 . . . . 284 F1
Broomlands La RH8 . . . 183 F8
Broomleigh ■ BR1 . . . . 52 A8
Broom Mead DA6 . . . . .14 A2
Broom Pk TN3 . . . . 284 E3
Broom Rd ME10 . . . . . 102 C5
Broomscroft Cotts
ME18 . . . . 159 C1
Broomshaw Rd ME16 . . 160 F3
Broomsleigh TN16 . . . . 118 E2
Broomwood Cl DA5 . . . 32 D6
Broomwood Rd BR5 . . .54 B7
Brotherhood Cl CT2 . . . 142 D4
Brougham Ct ■ DA2 . . .16 B1
Broughton By-Pass
ME13 . . . . 140 C2
Broughton Ct TN23 . . . 267 E1
Broughton Rd
Orpington BR6 . . . . . 86 D8
Otford TN14 . . . . 122 A3
Brow Cl BR5 . . . . 54 D2
Brow Cres BR5 . . . . . . 54 D2
Browndens Rd ME2 . . . .94 E4
Brownelow Copse ME5 . .97 B1
Brownhill Cl ME5 . . . . . 97 A4
Browning Cl
Bexley DA16 . . . . . . .12 E6
■ Lunsford ME20 . . . 127 F4
Browning Pl CT19 . . . . 335 E7
Browning Rd DA1 . . . . .15 F3
Brownings TN8 . . . . . . 217 C4
Browning Wlk RM18 . . . 19 C5
Browning Orch ME9 . . . 135 A7
Browning Wlk ME15 . . .195 C6
Brown Cl ME12 . . . . . . 28 H1
Brown Rd DA12 . . . . . .37 E7
Brownspring Dr SE9 . . . 30 B5
Browns Sch BR6 . . . . . .87 F5
Brown St ME8 . . . . .65 F1
Broxbourne Rd BR6 . . . .53 F2
Broxhall Rd CT4 . . . . . 208 B3
Bruce Cl Bexley DA16 . . .13 B6
Deal CT14 . . . . 215 B4
Bruce Ct DA15 . . . . 30 F4
Bruce Gr BR6 . . . . 54 A1
Bruces Wharf Rd RM17 . 18 A8
Brucks The ME18 . . . . . 192 E7
Bruges Ct ME10 . . . . . .68 F1
Brummel Cl DA7 . . . . . 14 C4
Brundell Terr CT4 . . . . 173 B2
Brunel Cl RM18 . . . . . . .19 B4
Brunel Way ME4 . . . . . 64 A7
Brungers Wlk TN10 . . . 222 B5
Brunswick Cl DA6 . . . . 13 D3
Brunswick Cotts ME9 . . 103 E6
Brunswick Ct ■ CT11 . . 117 E7
Brunswick Field ME9 . . 103 E6
Brunswick Gdns ■
CT16 . . . . 278 B3
Brunswick House Prim Sch
ME16 . . . . 161 E5
Brunswick Ind Ctr
TN23 . . . . 267 F2
Brunswick Rd
Ashford TN23 . . . . . . 267 F2
Bexley DA6 . . . . .13 E3
Birchington CT7 . . . . . 81 A5
Brunswick St E ME15 . . 162 A3
Brunswick Sq CT6 . . . . .76 E5
Brunswick St
Maidstone ME15 . . . . 162 A3
Ramsgate CT11 . . . . . 117 E7
Brunswick Terr TN1 . . . 286 A2
Brunswick Wlk ■
DA12 . . . . .37 D8
Brushwood Lodge ■
DA17 . . . . .4 A2
Bruton Cl BR7 . . . . 29 F1
Bryanston Rd RM18 . . . 19 C5
Bryant Cl ME18 . . . . . . 192 D6
Bryant Rd ME2 . . . . . . 63 A7
Bryant St ME4 . . . . 64 A3
Bryces Alley CT5 . . . . . 74 D2
Brymore Cl CT1 . . . . . . 143 B2
Brymore Rd CT1 . . . . . 143 B2
Bryony Dr TN23 . . . . . . 300 C3
Bryony Sch ME8 . . . . . .98 F5
Bubblestone Rd TN14 . . 122 B3
Bubhurst La TN17 . . . . 294 B7
Buckden Cl SE12 . . . . . 11 A1
Buckham Thorns Rd
TN16 . . . . 151 C1
Buckhole Farm Rd
ME23 . . . . 23 C4
Buckhurst Ave TN13 . . 154 C3
Buckhurst Dr CT9 . . . . .51 F2
Buckhurst La
Rockrobin TN5 . . . . . . 336 A6
Sevenoaks TN13 . . . . 154 C2
Buckhurst Pl TN5 . . . . 336 A6
Buckhurst Rd TN16 . . . 151 B7
Buckingham Ave DA16 . .12 E3
Buckingham Cl BR5 . . . 53 E2
Buckingham Dr BR7 . . . 30 C3
Buckingham Rd
■ Broadstairs CT10 . . 84 B4
Gillingham ME7 . . . . . 64 D5
Margate CT9 . . . . 50 I1
Northfleet DA11 . . . . . 36 D8
Royal Tunbridge Wells
TN1 . . . . 286 B2
Whitstable CT5 . . . . . .75 B2
Buckingham Row
ME15 . . . . 195 E7
Buckland Ave CT16 . . . 278 B2
Buckland Cl ME5 . . . . . 97 A2
Buckland Cotts ME13 . . 137 B8
Buckland Hill ME16 . . . 161 E6
Buckland Hospl CT17 . . 278 A1
Buckland La
Maidstone ME16 . . . . 161 D6
Staple CT3 . . . . 179 A4

Buckland Pl ME16 . . . . 161 E4
Buckland Rd
Cliffe Woods ME3 . . . . 40 A8
Luddesdown DA13 . . . 94 A7
Maidstone ME16 . . . . 161 E4
Orpington BR6 . . . . . .86 E6
Buckler Gdns SE9 . . . . .29 F5
Bucklers Cl
Royal Tunbridge Wells
TN2 . . . . 286 C3
Warden ME12 . . . . . . 49 E4
Buckles Ct DA17 . . . . . 3 D2
Buckley Cl DA1 . . . . . . 14 F5
Bucks Cross Rd
Chelsfield BR6 . . . . . .87 E5
Northfleet DA11 . . . . . 36 F5
Bucksford La TN23 . . . 299 C7
Buck St TN25 . . . . 203 C2
Buckthorn Cl CT14 . . . . 215 C2
Buckthorne Ho ME12 . . 47 A4
Buckthorne Rd ME12 . . 47 A4
Buckthorn House DA15 . .30 F5
Buckwheat Ct DA18 . . . 3 D3
Budd Ho ■ SE7 . . . . . . .1 C1
Buddle Dr ME2 . . . . . . 46 E7
Budd's Farm Cotts
TN30 . . . . 359 E2
Budd's La TN30 . . . . . . 359 F2
Budgin's Hill BR6 . . . . . 120 C8
Budleigh Cres ME16 . . . 13 C6
Buenos Ayres CT9 . . . . .50 H2
Buffs Ave CT20 . . . . . . 334 B6
Bugglesden Rd TN27,
TN30 . . . . 323 D5
Bugsby's Way SE10,SE7 . . .1 B2
Builders Sq CT3 . . . . . 177 A8
Bullace La ■ DA1 . . . . .15 E1
Bull Alley DA16 . . . . . .13 B4
Bullbanks Rd DA17 . . . .4 C2
Bulldog Rd ME5 . . . . . . 97 B2
Bulleid Pl TN24 . . . . . . 300 D1
Bullen La TN12 . . . . . . 224 E7
Buller Rd ME4 . . . . 63 F7
Buller's Ave CT6 . . . . . 76 E4
Bullers Cl DA14 . . . . . . 31 E3
Bullers Wood Dr BR7 . . .29 F1
Bullers Wood Sch BR7 . .52 E8
Bull Fields ME6 . . . . . . 128 A8
Bullfinch Cl
Paddock Wood TN12 . . 257 A5
Sevenoaks TN13 . . . . 153 D5
Bullfinch Cnr TN13 . . . 153 D5
Bullfinch Dene TN13 . . 153 D5
Bullfinch La TN13 . . . . 153 E5
Bull Hill
Horton Kirby DA4 . . . . 57 C5
Lenham Heath ME17 . . 200 A1
Bullingstone Cotts
TN3 . . . . 284 E7
Bullingstone La TN3 . . . 284 F7
Bullion Cl TN12 . . . . . . 256 F6
Bullivant Cl ■ DA9 . . . . 17 A2
Bull La
Bethersden TN26 . . . . 297 B4
Boughton Street ME13 . . 139 F4
Chislehurst BR7 . . . . . 30 D1
Eccles ME20 . . . . 128 F5
Lower Higham ME3 . . . .39 D7
Bull Lane Cotts
Hook Green TN3 . . . . . 316 C4
Yelsted ME9 . . . . .99 E1
Bull La Wrotham TN15 . .125 A3
Yelsted ME9 . . . . .99 E2
Bullockstone Rd CT6 . . 110 E7
Bull Orch ME16 . . . . . . 160 F2
Bull Rd ME19 . . . . 127 C5
Bulls Cl ■ CT21 . . . . . . 333 B2
Bulls Pl TN29 . . . . 287 D6
Bulltown Cnr TN25 . . . . 270 F3
Bullwark St CT17 . . . . . 310 D5
Bull Yd ■ DA11 . . . . . .19 B1
Bulrush Cl ME5 . . . . . . 96 F3
Bulrushes The TN23 . . . 299 D8
Bulwark Rd CT14 . . . . . 215 D7
Bumbles Cl ME1 . . . . . 96 D7
Bunce Court Rd ME13,
ME17 . . . . 200 D7
Bungalows The
Faversham ME13 . . . . 138 A4
Tenterden TN30 . . . . . 345 D7
Woodnesborough CT13 . . 180 B5
Bunkers Hill Ave CT17 . . 278 B1
Bunker's Hill
Dover CT17 . . . . 278 B2
Erith DA7 . . . . .4 A2
New Ash Green TN15 . . .92 B4
Bunkers Hill Rd CT17 . . 278 A1
Bunkers Hill DA14 . . . . .31 F5
Bunkley Mdw TN26 . . . 349 A7
Bunny La TN3 . . . . 313 E5
Bunters Hill Ave ME3 . . 40 B4
Bunton St SE18 . . . . . . 2 A3
Burberry La ME17 . . . . 197 B5
Burcharbro Rd SE2 . . . 13 D8
Burch Ave CT13 . . . . . 180 F8
Burch Rd DA11 . . . . . . .18 F1
Burdens TN27 . . . . 262 D5
Burdett Ave SE18,SE2 . . 3 C4
Burdett Cl DA14 . . . . . 31 E3
Burdett Rd TN4 . . . . . . 285 B4
Burdock Ct ME16 . . . . . 161 A3
Burdock Ho ■ ME15 . . . 195 D8
Burford's Alley CT3 . . . 147 D1
Burford Rd BR1 . . . . . . 52 E5
Burgate Cl CT1 . . . . . . 175 A8
Burgate Cl DA1 . . . . . . 14 F4
Burgate La ■ CT1 . . . . 175 A8
Burgate Terr TN25 . . . . 301 E4
Burgess Cl
Minster (Thanet) CT12 . .115 C7
Whitfield CT16 . . . . . . 278 B7
Burgess Gn CT14 . . . . . 214 C8
Burgess Hall Dr ME17 . . 196 F6

Burgess Rd
Aylesham CT3 . . . . . . 210 F6
Rochester ME2 . . . . . .63 B7
Burgess Row 10 TN30 . 345 A7
Burghclere Dr ME16 . . . 161 B2
Burghfield Rd DA13 . . . .36 F1
Burgoyne Ct ME14 . . . . 161 F7
Burgoyne Gr CT16 . . . . 278 A5
Burgoyne Hts CT15 . . . 278 E3
Burham CE Prim Sch
ME1 . . . . 128 F8
Burham Rd ME1 . . . . . . 95 E8
Burial Ground La
ME15 . . . . 161 E1
Burkeston Cl ME10 . . . . 102 A8
Burleigh Ave DA15 . . . . 12 F2
Burleigh Cl ME2 . . . . . .62 E8
Burleigh Dr ME14 . . . . 129 F1
Burleigh Rd TN27 . . . . 234 C7
Burley Rd Newham E16 . . .1 C8
Sittingbourne ME10 . . . 101 E4
Burlings La TN14 . . . . . 119 F2
Burlington Cl
6 Newham E6 . . . . . . .1 E7
Orpington BR6 . . . . . 86 B8
Burlington Dr CT6 . . . . 77 D5
Burlington Gdns
Gillingham ME8 . . . . . .98 E4
Margate CT9 . . . . 82 B8
Burlington Lodge BR7 . . 29 F1
Burma Cres CT1 . . . . . 143 D1
Burman Cl DA2 . . . . . . 34 C8
Burman Cl ME5 . . . . . . 97 B5
Burlington Ct ME5 . . . . 97 B5
Burmarsh Rd
Burmarsh TN29 . . . . . 352 C3
Hythe CT21 . . . . 353 C8
Burma Way ME5 . . . . . .96 F6
Burnaby Rd DA11 . . . . .18 E1
Burnan Ct CT5 . . . . . . 75 C2
Burnan Rd CT5 . . . . . . 75 C2
Burnell Ave DA16 . . . . 13 A5
Burnett Rd DA8 . . . . . . 15 D8
Burnham Cl ME10 . . . . 101 E8
Burnham Cres DA1 . . . . 15 C3
Burnham Rd
Dartford DA1 . . . . 15 C3
Sidcup DA14 . . . . 31 E6
Burnham Trad Est DA1 . . 15 D3
Burnham Wlk ME8 . . . . 98 E3
Burnley Rd RM20 . . . . . 17 A6
Burns Ave DA15 . . . . . 13 B1
Burns Cl Bexley DA16 . . .12 F6
Erith DA8 . . . . 14 F6
Burns Cres TN9 . . . . . . 254 A7
Burns Ho DA16 . . . . . . 13 C6
Burns Pl RM18 . . . . . . .19 B6
Burn's Rd ME7 . . . . . . 64 C7
Burns Rd ME1 . . . . 161 C2
Burnt Ash Heights BR1 . .29 B3
Burnt Ash Hill SE12 . . . 29 B3
Burnt Ash La BR1,SE12 . . 29 B3
Burnt Ash Prim Sch
BR1 . . . . 29 A3
Burntash Rd ME20 . . . . 160 F8
Burnt House Cl
Rochester ME2 . . . . . .40 C2
Sandhurst TN18 . . . . . 356 C5
Burnt House Hill CT3 . . 145 B5
Burnt House La
Dartford DA1 . . . . . . .33 F5
Hawley DA2 . . . . .33 F4
Langton Green TN3 . . . 285 A5
Burnthouse La TN27 . . . 263 D1
Burnt Lodge La TN5 . . . 338 B2
Burnt Oak Jun Sch
DA15 . . . . 31 A7
Burnt Oak La DA15 . . . 13 A1
Burnt Oak Terr ME7 . . . 64 D6
Burnt Oast Rd ME13 . . . 140 A3
Burntwick Dr ME9 . . . . .67 B3
Burntwood Gr TN13 . . . 187 B8
Burntwood Rd TN13 . . . 187 B7
Burnup Bank ME10 . . . 102 C5
Burrage Gr SE18 . . . . . .2 C2
Burrage Pl SE18 . . . . . .2 B1
Burrage Rd SE18 . . . . . .2 C1
Burrard Rd E16 . . . . . . .1 B7
Burr Bank Terr DA2 . . . 33 C4
Burr Cl DA7 . . . . .13 F4
Burrfield Dr BR5 . . . . . 54 D4
Burritt Mews ME1 . . . . 63 C3
Burrow Rd CT19 . . . . . 335 F6
Burrows La ME3 . . . . . 25 C3
Burrs Hill Cotts TN12 . . 289 D6
Burrs The ME10 . . . . . . 101 F3
Burrstock Way ME8 . . . .66 B2
Burrswood Villas TN3 . . 312 B7
Bursdon Cl DA15 . . . . . 30 F6
Bursill Cres CT12 . . . . .83 B1
Burslem Rd TN2 . . . . . 286 E7
Bursted Hill CT4 . . . . . 208 B2
Bursted Wood Prim Sch
DA7 . . . . 14 B5
Burston Rd ME17 . . . . . 194 B2
Burton Cl
Folkestone CT19 . . . . 335 A7
Rochester ME3 . . . . . .40 C3
Burton Fields CT6 . . . . .77 B4
Burton Rd TN24 . . . . . . 268 E6
Burt Rd E16 . . . . .1 C5
Burts Wharf DA17 . . . . .4 C5
Burwash Ct BR5 . . . . . 54 C4
Burwash Rd SE18 . . . . .2 D1
Burwood Ave BR2 . . . . .85 B8
Burwood Ho ME7 . . . . . 286 E5
Burwood Sch BR6 . . . . .87 D8
Bus Bridge Rd ME15 . . . 194 E6
Busbridge Rd ME6 . . . . 127 E7
Bush Ave CT12 . . . . . . .83 B1
Bush Cl ME9 . . . . 133 E5
Bushell Way BR7 . . . . . 30 A3
Bushey Ave BR5 . . . . . 53 D2
Bushey Rd ME13 . . . . . 139 F3

Bushey Ct DA8 .... 15 A6
Busheyfields Rd CT6 . 110 F6
Bushey Ho SE9 .... 29 C5
Bushey Lees DA15 .....12 F1
Bushfield Wlk DA10 ...35 E8
Bushmeadow Rd ME8 ..65 F2
Bushmoor Cres SE18 ..12 B6
Bush Rd Cuxton ME2 ....62 B2
  East Peckham TN12 .. 224 E8
Bush Row ME20 ...... 129 A3
Bushy Gill TN3 .... 285 A3
Bushy Gr ME17 .... 197 D2
Bushy Hill Rd CT2 .... 144 C7
Bushy Royds TN24 .... 300 D6
Bush The
  CT16 .... 277 D4
Business Acad Bexley Prim
  Section The DA18 ....3 B8
Buston Manor Farm Cotts
  ME18 .... 193 B2
Busty La TN15 .... 156 D6
Butcher Cl TN12 ..... 260 E3
Butcher's La ME19 ... 158 D1
Butchers La
  New Ash Green TN15 ... 91 D8
  Nonington CT15 .... 211 E5
Butchers Rd E16 ....1 A7
Butchers Yd BR6 .... 119 A8
Butcher Wlk DA10 ....35 E8
Butchery La 1 CT1 .. 175 A8
Butchery The 2 CT13 . 149 A1
Butler Ho 9 RM17 ....18 B8
Butler's Cotts DA7 .... 14 A5
Butler's Hill ME13 ... 140 D7
Butler's Pl DA3 ....91 E7
Buttercup Cl TN12 .. 257 A5
Butterfield Sq 10 E6 ....1 F7
Butterfly Ave DA1 ....33 F6
Butterfly Centre The ★
  CT15 .... 275 B3
Butterfly La SE9 .....12 B1
Buttermere
  Folkestone CT19 .... 335 B6
  Gillingham ME7 ..... 65 A5
Buttermere ME13 .... 188 A8
Buttermere Gdns CT3 . 210 F6
Buttermere Rd BR5 .. 54 D5
Butternut Copse
  TN23 .... 267 D3
Butterside Rd TN23 .. 300 C4
Butter St CT15 ...... 211 C4
Butt Field Rd TN23 .. 299 E2
Butt Green La ME17 .. 228 A7
Butt Haw Cl ME3 .....41 E5
Buttmarsh Cl SE18 ......2 B1
Button Dr ME3 .... 25 C5
Button Ho ME3 ....40 F6
Button La ME15 ...... 163 B2
Button St BR8,DA4 ... 56 C5
Butts Cl CT4 .... 208 A6
Butts Hill ME13 ..... 139 F5
Butts La TN5 .... 337 C7
Butts Mdw CT4 ...... 208 A6
Butts The Otford TN14 . 122 B2
  Sandwich CT13 ..... 148 F1
  Sittingbourne ME10 .. 101 F4
Buttway La ME3 .... A2
  Loose ME15 .... 195 A8
Buxton Cl Chatham ME5 . 97 D1
Buxton Rd Erith DA8 .. 14 D7
  Ramsgate CT12 ....83 B2
Buzzard Creek Ind Est
  IG11 ....3 A8
Bybrook Ct TN24 .... 268 C4
Bybrook Field CT20 .. 334 E3
Bybrook CT21 .... 333 D3
Bybrook Rd TN24 .... 268 C5
Bybrook Way CT20 .. 334 E4
Bychurch Pl 7 ME15 . 162 A3
Bycliffe Mews 2 DA11 ..36 F8
Bycliffe Terr 3 DA11 ..36 F8
Byland Cl SE3 ....3 B3
Byllan Rd CT17 ...... 277 E3
Byng Rd TN4 .... 285 F5
Bynon Ave DA7 ....13 F4
Byrneside TN11 ...... 221 E4
Byron Ave CT9 ....50 J1
Byron Cl
  Canterbury CT1 ..... 175 C7
  Woolwich SE28 ....3 C5
Byron Cres CT16 .... 278 B4
Byron Dr DA8 ....14 B7
Byron Gdns RM18 ... 19 C6
Byron Prim Sch ME7 .. 64 C3
Byron Rd Dartford DA1 .. 16 B3
  Gillingham ME7 ..... 64 C3
  Maidstone ME14 .... 162 B7
Bysing Wood Cotts
  ME13 .... 104 F1
Bysing Wood Prim Sch
  ME13 .... 138 A8
Bysing Wood Rd
  ME13 .... 138 B8
Bythorne Ct ME8 ......66 B1
Bywater Rd SE18 ....1 E3

C

Cabbage Stalk La TN4 . 285 E2
Cabin The TN24 ...... 268 D7
Cables Cl DA8 ....4 C3
Cacket's La TN14 .... 119 E4
Cade La TN13 .... 187 C7
Cade Rd TN23 .... 300 B7
Cades Orch ME13 ... 137 E3
Cadlocks Hill TN14 ....87 F1
Cadnam Cl
  Canterbury CT2 ..... 142 E3
  Rochester ME2 ....62 E8
Cadogan Ave DA2 .... 34 D8
Cadogan Gdns 6 TN1 . 286 B4
Cadogan Rd SE18 ....2 C3

Cadwallon Rd SE9 .... 30 C6
Caerleon Cl DA14 .... 31 C3
Caerleon Terr SE2 ......3 B2
Caernarvon Ct
  Erith DA8 .... 14 D7
  12 Orpington BR5 ... 54 C6
Caernarvon Dr ME15 . 161 F1
Caernarvon Gdns CT10 ..84 B5
Caesar Ave TN23 .... 299 F4
Caesar's Way CT19 .. 334 E7
Cage Green Prim Sch
  TN10 .... 222 D5
Cage Green Rd TN10 . 222 D5
Cage La TN27 .... 263 F1
Cagney Cl ME3 ...... 40 C3
Cairns Cl DA1 .... 15 D2
Cairns Mews SE18 .....11 E6
Caistor Rd TN9 ...... 222 A1
Caithness Gdns DA15 ..12 F1
Calais Cotts DA3 ..... 91 A8
Calais Hill CT2 ...... 142 E6
Calcraft Mews 6 CT1 . 148 B2
Calcott Wlk SE9 ..... 29 D4
Calcraft Ave DA9 .... 17 C2
Calcutta Ho 3 ME15 . 195 E5
Calcutta Rd RM18 ... 19 A5
Caldecote Cl ME8 .....66 B1
Caldecot La TN29 .... 372 D2
Caldecott Foundation Sch
  TN25 .... 302 B4
Calder Rd ME14 ..... 161 E7
Calderwood DA2 .....37 E2
Calderwood St SE18 ....2 A2
Caldew Ave ME8 ..... 65 C1
Caldew Gr ME10 ..... 102 A3
Caldy Rd DA1 ....4 B3
Caledonian Ct ME7 ...98 E8
Caledon Terr CT1 .... 175 A7
Calehill CT14 .... 162 C6
Caley Rd TN2 .... 286 D7
Calfstock La DA4 .....56 F5
Calgary Cres CT19 .. 335 E8
California Row
  Hawkenbury TN12 ... 261 C6
  Wingham CT3 ...... 177 E6
Caling Croft DA3 .....58 F1
Caliph Cl DA12 ....37 F5
Callams Cl ME8 ...... 98 D6
Calland TN25 .... 302 E5
Callaways La ME9 ... 100 B6
Calleywell La TN26 .. 330 A7
Callis Court Rd CT10 ..83 F6
Callis Grange Inf Sch
  CT10 ....83 F7
Callisto Ct ME16 .... 161 D3
Callis Way ME8 ...... 98 D5
Calshot Ct 17 DA2 ....16 B1
Calverden Rd CT12 ... 83 A1
Calverley Cl TN1 .... 286 C3
Calverley Park Cres 1
  TN1 .... 286 B3
Calverley Park Gdns
  TN1 .... 286 C4
Calverley Pk TN1 ... 286 B3
Calverley Rd
  Royal Tunbridge Wells
  TN1 .... 286 B3
Calverley St TN1 .... 286 B4
Calvert Cl Erith DA17 ....4 A2
  Sidcup DA14 ....31 E2
Calvert Dr DA2 ...... 32 D6
Calverton Prim Sch E16 ..1 D7
Calvin Cl BR5 .... 54 D6
Calydon Rd SE7 ....1 B1
Cambert Way SE3 ....11 B3
Camberwell La TN14 . 185 F4
Camborne Manor 2
  ME7 .... 64 C6
Camborne Rd
  Bexley DA16 ....12 F5
  Sidcup DA14 .... 31 C5
Cambourne Ave CT3 .. 81 D8
Cambrai Ct CT1 ..... 143 D1
Cambray Rd BR6 ......53 F2
Cambria Ave ME1 ....62 F2
Cambria Cl DA15 .....30 C7
Cambria Cres DA12 ...37 F4
Cambria Ho 2 DA8 ...14 E7
Cambrian Gr DA11 ... 37 A8
Cambrian Rd TN4 ... 286 C7
Cambridge Ave
  Bexley DA16 ....12 F5
  Sandwich CT13 .... 93 C6
Cambridge Barracks Rd 5
  SE18 ....1 F2
Cambridge Cl CT7 ......81 B7
Cambridge Cres
  ME15 .... 195 D7
Cambridge Dr SE12 .. 11 A2
Cambridge Gdns
  Folkestone CT20 .... 335 D6
  Royal Tunbridge Wells
  TN2 .... 286 B2
Cambridge Gn SE9 ...30 B7
Cambridge Ho 7 ME8 ....1 F2
Cambridge La ME9 .. 136 C8
Cambridge Mews
  CT14 .... 215 D3
Cambridge Rd
  Bromley BR1 ...... 29 A1
  Canterbury CT1 .... 174 F6
  Deal CT14 .... 215 D3
  Dover CT16 .... 310 D7
  Faversham ME13 ... 138 B6
  Gillingham ME8 .... 98 C6
  Rochester ME2 .... 63 A8
  Sidcup DA14 ....30 E4
  Sittingbourne ME10 . 102 B3
Cambridge Row SE18 ..2 B1
Cambridge St TN2 ... 286 C3

Cambridge Terr
  1 Chatham ME4 ......63 F4
  13 Dover CT16,CT17 .. 310 E7
  13 Folkestone CT20 .. 335 E5
  Margate CT9 ....51 B1
Cambridge Way CT1 . 174 F6
Cambus Rd E16 ....1 A8
Camdale Rd SE18 .....12 F7
Camden Ave TN2 .... 287 C6
Camden Cl
  Chatham ME5 ....97 B5
  Chislehurst BR7 .... 53 C8
  Northfleet DA11 .... 36 C7
Camden Cotts TN17 . 320 F8
Camden Cres SE18 .. 310 D2
Camden Ct 10 Erith DA17 ..4 A1
  Pembury TN2 ...... 287 D6
Camden Gr BR7 ...... 30 B2
Camden Hill TN2 ... 286 B5
Camden Park Rd BR7 . 30 A1
Camden Pk TN2 ..... 286 C2
Camden Rd
  Broadstairs CT10 .....83 E7
  Gillingham ME7 .... 64 D7
  Ramsgate CT11 .... 117 E6
  Royal Tunbridge Wells
  TN1 .... 286 B4
  Sevenoaks TN13 ... 154 B5
  Sidcup DA5 ....31 F8
Camden Sq 9 CT11 .. 117 E7
Camden St ME14 ... 162 A5
Camden Terr
  Ashford TN24 ...... 268 E1
  Seal TN15 .... 154 F6
  Sissinghurst TN17 .. 320 F8
Camden Way BR7 .... 30 A1
Camellia Cl
  Gillingham ME8 .... 98 D7
  4 Margate CT9 ....82 B8
Camelot Cl
  Biggin Hill TN16 ... 118 C3
  Woolwich SE28 ....2 D4
Camel Rd E16 ....1 E5
Camel Gdns DA13 ... 60 C3
Cameron Cl
  Chatham ME5 ....97 B8
  Joyden's Wood DA5 ..32 E5
Cameron Ct CT17 ... 310 A6
Cameron Ho ME3 .... 215 C1
Cameron Rd BR2 .... 52 A4
Camerons 4 TN18 .. 341 A2
Cameron Terr 10 SE12 ..29 B5
Campbell Cl
  Herne Bay CT6 ..... 77 C3
  Woolwich SE18 ..... 12 A6
Campbell Ho ME3 ....40 F6
Campbell Rd
  Deal CT14 .... 215 D4
  Maidstone ME15 ... 162 A3
  Northfleet DA11 .... 36 F8
  Royal Tunbridge Wells
  TN4 .... 286 A6
Camperdown Manor 5
  ME7 .... 64 A6
Campfield Rd SE9 ....29 D8
Camp Hill TN11 .... 220 A3
Camp Hill Cotts TN11 . 219 F2
Campion Cl
  Chatham ME5 ....96 E3
  Newham E6 ....1 A8
  Northfleet DA11 .... 36 E4
Campion Ct 6 RM17 . 18 D8
Campion Pl SE28 ......3 B5
Campleshon Rd ME8 . 98 D5
Camp Site The DA14 .. 32 A1
Campus Way ME8 ... 98 A8
Camp Way ME15 ... 195 C6
Camrose Ave DA8 ... 14 B8
Camrose St SE2 ....3 A2
Canada Cl CT19 .... 334 C6
Canada Farm Rd DA4 . 58 A6
Canada Mews CT14 . 215 C3
Canada Rd Deal CT14 . 215 D3
  Erith DA8 .... 14 B8
Canada Terr 3 ME14 . 162 A7
Canadian Ave ME7 ....64 C4
Canal Basin ME2 .... 19 D1
Canal Rd
  Gravesend DA12 .... 19 D1
  Higham ME3 .... 39 C8
  Rochester ME2 .... 63 C7
Canal Road Ind Pk 2
  DA12 .... 19 D1
Canberra Gdns ME10 . 101 C4
Canberra Rd
  Bexley DA7 .... 13 D8
  Greenwich SE7 .... 19 A5
Canberra Sq RM18 .. 19 A5
Canbury Path BR5 ... 54 A5
Candlers Way CT14 . 206 F8
Canning St ME14 ... 162 A6
Cannon Bridge Works
  TN9 .... 222 D2
Cannonbury Rd CT11 . 117 D6
Cannongate Ave CT21 . 333 D3
Cannongate Cl CT21 . 333 E2
Cannongate Gdns
  CT21 .... 333 E3
Cannongate Rd CT21 . 333 D3
Cannon La TN9 ..... 222 D2
Cannon Pl SE7 ....1 E1
Cannon Rd Bexley DA7 ..13 F6
  Ramsgate CT11 .... 117 D7
Cannon St 3 Deal CT14 . 215 C7

Cannon St continued
  Dover CT16 .... 310 D8
  Lydd TN29 .... 376 C6
  New Romney TN28 .. 373 B7
Canon Appleton Ct
  CT1 .... 174 E7
Canon Cl ME1 ....63 B2
Canon Gn CT3 ...... 178 A7
Canon La ME18 ..... 159 C1
Canon Rd BR1 ...... 52 D6
Canons Gate Rd CT16 . 310 E8
Canon Woods Way
  TN24 .... 268 F6
Cansiron La TN7,TN8 . 281 E2
Canterbury Ave DA15 . 31 C6
Canterbury Cathedral ★
  CT1 .... 175 A8
Canterbury Centre The
  (Mus) ★ CT1 ...... 142 F1
Canterbury Christ Church
  Univ Coll CT10 .... 83 C4
Canterbury Christ Church
  Univ Coll (The Mount)
  CT3 .... 143 F1
Canterbury Cl
  Broadstairs CT10 ... 83 D5
  Dartford DA1 ...... 34 A8
  2 Folkestone CT19 . 335 E6
  7 Newham E6 ....1 F7
Canterbury Coll CT1 . 175 B8
Canterbury Cres
  TN10 .... 222 D5
Canterbury Ct
  Ashford TN24 ...... 268 D2
  7 Lewisham SE12 ...29 B5
Canterbury East Sta
  CT1 .... 174 F7
Canterbury High Sch The
  CT2 .... 174 D8
Canterbury Hill CT2 . 142 E5
Canterbury Ho
  6 Erith DA8 ....14 F7
  2 Maidstone ME15 . 195 D7
Canterbury Ind Pk
  CT3 .... 145 A8
Canterbury La
  Canterbury CT1 .... 175 A8
  Gillingham ME8,ME9 . 66 C1
Canterbury Rd
  Ashford,Kennington
  TN24 .... 268 E5
  Ashford TN24 ..... 300 E6
  Barham CT4 .... 243 C5
  Boughton Aluph TN25 . 237 C5
  Boughton Street ME13 . 139 D4
  Brabourne Lees TN25 . 302 F6
  Brabourne TN25 ... 303 C8
  Chilham CT4 ...... 172 F1
  Denton CT4 .... 243 A1
  Dunkirk ME13 .... 140 C3
  Elham CT4 .... 273 E3
Canterbury Rd E CT11,
  CT12 .... 117 A6
Canterbury Rd
  Etchinghill CT18 ... 305 D4
  Faversham ME13 .. 138 C5
  Folkestone CT19 ... 335 D7
  Folkestone,Foord CT19 . 335 E6
  Gravesend DA12 ... 37 C6
  Hawkinge CT18,CT19,
  CT15,CT4 .... 307 B4
  Herne Bay CT6 .... 77 A3
  Herne CT3,CT6 .... 110 E5
  Littlebourne CT3 .. 176 C8
  Lydden CT15 ...... 276 E7
  Lyminge CT18 .... 305 C4
  Pembury TN2 ..... 287 E6
  Sarre CT7 .... 113 C7
  Sittingbourne ME10 . 102 B3
Canterbury Rd W
  CT12 .... 116 D7
Canterbury Rd
  Whitstable CT5 ... 108 D8
  Wingham CT3 ..... 178 A7
Canterbury Road
  Birchington CT7 ....81 B7
Canterbury Road Margate
  CT9 .... 50 G1
Canterbury Road Prim Sch
  ME10 .... 102 B3
Canterbury Road Westgate
  CT8,CT9 ....81 B8
Canterbury St ME7 ... 64 C4
Canterbury Tale The ★
  CT1 .... 174 F8
Canterbury Way DA1,
  DA2,RM20 .... 16 D5
Canterbury West Sta
  CT1 .... 142 F1
Cantwell Ho SE18 .....12 B7
Cantwell Rd SE18 .....12 B7
Canute Rd
  Birchington CT7 .... 80 D7
  Deal CT14 .... 182 C1
  Faversham ME13 .. 138 C6
Canute Wlk CT14 ... 182 D1
Capability Way DA9 .. 17 C3
Capelands DA3 ...... 92 A8
Capel Cl Ashford TN23 . 267 F1
  Broadstairs CT10 ... 51 F1
  Gillingham ME8 .... 98 D4
  Orpington BR2 .... 52 E1
Capel Court Pk CT18 . 308 D7
Capella Ho 1 SE7 ....11 B8
Capell Cl ME17 .... 194 C3
Capel-le-Ferne Prim Sch
  CT18 .... 308 C3
Capel Pl DA2 .... 33 C4
Capel Prim Sch TN12 . 255 F7
Capel Rd
  Bromley Green TN26 . 328 B4
  Faversham ME13 .. 138 B7

Capel Rd continued
  Petham CT4 .... 206 D7
  Sittingbourne ME10 . 101 E2
Capel St CT18 ...... 308 B3
Capetown Ho 1 ME15 . 195 F5
Capital Ind Est DA17 ....3 D3
Capstan Ct DA2 ..... 16 C3
Capstan Ctr RM18 ... 19 C2
Capstan Mews 4 DA11 . 36 E8
Capstan Row CT14 .. 215 D2
Capstone Farm Country
  Pk ★ ME7 .... 97 D5
Capstone Rd
  Chatham ME5 ...... 64 D1
  Gillingham ME7 .....97 F6
  Lewisham BR1 ..... 29 A4
Captain's Cl ME17 .. 229 E6
Captains Ct CT21 ... 333 C1
Capulet Mews E16 .....1 A5
Caraway Cl E13 ....1 B8
Cardens Rd ME3 .... 40 B8
Cardiff St SE18 ....12 E1
Cardigan Cl ME23 .....23 F3
Cardinal Cl
  Chislehurst BR7 .... 53 D8
  Minster (Sheppey) ME12 . 47 D7
  Tonbridge TN9 .... 254 D8
Cardinal Wlk ME18 . 159 C3
Cardwell Prim Sch SE18 ..1 F2
Carew Ho 18 SE18 ......1 F2
Carey Cl TN28 ...... 373 B6
Carey Ct DA6 ....14 B2
Carey Ho 5 CT1 .... 174 F7
Carey's Field TN13 .. 153 E7
Caring La ME14,ME17 . 163 E1
Caring Rd ME15,ME17 . 163 C5
Carisbrooke Ave DA5 . 31 D7
Carisbrooke Ct
  23 Dartford DA2 ....16 B1
  20 Sidcup DA14 ....31 A4
Carisbrooke Dr ME16 . 161 D4
Carisbrooke Rd
  Bromley BR2 ...... 52 C5
  Rochester ME2 .....39 E1
Carl Ekman Ho DA11 . 36 D8
Carleton Pl DA4 .... 57 C5
Carleton Rd CT1 .... 34 A8
Carlisle Cl ME2 ..... 62 C6
Carlisle Rd DA1 ..... 16 A1
Carlsden Cl CT17 ... 278 A3
Carlton Ave
  Broadstairs CT10 ... 84 A5
  Gillingham ME7 .... 97 F8
  Ramsgate CT11 .... 117 D6
  Sheerness ME12 ....28 B1
  Stone DA9 .... 16 E1
Carlton Cl
  Kings Hill ME18 ... 159 B3
  Tonbridge TN10 ... 222 E7
Carlton Cres
  Chatham ME5 ..... 97 D8
  Royal Tunbridge Wells
  TN1 .... 286 C4
Carlton Gdns ME15 . 195 B8
Carlton Gn DA14 .....30 F4
Carlton Hill CT6 .... 76 C4
Carlton Leas CT20 .. 335 C4
Carlton Mans CT9 ...51 A3
Carlton Par BR5 ......54 B2
Carlton Rd
  Ashford TN23 ..... 268 A2
  Bexley DA16 ....13 B4
  Erith DA8 .... 14 F7
Carlton Rd E CT8 ... 81 D8
Carlton Rd
  Kingsdown CT14 ... 248 C6
  Royal Tunbridge Wells
  TN1 .... 286 C4
  Sidcup DA14 .... 30 F3
  Whitstable CT5 .... 108 D2
Carlton Rd W CT8 ... 81 D8
Carlton St CT8 ...... 81 C8
Carlton Rise SE28 .....3 C6
Carlyle Ave BR1 .... 52 D6
Carlyle Rd SE28 ....3 C6
Carman's Cl ME15,
  ME17 .... 194 F3
Carmel Cl CT4 ...... 173 B2
Carmel Ct 2 CT7 ......80 F8
Carmelite Way DA3 ..58 F4
Carnation Cl 1 ME19 . 128 A1
Carnation Cres ME19 . 127 F1
Carnation Rd ME2 .. 62 D7
Carnation St SE2 ......3 B1
Carn Brae CT9 ....50 J2
Carnbrook Rd SE3 ... 11 D4
Carnecke Gdns SE9 ...11 E2
Carnet Cl DA1 ...... 32 E8
Carnoustie Cl Erith SE28 ..3 D7
Caroland Cl TN25 .. 302 D5
Caroline Cl CT5 .... 108 B6
Caroline Cres
  Broadstairs CT10 ...83 E6
  Maidstone ME16 .. 161 D7
Caroline Sq CT9 .....50 J3
Carolyn Dr BR6 ..... 87 A7
Carp Cl ME20 ...... 128 A4
Carpeaux Cl ME4 ... 64 A4
Carpenters Cl ME1 ...63 E2
Carpenters Ct BR1 .. 52 D7
Carpenters La
  Hadlow TN11 ...... 190 D2
  Staplehurst TN12 .. 260 C8
Carpinus Cl ME5 .....97 B1
Carrack Ho 1 DA8 .....4 E1
Carr Gr SE18 ....1 E2
Carr Ho DA1 ....14 E2
Carriage Ho ME13 .. 170 D5
Carriage Mews CT1 . 142 F1
Carriageway The
  TN16 .... 152 D3
Carrick Dr TN13 .... 154 B4

Carrie Ho 3 ME16 ... 161 E5
Carriers Pl TN3 .... 283 B4
Carriers Rd TN17 ... 320 D5
Carrill Way DA17 ......3 D3
Carrington Cl ME7 ....64 F6
Carrington Rd DA1 .. 16 A1
Carrington CT4 ..... 31 A3
Carroll Cl ME2 ..... 95 A4
Carroll Gdns ME20 . 127 F3
Carronade Pl SE28 .....2 D3
Carroway's Pl CT9 ....50 J2
Carsington Gdns DA1 . 33 D6
Carson Rd E16 ....1 A8
Carston Cl SE12 .... 11 A2
Carter La TN29 ..... 362 E2
Carter's Hill SE9 .... 29 C7
Carters Hill Cl SE9 .. 29 C7
Carters Hill La DA13 . 92 F2
Carter's Rd CT20 ... 334 F5
Carters Row DA11 ...36 F6
Carter's Wood TN26 . 349 B7
Cartmel Rd DA7 ..... 14 A6
Carton Cl ME1 ...... 63 D2
Carton Rd ME3 ..... 39 B3
Cartwright Cl CT3 .. 147 C2
Cartwright & Kelsey CE
  Prim Sch CT3 ..... 147 C2
Carville Ave TN4 .... 253 F1
Carvoran Way ME8 .. 98 C5
Cascade Cl BR5 .... 54 C6
Caslocke St 2 ME13 . 138 C7
Caspian Way DA10 ..17 E2
Caspian Wlk E16 ......1 D7
Cassilda Rd SE2 ......3 A2
Cassino Ho 16 CT1 .. 143 B2
Cassino Sq CT15 ... 278 E2
Casstine Cl BR8 ..... 32 F1
Castalia Ct DA1 .....15 F4
Castalia Cotts CT14 . 215 D3
Casterbridge Rd SE3 . 11 A4
Castfield Cl ME3 .....22 E1
Castile Rd 12 SE18 ....2 A2
Castilion Prim Sch SE28 ..3 C7
Castleacres Ind Pk
  ME10 .... 102 B6
Castle Ave
  Broadstairs CT10 ...84 B6
  Dover CT16 .... 278 D1
  Hythe CT21 .... 333 B4
  Rochester ME1 .... 63 C4
Castle Bay CT20 .... 334 D3
Castle Cl
  4 Folkestone CT20 . 334 E4
  Lympne CT21 ..... 331 F2
Castlecombe Prim Sch
  SE9 .... 29 E3
Castlecombe Rd SE9 . 29 E4
Castle Com Sch CT14 . 215 C4
Castle Cotts CT13 .. 148 E5
Castle Cres CT21 ... 333 C4
Castle Dene ME14 .. 161 F8
Castle Dr
  Kemsing TN15 .... 122 E2
  Whitfield CT16 .... 277 F7
Castle Farm Cotts
  TN11 .... 223 B4
Castle Farm Rd TN14 . 89 A3
Castlefields DA13 ....59 F8
Castle Glen 9 CT20 . 334 E3
Castle Hill Ave CT20 . 335 C4
Castle Hill Ct ME1 .. 63 C6
Castle Hill
  Folkestone CT19,CT18 . 335 A8
  Hartley DA3 ....58 E4
Castle Hill Rd 4 CT16 . 310 E8
Castle Hill
  Rochester ME1 .... 63 C6
  Thurnham ME14 .. 131 D1
  Tonbridge TN11 ... 254 F5
Castle Ho CT5 ....74 F7
Castle Hurst TN32 .. 355 B1
Castle La DA12 ......38 B6
Castlemaine Ave ME7 . 64 F6
Castle Mayne Ave CT7 . 81 B7
Castlemere Ave ME11 . 46 B5
Castle Mews CT14 .. 215 A4
Castlemount Ct CT16 . 310 E8
Castlemount Rd CT16 . 278 D1
Castle Rd Chatham ME4 . 64 B2
  Eynsford DA4 ..... 89 C5
  Folkestone CT20 .. 334 F3
  Grays RM17 ....17 F8
  Hythe CT21 .... 333 B4
  Maidstone ME16 .. 161 D7
  Royal Tunbridge Wells
  TN4 .... 286 A3
  Sittingbourne ME10 . 102 B5
  Swanscombe DA10 ..17 F1
  Whitstable CT5 .....74 F2
Castle Road Bsns Prec
  ME10 .... 102 B6
Castle Road Tech Ctr
  ME10 .... 102 B6
Castle Rough La ME10 . 68 F1
Castle Row CT1 .... 174 F7
Castle St
  6 Ashford TN23 ... 268 B2
  Canterbury CT1 ... 174 F8
  Dover CT16 .... 310 E8
  Queenborough ME11 . 46 A5
  Rochester ME2 .... 40 E1
  2 Royal Tunbridge
  Wells,Mount Sion TN1 . 286 A2
  2 Royal Tunbridge
  Wells,Southborough
  TN4 .... 253 F2
  Stone DA9 .... 17 A2

Castle St continued
Swanscombe DA10 . . . . . . .17 F1
Tonbridge TN9 . . . . 222 C2
Wouldham ME1 . . . . 95 C4
Castle Terr
Hadlow TN11 . . . . 223 E8
Hawkhurst TN18 . . . . 340 F3
Castleton Ave DA7 . . . . . 14 D5
Castleton Rd SE9 . . . . . . 29 C4
Castle View Bsns Ctr
ME1 . . . . 63 C6
Castleview Ct CT17 . . . . 278 B1
Castle View Mews ME1 . . 63 C6
Castle View Rd ME2 . . . . . 63 A7
Castle Way ME19 . . . . . 127 D2
Castle Wlk Deal CT14 . . 182 C1
Durgates TN5 . . . . 336 E4
Castlewood Day Hospl
SE18 . . . . 12 A6
Castlewood Dr SE9 . . . . . 11 F5
Castweazle TN30 . . . . . . 344 E6
Caterfield La RH7,RH8 . . 216 A5
Cates Ct TN12 . . . . 225 A7
Cathcart Dr BR6 . . . . 53 E1
Cathedral View CT2 . . . . 143 A2
Catherine Cl 2 ME16 . . . 161 A3
Catherine of Aragon Ct
DA15 . . . . 30 D8
Catherine Pl 7 TN1 . . . 286 B4
Catherine St ME1 . . . . . . 63 D3
Catherine Way CT10 . . . . 84 A6
Catkin Cl ME5 . . . . .96 F1
Catlyn Cl ME19 . . . . 160 A8
Catsole Hill CT3 . . . . . . 178 D2
Catterick Rd ME5 . . . . . . 97 D2
Cattistock Rd SE9 . . . . . . 29 F3
Cattle Market CT13 . . . . 148 F1
Catt's Hill TN30 . . . . . . 360 E3
Catts Pl TN12 . . . . 257 C4
Catt's Wood Rd CT4 . . . 207 F4
Cauldham Cl CT18 . . . . . 308 B1
Cauldham La CT18 . . . . . 308 B1
Caulkers Ho 7 ME4 . . . . 64 B2
Causeway The
Canterbury CT1 . . . . 142 F1
Sandwich CT13 . . . . 148 D2
Causton Rd TN17 . . . . . 320 C5
Cavalry Cl TN10 . . . . . . 222 E7
Cavalry Ct Deal CT14 . . 215 D3
Folkestone CT20 . . . . . . 334 D5
Cave Hill ME15 . . . . 161 F1
Cave La CT3 . . . . 178 D3
Cavell Cres DA1 . . . . 16 A3
Cavell Sq CT14 . . . . 215 A3
Cavell Way ME1 . . . . . . 101 D5
Cavenagh Rd CT15 . . . . 280 B6
Cavendish Ave
Bexley DA16 . . . . 12 F4
Erith DA8 . . . . 14 C8
Gillingham ME7 . . . . .64 E6
Sevenoaks TN13 . . . . . . 154 A5
Sidcup DA15 . . . . 31 A8
Cavendish Cl TN10 . . . . 222 D7
Cavendish Ct
Herne Bay CT6 . . . . 77 A5
Tonbridge TN9 . . . . 222 D3
Cavendish Dr TN2 . . . . . 286 B1
Cavendish Pl 2 CT11 . . . 117 E6
Cavendish Rd
Herne Bay CT6 . . . . 77 A5
Rochester ME1 . . . . 63 D3
Cavendish Sq DA3 . . . . . 58 D6
Cavendish St CT11 . . . . 117 E6
Cavendish Way ME15 . . 163 B3
Caversham Cl ME8 . . . . . 65 F1
Caveside Cl BR7 . . . . 53 A8
Cavour Rd
Faversham ME13 . . . . . . 138 C7
Sheerness ME12 . . . . 28 C2
Caxton Cl Hartley DA3 . . .58 F5
Tenterden TN30 . . . . . . 344 F7
Caxton Ho
Ashford TN24 . . . . 268 C3
The Chart RH8 . . . . 183 F3
Caxton La
Hadlow TN11 . . . . 223 E8
The Chart RH8 . . . . 183 E4
Caxton Rd CT9 . . . . 82 C8
Cayser Dr ME17 . . . . . . 197 E2
Caysers Croft TN12 . . . . 224 E6
Cazeneuve St ME1 . . . . . 63 C5

Cecil Ave
Gillingham ME8 . . . . 65 A2
Rochester ME2 . . . . .63 B8
Sheerness ME12 . . . . 28 B1
Cecil Burns Lodge
TN2 . . . . 286 D2
Cecil Ct Ashford TN24 . . 268 B3
Herne Bay CT6 . . . . 77 A4
Cecilia Gr CT10 . . . . .83 F6
Cecilia Rd CT11 . . . . 117 E8
Cecil Kidby Ho TN2 . . . 286 F6
Cecil Pk CT7 . . . . 77 A4
Cecil Rd
Kingsdown CT14 . . . . . . 248 D7
Northfleet DA11 . . . . .36 F7
Rochester ME1 . . . . 63 C3
Cecil Road Prim Sch
DA11 . . . . .36 F7
Cecil Sq CT9 . . . . .50 I2
Cecil St CT9 . . . . .50 I2
Cecil Way BR2 . . . . 52 A1
Cedar Ave
Gravesend DA12 . . . . 37 C4
Sidcup DA15 . . . . 31 A5
Cedar Cl Ashford TN23 . . 267 E3
Birchington CT8 . . . . .81 B7
Broadstairs CT10 . . . . . . .83 F7
Ditton ME20 . . . . 160 D8
Margate CT9 . . . . .51 B1

Cedar Cl continued
Meopham Station DA13 . . 60 A3
Orpington BR2 . . . . .85 E7
Sittingbourne ME10 . . . . 102 B2
Swanley BR8 . . . . 55 C7
Cedar Copse BR1 . . . . . . 52 F7
Cedar Cres
Orpington BR2 . . . . .85 E7
St Mary's Bay TN29 . . . . 365 F3
Cedar Ct Eltham SE9 . . . . 11 E1
Folkestone CT20 . . . . . . 334 E5
21 Greenwich SE7 . . . . . 11 C8
Maidstone ME14 . . . . . . 162 B5
Royal Tunbridge Wells
TN4 . . . . 286 A5
12 Tenterden TN30 . . . . 345 A7
Cedar Dr
Edenbridge TN8 . . . . . . 217 B2
Maidstone ME16 . . . . . . 160 E2
Sutton at H DA4 . . . . .57 B7
Cedar Gdns ME9 . . . . . . 132 E8
Cedar Gr Gillingham ME7 . . 98 A5
Sidcup DA5 . . . . 13 D1
Cedar Ho
Royal Tunbridge Wells
TN4 . . . . 285 E4
Sheerness ME12 . . . . . . .28 B2
Cedarhurst Cotts 5
DA5 . . . . 32 A8
Cedarhurst Dr SE9 . . . . . 11 C2
Cedar La TN27 . . . . 323 D7
Cedar Lodge TN4 . . . . . 285 F3
Cedarmore Ct BR7 . . . . . 53 C8
Cedar Mount SE9 . . . . . . 29 D7
Cedar Pl 6 SE7 . . . . 1 C1
Cedar Rd Bromley BR1 . . 52 C7
Dartford DA1 . . . . 26 E8
Erith DA8 . . . . .15 A6
Hoo St Werburgh ME3 . . .41 E3
Rochester ME2 . . . . .62 F6
Sturry CT2 . . . . 144 A6
Cedar Ridge TN2 . . . . . 286 D5
Cedars PRU The
ME16 . . . . 161 A2
Cedars Sch The ME1 . . . 63 C4
Cedars The
Barrowhill TN25 . . . . . . 331 D8
Paddock Wood TN12 . . . 257 A4
Sittingbourne ME10 . . . . 102 C5
Cedar Terrace Rd
TN13 . . . . 154 C4
Cedar Terr ME13 . . . . . 138 A4
Cedarview CT2 . . . . 142 C1
Cedarwood Ho ME15 . . 194 B6
Cedric Rd Eltham SE9 . . . 30 C5
Westgate-on-S CT8 . . . . . 50 C1
Ceil Villas CT14 . . . . . . 181 B4
Celandine Dr SE28 . . . . . 3 B5
Celestine Cl ME5 . . . . . . 97 A1
Cellar Hill ME9 . . . . 136 C8
Celt Cl ME10 . . . . 101 F8
Celtic Rd CT15 . . . . 215 A2
Cement Block Cotts 8
RM17 . . . . 18 C8
Cement Industry Heritage
Ctr★ DA11 . . . . .18 B2
Cemetery La
Ashford TN24 . . . . 268 C4
Hadlow TN11 . . . . 191 A1
Woolwich SE7 . . . . .11 E8
Cemetery Rd
Halling ME2 . . . . 95 A4
Snodland ME6 . . . . 94 F1
Woolwich SE2 . . . . .13 B7
Centenary Cl TN27 . . . . 234 C8
Centenary Ct DA4 . . . . . 57 A2
Centenary Gdns CT13 . . 180 A2
Central Ave
Bexley DA16 . . . . 13 A5
Chatham ME4 . . . . .64 B8
Gravesend DA12 . . . . 37 B5
Herne Bay CT6 . . . . 77 A6
Sittingbourne ME10 . . . . 101 F4
Tilbury RM18 . . . . 19 A6
Central Par
Rochester ME1 . . . . 63 D2
Sidcup DA15 . . . . 31 A5
Central Par BR5 . . . . 54 C7
Central Par TN5 . . . . . . 336 F4
Central Pk CT12 . . . . . . 114 D6
Central Rd Dartford DA1 . .15 C2
New Hythe ME20 . . . . . . 128 B4
Ramsgate CT11 . . . . 117 D8
Rochester ME2 . . . . 63 A7
Central Service Rd
CT16 . . . . 310 H8
Central Sta CT19 . . . . . 335 C5
Central Terr ME3 . . . . 40 F6
Central Way SE28 . . . . . . 3 B6
Centre 2000
Maidstone ME16 . . . . . . 161 C8
8 Sittingbourne ME10 . . 102 A4
Centre Common Rd
BR7 . . . . 30 C1
Centre Ct ME2 . . . . .63 E7
Centre Rd Dover CT17 . . 310 C6
New Ash Green DA3 . . . . . 91 E7
Centre The Margate CT9 . . 50 I2
Ramsgate CT11 . . . . 83 A1
Centurian Way DA18 . . . . 4 A3
Centurion Cl ME8 . . . . . . 64 F1
Centurion Wlk TN23 . . . 300 B4
Century Ct ME1 . . . . 63 C5
Century Rd
Faversham ME13 . . . . . 138 E7

Century Rd continued
Gillingham ME8 . . . . 98 D8
Century Wlk CT14 . . . . 215 C6
Ceres Ct ME10 . . . . 102 C5
Ceres Rd SE18 . . . . 2 F2
Cerne Rd DA12 . . . . 37 E5
Cervia Way DA12 . . . . . . .37 F5
Chada Ave ME7 . . . . .64 E3
Chadd Dr BR1 . . . . .52 E6
Chadfields RM18 . . . . . . 19 A7
Chadwell Hill RM17 . . . . 19 A8
Chadwick Cl DA11 . . . . . .36 E5
Chadwick Ct
2 Dartford DA1 . . . . 15 D1
4 Woolwich SE28 . . . . . . 3 B5
Chadwick Way SE28 . . . . 3 D6
Chadwin Rd E13 . . . . 1 B8
Chaffe's La ME9 . . . . . . .66 E3
Chaffes Terr ME9 . . . . . .66 E2
Chaffey Ho 6 SE7 . . . . . . 1 C1
Chaffinch Cl ME5 . . . . . . 97 A7
Chaffinch Dr TN23 . . . . 300 C3
Chaffinch Lodge 5
CT16 . . . . 278 B2
Chaffinch Way TN12 . . . 257 A5
Chafford La TN3 . . . . . . 283 F5
Chafy Cres CT2 . . . . 143 F5
Chain Gate ME17 . . . . . 232 A8
Chain The 6 CT13 . . . . . 149 A1
Chalcombe Rd SE2 . . . . . . 3 B3
Chalcroft Rd CT20 . . . . 334 E4
Chalet Cl DA5 . . . . 32 D4
Chalfont Ct 3 DA17 . . . . . 4 A1
Chalfont Dr
Gillingham ME8 . . . . 98 D6
Herne Bay CT6 . . . . 77 D2
Chalgrove Mews ME2 . . .95 A5
Chalice Way ME2 . . . . . . .16 F2
Chalk Ave TN30 . . . . . . 324 B2
Chalk Cl CT19 . . . . 335 A7
Chalk Rd RM17 . . . . 18 A8
Chalkenden Ave ME8 . . .65 A2
Chalkers Way ME8 . . . . .65 B4
Chalket La TN12 . . . . . . 287 C5
Chalk Hill CT11,CT12 . . 116 F6
Chalk Hill Rd CT14 . . . . 248 C5
Chalk La TN17 . . . . 319 E7
Chalk Pit Ave BR5 . . . . . 54 D6
Chalkpit Hill CT4 . . . . . 176 D3
Chalk Pit Hill
Chatham ME4 . . . . 64 A3
Staple CT3 . . . . 179 B5
Chalk Pit La CT13,CT3 . . 179 C5
Lower Higham ME3 . . . . . 39 C6
Newham E13 . . . . 1 C8
Queenborough ME11 . . . 46 A5
Chalksole Green La
CT15 . . . . 276 B2
Chalkstone Cl DA16 . . . . 13 A6
Chalkways TN15 . . . . . . 122 F3
Chalkwell Ct CT17 . . . . 310 A7
Chalkwell Rd ME10 . . . . 101 D5
Chalky Bank DA11 . . . . . 37 A3
Chalky Bank Rd ME8 . . . .65 F2
Chalky Rd ME9 . . . . 132 C6
Challenge Cl DA12 . . . . . 37 F4
Challenger Cl
Paddock Wood TN12 . . . 256 F6
Sittingbourne ME10 . . . . 101 E7
Challock Ct TN16 . . . . . 118 C3
Challock Ct CT9 . . . . .51 F2
Challock Ho
3 Erith DA8 . . . . .14 F7
3 Orpington BR5 . . . . . . 54 D1
Challock Prim Sch
TN25 . . . . 203 B1
Challock Wlk ME14 . . . . 162 C6
Chalmers Way ME8 . . . . 65 A4
Chamberlain Ave
ME16 . . . . 161 C2
Chamberlain Cl 5 SE28 . . .2 D3
Chamberlain Ct ME8 . . . .98 B5
Chamberlain Dr CT6 . . . . 76 B4
Chamberlain Rd
Chatham ME4 . . . . .64 B2
Dover CT17 . . . . 310 B8
Chambers Cl 2 DA9 . . . . 17 A2
Chancel Cl TN15 . . . . . . .90 E3
Chancel Ct CT12 . . . . . . 142 D1
Chancellor Ho TN4 . . . . 285 F3
Chancellor Way TN13 . . 154 A5
Chancelot Rd SE2 . . . . . . .3 B2
Chance Mdw CT15 . . . . 278 E6
Chancery Cl DA1 . . . . . . 34 A7
Chancery La ME15 . . . . 162 B3
Chancery Rd ME3 . . . . . .22 B5
Chanctonbury Chase
CT5 . . . . 108 A6
Chanctonbury Cl SE9 . . . 30 B5
Chandler Ave E16 . . . . . . 1 A8
Chandlers Dr DA8 . . . . . . .4 E2
Chandler's Hill DA13 . . . . 93 C5
Chandlers Mews DA9 . . . 17 C3
Chandler's Rd DA13 . . . . 93 C5
Chandlers Wharf ME1 . . . 63 B5
Chandos Rd
17 Broadstairs CT10 . . . .84 B4
Royal Tunbridge Wells
TN1 . . . . 286 C5
Chandos Sq 16 CT10 . . . .84 B4
Chandos Terr CT12 . . . . 117 E7
Channel Cl CT19 . . . . . . 335 F7
Channel Lea CT14 . . . . . 215 C1
Channel Rd CT9 . . . . 83 A6
Channel Sch The
CT19 . . . . 335 C7
Channel View Ct 19
CT11 . . . . 117 F7
Channel View 20 CT19 . 335 E5

Channel View Rd
CT17 . . . . 310 C5
Channel Watch TN28 . . . 373 E4
Channon Rd TN28 . . . . . 377 E7
Chantler's Hill TN12 . . . 257 A4
Chantlers Mead TN8 . . . 282 A5
Chantry Ave DA3 . . . . . . .58 E3
Chantry Cl DA14 . . . . 31 E3
Chantry Ct
15 Canterbury CT1 . . . . 142 F1
Gravesend DA12 . . . . . . 19 C1
Chantry La BR2 . . . . .52 D4
Chantry Pk CT7 . . . . . . 113 D7
Chantry Pl
Marden TN12 . . . . 259 C6
Sevenoaks TN13 . . . . . . 153 F5
Chantry Prim Sch
DA12 . . . . 19 C1
Chantry Rd TN12 . . . . . 259 C5
Chapel Alley Cotts
TN14 . . . . 122 A8
Chapel Cl Crayford DA1 . .14 E2
Etchinghill CT18 . . . . . . 305 D3
Ryarsh ME19 . . . . 126 F5
West Thurrock RM20 . . . .17 B8
Chapel Cotts ME17 . . . . 196 F5
Chapel Ct DA10 . . . . 17 C1
Chapel Farm Rd SE9 . . . .29 F6
Chapel Field Cotts DA4 . .57 B8
Chapel Hill Cl CT9 . . . . . .82 F7
Chapel Hill
Crayford DA1 . . . . .14 E2
Eythorne CT15 . . . . 245 C7
Margate CT9 . . . . 83 A6
Chapel Hos ME4 . . . . . . .94 E4
Chapel La Blean CT2 . . . 142 A7
Broad Oak CT2 . . . . 143 D7
18 Dover CT16 . . . . 310 D7
East Studdal CT15 . . . . . 246 C6
Egerton Forstal TN27 . . . 232 B2
Gillingham ME7 . . . . 98 A2
Gillingham ME8 . . . . 98 A4
Iden Green TN17 . . . . . . 342 C4
Maidstone ME14 . . . . . . 163 A5
Newchurch TN29 . . . . . . 351 C4
Rhodes Minnis CT4 . . . . 273 B4
Ripple CT14 . . . . 247 D8
St Margaret's at Cliffe
CT15 . . . . 279 D6
Sissinghurst TN17 . . . . . 321 D7
Staple CT3 . . . . 179 B6
Staplehurst TN12 . . . . . 260 F3
Sturry CT2 . . . . 143 F5
Upper Halling ME2 . . . . . 94 C4
Chapel Mews TN23 . . . . 268 C2
Chapel Place La CT11 . . 117 D7
Chapel Pl
16 Dover CT17 . . . . 310 D7
Ramsgate CT11 . . . . 117 D7
14 Royal Tunbridge Wells
TN1 . . . . 286 A2
Ticehurst TN5 . . . . 338 E1
Chapel Rd Bexley DA7 . . . 14 A3
Dymchurch TN29 . . . . . . 366 C7
Grain ME3 . . . . .27 B5
Limpsfield RH8 . . . . 183 C5
Ram Lane TN26 . . . . 234 F1
Ramsgate CT11 . . . . 117 C7
Snodland ME6 . . . . 128 A8
Sutton Valence ME17 . . . 229 E7
Tilmanstone CT14 . . . . . 213 A3
Whitfield CT16 . . . . 278 A8
Chapel Row Herne CT6 . . 111 A8
Ightham TN15 . . . . 156 C6
Kingsnorth TN23 . . . . . . 300 A3
Lydd TN29 . . . . 376 C6
Ram Lane TN26 . . . . 234 F1
Chapelsite Ct 6 CT17 . . . .4 A2
Chapel St Deal CT14 . . . 215 D6
East Malling ME19 . . . . . 160 A6
Faversham ME13 . . . . . . 138 D6
Herne Bay CT6 . . . . 77 A5
Hythe CT21 . . . . 333 B2
Minster (Sheppey) ME12 . .47 D6
Ryarsh ME19 . . . . 126 F5
Sheerness ME12 . . . . 28 A2
Chapel The
Chartham CT4 . . . . 173 F1
Maidstone ME16 . . . . . . 161 B3
Chapel View TN15 . . . . 156 C6
Chapel Wlk
Goathurst Common
TN14 . . . . 186 B5
Maypole DA2 . . . . .32 C6
Chapel Wood DA3 . . . . . . 57 A3
Chapel Wood Rd DA3,
TN15 . . . . .91 E8
Chaplains Wlk CT4 . . . . 173 E1
Chaplin Cl ME3 . . . . 40 C3
Chaplin Dr TN27 . . . . . . 262 D5
Chapman Ave ME15 . . . 195 E8
Chapman Ho CT14 . . . . 215 B3
Chapman Rd DA17 . . . . . . 4 B1
Chapmans Cl
Challock TN25 . . . . 203 C2
Sundridge TN14 . . . . . . 152 E3
Chapmans End BR5 . . . . .54 E7
Chapmans Hill CT15,
CT3 . . . . 211 B5
Chapman's Hill DA13,
TN15 . . . . .92 A4
Chapman's La
Orpington BR5,BR8 . . . . . 54 D7
Swanley BR8 . . . . 55 A7
Chapmans Rd TN14 . . . . 152 E3
Chapman Way
East Malling ME19 . . . . . 159 F6
Royal Tunbridge Wells
TN2 . . . . 286 C3
Chappell Way ME10 . . . 101 E6

Chapter Rd ME2 . . . . . . .62 F8
Chapter Sch ME2 . . . . . . 62 D7
Chardwell Cl E6 . . . . 1 F7
Charford Rd E16 . . . . 1 A8
Charing CE Prim Sch
TN27 . . . . 234 C8
Charing Cl
Orpington BR6 . . . . .86 F6
Ramsgate CT12 . . . . 117 C8
Charing Cres CT8 . . . . . . 81 D7
Charing Heath Rd
Charing Heath TN27 . . . 233 F8
Charing TN27 . . . . 234 A1
Charing Hill TN27 . . . . . 201 E1
Charing Ho 5 DA8 . . . . . .14 F7
Charing Rd ME8 . . . . 65 B3
Charing Sta TN27 . . . . . 234 B7
Chariot Way ME2 . . . . . . .62 F4
Charity Farm Cotts
TN17 . . . . 293 F7
Charlbury Rd ME16 . . . . 161 C3
Charldane Rd SE9 . . . . . . .30 B5
Charlecote Ct ME8 . . . . . 98 D8
Charles Busby Ct
ME20 . . . . 128 F1
Charles Cl Sidcup DA14 . . .31 A8
Snodland ME6 . . . . 128 A8
Charles Cres CT19 . . . . 334 E7
Charles Ct Erith DA8 . . . .14 E8
Royal Tunbridge Wells
TN2 . . . . 286 C3
Westgate-on-S CT8 . . . . .81 F8
Charles Darwin Ho 5
BR1 . . . . 29 B1
Charles Darwin Sch
TN16 . . . . 118 F3
Charles Dickens Ave
ME3 . . . . 39 C2
Charles Dickens Ctr
(Mus)★ ME1 . . . . 63 C5
Charles Dickens Sch The
CT10 . . . . .83 E4
Charles Drayson Ct
ME13 . . . . 138 E7
Charles Dr ME2 . . . . .62 B2
Charlesfield SE9 . . . . 29 C5
Charles Flemwell Mews
ME17 . . . . 197 D3
Charlesford Ave
ME17 . . . . 197 D3
Charles Garvice Ct SE3 . 11 D4
Charles Grinling Wlk
SE18 . . . . 2 A1
Charles Ho
CT17 . . . . 278 B1
Charles Lister Ct
CT17 . . . . 278 B1
Charles Rd
Badgers Mount TN14 . . . .88 B1
Deal CT14 . . . . 215 B4
Ramsgate CT11 . . . . 117 E8
Charles St Chatham ME4 . .64 E3
Grays RM17 . . . . 18 C8
Herne Bay CT6 . . . . 77 A5
Maidstone ME16 . . . . . . 161 E3
Newham E16 . . . . 1 C5
Charles Street Centre PRU
The TN4 . . . . 286 A8
Charles St
Rochester ME2 . . . . 63 A7
Royal Tunbridge Wells
TN4 . . . . 286 A8
Sheerness ME12 . . . . 28 A3
Stone DA9 . . . . .16 F2
Charleston Ct CT10 . . . . .84 B3
Charles Whincup Rd
E16 . . . . 1 B5
Charlesworth Dr CT7 . . . .81 B7
Charlieville Rd DA8 . . . . 14 C7
Charlock Cl ME16 . . . . . . 161 C5
Charlotte Cl Bexley DA6 . .13 C2
Chatham ME5 . . . . .97 B6
Charlotte Ct
Chislehurst BR7 . . . . 30 B2
4 Ramsgate CT11 . . . . . 117 E6
Charlotte Dr ME8 . . . . . . 65 C1
Charlotte Park Ave
BR1 . . . . .52 E6
Charlotte Pl
2 Margate CT9 . . . . .50 J1
West Thurrock RM20 . . . .17 B8
Charlottes Cotts TN11 . . 220 F1
Charlotte Sq 8 CT9 . . . . .50 J2
Charlotte St
13 Broadstairs CT10 . . . .84 B4
Folkestone CT20 . . . . . . 335 E5
Sittingbourne ME10 . . . . 101 B5
Charlton Ave CT16 . . . . 278 C1
Charlton CE Prim Sch
SE7 . . . . 1 C2
Charlton Church La SE7 . .1 C1
Charlton Cl
Ashford TN24 . . . . 301 A8
Ramsgate CT12 . . . . .83 B2
Charlton Cres 2 TN9 . . . 222 C2
Charlton Ctr 3 CT17 . . 310 C8
Charlton Dene SE7 . . . . . 11 D7
Charlton Dr TN16 . . . . . 118 D2
Charlton Gate Bsns Pk
SE7 . . . . 1 C2
Charlton Gn CT16 . . . . . 278 C1
Charlton La
Chartway Street ME17 . . 197 C1
Greenwich SE7 . . . . 1 D1
Sutton Valence ME17 . . . 230 C8
West Farleigh ME15 . . . . 193 C6
Charlton Manor ME7 . . . .64 B5
Charlton Manor Prim Sch
SE7 . . . . 11 D7
Charlton Park Rd SE7 . . . 11 D8
Charlton Rd SE3,SE7 . . . .11 B8
Charlton Sch SE7 . . . . . . 11 E8

Charlton Sta SE7 . . . . .1 C1
Charltons The ME13 . . . 139 F4
Charlton St RM20 . . . . . . 17 D8
Charlton St ME16 . . . . . 161 C2
Charlton's Way TN4 . . . . 285 E1
Charminster TN23 . . . . . 299 E6
Charmouth Rd DA16 . . . . 13 C6
Charnock BR8 . . . . .87 B1
Charnwood La BR6 . . . . . .87 B1
Charnwood Villas BR6 . . 87 C1
Charne The TN14 . . . . . 122 A2
Charnock BR8 . . . . .55 E5
Charnwood Rd CT6 . . . . . 77 B1
Charnwood CT5 . . . . 75 D1
Charollais Cl CT2 . . . . . . 143 A2
Chartam Terr CT11 . . . . 117 D5
Chart Cl ME13 . . . . 138 B7
Chart Cnr ME17 . . . . . . 196 B1
Charter Dr DA5 . . . . .31 E8
Charter Ho 11 CT16 . . . 310 E7
Charterhouse Dr
TN13 . . . . 154 A4
Charterhouse Rd BR6 . . . 87 A6
Charter St Chatham ME4 . .63 F2
Gillingham ME7 . . . . .64 C7
Chartham Downs Rd
CT4 . . . . 207 C7
Chartham Prim Sch
CT4 . . . . 173 C2
Chartham Sta CT4 . . . . . 173 D3
Chart Hill Rd
Chart Sutton ME17 . . . . 196 B1
Sutton Valence ME17 . . . 229 A4
Chart Hills Cl SE28 . . . . . 3 E7
Chart La TN16 . . . . 185 B7
Chart Mill Gun Powder
Mills★ ME13 . . . . 138 B7
Charton Cl 5 DA17 . . . . . .13 F8
Chart Pl ME8 . . . . 98 C3
Chart Rd
Ashford,Godinton Park
TN23 . . . . 267 F2
Ashford,Great Chart
TN23 . . . . 267 D1
Ashford,Stanhope TN23 . 299 D6
Folkestone CT19 . . . . . . 334 F6
Sutton Valence ME17 . . . 229 C7
Chart Road Ind Est
TN23 . . . . 268 A3
Chart View TN15 . . . . . . 123 B2
Chartway TN13 . . . . 154 C3
Chartway St ME17 . . . . 197 C1
Chartwell Ave CT6 . . . . . 77 C4
Chartwell Bsns Ctr
BR1 . . . . 52 D6
Chartwell Cl
Rochester ME2 . . . . .40 B1
Sidcup SE9 . . . . 30 D6
Chartwell Ct
Chatham ME4 . . . . .63 E4
Maidstone ME15 . . . . . . 162 B3
Chartwell Dr
Maidstone ME16 . . . . . . 161 B4
Orpington BR6 . . . . .86 D5
Chartwell Gr ME10 . . . . 101 C3
Chartwell★ TN16 . . . . . 184 F4
Chase Sq 14 DA11 . . . . . 19 B1
Chase The Bexley DA7 . . .14 B4
Bromley BR1 . . . . .52 B6
Chatham ME4 . . . . 63 D2
Gillingham ME8 . . . . 65 A2
Kemsing TN15 . . . . 122 E3
Pratt's Bottom BR6 . . . . . 87 A1
Ramsgate CT11 . . . . .83 F1
St Margaret's at Cliffe
CT15 . . . . 247 F1
Tonbridge TN10 . . . . . . 222 C5
West Thurrock RM20 . . . .17 D8
Chastilian Rd DA1 . . . . . . 33 A8
Chater Cl CT14 . . . . 215 C4
Chatfield Way ME19 . . . 128 B1
Chatham Ave BR2 . . . . . . 52 A2
Chatham Ct CT11 . . . . . 117 D8
Chatham Gram Sch for
Boys ME4 . . . . .96 F8
Chatham Gram Sch for
Girls ME5 . . . . 64 C2
Chatham Gr ME4 . . . . . . .63 F1
Chatham Hill ME4 . . . . . .64 B3
Chatham Hill Rd TN14 . . 154 C6
Chatham House Gram Sch
for Boys CT11 . . . . 117 E7
Chatham Ho 16 SE18 . . . .1 F2
Chatham Pl CT11 . . . . . . 117 E7
Chatham Rd
Kit's Coty ME20 . . . . 129 D6
Sandling ME14 . . . . 129 E1
Sandling ME20 . . . . 129 E4
Chatham Ski Ctr ME7 . . . .97 E6
Chatham South Sch
ME4 . . . . .96 F8
Chatham Sta ME4 . . . . . .63 E4
Chatham St CT11 . . . . . 117 E7
Chatsworth Ave
Bromley BR1 . . . . .29 B4
Sidcup DA15 . . . . 31 A4
Chatsworth Dr
Rochester ME2 . . . . .40 B1
Sittingbourne ME10 . . . . 101 B5
Chatsworth Ho 3 BR2 . . 52 A5
Chatsworth Inf Sch
DA15 . . . . 31 A7
Chatsworth Par BR5 . . . . 53 C4
Chatsworth Rd
Dartford DA1 . . . . 15 C3
10 Gillingham ME7 . . . . 64 C6
**Chattenden Barracks Royal
Sch of Military
Engineering** ME3 . . . . .40 F5
Chattenden Ct ME14 . . . 162 B6
Chattenden La ME3 . . . . . 40 F5
Chattenden Prim Sch
ME3 . . . . .40 F4

Chattenden Terr ME3 40 F4
Chatterton Rd BR2 52 D4
Chatwell Ct ME7 64 C5
Chaucer Ave CT5 75 B1
Chaucer Bsns Pk TN15 155 D8
Chaucer Cl
Canterbury CT1 175 C7
13 Maidstone ME15 195 E7
Rochester ME2 63 E8
Tilbury RM18 19 C5
Chaucer Coll CT2 142 D3
Chaucer Cres CT16 278 B3
Chaucer Ct CT1 175 B7
Chaucer Gdns TN9 253 F7
Chaucer Hospl CT4 175 A4
Chaucer Ind Pk TN15 155 D8
Chaucer Mews CT2 141 E1
Chaucer Pk DA1 33 F8
Chaucer Rd Bexley DA16 12 F6
Broadstairs CT10 84 A3
Canterbury CT1 143 C1
Elvington CT15 212 B2
Gillingham ME7 64 D3
Northfleet DA11 36 D5
Sidcup DA15 31 C7
Sittingbourne ME10 101 D3
Chaucer Tech Sch CT1 175 C7
Chaucer Way
Dartford DA1 16 A3
New Hythe ME20 128 A3
Chaucer Wood Ct CT1 143 B1
Chaundrye Cl SE9 11 F1
Chauntler Cl E16 1 B6
Chave Rd DA2 33 E5
Cheddar Cl TN24 268 B4
Cheeselands TN27 294 F2
Cheesmans Cl CT12 115 C5
Cheffins Ho ME7 64 E7
Chegwell Dr ME5 97 B4
Chegworth Gdns ME10 101 E1
Chegworth La ME17 198 A6
Chegworth Rd ME17 197 F5
Cheldoc Rise ME4 41 C2
Chellows La RH7 216 A1
Chelmar Rd ME7 64 B4
Chelmsford Cl E6 1 F7
Chelmsford Ho ME15 195 E6
Chelmsford Rd ME2 62 D6
Chelsea Ct
6 Bromley BR1 52 E6
Hythe CT21 333 C1
Chelsea Rd CT1 143 C4
Chelsfield Hill BR6 87 C2
Chelsfield Ho ME16 161 D5
Chelsfield La
Badgers Mount BR6,TN14 88 B2
Chelsfield BR5,BR6 87 D7
Orpington BR5 54 D1
Chelsfield Park Hospl BR6 87 F5
Chelsfield Prim Sch BR6 87 E5
Chelsfield Rd BR5 54 C3
Chelsfield Sta BR6 87 B5
Chelsiter Ct DA14 30 F4
Chelsworth Dr SE18 12 D8
Cheltenham Cl
Gravesend DA12 37 C3
Maidstone ME15 195 F6
Cheltenham Rd BR6 87 A7
Cheney Cl ME8 98 D5
Cheney Hill ME9 135 A5
Cheney Rd ME13 138 F7
Chenies Cl TN2 314 A8
Chenies The
Joyden's Wood DA2 32 E4
Orpington BR6 53 E3
Chennell Park Rd TN30 323 E1
Chennels The TN26 324 C7
Chepstow Ho 3 ME15 195 F6
Chequer La CT3 147 D2
Chequer's Terr ME12 48 A5
Chequers Cl
Chatham ME5 130 A8
Istead Rise DA13 59 F7
Orpington BR5 53 F5
Chequer's Cotts TN17 318 F8
Chequers Ctr ME15 162 A4
Chequers Ct ME2 40 A1
Chequers Hill Cotts TN8 219 A2
Chequers Hill CT4 207 C2
Chequers La RM9 3 F8
Chequers Pk TN25 237 E1
Chequers Rd ME12 47 E6
Chequertree TN25 329 B7
Cherbourg Cres ME5 96 F7
Cherbury Cl SE28 3 D7
Cheriton Apartments CT19 334 F6
Cheriton Ave Hayes BR2 52 A4
Ramsgate CT12 117 B8
Cheriton Court Rd CT20 334 C6
Cheriton Ct 12 SE12 29 A8
Cheriton Dr SE18 12 D8
Cheriton Gdns CT20 335 C4
Cheriton High St CT19 334 D6
Cheriton Intc CT19 334 C7
Cheriton Pl Deal CT14 215 D4
Folkestone CT20 335 D4
Cheriton Prim Sch CT20 334 C6
Cheriton Rd Deal CT14 215 D4
Folkestone CT19,CT20 335 B5
Folkestone, Morehall CT19 334 F6
Gillingham ME8 98 D8
Cheriton Way ME16 161 C7
Cheriton Wood Ho CT19 334 D7
Cherries The ME16 161 A2
Cherry Amber Cl ME8 98 F8
Cherry Ave
Canterbury CT2 142 D2
Swanley BR8 55 D5
Cherrybrook Rd CT20 334 D6
Cherry Cl
Lenham ME17 199 C5
Sittingbourne ME10 101 D6
Cherrycot Hill BR6 86 D6
Cherrycot Rise BR6 86 C6
Cherry Ct
Ashford TN23 268 B1
Broadstairs CT10 83 E7
Folkestone CT19 335 A6
Sidcup DA14 31 B5
Cherrydown Rd DA14 31 D6
Cherry Dr CT2 142 D2
Cherryfields TN17 342 D6
Cherry Fields ME10 101 A5
Cherry Garden Ave CT19 335 A7
Cherry Garden Cres TN25 237 F2
Cherry Garden La CT3 147 E1
Cherrygarden La CT15,CT3 211 E7
Cherry Garden La
Folkestone CT19 334 F7
Wye TN25 237 F2
Cherry Garden Rd CT2 142 D2
Cherry Gdns
Broadstairs CT10 83 C3
Elham CT4 273 F5
Herne Bay CT6 76 F4
Littlestone-on-Sea TN28 373 D6
Teynham ME9 103 C2
Cherry Glebe TN25 301 E3
Cherry Gr
Elvington CT15 212 B2
Tonbridge TN10 222 E5
Cherry Hill Ct ME9 100 B6
Cherry La CT14 214 D3
Cherry Orchard Cl BR5 54 C4
Cherry Orchard La TN25 329 E4
Cherry Orchard Mews CT3 144 F1
Cherry Orchard Prim Sch SE7 11 C7
Cherry Orchard Rd BR2 85 E8
Cherry Orchard Way ME16 161 B3
Cherry Orch
Ditton ME20 160 C8
Greenwich SE7 11 C8
Littlebourne CT3 144 F1
Old Wives Lees CT4 172 C2
Tenterden TN30 345 A6
Cherry Orch The TN11 190 E1
Cherry Orch
Whitstable CT5 109 C8
Woodchurch TN26 326 A3
Cherry Rd ME3 41 E3
Cherry Tree Ave CT16 278 C1
Cherry Tree Cl
Grays RM17 18 C8
Teynham ME9 103 D2
West Minst ME12 46 A8
Cherry Tree Ct 10 SE7 11 C8
Cherry Tree Dr ME13 104 F3
Cherry Tree Gdns CT12 83 B3
Cherry Tree Gr TN15 90 B1
Cherry Tree La DA2 32 F5
Cherry Tree Rd
Charing Heath TN27 233 E7
Gillingham ME8 98 F8
Royal Tunbridge Wells TN2 285 E1
Tonbridge TN10 222 D7
Cherry Trees DA3 58 F4
Cherry View ME17 195 B3
Cherry Waye CT15 245 D7
Cherry Wlk BR2 52 A1
Cherrywood Dr DA11 36 E5
Cherrywood Rise TN25 267 F4
Cherville La CT3 177 C7
Chervilles ME16 161 A2
Chervil Mews SE28 3 B5
Cherwell Cl TN10 222 B4
Chesfield Cl TN11 190 F1
Chesham Ave BR5 53 B3
Chesham Dr ME8 98 E6
Cheshire Rd
Maidstone ME15 195 E7
Maidstone,Willington ME15 162 E2
Cheshunt Cl DA13 60 A3
Cheshunt Rd DA17 4 A1
Chesil Ho 1 BR7 53 D8
Chessenden La TN27 264 A1
Chessington Ave DA7 13 E7
Chester Ave
Bethersden TN26 297 D5
Royal Tunbridge Wells TN2 286 D2
Chester Cl ME2 62 D6
Chesterfield Cl BR5 54 D5
Chesterfield Dr
Dartford DA1 15 B2
Sevenoaks TN13 153 D5
Chesterford Ho SE18 11 D7
Chester Rd
Gillingham ME7 64 D2
Sidcup DA15 12 E2
Westgate-on-S CT8 81 F8
Chesterton Rd
Cliffe ME3 22 B5
5 Lunsford ME20 127 F4
Chesterton Way RM18 19 C5
Chestfield Cl ME8 65 E2
Chestfield Rd CT5 109 C7
Chestfield & Swalecliffe Sta CT5 75 D2
Chestnut Ave
Blean CT2 142 A7
Chatham ME5 96 F3
Hill Park TN16 151 A6
Royal Tunbridge Wells TN4 286 B8
Staplehurst TN12 260 F4
Stone DA9 34 F8
Tatsfield TN16 150 E5
Chestnut Cl
Ashford TN23 267 E3
Chartham CT4 173 F1
Edenbridge TN8 217 B2
Frittenden TN17 293 E6
Hythe CT21 353 E8
Kings Hill ME19 159 A2
Northfleet DA11 18 F1
Orpington BR6 87 A5
Royal Tunbridge Wells TN4 286 B8
Sidcup DA15 31 A6
Tenterden TN30 324 C1
Ulcombe ME17 230 F6
Whitfield CT16 278 A8
Chestnut Copse RH8 183 B2
Chestnut Ct
Boughton Street ME13 140 A3
Royal Tunbridge Wells TN2 314 A8
Chestnut Dr Bexley DA7 13 E4
Broadstairs CT10 83 D4
Coxheath ME17 194 B3
Herne Bay CT6 76 D3
Kingswood ME17 197 D2
Sturry CT2 144 A7
Worth CT14 181 A4
Chestnut Gr DA2 32 E4
Chestnut Ho 5 ME16 161 A3
Chestnut La
Kingsnorth TN23 300 C4
Matfield TN12 256 D1
Sevenoaks TN13 154 B3
Vigo Village DA13 126 B8
Chestnut Pl TN8 282 A6
Chestnut Rd
Dartford DA1 33 D7
Dover CT17 310 B7
Rochester ME2 62 E6
Chestnut Rise SE18 2 E1
Chestnuts Royal BR7 30 D1
Chestnut St ME9 100 E4
Chestnuts The
Addington ME19 126 C3
Brabourne Lees TN25 302 D5
Chislehurst BR7 30 D1
7 Erith DA17 3 F1
Sellindge TN25 303 D1
The Moor TN18 354 F8
Woolwich SE18 12 B6
Chestnut Terr CT21 333 A1
Chestnut Wlk
Larkfield ME20 128 B2
Sevenoaks TN15 187 F6
Tonbridge TN9 221 F2
Chestnut Wood La ME9 100 E3
Cheswick Cl DA1 14 F3
Chesworth Cl DA8 14 E5
Chetney Cl ME2 62 C7
Chetney View ME9 68 D4
Chetwood Wlk 15 E6 1 E8
Chevalier Rd CT17 310 A7
Chevender BR7 30 B1
Cheveney Wlk 2 BR2 52 A6
Chevening CE Prim Sch TN13 153 B5
Chevening Cl ME5 97 A5
Chevening Ct BR6 87 A8
Chevening House BR5 54 A8
Chevening La TN14 120 E3
Chevening Rd
3 Greenwich SE10 1 A1
Sevenoaks TN13,TN14 153 B6
Sundridge TN14 152 F4
Chevenings The DA14 31 C5
Cheviot Cl Bexley DA7 14 E5
Tonbridge TN9 222 C4
Cheviot Ct CT10 84 B5
Cheviot Gdns ME15 163 A1
Cheviot Ho DA11 18 D1
Cheviot Way TN24 268 C4
Chevron Cl E16 1 A7
Chevron Ho RM17 18 B7
Cheyne Cl
Orpington BR2 85 E7
Sittingbourne ME10 101 F8
Cheyne Mid Sch The ME12 28 D2
Cheyne Rd ME12 48 D3
Cheyne Wlk
Longfield DA3 58 D6
Meopham DA13 93 A8
Chicago Ave ME7 64 F5
Chichester Cl
Ashford TN23 268 B1
Gillingham ME8 99 A8
Greenwich SE3 11 C6
Newham E6 1 E7
Chichester Ct 3 DA5 32 A8
Chichester Dr TN13 153 F2
Chichester Rd
Folkestone CT20 334 E4
Ramsgate CT12 83 B1
Stone DA9 16 F1
Tonbridge TN9 254 A8
Chichester Rise DA12 37 D4
Chichester Wharf 14 DA8 4 E1
Chichester Wlk CT12 83 B1
Chickenden La NT17 261 C4
Chickfield Gdns 4 ME5 64 C2
Chicks La TN17 317 F2
Chiddingfold Cl ME12 47 D6
Chiddingstone Ave DA7 13 F7
Chiddingstone Castle★ TN8 251 B7
Chiddingstone CE Prim Sch TN8 251 C7
Chiddingstone Cl ME15 195 F6
Chidley Cross Rd TN12 224 E6
Chieftain Cl ME7 65 B1
Chieveley Dr TN2 286 D1
Chieveley Par DA7 14 B4
Chieveley Rd DA7 14 B3
Chiffinch Gdns DA11 36 E5
Childgate Rd CT5 107 F2
Childsbridge La TN15 154 F7
Childsbridge Way TN15 154 F7
Childs Cres DA10 17 D1
Childscroft Rd ME8 65 F2
Childs Way TN15 124 F3
Chilham Ave CT8 81 D7
Chilham Cl
Chatham ME4 63 E3
Sidcup DA5 31 F8
West Minst ME12 46 B8
Chilham Ho
1 Maidstone ME15 195 E8
Rochester ME2 40 C1
Chilham Rd Bromley SE9 29 E4
Folkestone CT19 334 E6
Gillingham ME8 65 A3
Maidstone ME16 161 C7
Chilham Sta CT4 205 D8
Chilham Way BR2 52 A2
Chillenden Windmill★ CT3 178 F1
Chillington Cl ME2 94 E4
Chillington St ME14 161 F6
Chilliwack Rd ME3 40 F5
Chilston Cl TN4 286 A5
Chilston Rd
Lenham ME17 199 D5
Royal Tunbridge Wells TN4 286 A5
Chiltenhurst TN8 217 A2
Chiltern Cl Bexley DA7 14 E6
Maidstone ME15 162 F1
Chiltern Ct 11 SE9 12 A1
Chiltern End TN24 268 B3
Chiltern Rd DA11 36 E5
Chilterns DA14 31 A3
Chilterns, The BR1 52 B7
Chiltern Way TN9 222 C4
Chiltern Wlk TN2 286 D4
Chilton Ave
Sittingbourne ME10 102 A3
Temple Ewell CT16 277 C4
Chilton Ct
14 Folkestone CT20 335 E6
Gillingham ME8 65 E1
Chilton Dr ME3 39 B3
Chilton Field CT3 147 D2
Chilton Gdns CT3 147 D2
Chilton La CT11 117 A6
Chilton Pl CT3 147 D2
Chilton Prim Sch CT11 117 A6
Chilton Sq CT3 147 D2
Chilton Way CT17 277 D3
Chimes The
Ashford TN24 268 C3
Rochester ME1 63 C5
Chinbrook Cres 8 SE12 29 B5
Chinbrook Rd SE12 29 B5
Chine Farm Pl TN14 120 D3
Chineham Way CT1 174 F6
Chinnery Ct DA13 60 A2
Chippendale Cl ME5 96 F1
Chippendayle Dr ME17 198 D6
Chipperfield Rd
Orpington BR5 54 A7
Orpington BR5 54 B5
Chipstead Cl ME16 161 D6
Chipstead La TN13 153 D5
Chipstead Park Cl TN13 153 C5
Chipstead Pk TN13 153 D5
Chipstead Place Gdns TN13 153 D5
Chipstead Rd Erith DA8 14 E7
Gillingham ME8 98 D4
Chipstead Sq TN13 153 C5
Chislehurst Caves★ BR7 53 A8
Chislehurst Cl ME15 195 F6
Chislehurst High St BR7 30 B2
Chislehurst Rd
Bromley BR1,BR2 52 E8
Orpington BR6 54 A2
Orpington,Broom Hill BR6 53 F2
Orpington,Petts Wood BR5,BR6 53 E4
Sidcup DA14 31 A3
Chislehurst (St Nicholas) CE Prim Sch BR7 30 C1
Chislehurst & Sidcup Gram Sch DA15 31 B6
Chislehurst Sta BR7 53 A7
Chislet CE Prim Sch CT3 112 C5
Chislet Ct CT6 76 E5
Chislet Park Cotts CT3 111 F1
Chislet Park Farm Cotts CT3 111 F2
Chislett Cl TN25 303 E2
Chislet Wlk ME8 98 D5
Chisnall Rd CT17 277 E4
Chiswell Sq SE3 11 B5
Chittenden's La TN29 364 E5
Chitty La CT3 112 D6
Chorleywood Cres BR5 54 A7
Christchurch Ave DA8 14 E8
Christ Church Ave 1 TN1 286 A2
Christ Church CE High Sch TN23 299 F5
Christ Church CE Jun Sch CT11 117 C6
Christ Church CE Sch SE18 12 A6
Christ Church Coll CT1 175 B8
Christ Church Cres 2 DA12 37 C8
Christchurch Ct
3 Chatham ME5 64 C2
1 Dover CT17 310 D7
Christ Church Erith CE Prim Sch DA8 14 D8
Christchurch Ho 11 ME15 195 E5
Christchurch Rd
Ashford TN23 300 B8
Dartford DA1 15 C1
Christ Church Rd
Folkestone CT20 335 C4
3 Gravesend DA12 37 C8
Christchurch Rd
Sidcup DA15 30 F5
Tilbury RM18 19 A6
Christchurch Way CT16 278 B3
Christen Way ME15, ME17 195 F3
Christian Ct 3 ME2 63 C8
Christian Fields Ave DA12 37 C4
Christie Cl ME5 97 B6
Christie Dr 8 ME20 127 F4
Christie Ho DA6 14 B2
Christies Ave TN14 88 B1
Christmas La ME23 23 F3
Christmas St ME7 64 E7
Christopher Bushell Way TN24 268 E4
Christopher Cl DA15 12 F2
Christopher's Row ME9 136 A3
Christy Rd TN16 118 C4
Chrysler Ave CT6 76 B4
Chudleigh 7 DA14 31 B4
Chulkhurst TN27 294 F1
Chulkhurst Cl TN27 294 F1
Chunnel Ind Est TN23 268 B1
Church Alley 11 DA11 19 B1
Church App TN28 373 A6
Church Ave DA14 31 B3
Churchbury Rd SE9 29 D8
Church Cl
Brenchley TN12 289 C8
Cliffe ME3 22 B6
Church Cliff CT14 248 D6
Church Cl
Mereworth ME18 191 D8
Mersham TN25 301 E3
New Romney TN28 373 B6
Church Cotts
Cranbrook TN17 320 D5
Crockenhill BR8 55 D2
Rodmersham ME9 135 D8
Shoreham TN14 122 A8
Sutton Valence ME17 229 E7
Tenterden TN30 324 B3
Church Court Gr CT10 83 E6
Church Cres ME17 198 F6
Church Ct Dartford DA2 33 D5
Lyminge CT18 305 C6
Church Farm Cl
Crockenhill BR8 55 D3
Hoo St Werburgh ME3 41 E4
Church Farm Rd ME9 66 E3
Church Farm Way CT13 180 B6
Churchfield ME19 126 D3
Church Field Cotts TN15 154 F7
Church Field DA2 33 D6
Churchfield TN8 217 D1
Churchfield Pl CT9 50 I2
Churchfield Rd DA16 13 A4
Churchfields CT10 83 F7
Churchfield Sch SE2 3 A2
Church Field TN13 153 F5
Churchfields CT9 50 J1
Church Field
Snodland ME6 95 B1
Stanford TN25 304 B1
Churchfields Terr ME1 63 B4
Church Fields ME19 159 B8
Churchfield Way TN25 237 E2
Church Gn
Marden TN12 259 C6
Rochester ME2 63 C8
Staplehurst TN12 260 E2
Church Green ME17 164 E3
Church Haven CT14 247 F5
Church Hill
Bethersden TN26 297 D5
Boughton Street ME13 140 A5
Church Hill *continued*
Canterbury CT2 142 C1
Charing Heath ME17, TN27 233 C7
Chatham ME5 64 C2
Chilham CT4 205 B8
Crayford DA1 14 E3
Cudham TN14,TN16 119 C4
Dartford DA2 33 D6
Doddington ME9 167 F8
Eythorne CT15 245 C8
Hawkinge CT18 307 D4
High Halden TN26 324 E7
Hythe CT21 333 C2
Kingsnorth TN23 300 B3
Leigh TN11 220 F2
Linton ME17 228 B7
Loose ME17 195 C1
Orpington BR6 54 A2
Plaxtol TN15 189 E8
Ramsgate CT11 117 E7
Shepherdswell CT15 244 D4
Stockbury ME9 132 F7
Stone DA9 16 E2
Stone in Oxney TN30 360 F3
Sutton CT15 247 A7
Tatsfield TN16 150 D5
Temple Ewell CT16 277 D5
Church Hill Wood BR5 53 F4
Church Hill SE18 1 F3
Church Ho CT14 215 C7
Church Hts CT21 333 C2
Church Hyde SE18 12 E8
Churchill Ave
Chatham ME5 97 A7
Deal CT14 215 C2
Folkestone CT19 335 C8
Herne Bay CT6 77 D4
Churchill Bsns Ctr TN16 151 D1
Churchill CE Prim Sch TN16 151 C2
Churchill Cl
Bridge CT4 175 F1
Dartford DA1 34 B7
Folkestone CT19 335 D8
St Margaret's at Cliffe CT15 279 F5
Churchill Cotts ME17 196 F6
Churchill Ct
Hythe CT21 333 B1
4 Orpington BR6 86 C5
1 Ramsgate CT11 117 D7
Westerham TN16 151 D1
Churchill Ho
Benenden TN17 342 E6
Bridge CT4 175 F1
2 Folkestone CT20 334 F5
Maidstone ME16 161 B2
Sittingbourne ME10 102 C4
Teynham ME9 103 C3
1 Woolwich SE18 2 B2
Churchill Pk DA1 16 A2
Churchill Rd
Canterbury CT1 175 C6
Dover CT17 310 A6
Grays RM17 18 D8
Horton Kirby DA4 57 C5
Minster (Sheppey) ME12 47 D6
Newham E16 1 C7
Northfleet DA11 36 F7
Churchill Sch The CT18 307 A4
Churchill Sq ME19 159 A3
Churchills Ropewalk TN17 318 E8
Churchill St 7 CT16 278 C1
Churchill Way
Biggin Hill TN16 118 D4
Bromley BR1 52 A7
Faversham ME13 105 B1
Churchill Wlk CT18 306 F4
Church La
Adisham CT3 177 D1
Aldington TN25 330 D7
Barham CT4 209 F1
Boughton Aluph TN25 237 B4
Boyden Gate CT3 112 C7
Brenzett TN29 362 F5
Canterbury CT1 174 F8
21 Canterbury,Northgate CT1 143 A1
Capel TN12 255 F6
Chalk DA12 38 C6
Challock TN25 236 B8
Chartham CT4 173 D3
Chatham ME4 63 F6
Chislehurst BR7 53 C8
Church Hougham CT15 309 B5
Deal CT14 215 B6
East Peckham TN12 224 F7
Frant TN3 314 B4
Harrietsham ME17 198 E6
Iden TN31 368 B4
Kemsing TN15 123 B2
Kingston CT4 209 D3
Lower Hardres CT4 175 B2
Lydden CT15 276 E8
Maidstone,Bearsted ME14 163 C4
Maidstone ME16 160 E1
Churchlands Ho TN28 373 B6
Churchlands ME14 162 B5
Churchlands The TN28 373 B6
Church La
Newington ME9 100 B6
New Romney TN28 373 B5
Orpington BR2 52 E1
Peasmarsh TN31 367 C1

Church La *continued*
Petham CT4 .... 207 C3
Ringwould CT14 .... 247 F5
Ripple CT14 .... 214 D1
Selling ME13 .... 171 B6
Shadoxhurst TN26 ...... 327 A7
Stockbury ME9 .... 132 E8
Stourmouth CT3 .... 113 C2
Stowting TN25 .... 304 A6
Sturry CT2 .... 143 F5
Sutton Valence ME17 ... 230 B8
Tonbridge TN9 .... 222 C2
Trottiscliffe ME19 ...... 126 B5
Waltham CT4 .... 239 F5
Westbere CT2 .... 144 C7
West Farleigh ME15 .... 193 D7
West Langdon CT15 .... 246 D3
Whitstable CT5 .... 108 A6
Womenswold CT4 ...... 210 D2
Church Manorway DA8 ... 4 D3
Church Manor Way
SE18,SE2 .... 3 A2
Church Marshes Ctry Pk★
ME10 .... 102 A7
Church Mdws CT14 .... 215 A6
Church Meadow TN12 . 290 A7
Church Mews
Gillingham ME8 .... 98 F8
Iwade ME9 .... 68 E4
Church Path
Deal CT14 .... 215 B5
Gillingham ME7 .... 64 E6
Great Mongeham CT14 .. 214 D3
Lower Halstow ME9 ..... 67 C3
Northfleet DA11 .... 18 C1
Stone DA9 .... 16 F1
Church Rd
Ashford,Aylesford Green
TN24 .... 301 A7
Ashford,Kennington
TN24 .... 268 E6
Ashford TN23 .... 268 C2
Ashford,Willesborough
TN24 .... 301 A8
Bexley DA7,DA6 .... 13 F4
Bexley,Welling DA16 ...... 13 B3
Biggin Hill TN16 .... 118 E2
Bitchet Green TN15 ..... 155 E3
Boughton Malherbe
ME17 .... 232 A8
Brasted TN16 .... 152 B3
1 Broadstairs CT10 ...... 84 B4
Bromley BR1,BR2 .... 52 A7
Burmarsh TN29 .... 351 E4
Charing TN27 .... 201 D2
Chart Sutton ME17 ..... 196 C1
Chelsfield BR6 .... 87 D4
Coldred CT15 .... 245 A3
Crockenhill BR8 .... 55 D2
Dover CT17 .... 310 A7
Eastchurch ME12 .... 48 D2
Eastling ME13 .... 169 B2
Erith DA8 .... 4 D1
Faversham ME13 ...... 138 D7
Faversham,Oare ME13 .. 105 B3
Faversham,The Brents
ME13 .... 138 D8
Folkestone CT20 .... 334 C6
Goudhurst TN17 .... 318 F8
Grafty Green ME17 ..... 231 F7
Gravesend DA12,DA13 ... 37 D1
Halstead TN14 .... 120 F7
Harrietsham ME17 ..... 198 E6
Hartley DA3 .... 59 A2
Hawley DA4 .... 33 F1
Henhurst DA13 .... 60 C8
Hoath CT3 .... 111 E5
Hucking ME17 .... 132 E1
Hythe CT21 .... 333 C2
Kenardington TN26 ..... 348 A5
Kilndown TN17 .... 317 F3
Lamberhurst TN3 ...... 317 C6
Littlebourne CT3 .... 177 A8
Lydd TN29 .... 376 C6
Lyminge CT18 .... 305 C7
Maidstone ME15 .... 195 F7
Maidstone,Tovil ME15 ... 161 E2
Margate CT9 .... 50 J1
Mersham TN25 .... 301 E3
Molash CT4 .... 203 F5
New Romney TN28 ..... 373 A6
Northbourne,Betteshanger
CT14 .... 213 C6
Northbourne CT14 ..... 214 A5
Offham ME18 .... 158 D8
Orpington BR6 .... 86 D5
Orpington, Keston BR2 ... 85 D3
Paddock Wood TN12 .... 257 B6
Pembury TN2 .... 255 D1
Pembury TN2 .... 287 D8
Ramsgate CT11 .... 117 E7
Royal Tunbridge
Wells,Southborough
TN4 .... 253 F2
Royal Tunbridge Wells
TN1 .... 286 A3
Ryarsh ME19 .... 127 A3
Sandhurst Cross TN18 .. 355 F4
Seal TN15 .... 154 F6
Sevenoaks Weald TN14 .. 187 B3
Sevington TN24 .... 301 B6
Sidcup DA14 .... 31 A4
Sittingbourne ME9 ..... 102 E5
Sittingbourne,Murston
ME10 .... 102 B5
Smeeth TN25 .... 302 C4
Stalisfield Green ME13 .. 201 F5
Stone DA9 .... 16 F2
Sundridge TN14 .... 152 E2
Sutton at H DA4 .... 34 A2
Church Rd *continued*
Sutton Valence ME17 ... 229 C8
Swanley Village BR8 ..... 56 D8
Swanscombe DA10 .... 17 F1
Tenterden TN30 .... 345 A7
Tilbury RM18 .... 18 F6
Tonbridge TN11 .... 221 D6
West Kingsdown TN15 .... 90 E3
West Peckham ME18 ... 191 A6
West Tilbury RM18 .... 19 E8
Church Rise CT21 ...... 333 C2
Church Road Bsns Ctr
ME10 .... 102 B6
Church Row BR7 .... 53 C8
Church Row Mews BR7 . 30 C1
Church Row
Plaxtol TN15 .... 189 E8
Snodland ME6 .... 128 A7
West Peckham ME18 ... 191 B6
Churchsettle La TN5 .. 337 C1
Churchside Cl TN16 .. 118 C2
Churchside DA13 ...... 126 A8
Church Sq
2 Broadstairs CT10 ..... 84 B4
Lenham ME17 .... 199 D5
Church St
Broadstairs CT10 .... 83 E6
Burham ME1 .... 95 F1
Canterbury CT2 .... 142 E1
Chatham ME4 .... 64 A4
Cliffe ME3 .... 22 B5
Cowden TN8 .... 282 B5
Deal CT14 .... 215 B1
Dover CT16 .... 310 D7
Eastry CT13 .... 180 C2
Edenbridge TN8 .... 217 D1
Faversham ME13 ...... 138 D8
Folkestone CT20 .... 335 D4
Gillingham ME7 .... 64 E6
Gravesend DA11 .... 19 B1
Grays RM17 .... 18 C8
Hadlow TN11 .... 223 E8
Hoo St Werburgh ME3 .... 41 E5
Lower Higham ME3 ...... 39 D7
Maidstone, Boughton
Monchelsea ME17 .... 195 B2
Maidstone,Loose ME15 .. 194 F5
Maidstone ME14 .... 162 A4
Maidstone,Tovil ME15 ... 161 E2
Margate CT9 .... 50 J1
Minster (Thanet) CT12 .. 115 C5
Newham E16 .... 2 B5
Nonington CT15 .... 211 C5
Northfleet DA13 .... 36 A3
Church Street (St Pauls) 7
CT1 .... 175 A8
Church St
Rochester ME1 .... 63 D4
Rodmersham ME9 ...... 135 C8
7 Sandwich CT13 ...... 149 A1
3 Sandwich,The Butts
CT13 .... 148 F1
Seal TN15 .... 155 A7
Shoreham TN14 .... 122 A8
5 Sittingbourne ME10 .. 101 E4
Sittingbourne ME10 .... 101 E5
Teston ME18 .... 193 A8
Ticehurst TN5 .... 338 D1
Tonbridge TN9 .... 222 C2
Wadhurst TN5 .... 337 A4
Whitstable CT5 .... 74 F1
Woodnesborough CT13 .. 180 B6
Wye TN25 .... 237 E2
Church Terr
Chatham ME5 .... 64 C2
Minster (Sheppey) ME12 . 47 C7
Church Trad Est DA8 ... 15 A7
Church View
Aldington TN25 .... 330 A6
Biddenden TN27 .... 294 F2
4 Dartford DA1 .... 15 E1
Herne Bay CT6 .... 77 C4
Newchurch TN29 ...... 350 E3
Swanley BR8 .... 55 D6
Worth CT14 .... 181 B5
Church Way CT5 .... 75 D3
Church Whitfield Rd
CT16 .... 278 B8
Church Wlk
Dartford DA2 .... 33 D5
East Malling ME19 ..... 160 A7
Elham CT4 .... 273 F4
Eynsford DA4 .... 89 E7
Gravesend DA12 .... 37 D7
Gravesend DA12 .... 37 D8
Hawkhurst TN18 .... 341 A1
Headcorn TN27 .... 262 C5
Church Wood Cl CT2 .. 142 B2
Churchwood Dr CT5 .... 75 D1
Churchyard Cotts
TN3 .... 285 A8
Church Yard Pas 10
TN23 .... 268 B2
Church Yd TN23 .... 268 C2
Churn La TN12 .... 258 A2
Chute Cl ME8 .... 98 D4
Chyngton Cl DA15 ...... 30 F5
Cimba Wood DA12 ...... 37 E4
Cinder Hill La TN11 ... 220 C1
Cinderhill Wood Cvn Site
TN12 .... 256 C1
Cinderhill Wood TN12 . 256 C2
Cinder Path CT10 ...... 84 A4
Cinnabar Cl ME5 .... 97 A1
Cinnabar Dr ME10 .... 101 C6
Cinque Ports Ave
CT21 .... 333 B1
Cinque Ports Rd TN28 . 373 C5
Circle The RM18 .... 19 A6
Circuit Rd SE28 .... 3 A4
Circular Rd
Dover CT16 .... 279 B1
Finglesham CT14 .... 214 B7
Circular Way SE18 ..... 12 A8
Circus The CT6 .... 76 E4
Cirrus Cres DA12 .... 37 E3
Citadel Cres CT17 ..... 310 B6
Citadel Hts CT17 ...... 310 B6
Citadel Rd CT17 ...... 310 C6
Citadel The (Immigration
Removal Ctr) CT17 ... 310 B5
Citroen Cl CT6 .... 76 B4
City Bsns Pk CT1 ...... 143 C3
City Garden The 3
CT1 .... 175 A8
City View CT2 .... 174 C8
City Way ME1 .... 63 D2
Civic Sq RM18 .... 19 A5
Civic Way TN1 .... 286 A3
CJ Gallards Almshouses
TN4 .... 286 A8
Clacket La
Tatsfield TN16 .... 150 E2
Westerham TN16 ...... 184 A8
Clacketts Farm ME19 .. 127 B5
Claire Ct Birchington CT7 .. 80 F7
Broadstairs CT10 .... 84 B5
Claire Ho 4 ME16 ..... 161 E5
Clancy Gdns TN17 .... 320 B5
Clandon Ct BR1 .... 29 A2
Clandon Rd ME5 .... 97 D2
Clanricarde Gdns 1
TN1 .... 286 A3
Clanricarde Rd 2
TN1 .... 286 A3
Clanwilliam Rd CT14 .. 215 D5
Clapham Hill CT5 ..... 108 D5
Claphatch La TN5 ..... 338 A5
Clapper La TN12 ...... 260 D6
Clara Pl SE18 .... 2 A2
Clare Ave TN9 .... 221 F1
Clare Cnr SE9 .... 30 B8
Clare Cswy DA9 .... 16 F3
Clare Ct BR7 .... 52 F8
Clare Dr CT6 .... 76 C2
Clare La ME19 .... 159 E8
Claremont Cl
Kingsdown CT14 .... 248 C6
Newham E16 .... 2 A5
Orpington BR6 .... 86 A6
Claremont Cres DA1 .... 14 E3
Claremont Ct 4 TN2 .. 286 C7
Claremont Gdns
Ramsgate CT11 .... 117 C7
Royal Tunbridge Wells
TN2 .... 286 B2
Claremont Pl
Canterbury CT1 .... 174 F7
1 Gravesend DA11 ...... 37 B8
Iden Green TN17 ...... 342 C4
Marden TN12 .... 259 D4
Claremont Prim Sch
TN2 .... 286 B2
Claremont Rd
Bromley BR1 .... 52 F5
Deal CT14 .... 215 B5
Folkestone CT20 .... 335 C5
Hextable BR8 .... 32 E1
Kingsdown CT14 .... 248 C6
Maidstone ME14 .... 162 B5
Royal Tunbridge Wells
TN1 .... 286 B2
Claremont St
Herne Bay CT6 .... 76 C4
Newham E16 .... 2 A4
Claremont Terr CT13 .. 180 D7
Claremont Way 2 ME4 .. 63 F3
Clarence Ave
Bromley BR1 .... 52 E5
Margate CT9 .... 51 D2
Rochester ME1 .... 63 C4
Clarence Cres DA14 .... 31 B5
Clarence Ct
2 Grays RM17 .... 18 B8
Maidstone ME14 .... 162 E4
Pratt's Bottom BR6 ...... 87 C2
Clarence Gdns ME12 .... 49 E3
Clarence Lodge TN1 .. 286 A3
Clarence Pl Deal CT14 . 215 D7
Dover CT17 .... 310 D5
Gravesend DA12 .... 37 B7
Clarence Rd Bexley DA6 .. 13 E3
Biggin Hill TN16 .... 118 F1
Bromley,Mottingham SE9 .. 29 E6
Bromley,Widmore BR1 .... 52 E6
Capel-le-F CT18 .... 308 B2
Chatham ME4 .... 64 B2
Deal CT14 .... 215 D3
Grays RM17 .... 18 B8
Herne Bay CT6 .... 76 D5
Ramsgate CT11 .... 117 C6
Royal Tunbridge Wells
TN1 .... 286 A3
Sidcup DA14 .... 31 B5
Clarence Row
Gravesend DA12 .... 37 B8
Royal Tunbridge Wells
TN1 .... 286 A3
Sheerness ME12 .... 28 B2
Clarence St
Folkestone CT20 .... 335 D5
Herne Bay CT6 .... 76 E5
Clarendon Cl
Maidstone ME14 .... 163 A4
Orpington BR5 .... 54 A6
Sittingbourne ME10 .... 101 F1
Clarendon Ct TN13 .... 154 A2
Clarendon Dr ME2 ...... 40 A1
Clarendon Gdns
Dartford DA2 .... 34 D8
7 Ramsgate CT11 ...... 117 D6
Royal Tunbridge Wells
TN2 .... 286 A1
Clarendon Gn BR5 ...... 54 A5
Clarendon Gr BR5 ...... 54 A5
Clarendon House Gram Sch
CT11 .... 117 E6
Clarendon Mews
1 Broadstairs CT10 .... 84 A4
New Romney TN28 ..... 373 C8
Sidcup DA5 .... 32 B7
Clarendon Path BR5 .... 54 A6
Clarendon Pl
Dover CT17 .... 310 C7
Joyden's Wood DA2 ...... 32 E3
Maidstone ME14 .... 162 A4
Sevenoaks TN13 .... 154 A2
Clarendon Rd
Aylesham CT3 .... 210 F5
Broadstairs CT10 .... 84 A4
Dover CT17 .... 310 C7
Gravesend DA12 .... 19 C1
Margate CT9 .... 51 A2
Sevenoaks TN13 .... 154 A2
Clarendon St
Dover CT17 .... 310 C7
Herne Bay CT6 .... 76 C4
Clarendon Way
Royal Tunbridge Wells
TN2 .... 286 A1
St Paul's Cray BR5,BR7 .... 53 F6
Clare Rd CT5 .... 74 E2
Claret Ho TN13 .... 154 B3
Clareville Rd BR5 ...... 86 C8
Clare Way Bexley DA7 .... 13 E6
Sevenoaks TN13 .... 187 C8
Clarewood Dr ME19 ... 159 E8
Claridge Ct ME7 .... 97 F4
Claridge Mews CT21 .. 333 C2
Claridge TN4 .... 286 B6
Clarkbourne Dr RM17 .. 18 D8
Clark Cl DA8 .... 15 A6
Clarke Cres TN24 ..... 268 F4
Clarke's Cl CT14 ...... 214 F4
Clarkes Green Rd
TN15 .... 123 B5
Clarklands TN29 ...... 350 E3
Clark Mews ME20 ..... 128 F1
Clark Rd TN28 .... 373 E4
Clarks La
Halstead TN14 .... 120 F7
Titsey CR6,RH8,TN16 ... 150 C4
Clark's Yd TN5 .... 339 A3
Claston Cl DA1 .... 14 E3
Claudius Gr TN23 ..... 299 F5
Clavadal Rd TN12 ..... 257 A7
Clavell Cl ME8 .... 98 E4
Claxfield Cotts ME9 ... 103 A2
Claxfield Rd ME9 ..... 136 A8
Claybridge Rd SE12 .... 29 C4
Clay Cotts TN17 ...... 318 E8
Claydown Mews SE18 .... 2 A1
Clayfarm Rd SE9 .... 30 C6
Claygate TN23 .... 299 F5
Claygate Cross TN15 .. 157 A3
Claygate ME17 .... 164 D2
Claygate La TN11 ..... 189 F4
Claygate ME15 .... 162 D1
Claygate Rd TN12 ..... 226 B2
Clayhill Cres SE9 .... 29 D4
Clayhill TN17 .... 318 D8
Clay Hill Mount TN17 .. 318 E8
Clay Hill Rd TN3 ...... 316 D6
Claymill Ho 2 SE18 ...... 2 C1
Clayton Cl 3 E6 .... 1 F7
Clayton Croft Rd DA2 ... 33 A6
Clayton's La TN3 ..... 283 E2
Claytonville Terr DA17 .... 4 C4
Clay Wood Cl BR6 ...... 53 E2
Claywood La DA2 ...... 35 D5
Clayworth Cl DA15 ..... 13 B1
Cleanthus Cl SE18 ...... 12 B6
Cleanthus Rd SE18 ...... 12 B6
Clearmount Dr TN27 .. 234 C8
Clearmount Pk TN27 .. 234 D8
Clearways Bsns Est
TN15 .... 90 E3
Clearways Mobile Home Pk
TN15 .... 90 D3
Clearway ME19 .... 126 A1
Cleave Ave BR6 .... 86 E4
Cleave Rd ME7 .... 64 E3
Cleaver La CT11 .... 117 E7
Cleavers Cl TN17 ...... 321 A8
Cleavers TN17 .... 321 A8
Cleavesland ME18 ..... 225 E5
Cleeve Ave TN2 .... 286 D2
Cleeve Ct ME19 .... 159 B3
Cleeve Park Gdns
DA14 .... 31 B6
Cleeve Park Sch DA14 .. 31 C5
Clegg Ho SE3 .... 11 B3
Clematis Ave ME8 .... 98 B5
Clemens Pl ME18 ..... 159 C2
Clement Cl
Canterbury CT1 .... 143 B1
Sittingbourne ME10 .... 101 E8
Clement Ct ME16 ...... 161 D5
Clementine Cl CT6 ..... 77 D4
Clements Ave E16 .... 1 A6
Clement's Rd CT12 ..... 83 C2
Clement St BR8,DA4 ..... 33 E2
Cleminson Ct DA14 ..... 31 D2
Clenches Farm La
TN13 .... 154 A1
Clenches Farm Rd
TN13 .... 154 A1
Clendon Way SE18 .... 2 D2
Clerke Dr ME10 .... 102 A8
Clerks Field TN27 .... 262 D5
Clermont Cl ME7 .... 98 A4
Clevedon Ct TN25 .... 203 B2
Clevedon Ho BR1 .... 29 E1
Cleveland Cl CT16 .... 278 B3
Cleveland Ct CT9 .... 51 A3
Cleveland Ho
Maidstone ME16 .... 161 B2
Northfleet DA11 .... 18 D1
Cleveland Rd
Bexley DA16 .... 12 F5
Gillingham ME7 .... 64 D6
Cleveland TN2 .... 286 D4
Cleveley Lo CT11 .... 83 E2
Clevely Cl SE7 .... 1 D2
Cleven Lodge CT7 ..... 113 D6
Cleve Rd DA14 .... 31 D5
Cleves Rd TN15 .... 122 E2
Cleves View 4 DA1 .... 15 D1
Cleves Way TN23 ..... 299 E8
Clewer Ho 8 SE2 .... 3 D4
Clewer Lo CT5 .... 74 F2
Clewson Rise ME14 ... 162 B8
Cliff Ave CT6 .... 77 C5
Cliff Cl CT21 .... 333 D3
Cliff Cottage Chalet Pk
ME12 .... 48 F6
Cliff Dr Herne Bay CT6 ... 76 C4
Warden ME12 .... 49 E4
Cliffe Ave CT9 .... 50 F1
Cliffe Ct ME3 .... 22 B5
Cliffe Ho
Folkestone CT20 .... 335 A3
St Margaret's at Cliffe
CT15 .... 279 F6
Cliffe Pools Nature
Reserve★ ME3 .... 5 E1
Cliffe Rd Deal CT14 .... 248 D6
Rochester ME2 .... 40 A1
Cliffestone Ct CT20 ... 335 B5
Cliffe Woods Prim Sch
ME3 .... 40 C8
Cliff Field CT8 .... 81 C8
Cliff Gdns ME12 .... 47 E7
Cliff Hill ME17 .... 195 D4
Cliff Hill Rd ME17 ..... 195 C4
Clifford Ave BR7 .... 29 F2
Clifford Gdns CT14 ... 215 B2
Clifford Ho 6 ME14 ... 162 B4
Clifford Rd CT5 .... 108 F8
Cliff Prom CT10 .... 84 C7
Cliff Rd Birchington CT7 .. 80 F8
Broadstairs CT10 .... 84 B7
Dover CT15,CT16 ...... 279 C1
Folkestone CT20 .... 335 A3
Hythe CT21 .... 333 E3
Whitstable CT5 .... 74 F3
Cliff Reach DA9 .... 16 F6
Cliff Sea Gr CT6 .... 76 C4
Cliffs End Gr CT12 .... 116 D5
Cliffs End Rd CT12 .... 116 E5
Cliffside Dr CT10 ...... 84 A1
Cliff St CT11 .... 117 E6
Cliff Terr CT9 .... 50 J3
Clifftown Gdns CT6 .... 76 B4
Cliff View Gdns
Leysdown-on-S ME12 .... 49 D1
Warden ME12 .... 49 E4
Cliff View Rd CT12 .... 116 D6
Clifton Cl
Maidstone ME14 .... 162 B5
8 Orpington BR6 .... 86 C5
Rochester ME2 .... 62 F7
Clifton Cotts TN2 ..... 286 D8
Clifton Cres CT20 ..... 335 B3
Clifton Gdns
Canterbury CT2 .... 142 D2
Folkestone CT20 .... 335 C4
Margate CT9 .... 50 J3
Whitstable CT5 .... 108 D8
Clifton Gr DA11 .... 37 B8
Clifton Lawn CT11 .... 117 D5
Clifton Mans 7 CT20 .. 335 C4
Clifton Marine Par
DA11 .... 18 F1
Clifton Pl Margate CT9 ... 51 A3
Royal Tunbridge Wells
TN1 .... 286 B2
Clifton Rd Bexley DA16 .. 13 C4
Folkestone CT20 .... 335 C4
Gillingham ME7 .... 64 C7
Gravesend DA11 .... 19 A1
Margate CT9 .... 51 A2
Ramsgate CT11 .... 117 B8
Royal Tunbridge Wells
TN2 .... 286 C7
Sidcup DA14 .... 30 E4
Whitstable CT5 .... 74 D1
Clifton St CT9 .... 50 J3
Cliftonville Ave
Margate CT9 .... 51 A2
Ramsgate CT12 .... 83 B1
Cliftonville Ct
Lewisham SE12 .... 29 A7
Margate,Cliftonville CT9 .. 51 B3
Margate CT9 .... 51 A3
Cliftonville Mews CT9 .. 51 A3
Cliftonville Prim Sch
CT9 .... 51 C2
Clim Down CT14 ...... 248 D6
Clinch Ct 15 E16 .... 1 A8
Clinch St ME3 .... 24 A4
Clinton Ave Bexley DA16 . 13 A3
Rochester ME2 .... 62 E8
Clinton Bsns Ctr TN12 . 260 E5
Clinton Cl ME17 ...... 194 B3
Clinton La TN8 .... 218 E3
Clints La CT4 .... 243 D4
Clipper Bvd DA9 .... 16 E3
Clipper Bvd W DA2 ..... 16 D4
Clipper Cl ME2 .... 63 E7
Clipper Cres DA12 ...... 37 F4
Clipper Ct ME2 .... 63 E7
Clive Ave DA1 .... 14 F1
Clive Ct CT9 .... 51 B2
Cliveden Cl ME16 ..... 161 D7
Clive Dennis Ct TN24 .. 268 E1
Clive Ho ME20 .... 160 F8
Clive Rd
Cliffs End CT12 .... 116 D6
Erith DA17 .... 4 A2
Gravesend DA11 .... 19 B1
Clive Rd *continued*
Margate CT9 .... 83 A5
Rochester ME1 .... 63 C3
Sittingbourne ME10 .... 101 B5
Clock Ho The DA15 ..... 31 A7
Clockhouse TN23 ..... 267 F1
Clock House La TN13 .. 154 A4
Clockhouse Pk TN25 .. 203 C2
Clockhouse TN2 .... 286 F6
Clock Tower Mews
Snodland ME6 .... 95 A1
Woolwich SE28 .... 3 B6
Clocktower Par CT2 .. 142 A6
Cloisterham Rd ME1 ... 96 D7
Cloisters Ave BR2 .... 52 F4
Cloisters Ct DA7 .... 14 B4
Cloisters The
18 Canterbury CT1 ..... 142 F1
1 Dartford DA1 .... 15 E1
Lenham ME17 .... 199 C5
Ramsgate CT11 .... 117 D5
8 Sittingbourne ME10 .. 101 E4
Whitstable CT5 .... 74 F2
Cloke Mews TN15 ..... 156 F7
Cloonmore Ave BR6 ..... 86 F6
Clopton Ct ME8 .... 98 D8
Close The
Addington ME19 .... 126 C2
Ashford TN23 .... 299 F7
Birling ME19 .... 127 B5
Borough Green TN15 ... 157 A8
Bough Beech TN8 ...... 219 A2
Bridge CT4 .... 175 F1
Canterbury CT1 .... 174 D6
Canterbury,Hales Place
CT2 .... 142 F4
Canterbury,St Dunstan's
CT2 .... 142 C3
Cudham TN16 .... 119 B3
Dartford DA2 .... 33 D5
Faversham ME13 ...... 138 C6
Folkestone CT19 .... 335 E8
Groombridge TN3 ...... 312 C6
Hythe CT21 .... 333 B4
Ightham TN15 .... 156 D6
Lydden CT15 .... 276 F8
New Barn DA3 .... 59 B7
Orpington BR5 .... 53 E3
Rochester ME1 .... 63 C4
Royal Tunbridge Wells
TN2 .... 286 C8
Sevenoaks TN13 .... 153 E3
Sidcup DA14 .... 31 B3
1 Sidcup,Old Bexley
DA5 .... 32 A8
Wye TN25 .... 237 E2
Cloth Hall Gdns TN27 . 295 A2
Clothier Ho SE7 .... 1 E1
Clothworkers Rd SE18 .. 12 D7
Cloudberry Cl ME16 ... 161 D6
Cloudesley Cl ME1 ...... 63 B1
Cloudesley Rd
Bexley DA7 .... 13 F6
Erith DA8 .... 14 F6
Clouston Cl CT18 ..... 307 B5
Clovelly Dr ME12 .... 47 B8
Clovelly TN28 .... 373 E6
Clovelly Rd Bexley DA7 .. 13 E8
Whitstable CT5 .... 108 D7
Clovelly Way BR6 .... 53 F3
Clover Bank View ME5 .. 97 B6
Clover Ct
12 Grays RM17 .... 18 D8
Sittingbourne ME10 .... 102 B5
Cloverdale Gdns DA15 .. 12 F1
Clover Lay ME8 .... 66 B2
Cloverlay Ind Pk ME8 .. 66 C1
Clover Rd ME3 .... 41 E3
Clover Rise CT5 .... 75 B1
Clover St 3 ME4 .... 63 F4
Clovers The DA11 .... 36 E4
Clover Terr 4 ME15 ... 195 D8
Clover Way TN12 ...... 257 A5
Clover Wlk 13 TN8 .... 217 D3
Clowes Ct CT2 .... 142 C4
Clubb's La TN29 ...... 370 D7
Club Cotts TN11 ...... 221 D8
Club Gardens Rd BR2 ... 52 A2
Cluny Rd ME13 .... 138 F7
Clyde Rd TN10 .... 222 C6
Clydesdale Ho DA18 ..... 3 E4
Clyde St
1 Canterbury CT1 ..... 143 A1
Sheerness ME12 .... 28 D2
Clydon Cl DA8 .... 14 E8
Clynton Way TN23 ..... 300 A7
C M Booth Collection of
Historic Vehicles (Mus)★
TN17 .... 343 E4
Coach Dr TN26 .... 267 A7
Coach Dr The DA13 ... 125 E7
Coach & Horses Pas 18
TN2 .... 286 A2
Coach House Mews 8
BR1 .... 52 A6
Coach House Mews The
CT15 .... 245 D5
Coach Rd
Charing Heath TN27 .... 233 A6
Densole CT18 .... 306 F8
Egerton ME17,TN27 .... 232 E6
Ightham TN15 .... 156 B2
Rusthall TN4 .... 285 C3
Coach Yd The ME16 ... 161 B3
Coal Ct RM17 .... 18 A8
Coalhouse Fort★
RM18 .... 20 E6
Coalpit La ME9 .... 167 A6
Coast Dr
Greatstone-on-Sea
TN28 .... 373 E3
Lydd-on-S TN29 ...... 380 D8
St Mary's Bay TN29 .... 365 F2

Coastguard Alley CT5 .. 74 C1
Coastguard Cotts
 Birchington CT7 .... 80 C8
 Conyer ME9 .... 103 E6
 Dover CT16 .... 310 G8
 Grain ME3 .... 27 B5
 Herne Bay CT6 .... 75 F4
 Hythe CT21 .... 333 B1
 Kingsdown CT14 .... 248 D4
 Leysdown-on-S ME12 ....73 E4
 Lydd-on-S TN29 .... 380 D5
 Minster (Sheppey) ME12 . 48 C5
 23 Ramsgate,East Cliff
  CT11 .... 117 F7
 Ramsgate,Pegwell CT11 . 117 A5
 Sandwich CT13 .... 182 A8
Coastguard Cotts The
 ME12 .... 28 H1
Coastguard Hos ME12 .. 49 C5
Coast Rd TN28 .... 373 F7
Coates Hill Rd BR1 ..... 53 A7
Coats Ave ME12 .... 46 A8
Cobay CT21 .... 333 D2
Cobb CI ME2 .... 62 D8
Cobb Ct CT9 .... 50 I3
Cobbets Way TN8 ...... 249 C8
Cobbett CI ME19 .... 159 F8
Cobbett Rd SE9 .... 11 E4
Cobbett's Ride TN2 .... 285 F1
Cobblers Bridge Rd
 CT6 .... 76 D3
Cobblestones ME7 ...... 97 F5
Cobbs CI
 Paddock Wood TN12 .... 256 F6
 Wateringbury ME18 .... 192 E7
Cobbs Hill CT4 .... 172 C2
Cobbs Mews 3 CT20 ... 335 C4
Cobbs PI CT9 .... 50 I3
Cobbs Wood Ind Est
 TN23 .... 267 F2
Cobb Wlk ME13 .... 138 B8
Cobden Ct Bromley BR2 . 52 C5
 9 Woolwich SE28 .... 3 C5
Cobden PI 18 CT1 ..... 143 A1
Cobden Rd
 4 Chatham ME4 .... 64 B2
 Hythe CT21 .... 333 B1
 Orpington BR6 .... 86 D6
 Sevenoaks TN13 .... 154 C4
Cobdown CI ME20 ..... 128 C2
Cobdown Gr ME8 .... 66 A2
Cob Dr DA12 .... 38 E3
Cobfield ME17 .... 196 A1
Cobham Ave ME10 ..... 101 E1
Cobham Chase ME3 .... 138 B8
Cobham Cl Bromley BR2 . 52 E2
 Canterbury CT1 .... 175 C6
 Maidstone ME16 ...... 161 E4
 Rochester ME2 .... 62 E7
 2 Sidcup DA15 .... 13 B1
 Swanscombe DA9 .... 17 B1
Cobham Dr ME18 ...... 159 C3
Cobham Hall Sch DA12 . 61 C6
Cobham Ho 4 DA8 ..... 14 B7
Cobham PI DA6 .... 13 D2
Cobham Prim Sch
 DA12 .... 61 A8
Cobham Rise ME7 ...... 64 F5
Cobhams TN3 .... 285 A8
Cobham Terr DA9 .... 17 B1
Cobland Rd SE12 .... 29 C4
Cobs Cl TN15 .... 156 C6
Cobsden Cl TN29 ...... 366 A4
Cobsdene DA12 .... 37 D2
Cobsden Rd TN29 ..... 366 A4
Cobtree Cl ME5 .... 97 B3
Cobtree Rd ME17 ...... 194 C3
Cobtree Wharf ME20 .. 129 C2
Cobweb Cnr CT2 .... 142 B4
Cockerhurst Rd TN14 ...88 E2
Cockering Rd
 Canterbury CT1,CT4 ... 174 B4
 Chartham CT4 .... 173 E2
Cock La Elham CT4 .... 273 F4
 Hamstreet TN26 .... 349 A7
Cockmannings La BR5 .. 54 E1
Cockmannings Rd BR5 . 54 D2
Cockmount La TN5 .... 336 F5
Cockpit The TN12 ..... 259 C5
Cockreed La TN28 ..... 373 B7
Cocksett Ave BR6 ...... 86 E4
Cocksure La DA14 ...... 32 A4
Codrington Cres DA12 .. 37 D3
Codrington Gdns DA12 . 37 D3
Codrington Rd CT11 ... 117 D7
Cogans Terr CT1 ...... 174 E6
Cogate Rd TN12 .... 256 E6
Coggan Ho 7 CT1 .... 174 F7
Cokers Yd TN4 .... 254 A1
Colburn Rd CT10 ...... 84 A2
Colchester Cl ME5 ...... 97 A7
Cold Arbor Rd TN13 ... 153 D3
Cold Blow Cres DA5 .... 32 D7
Coldblow CT14 .... 215 A1
Coldblow La
 Hucking ME14 .... 132 A2
 Woodchurch TN26 ..... 168 B4
Coldbridge La TN27 ... 232 B5
Cold Harbour CT1 ..... 143 A2
Coldharbour Crest SE9 . 30 A5
Coldharbour La
 Aylesford ME20 .... 129 A1
 Bridge CT4,CT3 .... 209 D7
 Hucking ME14,ME9 .... 132 E7
Cold Harbour La ME9 .. 100 F6
Coldharbour La
 Old Romney TN29 .... 371 C5
 Peasmarsh TN31 ...... 367 E3
 Rainham RM13 .... 4 F6
 Shipbourne TN11 ..... 189 A2
 Sittingbourne ME10 ....68 F1

Coldharbour La continued
 Tonbridge TN11 ...... 221 E7
 Wye TN25 .... 238 A2
Coldharbour Rd
 Ashurst TN8,TN11 ..... 283 E8
 Gravesend DA11 .... 37 A4
 Iden Green TN17 ...... 342 B4
 Northfleet DA11 .... 36 F5
Cold Harbour Rd
 ME13 .... 201 A7
Coldharbour Sports Ctr
 SE9 .... 30 A6
Coldred Hill CT15 ..... 244 F1
Coldred Rd
 Coldred CT15 .... 245 B5
 Maidstone ME15 ...... 195 F4
 Shepherdswell CT15 .. 244 E3
Coldrum La ME19 ...... 126 C6
Coldshott RH8 .... 183 A2
Coldswood Rd CT12 ....82 F2
Colebrooke Ct DA14 ....31 B4
Colebrook Ind Est
 TN2 .... 254 E1
Colebrook Rd TN4 .... 286 C8
Colebrook St 1 DA8 ...14 F8
Cole Cl SE28 .... 3 B5
Colegate Dr ME14 .... 163 C4
Colegates Cl ME13 .... 105 B2
Colegates Ct ME13 .... 105 B2
Colegates Rd ME13 ... 105 A2
Coleman Cres CT12 .... 83 C1
Coleman Dr ME10 ...... 68 F1
Coleman Rd DA17 .... 4 A2
Colemans Cl TN29 .... 376 D7
Colemans Heath SE9 ...30 D5
Coleman's Stairs Rd
 CT7 .... 81 A8
Coleman's Yd 3 CT11 . 117 E6
Colepits Wood Rd SE9 . 12 D2
Coleraine Rd 1 SE3 ... 11 A8
Coleridge Cl 4 ME20 . 127 F4
Coleridge Gdns CT3 .. 210 F6
Coleridge Rd
 Dartford DA1 .... 16 B3
 Tilbury RM18 .... 19 C5
Coleridge Way BR6 .... 54 A3
Coles Ct TN2 .... 286 C3
Colesdane ME17 ...... 198 E8
Coleshall Cl ME15 .... 195 F6
Coleshall Cotts ME9 ... 68 D3
Coles La TN16 .... 152 C4
Cole Terr ME17 .... 199 C4
Colets Orch TN14 .... 122 B3
Colette CT CT10 .... 51 G2
Coleville Cres TN28 ... 377 E7
Colewood Dr ME2 ...... 62 B8
Colewood Rd CT5 ...... 75 E3
Colfe's Prep Sch SE12 ..11 B1
Colfe Way ME10 ...... 102 A8
Colin Blythe Rd TN10 . 222 F5
Colin Chapman Way
 DA3 .... 90 E6
Colin Cl DA2 .... 16 B1
Colin's Way CT21 ..... 334 A3
Collard Cl CT6 .... 77 A4
Collard Ho CT1 .... 175 C8
Collard Rd TN24 ...... 301 A6
Collards Cl CT12 ..... 114 D7
Collards La CT4 ...... 273 E3
College Ave
 Gillingham ME7 .... 64 B4
 Maidstone ME15 ..... 161 F3
 Tonbridge TN9 .... 254 A7
College Cotts ME16 .. 161 F3
College Ct
 Ashford TN23 .... 268 C2
 Canterbury CT1 ...... 143 B1
 6 Maidstone ME15 ... 162 A3
College Dr TN2 .... 286 D4
College Gn 10 BR1 .... 52 A8
College PI DA9 .... 17 C3
College Rd Bromley BR1 . 29 A1
 Canterbury CT1 ...... 143 B1
 Chatham ME4 .... 64 A7
 Deal CT14 .... 215 D8
 Hextable BR8 .... 32 F1
 Maidstone ME15 ..... 161 F2
 Margate CT9 .... 51 A1
 New Hythe ME20 ..... 128 B3
 Northfleet DA11 .... 18 B2
 Ramsgate CT11 .... 83 E1
 Sittingbourne ME10 .. 101 D3
College Row CT1 ...... 310 B7
College Sq 2 CT9 ..... 50 J2
College View SE9 ...... 29 D7
College Way CT3 ..... 178 A7
College Wlk
 4 Maidstone ME15 ... 162 A3
 3 Margate CT9 .... 50 J2
College Yd ME1 .... 63 C6
Coller Cres DA2 .... 34 E3
Collet Rd TN15 .... 122 E2
Collett Cl TN25 ...... 271 D8
Collet Wlk ME8 .... 98 D4
Collie Dr TN23 .... 299 E5
Collier Cl 2 .... 26 B2
Colliers' Green CE Prim
 Sch TN17 .... 291 F2
Colliers Shaw BR2 ..... 85 D5
Collindale Ave
 Erith DA8 .... 14 B8
 Sidcup DA15 .... 31 A7
Collingbourne TN23 .. 299 E6
Collinge ME19 .... 128 A1
Collings Wlk ME8 ...... 98 C4
Collington CI DA11 .....36 E8
Collington Ho 3 SE7 ...11 B8
Collington Terr ME15 . 195 E4
Collingwood Cl
 Broadstairs CT10 ......83 E4
 Westgate-on-S CT8 .... 81 D7

Collingwood Ct
 Folkestone CT20 ...... 334 E5
 7 Ramsgate CT11 .... 117 D7
Collingwood Ho DA9 ...17 D2
Collingwood Ind Ctr
 ME17 .... 196 E5
Collingwood Rd
 Kit's Coty ME20 ...... 129 C7
 St Margaret's at Cliffe
  CT15 .... 279 F8
 Whitstable CT5 .... 74 C1
Collingwood Rise
 CT20 .... 334 E5
Collingwood Wlk
 ME10 .... 101 B5
Collins Rd
 Herne Bay CT6 .... 76 C2
 New Romney TN28 ... 373 C5
Collison ME9 .... 345 D7
Collis St ME2 .... 63 A8
Colman Ho 4 ME14 ... 162 A4
Colman Rd E16 .... 1 C8
Colne Rd TN10 .... 222 B5
Colney Rd DA1 .... 15 F1
Colombo Sq CT12 ...... 83 A1
Colonade The 14
 TN18 .... 341 A2
Colonel's La TN30 .... 140 A3
Colonel Stephens Way
 TN30 .... 324 B2
Colonel's Way TN4 ... 254 A2
Colorado CT CT16 .... 278 B3
Colson Dr ME9 .... 68 E3
Coltness Cres SE2 ...... 3 B1
Colton Cres CT16 .... 278 A4
Coltsfoot Ct ME4 .... 161 B4
Coltsfoot Ct CT17 ..... 18 D8
Coltsfoot Ho E16 .... 1 B8
Coltsfoot La RH8 ..... 183 A1
Colts Hill PI TN12 .... 256 B5
Coltstead DA3 .... 91 E7
Columbia Ave CT5 ... 108 B7
Columbia Wharf Rd
 RM17 .... 18 A8
Columbine Ave E6 ...... 1 E8
Columbine Cl
 Rochester ME2 .... 62 E7
 West Malling ME19 ... 127 F1
 Whitstable CT5 ...... 108 C6
Columbine Rd
 East Malling ME19 ... 159 F8
 Rochester ME2 .... 62 E7
Columbus Ave CT12 ... 81 D1
Columbus Sq DA8 .... 14 F8
Colveiw Ct SE9 .... 29 D7
Colyer Cl SE9 .... 30 B6
Colyer Ho SE2 .... 3 D1
Colyer Rd DA11 .... 36 D6
Colyers Cl DA8 .... 14 D6
Colyers La DA8 .... 14 D6
Colyers Prim Sch DA8 . 14 D6
Colyers Wlk DA8 ...... 14 E6
Colyton Cl ME16 ..... 152 D5
Combe Bank Cotts
 TN14 .... 152 D5
Combe Bank Dr TN14 . 152 E4
Combe Bank Farm
 TN14 .... 152 D6
Combe Bank Sch
 TN14 .... 152 E4
Combedale Rd SE10 .....1 A1
Combeside SE18 .... 12 F7
Combwell Cres SE2 ..... 3 A3
Com Coll Whitstable The
 CT5 .... 108 F8
Comforts Farm Ave
 RH8 .... 183 A4
Comfrey Ct RM17 ...... 18 D8
Command Rd ME14 ... 161 F4
Commerce Way TN8 .. 217 C3
Commercial PI DA12 .. 19 C1
Commercial Rd
 Paddock Wood TN12 .. 256 F6
 Rochester ME2 .... 63 B7
 Royal Tunbridge Wells
  TN1 .... 286 B5
 Tonbridge TN9 .... 254 A7
Commissioners Ct ME4 . 63 F6
Commissioner's Rd
 ME2 .... 63 C8
Commodore Ct CT21 . 333 C4
Commodore Rd ME14 . 162 C5
Common La Cliffe ME3 . 22 C6
 Crabble CT17 .... 277 C3
 Dartford DA2 .... 33 B5
Common Rd
 Burham ME5 .... 96 B1
 Cliffe Woods ME3 ...... 40 B5
 Hadlow TN11 .... 190 D4
 Ightham TN15 .... 156 B4
 Sissinghurst TN17 ... 321 A8
Commonside BR2 ...... 85 C6
Common The CT1 ...... 63 C6
Common View TN4 ... 285 C4
Common Wall ME3 .... 22 D6
Common Way TN26 .. 267 A7
Commonwealth Cl
 ME10 .... 102 B3
Commonwealth Ho 5
 RM18 .... 19 A5
Commonwealth Way
 SE2 .... 3 C1
Commority Rd DA13 .. 126 B8
Compass Cl ME1 .... 63 C1
Compass Cl DA11 ......18 E1
Compass Ctr ME4 .....64 B8
Compasses Rd TN11 .. 220 B2
Compasses The TN11 . 220 B2
Comp La TN15 .... 157 E6
Compton Ct ME5 ...... 97 D2
Compton PI DA8 .... 14 E7
Concord Ave ME5 ...... 96 C5

Concord Cl
 Paddock Wood TN12 .. 256 E7
 Royal Tunbridge Wells
  TN2 .... 286 C4
Concorde Bsns Pk
 TN16 .... 118 D4
Concorde Dr E6 .... 1 F8
Concrete Cotts ME3 ... 22 A6
Condor Cl ME12 .... 49 E3
Condover Cres SE18 ... 12 B7
Condovers Cotts RM18 . 19 F8
Conduit Ho The ★
 CT1 .... 143 B1
Conduit Rd SE18 .... 2 B1
Conduit St ME13 ..... 138 D8
Coneyburrow Rd TN2 . 286 E5
Coney Mews ME4 ...... 64 A1
Conference Rd SE2 ..... 3 C2
Conference Wlk CT1 .. 175 C8
Conghurst La TN18 ... 355 B6
Congleton Gr SE18 ..... 2 C1
Congo Rd SE18 .... 2 D1
Congress Rd SE2 .... 3 C2
Congreve Rd SE9 ...... 11 F4
Congreve Wlk 6 E16 ....1 D8
Conifer Ave DA3 ...... 58 E3
Conifer Cl BR6 .... 86 D6
Conifer Ct CT8 .... 50 D1
Conifer Dr
 Chatham ME5 .... 97 C1
 Culverstone Green DA13 . .92 F1
Conifers The
 Deal CT14 .... 215 A2
 Shepherdswell CT15 .. 244 F2
Conifer Way BR8 ...... 55 C8
Conisborough Ct 13
 DA2 .... 16 B1
Coniscliffe Cl BR7 ..... 53 A8
Coniston Ave
 Bexley DA16 .... 12 E4
 Purfleet RM19 .... 16 C8
 Ramsgate CT11 ...... 117 A7
 Royal Tunbridge Wells
  TN4 .... 285 E5
Coniston Cl Bexley DA7 . 14 C6
 Dartford DA1 .... 33 B7
 Erith DA8 .... 14 C7
 Gillingham ME7 .... 65 A6
 Maidstone ME15 ..... 161 F2
 Otford TN14 .... 122 C4
Coniston Dr CT3 ...... 210 F6
Coniston Ho ME15 .... 195 E7
Coniston Rd Bexley DA7 . 14 C6
 Folkestone CT19 ..... 335 B7
Conker Cl TN23 ...... 300 C3
Connaught Barracks
 CT16 .... 278 E1
Connaught Bridge E16 . . 1 D6
Connaught Cl ME15 .. 196 A8
Connaught Gdns 9
 CT9 .... 50 J1
Connaught Mews
 2 Chatham ME4 ...... 64 C2
 Woolwich SE18 .... 2 A1
Connaught Rd
 Chatham ME4 .... 64 C2
 Dover CT16 .... 278 D1
 Folkestone CT20 ..... 335 D5
 Gillingham ME7 .... 64 D5
 Margate CT9 .... 50 J1
 Newham,Silvertown E16 . . 1 D5
 Sittingbourne ME10 .. 101 E3
 Woolwich SE18 .... 2 B1
Connaught Way TN4 .. 285 F5
Conquest Ind Est ME2 . 63 A5
Conrad Ave CT1 ...... 143 C3
Conrad Ct ME8 .... 98 C4
Consort Cl ME14 ..... 162 B5
Constable Ave E16 ...... 1 B5
Constable Rd
 Birchington CT7 .... 81 A8
 Northfleet DA11 .... 36 E5
 Tonbridge TN10 ..... 222 C5
Constable's Rd CT16 .. 310 E8
Constance St E16 ...... 1 E5
Constancia CT CT20 .. 335 C5
Constantine Rd TN23 . 299 F5
Constitutional Hill Rd
 TN4 .... 253 F1
Constitution Cres DA12 . .37 B7
Constitution Hill
 8 Chatham ME4 ...... 64 B3
 Gravesend DA12 ...... 37 C7
 Snodland ME6 .... 127 F6
Constitution Rd ME5 ..64 B2
Constitution Rise SE18 . 12 A6
Consul Cl CT6 .... 76 B4
Consul Gdns BR8 ...... 33 A1
Contessa Ct BR6 .... 86 E5
Continental App CT9 ..82 F6
Convalescent La TN17 . 292 F2
Convent Cl CT15 ..... 280 B6
Conventina Ho 3
 CT11 .... 117 D7
Convent Rd CT10 ...... 51 G1
Convent Wlk CT11 .... 117 B5
Conway Cl
 Birchington CT7 .... 80 C7
 Hythe CT21 .... 333 B4
 Rochester ME2 .... 39 C1
Conway Ct BR5 .... 54 C5
Conway Gdns RM17 ...18 B7
Conway Hall 16 ME7 ..64 A6
Conway Mews ME7 .... 64 A6
Conway Prim Sch SE18 . . 2 E2
Conway Rd
 Maidstone ME16 ..... 161 C6
 Woolwich SE18 .... 2 E2
Conyerd Rd TN15 .... 156 F6
Conyer Rd ME9 .... 103 F4
Conyers Wlk ME8 ...... 98 D4
Conyngham La CT4 ... 176 A2
Conyngham Rd
 Herne Bay CT6 .... 77 D5

Conyngham Rd continued
 Minster (Thanet) CT12 . 115 C9
Cooden Cl Bromley BR1 . 29 B1
 Gillingham ME8 .... 66 A2
Cook Cl ME5 .... 97 C6
Cookham Dene Cl BR7 . 53 D8
Cookham Hill ME1 ...... 63 A2
Cookham Rd DA14,DA8 . 55 A8
Cookham Wood Rd
 ME1 .... 96 B8
Cookhill Rd SE2 .... 3 B3
Cooks La ME10 .... 101 F6
Cook's Lea CT13 ...... 180 B2
Cookson Gr DA8 .... 14 B7
Cook Sq ME8 .... 65 F5
Cooks Wharf ME1 ...... 63 E4
Cookson Gr DA8 .... 14 B7
Cook Sq DA8 .... 14 B7
Cooks Wharf ME1 ...... 63 E4
Cooks Wharf ME1 ...... 63 E4
Cooling Castle ★ ME3 . .22 E4
Cooling Cl ME14 ..... 162 C6
Cooling Comm ME3 ... 40 D8
Coolinge La CT20 .... 334 F4
Coolinge Lea CT20 ... 335 D5
Cooling Rd Cliffe ME3 . 22 C4
 High Halstow ME23 ... 23 C4
 Rochester ME2 .... 40 B2
Cooling St ME3 .... 22 D4
Coombe Ave TN14 ... 154 B7
Coombe Cl
 Chatham ME5 .... 97 B3
 Dover CT17 .... 278 A1
 Snodland ME6 .... 128 A7
Coombe Ct Dover CT17 . 278 A1
 Sevenoaks TN14 ..... 154 B7
Coombe Dr ME10 ..... 102 C4
Coombe Farm La ME4 . 24 E6
Coombe La TN13,CT3 . 179 E8
Coombe Lands TN30 .. 359 D4
Coombe La TN30 ..... 345 A4
Coombe Lea BR1 ...... 52 E6
Coombe Lodge SE7 .... 11 C8
Coombe Rd
 Crabble CT17 .... 277 F1
 Dover CT15,CT17 .... 309 E8
 Folkestone CT19 ..... 334 F6
 Gravesend DA12 ...... 37 C6
 Hoo St Werburgh ME3 . .41 E5
 Maidstone ME15 ..... 161 F2
 Otford TN14 .... 122 C4
Coombe Valley Rd
 CT17 .... 278 A1
Coombe Way CT18 ... 307 C4
Coombe Wlk CT5 ..... 108 A2
Coombe Wood La
 CT18 .... 307 C4
Coombfield Dr DA2 .... 34 D4
Coomb Field TN8 .... 249 C8
Cooper Cl DA9 .... 16 F2
Cooper Ct SE18 .... 12 B8
Cooper Rd Chatham ME5 . .97 B3
 Snodland ME6 .... 127 F6
Coopers Cl DA4 .... 55 D8
Coopers Cotts DA2 .... 34 A4
Coopers Dr DA2 .... 32 E6
Cooper Shaw Rd RM18 . 19 E7
Cooper's Hill CT6 ...... 76 F5
Cooper's La TN25 .... 302 F2
Coopers La
 Canterbury CT1 ...... 174 E7
 Lewisham SE12 .... 29 B6
Coopers' Lane Prim Sch
 SE12 .... 29 B6
Coopers La TN11,TN3 . 284 C7
Cooper's Rd DA11 .... 36 E7
Coopers Tech Coll BR7 . 53 C8
Cooper Street Dro
 CT3 .... 148 B4
Coote Rd DA7 .... 13 F6
Cooting La CT3 ...... 210 D8
Cooting Rd CT3 ...... 210 D8
Copenhagen Rd ME7 .. 64 C4
Copinger Cl CT2 ...... 143 A4
Copland Ave ME12 .... 47 C6
Copley Dene BR1 ...... 52 D8
Coppards La TN31 .... 357 D1
Copper Beech Cl
 Gravesend DA12 ...... 37 D8
 7 Orpington BR5 ...... 54 C4
Copper Beech View
 TN9 .... 254 A8
Copperfield Cl
 Ashford TN24 .... 268 C6
 Chalk DA12 .... 38 A7
 Kingswood ME17 ..... 197 D2
Copperfield Cres ME3 . 39 C2
Copperfield Ct
 Broadstairs CT10 ......84 B5
 Crayford DA1 .... 14 E2
Copperfield Dr ME17 . 198 F4
Copperfield Ho 6 ME4 . 63 F4
Copperfield Rd
 Erith SE28 .... 3 C7
 Rochester ME1 .... 63 B4
Copperfields Cl TN15 . 122 F2
Copperfields
 2 Dartford DA1 .... 15 E1
 Kemsing TN15 .... 122 F2
 Lydd TN29 .... 376 B6
Copperfields Orch
 TN15 .... 122 F2
Copperfields The ME1 . 63 B4
Copperfields Wlk
 TN15 .... 122 F2
Copperfield Way BR7 .. 30 C2
Coppergate CT2 ...... 142 F2
Coppergate Cl ME1 ... 52 B8
Coppergate ME7 .... 97 F5
Copperhouse La ME7 . 64 F4
Copperhouse Rd ME2 . 62 C7
Copperhurst Wlk CT9 . 51 F8
Copper La TN12 ...... 259 E5
Copperpenny Dr ME7 . .98 B3
Coppers Ct TN4 ...... 286 A8

Coppers La TN12 ..... 256 E1
Copper Tree Ct ME15 . 195 A5
Copper Tree Wlk ME5 . 97 C1
Copperwood TN24 ... 268 C4
Coppice Ct ME7 .... 98 B4
Coppice Rd ME5 .... 97 C2
Coppice The
 Aylesford ME20 ..... 128 C3
 Bitchet Green TN15 .. 155 D1
 Hythe CT21 .... 333 B4
 Joyden's Wood DA5 ... 32 D5
 Pembury TN2 .... 287 D7
 Sturry CT2 .... 143 F6
 Vigo Village DA13 ... 126 B8
Coppice View ME14 .. 162 E6
Copping's Rd TN11 ... 220 C4
Coppins La ME9 ...... 101 B2
Coppin St CT14 ...... 215 D6
Coppock Cl CT12 ...... 83 B1
Copse Bank TN15 .... 154 F7
Copse Cl Greenwich SE7 . .11 B8
 Rochester ME1 .... 63 E1
Copsehill TN12 .... 127 E2
Copse Rd TN11 ...... 221 E4
Copse Side DA3 .... 58 E6
Copse The
 Ashford TN23 .... 267 D3
 Hoo St Werburgh ME3 . .41 E3
Copsewood Cl DA15 ...12 E1
Copsewood Way
 ME15 .... 163 A3
Cop Street Rd CT3 .... 147 D3
Copt Cl CT2 .... 143 F7
Coptefield Dr DA17 ..... 3 E3
Copthall Ave TN18 ... 341 A1
Copthall Gdns 13
 CT20 .... 335 D5
Copt Hall TN18 ...... 357 D3
Copt Hall Rd
 Ightham TN15 .... 156 A4
 Sole Street DA13 ..... 60 B5
Copthorne Ave BR2 .... 85 F8
Coralline Wlk 4 SE2 .... 3 C4
Corben Cl ME16 ..... 161 B6
Corbridge Ho SE2 ...... 3 C3
Corbylands Rd DA15 ...30 E7
Cordelia Cres ME1 ..... 62 F2
Cordingham Rd CT5 .. 108 A4
Cordova Ct CT20 ..... 335 B4
Corelli Rd SE18,SE3 ....11 E6
Corhaven Ho 3 DA8 .. 14 E7
Corinthian CT ME3 .... 27 B5
Corinthian Manorway
 DA8 .... 4 D2
Corinthian Rd DA8 ..... 4 D2
Cork Ho BR5 .... 54 B6
Cork La TN12 .... 292 D8
Cork St ME20 .... 128 F6
Corkwell St ME4 .... 63 E3
Cormorant Cl ME2 .... 62 C7
Cormorant Way CT6 ...77 F4
Cornbrook Rd CT21 .. 353 D8
Cornel Ho 4 DA15 ..... 31 A5
Cornelia Cres ME1 ..... 62 F2
Cornelis Dr CT12 .... 115 B5
Cornell Cl DA14 .... 31 E2
Corner Cotts TN26 ... 348 A6
Corner Farm Rd TN12 . 260 E6
Corner Field TN23 .... 300 B5
Corner Gn SE3 .... 11 A5
Cornes Ct TN2 .... 269 A1
Cornfield Way TN10 . 222 D6
Cornflower Cl ME14 .. 162 E4
Cornford Cl Hayes BR2 . 52 A4
 Pembury TN2 .... 287 B6
Cornford La TN2 ..... 287 B5
Cornford Pk TN2 ..... 287 C6
Cornford Rd DA7 ...... 81 A7
Cornforth Cl TN12 ... 260 F4
Cornhill 15 CT11 ..... 117 E6
Corniche The CT20 ... 334 C3
Corn Mill Dr BR6 ...... 54 A2
Cornwall Ave
 Bexley DA16 .... 12 C4
 Ramsgate CT11 ...... 117 F8
Cornwall Cl ME15 .... 195 E7
Cornwall Cres ME1 .... 95 D4
Cornwall Dr BR5 ...... 31 C1
Cornwall Gdns
 Canterbury CT1 ...... 175 D7
 Margate CT9 .... 51 B3
Cornwall Ho
 Deal CT14 .... 215 A5
 5 Dover CT17 .... 310 D7
Cornwallis Ave
 Aylesham CT3 .... 210 F6
 Chatham ME4 .... 63 E1
 Folkestone CT19 ..... 335 B6
 Gillingham ME8 .... 65 A4
 Herne Bay CT6 .... 77 C3
 Linton ME17 .... 227 E8
 Sidcup SE9 .... 30 D6
 Tonbridge TN10 ..... 222 F4
Cornwallis Circ CT5 ... 74 D1
Cornwallis Cl
 Ashford TN24 .... 301 B7
 Erith DA8 .... 14 F8
 Folkestone CT19 ..... 335 B6
Cornwallis Cotts
 ME17 .... 194 E2
Cornwallis Gdns CT10 . 84 A6
Cornwallis Rdbt ME8 . 65 A4
Cornwallis Rd
 Maidstone ME16 ..... 161 D4
 Woolwich SE18 .... 2 B3
 Woolwich SE18 .... 2 C3
Cornwallis Sch The
 ME15 .... 194 F2
Cornwallis Wlk SE9 ....11 F4

Cornwall Rd
Dartford DA1 . . . . .15 F4
Deal CT14 . . . . 215 C3
Gillingham ME7 . . . . . . 64 D6
Herne Bay CT6 . . . . . . .76 B2
Rochester ME1 . . . . . . 63 C3
Cornwall Ave DA12 . . 37 C5
Corona Rd SE12 . . . . . 29 A8
Corona Terr ME6 . . . . 127 F6
Coronation Cl
Bexley DA5 . . . . 13 D1
Broadstairs CT10 . . . . . .83 E7
Coronation Cotts
Folkestone CT19 . . . . 334 D6
Stoke ME3 . . . . 25 A3
Ticehurst TN5 . . . . . . 338 F2
Coronation Cres
Margate CT9 . . . . .82 B8
Queenborough ME11 . . .45 F5
Coronation Ct DA8 . . . 14 D7
Coronation Dr
Ashford TN23 . . . . 267 C1
Leysdown-on-S ME12 . . 49 D2
Coronation Flats 5
ME4 . . . . .63 F3
Coronation Rd
Chatham ME5 . . . . 64 C2
Grain ME3 . . . . 27 B5
Ramsgate CT11 . . . . . 117 D6
Sheerness ME12 . . . . . . 28 D1
Coronation Sq TN29 . . 376 C6
Corone Cl CT19 . . . . . 335 A7
Corporation Rd ME7 . . 64 D7
Corporation St ME1 . . . 63 A6
Corral Cl ME5 . . . . 64 D2
Corral Hts 11 DA8 . . . . .4 E1
Corrall Almshouses 5
ME15 . . . . 162 A3
Corrance Gn ME15 . . . 195 A8
Correnden Rd TN10 . . 222 A3
Corseley Rd TN3 . . . . 312 B5
Corsican Wlk CT6 . . . . 77 C3
Cortanore ME10 . . . . . 101 E2
Cortland Cl
Crayford DA1 . . . . .14 E1
Sittingbourne ME10 . . . 101 E6
Cortland Mews ME10 . . 101 E6
Corunna Cl CT21 . . . . 333 A2
Corunna Pl CT15 . . . . 278 E8
Corylus Dr CT5 . . . . . 108 A7
Cory's Rd ME1 . . . . . . 63 D6
Cossack St ME1 . . . . . 63 D3
Cossington Rd
Canterbury CT1 . . . . . 175 A7
Chatham ME5 . . . . .97 B1
Costells Mdw TN16 . . 151 D1
Cosway Cotts TN25 . . 329 C1
Cot La TN27 . . . . 295 B3
Cotleigh Ave DA5 . . . . 31 D6
Cotmandene Cres BR5 . 54 A7
Cotman's Ash La
TN15 . . . . 123 D4
Cotman Way TN12 . . . 224 E6
Coton Rd DA16 . . . . . . 13 A4
Cotswold Cl
Ashford TN24 . . . . 268 B4
Bexley DA7 . . . . .14 E5
Cotswold Gdns ME15 . 163 A2
Cotswold Rd DA11 . . . .36 E5
Cotswold Rise BR6 . . . .53 F3
Cottage Ave BR2 . . . . . 52 E1
Cottage Field Cl DA14 . 31 C7
Cottage Rd
Chatham ME4 . . . . .63 F6
Ramsgate CT11 . . . . . 117 E6
Cottage Row CT13 . . . 148 F1
Cottall Ave ME4 . . . . . .63 F2
Cottenham Cl ME17 . . 159 F7
Cottington Ct CT12 . . 116 B5
Cotton Hill Ho TN26 . . 349 A7
Cotton Hill Wlk TN26 . 349 A7
Cotton La DA2,DA9 . . . 16 C2
Cotton Rd CT1 . . . . . . 174 E7
Couchman Green La
TN12 . . . . 260 F7
Coulman St ME7 . . . . . 64 D5
Coulson Gr CT14 . . . . 214 A5
Coulter Ho DA9 . . . . . . 17 C2
Coulter Rd
Ashford TN23 . . . . 299 E5
Herne Bay CT6 . . . . . . .76 B2
Coulters Cl ME14 . . . . 162 D5
Coulton Ave DA11 . . . . .36 E7
Coultrip Cl ME12 . . . . .48 B5
Council Ave DA11 . . . . 18 C1
Council Cotts
Chainhurst ME15 . . . . 227 A7
Chiddingstone Causeway
TN11 . . . . 252 A8
Coxheath ME15 . . . . . 194 A4
Council Hos TN15 . . . . 190 A8
Countess Mountbatten Ct
CT8 . . . . .81 E8
Countess of Thanet's
Almshouses TN8 . . . 281 F3
Country's Field TN29 . 366 C8
Country Ways ME17 . . 200 D3
County Gate SE9 . . . . 30 C5
County Gr ME19 . . . . 159 B8
County Ho SE18 . . . . . 12 A8
County Rd
Maidstone ME14 . . . . . 162 A5
Newham E6 . . . . .2 B8
County Sq 8 TN23 . . . 268 B2
Coupland Pl SE18 . . . . .2 C1
Courier Rd RM13 . . . . . .4 D8
Course The SE9 . . . . . 30 A5
Courtaulds Cl SE28 . . . .3 A8
Court Ave DA17 . . . . . .3 F1
Court Broomes ME17 . 230 C8

Court Cotts
St Nicholas at Wade CT7 .79 E2
Wingham CT3 . . . . 178 A7
Court Cres BR8 . . . . . . 55 E5
Court Dr ME16 . . . . . . 161 D4
Courtenay Ho ME13 . . 140 C3
Courtenay Rd
Boughton Street CT2,
ME13 . . . . 140 E5
Deal CT14 . . . . 215 C8
Maidstone ME15 . . . . . 161 F2
Courtenay Rd ME8 . . . . .98 B8
Courtenwell TN3 . . . . . 284 F4
Court Farm Rd SE9 . . . .29 E5
Courtfield Ave ME5 . . . .97 B3
Court Flats CT3 . . . . . 178 A7
Court Hall Mus ★
ME10 . . . . 101 E6
Court Hall ME11 . . . . . .45 F5
Court Hill Ho CT16 . . . 277 E4
Court Hill CT3 . . . . . . 144 E2
Courthope Ave TN5 . . 336 F4
Courthope TN12 . . . . . 257 A6
Court La Detling ME14 . 131 C5
Hadlow TN11 . . . . 224 B7
Courtland Ave CT16 . . 278 A6
Courtland Dr CT16 . . . 277 A6
Courtland Gr SE28 . . . . .3 D6
Courtlands Ave SE12 . . .11 B2
Courtlands BR7 . . . . . . .30 B2
Courtlands Cl
Cliffs End CT12 . . . . . . 116 E5
Teston ME18 . . . . 193 A8
Courtlands CT14 . . . . . 248 D6
Courtlands Farm
TN17 . . . . 320 A3
Courtlands
Herne Bay CT6 . . . . . . .77 B3
Teston ME18 . . . . 193 A8
Tonbridge TN10 . . . . . 222 A3
Courtlands Way CT8 . . . 50 D1
Court Lane Pl TN11 . . . 223 F8
Court La CT3 . . . . 146 B6
Courtleet Dr DA8 . . . . . .14 B6
Court Lodge
Deal CT14 . . . . 215 B6
Erith DA17 . . . . .4 A1
Court Lodge Cotts
East Farleigh ME15 . . . 194 A7
Horton Kirby DA4 . . . . . 57 C6
Mereworth ME18 . . . . 191 E4
West Farleigh ME15 . . . 193 D7
Court Lodge Farm
ME18 . . . . 193 B7
Court Lodge Flats
TN3 . . . . 317 C6
Court Lodge Rd
Appledore TN26 . . . . . 361 C7
Gillingham ME7 . . . . . .64 F6
Court Lodge DA12 . . . . .38 E2
Court Mdws CT3 . . . . . 176 F8
Court Mdw TN15 . . . . 124 F3
Court Meadow ME8 . . . .65 B2
Court Mews DA11 . . . . .18 B1
Court Mount CT7 . . . . . 81 A6
Court Pl 5 CT20 . . . . 335 C4
Court Pl Burham ME1 . 128 F8
Dartford DA2 . . . . .34 E3
Deal CT14 . . . . 215 B1
Eltham SE9 . . . . .29 F7
Court Road (Orpington
By-Pass)
Chelsfield BR6,TN14 . . . 87 D5
Orpington BR6 . . . . . . .54 B2
Court Royal TN2 . . . . . 313 E8
Court St Bromley BR1 . . 52 A7
Faversham ME13 . . . . 138 D7
Courts The CT9 . . . . . . 50 E1
Court Tree Dr ME12 . . .48 B5
Courtwood Dr TN13 . . 154 A3
Court Wurtin TN3 . . . . 300 A7
Courtyard Gdns TN15 . 124 F3
Courtyard The
Ashford TN24 . . . . 300 F6
Gillingham ME8 . . . . . . 98 A8
Staple CT3 . . . . 179 A6
Watts's Cross TN11 . . . 221 A7
Westerham TN16 . . . . . 184 D8
Court Yd SE9 . . . . .11 F1
Cousley Wood Rd
TN5 . . . . 337 C7
Couthurst Rd SE3 . . . . .11 B7
Coutts Ave DA12 . . . . .38 E4
Covelees Wall E6 . . . . .2 A7
Coventon La CT14 . . . 181 A5
Coventry Cl
9 Newham E6 . . . . .1 F7
Rochester ME2 . . . . . . 62 D6
Coventry Gdns CT6 . . . .77 E5
Coventry Rd TN10 . . . 222 D5
Coverdale Ave ME15 . . 195 D6
Coverdale Cl ME5 . . . . .97 B7
Covert TN23 . . . . 267 E1
Covert Rd CT3 . . . . . . 210 E4
Covert The
Chatham ME5 . . . . .97 B1
Orpington BR6 . . . . . . .53 E3
Vigo Village DA13 . . . . 125 E7
Covesfield DA11 . . . . . .36 F8
Covet La CT4 . . . . 209 C2
Covet Wood Cl BR5 . . . .53 F3
Covey Hall Rd ME6 . . . . 95 A1
Cowan La CT4 . . . . 1 E8
Cowbeck Cl ME8 . . . . . 98 D6
Cowden Cl TN18 . . . . . 354 E8
Cowden Cross TN8 . . . 282 C7
Cowden La TN18 . . . . . 354 E7
Cowden Mews TN8 . . . 282 A6

Cowden Rd
Maidstone ME14 . . . . . 162 C5
Orpington BR6 . . . . . . .53 F2
Cowden Sta TN8 . . . . . 282 D8
Cowdray Rd CT14 . . . . 215 A3
Cowdray Sq CT14 . . . . 215 A3
Cowdrey Cl
Ashford TN24 . . . . 301 A7
Maidstone ME16 . . . . . 161 B2
Rochester ME1 . . . . . . .63 B2
Cowdrey Ct DA1 . . . . . .33 B8
Cowdrey Pl CT1 . . . . . 175 B6
Cowdreys TN9 . . . . . . 254 C8
Cowen Ho 4 SE18 . . . .12 B8
Cowgate Hill CT17 . . . 310 D7
Cowgate La CT18 . . . . 307 C5
Cow La Canterbury CT1 . 174 D7
Dover CT17 . . . . 310 A7
Horseshoe Green TN8 . . 250 D1
Cow Leaze E6 . . . . .2 A7
Cowley Ave DA9 . . . . . .17 A2
Cowley Rise CT9 . . . . . 83 C8
Cowper Ave RM18 . . . . .19 B6
Cowper Cl Bexley DA16 . 13 A2
Bromley BR2 . . . . 52 B5
Whitstable CT5 . . . . 75 D3
Cowper Rd Bromley BR2 . 52 D5
Crabble CT17 . . . . 277 E3
Deal CT14 . . . . 215 C5
Erith DA17 . . . . .4 A2
Gillingham ME7 . . . . . . 64 D3
Margate CT9 . . . . .50 J1
Sittingbourne ME10 . . . 102 B4
Cowstead Rd ME9 . . . . 99 D2
Coxes Ave CT12 . . . . . .83 B3
Coxes La CT12 . . . . . . .83 B3
Coxett Hill ME13 . . . . 137 D5
Cox Gdns ME8 . . . . . . 65 A2
Coxheath Prim Sch
ME7 . . . . 194 C3
Coxhill Cres CT17 . . . . 277 D3
Coxhill Gdns CT17 . . . 277 D3
Coxhill CT15 . . . . 244 C3
Coxland Cotts TN26 . . 347 B1
Coxmount Rd SE7 . . . . .1 D1
Crabble Ave CT17 . . . . 278 A2
Crabble Cl CT17 . . . . . 277 F2
Crabble Corn Mill ★
CT17 . . . . 277 F3
Crabble Hill CT16,
CT17 . . . . 278 A2
Crabble La CT17 . . . . . 277 E2
Crabble Mdws CT17 . . 278 A2
Crabble Rd CT17 . . . . . 278 A3
Crabbs Croft Cl 7 BR6 . 86 C5
Crabtree Cl ME19 . . . . 159 A4
Crabtree La ME17 . . . . 233 B8
Crabtree Manorway N
DA17 . . . . .4 C5
Crabtree Manorway S
DA17 . . . . .4 C3
Crabtree Rdbt ME14 . . 129 E2
Crabtree Rd ME8 . . . . . 98 D8
Craddock Dr 8 CT1 . . 143 B1
Craddock Ho CT1 . . . . 143 B1
Craddock Rd CT1 . . . . 143 B1
Craddock Way ME8 . . . 98 D5
Cradducks La TN12 . . . 261 B4
Cradle Bridge Dr
TN24 . . . . 268 F2
Cradles Rd ME9 . . . . . . 99 C2
Cradley Rd SE9 . . . . . . 30 D7
Crafford St CT16 . . . . 278 D1
Craft Workshops
TN27 . . . . 230 C1
Cragie Wlk ME8 . . . . . .98 E4
Craigerne Rd SE3 . . . . .11 B7
Craig Ho SE3 . . . . .11 B7
Craigholm SE18 . . . . . 12 A6
Craig Ho ME1 . . . . .63 E1
Craighton Ho 2 CT16 . 310 D7
Craigie Ct DA1 . . . . . . 34 A8
Craigton Rd SE9 . . . . . .11 F3
Crales Ho SE18 . . . . . . 1 E3
Cramonde Pl DA16 . . . . 13 A5
Crampton Ct CT10 . . . . 84 A4
Crampton's Rd TN14 . . 154 B7
Cramptons TN17 . . . . . 320 F8
Cranborne Ave ME15 . . 162 C1
Cranborne Wlk CT2 . . 142 E3
Cranbourne Ave ME15 . 195 B8
Cranbourne Cotts CT11 . 117 F8
Cranbrook CE Prim Sch
TN17 . . . . 320 D5
Cranbrook Cl
Gillingham ME8 . . . . . . 65 C3
Hayes BR2 . . . . 52 A3
Maidstone ME15 . . . . . 195 F7
Margate CT9 . . . . .51 E1
Cranbrook Dr ME10 . . . 101 D1
Cranbrook Ho 1 DA8 . .14 F7
Cranbrook Mews 1
TN8 . . . . 217 C1
Cranbrook Mus ★
TN17 . . . . 320 D5
Cranbrook Rd
Benenden TN17 . . . . . 341 F8
Bexley DA7 . . . . .13 F6
Fosten Green TN27 . . . 322 C6
Goudhurst TN17 . . . . . 319 A8
Hawkhurst TN18 . . . . . 340 F4
Knox Bridge TN12,TN17 . 292 F7
Parkgate TN30 . . . . . . 323 C1
Tenterden TN30 . . . . . 344 E7
Cranbrook Sch TN17 . . 320 D5
Cranbrooks TN25 . . . . 301 D4
Cranbrook Union Mill ★
TN17 . . . . 320 D4
Crandalls TN11 . . . . . . 220 F1

Cranden Wlk DA4 . . . . .57 E7
Crane Ho 11 TN18 . . . . 340 F2
Crane House Gdns 10
TN18 . . . . 340 F2
Crane La TN17 . . . . . . 320 D5
Cranford Cl ME8 . . . . . . 65 D1
Cranford Ho DA1 . . . . . 15 A7
Cranford Rd
Dartford DA1 . . . . .33 E7
Tonbridge TN10 . . . . . 223 A5
Cranham Sq TN12 . . . 259 C5
Cranleigh Cl
Orpington BR6 . . . . . . 87 A7
Sidcup DA5 . . . . .14 B1
Cranleigh Ct CT5 . . . . 108 E8
Cranleigh Dr
Swanley BR8 . . . . 55 E5
Whitfield CT16 . . . . . . 278 B7
Cranleigh Gdns
Chatham ME4 . . . . 63 D3
Maidstone ME16 . . . . . 161 C7
Whitstable CT5 . . . . . . 108 E8
Cranley Par SE9 . . . . . . 29 E4
Cranley Rd E13 . . . . . . .1 B8
Cranmer Cl CT4 . . . . . 176 B4
Cranmer Ct ME15 . . . . 195 B8
Cranmer Ct ME2 . . . . . 63 C8
Cranmer Ho 6 CT2 . . 142 E1
Cranmer Rd TN13 . . . . 153 E4
Cranmore Rd BR7 . . . . . 23 A7
Cranstone Ct 12 DA14 . .31 B4
Cranswick Cotts CT14 . 247 C8
Cranwell Rd TN4 . . . . . 285 C4
Crates Yd TN4 . . . . 286 A5
Crathie Rd SE12 . . . . . .11 B1
Craufurd Gn CT20 . . . . 334 D5
Craven Cl CT9 . . . . 82 C8
Craven Rd BR6 . . . . . . 87 D7
Crawford St SE18 . . . . 13 A8
Crawford Gdns CT9 . . . .51 B2
Crawford Rd CT10 . . . . .83 F5
Crawfords BR8 . . . . . . .32 E1
Crawley Ct 1 DA11 . . . .19 B1
Crawshay Ct TN13 . . . 154 A4
Cray Ave BR5 . . . . 54 B4
Cray Bldgs DA14 . . . . . 31 C2
Craybrooke Rd DA14 . . 31 B4
Crayburne DA13 . . . . . .35 F4
Craybury End SE9 . . . . 30 C6
Cray Cl DA1 . . . . 15 A3
Craydene Rd DA8 . . . . .14 F6
Crayfields Bsns Pk BR5 . 54 C8
Crayfields Ind Pk BR5 . . 54 C7
Crayford Cl
Maidstone ME14 . . . . . 162 C6
Newham E6 . . . . 1 F7
Crayford Commercial Ctr
DA1 . . . . .14 E1
Crayford High St DA1 . . 14 F2
Crayford Ind Est DA1 . . 14 F2
Crayford Rd DA1 . . . . . .14 E1
Crayford Sta DA1 . . . . .14 E1
Crayford Way DA1 . . . . 15 A3
Craylands La DA10 . . . . 17 C2
Craylands BR5 . . . . 54 C6
Craylands Sq DA10 . . . 17 C2
Crayleigh Terr DA14 . . 31 C2
Craymill Sq DA1 . . . . . .14 F5
Cray Rd Crockenhill BR8 . 55 C3
Erith DA17 . . . . .14 A8
Sidcup DA14 . . . . 31 C2
Crayside Ind Est DA1 . . 15 B5
Crays Par The BR5 . . . . 54 C7
Craythorne Cl
Hythe CT21 . . . . 334 B4
New Romney TN28 . . . 373 B8
Craythorne Ho TN30 . . 345 B8
Craythorne La TN28 . . 373 B7
Craythorne TN30 . . . . . 345 B8
Cray Valley Rd BR5 . . . .54 B4
Creasey's Row TN14 . . 185 E5
Credenhall Dr BR2 . . . . 52 F1
Crediton Rd E16 . . . . . .1 A7
Credo Way RM20 . . . . . .17 B8
Creek La ME3 . . . . .25 B2
Creek The DA11 . . . . . .18 B2
Creek Way RM13 . . . . . .4 E8
Creighton Flats 2
CT13 . . . . 148 F1
Cremer Cl CT4 . . . . . . 173 C2
Cremer Pl ME13 . . . . . 138 A8
Cremers Rd ME10 . . . . 102 B5
Cremorne Rd 1 DA11 . .36 F8
Crendon Pk TN4 . . . . . 286 A8
Crescent Ave RM17 . . . 18 D8
Crescent Cotts TN13 . . 153 E7
Crescent Ct
1 Grays RM17 . . . . 18 D8
Sidcup DA15 . . . . 31 A5
Crescent Dr BR5 . . . . . 53 C3
Crescent Gdns BR8 . . . 55 C7
Crescent Ho
Margate CT9 . . . . 51 A2
Ramsgate CT12 . . . . . 117 C7
Rochester ME2 . . . . . . 63 C7
Crescent Rd
Birchington CT7 . . . . . .81 A7
Broadstairs CT10 . . . . . 84 C8
Bromley BR1 . . . . 29 A1
Erith DA8 . . . . .14 F8
Faversham ME13 . . . . 138 D7
Margate CT9 . . . . 50 H2
Ramsgate CT11 . . . . . 117 D7
Royal Tunbridge Wells
TN1 . . . . 286 B3
Sidcup DA15 . . . . 30 F5
Woolwich SE18 . . . . . . .2 B1
Crescent The
Aylesham CT15 . . . . . 211 A3
Bidborough TN4 . . . . . 253 E4
Borough Green TN15 . . 157 A8
Boughton Street ME13 . 140 A3

Crescent The continued
Canterbury CT2 . . . . . 142 F4
Chartham CT4 . . . . . . 173 D1
Eythorne CT15 . . . . . . 245 C7
Folkestone CT20 . . . . 334 E3
Groombridge TN3 . . . . 312 C2
Halfway Houses ME12 . .46 E6
Longfield DA3 . . . . 58 E6
Lower Halstow ME9 . . . 67 C3
Maidstone ME14 . . . . . 161 F8
Northfleet DA11 . . . . . .36 F6
St Margaret's at Cliffe
CT15 . . . . 280 A5
St Mary's Island ME4 . . 41 B1
Sandwich CT13 . . . . . 180 E6
Sevenoaks TN13 . . . . . 154 D6
Sheerness ME12 . . . . . 28 C2
Sidcup DA14 . . . . 30 F4
Stoke ME3 . . . . 31 C8
Sittingbourne ME10 . . . 69 A1
Swanscombe DA9 . . . . 17 C2
Teynham ME9 . . . . . . 103 D3
Tonbridge TN9 . . . . . . 222 B2
Crescent Way
Chatham ME5 . . . . 96 D5
Orpington BR6 . . . . . . .86 E5
Cressey Ct 7 ME4 . . . . .63 E4
Cressfield TN23 . . . . . 267 F1
Cressingham Ct 1 DA17 . .4 A2
Cress Way ME13 . . . . . 138 A7
Cresta Cl CT6 . . . . .75 F4
Crest Ave RM17 . . . . . .18 B7
Crest La CT14 . . . . 121 B8
Crest Ind Est TN12 . . . 259 C6
Crest Rd ME1 . . . . 63 C1
Crest View Dr BR5 . . . . 53 C4
Crest View DA9 . . . . . . 17 A3
Crestway ME5 . . . . .97 B8
Crete Hall Rd DA11 . . . .18 E1
Crete Rd E CT18,CT19 . 307 D1
Crete Rd W CT18 . . . . 307 B1
Creteway CT19 . . . . . . 335 E8
Creton St SE18 . . . . . . .2 A3
Creve Coeur Cl ME14 . . 163 A5
Crevequer Chambers 11
ME8 . . . . .65 F1
Cricketers
Bells Yew Green TN3 . . 315 A5
Erith DA8 . . . . .4 E1
Harrietsham ME17 . . . 198 D6
Hawkinge CT18 . . . . . 307 B6
Sittingbourne ME10 . . . 101 F8
Cricketers Dr DA13 . . . 93 A7
Cricket Ground Rd BR7 . 23 B8
Crimond Ave TN29 . . . 353 A4
Criol Rd TN26 . . . . 299 A2
Cripple Hill TN26 . . . . 296 D1
Cripple St ME15 . . . . . 195 A7
Cripps Cl CT3 . . . . 210 E5
Cripps' La CT15 . . . . . 279 F6
Crisfield Ct TN30 . . . . 324 B2
Crispe Cl ME8 . . . . 98 D4
Crispe Park Cl CT7 . . . .81 A3
Crispin Cl ME13 . . . . . 138 D8
Crispin Ct ME17 . . . . . 194 C3
Crispin Rd ME2 . . . . . .62 E8
Crispin Way ME19 . . . 159 A4
Crittall's Cnr DA14 . . . 31 C1
Crittenden Bglws
ME15 . . . . 194 A4
Crittenden Cotts
ME15 . . . . 194 A4
Crittenden Rd TN12 . . 256 D3
Crittle's Ct TN5 . . . . . 336 F4
Crockenhill Way DA13 . .36 E1
Crockenhill Hill BR5 . . . 54 D4
Crockenhill La BR8,DA4 . 56 C2
Crockenhill Prim Sch
BR8 . . . . 55 C3
Crocken Hill Rd TN27 . 232 C2
Crockenhill Rd BR5,BR8 . 54 E4
Crockers Hatch Cnr
TN3 . . . . 284 D2
Crockford Cl TN10 . . . 222 F7
Crockham Hill CE Prim Sch
TN8 . . . . 184 C2
Crockham La ME13 . . . 140 B6
Crockham Rd ME13 . . . 140 C6
Crockham Way SE9 . . . 30 A4
Crockshard Hill CT3 . . 178 B4
Crockshard La CT3 . . . 178 B4
Croft Cl Bromley BR7 . . 29 F3
Chatham ME5 . . . . 97 C1
Erith DA17 . . . . .3 F1
Tonbridge TN10 . . . . . 222 F5
Croft Ct TN8 . . . . 217 C1
Crofters Cl CT21 . . . . . 353 E8
Crofters The ME8 . . . . .98 F7
Croft Gdns ME17 . . . . 199 D4
Croft La
Edenbridge TN8 . . . . . 217 C1
Folkestone CT20 . . . . 334 F5
Crofton Ave
Orpington BR5,BR6 . . . 86 C8
Sidcup DA5 . . . . 31 D8
Crofton Cl TN24 . . . . . 268 C6
Crofton Inf Sch BR5 . . . 53 D2
Crofton Jun Sch BR5 . . 53 D2
Crofton La BR5,BR6 . . . 53 D2
Crofton Rd
Orpington BR6 . . . . . . .86 B8
Westgate-on-S CT8 . . . .81 E7
Croft Rd Ashford TN24 . 268 D2
Bromley BR1 . . . . 29 A1
Westerham TN16 . . . . 151 C1
Croftside DA13 . . . . . . 126 A8
Croft's Pl 8 CT10 . . . . .84 B4
Croft The
Leybourne ME19 . . . . 127 E2
Swanley BR8 . . . . 55 C6

Croft The continued
Tenterden TN30 . . . . . 345 B7
Croft Way
Sevenoaks TN13 . . . . . 153 F2
Sidcup DA15 . . . . .30 E5
Croftwood TN23 . . . . . 299 D6
Croidene Ct ME12 . . . . 47 A6
Cromarty Ct 8 BR1 . . . 52 C7
Crombie Cl CT18 . . . . . 307 B5
Crombie Rd DA15 . . . . 30 D7
Cromer Pl 5 BR6 . . . . 53 D1
Cromer Rd
Rochester ME2 . . . . . . .63 B8
Sittingbourne ME9,
ME10 . . . . 134 F8
Cromer St TN9 . . . . . . 222 A1
Cromford Ct BR1 . . . . . .86 E7
Cromlix Cl BR7 . . . . . . .53 B7
Crompton Gdns ME15 . 162 B3
Crompton Tower Rly Mus ★
CT10 . . . . 84 A4
Cromwell Ave BR2 . . . . 52 B5
Cromwell Cl BR2 . . . . . 52 B5
Cromwell Mews BR7 . . 53 A8
Cromwell Park Pl
CT20 . . . . 334 D4
Cromwell Rd
Canterbury CT1 . . . . . 175 A6
Maidstone ME14 . . . . . 162 B5
Royal Tunbridge Wells
TN2 . . . . 286 C3
West Minst ME11 . . . . .45 F7
Whitstable CT5 . . . . . . .74 C1
Cromwell Terr ME4 . . . . 64 A3
Cronin Cl 2 ME20 . . . 127 F4
Crooked La DA11,DA12 . .19 B1
Crooked S Rd CT14 . . . 247 C2
Crookenden Pl CT4 . . . 242 F8
Crook Log DA6 . . . . 13 D3
Crook Log Prim Sch
DA6 . . . . 13 D3
Crook Rd TN12 . . . . . . 257 D1
Crook's Court La
CT15 . . . . 308 F4
Crookston Rd SE9 . . . . 12 A4
Croombs Rd E16 . . . . . .1 C8
Crosby House DA1 . . . . 15 A1
Crosier Cl SE3 . . . . . . .11 E6
Crosier Ct ME9 . . . . . . .66 E3
Crosley Rd ME7 . . . . . . 64 D3
Cross-at-Hand Cotts
TN12 . . . . 228 E2
Crossbrook Rd SE3 . . . .11 E4
Cross Ct 11 SE28 . . . . .3 B6
Cross Dr ME17 . . . . . . 197 B1
Cross Keys Cl TN13 . . . 187 A8
Cross Keys
Maidstone ME14 . . . . . 163 C4
Sevenoaks TN13 . . . . . 187 A8
Cross La 7 ME13 . . . . 138 D7
Cross Lane E DA12 . . . . 37 B6
Cross Lane Gdns TN5 . 338 D1
Cross Lane W DA11 . . . 37 B6
Cross La Sidcup DA5 . . . 31 F8
Sittingbourne ME10 . . . 101 E6
Throwley Forstal ME13 . 202 C7
Ticehurst TN5 . . . . . . 338 D2
Crossley Ave CT6 . . . . .75 F4
Crossley Cl TN16 . . . . 118 D4
Crossmead SE9 . . . . . .29 F7
Cross Rd Birchington CT7 . 81 B8
Dartford DA1 . . . . 15 C1
Deal CT14 . . . . 215 A2
Hawley DA2 . . . . 33 F4
Northfleet DA11 . . . . . .18 F1
Orpington,Keston Mark
BR2 . . . . .85 E8
Orpington,St Mary Cray
BR5 . . . . 54 B4
Sidcup DA14 . . . . .31 B4
Cross St
2 Canterbury CT2 . . . 142 E1
Chatham ME4 . . . . 64 A4
Erith DA8 . . . . .14 E8
Gillingham ME7 . . . . . . 64 C6
Herne Bay CT6 . . . . . . 76 D3
Cross Stile TN23 . . . . . 299 F8
Cross St
Maidstone ME14 . . . . . 162 A6
Rochester ME2 . . . . . . .63 B8
Cross The CT13 . . . . . 180 B2
Crossway Chatham ME5 . .96 E6
Erith SE28 . . . . .3 D7
Orpington BR5 . . . . . . 53 D4
Cross Way ME1 . . . . . . 63 C3
Crossways Ave CT9 . . . 83 A5
Crossways Bvd DA2,
DA9 . . . . .16 E3
Crossways
Canterbury CT2 . . . . . 142 F4
Chart Sutton ME17 . . . 196 B1
Crossways Cl TN29 . . . 352 E2
Crossways Cl TN16 . . . 150 C7
Crossways Hextable BR8 . .32 F1
Sittingbourne ME10 . . . 101 C1
Tatsfield TN16 . . . . . . 150 C7
Crossway The
Bromley SE9 . . . . 29 D6
Royal Tunbridge Wells
TN4 . . . . 285 D2
Crouch Cotts ME13 . . . 171 E8
Crouch Croft SE9 . . . . . 30 A5
Crouch Hill Ct ME9 . . . 67 C3
Crouch House Cotts
TN8 . . . . 217 B2
Crouch House Rd TN8 . 217 B2
Crouch La
Crouch TN15 . . . . 157 B6
Linkhill TN18 . . . . 356 D6
Selling ME13 . . . . 171 E8
Crowbridge Link
TN24 . . . . 300 F7

Crowbridge Rd TN24 .. 300 F6
Crow Cnr
  Brabourne TN25 ..... 270 E1
  Rochester ME1 .... 63 C5
Crowden Way SE28 ....3 C6
Crow Dr TN14 .... 121 C4
Crowfoot Cl SE28 ......2 E5
Crow Hill
  Borough Green TN15 ... 157 A7
  Broadstairs CT10 ....84 B5
Crow Hill Rd
  Borough Green TN15 ... 157 A7
  Margate CT9 ....82 B8
Crowhurst La
  Basted TN15 .... 156 E4
  West Kingsdown TN15 ..91 B4
Crowhurst Oast TN12 . 191 D1
Crowhurst Rd TN15 ... 156 F6
Crowhurst Way BR5 .... 54 C4
Crow La ME1 .... 63 C5
Crown Acres CT12 .... 225 A6
Crown Cl BR6 .... 87 A6
Crown Ct Bromley BR2 .. 52 E4
  Cranbrook TN17 ..... 320 C5
  Deal CT14 .... 215 D6
  Eltham SE12 .... 11 B1
  Tilbury RM18 .... 19 A5
Crownfield Rd TN23 ... 299 F8
Crownfields
  Maidstone ME14 ..... 162 F4
  Sevenoaks TN13 ..... 154 B2
Crown Gdns CT2 ..... 142 E1
Crown Gn DA12 ....38 E3
Crown Hill Rd CT6 .... 76 C4
Crown Ho
  Lamberhurst TN3 .... 317 B5
  Rochester ME1 ....63 B4
Crown La Bromley BR2 .. 52 D4
  Chislehurst BR7 ..... 53 C8
Crown Lane Spur BR2 .. 52 D3
Crown La Shorne DA12 .. 34 C8
  Stelling Minnis CT4 .. 240 E3
Crown Quay La 5
  ME10 .... 102 A4
Crown Rd Grays RM17 .. 18 A8
  Marlpit Hill TN8 .... 217 D2
  Orpington BR6 .... 87 A5
  Shoreham TN14 ....88 F1
  Sittingbourne ME10 .. 101 E6
Crown St ME7 .... 64 D6
Crown Woods Sch SE9 . 12 C2
Crown Woods Way
  SE9 .... 12 D2
Crows Camp Rd CT4 .. 209 A5
Crowther Cl TN12 .... 260 E4
Croxley Cl BR5 ....54 B7
Croxley Gn BR5 ....54 B8
Croyde Cl DA15 ...... 30 D8
Croydon Cl ME5 ..... 97 C4
Croydon Rd
  Hayes BR2,BR4,BR6 .... 85 C7
  Tatsfield TN16 ...... 150 F3
  Westerham TN16 .... 151 B2
Crozier Ho SE3 .... 11 B4
Cruden Rd DA12 ......37 F6
Cruise Liner Terminal
  CT17 .... 310 E4
Crumpsall St SE2 ......3 C2
Crump's La ME17 .... 231 B4
Crundale 2 ME14 .... 162 A5
Crundale Rd ME8 .... 65 C3
Crundale Tower BR5 ... 54 C1
Crundale Way CT9 .... 51 E1
Crundwell Rd TN4 .... 253 F1
Crusader Cl ME8 ......98 B8
Crusader Ct DA1 ......15 F3
Crusoe Rd DA8 ....4 D1
Crutches La ME3,ME2 .. 39 B1
Cryalls Bsns Est ME10 . 101 C4
Cryalls La ME10,ME9 .. 101 C3
Cryals Ct TN12 ...... 288 E5
Cryals Rd TN12 ..... 288 D5
Cryol Rd TN23 ...... 300 A7
Crystal Bsns Ctr CT13 . 149 B2
Crystal Ho 2 SE18 ....2 F2
Ctr for European
  Agri-Enviromental
  Studies TN25 .... 238 A1
Cubitt Ho CT19 ...... 335 D6
Cuckmere Ct 18 BR5 ... 54 C1
Cuckold's Cnr
  High Halden TN26 ... 325 E1
  Lower Higham ME3 ... 39 C6
Cuckolds Cnr
  New Ash Green DA3 ...92 B7
  Snargate TN29 ...... 362 E7
  Cuckold's Cnr TN12 .. 260 F4
Cuckolds Green Rd
  ME3 .... 25 B5
Cuckoo La
  Ashford,Singleton TN23 . 299 E7
  Ashford TN23 ...... 299 D6
  Lamberhurst TN12 ... 289 A2
  Postling CT21 ...... 304 F2
  Tonbridge TN11 ..... 223 A7
Cuckoowood Ave
  ME14 .... 129 F1
Cudham CE Prim Sch
  TN16 .... 119 A3
Cudham Cl ME14 .... 162 C6
Cudham Gdns CT9 .... 51 E2
Cudham La N TN14 ... 119 D7
Cudham La S TN14 ... 119 D2
Cudham Park Rd TN14 . 86 E1
Cudham Rd
  Downe BR6 .... 119 B7
  Tatsfield TN16 ...... 150 E8
Cudworth Rd TN24 ... 300 F7
Cuff Cres SE9 .... 11 D1
Cugley Rd DA2 ...... 34 C8
Culcroft DA3 ....58 F6

Cullens Hill CT4 ..... 273 F4
Cullet Dr ME11 ...... 46 A3
Culling's Hill CT4 .... 273 F4
Culmers Terr ME13 ... 139 E8
Culpeper Cl
  Hollingbourne ME17 .. 164 E2
  Rochester ME2 ......63 E6
Culpepers TN17 ..... 318 E7
Culpepper Cl CT2 .... 143 A4
Culpepper Rd
  Coxheath ME17 ..... 194 B3
  Gillingham ME8 ..... 99 E3
Culter Field TN23 .... 299 E8
Culverden Ave ME12 .. 47 F6
Culverden Down TN4 .. 285 F5
Culverden Park Rd
  TN4 .... 285 F5
Culverden Pk TN4 .... 285 F5
Culverden Sq TN4 .... 286 A5
Culverden St TN1 .... 286 A4
Culver's La TN12 .... 376 D5
Culverstone Green Prim
  Sch DA13 ....92 F4
Culverstone Ho BR5 ...54 B6
Culverton Ct 18 DA14 .. 31 A4
Culvey Cl DA3 ....58 E4
Cumberland Ave
  Bexley DA16 .... 12 F3
  Broadstairs CT10 .... 84 A5
  Canterbury CT1 ..... 175 D7
  Gravesend DA12 ..... 37 C8
  Maidstone ME15 .... 195 D8
Cumberland Cotts 23
  TN1 .... 286 A2
Cumberland Ct
  Sevenoaks TN13 ..... 153 E7
  Tonbridge TN10 ..... 222 A4
Cumberland Dr
  Dartford DA1 ....33 F8
  Erith DA7 .... 13 E7
  Lower Halstow ME9 ... 67 C3
Cumberland Gdns 10
  TN1 .... 286 A2
Cumberland Ho SE28 ...2 D4
Cumberland Mews 12
  TN1 .... 286 A2
Cumberland Rd
  Chatham ME4,ME7 .....64 B7
  Gillingham ME7 ..... 64 C7
  Margate CT9 .... 51 B3
  Newham E13 ....1 B8
  1 Ramsgate CT11 ... 117 D6
Cumberland Sch E16 ...1 A8
Cumberland Villas 5
  DA12 .... 37 C8
Cumberland Wlk TN1 . 286 A2
Cumberland Yd 11
  TN1 .... 286 A2
Cumbrian Ave DA7 ....14 E5
Cundishall Cl CT5 .... 108 C8
Cundy Rd E16 ....1 C7
Cunningham Cl TN4 .. 286 B7
Cunningham Cres
  Birchington CT7 ......80 E7
  Chatham ME5 ....97 B7
Cunningham Ho ME1 ...63 B4
Cunningham Rd TN4 .. 286 B7
Cupola Cl BR1 ....29 B3
Curates Wlk DA2 ..... 33 D5
Curlew Ave ME9 ......67 B3
Curlew Cl Erith SE28 ...3 D6
  Herne Bay CT6 ...... 77 C2
Curlew Cres ME2 ..... 62 C6
Curlew Pl CT18 ..... 307 A3
Curlews The DA12 .... 37 D6
Curlinge Ct CT14 .... 117 A6
Curran Ave DA15 ..... 12 F2
Currie Rd TN4 ...... 286 A5
Curteis Rd TN30 .... 324 B1
Curtis Ct BR6 .... 54 A2
Curtis La CT4 .... 240 D2
Curtismill Cl BR5 .... 54 B6
Curtismill Way BR5 ... 54 B6
Curtis Rd TN24 ..... 300 E7
Curtis Way
  1 Faversham ME13 .. 138 C7
  Rochester ME1 ...... 96 D7
  7 Woolwich SE28 .....3 B6
Curtis Wood Park Rd
  CT6 .... 111 A7
Curtis Wood Rd CT6 .. 110 F7
Curzon Cl Deal CT14 . 215 C3
  Orpington BR6 ...... 86 D6
Curzon Cres SE9 ..... 30 C5
Curzon Dr RM17 ..... 18 C7
Curzon Ho 5 CT11 ... 117 A6
  Dover CT17 .... 310 B8
Curzon Rd Chatham ME4 .63 F3
  Maidstone ME14 .... 162 A6
Cushings Wlk 18 CT5 .. 74 D2
Cushman Rd CT1 .... 174 E7
Custom House for Excel Sta
  E16 ....1 B6
Cutbush Almshouses
  3 Maidstone ME14 ... 162 A4
  1 Maidstone ME15 ... 162 A3
Cutbush and Corrall Ct 1
  ME14 .... 162 B4
Cutbush Cl ME17 .... 198 D6
Cutbush Ho 2 ME15 .. 162 A3
Cuthbert Rd CT8 .....81 E8
Cutmore St DA11 ..... 37 B8
Cutter Cl ME2 .... 40 F3
Cutter Ho 6 DA8 ......4 E1
Cutter Ridge Rd DA13 . 61 A1
Cut The TN27 ...... 295 E8
Cuttings The CT12 ... 117 C8
Cutty Sark Ct DA9 ... 27 E2
Cuxton Cl DA6 ....13 C2

Cuxton Ind Est ME2 ... 62 C2
Cuxton BR5 .... 53 C4
Cuxton Rd
  Maidstone ME15 .... 195 F5
  Rochester ME2 ...... 62 F5
Cuxton Sta ME2 ..... 62 C2
Cyclamen Rd BR8 .... 55 D5
Cygnet Cl ME20 ..... 128 A2
Cygnet Gdns DA11 ....36 F6
Cygnet L Ctr DA11 ....36 E6
Cygnet Rd ME5 ...... 97 C2
Cygnet Way TN21 ... 267 F1
Cylinder Rd CT21 .... 333 B4
Cypress Ave
  Ashford TN23 ...... 267 E2
  Hoo St Werburgh ME3 .41 E3
Cypress Ct CT5 ..... 108 C4
Cypress Ct ME7 ......64 F6
Cypress Gr
  Elvington CT15 ..... 212 B2
  Royal Tunbridge Wells
  TN2 .... 314 C8
Cypress Rd ME2 ..... 40 C1
Cypress Tree Cl DA15 ..30 F7
Cyprus Ct ME13 ..... 138 E7
Cyprus Pl E6 ....2 A6
Cyprus Rd ME13 .... 138 E7
Cyprus Sta E6 ....2 A6
Cyril Hall Ct DA11 .... 18 F1
Cyril John Gange Lodge
  TN2 .... 286 D2
Cyril Lodge 3 CT14 ... 31 A4
Cyril Rd Bexley DA7 ... 13 E5
  Orpington BR6 ...... 54 A2

D

D2 Trad Est ME10 .... 102 B6
Dabbling Cl DA8 ......15 B7
Daerwood Cl BR2 .... 52 F1
Daffodil Rd ME2 ......62 E7
Daglish Cl TN28 .... 373 B6
Dagmar Rd ME4 ......64 B2
Dagonet Gdns BR1 ... 29 A5
Dagonet Rd BR1 ..... 29 A5
Dahlia Dr BR8 .... 55 F7
Dahlia Rd SE2 ....3 B2
Daimler Ave CT6 .....76 B3
Dainton Cl 2 BR1 .... 52 B8
Daintons Cotts 2
  TN18 .... 340 F2
Dairsie Ct 4 BR1 .... 52 C7
Dairsie Rd SE9 ...... 12 A4
Dairy Cl 3 Bromley BR1 .29 B1
  Sutton at H DA4 ..... 34 B1
Dairy La
  Chainhurst TN12 .... 226 F4
  Crockham Hill TN8 .. 184 B1
  Woolwich SE18 ....1 F2
Dairy Pl TN11 .... 226 F4
Daisy Munns Ho SE9 .. 30 C7
Dajen Bsns Pk ME4 ... 64 C1
Dalberg Way SE2 ......3 D3
Dalby Rd CT9 .... 51 A3
Dalby Sq CT9 .... 51 A3
Daleacres Cvn Pk
  CT21 .... 352 E7
Dale Cl Crayford DA1 .. 14 F1
  Greenwich SE3 ...... 11 A4
Dale Ct Bromley BR1 .. 52 D6
  Chatham ME5 .... 97 A2
Dale End DA1 .... 14 F1
Dalemain Mews E16 ...1 A5
Dale Rd Crayford DA1 .. 14 F1
  Northfleet DA13 ..... 36 A4
  Rochester ME1 ...... 63 C3
  Swanley BR8 .... 55 C6
Daleside Cl BR6 ..... 87 A4
Daleside Rd BR6 .... 87 A5
Dale St Chatham ME4 .. 63 E2
  Royal Tunbridge Wells
  TN1 .... 286 B4
Dale The BR2 .... 85 D6
Dale View DA8 ...... 14 F5
Dale Wlk Ashford TN24 . 268 C7
  Dartford DA2 .... 34 C7
Dale Wood Rd BR6 ... 53 E1
Dalewood ME10 ..... 102 A2
Dalison Ct ME2 ...... 95 B4
Dallas-Brett Cres
  CT19 .... 335 E4
Dallinger Rd 1 CT7 ...80 F8
Dallin Rd Bexley DA6 .. 13 D3
  Woolwich SE18 ...... 12 B7
Dalmatia Ct CT17 ... 278 A1
Dalmeny Ave CT9 .... 51 D1
Dalmeny Rd DA8 .... 14 B6
Dalmeny Terr CT21 .. 333 A1
Dalton Cl BR6 ....86 E7
Dalton Ct 7 CT11 ... 117 E7
Daltons Rd BR6,BR8 .. 88 C7
Dalton St SE27 ...... 64 C6
Dalwood TN28 ...... 373 A4
Dalycross Cvn Pk
  CT21 .... 352 E7
Damask Cl CT2 ..... 142 E3
Damerham Cl CT2 ... 142 E3
Damiem Cl ME4 ..... 64 A2
Damigos Rd DA12 ....37 F7
Damon Cl DA14 ...... 31 B5
Damon Ct DA14 ..... 31 B5
Damson Ct BR8 ..... 55 D5
Damson Dr ME3 ..... 41 E3
Danaway Cotts ME9 .. 100 C3
Dando Cres SE3 ..... 11 B4
Dan Dr ME13 .... 138 A8
Dane Cl Chatham ME5 .. 96 F7
  Hartlip ME9 .... 99 D6
  Orpington BR6 ..... 51 A4
  Sidcup DA5 .... 32 A8
Danecourt Com Sch
  ME8 .... 65 A2

Dane Court Gdns CT10 . 83 D5
Dane Court Gram Sch
  CT10 .... 83 E4
Dane Court Rd CT10 .. 83 C6
Dane Cres CT11 .... 117 E8
Dane Ct
  Coxheath ME17 .... 194 C2
  Tilmanstone CT14 .. 212 F4
Danedale Ave ME12 .. 47 F6
Dane End Rd CT8 .... 81 D8
Danefield Ct ME14 .. 163 B4
Dane Gdns CT9 ......83 B8
Dane Hill Gr CT9 .... 50 J3
Dane Hill CT9 ...... 50 J3
Dane Hill Row CT9 ... 50 J2
Danehill Wlk DA14 ... 31 A5
Dane Ho CT14 ..... 215 D8
Danehurst CT8 ..... 50 C1
Dane John Ct 3 CT1 . 174 F7
Dane John Mews 1
  CT1 .... 174 F7
Dane La ME9 .... 99 D6
Danemore TN30 .... 345 B8
Dane Mount CT9 .... 83 C8
Dane Park Rd
  Margate CT9 .... 50 J2
  Ramsgate CT11 .... 117 E8
Dane Park Villas CT9 .. 51 A2
Dane Pk ME15 ..... 194 C6
Dane Rd Birchington CT7 . 80 D7
  Margate CT9 .... 51 A2
  Otford TN14 .... 121 F2
  Ramsgate CT11 .... 117 E8
Danes Cl ME13 ..... 36 C5
Danes Ct CT16 ..... 278 D2
Danes Dr ME12 ..... 49 D2
Danes Hill ME7 ..... 65 A6
Danes Mead ME10 ... 68 F1
Danesmead Terr CT9 .. 50 J2
Dane Valley Rd CT10,
  CT9 .... 83 C8
Daniel Ho 5 ME16 ... 161 E5
Daniels Ct CT5 ...... 74 C1
Danley Mid Sch ME12 . 46 F7
Danley Rd ME12 ..... 46 E7
Danns La ME18,ME19 . 159 A1
Dansington Rd DA16 .. 13 A3
Danson House ★ DA6 . 13 C3
Danson Cl ME16 .... 13 B3
Danson Mead DA16 ... 13 B3
Danson Prim Sch DA16 . 13 A3
Danson Rd Bexley DA5 . 13 C2
  Bexley DA5,DA6 .... 13 D2
Danson Underpass
  DA5 .... 13 C1
Danson Way ME8 .... 65 D2
Danton La CT18 .... 306 C1
Danvers Rd TN9 .... 222 B1
Darby Gdns ME3 ..... 39 B3
Darby Pl CT20 ...... 335 D5
Darby Rd CT20 ..... 335 D5
Darby's La TN5 ..... 337 B2
D'arcy Pl BR2 ...... 52 A5
Darcy Sq TN28 ..... 373 E5
Darent Cl TN13 .... 153 C5
Darenth Ave TN10 .. 222 C5
Darenth Cl CT6 ..... 77 B3
Darenth Cotts TN14 . 121 F8
Darenth Ct 18 BR5 ... 54 D1
Darenth Dr DA12 .... 38 B7
Darenth Gdns TN16 .. 151 D1
Darenth Hill DA2 .... 34 C3
Darenth La TN13 ... 153 E6
Darenth Park Ave DA2 . 34 F5
Darenth Prim Sch DA2 . 34 E2
Darenth Rd Bexley DA16 . 13 A6
  Dartford DA1 ....33 F7
Darenth Rd S DA2 ... 34 B4
Darenth Rise ME5 .... 97 B3
Darenth Wood Rd DA2 . 34 D6
Darent Ind Pk DA8 ... 15 D8
Darent Mead DA4 .... 57 B8
Darent Valley Hospl
  DA2 .... 34 E7
Dargate Cl ME16 .... 161 D7
Dargate Rd
  Dargate CT2,ME13 .. 140 F7
  Yorkletts CT5 ...... 108 A3
Dargets Rd ME5 ..... 97 A3
Dark Hill ME13 ..... 138 C7
Darland Ave ME7 .... 64 E1
Darland Ho SE9 ..... 12 D1
Darlinghurst Rd TN19 . 334 E7
Darlington Dr ME12 ... 47 A6
Darlington St CT20 .. 335 D5
Darlton Cl DA1 ...... 14 F4
Darman La TN18,ME18 . 225 D3
Darnets Field TN14 .. 121 F2
Darnley Cl
  Broadstairs CT10 ....83 B7
  Folkestone CT20 ... 334 F4
  Rochester ME2 ..... 62 D6
Darnley Dr CT11 ..... 37 A8
Darnley Rd TN4 .... 253 E4
Darnley Rd
  Gravesend DA11 ..... 37 A8
  Rochester ME2 ......62 F6
  Sittingbourne ME10 . 101 E6
  Woolwich SE28 ....3 A6
Darnley St DA11 ..... 37 B8
Darns Hill BR8 ...... 55 C2
Darracott Cl CT14 .. 215 B5
Darrell Cl CT6 ...... 76 C3
Darren Gdns CT10 ...83 F2
Darrick Wood Rd BR6 . 86 C7
Darrick Wood Inf & Jun
  Schs BR6 .... 86 B6
Darrick Wood Rd BR6 . 86 B7
Darrick Wood Sch BR6 . 86 B7
Darrick Wood Sports Ctr
  BR6 .... 86 B7

Dart Cl ME2 ....62 F7
Dartford Borough Mus ★
  DA1 .... 33 B8
Dartford Gram Sch
  DA1 .... 15 C1
Dartford Gram Sch for Girls
  DA1 .... 33 C8
Dartford Hospl Specl Sch
  DA3 .... 59 A6
Dartford Rd
  Coldblow DA5 ...... 32 C7
  Dartford DA1 .... 15 B1
  Farningham DA4 .... 57 A5
  Sevenoaks TN13 .... 154 C3
Dartford Sta DA1 .... 15 E1
Dartford Technology Coll
  DA1 .... 33 D8
Dartford Trad Pk DA1 . 33 F6
Dartford West Technology
  Coll for Girls DA1 .. 33 C8
Dartmouth Rd BR2 ... 52 A2
Darwin Cl BR6 ...... 86 D5
Darwin Coll CT2 .... 142 C5
Darwin Ct Eltham SE9 . 12 A1
  Rochester ME1 ..... 63 D5
Darwin Dr TN10 .... 222 D6
Darwin Rd Bexley DA16 . 12 F4
  Birchington CT7 ......80 F8
  Canterbury CT2 .... 142 E5
  Tilbury RM18 ...... 18 F6
Daryngton Ave CT7 ... 80 C7
Dashmonden Cl ME2 .. 40 C2
Dashwood Cl DA6 ... 14 A2
Dashwood Rd DA11 .. 37 A6
Davall Ho 10 RM17 ... 18 B8
Davema Cl BR7 ..... 53 A8
Davenport Ave ME7 .. 64 E7
Davenport Rd DA14 .. 31 E6
Davey Cl ME1 ...... 63 C5
David Ave ME12 ..... 51 D2
David Coffer Ct CT17 .. 4 B2
David Dr 28 DA14 ... 31 A5
David Ho 28 DA14 ... 31 A5
David Ramsey Ho SE3 . 11 D2
Davids Cl CT10 ......84 B3
Davidson Ho DA9 .... 17 C2
Davidson Rd CT2 ... 142 D1
Davie Cl ME12 ...... 46 B8
Davie Ct ME12 ..... 46 B8
Davington Hill ME13 . 138 C8
Davington Prim Sch
  ME13 .... 138 C8
Davis Ave Deal CT14 .. 215 A4
  Northfleet DA11 ..... 36 F7
Davis Cl TN13 ..... 154 C5
Davy's Pl DA12 ...... 37 E2
Dawbourne TN30 ... 324 B3
Dawell Dr TN16 .... 118 C2
Dawes Cl DA9 ....16 F2
Dawes Rd CT2,ME13 . 140 C4
Dawes St ME7 ...... 64 C5
Dawn La ME18 ..... 159 D3
Dawn Rise ME12 ..... 48 F6
Dawson Ave BR5 .....54 B7
Dawson Cl SE18 ......2 C2
Dawson Ct 7 ME7 ... 64 A6
Dawson Dr BR8 ..... 32 E1
Dawson Rd CT19 ... 335 B6
Dawson's Row 5 .... 138 A6
Day Ho 2 ME14 .... 162 B4
Days Lane Prim Sch
  DA15 .... 12 F1
Days La DA15 .... 30 E8
Daytona Way CT6 .... 76 A4
Dayton Dr DA8 ...... 15 D8
Dayton Rd ME13 .... 170 C3
Deacon Cl ME2 ......62 E8
Deacon Est The ME20 . 129 A2
Deacons Leas BR6 ... 86 D6
Deacon Trad Est TN9 . 222 D1
Deakin Leas TN9 .... 254 B7
Deakins Terr BR6 .... 54 A2
Deal Castle ★ CT14 .. 215 D5
Deal Castle Rd CT14 . 215 D5
Deal Ct Ent Ctr CT14 . 215 C7
Deal Ho ME15 ..... 195 E8
Deal Maritime & Local
  History Mus ★ CT14 . 215 D6
Deal Parochial CE Prim Sch
  CT14 .... 215 C5
Deal Rd
  Northbourne CT14 ... 214 A4
  Sandwich CT13,CT14 . 180 F5
  Deal Sta CT14 ..... 215 C6
Dean & Chapter Cotts
  DA13 .... 36 B2
Dean Croft CT6 ......77 B2
Dean Ct 14 CT1 .... 143 A1
Deane Ct CT5 ...... 108 E7
Deane Ct 8 ME7 .... 64 C6
Deanery Rd TN8 .... 184 C2
Dean Hill CT4,TN25 .. 240 B2
Dean La DA13 ...... 93 C5
Dean Mead CT19 ... 335 B7
Dean Rd
  Luddesdown DA13 ... 93 B8
  Rochester ME2 ......62 F8
  Sittingbourne ME10 . 101 E6
  Woolwich SE28 ....3 A6
Deans Ct 7 TN9 .... 254 B8
Deansfield Prim Sch
  SE9 .... 12 A4
Deans Hill Rd ME9 .. 133 C6
Deans Mill Ct CT1 .. 142 F1
Dean St ME15 ..... 194 C6
Deansway Ave CT3 .. 143 F7
Dean's Wlk TN23 ... 299 F7
Deanwood Cl ME8 ... 98 D6
Deanwood Dr ME8 ... 98 E6
Deanwood Prim Education
  Tech Sch ME8 ..... 98 D3

Deanwood Rd CT17 .. 277 E2
Deborah Cl CT5 .... 108 F7
Debrabant Cl DA8 ... 14 D8
De Burgh Hill CT17 .. 278 C1
De Burgh St 2 CT17 . 310 C8
Decimus Pl ME4 .... 286 B4
Decoy Hill Rd ME23 .. 42 B5
Deedes Cl CT21 .... 333 C3
Deepdene Rd DA16 .. 13 A4
Deepdene TN5 ..... 337 A6
Deerhurst Ct DA3 ... 59 C6
Deerhurst Gdns ME16 . 161 D4
Deering Cl ME4 ..... 41 B2
Deerleap La TN14 ... 120 E6
Deerson La CT3 .... 146 A4
Deerton St ME9 .... 104 A2
Defiance Wlk SE18 ...1 F3
Defiant Cl ME5 ......97 B6
Defoe Cl Chatham ME5 . 97 B6
  Erith DA8 .... 14 F6
Degema Rd BR7 ..... 30 B3
Deham Ho ME10 .... 101 D5
De Havilland Cl CT18 . 307 B4
De Havillands CT4 .. 176 E3
Deidre Chapman Ho
  DA10 .... 17 E1
Delacourt Cl CT12 .. 116 D5
Delacourt Rd SE3 ... 11 B7
Delafield Rd SE7 .....1 C1
Delagarde Rd TN16 . 151 C1
Delamark Rd ME1 ... 28 C2
Delamere Gdns 3
  ME6 .... 128 A8
Delamere Rd ME6 ... 128 A8
Delane Rd CT14 .... 215 A5
De L'angle Row CT4 . 173 D3
De Lapre Cl BR5 .... 54 D2
Delarue Cl TN11 .... 222 D8
Delaware Cl CT2 .... 143 F6
Delaware Cotts TN8 . 249 F8
Delce Jun & Inf Schs
  ME1 .... 63 D2
Delce Rd ME1 ...... 63 D4
Delfside CT13 ..... 181 A8
Delf St CT13 .... 148 F1
Delisle Rd SE28 ....2 E4
Delius Dr TN10 .... 222 F6
Delvan Cl SE18 ..... 12 A7
Delves Ave TN2 .... 286 C1
Demelza Cl ME2 ..... 62 A2
Demelza House Hospice
  ME9 .... 100 D3
De Mere Cl ME8 ..... 98 D6
Demozay Cl CT18 ... 307 A4
Denbeigh Dr TN10 .. 222 C6
Denberry Dr DA14 ... 31 B5
Denbigh Ave ME9 ... 65 C1
Denbigh Cl Bromley BR7 . 29 C2
  Sittingbourne ME10 . 101 E7
Denbigh Rd
  Ramsgate CT12 ......83 A1
  Royal Tunbridge Wells
  TN4 .... 286 C7
Denbridge Rd BR1 ...52 F7
Dence Cl CT6 .... 77 B5
Dence Pk CT6 ...... 77 B4
Dencorra Way TN23 . 268 A1
Dene Ave DA15 ..... 31 B8
Dene Cl DA2 .... 32 E4
Denecourt BR5 ..... 54 B8
Dene Dr New Barn DA3 . 59 B7
  Orpington BR6 ..... 87 B7
Dene Farm Barns CT3 . 178 A4
Dene Farm La CT3 .. 178 A4
Dene Holm Rd DA11 .. 36 C5
Dene Lodge Cl TN15 . 156 F7
Dene Rd DA1 .... 33 F8
Denesfield Ct TN13 . 153 C4
Denesway DA13 ......60 D3
Dene The
  Bethersden TN26 ... 297 D5
  Canterbury CT1 .... 175 B5
  Hythe CT21 .... 333 C2
  Sevenoaks TN13 .... 154 B1
Dene Way TN3 ..... 285 A7
Dene Wlk Longfield DA3 . 58 E6
  Margate CT9 .... 82 F7
Dengemarsh Rd TN29 . 379 A7
Dengrove Cvn Site
  CT2 .... 143 D6
Denham Cl Bexley DA16 . 13 C4
  Dymchurch TN29 ... 353 B4
Denham Rd ME9 .... 100 B7
Denham St 2 SE10 ...1 A1
Denison Mews ME3 .. 25 C4
Deniston Ave DA5 ... 31 F7
Den La TN12 ...... 226 C3
Denmark Ho 10 SE18 ..1 E2
Denmark Rd
  Bromley BR1 ....52 B8
  Ramsgate CT11 .... 117 E8
Denmark St
  Folkestone CT19 ... 335 E6
  Newham E13 ....1 B8
Dennard Way BR6 .... 86 A6
Denne Cl CT2 ...... 143 F7

Denne Manor La CT4 .. 204 C8
Dennes La TN29 ... 376 C8
Dennes Mill Cl TN25 .. 237 D2
Denness Rd TN23 ... 300 B7
Dennettsland Rd TN8 . 184 C1
Denning Cl ME16 ... 161 B4
Dennington Ct TN4 ... 254 A2
Dennis Cadman Ho
ME20 ... 128 F1
Dennis Rd DA11 ... 37 B5
Dennis Way CT19 ... 334 E7
Dennis Wilcocks Cl
ME9 ... 100 B6
Denny Cl 13 E6 ... 1 E8
Denny Ct 3 DA2 ... 16 B1
Densole La CT18 ... 307 A8
Densole Way CT18 ... 307 A8
Denstead Cotts CT4 ... 173 B8
Denstead Ct CT2 ... 142 C4
Denstead La CT4,ME13 . 173 C7
Denstead Oast CT4 ... 173 B8
Denstead Wlk 11
ME15 ... 195 F6
Denstroude La CT2 ... 141 D8
Dental Cl ME10 ... 101 A5
Dental St CT21 ... 333 C2
Dent-De-Lion Ct CT9 .. 82 A8
Dent-De-Lion Rd
Margate CT9 ... 82 A8
Westgate-on-S CT8 ... 50 C1
Denton Cl ME15 ... 195 E8
Denton Court Rd DA12 .. 37 E8
Denton Ct BR2 ... 53 A2
Denton Gn ME8 ... 65 B4
Denton Rd Bexley DA16 . 13 C7
Dartford DA1 ... 32 E8
Maypole DA5 ... 32 E7
Denton St DA12 ... 37 E8
Denton Terr DA5 ... 32 E6
Denton Way CT9 ... 51 C1
Denver Cl BR6 ... 53 E3
Denver Ind Est RM13 ... 4 F8
Denver Rd DA1 ... 33 A8
De Quincey Mews E16 ... 1 A5
Derby Cl
Sittingbourne ME10 ... 101 D6
Tonbridge TN11 ... 221 E6
Derby Rd Gillingham ME5 . 64 E2
Grays RM17 ... 18 B8
Maidstone ME15 ... 195 C8
Derby Road Bridge
RM17 ... 18 B8
Derifall Cl E6 ... 1 F8
Dering Cl Bridge CT4 ... 175 F1
Pluckley TN27 ... 265 C4
Dering Rd
Ashford TN24 ... 268 D2
Bridge CT4 ... 176 A1
Herne Bay CT6 ... 76 F4
Derings The TN29 ... 376 B6
Dering Terr TN27 ... 265 C3
Dering Way DA12 ... 37 F7
Deringwood Dr ME15 .. 162 F1
Dernier Rd TN10,TN9 .. 222 C4
Derrick Gdns SE7 ... 1 C3
Derringstone Downs
CT4 ... 242 F6
Derringstone Hill CT4 . 242 F6
Derringstone St CT4 .. 242 F7
Derry Downs BR5 ... 54 C3
Derville Ho TN28 ... 373 B6
Derville Rd TN29 ... 377 E7
Derwent Ave CT11 ... 117 A7
Derwent Cl DA1 ... 33 B7
Derwent Cres DA7 ... 14 A5
Derwent Dr
Orpington BR5 ... 53 D2
Royal Tunbridge Wells
TN4 ... 285 E5
Derwent Ho 3 ME15 .. 195 E7
Derwent Rd TN10 ... 222 C5
Derwent Way
Aylesham CT3 ... 210 F6
Gillingham ME8 ... 98 D8
Desmond Cres ME13 .. 139 A5
D'este Rd CT11 ... 117 F7
Detillens La RH8 ... 183 A6
Detling Ave CT10 ... 84 A1
Detling CE Prim Sch
ME14 ... 131 A1
Detling Cl
Gillingham ME8 ... 65 C2
West Minst ME12 ... 46 B7
Detling Hill ME14 ... 131 B2
Detling Rd Bromley BR1 . 29 A3
Erith DA8 ... 14 D7
Northfleet DA11 ... 36 D7
Devalls Cl E6 ... 2 A6
Devenish Rd SE2 ... 3 A4
Devon Ave CT14 ... 215 C3
Devon Cl Chatham ME5 .. 97 C7
Rainham ME8 ... 65 F1
Devon Ct Ramsgate CT12 . 83 B2
Sutton at H DA4 ... 57 B8
Devon Gdns CT7 ... 80 F7
Devon Rd
Canterbury CT1 ... 175 D8
Folkestone CT19 ... 335 D5
Maidstone ME15 ... 195 C8
Sutton at H DA4 ... 57 C8
Devonshire Ave DA1 ... 15 B1
Devonshire Cl TN2 ... 313 F8
Devonshire Gdns CT9 .. 51 C3
Devonshire Rd
Bexley DA6 ... 13 E3
Bromley SE9 ... 29 E6
Dover CT17 ... 310 B8
Gillingham ME7 ... 64 D7
Gravesend DA12 ... 37 B6
Newham E16 ... 1 B7
Devonshire Rd *continued*
Orpington BR6 ... 54 A2
West Thurrock RM20 ... 17 E8
Devonshire Sq BR2 ... 52 B5
Devonshire Terr CT10 ... 84 B5
De Warren Ho DA11 ... 18 D1
Dewberry Cl ME4 ... 41 B1
Dewberry Gdns E6 ... 1 E8
Dewhurst Cotts TN5 ... 336 A8
Dewhurst La TN5 ... 336 B8
DeWinter Ho TN13 ... 154 A3
Dewlands Ave DA2 ... 34 B8
Dew La TN31 ... 367 A1
Dexter Cl TN25 ... 268 C8
Dexter Ho 2 DA18 ... 3 E3
Deyley Way TN23 ... 299 C8
Dhekelia Cl ME14 ... 162 A7
Dial Cl Gillingham ME7 ... 64 F6
Swanscombe DA9 ... 17 D2
Dial Rd ME7 ... 64 F6
Diameter Rd BR5 ... 53 C3
Diamond Cotts TN12 .. 256 B7
Diamond Ct ME12 ... 28 B1
Diamond Field TN12 .. 289 F3
Diamond Rd CT5 ... 74 E2
Diana Ct DA8 ... 14 E8
Diana Gdns CT14 ... 215 A5
Diana Rd ME4 ... 64 A2
Dianne Ct SE12 ... 29 A7
Dianthus Cl SE2 ... 3 B1
Dibden La TN13,TN14 .. 186 E8
Dibdin Rd CT14 ... 215 D7
Dickens Ave
Canterbury CT1 ... 143 D2
Dartford DA1 ... 16 A3
Tilbury RM18 ... 19 B6
Dickens Cl Erith DA8 ... 14 B7
Hartley DA3 ... 58 F4
Langley Heath ME17 ... 196 E4
Dickens Ct Higham ME3 . 39 C4
Rochester ME2 ... 63 D8
Staplehurst TN12 ... 260 F5
Dickens Dr
Chislehurst BR7 ... 30 C2
West Malling ME19 ... 127 F1
Dickens Ho 3 DA17 ... 3 F1
Dickens House Mus★
CT10 ... 84 B4
Dickensian Cl ME3 ... 25 A2
Dickens Rd
Broadstairs CT10 ... 84 B5
Gravesend DA12 ... 37 E7
Maidstone ME14 ... 161 E8
Rochester ME1 ... 63 C3
Dickens Way TN18 ... 341 A2
Dickens Wlk CT10 ... 84 B4
Dickley La ME17 ... 199 A6
Dickson Ct 7 ME10 ... 102 B4
Dickson Ho SE18 ... 11 E6
Dickson Rd
Dover CT17 ... 310 C8
Eltham SE9 ... 11 E4
Dicksons Bourne
TN25 ... 329 F6
Dickson's Cnr CT13 ... 182 A6
Dieu Stone La CT16 ... 310 E8
Digby Rd CT20 ... 334 E5
Digdog La TN12,TN17 .. 293 D3
Diggerland★ ME2 ... 62 F4
Dignals Cl ME8 ... 65 F2
Dignash TN25 ... 235 E2
Dilhorne Cl SE12 ... 29 B5
Diligent Dr ME10 ... 101 F7
Dillon Way TN2 ... 286 D7
Dillywood Cotts ME3 ... 39 F2
Dilly Wood Fields ME3 . 40 A3
Dillywood La ME3 ... 39 F2
Dilnot La CT7 ... 81 B3
Dimmock Cl TN12 ... 257 B7
Dingleden La TN17 ... 342 F2
Diocesan & Payne Smith CE
Prim Sch CT1 ... 143 A1
Dippers Cl TN15 ... 122 F2
Discovery Dr ME19 ... 159 B3
Discovery Rd ME15 ... 163 B2
Discovery Sch The
ME18 ... 159 D3
Discovery Wlk CT1 ... 175 C7
Dislingbury Rd TN11 .. 255 C4
Disraeli Cl
Maidstone ME15 ... 195 E5
Woolwich SE28 ... 3 C5
Dittisham Rd SE9 ... 29 E4
Ditton CE Jun Sch
ME20 ... 128 C1
Ditton Court Cl ME20 .. 128 B1
Ditton Inf Sch ME20 ... 128 C1
Ditton Pl ME20 ... 128 B1
Ditton Rd DA6 ... 13 E2
Dixon Cl
Maidstone ME15 ... 161 F2
4 Newham E6 ... 1 F7
Dixon Ho SE2 ... 3 C1
Dixwell Cl ME8 ... 98 D5
Dixwell Rd CT20 ... 335 A4
Dobbie Cl ME10 ... 101 E6
Dobell Rd SE9 ... 11 F2
Dobells TN17 ... 320 D4
Dobson Rd DA12 ... 37 E3
Dock Approach Rd
RM17 ... 18 E8
Dock Exit Rd CT16 ... 310 F8
Dock Head Rd
Chatham ME4 ... 64 A8
St Mary's Island ME4 ... 41 A1
Dockland St E16 ... 2 A5
Dock Rd Chatham ME4 ... 63 F6
Chatham ME4 ... 64 A7
Grays RM17 ... 18 D8
Grays RM17 ... 18 E7
Tilbury RM18 ... 18 E5
Dockside Outlet Ctr
ME4 ... 64 A8
Dockside Rd E16 ... 1 D6
Doctor Hope's Rd
TN17 ... 320 D4
Doctor's La CT15 ... 309 B5
Doddington Ct ME16 .. 161 E5
Doddington Place Gdns★
ME9 ... 168 A7
Doddington Prim Sch
ME9 ... 167 F7
Doddington Rd ME8 ... 65 D3
Dodd Rd TN10 ... 222 E5
Dodd's La CT16 ... 278 A3
Doebury Wlk SE18 ... 13 A8
Does Alley 4 ME10 ... 101 F4
Dog Cotts RH19 ... 281 B1
Doggerel Acre CT5 ... 108 F7
Doggetts Cl TN8 ... 249 C8
Doggetts Row ME3 ... 27 B6
Dog Kennel La CT18 ... 305 B7
Dogwood Cl
Chatham ME5 ... 97 D1
Northfleet DA11 ... 36 F4
Dola Ave CT14 ... 215 B6
Dolphin Cl
Broadstairs CT10 ... 51 G3
Erith SE28 ... 3 D7
Dolphin Dr ME8 ... 98 E5
Dolphin Ho
1 Dover CT16 ... 310 E7
Rochester ME1 ... 63 E5
Dolphin La CT16 ... 310 E7
Dolphin Pas 3 CT16 ... 310 E7
Dolphin Pk ME10 ... 102 B5
Dolphin Pl 5 CT16 ... 310 E7
Dolphin Rd Lydd TN29 . 376 C6
Sittingbourne ME10 ... 102 B5
Dolphins Rd CT19 ... 335 D7
Dolphin St Deal CT14 .. 215 D7
Herne Bay CT6 ... 76 E5
Dolphin Yard Sailing Barge
Mus★ ME10 ... 102 A5
Dombey Cl Higham ME3 . 39 C3
Rochester ME1 ... 63 C3
Domneva Rd
Minster (Thanet) CT12 .. 115 B6
Westgate-on-S CT8 ... 81 D8
Domonic Dr SE9 ... 30 B5
Donald Biggs Dr DA12 .. 37 D8
Donald Moor Ave
ME9 ... 103 C2
Donaldson Rd SE18 ... 12 A6
Donald Troup Ho ME1 .. 63 C4
Doncaster Cl 7 ME15 . 195 F6
Donegal Rd CT1 ... 175 C8
Donemowe Dr ME10 .. 101 F8
Donet Cl ME8 ... 98 C5
Dongola Rd ME2 ... 40 B1
Donkey Field TN11 ... 220 E1
Donkey La
Adisham CT3 ... 210 C8
Appledore Heath TN26 .. 347 C2
Maplescombe DA4 ... 90 B8
Donkey St CT21,TN29 .. 352 E5
Donnahay Rd CT12 ... 83 C3
Donnington Ct 1 DA2 ... 16 B1
Donnington Rd TN13 . 153 D7
Donnithorne Ho CT6 ... 76 E5
Doon Brae TN4 ... 254 A2
Dorado Gdns BR6 ... 87 D7
Doran Gr SE18 ... 12 E7
Dorcas Gdns CT10 ... 84 A6
Dorchester Ave DA5 ... 31 D8
Dorchester Cl
Cliffe Woods ME3 ... 40 B7
Dartford DA1 ... 33 F7
Orpington BR5 ... 31 B1
Dorchester Rd DA12 ... 37 D5
Dorchester TN1 ... 286 B6
Dorcis Ave DA7 ... 13 E5
Doreen Bird Coll (Birbeck
Ctr) DA15 ... 31 A5
Doreen Bird Coll (Studio
Ho) DA15 ... 31 A5
Doria Dr DA12 ... 37 F5
Doric Ave TN4 ... 253 F1
Doric Cl TN4 ... 253 F1
Doric Ct CT11 ... 117 C5
Dorin Ct TN2 ... 286 C3
Doris Ave DA8 ... 14 C6
Dorking Rd TN1 ... 286 C6
Dorman Ave N CT3 ... 210 E6
Dorman Ave S CT3 ... 210 F5
Dormers Dr DA13 ... 60 B2
Dornberg Cl SE3 ... 11 A7
Dornberg Rd SE3 ... 11 B7
Dornden Dr TN3 ... 285 A4
Dornden Gdns ME5 ... 97 B2
Dorne Cotts TN27 ... 232 E6
Dorney Rise BR5 ... 53 F5
Dorothy Ave TN17 ... 320 E4
Dorothy Dr CT12 ... 83 C2
Dorothy Evans Cl DA7 ... 14 B3
Dorrit Way
Chislehurst BR7 ... 30 C2
Rochester ME1 ... 63 D2
Dorset Ave DA16 ... 12 F3
Dorset Cl CT5 ... 108 B7
Dorset Cotts TN7 ... 311 B4
Dorset Cres DA12 ... 37 E4
Dorset Ct Deal CT14 .. 215 D2
Ramsgate CT12 ... 83 B2
Dorset Gdns
Birchington CT7 ... 80 F7
Deal CT14 ... 215 C2
Dorset Pl ME13 ... 138 C7
Dorset Rd Bromley SE9 ... 29 E6
Canterbury CT1 ... 175 D7
Royal Tunbridge Wells
TN2 ... 286 D2
West Minst ME12 ... 46 A8
Dorset Road Inf Sch
SE9 ... 29 E6
Dorset Sq ME8 ... 65 D1
Dorset St TN13 ... 154 C2
Dorset Way ME15 ... 195 C8
Dorton Dr TN15 ... 154 F5
Dorton House (Royal
London Society Sch for
the Blind) TN15 ... 154 F5
Dorton House Sch
TN15 ... 154 F5
Dorville Rd SE12 ... 11 A2
Dossett Ct CT14 ... 215 A2
Dothill Rd SE18 ... 12 C7
Dotterel Cl ME5 ... 97 D2
Doubleday Dr ME9 ... 102 E2
Doubleton La TN11 ... 252 A5
Douglas Almshouses
ME17 ... 199 D5
Douglas Ave
Hythe CT21 ... 333 C2
Whitstable CT5 ... 74 E1
Douglas Bglws CT15 .. 246 E8
Douglas Bldgs TN12 .. 260 E5
Douglas Cl CT10 ... 83 E5
Douglas Ct TN16 ... 118 E2
Douglas Rd Bexley DA16 . 13 B6
Deal CT14 ... 215 A3
Dover CT17 ... 310 B8
Herne Bay CT6 ... 77 A4
Lenham ME17 ... 199 D5
Maidstone ME16 ... 161 E3
8 Newham E16 ... 1 A8
Tonbridge TN9 ... 254 A8
Douglas Terr CT14 ... 215 D5
Doug Siddons Ct 12
RM17 ... 18 C8
Dour Ho The 13 CT16 .. 310 D8
Dour Mews 12 CT16 ... 278 C1
Douro Cl CT1 ... 143 D1
Douro Pl CT16 ... 310 E7
Douro Stables TN4 ... 286 A4
Dour Side CT17 ... 277 F3
Dour St CT16 ... 310 D8
Doust Way ME1 ... 63 D5
Dove App E6 ... 1 E8
Dove Cl Chatham ME5 ... 97 B6
Herne CT6 ... 110 E7
Hythe CT21 ... 353 D8
Kingsnorth TN23 ... 300 C3
Whitstable CT5 ... 108 C7
Dovecote Ct CT4 ... 205 B8
Dove Ct 6 CT11 ... 117 E7
Dovedale CT7 ... 81 B7
Dovedale Cl DA16 ... 13 A5
Dovedale Ct
Ashford TN24 ... 268 B4
Birchington CT7 ... 81 B7
Dovedale Rd DA2 ... 34 C7
Dove Lea Gdns CT17 .. 277 E3
Doveney Cl BR5 ... 54 D6
Dover Castle & Princess of
Wales Regiment Mus★
CT16 ... 310 F8
Dover Coll CT17 ... 310 C8
Dove Rd TN10 ... 222 C6
Dover Gram Sch for Boys
CT17 ... 310 A8
Dover Gram Sch for Girls
CT16 ... 278 C1
Dover Hill CT19 ... 335 F8
Dover Ho
2 Maidstone ME15 ... 195 E8
Rochester ME2 ... 40 C1
Dover Mus★ CT16 ... 310 D7
Dover Patrol SE3 ... 11 B5
Dover Patrol Meml★
CT15 ... 280 C7
Dover Pl TN23 ... 268 C1
Dover Priory Sta
CT17 ... 310 C8
Dover Rd Barham CT4 .. 210 A1
Bishopsbourne CT4 ... 209 D5
Dover CT15 ... 278 E4
Dover Rd E DA11 ... 36 F7
Dover Rd
Folkestone CT19,CT20 .. 335 E7
Northfleet DA11 ... 36 D8
Ringwould CT14 ... 248 A6
St Margaret's at Cliffe
CT15 ... 279 D6
Sandwich CT13 ... 180 F6
Tilmanstone CT13,CT14 . 213 B5
Woolage Green CT4 ... 243 D6
Woolwich DA16 ... 12 C5
Dover Road Com Prim Sch
DA11 ... 36 E7
Dover St
Canterbury CT1 ... 175 A7
Maidstone ME16 ... 161 C2
1 Sittingbourne ME10 .. 101 E4
Doves Cl BR2 ... 85 E8
Doves Cnr CT14 ... 213 A4
Dowding Ho TN12 ... 256 F6
Dowding Rd TN16 ... 118 D4
Dowding Way TN2 ... 254 E1
Dowding Wlk 3 DA11 ... 36 E5
Dowell Mews CT14 ... 215 C3
Dower Ho The DA14 ... 31 F5
Dower House Cres
TN4 ... 253 E3
Dowgate Cl TN9 ... 254 D7
Dowle Cl TN29 ... 372 A7
Dowlerville Rd BR6 ... 86 F4
Dowling Cl ME6 ... 127 E7
Dowling Ho DA17 ... 3 F3
Downage The DA11 ... 37 A6
Downash Ct TN5 ... 339 A3
Downash Ho TN5 ... 339 A3
Down Ave TN3 ... 317 A4
Downbank Ave DA7 ... 14 D5
Down Barton Farm Cotts
CT7 ... 79 D1
Down Barton Rd CT7 ... 79 E1
Down Court Rd ME9 ... 135 C1
Down Ct TN23 ... 299 E5
Downderry Way ME20 . 128 B1
Downe Ave TN14 ... 119 D8
Downe Cl DA16 ... 13 C7
Downe Ho 10 SE7 ... 11 C8
Downend SE18 ... 12 B7
Downe Prim Sch BR6 . 119 A8
Downer Ct ME1 ... 96 E8
Downe Rd
Cudham BR6,TN14 ... 119 C5
Farthing Street BR2 ... 85 E2
Downham Way BR1 ... 29 A4
Downhill Cl CT16 ... 277 D6
Down House Mus★
BR6 ... 119 A7
Downings E6 ... 2 A7
Downings The CT6 ... 77 A2
Down La TN3 ... 314 B1
Downland Ct TN24 ... 268 B3
Downlands Deal CT14 .. 248 B8
Harrietsham ME17 ... 198 F6
Downleys Cl SE9 ... 29 F6
Downman Rd SE9 ... 11 E4
Downs Ave Bromley BR7 .. 29 F3
Dartford DA1 ... 34 A8
Whitstable CT5 ... 74 E1
Downs CE Prim Sch The
CT14 ... 215 B2
Downs Cl Charing TN27 . 234 C8
East Studdal CT15 ... 246 D8
Hawkinge CT18 ... 307 A4
Down's Cl TN27 ... 262 E5
Downs Cl
Maidstone ME14 ... 162 B8
Sittingbourne ME10 ... 101 D2
Downs Ct ME18 ... 193 B3
Downside
Bekesbourne CT4 ... 176 E3
Folkestone CT19 ... 335 C7
Downside Rd CT16 ... 278 B7
Downside
Rochester ME2 ... 63 A7
St Margaret's at Cliffe
CT15 ... 280 A6
Downsland Ho ME2 ... 62 C2
Downs Pk CT6 ... 77 A5
Downs Rd
Canterbury CT2 ... 142 F4
Deal CT14 ... 215 C3
East Studdal CT15 ... 246 E8
Folkestone CT19 ... 335 C7
Istead Rise DA13 ... 36 D3
Maidstone ME14 ... 162 B8
Ramsgate CT11 ... 117 B6
Yalding ME18 ... 193 A1
Downs The
Chartham CT4 ... 173 E1
Chatham ME5 ... 96 D1
Preston CT3 ... 146 C6
Ramsgate CT11 ... 117 D5
Downs Valley DA3 ... 58 E5
Downs View ME1 ... 95 F1
Downsview ME5 ... 97 C8
Downs View Cl BR6 ... 87 C1
Downsview Cl BR8 ... 55 F6
Downs View Inf Sch
TN24 ... 268 E7
Downsview Prim Sch
BR8 ... 56 A6
Downs View Rd ME14 .. 162 B8
Downsview Rd TN13 ... 153 F2
Downsview ME19 ... 126 A5
Downs View ME19 ... 159 B8
Downs Way TN27 ... 234 C8
Downsway BR6 ... 86 E5
Downs Way TN25 ... 303 C1
Downs Wood DA13 ... 125 F8
Downton Cotts TN18 ... 355 F4
Doyle Cl DA8 ... 14 E6
Doyle Way RM18 ... 19 C5
Drage Rd TN12 ... 224 E6
Dragonfly Cl TN23 ... 299 D8
Dragonfly Way CT18 ... 306 F4
Dragoon Ho 10 CT1 ... 143 A1
Drainless Rd CT13 ... 180 A5
Drake Ave ME12 ... 47 D5
Drake Cres SE28 ... 3 C7
Drake Ct Orpington BR5 .. 54 B3
3 Ramsgate CT11 ... 117 F8
Drake Hall E16 ... 1 B5
Drake Mews BR2 ... 52 C5
Drake Point 12 DA8 ... 4 E1
Drake Rd TN24 ... 301 B7
Drake's Ave ME2 ... 62 F8
Drakes Cl ME9 ... 66 E2
Drakes Lee TN28 ... 373 E5
Draper Cl DA17 ... 3 F2
Draper Ct BR1 ... 52 E5
Drapers Almshouses
CT9 ... 83 A8
Drapers Ave CT9 ... 82 F8
Drapers Cl CT9 ... 83 A8
Drapers Mills Prim Sch
CT9 ... 83 A8
Draper St 3 TN4 ... 253 F2
Drapers Windmill★
CT9 ... 51 A1
Drawbridge Cl ME15 ... 195 E8
Drawell Cl SE18 ... 2 E1
Dray Corner Rd TN27 .. 261 F7
Dray Ct TN11 ... 223 E8
Drays Cotts DA4 ... 57 B5
Dray's Field ME9 ... 166 A7
Drayton Ave BR6 ... 53 B1
Drayton Cl ME23 ... 23 E4
Drayton Rd TN9 ... 254 C8
Dreadnought Ave
ME12 ... 47 A6
Dreamland Family Fun
Pk★ CT9 ... 50 I2
Dresden Ct CT8 ... 81 D8
Drewery Dr ME8 ... 98 C5
Drew La CT14 ... 215 C4
Drew Prim Sch E16 ... 1 E5
Drew Rd E16 ... 1 E5
Driffield Gdns TN9 ... 253 F7
Drift The BR2 ... 85 D7
Drill La CT3 ... 145 B1
Drive The Ashurst TN3 .. 283 F5
Bexley DA5 ... 31 D8
Broadstairs CT10 ... 83 F6
Canterbury CT1 ... 175 B6
Chislehurst BR7 ... 53 E8
Deal CT14 ... 215 C5
Erith DA8 ... 14 B8
Gravesend DA12 ... 37 E4
New Barn DA3 ... 59 B6
Orpington BR6 ... 86 F8
Royal Tunbridge Wells
TN2 ... 286 B1
St Paul's Cray BR7 ... 53 F6
Sevenoaks TN13 ... 154 B3
Sidcup DA14 ... 31 B4
Tonbridge TN9 ... 254 B7
Whitstable CT5 ... 109 D8
Drop Redoubt Fort★
CT17 ... 310 D7
Drop Redoubt Rd
CT17 ... 310 D7
Drove Rd ME12 ... 46 E7
Drovers Rdbt TN24 ... 268 A4
Drove The
Fordwich CT2 ... 144 A4
Monkton CT12 ... 114 B6
Northbourne CT14 ... 214 A5
Whitfield CT16 ... 278 A8
Whitstable CT5 ... 109 D8
Droveway Gdns CT15 .. 280 A6
Drove Way The DA13 ... 36 E1
Droveway The CT15 ... 280 B6
Drudgeon Way DA2 ... 35 B5
Druidstone Wildlife Pk★
CT2 ... 141 F7
Drum La TN23 ... 268 B2
Drum Major Dr CT14 .. 215 B3
Drummond Cl DA8 ... 14 E6
Drury Rd TN30 ... 324 B1
Dry Bank Ct TN10 ... 222 C4
Dry Bank Rd TN10 ... 222 C4
Drybeck Ave CT11 ... 116 F7
Dryden Cl CT1 ... 175 C7
Dryden Ho BR2 ... 52 D4
Dryden Pl RM18 ... 19 B6
Dryden Rd Bexley DA16 ... 12 F6
Dover CT16 ... 278 B3
Dryden Way BR6 ... 54 A1
Dry End Rd ME20 ... 128 C3
Dryhill La TN14 ... 153 B3
Dry Hill Park Cres
TN10 ... 222 C3
Dry Hill Park Rd TN10 . 222 B3
Dryhill Rd DA17 ... 13 F8
Dry Hill Rd TN9 ... 222 B3
Dryland Ave 6 BR6 ... 86 F6
Dryland Rd
Borough Green TN15 ... 156 F6
Snodland ME6 ... 127 F8
Drywall Ind Est ME10 .. 102 B6
Dublin Ho 18 ME15 ... 195 E7
Duchess Cl ME2 ... 62 E8
Duchess of Kent Ct The
ME20 ... 128 F1
Duchess Of Kent Dr
ME5 ... 97 B3
Duchess' Wlk TN15 ... 154 E2
Ducie Ho 9 SE7 ... 11 C8
Ducketts Rd DA1 ... 14 F2
Duck La
Canterbury CT1 ... 143 A1
Shadoxhurst TN26 ... 326 F7
Duckpits Rd CT4 ... 240 A6
Duck St CT4 ... 273 F4
Duckworth Cl TN24 ... 301 B7
Duddington Cl SE9 ... 29 D4
Dudely Rd DA11 ... 36 E8
Dudley Ave CT8 ... 81 C8
Dudley Keen Ct TN9 ... 254 E8
Dudley Lodge TN2 ... 286 C4
Dudley Rd
Ashford TN24 ... 268 E5
Folkestone CT19 ... 335 E5
Royal Tunbridge Wells
TN1 ... 286 A4
Dudsbury Rd
Dartford DA1 ... 15 B2
Sidcup DA14 ... 31 B2
Duggan Dr BR7 ... 29 E2
Duke of Clarence Trad Est
The ME12 ... 28 A3
Duke Of Wellington Ave
SE18,SE28 ... 2 C3
Duke of York's Royal
Military Sch CT15 ... 278 F4
Dukes Mdw TN26 ... 349 A7
Dukes Meadow TN11 .. 219 F2
Dukes Meadow Dr ME7 .. 97 F6
Dukes Orch DA5 ... 32 C7
Dukes Rd TN1 ... 286 C5
Duke St Deal CT14 ... 215 D7
Margate CT9 ... 50 I3
Dukes Wlk 7 ME15 ... 162 A4
Dukeswood CT5 ... 109 D6
Dully Rd Lynsted ME9 .. 135 E6
Sittingbourne ME9 ... 102 E1
Dulverton Prim Sch
SE9 ... 30 D6
Dulverton Rd SE9 ... 30 D6
Dulwich Prep Sch
TN17 ... 321 A4
Dumbourne La TN30 .. 345 D2
Dumbreck Rd SE9 ... 12 A4
Dumergue Ave ME11 ... 46 B5
Dumpton Gap Rd CT10 . 84 A2
Dumpton La CT11 ... 83 E1
Dumpton Park Dr CT10,
CT11 ... 84 A2

Dumpton Park Rd
CT11 ... 117 E8
Dumpton Park Sta
CT11 ... 83 F1
Dunbar Ct BR2 ... 52 A5
Dunblane Rd SE9 ... 11 E5
Duncan Cl CT5 ... 108 D7
Duncan Dr CT7 ... 80 E8
Duncan Ho 2 SE7 ... 11 B8
Duncan Rd
Gillingham ME7 ... 64 D5
Ramsgate CT11 ... 117 D7
Whitstable CT5 ... 108 D7
Duncans Cotts 6
TN16 ... 151 D1
Duncroft SE18 ... 12 E7
Dundale Rd TN12,TN3 .. 288 A3
Dundonald Cl 7 E6 ... 1 E7
Dundonald Rd
11 Broadstairs CT10 ... 84 B4
Ramsgate CT11 ... 117 C7
Dunedin Cl ME10 ... 101 C3
Dunedin Dr CT16 ... 278 B3
Dunedin Ho
9 Maidstone ME15 ... 195 E5
Newham E16 ... 1 F5
2 Tilbury RM18 ... 19 A5
Dunedin Rd CT12 ... 83 A1
Dunera Dr ME14 ... 162 A7
Dunes Rd TN28 ... 373 D3
Dunes The CT13 ... 182 A7
Dungeness Nature National
Reserve★ TN29 ... 380 B4
Dungeness Rd TN29 ... 380 A7
Dungeness Sta★
TN29 ... 380 D2
Dunkeld Ho 6 ME15 .. 195 E7
Dunkery Rd SE9 ... 29 E5
Dunkery Rise TN24 ... 268 B4
Dunkin Rd DA1 ... 16 A3
Dunkirk Cl
Dymchurch TN29 ... 366 B7
Gravesend DA12 ... 37 C3
Dunkirk Dr ME5 ... 96 F6
Dunkirk Rd N ME13 ... 140 B2
Dunkirk Rd S ME13 ... 140 B1
Dunkirk Sq CT15 ... 278 F3
Dunkirk Village Sch
ME13 ... 140 D2
Dunkley Villas TN15 ... 125 F1
Dunk's Green Rd
TN11 ... 190 A5
Dunlin Ct TN29 ... 366 A3
Dunlin Dr ME4 ... 41 C2
Dunlop Ct 7 TN18 ... 341 A2
Dunlop Rd RM18 ... 18 F6
Dunnett Rd CT19 ... 334 E6
Dunning's La ME1 ... 63 C4
Dunnings The ME16 ... 161 A2
Dunn Lodge TN2 ... 286 D2
Dunnock Rd
Ashford TN25 ... 268 B7
Newham E6 ... 1 E7
Dunnose Ct RM19 ... 16 B8
Dunn Street Rd ME7 ... 131 A8
Dunoon Cotts BR6 ... 119 A5
Dunoon Ct CT11 ... 83 F1
Dunorlan Farm Cotts
TN2 ... 286 E4
Dunorlan Farm TN2 ... 286 E4
Dunstable Ct 5 SE3 ... 11 A7
Dunstall Cl TN29 ... 366 A5
Dunstall Gdns TN29 ... 366 A5
Dunstall La TN29 ... 366 A5
Dunstall Welling Est
DA16 ... 13 B5
Dunstan Ave CT8 ... 81 D7
Dunstan Glade BR5 ... 53 D3
Dunstan Gr TN4 ... 286 B6
Dunstan Ho CT14 ... 215 D8
Dunstan Rd TN4 ... 286 B6
Dunster Ct 16 DA2 ... 16 B1
Dunster Terr 3 ME15 .. 195 E8
Dunton Green Prim Sch
TN13 ... 153 E7
Dunton Green Sta
TN13 ... 153 E7
Dunvegan Rd SE9 ... 11 F3
Dunwich Rd DA7 ... 13 F6
Dupree Rd SE7 ... 1 B1
Durant Rd BR8 ... 33 A2
Durban Cl CT12 ... 83 A2
Durban Cres CT16 ... 278 C4
Durban Ho 7 ME15 ... 195 E5
Durban Rd CT9 ... 51 A1
Durham Cl
Canterbury CT1 ... 174 F6
9 Dover CT17 ... 310 D7
Maidstone ME15 ... 162 E1
Durham Hill CT17 ... 310 D7
Durham Rd Bromley BR2 . 52 A5
Gillingham ME8 ... 98 C7
Sidcup DA14 ... 31 B3
Durham Rise SE18 ... 2 D1
Duriun Way DA8 ... 15 B7
Durley Gdns BR6 ... 87 B7
Durling Ct ME8 ... 66 A1
Durlings Orch TN15 ... 156 D6
Durlock Ave CT11 ... 117 B5
Durlock CT12 ... 115 C5
Durlock Rd CT3 ... 179 B7
Durlocks The CT19 ... 335 E5
Durndale La
Northfleet DA11 ... 36 E4
Northfleet DA11 ... 36 F5
Durnford Cl CT2 ... 142 E2
Durovernum Ct CT1 ... 175 A7
Durrant Way
Orpington BR6 ... 86 D5
Swanscombe DA10 ... 35 E8
Durrell Gdns ME5 ... 64 C1
Dursley Cl SE3 ... 11 C5
Dursley Gdns SE3 ... 11 D6
Dursley Rd SE3 ... 11 C5
Duval Dr ME1 ... 96 E8
Duvard's Pl ME9 ... 100 F1
Duxberry Cl BR2 ... 52 E4
Dux Court Rd ME23 ... 23 D2
Duxford Ho 12 SE2 ... 3 D4
Dux Hill TN15 ... 189 F8
Dux La TN15 ... 156 F1
Dwelly La TN8 ... 216 D3
Dyke Dr BR5 ... 54 C2
Dyke Rd CT19 ... 335 E5
Dykewood Cl DA5 ... 32 E5
Dylan Rd DA17 ... 4 A3
Dymchurch Cl BR6 ... 86 E6
Dymchurch Ho 1
CT1 ... 175 B8
Dymchurch Prim Sch
TN29 ... 366 C8
Dymchurch Rd
Hythe CT21,TN29 ... 353 C6
St Mary's Bay TN29,
TN28 ... 366 A5
Dymchurch Sta★
TN29 ... 366 B7
Dyneley Rd SE12 ... 29 C5
Dynes Rd TN15 ... 122 E2
Dynevor Rd TN4 ... 286 C7
Dyngley Cl ME10 ... 101 E6

E

Eadred Way ME10 ... 69 A1
Eagle Cl ME20 ... 128 A2
Eagle Cotts 8 CT11 ... 117 D7
Eagle Heights Bird of Prey
Ctr★ DA4 ... 89 B8
Eagle Hill CT11 ... 117 D7
Eagle Ho RM17 ... 17 F8
Eagles Cl ME10 ... 102 C4
Eagles Dr TN16 ... 118 D1
Eaglesfield Rd SE18 ... 12 B6
Eaglesfield Sch SE18 ... 12 A6
Eagles Rd DA9 ... 17 B2
Eaglestone Cl TN15 ... 157 A8
Eagle Way DA11 ... 18 A2
Ealdham Prim Sch SE9 . 11 C3
Ealdham Sq SE9 ... 11 C3
Ealham Cl
Ashford TN24 ... 301 A8
Canterbury CT4 ... 175 B5
Ealing Cl ME5 ... 97 C4
Eardemont Cl DA1 ... 14 F3
Eardley Point 7 SE18 ... 2 B2
Eardley Rd Erith DA17 ... 4 A1
Sevenoaks TN13 ... 154 B3
Earl Cl ME5 ... 97 B4
Earl Rd DA11 ... 36 E6
Earl Rise SE18 ... 2 D2
Earls Ave TN24 ... 268 F1
Earl's Ave CT20 ... 335 B4
Earlsfield TN25 ... 330 A6
Earlsfield Rd CT21 ... 333 D2
Earlshall Rd SE9 ... 12 A3
Earlsmead Cres CT12 .. 116 C5
Earl's Rd TN4 ... 285 F4
Earl St ME14 ... 161 F4
Earlsworth Ct TN24 ... 300 E6
Earlsworth Rd TN24 ... 300 D6
Easole Hts CT15 ... 211 D5
Easole St CT15 ... 211 D5
Eason Villas TN12 ... 259 D6
East Beckton District Ctr
E6 ... 1 F8
East Blean Wood (Nature
Reserve)★ CT3,CT6 .. 111 B6
East Borough Prim Sch
ME14 ... 162 B5
Eastbridge Rd TN29 ... 366 B8
Eastbrook Pl CT16 ... 310 E8
Eastbrook Rd SE3 ... 11 B6
Eastbury Rd Newham E6 ... 2 A8
Orpington BR5 ... 53 D3
Eastchurch CE Prim Sch
ME12 ... 48 E4
Eastchurch Holiday Camp
ME12 ... 48 F5
Eastchurch Rd
Margate CT9 ... 51 E3
Minster (Sheppey) ME12 .. 48 B5
East Cliff CT16 ... 310 F8
Eastcliffe Hts 7 CT20 . 335 E5
East Cliff CT19 ... 335 E5
East Cliff Gdns 22
CT19 ... 335 E5
East Cliff Par CT6 ... 77 A5
East Cliff Pas 23 CT19 . 335 E5
East Cliff Rd TN4 ... 286 A6
East Cliff & Warren Ctry
Pk★ CT18 ... 308 D1
Eastcombe Ave SE7 ... 11 B8
Eastcote BR6 ... 53 F1
Eastcote Prim Sch
DA16 ... 12 D4
Eastcote Rd DA16 ... 12 D5
Eastcourt Gn ME8 ... 65 B4
Eastcourt La
Gillingham ME7,ME8 ... 65 B4
Gillingham ME8 ... 65 B3
East Court Sch CT11 ... 117 G7
East Crescent Rd DA12 . 19 C1
East Cross TN30 ... 345 B7
East Ct 4 ME15 ... 162 A1
East Dr BR5 ... 54 B3
East End Rd ME4,ME7 ... 64 D8
Easterfields ME19 ... 160 C5
Eastern Arm N CT16 ... 310 H8
Eastern Arm S CT16 ... 310 H8
Eastern Ave
Ashford TN23 ... 268 A2
Halfway Houses ME12 ... 46 D6
Queenborough ME11 ... 46 B4
West Thurrock RM20 ... 16 F8
Eastern Espl
Broadstairs CT10 ... 84 B5
Margate CT9 ... 51 B3
Eastern Gdns TN24 ... 300 E8
Eastern Holiday Camp
ME12 ... 49 G2
Eastern Rd
Gillingham ME7 ... 64 F6
Leysdown-on-S ME12 ... 49 G2
Lydd TN29 ... 376 D7
Eastern Service Rd
CT16 ... 310 H8
Eastern View TN16 ... 118 C2
Eastern Way Erith SE28 ... 3 D5
1 Grays RM17 ... 18 A8
East Farleigh Prim Sch
ME15 ... 194 B6
East Farleigh Sta
ME16 ... 194 B8
Eastfield Gdns TN10 ... 222 E5
Eastfield Ho ME16 ... 161 B2
Eastfield Rd 1 CT7 ... 81 A7
Eastfields CT19 ... 335 D6
East Fleet Cvn Pk
TN29 ... 353 A4
Eastgate Cl Erith SE28 ... 3 D7
Herne Bay CT6 ... 77 B3
Eastgate Ct ME1 ... 63 C5
Eastgate Rd TN30 ... 345 C8
Eastgate ME1 ... 63 C5
Eastgate Terr ME1 ... 63 C5
East Gn ME10 ... 69 A1
East Hall Hill ME17 ... 228 E7
East Hall La ME10 ... 102 C5
East Hall Rd BR5 ... 54 F2
East Ham Ind Est E6 ... 1 E8
East Ham Manor Way
E6 ... 2 A7
East Hill Ashford TN24 .. 268 C2
Biggin Hill TN16 ... 118 B1
Dartford DA1 ... 33 F8
East Hill Dr DA1 ... 33 F8
East Hill Farm Cvn Pk
TN15 ... 90 C1
East Hill Farm Pk TN15 .. 90 B1
East Hill Rd TN15 ... 123 B7
East Hill Sutton at H DA4 . 57 D7
Tenterden TN30 ... 345 B8
East Ho DA1 ... 15 F4
East Holme DA8 ... 14 D6
East Kent Ave DA11 ... 18 C1
East Kent Light Rly★
CT15 ... 245 A7
East Kent Light Rly★
CT15 ... 244 E6
East Kent Ret Pk CT10 ... 83 B4
Eastland Ct 3 BR1 ... 52 C7
Eastlands Cl TN4 ... 313 E8
Eastlands Rd TN4 ... 285 E1
East Langdon Rd
Guston CT15 ... 278 F7
Martin Mill CT15 ... 247 B2
East La Sheerness ME12 . 28 A2
Sutton at H DA4 ... 57 D7
Eastleigh Rd DA7 ... 14 C4
Eastling Cl ME8 ... 65 D3
Eastling Ho 8 BR5 ... 54 D1
Eastling Prim Sch
ME13 ... 168 F5
Eastling Rd
Eastling ME13 ... 168 F7
Painters Forstal ME13 ... 137 D2
East Lodge Rd TN23 ... 267 F3
East Malling Research Sta
(Horticultural) ME19 . 160 C6
East Malling Sta
ME19 ... 160 A6
East Mascalls 17 SE7 ... 11 C8
Eastmead Ave TN23 ... 300 C8
Eastmead Cl BR1 ... 52 E7
East Mill DA11 ... 18 F1
East Milton Rd DA12 ... 37 D8
Eastmoor Pl SE7 ... 1 D3
Eastmoor St SE7 ... 1 D3
East Mountain La
TN24 ... 268 F7
East Norman Rd CT16 . 278 E1
Eastnor Rd SE9 ... 30 C7
East Northdown Cl CT9 . 51 E1
Easton's Cnr TN25 ... 329 F4
East Park Rd ME20 ... 161 A8
East Peckham Prim Sch
TN12 ... 224 E7
East Point TN15 ... 155 A6
East Ramp CT16 ... 310 G8
East Rd Bexley DA16 ... 13 B5
Chatham ME4 ... 64 A7
Folkestone CT20 ... 334 D4
Sandwich CT13 ... 149 A8
East Rochester Way
Coldblow DA1 ... 32 D8
Sidcup DA5,DA15 ... 13 C1
East Roman Ditch
CT16 ... 310 F8
East Row ME1 ... 63 C5
Eastry CE Prim Sch
CT13 ... 180 B2
Eastry Cl Ashford TN23 . 300 A6
Maidstone ME16 ... 161 C7
Eastry Ct CT3 ... 210 F5
Eastry Mews CT13 ... 180 B2
Eastry Pk CT13 ... 180 C1
Eastry Rd DA8 ... 14 A7
East St Addington ME19 . 126 D3
Ashford TN23 ... 268 B2
Bexley DA7 ... 14 A3
Bromley BR1 ... 52 A7
Canterbury CT1 ... 143 C3
Chatham ME4 ... 64 A3
Dover CT17 ... 310 C8
Faversham ME13 ... 138 D7
Folkestone CT19 ... 335 E5
Gillingham ME7 ... 64 D6
East St *continued*
Grays RM20 ... 17 E8
Harrietsham ME17 ... 198 E5
Herne Bay CT6 ... 77 A5
Hunton ME15 ... 226 F7
Hythe CT21 ... 333 D2
East Stour Ct TN24 ... 268 D1
East Stour Prim Sch
TN24 ... 300 D6
East Stour Way TN24 .. 300 D6
East Street N ME19 ... 126 D3
East St
Sittingbourne ME10 ... 102 A4
Snodland ME6 ... 128 B8
Tonbridge TN9 ... 222 C2
East Sutton Park (HM
Young Offender Inst &
Prison) ME17 ... 230 B7
East Sutton Rd
Sutton Valence ME17 ... 230 A7
Sutton Valence ME17,
TN27 ... 230 C4
East Terr
Gravesend DA12 ... 19 C1
Sidcup DA15 ... 30 E7
East Thamesmead Bsns Pk
DA18 ... 3 F4
East Thurrock Rd
RM17 ... 18 C8
Eastview Ave SE18 ... 12 E7
East View
Brookland TN29 ... 370 D8
Hersden CT3 ... 111 F1
Eastway BR2 ... 52 A2
East Weald Dr TN30 ... 324 B1
Eastwell Barn Mews
TN30 ... 345 A8
Eastwell Cl
Maidstone ME14 ... 162 C5
Paddock Wood TN12 ... 256 E6
Shadoxhurst TN26 ... 299 B1
Eastwell Mdws TN30 ... 345 A8
Eastwell 5 TN30 ... 345 A7
Eastwell Terr TN25 ... 236 E3
East Wickham Inf Sch
DA16 ... 12 F6
East Wickham Jun Sch
DA16 ... 13 A6
Eastwood Cotts ME9 .. 103 E6
Eastwood Rd
Eastwood ME17 ... 231 C5
Sittingbourne ME10 ... 101 D5
East Woodside DA5 ... 31 E7
East Wootton Cotts
CT4 ... 207 A4
Eaton Ct BR7 ... 30 C2
Eaton Hill CT9 ... 50 I2
Eaton Rd Dover CT17 ... 310 B7
Margate CT9 ... 50 I1
Sidcup DA14 ... 31 D6
Eaton Sq DA3 ... 58 D6
Eaves Ct ME10 ... 102 B5
Eaves Rd CT17 ... 310 A7
Ebbsfleet Ind Est DA11 . 18 A2
Ebbsfleet La CT12 ... 116 A3
Ebbsfleet Wlk DA11 ... 18 B1
Ebdon Way SE3 ... 11 B4
Ebony Cotts TN30 ... 360 A6
Ebony Wlk ME16 ... 161 B3
Ebury Cl BR2 ... 85 E7
Eccles Row ME20 ... 128 F6
Eccleston Cl BR6 ... 53 D1
Eccleston Rd ME15 ... 161 F2
Echo Cl ME15 ... 195 F6
Echo Ct DA12 ... 37 C6
Echo Ho ME10 ... 102 B3
Echo Sq DA12 ... 37 C6
Echo Wlk ME12 ... 47 D6
Eckford Cl CT18 ... 306 F4
Eclipse Dr ME10 ... 101 E8
Eclipse Rd E13 ... 1 B8
Edam Ct 11 DA14 ... 31 A5
Eddie Willet Rd CT6 ... 76 B3
Eddington Cl ME15 ... 195 B6
Eddington La CT6 ... 76 F3
Eddington Way CT6 ... 76 E3
Eden Ave ME5 ... 97 A7
Edenbridge Cl BR5 ... 54 D5
Edenbridge & District War
Meml Hospl TN8 ... 249 D7
Edenbridge Dr ME12 ... 46 B8
Edenbridge Ho 2
CT1 ... 175 B8
Edenbridge Prim Sch
TN8 ... 217 D1
Edenbridge Rd TN7 ... 282 E1
Edenbridge Sta TN8 ... 217 C3
Edenbridge Town Sta
TN8 ... 217 D2
Edenbridge Trad Ctr
TN8 ... 249 D8
Eden Cl DA5 ... 32 D4
Eden Ct
1 Hawkhurst TN18 ... 340 F2
17 Orpington BR5 ... 54 D1
Tonbridge TN10 ... 222 C5
Edendale Rd DA7 ... 14 D5
Eden Farm La ME19 ... 159 D8
Edenfield CT7 ... 81 B7
Eden Ho TN23 ... 300 C8
Eden Holiday Camp
ME12 ... 49 A5
Edenhurst TN13 ... 154 A2
Eden Pl DA12 ... 37 B8
Eden Rd
High Halstow ME23 ... 23 E4
Joyden's Wood DA5 ... 32 D4
Royal Tunbridge Wells
TN1 ... 286 A2
Whitstable CT5 ... 108 A7
Edensmuir Ct SE3 ... 11 A7
Eden Valley Mus★
TN8 ... 217 C1
Eden Villas TN8 ... 249 D7
Eden Wlk 9 TN1 ... 286 A2
Edgar Cl Swanley BR8 ... 55 F6
Whitstable CT5 ... 75 D3
Edgar Ho CT14 ... 215 B3
Edgar Rd
Canterbury CT1 ... 143 B1
Dover CT17 ... 278 B1
Kemsing TN15 ... 122 E2
Margate CT9 ... 51 A3
Minster (Thanet) CT12 .. 115 B6
Tatsfield TN16 ... 150 D6
Edgeborough Way BR1 . 52 D8
Edgebury BR7,SE9 ... 30 B4
Edgebury Prim Sch
BR7 ... 30 C4
Edgebury Wlk BR7 ... 30 C5
Edge End Rd CT10 ... 83 F4
Edgefield Cl DA1 ... 34 B7
Edgehill Cl CT20 ... 334 D4
Edge Hill Ct DA14 ... 30 F4
Edgehill Gdns DA13 ... 59 F8
Edgehill Rd BR7 ... 30 C4
Edge Hill SE18 ... 12 B8
Edgeler Ct ME6 ... 127 F7
Edger Pl 5 ME15 ... 162 A4
Edgeway ME4 ... 41 B2
Edgewood Dr BR6 ... 87 A5
Edgeworth Rd SE9 ... 11 D3
Edgington Way DA14 ... 31 D1
Edinburgh Ct DA8 ... 14 D7
Edinburgh Ho
Deal CT14 ... 215 A5
7 Dover CT17 ... 310 D7
Edinburgh Mews RM18 .. 19 B5
Edinburgh Pl 7 CT20 . 335 B3
Edinburgh Rd
Ashford TN24 ... 268 B2
Chatham ME4 ... 64 C2
Gillingham ME7 ... 64 D5
Grain ME3 ... 27 B5
Margate CT9 ... 82 B8
Edinburgh Sq ME15 ... 195 C7
Edinburgh Wlk 5 CT9 ... 82 B8
Edington Rd SE2 ... 3 B3
Edisbury Wlk ME8 ... 98 D5
Edison Gr SE18 ... 12 F7
Edison Rd Bexley DA16 ... 12 F6
2 Bromley BR2 ... 52 A7
Edith Cavell Way SE18 ... 11 E6
Edith Ct BR1 ... 52 D6
Edith Pond Ct SE9 ... 30 B6
Edith Rd
Faversham ME13 ... 138 C6
Orpington BR6 ... 87 A5
Ramsgate CT11 ... 117 C6
Westgate-on-S CT8 ... 50 D1
Ediva Rd DA13 ... 60 A4
Edmanson Ave CT9 ... 50 E1
Edmund Cl
Maidstone ME16 ... 161 A3
Meopham Station DA13 ... 60 A4
Edmund Hurst Dr E6 ... 2 B8
Edmund Rd Bexley DA16 . 13 A4
Orpington BR5 ... 54 C3
Edmunds Ave BR5 ... 54 D6
Edmund St CT3 ... 178 A8
Edna Rd ME14 ... 161 F8
Edred Rd CT17 ... 310 B8
Edward Ct Chatham ME5 . 64 C1
2 Newham E16 ... 1 A8
Edward Dr CT7 ... 81 B7
Edward Harvey Ct DA17 .. 3 F1
Edward Rd
Biggin Hill TN16 ... 118 E1
Bromley BR1 ... 29 C1
Canterbury CT1 ... 175 A8
Chislehurst BR7 ... 30 B3
Folkestone CT19 ... 335 D6
Kingsdown CT14 ... 248 C6
Queenborough ME11 ... 46 B5
Edwards Cl ME8 ... 98 C5
Edwards Ct DA4 ... 89 E7
Edwards Gdns BR8 ... 55 D5
Edwards Rd
Dover CT16 ... 310 D8
Erith DA17 ... 4 A2
Edward St Chatham ME4 . 64 A3
Rochester ME2 ... 63 B7
Royal Tunbridge Wells
TN4 ... 285 F8
Rusthall TN4 ... 285 C4
Sheerness ME12 ... 28 A3
Edward Terr 9 CT20 ... 335 E6
Edward Tyler Rd SE12 .. 29 C6
Edward Wlk ME19 ... 159 F8
Edwina Ave ME12 ... 47 A7
Edwin Arnold Ct DA15 ... 30 F4
Edwin Cl DA7 ... 13 F8
Edwin Petty Pl DA2 ... 34 C8
Edwin Rd Dartford DA2 .. 33 C5
Gillingham ME8 ... 98 C8
Edwins Pl ME9 ... 100 C7
Edwin St
Gravesend DA12 ... 37 B8
Newham E16 ... 1 A8
Edyngham Cl ME10 ... 102 A8
Effingham Cres CT17 .. 310 D8
Effingham St
Dover CT17 ... 310 D8
Ramsgate CT11 ... 117 E6
Egbert Rd
Birchington CT7 ... 80 D8
Faversham ME13 ... 138 C6
Minster (Thanet) CT12 .. 115 B6
Westgate-on-S CT8 ... 50 C1
Egdean Wlk TN13 ... 154 C4
Egerton Ave BR8 ... 55 F8
Egerton CE Prim Sch
TN27 ... 232 F3
Egerton Cl DA1 ... 33 B7
Egerton Dr CT9 ... 51 E2
Egerton House Rd
TN27 ... 232 E4
Egerton Rd
Charing Heath TN27 ... 233 C7
Maidstone ME14 ... 161 E7
Pluckley TN27 ... 233 B1
Temple Ewell CT16 ... 277 E5
Eggarton La CT4 ... 205 C2
Eggpie La TN11,TN14 ... 220 E7
Eggringe TN23 ... 267 E1
Egham Rd E13 ... 1 B8
Eglantine La DA4 ... 57 B3
Eglinton Hill SE18 ... 12 B7
Eglinton Prim Sch
SE18 ... 12 A8
Eglinton Rd
Swanscombe DA10 ... 17 F1
Woolwich SE18 ... 12 B8
Egremont Rd ME15 ... 162 F2
Egret Cl ME4 ... 41 B2
Eider Cl CT6 ... 76 D2
Eighteen Acre La
TN29 ... 371 D8
Eileen Ct BR7 ... 30 A3
Eisenhower Dr E6 ... 1 E8
Elaine Ave ME2 ... 62 E7
Elaine Ct ME2 ... 62 E6
Elaine Prim Sch ME2 ... 62 E6
Elbourne Trad Est DA17 .. 4 B3
Elbury Dr E16 ... 1 A7
Elder Cl
Kingswood ME17 ... 197 D2
Sidcup DA15 ... 30 F7
Elder Ct ME8 ... 98 B6
Elderslie Rd SE9 ... 12 A2
Elders The CT3 ... 144 F1
Eldon Pl 4 CT10 ... 84 B4
Eldon St ME4 ... 64 A4
Eldon Way TN12 ... 256 F7
Eldred Dr BR5 ... 87 D8
Eleanor Dr ME10 ... 101 E8
Eleanor Smith Sch E16 .. 1 C8
Eleanor Wlk 19 SE18 ... 1 F2
Elford Cl SE3 ... 11 C3
Elford Rd ME3 ... 22 B5
Elfrida Cl CT9 ... 83 C8
Elgal Cl BR6 ... 86 B5
Elgar Bretts Ct 10 CT1 . 174 F7
Elgar Cl TN10 ... 222 E6
Elgar Gdns RM18 ... 19 B6
Elgar Pl CT11 ... 117 D7
Elgin Gdns ME2 ... 62 D5
Elham CE Prim Sch
CT4 ... 273 F4
Elham Cl Bromley BR1 ... 29 D1
Gillingham ME8 ... 65 B3
Margate CT9 ... 51 C1
Elham Rd CT1 ... 174 E6
Elham Valley Railway
Mus★ CT18 ... 334 A8
Elham Valley Vineyards★
CT4 ... 242 D4
Elham Way CT10 ... 84 A2
Elibank Rd SE9 ... 12 A3
Eling Ct ME15 ... 195 A8
Eliot Coll CT2 ... 142 E4
Eliot Rd DA1 ... 16 B2
Elizabethan Ct TN27 ... 234 C7
Elizabeth Carter Ave
CT14 ... 214 F4
Elizabeth Cl RM18 ... 19 B5
Elizabeth Cotts DA4 ... 89 E8
Elizabeth Ct
Broadstairs CT10 ... 84 B6
Canterbury CT1 ... 175 B6
Chatham ME5 ... 97 A7
Dartford DA2 ... 34 D3
Erith DA8 ... 14 D7
Gillingham ME8 ... 65 C1
6 Gravesend DA11 ... 19 A1
Herne Bay CT6 ... 76 F5
Elizabeth Dr CT18 ... 308 B2
Elizabeth Fry Pl SE18 ... 11 E6
Elizabeth Garlick Ct 1
TN1 ... 286 B4
Elizabeth Garrett Anderson
Ho 9 DA17 ... 4 A3
Elizabeth Gdns CT21 .. 333 B1
Elizabeth Ho
Maidstone ME14 ... 162 A6
Rochester ME1 ... 63 C4
Elizabeth Huggins Cotts
DA11 ... 37 B6
Elizabeth Kemp Ct
CT12 ... 83 C1
Elizabeth Pl DA4 ... 56 E3
Elizabeth Rd CT11 ... 117 F6
Elizabeth Smith's Ct
ME19 ... 159 F7
Elizabeth St
Dover CT17 ... 310 D6
Stone DA9 ... 16 E2
Elizabeth Terr SE9 ... 11 F1
Elizabeth Way
Herne Bay CT6 ... 77 B3
Orpington BR5 ... 54 C4
Eliza Cook Cl DA9 ... 17 B3
Ellard Ct DA16 ... 13 C4
Ellen Ave CT11 ... 83 E2
Ellenborough Rd DA14 .. 31 E3
Ellen Cl BR1 ... 52 D6
Ellen Ct CT3 ... 176 F8
Ellenden Ct CT2 ... 142 C4
Ellen's Hill CT14 ... 214 E3
Ellen's Pl ME9 ... 100 C6
Ellens Rd CT14 ... 214 F2
Ellenswood Cl ME15 ... 163 A1
Ellen Wilkinson Prim Sch
E6 ... 1 E8
Ellerman Rd RM18 ... 18 F5

Ellerslie Ct 🔳 DA12 .... 37 D8
Ellerslie DA12 .... 37 D8
Ellesmere Ct SE12 ...... 29 A7
Ellesmere Mews
TN28 .... 373 C8
Ellingham Leas ME15 ... 195 C7
Ellingham Way TN23 .... 300 A5
Ellington Ave CT9 ......82 B8
Ellington Inf Sch
CT11 .... 117 C7
Ellington Pl CT11 .... 117 C7
Ellington Rd CT11 ...... 117 D7
Ellington Sch for Girls
CT11 .... 117 C7
Elliot Cl CT1 .... 143 C3
Elliot Ct CT6 .... 77 C4
Elliots Pl ME13 .... 138 D7
Elliott Park Sch ME12 ... 47 A7
Elliott Rd BR2 .... 52 D5
Elliotts La TN16 .... 152 C3
Elliott St DA12 .... 37 D8
Ellis Cl Eltham SE9 ..... 30 C6
Swanley BR8 .... 55 D5
Elliscombe Mount SE7 .. 11 C8
Elliscombe Rd SE7 ..... 11 C8
Ellis Ct DA1 ....34 B7
Ellis Dr TN28 .... 373 C8
Ellis Ho 🔳 ME14 ...... 162 B4
Ellison Cl CT5 .... 75 C1
Ellison Ct ME13 .... 138 E6
Ellison Rd DA15 .... 30 D7
Ellisons Wlk CT1 ...... 175 C8
Ellison Way ME8 .... 66 A2
Ellis Rd CT5 .... 75 A3
Elliston Ho 🔳 SE18 .... 2 A2
Ellis Way Dartford DA1 .. 33 F6
Herne Bay CT6 .... 77 C2
Elm Ave Chatham ME4 ... 63 E1
Chattenden ME3 .... 41 A4
Elmbank Dr BR1 .... 52 D7
Elmbourne Dr DA17 .....4 B2
Elmbrook Gdns SE9 .... 11 E3
Elm Cl Dartford DA1 .... 33 C7
Egerton TN27 .... 232 F3
Higham ME3 .... 39 C3
Elm Cotts
Boughton Lees TN25 ... 236 E3
Swanley Village BR8 ....56 B8
Elm Court Ind Est ME7 .. 97 E3
Elm Cres ME19 .... 159 F8
Elmcroft Ave DA15 ..... 13 A1
Elmcroft Rd BR6 .... 54 A2
Elm Ct CT8 ....81 E8
Elmdene Rd SE18 ....2 B1
Elm Dr BR8 .... 55 D7
Elmfield Cl
Gravesend DA11 .... 37 B7
Sevenoaks Weald TN14 . 187 B2
Elmfield Ct Bexley DA16 . 13 B6
Coxheath ME17 .... 194 C3
Tenterden TN30 .... 345 B8
Elmfield ME8 .... 65 A3
Elmfield Pk BR1 .... 52 A6
Elmfield Rd BR1 .... 52 A6
Elm Fields TN29 .... 372 A6
Elmfield TN30 .... 345 B8
Elm Gdns CT21 .... 333 E2
Elm Gr Erith DA8 .... 14 D7
Maidstone ME15 ...... 162 B3
Manston CT12 .... 82 D1
Orpington BR6 .... 53 F1
Sittingbourne ME10 .... 102 B4
Tonbridge TN11 .... 221 F5
Westgate-on-S CT8 .....81 E8
Elm Ho 🔳 CT21 .... 333 B2
Elmhurst Ave TN2 ..... 287 D8
Elmhurst DA17 .... 13 E8
Elmhurst Cl TN25 ..... 267 F4
Elmhurst Cvn Pk ME12 . 48 F6
Elmhurst Gdns ME4 .... 63 E3
Elmhurst Rd SE9 ...... 29 E5
Elmhurst DA9 .... 27 E1
Elmington Cl DA5 ...... 14 B1
Elm La
Minster (Sheppey) ME12 .47 E5
Tonbridge TN10 ...... 222 C3
Elmlee Cl BR7 .... 29 F2
Elmleigh Rd CT3 ...... 177 A8
Elmley Cl 🔳 E6 ....1 E8
Elmley Ind Est ME11 ... 46 A2
Elmley Marshes Nature
Reserve ★ ME12 ......70 F4
Elmley Rd ME12 .... 47 D3
Elmley St SE18 ....2 D2
Elmley Way CT9 .... 82 E8
Elm Park Gdns CT17 ... 309 F7
Elm Par 🔟 DA14 ...... 31 A4
Elm Pl TN23 .... 299 F7
Elm Rd Aylesham CT3 ... 210 E5
Dartford DA1 .... 33 D7
Erith DA8 .... 15 A6
🔳 Folkestone CT19 ... 335 E6
Gillingham ME7 ....64 E6
Gravesend DA12 ...... 37 C5
Grays RM17 .... 18 C8
Hoo St Werburgh ME3 .. 41 E3
Orpington BR6 .... 87 A3
Royal Tunbridge Wells
TN4 .... 253 F1
St Mary's Bay TN29 .... 365 F3
Sidcup DA14 .... 31 A4
Stone DA9 ....16 E1
Westerham TN16 ...... 151 E2
Elms Ave CT11 .... 117 D6
Elms Hill CT15 .... 309 D8
Elmshurst Gdns TN10 .. 222 C4
Elmslie Ct SE9 .... 12 A1
Elmsmead TN31 .... 368 B4
Elmstead Ave BR7 ..... 29 F3
Elmstead 🔳 TN13 .... 153 E5

Elmstead Glade BR7 ....29 F2
Elmstead La BR7 ...... 29 F3
Elmstead Pl 🔢 CT20 .. 335 E5
Elmstead Rd 14 E6
Elmstead Woods Sta
BR7 ....29 E2
Elmsted Cres DA16 .... 13 C8
Elms The Hersden CT3 . 111 E1
Teynham ME9 .... 104 A2
Elmstone Cotts ME13 .. 120 D4
Elmstone Gdns CT9 ....51 E2
Elmstone La ME16 .... 161 B2
Elmstone Rd
Gillingham ME8 .... 98 D7
Ramsgate CT11 ...... 117 D7
Elmstone Terr 🔳 BR5 .. 54 C5
Elms Vale Rd CT15,
CT17 .... 309 E7
Elm Terr 🔳 Eltham SE9 . 12 A1
West Thurrock RM20 .... 17 B8
Elmton La CT15 .... 212 C1
Elmtree TN20 .... 347 C1
Elm Tree Ave ME9 ..... 68 D4
Elmtree Cotts TN14 ... 120 D4
Elm Tree Cotts ME3 ... 25 A3
Elm Tree Ct 🔳 SE7 .... 11 C8
Elm Tree Dr ME1 ...... 63 A2
Elmway ME12 .... 48 F6
Elm Wlk
Aylesford ME20 ...... 128 E1
Orpington BR6 ....85 F7
Elmwood Ave CT10 .... 84 A8
Elmwood Cl CT10 ..... 84 A7
Elm Wood Cl CT5 ...... 75 C2
Elmwood Dr DA5 ...... 31 E8
Elmwood Rd ME3 ..... 40 F6
Elm Wood W CT5 ...... 75 C2
Elphick's Pl TN2 ...... 314 B8
Elrick Cl DA8 ....14 E8
Elsa Rd DA16 .... 13 C5
Elsinore Ho 🔳 SE18 ....1 E2
Elster Pl ME19 .... 159 B3
Elstow Ct Eltham SE9 ...11 F7
Eltham SE9 .... 12 A2
Elstree Gdns DA17 ......3 E2
Elswyn Ho 🔢 DA14 ... 31 A5
Eltham CE Prim Sch
SE9 ....11 F2
Eltham Coll SE9 ...... 29 D6
Eltham Green Rd SE9 .. 11 D3
Eltham Green Sch SE9 . 11 D1
Eltham High St SE9 .... 11 F1
Eltham Hill SE9 .... 11 E2
Eltham Hill Tech Coll for
Girls SE9 ....11 E1
Eltham Palace SE9 ....11 E1
Eltham Palace Rd SE9 .. 11 D1
Eltham Park Gdns SE9 . 12 A3
Eltham Rd SE12,SE9 ... 11 B2
Eltham Sta SE9 ....11 F2
Elventon Cl CT19 ..... 334 E7
Elverland La ME13,
ME9 .... 137 B2
Elveys Cotts ME18 .... 192 F1
Elvington Cl ME16 .... 161 D5
Elvington La CT18 .... 306 E2
Elwick Ct DA1 .... 15 A3
Elwick La 🔳 TN23 .... 268 B2
Elwick Rd TN23 ...... 268 B2
Elwill Way DA13 ....59 F8
Elwyn Gdns SE12 ..... 29 A8
Ely Cl Erith DA8 ....14 F5
Gillingham ME8 ....65 E2
Ely Ct TN1 .... 286 B4
Ely Gdns TN10 .... 222 D4
Elysian Ave BR5 ....53 F3
Embassy Cl ME7 ......64 F1
Embassy Ct Bexley DA16 . 13 B4
Sidcup DA14 .... 31 B5
Ember Cl BR5 .... 53 C2
Emblin Ct 🔳 DA14 .... 31 A4
Emelina Way CT5 ..... 108 B6
Emerald Ct 🔳 Newham E16 . 1 E7
Rochester ME1 .... 96 F7
Emerald Cres ME10 ... 101 D6
Emerald View ME12 ....49 E4
Emersons Ave BR8 .... 32 F1
Emerton Cl DA6 .... 13 E3
Emes Rd DA8 .... 14 C7
Emily Jackson Cl
TN13 .... 154 B3
Emily Jackson Ho
TN13 .... 154 B3
Emily Rd ME5 ....97 B6
Emmanuel Ho 🔳 SE18 ...2 D1
Emmerson Gdns CT5 .. 75 D3
Emmet Hill La ME18 .. 225 F5
Emmetts Garden ★
TN14 .... 185 D5
Emmetts La TN14,
TN16 .... 185 D6
Emperor Way TN23 .... 299 F4
Empire Terr CT9 ....82 E8
Empress Dr BR7 ...... 30 B2
Empress Gdns ME12 ...49 D4
Empress Rd DA12 ..... 37 E8
Emsworth Gr ME14 ... 162 D6
Enbrook Rd CT20 ..... 334 E5
Enbrook Valley CT20 .. 334 E5
Encombe CT20 .... 334 D3
Endeavour Foyer The 🔳
ME4 ....64 B2
Enderfield Ct BR7 ..... 53 A8
Enfield Rd CT14 ...... 215 D7
Engineer Cl SE18 ..... 12 A8
Engineers Ct 🔳 TN23 . 268 B2
Englefield Cl BR5 ...... 53 F5
Englefield Cres
Cliffe Woods ME3 ......40 B7
Orpington BR5 .... 54 A5

Englefield Path BR5 ... 54 A5
English Martyrs' RC Prim
Sch ME2 ....63 B8
Ennerdale ME13 ...... 138 E6
Ennerdale Gdns CT3 .. 210 F6
Ennerdale Ho ME15 ... 195 E7
Ennerdale Rd DA7 .... 14 A6
Ennis Rd SE18 .... 12 C8
Ensfield Rd Leigh TN11 . 220 E1
Tonbridge TN11 ...... 253 A6
Ensign Ho RM17 ....17 F8
Enslin Rd SE9 .... 30 A8
Enterprise Bsns Est
ME2 ....63 D8
Enterprise Cl ME2 ..... 63 D8
Enterprise Ctr TN24 .. 300 E7
Enterprise Ctr The
ME5 .... 130 C8
Enterprise Rd
Maidstone ME15 ...... 162 A1
Margate CT9 .... 82 E8
Enterprise Way TN8 .. 217 C3
Enticott Cl CT5 .... 75 A1
Entick Cl ME2 .... 63 C6
Eppe Cl ME7 ....63 B8
Epping Cl CT6 .... 77 B2
Epple Bay Ave CT7 .....81 B8
Epple Bay Rd CT7 ......81 A8
Epple Rd CT7 ....81 B8
Epps Rd ME10 .... 101 E3
Epsom Cl Bexley DA7 ...14 B4
Maidstone ME15 ...... 195 F6
West Malling ME19 .... 159 B8
Epstein Rd SE28 ....3 B5
Erebus Dr SE28 ....2 C4
Erica Ct BR8 .... 55 E5
Eric Rd CT17 .... 278 B2
Eridge Ct TN2 .... 285 F1
Eridge Green Cl BR5 .. 54 C1
Eridge Rd
Groombridge TN3 .... 312 D5
Royal Tunbridge Wells
TN2,TN4 .... 285 E1
Eridge Sta TN3 ...... 312 E2
Erindale Terr SE18 .... 12 D8
Erindale SE18 .... 12 D8
Erith Cl ME14 .... 162 A8
Erith & District Hospl
DA8 .... 14 D8
Erith High St DA8 ......4 E1
Erith Mus ★ DA8 ....4 E1
Erith DA8,DA17 ....4 B1
Erith Sch DA8 .... 14 D7
Erith Small Bsns Ctr 🔳
DA8 ....14 F8
Erith Sta DA8 ....4 E1
Erith St CT17 .... 278 B1
Ermington Rd SE9 .... 30 C6
Ernest Dr ME16 ...... 161 B5
Ernest Rd ME4 .... 64 A3
Ernwell Rd CT19 ..... 335 D6
Ersham Rd CT1 ...... 175 A7
Erskine Ho 🔳 SE7 ..... 11 C8
Erskine Park Rd TN4 .. 285 C7
Erskine Rd DA13 ..... 126 B8
Erwood Rd SE7 ....1 E1
Escott Gdns SE9 ..... 29 E4
Escreet Gr SE18 ....2 A2
Eshcol Rd ME3 .... 42 C6
Esher Cl DA5 .... 31 E7
Eskdale Ave CT11 .... 117 A7
Eskdale Cl DA2 .... 34 C7
Eskdale Rd DA7 .... 14 A5
Esmonde Dr CT12 .....81 F2
Esmonde Ho 🔳 ME7 ... 64 A6
Esplanade Dover CT17 . 310 C6
Rochester ME1 .... 63 B5
Westgate-on-S CT8 .... 50 C1
Essella Pk TN24 ..... 268 E1
Essella Rd TN24 ..... 268 E1
Essenden Rd DA17 .....4 A1
Essetford Rd TN23 ... 300 A7
Essex Ave CT6 ....76 B4
Essex Cl TN12 .... 313 F8
Essex Gdns CT7 .... 80 F6
Essex Rd
Canterbury CT1 ...... 175 D7
🔳 Dartford DA1 ...... 15 D1
Gravesend DA11 ...... 37 A7
Halling ME2 .... 95 A6
Longfield DA3 ....58 D7
Maidstone ME15 ...... 195 E6
Westgate-on-S CT8 .....81 E8
West Thurrock RM20 ... 17 A8
Essex St CT5 .... 108 D8
Estelle Ct ME1 .... 96 D7
Esther Ct ME10 ...... 101 E8
Estridge Way TN10 ... 222 F5
Estuary Cotts RM18 ... 20 D7
Estuary Rd ME12 ......28 B1
Estuary Way CT5 ...... 75 D3
Etchden Rd TN26 .... 298 A8
Etfield Gr DA14 .... 31 B3
Ethelbert Cres CT9 .... 51 A3
Ethelbert Gdns CT9 ... 50 J3
Ethelbert Rd
Birchington CT7 .... 80 D8
Bromley BR1 .... 52 A6
Canterbury CT1 ...... 175 B6
Deal CT14 .... 182 C1
Dover CT17 .... 310 C8
Erith DA8 .... 14 C7
Faversham ME13 .... 138 C6
Folkestone CT19 ..... 335 D7
Hawley DA2 .... 33 E3
Margate CT9 .... 50 J3
Orpington BR5 .... 54 B4
Ramsgate CT11 ...... 117 D6
Rochester ME1 .... 63 C4
Ethelbert Road Inf Sch
ME13 .... 138 C6
Ethelbert Sq CT8 ..... 50 C1

Ethelbert Terr
Margate CT9 .... 51 A3
Westgate-on-S CT8 .... 50 C1
Ethel Brooks Ho SE18 . 12 B8
Ethelburga Dr CT18 .. 305 B7
Ethel-Maud Ct ME7 ... 64 D7
Ethel Rd
Broadstairs CT10 ......83 F5
Newham E16 ....1 B7
Ethelred Cl ME13 .... 138 C6
Ethelred Ct CT8 ...... 50 C1
Ethel Terr BR6 .... 87 C2
Etherington Hill TN3 .. 285 C6
Ethnam La TN18 ..... 356 E4
Ethronvi Rd DA7 ......13 E4
Eton Cl ME5 ....96 F4
Eton Ct TN13 .... 154 B4
Eton Rd BR6 ....87 B6
Eton Way DA1 .... 15 C3
Ettrick Terr CT21 .... 333 A2
Eugenie Mews BR7 ....53 B8
Eurogate Bsns Pk
TN24 .... 268 B5
Eurolink Bsns Pk
ME10 .... 102 B5
Eurolink Way ME10 ... 101 F4
Europa Pk RM20 ...... 17 C8
Europa Trad Est DA8 ...4 D1
Europe Rd SE18 ....1 F3
Euroway ME20 .... 160 E8
Eustace Pl 🔳 SE18 ....1 F2
Evanlode Ho 🔳 SE2 ....3 C4
Evans Cl ME2 .... 17 A2
Evans Ct SE9 .... 29 E6
Evans Rd TN24 ...... 301 A7
Eva Rd ME7 .... 64 D3
Evelings Alley 🔢 CT5 . 74 D2
Evelyn Cl ME2 .... 63 C8
Evelyn Gdns SE3 ..... 11 C6
Evelyn Ct CT21 ...... 334 A2
Evelyn Denington Rd E6 .. 1 F8
Evelyn Ho
🔳 Folkestone CT20 . 335 D5
🔳 Rochester ME2 ... 63 C8
Evelyn Rd
Maidstone ME16 ..... 161 E3
Newham E16 ....1 B5
Otford TN14 .... 122 C2
Evenden Ho TN17 ... 320 D5
Evenden Rd DA13 .... 60 A2
Evenhill Rd CT3 ..... 176 E8
Everard Ave BR2 ..... 52 A1
Everard Way ME13 .. 138 B8
Everest Cl 🔳 DA11 ... 36 E5
Everest Ct SE9 .... 29 E6
Everest Dr ME3 ...... 41 E4
Everest La ME2 ...... 40 B1
Everest Mews ME3 ... 41 E4
Everest Pl BR8 .... 55 D5
Everest Rd SE9 ....11 F2
Everett Wlk DA17 ......3 F1
Everglade TN16 ..... 118 D1
Everglade Cl DA3 .....58 F5
Everglades The ME7 ...97 F6
Evergreen Cl
Gillingham ME7 .... 98 A5
Higham ME3 .... 39 B3
Iwade ME9 .... 68 D4
Leybourne ME19 ..... 127 E2
Everist Ct SE18 ..... 305 C6
Eversfield Ct SE12 ....29 B6
Eversleigh Rise CT5 .. 108 F7
Eversley Ave DA7,DA8 . 14 E5
Eversley Cl ME16 .... 161 C6
Eversley Coll CT20 .... 334 F4
Eversley Cross DA7 ... 14 E5
Eversley Rd
Greenwich SE7 ....11 B8
Hythe CT21 .... 334 B3
Eversley Way CT20 ... 334 F5
Evesham Rd DA12 .... 37 D6
Evington Pottery ★
TN25 .... 271 D7
Evison Cl CT16 ...... 278 B2
Evorg Ho 🔳 ME4 ......64 B2
Evry Rd DA14 .... 31 C2
Ewart Rd ME4 ....63 E1
Ewehurst La TN3 ..... 284 F6
Ewell Ave ME19 ..... 159 A8
Ewell La ME15 ...... 193 D5
Ewins Cl TN12 ...... 257 A6
Excel Waterfront E16 ...1 A6
Exchange St CT14 ... 215 D7
Exchange The CT5 .....74 E3
Exedown Rd TN15 .... 124 C4
Exeter Cl
Folkestone CT19 ..... 334 D6
Newham E6 ....1 F7
Tonbridge TN10 ..... 222 D4
Exeter Rd Bexley DA16 .12 F5
Gravesend DA12 ..... 37 D5
Newham E16 ....1 A8
Exeter Wlk ME1 ...... 96 C7
Exford Gdns SE12 .... 29 B7
Exford Rd SE12 ...... 29 B7
Exmoor Rise TN24 ... 268 B4
Exmouth Rd
Bexley DA16 .... 13 C7
Gillingham ME7 ...... 64 C7
Grays RM17 .... 18 B8
Exton Cl ME5 .... 97 C2
Exton Gdns ME14 ... 162 F5
Eye The ME4 ....63 F5
Eyhorne St ME17 .... 164 D2
Eynsford Castle ★ DA4 .89 E8
Eynsford Cl Margate CT9 .51 F2
Orpington BR5 .... 53 C3
Eynsford Cres DA5 ... 31 D7
Eynsford Rd
Crockenhill BR8 ...... 55 E3
Eynsford DA4 ....56 F1
Maidstone ME16 ..... 161 D7
Swanscombe DA9 .... 17 C2
Eynsford Rise DA4 .... 89 D6

Eynsford Sta DA4 .... 89 D6
Eynsham Dr SE2 ....3 B3
Eynswood Dr DA14 ... 31 C3
Eythorne Court Barn
CT15 .... 245 B7
Eythorne Cl TN24 .... 268 D5
Eythorne Elvington Com
Prim Sch CT15 ..... 245 C8
Eythorne Rd CT15 ... 244 E6
Eythorne Sta CT15 .. 245 C8

F

Fackenden La TN14 ... 122 C7
Factory Rd Newham E16 .. 1 E5
Northfleet DA11 ...... 18 C1
Faesten Way DA5 ..... 32 C5
Fagus Wood Forest Wlks ★
TN26 .... 327 D2
Fagus Rd ME5 ....97 B1
Fairacre CT10 ....83 E4
Fairacre Pl DA3 ....58 E6
Fairacres Cl CT6 ...... 77 C4
Fair Acres BR2 .... 52 A4
Fairbank Ave BR6 .....86 B8
Fairbourne Heath Cotts
ME17 .... 198 B1
Fairbourne La ME17 .. 198 C4
Fairby La DA3 ....58 C2
Fairby Rd SE12 ....11 B2
Faircrouch La TN5 ... 336 B5
Fairfax Bsns Ctr ME15 . 195 F4
Fairfax Cl
Folkestone CT20 ..... 334 D5
Gillingham ME8 .... 98 D5
Fairfax Dr CT6 ....77 F5
Fairfax Gdns SE3 ..... 11 C6
Fairfax Ho ME15 .... 195 F5
Fairfax Mews CT6 .....1 B5
Fairfax Rd RM18 ..... 18 F6
Fairfield Ave TN2 .... 286 C5
Fairfield Cl
Kemsing TN15 ...... 123 A1
New Romney TN28 ... 373 B7
Sidcup DA15 .... 12 F1
Fairfield Cres TN9 ... 254 C8
Eltham CT4 .... 273 F5
Fairfield Deal CT14 ... 214 F6
Fairfield Gr SE7 ...... 11 B8
Fairfield Pk CT10 .....83 E4
Fairfield Rd Bexley DA7 .13 F5
Borough Green TN15 .. 156 F8
Broadstairs CT10 ......83 E4
Bromley BR1 .... 29 A1
Minster (Thanet) CT12 . 115 B7
New Romney TN28 ... 373 B7
Orpington BR5 .... 53 D3
Ramsgate CT11 ....83 E2
Fairfields DA12 ...... 37 E3
Fairfield Terr TN26 ... 349 E4
Fairfield Way TN11 ... 221 F5
Fairford Ave DA7 ..... 14 D6
Fairglen Cotts TN5 ... 336 B3
Fairglen Rd TN5 ..... 336 B4
Fairhurst Dr ME15 ... 194 B4
Fairings The TN30 ... 345 B8
Fairland Ho BR2 ......52 B5
Fairlands Ct 🔳 SE9 ... 12 A1
Fairlawn Ave DA7 .... 13 D5
Fairlawn Cl ME18 .... 193 A8
Fairlawn Ct SE7 ...... 11 C7
Fairlawn SE7 .... 11 C8
Fairlawn Rd CT12 .....83 B3
Fairlawn CT5 .... 75 D1
Fairlead Rd ME1 ..... 63 D1
Fairleas ME10 .... 102 B2
Fairlight Ave CT12 ... 117 B8
Fairlight Cl TN4 ..... 254 A2
Fairlight Cotts 🔳
ME13 .... 138 C7
Fairlight Cross DA3 .. 59 C6
Fairlight Rd CT10 .... 222 B4
Fairlight Rd CT21 .... 333 A3
Fair St CT10 ....83 E4
Fairthorn Rd SE7 ......1 A1
Fairtrough Rd BR6 ... 120 B7
Fairview Ave ME8 .....98 B5
Fairview Cl Margate CT9 . 51 A2
Tonbridge TN9 ...... 254 B7
Fairview Com Inf Sch
ME8 .... 98 C5
Fair View Com Jun Sch
ME8 .... 98 C5
Fairview Cotts ME15 . 194 F5
Fair View Cotts TN5 .. 337 A6
Fairview Cotts ME9 .. 166 C7
Fairview Dr
Ashford TN24 .... 300 D6
Higham ME3 .... 39 B4
Orpington BR6 .... 86 D6
Fairview DA8 ....14 F7
Fairview Gdns
Deal CT14 .... 215 A4
Meopham Station DA13 . 60 A4
Sturry CT2 .... 144 A6
Fairview TN18 .... 340 F1

Fairview Ind PK
Rainham RM13 ....4 D8
Ruckinge TN26 ...... 349 D7
New Ash Green DA3 ...91 B7
Fairview Lympne CT21 . 332 A3
Fairview Rd
Elvington CT15 ...... 212 B1
Istead Rise DA13 ......36 E1
Sittingbourne ME10 .. 102 A3
Fairview Trad Est
RH8 .... 183 A2
Fairwater Ave DA16 .. 13 A3
Fairway Ave CT19 ... 335 A7
Fairway DA6 ....13 E2
Fairway Cl
Rochester ME1 .... 63 C1
St Mary's Bay TN29 ... 365 F3
Fairway Cres CT5 .... 108 A7
Fairway Ct 🔢 SE9 .... 12 A1
Fairway Dr Dartford DA2 .34 B8
🔳 Deal SE28 ....3 E7
Fairway Orpington BR5 .. 53 D4
Sandwich CT13 ...... 182 A7
Fairways Ct 🔳 DA11 .. 37 B8
Fairways The
Faversham ME13 .... 138 A6
Royal Tunbridge Wells
TN4 .... 286 A7
Fairway The
Bromley,Southborough
BR1 .... 52 F4
🔳 Bromley,Sundridge
BR1 .... 29 B1
Deal CT14 .... 215 C8
Gravesend DA11 ..... 37 B6
Herne Bay CT6 ....76 D2
Hythe CT21 .... 333 C1
Littlestone-on-Sea TN28 . 373 D6
Rochester ME1 .... 63 C1
St Mary's Bay TN29 ... 366 A5
Sittingbourne ME10 .. 101 E1
Fairwood Ind Est
TN23 .... 268 A1
Fairwood Ind Pk TN23 . 267 F2
Falcon Ave Bromley BR1 .52 E5
Grays RM17 .... 18 C7
Falcon Cl Dartford DA1 . 15 F2
Herne CT6 .... 110 F7
Falcon Ct ME1 ...... 102 A2
Falcon Gdns ME12 ... 47 D7
Falcon Gn ME20 .... 127 F1
Falcon Ho 🔳 ME10 .. 102 A4
Falcon Mews ME1 .....36 E7
Falcons Cl TN16 ..... 118 D2
Falcon Way TN23 ... 299 E7
Falconwood Ave DA16 .12 E5
Falconwood Par DA16 . 12 E3
Falconwood Sta SE9 .. 12 D3
Falkland Pl ME5 ....96 E1
Fallowfield Bean DA2 ... 35 B5
Chatham ME5 ....97 B8
Fallowfield Cl ME14 .. 162 E4
Fallowfield ME10 .... 102 A2
Falmouth Pl TN12 ... 256 C7
Falstaff Cl DA1 ....32 E8
Fanconi Rd ME5 ......97 B3
Fancy Row ME14 .... 163 C5
Fane Way ME8 .... 98 D4
Fans La ME9 .... 68 D4
Fantail Cl SE28 ....3 C7
Fan The CT16 .... 310 H8
Fant La ME16 .... 161 B2
Fant St ME16 .... 161 A2
Faraday Ave DA14 .....31 B6
Faraday Ho Erith DA17 ...4 A3
Rochester ME1 .... 63 D5
Faraday Lodge TN2 .. 286 E5
Faraday Rd Bexley DA16 . 13 A4
Maidstone ME14 .... 162 C7
Faraday Ride TN10 ... 222 D7
Faraday Way
Greenwich SE18 ....1 D3
Orpington BR5 .... 54 B8
Fareham Wlk 🔟 ME15 . 195 F6
Faringdon Ave BR2 ... 53 A3
Farington Cl ME16 ... 161 B4
Farjeon Rd SE18,SE3 .. 11 D6
Farleigh Ave BR2 ..... 52 A2
Farleigh Ct ME16 .... 161 A2
Farleigh Hill ME15 ... 161 E1
Farleigh Hill Ret Pk
ME15 .... 161 E1
Farleigh La ME16 .... 161 A1
Farleigh Trad Est
ME15 .... 161 E1
Farley Cl Chatham ME5 . 97 D2
Shadoxhurst TN26 ... 299 A1
Farleycroft TN16 ..... 151 C1
Farley La TN16 ...... 184 B8
Farley Nursery TN16 . 184 C8
Farley Rd
Gravesend DA12 ......37 F7
Margate CT9 ....82 F7
Farleys Way TN31 ... 367 B2
Farlow Cl DA11 ....36 F5
Farm Ave BR8 .... 55 C6
Farm Cl TN23 .... 299 E7
Farmcombe Cl TN2 .. 286 B2
Farmcombe La TN2 .. 286 C2
Farmcombe Rd TN2 .. 286 C2
Farmcote Rd SE12 .... 29 A7
Farmcroft DA11 ......37 A6
Farmdale Ave ME1 ....62 F2
Farmdale Rd SE10 ......1 A1
Farmer Cl Hythe CT21 . 333 D3
Leeds ME17 .... 197 A6
Farm Gdns TN31 .... 367 C2
Farm Ground Cl TN9 . 254 E8
Farm Hill Ave ME2 ....39 F1
Farm Holt DA3 ....58 F1
Farmhouse Cl CT4 ... 242 F7
Farm House Cl CT5 .. 108 F8

Farm La CT14 . . . . 214 F6
Farmland Wlk BR7 . . . . . 30 B3
Farm La TN10 . . . . 222 A4
Farm Pl DA1 . . . . 15 A3
Farm Rd Chatham ME5 . . . 96 E5
  Hamstreet TN26 . . . . . . 349 A4
  Sevenoaks TN14 . . . . . . 154 C7
Farmstead Dr TN8 . . . . . . 217 D3
Farm Vale DA5 . . . . 14 B1
Farnaby Dr TN13 . . . . . . 154 A1
Farnaby Rd SE9 . . . . 11 C3
Farnborough Cl ME16 . . 161 C2
Farnborough Comm
  BR6 . . . . 86 A6
Farnborough Ct 2
  BR6 . . . . 86 C5
Farnborough Hill BR6 . . 86 C5
Farnborough Prim Sch
  BR6 . . . . 86 C5
Farnborough Way BR6 . . 86 D5
Farncombe Way CT16 . . 278 B2
Farne Cl ME15 . . . . 195 A6
Farnham Beeches
  TN3 . . . . 285 A4
Farnham Cl
  Gillingham ME8 . . . . 66 B1
  Gillingham ME8 . . . . 99 A8
  Langton Green TN3 . . . . 285 A3
Farnham La TN3 . . . . 285 A4
Farnham Pl TN3 . . . . 285 A3
Farnham Rd DA16 . . . . . . 13 C5
Farningham Cl ME14 . . . 162 C6
Farningham Hill Rd
  DA4 . . . . 56 D4
Farningham Road Sta
  DA4 . . . . 57 B7
Farningham Wood (Nature
  Reserve)★ BR8,DA4 . . 56 D5
Farnol Rd DA1 . . . . 16 A3
Faro Cl BR1 . . . . 53 A7
Farraday Cl ME1 . . . . 96 D8
Farrance Ct TN1 . . . . . . 286 B4
Farrant Cl BR6 . . . . 87 A3
Farrants Ct BR1 . . . . 52 F7
Farrar Rd CT7 . . . . 81 A6
Farrell Ct DA2 . . . . 33 C5
Farrers Wlk TN23 . . . . . 300 B4
Farrier Cl
  Ashford TN23 . . . . 267 F5
  Bromley BR1 . . . . 52 D6
  Maidstone ME14 . . . . . . 162 E5
Farriers Cl DA12 . . . . . . 37 F7
Farriers Ct ME8 . . . . 99 C8
Farrier St CT14 . . . . 215 D7
Farrington Ave BR5 . . . . 54 B6
Farrington Pl BR7 . . . . . . 30 D1
Farringtons & Stratford Ho
  Sch BR7 . . . . 30 D1
Farrow Ct TN23 . . . . 300 A6
Fartherwell Ave ME19 . . 159 A8
Fartherwell Rd ME19 . . 159 A8
Farthing Cl DA1 . . . . 15 F3
Farthing Cnr ME9 . . . . . . 98 E3
Farthingfield TN15 . . . . 125 A3
Farthing Hill TN5 . . . . . 338 E1
Farthingloe Cotts
  CT15 . . . . 309 F5
Farthingloe Ct CT17 . . . 310 A4
Farthingloe Rd CT17 . . . 310 A6
Farthings Cotts ME14 . . 129 F1
Farthings Ct CT2 . . . . . . 142 C4
Farthing St BR6 . . . . 85 F2
Farwell Rd DA14 . . . . 31 C4
Farwig La BR1 . . . . 52 A8
Fashoda Rd BR2 . . . . 52 D5
Fauchon's Cl ME14 . . . . 162 F3
Fauchon's La ME14 . . . . 162 F4
Faulkners La CT2 . . . . . 142 A1
Faussett Hill CT4 . . . . . 207 F8
Faustina Dr TN23 . . . . . 299 F4
Faversham Cottage Hospl
  ME13 . . . . 138 C7
Faversham Ind Est
  ME13 . . . . 138 C8
Faversham Miniature Rly★
  ME13 . . . . 138 B4
Faversham Rd
  Boughton Lees TN24,
  TN25 . . . . 236 E5
  Challock ME13,TN27 . . . 202 C3
  Charing TN27 . . . . 201 E1
  Lenham ME17 . . . . 199 E7
  Lewson Street ME13,
  ME9 . . . . 137 B5
  Pested TN25,ME13 . . . . 203 B4
  Whitstable CT5 . . . . . . 107 C6
  Wichling ME17,ME9 . . . 167 B4
Faversham Reach
  ME13 . . . . 138 D8
Faversham Sta ME13 . . 138 D6
Faversham Stone Chap★
  ME13 . . . . 137 E7
F Ave SE18 . . . . 2 B3
Favourite Rd CT5 . . . . . 108 B6
Fawkes Ave DA1 . . . . 33 F6
Fawkham Ave DA3 . . . . . 59 C6
Fawkham CE Prim Sch
  DA3 . . . . 58 B1
Fawkham Green Rd
  DA3 . . . . 91 B7
Fawkham Ho 10 BR5 . . . 54 D1
Fawkham Manor Hospl
  DA3 . . . . 58 C1
Fawkham Rd
  Longfield DA3 . . . . 58 D6
  West Kingsdown TN15 . . 91 A4
Fawley CT ME14 . . . . . . 161 E7
Fay Cl ME1 . . . . 63 B3
Fazan Ct TN5 . . . . 336 F4
Fearon St SE10 . . . . 1 A1
Featherbed La
  Iwade ME9 . . . . 68 E2

Featherbed La continued
  Selling ME13 . . . . 171 A7
Featherby Cotts ME7 . . . 64 F6
Featherby Inf Sch ME8 . . 65 A3
Featherby Jun Sch
  ME8 . . . . 65 A3
Featherby Rd
  Gillingham,Grange ME7 . 65 A5
  Gillingham,Twydall ME8 . 65 A7
Federation Rd SE2 . . . . . 3 C2
Feenan Highway RM18 . . 19 B6
Felborough Cl CT4 . . . . 205 C8
Felderland Cl
  Maidstone ME17 . . . . . 195 E5
  Sandwich CT14 . . . . . . 180 F5
Felderland Dr ME17 . . . 195 E5
Felderland La CT14 . . . . 180 E4
Felderland Rd ME17 . . . 195 E5
Feldspar Cl
  Chatham ME5 . . . . 97 A1
  Sittingbourne ME10 . . . 101 D6
Felhampton Rd SE9 . . . . 30 B5
Felix Manor BR7 . . . . 30 E2
Felixstowe Ct E16 . . . . . 2 B3
Felixstowe Rd SE2 . . . . . 3 B3
Fell Mead TN12 . . . . . . 224 F6
Fellowes Way TN11 . . . 221 E5
Fellows Cl ME8 . . . . 98 B6
Felltram Way SE7 . . . . . . 1 A1
Felma Ho 12 SE7 . . . . . . 11 C8
Felspar Cl SE18 . . . . 2 F1
Felstead Br BR6 . . . . 87 B8
Felsted Rd E16 . . . . 1 D7
Felton Cl BR5 . . . . 53 B3
Felton Ho SE3 . . . . 11 C3
Felton Lea DA14 . . . . . . 30 F3
Fendyke Rd DA17 . . . . . . 3 D3
Fen Gr DA15 . . . . 12 F1
Fen Mdw TN15 . . . . 124 C1
Fenn Cl BR1 . . . . 29 A2
Fennel Cl ME16 . . . . . . 161 B3
Fennell Cl ME1 . . . . 63 B3
Fennell St SE18 . . . . 12 A8
Fenner Cl CT20 . . . . . . 334 E4
Fenn St ME3 . . . . 24 B4
Fenoulhet Way CT6 . . . . 77 A5
Fen Pond Rd TN15 . . . . 156 C7
Fens Way BR8 . . . . 33 A2
Fenton Cl BR7 . . . . 29 F3
Fenton Ct CT14 . . . . . . 215 B6
Fenwick Cl 16 SE18 . . . . 12 A8
Feoffe Cotts TN17 . . . . 342 E7
Ferbies TN3 . . . . 285 A7
Ferbies TN3 . . . . 285 A7
Ferby Ct DA15 . . . . 30 F4
Ferdi Lethert Ho
  TN24 . . . . 268 E5
Ferdinand Terr TN3 . . . 312 C7
Ferguson Ave DA12 . . . . 37 C4
Ferguson Cl CT21 . . . . 333 F2
Ferguson Rd TN29 . . . . 378 E6
Ferguson Way CT21 . . . 333 A1
Fernbank Cl ME5 . . . . . . 96 F3
Fern Bank Cres CT19 . . 335 D6
Fern Bank DA4 . . . . 89 E8
Fern Cl Erith DA8 . . . . . 15 B6
  Hawkinge CT18 . . . . . . 307 C6
  Whitstable CT5 . . . . 75 C1
Fern Ct Bexley DA7 . . . . 14 A3
  Broadstairs CT10 . . . . . 84 B5
  Dover CT17 . . . . 278 D1
Ferndale BR1 . . . . 52 C7
Ferndale Cl Bexley DA7 . 13 E6
  Halfway Houses ME12 . . 46 D6
  Royal Tunbridge Wells
  TN2 . . . . 286 C4
Ferndale Ct CT7 . . . . 81 A6
Ferndale Point TN2 . . . 286 C4
Ferndale Rd
  Gillingham ME7 . . . . 64 E5
  Gravesend DA12 . . . . . . 37 B6
Ferndale
  Royal Tunbridge Wells
  TN2 . . . . 286 D5
  Sevenoaks TN13 . . . . . 154 C5
Ferndale St E6 . . . . 2 B7
Ferndale Way BR6 . . . . . 86 D5
Ferndene DA3 . . . . 59 D6
Ferndown Ave BR6 . . . . . 53 D1
Ferndown CT7 . . . . 80 D8
Ferndown ME7 . . . . 98 A5
Ferndown Rd SE9 . . . . . . 29 D8
Fern Down DA13 . . . . . . 126 B8
Ferne La CT15 . . . . 276 D3
Ferne Way CT20 . . . . . . 334 E6
Fernfield CT18 . . . . 307 C6
Fernfield La CT18 . . . . . 307 C7
Fernheath Way DA2 . . . . 32 D3
Fern Hill Pl 3 BR6 . . . . . 86 C5
Fernhill Rd ME16 . . . . . 161 A2
Fernhill St E16 . . . . 1 F5
Fernholt TN10 . . . . 222 C7
Fernhurst Cres TN4 . . . 254 A2
Fernlea Ave CT6 . . . . 76 A4
Fernleigh Cl ME13 . . . . 140 B3
Fernleigh Rise ME20 . . 128 B2
Fernley Ct 11 CT20 . . . . 335 D5
Fernside La TN13 . . . . . 187 D6
Ferns The
  Larkfield ME20 . . . . . . 128 B1
  Platt TN15 . . . . 157 C7
  Royal Tunbridge Wells
  TN1 . . . . 286 C4
Fern Wlk ME10 . . . . . . 102 C5
Fernwood Cl BR1 . . . . . . 52 C7
Ferranti Cl SE18 . . . . 1 D3
Ferrier Cl ME8 . . . . 98 E4
Ferrier Point 8 E16 . . . . 1 A8
Ferringham TN4 . . . . . . 285 F4
Ferry La Ind Est RM13 . . 4 F8
Ferry La Rainham RM13 . . 4 E7
  Wouldham ME1 . . . . 95 C4

Ferry Pl SE18 . . . . 2 A3
Ferry Rd Halling ME2 . . . 95 B4
  Iwade ME9 . . . . 68 E4
  Queenborough ME11,
  ME12 . . . . 46 D1
  Tilbury RM18 . . . . 19 A4
Ferry View ME11 . . . . . . 45 F3
Festival Ave DA3 . . . . . . 59 D6
Festival Cl Erith DA8 . . . 15 A7
  Sidcup DA5 . . . . 31 D7
Festoon Way E16 . . . . . . 1 D6
Ffinch Cl ME20 . . . . . . 160 D8
Fiddlers Cl DA9 . . . . 17 B3
Fiddling La TN25 . . . . . 303 E6
Field Ave CT1 . . . . 143 D3
Field Cl Bromley BR1 . . . 52 C7
  Chatham ME5 . . . . 96 E6
Field Dr TN8 . . . . 217 D3
Field End TN24 . . . . 269 A1
Field End Pl ME13 . . . . 140 A3
Fielder CT ME10 . . . . . . 102 C5
Fieldfare Rd SE28 . . . . . 3 C6
Fielding Ave RM18 . . . . . 19 B6
Fielding Dr ME20 . . . . . 128 A3
Fielding St ME13 . . . . . 138 C7
Fieldings The ME10 . . . 101 E8
Field Mill Rd TN27 . . . . 233 B5
Fieldside Cl BR6 . . . . 86 C6
Fields La ME18 . . . . 192 E7
Fieldview Cl ME12 . . . . . 46 C6
Field View
  Kingsnorth TN23 . . . . . 300 B4
  Whitstable CT5 . . . . . . 108 B7
Fieldway BR5 . . . . 53 D3
Fieldways TN18 . . . . . . 341 A1
Field Way CT2 . . . . 143 F5
Fieldworks Rd ME7 . . . . 64 A7
Fiennes Way TN13 . . . . 187 C8
Fiesta Dr RM9 . . . . 4 C8
Fiesta Wlk CT1 . . . . 175 C7
Fife Rd Herne Bay CT6 . . 76 B3
  Newham E16 . . . . 1 A8
Fifteenpenny Fields
  SE9 . . . . 12 A2
Fifth Ave Margate CT9 . . 51 B3
  West Thurrock RM20 . . . 17 A8
Fig Tree Cl CT10 . . . . . . 83 F7
Fig Tree Wlk CT15 . . . . 245 C7
Fiji Terr ME14 . . . . 162 A7
Filborough Way DA12 . . 38 B6
Filer Rd ME12 . . . . 46 E7
Filey Cl TN16 . . . . 150 B8
Filmer La TN14 . . . . . . 154 E6
Filmer Rd CT4 . . . . 175 F1
Filston La TN14 . . . . . . 121 E5
Filston Rd DA8 . . . . 4 C1
Finchale Rd SE2 . . . . 3 A3
Finch Cl
  St Nicholas at Wade CT7 . 79 E2
  Sittingbourne ME10 . . . 101 F3
Finch Gr CT21 . . . . 353 D8
Finchley Cl DA1 . . . . 16 A1
Finchley Rd RM17 . . . . . 18 B8
Finch Mews CT14 . . . . . 215 C4
Finch's Cross RH8 . . . . 216 A8
Findlay Cl ME8 . . . . 98 D6
Findlay Ct 9 CT21 . . . . 333 B2
Finglesham Ct ME8 . . . . 13 E6
Finglesham Ct ME15 . . 195 C8
Finglesham Farm Barns
  CT14 . . . . 214 A8
Finlay Cl ME13 . . . . 138 B7
Finn Farm Ct TN23 . . . 300 D1
Finn Farm Rd TN23 . . . 300 C2
Finsbury Ct TN11 . . . . . 117 E8
Finsbury Pl TN11 . . . . . 117 E8
Finsbury Way DA5 . . . . . 13 F1
Fintonagh Dr ME14 . . . 162 B6
Finucane Dr BR5 . . . . . . 54 C2
Finwell Rd ME8 . . . . 66 A2
Firbank Cl E16 . . . . 1 D8
Firbank Gdns CT9 . . . . . 82 D7
Firbanks CT5 . . . . 108 F8
Fircroft Way TN8 . . . . . 217 C3
Fir Ct TN24 . . . . 268 F1
Fir Dene BR6 . . . . 86 A7
Firecrest Cl DA3 . . . . . . 59 B6
Firepower (Mus)★ SE18 . 2 B3
Firethorn Cl ME7 . . . . . . 64 E6
Firmin Ave ME17 . . . . . 195 D5
Firmingers Rd BR6 . . . . 88 C5
Firmin Rd DA1 . . . . 15 C2
Firs Cl Aylesford ME20 . 128 E1
  Folkestone CT19 . . . . . 334 D7
Firs Ct TN4 . . . . 285 F6
Firside Gr DA15 . . . . 30 F7
Firs La CT19 . . . . 334 D7
Firs Rd CT4 . . . . 210 F1
First Ave Bexley DA7 . . . 13 C7
  Broadstairs CT10 . . . . . 51 F2
  Chatham ME4 . . . . 64 C2
  Eastchurch ME12 . . . . . 48 E5
  Gillingham ME7 . . . . 64 E3
  Margate CT9 . . . . 51 B3
  Northfleet DA11 . . . . . . 36 E7
  Rushenden ME11 . . . . . 45 F3
  Sheerness ME12 . . . . . . 28 C1
  West Thurrock RM20 . . . 17 A8
Firs The Coldblow DA5 . . 32 D7
  Deal CT14 . . . . 215 C8
  Hersden CT3 . . . . 111 E1
  Sidcup DA15 . . . . 30 F5
First La ME17 . . . . 163 E2
First St TN3 . . . . 284 F1
Fir Tree Cl Grays RM17 . 18 B8
  5 Orpington BR6 . . . . . 86 F5
  Ramsgate CT11 . . . . . . 117 C6
Firtree Cl CT2 . . . . 142 B3

Fir Tree Cl
  Staplehurst TN12 . . . . 260 F3
  Tonbridge TN11 . . . . . . 221 E5
Fir Tree Gr
  Bredhurst ME7 . . . . 98 B1
  Chatham ME5 . . . . 97 D1
Fir Tree Hill CT13 . . . . 180 B6
Fir Tree Rd TN4 . . . . . . 285 F3
Fisher Cl CT21 . . . . 333 D1
Fisherman's Wharf
  CT13 . . . . 149 A1
Fishermans Ctyd
  CT14 . . . . 215 D3
Fishermans Wlk SE28 . . 2 A1
Fishermen's Hill DA11 . 18 B2
Fisher Rd
  Canterbury CT2 . . . . . . 142 D1
  Chatham ME5 . . . . 97 B7
Fishers Cl TN12 . . . . . . 260 F5
Fisher's Gate Cotts
  TN7 . . . . 311 A1
Fishers CT14 . . . . 215 D3
Fishers Rd TN12 . . . . . . 260 F5
Fisher St
  Maidstone ME14 . . . . . 162 A6
  Newham E16 . . . . 1 A8
Fisher Street Rd
  ME13 . . . . 170 E2
Fisher St CT13 . . . . 149 A1
Fisher's Way DA17 . . . . . 4 C5
Fishguard Way E16 . . . . 2 B5
Fish Market CT19 . . . . . 335 E5
Fishmonger's La 8
  CT16 . . . . 310 E7
Fishponds Rd BR2 . . . . . 85 D5
Fitzgerald Ave CT6 . . . . 76 C4
Fitzmary Ave CT9 . . . . . 50 E1
Fitzroy Ave
  Broadstairs CT10 . . . . . 51 G2
  Margate CT9 . . . . 51 B3
  Ramsgate CT12 . . . . . . 83 B2
Fitzroy Ct DA1 . . . . 34 B7
Fitzroy Rd CT5 . . . . 74 F2
Fitzthorold Ho ME7 . . . . 64 E7
Fitzwalter Ct 1 CT16 . . 278 B3
Fitzwilliam Mews E16 . . 1 A5
Fitzwilliam Rd ME14 . . 162 F5
Five Acre Wood Sch
  ME15 . . . . 195 B7
Five Arches Bsns Est
  DA14 . . . . 31 D3
Fiveash Rd DA11 . . . . . . 36 F8
Five Bells La 5 ME1 . . . 63 D4
Five Elms Rd BR2 . . . . . 85 C7
Five Fields La TN8 . . . . 218 B4
Five Oak Green Rd
  Capel TN11,TN12 . . . . 255 D6
  Tonbridge TN11 . . . . . . 254 F7
Five Oak La TN12 . . . . . 260 B1
Five Oaks Mews BR1 . . 29 A5
Five Vents La TN29 . . . 372 B8
Five Ways St ME4 . . . . . 64 A4
Fiveways 6 CT17 . . . . . 310 C8
Fiveways L Ctr ME4 . . . 64 A4
Fiveways Rise CT14 . . . 214 F5
Five Ways TN1 . . . . 286 B4
Five Wents BR8 . . . . 56 A7
Flack Gdns ME3 . . . . 41 E5
Flamborough CT TN16 . 150 B8
Flamingo Cl ME5 . . . . . . 97 A7
Flamingo Dr CT6 . . . . . . 76 E3
Flamsteed Rd SE7 . . . . . 1 E1
Flanders Cl ME10 . . . . . 68 F1
Flanders Field TN25 . . . 301 A4
Flats The
  Gravesend DA12 . . . . . . 37 E8
  Swanscombe DA9 . . . . . 17 C2
Flax Court La CT15 . . . . 245 C7
Flaxman Cl 13 ME7 . . . . 64 A6
Flaxman Ct DA1 . . . . 4 A1
Flaxman Dr ME16 . . . . . 161 C6
Flaxmore Cl DA7 . . . . . . 14 B4
Flaxmore Pl TN4 . . . . . 254 A2
Flaxpond Rd ME15 . . . . 161 B2
Flaxton Rd SE18 . . . . . . 12 E7
Fleet Ave Dartford DA2 . 34 C7
  Sheerness ME12 . . . . . . 28 B1
Fleet Dale Par DA2 . . . . 34 C7
Fleet Ho DA13 . . . . 36 B2
Fleet Rd Dartford DA2 . . 34 C7
  Northfleet DA11 . . . . . . 36 C5
  Rochester ME1 . . . . 63 D1
Fleets La CT2 . . . . 142 D7
Fleet Terr DA11 . . . . 36 D7
Fleet Villas TN24 . . . . . 268 D7
Fleetwood Cl CT6 . . . . . 76 D4
Fleetwood Ct
  1 Newham E6 . . . . 1 F8
  Orpington BR6 . . . . 86 A6
Fleming Gdns RM18 . . . 19 C6
Fleming Ho SE2 . . . . 3 C1
Fleming Rd CT13,CT3 . . 179 D6
Fleming Way Erith SE28 . 3 D6
  Folkestone CT19 . . . . . 335 E8
  Tonbridge TN10 . . . . . . 222 C7
Fletcher Battery Camp Site
  ME12 . . . . 49 A6
Fletcher Cl E6 . . . . 2 B6
Fletcher Rd
  Staplehurst TN12 . . . . 260 E3
  Whitstable CT5 . . . . 75 B1
Fletchers CT5 . . . . 82 B5
Fletchers Way CT14 . . . 215 A5
Fletching Rd SE7 . . . . . . 11 D8
Flete Rd CT9 . . . . 82 D5

Fleur de Lis Heritage Ctr★
  ME13 . . . . 138 D7
Flimwell TN23 . . . . 299 D6
Flimwell Cl TN5 . . . . . . 339 E5
Flint Cl 8 Orpington BR6 . 86 F4
  Sittingbourne ME10 . . . 101 E8
Flint Cotts CT7 . . . . 80 F6
Flint Down Cl BR5 . . . . . 54 A8
Flint Gn ME5 . . . . 97 C3
Flint Gr ME7 . . . . 98 D8
Flint Ho CT9 . . . . 50 J3
Flint La ME17 . . . . 166 C1
Flintmill Cres SE3,SE9 . . 11 E5
Flint St RM20 . . . . 17 B8
Floathaven Cl SE28 . . . . 3 A5
Floats The TN13 . . . . . . 153 E6
Flodden Rd CT14 . . . . . 214 F3
Flood Hatch ME15 . . . . 161 D2
Flood La ME13 . . . . 138 C8
Flood St TN25 . . . . 301 D2
Florance La TN3 . . . . . . 312 B6
Flora Rd CT11 . . . . 117 E8
Flora St DA17 . . . . 3 F1
Florence Ave CT5 . . . . . 108 B7
Florence CT RM17,RM20 . 17 E8
Florence Cotts
  5 Edenbridge TN8 . . . . 217 C1
  Ramsgate CT11 . . . . . . 117 D6
Florence Ct CT9 . . . . . . 51 B3
Florence Farm Mobile
  Home Pk TN15 . . . . . . 90 D4
Florence Ho SE18 . . . . . 11 F6
Florence Rd
  4 Bromley BR1 . . . . . . 52 A8
  Erith DA17,SE2 . . . . . . 3 C2
  Maidstone ME16 . . . . . 161 F8
  3 Ramsgate CT11 . . . . 117 D6
Florence St 3 ME2 . . . . 63 B8
Florida Cl CT16 . . . . . . 278 B3
Florin Dr ME1 . . . . 63 B4
Flowerfield TN14 . . . . . 121 F2
Flowerhill Way DA13 . . . 36 E1
Flower Rise ME14 . . . . 161 F7
Floyd Cl TN4 . . . . 286 A7
Floyd Rd SE7 . . . . 1 C1
Flume End ME15 . . . . . 161 D2
Flyers Way The TN16 . . 151 D1
Flying Horse La 6
  CT16 . . . . 310 E7
Foads Hill CT12 . . . . . . 116 B6
Foads La CT12 . . . . 116 D5
Foalhurst Cl TN10 . . . . 222 E4
Focal Point Rd CT16 . . 277 F4
Fodbury Ct CT16 . . . . . 50 C1
Foley Cl ME24 . . . . 301 A7
Foley Ct DA1 . . . . 34 B7
Foley Rd TN16 . . . . 118 D1
Foley St ME14 . . . . 162 A5
Folkestone, Christ Church
  CE Prim Sch CT20 . . . 335 C5
Folkestone Ent Ctr
  CT19 . . . . 334 F8
Folkestone Harbour Sta
  CT20 . . . . 335 E4
Folkestone Mus★
  CT20 . . . . 335 D5
Folkestone Race Course
  CT21 . . . . 332 A6
Folkestone Rd
  Brookland TN31 . . . . . . 369 B3
  Church Hougham CT15 . 309 D4
  Dover CT17,CT15 . . . . 310 B7
Folkestone, St Mary's CE
  Prim Sch CT20 . . . . . . 335 F6
Folkestone, St Peter's CE
  Prim Sch CT19 . . . . . . 335 E6
Folkestone Sch for Girls
  The CT20 . . . . 334 F4
Folkestone West Sta
  CT18 . . . . 334 F5
Folkstone Ho 4 ME15 . 195 F6
Folkstone, St Martin's CE
  Prim Sch CT18 . . . . . . 334 F1
Folks Wood Way
  CT21 . . . . 332 A4
Folly Rd CT20 . . . . 335 E6
Fonblanque Rd ME12 . . 28 C2
Fontwell Cl ME15 . . . . . 195 F6
Fontwell Dr BR2 . . . . . . 53 A4
Foord Almshouses
  ME1 . . . . 63 B3
Foord Cl DA2 . . . . 34 E6
Foord Rd ME17 . . . . . . 199 E8
Foord Rd N CT19,CT20 . 335 D5
Foord Rd S 14 CT20 . . . 335 D5
Foord St ME1 . . . . 63 D4
Footbury Hill Rd BR6 . . 54 A2
Foots Cray High St
  DA14 . . . . 31 D2
Foots Cray La DA14 . . . 31 C7
Footscray Rd SE9 . . . . . 30 C7
Forbes Rd ME13 . . . . . 138 C6
Force Green Farm Cotts
  TN16 . . . . 151 E4
Force Green La TN16 . . 151 E4
Ford Cl Bridge CT4 . . . . 175 F1
  Herne Bay CT6 . . . . 76 A4
Fordcombe CE Prim Sch
  TN3 . . . . 284 C4
Fordcombe Cl ME15 . . . 195 F7
Fordcombe Rd
  Fordcombe TN3 . . . . . . 284 C4
  Penshurst TN11 . . . . . . 252 A3
Fordcroft Rd BR5 . . . . . 54 B4
Forde Ave BR1 . . . . 52 C6
Fordgate Bsns Pk DA17 . 4 C4
Ford Hill CT3,CT6 . . . . 111 E8
Ford Ho 2 SE18 . . . . . . 2 B1
Ford La
  Trottiscliffe ME19 . . . . 126 A4

Ford La continued
  Wrotham Heath TN15,
  ME19 . . . . 125 F2
Fordoun Rd CT10 . . . . . 83 F5
Ford Rd DA11 . . . . 18 B2
Fords Park Rd E16 . . . . . 1 A7
Ford Way TN23 . . . . 267 F1
Fordwich Cl
  Maidstone ME16 . . . . . 161 B7
  Orpington BR6 . . . . 53 F2
Fordwich Dr ME2 . . . . . . 40 A2
Fordwich Gn ME8 . . . . . 65 C3
Fordwich Gr CT10 . . . . . 83 E7
Fordwich Pl CT13 . . . . . 180 F8
Fordwich Rd CT2 . . . . . 143 F4
Fordwich TH★ CT2 . . . . 144 A4
Ford Wlk CT5 . . . . 108 A3
Foreland Ave
  Folkestone CT19 . . . . . 335 F6
  Margate CT9 . . . . 51 D1
Foreland Ct
  Birchington CT7 . . . . . . 80 D8
  Ramsgate CT11 . . . . . . 117 D5
St Margaret's at Cliffe
  CT15 . . . . 280 A5
Foreland Hts CT10 . . . . 84 B7
Foreland Park Ho CT10 . 84 B7
Foreland Rd CT15 . . . . 280 A4
Foreland Sch The CT10 . 84 A6
Forelands Sq CT14 . . . . 215 B3
Foreland St SE18 . . . . . 2 D2
Foreland The CT1 . . . . . 175 B5
Foreman Ctr TN27 . . . . 262 D5
Foremans Barn Rd
  ME15 . . . . 193 F3
Foreman's Wlk TN27 . . 262 D5
Foreness CI CT10 . . . . . 51 G3
Forestall Mdw TN23 . . 300 B4
Forest Ave TN25 . . . . . . 267 E4
Forest Cl BR7 . . . . 53 A8
Forest Cotts TN25 . . . . 203 C2
Forestdale Rd ME5 . . . . 130 A8
Forest Dene TN2 . . . . . . 286 C1
Forest Dr Chatham ME5 . 96 F2
  Orpington BR2 . . . . 85 E6
Foresters Cl ME5 . . . . . . 96 F2
Foresters Cres DA7 . . . . 14 B3
Foresters Homes The
  DA7 . . . . 14 B3
Foresters Way CT20 . . . 335 D5
Forest Gr TN10 . . . . . . 222 C5
Forest Hill ME15 . . . . . 161 F1
Forest Lawns BR1 . . . . . 52 C8
Forest Rd Erith DA8 . . . . 15 A6
  Paddock Wood TN12 . . 257 A6
  Royal Tunbridge Wells
  TN2 . . . . 286 C1
Forest Ridge BR2 . . . . . 85 E9
Forestry Cotts CT4 . . . . 239 B7
Forest Way
  Eltham DA15 . . . . 30 D8
  Kings Hill ME19 . . . . . . 159 A3
  Orpington BR5 . . . . 53 F4
  Pembury TN2 . . . . 287 D8
  Royal Tunbridge Wells
  TN2 . . . . 286 D1
Forge Cl Eythorne CT15 . 245 C7
  Five Oak Green TN12 . . 256 B7
  Hayes BR2 . . . . 52 A1
  Penshurst TN11 . . . . . . 252 B4
  Sellindge TN25 . . . . . . 303 D1
  Sturry CT2 . . . . 143 F5
Forge Cotts
  Boyden Gate CT3 . . . . 112 C8
  Broadstairs CT10 . . . . . 84 B5
  Faversham ME13 . . . . . 139 D8
  Flimwell TN5 . . . . 339 C3
  Nettlestead Green
  ME18 . . . . 192 C2
  Wrotham Heath TN15 . . 125 E1
Forge Croft TN8 . . . . . . 217 D1
Forgefield
  Bethersden TN26 . . . . 297 D5
  Biggin Hill TN16 . . . . . 118 D3
Forgefield Cotts TN18 . 356 A4
Forgefield Ct BR5 . . . . . 54 C4
Forgefields CT6 . . . . . . 111 B8
Forge Field CT15 . . . . . 308 E5
Forge Hill
  Aldington TN25 . . . . . . 330 A5
  Bethersden TN26 . . . . 297 C5
Forge Ho
  Canterbury CT1 . . . . . . 174 E6
  Ickham CT3 . . . . 145 C1
Forge La Ashford TN23 . 268 B2
  Benover ME18 . . . . . . 226 B4
  Boxley ME14 . . . . 130 C2
  Boyden Gate CT3 . . . . 112 C8
  Bredhurst ME7 . . . . 98 A1
  East Farleigh ME15 . . . 194 C7
  Egerton Forstal TN27 . 232 C1
  Gillingham ME7 . . . . 64 E7
  Gravesend DA12 . . . . . . 37 F6
  Headcorn TN27 . . . . . . 262 D5
  Higham ME3 . . . . 39 C3
  High Halstow ME23 . . . . 23 E3
  Horton Kirby DA4 . . . . . 57 C5
  Leeds ME17 . . . . 196 F7
  Maidstone ME14 . . . . . 163 C4
  Rabbit's Cross ME17,
  TN12 . . . . 228 F3
  Ramsgate CT11 . . . . . . 117 C7
  Shorne DA12 . . . . 38 E3
  Sutton CT15 . . . . 247 A6
  Upchurch ME9 . . . . 66 F3
  West Kingsdown TN15 . . 91 A1
  West Peckham ME18 . . 191 A6
  Whitfield CT16 . . . . . . 278 A8
  Whitstable CT5 . . . . . . 108 D8

402 For–Geo

Forge Mdw
Harrietsham ME17 198 D6
Stone in Oxney TN30 361 A4
Forge Meadows TN27 262 D5
Forge Meads TN30 359 E3
Forge Path CT16 278 A8
Forge Pl DA12 37 F7
Forge Rd Cobbarn TN3 312 C2
Royal Tunbridge Wells TN4 254 A1
Sittingbourne ME10 101 E6
Forge Sq TN11 220 F2
Forge The TN12 256 B7
Forge View TN15 188 B5
Forge Way
Paddock Wood TN12 257 A7
Shoreham TN14 121 F8
Formation The E16 2 B4
Formby Rd ME2 95 A7
Formby Terr ME2 95 A6
Forrens The 15 CT1 143 A1
Forrester Cl CT1 143 C2
Forsham La ME17 229 C5
Forson Cl TN30 345 B8
Forstal Cl BR2 52 A6
Forstal Cotts
Forstal ME20 129 B2
Lenham Heath ME17 200 A1
Forstal La ME17 194 D4
Forstall TN3 285 A4
Forstall The TN11 221 A2
Forstal Rd
Egerton Forstal TN27 232 C1
Forstal ME20 129 C2
Woolage Village CT4 210 E1
Forstal The
Cobbarn TN3 312 F3
Hadlow TN11 223 F8
Lenham Heath ME17 200 A1
Pembury TN2 287 E8
Preston CT3 146 B6
Wye TN25 237 E2
Forsters ME17 196 E4
Forsyth Cl ME19 128 A1
Forsyth Ct 7 ME7 64 C7
Fort Amherst Heritage Pk & Caverns★ ME4 63 F5
Fort Burgoyne (Casemated Barracks) CT15 278 E2
Fort Burgoyne Rd CT16 278 E1
Fort Cl TN29 377 E6
Fort Cotts CT10 84 B4
Fort Cres CT9 50 J3
Fort Hill CT9 50 I3
Fortis Cl E16 1 C7
Fort Lower Prom CT9 50 J3
Fort Luton (Mus)★ ME4 64 A1
Fort Paragon CT9 50 J3
Fort Pitt Gram Sch ME4 63 E4
Fort Pitt Hill ME1,ME4 63 E4
Fort Pitt St ME4 63 E3
Fort Prom CT9 50 J3
Fort Rd
Badgers Mount TN14 121 C4
Broadstairs CT10 84 B4
Hythe CT21 333 A2
Margate CT9 50 I3
Tilbury RM18 19 C5
Fortrye Cl DA11 36 E6
Fort St Newham E16 1 B5
Rochester ME1 63 D4
Fortuna Cl DA3 58 F5
Fortuna Ct CT11 117 D7
Fortune Way ME18 159 B3
Fortune Wlk 7 SE28 2 D3
Forty Acre La E16 1 A8
Forty Acres Hill ME12 47 C4
Forty Acres Rd CT2 142 E2
Forum The 2 ME10 101 F4
Forum Way TN23 299 E5
Forward Way ME1 96 C6
Fossdene Prim Sch SE7 1 B1
Fossdene Rd SE7 1 B1
Fosse Bank Cl TN9 254 A7
Fosse Bank New Sch TN11 221 E7
Fosse Rd TN9 222 B2
Fossett Lodge DA7 14 C6
Fossington Rd DA17 3 D2
Fostall Gn TN23 299 F7
Fostall Rd ME13 105 C1
Fosten La TN27 322 E7
Foster Clarke Dr ME17 195 D5
Foster Clark Est ME15 162 B2
Foster Cl CT19 334 E7
Foster Rd TN24 301 A6
Foster's Ave CT10 83 E7
Fosters Cl BR7 29 F3
Foster's Ct CT13 181 A7
Fosters Mews DA3 58 E7
Fosters Old School DA16 13 B5
Fosters Prim Sch DA16 13 B4
Foster St ME15 162 A3
Foster Way CT14 215 B5
Fostington Way ME5 96 F1
Fougeres Way TN24 268 A4
Foulds Cl ME8 98 B5
Founder Cl E6 2 B7
Foundry Wharf ME1 63 E4
Fountain Ct
Eynsford DA4 89 E8
Sidcup DA15 13 B1
Fountain Inn Ct CT9 50 I3
Fountain La
Maidstone ME16 161 A2
Fountain La *continued*
Sheerness ME12 28 A2
Fountain Rd ME2 39 E1
Fountains Cl TN24 269 A1
Fountain St
2 Sittingbourne ME10 101 E4
3 Whitstable CT5 74 D2
Fountain Wlk DA11 18 F1
Fouracre Cotts ME9 99 E6
Four Acres ME19 160 B5
Four Elms Hill ME3 40 E4
Four Elms Prim Sch TN8 218 B5
Four Elms Rdbt ME3 40 E3
Four Elms Rd TN8 217 D4
Four Horseshoes Pk ME13 106 D1
Four Oaks ME13 137 E8
Four Oaks Rd TN12, TN27 261 E7
Fourth Ave
Eastchurch ME12 48 F5
Gillingham ME7 64 E4
West Thurrock RM20 17 A8
Four Trees TN8 217 C3
Four Turnings CT3 146 B3
Four Wents
Langley Heath ME17 196 E3
Maidstone ME17 195 F2
Fourwents Rd ME3 41 D7
Fowey Cl ME5 97 C5
Fowler Cl
Gillingham ME8 98 C3
Sidcup DA14 31 E3
Foxborough Cl CT13 180 B6
Foxborough Hill CT13 180 B5
Foxborough La CT12 115 C6
Foxburrow Cl ME8 98 D5
Foxbury Ave BR7 30 D2
Foxbury Cl Bromley BR1 29 B2
Orpington BR6 87 A5
Foxbury Dr BR6 87 A4
Foxbury DA3 91 E7
Foxbury Rd BR1 29 B2
Foxbury Wlk DA11 36 D4
Foxbush TN11 221 C6
Fox Cl Lyminge CT18 305 B7
Newham E16 1 A8
Orpington BR6 87 A5
Foxcroft Rd SE18 12 B6
Foxden Dr ME15 162 F1
Foxdene Ct CT5 107 F6
Foxdene Rd CT5 107 F6
Foxdown Cl CT2 142 E2
Foxearth Cl TN16 118 E1
Foxendown La DA13 60 B1
Foxes Dale SE3 11 A4
Foxfield Prim Sch SE18 2 C1
Foxfield Rd BR6 86 D8
Foxglove Cl
9 Marlpit Hill TN8 217 D3
Sidcup DA15 13 A1
Foxglove Cres ME5 96 E4
Foxglove Gn TN24 268 F2
Foxglove Rd TN24 268 E1
Foxglove Rise ME14 161 E7
Foxgloves The TN12 257 B5
Foxgrove Path SE28 2 E5
Foxgrove Rd CT5 75 A1
Foxgrove ME10 101 E7
Fox Hill Keston BR2 85 C5
Sittingbourne ME10, ME9 102 D3
Foxhole La
Four Throws TN18 355 D8
Hawkhurst TN18 341 E1
Matfield TN12 288 C8
Wadhurst TN5 337 B4
Foxhole Rd SE9 11 E2
Fox Hollow Cl 2 SE18 2 E1
Fox Hollow Dr DA7 13 D4
Fox Holt Rd CT15 275 B2
Foxhome Cl BR7 30 A2
Fox House Rd DA17 4 B1
Foxhunter Pk The CT12 114 D6
Fox in the Wood TN5 336 C6
Fox La BR2 85 C5
Fox Lea TN15 156 F7
Foxley Rd ME11 46 A5
Fox Manor Way RM20 17 B8
Fox's Cross Hill CT5 108 A3
Fox's Cross Rd CT5 108 C3
Fox's Cross CT5 108 B4
Fox St ME7 64 C6
Foxtail Cl ME4 41 B2
Foxton Ho E16 2 A4
Foxton Rd RM20 17 D8
Fox Way CT4 242 F8
Foxwood Gr
Northfleet DA11 36 E7
Pratt's Bottom BR6 87 C1
Foxwood Rd DA2 35 B5
Foxwood Way DA3 59 D7
Framley Rd TN10 222 F5
Framlingham Cres SE9 29 F4
Frampton Rd CT21 333 A2
France Rd CT16 278 A5
Frances Gdns CT11 117 F8
Frances St SE18 1 F2
Francis Ave DA7 14 A5
Francis Cl CT12 116 D5
Francis Ct 7 DA8 4 E1
Francis Dr ME5 97 A2
Francis La ME15 195 F5
Francis Rd
Ashford TN23 300 B8
Broadstairs CT10 84 B7
Dartford DA1 15 B2
Orpington BR5 54 D6
Tonbridge TN11 221 D6
Frankapps Cl ME9 100 B6
Frank Burton Cl 5 SE7 1 B1
Frank Edinger Cl TN24 268 D4
Frankfield Rise TN2 286 A1
Frank Godley Ct DA14 31 B3
Franklin Dr ME14 162 D4
Franklin Pas SE9 11 E4
Franklin Rd Bexley DA7 13 F6
Gillingham ME7 64 D5
Gravesend DA12 37 D3
Maypole DA2 32 E6
Franklins Cotts ME15 194 C5
Franklyn Ho CT2 143 F5
Franklyn Rd CT2 174 C8
Franks Ct ME8 65 B2
Frank's Hollow Rd TN3 253 C2
Franks La DA4 57 B4
Frankswood Ave BR5 53 C4
Frank Walters Bsns Pk The CT10 83 D3
Frank Woolley Rd TN10 222 F5
Frant CE Prim Sch TN3 314 B4
Frant Cotts TN5 338 E1
Frant Ct TN3 314 B3
Frant Field TN8 217 C1
Frant Green Rd TN3 314 B3
Frant Rd TN2,TN3 314 A7
Frant Sta TN3 314 F5
Fraser Cl Coldblow DA5 32 C7
4 Newham E6 1 E7
Fraser Ho 3 SE18 2 A2
Fraser Rd DA8 4 D1
Freathy La TN25 268 C8
Freda Cl CT10 83 F1
Frederick Andrews Ct RM17 18 D8
Frederick Ho 4 SE18 1 E3
Frederick Pl SE18 2 B1
Frederick Rd
Deal CT14 215 A3
Gillingham ME7 64 C4
Frederick St ME10 101 E4
Freedown The CT15 280 A7
Free Heath Rd TN3, TN5 316 C3
Freehold The
East Peckham TN12 224 F6
Hadlow TN11 190 D1
Freeland Ct 24 DA14 31 A5
Freelands Gr BR1 52 B8
Freelands Rd
Bromley BR1 52 B8
Snodland ME6 127 F8
Freeland Way DA8 15 A6
Freeman Ct 3 ME10 101 E4
Freeman Gdns ME4 63 F2
Freeman Rd DA12 37 E5
Freeman's Cl CT5 108 A6
Freeman's Rd CT12 115 B6
Freeman Way ME15 195 E7
Freemasons Rd E16 1 B7
Freemen's Way CT14 215 B3
Freesia Cl
Gillingham ME7 64 F6
Orpington BR6 86 F5
Freight La TN17 320 C3
Fremantle Ho RM18 18 F6
Fremantle Rd Erith DA17 4 A2
Folkestone CT20 334 E5
Fremlin Cl TN4 285 B4
Fremlins Rd ME14 163 C4
Frencham Cl CT2 143 A4
French's Row ME9 103 D2
Frensham Cl ME10 102 B4
Frensham Rd
Rolvenden TN17 344 A1
Sidcup SE9 30 D6
Frensham Wlk ME5 96 F1
Freshfield La CT21 333 B4
Freshland Rd ME16 161 B4
Freshlands CT6 77 E5
Freshwater Cl CT6 76 B3
Freshwater Rd ME5 97 B7
Freta Rd DA6 13 F2
Frewing Cl BR7 30 A3
Friar Rd BR5 54 A4
Friars Ave ME5 96 F2
Friars Cl CT5 75 A1
Friars Mews SE9 12 A2
Friars Pk ME20 128 E2
Friars Sch TN23 299 B8
Friars The★ ME20 128 E2
Canterbury CT1 142 F1
Friars Way Dover CT16 278 A3
Royal Tunbridge Wells TN2 286 D6
Friars Wlk SE2 3 D1
Friary Pl 3 ME2 63 B7
Friary Prec ME2 63 B7
Friary Way CT2 142 D2
Friday Rd DA8 4 D1
Friday St ME17 230 B6
Frid Cnr TN26 297 E7
Friendly Cl CT9 51 D1
Friends Ave CT9 83 B8
Friesian Way TN24 268 C8
Friezland Rd TN4 285 D1
Friezley La TN17 292 C1
Frimley Ct DA14 31 C3
Frindsbury Hill ME2 40 C1
Frindsbury Rd ME2 63 B8
Frinstead Gr BR5 54 D5
Frinstead Wlk ME16 161 B7
Frinsted Cl ME8 65 C3
Frinsted Rd Erith DA8 14 D7
Milstead ME9 134 E2
Frinton Rd DA14 31 E6
Friston Way ME1 96 D8
Friswell Pl 1 DA6 14 A3
Frith Bsns Pk TN25 329 B6
Frith Rd
Aldington Frith TN25 329 C6
Dover CT16 278 C1
Frithwood Cl ME15 162 F1
Frittenden CE Prim Sch TN17 293 E6
Frittenden Cl TN23 299 E6
Frittenden Rd
Rochester ME2 40 D2
Staplehurst TN12 261 B2
Frobisher Cl ME10 101 E7
Frobisher Ct
3 Dartford DA1 15 D1
2 Ramsgate CT11 117 F8
Frobisher Gdns ME1 63 C2
Frobisher Rd Erith DA8 15 A7
Newham E6 2 A7
Frobisher Way
Gravesend DA12 37 E3
Swanscombe DA9 17 B3
Frog Farm Cotts ME9 67 A4
Frog Hole La TN8, TN16 184 D2
Frog La
Bishopsbourne CT4 209 C6
Rainham RM13 4 D8
Royal Tunbridge Wells TN1 286 A2
West Malling ME19 159 C8
Frogmore Wlk ME17 199 C5
Frognal Ave DA14 31 A2
Frognal Cl ME9 103 B2
Frognal Cnr BR7 30 F2
Frognal Gdns ME9 103 C2
Frognal La ME9 103 B2
Frognal Pl DA14 31 A3
Frogs Hole La TN17, TN27 322 E3
Frog's La TN17 343 E1
Froissart Rd SE9 11 E2
Fromandez Dr TN12 289 F5
Frome Ct TN10 222 B5
Front Brents ME13 138 D8
Front Rd TN26 326 A1
Front St CT14 247 F5
Front The CT15 280 A4
Frost Cres ME5 97 A7
Frostland La TN26, TN29 350 C1
Froyle Cl ME16 161 C6
Fruiterer's Cl ME9 135 B7
Fruitfields TN5 339 C3
Fry Cl ME3 27 A6
Fry's Cotts ME3 25 C4
Frythe Cl TN17 320 D4
Frythe Cres TN17 320 D4
Frythe Way TN17 320 D4
Frythe Wlk TN17 320 D4
Fuchsia St SE2 3 B1
Fuggles Cl TN12 256 E6
Fuggles Ct TN17 342 D6
Fulbert Dr ME14 162 F5
Fulbert Rd CT16 278 B5
Fulham Ave CT9 82 C7
Fuller Cl Durgates TN5 336 E5
Orpington BR6 86 F5
Fullers Cl ME14 163 A4
Fullers Hill 7 TN16 151 D1
Fullers Yd CT9 50 J2
Fulmar Ct TN29 365 F3
Fulmar Mews CT18 307 A3
Fulmar Rd ME2 62 D6
Fulmar Way CT6 77 F4
Fulmer Rd E16 1 D8
Fulsam Pl CT9 50 H1
Fulston Manor Sch ME10 101 F2
Fulston Pl ME10 102 A3
Fulthorp Rd SE3 11 A5
Fulwich Rd DA1 15 F1
Furfield Cl ME17 195 E5
Furley Park Prim Sch TN23 300 C2
Furnace Ave TN3 317 A3
Furnace La
Hook Green TN3 316 E4
Horsmonden TN12 289 F7
Furner Cl DA1 14 F4
Furness Sch BR8 32 F2
Furnival Ct TN2 313 F8
Furrell's Rd ME1 63 D5
Further Field TN12 260 E5
Furze Bank TN8 218 B5
Furzefield Ave TN3 285 A8
Furzefield Cl BR7 30 B2
Furzefield Rd SE3 11 B7
Furze Hill Cres ME12 46 E6
Furzehill Sq BR5 54 B5
Fusilier Ave CT20 334 B5
Fyfe Way BR1 52 A7
Fyndon Ho CT1 175 C7

G

Gable Cl DA1 15 A2
Gables Cl SE12 29 A7
Gables The
11 Bromley BR1 29 B1
New Barn DA3 59 C6
Gabriel Gdns DA12 37 E3
Gabriel's Hill ME15 162 A4
Gabrielspring Rd DA3 90 D8
Gabriel Spring Road (East) DA3 90 F8
Gadby Rd ME10 101 C5
Gadsby La TN26 297 A3
Gads Hill ME7 64 F6
Gads Hill Sch ME3 39 C2
Gadwall Cl E16 1 B7
Gadwall Way SE28 2 D4
Gafford's Bridge Cotts TN12 258 C4
Gagetown Terr 1 ME14 161 F7
Gainsboro Rd 4 CT7 80 F8
Gainsborough Ave
Dartford DA1 15 C2
Margate CT9 83 C8
Tilbury RM18 19 B6
Gainsborough Cl
Folkestone CT19 335 A7
Gillingham ME8 98 D6
Sittingbourne ME10 101 B5
Gainsborough Ct 3 BR2 52 C5
Gainsborough Dr
Herne Bay CT6 77 E5
Maidstone ME16 161 B4
Northfleet DA11 36 D5
Gainsborough Gdns TN10 222 E5
Gainsborough Ho ME1 63 D5
Gainsborough Sq DA7 13 D4
Gaitskell Rd SE9 30 C7
Galahad Ave ME2 62 E6
Galahad Rd BR1 29 A4
Galena Cl Chatham ME5 97 A1
Sittingbourne ME10 101 C6
Galena Ho 4 SE18 2 F1
Gallants La
Coxheath ME15 194 A2
East Farleigh ME15 193 F6
Galleon Bvd DA2 16 D3
Galleon Cl Erith DA8 4 D2
Rochester ME1 96 C8
Galleon Mews 3 DA11 36 E8
Galleon Way ME2 40 F3
Galley Hill Rd DA11, DA10 17 F2
Galley Hill Trad Est DA10 17 E2
Galliard St CT13 181 A8
Gallions Mount Prim Sch SE18 2 F1
Gallions Prim Sch E6 2 B7
Gallions Rd SE7 1 B2
Gallions Reach Sh Pk E6 2 C8
Gallions Reach Sta E6 2 B6
Gallions View Rd SE28 2 E4
Gallon Cl SE7 1 C2
Gallops The DA13 125 F7
Gallosson Rd SE18 2 E2
Galloway Dr
Ashford TN25 268 C8
Dartford DA1 32 E8
Galloways Rd TN29 376 C5
Gallow's Cnr CT21 333 A2
Gallows Wood DA3 91 A6
Gallus Sq SE3 11 B4
Gallwey Ave CT7 80 E7
Galsworthy Cl SE28 3 B5
Galsworthy Cres SE3 11 C6
Galsworthy Rd RM18 19 C6
Galton Ho SE18 11 F6
Galway Rd ME12 28 C1
Games Ho 7 SE7 11 C8
Gamma Rd ME3 42 D7
Gammon's Farm La TN29 351 B3
Gammons Yd 6 CT2 142 F1
Gandy's La ME17 195 C2
Gange Mews 3 ME13 138 D7
Gann Rd CT5 74 F2
Gaol La 13 CT16 310 D7
Gap House Sch CT10 84 B2
Gap The Blean CT2 142 A7
Canterbury CT1 175 B5
Garden Ave DA7 14 A4
Garden Cl
Lewisham SE12 29 B5
Maidstone ME15 195 E7
Rough Common CT2 142 A2
Staplehurst TN12 260 F1
Toy's Hill TN16 185 C3
Garden Cotts
Leigh TN11 221 A2
Orpington BR5 54 C7
Wingham CT3 178 A7
Garden Ct
10 Eltham SE9 12 A1
Sevenoaks TN13 154 D5
Wouldham ME1 95 C5
Gardeners Cl SE9 29 E5
Gardeners Pl CT4 173 F1
Garden Hall The TN25 238 A1
Garden Ho 9 TN1 286 B4
Gardenia Cl ME2 40 B2
Garden La BR1 29 B2
Garden of England Pk (Mobile Home Pk) ME17 198 B7
Garden Pl
Ashford TN24 268 E6
Dartford DA2 33 D5
Garden Rd Bromley BR1 29 B2
Folkestone CT19 335 D6
Royal Tunbridge Wells TN1 286 B4
Sevenoaks TN13 154 D5
Tonbridge TN9 222 D2
Garden Row DA11 36 F5
Garden St ME7 64 A6
Gardens The
Coxheath ME17 194 C3
Ivychurch TN29 363 F4
Garden St TN1 286 B4
Garden Terr TN15 155 A6
Garden Way ME19 158 F2
Gardiner Cl BR5 54 C7
Gardiner Ho SE18 11 E7
Gardiner's Hill TN31 368 B6
Gardiner St ME7 64 C6
Gardner Cl CT18 306 F3
Gardyne Mews 12 TN9 254 B8
Gareth Gr BR1 29 A4
Garfield Pl 4 ME13 138 D7
Garfield Rd
Gillingham ME7 64 D6
Margate CT9 50 H2
Garganey Wlk SE28 3 D6
Gargery Cl DA12 37 F7
Garibaldi St SE18 2 E2
Garland Rd SE18 12 D7
Garlands TN11 221 D8
Garlinge Green Rd CT4 206 E6
Garlinge Inf Sch CT9 82 C8
Garlinge Jun Sch CT9 82 B8
Garlinge Rd TN4 254 A1
Garner Ct RM18 18 F5
Garner Dr ME19 128 A1
Garnett Cl SE9 11 F4
Garnet Wlk 9 E6 1 E8
Garrard Ave CT9 82 B8
Garrard Cl Bexley DA7 14 A4
Chislehurst BR7 30 B3
Garrick Cl TN10 222 E7
Garrick Dr SE28 2 D3
Garrick St 18 DA11 19 B1
Garrington Cl ME14 162 C6
Garrison Cl SE18 12 A7
Garrison Rd ME12 28 A3
Garrolds Cl BR8 55 D7
Garrow DA3 59 B6
Garside Cl SE28 2 D3
Garth Rd TN13 187 C7
Gartly Cotts DA1 15 C1
Garton Way TN23 299 C7
Garvary Rd E16 1 B7
Garvock Dr TN13 154 A1
Gascoyne Cl ME15 163 B2
Gascoyne Dr DA1 14 F4
Gas House Rd ME1 63 C6
Gas La ME13 139 F3
Gasoline Alley TN15 125 D2
Gas Rd
Sittingbourne ME10 101 F5
Sittingbourne,Murston ME10 102 B6
Gasson Rd DA10 17 E1
Gassons Rd ME6 127 E8
Gas St CT1 174 F7
Gasworks La TN23 268 B2
Gatcombe Cl
Chatham ME5 97 A5
Maidstone ME16 161 B5
Gatcombe Rd E16 1 A5
Gateacre Ct 14 DA14 31 B4
Gateacre Rd CT5 108 A6
Gate Farm Rd TN3, TN11 253 C4
Gatefield Cotts TN17 343 F4
Gatefield La 9 ME13 138 D7
Gate House Cotts SE12 29 B6
Gatehouse Farm Cotts TN3 253 C4
Gatekeeper Chase ME8 98 F8
Gate La CT4 273 A4
Gate Quays CT9 50 I2
Gates Green Rd BR2, BR4 85 A6
Gateway Ct 21 CT11 117 F7
Gateway Par DA12 37 F4
Gateway Prim Sch The DA2 16 B1
Gateway The CT16 310 E7
Gatland La ME16 161 B2
Gatling Rd SE2 3 A1
Gattons Way DA14 31 F4
Gatwick Farm Cotts RH19 281 A4
Gatwick Rd DA12 37 B6
Gault Cl ME15 163 A2
Gaunt's Cl CT14 215 A4
Gautrey Sq 5 E6 1 F7
Gavestone Cres SE12 29 B8
Gavestone Rd SE12 29 B8
Gavestone Terr SE12 29 B8
Gavin Ho SE18 2 E2
Gayhurst Cl ME8 98 D6
Gayhurst Dr ME10 101 C5
Gaylor Rd RM18 18 F6
Gayton Rd SE2 3 C3
Gaza Trad Est TN11 220 D7
Gazedown TN29 365 F3
Gaze Hill Ave ME10 102 A3
Gazelle Glade DA12 37 F3
Gean Cl ME5 130 A8
Geddes Cl CT18 306 F3
Geddes Pl 3 DA6 14 A3
Gedge's Hill TN12 256 F3
Geffery's Ct SE9 29 E5
General Gordon Pl 2 SE18 2 B2
Genesta Ave CT5 108 B7
Genesta Cl ME10 101 E7
Genesta Glade DA12 38 A3
Genesta Rd SE18 12 C8
Geneva Ave ME8 65 A2
Gentian Cl
4 Chatham ME5 96 E4
Maidstone ME14 162 E5
Geoffrey Ct CT7 81 A7
George Akass Ho 3 SE18 2 C1
George Alley CT14 215 D6
George Cooper Ho 11 CT20 335 C4
George Crooks Ho 7 RM17 18 B8
George Gurr Cres CT19 335 D8
George Hill Rd CT10, CT9 51 E1

George La
Boughton Street ME13 .. 139 F3
Folkestone CT20 .... 335 D4
Hayes BR2 .... 52 B1
Leeds ME17 .... 197 B7
New Romney TN28 ...... 373 B7
Rochester ME1 .... 63 C6
George Marsham Ho
ME15 .... 194 F3
George Parris Ct ME12 . 47 C6
George Pk CT9 .... 50 F1
George Roche Rd
CT1 .... 175 A6
George's Ave CT5 ..... 108 A7
Georges Cl BR5 .... 54 C6
George Spurgen Com Prim
Sch CT19 .... 335 E7
George's Rd TN16 ..... 150 D7
George St
Ashford TN23 .... 268 B1
Chainhurst ME15 .... 227 A7
Deal CT14 .... 215 D7
Dover CT17 .... 278 C1
Grays RM17 .... 18 A8
Maidstone ME15 .... 162 A3
George Stone Ho 25
CT20 .... 335 E5
George St
Ramsgate CT11 .... 117 E7
Royal Tunbridge Wells
TN2 .... 286 C3
Sittingbourne ME10 .... 102 B4
Sparrow's Green TN5 ... 336 F5
Staplehurst TN12 ...... 260 E6
Tonbridge TN9 .... 254 B8
George Summers Cl
ME2 .... 63 E8
George V Ave CT9 ...... 82 C8
George Warren Ct 1
CT9 .... 50 J1
George Williams Way
TN24 .... 268 E5
George Wood Cl
TN29 .... 376 C6
Georgian Cl Hayes BR2 .. 52 B1
Rushenden ME11 .... 46 A3
Georgian Dr ME17 ..... 194 D3
Georgian Way ME8 ...... 98 C4
Georgia Pl TN2 .... 286 C4
Geraint Rd BR1 .... 29 A4
Gerald Ave ME4 .... 63 F2
Geraldine Rd CT19 .... 334 F6
Gerald Palmby Ct
CT14 .... 215 C7
Gerald Rd DA12 .... 37 E8
Gerda Rd SE9 .... 30 C6
Gerdview Dr DA2 .... 33 C4
Gerlac Ho TN24 .... 268 C5
Gerrard Ave ME1 .... 96 E8
Gerrard Ho 4 BR2 ...... 52 C5
Gerrards Dr ME10 ..... 101 F2
Gertrude Rd DA17 .... 4 A2
Gibbet La TN12 .... 289 F6
Gibbetts TN3 .... 284 F3
Gibbons Rd ME10 ...... 101 B5
Gibbs Hill
Headcorn TN27 .... 262 E5
Nettlestead ME18 ...... 192 B5
Gibraltar Ave ME7 ...... 64 B7
Gibraltar Hill ME4 ...... 63 F4
Gibraltar La
Hawkinge CT18 .... 307 A2
Maidstone ME14 .... 161 F8
Gibraltar Sq CT15 ..... 278 E3
Gibson Cl DA11 .... 36 F5
Gibson Dr ME19 .... 158 F4
Gibson Ho ME3 .... 40 F6
Gibson St ME10 .... 101 E4
Gidd's Pond Cotts
ME14 .... 162 E6
Giddyhorn La ME16 .... 161 C5
Gideon Cl DA17 .... 4 B2
Gifford Cl ME8 .... 65 C3
Gigger's Green Rd
TN25 .... 351 C7
Giggs Hill BR5 .... 54 A8
Gighill Rd ME20 ...... 127 F4
Gilbert Cl
Gillingham ME7 .... 98 A5
Swanscombe DA10 ...... 17 D1
Woolwich SE18 .... 11 F6
Gilbert Pl 9 CT20 ..... 334 E3
Gilbert Rd
4 Ashford TN24 .... 268 B2
Bromley BR1 .... 29 A1
Erith DA17 .... 4 A3
Ramsgate CT11 .... 117 D8
Gilbert Terr 2 ME14 ... 161 F7
Gilbert Way CT1 ...... 174 E6
Gilbourne Rd SE18 ...... 12 F8
Gilchrist Ave CT6 ...... 76 C2
Gilchrist Cotts TN14 ... 187 C2
Gildenhill Rd BR8 ...... 33 C1
Gildersome St SE18 ..... 12 A8
Giles Field DA12 .... 37 F7
Giles Gdns CT9 .... 82 F8
Giles La CT2 .... 142 D4
Giles-Young Ct 7
ME10 .... 101 E5
Gilford Rd CT14 ...... 215 D5
Gilham Gr CT14 ...... 215 A8
Gillan Ct 1 SE12 .... 29 B5
Gill Ave Newham E16 ...... 1 A7
Rochester ME2 .... 40 D2
Gill Cres DA11 .... 36 F5
Gill Ct SE18 .... 2 C2
Gillett Rd TN29 .... 376 D7
Gilletts La ME19 ...... 160 A6
Gillies Ct DA14 .... 30 E4
Gillies Rd TN15 .... 90 E5
Gillingham Coll The
ME7 .... 64 F4
Gillingham Gate ME7 ... 64 C8
Gillingham Gate Rd
ME7 .... 64 C8
Gillingham Gn ME7 ...... 64 E6
Gillingham Rd ME7 ...... 64 D5
Gillingham Sta ME7 ..... 64 D5
Gill La
Aldington Frith TN25 ... 329 A8
Ruckinge TN26 .... 328 C2
Gillman Cl CT18 .... 306 F4
Gillmans Rd BR5 .... 54 B1
Gillon Mews 9 CT1 ... 143 B2
Gill's Rd
Green Street Green DA2 ... 35 B1
Sutton at H DA4 .... 57 F8
Gills Terr ME8 .... 66 C3
Gill The TN2 .... 287 E8
Gilroy Way BR5 .... 54 B2
Gimble Way TN2 .... 255 D1
Gingerbread La TN18 .. 339 F2
Ginsbury Cl ME2 .... 63 E6
Gipps Cross La TN3 ... 284 F3
Gipsy La RM17 .... 18 C8
Gipsy Rd DA16 .... 13 D5
Giralda Cl E16 .... 1 D8
Giraud Dr ME13 .... 138 B8
Glack Rd CT14 .... 214 F4
Glade Bsns Ctr The
RM20 .... 16 F8
Glades Sh Ctr The BR1 . 52 A7
Glades The DA12 .... 37 D2
Gladeswood Rd DA17 ..... 4 B2
Glade The Bromley BR1 .. 52 D7
Chatham ME5 .... 97 A2
Deal CT14 .... 214 F6
Greenwich SE7 .... 11 C7
Sevenoaks TN13 .... 154 B4
Tonbridge TN10 .... 222 E7
Gladstone Ct CT10 ...... 83 F4
Gladstone Dr ME10 .... 102 C4
Gladstone Rd
Ashford TN24 .... 300 E7
Broadstairs CT10 .... 83 F4
Chatham ME4 .... 63 E2
Dartford DA1 .... 15 F1
Deal CT14 .... 215 C4
Folkestone CT19 .... 335 E6
Maidstone ME14 .... 162 A6
Margate CT9 .... 50 I1
Orpington BR6 .... 86 C5
Rusthall TN4 .... 285 B4
Tonbridge TN9 .... 222 B1
Whitstable CT5 .... 74 D2
Gladwell Rd BR1 .... 29 A2
Gladwyn Cl ME8 .... 98 D4
Glamford Rd ME2 .... 62 D5
Glamis Cl ME5 .... 97 A5
Glanfield Ct TN1 ...... 286 C5
Glanville Rd
Bromley BR2 .... 52 B6
Gillingham ME7 .... 64 D5
Rochester ME2 .... 63 A8
Glasbrook Rd SE9 .... 29 D8
Glasgow Ho 8 ME15 .. 195 E7
Glassenbury Rd TN17 .. 319 E4
Glassmill La BR2 .... 52 A7
Glass Yd SE18 .... 2 A3
Glastonbury Cl BR5 ..... 54 C1
Gleaming Wood Dr
ME5 .... 130 D8
Gleaners Cl ME14 ..... 162 E4
Gleanings Mews ME1 ... 63 C5
Glebe Cl
St Margaret's at Cliffe
CT15 .... 279 F6
Smarden TN27 .... 264 B2
Glebe Cotts
Brasted TN16 .... 152 B4
Eastling ME13 .... 168 E7
Glebe Ct CT12 .... 115 B5
Glebefield The TN13 ... 153 F4
Glebe Gdns
Lenham ME17 .... 199 E5
6 Margate CT9 .... 82 B8
Glebe House Dr BR2 .... 52 B1
Glebe Ho 7 SE18 .... 2 A2
Glebe La ME16 .... 161 A1
Glebeland TN27 .... 232 F4
Glebelands
Alkham CT15 .... 276 D1
Ash CT3 .... 147 C2
Bidborough TN3 .... 253 C3
Biddenden TN27 .... 294 F1
Crayford DA1 .... 14 F3
Mersham TN25 .... 301 E4
Penshurst TN11 .... 252 A3
Glebe La
Sevenoaks TN13 .... 154 B1
Sittingbourne ME10 .... 102 B2
Glebe Mdw ME18 ...... 192 E7
Glebe Pl DA4 .... 57 C5
Glebe Rd Bromley BR1 .... 52 A8
Gillingham ME7 .... 64 E3
Margate CT9 .... 82 B8
Northfleet DA11 .... 36 F7
Sevenoaks Weald TN14 .. 187 B3
Glebe The
Bidborough TN3 .... 253 D3
Charing TN27 .... 234 D7
Chislehurst BR7 .... 53 C8
Cuxton ME2 .... 62 C2
Pembury TN2 .... 287 D8
Penshurst TN11 .... 252 A3
Glebe Way
Ashford TN24 .... 268 D6
Erith DA8 .... 14 E8
Whitstable CT5 .... 108 D8
Gleeson Dr BR6 .... 86 F6
Glemsford Cotts CT2 .. 141 E1
Glenalvon Way 7 SE18 .... 1 E2
Glen Ave CT6 .... 77 C5
Glenavon Ho CT10 ...... 84 B7
Glenbarr Cl SE9 .... 12 B4
Glenbervie Dr CT6 ...... 77 E5
Glenbrook Cl CT6 ...... 77 D5
Glenbrook Gr ME10 ... 101 E7
Glencairne Cl E16 .... 1 D8
Glencoe Jun Sch ME4 .. 64 A2
Glencoe Rd
Chatham ME4 .... 64 A2
Margate CT9 .... 51 A1
Glen Ct Lewisham SE12 .. 29 A8
Sidcup DA14 .... 31 A4
Glendale Cl SE9 .... 12 A4
Glendale Ct TN2 ...... 286 D6
Glendale CT20 .... 335 E4
Glendale Rd Erith DA8 .... 4 C2
Minster (Sheppey) ME12 .. 47 B7
Northfleet DA11 .... 36 E5
Glendale BR8 .... 55 F4
Glendale Way SE28 .... 3 C6
Glendower Cres BR6 .... 54 A3
Glendown Rd SE2 .... 3 A1
Glen Dunlop Ho The
TN13 .... 154 C5
Gleneagles Cl BR6 ...... 53 D1
Gleneagles Ct ME5 ...... 96 F2
Gleneagles Dr ME15 ... 162 A1
Gleneagles Gn 1 BR6 .. 53 D1
Glenesk Rd SE9 .... 12 B3
Glenfield Rd CT16 ..... 278 B3
Glengall Rd DA7 .... 13 E4
Glen Gr CT17 .... 310 B7
Glenhead Cl SE9 .... 12 B4
Glen Ho 6 E16 .... 2 A5
Glenhouse Rd SE9 .... 12 A2
Glenhurst Ave DA5 ...... 31 F7
Glen Iris Ave CT2 ..... 142 C2
Glen Iris Cl CT2 ...... 142 C2
Glenister St E16 .... 2 A4
Glenlea Rd SE9 .... 12 A3
Glenleigh Rd ME18 .... 192 D6
Glenluce Rd SE3 .... 11 A8
Glenlyon Rd SE9 .... 12 A2
Glenmore Pk TN2 ...... 313 F8
Glenmore Rd DA16 ...... 12 F6
Glenmount Path 1
SE18 .... 2 C1
Glen Rd CT14 .... 248 C6
Glenrose Ct DA14 .... 31 B3
Glenshiel Rd SE9 .... 12 A2
Glenside Ave CT1 ..... 143 B2
Glenside CT5 .... 109 A8
Glen The
Minster (Sheppey) ME12 .. 47 B7
Orpington BR6 .... 86 A7
Shepherdswell CT15 .... 244 D5
Upstreet CT3 .... 112 D3
Glentrammon Ave BR6 .. 86 F4
Glentrammon Cl BR6 .... 86 F5
Glentrammon Gdns
BR6 .... 86 F4
Glentrammon Rd
Orpington BR6 .... 86 F4
Orpington BR6 .... 87 A4
Glenure Rd SE9 .... 12 A2
Glenview SE2 .... 13 D8
Glen View DA12 .... 37 C7
Glen View Rd BR1 ...... 52 D7
Glen Wlk CT5 .... 108 A3
Glenwood Cl
Chatham ME5 .... 64 C1
Gillingham ME7 .... 98 A7
Maidstone ME16 .... 161 C5
Tenterden TN30 .... 324 B3
Glenwood Ct 18 DA14 ... 31 A4
Glenwood Dr ME12 ...... 47 C6
Glenwood TN30 .... 324 B3
Glimpsing Gn DA18 .... 3 E3
Glistening Glade ME8 ... 98 E6
Gload Cres BR5 .... 87 D8
Globe Ct SE18 .... 12 C8
Globe La ME4 .... 63 F5
Globe Yd 13 DA11 .... 19 B1
Gloster Cl CT18 .... 307 B3
Gloster Ropewalk
CT17 .... 310 C5
Gloster Way CT17 ..... 310 C5
Gloucester Ave
Bexley DA16 .... 12 F3
Broadstairs CT10 .... 83 F3
Margate CT9 .... 51 D2
Sidcup DA15 .... 30 E6
Gloucester Cl ME8 ...... 99 A8
Gloucester Ct RM18 ..... 18 F5
Gloucester Mews
TN28 .... 373 C8
Gloucester Par DA15 ... 13 A2
Gloucester Pl 17
CT20 .... 335 D5
Gloucester Rd
Dartford DA1 .... 33 B8
Erith DA17 .... 3 F1
Gravesend DA12 .... 37 C4
Maidstone ME15 .... 195 D8
Turner's Green TN5 .... 336 F6
Whitstable CT5 .... 74 F2
Glover Cl
Sittingbourne ME10 ..... 68 F1
Woolwich SE2 .... 3 C2
Glover Rd TN24 .... 268 E1
Glovers Cl TN16 ...... 118 B3
Glovers Cres ME10 .... 101 F3
Glovers Mill ME4 .... 63 D3
Gloxinia Rd DA13 .... 36 B2
Glyn Davies Cl TN13 .. 153 E7
Glyndebourne Pk BR6 ... 86 B8
Glynde Rd DA7 .... 13 E4
Glyndon Rd SE18 .... 2 D2
Glyn Dr DA14 .... 31 B4
Glynne Cl ME8 .... 98 D6
Goad Ave ME5 .... 97 B3
Goat Lees La TN25 .... 268 D8
Goatsfield Rd TN16 ... 150 C7
Gobery Hill CT3 .... 146 B1
Goddards Cl TN17 ..... 320 B4
Goddard's Green Cotts
TN17 .... 321 F1
Godden Rd
Canterbury CT2 .... 143 A4
Snodland ME6 .... 127 F8
Godden Way ME8 .... 65 A4
Goddings Dr ME1 .... 63 C3
Goddington Chase BR6 .. 87 B6
Goddington Ho BR6 ..... 87 C7
Goddington La
Harrietsham ME17 ..... 198 B6
Orpington BR6 .... 87 A7
Goddington Rd ME2 ..... 63 B8
Godfrey Cl ME2 .... 39 F1
Godfrey Evans Cl
TN10 .... 222 F5
Godfrey Gdns CT4 ..... 173 F1
Godfrey Hill SE18 .... 1 E2
Godfrey Ho CT5 .... 108 E8
Godfrey's Grave ME13 . 140 B7
Godfrey Rd SE18 .... 1 F2
Godfreys Cotts ME13 .. 203 C8
Godfrey Wlk TN23 ..... 300 B8
Godinton★ TN23 .... 267 C4
Godinton La TN23,
TN26 .... 267 D5
Godinton Prim Sch
TN23 .... 267 D3
Godinton Rd TN23 ..... 268 A2
Godinton Way TN23 ... 268 A2
Godinton Way Ind Est
TN23 .... 268 B2
Godstow Rd SE2 .... 3 C4
Godwin Bglws CT9 ...... 51 B3
Godwin Cl ME10 .... 68 F1
Godwin Cotts CT9 ...... 51 A3
Godwin Ho SE18 .... 11 F6
Godwin Rd Bromley BR2 . 52 C6
Canterbury CT1 .... 174 C6
Dover CT16 .... 310 F8
Margate CT9 .... 51 A3
Godwyne Cl CT16 ...... 310 D8
Godwyne Ct CT16 ...... 278 D1
Godwyne Rd CT16 ...... 278 D1
Godwyn Gdns CT20 .... 335 A4
Godwyn Rd Deal CT14 .. 215 C8
Folkestone CT20 .... 335 A4
Gogway CT4 .... 240 B4
Goldace RM17 .... 17 F8
Goldcrest Cl
Newham E16 .... 1 D8
Woolwich SE28 .... 3 C6
Goldcrest Dr ME4 .... 41 C2
Goldcrest Wlk CT5 .... 108 B6
Golden Acre La CT8 ..... 81 D7
Golden Cl CT8 .... 81 D7
Golden Hill CT5 .... 108 F6
Golden Plover Cl E16 .... 1 A7
Golden Sq
New Romney TN28 ..... 373 A6
Tenterden TN30 .... 345 B8
Golden St CT14 .... 215 D7
Golden Wood Cl ME5 .. 130 D8
Goldfinch Cl
Faversham ME13 ...... 105 C1
Herne Bay CT6 .... 77 C2
Larkfield ME20 .... 128 A2
Orpington BR6 .... 87 A5
Paddock Wood TN12 .... 257 A5
Goldfinch Rd SE28 .... 2 D3
Gold Hill TN25 .... 235 D4
Goldie Leigh Hospl
SE2 .... 13 C8
Golding Cl Ditton ME20 . 128 C1
Rochester ME1 .... 63 E1
Golding Gdns TN12 .... 225 A6
Golding Rd TN13 ...... 154 C5
Goldings Cl ME19 ..... 159 A3
Goldings TN12 .... 256 E5
Goldings The ME8 ...... 98 C8
Goldmark Ho SE3 .... 11 B4
Goldsel Rd BR8 .... 55 E5
Goldsmid Rd TN9 ...... 254 C8
Goldsmid St 3 SE18 ...... 2 E1
Goldsmith Ct TN30 .... 324 B1
Goldsmith RM17 .... 17 F8
Goldsmith Rd ME8 ...... 98 E5
Goldstone Dro CT3 .... 147 E7
Goldstone Wlk ME5 ..... 97 A1
Gold St DA12,DA13 ...... 60 E4
Goldsworth Dr ME2 ...... 40 A1
Goldthorne Cl ME14 ... 162 C5
Goldups Lane Cotts
CT4 .... 171 C1
Goldups La CT4 .... 171 C1
Goldwell Cl TN25 ..... 330 A6
Goldwell Hos TN25 .... 330 A6
Goldwell La
Aldington TN25 .... 330 B7
Great Chart TN23,TN26 .. 298 F8
Goldwing Cl E16 .... 1 A7
Golf Ct CT14 .... 182 C1
Golf Links Ave DA11 .... 37 B3
Golford Rd TN17 ...... 320 F4
Golf Rd Bromley BR1 .... 53 A6
Deal CT14 .... 215 C8
Golf Road Pl CT14 ..... 215 C8
Gollogly Terr 8 SE7 ...... 1 C1
Gooch Cl ME16 .... 161 D8
Goodall Cl ME8 .... 98 E5
Goodban Sq CT3 .... 147 D1
Goodbury Rd TN15 ..... 123 B6
Goodcheap La TN25 ... 269 D2
Goodensfield TN5 ..... 336 E5
Goodfellow Way 3
CT16 .... 310 D8
Good Hope CT14 ...... 214 F4
Gooding Ho SE7 .... 1 C1
Good Intent Cotts
TN27 .... 233 A5
Goodley Stock Rd
TN8,TN16 .... 184 B6
Goodmead Rd BR6 ...... 54 A2
Goodnestone CE Prim Sch
CT3 .... 178 C2
Goodnestone Gdns★
CT3 .... 178 C1
Goodnestone Hill CT3 . 178 D2
Goodnestone Rd
Sittingbourne ME10 ... 102 B4
Wingham CT3 .... 178 B5
Goods Hill TN30 .... 344 D8
Goods Station Rd TN1 . 286 B4
Goodtrees La TN8 ..... 282 B2
Goodwin Ave CT5 .... 75 E2
Goodwin Cl TN8 .... 217 B2
Goodwin Ct CT9 .... 51 D3
Goodwin Dr
Maidstone ME14 .... 162 B8
Sidcup DA14 .... 31 D6
Goodwin Pk CT9 .... 83 A5
Goodwin Rd
Cliffe Woods ME3 .... 40 B7
Ramsgate CT11 .... 117 B5
St Margaret's at Cliffe
CT15 .... 280 A4
Goodwins The TN2 .... 285 F1
Goodwood Cl
High Halstow ME23 ..... 23 E4
Maidstone ME15 .... 195 F6
Goodwood Cres DA12 .. 37 C2
Goodworth Rd TN15 ... 124 F3
Goosander Way SE28 ..... 2 D3
Goose Cl ME5 .... 97 A7
Goose Farm CT2 .... 143 D7
Goosefields ME13 ..... 106 E1
Goose Green Cl BR5 .... 54 A7
Gooseneck La TN27 ... 262 C5
Goose Sq 8 E6 .... 1 F7
Gordon Ave ME11 .... 46 A4
Gordon Cl
Ashford TN24 .... 268 D2
East Tilbury RM18 ...... 20 D7
Sittingbourne ME10 .... 102 C4
Gordon Cotts ME9 ..... 134 B6
Gordon Ct ME17 .... 194 E3
Gordon Gr CT8 .... 50 C1
Gordon Ho SE12 .... 29 A8
Gordon Inf Sch ME2 .... 63 A8
Gordon Jun Sch ME2 .... 63 A8
Gordon Pl DA12 .... 19 C1
Gordon Prim Sch SE9 ... 11 F3
Gordon Promenade E
DA12 .... 19 D1
Gordon Rd
Canterbury CT1 .... 174 F7
Chatham,Luton ME4 ..... 64 B2
Chatham ME4 .... 64 A7
Dartford DA1 .... 33 D8
Dover CT16 .... 278 A5
Erith DA17 .... 4 C2
Faversham ME13 ...... 138 E8
Folkestone CT20 .... 334 D6
Gillingham ME7 .... 64 E5
Herne Bay CT6 .... 76 F4
Hoo St Werburgh ME3 ... 41 D5
Margate CT9 .... 51 A3
Margate, Westwood CT9 .. 83 A5
Northfleet DA11 .... 36 E8
Ramsgate CT11 .... 117 D8
Rochester ME2 .... 63 A8
Royal Tunbridge Wells
TN4 .... 286 C7
Sevenoaks TN13 .... 154 B2
Sidcup DA15 .... 12 E2
Whitstable CT5 .... 108 D8
Gordon Sq
Birchington CT7 .... 80 F7
Faversham ME13 ...... 138 E7
Gordon Terr
Lydd TN29 .... 376 C5
Rochester ME1 .... 63 C4
Gordon Way BR1 .... 52 A8
Gore Cl CT13 .... 180 B3
Gore Cotts Dartford DA2 . 34 C4
Upchurch ME9 .... 66 E1
Gore Court Rd
Maidstone ME15 .... 195 F5
Sittingbourne ME10 .... 101 E2
Gore Ct TN24 .... 268 C3
Gore End Cl CT7 .... 80 F7
Gore Farm Cotts DA2 ... 34 C5
Gore Farm CT13 .... 180 B3
Gore Farm Trails★
ME9 .... 66 D1
Gore Green Rd ME3 ..... 39 E7
Gore La Brandfold TN17 . 290 E4
Eastry CT13 .... 180 B2
Gorely Ho 14 CT17 .... 310 D7
Gore Mews 3 CT1 ..... 143 B2
Gore Rd Dartford DA2 ... 34 C6
Eastry CT13 .... 180 B3
Silver Street ME9 ...... 133 F5
Gore Street Farm Cotts
CT12 .... 114 A7
Gore Terr CT13 .... 180 B3
Goretop La CT14 ...... 181 C6
Gorham Cl ME6 .... 127 F7
Gorham Dr
Maidstone ME15 .... 163 A1
Tonbridge TN9 .... 254 E8
Gorman Rd SE18 .... 1 F2
Gorrell Rd CT5 .... 74 E1
Gorringe Ave DA4 ...... 57 D7
Gorse Ave ME5 .... 96 F5
Gorse Cl E16 .... 1 A7
Gorse Cres ME20 ...... 160 D8
Gorse La CT6 .... 77 C2
Gorse Mead TN23 ..... 299 F8
Gorse Rd Orpington BR5 .. 88 A8
Rochester ME2 .... 62 F8
Royal Tunbridge Wells
TN2 .... 286 E5
Sittingbourne ME10 .... 102 C5
Gorse Way DA3 .... 59 A4
Gorse Wood Rd
Hartley DA3 .... 59 A5
New Barn DA3 .... 59 A6
Gorst St ME7 .... 64 C5
Goschen Rd CT17 ..... 310 B8
Gosfield Rd CT6 .... 77 A4
Goshawk Ho 1 ME10 .. 102 A4
Gosmere Farm Barns
Doddington ME13 ...... 167 E7
Sheldwich ME13 .... 170 E7
Gossage Rd SE18 .... 2 D1
Gosselin St CT5 .... 108 E8
Goss Hall La CT3 ..... 148 A2
Goss Hill BR8,DA2 ...... 33 C2
Gosshill Rd BR7 .... 53 A7
Gossington Cl BR7 ...... 30 B4
Goteley Mere TN24 .... 268 C7
Gothic Cl Dartford DA1 .. 33 D5
Deal CT14 .... 215 B1
Gothic Cotts TN26 ..... 235 A1
Goudhurst Cl
Canterbury CT2 .... 143 A4
Maidstone ME16 .... 161 E4
Goudhurst & Kilndown CE
Prim Sch TN17 .... 318 F8
Goudhurst Rd
Cranbrook TN17 .... 320 D8
Gillingham ME8 .... 65 B3
Horsmonden TN12 ..... 290 B5
Knox Bridge TN12,TN17 . 292 C6
Marden TN12 .... 259 B5
Gouge Ave DA11 .... 36 E7
Gough Rd CT20 .... 334 E3
Gould Rd ME5 .... 97 B3
Gourock Rd SE9 .... 12 A2
Gover Hill TN11,ME18 .. 190 E6
Gover View TN11 ...... 190 E7
Gower Ho ME14 .... 162 A6
Grace Ave Bexley DA7 .... 13 F5
Maidstone ME16 .... 161 D6
Grace Cl SE9 .... 29 D5
Grace Ct 16 CT20 ...... 335 D5
Grace Hill CT20 .... 335 D5
Grace Mdw CT16 ...... 278 A7
Grace Rd ME12 .... 28 A1
Grace Sch CT20 ...... 335 D5
Grace Wlk CT14 .... 215 A5
Gracious Lane Bridge
TN13 .... 187 A6
Gracious Lane End
TN14 .... 186 F5
Gracious La TN13 ..... 187 B5
Grafton Ave ME1 .... 96 E8
Grafton Rd
Broadstairs CT10 .... 83 F8
Sittingbourne ME10 .... 101 F4
Grafton Rise CT6 .... 76 C4
Graham Cl ME4 .... 63 F6
Graham Ct 12 BR1 ...... 29 B1
Graham Ho SE18 .... 12 B7
Graham Rd DA7 .... 14 A3
Grainey Field ME9 ...... 99 E4
Grainger Wlk TN10 .... 222 E6
Grain Rd Gillingham ME8 . 98 C3
Grain ME3 .... 26 D3
Grampian Cl
Orpington BR6 .... 53 F3
Royal Tunbridge Wells
TN2 .... 286 D5
Grampian Way ME15 .. 163 A1
Grampion Cl TN24 ..... 268 C4
Gram Sch for Girls
Wilmington The DA2 ... 33 B5
Gram's Rd CT14 .... 248 C8
Granada Ho 8 ME15 ... 162 A4
Granada St 9 ME15 ... 162 A4
Granary Cl
Maidstone ME14 .... 162 E5
Rainham ME8 .... 65 F1
Granary Cotts TN16 ... 152 C3
Granary Court Rd
TN25 .... 303 A4
Granary TN12 .... 257 B6
Granary Pl CT5 .... 108 D8
Granby Ho 8 SE18 .... 1 F2
Granby Rd Eltham SE9 .... 11 F4
Northfleet DA11 .... 18 D1
Woolwich SE18 .... 2 B3
Grand Ct
6 Folkestone CT20 .... 335 B3
7 Gillingham ME7 ...... 64 C6
Littlestone-on-Sea TN28 . 373 E5
Grand Depot Rd SE18 .... 2 A1
Grand Dr CT6 .... 76 C4
Grand Mans CT10 ...... 84 B3
Grand Par TN28 .... 373 E5
Grand Pavilion CT5 ..... 74 F3
Grandshore La TN17 ... 293 B5
Grandsire Gdns ME3 .... 41 E6
Grand The 4 CT20 ..... 335 B3
Grand View Ave TN16 .. 118 C3
Grange Cl
Edenbridge TN8 .... 217 C1
Leybourne ME19 ...... 127 C2
Sidcup DA15 .... 31 A5
Westerham TN16 ...... 151 C1
Grange Cres
6 Dartford DA2 .... 16 B1
Erith SE28 .... 3 C7
Tenterden TN30 .... 324 A3
Grange Ct
1 Folkestone CT20 .... 335 C4
9 Ramsgate CT11 ..... 117 C6
Grange Dr Bromley BR7 .. 29 F2
Pratt's Bottom BR6 ..... 87 C2
Grange Gdns TN4 ..... 285 D4
Grange Hill
Chatham ME5 .... 64 B3
Plaxtol TN15 .... 189 E8
Grangehill Pl SE9 .... 11 F4

Grangehill Rd SE9 11 F3
Grange Ho Erith DA8 15 A5
Gravesend DA11 37 A8
Maidstone ME16 161 A2
Grange La
Boxley ME14 130 A1
Hartley DA3 59 B2
Grange Park Sch ME19 127 B3
Grange Rd CT10 83 F6
Grange Rdbt ME7 65 A6
Grange Rd Deal CT14 215 B5
Folkestone CT19 334 E6
Gillingham ME7 65 A6
Gravesend DA11 37 A8
Grays RM17 18 B8
Herne Bay CT6 77 C4
Hythe CT21 333 B4
Orpington BR6 86 C8
Platt TN15 157 C7
Ramsgate CT11 117 C6
Rochester ME2 63 B7
Rusthall TN4 285 D4
Sevenoaks TN13 187 A8
Tenterden TN30 323 F3
Tenterden TN30 324 A3
Grange The
East Malling ME19 160 A7
Shepherdswell CT15 244 D5
Sutton at H DA4 57 D8
Westerham TN16 151 C1
West Kingsdown TN15 90 F2
Whitstable CT5 108 A6
Grange Way
Broadstairs CT10 83 F2
Erith DA8 15 B7
Hartley DA3 58 F3
Rochester ME1 63 C3
Grangeways Cl DA11 36 F4
Grangewood DA5 31 F7
Granite St SE18 2 F1
Grant Cl
Broadstairs CT10 83 E6
Rainham ME7 65 B1
Grant Dr ME15 195 D6
Grantham Ave CT14 215 A5
Grantley Cl TN23 300 A8
Granton Rd DA14 31 C2
Grant's Cotts ME17 199 B5
Grant Rd ME3 40 C3
Grants La TN8,RH8 216 C6
Granville Ave
Broadstairs CT10 84 B3
Ramsgate CT12 83 B1
Granville Cl ME13 138 C7
Granville Ct Deal CT14 215 C2
Erith SE2 3 D1
Maidstone ME14 162 A6
Sevenoaks TN13 154 A3
Granville Dr CT6 76 B2
Granville Farm Mews 24 CT11 117 F7
Granville Ho 18 CT11 117 F7
Granville Marina 20 CT11 117 F7
Granville Mews DA14 31 A4
Granville Par CT20 334 E3
Granville Pl
Folkestone CT20 334 F3
Sheerness ME12 28 C2
Granville Rd
Bexley DA16 13 C4
Broadstairs CT10 84 B3
Deal CT14 215 C2
Granville Rd E CT20 334 F3
Granville Rd
Gillingham ME7 64 E5
Kingsdown CT14 248 D3
Limpsfield RH8 183 A7
Maidstone ME14 162 A6
Northfleet DA11 36 F7
Royal Tunbridge Wells TN1 286 C5
St Margaret's at Cliffe CT15 280 B6
Sevenoaks TN13 154 A3
Sheerness ME12 28 C2
Sidcup DA14 31 B4
Westerham TN16 151 C1
Granville Sch The TN13 154 A4
Granville St Deal CT14 215 D5
Dover CT16 278 C1
Granville The CT15 280 B6
Grapple Rd ME14 162 A7
Grasdene Rd SE18 13 A7
Grasmere Ave
Orpington BR6 86 B7
Ramsgate CT11 117 A7
Grasmere Gdns
Folkestone CT19 335 B7
Orpington BR6 86 B7
Grasmere Gr ME2 40 C2
Grasmere Pk CT5 109 B8
Grasmere Rd
Ashford TN24 268 C6
Bexley DA7 14 C5
Orpington BR6 86 B7
Whitstable CT5 109 B8
Grasmere Way CT3 210 F6
Grasshaven Way SE28 2 F5
Grassington Rd 11 DA14 31 A4
Grasslands
Ashford TN23 299 D7
Langley Heath ME17 196 E4
Grassmere
Leybourne ME19 127 F2
St Mary's Bay TN29 365 E3
Grassy Glade ME7 98 B6
Grassy La TN13 187 B8
Gravel Castle Rd CT4 243 A8
Gravel Hill DA6 14 B2
Gravel Hill Cl DA6 14 B1
Gravel Hill Prim Sch DA6 14 B3
Gravel Hill ME13 201 C8
Gravel La CT15 309 A4
Gravelly Bottom Rd ME17 197 B2
Gravelly Field TN23 299 C8
Gravelly Ways TN12 225 D5
Gravel Pit Way BR6 54 A1
Gravel Rd Orpington BR2 85 E8
Sutton at H DA4 34 B1
Gravel Wlk
3 Ashford TN23 268 B3
12 Canterbury CT1 174 F8
Rochester ME1 63 D5
Gravelwood Cl BR7 30 C5
Graveney Cl ME3 40 C7
Graveney Prim Sch ME13 106 E1
Graveney Rd
Faversham ME13 138 F7
Maidstone ME15 195 F7
Gravesend Gram Sch for Girls DA11 37 A7
Gravesend Gram Sch DA12 37 D8
Gravesend & North Kent Hospl DA11 19 A1
Gravesend Rd
Higham ME2,ME3,DA12 39 C2
Rochester ME2 62 F8
Shorne DA12 38 D5
Vigo Village TN15 125 D6
Gravesend Sta DA11 19 B1
Graves Est DA16 13 B5
Gravesham Ct 8 DA12 37 B8
Gravesham Mus★ DA11 19 B1
Gray Cl CT18 307 C5
Gray Ho SE2 3 D1
Grayland Cl BR1 52 D8
Graylands RM17 17 E8
Graylen Cl CT14 215 C7
Graylings Ct ME10 101 C2
Graylings The ME1 63 B3
Grayne Ave ME3 27 B5
Grays Farm Prim Sch BR5 54 B8
Grays Farm Production Village BR5 54 B8
Grays Farm Rd BR5 54 B8
Grayshott Cl ME10 101 F3
Grays Rd TN16 151 D7
Grays Sh Ctr RM17 18 A8
Grays Sta RM17 18 A8
Graystone Rd CT5 75 A2
Grays Way CT1 174 B6
Grazeley Cl DA6 14 C2
Great Ash BR7 30 A1
Great Basin Rd ME12 27 F2
Great Bounds Dr TN4 253 E3
Great Brooms Rd TN4 286 C8
Great Burton Ho TN24 268 E5
Great Chart Prim Sch TN23 299 D8
Great Conduit St CT21 333 C2
Great Courtlands TN3 285 A3
Great Elms TN11 190 E1
Great Elms Rd BR2 52 C5
Great Footway TN3 284 F3
Great Hall Arc 3 TN1 286 B3
Great Harry Dr SE9 30 A5
Great Ivy Mill Cotts ME15 194 F7
Great Lines ME7 64 B5
Great Lodge Ret Pk TN2 254 E1
Great Maytham Hall★ TN17 343 F2
Great Mead TN8 217 C3
Greatness La TN14 154 C6
Greatness Rd TN14 154 C6
Great Oak
Hurst Green TN19 354 A3
Royal Tunbridge Wells TN2 286 D6
Great Oaks Small Sch CT13 180 B2
Great Queen St DA1 15 F1
Great South Ave ME4 64 A1
Greatstone Prim Sch TN28 373 D2
Great Stour Pl 3 CT2 142 F1
Great Thrift BR5 53 C5
Great Till Cl TN14 121 E3
Greatwood BR7 30 A1
Grebe Apartments 15 ME15 195 E5
Grebe Cl
Hawkinge CT18 307 A4
Lower Stoke ME3 25 C4
Grebe Cres CT21 353 C8
Grebe Ct ME20 127 F1
Grecian Rd TN1 286 B2
Grecian St ME14 162 A6
Greenacre Cl
Chatham ME5 97 A5
Swanley BR8 55 E5
Greenacre DA1 33 D6
Greenacre Dr CT14 215 C1
Greenacre CT4 209 D3
Greenacre Sch ME5 96 F5
Green Acres Cl CT6 77 B3
Greenacres Cl BR6 86 C6
Greenacres Deal CT14 182 B4
Eltham SE9 12 A1
Green Acres CT15 245 D7
Greenacres Prim Sch & Language Impairment Unit SE9 30 A6
Green Acres DA14 30 F4
Greenbank
Ashford TN24 268 D6
Chatham ME5 97 B8
Green Bank Cl ME7 98 A5
Greenbank Lodge 2 BR7 53 A8
Greenbanks
Dartford DA1 33 E6
Lyminge CT18 305 C6
Greenbay Rd SE7 11 D7
Greenborough Cl ME15 195 E6
Green Cl CT18 307 B4
Green Cloth Mews 2 CT1 143 B2
Green Cl ME1 63 D2
Green Court Rd BR8 55 D3
Greencourt Rd BR5 53 E4
Greencroft TN23 299 E6
Greencroft Cl E6 1 D8
Green Ct Bridge CT4 176 A1
Folkestone CT19 335 E7
Greendale Wlk 4 DA11 36 E5
Green Dell CT2 142 F4
Green Farm Cl BR6 86 F5
Green Farm La DA12 38 E5
Greenfield Cl
Eccles ME20 129 A6
Rusthall TN4 285 C5
Greenfield Cotts
Boxley ME14 130 C3
9 Canterbury CT1 174 F7
Greenfield Ct SE9 29 E5
Greenfield Dr BR1 52 C7
Greenfield TN8 217 D1
Greenfield Gdns BR5 53 D2
Greenfield Rd
Folkestone CT19 335 E7
Gillingham ME7 64 D6
Joyden's Wood DA2 32 D3
Ramsgate CT12 83 C2
Greenfields Cl ME3 40 D3
Greenfields
Maidstone ME15 195 E8
Sellindge TN25 303 E2
Greenfinches
Gillingham ME7 97 F6
New Barn DA3 59 B6
Greenfrith Dr TN10 222 B6
Green Gates CT16 278 A8
Green Gdns BR6 86 C5
Greenhaven Dr SE28 3 B7
Green Hedges TN30 345 B8
Green Hill BR6 118 F7
Greenhill Bridge Rd CT6 76 D3
Greenhill Cl CT12 115 B7
Greenhill Cts SE18 1 F1
Greenhill Gdns
Herne Bay CT6 76 D3
Minster (Thanet) CT12 115 B7
Green Hill La ME17 198 D1
Greenhill La TN27 264 F7
Green Hill ME15 163 B1
Greenhill Rd
Herne Bay CT6 76 C2
Northfleet DA11 36 F6
Otford TN14 122 C5
Green Hills CT4 242 D8
Greenhill TN12 260 E5
Greenhill Terr SE18 1 F1
Green Hill SE18 1 F1
Greenhithe Cl DA15 30 E8
Greenhithe for Bluewater Sta DA9 17 A2
Greenhithe 3 ME15 162 A3
Greenholm Rd SE9 12 B2
Greenhouse La CT2 142 E2
Greenhurst La
Limpsfield RH8 183 A4
Oxted RH8 183 A3
Greening St SE2 3 C2
Green La Alkham CT15 276 D3
Ashford TN23 299 E5
Bethersden TN26 297 A2
Broadstairs CT10 83 E5
Capel-le-F CT18 308 B3
Challock TN25 203 A2
Cliffe ME3 22 B6
Collier Street TN12 258 E8
Deal CT14 215 B1
Dover CT16 278 B3
East End TN17 322 C2
Eltham BR7,SE9 30 B5
Eythorne CT15 245 D7
Folkestone CT19 335 E7
Four Elms TN8 218 C7
Goodnestone CT3 179 B3
Grain ME3 27 B5
Hythe CT21 333 A2
Langley Heath ME17 196 E3
Maidstone ME17 195 C3
Margate CT9 83 E8
Meopham Station DA13 60 B2
Greenlands TN15 157 C7
Greenlands Rd TN15 155 B8
Greenlands DA12 60 D4
Green Lane Ave CT21 333 A2
Green Lane Bsns Pk SE9 30 A6
Green Lane Cotts
Collier Street TN12 226 D1
Langley Heath ME17 196 E3
Green La
Old Wives Lees CT4 172 C2
Paddock Wood TN12 257 A5
Platt's Heath ME17 198 F2
Green La *continued*
Rhodes Minnis CT4, CT18 272 E2
Rodmersham ME9 135 B7
St Margaret's at Cliffe CT15 247 F1
Smarden TN27 264 A1
Sutton Valence ME17 229 B4
Temple Ewell CT16 277 E6
Green La The TN11 220 F1
Green La
Trottiscliffe ME19 126 A5
Whitfield CT16 277 E7
Whitstable CT5 108 D8
Green Lawns 10 SE18 2 B2
Greenlaw St SE18 2 A3
Green La ME9 99 F1
Greenleas
1 Folkestone CT20 335 B3
Pembury TN2 287 C6
Green Leas CT5 75 D1
Greenlees Cl ME10 101 B5
Green Lees ME13 137 E2
Greenleigh Ave BR5 54 B5
Greenly Way TN28 373 C6
Green Mdws TN29 352 D2
Greenoak Rise TN16 118 C1
Green Pl DA1 14 E2
Green Porch Cl ME10 101 F7
Green Rd
Birchington CT7 80 F8
Horsmonden TN12 290 A6
Stalisfield Green ME13 201 C6
Greensand Rd ME15 163 A2
Green Sands ME5 130 C8
Green's Cotts ME15 194 A4
Greens End SE18 2 B2
Greenshields Ind Est E16 1 A4
Greenside TN26 324 E7
Greenside Ho CT9 50 F1
Greenside
Maidstone ME15 162 B3
Sidcup DA5 31 E7
Swanley BR8 55 D7
Greenside Wlk TN16 118 B1
Greenslade Prim Sch SE18 12 D8
Greensleeves Way ME18 159 C3
Greensole La CT12 82 E1
Green Sq TN5 336 F5
Green St ME7 64 C5
Green Street Green Prim Sch BR6 86 F4
Green Street Green Rd DA1,DA2 34 D4
Green The
Bexley,Bexleyheath DA7 14 A6
Bexley,Falconwood DA16 12 E3
Biddenden TN27 323 D6
Blean CT2 142 A6
Burmarsh TN29 352 C4
Chartham CT4 173 D3
Dartford DA2 34 D6
East Farleigh ME15 194 B7
Frant TN3 314 B3
Harbledown CT2 141 E1
Hayes BR2 52 A2
Hythe CT21 333 B4
Langton Green TN3 284 E3
Leigh TN11 220 F1
Lewisham BR1 29 A5
Littlebourne CT3 176 F7
Lower Halstow ME9 67 B3
Lydd TN29 376 B5
Manston CT12 82 D1
Orpington BR5 31 B1
Sevenoaks TN13 154 D5
Sheerness ME12 28 H1
Sidcup DA14 31 A4
Warehorne TN26 348 D6
Westerham TN16 151 D1
West Tilbury RM18 19 E8
Woodchurch TN26 326 A2
Woolage Village CT4 210 E1
Wye TN25 237 E2
Greentrees Ave TN10 222 F5
Green Vale DA6 13 D2
Greenvale Gdns ME8 65 B2
Greenvale Inf Sch ME4 64 A2
Greenvale Rd SE9 12 A3
Green View Ave TN11 221 A1
Greenview Cres TN11 221 E4
Greenview Wlk ME8 65 A4
Green Way BR2 52 E3
Greenway Chatham ME5 96 D6
Chislehurst BR7 30 B3
Greenway Court Farm Cotts ME17 165 A1
Greenway Court Rd ME17 165 A1
Greenway TN17 320 B4
Green Way SE9 11 D2
Greenway ME13 138 B8
Green Way DA3 58 E4
Greenway La ME17 198 A7
Green Way Lydd TN29 376 C5
Maidstone ME16 161 B3
Royal Tunbridge Wells TN2 286 E8
Greenways
Addington ME19 126 E2
Lower Halstow ME9 67 B3
Maidstone ME14 162 F5
New Barn DA3 59 D6
Sittingbourne ME10 102 B3
Greenways The TN12 256 F5
Greenway TN16 150 C7
Greenway The
Orpington BR5 54 B3
Oxted RH8 183 B2
Greenwich Cl
Chatham ME5 97 B4
Maidstone ME16 161 D4
Greenwich Com Coll SE18 2 C2
Greenwich Cres E6 1 E8
Greenwich Hts SE18 11 E7
Greenwich Sh Pk SE7 1 B2
Green Wlk DA1 14 F3
Greenwood Cl
Orpington BR5 53 E3
Sidcup DA15 31 A6
Greenwood Gdns RH8 183 A1
Greenwood Ho 8 RM17 18 B8
Greenwood Pl TN15 125 A2
Greenwood Rd DA5 32 D4
Greenwood Way TN13 153 F2
Greggs Wood Rd TN2 286 E7
Gregor Mews SE3 11 A7
Gregory Cl
Gillingham ME8 98 E4
Sittingbourne ME10 102 A8
Gregory Cres SE9 29 D8
Gregory Ct TN25 237 E2
Gregory Ho SE3 11 B5
Grenada Rd SE7 11 C7
Grenadier Cl
Gillingham ME8 66 B2
Maidstone ME15 162 F2
Grenadier St E16 2 A5
Grenfell Cl TN16 118 C7
Grenham Bay Ave CT7 80 E8
Grenham Rd CT7 80 F8
Grenville Cl DA13 93 A8
Grenville Gdns CT7 80 E8
Grenville Way CT10 83 E4
Gresham Ave
Hartley DA3 58 F4
Margate CT9 50 E1
Gresham Cl
3 Rainham ME8 65 F1
Sidcup DA5 13 F1
Tonbridge TN10 222 E7
Gresham Rd
Coxheath ME17 194 D3
Newham E16 1 B7
Greshams Way TN8 217 A2
Gresswell Cl DA14 31 A5
Greville Ho CT17 310 C7
Greville Homes CT13 180 B2
Greybury La TN8 249 B3
Greyfriars Cl ME16 161 D5
Grey Friars Cotts 8 CT1 174 F8
Greyfriars Ct CT10 51 F1
Greyhound Way DA1 14 E1
Grey Ladies Oasts TN15 157 B3
Greys Park Cl BR2 85 D5
Greystone Pk TN14 152 E2
Greystones Cl TN15 122 E2
Greystones Rd
Cliffs End CT12 116 D5
Maidstone ME15 163 A2
Grey Wethers ME14 129 E4
Grey Willow Gdns TN23 299 D8
Gribble Bridge La TN27 323 B5
Grice Ave TN16 118 C6
Grice Cl CT18 306 F3
Grieveson Ho ME4 64 A4
Grieves Rd DA11 36 F5
Griffin Cotts TN26 347 C2
Griffin Manor Way SE28 2 D3
Griffin Rd SE18 2 D2
Griffin's Cnr TN25 269 E7
Griffin St CT14 215 D7
Griffin Way SE28 2 E3
Griffin Wlk DA9 16 F2
Griffiths Ho 2 SE18 12 B8
Grigg La TN27 263 C7
Grigg's Cross BR5 54 D3
Griggs Way TN15 157 A7
Grimsby Gr E16 2 B4
Grimshill Ct CT2 142 C4
Grimshill Rd CT5 108 E8
Grimston Ave CT20 335 B4
Grimston Gdns CT20 335 B4
Grimthorpe Ave CT5 108 C7
Grinling Ho 6 SE18 2 A2
Grinsell Hill CT12 115 E6
Grisbrook Farm Cl TN29 376 D6
Grisbrook Rd TN29 376 D6
Grizedale Cl ME1 96 D8
Gromenfield TN3 312 C7
Groombridge Cl DA16 13 A2
Groombridge Hill TN3 284 D1
Groombridge Place Gdns★ TN3 312 C8
Groombridge Place★ TN3 312 C8
Groombridge Rd TN3 284 A1
Groombridge St Thomas' CE Prim Sch TN3 312 C6
Groombridge Sq 13 ME15 195 F6
Groombridge Station★ TN3 312 C7
Groom Cl BR2 52 B5
Groom Way ME17 199 E6
Grosmont Rd SE18 2 F1
Grosvenor Ave ME4 63 E3
Grosvenor Bridge TN1 286 B5
Grosvenor Cotts CT7 81 B3
Grosvenor Cres DA1 15 D2
Grosvenor Gdns CT9 50 I1
Grosvenor Hill CT9 50 I2
Grosvenor Ho 5 ME15 195 F5
Grosvenor Manor DA5 32 D6
Grosvenor Pk TN1 286 A4
Grosvenor Pl CT9 50 I2
Grosvenor Rd
Ashford TN24 268 D7
Bexley DA6 13 E2
Broadstairs CT10 84 A4
Erith DA17 14 A8
Gillingham ME7 65 A1
Orpington BR5 53 E3
Ramsgate CT11 117 C7
Royal Tunbridge Wells TN1 286 A4
Whitstable CT5 108 D7
Grosvenor Sq DA3 58 E6
Grosvenor Wlk TN1 286 A4
Grotto Gdns 6 CT9 50 J2
Grotto Hill CT9 50 J2
Grotto Rd 5 CT9 50 J2
Grove Ave
Leysdown-on-S ME12 49 G2
Royal Tunbridge Wells TN1 286 A2
Grovebury Cl DA8 14 D8
Grovebury Ct DA6 14 B2
Grovebury Rd SE2 3 B4
Grove Cl
Faversham ME13 138 A6
Goose Green TN11 191 C3
Hayes BR2 85 A8
Grove Cotts TN30 345 B6
Grove Court Farm ME13 140 A3
Grove Ct Greenwich SE3 11 A6
4 Rochester ME2 63 B7
Grove Dairy Farm ME9 101 A6
Grove Ferry Hill CT3 112 E3
Grove Ferry Rd CT3 113 A2
Grove Gdns 6 CT9 50 G1
Grove Green La ME14 162 E5
Grove Green Rd ME14 162 F5
Groveherst Rd DA1 15 F4
Grove Hill Gdns TN1 286 B2
Grove Hill Ho TN1 286 B3
Grove Hill Rd TN1 286 B3
Grove Ho TN27 265 C3
Grovehurst Ave ME10 68 F1
Grovehurst La TN12 290 C5
Grovehurst Rd ME10, ME9 68 E2
Grove La
Brookland TN29 362 D3
Hunton ME15 226 D7
Iden TN31 368 C4
Grovelands ME17 199 E5
Grovelands Rd BR5 31 A1
Grovelands Way RM17 17 F8
Grove Market Pl SE9 11 F1
Grove Park Ave ME10 101 B5
Grove Park Prim Sch ME10 101 B6
Grove Park Rd SE9 29 D6
Grove Park Sta SE12 29 B5
Grove Pl ME13 138 A6
Grove Rd
Bexley,Bexleyheath DA7 14 C3
8 Bexley,West Heath DA17 13 F8
Chatham ME4 64 B2
Deal CT14 215 D3
Folkestone CT20 335 E6
Gillingham ME7 65 A6
Grays RM17 18 C8
Maidstone ME15 195 C7
Northfleet DA11 18 B2
Penshurst TN11,TN8 251 E2
Preston CT3 146 B8
Ramsgate CT11 117 D6
Rochester ME2 63 B8
Seal TN15 155 B5
Selling ME13 171 B4
Sevenoaks TN14 154 C6
Staple CT3 178 F6
Tatsfield TN16 150 C7
Upper Halling ME2 94 E5
Wickhambreaux CT3 145 D6
Grove Road Cotts
Wickhambreaux CT3 145 C2
Wickhambreaux,Frognall CT3 145 C3
Grover St 3 TN1 286 B4
Groves The ME6 127 F7
Grove Terr CT1 174 E7
Grove The
Ashford TN24 268 E6
Barham CT4 242 F8
Bexley DA6 13 D3
Biggin Hill TN16 118 E1
Deal CT14 215 C6
Dover CT16 278 C1
Fawkham Green DA3 58 A2
Gravesend DA12 37 B8
Herne Bay CT6 76 C2
Maidstone ME14 163 A3
Pembury TN2 287 D8
Sidcup DA14 31 E4
Swanley BR8 55 F6
Swanscombe DA10 17 F2
Westgate-on-S CT8 81 F8
West Kingsdown TN15 90 F1
Grove Vale BR7 30 A2
Groveway ME12 49 F2
Grove Way CT3 146 C7
Grove Wood Cotts TN11 188 A1
Grovewood Ct ME14 162 E4
Grovewood Dr ME14 162 E4
Grub St RH8 183 C6
Grummock Ave CT11 117 B7
Grundy's Hill 13 CT11 117 E6

Guardian Ct ME8 ...... 65 C1
Guardian Ind Est
  TN12 .... 259 C7
Guards Cl TN10 .. 222 V6
Guernsey Way TN24 .. 268 C7
Guestling Mill Ct 1
  CT13 .... 148 F1
Guestwick TN10 .. 222 F5
Guibal Rd SE12 .....29 B7
Guildables La RH8,
  TN8 .... 216 E7
Guildcount La 5
  CT13 .... 148 F1
Guildford Ave CT8 ...81 E8
Guildford Gdns ME2 .. 62 C6
Guildford Lawn 1
  CT11 .... 117 E6
Guildford Rd
  Canterbury CT1 .. 174 F6
  Newham E6 ....1 F7
  7 Royal Tunbridge Wells
  TN1 .... 286 B3
Guildhall 10 CT20 .. 335 D5
Guildhall Mus ★ ME11 ...45 F5
Guildhall Mus The ★
  ME1 .... 63 C6
Guildhall St N CT19,
  CT20 .... 335 D5
Guildhall St
  4 Canterbury CT1 ..... 174 F6
  18 Folkestone CT20 .. 335 D5
Guild Rd Erith DA8 .....14 F7
  Greenwich SE7 ..... 11 D8
Guilford Ave CT16 .. 278 A6
Guilford Ct CT14 .. 215 D2
Guilford Ho CT13 .. 182 A7
Guilford Rd CT13 .. 181 E8
Guilton CT3 .... 147 B1
Guiness Dr ME2 .....40 B2
Guldeford La TN29,
  TN31 .... 369 F3
Guldeford Lane Cnr
  TN31 .... 369 D2
Gulland Ho 4 ME14 .. 162 B4
Gullands ME17 .. 196 E4
Gulliver Rd DA15 .....30 E6
Gumley Rd RM20 .....17 E8
Gumping Rd BR5,BR6 .. 86 C8
Gun Back La TN12 .. 290 A5
Gundulph Ho TN10 .. 222 C3
Gundulph Rd
  Bromley BR2 .... 52 C6
  Rochester ME1 .... 63 E4
Gundulph Sq ME1 .. 63 C6
Gunfleet Cl DA12 .....37 E8
Gun Hill RM18 ..... 19 D8
Gunlands TN12 .. 290 A6
Gun La ME2 ....63 B7
Gunner La SE18 .....2 A1
Gunnery Terr SE18 .....2 C3
Gunning St SE18 .....2 E2
Gunnis Cl ME8 ..... 98 D4
Gunn Rd DA10 .....17 E1
Gun Tower Mews ME1 ...63 B4
Gurdon Rd SE7 .....1 B1
Gurling Rd CT15 .. 247 F1
Guston CE Prim Sch
  CT15 .... 278 E3
Guston Rd
  East Langdon CT15 .. 279 A8
  Maidstone ME14 .. 162 C6
Guthrie Gdns CT17 .. 277 E3
Guy Barnett Gr SE3 .. 11 A4
Guy Cl CT10 ....84 A7
Gwillim Cl DA15 ..... 13 A2
Gwyn Rd DA11 .....36 C6
Gwyn Rd CT12 .....83 C2
Gybbon Rise TN12 .. 260 E3
Gybbons Rd TN17 .. 343 F3
Gypsy Cnr CT5 .. 109 D3
Gypsy Way ME23 .....23 E5

H

Hackfield TN23 .. 267 F1
Hackington Cl CT2 .. 142 E4
Hackington Pl CT2 .. 142 F2
Hackington Rd CT2 .. 142 E7
Hackington Terr CT2 .. 142 F2
Hacklinge Hill CT14 .. 181 B2
Hackney Rd ME16 .. 161 C2
Hadden Rd SE28 ....3 C4
Haddon Dene Sch CT10 .83 F4
Haddon Gr DA15 .. 31 A8
Haddon Rd BR5 .. 54 C4
Hadleigh Cl ME7 .. 98 A3
Hadleigh Gdns CT6 ....77 B5
Hadleigh Wlk 1 E6 ... 1 E7
Hadley Ct DA13 .....93 B8
Hadley Gdns ME17 .. 164 E2
Hadley House BR5 .....53 F7
Hadley Rd DA17 ....3 F2
Hadlow Coll
  Canterbury CT1 .. 175 B8
  Hadlow TN11 .... 223 D8
Hadlow Coll Mottingham
  Ctr SE12 .... 29 C7
Hadlow Coll Nature
  Reserve ★ SE12 ....29 C7
Hadlow Ct TN9 .. 222 C2
Hadlow Dr CT9 .....51 E2
Hadlow Pk TN11 .. 190 E1
Hadlow Rd DA16 .. 13 C7
Hadlow Rd E TN10,
  TN11 .... 223 A5
Hadlow Rd
  Maidstone ME14 .. 162 C5
  Sidcup DA14 ..... 31 A4
  Tonbridge TN9 .. 222 D3
Hadlow Sch TN11 .. 223 E8
Hadlow Stair Rd TN10 .. 222 F4

Hadlow Way DA13 .....36 E1
Hadrian Gdns TN23 .. 299 F5
Haffenden Cl TN12 .. 259 D6
Haffenden Mdw TN27 .. 234 C8
Haffenden Rd TN30 .. 324 B1
Ha-Ha Rd SE18 ....11 F8
Haig Ave Chatham ME1 .. 63 D1
  Chatham ME4 ..... 64 A2
  Gillingham ME7 .....64 E4
Haig Ct BR7 .... 30 B3
Haig Gdns DA12 .. 37 C8
Haig Rd TN16 .. 118 E2
Haig Villas ME3 .. 41 A5
Haileybury Rd BR6 .. 87 A6
Hailey Rd Bsns Pk DA18 ..4 A4
Hailing Mews BR2 .....52 B6
Hailstone Cl TN11 .. 223 E8
Haimo Prim Sch SE9 .. 11 D2
Haimo Rd SE9 .. 11 D2
Hainault St SE9 .....30 B7
Haine Ind Est CT12 ....82 F1
Haine Rd CT12,CT10 ...82 F2
Halcot Ave DA6 .. 14 C2
Haldane Gdns DA11 .. 36 C7
Haldane Rd SE28 ....3 D6
Halden Cl ME15 .. 195 F6
Halden La TN17 .. 343 F6
Hale Cl BR6 .... 86 C6
Hale Cotts DA9 .. 17 C2
Hale La TN12 .. 225 A7
Hale La TN14 .. 121 F2
Hale Oak Rd
  Hall's Green TN8,TN14 .. 219 E4
  Sevenoaks Weald TN14 .. 187 B1
Hale Rd ME3 .. 40 C7
Hales Cl TN30 .. 345 B8
Hales Cl TN30 .. 345 B8
Hales Dr CT2 .. 142 F3
Hales Rd ME10 .. 101 D1
Haleys Pl ME1 .. 129 A8
Halfmile Ride CT9 .....82 E6
Half Moon La TN11 .. 221 D6
Half Moon Way ME23 ...23 E3
Halford Cl CT6 ....77 B2
Halfpence La DA12 .....61 B7
Halfpenny Cl ME16 .. 161 A2
Halfway Houses Prim Sch
  ME12 .... 46 D6
Halfway Rd ME12 .. 46 D8
Halfway St DA15 .....30 E7
Halifax Cl ME5 ....97 B6
Halifield Dr DA17 ....3 E3
Hallam Cl BR7 .. 286 E4
Hall Ave TN24 .. 300 F6
Hall By The Sea Rd
  CT9 .... 50 H2
Hall Cl ME10 .. 101 E6
Hall Cres CT14 .. 214 F5
Hallcroft Cl CT11 .. 117 C7
Hallett Wlk 10 CT1 .. 143 B2
Hallford Way DA1 .. 15 C2
Hallgate SE3 .. 11 A4
Hall Hill TN15 .. 155 C4
Halliday Ct CT21 .. 333 A2
Halliday Dr CT14 .. 215 D3
Halling Prim Sch ME2 ..95 B3
Halling Sta ME2 .. 95 A5
Hall Place ★ DA5 .. 14 C1
Hall Place Cres DA1,
  DA5 .... 14 D2
Hall Rd Aylesford ME20 .. 128 F1
  Chatham ME5 .. 97 C3
  Dartford DA1 .....15 F3
  High Halstow ME3 .. 24 C6
  Northfleet,Pepper Hill
  DA11 .... 36 C5
  Northfleet,Wombwell Park
  DA11 .... 36 D6
  Wouldham ME1 .. 95 C3
Halls Cotts TN5 .. 336 F5
Hallsfield Rd ME5 .. 96 D2
Hall's Hole Rd TN2 .. 289 B5
Hallsville Prim Sch E16 ..1 A7
Hall The SE3 .. 11 A4
Hall View SE9 .. 29 D6
Hallwards TN12 .. 260 E2
Hallwood Cl ME8 .. 98 D5
Hallwood Ho ME5 .. 97 C2
Hallywell Cres E6 ....1 F8
Halons Rd SE9 .. 30 A8
Halsbrook Rd SE3 .. 11 D4
Halstatt Rd CT14 .. 215 A3
Halstead Cl CT2 .. 143 B4
Halstead Com Prim Sch
  TN14 .... 120 F7
Halstead Gdns CT9 ....51 F3
Halstead La TN14 .. 120 E5
Halstead Rd DA8 .....14 E6
Halstead Wlk ME16 .. 161 C7
Halstow Cl ME15 .. 195 F6
Halstow Prim Sch SE10 ..1 A1
Halstow Rd SE10,SE3 ....1 A1
Halstow Way TN23 .. 299 F8
Halt Cvn Pk The TN15 ...90 E1
Halt Robin La DA17 .....4 B2
Halt Robin Rd DA17 .....4 B2
Halt The Elham CT4 .. 273 F4
  Whitstable CT5 .. 109 A7
Hambledon Ct ME16 .. 161 B3
Hambledown Rd DA15 ...30 D8
Hamble Rd TN10 .. 222 B5
Hambro Ave BR2 .. 52 A1
Hambrook Cl CT4 .. 205 B8
Hambrook La CT4 .. 205 C8
Hambrook Wlk ME10 .. 101 F8
Hamele The CT3 .. 143 F5
Hamelin Rd ME7 .....97 F8
Hamerton Rd DA11 ...18 B2
Ham Farm Cotts CT14 .. 180 F2
Hamill Terr CT1 .. 143 B2

Hamilton Cl
  Littlestone-on-Sea TN28 .. 373 E5
  Ramsgate CT12 ....83 B1
Hamilton Cres ME10 .. 101 C3
Hamilton Ct
  Chatham ME5 .. 64 C1
  Rochester ME1 ....63 B4
  Royal Tunbridge Wells
  TN4 .... 286 A5
Hamilton Ho
  Coxheath ME17 .. 194 C3
  Maidstone ME15 .. 195 F5
  Royal Tunbridge Wells
  TN4 .... 286 A5
Hamilton Rd
  Ashford TN24 .. 300 D4
  Bexley DA7 .. 13 D5
  Deal CT14 .. 215 C4
  Dover CT17 .. 310 B8
  Gillingham ME7 .. 64 D7
  Lydd TN29 .. 376 C6
  Sidcup DA15 .. 31 A4
  Whitstable CT5 .. 75 A1
Hamilton Wlk DA8 .....14 F7
Ham La Gillingham ME7 ..97 E3
  Lenham ME17 .. 199 C5
Hamlea Cl SE12 .. 11 A2
Hamlet Est DA8 ....4 D1
Hamlet Ho Eltham SE9 .. 12 A2
  5 Erith DA8 .... 14 E7
Hamlin Rd TN13 .. 153 E6
Hamlyn Rd TN13 .. 153 E6
Hammelton Rd 2 BR1 .. 52 A8
Hammerwood Pk ★
  RH19 .... 281 C2
Ham Mill La TN26,
  TN29 .... 349 A2
Hammond Cl TN28 .. 211 E5
Hammond's Cnr TN29 .. 372 E6
Hammonds 9 ME16 .. 341 A2
Hammond's Rd CT20 .. 334 E5
Hammond Way 2 SE28 ...3 B6
Hamond Hill 6 ME4 ....63 E4
Hampden La TN23 .. 300 A7
Hampden Mews TN23 .. 300 A7
Hampden Rd TN23 .. 300 A6
Hampden Way ME19 .. 158 F3
Hampshire Cl ME5 .....97 C7
Hampshire Dr ME15 .. 195 C8
Hampshire Rd CT1 .. 175 D7
Hampshires The
  ME17 .... 198 C6
Hampson Way ME14 .. 163 A4
Hampstead Cl SE28 .....3 B5
Hampstead La TN17 .. 192 C1
Hampton Cl
  Chatham ME5 .. 97 A5
  Herne Bay CT6 .. 76 A3
Hampton Cotts TN14 .. 120 F7
Hampton Cres CT2 .....37 E6
Hampton Ct DA8 .. 14 D7
Hampton Gdns CT6 .. 76 A3
Hampton Ho DA7 .. 14 B5
Hampton La TN25 .. 270 C3
Hampton Pier Ave CT6 ..76 B4
Hampton Prim Sch
  CT6 .... 76 C4
Hampton Rd ME14 .. 162 C6
Hampton Rd TN11 .. 190 B5
Hampton Vale CT21 .. 334 B4
Ham Rd ME13 .. 105 C1
Ham River Mill ME3 .. 40 A6
Ham Shades Cl 1
  DA15 .... 31 A5
Ham Shades La CT5 .. 75 A1
Hamstreet Prim Sch
  TN26 .... 348 F8
Hamstreet Rd
  Bromley Green TN26 .. 327 E5
  Hamstreet TN26 .. 349 C7
Ham Street Sta TN26 .. 349 A8
Hamwick Gn ME5 .. 97 C1
Hanameel St E16 ....1 B5
Hanbury Cl ME18 .. 192 E7
Hanbury Dr TN16 .. 118 B6
Hanbury Wlk DA5 .....32 E5
Hancock Cl ME3 ....40 B1
Hancocks Field CT14 .. 215 A5
Handel Cres RM18 .. 19 A7
Handel Wlk TN10 .. 222 E6
Hands Wlk E16 ....1 A7
Hanes Dene ME2 .. 94 F5
Hang Grove Hill BR6 .. 119 B6
Hanging Bank TN14 .. 185 F3
Hangmans Cnr BR7 .....53 B8
Hangman's La CT14 .. 247 F5
Hanley Ct TN13 .. 154 B4
Hanmer Way TN12 .. 260 E2
Hanover Ave E16 ....1 A5
Hanover Cl
  Ashford TN23 .. 267 F2
  Deal CT14 .. 215 D2
  Margate CT9 ....51 E2
  Sittingbourne ME10 .. 101 C2
Hanover Ct
  Broadstairs CT10 .....83 F4
  10 Bromley BR2 .. 52 A6
  Faversham ME13 .. 138 B8
  Hythe CT21 .. 333 C1
  Maidstone ME14 .. 162 B5
Hanover Dr
  Chislehurst BR7 .. 30 C4
  Gillingham ME8 .. 98 C4
Hanover Gn ME20 .. 127 F3
Hanover Ho 2 CT20 .. 335 C4
Hanover Pl
  Canterbury CT2 .. 142 F2
  New Ash Green DA3 ...91 F8

Hanover Sq CT6 ....76 F5
Hanover St CT6 ....76 F5
Hanover Way DA7 .. 13 D4
Hanscomb Ho CT2 .. 142 E2
Hanslett's La ME13 .. 137 D3
Hansol Rd DA6 ....13 E2
Hansom Terr 1 BR1 .. 52 B8
Hanson Dr ME15 .. 194 F3
Hanway ME8 .. 65 A2
Happy Valley Holiday Camp
  ME12 .... 49 E2
Harbex Cl DA5 ....32 B8
Harbledown Gdns CT9 ..51 E3
Harbledown Ho ME16 .. 161 B2
Harbledown Manor
  ME8 .... 65 D3
Harbledown Pk CT2 .. 142 C1
Harbledown Pl BR5 .. 54 C5
Harborough Ave DA15 ...30 F8
Harbour Approach Rd
  CT20 .... 335 E4
Harbourland Cl ME14 .. 162 B8
Harbourne La TN26,
  TN30 .... 324 E5
Harbour Par CT11 .. 117 E6
Harbour Point CT19 .. 335 F5
Harbour Sch CT15 .. 309 E7
Harbour St
  Broadstairs CT10 .....84 B4
  Folkestone CT20 .. 335 E5
  Ramsgate CT11 .. 117 E6
  Whitstable CT5 .. 74 D2
Harbour The ME17 .. 229 E5
Harbour Twrs 16 CT11 .. 117 E6
Harbour View Rd
  CT17 .... 310 B8
Harbour Way CT20 .. 335 E4
Harcourt Ave DA15 .. 31 C8
Harcourt Dr
  Canterbury CT2 .. 142 D2
  Herne Bay CT6 ....76 B5
Harcourt Gdns ME8 .....98 E4
Harcourt Prim Sch
  CT19 .... 334 E7
Harcourt Rd Bexley DA6 ..13 E3
  Folkestone CT19 .. 334 F7
Harden Ct 1 SE18 ....1 E2
Harden's View TN26 .. 348 D6
Harden Rd Lydd TN29 .. 376 D7
  Northfleet DA11 .....36 F6
Hardie Cl ME19 .. 127 F1
Hardinge Ave TN4 .. 253 E3
Hardinge Cres SE18 .....2 C3
Hardinge Rd TN24 .. 268 C3
Hardinge St SE18 ....2 B3
Harding Ho 9 SE18 .....1 F2
Harding Rd DA7 .. 13 F5
Hardman Rd SE7 ....1 B1
Hardres Court Rd CT4 .. 208 A3
Hardres Rd CT11 .. 117 E8
Hardres St CT11 .. 117 E7
Hardres Terr BR5 .. 87 D8
Hards Town ME4 .. 64 A4
Hardwick Cres 2 DA2 ..16 B1
Hardwick Ct DA8 .. 14 D8
Hardwicke Ho TN27 .. 234 B7
Hardwicke Rd CT17 .. 310 B6
Hardwick Ho ME15 .. 195 E8
Hardwick Rd
  Folkestone CT20 .. 335 A4
  Tonbridge TN11 .. 221 E6
Hardy Ave Newham E16 ...1 A5
  Northfleet DA11 .....36 E6
Hardy Cl Ashford TN24 .. 301 A7
  Canterbury CT2 .. 142 C1
  Chatham ME5 ....97 B6
Hardy Gr DA1 .. 16 A4
Hardy Lodge ME1 .....63 B4
Hardy Rd
  Greatstone-on-Sea
  TN28 .... 373 D3
  2 Greenwich SE3 .. 11 A8
  St Margaret's at Cliffe
  CT15 .... 279 E8
Hardy St ME14 .. 162 A6
Harebell Cl
  3 Chatham ME5 ....96 F4
  Maidstone ME14 .. 162 E5
  Minster (Sheppey) ME12 .. 47 A4
Harebell Dr E6 ....1 E8
Harebrook CT11 ....83 F1
Haredale Cl ME1 .. 96 F3
Harefield Rd DA14 .. 31 D5
Harenc Sch DA14 .. 31 C3
Harescroft TN2 .. 313 F7
Hare St 2 Chatham ME4 ..64 B3
  Woolwich SE18 ....2 A3
Harewood Lincoln Ho
  DA11 .... 18 D1
Harfst Way BR8 .. 55 C8
Hargate Cl TN2 .. 313 F8
Hargood Rd SE3 .. 11 C6
Harkness Ct 6 ME10 .. 102 B4
Harkness Dr CT2 .. 142 E2
Harland Ave DA15 .....30 E6
Harland Rd SE12 .. 29 A7
Harlands Gr BR6 ....86 B6
Harland Way TN4 .. 253 F4
Harlech Cl ME2 ....39 F1
Harlequin Ho 1 DA18 ...3 E3
Harley 5 BR7 .. 53 D8
Harleyford Rd ME1 .. 52 C8
Harley Gdns BR6 ....86 E6
Harling Cl ME17 .. 195 D5
Harlinger St SE18 .. 1 E3
Harlington Rd DA7 .....13 E4
Harman Ave
  Gravesend DA11 ....37 B3
  Lympne CT21 .. 333 A3
Harman Ct ME5 ....97 B3
Harman Dr DA15 .....12 F1

Harmer Ct
  Royal Tunbridge Wells
  TN4 .... 254 A2
  Swanscombe DA10 .....17 F1
Harmer Rd DA10 .....17 F1
Harmer St DA12 .. 19 C1
Harmers Way TN27 .. 232 F3
Harmony St TN4 .. 285 D4
Harmony Way 1 BR1,
  BR2 .... 52 A7
Harmsworth Ct TN17 .. 342 E6
Harmsworth Gdns
  CT10 .... 84 A5
Harness Rd SE28 ....3 A4
Harnet St 6 CT13 .. 148 F1
Harnetts Cl BR8 .. 55 D2
Harold Ave Erith DA17 ...3 F1
  Gillingham ME7 ....64 E4
  Westgate-on-S CT8 .....81 E8
Harold Campbell Ct
  DA1 .... 33 D8
Harold Ct ME13 .. 138 C6
Harold Gibbons Ct SE7 .. 11 C8
Harold Ho 2 TN2 .. 286 C7
Harold Rd
  Birchington CT7 .....80 E8
  Cuxton ME2 .. 62 C3
  Deal CT14 .. 215 D8
  Hawley DA2 .. 33 F4
  Margate CT9 .. 51 B3
  Sittingbourne ME10 .. 102 B4
Harold's Rd CT16 .. 310 E8
Harold St Dover CT16 .. 310 D8
  Queenborough ME11 .. 46 A4
Harper Rd
  Ashford TN23 .. 299 F8
  Newham E6 .... 1 F7
Harp Farm Rd ME14 .. 130 C6
Harple La ME14 .. 130 F1
Harps Ave ME12 .. 47 C6
Harpswood ME17 .. 164 F1
Harpswood La CT21 .. 333 A4
Harptree Dr ME5 ....96 F5
Harraden Rd SE3 .. 11 C6
Harrier Dr ME10 .. 102 A2
Harrier Mews SE28 .....2 D4
Harrier Way E6 ....1 F8
Harries Rd TN2 .. 286 E7
Harriestsham Sta
  ME17 .... 198 D6
Harriet Dr ME17 .....63 B3
Harriets Cnr CT5 .. 108 B5
Harrietsham Ho 18
  ME16 .... 161 A3
Harrietsham Prim Sch
  ME17 .... 198 E6
Harringe La CT21,
  TN25 .... 331 A6
Harrington Ho 7 BR1 .. 52 A8
Harrington Way SE18 ....1 D3
Harriot Cl CT19 .. 335 B7
Harris Cl DA11 ....36 F5
Harris Gdns ME10 .. 102 C5
Harris Ho ME2 ....95 B4
Harrison Ct 4 ME8 .....65 F1
Harrison Dr
  Harrietsham ME17 .. 198 E6
  High Halstow ME23 .....23 E4
Harrison Rd
  Borough Green TN15 .. 156 F7
  4 Ramsgate CT11 .. 117 D6
Harrison Terr ME13 .. 105 A2
Harrison Way TN13 .. 154 A5
Harris Rd Bexley DA7 .. 13 F6
  Sheerness ME12 .. 28 C2
Harris's Alley CT3 .. 178 A7
Harrogate Ct 6 SE12 .. 29 A8
Harrowby Gdns DA11 ...36 E6
Harrow Ct TN8 .. 217 D3
Harrow Ct Chatham ME5 ...97 C4
  Stockbury ME9 .. 132 D8
Harrow Dene CT10 .....83 E6
Harrow Gdns BR6 ....87 B6
Harrow Manor Way SE2 ..3 C3
Harrow Rd
  Gillingham ME7 ....97 F6
  Halstead TN14 .. 120 E4
Harrow Way
  Ashford TN23 .. 299 E5
  Maidstone ME14 .. 162 E5
Harry Pay Cl TN24 .. 268 F4
Harrys Rd ME9 .. 103 D3
Harry Wells Rd CT6 .....76 B3
Hart Cl CT18 .. 307 F4
Hart Dyke Cres BR8 .. 55 D6
Hart Hill TN27 .. 201 E4
Hart Ho BR6 .. 54 A2
Harting Rd SE9 .. 29 E5
Hartington Cl BR6 .. 86 C5
Hartington Rd E16 ....1 B7
Hartington St ME4 .. 64 A3
Hartlake Rd TN11 .. 223 D3
Hartlands Cl DA5 .. 13 F1
Hartlepool Ct E16 ....2 B4
Hartley Bottom Rd
  TN17 .... 320 A3
Hartley Cl Bromley BR1 ..52 F7
  Maidstone ME15 .. 195 F6
Hartley Court Gdns
  TN17 .... 320 A3
Hartley Hill DA3 .. 59 A1

Hartley Mews ME8 .....65 B3
Hartley Prim Sch DA3 ..58 E3
Hartley Rd Bexley DA16 .. 13 C7
  Hartley TN17 .... 320 A3
  Longfield DA3 ....58 E7
  Westerham TN16 .. 151 D2
Hartlip CE Prim Sch
  ME9 .... 99 D5
Hartlip Cl ME9 ....46 B7
Hartlip Hill ME9 ....99 F7
Hartmann Rd E16 ....1 E5
Hartnokes TN18 .. 341 A2
Hartnup St ME16 .. 161 C2
Harton Cl BR1 .. 52 D8
Hartpiece Cl ME8 ....65 F2
Hartridge Farm ME15 .. 194 A7
Harts Cotts TN26 .. 349 A8
Hartsdown Rd CT9 .. 82 D8
Hartsdown Tech Coll
  CT9 .... 82 D8
Hart Shaw DA3 ....59 B7
Hartshill Rd DA11 .....36 F6
Harts Holiday Camp
  ME12 .... 49 G1
Hartslands Rd TN13 .. 154 C4
Harts La 6 CT5 .. 74 D2
Hartslock Dr DA18,SE2 ...3 B4
Hartsmead Rd SE9 .....29 F6
Hart St ME16 .. 161 F3
Hart Street Bsns Ctr
  ME16 .... 161 F3
Hartville Rd SE18 ....2 E2
Hartwell Ho 2 SE7 ....1 B1
Harty Ave ME8 ....98 B3
Harty Ferry Cotts
  ME13 .... 105 C5
Harty Ferry Rd ME12 ...72 E4
Harty Ferry View CT5 .. 108 C6
Harty Terr ME12 .. 48 A5
Harvard Ct 9 SE9 .. 12 A1
Harvel Ave ME2 ....62 F7
Harvel Cl BR5,BR7 .. 54 A6
Harvel Cres SE2 ....3 D1
Harvel La DA13 ....93 B2
Harvel Rd DA13 .. 126 A8
Harvel St DA13 .. 93 C3
Harvest Bank Rd BR4 .. 85 A7
Harvesters Cl ME8 .....98 E7
Harvesters Way ME14 .. 162 E4
Harvest La CT4 .. 240 E5
Harvest Rd TN10 .. 222 D6
Harvest Ridge ME19 .. 127 D2
Harvest Way
  Ashford TN23 .. 299 D7
  Crockenhill BR8 .. 55 D2
  Hawkinge CT18 .. 307 B4
Harvey Ave CT14 .. 215 C3
Harvey Ct CT19 .. 335 A6
Harvey Dr
  Sittingbourne ME10 .. 102 A2
  Whitstable CT5 ....75 B1
Harvey Gdns SE7 ....1 C1
Harvey Gram Sch The
  CT19 .... 335 A6
Harvey Pl
  21 Folkestone CT20 .. 335 D5
  9 Folkestone CT20 .. 335 E5
Harvey Point 9 E16 .....1 A8
Harvey Rd
  Ashford TN24 .. 268 F1
  Gillingham ME8 ....98 E8
Harvey St CT20 .. 335 E5
Harville Rd TN25 .. 237 C2
Harvill Rd DA14 .. 31 E3
Harwich St CT5 .. 108 D8
Harwick Dr TN28 .. 373 C8
Harwood Ave ME1 .....52 B7
Harwood Ct 3 RM17 .. 18 C8
Harwood Ho TN25 .. 237 E1
Harwood Rd ME8 ....66 B1
Hasborough Rd CT19 .. 335 F6
Haskard Cl CT18 .. 306 F4
Haslemere Est ME15 .. 195 F5
Haslemere Rd DA7 .. 14 A5
Hasler Cl SE28 ....3 C6
Hasletts Cl TN1 .. 286 B6
Haslewood Cl TN27 .. 264 B2
Hassall Reach CT1 .. 174 B6
Hassell St TN25 .. 238 F2
Hassendean Rd SE3 .....11 B7
Hassock Wood BR2 .....85 E6
Hassop Wlk SE9 ....29 E4
Hasted Cl DA9 .. 17 C1
Hasted Rd Greenwich SE7 ..1 D1
  Newington ME9 .. 100 B7
Hasteds ME17 .. 164 D2
Haste Hill Cl ME17 .. 195 B3
Haste Hill Rd ME17 .. 195 B3
Hast Hill Ho BR2 ....85 B6
Hastings Ave CT9 .. 51 A1
Hastings Ct RM17 .....17 E8
Hastings Ho SE18 ....1 F2
Hastings Pl CT13 .. 180 F8
Hastings Rd
  Maidstone ME15 .. 162 B3
  Newenden TN17,TN18 .. 357 C6
  Orpington BR2 ....85 E8
  Pembury,Kipping's Cross
  TN2 .... 287 F5
  Pembury TN2 .. 287 D6
  The Moor TN18 .. 354 F6
Hastings St 3 SE18 ....2 C3
Hatches La TN11,TN12 .. 224 D6
Hatch La CT4 .. 173 C5
Hatch Rd ME17 .. 199 C5
Hatch St 3 ME13 .. 138 C7
Hatfield Ct SE3 .. 11 A7
Hatfield Rd
  Margate CT9 .. 50 G2
  Ramsgate CT11 .. 117 D7

Hatfield Rd continued
Rochester ME2 .... 63 A8
Hatham Green La TN15 . 91 D1
Hathaway Cl BR2 ....52 F1
Hathaway Ct
Gillingham ME8 .... 98 D8
Rochester ME1 ....83 B5
Hatherall Rd ME14 .. 162 B6
Hatherley Cres DA14 ... 31 A6
Hatherley Ct CT9 ...... 51 A3
Hatherley Rd DA14 .... 31 A5
Hathern Gdns SE9 ..... 30 A4
Hatmill La TN12 ...... 289 A7
Hattersfield Cl DA17 ... 3 F2
Hatton Cl
Northfleet DA11 ....36 E5
Woolwich SE18 .... 12 D7
Hatton Ct BR7 ....29 F1
Hatton Rd ME5 .... 97 C3
Havant Ave ME15 .... 195 F6
Havelock Pl CT3 ...... 147 E1
Havelock Rd
Bromley BR2 .... 52 C5
Dartford DA1 ....15 B1
Deal CT14 .... 215 C3
Erith DA17 ....3 F2
Northfleet DA11 ....36 F7
Tonbridge TN9 .... 222 B2
Havelock St CT1 ..... 143 A1
Haven Cl
Eltham SE9 ....29 F5
Istead Rise DA13 ....59 F8
Rochester ME1 .... 63 C2
Sidcup DA14 .... 31 C2
Swanley BR8 ....55 F7
Haven Dr
Hawkinge CT18 .... 307 A4
Herne Bay CT6 ....77 F6
Havengore Ave DA12 ...37 E8
Haven Hill TN15 .... 92 A3
Haven Lodge ◘ SE18 ..2 B2
Haven St ME3 .... 40 C5
Haven The
Ashford TN24 .... 299 F5
Brenzett TN29 .... 363 A3
Hythe CT21 .... 353 C8
Haventhorpe TN24 .... 268 C3
Haven Way ME4 ....41 B1
Havering Cl TN24 ..... 286 F6
Haverstock Ct ◙ BR5 ...54 B7
Haverthwaite Rd BR6 .. 86 F7
Havisham Cl ME1 ...... 63 D2
Havisham Rd DA12 .... 38 A7
Hawbeck Rd ME8 ...... 98 C3
Hawden Cl TN11 ...... 221 F4
Hawden La TN11 ..... 221 F4
Hawden Rd TN9 ...... 222 B2
Hawe Cl CT2 .... 143 A4
Hawe Farm Way CT6 ...77 B2
Hawe La CT2 .... 144 A7
Hawes Ave CT11 ..... 117 F5
Hawes Rd BR1 ....52 B8
Hawfield Bank BR6 ..... 87 D7
Hawk Cl CT5 .... 108 C7
Hawkenbury Cl TN2 .. 286 D2
Hawkenbury Mead
TN2 .... 286 D1
Hawkenbury Rd
Hawkenbury TN2 ...... 261 C6
Royal Tunbridge Wells
TN2, TN3 .... 286 E1
Hawkenbury Rise ME2 ..40 B2
Hawkesbury St CT17 .. 310 D5
Hawkes Cl RM17 ....18 B8
Hawkes Pl TN13 ...... 187 A8
Hawkes Rd ME20 .... 128 F5
Hawkhurst CE Prim Sch
TN18 .... 341 B2
Hawkhurst Cl CT7 ....81 B8
Hawkhurst Cottage Hospl
TN18 .... 340 D2
Hawkhurst Rd
Flimwell TN5,TN18 .... 339 E2
Gillingham ME8 ....65 B3
Gill's Green TN17,TN18 .. 340 F7
Hawkhurst Way TN10 ...84 A2
Hawkinge Prim Sch
CT18 .... 307 B4
Hawkinge Wlk BR5 .....54 B6
Hawkins Ave DA12 .... 37 C4
Hawkins Cl
Chatham ME7 .... 64 A6
Sittingbourne ME10 ... 101 E7
Hawkins Rd CT19 .... 334 D6
Hawkridge Gr ME8 ... 159 A3
Hawksdown CT14 .... 248 B8
Hawksdown Rd CT14 .. 248 C8
Hawks Hill La ME9 ... 134 C4
Hawkshill Rd CT14 ... 248 D8
Hawk's La CT1 .... 174 F8
Hawksmoor Cl
◘ Newham E6 ....1 E7
Woolwich SE18 ....2 E1
Hawksmoor Sch SE28 ...3 B6
Hawks Rd CT6 ....76 B2
Hawks Way TN23 .... 299 E7
Hawkwell Bsns Ctr
TN2 .... 255 F2
Hawkwell Cotts TN2 .. 255 F2
Hawkwood Cl ME1 .... 63 D5
Hawkwood La BR7 .... 53 C8
Hawkwood ME16 ..... 161 B5
Hawley Cl ME16 ..... 161 E4
Hawley Rd DA1,DA2,DA4 .. 34 A4
Hawley Sq CT9 ....50 J2
Hawley St CT9 ....50 I2
Hawley Terr DA2 ..... 34 A4
Hawley Vale DA2 ..... 34 A4
Hawser Rd ME1 ...... 63 C1
Hawstead La BR6 ....87 F5

Hawthorn TN26 ...... 361 D8
Hawthorn Ave
Canterbury CT2 .... 143 A2
West Minst ME12 ....46 A8
Hawthorn Cl
Aylesham CT3 .... 210 E4
Crabble CT17 .... 277 E2
Edenbridge TN8 ...... 217 C2
Gravesend DA12 .... 37 C4
Hythe CT21 .... 353 E8
Orpington BR5 .... 53 D3
Ramsgate CT11 ....83 E1
St Mary's Bay TN29 .. 365 F3
Hawthorn Cnr
Herne Bay CT6 .... 78 A3
Old Romney TN29 .... 371 E3
Hawthorn Cotts ◘
DA16 .... 13 A4
Hawthornden Cl
ME18 .... 159 C3
Hawthornden Ct BR2 .. 85 A8
Hawthornden Rd BR2 .. 85 A8
Hawthorne Ave
Biggin Hill TN16 ...... 118 D4
Gillingham ME8 .... 65 C2
Hawthorne Cl
Bromley BR1 ....52 F6
Eythorne CT15 .... 245 D7
Hawthorne Ho ◙
ME16 .... 161 A3
Hawthorne Rd BR1 .....52 F6
**Hawthorn Farm Cvn &
Camping Site** CT15 .. 247 C1
Hawthorn Ho
◘ Chatham ME5 ....96 F5
◙ Sittingbourne ME10 101 E4
Hawthorn La TN13 ... 153 F5
Hawthorn Pl DA8 ....4 C1
Hawthorn Rd
Bexley DA6 ....13 F3
Dartford DA1 ....33 D7
Kingsnorth TN23 ..... 300 B4
Rochester ME7 ....62 E6
Sittingbourne ME10 .. 101 E4
Hawthorns
Chatham ME5 ....96 F1
Hartley BR3 ....58 F5
Hawthorns The
Aylesford ME20 ...... 128 E1
Broadstairs CT10 ...... 83 C4
Chatham ME5 ....96 F6
Oxted RH8 .... 183 A2
The Moor TN18 .... 354 F8
Hawthorn Terr DA15 ...12 F2
Hawthorn Wlk
Royal Tunbridge Wells
TN2 .... 286 E8
Tonbridge TN10 ...... 222 C7
Haxted Rd BR1 ....52 B8
Hayday Rd E16 ....1 A8
Haydens Cl BR5 ...... 54 C3
Haydens Mews TN9 .. 222 C3
Haydens The TN9 .... 222 C3
Haydon Cl ME16 ..... 161 B4
Hayes Alley ◙ CT5 .....74 D2
Hayesbrook Sch TN9 . 254 A8
Hayes Cl Hayes BR2 .....52 A1
Higham ME3 ....39 C3
West Thurrock RM20 ...17 C8
Hayes Cotts ME19 ... 158 D7
Hayesden La TN11,TN3 . 253 B5
Hayesford Park Dr BR2 . 52 A4
Hayes Gdn BR2 .... 52 A1
Hayes La Hayes BR2 ....52 A4
Stockbury ME9 .... 132 F6
Hayes Prim Sch BR2 ...52 B1
Stone DA9 ....34 E8
Hayes Rd Bromley BR2 ..52 A5
Hayes Sch BR2 ....85 B8
Hayes Sta BR2 ....52 A1
Hayes St BR2 ....52 B1
Hayes Terr DA12 ......38 E3
Hayes Wlk ME19 .... 159 A2
Hayes Wood Ave BR2 ..52 B1
Hayfield ME19 ...... 127 E2
Hayfield Rd BR5 ...... 54 A4
Hayfields ME5 ....97 C2
Haygate Ho ME1 ..... 63 C4
Hay Hill CT13,CT14 .. 180 D2
Hay Ho CT21 .... 333 B2
Hay La CT14 .... 180 F2
Hayle Mill Cotts ME15 194 F8
Hayle Mill Rd ME15 .. 194 F8
Hayle Rd ME15 ...... 162 A3
Hayley Cl ME2 .... 62 C2
Hayley Ho DA17 ....14 A8
Haymakers La TN23 .. 299 D8
Haymans Hill TN12 .. 290 C7
Hayman Wlk ME20 ... 128 F6
Haymen St ME4 ...... 63 E3
Haynes Ho ◙ ME14 .. 162 B4
Haynes Rd
Gravesend DA11 .... 37 A6
Northfleet DA11 ....36 F5
Hayrick Cl ME14 .... 162 E5
Haysden Ctry Pk★
TN11 .... 253 D8
Haysel ME10 .... 102 A2
Hay's Mead DA13 .....60 F3
Hays Rd ME6 .... 127 F6
Hayton Rd TN25 .... 304 A2
Haywain Cl
Ashford TN23 .... 299 E5
Maidstone ME14 ..... 162 F4
Paddock Wood TN12 .. 257 A5
Hayward Ave ME4 .....63 B8
Hayward Cl
Ashford TN24 .... 301 A8
Crayford DA1 .... 14 D2
Deal CT14 .... 215 A4
Hayward Dr DA1 ....33 F4
Hayward's Cl TN28 .. 373 B6
Hayward's Hill ME13 169 C4

Hayward's Ho ME1 .... 63 C6
Haywood Rd BR2 ......52 D5
Haywood Rise BR6 .....86 E5
Hazard Ho ◘ DA1 .... 19 A1
Hazebrouck Rd ME13 138 A7
Hazel Ave
Hoo St Werburgh ME3 ...41 E3
Maidstone ME16 ..... 161 C5
Hazelbank TN3 ...... 284 F3
Hazel Cl CT5 .... 245 C7
Hazel Cotts TN14 ... 121 A6
Hazel Ct Birchington CT7 . 80 D8
Hersden CT3 .... 144 D8
Hazelden Cl TN15 .... 91 A2
Hazelden Cotts ME2 .. 39 C6
Hazeldene Chalet Pk
ME12 ....48 F5
Hazeldene Rd DA16 .. 13 C5
Hazelwood Cl CT17 .. 277 E6
Hazel Dr DA8 ....15 B6
Hazel End RH8 ...... 183 B3
Hazel Gr Chatham ME5 ..97 B8
Orpington BR6 ....86 B8
Sheerness ME12 .... 28 G1
Hazel Hts TN25 ..... 267 E5
Hazelmere Rd BR5 ... 53 D5
Hazelmere ◙ DA1 .... 31 A4
Hazelmere Way BR2 .. 52 A3
Hazel Rd Dartford DA1 .. 33 D6
Erith DA8 ....15 A6
Hazel Shaw TN10 ... 222 D7
Hazels The ME8 ...... 98 B5
Hazel Street Rd ME9 . 133 A4
Hazelview ME19 ..... 126 E3
Hazel Wlk
Broadstairs CT10 ..... 83 C4
Bromley BR2 ....53 A3
Hazelwood Cl TN2 .. 286 D8
Hazelwood Cotts TN5 338 D1
Hazelwood Dr ME16 .. 161 B4
Hazelwood Hts RH8 .. 183 A4
Hazelwood Mdw CT13 180 F7
Hazelwood Rd
Downe TN14 .... 119 D8
Oxted RH8 .... 183 B3
Hazelwood Sch RH8 .. 183 A4
Hazen Rd ME18 ..... 159 B3
Hazlemere Dr
Gillingham ME7 .... 65 A5
Herne Bay CT6 .... 77 D5
Hazlemere Rd CT5 ... 108 A7
Hazling Dane CT15 .. 244 F5
Hazlitt Ct ◙ SE28 .....3 C5
Hazlitt Dr ME16 ..... 161 D5
Headcorn Dr CT2 .... 143 B4
Headcorn Gdns CT9 ...51 E2
Headcorn Prim Sch
TN27 .... 262 C5
Headcorn Rd
Bromley BR1 .... 29 A3
Gillingham ME8 ....65 B4
Lashenden TN27 ..... 295 A5
Platt's Heath ME17 .. 198 F1
Smarden Bell TN27 .. 263 C3
Staplehurst TN12 .... 261 B4
Sutton Valence ME17 . 229 E4
Ulcombe ME17 ...... 230 F5
Headcorn Sta TN27 .. 262 D4
Head Hill ME13 ..... 139 D7
Head Hill Rd ME13 .. 139 D8
Headingley Rd ME16 .. 161 B6
Headley Cl TN8 ..... 217 C2
Headley Ho ◙ BR5 ....54 B7
Head Race The ME15 .. 161 D2
Healy Dr ◘ BR6 ....86 F6
Heansill La TN18 .... 354 E8
Heard Way ME10 .... 102 B5
Hearne Cl ME10 ..... 102 B5
Hearns Rd BR5 ...... 54 C5
Heartenoak Rd TN18 . 341 B3
Heart In Hand Cnr CT3 . 67 F2
Heart In Hand Rd CT6 ..77 F2
Heart's Delight La
CT3 .... 146 B3
Hearts Delight ME9 .. 101 B1
Hearts Delight Rd
ME9 .... 101 B1
Heath Ave DA7 ...... 13 D8
Heath Cl BR5 .... 54 C3
Heathclose Ave DA1 ...33 B8
Heathclose Rd DA1 ....33 B7
Heath Cl Sturry CT2 .. 143 F7
Swanley BR8 ....55 E7
Heathcote Cl ME20 .. 128 F2
Heath Ct
Horsmonden TN12 ... 289 F6
St Margaret's at Cliffe
CT15 .... 279 F6
Heathdene Dr DA17 ....4 B2
Heathend Rd DA5 .....32 E7
Heatherbank BR7 .... 53 A7
Heatherbank DA14 ....11 C1
Heatherbank Sch SE9 ..11 F5
Heather Bank TN12 .. 257 B6
Heather Cl Chatham ME5 . 94 F6
Margate CT9 ....82 C8
Newham E6 ....2 A7
Sittingbourne ME10 .. 102 A3
Heather Dr
Dartford DA1 .... 33 A8
Maidstone ME15 ..... 162 B2
Tenterden TN30 ...... 324 B3
Heather End BR8 ..... 55 D5
Heather Rd SE12 ......29 A7
Heatherside Rd DA14 .. 31 C5
Heathers The TN17 .. 320 A3
Heather Wlk TN10 .. 222 B6
Heatherwood Cl ME17 . 197 E2
Heathfield Ave
Dover CT16 .... 278 B2
Maidstone ME14 ..... 162 C7

Heathfield Bglws
ME17 .... 200 B1
Heathfield BR7 .... 30 C2
Heathfield Cl
Chatham ME5 ....97 B7
Maidstone ME14 ..... 162 B7
Newham E16 ....1 D8
Orpington BR2 .... 85 C5
Heathfield Ct DA14 ....31 B3
Heathfield La BR7 .... 30 C2
Heathfield ME17 ..... 196 E4
Heathfield Rd
Ashford TN24 .... 268 C3
Bexley DA6 ....13 F3
Maidstone ME14 ..... 162 C7
Orpington BR2 .... 85 D5
Sevenoaks TN13 ..... 153 F5
Heathfields TN2 ..... 286 D4
Heathfield Terr
Bexley SE18 ....12 F8
Swanley BR8 ....55 F7
Heathfield Way CT4 .. 242 F8
Heath Gdns DA1 ..... 33 C7
Heath Gr ME16 ...... 161 A2
Heath Ho CT3 .... 111 E5
Heath House DA15 .....30 F4
Heath La Dartford DA1 . 33 C7
Dartford DA1,DA2 .....33 B7
Heathlands Rise DA1 .. 15 B1
Heathlee Rd DA1 ..... 14 E1
Heathley End ME7 .... 30 C2
Heathorn St ME14 ... 162 B5
Heath Park Dr BR1 ....52 E6
Heath Rd Coldblow DA5 . 32 C7
Coxheath ME17 ...... 194 C3
Crayford DA1 ....14 F1
East Farleigh ME15 .. 193 E4
Langley Heath ME17 . 196 E4
Maidstone,Cock Street
ME17 .... 195 C2
Maidstone,East Barming
ME16 .... 160 F3
Heath Rise BR2 ...... 52 A3
Heathside TN26 ..... 347 C1
Heathside Ave
Bexley DA7 ....13 E5
Coxheath ME17 ...... 194 C4
Heath Side BR5 ...... 53 C2
Heath St DA1 .... 33 D8
Heath Terr TN12 .... 290 A6
Heath The
Appledore Heath TN26 . 347 C1
Well Street ME19 .... 159 F5
Whitstable CT5 ....75 B1
Heathview Ave DA1 ...14 E1
Heathview Cres DA1 ...33 B7
Heath View Dr SE2 .. 13 D8
Heathview TN4 ...... 253 F2
Heath Villas
Appledore Heath TN26 . 347 C2
Woolwich SE18 ....2 F1
Heath Way DA7,DA8 .. 14 D6
Heathway SE3 ....11 A7
Heathwood Dr CT11 ...83 E1
Heathwood Gdns
Swanley BR8 .... 55 C7
Woolwich SE7 ....1 E1
Heathwood Wlk DA5 .. 32 E7
Heaton Rd CT1 ...... 174 F6
Heaverham Rd TN15 . 123 C2
Heavitree Cl ◙ SE18 ...2 D1
Heavitree Rd SE18 .....2 D1
Hectorage Rd TN9 ... 254 D8
Hector St SE18 ....2 E2
Hedge Barton Trailer Pk
TN3 .... 283 F5
Hedgend Ind Est CT7 ..79 F3
Hedge Place Rd DA9 .. 17 F1
Hedgerows TN23 .... 299 D7
Hedgerows The DA11 ..36 E6
Hedgerow The ME14 . 162 E5
Hedges The ME14 ... 162 A7
Hedley Ave RM20 .... 17 C8
Hedley St ME14 ..... 162 A5
Heel La CT2 .... 143 C8
Heel Rd ME13 ...... 202 B7
Heights Terr CT17 .. 310 C6
Heights The
Greenwich SE7 ....1 C1
Whitstable CT5 .... 108 C6
Helding Cl CT6 ....77 B2
Helegan Cl BR6 ....86 F6
Helena Ave CT9 ....82 E8
Helena Corniche
CT20 .... 334 C3
Helen Allison Sch
DA13 .... 60 A2
Helena Rd CT18 .... 308 C2
Helena Villas CT21 .. 334 B3
Helen Cl DA1 ....33 B8
Helen Ct ◙ DA14 .....31 B4
Helen Keller Cl TN10 . 222 D4
Helen St SE18 ....2 C2
Helen Thompson Cl
ME9 ....68 E4
Hellyar Ct ME1 ...... 63 C4
Helmdon Cl CT12 ... 83 C2
Helvellyn Ave CT11 .. 117 B7
Hemmings Cl DA14 ...31 B6
Hempstead Inf Sch
ME7 .... 98 A5
Hempstead Jun Sch
ME7 .... 98 A5
Hempstead La ME9 .. 102 E3
Hempstead Rd
Gillingham ME7 .... 98 A5
Gillingham ME7,ME8 ...98 B6
Hempstead St ◘ TN23 268 B2
Hempton Hill TN25 .. 304 C5

Hemstead Forest Walks★
TN27 .... 322 A7
Hemstead Forest Walks★
.... 322 C5
Hemstead Forest Walks★
TN17 .... 321 E2
Hemsted Rd DA16 .... 14 E7
Henbane Cl ME14 ... 162 E5
Henderson Dr DA1 ... 16 A3
Henderson Rd TN16 . 118 C7
Hendley Dr TN17 .... 320 C5
Hendry Ho ME3 ....40 F6
Hendy Rd ME6 ...... 128 B8
Henfield Cl DA5 ...... 14 A1
Hengist Ave CT9 ......51 B1
Hengist Rd
Birchington CT7 ...... 80 C7
Deal CT14 .... 215 D7
Eltham SE12 ....29 B8
Erith DA8 ....14 C7
Westgate-on-S CT8 ... 81 D8
Westgate-on-S CT8 ... 81 E8
Hengrove Ct DA5 ......31 C7
Henham Gdns TN12 .. 225 A6
Henhurst Hill DA12 .. 60 D8
Henhurst Rd
Gravesend DA13 ....37 E1
Henhurst DA12 ....60 E8
Heniker La ME17 .... 230 A4
Henley Bsns Pk ME2 . 63 D7
Henley Cl Chatham ME5 . 97 A6
Gillingham ME8 .... 98 C8
Royal Tunbridge Wells
TN2 .... 286 C4
Henley Ct DA5 ....31 F8
Henley Deane DA11 .. 36 E4
Henley Fields
Maidstone ME14 ..... 162 E6
Tenterden TN30 ..... 324 B2
Henley Mdws TN30 .. 324 A2
Henley Rd Newham E16 ..1 F4
Paddock Wood TN12 . 257 A7
Henley St DA13 ....60 F3
Henley View TN30 ... 324 B2
Henniker Cl CT16 ... 278 A5
Henniker Cotts TN17 . 320 A3
Henry Addlington Cl SE6 . 2 B8
Henry Cooper Way SE9 . 29 D4
Henry Ct CT1 .... 174 F7
Henry St Bromley BR1 ..52 B8
Chatham ME4 ....64 B3
Gillingham ME8 .... 66 A1
◙ Grays RM17 .... 18 C8
Henson Cl BR6 ...... 86 B8
Henville Rd BR1 ......52 B8
Henwick Prim Sch SE9 . 11 E4
Henwick Rd SE9 ..... 11 E4
Henwood TN24 ..... 268 D3
Henwood Bsns Ctr
TN24 .... 268 D2
Henwood Green Rd
TN2 .... 287 E6
Henwoods Cres TN2 . 287 D6
Henwoods Mount
TN2 .... 287 E6
Herald Wlk DA1 ......15 F2
Herbert Dane Ct ◘
ME13 .... 138 D7
Herbert Pl SE18 ......12 B8
Herbert Rd
Ashford TN24 .... 300 D6
Bexley DA7 ....13 E5
Bromley BR2 ....52 E4
Chatham ME4 ....64 A3
Gillingham ME8 .... 65 D2
Hextable BR8 ....33 B2
Ramsgate CT11 ...... 117 C6
Swanscombe DA10 ....17 F1
Woolwich SE18 ....12 B8
Herbert St CT17 .... 278 B1
Herdsdown ME3 ...... 41 D5
Herdson Rd CT20 ... 335 A5
Hereford Cl
Ashford TN24 .... 268 C7
Gillingham ME8 ....65 D2
Hereford Gdns CT7 ...80 F6
Hereford Rd ME15 .. 195 D7
Hereson Rd CT11 ... 117 F8
Hereson Sch The CT10 . 84 A3
Hereward Ave CT7 ....80 E8
Heritage Cl CT5 ..... 108 A6
Heritage Ct CT11 ... 174 F8
Heritage Dr ME7 .....64 F1
Heritage Gdns CT16 . 310 E8
Heritage Hill BR2 .... 85 C5
Heritage Quay DA12 . 19 C1
Heritage Rd
Chatham ME5 ....97 A6
Folkestone CT20 .... 334 D6
Heritage The BR6 .... 54 A2
Herman Terr ME4 .... 64 A3
Hermitage Cl
Hythe CT21 .... 333 B2
Woolwich SE2 ....3 C3
Hermitage Cnr ME17 . 228 F6
Hermitage Ct
Maidstone ME16 ..... 160 F5
Tonbridge ME9 ...... 222 C2
Hermitage Farm
ME19 .... 159 C8
Hermitage La
Detling ME14 .... 131 B4
Maidstone ME16,ME20 . 160 F6
Rabbit's Cross ME17 .. 228 F6
Hermitage Rd ME3 ....39 E4
Hermitage The ME19 . 159 E8
Herne Ave CT6 ...... 77 A4
Herne Bay High Sch
CT6 ....76 D3
Herne Bay Inf Sch CT6 . 76 F4
Herne Bay Jun Sch
CT6 ....76 F4

Herne Bay Mus★ CT6 ..76 F5
Herne Bay Rd
Sturry CT3 .... 110 E2
Whitstable CT5 .... 75 C3
Herne Bay Sta CT6 ... 76 E3
Herne Bay West Ind Est
CT6 ....76 C3
Herne CE Inf Sch CT6 . 111 B8
Herne CE Jun Sch
CT6 .... 111 A8
Herne Ct CT19 ..... 334 C6
Herne Dr CT6 .... 76 C2
Herne Rd ME8 .... 65 C2
Herne St CT6 .... 111 A8
Herneville Gdns CT6 ...77 B4
Herne Windmill★ CT6 ..77 A4
Hernhill CE Prim Sch
ME13 .... 140 B7
Hern The TN15 ..... 157 C5
Hero Ho ME12 ....28 B2
Heron Apartments ◙
ME15 .... 195 F5
Heron Cl
Lower Halstow ME9 ...67 B3
Marlpit Hill CT18 .... 217 C3
Heron Cotts TN18 ... 357 D3
Heron Cres DA14 .... 30 E4
Heron Ct BR2 .... 52 C5
Heronden Rd
Eastry CT13 .... 179 F1
Maidstone ME15 ..... 195 F4
Heronden View CT13 . 180 A2
Heron Dr ME12 ......47 B5
Heron Forestall Ave
CT18 .... 307 B4
Herongate Rd BR8 ....32 E2
Heron Hill DA17 ....3 F2
Heron Hill La DA13 ... 93 A4
Heron Ho Ashford TN23 . 267 F1
Sidcup DA14 ....30 F4
Heron Lodge ◘ CT16 . 278 B2
Heron Rd ME20 ..... 127 F1
Heron's Brook TN25 . 269 E6
Herons Cl CT4 ...... 205 C8
Heronsgate Prim Sch
SE28 ....2 D3
Heron's Way CT21 .. 353 D8
Herons Way TN2 .... 287 E8
Heron Way
Chatham ME5 ....97 B7
Lower Stoke ME3 ..... 25 C4
Heron Wlk TN23 .... 299 E8
Hero Wlk ME1 .... 96 C7
Herringham Rd SE7 ....1 C3
Herschell Rd CT7 .....80 F8
Herschell Rd E CT14 . 215 C3
Herschell Rd W CT14 . 215 C3
Herschell Sq CT14 .. 215 C3
Hersden Com Prim Sch
CT3 .... 111 E1
Hertford Ct CT1 ..... 175 C8
Hertford Ho
Herne Bay CT6 .... 77 A5
◙ Ramsgate CT11 ... 117 E6
Hertford Pl CT11 .... 117 E6
Hertford Rd CT9 ..... 83 C8
Hertford St CT11 .... 117 E6
Herts Cres ME15 .... 194 F3
Hertsfield Ave ME2 .. 40 A2
Hertsfield Farm Cotts
TN12 .... 228 B4
Hervey Rd SE3 ....11 B6
Herying Cl ME2 ....95 B4
Hesketh Ave DA2 .....34 B7
Hesketh Pk TN2 .... 287 E6
Hestia Way TN23 ... 299 E5
Hever Ave TN15 ..... 90 E4
Hever Castle★ TN8 .. 250 D7
Hever CE Prim Sch
TN8 .... 250 D6
Hever Cl ME15 ...... 195 F6
Hever Court Rd DA12 . 37 D2
Hever Croft Eltham SE9 . 30 A4
Rochester ME2 ....62 F5
Hever Gdns
Bromley BR1 .... 53 A7
Maidstone ME16 ..... 161 E3
Heverham Rd DA7 ... 14 A6
Hever Ho ME2 .... 40 C1
Hever Pl
Canterbury CT2 ...... 143 A3
Sittingbourne ME10 .. 101 D3
Hever Rd
Bough Beech TN8 .... 218 D2
Hever TN8 .... 250 B7
West Kingsdown TN15 . 90 E4
Hever Road Cotts TN8 218 E2
Heversham Rd DA7 ... 14 A6
Hever Sta TN8 ...... 250 B6
Heverswood TN14 .... 88 A2
Hever Wood Rd TN15 . 90 E4
Hewett Ho ◘ SE18 ....2 A2
Hewett Pl BR8 .... 55 D5
Hewitt Cl Gillingham ME7 . 64 F6
Maidstone ME16 ..... 161 D1
Hewitt Rd ◘ CT16 .. 310 D8
Hewitts Pl TN24 .... 268 F1
Hewitts Rd BR6,TN14 ..87 F3
Hextable Cl
Ashford TN23 .... 299 F6
Maidstone ME16 ..... 161 D7
Hextable Inf Sch BR8 .. 32 E2
Hextable Jun Sch BR8 . 32 F2
Hextable Sch BR8 .....55 F8
Heyford Cl CT18 .... 307 B4
Hibbs Cl BR8 .... 55 D7
Hibernia Dr DA12 .... 37 F5
Hibernia Point ◘◘ SE2 .. 3 D4
Hibernia Rd ◙ CT11 . 117 E6
Hickin Cl SE7 .... 1 D2
Hickman Cl E16 ....1 D8
Hickory Dell ME7 .... 98 A5
Hicks Forstall Rd CT3 . 111 B5

Hide E6 2 A7
Higgins' La ME4 63 F5
Higham Cl ME15 161 E2
Higham Gdns TN10 222 F5
Higham La Bridge CT4 209 B8
Tonbridge TN10,TN11 222 F6
Higham Park & Gdns★ CT4 209 C8
Higham Prim Sch ME3 39 C5
Higham Rd Cliffe ME3 22 A4
Rochester ME3 40 C3
Higham School Rd TN10 222 E6
Higham Sta ME3 39 D6
Higham View ME14 129 E4
High Bank ME1 63 D2
Highbanks Cl DA16 13 B7
High Banks ME15 194 F5
High Beeches
Orpington BR6 87 A4
Royal Tunbridge Wells TN2 286 D6
Sidcup DA14 31 E3
Highberry ME19 127 E2
Highbrook Rd SE3 11 D4
High Brooms Ind Pk TN2 286 C8
High Brooms Rd TN4 286 C7
High Brooms Sta TN4 286 C7
Highbury Gdns CT12 83 B3
Highbury La TN30 345 A7
Highbury Pl TN5 336 F5
Highbury Wlk CT12 83 B2
Highcombe Cl SE9 29 E7
Highcombe SE7 11 B8
High Croft Cotts BR8 56 A5
Highcroft Gn ME15 195 F4
Highcroft Hall BR8 55 D1
Highcross Rd DA13 35 D2
High Cross Rd TN15 156 B1
High Dewar Rd ME8 99 A8
Highdown Cotts TN17 317 F3
High Elms Ctry Pk★ BR6 86 D3
High Elms ME8 65 E1
High Elms Rd BR6 86 C2
Highfield Ave Erith DA8 14 B8
Orpington BR6 86 F5
Highfield Cl
Gillingham ME8 98 D7
Hawkhurst TN18 341 A1
Hythe CT21 333 A4
Pembury TN2 287 D6
Ramsgate CT12 83 B3
Rough Common CT2 142 B3
Highfield Cotts DA2 33 B2
Highfield Ct
Dartford DA1 33 D8
Herne Bay CT6 76 E4
5 Margate CT9 51 B2
Ramsgate CT12 83 B2
Highfield Gdns CT9 50 H1
Highfield Ind Est CT19 335 F6
Highfield La TN24, TN25 301 C6
Highfield Rd
Ashford TN24 301 A8
Bexley DA6 13 F2
Biggin Hill TN16 118 C3
Bromley BR1 52 F5
Dartford DA1 33 D8
Gillingham ME8 98 D7
Halfway Houses ME12 46 E6
Kemsing TN15 122 F3
Highfield Rd N DA1 15 D1
Highfield Rd
Ramsgate CT12 83 B3
Royal Tunbridge Wells TN4 286 C7
St Paul's Cray BR7 53 F6
Highfield Rd S DA1 33 D7
Highfields Ave CT6 77 D4
Highfields Rd TN8 217 C4
Highfields View CT6 77 C4
High Firs Prim Sch BR8 55 F5
High Firs BR8 55 E5
Highgate Ct 8 TN18 340 F2
Highgate Hill TN18 340 F1
Highgate Rd CT5 75 B1
High Gr BR1 52 D8
Highgrove Cl BR7 52 E8
Highgrove Rd ME5 97 A5
Highgrove TN2 314 A8
High Gr SE18 12 D6
High Halden CE Prim Sch TN26 324 E7
High Halden Rd TN26, TN27 295 C2
High Halstow Prim Sch ME23 23 E3
High Hilden Cl TN10 222 A4
High House La TN11 190 C2
High Knocke TN29 366 B6
Highland Cl CT20 334 F4
Highland Rd
Badgers Mount TN14 121 B8
Bexley DA6 14 A3
Chartham CT4 173 D1
Maidstone ME15 195 E6
Highlands Cl ME2 62 D5
Highlands Cres TN29 366 A4
Highlands DA1 33 C8
Highlands Glade CT12 82 E1
Highlands Hill BR8 56 A8
Highlands Pk TN15 154 E6
Highlands Rd BR5 54 C2
Highlands TN2 286 D7
High Mdw CT17 278 C1
Highmead SE18 12 F7
High Meads Rd E16 1 D7
High Minnis CT4 272 F8
High Oak Hill ME9 100 D8
Highpoint TN24 268 D3
High Point SE9 30 B5
High Rd DA2 33 C5
High Ridge TN23 299 C7
Highridge Cl ME14 162 F5
Highridge ME7 64 F1
High Ridge TN17 318 E8
Highridge CT21 334 A3
High Rocks La TN3, TN4 285 C1
High Rocks★ TN3 285 B1
High Rocks Sta★ TN3 285 B1
High St The TN27 234 C7
High Snoad Wood TN25 203 A1
High St Ashford TN23 268 C2
Aylesford ME20 128 F3
Bean DA2 35 B5
Bidborough TN3 253 C3
Biddenden TN27 294 F1
Borough Green TN15 156 F7
Brasted TN14,TN16 152 C3
Brenchley TN12 289 B8
Bridge CT4 176 A1
Broadstairs CT10 83 E5
Broadstairs,St Peter's CT10 84 A4
Bromley BR1 52 A6
Bromley BR1 52 A7
Brookland TN29 370 E8
Canterbury CT1 174 F8
8 Canterbury,Northgate CT1 143 A1
Chatham ME4 64 A4
Chatham ME7 64 A6
Cowden TN8 282 B5
Cranbrook TN17 320 C4
Dartford DA1 15 E1
Deal CT14 215 D6
Dover CT16 310 C8
Downe BR6 119 A8
Dymchurch TN29 366 C8
Highstead Cres DA8 14 E7
High St Eastchurch ME12 48 D3
East Malling ME19 160 A6
Eastry CT13 180 B2
Edenbridge TN8 217 C1
Highsted Gram Sch ME10 101 F2
Highsted Rd ME9, ME10 101 F1
High St Elham CT4 273 F5
Eynsford DA4 89 E8
Farningham DA4 56 F2
Flimwell TN5 339 C3
Fordwich CT2 144 A4
Frant TN3 314 C4
Gillingham ME7 64 C5
Gillingham,Rainham ME8 98 F8
Goudhurst TN17 318 E8
Grain ME3 27 B6
Gravesend DA11 19 B1
2 Grays RM17 18 A8
Hadlow TN11 223 E8
Halling ME2 95 A4
Hawkhurst TN18 340 E2
Headcorn TN27 262 C5
Herne Bay CT6 76 F5
Hythe CT21 333 C2
Kemsing TN15 123 B2
Lamberhurst TN3 317 B5
Leigh TN11 220 F1
Lenham ME17 199 D5
Limpsfield RH8 183 B7
Littlebourne CT3 176 F7
Lower Stoke ME3 25 C4
Lydd TN29 376 C6
Lyminge CT18 305 C6
Maidstone ME14 161 F4
Manston CT12 116 D8
Marden TN12 259 D6
Margate CT9 50 I2
Margate,Garlinge CT9 82 B7
Minster (Sheppey) ME12 47 D6
Minster (Thanet) CT12 115 C6
Newington ME9 100 C6
New Romney TN28 373 B6
Northfleet DA11 18 C1
Orpington,Broom Hill BR6 54 A1
Orpington,Farnborough BR6 86 C5
Orpington,Green Street Green BR6 86 F4
Orpington,St Mary Cray BR5 54 C4
Otford TN14 122 A3
Pembury TN2 287 C6
Penshurst TN11 252 B4
Queenborough ME11 45 F5
Ramsgate CT11 117 E7
Highstreet Rd
Waterham ME13 107 D2
Yorkletts CT5,ME13 107 E2
High Street St Lawrence CT11 117 B7
High St Rochester ME1 63 C6
Rochester,Strood ME2 63 B7
Rochester,Upper Upnor ME2 40 F1
Rolvenden TN17 343 E4
Royal Tunbridge Wells TN1 286 A2
Rusthall TN4 285 C4
St Margaret's at Cliffe CT15 279 F6
Sandwich CT13 149 A1
Seal TN15 154 F6
Sevenoaks,Chipstead TN13 153 C5
Sevenoaks TN13 154 C2
Sheerness,Blue Town ME12 28 A3
High St *continued*
Sheerness ME12 28 C2
Shoreham TN14 88 F1
Sidcup DA14 31 A4
Sittingbourne ME10 101 F4
Sittingbourne,Milton Regis ME10 101 E6
Snodland ME6 128 A8
Staplehurst TN12 260 F3
Sturry CT2 143 F5
Sutton Valence ME17 229 E7
Swanley BR8 55 F5
Swanscombe DA10 17 F2
Swanscombe,Greenhithe DA9 17 B3
Temple Ewell CT16 277 D5
Tenterden TN30 345 A7
Ticehurst TN5 338 C1
Tonbridge TN9 222 C2
Wadhurst TN5 336 F4
Westerham TN16 184 C8
West Malling ME19 159 C8
Whitstable CT5 74 D2
Wingham CT3 178 A8
Wouldham ME1 95 C5
Wrotham TN15 125 A3
Wye TN25 237 E2
Yalding ME18 192 F1
High Tor Cl BR1 29 B1
High Tor View SE28 2 E5
High Trees Cl TN24 301 A8
High Trees DA2 16 B1
High View Ave CT6 76 B5
Highview Cl
Boughton Street ME13 140 B3
Loose ME15 195 A8
Highview Dr ME5 96 D5
High View ME3 39 C4
Highview Pk Cvn Pk CT18 335 G8
Highview Rd
Minster (Sheppey) ME12 47 C7
Sidcup DA14 31 B4
Highview Sch CT19 335 D6
Highview
Vigo Village DA13 126 B8
Woolwich SE18 12 B7
Highway Prim Sch The BR6 87 C5
Highway The BR6 87 C5
Highwood Cl BR6 86 C8
Highwood Dr BR6 86 C8
Highwoods Cl ME3 39 C4
High Woods La TN3 287 B3
Highworth Gram Sch for Girls TN24 268 A3
Hilary Cl Bexley DA8 14 C6
Herne Bay CT6 77 C4
Hilary Gdns ME1 62 F2
Hilbert Cl TN2 286 C5
Hilbert Rd TN2 286 C5
Hilborough Way BR6 86 D5
Hilda May Ave BR8 55 E7
Hilda Rd Chatham ME4 64 A3
Halfway Houses ME12 46 D6
Hilda Vale Cl BR6 86 A6
Hilda Vale Rd BR6 86 B6
Hilden Ave TN11 221 F4
Hildenborough CE Prim Sch TN11 221 D6
Hildenborough Cres ME16 161 C7
Hildenborough Rd
Leigh TN11 221 A3
Shipbourne TN11,TN15 188 E4
Hildenborough Sta TN11 221 B6
Hildenbrook Farm TN11 188 E2
Hilden Dr DA8 15 B7
Hildenfields TN10 222 A4
Hilden Grange Sch TN10 222 B3
Hilden Oaks Sch TN10 222 B3
Hilden Park Rd TN11 221 F4
Hilders Cl TN8 217 B4
Hildersham Cl CT10 83 E5
Hilders La TN8 217 A4
Hillary Ave DA11 36 E5
Hillary Ct SE9 29 E6
Hillary Rd ME14 162 A7
Hill Ave CT15 244 E5
Hillborough Ave TN13 154 D5
Hillborough Bsns Pk CT6 77 F4
Hillborough Dr CT6 77 F5
Hillborough Gr ME5 97 A3
Hillborough Rd CT6 77 B5
Hillbrow Ave
Herne Bay CT6 77 B2
Sturry CT2 143 F7
Hill Brow BR1 52 D8
Hillbrow Cl DA5 32 D4
Hill Brow DA1 14 F1
Hillbrow La TN23 267 F1
Hill Brow ME14 163 A5
Hillbrow Rd
Ashford TN23 268 A1
Ramsgate CT11 117 D8
Hill Brow ME10 101 D2
Hillbury Gdns TN5 338 D1
Hill Chase ME5 96 E3
Hill Cl Chislehurst BR7 30 B3
Istead Rise DA13 36 E1
Hill Cres Aylesham CT3 210 E5
Coldblow DA5 32 C7
Lenham ME17 199 D5
Hillcrest TN23 299 B8
Hillcrest Ave RM20 17 A8
Hillcrest Cl TN24 268 E6
Hillcrest Dr Cuxton ME2 62 C2
Royal Tunbridge Wells TN2 286 D7
Hillcrest Dr *continued*
Stone DA9 17 A2
Hillcrest TN8 218 B5
Hillcrest Gdns
Deal CT14 215 A2
Ramsgate CT11 117 B6
Hillcrest Rd
Biggin Hill TN16 118 D3
Bromley BR1 29 A4
Chatham ME4 63 F2
Dartford DA1 32 F8
Hythe CT21 333 B3
Kingsdown CT14 248 D4
Littlebourne CT3 176 E8
Marlpit Hill TN8 217 C4
Orpington BR6 87 A8
Hill Crest
Royal Tunbridge Wells TN4 286 B8
Sevenoaks TN13 154 A5
Sidcup DA15 31 B8
Hillcroft DA4 89 D7
Hillcroft Rd
Herne Bay CT6 77 B3
Newham E6 2 B8
Hill Ct Charing TN27 201 E1
Chattenden ME3 40 F4
Hillden Shaw ME15 195 A8
Hilldown Lodge BR6 87 B8
Hill Dr CT13 180 B3
Hilldrop Rd BR1 29 B2
Hill End Orpington BR6 86 F8
Woolwich SE18 12 A6
Hiller Cl CT10 84 A6
Hill Farm Cl ME23 23 E3
Hillfield Rd TN13 153 E7
Hillfield Villas TN26 324 F8
Hillgarth TN4 286 A8
Hill Green Rd ME9 132 D8
Hill House Dr CT12 115 C7
Hill House Rd DA2 34 C8
Hillingdale TN16 118 B1
Hillingdon Ave TN13 154 D6
Hillingdon Rd
Bexley DA7 14 C4
Gravesend DA11 37 B6
Hillingdon Rise TN13 154 D5
Hill La CT18 306 B1
Hillman Ave CT6 76 A4
Hill Rd Dartford DA2 33 E6
Folkestone CT19 335 E8
Folkestone,Foord CT19 335 E7
Rochester ME1 63 A2
Wouldham ME1 95 F5
Hillreach SE18 1 F1
Hill Rise Ashford TN25 267 E5
Dartford DA2 34 E3
Hill Sch The TN16 151 B4
Hillsgrove Cl DA16 13 C7
Hillsgrove Prim Sch DA16 13 C7
Hillshaw Cres ME2 62 D5
Hill Shaw DA3 58 F3
Hillside Ave
Canterbury CT2 142 C2
Gravesend DA12 37 D6
Rochester ME2 63 B8
Rushenden ME11 45 F3
Hillside Cotts
Newbury's TN5 337 B8
Wingham CT3 146 A1
Hillside Ct Hythe CT21 333 C2
2 Rochester ME2 63 A7
Swanley BR8 56 A5
Wateringbury ME18 192 E7
Hillside DA2 34 E3
Hillside Dr DA12 37 D6
Hillside Erith DA17 4 C2
Farningham DA4 56 F2
1 Folkestone CT20 334 E3
Hillside Ind Est CT20 334 E4
Hillside La BR2 85 A8
Hillside Prim Sch BR5 54 C2
Hillside Rd
Chatham ME4 64 A4
Dartford DA1 15 A1
Dover CT17 278 A2
Kemsing TN15 122 F2
Minster (Sheppey) ME12 47 B7
Sevenoaks TN13 154 D4
Stalisfield Green ME13 201 E6
Tatsfield TN16 150 E8
Whitstable CT5 75 A1
Hillside ME1 63 A2
Hillside St CT21 333 C2
Hillside Terr DA12 37 B7
Hillside The BR6 87 B2
Hillside TN9 254 A7
Hills La TN15 123 C7
Hillsley Ct 13 DA14 31 A4
Hill's Terr ME4 63 F3
Hillstone Ct 5 CT16 310 E8
Hill St TN1 286 B5
Hill The Charing TN27 234 D8
Cranbrook TN17 320 D4
Littlebourne CT3 176 F8
Northfleet DA11 18 C1
Hill Top Cotts ME17 194 E2
Hilltop Gdns
Dartford DA1 15 F2
Orpington BR6 86 E8
Hilltop Ho CT2 142 C3
Hill Top TN17 291 E5
Hilltop Prim Sch ME2 40 C1
Hill Top Rd CT6 77 B5
Hilltop Rd
Minster (Sheppey) ME12 47 A5
Rochester ME2 40 C1
West Thurrock RM20 17 B8
Hilltop Tonbridge TN9 254 B7
West Farleigh ME15 193 D3
Whitstable CT5 108 D7
Hill View Ashford TN24 268 C3
Hill View *continued*
Basted TN15 156 F4
Borough Green TN15 157 A7
Hill View Cl TN15 157 A7
Hillview Cres BR6 53 F1
Hill View Ct CT4 209 E2
Hill View Dr
Bexley DA16 12 E5
Woolwich SE28 2 E5
Hillview Ho DA12 37 C7
Hill View CT9 82 D7
Hillview Rd
Canterbury CT2 142 C2
Eltham BR7 30 A4
Hill View Rd
New Barn DA3 59 B6
Orpington BR6 86 F8
Rusthall TN4 285 C4
Tonbridge TN11 221 F5
Hillview Rd CT5 108 D8
Hillview Sch for Girls TN9 254 D8
Hill View Terr CT18 305 D3
Hill View Way ME5 96 E5
Hillydeal Rd TN14 122 C4
Hillyfield Cl ME2 39 F1
Hillyfield Rd TN23 300 A8
Hillyfields Rise TN23 268 A1
Hilton Bsns Ctr TN23 300 B6
Hilton Cl ME13 138 D6
Hilton Dr ME10 101 B6
Hilton Rd Ashford TN23 267 F2
Cliffe Woods ME3 40 B7
Hinchliffe Way CT9 83 D8
Hind Cl TN29 366 C8
Hind Cres DA8 14 D7
Hinde Cl ME10 101 F7
Hinde Ho ME10 101 E6
Hines Terr ME5 64 C1
Hinksden Rd TN17, TN18 341 F3
Hinksey Path SE2 3 D3
Hinstock Rd SE18 12 C7
Hinton Cl SE9 29 E7
Hinton Cres ME7 98 A6
Hinxhill Rd TN24,TN25 269 D1
Hirst Cl CT16 278 B4
Historic Dockyard The★ ME4 64 A8
Hitchen Hatch La TN13 154 B4
Hither Chantlers TN3 285 A2
Hither Farm Rd SE3 11 C4
Hither Field TN27 234 C7
Hive La DA11 18 B2
Hive The DA11 18 B2
Hoades Wood Rd CT2 144 A7
Hoad Rd CT15,CT18 275 A2
Hoads Wood Gdns TN25 267 E6
Hoath Cl ME8 98 B7
Hoath Farm The CT3 175 F7
Hoath La ME8 98 B7
Hoath Mdw TN12 290 A6
Hoath Prim Sch CT3 111 E5
Hoath Rd CT3 111 C3
Hoath Way ME7,ME8 98 B5
Hobart Cres CT16 278 C3
Hobart Gdns ME10 101 C4
Hobart Rd
Ramsgate CT12 83 A1
Tilbury RM18 19 A6
Hoblands End BR7 30 E2
Hockenden La BR8 55 B7
Hockeredge Gdns CT8 81 F8
Hockers Cl ME14 163 A8
Hockers La ME14 163 A8
Hoddesdon Rd DA17 4 A1
Hodge's Gap CT9 51 C3
Hodgkins Cl SE28 3 D6
Hodgson Cres ME6 95 A1
Hodgson Rd CT5 107 F7
Hodsoll Ct BR5 54 D4
Hodsoll St TN15 92 D1
Hodson Cres BR5 54 D3
Hogarth Cl
Herne Bay CT6 77 E5
Newham E16 1 D8
Hogarth Ho ME11 45 F5
Hogbarn La ME17 165 F2
Hogben Cl CT18 305 B7
Hogben's Hill ME13 171 A6
Hogbrook Hill La CT15 308 D8
Hogg La CT4 207 E2
Hog Gn CT4 273 F4
Hog Hill ME14 163 B5
Hog Hole La TN3 316 F2
Hog La DA11 36 D5
Hognore La TN15 125 D6
Hogpound Cnr TN30 360 B6
Hogs Orch BR8 56 B8
Hogtrough Hill TN16 152 A5
Holbeach Gdns DA15 12 F1
Holbeam Rd ME13 169 A1
Holborn La ME4 63 F5
Holborn Rd E13 1 B8
Holborough Rd ME6 95 A1
Holbourn Cl CT6 111 B8
Holbrook Dr CT12 83 B1
Holbrook Ho BR7 53 D8
Holbrook La BR7 30 D1
Holbrook Way BR2 52 F4
Holburne Cl SE3 11 C6
Holburne Gdns SE3 11 D6
Holburne Rd SE3 11 D6
Holcombe Cl TN16 151 D1
Holcombe Rd
Chatham ME4 63 F2
Rochester ME1 63 C3
Holcote Cl DA17 3 E3
Holden Cnr TN4 253 F1
Holdenhurst TN23 299 E6
Holden Park Rd TN4 286 A8
Holden Rd TN4 253 F1
Holder Cl ME5 97 C6
Holding St ME8 65 F1
Hole La TN8 217 A6
Holford St 1 TN9 222 B1
Holgate St SE7 1 D3
Hollandbury Pk ME18 159 C2
Holland Cl
Broadstairs CT10 51 G2
Sheerness ME12 28 B1
Holland Cres RH8 183 A2
Holland Ho ME1 63 D5
Holland Jun Sch RH8 183 A1
Holland La RH8 183 A2
Holland Rd
Chatham ME5 96 E4
Maidstone ME14 162 B5
Oxted RH8 183 A1
Hollands Ave CT19 335 F7
Hollands Cl DA12 38 E3
Hollicondane Rd CT11 117 E8
Hollies Ave DA15 30 F7
Hollies The
Gravesend DA12 37 D2
New Barn DA3 59 C6
Sidcup DA15 31 A8
Holligrave Rd BR1 52 A8
Hollin Cl TN4 285 F4
Hollingbourne Ave DA7 13 F6
Hollingbourne Hill ME17 164 F4
Hollingbourne Prim Sch ME17 164 E2
Hollingbourne Rd ME8 65 C2
Hollingbourne Sta ME17 164 C3
Hollingbourne Tower 4 BR5 54 D1
Hollington Ct BR7 30 B2
Hollington Pl TN24 268 B3
Hollingworth Ct ME14 162 C3
Hollingworth Rd
Maidstone ME15 195 F5
Orpington BR2,BR5 53 B2
Hollingworth Way TN16 151 D1
Hollow La
Canterbury CT1 174 E5
Hartlip ME9 99 E5
Snodland ME6 127 F6
Hollowmede CT1 174 E6
Hollow Rd CT3 112 B6
Hollow St CT3 112 C5
Hollow Trees Dr TN11 221 A1
Hollow Wood Rd CT17 309 E8
Holly Bank TN12 289 B8
Hollybank Hill ME10 101 D4
Hollybrake Cl BR7 30 D1
Hollybush Cl TN13 154 C3
Hollybush Cnr CT4 177 A3
Hollybush Ct TN13 154 C3
Hollybush La BR6 88 A4
Holly Bush La TN13 154 C3
Hollybush La CT3 145 A4
Hollybush Rd DA12 37 C6
Holly Cl
Broadstairs CT10 83 C4
Chatham ME5 97 C8
Eastry CT13 180 B2
Folkestone CT19 335 E7
Gillingham ME7 64 E6
Hythe CT21 333 D3
Holly Cotts TN8 217 B2
Hollycroft ME2 62 C2
Holly Ct 1 DA14 31 B4
Hollydale Dr BR2 85 F7
Hollydene Rd TN5 336 F6
Holly Farm Rd ME15 196 C6
Holly Gdns Bexley DA7 14 C3
Maidstone ME14 162 B7
Margate CT9 51 C2
Holly Hill DA13 93 F3
Holly Hill Rd
Erith DA8,DA17 4 B1
Hernhill ME13 140 D5
Holly La CT9 51 C2
Holly Mdws TN23 267 D3
Holly Rd Dartford DA1 33 D7
Orpington BR6 87 A3
Ramsgate CT11 117 E8
Rochester ME2 40 D2
Rochester,Strood ME2 62 E5
St Mary's Bay TN29 365 F4
Hollyshaw Cl TN2 286 C2
Hollyshaw TN2 286 C2
Hollytree Ave BR8 55 E7
Holly Tree Cl ME17 197 E2
Hollytree Dr ME3 39 B3
Hollytree Par DA14 31 C2
Hollywood La
Knockmill TN15 123 F8
Rochester ME2 40 C2
Hollywood Way DA8 15 B6
Holman Mews CT1 175 A7
Holmbury Manor 21 DA14 31 A4
Holmbury Pk BR7 29 E1
Holmcroft Way BR2 52 F4
Holm Ct 5 SE12 29 B5
Holmdale Rd BR7 30 C3
Holmden Ct 2 TN8 217 C1
Holmdene Ct 5 BR1 52 E6
Holme Oak Cl CT1 174 F6
Holmes Cl ME23 23 E3
Holmes Ct
5 Canterbury CT1 175 B8
Ryarsh ME19 126 F4

Holmesdale Cl
Durgates TN5 ... 336 E5
Maidstone ME15 ... 194 F3
Holmesdale Hill DA4 ... 57 D8
Holmesdale Rd
Bexley DA7 ... 13 D5
Sevenoaks TN13 ... 154 D4
Sutton at H DA4 ... 57 C8
Holmesdale Tech Coll ME6 ... 127 F7
Holmesdale Terr 14 CT20 ... 335 D4
Holmestone Rd CT17 ... 277 E1
Holmes Way CT12 ... 83 A3
Holmewood House Sch TN3 ... 285 A2
Holmewood Rd TN4 ... 286 C7
Holmewood Ridge TN3 ... 284 F3
Holmhurst Cl TN4 ... 285 F4
Holmhurst Rd DA17 ... 4 B1
Holmlea Cl TN24 ... 268 E1
Holmleigh Ave DA1 ... 15 C2
Holm Mill La ME17 ... 198 B6
Holm Oak Gdns CT10 ... 83 F4
Holmoaks
Gillingham ME8 ... 65 E2
Maidstone ME14 ... 162 C5
Holmscroft Rd CT6 ... 77 D5
Holmsdale Gr DA1,DA7 ... 14 E4
Holmside Ave ME12 ... 46 D6
Holmside ME7 ... 64 E3
Holm Wlk SE3 ... 11 A5
Holmwood Cotts BR6 ... 87 C1
Holmwood Ct DA14 ... 30 F3
Holmwood Rd TN23 ... 299 E7
Holness Rd CT3 ... 147 D2
Holstein Way 6 DA18 ... 3 E3
Holt Cl SE28 ... 3 C6
Holters Mews 13 CT1 ... 175 A8
Holters Mill CT2 ... 142 F2
Holton Cl CT7 ... 81 A6
Holt Rd E16 ... 1 E5
Holt St CT15 ... 211 C4
Holt Wood Ave ME20 ... 160 E8
Holtwood Cl ME8 ... 98 D6
Holtye Cres ME15 ... 162 B2
Holtye Rd RH19 ... 281 A4
Holwood Park Ave BR2, BR4 ... 85 F6
Holy Family RC Prim Sch
Eltham SE3 ... 11 C3
Maidstone ME15 ... 195 F4
Holyhead Cl 3 E6 ... 1 F8
Holy Innocents RC Prim Sch BR6 ... 86 F7
Holyoake Terr TN13 ... 154 A3
Holyrood Dr ME12 ... 47 A5
Holyrood Mews E16 ... 1 A5
Holy Trinity CE Prim Sch
Broadstairs CT10 ... 84 A1
Dartford DA1 ... 15 C2
Gravesend DA12 ... 37 C8
Holy Trinity Coll Prep Sch BR1 ... 52 C8
Holy Trinity Lamorbey CE Prim Sch DA15 ... 31 A7
Holy Trinity & St John's CE Prim Sch CT9 ... 50 J2
Holywell Ave CT19 ... 335 D8
Holywell Cl
Greenwich SE3 ... 11 A8
Orpington BR6 ... 87 A6
Holywell Ho CT19 ... 335 D8
Holywell La ME9 ... 66 F2
Holywell Prim Sch ME9 ... 66 F3
Homebirch Ho 6 CT7 ... 80 F8
Homedean Rd TN13 ... 153 C4
Home Farm BR6 ... 88 A5
Home Farm Cl TN11 ... 221 A3
Home Farm Cotts
East Studdal CT14 ... 213 E6
Orpington BR5 ... 54 D8
Home Farm Ct TN3 ... 314 C4
Homefarm Est ME20 ... 128 F1
Home Farm La TN2 ... 286 E8
Homefern Ho CT9 ... 50 I3
Homefield Ave CT14 ... 215 B6
Homefield Cl
Orpington BR5 ... 54 B5
Swanley BR8 ... 55 F6
Homefield Dr ME8 ... 66 B2
Homefield Rd
Bromley BR1 ... 52 C8
Sevenoaks TN13 ... 153 E5
Homefield Rise BR6 ... 54 A1
Homefield Row CT14 ... 215 B6
Homefleet Ho 13 CT11 ... 117 F7
Home Gdns DA1 ... 15 E1
Home Hill BR8 ... 32 F1
Homelands Cl TN25 ... 303 E1
Home Lea BR6 ... 86 F5
Homeleigh Rd CT12 ... 83 B3
Home Mead Cl 6 DA12 ... 37 B8
Homemead 7 DA12 ... 37 B8
Homemead Rd BR2 ... 52 F4
Homemead DA9 ... 17 B1
Homepeak Ho 12 CT21 ... 333 B2
Homepine Ho 8 CT20 ... 335 C4
Home Pk RH8 ... 183 A4
Homer Cl DA7 ... 14 C6
Homersham CT1 ... 174 D6
Homesdale Bsns Ctr BR1 ... 52 D6
Homesdale Rd
Bromley BR1,BR2 ... 52 C6
Orpington BR5 ... 53 E2
Homeside Farm CT4 ... 240 F6
Homespire Ho 19 CT1 ... 143 A1
Homestall Ct CT2 ... 142 C4
Homestall La ME13 ... 139 B5
Homestall Rd ME9 ... 136 D3
Homestead TN23 ... 299 D8
Homestead Cl 7 CT9 ... 50 J1
Homestead Ct CT14 ... 215 A4
Homestead La CT15 ... 246 C7
Homestead Rd
Marlpit Hill TN8 ... 217 B5
Orpington BR6 ... 87 B4
Homestead The
Crayford DA1 ... 14 E2
Dartford DA1 ... 15 C1
Groombridge TN3 ... 312 C7
Homestead View ME9 ... 101 B2
Homestead Village CT11 ... 117 C5
Homevale Cotts TN14 ... 120 E4
Homevale Ho 3 CT20 ... 334 E3
Homeview 3 ME10 ... 102 B4
Homeview Terr 2 ME10 ... 102 B4
Homewards Rd ME3 ... 9 B2
Homewood Ave ME10 ... 101 D3
Homewood Cotts DA12 ... 38 E1
Homewood Cres BR7 ... 30 E2
Homewood Inf Sch ME10 ... 101 D4
Homewood Rd
Langton Green TN3 ... 284 F3
Sturry CT2 ... 144 A6
Tenterden TN30 ... 324 B1
Homewood Sch & Sixth Form Ctr TN30 ... 324 B1
Homlesdale Bsns Ctr TN15 ... 157 C8
Homoeopathic Hospl TN1 ... 286 A3
Honduras Terr 8 ME14 ... 162 A7
Hone St ME2 ... 63 B8
Honeyball Wlk ME9 ... 103 C2
Honey Bee Glade ME8 ... 98 E6
Honeybourne Way BR5 ... 53 D1
Honey Cl ME7 ... 98 A5
Honeycombe Lodge DA11 ... 18 D1
Honeycrest Ind Pk TN12 ... 260 E5
Honeycrock Hill ME9 ... 132 F8
Honeyden Rd DA14 ... 31 E2
Honeyfield TN23 ... 267 E1
Honey Hill CT2,CT5 ... 141 F8
Honey La ME15 ... 196 B6
Honeypot Cl ME2 ... 63 B8
Honeypot La
Hodsoll Street TN15 ... 92 D2
Kemsing TN15 ... 155 C8
Limpsfield TN8 ... 216 D4
Honeysuckle Cl
3 Chatham ME5 ... 96 E4
Gillingham ME7 ... 97 F4
Margate CT9 ... 82 C8
Honeysuckle Ct
4 Lewisham SE12 ... 29 A8
Sittingbourne ME10 ... 102 B5
Honeysuckle Rd CT11 ... 117 F8
Honeysuckle Way CT6 ... 77 D2
Honeywood Cl
Canterbury CT1 ... 143 B2
Dover CT16 ... 278 A6
Lympne CT21 ... 332 A4
Honeywood Ho CT16 ... 278 A6
Honeywood Parkway CT16 ... 278 B5
Honeywood Rd CT16 ... 278 A6
Honfleur Rd CT13 ... 180 F8
Honiton House Sch CT9 ... 51 A3
Honiton Rd DA16 ... 12 F5
Honner Cl CT18 ... 306 F3
Honywood Rd ME17 ... 199 C4
Hoo Comm ME3 ... 41 A4
Hood Ave BR5 ... 54 B4
Hoo Farm CT12 ... 114 F6
Hook Cl Chatham ME5 ... 96 E5
Folkestone CT20 ... 334 F5
Hook Farm Rd BR2 ... 52 D4
Hookfields DA11 ... 36 E5
Hook Green Ct DA13 ... 60 A4
Hook Green La DA2 ... 32 F5
Hook Green Rd DA13 ... 35 F1
Hook Hill TN5 ... 338 A6
Hook La Bexley DA16 ... 13 A4
Brookland TN29 ... 370 C6
Charing TN27 ... 234 A7
Harrietsham ME17 ... 198 C6
Hook Lane Prim Sch DA16 ... 13 A4
Hook Place Cotts DA13 ... 36 A2
Hook Rd ME6 ... 127 F8
Hookstead TN26 ... 324 C7
Hook Wall TN29 ... 370 E5
Hookwood Bglws RH8 ... 183 B7
Hookwood Cnr RH8 ... 183 B7
Hookwood Cotts TN14 ... 120 C8
Hookwood Rd BR6, TN14 ... 120 C7
Hooper Rd E16 ... 1 A7
Hoopers La
Herne Bay CT6 ... 77 D3
St Mary Hoo ME3 ... 24 F5
Hooper's Pl ME1 ... 63 C4
Hooper's Rd ME1 ... 63 C4
Hoopers Yd TN13 ... 154 C1
Hoo Rd ME2,ME3 ... 40 D3
Hoo St Werburgh Prim Sch ME3 ... 41 D5
Hop Bine Cl TN12 ... 225 A7
Hope Ave TN11 ... 190 E1
Hope Cl SE12 ... 29 B5
Hope Cotts DA2 ... 35 B6
Hopedale Rd SE7 ... 11 B8
Hopehouse La TN17, TN18 ... 356 E7
Hope La
New Romney TN28 ... 373 A8
St Mary in the Marsh TN29 ... 364 F2
Hope Rd Deal CT14 ... 215 D5
Swanscombe DA10 ... 17 F1
Hopes Gr TN26 ... 324 D7
Hope's La CT12 ... 83 C3
Hope St Chatham ME4 ... 64 A3
Maidstone ME14 ... 161 F6
Sheerness ME12 ... 28 B2
Hope Terr ME3 ... 39 D7
Hope Villas CT1 ... 174 D6
Hopeville Ave CT10 ... 83 E6
Hopewell Bsns Ctr ME5 ... 97 C8
Hopewell Dr
Chatham ME5 ... 97 C8
Gravesend DA12 ... 37 F3
Hopewell Sch TN23 ... 299 E7
Hop Farm Country Pk★ TN12 ... 225 A3
Hopgarden Cl 12 TN8 ... 217 D3
Hopgarden La TN13 ... 187 A8
Hopgarden Oast ME18 ... 192 F1
Hopgarden Rd TN10 ... 222 D6
Hop Garden Way CT1 ... 174 E6
Hop Gdn TN26 ... 347 C1
Hoppers Cnr ME15 ... 193 D7
Hoppers Way TN23 ... 299 D8
Hop Pocket Cl TN17 ... 321 A8
Hop Pocket La TN12 ... 256 F7
Hopsons Pl ME12 ... 47 C5
Hopton Ct BR2 ... 52 A1
Hopton Rd SE18 ... 2 B3
Hopwood Gdns TN4 ... 286 A6
Horatio Pl ME1 ... 63 B4
Horizon Cl TN4 ... 286 B8
Horley Cl DA6 ... 14 A2
Horley Rd SE9 ... 29 E4
Hornash La TN26 ... 327 D8
Hornbeam Ave
Chatham ME5 ... 97 B2
Royal Tunbridge Wells TN4 ... 254 D1
Hornbeam Cl
Ashford TN23 ... 267 F3
Larkfield ME20 ... 128 B2
Paddock Wood TN12 ... 256 F5
Hornbeam Ho 6 DA15 ... 31 A5
Hornbeam La DA7 ... 14 C5
Hornbeams DA13 ... 126 B8
Hornbeam Way BR2 ... 53 A3
Hornbrook La TN26 ... 347 C7
Horncastle Cl SE12 ... 29 A8
Horncastle Rd SE12 ... 29 A8
Horne Ho SE18 ... 11 E6
Hornes Place Chapel★ TN26 ... 347 D2
Hornet Cl CT10 ... 83 D3
Hornfair Rd SE7 ... 11 D7
Hornfield Cotts DA13 ... 93 C3
Horn Hill ME9 ... 134 E2
Horning Cl SE9 ... 29 E4
Horn La SE10 ... 1 A2
Horn Link Way SE10 ... 1 A2
Horn Park Cl SE12 ... 11 B2
Horn Park La SE12 ... 11 B1
Horn Park Prim Sch SE12 ... 29 B8
Horns La ME18 ... 158 D1
Horns Lodge Farm TN11 ... 222 C8
Horns Lodge La TN11 ... 222 A8
Horn's Oak Rd DA13 ... 93 B6
Horns Rd
The Moor TN18 ... 354 B8
The Moor TN18 ... 354 D8
The Moor TN18 ... 354 F7
Horn St CT19,CT20, CT21 ... 334 B4
Horn Yd 7 DA11 ... 19 B1
Horsa Rd
Birchington CT7 ... 80 D7
Deal CT14 ... 215 D8
Eltham SE12 ... 29 C8
Erith DA8 ... 14 C7
Horsebridge Rd CT5 ... 74 D2
Horsecroft Cl BR6 ... 54 B1
Horsegrove Ave TN5 ... 338 F1
Horse Leaze E6 ... 2 A7
Horselees Rd ME13 ... 140 A2
Horsell Rd BR5 ... 54 B8
Horseshoe Cl
Gillingham ME7 ... 97 F5
Maidstone ME14 ... 162 E5
Horseshoes La ME17 ... 196 E4
Horse Wash La ME1 ... 63 C6
Horsfeld Gdns SE9 ... 11 E2
Horsfeld Rd SE9 ... 11 D2
Horsfield Cl DA2 ... 34 C8
Horsford Wlk ME13 ... 138 A8
Horsham Hill ME9 ... 66 E4
Horsham La ME8,ME9 ... 66 D3
Horsham Rd DA6 ... 14 A2
Horshams The CT6 ... 77 D5
Horsley Cl CT18 ... 307 B4
Horsley Ho SE18 ... 12 A7
Horsley Rd Bromley BR1 ... 52 B8
Rochester ME1 ... 63 B4
Horsmonden Cl BR6 ... 53 F2
Horsmonden Prim Sch TN12 ... 290 A6
Horsmonden Rd TN12 ... 289 D6
Horsted Ave ME4 ... 63 E1
Horsted Inf Sch ME4 ... 96 D5
Horsted Jun Sch ME5 ... 96 D5
Horsted Ret Pk ME5 ... 96 D5
Horsted Way ME1 ... 96 D7
Horton Cotts CT4 ... 173 E4
Horton Downs ME15 ... 162 F1
Horton Gdns CT4 ... 173 E4
Horton Kirby CE Prim Sch DA4 ... 57 C6
Horton Pl TN16 ... 151 D1
Horton Rd DA4 ... 57 C6
Hortons Cl TN17 ... 342 D7
Hortons Way 1 TN16 ... 151 D1
Horton Tower 2 BR5 ... 54 C5
Horton Way DA4 ... 56 F2
Horwood Cl ME1 ... 96 B8
Hoselands View DA3 ... 58 E5
Hoser Ave SE12 ... 29 A6
Hoser Gdns CT7 ... 81 A7
Hosey Common La TN16 ... 184 F5
Hosey Common Rd TN8,TN16 ... 184 D5
Hosey Hill TN16 ... 184 E8
Hoskin's Cl E16 ... 1 C7
Hospital Hill CT20, CT21 ... 334 C3
Hospital La
Canterbury CT1 ... 174 F8
3 Chatham ME1 ... 63 E4
Hospital Meadow Cotts CT3 ... 178 D2
Hospital of Thomas the Martyr Eastbridge The★ CT1 ... 174 F8
Hospital Rd
Hollingbourne ME17 ... 197 E8
Sevenoaks TN13 ... 154 C6
Hostier Cl ME2 ... 95 B4
Hotel Rd Gillingham ME8 ... 65 A2
St Margaret's at Cliffe CT15 ... 280 B6
Hotham Cl
Sutton at H DA4 ... 34 B1
Swanley Village BR8 ... 56 B8
Hothfield Common Nature Reserve★ TN26 ... 266 F8
Hothfield Rd ME8 ... 65 F1
Hothfield Village Prim Sch TN26 ... 266 F7
Hottsfield DA3 ... 58 E6
Hougham Court La CT15 ... 309 A3
Hougham Ho 11 BR5 ... 54 D1
Houghton Ave ME7 ... 98 B3
Houghton Green La TN31 ... 368 C2
Houghton Ho CT19 ... 335 C5
Houghton La TN31 ... 368 C3
Housefield TN24 ... 268 F2
Housefield Rd ME13 ... 202 C6
Houselands Rd TN9 ... 222 B2
House Mdw TN23 ... 299 C7
Hove Cl RM17 ... 18 A8
Hovenden Cl CT2 ... 143 A4
Hovendens TN17 ... 321 A8
Hoveton Rd SE28 ... 3 C7
Howard Ave
Rochester ME1 ... 63 D3
Sidcup DA5 ... 31 C8
Sittingbourne ME10 ... 101 D6
Howard Cl ME12 ... 47 C7
Howard Dr ME16 ... 161 B5
Howard Gdns TN2 ... 286 A1
Howard Rd
Broadstairs CT10 ... 84 A3
Bromley BR1 ... 29 A1
Dartford DA1 ... 16 A1
East Malling ME19 ... 159 F8
Howard Sch The ME8 ... 98 D8
Howarth Rd SE2 ... 3 A2
Howbury Ctr PRU The DA8 ... 15 A7
Howbury La DA8 ... 15 A5
Howbury Wlk ME8 ... 98 D4
Howden Cl SE28 ... 3 D6
Howells Cl TN15 ... 90 E4
Howerd Way SE18 ... 11 E6
Howes Cotts TN18 ... 354 F8
Howfield La CT4 ... 173 E5
How Green La TN8 ... 218 C2
Howick Cl ME20 ... 160 F8
Howick Mans SE18 ... 1 E3
Howland Cotts TN12 ... 259 E6
Howland Mews CT1 ... 174 E6
Howland Rd TN12 ... 259 E6
Howlands Ct TN15 ... 124 F4
Howlands TN15 ... 124 F4
Howletts Oast CT4 ... 176 C5
Howletts Wild Animal Pk★ CT4 ... 176 D6
Howlsmere Cl ME2 ... 95 B3
Hoxton Cl TN23 ... 299 D8
Hoystings Cl The CT1 ... 175 A7
Hubbards Cotts ME8 ... 66 C2
Hubbard's Hill TN13, TN14 ... 187 B4
Hubbards Hill ME17 ... 200 B6
Hubbard's La ME15 ... 195 A3
Hubble Dr ME15 ... 195 E7
Hubert Way CT10 ... 83 E6
Huckleberry Cl ME5 ... 97 B3
Hudson Cl
7 Dover CT16 ... 278 B3
Rainham ME8 ... 65 C1
Sturry CT2 ... 143 F6
Hudson Ho DA4 ... 57 D7
Hudson Pl SE18 ... 2 C1
Hudson Rd Bexley DA7 ... 13 F6
Canterbury CT1 ... 143 B2
Huggen's College Almshouses DA11 ... 18 B2
Hugh Christie Tech Coll TN10 ... 222 D6
Hughes Dr ME2 ... 40 D2
Hugh Pl 5 ME13 ... 138 D7
Hugh Price Cl ME10 ... 102 C5
Hugin Ave CT10 ... 83 E7
Hulberry Farm DA4 ... 89 B8
Hulkes La ME1 ... 63 E4
Hull Pl Deal CT14 ... 214 F6
Newham E16 ... 2 C5
Hull Rd TN29 ... 377 E6
Hulsewood Cl DA2 ... 33 B5
Hulsons Ct 1 TN18 ... 341 A2
Humber Ave CT6 ... 75 F4
Humber Cres ME2 ... 62 F7
Humber Rd
Dartford DA1 ... 15 D2
Greenwich SE3 ... 11 A8
Humboldt Ct TN2 ... 286 D5
Hume Ave RM18 ... 19 B5
Hume Cl RM18 ... 19 A4
Hume Ct CT21 ... 333 D1
Hume Terr E16 ... 1 B7
Humphreys TN12 ... 288 F6
Humphrey Terr CT18 ... 306 F4
Hundred of Hoo Comp Sch The ME3 ... 41 C5
Hundreds Cl CT8 ... 81 D7
Hunger Hatch La TN27 ... 233 F4
Hungershall Park Cl TN4 ... 285 E1
Hungershall Pk TN4 ... 285 E2
Hunsdon Dr TN13 ... 154 B4
Hunstanton Cl ME8 ... 98 E3
Hunt Cl CT18 ... 307 A4
Hunter Ave TN24 ... 300 E8
Hunter Cl TN24 ... 300 E8
Hunter Rd TN24 ... 268 E1
Hunters Bank CT4 ... 273 F4
Hunters Chase
Herne Bay CT6 ... 77 C2
Whitstable CT5 ... 108 E7
Hunters Cl DA5 ... 32 E5
Hunters Ct 5 ME7 ... 64 C7
Hunter Seal TN11 ... 221 E2
Huntersfield Cl ME5 ... 97 C1
Hunters Forstal Rd CT6 ... 77 C2
Hunter's Gr BR6 ... 86 C6
Hunters Lodge 10 DA15 ... 31 A5
Hunters Way
Gillingham ME7 ... 64 E1
Royal Tunbridge Wells TN2 ... 285 F1
Sheldwich ME13 ... 170 C5
Hunters Way W ME5 ... 64 E1
Hunters Wlk
Deal CT14 ... 215 B6
Knockholt TN14 ... 120 E5
Huntingdon Wlk 2 ME15 ... 195 E7
Huntingfield Rd DA13 ... 60 A2
Hunting Gate CT7 ... 80 F8
Huntington Cl TN17 ... 320 D4
Huntington Rd ME17 ... 194 B3
Huntley Ave DA11 ... 18 C1
Huntley Mill Rd TN5 ... 338 E3
Huntleys Pk TN4 ... 285 F5
Hunton CE Prim Sch ME15 ... 226 D7
Hunton Gdns CT2 ... 143 A4
Hunton Hill
Coxheath ME15 ... 194 A2
Hunton ME15 ... 193 F1
Hunton Ho 4 BR5 ... 54 C4
Hunton Rd TN12 ... 227 A3
Hunt Rd Northfleet DA11 ... 36 F5
Tonbridge TN10 ... 222 E6
Hunts Farm Cl TN15 ... 157 A7
Huntsfield Ind Est CT20 ... 334 D4
Hunts La TN17 ... 318 E8
Huntsman Ho 2 DA11 ... 36 F8
Huntsman La
Maidstone ME14 ... 162 B4
Wrotham Heath TN15 ... 125 E1
Huntsmans Cl ME1 ... 63 E1
Huntsman's Cnr ME4 ... 96 E8
Hunts Mede Cl BR7 ... 29 F1
Huntsmoor House BR5 ... 54 B5
Hunt St
Nettlestead ME15,ME18 ... 192 F5
West Farleigh ME15 ... 193 B5
Huntswood TN23 ... 267 E1
Hurlfield DA2 ... 33 C5
Hurlingham Cl TN10 ... 222 E7
Hurlingham Rd DA7 ... 13 F7
Huron Cl 5 BR6 ... 86 F4
Hurricane Rd ME19 ... 158 F3
Hurstbourne Cotts DA5 ... 32 B8
Hurst Cl Chatham ME5 ... 96 E6
Staplehurst TN12 ... 260 F4
Tenterden TN30 ... 344 F7
Hurst Ct Newham E6 ... 1 D8
Sidcup DA15 ... 31 A6
Hurst Farm Rd TN14 ... 187 B3
Hurstfield BR2 ... 52 A4
Hurstford La TN26, TN27 ... 234 C2
Hurst Green CE Prim Sch TN19 ... 354 A2
Hurst Green Cl RH8 ... 183 A3
Hurst Green Inf Sch RH8 ... 183 A3
Hurst Green Rd RH8 ... 183 A3
Hurst Gr CT12 ... 83 C1
Hurst Hill ME5 ... 96 E2
Hurst Ho SE2 ... 3 D1
Hurstings The ME15 ... 161 D2
Hurst La
Capel-le-F CT18 ... 308 B4
Charing Heath TN27 ... 233 E6
Erith SE2 ... 3 D1
Hurstlands RH8 ... 183 A3
Hurst La
Sevenoaks Weald TN14 ... 187 B2
Sittingbourne ME10 ... 68 F1
Hurstmere Foundation Sch for Boys DA15 ... 31 C7
Hurst Pl Gillingham ME8 ... 98 F8
Woolwich SE2 ... 3 C1
Hurst Prim Sch DA5 ... 31 D7
Hurst Rd Ashford TN24 ... 268 C7
Erith DA8 ... 14 C7
Sidcup DA5 ... 31 D7
Hurst Springs DA5 ... 31 E7
Hurst The Crouch TN11 ... 190 D7
Plaxtol Spoute TN15 ... 157 C1
Royal Tunbridge Wells TN2 ... 286 E7
Hurst Way
Maidstone ME16 ... 160 F2
Sevenoaks TN13 ... 187 C8
Hurstwood Ave
Bexley DA7,DA8 ... 14 E6
Sidcup DA5 ... 31 E7
Hurstwood ME5 ... 96 E4
Hurstwood Dr BR1 ... 52 F6
Hurstwood La TN4 ... 285 F3
Hurstwood Pk TN4 ... 285 F3
Hurstwood Rd
Bredhurst,Bredhurst Hurst ME14 ... 131 B7
Bredhurst ME7 ... 98 B1
Warren Street ME13 ... 200 E8
Husheath Hill TN17 ... 291 F6
Hussar Ho ME1 ... 63 C3
Husseywell Cres BR2 ... 52 A1
Hustlings Dr ME12 ... 48 B5
Hutchings Cl ME10 ... 102 C5
Hutchins Rd SE28 ... 3 A5
Hutsford Cl ME8 ... 98 D5
Hutson Terr RM19 ... 16 D8
Huxley Ct 3 ME1 ... 63 D4
Huxley Ho SE2 ... 3 D1
Huxley Rd DA16 ... 12 F4
Hyacinth Rd ME2 ... 62 E6
Hybrid Cl ME1 ... 63 D1
Hyde Ct CT17 ... 310 C7
Hyde Dr BR5 ... 54 B5
Hyde Pl CT3 ... 210 F5
Hyde Rd Bexley DA7 ... 13 F5
Maidstone ME16 ... 161 D6
Hyders Forge TN15 ... 190 A8
Hyde's Orch TN27 ... 262 E5
Hyde The CT4 ... 173 B2
Hylands Cotts TN26 ... 326 A2
Hylton St SE18 ... 2 F2
Hyndford Cres DA9 ... 17 C2
Hyperion Dr ME2 ... 39 F1
Hythe Ave DA7 ... 13 F7
Hythe Cl
Folkestone CT20 ... 334 F5
Orpington BR5 ... 54 C5
Royal Tunbridge Wells TN4 ... 254 A1
Hythe Com Sch CT21 ... 333 B1
Hythe Pl CT13 ... 181 A8
Hythe Rd Ashford TN24 ... 268 E1
Dymchurch TN29 ... 352 E1
Lympne CT21 ... 332 D4
Sittingbourne ME10 ... 101 D5
Smeeth TN25,TN24 ... 302 C3
Hythe, St Leonard's CE Jun Sch CT21 ... 333 B2
Hythe Sta★ CT21 ... 333 A2
Hythe St Dartford DA1 ... 15 E1
Dartford DA1 ... 15 E2
Hyton Dr CT14 ... 215 B6

I

Ian's Wlk CT21 ... 334 A3
Ibis Cl CT5 ... 108 B6
Ice Bowl The★ ME8 ... 65 A1
Ickham Court Farm CT3 ... 145 C1
Ickleton Rd SE9 ... 29 E4
Icough Ct SE3 ... 11 B7
Iddenden Cotts TN18 ... 340 D2
Ide Hill CE Prim Sch TN14 ... 185 F4
Ide Hill Rd
Bough Beech TN8,TN14 ... 218 F5
Ide Hill TN14 ... 185 F2
Iden Cres TN12 ... 260 F2
Iden Croft Herbs★ TN12 ... 261 A1
Iden Green Cotts TN17 ... 319 C8
Iden La TN27 ... 233 B4
Iden Rd Iden TN31 ... 368 B3
Rochester ME2 ... 40 C1
Idenwood Cl ME8 ... 98 D6
Idleigh Court Rd DA3, DA13 ... 92 C8
Iffin La CT4 ... 174 E2
Ifield Cl ME15 ... 195 F7
Ifield Sch The DA12 ... 37 C3
Ifield Way DA12 ... 37 D2
Ightham By-Pass TN15 ... 156 C7
Ightham Cotts DA2 ... 35 B6
Ightham Mote★ TN15 ... 189 A7
Ightham Prim Sch TN15 ... 156 B6
Ightham Rd Bexley DA8 ... 14 A7
Shipbourne TN11,TN15 ... 189 C5
Ilex Rd CT19 ... 334 F6
Ilkley Rd E16 ... 1 C8
Illustrious Cl ME5 ... 97 A6
Imber Ct 4 SE9 ... 12 A1
Imbert Cl TN28 ... 373 C6
Impala Gdns TN4 ... 286 B6
Imperial Ave ME12 ... 47 D7
Imperial Bsns Pk DA11 ... 18 F1

Imperial Ct BR7 . . . . .30 B2
Imperial Dr
  Gravesend DA12 . . . . .37 F3
  Warden ME12 . . . . .49 E4
Imperial Pl BR7 . . . . .53 A8
Imperial Rd ME7 . . . . .64 C3
Imperial Ret Pk DA11 . . .19 A1
Imperial Way
  Ashford TN23 . . . . .299 C8
  Chislehurst BR7 . . . . .30 C5
Impton La ME5 . . . . .97 A1
Inca Dr SE9 . . . . .30 B8
Ince Rd CT2 . . . . .143 F7
Indus Rd SE7 . . . . .11 C7
Industrial Est The
  TN8 . . . . .217 B3
Ingleborough La
  TN15 . . . . .157 C8
Ingleby Way BR7 . . . . .30 A3
Ingle Cl CT7 . . . . .81 B7
Ingleden Cl ME10 . . . . . . .101 F8
Ingleden Park Rd
  TN30 . . . . .324 C1
Ingledew Rd SE18 . . . . .2 D1
Ingle Pl ME18 . . . . .159 A2
Ingle Rd ME4 . . . . .63 F2
Ingleside Gr 3 SE3 . . . . . .11 A8
Ingles La 3 CT20 . . . . . . .335 D5
Ingles Mews 4 CT20 . . . .335 C4
Ingles Rd CT20 . . . . .335 C4
Ingleton Ave DA16 . . . . . . .13 A2
Inglewood BR7 . . . . .30 D2
Inglewood Copse BR1 . . . .52 F7
Inglewood Rd DA7 . . . . . . .14 D3
Inglewood BR8 . . . . .55 E7
Ingoldsby Rd
  Birchington CT7 . . . . .80 E7
  Canterbury CT1 . . . . . . .174 D6
  Folkestone CT19 . . . . . . .335 E7
  Gravesend DA12 . . . . .37 F7
Ingram Cl CT18 . . . . .306 F3
Ingram Rd Dartford DA1 . .33 E7
  Gillingham ME7 . . . . .64 E6
Ingress Gdns DA9 . . . . . . .17 D2
Ingress Park Ave DA9 . . . .17 C3
Ingress Terr DA13 . . . . . . .35 E4
Inigo Jones Rd SE7 . . . . . .11 E7
Inner Lines ME7 . . . . .64 A6
Institute Rd
  Chatham ME4 . . . . .64 A4
  Faversham ME13 . . . . . . .138 D7
Instone Rd DA1 . . . . .33 D8
Inverary Ct CT11 . . . . .83 E1
Inverary Pl SE18 . . . . .12 D8
Inverine Rd SE7 . . . . .1 B1
Invermore Pl SE18 . . . . .2 C2
Inverness Ho 7 ME15 . . .195 E7
Inverness Mews E16 . . . . . .2 C5
Inverness Terr CT10 . . . . . .84 A3
Invicta Bsns Pk TN15 . . .125 C2
Invicta Cl BR7 . . . . .30 A3
Invicta Cl ME10 . . . . .101 F7
Invicta Gram Sch
  ME14 . . . . .162 C4
Invicta Ho
  Canterbury CT1 . . . . . . .174 F7
  Margate CT9 . . . . .51 C1
Invicta Par 3 DA14 . . . . . .31 B4
Invicta Prim Sch SE3 . . . .11 A7
Invicta Rd Dartford DA2 . .16 B1
  Folkestone CT19 . . . . . . .335 E7
  Greenwich SE3 . . . . .11 A8
  Lydd TN29 . . . . .378 I6
  Margate CT9 . . . . .83 B8
  Sheerness ME12 . . . . .28 C2
  Whitstable CT5 . . . . .108 F8
Invicta Villas ME14 . . . . .163 C4
Inward Car Lanes
  CT16 . . . . .310 G8
Inward Freight Lanes
  CT16 . . . . .310 G8
Io Ctr SE18 . . . . .2 C3
Iona Cl ME5 . . . . .97 D1
Iona Rd ME15 . . . . .195 A4
Ionia Wlk DA12 . . . . .37 F5
Irchester St 11 CT11 . . . .117 F7
Ireland Cl E6 . . . . .1 F8
Ireland Ct TN24 . . . . .268 D2
Irene Astor Ct 7
  CT20 . . . . .335 D5
Irene Rd BR6 . . . . .53 F2
Iris Ave DA5 . . . . .13 E1
Iris Cl ME5 . . . . .130 A8
Iris Cres DA7 . . . . .13 F8
Iron Bar La 4 CT1 . . . . . .175 A8
Iron Mill La DA1 . . . . .14 F3
Iron Mill Pl DA1 . . . . .14 F3
Ironside Cl ME5 . . . . .97 A8
Ironstones TN3 . . . . .285 B3
Irvine Dr CT9 . . . . .83 C8
Irvine Rd ME3 . . . . .39 B3
Irvine Way BR6 . . . . .53 F2
Irving Ho TN1 . . . . .286 B5
Irving Way BR1 . . . . .55 D7
Irving Wlk DA10 . . . . .35 E8
Irwin Ave SE18 . . . . .12 E7
Isabella Dr BR6 . . . . .86 C6
Isis Cl CT21 . . . . .332 A3
Island Rd
  Upstreet CT3,CT7 . . . . . .112 D2
  Westbere CT2,CT3 . . . . . .144 C7
Island Wall CT5 . . . . .74 C1
Island Way E ME4 . . . . . . .41 C1
Island Way W ME4 . . . . . .41 B2
Isla Rd SE18 . . . . .12 C8
Islehurst Cl BR7 . . . . .53 A8
Isle of Sheppey Holiday
  Village ME12 . . . . .49 F2
Islington Farm Rd
  ME3 . . . . .40 D4
Ismays Rd TN15 . . . . .156 C3
Istead Rise DA13 . . . . .36 F1

Istead Rise Prim Sch
  DA13 . . . . .59 E8
Itchingwood Common Rd
  RH8 . . . . .183 E2
Ito Way ME8 . . . . .65 A3
Ivanhoe Rd
  Herne Bay CT6 . . . . .77 A4
  Westgate-on-S CT8 . . . . . .50 C1
Ivedon Rd DA16 . . . . .13 C5
Ivens Way ME17 . . . . .198 D6
Iverhurst Cl ME8 . . . . .13 D2
Iversgate Cl ME8 . . . . .65 F2
Ives Holiday Camp
  ME12 . . . . .49 G1
Ives Rd TN9 . . . . .221 F1
Ivor Gr SE9 . . . . .30 B7
Ivor Ho DA14 . . . . .31 C3
Ivory Cl ME13 . . . . .105 A1
Ivorydown BR1 . . . . .29 A4
Ivy Bower Cl DA9 . . . . .17 B2
Ivybridge Ct 1 BR7 . . . . .53 A8
Ivychurch Gdns CT9 . . . . .51 E2
Ivychurch Rd TN29 . . . . . .363 B3
Ivy Cl Dartford DA1 . . . . . .34 A8
  Etchinghill CT18 . . . . . . .305 D3
  Gravesend DA12 . . . . .37 D5
  Kingswood ME17 . . . . . . .197 D2
Ivy Cottage Hill CT12 . . .115 E7
Ivy Cotts TN23 . . . . .299 C8
Ivy Ct CT2 . . . . .142 E6
Ivy House La TN13,
  TN14 . . . . .121 E2
Ivy House Rd CT5 . . . . . . .74 F1
Ivy La
  Bells Yew Green TN3 . . . .315 A5
  Canterbury CT1 . . . . . . .175 A8
  Knockholt TN14 . . . . .120 E3
  Ramsgate CT11 . . . . .117 D6
Ivy Mews ME17 . . . . .197 E2
Ivy Pl Canterbury CT1 . . . .174 E7
  Deal CT14 . . . . .215 D7
  Rochester ME1 . . . . .63 A2
Ivy Rd E16 . . . . .1 A7
Ivyside CT8 . . . . .50 C1
Ivy St ME8 . . . . .98 F8
Ivy Villas DA9 . . . . .17 A2
Ivy Way CT19 . . . . .335 E7
Iwade Com Prim Sch
  ME9 . . . . .68 D4
Izane Rd DA6 . . . . .13 F3

Jaarlen Rd TN29 . . . . . . .376 B6
Jacinth Dr ME10 . . . . . . .101 C6
Jackass La BR2 . . . . .85 C4
Jacklin Cl ME5 . . . . .96 F2
Jackson Ave ME1 . . . . .96 E8
Jackson Cl
  Rainham ME8 . . . . .65 C1
  1 Stone DA9 . . . . .17 A2
Jackson Ho 4 SE7 . . . . . . .11 B8
Jackson Rd
  Canterbury CT1 . . . . . . .174 E7
  Orpington BR2 . . . . .85 F8
Jackson's Cnr ME3 . . . . . .24 A3
Jacksons La 8 TN30 . . . .345 A7
Jacksons Stables CT8 . . . .50 D1
Jackson St SE18 . . . . .12 A8
Jackson Way TN17 . . . . . .322 C3
Jacob Cl CT19 . . . . .82 E7
Jacobs Ho ME12 . . . . .28 C2
Jacob Ho 5 DA18 . . . . .3 D4
Jacob's La ME3 . . . . .42 B6
Jacobs Oak TN24 . . . . . . .300 D6
Jacob Yd 8 ME3 . . . . .138 D7
Jade Cl Newham E16 . . . . . .1 D7
  Sittingbourne ME10 . . . . .101 C7
Jade Hill ME2 . . . . .95 A6
Jaffa Ct CT5 . . . . .108 D8
Jaffray Rd BR2 . . . . .52 D5
Jaggard Way TN12 . . . . . .260 E3
Jagger Cl DA2 . . . . .34 C8
Jago Cl SE18 . . . . .12 C8
Jail La Biggin Hill TN16 . .118 E3
  Cudham TN16 . . . . .119 A3
Jamaica Terr ME14 . . . . . .162 C4
James Allchin Gdns
  TN24 . . . . .268 F4
James Cl Ash CT3 . . . . . . .147 D2
  Lyminge CT18 . . . . .305 C7
James Ct
  Folkestone CT20 . . . . . . .335 A4
  2 Margate CT9 . . . . .51 B2
James Hall Gdns
  CT14 . . . . .215 C3
James Haney Dr TN24 . . .268 F5
James Morris Ct 3
  CT20 . . . . .334 F3
James Newman Ct SE9 . .30 A5
James Rd Cuxton ME2 . . . .62 C2
  Dartford DA1 . . . . .9 B3
James St Ashford TN23 . . .268 A2
  5 Chatham ME4 . . . . . . .63 F4
  Folkestone CT19 . . . . . . .335 D6
  Gillingham ME7 . . . . .64 C6
  Maidstone ME14 . . . . . . .162 A5
  8 Ramsgate CT11 . . . . . .117 D6
  Rochester ME1 . . . . .63 C4
  Sheerness ME12 . . . . .28 D2
James Watt Way DA8 . . . .14 F8
James Whath an Way
  ME14 . . . . .162 C6
Jane Seymour Ct DA15 . .30 D8
Janet Ct 4 DA7 . . . . .14 A3
Janson Ct 11 DA14 . . . . . .31 B4
Japonica Cl ME5 . . . . .32 A6
Jaquets Ct DA8 . . . . .14 F8
Jarman's Field TN25 . . . .237 F2
Jarrah Cotts RM19 . . . . . .16 D8
Jarrett Ave ME4 . . . . .40 C2
Jarrett Ho 10 CT20 . . . . . .335 C4

Jarrett's Ct 1 ME10 . . . .102 B4
Jarvis Dr TN24 . . . . .301 A7
Jarvis La TN17 . . . . .291 B3
Jarvis Pl TN30 . . . . .324 B3
Jarvist Pl CT14 . . . . .248 D6
Jasmine Cl
  Chartham CT4 . . . . .173 E1
  2 Chatham ME5 . . . . . . .96 F4
  East Malling ME19 . . . . . .159 F8
  Orpington BR6 . . . . .86 B8
Jasmine Cotts
  Borough Green TN15 . . . .156 F7
  Groombridge TN3 . . . . . .312 C7
Jasmine Ct SE12 . . . . .11 A1
Jasmine Rd ME19 . . . . . . .159 F8
Jason Wlk SE9 . . . . .30 A4
Jasper Ave ME1 . . . . .63 D2
Jasper Rd E16 . . . . .1 D7
Javelin Rd ME19 . . . . .158 F3
Jay Gdns BR7 . . . . .29 F4
Jayne Wlk CT5 . . . . .108 B6
Jefferson Cl TN23 . . . . . . .267 F1
Jefferson Dr ME8 . . . . .65 C1
Jefferson Rd ME2 . . . . .28 D2
Jefferson Wlk 13 SE18 . . .12 A8
Jefferstone Gdns
  TN29 . . . . .365 E4
Jefferstone La TN29 . . . . .365 E4
Jeffery La ME7 . . . . .64 C6
Jeffrey Cl TN12 . . . . .260 E4
Jeffrey Ct DA8 . . . . .14 C7
Jeffrey Row SE12 . . . . .11 B2
Jeffrey St ME14 . . . . .162 A5
Jeken Rd SE9 . . . . .11 C3
Jellicoe Ave DA12 . . . . . . .37 C5
Jellicoe Ave W DA12 . . . . .37 C5
Jellicoe Ct TN24 . . . . .301 A7
Jemmett Rd TN23 . . . . . .300 A8
Jenkins' Dale ME4 . . . . . . .63 F3
Jenkins Dr ME15 . . . . .195 E5
Jenner Cl DA14 . . . . .31 A4
Jenner Ho 4 DA17 . . . . . . .4 A3
Jenner Rd ME1 . . . . .63 C4
Jenner's Way TN29 . . . . . .365 F3
Jenner Way ME20 . . . . . . .128 F6
Jennifer Ct ME3 . . . . .42 A5
Jennifer Gdns CT9 . . . . . . .83 C8
Jenningtree Rd DA8 . . . . . .15 B7
Jenningtree Way DA17 . . . .4 C4
Jenton Ave DA7 . . . . .13 E5
Jerome Ave ME20 . . . . . . .127 F4
Jersey Cl TN24 . . . . .268 C8
Jersey Dr BR5 . . . . .53 D3
Jersey La CT4 . . . . .207 C6
Jersey Rd Newham E16 . . . .1 F8
  Rochester ME2 . . . . .63 A8
Jervis Rd TN29 . . . . .365 F4
Jesmond St 3 CT19 . . . . .335 D6
Jessamine Pl DA2 . . . . . . .34 E8
Jessamine Terr BR8 . . . . . .55 C8
Jesse's Hill CT4 . . . . .209 B1
Jessett Cl DA8 . . . . .4 D2
Jessica Mews
  2 Canterbury CT1 . . . . . .143 B1
  Sittingbourne ME10 . . . . .101 E7
Jesson Ct TN29 . . . . .366 A4
Jesson Court Cvn Pk
  TN29 . . . . .365 F4
Jessup Cl SE18 . . . . .2 C2
Jesuit Cl CT2 . . . . .143 A4
Jesus Hospl CT1 . . . . .143 A1
Jetty Rd Kingsnorth ME3 . .24 A7
  Sheerness ME12 . . . . .28 A3
  Warden ME12 . . . . .49 D4
Jetty Wlk 8 RM17 . . . . . . .18 A8
Jevington Way SE12 . . . . .29 B7
Jewell Gr TN12 . . . . .259 D5
Jewels Hill TN16 . . . . .118 A6
Jewry La CT1 . . . . .174 F8
Jeyes Rd ME7 . . . . .64 C4
Jezreels Rd ME7 . . . . .64 D3
Jillian Way TN23 . . . . . . .299 E7
Jim Bradley Cl 10 SE18 . .2 A2
Jiniwin Rd ME1 . . . . .96 D7
Joan Cres SE9 . . . . .29 D8
Jo-Ann's Ct 5 CT10 . . . . .84 A4
Jockey La TN17 . . . . .320 D5
Johannesburg Ho 2
  ME15 . . . . .195 F5
Johannesburg Rd
  CT16 . . . . .278 C4
John Anderson Ct 11
  ME13 . . . . .138 D7
John Badger Cl TN24 . . . .268 C5
John Bowley Ho CT19 . . .334 F6
John Brunt Ct TN12 . . . . .257 A7
John Burns Cotts RH8 . . .183 E5
John Dutton Way
  TN24 . . . . .268 E4
John Graham Ct CT1 . . . .175 A6
John Hall Cl ME13 . . . . . .105 B2
John Hunt Ct SE9 . . . . . . .29 E6
John Mayne CE Prim Sch
  TN27 . . . . .294 F1
John Nash Cl ME9 . . . . . .136 B8
John Newington Cl
  TN24 . . . . .268 F5
John Newton Ct DA16 . . .13 B4
Johns Cl DA3 . . . . .58 F4
John's Gn CT13 . . . . .180 E6
Johnson Ave ME7 . . . . .64 C7
Johnson Rd
  Bromley BR2 . . . . .52 D4
  Sittingbourne ME10 . . . . .101 F7
Johnsons Ave TN14 . . . . . .88 B1
Johnsons Ct TN15 . . . . . .154 E4

Johnsons Way DA9 . . . . . .17 C1
Johnson Way ME12 . . . . . .47 A7
John Spare Ct TN4 . . . . . .286 A6
Johns Rd TN16 . . . . .119 B3
John's Rd
  Meopham Station DA13 . . .59 F4
  Tatsfield TN16 . . . . .150 D7
John St Broadstairs CT10 . .84 A4
  Grays RM17 . . . . .18 C8
  Maidstone ME14 . . . . . . .162 A6
  Rochester ME1 . . . . .63 C4
  Royal Tunbridge Wells
  TN4 . . . . .286 A5
John Tapping Cl CT14 . . .215 B1
John Wesley Ct SE9 . . . . .12 A3
John Wilson Bsns Pk
  CT5 . . . . .75 B1
John Wilson St SE18 . . . . .2 A2
Joiners Ct ME4 . . . . .64 B2
Jointon Rd CT20 . . . . .335 B4
Jonas Dr TN5 . . . . .336 E5
Jonas La TN5 . . . . .336 E5
Jordan Cl ME15 . . . . .195 E5
Joseph Conrad Ho
  CT2 . . . . .142 D1
Joseph Wilson Ind Est
  CT5 . . . . .109 A7
Josling Cl RM17 . . . . .17 F8
Joss Gap Rd CT10 . . . . . . .51 H1
Joyce Cl TN17 . . . . .320 C5
Joyce Dawson Way
  SE28 . . . . .3 A6
Joyce Green La
  Dartford DA1 . . . . .15 E6
  Dartford,Temple Hill DA1 . .15 E4
Joyce Green Rd DA1 . . . . .15 E4
Joyce Green Wlk DA1 . . . .15 F3
Joyce Page Cl 7 SE7 . . . .11 D8
Joyden's Wood Rd DA5 . .32 E5
Joyes Cl
  Folkestone CT19 . . . . . . .335 E7
  Whitfield CT16 . . . . .278 B7
Joyes Rd
  Folkestone CT19 . . . . . . .335 E7
  Whitfield CT16 . . . . .278 B7
Joy Lane Inf Sch CT5 . . .108 C7
Joy Lane Jun Sch
  CT5 . . . . .108 C7
Joy La CT5 . . . . .108 B8
Joy Rd DA12 . . . . .37 C7
Joy Wood ME17 . . . . .195 D5
Jubilee Cl TN21,CT21 . . .353 D8
  Swanscombe DA9 . . . . . . .17 C1
Jubilee Cnr ME17 . . . . . . .230 E3
Jubilee Cotts
  Sevenoaks TN14 . . . . . . .154 B7
  Staple CT3 . . . . .179 B6
  Sutton Valence ME17 . . . .229 E7
  Throwley ME13 . . . . .169 D1
  Worth CT14 . . . . .181 B4
Jubilee Cres
  Gravesend DA12 . . . . .37 E6
  Ightham TN15 . . . . .156 C6
  Queenborough ME11 . . . . .45 F5
Jubilee Ct
  12 Broadstairs CT10 . . . . .84 B4
  Dartford DA1 . . . . .33 D8
  17 Ramsgate CT11 . . . . .117 F7
  Whitstable CT5 . . . . .75 A3
Jubilee Dr CT14 . . . . .215 D3
Jubilee Fields ME8 . . . . . .66 D2
Jubilee Field TN30 . . . . . .359 E4
Jubilee Ho CT20 . . . . .335 B4
Jubilee Park Cntry Pk ★
  BR1,BR5 . . . . .53 B5
Jubilee Prim Sch SE28 . . .3 C6
Jubilee Rd
  Chelsfield BR6 . . . . .88 A4
  Littlebourne CT3 . . . . . . .176 F8
  Sandwich CT13 . . . . .180 F8
  West Thurrock RM20 . . . . .17 B8
  Worth CT14 . . . . .181 B4
Jubilee Rise TN15 . . . . . .154 E6
Jubilee St ME10 . . . . .101 E5
Jubilee Terr
  Gillingham ME7 . . . . .64 C6
  Knockholt TN14 . . . . .120 E4
Jubilee Way
  Dover CT15,CT16 . . . . . .279 A2
  Sidcup DA14 . . . . .31 A6
Judd Rd
  Faversham ME13 . . . . . . .138 A7
  Tonbridge TN9 . . . . .254 B7
Judd Sch The TN9 . . . . . .254 A8
Judeth Gdns DA12 . . . . . .37 E3
Judkins Cl ME5 . . . . .97 C6
Juglans Rd BR6 . . . . .54 A1
Julia Garfield Mews E16 . .1 B8
Julian Ct
  Folkestone CT19 . . . . . . .335 B5
  3 Sidcup DA14 . . . . .31 A4
Julian Rd
  Folkestone CT19 . . . . . . .335 B5
  Orpington BR6 . . . . .87 A4
Julians Cl TN13 . . . . .187 A8
Julians Way TN13 . . . . . .187 A8
Julie Cl CT10 . . . . .84 A7
Julien Pl TN24 . . . . .301 A8
Junction Rd
  Bodiam TN18,TN32 . . . . .355 A3
  Dartford DA1 . . . . .15 D1
  Gillingham ME7 . . . . .64 D4
  Herne Bay CT6 . . . . .76 C2
Junior King's Sch
  CT2 . . . . .143 E5
Juniper Cl
  Ashford TN23 . . . . .267 E2
  Biggin Hill TN16 . . . . . . .118 E2

Juniper Cl continued
  Canterbury CT1 . . . . .175 A6
  Chatham ME5 . . . . .97 A4
  Maidstone ME16 . . . . . . .161 B6
  Royal Tunbridge Wells
  TN4 . . . . .254 D1
  Whitstable CT5 . . . . .74 F1
Juniper La E6 . . . . .1 B8
Juniper Wlk BR8 . . . . .55 D7
Jupiter La TN23 . . . . .299 E5
Jury's Gap Coastguard
  Cotts TN31 . . . . .374 E1
Jury's Gap Rd TN29 . . . .376 A5
Jury St 12 DA11 . . . . .19 B1
Jutland Cl ME3 . . . . .9 C1
Jutland Ho SE18 . . . . .1 E2

K

K9 Est RM13 . . . . .4 E7
Kain Ct CT12 . . . . .83 B1
Kake St CT4 . . . . .239 E7
Kale Rd DA18 . . . . .3 E4
Karloff Way ME2 . . . . .40 B2
Kashgar Rd SE18 . . . . .2 F2
Kashmir Rd SE7 . . . . .11 D7
Katherine Ct ME5 . . . . . . .97 B2
Katherine Gdns SE9 . . . . .11 D3
Katherine Rd TN8 . . . . . . .249 C8
Katherine Villas TN8 . . . .249 C8
Kay St ME14 . . . . .13 B6
Kearsney Abbey ★
  CT16 . . . . .277 D4
Kearsney Ave CT16 . . . . . .277 E4
Kearsney Cl CT16 . . . . . . .277 D4
Kearsney Sta CT16 . . . . . .277 D4
Keary Rd DA10 . . . . .35 F8
Keat Farm Cl CT6 . . . . . . .77 F5
Keating Cl ME1 . . . . .63 A3
Keats Ave E16 . . . . .1 B5
Keats Gdns RM18 . . . . . . .19 B5
Keats Ho DA1 . . . . .14 E2
Keats Rd Bexley DA16 . . . .12 F6
  Erith DA17 . . . . .4 C3
  Lunsford ME20 . . . . .127 F3
Kechill Gdns BR2 . . . . .52 A2
Keddow's Cl CT21 . . . . . .353 D8
Kedleston Dr BR5 . . . . . . .53 F4
Kedleston Rd CT16 . . . . . .278 C5
Keeble Cl SE18 . . . . .12 B8
Keedonwood Rd BR1 . . . . .29 A3
Keefe Cl ME5 . . . . .96 D1
Keeley Mews ME7 . . . . . . .64 E3
Keel Gdns TN4 . . . . .285 E8
Keeling Rd SE9 . . . . .11 D2
Keemor Cl SE18 . . . . .12 A7
Keeper's Hill CT4 . . . . . . .176 D2
Keep The SE3 . . . . .11 A5
Keightley Dr SE9 . . . . .30 C7
Keir Hardie Prim Sch
  E16 . . . . .1 A8
Keir Hardy Ho 7 DA17 . . .4 A3
Keith Ave
  Ramsgate CT12 . . . . .117 A8
  Sutton at H DA4 . . . . .34 B2
Keith Park Cres TN16 . . .118 C7
Keith Sutton House
  SE9 . . . . .30 C6
Kelbrook Rd SE3 . . . . .11 E4
Kelchers La TN11 . . . . . . .223 F5
Kelham Ho 10 SE18 . . . . .12 B8
Kellaway Rd
  Chatham ME5 . . . . .97 A2
  Greenwich SE3 . . . . .11 D5
Kellner Rd SE28 . . . . .2 F3
Kelly Dr ME7 . . . . .64 C7
Kelly Ho
  15 Greenwich SE7 . . . . .11 C8
  Rochester ME1 . . . . .96 C7
Kelsall Cl SE3 . . . . .11 B5
Kelsey Cl BR5 . . . . .54 B7
Kelso Dr DA12 . . . . .37 F4
Kelvedon Rd CT14 . . . . . .215 C2
Kelvin Cl TN10 . . . . .222 D7
Kelvin Ho 3 DA17 . . . . . . .4 A3
Kelvin Par BR6 . . . . .53 E1
Kelvin Rd Bexley DA16 . . . .13 A4
  Tilbury RM18 . . . . .19 A5
Kemble Cl TN2 . . . . .286 E7
Kemble Dr BR2 . . . . .85 E7
Kembleside Rd TN16 . . . .118 C1
Kemnal Rd BR7 . . . . .30 D3
Kemnal Tech Coll BR5 . . .31 B1
Kemnal Warren BR7 . . . . .30 D2
Kemp Alley 2 CT5 . . . . . . .74 D1
Kemp Cl ME5 . . . . .96 E4
Kempes Pl TN25 . . . . .237 E2
Kempley Ct 2 RM17 . . . . .18 D8
Kemp Rd CT5 . . . . .75 C2
Kempton Cl
  Chatham ME5 . . . . .97 C2
  Erith DA8 . . . . .14 C8
Kempt St SE18 . . . . .12 A8
Kemsdale Rd ME13 . . . . . .139 F6
Kemsing Cl DA5 . . . . .31 E8
Kemsing Gdns CT2 . . . . . .143 B4
Kemsing Prim Sch
  TN15 . . . . .123 A2
Kemsing Rd
  Greenwich SE10 . . . . .1 A1
  Wrotham TN15 . . . . .124 C3
Kemsing Sta TN15 . . . . . .155 D8
Kemsley Cl
  Northfleet DA11 . . . . .36 F4
  Swanscombe DA9 . . . . . . .17 B1
Kemsley Ct BR5 . . . . .54 B8
Kemsley Down Sta
  ME10 . . . . .69 C1
Kemsley Mill Railway
  Mus ★ ME10 . . . . .69 C1
Kemsley Rd TN16 . . . . . . .150 D8
Kemsley Sta ME10 . . . . . . .68 E1

Kemsley Street Rd
  ME7 . . . . .98 C1
Kenardington Rd
  TN26 . . . . .347 E3
Kenbrook TN24 . . . . .268 C7
Kencot Cl DA18 . . . . .3 F4
Kendal Cl
  Ramsgate CT11 . . . . .117 B6
  Tonbridge TN9 . . . . .222 C2
Kendal Dr TN9 . . . . .222 C2
Kendall Ave ME18 . . . . . .159 C3
Kendall Ct DA15 . . . . .31 A5
Kendall Gdns DA11 . . . . . .36 F8
Kendall Lodge 9 BR1 . . .52 B8
Kendall Pl 1 ME15 . . . . .195 D8
Kendall Rd SE18 . . . . .11 E6
Kendal Mdw CT5 . . . . .75 E1
Kendal Pk TN4 . . . . .285 E5
Kendal Rise CT10 . . . . .84 A5
Kendal Way ME8 . . . . .98 D8
Kendon Bsns Pk ME2 . . . .63 D8
Kenfield Rd CT4 . . . . .207 A6
Kengate Ind Est CT21 . . .332 F1
Kenia Wlk DA12 . . . . .37 F5
Kenilworth Cl CT15 . . . . .280 A6
Kenilworth Ct
  10 Dartford DA2 . . . . . . .16 B1
  Sittingbourne ME10 . . . . .101 C5
Kenilworth Dr ME8 . . . . . .98 D6
Kenilworth Gdns
  Gillingham ME8 . . . . .98 D7
  Woolwich SE18 . . . . .12 B5
Kenilworth Ho ME16 . . . .161 B2
Kenilworth Rd BR5 . . . . . .53 C3
Kenley Cl
  St Paul's Cray BR7 . . . . . .53 E6
  Sidcup DA14 . . . . .32 A8
Kenley Ho 6 BR5 . . . . .54 B7
Kenmere Rd DA16 . . . . . . .13 C5
Kennacraig Cl E16 . . . . .1 A5
Kennard Cl ME1 . . . . .62 F2
Kennard St E16 . . . . .1 F5
Kennedy Cl
  Faversham ME13 . . . . . . .138 D8
  Orpington BR5 . . . . .53 D1
Kennedy Dr CT14 . . . . . . .215 B2
Kennedy Gdns TN13 . . . .154 D3
Kennedy Ho
  Benenden TN17 . . . . .342 E6
  Northfleet DA11 . . . . .36 D5
  8 Ramsgate CT11 . . . . . .117 F7
Kennel Barn Rd ME9 . . . .133 C5
Kennel Hill CT15 . . . . . . .245 E6
Kennelling Rd ME13,
  TN27 . . . . .201 D5
Kennels The CT15 . . . . . . .245 E6
Kennet Cl 2 BR8 . . . . .55 E6
Kennet Rd Crayford DA1 . .15 A4
  Tonbridge TN10 . . . . . . .222 C2
Kennett Ct 10 BR5 . . . . . .54 D1
Kennett Dr CT14 . . . . . . .215 A2
Kennett Lane Cotts
  TN25 . . . . .332 B8
Kennett La TN25 . . . . . . .332 B8
Kennington CE Jun Sch
  TN24 . . . . .268 C7
Kennington Cl
  Gillingham ME8 . . . . .65 B4
  Maidstone ME15 . . . . . . .195 F7
Kennington Pl TN24 . . . . .268 D7
Kennington Rd TN24 . . . .269 A1
Kensington Ct 5 RM17 . .18 C8
Kensington Ho ME16 . . . .161 A2
Kensington Rd CT1 . . . . .143 C4
Kent Ave Ashford TN24 . . .268 D3
  Bexley DA16 . . . . .12 F2
  Canterbury CT1 . . . . . . .175 D8
  Maidstone ME15 . . . . . . .162 C1
  Minster (Sheppey) ME12 . .47 B6
  Sittingbourne ME10 . . . . .101 D3
Kent Battle of Britain
  Mus ★ CT18 . . . . .306 F4
Kent & Canterbury Hospl
  CT1 . . . . .175 A5
Kent Cl Orpington BR6 . . . .86 E4
  Paddock Wood TN12 . . . .257 A6
  Rochester ME1 . . . . .96 C8
Kent Coll CT2 . . . . .142 C3
Kent Coll Inf & Jun Sch
  CT2 . . . . .142 A1
Kent Coll TN2 . . . . .142 A1
Kent County Optholmic &
  Aural Hospl ME14 . . . . .162 A4
Kent County Show Gd
  ME14 . . . . .131 C3
Kent & East Sussex Rly
  Mus ★ TN30 . . . . .345 A8
Kent & East Sussex Rly★
  TN17 . . . . .344 C1
Kent & East Sussex Steam
  Rly★ TN17 . . . . .358 C1
Kent Gdns CT7 . . . . .80 F7
Kent Hatch Rd
  Crockham Hill RH8,TN8 . .184 B4
  The Chart RH8,TN8 . . . . .183 D4
Kent Ho
  4 Broadstairs CT10 . . . . .84 A4
  Folkestone CT20 . . . . . . .335 B4
  10 Hawkhurst TN18 . . . .341 A2
  Royal Tunbridge Wells
  TN1 . . . . .286 C2
  Sutton at H DA4 . . . . .57 D7
Kent Inst of Art & Design
  Canterbury CT1 . . . . . . .175 B7
  Maidstone ME16 . . . . . . .161 C3
  Rochester ME1 . . . . .63 C4
Kent International Airport
  CT12 . . . . .82 B1
Kentish Ct 8 ME16 . . . . . .161 E4
Kentish Gdns TN2 . . . . . .313 E8

Kentish Mans **15** TN1 . . . 286 A2
Kentish Rd DA17 . . . . .4 A2
Kentish Way BR1,BR2 . . . .52 B6
Kent Kraft Ind Est
  DA11 . . . . .17 F2
Kentlea Rd SE28 . . . . .2 E4
Kentmere Ave CT11 . . . 116 F7
Kentmere Rd SE18 . . . . . . .2 E2
Kent Music Sch CT1 . . . 142 F1
Kenton Gdns CT12 . . . . 115 B6
Kent Pl CT11 . . . . 117 F6
Kent Rd Dartford DA1 . . . .15 E1
  Folkestone CT19 . . . . . 334 E2
  Gravesend DA11 . . . . . . .37 A7
  4 Grays RM17 . . . . .18 C8
  Halling ME2 . . . . .95 A6
  Longfield DA3 . . . . .58 D7
  Margate CT9 . . . . .83 B8
  Orpington BR5 . . . . .54 B3
  Royal Tunbridge Wells
    TN4 . . . . 286 A4
  Sheerness ME12 . . . . . . .28 B1
  Snodland ME6 . . . . 128 A6
Kent Science Pk ME9 . 134 D6
Kent St ME18 . . . . 158 E2
Kentstone Ct ME4 . . . . . .64 A4
Kent St CT5 . . . . 108 D8
Kent & Sussex Hospl
  TN4 . . . . 286 A4
Kent Terr
  Gillingham ME8 . . . . . . .66 C2
  Lower Higham ME3 . . . . .39 D7
  Meopham DA13 . . . . .93 A7
  Ramsgate CT11 . . . . . . 117 F6
Kent View Dr ME12 . . . . .48 D1
Kenward Ct TN11 . . . . . 223 E8
Kenward Rd Eltham SE9 . .11 D2
  Maidstone ME16 . . . . . 161 C5
  Yalding ME18 . . . . 192 E2
Kenwood Ave
  Chatham ME5 . . . . .97 A4
  New Barn DA3 . . . . .59 C6
Kenwyn Rd DA1 . . . . .15 D2
Kenya Rd SE7 . . . . .1 B6
Kenya Terr **7** ME14 . . . 162 A7
Kenyon Wlk ME8 . . . . . . .98 B3
Kerry Cl E16 . . . . .1 B7
Kerry Hill Way ME14 . . 161 E6
Kersey Gdns SE9 . . . . . . .29 E4
Kerton Rd TN29 . . . . . . 380 D2
Kesteven Ct ME2 . . . . . . .95 B5
Kestlake Rd DA5 . . . . . . .13 C1
Keston Ave BR2 . . . . .85 C5
Keston CE Prim Sch
  BR2 . . . . .85 D5
Keston Cl DA16 . . . . .13 C7
Keston Ct
  Gillingham ME8 . . . . . . .65 A2
  Sidcup DA5 . . . . .31 F8
Keston Gdns BR2 . . . . . .85 C6
Keston Park Cl BR2 . . . .85 F7
Kestrel Ave E6 . . . . .1 E8
Kestrel Cl
  Kingsnorth TN23 . . . . . 300 C3
  Marlpit Hill TN8 . . . . . . 217 D3
  Sittingbourne ME10 . . . 102 A2
Kestrel Ct
  4 Sittingbourne ME10 . 102 A4
  Whitstable CT5 . . . . .75 A3
Kestrel Ho ME7 . . . . .64 B6
Kestrel Rd ME5 . . . . .97 C2
Keswick Ave ME10 . . . . 102 C3
Keswick Cl TN9 . . . . 222 C2
Keswick Ct ME7 . . . . .65 A5
Keswick Dr ME16 . . . . . 161 B8
Keswick Gdns RM19 . . . .16 C8
Keswick Rd Bexley DA7 . .14 A6
  Orpington BR6 . . . . .54 A2
Ketridge La ME18 . . . . . 159 D2
Kettle Dr CT18 . . . . 307 B5
Kettle Hill ME13 . . . . . . 168 F4
Kettle Hill Rd
  Eastling ME13 . . . . 168 F5
  Throwley ME13 . . . . 169 A4
Kettle La ME15 . . . . 193 E6
Kettlewell Ct BR8 . . . . . .55 F7
Kevin Dr CT11 . . . . 117 B6
Kevington Cl BR5 . . . . . .53 F5
Kevington Dr BR7 . . . . . .53 F5
Kewlands ME14 . . . . 162 C6
Keycol Hill ME9 . . . . . . 100 F5
Keyes Ave ME4 . . . . .63 F2
Keyes Gdns TN9 . . . . . . 253 F7
Keyes Pl CT19 . . . . 335 E2
Keyes Rd DA1 . . . . .16 A3
Keymer Cl TN16 . . . . . . 118 D3
Keynes Coll CT2 . . . . . . 142 D4
Keynes **9** SE28 . . . . .3 B6
Keynsham Gdns SE9 . . . .11 C2
Keynsham Rd SE9 . . . . . .11 C2
Keys The CT18 . . . . 307 C5
Key St ME10 . . . . 101 A5
Keyworth Cl TN12 . . . . 256 F6
Keyworth Mews **7**
  CT1 . . . . 143 B2
Khalsa Ave DA12 . . . . . . .37 C8
Khartoum Pl DA12 . . . . .19 C1
Khartoum Rd ME4 . . . . . .63 F6
Khartoum Sq CT16 . . . . 278 A6
Khyber Rd ME4,ME7 . . . .64 A7
Kibbles La TN4 . . . . 285 E8
Kidbrooke Gdns SE3 . . . .11 A6
Kidbrooke Gr SE3 . . . . . .11 B6
Kidbrooke La SE9 . . . . . .11 C3
Kidbrooke Park Cl SE3 . .11 C6
Kidbrooke Park Prim Sch
  SE3 . . . . .11 C6
Kidbrooke Sch SE3 . . . . .11 D5

Kidbrooke Sta SE3 . . . . .11 B4
Kidbrooke Way SE3 . . . . .11 B5
Kiddens BR8 . . . . .55 B7
Kidd Pl SE7 . . . . .1 E1
Kidds Cotts BR8 . . . . 55 D3
Kierbeck Bsns Complex
  E16 . . . . .1 B4
Kilbride Ct CT11 . . . . . . .83 F1
Kilburn Ho **6** ME14 . . . 162 A5
Kildare Rd E16 . . . . .1 A7
Killewarren Way BR5 . . .54 C3
Killick Cl TN13 . . . . 153 E6
Killick Rd ME3 . . . . .41 D5
Killicks Cotts ME14 . . . 225 F8
Killigarth Ct **22** DA14 . . .31 A4
Kilnbank TN2 . . . . 286 C7
Kiln Barn Rd ME19,ME
  20 . . . . 160 C7
Kilnbridge Cl ME15 . . . 194 B7
Kilnbridge Wks ME15 . . 194 B7
Kiln Cl Challock TN25 . . 203 B1
  Sittingbourne ME10 . . . 102 A3
Kiln Cnr CT21 . . . . 333 B4
Kilndown Cl
  Ashford TN23 . . . . 299 E6
  Maidstone ME16 . . . . . 161 C7
Kilndown Gdns
  Canterbury CT2 . . . . . . 143 A4
  Margate CT9 . . . . .51 E2
Kilndown DA12 . . . . .37 D2
Kilnfields BR6 . . . . .88 A4
Kiln Field TN30 . . . . 345 C2
Kiln La
  Bethersden TN26 . . . . . 297 F5
  Leigh TN11 . . . . 220 F1
Kiln Rd TN25 . . . . 329 F4
Kiln Way TN12 . . . . 257 A5
Kilnwood TN14 . . . . 120 F6
Kimbell Pl SE3 . . . . .11 C3
Kimber Ho **1** SE18 . . . . .12 B8
Kimberley Cl E16 . . . . . 278 C3
Kimberley Cnr CT10 . . . .83 F8
Kimberley Ct CT8 . . . . . .50 C1
Kimberley Dr DA14 . . . . .31 D6
Kimberley Gr CT5 . . . . . 107 F6
Kimberley Rd
  Gillingham ME7 . . . . . . .64 D3
  Ramsgate CT12 . . . . . . .83 A1
Kimberley Way TN24 . . 300 C7
Kimberly Cl DA17 . . . . . . .3 F2
Kimberly Terr CT18 . . . 305 C7
Kimmeridge Ave ME8 . . .11 C3
Kimmeridge Rd SE9 . . . .29 E4
Kincraig BR7 . . . . .53 A8
Kincraig Dr TN13 . . . . . 154 B4
Kinder Cl SE28 . . . . .3 D6
King and Queen Cl SE9 . .29 E4
King Arthur Ct ME10 . . 101 E3
King Arthur Ct CT12 . . 116 D7
King Arthur's Dr ME2 . . .40 A1
King Charles Ct CT14 . . 215 D2
King Edward Ave
  Broadstairs CT10 . . . . . .84 A4
  Dartford DA1 . . . . .15 D1
  Herne Bay CT6 . . . . .77 B4
King Edward Ct CT6 . . . .77 B4
King Edward Rd
  Birchington CT7 . . . . . . .81 A5
  Chatham ME4 . . . . .63 F2
  Deal CT14 . . . . 215 D8
  Gillingham ME7 . . . . . . .64 F6
  Maidstone ME15 . . . . . 161 F2
  1 Ramsgate CT11 . . . 117 C6
  Rochester ME1 . . . . .63 C5
  Stone DA9 . . . . .17 A2
King Edward St CT5 . . . .74 D1
King Ethelbert Sch
  CT7 . . . . .81 C7
Kingfisher Apartments **13**
  ME15 . . . . 195 E5
Kingfisher Ave CT21 . . . 353 D8
Kingfisher Cl
  Ashford TN24 . . . . 301 A7
  Erith SE28 . . . . .3 C6
  Iwade ME9 . . . . .68 E4
  Margate CT9 . . . . .82 B8
  Orpington BR5 . . . . .54 D5
  Whitstable CT5 . . . . . . 108 C7
Kingfisher Com Prim Sch
  ME5 . . . . .97 B7
Kingfisher Dr
  Chatham ME5 . . . . .97 C7
  Swanscombe DA9 . . . . . .17 A1
Kingfisher Gdns CT21 . . 353 C8
Kingfisher Ho
  Ashford TN23 . . . . 267 F1
  Orpington BR5 . . . . .54 C8
Kingfisher Pl DA4 . . . . . .57 C7
Kingfisher Rd ME20 . . . 128 A2
Kingfisher St E6 . . . . .1 E8
Kingfisher Wlk CT10 . . . .83 F5
King George Ave E16 . . . .1 D7
King George Rd ME5 . . . .96 E4
King George Villas
  CT14 . . . . 181 B3
King George V Memorial
  Houses ME8 . . . . .65 C2
King Harolds Way ME7 . .13 E7
King Henry Mews **7**
  BR6 . . . . .86 F5
King Hill ME19 . . . . 159 A5
King John's Wlk SE9 . . . .11 B1
King Lear's Way CT17 . . 310 B5
Kingly Way CT17 . . . . . . 310 A7
King's Prospect TN24 . . 300 E6

Kings Acre ME15 . . . . . . 163 A1
Kingsand Rd SE12 . . . . . .29 A6
King's Ave
  Ashford TN23 . . . . 268 A2
  Birchington CT7 . . . . . . .80 D7
  Broadstairs CT10 . . . . . .84 B6
Kings Ave BR1 . . . . .29 A2
King's Ave
  Ramsgate CT12 . . . . . . .83 B1
  Rochester ME1 . . . . .63 C3
  Sandwich CT13 . . . . . . 182 A8
  Whitstable CT5 . . . . .74 E1
King's Bastion ME7 . . . . .64 A5
Kingsbridge Ct **11**
  CT20 . . . . 335 E5
Kings Chase TN24 . . . . . 269 A2
King's Cl DA1 . . . . .14 E3
King's Cl CT14 . . . . 248 D6
Kings Cotts
  Cranbrook CT17 . . . . . . 320 D6
  Leeds ME17 . . . . 196 F6
King's Cotts
  Wateringbury ME18 . . . 192 D6
  Yalding ME18 . . . . 193 A1
Kings Ct Deal CT14 . . . . 215 D3
  Horsmonden TN12 . . . . 290 A6
  21 Sidcup DA14 . . . . . .31 A5
Kingsdale Ct
  Chatham ME5 . . . . .64 C1
  Swanscombe DA10 . . . . .17 C1
Kingsdale Rd SE18 . . . . .12 F8
Kingsdown Cl
  Gillingham ME7 . . . . . . .98 B4
  Gravesend DA12 . . . . . . .37 F7
  Maidstone ME16 . . . . . 161 E4
Kingsdown Cotts ME9 . 135 C4
Kingsdown Hill CT14 . . 248 D4
Kingsdown Ind Est
  ME20 . . . . 160 B8
Kingsdown Park Holiday
  Village CT14 . . . . 248 D5
Kingsdown Pk CT5 . . . . .74 F2
Kingsdown Rd
  Kingsdown CT14 . . . . . 248 D7
  Lynsted ME9 . . . . 135 D4
  St Margaret's at Cliffe
    CT15 . . . . 280 A7
Kingsdown & Ringwould CE
  Prim Sch CT14 . . . . . . 248 C5
Kingsdown Way BR2 . . . .52 A3
Kings Dr DA12 . . . . .37 B5
Kings Farm Prim Sch
  DA11 . . . . .37 C3
Kingsfield Ho SE9 . . . . . .29 D5
Kingsfield Rd CT6 . . . . . .77 B2
Kingsford Cl TN25 . . . . 301 E4
Kingsford Com Sch E6 . . .1 F7
Kingsford Cotts TN17 . . 342 D6
Kingsford Ct CT17 . . . . 278 B1
Kingsford St TN25 . . . . 301 D5
Kingsford Way E6 . . . . . . .1 F8
Kingsgate Ave CT10 . . . .51 F1
Kingsgate Bay Rd CT10 . .51 H2
Kingsgate Castle CT10 . .51 H2
Kingsgate Cl Bexley DA7 .13 C6
  Maidstone ME16 . . . . . 161 C4
  Orpington BR5 . . . . .54 C6
Kingsgate Coll CT10 . . . .84 A8
Kingsgate La TN30 . . . . 359 C5
Kingsground SE9 . . . . . . .11 E1
King's Head Alley
  ME12 . . . . .28 A3
King's Highway SE18,
  SE2 . . . . .12 F8
Kings Hill Ave ME19 . . . 159 A4
Kingshill Dr ME3 . . . . . . .41 D6
Kings Hill Sch ME19 . . . 159 A3
Kingsholm Gdns SE9 . . . .11 E3
Kingshurst Rd SE12 . . . .29 A8
Kingsingfield Cl TN15 . . .90 E3
Kingsingfield Rd TN15 . .90 E2
Kings La TN12 . . . . 258 C7
Kingsland Gdns CT14 . . 215 D2
Kingsland Gr TN27 . . . . 262 D5
Kingsland Hollow
  TN29 . . . . 366 A4
Kingsland La
  Egerton Forstal TN27 . . 232 E1
  Westwell TN25 . . . . 235 F1
Kingsley Ave DA1 . . . . . .16 A2
Kingsley Ct Bexley DA6 . .14 A3
  Wadhurst TN5 . . . . 337 A4
  1 Woolwich SE28 . . . . .3 C5
Kingsley Mews BR7 . . . .30 B2
Kingsley Rd
  Maidstone ME15 . . . . . 162 A3
  Orpington BR6 . . . . .86 F3
  Whitstable CT5 . . . . . . 108 E8
Kingsley Wood Dr SE9 . .29 F5
Kingsman Par SE18 . . . . .1 F3
Kingsman St SE18 . . . . . . .1 F2
Kingsmarsh La TN29 . . 372 C5
Kings Mdw TN24 . . . . . 268 E7
Kingsmead TN16 . . . . . . 118 D3
Kingsmead Cl DA15 . . . .31 A6
Kingsmead Cotts BR2 . . .52 E1
Kingsmead Ct CT19 . . . 335 B8
Kingsmead Pk
  Allhallows-on-S ME3 . . . .9 E3
  Paddock Wood TN12 . . 257 A6
Kingsmead Prim Sch
  CT1 . . . . 143 A1
Kingsmead Rd CT1,
  CT2 . . . . 143 A2
Kingsmead CT8 . . . . .50 C1
Kingsmere BR7 . . . . .52 E8
Kings Mews **7** CT1 . . . 143 A1
Kings Mill Cl ME9 . . . . . 101 C6
Kingsnorth CE Prim Sch
  TN23 . . . . 300 B3
Kingsnorth Cl ME3 . . . . .41 E6
Kingsnorth Ct
  Crockenhill BR8 . . . . . . .55 C3

Kingsnorth Ct continued
  2 Folkestone CT20 . . 335 B5
Kingsnorth Gdns
  CT20 . . . . 335 C5
Kingsnorth Ind Est
  ME3 . . . . .42 D7
Kingsnorth Rd
  Ashford TN23 . . . . 300 A6
  Faversham ME13 . . . . . 138 C6
  Gillingham ME8 . . . . . . .65 C4
Kings Oak Mews ME5 . . .96 F4
King's Orch Eltham SE9 . .11 E1
  Rochester ME1 . . . . .63 C5
Kings Par **7** TN24 . . . . 268 B2
King's Pk CT1 . . . . 143 B1
Kings Pk TN2 . . . . 286 D3
King's Pl **5** CT1 . . . . . . 117 E6
Kings Rd Aylesham CT3 . 210 F6
  Biggin Hill TN16 . . . . . . 118 C2
King's Rd
  Birchington CT7 . . . . . . .81 A6
  Chatham ME5 . . . . .64 D1
Kings Rd CT17 . . . . 310 A7
King's Rd ME13 . . . . 138 C7
Kings Rd
  Folkestone CT20 . . . . . 334 C6
  Headcorn TN27 . . . . . . 262 C5
King's Rd CT5 . . . . .76 F5
Kings Rd
  Minster (Sheppey) ME12 . .47 D7
  Orpington BR6 . . . . .86 F6
King's Rd
  Ramsgate CT11 . . . . . . 117 D8
  Tonbridge TN9 . . . . 254 D7
Kings Reach ME15 . . . . 195 D8
Kingsridge Gdns DA1 . . .15 D1
Kings Ropewalk CT17 . . 310 B5
Kings Row
  1 Maidstone ME15 . . . 162 A1
  Rochester ME1 . . . . .63 B4
King's Sch Canterbury The
  CT1 . . . . 143 A1
King's Sch ME1 . . . . .63 C5
King's Sch The CT1 . . . 175 A8
King's Standing Ind Est
  TN2 . . . . 254 F2
Kings Standing Way
  TN2 . . . . 254 F1
King St Brookland TN29 . 362 D2
  Canterbury CT1 . . . . . . 142 F1
  Chatham ME4 . . . . .64 A4
  Deal CT14 . . . . 215 D6
  Deal, Walmer CT14 . . . 215 D3
  Dover CT16 . . . . 310 D7
  Fordwich CT2 . . . . 144 A4
  Gillingham ME7 . . . . . . .64 C6
  Gravesend DA12 . . . . . . .19 B1
  Maidstone ME14 . . . . . 162 A4
  Margate CT9 . . . . .50 J3
Kings Toll Rd TN2 . . . . . 288 A6
Kingston Ave CT9 . . . . . .82 C7
Kingston Cl
  Crabble CT17 . . . . 277 F3
  Herne Bay CT6 . . . . .77 F5
  Ramsgate CT12 . . . . . . .83 B2
Kingston Cres ME5 . . . . .97 C4
Kingston Ct DA11 . . . . . .18 B1
Kingston Dr ME15 . . . . . 195 A8
Kingstone Ct **3** CT20 . . 335 B5
King St Ramsgate CT11 . 117 E7
  Rochester ME1 . . . . .63 C4
  Sandwich CT13 . . . . . . 149 A1
  Sheerness ME12 . . . . . . .28 A2
  Sittingbourne ME10 . . . 101 E5
  West Malling ME19 . . . 159 C8
Kingsway Chatham ME5 . .64 D1
  Dymchurch TN29 . . . . . 352 E2
  Gillingham ME7 . . . . . . .64 E1
  Orpington BR5 . . . . .53 D4
Kingswear Gdns ME2 . . .63 C7
Kings Wlk Grays RM17 . .18 A8
  Maidstone ME14 . . . . . 162 B5
Kingswood Ave
  Chatham ME4 . . . . .63 F2
  Erith DA17 . . . . .3 F2
  Swanley BR8 . . . . .55 F6
Kingswood Cl
  Ashford TN24 . . . . 268 D5
  Dartford DA1 . . . . .15 C1
  Orpington BR6 . . . . .53 D2
  Royal Tunbridge Wells
    TN2 . . . . 286 C3
Kingswood Ho
  12 Maidstone ME16 . . 161 A3
  16 Sidcup DA14 . . . . . .31 B4
Kingswood Prim Sch
  ME17 . . . . 197 E2
Kingswood Rd
  Gillingham ME7 . . . . . . .64 D6
  Kit's Coty ME20 . . . . . . 129 D8
  Royal Tunbridge Wells
    TN2 . . . . 286 C3
  Sevenoaks TN13 . . . . . 153 E7
Kingswood Villas
  CT17 . . . . 278 A2
King William Rd **6**
  ME7 . . . . .64 C7
Kinlet Rd SE18 . . . . .12 C6
Kinnell Ct **13** DA14 . . . .31 B4
Kinnings Row TN9 . . . . 222 C2
Kinross Cl ME5 . . . . .97 B7
Kinveachy Gdns SE7 . . . .1 E1
Kipling Ave RM18 . . . . . .19 C6
Kipling Dr ME20 . . . . . . 127 F4
Kipling Rd
  Ashford TN23 . . . . 268 B2
  Bexley DA7 . . . . .13 E6
Kipping Cl CT18 . . . . . . 307 A4
Kippington Cl TN13 . . . 153 F3
Kippington Dr SE9 . . . . .29 D7

Kippington Rd TN13 . . . 154 A2
Kirby Cl TN17 . . . . 320 D4
Kirby's Hts **8** CT2 . . . . 142 F1
Kirby Rd Chattenden ME3 . 40 F5
  Dartford DA2 . . . . .34 D8
Kirby's La CT1 . . . . 142 F1
Kirkcourt TN13 . . . . 154 A4
Kirkdale Cl ME15 . . . . . . .97 D1
Kirkdale Cotts ME15 . . 194 F5
Kirkdale ME15 . . . . 194 F5
Kirkdale Rd
  Maidstone ME15 . . . . . 194 F6
  Royal Tunbridge Wells
    TN1 . . . . 286 B4
Kirk Gdns CT14 . . . . 215 B2
Kirkham Rd E6 . . . . .1 E7
Kirkham St SE18 . . . . . . .12 E8
Kirkins Cl TN12 . . . . . . 290 A6
Kirkland Cl DA15 . . . . . . .12 E1
Kirk La SE18 . . . . .12 C6
Kirkman Ct TN12 . . . . . 260 E3
Kirkside Rd SE3 . . . . . . .11 A8
Kirkstone Ave CT11 . . . 116 F7
Kirk View TN13 . . . . 299 C8
Kirkwood Ave TN26 . . . 326 A1
Kirton Cl CT18 . . . . 306 F4
Kitchener Ave
  Chatham ME4 . . . . .64 A1
  Gravesend DA12 . . . . . . .37 C5
Kitchener Ct CT4 . . . . . 242 F8
Kitchener Cotts ME3 . . .25 C4
Kitchener Rd
  Chattenden ME3 . . . . . .40 F1
  Dover CT17 . . . . 310 A7
  Rochester ME2 . . . . .63 A8
Kitchener Sq CT19 . . . . 335 E8
Kite Farm CT5 . . . . .75 D3
Kite La TN12 . . . . 289 A6
Kitewell La TN29 . . . . . 376 D8
Kither Rd TN23 . . . . 300 A4
Kit Hill Ave ME5 . . . . . . .96 E3
Kit Hill ME13 . . . . 171 D8
Kitsbridge La
  Hamstreet TN26 . . . . . 349 C4
  Ruckinge TN25,TN26 . . 350 B6
Kit's Coty House ★
  ME20 . . . . 129 C6
Kittiwake Cl CT6 . . . . . . .77 F5
Klondike Ind Est ME11 . .45 F4
Knatchbull Way TN25 . . 302 E5
Knatts La TN15 . . . . 123 E8
Knatts Valley Rd TN15 . .90 D2
Knaves Acre TN27 . . . . 262 D5
Knave Wood Rd TN15 . 122 E2
Knee Hill Cres SE2 . . . . . .3 C2
Knee Hill SE2 . . . . .3 C1
Knell La CT3 . . . . 147 C3
Knight Ave
  Canterbury CT2 . . . . . . 174 C8
  Gillingham ME7 . . . . . . .64 D7
Knighton Rd TN14 . . . . 121 F2
Knight Rd
  Rochester ME2 . . . . .63 A6
  Tonbridge TN10 . . . . . . 222 E6
Knightrider Ct ME15 . . . 162 A3
Knightrider St
  Maidstone ME15 . . . . . 162 A4
  Sandwich CT13 . . . . . . 149 A1
Knights Alley **20** CT5 . . .74 D2
Knight's Ave CT10 . . . . . .84 B6
Knightsbridge Cl TN4 . . 286 B6
Knightsbridge Mews
  BR7 . . . . .29 F1
Knights Cl
  Hoo St Werburgh ME3 . .41 E1
  Pembury TN2 . . . . 287 D7
Knights Croft DA3 . . . . . .91 F7
Knight's Ct CT17 . . . . . 278 B1
Knight's Ct **7** ME10 . . .14 F7
Knights Ct ME10 . . . . . . 101 E3
Knights Field ME4 . . . . . .89 E7
Knightsfield Rd ME10 . . 101 D7
Knights Manor Way
  DA1 . . . . .15 F1
Knights Pk
  Rochester ME2 . . . . .63 A6
  Royal Tunbridge Wells
    TN11 . . . . 254 F1
Knight's Rd CT16 . . . . . 310 E8
Knights Rd
  Hoo St Werburgh ME3 . .41 D5
  Newham E16 . . . . .1 A4
Knights Ridge BR6 . . . . .87 B5
Knight's Ridge TN2 . . . 287 D7
Knights Templars
  CT17 . . . . 310 C6
Knights Way CT16 . . . . 278 A6
Knight's Way TN2 . . . . . 262 D6
Knights Way TN2,TN11 . 254 F1
Knockhall Chase DA9 . . .17 C2
Knockhall Com Prim Sch
  DA9 . . . . .17 C2
Knockhall Rd DA9 . . . . . .17 C2
Knock Hill TN30 . . . . . . 361 A2
Knockholt Rd
  Eltham SE9 . . . . .11 D2
  Halstead TN14 . . . . 120 F6
  Margate CT9 . . . . .51 E2
Knockholt Sta TN14 . . . .87 E2
Knockhurst Ct TN30 . . . 324 C1
Knock Mill La TN15 . . . 124 A5
Knock Rd TN23 . . . . 300 A7
Knockwood Rd TN30 . . 324 C1
Knold Pk CT9 . . . . .82 E8
Knole Cl TN14 . . . . 187 B2
Knole Gate DA15 . . . . . .30 E5
Knole House ★ TN15 . . 154 C1
Knole La TN13,TN15 . . 154 C1
Knole Rd Chatham ME5 . .97 C3
  Dartford DA1 . . . . .33 D8
  Sevenoaks TN13 . . . . . 154 D1

Knole The Eltham SE9 . . .30 A4
  Faversham ME13 . . . . . 138 B7
  Istead Rise DA13 . . . . . .36 E1
Knole Way TN13 . . . . . . 154 C2
Knoll Ct
  Folkestone CT20 . . . . . 335 C4
  Orpington BR6 . . . . .86 F8
Knoll Hill TN25 . . . . 330 C3
Knoll La CT15 . . . . 299 E7
Knoll Pl CT14 . . . . 215 C2
Knoll Rd Sidcup DA14 . . .31 B4
  Sidcup,Old Bexley DA5 . .14 A1
Knoll Rise BR6 . . . . .53 F1
Knoll The Hayes BR2 . . . .52 A1
Knotley Hall Cotts
  TN11 . . . . 220 A2
Knott Cres TN24 . . . . . . 301 A7
Knott Ct ME14 . . . . 161 F6
Knott's La CT15 . . . . . . 279 F6
Knotts La CT1 . . . . 143 A3
Knotts Pl TN13 . . . . 154 A3
Knotts Sq TN23 . . . . . . 268 C2
Knowle Ave ME4 . . . . . . .13 F7
Knowle Cl TN3 . . . . 284 F5
Knowle Cott TN3 . . . . . 314 E1
Knowle Cotts TN3 . . . . 314 E1
Knowle La TN12 . . . . . . 257 C3
Knowle Lodge BR7 . . . . .29 F2
Knowle Rd
  Maidstone ME14 . . . . . 162 B6
  Orpington BR2 . . . . .85 E8
  Paddock Wood TN12 . . 257 D3
  Wouldham ME1 . . . . .95 D4
Knowler Way CT6 . . . . . .77 C5
Knowles Gdns TN7 . . . . 262 D5
Knowles Wlk TN12 . . . . 260 F4
Knowlton Gdns ME16 . . 161 B2
Knowlton Gn BR2 . . . . . .52 A4
Knowlton Wlk **1** CT1 . . 143 B1
Knowsley Way TN11 . . . 221 D6
Knox Ct TN15 . . . . 154 F6
Kohima Pl CT15 . . . . . . 278 F2
Koonowla Ct TN16 . . . . 118 D4
Kydbrook Cl BR5 . . . . . . .53 C2
Kyetop Wlk ME8 . . . . . . .98 D6
Kynaston Rd
  Bromley BR1 . . . . .29 A3
  Orpington BR5 . . . . .54 B2

L

La Belle Alliance Sq **9**
  CT11 . . . . 117 E7
Labour-in-vain Rd
  TN15 . . . . 124 E5
Laburnham Pl SE9 . . . . .12 A2
Laburnum Ave
  Dartford DA1 . . . . .33 D7
  Sandwich CT13 . . . . . . 180 F8
  Swanley BR8 . . . . .55 D6
Laburnum Cl CT16 . . . . 277 E4
Laburnum Dr ME20 . . . 128 A2
Laburnum Gr
  Northfleet DA11 . . . . . . .36 D8
  Sheerness ME12 . . . . . . .28 H1
Laburnum Ho ME12 . . . .28 B2
Laburnum La CT2 . . . . . 144 B7
Laburnum Pl ME10 . . . . 101 E4
Laburnum Rd ME2 . . . . .62 E5
Laburnum Way BR2 . . . .53 B2
Labworth Ct ME12 . . . . .46 E6
Lacebark Cl DA15 . . . . . .30 F8
Lacey Cl ME17 . . . . 196 E4
Laceys La ME17 . . . . . . 227 C7
Lachlan Way **2** CT20 . . 334 F3
Lackenden Cotts CT3 . . 176 D6
Lacknut Cotts DA13 . . . .92 E2
Lacock Gdns
  Loose ME15 . . . . 195 A8
  Maidstone ME15 . . . . . 162 A1
Lacton Oast TN24 . . . . 301 B8
Lacton Way TN24 . . . . . 301 A8
Lacy Cl ME16 . . . . 161 D7
Ladbrooke Cres DA14 . . 31 D5
Ladbrooke Ho **7**
  ME14 . . . . 162 A5
Laddingford Farm Ind Est
  ME18 . . . . 225 D4
Laddingford St Mary's CE
  Prim Sch ME18 . . . . . 225 E4
Ladds Cnr ME7 . . . . .65 B5
Ladds La ME6 . . . . .95 A2
Ladds Way BR8 . . . . .55 D5
Lade Fort Cotts TN29 . . 377 E6
Lade Fort Cres TN29 . . 377 E6
Ladham Rd TN17 . . . . . 291 A2
Ladies Mile TN6,TN7 . . 311 D4
Ladies Wlk CT21 . . . . . 333 C1
Lady Boswell's CE Prim Sch
  TN13 . . . . 154 C2
Ladyclose Ave ME3 . . . . .40 A7
Ladycroft Gdns **6** BR6 . .86 C5
Ladycroft Way BR6 . . . . .86 C5
Ladyfern Cl TN2 . . . . . . 286 C4
Ladyfields ME5 . . . . .97 D2
Ladyfields Cl ME9 . . . . 100 F5
Ladyfields
  Herne Bay CT6 . . . . .77 D2
  Northfleet DA11 . . . . . . .36 H4
Lady Garne Rd CT15 . . 308 F5
Lady Joanna Thornhill
  Endowed Prim Sch
  TN25 . . . . 237 E2
Lady Oak La TN5,TN17 . 339 C7
Lady's Gift Rd TN4 . . . . 285 F8
Ladysmith Gr CT5 . . . . 107 F6
Ladysmith Rd
  Eltham SE9 . . . . .12 A1

Ladysmith Rd continued
Whitstable CT5 ....108 C5
Lady Vane Cl TN11 .....189 C5
Ladywell 7 CT16 ....310 D8
Ladywell Ho
2 Dover CT16 ....310 D8
7 Orpington BR5 ....54 B7
Ladywood Ave BR5 ......53 E4
Ladywood Rd
Cuxton ME2 ....62 B2
Dartford DA2 ....34 E3
Sturry CT2 ....143 F7
Lady Wootton's Gn 6
CT1 ....175 A8
La Galamina TN28 ......377 E8
Lagonda Way DA1 ....15 C3
Lagoon Rd BR5 ....54 B4
Lagos Ave CT12 ....83 A1
Lake Ave BR1 ....29 A2
Lakedale Rd SE18 ....2 E1
Lake Dr ME3 ....39 C6
Lakelands
Harrietsham ME17 .....198 E6
Loose ME15 ....195 A7
Lakeman Way TN4 ......286 B7
Lakemead TN23 ....299 E8
Lake Rd Ditton ME20 ...160 E8
TN4 ....285 E4
Laker Ho ME14 ....162 A6
Laker Rd ME1 ....96 C6
Lakeside Ave SE28 ......3 A5
Lakeside Cl
Bexley DA5,DA15 ......13 C2
Bough Beech TN8 .....218 F4
Lakeside Dr BR2 ....85 E7
Lakeside Gdns TN26 ...234 F1
Lakeside Pk ME2 ....63 E7
Lakeside
Royal Tunbridge Wells
TN2 ....286 C6
Snodland ME6 ....127 F6
Lakes Rd BR2 ....85 C5
Lakes The ME20 ....128 A4
Lakesview International
Bsns Pk CT3 ....112 A1
Lakeswood Rd BR5 .....53 C3
Lakeview Cl ME6 ......128 A6
Lakeview Rd DA16 ......13 B3
Lake View Rd TN13 ....154 A4
Lake Wlk ME20 ....128 A5
Lakewood Dr ME8 ......98 C6
Laking Ave CT10 ....84 B7
Laleham Gdns CT9 .....51 B2
Laleham Rd CT9 ....51 B1
Laleham Sch CT9 ......51 B1
Laleham Wlk CT9 ......51 B1
Lambarde Ave SE9 ......30 A4
Lambarde Cl ME2 ......95 A4
Lambarde Dr TN13 ....154 A4
Lambarde Rd TN13 ....154 A5
Lambardes Cl TN14 ...120 C8
Lambardes DA3 ....91 F7
Lambard Ho 8 ME14 ...162 A5
Lamb Cl RM18 ....19 C5
Lambden Rd TN27 .....265 C6
Lamberhurst Cl 14 BR5 .54 D1
Lamberhurst Farm
ME13 ....107 F1
Lamberhurst Gn ME8 ...65 B3
Lamberhurst Rd
Horsmonden TN12,TN3 .289 C3
Lamberhurst TN3,TN12 .317 C2
Maidstone ME16 ......161 B7
Lamberhurst St Mary's CE
Prim Sch TN3 ....317 B6
Lamberhurst Vineyard ★
TN3 ....317 A4
Lamberhurst Way CT9 ..51 F3
Lambersart Cl TN4 ....254 D1
Lambert Cl TN16 ......118 D3
Lambert Ct DA8 ....14 C8
Lambert Ho CT14 .....215 B3
Lambert Mews 4
ME6 ....128 A8
Lambert Rd E16 ....1 B7
Lamberts Pl TN12 .....290 B5
Lamberts Rd TN2 .....286 D8
Lambert's Yd TN9 .....222 B1
Lambes Ct ME8 ....98 D5
Lambeth Cl ME5 ....97 B4
Lambeth Rd CT1 ......143 C4
Lambourn Dr ME19 ....159 A2
Lambourne Pl
Gillingham ME8 ....66 A2
Greenwich SE3 ....11 B6
Lambourne Rd ME15 ..162 F2
Lambourne Wlk CT1 ...175 C8
Lambourn Ho BR1 ......29 C1
Lambourn Way
Chatham ME5 ....97 C2
Royal Tunbridge Wells
TN2 ....286 D1
Lambs Bank TN9 ......254 B7
Lambscroft Ave SE9 ....29 D5
Lamb's Cross ME17 ....229 A5
Lambsfrith Gr ME7 ....98 B3
Lamb's Mobile Home Pk
TN12 ....257 A7
Lamb's Wlk CT5 ......108 C6
Lambton Rd CT17 ....278 A1
Laming Rd CT7 ....81 B6
Lammas Dr ME10 .....101 E6
Lammas Gate ME14 ...138 D8
Lamorbey Cl DA15 .....30 F6
Lamorna Ave ME12 .....37 D6
Lamorna Cl BR6 ....54 A2
Lampington Row TN3 .284 E3
Lamplighters Cl
2 Dartford DA1 ....15 F1
Gillingham ME7 ....97 F5
Lamport Cl SE18 ....1 F2

Lamson Rd RM13 ....4 F8
Lancashire Rd ME15 ...195 E7
Lancaster Ave CT18 ...308 C2
Lancaster Cl
Hamstreet TN26 ......349 A8
Ramsgate CT12 ....83 B1
Lancaster Ct
Gillingham ME8 ....98 C7
Gravesend DA12 ....37 C5
Lancaster Gdns
Birchington CT7 ....80 F6
Bromley BR1 ....52 E4
Herne Bay CT6 ....77 D5
Lancaster Ho
Deal CT14 ....215 A5
3 Dover CT17 ....310 D7
Lancaster Rd
Canterbury CT1 ......174 F6
Dover CT17 ....310 D7
Lancaster The CT10 ....84 B3
Lancaster Way ME19 ..158 F3
Lance Cl ME10 ....101 F8
Lance Croft DA3 ....91 F8
Lancelot Cl Deal CT14 .215 A3
Rochester ME2 ....62 E6
Lancelot Ct BR6 ....87 B8
Lancelot Rd DA16 ......13 A4
Lancer Ho ME1 ....63 C3
Lances Cl DA13 ....60 A2
Lancet La ME15 ....195 A6
Lancey Cl SE7 ....1 E2
Lanchester Ct TN6 ......76 A3
Lancing Rd BR6 ....87 B8
Landale Gdns DA1 .....33 C8
Landbury Wlk TN23 ...267 F4
Landon Rd CT6 ....77 C4
Landor Ct ME7 ....98 A3
Landrail Rd ME9 ....67 B3
Landseer Ave ME4 .....36 D5
Landseer Cl TN10 ....222 E6
Landstead Rd SE18 ....12 D7
Land Way ME3 ....39 D5
Landway TN15 ....154 F7
Landway The
Borough Green TN15 ..156 F7
Kemsing TN15 ....123 A2
Maidstone ME14 .....163 A4
Orpington BR5 ....54 C6
Lane Ave DA9 ....17 C1
Lane End Bexley DA7 ...14 B4
Herne Bay CT6 ....76 D5
Lanes Ave DA11 ....37 A5
Laneside BR7 ....30 C3
Lanes The CT12 ......115 D6
Lane's Wlk CT5 ....74 E2
Lane The
Fordcombe TN3 ......284 C5
Greenwich SE3 ....11 A4
Guston CT15 ....278 F6
Lanfranc Gdns CT2 ...142 C1
Lanfranc Ho 5 CT1 ...143 A1
Lanfranc Rd CT14 ....215 C8
Langafel CE Prim Sch
DA3 ....59 A6
Langafel Cl DA3 ....58 E7
Langbrook Rd SE3 .....11 D5
Lang Ct CT5 ....75 C3
Langdale TN23 ....299 E8
Langdale Ave CT11 ...117 A7
Langdale Cl
Gillingham ME8 ....65 D1
Orpington BR6 ....86 B7
Langdale Cres DA7 .....14 A6
Langdale Rise ME4 .....54 D7
Langdale Wlk 5 DA11 ..36 E5
Langdon Ave CT3 .....147 F1
Langdon Cl CT15 .....279 F5
Langdon Cross CT15 ..279 C7
Langdon Prim Sch
CT15 ....247 A1
Langdon Rd
Bromley BR2 ....52 B6
Folkestone CT19 .....334 D7
Rochester ME1 ....63 C4
Langdon Shaw DA14 ...30 F3
Langford Pl DA14 ......31 A5
Langham Ct CT19 ......50 F1
Langham Gr ME16 ....161 C4
Langholm Rd
Ashford TN23 ....300 A7
Langton Green TN3 ...284 F3
Langhorne Gdns 9
CT20 ....335 C4
Langhorne Ho 6 SE7 ..11 C8
Langlands Dr DA2 .....34 E3
Langley Ct 13 SE9 ....12 A1
Langley Gdns
2 Bromley BR2 ....52 C5
Margate CT9 ....51 E3
Orpington BR5 ....53 B3
Langley Ho
6 Bromley BR1 ......29 B1
11 Maidstone ME16 ..161 A3
Langley Rd Bexley DA16 .13 C8
Sittingbourne ME10 ..101 F7
Langmore Ct DA7 .....13 D4
Langney Dr TN23 .....299 E6
Langport Rd TN28 ....373 C6
Langton Cl ME14 .....162 C5
Langton Cotts CT3 ...146 B5
Langton Green Prim Sch
TN3 ....284 E4
Langton La CT4 ....175 A4
Langton Rd
Rusthall TN3,TN4 ....285 C3
Speldhurst TN3 ......285 A7
Langton Ridge TN3 ...285 B3
Langton Way SE3 ......11 A2
Langworth Cl DA2 .....33 D5
Lankester Parker Rd
ME1 ....96 C6
Lannoy Rd SE9 ....30 C7

Lanridge Rd SE2 ....3 D3
Lansbury Cres DA1 ....16 A2
Lansbury Gdns
Lansbury Ct 4 SE28 ....3 B6
Lansbury Gdns RM18 ..19 A6
Lansbury Ho 5 DA17 ...3 F1
Lansdowne Ave
Bexley DA7 ....13 D7
Maidstone ME15 .....195 C6
Orpington BR6 ....53 B1
Lansdowne Ct 9 ME4 ..63 F4
Lansdowne La SE7 ......1 D1
Lansdowne Mews SE7 ...1 D1
Lansdowne Prim Sch
Sittingbourne ME10 ..102 C3
Tilbury RM18 ....18 F5
Lansdowne Rd
Bromley BR1 ....29 B1
Chatham ME4 ....63 E2
Royal Tunbridge Wells
TN1 ....286 B4
Sevenoaks TN13 .....154 D5
Tonbridge TN9 ....222 B2
Lansdowne Sq
Northfleet DA11 ....18 F1
2 Royal Tunbridge Wells
TN1 ....286 B4
Lansdown Pl DA11 .....36 F7
Lansdown Rd
Canterbury CT1 ......175 A7
Sidcup DA14 ....31 B5
Sittingbourne ME10 ..102 C3
Tilbury RM18 ....18 F5
Lantern Ho SE18 ......2 A1
Lanthorne Mews
Royal Tunbridge
Wells,Calverley Park
TN1 ....286 B3
Lanthorne Rd CT10 ....84 A4
Lapins La ME19 ......158 F2
Lapis Cl DA12 ....38 B7
La Providence ME1 ....63 C5
Lapwing Cl Erith DA8 ..15 B7
Hawkinge CT18 ......307 A3
Minster (Sheppey) ME12 .47 B5
Lapwing Dr
Ashford TN23 ....300 D3
Lower Halstow ME9 ...67 B3
Lapwing Rd ME3 ......27 B5
Lapwings DA3 ....59 B6
Lapwings The DA12 ...37 D6
Lapworth Ct BR6 ......87 C8
Larch Cl
Broadstairs CT10 .....83 D4
Larkfield ME20 ......128 B2
Larch Cres
Hoo St Werburgh ME3 .41 E3
Tonbridge TN10 .....222 C6
Larchcroft ME5 ....97 A4
Larch Dene BR6 ....86 A8
Larches The
Faversham ME13 .....138 A8
Higham ME3 ....39 C3
Whitstable CT5 ......108 C8
Larch Gr
Paddock Wood TN12 ..256 F6
Sidcup DA15 ....30 A3
Larch Rd Dartford DA1 .33 D7
Elvington CT15 ......212 B1
Larch Terr ME12 ......46 A8
Larch Way BR2 ....53 A2
Larch Wlk
Ashford TN24 ....268 C6
Swanley BR8 ....59 D7
Larch Wood Cl ME5 ...97 D1
Larchwood Rd SE9 ....30 B6
Largo Wlk DA8 ....14 E6
Larkey View CT4 .....173 E1
Larkfield
Gillingham ME7 ......64 E4
Sittingbourne ME10 ..101 B3
Larkfield Cl Hayes BR2 .85 A8
Larkfield ME20 ......128 A1
Larkfield TN12 ......256 A1
Larkfield Rd
Larkfield ME20 ......128 B1
Sevenoaks TN13 ....153 C4
Sidcup DA14 ....30 F5
Larkfields DA11 ....36 E5
Larkfield Trad Est
ME20 ....128 B5
Larkin Cl ME2 ....40 B2
Larking Dr ME16 .....161 D7
Larkscliff Ct CT7 ......80 D8
Larks Field DA3 ....58 F5
Larksfield Rd ME13 ..105 C1
Larkspur Cl
2 East Malling ME19 ..128 A1
4 Newham E6 ....1 E8
Orpington BR5 ....87 C7
Larkspur Lodge DA14 ..31 B5
Larkspur Rd
Chatham ME5 ....96 E4
West Malling ME19 ..127 F1
Larkstore Pk TN12 ...260 D5
Larkswood Cl DA8 ....15 A6
Larkwell La DA3 ......58 F5
Larner Rd DA8 ....14 E7
La Rocco DA12 ......377 E8
Lascelles Rd CT17 ...310 A4
Laser Quay ME2 ......63 D6
Lashenden Air Warfare
Mus ★ TN27 ....263 A2
Lassa Rd SE9 ....11 F2
La Tausco TN28 .....377 D8
Latchgate CT20 .....334 C3
La-Tene CT14 ....215 B2
Latham Cl
Biggin Hill TN16 .....118 C3
Dartford DA2 ....34 E6
Newham E6 ....1 E7
Latham Rd DA6 ....14 A2

Lathe Barn ★ TN29 ...352 D5
Latimer Cl CT16 ....76 B2
Latimer Pl 4 ME7 .....64 C7
Latona Dr DA12 ......37 F3
La Tourne Gdns BR6 ...86 C7
Latymers TN11 ......252 B4
Launcelot Prim Sch
BR1 ....29 A4
Launcelot Rd BR1 .....29 A4
Launcelot Way ME15 .161 E2
Launder Way ME15 ...161 E2
Laundry Rd CT12 ....115 D7
Launton Dr DA6 ......13 D3
Laura Dr BR8 ....33 A1
Laura Pl ME1 ....63 A2
Laura Villas CT6 ......76 E5
Laureate Cl CT9 ......51 B2
Laurel Ave
Gravesend DA12 ......37 C6
St Mary's Bay TN29 .365 F4
Laurel Bank
Royal Tunbridge Wells
TN4 ....286 B6
Wadhurst TN5 ....337 A4
Laurel Cl Dartford DA1 .33 C7
Folkestone CT20 .....334 E6
Sidcup DA14 ....31 A5
Laurel Gdns BR1 ......52 E5
Laurel Gr ME17 ......197 D2
Laurel Ho
Greenwich SE7 ....11 C8
Sheerness ME12 ......28 B2
Laurel Rd
Gillingham ME7 ....64 C7
Royal Tunbridge Wells
TN2 ....286 D7
Laurels The
12 Bromley BR1 ......52 B8
Bromley BR2 ....52 A5
Dartford DA2 ....33 C5
18 Erith DA17 ....4 A1
Maidstone ME16 .....161 C2
New Barn DA3 ....59 D6
Laurel Way
Chartham CT4 ....173 E1
Royal Tunbridge Wells
TN2 ....286 D7
Laurel Wlk ME8 ......98 C6
Laurensfield CT12 ...115 C7
Laureston Pl CT16 ...310 E8
Laurice Ct 6 CT11 ...117 C6
Laurie Gray Ave ME5 ..96 D1
Lauriston Cl CT11 ...117 A5
Lauriston Mount CT10 .84 A5
Lausanne Rd CT10 ....50 J2
Lausanne Terr 11 CT9 ..50 J2
Lavenda Cl ME7 ......98 A4
Lavender Cl
Bromley BR2 ....52 E3
1 Chatham ME5 ......96 E4
East Malling ME19 ..159 F8
Margate CT9 ....82 C8
Whitstable CT5 ......75 C2
Lavender Ct ME10 ....102 A3
Lavender Gdns TN5 ..338 E1
Lavender Hill
Swanley BR8 ....55 D6
Tonbridge TN9 ......254 C8
Lavender Ho 3 ME15 .195 D8
Lavender La CT12 ...116 C5
Lavender Mews CT1 ..174 F8
Lavender Rd ME19 ...159 F8
Lavender Sq 6 TN18 .341 A2
Lavenders Rd ME19 ..159 C6
Lavender Wlk ME19 ..159 F8
Lavernock Rd DA7 ....14 A5
Laverstoke Rd ME16 .161 C8
Lavidge Rd SE9 ....29 F6
Lavinia Rd 1 DA1 .....15 F1
Lavisham Ho BR1 .....29 B3
Lawford Gdns DA1 ....15 C2
Lawley Cl CT12 ......83 C1
Lawn Cl Bromley BR1 ..29 B1
Chatham ME4 ....64 B2
Swanley BR8 ....55 C7
Tenterden TN30 .....344 F7
Lawn Pk TN13 ....187 B8
Lawn Prim Sch DA11 ..18 C1
Lawn Rd
Broadstairs CT10 .....84 A4
Deal CT14 ....215 C1
Northfleet DA11 ......18 C1
Tonbridge TN9 ......254 B8
Lawn Villas CT11 ....117 C6
Lawns Cres RM17 .....18 D8
Lawns The
Brenchley TN12 .....289 B8
15 Ramsgate CT11 ..117 F7
Sidcup DA14 ....31 B4
Lawn Villas DA11 ....36 F5
Lawrance Sq DA11 ...36 F5
Lawrence Cl
Folkestone CT19 ....334 F6
Loose ME15 ....195 A7
Lawrence Ct CT19 ...335 E6
Lawrence Dr DA12 ....61 A5
Lawrence Gdns
Herne Bay CT6 ....77 C4
Tilbury RM18 ....19 B7
Lawrence Hill Gdns
DA1 ....15 C1
Lawrence Hill Rd DA1 .15 C1
Lawrence Rd Erith DA8 .14 B7
Hayes BR4 ....85 A6
Tonbridge TN10 .....222 E6
Lawrence St ME7 ......64 C5
Laws La TN25 ....329 D7
Lawson Cl
Chatham CT4 ....173 D2
Newham E16 ....1 C8
Lawson Gdns DA1 .....15 D3
Lawson Ho 1 SE18 ...12 A8
Lawson Rd DA1 ......15 D3
Lawsons Mews TN9 ..222 C2
Laxey Rd BR6 ....86 F4

Laxey The ME15 ......161 E1
Laxton Cl ME15 ......162 F3
Laxton Dr ME17 .....196 A1
Laxton Gdns TN12 ...256 E7
Laxton Way
Canterbury CT1 .....175 C7
Faversham ME13 ....138 C5
Sittingbourne ME10 ..101 D6
Whitstable CT5 ....75 C1
Layfield Cotts ME9 ....68 D1
Layfield Ho 4 SE10 ....1 A1
Layfield Rd ME7 ......64 F7
Layhams Rd BR2 ......85 A3
Lay La CT3 ....147 D2
Laylam Cl CT10 ....83 D5
Laymarsh Cl DA17 .....3 F3
Layzell Wlk SE9 ......29 B5
Lazarus Hart Havens of
Rest The 4 CT11 ...117 C8
Leach Ho ME13 ......140 A3
Lea Cl CT21 ....333 B4
Leacon Cotts The
TN27 ....234 E4
Leacon Cotts TN27 ...234 E4
Leacon Rd TN23 .....267 F2
Lea Ct ME4 ....63 E1
Leafield Cl TN23 .....31 F5
Leafield TN25 ....303 D1
Leafy Glade ME8 .....98 B6
Leafy Gr BR2 ....85 C5
Leafy La DA13 ....93 A3
Leafy Oak Rd SE12 ...29 C5
Leahurst Ct CT16 ....277 E4
Leake Ho 2 ME1 .....63 C1
Lealands Ave TN11 ...221 A1
Lealands Cl TN3 .....312 C6
Leaman Ct ME4 ......23 E4
Leamington Ave
Bromley BR1 ....29 C3
Orpington BR6 ....86 E6
Leamington Cl BR1 ...29 C3
Leamington Dr ME16 .161 B4
Leamouth Rd E6 ....1 E8
Leander Dr DA12 ......37 F4
Leander Rd ME1 ....96 C7
Lea Rd TN13 ....187 C8
Learoyd Gdns E6 ......2 A6
Learoyd Rd TN28 ....373 C6
Leas Dale SE9 ....30 A5
Leas Green BR7 ....30 F2
Leas Rd CT14 ....215 B4
Leas The
Faversham ME13 ....138 B8
Folkestone CT20 ....335 C4
Kingsdown CT14 ....248 D5
Minster (Sheppey) ME12 .47 C8
Sheerness ME12 ......28 A1
Whitstable CT5 ....75 D1
Woolwich SE18 ......12 B6
Leatherbottle Gn DA18 .3 F3
Leather Cl TN8 ......249 C8
Leatt Cl CT10 ....83 F4
Lea Vale DA8 ....14 D3
Leaveland Cl TN23 ...299 E6
Leaveland Cotts ME13 .170 B2
Leaves Gn Br2 ......118 D8
Leaves Green Cres
BR2 ....118 C8
Leaves Green Rd
Biggin Hill BR2 ......118 D8
Keston BR2 ....85 D1
Lebanon Gdns TN16 .118 D2
Lebrun Sq SE3 ....11 B4
Leckwith Ave DA7 ....13 E8
Leclair Ho SE3 ....11 B4
Leconfield Cl TN9 ...253 F7
Leda Cotts TN25 .....234 F3
Leda Rd SE18 ....1 F1
Leeds & Broomfield CE
Prim Sch ME17 .....197 A4
Leeds Castle ★ ME17 .197 D7
Leeds Cl BR6 ....87 B8
Leeds Ho ME2 ....40 C1
Leeds Rd ME17 .....196 E3
Leeds Sq ME8 ....65 B3
Lee Gn BR5 ....54 A4
Lee Green Rd ME3 ....40 B6
Lee Ho CT14 ....215 C1
Leelands Ho CT14 ...215 B1
Lee Rd ME6 ....128 A8
Lees Cl The TN25 ...302 C5
Lees Court Rd ME13 .170 C5
Leeson Hill BR5,BR7 ..54 A6
Leesons Prim Sch BR5 .54 B6
Leesons Way BR5 .....53 F7
Lees Rd Ashford TN24 .269 A1
Brabourne Lees TN25 .302 E6
Congelow ME18 .....225 E7
Lee Sta SE12 ....11 A1
Lees Terr CT4 ....172 C2
Lees The CT6 ....77 C5
Leeswood TN24 .....269 B1
Leet Cl Gillingham ME7 .64 E6
Minster (Sheppey) ME12 .48 B5
Leeward Rd ME1 ......63 C1
Leewood Cl SE12 ......11 A1
Leewood Pl BR8 ......55 D5
Legatt Rd SE9 ....11 D2
Legge La ME19 ......127 D6
Leggett's La TN4 ....284 E5
Leggs' La TN3 ....284 E5
Leghorn Rd SE18 ......2 C1
Leicester Ave CT9 ....51 C2
Leicester Ct CT9 .....51 D3

Leicester Dr TN2 .....313 F8
Leicester Gdns ME12 ..49 E3
Leicester Rd
Maidstone ME15 .....195 D7
Tilbury RM18 ....18 F6
Leigh Ave ME15 .....195 B6
Leigh City Tech Coll The
DA1 ....34 A7
Leigh Ct ME12 ....46 F5
Leigh Green Ind Est
TN30 ....345 E6
Leigh Halt TN11 .....220 F1
Leigh Pl DA16 ....13 A5
Leigh Prim Sch TN11 .220 F1
Leigh Rd
Gravesend DA11 ......37 B6
Ramsgate CT12 ....82 F1
Rochester ME3 ....40 C3
Tonbridge TN11 .....221 D3
Leigh Terr
6 Orpington BR5 .....54 B6
Teston ME18 ....160 A1
Leighton Cl TN4 .....286 A7
Leighton Ct 3 CT16 ..278 C1
Leighton Gdns RM18 ..19 A7
Leighton Rd CT16 ...278 C1
Leighville Dr CT6 .....76 D4
Leila Parnell Pl 22 SE7 .11 C8
Leitch Row ME7 ......64 A7
Leith Hill Gn BR5 ....54 A8
Leith Hill BR5 ....54 A8
Leith Park Rd DA12 ...37 B7
Leivers Rd CT14 .....215 A3
Le May Ave SE12 .....29 B5
Lemonwell Ct SE9 ....12 C2
Lemonwell Dr SE9 ....12 C2
Lenacre Ave CT16 ...277 F7
Lenacre La CT16 ....277 F8
Lenacre St TN25,TN26 .236 B2
Len Clifton Ho 6 SE18 ..1 F2
Lenderyou Cl DA11 ...33 E8
Lendon Rd TN15 .....156 F6
Lendrim Cl 11 ME7 ...64 A6
Leneda Dr TN2 ......313 E8
Leney Rd ME18 ......192 E7
Lenfield Ave ME14 ...162 B4
Length The CT7 ....79 F2
Lenham Cl CT10 ......84 A2
Lenham Ct 15 ME16 ..162 B4
Lenham Forstal Rd
ME17 ....233 B8
Lenham Gdns CT9 ....82 B8
Lenham Heath Rd
ME17 ....199 C2
Lenham Ho
Lenham ME17 ....199 E5
18 Orpington BR5 ....54 D1
Lenham Prim Sch
ME17 ....199 C5
Lenham Rd Bexley DA7 .14 B1
Broadstone TN27,ME17 .231 D3
Fairbourne Heath ME17 .198 C1
Headcorn ME17 .....262 E6
Lenham Sta ME17 ...199 C4
Lenham Way ME8 ....65 A3
Lennard Ct 4 CT20 ..335 E5
Lennard Rd
Folkestone CT20 ....335 E5
Orpington BR2 ....52 F1
Sevenoaks TN13 ....153 C7
Lennox Ave DA11 ....19 A1
Lennox Ho 6 DA17 ....4 A3
Lennox Rd E DA11 ...37 A8
Lennox Rd
Gravesend DA11 ......37 A8
Northfleet DA11 ......36 F8
Lenor Cl DA6 ....13 E3
Lensbury Way SE2 .....3 D3
Lenside Dr ME15 ....163 A2
Lenton St SE18 ....2 D2
Len Valley Wlk ME15 .162 F1
Leona Ct 8 CT9 ......51 B2
Leonard Ave
Otford TN14 ....122 B3
Swanscombe DA10 ...35 A8
Leonard Cl ME16 ....161 B6
Leonard Ct DA14 .....31 B5
Leonard Judge Ho DA2 .34 E3
Leonard Pl BR2 ......85 E7
Leonard Rd
7 Chatham ME4 .....64 B3
Greatstone-on-S TN28 .377 E7
Leonard Robbins Path 3
SE28 ....3 B6
Leonard's Ave CT11 ..83 E1
Leonard St E16 ....1 E5
Leonie Ct CT6 ....76 D4
Leopold Rd
2 Chatham ME4 .....64 A3
Ramsgate CT11 .....117 E8
Leopold St CT11 ....117 E6
Le Roux Cl CT18 ....306 F4
Lerryn Gdns CT10 ...83 F8
Lesley Ave CT1 ......175 A6
Lesley Chalk Ho 3 TN28 .268 C2
Lesley Cl
Istead Rise DA13 .....59 F8
Sidcup DA5 ....32 B8
Swanley BR8 ....55 D6
Lesley Pl ME16 ......161 E5
Lesley Tew Ct TN10 .222 C5
Leslie Ave CT9 ....82 B8
Leslie Cres TN30 ....324 E2
Leslie Rd
Birchington CT7 ......81 A8
Gillingham ME7 ......64 D7
Newham E16 ....1 B7
Leslie Smith Dr ME13 .138 C7

Leslie Smith Sq 7
  SE18 . . . . 12 A8
Lesnes Abbey (remains
  of)★ SE2 . . . . .3 D2
Lesney Park Rd DA8 . . . . 14 D8
Lesney Pk DA8 . . . . 14 D8
Lessness Ave DA7 . . . . . 13 D7
Lessness Heath Prim Sch
  DA17 . . . . .4 A1
Lessness Pk DA17 . . . . . .4 A1
Lessness Rd 12 DA17 . . . .4 A1
Les Spickett Cl ME13 . . 138 E6
Lested La ME17 . . . . . . 196 B1
Lestock Ho SE3 . . . . 11 B8
Lester Rd ME4 . . . . 64 A3
Letchworth Ave ME4 . . . .63 F1
Letchworth Cl BR2 . . . . 52 A4
Letchworth Dr BR2 . . . . 52 A4
Le Temple Rd TN12 . . . 257 B6
Letter Box La TN13 . . . 187 C6
Leverholme Gdns SE9 . . 30 A4
Levett Cl ME3 . . . . .27 B6
Levetts La TN32 . . . . . 355 D1
Leviathan Way ME4 . . . . 41 A1
Lewd La TN27 . . . . 264 A3
Lewes Cl RM17 . . . . 18 A8
Lewes Rd BR1 . . . . 52 D7
Lewin Cl SE18 . . . . .2 E2
Lewing Cl BR6 . . . . .53 E1
Lewin Rd DA6 . . . . 13 E3
Lewis Ave ME8 . . . . .65 B2
Lewis Cl ME13 . . . . 138 A7
Lewis Court Dr ME17 . . 195 C3
Lewis Cres CT9 . . . . 51 B3
Lewis Ct Ashford TN23 . . 299 F7
  Northfleet DA11 . . . . . .36 F6
Lewisham Rd CT17 . . . . 277 E3
Lewis King Ho 7 BR1 . . 29 B1
Lewis Mews ME6 . . . . . 127 E6
Lewis Rd Bexley DA16 . . 13 C4
  Istead Rise DA13 . . . . . 59 F8
  Sidcup DA14 . . . . 31 C5
  Swanscombe DA10 . . . . .17 E1
Lewis Row ME17 . . . . . 228 C6
Lewson Street Rd
  ME9 . . . . 136 E8
Leybank TN11 . . . . 221 F4
Leybourne Cl
  Chatham ME5 . . . . 97 A2
  Hayes BR2 . . . . 52 A3
Leybourne Dell TN17 . . 342 E6
Leybourne Dr CT9 . . . . .82 B8
Leybourne Rd ME2 . . . . .62 F8
Leybourne, St Peter & St
  Paul CE Prim Sch
  ME19 . . . . 127 E2
Leybourne Way ME19 . . 127 F4
Leybourn Rd CT10 . . . . .84 B2
Leybridge Ct SE12 . . . . 11 A2
Leyburn Ct TN9 . . . . . . 222 C3
Leyburne Rd CT16 . . . . 310 D8
Leyburn Ho SE18 . . . . . .11 E7
Leycroft Cl CT2 . . . . . . 142 E3
Leycroft Gdns DA8 . . . . .15 B6
Leydenhatch La BR8 . . . 55 D8
Leyes Rd E16 . . . . .1 D7
Leyhill Cl BR8 . . . . .55 E4
Leyland Rd SE12 . . . . . 11 A2
Leysdown Ave DA7 . . . . 14 C3
Leysdown Rd
  Eastchurch ME12 . . . . .48 E3
  Eltham SE9 . . . . .29 F6
  Leysdown-on-S ME12 . . 49 C1
Leysdown View CT5 . . . 108 C6
Leys The CT12 . . . . 82 D1
Leyton Ave ME7 . . . . . . .64 E1
Leyton Cross DA2 . . . . . 33 A6
Leyton Cross Rd DA2 . . .32 F5
Leywood Rd DA13 . . . . . 93 D3
Lezayre Rd BR6 . . . . . . .86 F4
Liberty Mews BR6 . . . . .86 F4
Library Rd CT2 . . . . 142 D4
Libya Terr 6 ME14 . . . . 162 A7
Lichdale Cl 8 BR6 . . . . .86 F6
Lichfield Ave CT1 . . . . . 175 B6
Lichfield Cl ME8 . . . . . . 65 D2
Lichfield Ho 12 ME15 . . 195 E7
Liddon Rd BR1 . . . . 52 D6
Lidsing Rd ME14 . . . . . 130 E6
Lidwells La TN17 . . . . . 290 E1
Liege Cl ME10 . . . . .68 F1
Lieth Park Rd DA12 . . . 37 C7
Liffler Rd SE18 . . . . .2 E1
Lighterman's Mews 2
  DA11 . . . . .36 E8
Lightermans Way DA9 . . 17 C3
Lightfoot Gn TN18 . . . . 340 E3
Lighthouse Rd CT15 . . . 280 A5
Lilac Cres ME2 . . . . .62 E6
Lilac Ct TN23 . . . . 267 E3
Lilac Gdns BR8 . . . . 55 D6
Lilac Gn 4 ME19 . . . . . 128 A1
Lilac Pl DA13 . . . . .60 B2
Lilac Rd ME2 . . . . .62 E5
Lila Pl BR8 . . . . .55 E5
Lilburne Gdns SE9 . . . . .11 E2
Lilburne Rd SE9 . . . . . . .11 E2
Lilian Barker Cl SE12 . . 11 A2
Lilk Hill ME14 . . . . 163 C3
Lillechurch Rd ME3 . . . .39 F7
Lillian Rd CT11 . . . . . . 117 F8
Lillieburn ME19 . . . . . . 127 D2
Lillie Rd TN16 . . . . 118 D1
Lily Nichols Ho E16 . . . .1 E5
Lilyvale Cotts TN25 . . . 302 F4
Lilyvale Rd TN25 . . . . . 302 F4
Lime Ave
  Benenden TN17 . . . . . 342 C8
  Northfleet DA11 . . . . . 36 D8

Lime Cl Ashford TN23 . . 267 F3
  Bromley BR1 . . . . .52 E5
  Chartham CT4 . . . . . . 173 E1
  Frant TN3 . . . . 314 B3
  Marden TN12 . . . . 259 C6
Lime Cotts TN12 . . . . . 260 F3
Lime Cres ME19 . . . . . . 160 A7
Lime Ct Eltham SE9 . . . .30 B6
  Gillingham ME8 . . . . . . 98 C3
Lime Gr
  Biddenden TN27 . . . . . 323 D7
  Halfway Houses ME12 . . 46 D5
  Orpington BR6 . . . . . . .86 B8
  Sidcup DA15 . . . . .12 F1
  Sittingbourne ME10 . . 102 A4
Lime Hill Rd TN1 . . . . . 286 A4
Lime Kiln Dr SE7 . . . . . .11 B8
Limekiln Rdbt CT17 . . . 310 D6
Lime Kiln Rd CT1 . . . . . 174 F6
Limekiln St CT17 . . . . . 310 D5
Lime Kiln Wharf ME11 . . 46 A5
Lime Pit La TN13,TN14 . 121 C2
Limepits Cross ME9 . . . 100 F3
Lime Rd BR8 . . . . 55 D6
Lime Row DA18 . . . . .3 F3
Limes Cl TN30 . . . . 345 C8
Limes Gr TN18 . . . . 340 F5
Limes Pl 15 ME13 . . . . 138 D7
Limes Rd Dover CT16 . . 278 C1
  Folkestone CT19 . . . . 334 F6
Limes Row BR6 . . . . .86 B5
Limes The
  Ashford TN23 . . . . . . 300 A5
  Edenbridge TN8 . . . . . 217 C1
  Frittenden TN17 . . . . . 293 E6
  Lenham ME17 . . . . . . 199 D5
  Old Romney TN29 . . . . 372 A7
  Orpington BR2 . . . . . . .85 E8
Lime Tree Ave DA9 . . . . 35 A7
Limetree Cl ME5 . . . . . . .97 B8
Lime Tree Cl TN9 . . . . . 222 C2
Lime Trees TN12 . . . . . 260 E4
Limetree Terr
  5 Bexley DA16 . . . . . 13 A4
  Lenham ME17 . . . . . . 199 E6
Lime Tree Wlk TN13 . . 154 B2
Lime Villas CT4 . . . . . . 273 F5
Limewood Rd DA8 . . . . 14 C7
Limpsfield CE Inf Sch
  RH8 . . . . 183 C6
Limpsfield Grange Sch
  RH8 . . . . 183 A8
Linces The TN18 . . . . . . 279 A4
Linchmere Rd 7 SE12 . . 11 A8
Lincoln Ave CT1 . . . . . . 175 B7
  Rochester ME2 . . . . . . 62 D6
  Whitstable CT5 . . . . . . 75 D3
Lincoln Cl 3 SE12 . . . . 29 C5
Lincoln Gdns CT7 . . . . . .80 F7
Lincoln Green Rd BR5 . . 53 F4
Lincol n Rd ME7 . . . . . . 64 D7
Lincoln Rd
  Maidstone ME15 . . . . . 195 D8
  Sidcup DA14 . . . . .31 B3
Lincolnshire Terr DA2 . . 34 D4
Lincolnshott DA13 . . . . .36 B3
Lindale Flats CT14 . . . . 215 C2
Lindel Ct ME18 . . . . . . 159 B3
Linden Ave
  Broadstairs CT10 . . . . .84 B5
  Dartford DA1 . . . . 33 C7
  Herne Bay CT6 . . . . . . .76 E4
  Whitstable CT5 . . . . . . .74 F1
Linden Chase
  Canterbury CT2 . . . . . 142 E1
  Sevenoaks TN13 . . . . . 154 B5
Linden Cl Orpington BR6 . 87 A5
  Paddock Wood TN12 . . 257 A6
  Purfleet RM19 . . . . 16 C8
  Royal Tunbridge Wells
  TN4 . . . . 286 A2
  Sittingbourne ME10 . . 101 D3
  Westgate-on-S CT8 . . . .81 E7
Linden Cres CT19 . . . . . 335 D6
Linden Ct Sidcup DA14 . . 30 E4
  Tonbridge TN10 . . . . . 222 B7
Linden Dr ME12 . . . . . . 46 A7
Lindenfield BR7 . . . . . . .53 B7
Linden Gdns TN2 . . . . . 285 E1
Linden Gr CT2 . . . . 142 E1
Linden Grove Prim Sch
  TN23 . . . . 299 F6
Linden Ho
  4 Bromley BR1 . . . . . .29 B1
  5 Chatham ME5 . . . . . .96 F4
Linden Park Rd TN2 . . . 286 A2
Linden Rd
  Ashford TN24 . . . . . . 268 D1
  Chartham CT4 . . . . . . 173 E1
  Coxheath ME17 . . . . . 194 C4
  Gillingham ME7 . . . . . .64 E5
  Westgate-on-S CT8 . . . .81 F8
Lindens CT21 . . . . 333 D2
Linden Sq TN13 . . . . . . 153 E5
Lindens The ME20 . . . . 128 E1
Lindenthorpe Rd CT10 . . 84 A6
Lindfield Cotts ME13 . . 138 A6
Lindisfarne Cl DA12 . . . .37 E6
Lindisfarne Gdns
  ME16 . . . . 161 E3
Lindridge Cl CT6 . . . . . 111 A8
Lindridge La TN12 . . . . 260 C5
Lindsay Ho 2 SE18 . . . . .2 A2
Lindsey Cl BR1 . . . . .52 E6
Lindwood Cl 8 E6 . . . . . .1 F8
Lineacre Cl ME8 . . . . . . 98 D6
Linen Ct CT1 . . . . 174 F8
Lingey Cl DA15 . . . . 23 F6
Lingfield Ave DA2 . . . . .34 B8
Lingfield Cres SE9 . . . . 12 D3

Lingfield Mews 4
  TN8 . . . . 217 C1
Lingfield Rd
  Borough Green TN15 . . 157 B7
  Edenbridge TN8 . . . . . 249 A8
  Gravesend DA12 . . . . . .37 B6
Lingley Rd Erith DA8 . . . 14 C8
Lingwood DA7 . . . . .14 B5
Linington Rd CT7 . . . . . . 81 A6
Link 20 Bsns Pk
  ME20 . . . . .49 F2
Linkden Cotts TN18 . . . 356 E5
Link Field BR2 . . . . .52 A3
Link Hill La TN27 . . . . . 232 D3
Link La SE18 . . . . 175 A8
Link Rd Broadstairs CT10 . 83 F7
  Tyler Hill CT2 . . . . . . 142 E6
Links Cl CT6 . . . . 77 A3
Links Cres TN29 . . . . . . 366 A4
Links Ct Deal CT14 . . . . 182 C1
  Eltham SE9 . . . . .30 B7
Linksfield Cl CT8 . . . . . . 81 D7
Linksfield Rd CT8 . . . . . . 81 D7
Links Rd CT14 . . . . 215 C8
Links The
  Addington ME19 . . . . . 126 E2
  Chatham ME5 . . . . .97 B8
Links View
  Dartford DA1 . . . . 33 C7
  Woolwich SE18 . . . . .1 E7
Linksway Cl CT19 . . . . . 335 B8
Linksway CT19 . . . . 335 B8
Links Way TN28 . . . . . . 373 D6
Link The Ashford TN23 . 299 F7
  Eltham SE9 . . . . .30 A5
  New Ash Green DA3 . . . .91 F8
Link Way BR2 . . . . .52 E2
Linkway Ditton ME20 . . 128 C1
  Iwade ME9 . . . . 68 D4
Link Way TN2 . . . . 286 E8
Linley Cl RM18 . . . . 20 D7
Linley Rd CT10 . . . . .83 E7
Linnet Ave
  Paddock Wood TN12 . . 257 A5
  Whitstable CT5 . . . . . . 108 B6
Linnet Cl SE28 . . . . .3 C6
Linslade Rd BR6 . . . . . . 87 A4
Linsted Ct SE9 . . . . .12 E1
Linton Cl Bexley DA16 . . .13 B6
  2 Greenwich SE7 . . . . . .1 C1
Linton Dann Cl ME3 . . . 41 D6
Linton Gdns ME6 . . . . . . .1 F
Linton Gore ME17 . . . . 194 D3
Linton Hill TN12 . . . . . 227 F6
Linton Mead Prim Sch
  SE28 . . . . .3 B6
Linton Rd ME15 . . . . . . 194 F4
Lintorn Symonds Rd
  ME3 . . . . .40 F5
Linwood Ave ME2 . . . . .62 E8
Lionard Ho 3 CT2 . . . . 142 E1
Lion Ct CT14 . . . . 215 C5
Lionel Gdns SE9 . . . . . . 11 A2
Lionel Oxley Ho 5
  RM17 . . . . .18 B8
Lionel Rd Eltham SE9 . . . 11 D2
  Tonbridge TN9 . . . . . . 254 A8
Lion Field ME13 . . . . . . 138 B7
Lion Rd Bexley DA6 . . . . .13 F3
  Newham E6 . . . . .1 F8
Lions Cl SE9 . . . . 29 D5
Lion's Rd TN28 . . . . . . 373 A6
Lion Yd
  Faversham ME13 . . . . . 138 A6
  3 Sittingbourne ME10 . 101 F4
Liphook Way ME16 . . . . 161 C8
Lipscombe Rd TN2 . . . . 286 D6
Lipton Cl SE28 . . . . .3 C6
Liptraps La TN2 . . . . . . 286 D7
Lipwell Hill ME23 . . . . . .23 B4
Lisa Ct CT5 . . . . .75 A2
Liskeard Cl BR7 . . . . . . 30 C2
Liskeard Gdns SE3 . . . . 11 A6
Lisle Cl DA12 . . . . .38 B6
Lismore Cl ME15 . . . . . 195 A7
Lismore Rd
  Herne Bay CT6 . . . . . . 77 D5
  Whitstable CT5 . . . . . . 109 B8
Liss Rd CT13 . . . . 180 A1
Lister Cl Deal CT14 . . . . 215 C5
  Dover CT17 . . . . 278 B1
  East Malling ME19 . . . 159 F8
Lister Ho Erith SE2 . . . . .3 D1
  Margate CT9 . . . . .83 A8
Lister Rd Margate CT9 . . .83 A8
  Tilbury RM18 . . . . 19 A5
Lister Way CT20 . . . . . . 334 F3
Lister Wlk SE28 . . . . . . .3 D6
Listmas Rd ME4 . . . . . . .64 B3
List The CT3 . . . . 145 C2
Listways Cotts CT3 . . . . 211 B6
Little Acres TN25 . . . . . 328 E7
Little Alley TN8 . . . . . . 249 B5
Little Ave CT14 . . . . . . 214 F3
Little Bayham Cotts
  TN3 . . . . 315 F4
Little Birches DA15 . . . .30 E6
Little Boundes Cl TN4 . . 253 F3
Littlebourne Ave 8 . . . . .65 B4
Littlebourne CE Prim Sch
  CT3 . . . . 176 F8
Littlebourne Rd
  Canterbury CT1,CT3 . . 175 E8
  Maidstone ME14 . . . . . 162 C6
Little Brook Rd TN23 . . 268 A3
Little Brook Hospl DA2 . 16 C1
Littlebrook Manor Way
  DA1 . . . . .16 A2
Little Brook Rd TN23 . . 268 A3
Little Browns La TN8 . . 216 F4
Little Buckland Ave
  ME16 . . . . 161 D6

Little Charles St CT6 . . .76 F5
Little Chequers TN25 . . 237 E2
Littlecombe SE7 . . . . . . .11 B8
Little Copse Cl CT4 . . . . 173 E1
Littlecourt Rd TN13 . . . 154 A3
Littlecroft Eltham SE9 . . 12 A4
  Istead Rise DA13 . . . . . .36 E1
Littledale CT2 . . . . 34 C5
Littlefield TN11 . . . . . . 223 E8
Littlefield Rd ME8 . . . . . .66 B2
Little Field TN12 . . . . . 260 E5
Little Footway TN3 . . . . 284 F3
Little Glovers ME10 . . . 101 F3
Little Groves Cvn & Chalet
  Pk ME12 . . . . .49 F2
Little Groves Holiday Camp
  ME12 . . . . .49 F2
Little Heath Rd DA7 . . . .13 F7
Little Heath SE7 . . . . .1 E1
Little Hempen TN23 . . . 299 D8
Little Hill TN30 . . . . . . 324 B2
Little Job's Cross
  TN17 . . . . 343 F1
Little John Ave ME5 . . . . 96 F2
Littlejohn Rd BR5 . . . . . 54 B4
Little Julians Hill
  TN13 . . . . 187 A8
Little Kit's Coty House★
  ME20 . . . . 129 C5
Little Knoll TN23 . . . . . 299 F8
Little Mallett TN3 . . . . . 284 F3
Little Market Row
  ME19 . . . . 127 E2
Little Mdw CT2 . . . . . . 141 E1
Littlemead CT19 . . . . . . 335 A7
Littlemede SE9 . . . . .29 F5
Little Mill Farm Cotts
  TN12 . . . . 259 C8
Little Mount Sion
  TN1 . . . . 286 A2
Little Oakham Ct ME3 . . 25 C4
Little Orch ME17 . . . . . 194 D3
Little Oxley ME19 . . . . . 127 E2
Little Paddocks CT5 . . . 109 D7
Little Pk TN5 . . . . 336 E5
Little Queen St DA1 . . . .33 F8
Little Redlands BR1 . . . . 52 E7
Little Robhurst TN26 . . 324 D8
Little Sheephurst Cotts
  TN12 . . . . 258 E5
Littlestone Ct TN28 . . . 373 E5
Littlestone Ho TN28 . . . 373 E5
Littlestone Rd TN28 . . . 373 D6
Little Stone Stile Cotts
  ME13 . . . . 171 F4
Little Switzerland
  CT19 . . . . 335 G8
Little Thrift BR5 . . . . . . 53 C5
Little Walton CT13 . . . . 180 C3
Little Wood Cl BR5 . . . . 54 A8
Little Wood TN13 . . . . . 154 D5
Little York Mdws ME7 . . 65 C4
Liverpool Lawn 18
  CT11 . . . . 117 E6
Liverpool Rd CT14 . . . . 215 D2
Liverman Wlk DA9 . . . . .17 C3
Livesey Cl SE28 . . . . .2 C3
Livesey St ME18 . . . . . . 160 A1
Livingstone Bldgs ME7 . 64 D5
Livingstone Circ ME7 . . .64 D5
Livingstone Ct TN29 . . . 353 E4
Livingstone Gdns DA12 . .37 C7
Livingstone Hospl DA1 . .33 F7
Livingstone Rd
  Broadstairs CT10 . . . . .83 E6
  Gillingham ME7 . . . . . .64 E5
  Gravesend DA12 . . . . . 37 D3
Livingstone Wlk 6
  ME15 . . . . 195 F5
Lizban St SE3 . . . . 11 B7
Llanover Rd SE18 . . . . . 12 A7
Lloyd Ct CT14 . . . . 215 D7
Lloyd Ho BR1 . . . . .29 B3
Lloyd Rd CT10 . . . . 84 A5
Lloyds Gn TN30 . . . . . . 359 D4
Loading Bay App
  CT13 . . . . 149 A8
Loaland Bsns Ctr ME2 . . 63 D8
Loam Ct DA1 . . . . .33 C7
Loampits Cl TN9 . . . . . 222 D3
Lobelia Cl
  Gillingham ME7 . . . . . .64 C6
  5 Newham E6 . . . . .1 E8
Locarno Ave ME8 . . . . . 65 A2
Lochat Rd ME3 . . . . .40 E6
Lochmere Cl DA8 . . . . . .14 B8
Lockesley Dr BR5 . . . . . 54 A3
Lockham Farm Ave
  ME17 . . . . 195 D5
Lockholt Cl TN23 . . . . . 267 E3
Lockington Ct TN9 . . . . 253 F7
Lockington Gr ME1 . . . . 63 C5
Lock La ME14 . . . . 129 D1
Lockside TN9 . . . . 222 C2
Locksley Cl ME5 . . . . . . .96 E2
Lock St ME7 . . . . 64 C5
Lockwood Ho E16 . . . . . 161 D7
Lock's Yd TN13 . . . . . . 154 C2
Lockyer Rd RM19 . . . . . 16 C8
Lockyers Hill DA13 . . . . .93 F5
Lodden Ct 15 BR5 . . . . . 54 D1
Loddington La
  Linton ME17 . . . . 228 A8
  Maidstone,Boughton
  Monchelsea ME17 . . . 195 A1
Loder Cl ME17 . . . . 199 B5
Lodge Ave DA1 . . . . 15 C1
Lodge Cl Orpington BR6 . 87 A7
  Wateringbury ME18 . . 192 D8
Lodge Cres BR6 . . . . . . .54 B1

Lodge Farmhouse
  ME20 . . . . 128 E3
Lodge Field Rd CT5 . . . .75 D1
Lodge Gdns ME17 . . . . . 230 F6
Lodge Hill DA16 . . . . . . .13 B7
Lodge Hill La ME3 . . . . .40 F7
Lodge La Cobham DA12 . .61 B5
  Royal Tunbridge Wells
  TN3 . . . . 313 A8
  Sidcup DA5 . . . . 13 D1
  Westerham TN16 . . . . . 184 C8
Lodge Oak La TN9 . . . . 254 D8
Lodge Rd Bromley BR1 . . 29 C1
  Maidstone ME14 . . . . . 162 D5
  Staplehurst TN12 . . . . 260 E5
  Tonbridge TN9 . . . . . . 222 B2
Lodgewood Cotts
  TN8 . . . . 218 D2
Lodge Wood Dr TN25 . . 267 E5
Logs Hill BR1,BR2 . . . . .52 E8
Logs Hill Cl BR7 . . . . . .52 E8
Lolland Ho 9 SE1 . . . . . . .1 F7
Lomaria Ct TN2 . . . . . . 286 C4
Lomas La TN18 . . . . . . 356 F5
Lomas Rd ME10,ME9 . . 102 D4
Lombard St
  Horton Kirby DA4 . . . . 57 C5
  Margate CT9 . . . . .50 J3
Lombard Trad Est SE7 . . .1 B2
Lombard Wall SE7 . . . . . .1 B2
Lombardy Cl ME7 . . . . . 98 A6
Lombardy Dr ME14 . . . . 162 C5
Lomer Farm DA13 . . . . . 93 A8
Londonderry Ho 15
  ME15 . . . . 195 E7
Londonderry Par DA8 . . 14 D7
London Ind Pk E6 E2 . . . .2 C1
London La Bromley BR1 . 29 A1
  Sissinghurst TN12 . . . 293 A2
London Pl 20 CT20 . . . . 335 E5
London Rd
  Addington ME19 . . . . . 126 D2
  Badgers Mount TN14 . 121 C6
  Bidborough TN4 . . . . . 253 F3
  Bromley BR1 . . . . 52 A8
  Canterbury CT2 . . . . . 142 D1
  Chelsfield TN14 . . . . . .87 F2
  Crayford DA1 . . . . 14 D2
  Deal CT14 . . . . 215 B5
  Ditton ME20 . . . . 128 C1
  Dover CT16,CT17 . . . . 278 B1
  Dunkirk ME13 . . . . . . 140 E2
London Rd E ME20 . . . . 160 F8
London Rd
  Farningham BR8,DA4 . . 56 D3
  Faversham ME13 . . . . . 138 B6
  Flimwell TN5 . . . . 339 D3
  Gillingham ME8 . . . . . . 65 C1
  Grays RM17,RM20 . . . . .17 E8
  Hartlip ME8,ME9 . . . . . 99 D7
  Hildenborough TN11,
  Hurst Green TN19 . . . 354 A3
  Hythe CT21 . . . . 332 F3
  Maidstone ME16 . . . . . 161 C6
  Newington ME9 . . . . . 100 A6
  Northfleet DA11 . . . . . .18 E1
  Otford TN13 . . . . 121 D1
  Ramsgate CT11 . . . . . 117 B6
  Rochester ME2 . . . . . . 63 A7
  Royal Tunbridge
  Wells,Mount Sion TN1 . 286 A3
  Royal Tunbridge Wells
  TN4 . . . . 286 A8
  Sevenoaks,Dunton Green
  TN13 . . . . 153 E7
  Sevenoaks TN13 . . . . . 154 B2
  Sittingbourne ME10 . . 101 C4
  Stone DA2,DA9 . . . . . . .16 E1
  Swanley BR8 . . . . 55 D7
  Swanley BR8 . . . . 55 E6
  Swanscombe DA9 . . . . 17 C2
  Temple Ewell CT15,
  CT16 . . . . 277 B6
  Teynham ME9 . . . . . . 103 C1
  Tilbury RM18 . . . . .19 B5
  Tonbridge TN10,TN11, . 222 B3
  West Kingsdown TN15 . .91 A1
  Wrotham Heath TN15,
  ME19 . . . . 125 F1
  Wrotham TN15 . . . . . . 125 B3
London Road Purfleet
  RM19 . . . . 16 C8
London Road (River)
  CT16,CT17 . . . . 277 F4
London Road Temple Ewell
  CT16 . . . . 277 D5
London Road Trad Est
  ME10 . . . . 101 D4
London Road West
  Thurrock RM20 . . . . . . 17 A8
London St CT20 . . . . . . 335 E5
Lone Barn Rd ME17 . . . 200 B8
Lonefield TN26 . . . . . . 299 B1
Lonewood Way TN11 . . 190 F2
Long Acre Cl CT2 . . . . . 142 E2
Long Acre Rd TN23 . . . . 87 D8
Longacre CT5 . . . . 75 D1
Longage Hill CT18,CT4 . 273 A1
Long Barn Rd TN14 . . . 187 B2
Long Barrow The
  TN24 . . . . 300 E6
Long Beech TN25 . . . . . 267 E1
Longbridge Rd TN24 . . . 269 B1
Longbridge Terr CT21 . . 332 F1
Longbury Cl BR5 . . . . . . 54 B6
Longbury Dr BR5 . . . . . .54 B6
Long Catlis Rd ME8 . . . . 98 D4
Longcroft SE9 . . . . 30 A5
Longdon Wood BR2 . . . . 85 E6
Longdown Ho ME5 . . . . .96 F6

Long Dr CT13 . . . . 180 C2
Longfellow Rd ME7 . . . .64 C3
Longfield Ave
  High Halstow ME23 . . . .23 E4
  New Barn DA3,DA13 . . . 59 D7
Longfield Ct CT5 . . . . . .75 D2
Longfield Ct CT5 . . . . . .75 D2
Longfield Pl ME15 . . . . 195 C8
Longfield Rd
  Dover CT17 . . . . 310 B7
  Meopham Station DA3,
  DA13 . . . . .59 E3
  Royal Tunbridge Wells
  TN1,TN2,TN11 . . . . . . 254 E1
Longfields Sta DA3 . . . . .58 F5
Longfield TN30 . . . . . . 345 A6
Longford Cl ME8 . . . . . . 99 A8
Longford Ct ME8 . . . . . . 99 A8
Longford Terr 9
  CT20 . . . . 335 D4
Longford Way 10
  CT20 . . . . 335 D4
Longham Copse ME15 . 162 F1
Longhill Ave ME5 . . . . . .64 B3
Long Hill CT4 . . . . 172 C1
Longhurst Dr ME5 . . . . .96 F2
Long La DA7 . . . . .13 E6
Longlands Park Cres
  DA15 . . . . .30 E6
Longlands Prim Sch
  DA15 . . . . .30 E6
Longlands Rd DA15 . . . .30 F5
Long La
  Rabbit's Cross ME17 . . 228 D5
  Shepherdswell CT15 . . 244 D7
Longleat 3 DA6 . . . . . . .13 E3
Longleigh La SE2,DA7 . . 13 C8
Long Length TN23 . . . . 299 D4
Longley Rd
  Rainham ME8 . . . . .65 F1
  Rochester ME1 . . . . . . 63 C4
Longmarket 2 CT1 . . . . 175 A8
Long Mark Rd 5 E16 . . . 1 D8
Longmarsh La CT20 . . . 335 C5
Longmarsh View DA4 . . .57 B8
Long Mdw CT12 . . . . . . 114 D6
Longmead BR7 . . . . 53 A7
Longmead Cl CT6 . . . . . 76 C3
Long Mead Com Prim Sch
  TN10 . . . . 222 B5
Longmead Dr DA14 . . . . 31 D6
Longmeade DA12 . . . . . .37 F7
Longmeadow Rd DA15 . .30 E7
Longmeadow TN13 . . . . 153 D6
Long Meadow Way
  CT2 . . . . 143 A4
Long Meads TN3 . . . . . 285 B4
Long Mead Way TN10 . . 222 B4
Longmete Rd CT3 . . . . . 146 C5
Long Mill La
  Crouch TN15 . . . . 157 B3
  Platt TN15 . . . . 157 C2
Longmore Dr ME12 . . . . 48 C1
Longparish Cl ME15 . . . 195 F6
Longport CT1 . . . . 175 B8
Long Reach Cl CT5 . . . . 108 C6
Long Reach Rd DA8 . . . .15 B7
Long Rede La ME16 . . . 160 F2
Longridge ME10 . . . . . . 102 B2
Long Rock CT5 . . . . .75 D3
Long Row TN25 . . . . . . 301 D2
Long's Acre TN25 . . . . . 237 E1
Longsfield TN25 . . . . . . 330 A6
Longshaw Rd ME15 . . . 195 F5
Long Slip TN3 . . . . 285 A3
Longtail Rise CT6 . . . . . .76 E2
Longten's Cotts DA12 . . .38 E6
Longtown CT19 E9 DA2 . 16 B1
Longtye Dr CT5 . . . . . . 109 C7
Longview Way TN2 . . . . 286 D7
Longwalk DA13 . . . . . . .59 D8
Long Wlk Ashford TN23 . 267 E4
  Woolwich SE18 . . . . . . .12 B8
Longwood ME5 . . . . 97 B1
Longworth Cl SE28 . . . . .3 D7
Lonsdale Ave CT9 . . . . . 51 C3
Lonsdale Cl SE9 . . . . . . 29 D5
Lonsdale Cres DA2 . . . . 34 C7
Lonsdale Ct CT16 . . . . . 278 D1
Lonsdale Dr
  Gillingham ME8 . . . . . .98 E7
  Herne Bay CT6 . . . . . . .76 B5
  Sittingbourne ME10 . . 101 C5
Lonsdale Gdns TN1 . . . . 286 A3
Lonsdale Rd DA7 . . . . . .13 F5
Lookers La CT21 . . . . . . 333 B3
Loop Court Mews 9
  CT13 . . . . 148 F1
Loop Rd BR7 . . . . 30 C2
Loop St CT13 . . . . 148 F1
Loose Down Rd ME13 . . 202 F7
Loose Inf & Jun Schs
  ME15 . . . . 195 A6
Loose Rd ME15 . . . . 195 A7
Loraine Ct BR7 . . . . .30 B3
Lord Chatham's Ride
  TN14 . . . . 120 D2
Lord Cornwallis Ct
  CT19 . . . . 335 C8
Lord Roberts Terr SE18 . .2 C1
Lord Romney's Hill
  ME14 . . . . 162 F3
Lords Cl ME9 . . . . 102 E2
Lords Cotts ME13 . . . . . 170 C4
Lord St Gravesend DA12 . .37 B8
  Newham E6 . . . . .1 E5
Lords Wood Cl ME5 . . . .97 B2
Lordswood Cl DA2 . . . . .34 E4
Lordswood Ind Est
  ME5 . . . . 130 C8

Lordswood Inf & Jun Sch
ME5 97 B3
Lords Wood La ME5 97 B3
Lord Warden Ave
CT14 215 D2
Lord Warden Ho
CT17 310 D5
Lord Warden Sq CT17 310 D5
Lord Warwick St SE18 1 F3
Lorenden Park Nature
Reserve★ ME13 137 F3
Lorenden Pk TN18 340 F1
Lorenden Prep Sch
ME13 137 E3
Lorien Flats TN24 268 D7
Lorimar Bsns Ctr RM13 4 E8
Lorimar Ct ME10 101 C7
Lorina Rd CT12 117 C8
Lorne Cotts CT14 215 C7
Lorne Rd
Dover CT16,CT17 278 B2
Ramsgate CT11 117 C6
Lorraine Ct
1 Folkestone CT19 335 E6
Swanscombe DA9 17 B1
Lorton Cl DA12 37 E6
Lossenham La TN18 357 D3
Lotus Rd TN16 118 F1
Loudon Ct TN23 267 E3
Loudon Path TN23 267 E3
Loudon Way TN23 267 E3
Loughborough Ct 2
CT11 117 E7
Louise Ct 8 DA6 13 E3
Louis Gdns BR7 29 F4
Louisville Ave ME7 64 D4
Lourdes Manor Cl
TN25 303 D1
Louvain Rd DA9 34 E8
Lovage App E6 1 E8
Love La Adisham CT3 177 F2
12 Canterbury CT1 175 A8
Lovelace Ave BR2 53 A3
Lovelace Cl
Gillingham ME8 98 D4
West Kingsdown TN15 90 E4
Lovelace Ct TN26 297 C5
Lovelace Gn SE9 11 F4
Love La
East Tilbury RM18 20 C8
Faversham ME13 138 F6
Margate CT9 50 I3
Minster (Sheppey) ME12 47 D7
Rochester ME1 63 C5
Sidcup DA5 14 A1
Swift's Green TN27 263 B5
Lovel Ave DA16 13 A5
Love La
Wateringbury ME18 192 D7
Woolwich SE18 2 B2
Lovell Rd
Minster (Sheppey) ME12 47 A5
Rough Common CT2 142 B3
Lovers La TN17 290 F1
Lover's La DA9,DA10 17 D3
Loves Holiday Camp
ME12 49 F3
Love Street Cl CT6 76 C2
Lovibonds Ave BR6 86 B7
Low Cl DA9 17 A2
Lowe Ave E16 1 A8
Lower Bannister Cotts
ME9 101 B2
Lower Bell La ME20 128 B2
Lower Blackhouse Hill
CT21 333 D3
Lower Bloors La ME8 65 E3
Lower Boxley Rd 10
ME14 162 A5
Lower Bridge St CT1 175 A8
Lower Camden BR7 52 F8
Lower Chantry La
CT1 175 A8
Lower Church Hill DA9 16 E2
Lower Croft BR8 55 F5
Lower Denmark Rd
TN23 300 C8
Lower Ensden Rd CT4 172 D4
Lower Fant Rd ME16 161 D2
Lower Farm Rd ME17 228 D5
Lower Gn TN11 220 F1
Lower Gore La CT13 180 B3
Lower Gravel Rd BR2 52 F1
Lower Green Rd
Pembury TN2 287 D7
Rusthall TN3,TN4 285 C6
Lower Halstow Prim Sch
ME9 67 B2
Lower Hartlip Rd ME9 99 E5
Lower Haysden La
TN11,TN9 253 D8
Lower Hazelhurst
Ticehurst TN5 338 A4
Ticehurst TN5 338 B4
Lower Herne Rd CT6 110 E8
Lower Higham Rd
DA12 38 B7
Lower High St TN5 337 A4
Lower Lees Rd CT4 172 D2
Lower Mill La CT14 215 C5
Lower Northdown Ave
CT9 51 B2
Lower Norton La ME9 104 A1
Lower Park Rd DA17 4 A2
Lower Platts TN5 338 F1
Lower Queens Rd
TN24 268 C3
Lower Rainham Rd
Gillingham,Lower Rainham
ME8 66 A3
Gillingham ME7 65 D5
Lower Range Rd DA12 37 E8
Lower Rd
Eastchurch ME12 48 B3
East Farleigh ME15 194 B7
Lower Rd E CT16 310 H8
Lower Rd Erith DA17 4 B3
Lower Rd
Erith DA8 4 D2
Faversham ME13 137 C8
Hextable BR8 33 B1
Higham DA12,ME3 39 B6
Maidstone ME15 162 B3
Minster (Sheppey) ME12 46 E4
Northfleet DA11 18 A3
Orpington BR5 54 B3
River CT17 277 E3
Shorne DA12 38 E6
Staple CT3 179 B6
Stone in Oxney TN30 360 D5
Sutton Valence ME17 229 E7
Temple Ewell CT16 277 D5
Teynham,Lower Newlands
ME9,ME13 103 E2
Teynham ME9 103 B3
Lower Rd W CT16 310 G8
Lower Rd
West Farleigh ME15 193 D7
Woodchurch TN26 326 B1
Lower Rochester Rd
ME3 39 E6
Lower Rowling Cotts
CT3 179 B2
Lower Sandgate Rd
CT20 335 C3
Lower Sands TN29 352 E2
Lower Santon La CT3 146 D7
Lower Station Rd DA1 14 E1
Lower St Eastry CT13 180 B1
Leeds ME17 197 A7
Lower Stone St ME15 162 A3
Lower St
Tilmanstone CT14 213 A2
Tonbridge TN11 220 B5
Lower Tovil ME15 161 E2
Lower Twydall La ME7,
ME8 65 C4
Lower Vicarage Rd
TN24 268 D7
Lower Wall Rd
Burmarsh CT21 352 D8
Dymchurch CT21 353 A7
Lower Warren Rd
ME20 129 E6
Lower Woodlands Rd
ME7 65 A6
Lowestoft Mews E16 2 B4
Lowfield Rd ME12 46 E6
Lowfield St DA1 33 E8
Low Meadow ME2 95 B5
Lownds Ct BR1 52 A7
Lowry Cl DA8 4 D2
Lowry The 4 TN9 254 B8
Lowslip Hill CT15 309 A5
Low Street La RM18 19 F8
Lowther Rd CT17 310 B8
Loxwood Cl
Orpington BR5,BR6 87 D8
Whitfield CT16 278 B7
Lubbock Cl ME15 195 E5
Lubbock Ct BR7 29 F1
Lubbock Ho BR6 86 E8
Lubbock Rd BR7 29 F1
Lubbock Wlk ME8 98 D5
Lucas Cres DA9 17 C3
Lucas Rd ME6 127 E7
Lucerne Ct 5 Erith DA18 3 E3
Whitstable CT5 107 F6
Lucerne Dr CT5 107 F6
Lucerne La CT15 247 C2
Lucerne Rd BR6 53 F1
Lucerne St ME14 162 A5
Lucilina Dr TN8 249 C8
Lucilla Ave TN23 299 F4
Luckhurst Gdns CT9 51 E3
Luckhurst Rd
Ashford TN24 301 A7
Crabble CT17 277 E3
Luckley Ho TN25 237 E2
Lucknow Cl CT15 278 F3
Lucknow Rd TN12 257 A8
Lucknow St SE18 12 E7
Lucks Hill ME19 159 D8
Lucks La
Paddock Wood TN12 257 B8
Rabbit's Cross ME17 228 F6
Lucks Way TN12 259 B6
Lucy Ave CT19 335 B7
Lucy's Hill CT21 333 B2
Luddenham Cl
Ashford TN23 299 F6
Maidstone ME14 162 C6
Luddenham Sch ME13 104 E1
Luddesdon Rd DA8 14 A7
Luddesdown Ho 5
BR5 54 C4
Luddesdown Rd DA13 61 A2
Ludgate Rd ME9 135 F5
Ludham Cl SE28 3 C7
Ludlow Cl BR2 52 A6
Luffield Rd SE2 3 B3
Luffman Rd SE12 29 B5
Lughorse La ME15,
ME18 193 C1
Lukes Cl CT17 278 B1
Lukin Ho CT21 332 F1
Lullarook Cl TN16 118 C3
Lullingstone Ave BR8 55 F6
Lullingstone Castle★
DA4 89 B5
Lullingstone Cl
Gillingham ME7 98 B3
Orpington BR5 31 B1
Lullingstone Cres BR5 31 B1
Lullingstone Ct 15
CT1 174 F8
Lullingstone La DA4 89 C8
Lullingstone Pk★ DA4 88 F6
Lullingstone Pk Visitor
Ctr★ DA4 89 B4
Lullingstone Rd
3 Bexley DA17 13 F8
Maidstone ME16 161 C7
Lullingstone Roman Villa
(rems of)★ DA4 89 B7
Lulworth Rd
Bexley DA16 12 F5
Bromley SE9 29 E6
Lumley Cl DA17 4 A1
Lumsden Terr 8 ME4 63 E4
Lunar Cl TN16 118 D3
Lunedale Rd DA2 34 C7
Lunsford District Ctr
ME20 128 A4
Lunsford La ME20 127 F2
Lunsford Prim Sch
ME20 128 A2
Lupton Cl SE12 29 B4
Lurkins Rise TN17 318 D7
Lushington Rd ME14 161 E7
Lusted Hall La TN16 150 C7
Lusted Rd TN13 153 E7
Luton Ave CT10 83 F3
Luton Ct CT10 83 F3
Luton High St ME5 64 C2
Luton Inf Sch ME5 64 C2
Luton Jun Sch ME4 64 C2
Luton Rd
Chatham ME4,ME5 64 B2
Faversham ME13 138 E7
Sidcup DA14 31 C5
Luxfield Rd SE9 29 E7
Luxon Rd DA13 93 E4
Luxted Rd BR6 119 A6
Lyall Way ME8 98 E4
Lychfield Dr ME2 63 A8
Lych Gate Rd BR6 54 A1
Lydbrook Cl ME10 101 D4
Lydd Airport TN29 377 A7
Lydd Cl DA14 30 E5
Lydden Ct SE9 12 E1
Lydden Hill CT15 244 C1
Lydden International Motor
Racing Circuit CT4 243 F3
Lydden Prim Sch
CT15 276 F8
Lydd Prim Sch TN29 376 C6
Lydd Rd Bexley DA7 13 F7
Chatham ME5 97 B5
New Romney TN28,
TN29 372 F6
Lydd Town Crossing
TN29 376 D8
Lydd Town Mus★
TN29 376 C6
Lydens La TN8 249 F6
Lydford Ct 18 DA2 16 B1
Lydia Cotts 2 DA11 37 B8
Lydia Rd Deal CT14 215 A2
Erith DA8 14 F8
Lydos Cl TN29 377 E5
Lydstep Rd BR7 30 A4
Lyell Ct CT2 142 C4
Lyell Cl CT21 333 A1
Lyell Ct 5 CT7 80 F8
Lyell Rd CT7 80 F8
Lyford St SE18 1 E2
Lyle Cl ME2 63 B8
Lyle Ct ME16 161 C5
Lyle Pk TN13 154 B4
Lyme Farm Rd SE12 11 B3
Lyme Rd DA16 13 B6
Lyminge CE Prim Sch
CT18 305 C7
Lyminge Cl
Gillingham ME8 65 C2
Sidcup DA14 30 F4
Lyminge Way CT9 51 C1
Lymington Cl 2 E6 1 F8
Lymington Ct ME15 195 F4
Lymington Rd CT8 81 E7
Lympne Castle★
CT21 331 F2
Lympne CE Prim Sch
CT21 332 A3
Lympne Hill CT21 332 A2
Lympne Ind Pk CT21 331 E3
Lynacre CT2 142 C1
Lyn Ct CT20 335 A5
Lyndale Est RM20 17 B8
Lyndean Ind Est SE2 3 C3
Lynden Way BR8 55 D6
Lyndhurst Ave
Gillingham ME8 98 C7
Margate CT9 51 B2
Lyndhurst BR7 30 B2
Lyndhurst Cl Bexley DA7 14 B4
Canterbury CT2 142 E3
Orpington BR6 86 B6
Lyndhurst Dr TN13 153 E3
Lyndhurst Gr ME10 101 E2
Lyndhurst Rd
Bexley DA7 14 B4
Broadstairs CT10 84 A6
Crabble CT17 277 E2
Dymchurch TN29 366 C8
Maidstone ME15 195 C8
Ramsgate CT11 117 F7
Lyndhurst Way DA13 59 F8
Lyndon Ave DA15 12 F2
Lyndon Rd DA17 4 A2
Lyndon Way CT18 305 C7
Lynette Ave ME2 40 A1
Lyngate Ct CT9 51 D2
Lyngs Cl ME18 225 F8
Lynmead Cl TN8 217 B4
Lynmere Rd DA16 13 B5
Lynmouth Dr ME12 47 C7
Lynmouth Rise BR5 54 B5
Lynne Cl 7 BR6 86 F4
Lynors Ave ME2 40 A1
Lynstead Cl BR1 52 C7
Lynstead Ho ME16 161 A1
Lynsted Cl
Ashford TN23 299 F6
Bexley DA6 14 B2
Lynsted Gdns SE9 11 D4
Lynsted La ME9 136 B7
Lynsted & Norton Prim Sch
ME9 136 A7
Lynsted Rd
Gillingham ME8 65 B3
Halfway Houses ME12 46 E7
Lynton Ave BR5 54 B5
Lynton Court Mans
CT9 51 B3
Lynton Dr ME5 97 B3
Lynton Pl CT4 176 A1
Lynton Rd
Gravesend DA11 37 A7
Hythe CT21 333 C1
Lynton Rd S DA11 37 A7
Lynwood
Folkestone CT19 335 C7
Groombridge TN3 312 C6
Lynwood Gr BR6 53 E1
Lynx Way E16 1 D6
Lyons Cres TN9 222 C2
Lyons The TN9 222 C2
Lyoth Rd BR5 86 C8
Lysander Cl
Broadstairs CT10 83 C3
Littlebourne CT4 176 E4
Lysander Rd ME19 158 F3
Lysander Way BR6 86 C7
Lysander Wlk CT18 307 A4
Lytchet Rd BR1 29 B1
Lytham Ave CT6 76 D1
Lytham Cl SE28 3 E7
Lytton Strachey Path 8
SE28 3 B6
Lyveden Rd SE3 11 B7

M

Mabbett Ho 2 SE18 12 A8
Mabel Cotts DA3 59 A6
Mabel Rd BR8 33 A2
Mabledon Ave TN24 268 D1
Mabledon Cl TN28 373 B6
Mabledon Rd TN9 254 A8
Macallister Ho 8 SE18 12 B8
Macaulay Cl ME20 128 A4
Macaulay Way 2 SE28 3 B5
Macbean St SE18 2 B3
Macdonald Ct TN12 257 A6
Macdonald Par CT5 108 A6
Macdonald Rd
Dover CT17 278 A1
Gillingham ME7 64 D6
Mace Ct RM17 18 E8
Mace Farm Cotts
TN14 119 E6
Mace Ind Est TN24 268 C3
Mace La Ashford TN24 268 C2
Downe TN14 119 D6
Mace Terr TN26 299 A1
Macgregor Rd E16 1 C8
Mackenders Cl ME20 129 A6
Mackenders Gn ME20 129 A6
Mackenders La ME20 129 A6
Mackenzie Dr CT20 334 E5
Mackenzie Way DA12 37 D2
Mackeson Ct 8 CT21 333 B2
Mackintosh Cl ME23 23 F3
Macklands Ho ME8 66 A2
Macklands Way ME8 66 A2
Macleod Ho SE18 11 E6
Macmillan Gdns 2
DA1 16 A3
Macoma Rd SE18 12 D8
Macoma Terr SE18 12 D8
Madan Cl TN16 151 E2
Madan Rd TN16 151 E2
Mada Rd BR6 86 B7
Madden Ave ME5 96 E5
Madden Cl DA10 17 E1
Maddocks Cl DA14 31 E3
Madeira Ct CT20 335 B3
Madeira Pk TN2 286 B2
Madeira Rd
Littlestone-on-Sea TN28 373 E6
Margate CT9 51 A2
Madeira Wlk CT11 117 E6
Madginford Cl ME15 163 A2
Madginford Park Inf Sch
ME15 163 A2
Madginford Park Jun Sch
ME15 163 A2
Madginford Rd ME15 162 F2
Madison Cres DA7 13 C7
Madison Gdns DA7 13 C7
Madison Way TN13 153 F4
Madras Ho 2 ME15 195 E5
Maesmaur Rd TN16 150 D6
Mafeking Rd ME5 96 F3
Magazine Rd TN24 268 B3
Magdala Rd
Broadstairs CT10 83 E6
Dover CT17 278 B1
Magdalen Cl ME7 98 A4
Magdalen Ct
Broadstairs CT10 84 A6
Canterbury CT1 175 B7
Magdelan Gr BR6 87 B6
Magness Rd CT14 215 A2
Magnet Rd RM20 17 C8
Magnolia Ave
Gillingham ME8 98 B5
Margate CT9 51 D2
Magnolia Cl TN9 254 C7
Magnolia Dr
Biggin Hill TN16 118 E3
Chartham CT4 173 E1
Magnolia Ho 3 ME16 161 A3
Magnolia Rise CT6 77 D2
Magpie Bottom TN15 122 E6
Magpie Cl ME20 128 A1
Magpie Ct ME12 47 A6
Magpie Gn 3 TN8 217 D3
Magpie Hall Cl BR2 52 E3
Magpie Hall La BR2 52 F3
Magpie Hall Rd
Chatham ME4 64 A2
Stubb's Cross TN26 299 E2
Magpie La
Rhodes Minnis CT4 273 B3
Yelsted ME9,ME14 98 F1
Magpie Lodge 4
CT16 278 B2
Magwitch Cl ME1 63 B4
Maida Rd Chatham ME4 64 B2
Erith DA17 4 A3
Maida Vale Rd DA1 15 A2
Maiden Erlegh Ave
DA5 31 E7
Maiden La
Canterbury CT1 174 D6
Crayford DA1 15 A3
Maidstone Barracks Sta
ME16 161 E5
Maidstone East Sta
ME14 161 F5
Maidstone Gram Sch for
Girls ME16 161 E5
Maidstone Gram Sch
ME15 162 B2
Maidstone Hospl The
ME16 161 A4
Maidstone Ind Ctr
ME14 161 F5
Maidstone L Ctr ME15 162 C2
Maidstone Mus & Bentlif
Art Gallery★ ME14 161 F5
Maidstone Rd
Bredhurst ME7,ME8 98 B2
Charing TN25,TN26,
TN27 234 D6
Chatham ME4 63 F2
Chatham ME5 96 D4
Colt's Hill TN12,TN2 256 B4
Danaway ME9 100 D4
Five Wents ME17 196 E2
Gillingham ME8 98 C6
Goose Green ME18,
TN11 191 C3
Grays RM17 18 A8
Headcorn TN27 262 B7
Horsmonden,Claygate
TN12 258 C3
Horsmonden TN12 290 A7
Lenham ME17 199 D5
Matfield TN12 288 C6
Nettlestead Green
ME18 192 C3
Pembury TN2 255 E1
Platt TN15 157 C7
Potters Corner TN25,
TN26 267 D7
Rochester ME1 63 C3
Seal TN15 155 C5
Sevenoaks TN13 153 E5
Sidcup DA14 31 F1
Staplehurst TN12 260 E7
Swanley DA14,BR8 55 B8
Underling Green TN12 227 F2
Maidstone St Michaels CE
Jun Sch ME16 161 E3
Maidstone West Sta
ME16 161 F3
Mailyns The ME8 98 D7
Maine Cl CT16 278 B3
Main Gate Rd ME4 63 F7
Main Rd
Biggin Hill TN16 118 C5
Chattenden ME3 40 F4
Cooling ME3 22 F4
Crockenhill BR8 55 D3
Crockham Hill TN8 184 C1
Cudham TN16 151 A7
Farningham DA4 56 F3
Halstead TN14 120 C3
Hoo St Werburgh ME3 41 C5
Kingsnorth ME3 42 D7
Longfield DA3 58 E7
Marlpit Hill TN8 217 B6
Orpington BR5 54 C7
Queenborough ME11,
ME12 46 B5
Sellindge TN25 303 C1
Sheerness ME12 28 A3
Sidcup DA14,DA15 30 E5
Sundridge TN14 152 E3
Sutton at H DA4 34 B1
Swanley BR8 55 F8
Mainridge Rd BR7 30 A4
Main Road Gorse Hill
DA4 90 D7
Main St Iden TN31 368 B4
Peasmarsh TN31 367 B2
St Mary's Island ME4 41 B2
Maison Des Fleurs
ME16 161 C2
Maison Dieu★ ME13 138 A6
Maison Dieu Pl 4
CT16 310 D8
Maison Dieu Rd CT16 310 D8
Maitland Ct ME13 105 B1
Majendie Rd SE18 2 D1
Majestic Par CT20 335 C4
Major Clark Ho TN17 320 C5
Major Cl CT5 108 B6
Major York's Rd TN4 285 F2
Makenade Ave ME13 138 E6
Malan Cl TN16 118 E2
Malcolm Sargent Rd
TN23 300 B5
Malden Dr ME14 162 A8
Malham Dr CT9 51 A1
Mallard Apartments 14
ME15 195 E5
Mallard Cl Dartford DA1 15 F2
Herne Bay CT6 76 E2
Mallard Cres ME9 68 D4
Mallard Ct ME12 47 A6
Mallard Path 6 SE28 2 D3
Mallards TN24 300 D7
Mallards Way ME15 163 A1
Mallard Way
Lower Stoke ME3 25 C4
Marlpit Hill TN8 217 C3
Mallard Wlk
Larkfield ME20 127 F2
Sidcup DA14 31 C2
Malling Ct ME19 159 F7
Mallingdene Cl ME3 40 B8
Malling Rd
Kings Hill M18,ME19 158 F2
Lunsford ME6,ME20 127 F5
Snodland ME6 128 A7
Teston ME18 160 A1
Malling Sch The ME19 159 F7
Mallings Dr ME14 163 C4
Mallings La ME14 163 C4
Malling Terr ME16 161 C4
Mallory Cl CT12 83 C2
Mallow Cl DA11 36 E4
Mallow Ct RM17 18 D8
Mallows The ME14 161 E7
Mallow Way 1 ME5 96 F4
Mall The 6 Bexley DA6 14 A3
4 Bromley BR1 52 A6
Faversham ME13 138 C6
Mallys Pl DA4 57 C8
Malmains Rd CT17 310 A6
Malmaynes Hall Rd
ME3 24 D3
Malmedy Ct CT14 215 A1
Malory Sch BR1 29 A4
Malta Ave ME5 97 A7
Malta Ho 17 CT1 143 B2
Malta Rd RM18 18 F5
Malta Terr 5 ME14 162 A7
Maltby Cl BR6 54 A1
Malthouse Cl ME17 199 D5
Malthouse Cotts
Boughton Lees TN25 236 F4
New Romney TN28 373 A6
Malthouse Hill
10 Hythe CT21 333 B2
Maidstone ME15 194 F4
Malthouse La
Hamstreet TN26 327 D1
Peasmarsh TN31 367 D2
Shorne DA12 38 E3
Malt House La TN30 345 A7
Malthouse Rd
Canterbury CT2 142 F2
Stansted TN15 91 F2
Malthouses The
Birchington CT7 80 F7
Brabourne TN25 303 B8
Malthouse The ME16 194 A8
Malthus Path 7 SE28 3 C5
Maltings Bsns Pk The
TN31 367 C2
Maltings Cl TN11 223 E8
Maltings Ent Ctr The
DA12 37 F7
Maltings Hall The
CT11 117 D7
Maltings The
7 Canterbury,St Dunstan's
CT2 142 E1
10 Canterbury,St Martin's
CT1 175 A8
Deal CT14 248 B8
Faversham ME13 138 D8
Gillingham ME8 99 A8
3 Gravesend DA11 19 A1
Hadlow TN11 223 E8
Littlebourne CT3 176 F7
Loose ME17 195 B4
Maidstone, Grove Green
ME14 162 E5
Orpington BR6 53 F1
Peasmarsh TN31 367 C2
Westerham TN16 184 C8
Malt Mews ME1 63 C5
Malton Mews SE18 12 E8
Malton St SE18 12 E8
Malton Way TN2 286 F7
Malt Shovel Cotts DA4 89 D7
Malus Cl ME5 97 B1
Malvern Ave DA7 13 E7
Malvern Ho DA11 18 D1
Malvern Mdw CT16 277 E5
Malvern Pk CT6 77 D4
Malvern Rd
Ashford TN24 268 B4
Dover CT17 310 C7
Gillingham ME7 64 E3
Orpington BR6 87 B6
Temple Ewell CT16 277 E5
Malvina Ave DA12 37 C6
Malyons Rd BR8 32 F1
Mamignot Cl ME14 163 A5
Manchester Cl ME5 97 C6
Manchester Ct E16 1 B7
Manciple Cl CT2 174 C8
Mandarin La CT6 76 E2
Mandela Ho SE18 12 D8
Mandela Rd E16 1 A7
Mandeville Cl 1 SE3 11 A7

Mandeville Ct 🔳
 ME14 . . . . **162** A5
Mandeville Rd CT2 . . . . . **142** E2
Manford Ind Est DA8 . . . **15** B8
Mangers La CT16 . . . . . . **278** A4
Mangers Pl CT16 . . . . . . **278** A3
Mangold Way 🔳 DA18 . . . .3 E3
Mangravet Ave ME15 . . **195** C7
Manister Rd SE2 . . . . .3 A3
Manitoba Gdns 🔳 BR6 . .**86** F4
Manktelow Ct CT16 . . . . . .**83** F2
Manley Cl CT16 . . . . . . **278** A7
Manley Ho CT16 . . . . . . **278** A7
Manning Ct 🔳 SE28 . . . . .3 B5
Manningham Ho
 ME19 . . . . **160** A6
Manning Rd BR5 . . . .**54** D4
Mannock Ho 🔳 CT1 . . **143** B1
Mannock Rd DA1 . . . .**15** F4
Manns Hill CT14 . . . . . **241** A6
Mann Sq TN9 . . . . **254** D7
Manor Ave CT14 . . . . . . **215** B4
Manorbrook SE3 . . . . . . **11** A3
Manor Cl
 Canterbury CT1 . . . . . **174** C5
 Chalk DA12 . . . .**38** B6
 Crayford DA1 . . . .**14** E3
 Dartford DA2 . . . . **33** A5
 Deal CT14 . . . . **215** A4
 Erith SE28 . . . . .3 C7
 Herne Bay CT6 . . . .**77** F6
 Maidstone ME14 . . . . . **163** B3
 Royal Tunbridge Wells
 TN4 . . . . **285** E3
 Rushenden ME11 . . . . . . **46** A3
Manor Cotts
 Hernhill ME13 . . . . **140** B6
 Lamberhurst TN3 . . . . . . **317** B5
 Langley ME17 . . . . **196** C5
Manor Ct
 Canterbury CT1 . . . . . . **174** F7
 Gillingham ME7 . . . .**65** C4
 Maidstone ME14 . . . . . **163** B3
 Sole Street DA13 . . . . . . **60** D4
Manordene Rd SE28 . . . . .3 D7
Manor Dr
 Birchington CT7 . . . .**80** F6
 Hartley DA3 . . . .**59** A3
Manor Farm Cl CT21 . . **332** A4
Manor Farm Cotts
 TN15 . . . . **156** A6
Manorfield
 Ashford TN23 . . . . **299** E8
 Elham CT4 . . . . **273** F4
Manorfields Cl BR7 . . . . .**53** F6
Manor Field DA12 . . . . . . **38** E3
Manor Forstal DA3 . . . . . .**91** F7
Manor Gdns
 Chatham ME5 . . . .**96** A4
 Whitfield CT16 . . . . **278** A8
Manor Gr
 Sittingbourne ME10 . . . . **101** D3
 Tonbridge TN10 . . . . . . **222** C3
Manor Ho
 🔳 Chatham ME7 . . . .**64** A6
 Chislehurst BR7 . . . . **53** D8
Manor Ho The
 Canterbury CT2 . . . . . . **142** F2
 🔳 Folkestone CT20 . . **335** B3
 Limpsfield RH8 . . . . **183** B3
 Sarre CT7 . . . . **113** D6
 Sidcup DA15 . . . .**31** A7
 Sidcup,Old Bexley DA5 . . . **32** B7
Manor House Dr
 Ashford TN23 . . . . **300** D3
 Maidstone ME16 . . . . . **161** D3
Manor House Gdns
 TN8 . . . . **217** C1
Manor La
 Fawkham Green DA3 . . . . **58** C2
 Hartley DA3 . . . . **59** A3
 Rochester ME1 . . . .**62** F3
Manor Lea Rd CT17 . . . . . .**79** F1
Manor Leaze TN25 . . . . **302** F5
Manor Mews CT14 . . . . **247** F5
Manor Oak Prim Sch
 BR5 . . . .**54** D4
Manor Park Ctry Pk ★
 ME19 . . . . **159** B7
Manor Park Rd BR7 . . . . .**53** D8
Manor Pk
 Chislehurst BR7 . . . . **53** D8
 Erith DA8 . . . . **15** A8
 Royal Tunbridge Wells
 TN4 . . . . **285** E3
Manor Pl Bromley BR1 . . .**52** E8
 Chislehurst BR7 . . . . **53** D7
Manor Pound La TN25 . **302** F7
Manor Rd
 🔳 Broadstairs CT10 . . . .**84** A4
 Chatham ME4 . . . .**63** F4
 Crayford DA1 . . . .**14** E3
 Deal CT14 . . . . **215** A4
 Dover CT17 . . . . **310** A6
 Edenbridge TN8 . . . . . . **217** B1
 Erith DA8 . . . . **15** A8
 Folkestone CT20 . . . . . **335** C4
 🔳 Gravesend DA12 . . . . .**19** B1
 Grays RM17 . . . . **18** C8
 Herne Bay CT6 . . . .**77** F6
 Knockmill TN15 . . . . . . **123** F8
 Lydd TN29 . . . . **376** C6
 Milstead ME9 . . . . **134** F2
 New Barn DA3 . . . . **59** C4
 Royal Tunbridge Wells
 TN4 . . . . **253** E1
 Rushenden ME11 . . . . . . **46** A3
 Rusthall TN4 . . . . **285** C4
 St Nicholas at Wade CT7 . .**79** F1

 Sidcup DA15 . . . .**31** A5
 Sidcup,Old Bexley DA5 . . . **32** B7
 Sole Street DA13 . . . . . . **60** D4
 Sundridge TN14 . . . . . . **152** D3
 Swanscombe DA10 . . . . . .**35** E8
 Tatsfield TN16 . . . . **150** E7
 Tilbury RM18 . . . . **19** A5
 West Thurrock RM20 . . . . **17** C8
 Whitstable CT5 . . . . **75** A2
Manor Rise
 Dover CT17 . . . . **310** A6
 Maidstone ME14 . . . . . **163** B3
Manorside Cl SE2 . . . . .3 D2
Manor St ME7 . . . .**64** A6
Manor The TN2 . . . . . . **286** E5
Manor Way
 Ashford TN23 . . . . **267** F4
 Bexley DA7 . . . . **14** D4
 Bromley BR2 . . . .**52** E3
Manor Way Bsns Ctr
 RM13 . . . . .4 D8
Manor Way Eltham SE3 . . **11** A3
 Grays RM17 . . . . **18** D7
 Grays RM17 . . . . **18** D7
 Leysdown-on-S ME12 . . . . **49** H2
 Northfleet DA11 . . . . **18** A3
 Orpington BR5 . . . . **53** C5
 Sidcup DA15 . . . .**32** A7
 Swanscombe DA10 . . . . . .**17** E3
 Warden ME12 . . . . **49** D6
Manse Ct DA14 . . . . **31** C3
Manse Field CT16 . . . . . **278** B2
Mansel Dr ME1 . . . .**63** A2
Mansell La CT15 . . . . . . **275** B4
Manse Par BR8 . . . . **56** A5
Manse Way BR8 . . . . **56** A5
Mansfield Cl BR5 . . . . **54** D2
Mansfield Dr ME9 . . . .**68** D3
Mansfield Rd BR8 . . . . . . **32** F2
Mansfield Wlk ME14 . . . **161** E3
Mansion Gdns CT16 . . . **278** A4
Mansion House Cl
 TN27 . . . . **295** A2
Mansion Row ME7 . . . . . . **64** A6
Mansions The CT10 . . . . . .**83** E4
Mansion St CT9 . . . . **50** I3
Manston Court Cotts
 CT12 . . . .**82** C2
Manston Court Rd
 CT12,CT9 . . . .**82** D3
Manston Pk CT12 . . . .**81** D2
Manston Rd
 Acol CT12,CT7 . . . . **81** D4
 Margate CT12,CT9 . . . . . . **82** C4
 Ramsgate CT11,CT12 . . . **117** A8
Mansum Ct CT7 . . . . **79** F2
Manthorpe Rd SE18 . . . . .2 C1
Mantles Hill CT14 . . . . . **214** D1
Manton Rd SE2 . . . . .3 A2
Manwarings The
 TN12 . . . . **290** A6
Manwood Almshouse
 CT2 . . . . **142** F3
Manwood Ave CT2 . . . . . **142** F3
Manwood Cl ME10 . . . . . **101** F2
Manwood Rd CT13 . . . . . **181** A8
Manwood St E16 . . . . .1 F5
Maple Ave
 Gillingham ME7 . . . .**64** E6
 Maidstone ME16 . . . . . **161** C6
Maple Cl Ashford TN23 . . **267** E3
 Broadstairs CT10 . . . . **51** E1
 Larkfield ME20 . . . . **128** A2
 Orpington BR5 . . . . **53** D4
 Rough Common CT2 . . . . **142** B3
 Royal Tunbridge Wells
 TN2 . . . . **286** A1
 Swanley BR8 . . . .**55** E7
Maple Cres DA15 . . . . . . **13** A1
Maplecroft Cl E6 . . . . .1 E7
Maple Ct Erith DA8 . . . . . .**14** F7
 Hersden CT3 . . . . **144** E8
 Newham E6 . . . . .2 A8
 Royal Tunbridge Wells
 TN4 . . . . **285** E4
 Sidcup DA14 . . . . **31** C3
 Stone DA9 . . . .**34** E8
Mapledene BR7 . . . . **30** C3
Maple Dr
 Hawkinge CT18 . . . . . . **307** C5
 St Mary's Bay TN29 . . . . **365** F4
Maplefields Gdns
 CT18 . . . . **307** C5
Maple Gdns CT3 . . . . . . **144** E8
Maplehurst Cl DA2 . . . . . . **32** E6
Maple Leaf Cl TN16 . . . . **118** D3
Maple Leaf Dr DA15 . . . . .**30** F7
Maple Rd Dartford DA3 . . . **33** C7
 Gravesend DA12 . . . . **37** C4
 Grays RM17 . . . . **18** C8
 Hoo St Werburgh ME3 . . .**41** E3
 Rochester ME2 . . . . **63** A7
Maplescombe Farm Cotts
 DA4 . . . .**90** B6
Maplescombe La DA4 . . . .**90** B6
Maplesden Cl ME16 . . . **160** F3
Maplesden TN12 . . . . . . **259** D5
Maplesden Noakes Sch The
 ME16 . . . . **161** E6
Maples The
 Broadstairs CT10 . . . . **83** D4
 Minster (Sheppey) ME12 . .**47** B6
 New Barn DA3 . . . . **59** B6
Maple St ME12 . . . . **28** C1
Mapleton Cl BR2 . . . .**52** A3
Mapleton TN8 . . . . **218** A7
Mapleton Rd
 Four Elms TN8 . . . . **218** A8
 Westerham TN8,TN16 . . **184** E3
Maple Tree Pl SE3 . . . . . . **11** E6
Maplin Ho 🔳 SE2 . . . . . . .3 D4

Maplin Rd E16 . . . . .1 B7
Maplins Cl 🔳 ME8 . . . . . . **65** F1
Mara Ct ME4 . . . .**63** F1
Maran Way DA18 . . . . .3 D3
Marathon Paddock
 ME7 . . . .**64** D4
Marathon Way SE28 . . . . . .2 F4
Marble Ho 🔳 SE18 . . . . . . .2 F1
Marbrook Ct SE12 . . . . . . **29** C5
Marc Brunel Way ME4 . . . **64** A7
Marcellina Way BR6 . . . . . .**86** F7
Marcet Rd DA1 . . . . **15** C2
Marconi Ho SE2 . . . . .3 C1
Marconi Rd DA11 . . . . **36** D5
Marconi Way ME1 . . . .**96** D7
Marcroft CT10 . . . . **84** B7
Marcus Rd DA1 . . . . **33** A8
Mardale Ct ME8 . . . . **66** A1
Marden Ave Hayes BR2 . . **52** A3
 Ramsgate CT12 . . . . **117** D8
Marden Cres DA5 . . . . . . **14** C2
Marden Prim Sch
 TN12 . . . . **259** B5
Marden Rd
 Rochester ME2 . . . .**40** C1
 Staplehurst TN12 . . . . . **260** C5
Marden Sta TN12 . . . . . . **259** C6
Mardol Rd TN24 . . . . **268** C5
Marechal Niel Ave
 DA15 . . . . **30** D5
Marechal Niel Par
 DA15 . . . . **30** D5
Maresfield Cl CT16 . . . . . **278** B2
Margaret Barr Row
 DA10 . . . . **35** E8
Margaret Ct CT6 . . . .**76** F4
Margaret Gardner Dr
 SE9 . . . .**29** F6
Margaret Rd DA5 . . . . **13** D1
Margaret St CT20 . . . . . . **335** E5
Margate Caves ★ CT9 . . .**50** J3
Margate Cl ME7 . . . .**64** E6
Margate Hill CT7 . . . . **81** C4
Margate Rd
 Herne Bay,Broomfield
 CT6 . . . .**77** D2
 Herne Bay CT6 . . . . **77** C3
 Ramsgate CT10,CT12,
 CT11 . . . .**83** B3
Margate Sta CT9 . . . . **50** H2
Margetts La ME1 . . . .**95** D5
Margetts Pl ME2 . . . . **41** A3
Mar Ho 🔳 SE7 . . . . **11** C8
Marian Ave ME12 . . . . **47** A7
Marian Sq TN12 . . . . **260** F4
Marigold Way ME16 . . . **161** A3
Marilyn Cres CT7 . . . .**81** B7
Marina Cl 🔳 BR2 . . . .**52** A6
Marina Ct Deal CT14 . . . **215** D8
 Hythe CT21 . . . . **333** C1
Marina Dr Bexley DA16 . . . **12** E5
 Dartford DA1 . . . . **34** A7
 Minster (Sheppey) ME12 . **47** A7
 Northfleet DA11 . . . . **18** F1
Marina Espl CT11 . . . . . . **117** F7
Marina Rd CT11 . . . . **117** F7
Marina The CT14 . . . . . . **215** D8
Marine Ave TN29 . . . . . . **352** F3
Marine Cres
 🔳 Folkestone CT20 . . **335** D4
 Whitstable CT5 . . . . **75** B3
Marine Ct
 🔳 Dover CT16 . . . . **310** E7
 Whitstable CT5 . . . . **74** F3
Marine Dr
 Broadstairs CT10 . . . . **51** G3
 Hoo St Werburgh ME3 . . .**41** E3
 Margate CT9 . . . . **50** I2
 Woolwich SE18 . . . . .1 F2
Marine Gap CT5 . . . . **74** C1
Marine Gdns CT9 . . . . **50** I2
Marine Ho CT5 . . . . **74** C1
Marine Hts CT8 . . . . **50** D1
Marine Parade Mews
 CT20 . . . . **335** E4
Marine Par Dover CT16 . . **310** E7
 Folkestone CT20 . . . . . . **335** E4
 Hythe CT21 . . . . **333** C1
 Littlestone-on-Sea TN28 . **373** E5
 Sheerness ME12 . . . . **28** E2
 Whitstable CT5 . . . . **75** A3
Marine Point CT20 . . . . . **335** A3
Marine Rd CT14 . . . . **215** D4
Mariners Ct
 Swanscombe DA9 . . . . . . **17** B8
 Whitstable CT5 . . . . **108** D8
Mariners Lea CT10 . . . . . . **83** D4
Mariners Lee CT5 . . . . **74** E3
Mariners The ME1 . . . . . . **63** B4
Mariners View ME7 . . . . . . **64** F7
Mariners Way 🔳 DA11 . . .**36** E8
Mariners Wlk DA8 . . . . **14** F8
Marine Terr
 Folkestone CT20 . . . . . . **335** E4
 Margate CT9 . . . . **50** H2
 Whitstable CT5 . . . . **74** F3
Marine View ME4 . . . .**41** B1
Marine Walk St CT21 . . . **333** C2
Marion Cl ME5 . . . .**97** A2
Marion Cotts TN15 . . . . . **157** E8
Marion Cres
 Maidstone ME15 . . . . . **195** B8
 Orpington BR5 . . . . **54** B4
Maritime Ave CT6 . . . . **77** C4
Maritime Cl
 Rochester ME2 . . . .**63** D8
 Swanscombe DA9 . . . .**17** B2
Maritime Est ME2 . . . . **63** D8
Maritime Gate DA11 . . . . .**36** E8
Maritime Ind Est SE7 . . . . .1 B2
Maritime Pl CT14 . . . . . . **215** D7
Maritime Way ME4 . . . . . . **64** A8
Marjan Ct CT17 . . . . **278** A1

Marjorie McClure Sch
 BR7 . . . . **53** C8
Marjory Pease Cotts
 RH8 . . . . **183** E5
Mark Ave CT11 . . . . **117** B5
Mark Cl Bexley DA7 . . . . . **13** E6
 Orpington BR2 . . . . **85** E6
Markers Lodge DA12 . . . . .**37** E8
Market Alley 🔳 DA11 . . . **19** B1
Market Bldgs 🔳 ME14 . . **161** F4
Market Colonnade 🔳
 ME14 . . . . **161** F4
Market Hill CT21 . . . . . . **333** C2
Market La 🔳 TN23 . . . . **268** B2
Market Mdw BR5 . . . . **54** C5
Market Par
 Bromley BR1 . . . . **52** A8
 🔳 Sidcup DA14 . . . . **31** B4
Market Pl
 Aylesham CT3 . . . . **210** F5
 🔳 Bexley DA6 . . . . **14** A3
 Charing TN27 . . . . **234** C7
 Dartford DA1 . . . . **33** E8
 🔳 Faversham ME13 . . . **138** D7
 🔟 Folkestone CT20 . . **335** D5
 Margate CT9 . . . . **50** I3
 🔟 Royal Tunbridge Wells
 TN2 . . . . **286** A2
 Sandwich CT13 . . . . **149** A1
 Staplehurst TN12 . . . . . **260** F5
 Woolwich SE18 . . . . .2 A2
Market View CT3 . . . . . . **210** F5
Market Way
 Canterbury CT2 . . . . . . **143** A2
 🔳 Westerham TN16 . . . **151** D1
Mark La DA12 . . . . **19** E1
Markland Rd CT17 . . . . . **309** F7
Marks Sq DA11 . . . . **36** F4
Mark St ME4 . . . . **64** A2
Mark Way BR8 . . . . **56** A4
Marlborough Cl
 Broadstairs CT10 . . . . **83** E3
 Littlestone-on-Sea TN28 . **373** D6
 Orpington BR6 . . . . **53** F3
 Royal Tunbridge Wells
 TN4 . . . . **285** E4
Marlborough Cres
 TN13 . . . . **153** E3
Marlborough Ct
 Folkestone CT20 . . . . . **335** B4
 Hythe CT21 . . . . **333** D1
 Westerham TN16 . . . . . **151** C1
Marlborough Ho
 🔳 Gillingham ME8 . . . . . **98** E8
 Margate CT9 . . . . **51** C3
Marlborough House Sch
 TN18 . . . . **340** E2
Marlborough La SE7 . . . . **11** C7
Marlborough Park Ave
 DA15 . . . . **31** A7
Marlborough Par
 ME16 . . . . **160** F2
Marlborough Rd
 Bexley DA7 . . . . **13** D4
 Bromley BR2 . . . .**52** C5
 Dartford DA1 . . . . **15** C1
 Deal CT14 . . . . **215** A2
 Dover CT17 . . . . **309** F7
 Gillingham ME7 . . . .**64** B5
 Margate CT9 . . . . **50** I1
 🔳 Ramsgate CT11 . . . . **117** D6
 Whitstable CT5 . . . . **108** D5
 Woolwich SE18 . . . . .2 C2
Marlborough Road Ind Est
 CT14 . . . . **215** A3
Marlborough Sch DA15 . **31** A8
Marlborough Way
 ME14 . . . . **268** F7
Marle Place Gdns ★
 TN12 . . . . **289** C4
Marle Place Rd TN12 . . **289** C4
Marler Ho DA8 . . . . **14** F5
Marler Rd CT19 . . . . **334** E6
Marley Ave DA7 . . . . **13** D8
Marley Ct CT2 . . . . **142** C4
Marley La Chislet CT3 . . **112** A5
 Finglesham CT14 . . . . . **214** A8
 Kingston CT4 . . . . **209** B1
 Smarden Bell TN27 . . . . **263** C3
Marley Rd
 Harrietsham ME17 . . . . **198** F6
 Hoo St Werburgh ME3 . . .**41** D6
Marley Way ME1 . . . . **63** C2
Marlfield TN12 . . . . **260** E4
Marlhurst TN8 . . . . **217** B4
Marlin Ct 🔳 DA14 . . . . . . **31** A4
Marling Cross DA12 . . . . . .**37** E1
Marlings Cl BR7 . . . . **53** E5
Marlings Park Ave BR7 . . **53** E6
Marling Way DA12 . . . .**37** E3
Marlow Cl CT5 . . . . **75** B1
Marlow Copse ME5 . . . . . .**96** F1
Marlow Ct TN13 . . . . **154** B4
Marlowe Arc 🔳 CT1 . . . **174** F8
Marlowe Ave CT1 . . . . . . **174** F8
Marlowe Ct BR7 . . . . **30** D2
Marlowe Ct 🔳 CT1 . . . . **174** F8
Marlowe Gdns SE9 . . . . **12** A1
Marlowe Rd
 Ashford TN23 . . . . **268** B2

 Dover CT16 . . . . **278** B3
 Margate CT9 . . . . **83** C8
 New Hythe ME20 . . . . . . **128** A3
Marlowes The DA1 . . . . . . **14** D3
Marlow Ho CT7 . . . .**81** B7
Marlow Mdws CT7 . . . . . **143** F5
Marlpit Cl TN8 . . . . **217** C4
Marlpit Cotts ME17 . . . . **195** E2
Marlpit Gdns TN5 . . . . . . **338** E1
Marlpits The TN5 . . . . . . **336** E5
Marlwood Cl DA15 . . . . . . **30** E6
Marmadon Rd SE18 . . . . . .2 F2
Marmion Way TN23 . . . . **299** C8
Marne Ave DA16 . . . . **13** A4
Marquis Dr ME7 . . . .**98** B3
Marrabon Cl DA15 . . . . . . **31** A7
Marram Ct RM17 . . . . **18** E8
Marr Cl ME12 . . . .**46** F7
Marrians Way 🔳 ME5 . . . **64** C2
Marriott Rd DA1 . . . . **34** A8
Marriotts Wharf 🔳
 DA11 . . . . **19** B1
Marrose Ave CT12 . . . . . . **83** B3
Marrowbone Hill ME12 . . .**48** B5
Marsden Way 🔳 BR6 . . . **86** F6
Marshall Cres
 Broadstairs CT10 . . . . **83** E4
 Rushenden ME11 . . . . . . **45** F3
Marshall Gdns TN11 . . . **190** E1
Marshall Path SE28 . . . . . .3 B6
Marshall Rd ME8 . . . . **98** C8
Marshalls Gr SE18 . . . . .1 E2
Marshalls Land TN30 . . . **324** A3
Marshall St CT19 . . . . . . **335** E7
Marsham Cl BR7 . . . . **30** B3
Marsham Cres ME17 . . . **196** B1
Marsham St ME14 . . . . . **162** A4
Marsham Way ME2 . . . . . .**95** A5
Marshborough Rd
 CT13 . . . . **180** B7
Marshbrook Cl SE3 . . . . . **11** D4
Marsh Cres
 High Halstow ME23 . . . . . **23** E4
 New Romney TN28 . . . . **373** B6
Marsh Farm Rd CT12 . . . **115** B4
Marsh Green Rd TN8 . . . **249** C5
Marsh La Cliffe ME3 . . . . . .**22** B6
 Deal CT14 . . . . **215** A7
Marshlands CT1 TN29 . . . **366** B7
Marshlands TN29 . . . . . . **366** B7
Marshland View ME3 . . . . **25** C5
Marsh La ME9 . . . . **104** A4
Marsh Quarter La
 TN18 . . . . **356** C3
Marsh Rd Halling ME2 . . . .**95** B5
 Ruckinge TN26 . . . . **349** F6
Marsh Rise ME10 . . . . **69** A1
Marsh St Dartford DA1 . . **16** A3
 Dartford DA1 . . . . **16** A5
 Rochester ME2 . . . .**63** B7
Marsh View
 Gravesend DA12 . . . .**37** F7
 Hythe CT21 . . . . **353** C8
Marsh Way
 New Hythe ME20 . . . . . . **128** A4
 Rainham RM13 . . . . .4 D8
Marshwood Cl CT1 . . . . . **143** C3
Marstan Cl ME9 . . . .**66** E2
Marston Cl ME5 . . . .**96** E3
Marston Ct DA14 . . . . **30** F4
Marston Dr ME14 . . . . . . **162** C5
Marston Ho RM17 . . . . . . **18** A8
Marston Wlk ME5 . . . .**96** E3
Martello Cotts CT21 . . . . **353** E8
Martello Dr CT21 . . . . . . **332** F1
Martello Ind Ctr CT19 . . **335** F6
Martello Rd
 Folkestone CT20 . . . . . **335** E6
 Folkestone, Sandgate
 CT20 . . . . **334** E3
Martello Terr 🔳 CT20 . . **334** F3
Martello Tower Mus
 TN29 . . . . **366** C7
Martello Tower Visitor
 Ctr ★ CT19 . . . . **335** A6
Martello Twr ★ TN29 . . **366** C7
Marten Rd CT20 . . . . **335** B5
Martens Ave DA7 . . . . **14** C3
Martens Cl DA7 . . . . **14** C3
Martha Ct CT19 . . . . **335** B7
Martham Ct SE28 . . . . .3 D6
Martin Bowes Rd SE9 . . **11** F4
Martin Ct ME7 . . . . **98** A3
Martindale Ave
 Newham E16 . . . . .1 A6
 Orpington BR6 . . . .**87** A5
Martindale Cl CT1 . . . . . **175** A7
Martin Dale Cres
 CT15 . . . . **247** C2
Martin Dene DA6 . . . . **13** C4
Martindown Rd CT5 . . . . **108** C7
Martin Dr DA2 . . . . **16** C1
Martin Hardie Way
 TN10 . . . . **222** E6
Martin Ho Dartford DA2 . **34** C8
 Gravesend DA11 . . . .**37** A5
Martin House DA11 . . . . . . **36** F6
Martin Ho TN25 . . . . **237** E2
Martin Mill Sta CT15 . . . **247** C2
Martin Rd Dartford DA2 . . **33** C8
 Rochester ME2 . . . . **63** B8
Martin Rise DA6 . . . . **13** C3
Martins Cl
 Lower Higham ME3 . . . . . **39** D6
 Orpington BR5 . . . . **54** D6
Martin's Cl CT12 . . . . **83** C2
Martins Cl TN30 . . . . **345** C8
Martins La TN12 . . . . **191** E2
Martins Pl SE28 . . . . .2 E7
Martin Sq ME20 . . . . **128** A2
Martin's Shaw TN13 . . . **153** C5
Martins The TN26 . . . . . **325** A8

Martin St SE28 . . . . .2 E5
Martin's Way CT21 . . . . . **353** D8
Martins Wlk SE28 . . . . .2 E7
Martyn Ho SE2 . . . . **13** D8
Martyrs' Field Rd CT1 . . **174** F7
Marvels Cl SE12 . . . . **29** B6
Marvels La SE12 . . . . **29** C5
Marvels Lane Prim Sch
 SE12 . . . . **29** C4
Marvillion Ct TN12 . . . . . **224** F6
Marvin Ho 🔳 SE18 . . . . . . **12** B8
Marwell TN16 . . . . **151** B1
Marwood Cl DA16 . . . . **13** B4
Marybank SE18 . . . . .1 F2
Mary Burrows Gdns
 TN15 . . . . **123** B2
Mary Cl ME4 . . . . **64** A2
Mary Day's TN7 . . . . **318** E7
Maryfield Cl DA5 . . . . **32** E5
Mary Green Wlk 🔳
 CT1 . . . . **143** B2
Mary Hougham Almshouses
 CT14 . . . . **215** D7
Maryland Ct
 Gillingham ME8 . . . .**98** E5
 Hythe CT21 . . . . **333** D3
Maryland Dr ME16 . . . . . **160** F2
Maryland Gr CT1 . . . . . . **175** C6
Maryland Rd ME2 . . . . . . **286** D1
Mary Last Cl ME6 . . . . . . **127** E7
Mary Lawrenson Pl 🔳
 SE3 . . . . **11** A7
Mary Macarthur Ho 🔳
 DA17 . . . . .4 A3
Mary Magdalene Ho 🔳
 TN9 . . . . **254** B8
Maryon Ct BR5 . . . .**54** B5
Maryon Gr SE7 . . . . .1 E2
Maryon Rd SE7,SE18 . . . . . .1 E2
Mary Rd CT14 . . . . **215** A3
Mary Rose Mall E6 . . . . . . .1 F8
Mary Slessor Ho 🔳
 DA17 . . . . .4 A3
Maryville DA16 . . . . **12** F5
Mascall's Court La
 TN12 . . . . **257** B4
Mascall's Court Rd
 TN12 . . . . **257** A4
Mascalls Ct 🔳 SE7 . . . . . **11** C8
Mascalls Pk TN12 . . . . . **256** F5
Mascalls Rd SE7 . . . . **11** C8
Mascalls Sec Sch
 TN12 . . . . **257** A4
Masefield Cl DA8 . . . .**14** F6
Masefield Dr ME3 . . . . **40** B8
Masefield Rd
 Dartford DA1 . . . . **16** B2
 Lunsford ME20 . . . . **127** F4
 Northfleet DA11 . . . . **36** D5
Masefield View BR6 . . . . . **86** C7
Masefield Way TN9 . . . . **253** F7
Masham Ho 🔳 DA18 . . . . .3 D4
Mason Cl Bexley DA7 . . . . **14** B4
 Newham E16 . . . . .1 A6
Masons Hill
 Bromley BR2 . . . .**52** B5
 Woolwich SE18 . . . . .2 B2
Masons Rd CT17 . . . . **278** B1
Mason's Rise CT10 . . . . . . **84** A5
Mason Way ME2 . . . .**40** B2
Master Gunner Pl SE18 . . .1 E8
Masters La ME19 . . . . . . **127** B5
Masterson Ho DA4 . . . . . . **57** D7
Masthead Ct ME2 . . . . **16** C3
Matchless Dr SE18 . . . . . . **12** A7
Matfield Cl BR2 . . . . **52** A4
Matfield Cres ME14 . . . . **162** C5
Matfield Rd DA17 . . . . **14** A8
Matilda Cl ME8 . . . .**98** B8
Matrix Bsns Ctr DA1 . . . . . **15** E3
Matterdale Gdns
 ME16 . . . . **160** E2
Matthews Cl CT14 . . . . . **215** C6
Matthews Ho 🔳 SE7 . . . **11** C8
Matthews La TN11,
 ME18 . . . . **190** E1
Matthew's Pl 🔳 CT16 . . **278** C1
Matthews Rd CT6 . . . . **76** C2
Mattinson Pl ME9 . . . . . . **165** F7
Matts Hill Rd ME9 . . . .**98** E2
Maud Cashmore Way
 SE18 . . . . .1 F3
Maude Rd BR8 . . . . **33** A2
Maudslay Rd SE9 . . . .**11** F4
Maugham Ct CT5 . . . . . . **108** D8
Maundene Sch ME5 . . . . . .**97** B5
Maunders Ct ME5 . . . .**97** C8
Maurice Ct CT9 . . . .**51** B3
Mavelstone Cl BR1 . . . . . . **52** E8
Mavelstone Rd BR1 . . . . . .**52** E8
Mavis Wlk 🔳 E6 . . . . .1 E8
Maxey Rd SE18 . . . . .2 C2
Maximfeldt Rd DA8 . . . . . . .4 E1
Maximilian Dr ME2 . . . . . . **95** B4
Maxim Rd Crayford DA1 . . .**14** E2
 Erith DA8 . . . . .4 E2
Maxine Gdns CT10 . . . . . . **83** F5
Maxted Ct CT6 . . . . **77** C4
Maxton Cl Dover CT17 . . **310** A6
 Maidstone ME14 . . . . . **162** F5
Maxton Ct CT17 . . . . **310** A6
Maxton Rd CT17 . . . . **310** A6
Maxwell Dr ME16 . . . . . . **161** B6
Maxwell Gdns BR6 . . . .**87** C2
Maxwell House DA17 . . . . .**30** B1
Maxwell Ho SE18 . . . . **12** B8
Maxwell Pl CT14 . . . . **215** C4
Maxwell Rd Bexley DA16 . . **13** A4
 Chatham ME7 . . . .**64** A6
May Ave DA11 . . . . **36** F7
May Avenue Est 🔳
 DA11 . . . .**36** F7

May Ave BR5 .... 54 B4
Maybrook Ind Est
CT1 .... 143 D4
Maybury Ave DA2 ...... 34 C7
Maybury Cl BR5 .... 53 B4
Maycotts La TN12 ... 256 D1
May Ct MR17 .... 18 E8
Mayday Gdns SE3 ..... 11 E5
Maydowns Rd CT5 ..... 75 D2
Mayerne Rd SE9 ...... 11 D2
Mayers Rd CT14 ...... 215 A1
Mayes Cl BR8 .... 56 A5
Mayeswood Rd SE12 ... 29 C4
Mayfair Ave Bexley DA7 . 13 C6
Loose ME15 .... 195 A8
Mayfair Rd DA1 ...... 15 D2
Mayfair 2 ME2 .... 63 C8
Mayfield Ave
Dover CT16 .... 278 C2
Orpington BR6 .... 53 F2
Mayfield DA7 .... 13 F4
Mayfield Cl
Chatham ME5 .... 97 A1
Gillingham ME8 ...... 65 E5
Mayfield Ct
3 Dover CT16 .... 278 B2
Sidcup DA14 .... 31 B3
Mayfield Gdns CT16 .. 278 C2
Mayfield La TN5 ..... 336 D4
Mayfield Pk TN5 ..... 336 E5
Mayfield Rd
Bromley BR1 .... 52 E4
Erith DA17 .... 4 C2
Herne Bay CT6 .... 77 A3
Lyminge CT18 .... 305 C6
Northfleet DA11 ...... 36 F8
Royal Tunbridge Wells
TN4 .... 285 F4
Whitfield CT16 ...... 278 A7
Mayfield
Sevenoaks TN13 ..... 153 E7
Swanscombe DA10 .... 17 E1
Mayfield Villas DA14 . 31 C2
Mayflower Ho ME1 .... 63 B4
Mayfly Cl BR5 .... 54 D5
Mayfly Dr CT18 ...... 307 A4
Mayford Rd ME5 ...... 97 D2
Mayforth Gdns CT11 .. 117 B6
Mayhew Cl TN23 ..... 300 A8
Mayhill Rd SE7 .... 11 B8
Maylam Ct TN10 ..... 222 C1
Maylam Gdns ME10 ... 101 B4
Maylands Dr DA14 .... 31 D5
May Lodge CT14 ..... 215 D5
Maymills Cotts CT13 .. 180 B2
Maynard Ave CT9 ..... 82 B8
Maynard Cl DA8 ...... 14 C7
Maynard & Cotton's Spital
9 CT1 .... 174 F8
Maynard Ho SE18 ...... 2 C2
Maynard Pl ME5 ...... 64 D2
Maynard Rd CT1 ..... 174 E7
Maynards TN12 ...... 259 C5
Mayor's La DA2 .... 33 C3
Mayor's Pl 11 TN30 . 345 A7
Maypits TN23 .... 299 F8
Mayplace Ave SE18 ... 15 A3
Mayplace Cl DA7 ..... 14 B4
Mayplace La
Woolwich SE18 ...... 12 B7
Woolwich SE18 ...... 12 B8
Mayplace Prim Sch
DA7 .... 14 D3
Mayplace Rd E DA7 ... 14 C4
Mayplace Rd W DA7 .. 14 A3
May Pl DA12 .... 60 D4
Maypole Cotts BR6 ... 88 A4
Maypole Cres DA8 .... 15 D8
Maypole Dr ME18 .... 159 C3
Maypole La
Goudhurst TN17 ..... 318 F8
Hoath CT3 .... 111 E6
Maypole Prim Sch DA5 . 32 E5
Maypole Rd
Chelsfield BR6 .... 87 F4
Gravesend DA12 ...... 37 F7
Hoath CT3 .... 111 E6
May Rd Gillingham ME7 . 64 C4
Hawley DA2 .... 33 F4
Rochester ME1 .... 63 C3
Mays Rd 3 CT11 ..... 117 C6
May St Cuxton ME2 ... 62 B2
Herne Bay CT6 .... 77 F4
Mayston Mews 6 SE10 . 1 A1
Maystreet Cross CT6 .. 77 F3
May St ME6 .... 128 B8
Maytham Bglws TN17 . 344 A1
Maytham Rd TN17 .... 358 C7
Mayton La CT2 .... 110 C1
Maytree Cotts CT14 .. 247 D8
Mayview DA1 .... 33 E7
Mayville Rd CT10 ..... 83 E6
Mayweed Ave ME5 .... 96 E4
May Wynne Ho E16 .... 1 B7
McAlpine Cres ME15 . 194 F3
McAuley Cl SE9 ...... 12 A2
McCabe Cl TN12 ..... 260 E2
McCall Cres SE7 .... 1 E1
McCarthy Ave CT2 ... 143 F7
McClean Wlk ME12 ... 71 C8
McCudden Rd DA1 .... 15 F4
McCudden Row 8
ME7 .... 64 A6
McDermott Rd TN15 . 156 F7
McDowall Cl 11 E16 ... 1 A8
McIntyre Ct 6 SE18 .... 1 E7
McKenzie Cl ME6 .... 160 F8
McKenzie Rd ME5 .... 97 A3
McKillop Way DA14 ... 31 C1
McKinlay Ct
Bexley DA16 .... 13 C4
Birchington CT7 ...... 80 D8

McLeod Rd SE2 .... 3 B2
McMichaels Way
TN19 .... 354 A3
McMillan Cl DA12 .... 37 C4
Mead Cl BR8 .... 56 A4
Mead Cres DA1 .... 33 D7
Meades Cl TN12 ..... 259 B6
Meade The CT18 ..... 306 F4
Mead Gn ME5 .... 97 C3
Mead Ho TN16 ...... 118 D3
Mead Rd Chatham ME4 . 64 A1
Mead Rd Ashford TN15 . 90 F2
Meadowbank Ct
ME19 .... 159 C8
Meadow Bank TN11 . 220 F1
Meadow Bank Mews
ME19 .... 159 C8
Meadow Bank ME13 . 137 F2
Meadowbank Rd ME4 . 64 A4
Meadow Bank ME19 . 159 C8
Meadowbrook Cl
TN24 .... 268 D6
Meadow Brook Ct
CT20 .... 334 E4
Meadowbrook CT20 . 334 E4
Meadowbrook Rd
TN24 .... 268 D6
Meadow Cl Bexley DA6 . 13 F2
Bridge CT4 .... 176 A1
Chatham ME5 .... 96 F5
Chilham CT4 .... 205 E8
Chislehurst BR7 ...... 30 B3
Hawkinge CT18 ..... 307 A4
Herne Bay CT6 .... 77 C4
Iwade ME9 .... 68 D4
Sevenoaks TN13 ..... 154 A4
Upper Halling ME2 ... 94 E4
Meadow Cotts
East Studdal CT15 .. 246 D8
Goodnestone CT3 ... 179 A2
Meadow Cres ME2 .... 96 E4
Meadow Croft BR1 .... 52 F6
Meadow Ct Margate CT9 . 83 B8
Westenhanger TN21 . 332 B6
Meadowdown Cl ME7 . 98 A4
Meadowdown ME14 . 162 E4
Meadow Dr CT5 ..... 109 D8
Meadowford Cl SE28 .. 3 A6
Meadow Gr TN25 .... 331 D8
Meadow Hill Cotts
CT15 .... 276 D1
Meadow Hill Rd 6
TN1 .... 286 B3
Meadow Ho ME9 .... 101 B2
Meadow La
Culverstone Green DA13 . 93 A1
Lewisham SE12 ...... 29 B5
Marlpit Hill TN8 .... 217 B4
Meadowlands
Oxted RH8 .... 183 A1
Seal TN15 .... 154 F7
Meadow Rd
Ashford TN23 .... 268 A4
Canterbury CT2 ..... 142 C2
Gravesend DA11 ...... 37 A6
Groombridge TN3 ... 312 C2
Northfleet DA11 ...... 36 C7
Royal Tunbridge
Wells,Southborough
TN4 .... 253 F1
Royal Tunbridge Wells
TN1 .... 286 A4
Rusthall TN4 .... 285 C4
Sturry CT2 .... 143 F6
Tonbridge TN9 ...... 254 B8
Meadow Rise ME9 .... 68 D4
Meadows Ct DA14 .... 31 B2
Meadows TN17 ...... 321 D1
Meadowside Cotts
TN5 .... 338 F1
Meadowside
Dartford DA1 .... 33 E7
Eltham SE3,SE9 ...... 11 C3
Meadows Sch TN4 .. 253 F2
Meadowside The
Biddenden TN27 .... 294 F2
Halstead TN14 ...... 120 F4
Herne Bay CT6 .... 77 D2
3 Maidstone ME15 . 161 E2
New Romney TN28 .. 373 C6
Orpington BR6 .... 87 C4
Sittingbourne ME10 . 101 F2
Wittersham TN30 ... 359 D4
Meadowsweet Cl 3 E16 .. 1 D8
Meadowsweet Ho
TN23 .... 267 F1
Meadowsweet View
ME4 ....41 B2
Meadow The
Chislehurst BR7 ..... 30 C2
Pembury TN2 .... 287 E8
Meadow View Cotts
Hurst Green TN19 ... 354 A3
Laddingford ME18 .. 225 E5
Meadow View
Flimwell TN5 .... 339 A3
Hothfield TN26 ..... 267 A6
Meadow View Ind Est
TN26 .... 349 C7
Meadowview CT12 .. 114 D6
Meadowview BR5 .... 54 C6
Meadow View Rd
Maidstone ME17 .... 195 B3
Shepherdswell CT15 . 244 E5
Meadowview Rd DA5 . 13 F1
Meadow View DA15 .. 31 B8
Meadow Way
Dartford DA1 .... 34 C8
Eythorne CT15 ..... 245 C8
Hythe CT21 .... 353 D8
Marden TN12 ...... 259 E6
Orpington BR6 ...... 86 A7

Wouldham ME1 ...... 95 C5
Meadow Wlk
Dartford DA2 .... 33 C4
Maidstone ME15 .... 162 B3
Snodland ME6 ...... 127 F7
Whitstable CT5 ..... 108 C6
Mead Rd Ashford TN24 . 300 E7
Chislehurst BR7 ..... 30 C2
Dartford DA1 .... 33 D7
Edenbridge TN8 .... 249 D7
Folkestone CT19 ... 335 D6
Gravesend DA11 ..... 37 B6
Mead Road Inf Sch
BR7 .... 30 C2
Meads Ave The ME10 . 101 D7
Mead Sch The TN2 .. 286 A1
Meadside Wlk ME5 ...96 F6
Meads The
Hartley TN17 .... 319 F1
Royal Tunbridge Wells
TN2 .... 286 C2
Meads Way TN29 ... 365 E3
Mead The
Leybourne ME19 .... 127 E2
New Ash Green DA3 ..91 E8
Mead Wall ME3 .... 5 F2
Mead Way CT2 ...... 142 E1
Meadway TN14 ..... 120 F6
Mead Way BR2 .... 52 A3
Meadway CT17 ..... 277 E3
Meadway The
Orpington BR6 .... 87 B4
Sevenoaks TN13 .... 153 F5
Meadway TN11 ..... 221 E5
Mead Wlk TN3 ...... 299 E8
Meath Cl BR5 .... 54 B4
Medbury Rd DA12 .... 37 F7
Medebourne Cl SE3 .. 11 A4
Mede Ho BR1 .... 29 B3
Medhurst Cres DA12 . 37 F6
Medhurst Gdns DA12 . 37 F5
Medick Ct MR17 .... 18 E8
Medina Ave CT5 ..... 108 B7
Medina Ho 6 DA8 .... 14 C7
Medina Rd
Ditton ME20 .... 128 C1
Tonbridge TN10 .... 222 C6
Medlar Cl ME9 ...... 134 A6
Medlar Gr ME7 .... 98 A4
Medlar Ho 3 DA15 ... 31 A5
Medlar Rd RM17 .... 18 E8
Medlars The
Maidstone ME14 ... 162 D6
Meopham Station DA13 . 60 A3
Medway Ave
High Halstow ME23 ..23 E4
Yalding ME18 .... 192 F1
Medway City Est ME2 . 63 D7
Medway Com Coll ME4 . 64 A1
Medway Cotts
Iden Green TN17 .... 342 D3
Marden TN12 ...... 259 C6
Medway Ct
Aylesford ME20 .... 128 F2
20 Orpington BR5 .. 54 D1
Mercer St TN1 ...... 286 B5
Medway Ent Ctr ME2 . 63 D8
Medway Gdns ME4 ...63 F7
Medway Heights 5
ME4 ....63 E4
Medway Heritage Ctr *
ME4 ....63 F5
Medway Ho 7 ME4 .. 161 F4
Medway Maritime Hospl
ME7 ....64 B4
Medway Mdws TN12 . 225 A6
Medway Rd
Crayford DA1 .... 15 A4
Gillingham ME7 ..... 64 C7
Royal Tunbridge Wells
TN1 .... 286 B5
Sheerness ME12 .....28 B1
Medway St
Chatham ME4 .... 63 F3
Maidstone ME14 ... 161 F4
Medway Trad Est
ME16 .... 161 F3
Medway View
Barnes Street TN11 .. 224 A5
Middle Stoke ME3 ... 25 C3
Medway Villas ME15 . 194 B3
Medway Wharf Rd
TN9 .... 222 C1
Meehan Rd TN28 ... 373 E4
Meehan Rd S TN28 . 373 E3
Meerbrook Rd SE3 .. 11 C4
Meeres Court La
ME10 .... 102 C5
Meeson's Cl ME13 ... 168 E6
Meeson's La RM17 .. 17 F8
Meeting Ct CT9 ....50 I3
Meeting House La 2
ME4 ....63 F4
Meeting St CT11 .... 117 E7
Megan Ct TN29 .... 376 D7
Megby Cl ME8 .... 98 D6
Meggett La CT15 .... 308 C7
Megone Cl CT18 .... 307 A4
Megrims Hill TN18 .. 356 A6
Meirs Court Rd ME8 . 98 E6
Melanda Cl BR7 ..... 29 F3
Melanie Cl DA7 ...... 13 E6
Melba Gdns RM18 ... 19 A7
Melbourne Ave
Dover CT16 .... 278 C4
Ramsgate CT12 ......83 B1
Melbourne Com Prim Sch
CT16 .... 278 C4
Melbourne Ct RM18 .. 18 E6
Melbourne Quay 4
DA11 ....19 B1

Melbourne Rd
Chatham ME4 .... 64 A3
Tilbury RM18 ....18 E6
Melbury Cl BR7 ...... 29 F2
Melbury Grange BR1 . 52 E8
Melbury Mews TN28 . 373 C8
Meldrum Cl
Orpington BR5 ...... 54 C3
Oxted RH8 .... 183 A3
Melford Dr ME16 ... 161 C4
Mellanby Cl CT7 ..... 81 A6
Melliker La DA13 .... 60 A3
Melling St SE18 ...... 12 E8
Mellish Ind Est SE18 ... 1 D3
Mellor Row ME10 .... 68 F1
Mells Cres SE9 ...... 29 F4
Melody Cl
Gillingham ME8 ..... 98 C4
Warden ME12 .... 49 E4
Melody Rd TN16 ... 118 C5
Melon La TN26,TN29 . 364 B6
Melrose Ave
Dartford DA1 .... 32 E8
Kings Hill ME19 .... 159 C3
Melrose Cl
Lewisham SE12 ...... 29 B7
Loose ME15 .... 195 A7
Melrose Cres BR6 ... 86 D5
Melrose Rd TN16 ... 118 C3
Melsetter Cl CT7 .....81 B7
Melthorpe Gdns SE3 . 11 E6
Melville Ct ME4 ...... 63 F6
Melville Lea CT13 ... 180 C7
Melville Rd
Maidstone ME15 ... 162 A3
Sidcup DA14 .... 31 C6
Memess Path 4 SE18 . 12 A8
Memorial (General) Hospl
ME10 .... 101 F3
Memorial Hospl SE18 . 12 A5
Mendfield St 5 ME13 . 138 C7
Mendip Ho ME18 .... 18 D1
Mendip Rd DA7 ...... 14 E6
Mendip Rise TN24 .. 268 B4
Mendip Wlk TN2 ... 286 D5
Menin Rd ME10 ..... 68 F1
Mennie Ho SE18 .... 11 F6
Mentmore Ho CT12 . 83 C3
Mentmore Rd CT12 . 83 C3
Menzies Ct CT14 ... 215 B1
Menzies Ct ME12 .... 47 A5
Menzies Rd CT16 .. 278 A5
Meon Ct 21 BR5 ..... 54 D1
Meopham Com Prim Sch
Meopham DA13 ..... 93 A8
Meopham Station DA13 . 60 A2
Meopham Sta DA13 . 60 A4
Mera Dr DA7 .... 14 A3
Merbury Rd SE28 ..... 2 E4
Mercer Cl ME20 .... 128 B4
Mercer Dr ME17 .... 198 F6
Mercers Cl TN12 ... 256 E6
Mercers
Hawkhurst TN18 ... 341 A1
Langton Green TN3 . 285 A3
Mercers Pl ME19 ... 159 A2
Mercer St TN1 ...... 286 B5
Mercer Way ME17 .. 196 B1
Mercery La 5 CT1 ... 174 F8
Merchant Pl TN12 .. 259 C5
Merchant Store The 7
CT2 .... 142 F1
Merchants Way CT2 . 174 C8
Merchland Rd SE9 ... 30 C7
Mercury Cl ME1 ..... 63 A3
Mere Cl BR6 ....86 B8
Meredale Sch ME8 ... 66 A1
Meredith Cl ME17 ... 196 F7
Mere Gate CT9 ...... 50 I1
Meresborough Cotts
ME8 ....98 F5
Meresborough La ME8,
ME9 ....99 B5
Meresborough Rd ME8 . 99 A7
Mereside 86 A8
Merevale Ho 3 TN1 . 286 A3
Merewood Cl 1 BR1 . 53 A7
Merewood Rd DA7 ... 14 C5
Mereworth Cl ME8 .. 65 A3
Mereworth Com Prim Sch
ME18 .... 191 D8
Mereworth Dr SE18 . 12 C7
Mereworth Ho ME2 . 40 C1
Mereworth Rd
Royal Tunbridge Wells
TN4 .... 286 A6
West Peckham ME18 . 191 C7
Merganser Gdns SE28 .. 2 D3
Meriden Cl BR1 ..... 29 D1
Meriden Wlk CT18 .. 305 D3
Meridian Ct
Ashford TN23 ...... 299 E7
Maidstone ME16 ... 161 E4
Meridian Pk ME2 .....63 E6
Meridian Rd SE7 .... 11 D7
Meridian Trad Est SE7 ... 1 B2
Meriel Wk DA9 ....17 B3
Merifield Rd SE9 .... 11 C3
Merileys Cl DA3 ..... 59 C6
Merino Pl DA15 ..... 13 A2
Merino Way TN23 .. 299 E5
Merivale Gr ME5 .....97 B4
Merleburgh Dr ME10 . 101 F8
Merle Common Rd
RH8 .... 216 B7
Merlewood Dr BR7 .. 52 F8
Merlewood TN13 ... 154 B4
Merlin Ave ME20 ... 127 F2
Merlin Cl
Sittingbourne ME10 . 102 A3
Tonbridge TN10 .... 222 B5
Merlin Gdns BR1 .... 29 A5
Merlin Ho Chatham ME4 . 64 B8

Merlin Ho continued
2 Sittingbourne ME10 . 102 A3
Merlin Prim Sch BR1 . 29 A5
Merlin Rd DA16 ..... 13 A3
Merlin Rd N DA16 ... 13 A3
Mermaid Cl
Chatham ME5 .... 97 A6
Northfleet DA11 ..... 36 D8
Mermerus Gdns DA12 . 37 F4
Merrals Wood Rd ME2 . 62 D5
Merrilees Rd DA15 ...30 E8
Merriman Ho ME2 .... 40 F6
Merriman Rd SE3 .... 11 C4
Merriments Gdns *
ME19 .... 354 B5
Merriments La
Hurst Green TN19,
TN19 .... 354 D5
Hurst Green TN19 . 354 B5
Merrion Cl TN4 .... 286 B5
Merrion Way TN4 ... 286 B5
Merritt Rd TN28 ... 373 E4
Merrivale Hts CT10 .. 84 A2
Merry Boys Rd ME3 . 40 B8
Merrydown Way BR7 . 52 F8
Merryfield Ct 9 TN9 . 254 B8
Merryfield SE3 ...... 11 A5
Merryfield Ho 4 SE9 . 29 C5
Merryfields Cl DA3 .. 58 F5
Merryfields ME2 .... 40 A1
Merryhills Cl TN16 .. 118 D3
Merryweather Cl DA1 . 15 F1
Merryweather Gr CT6 . 77 D2
Mersey Rd ME10 ... 222 B5
Mersham Prim Sch
TN25 .... 301 E3
Merston Ct ME3 ..... 39 C4
Merton Ave DA3 .... 58 F5
Merton Ct ME5 ...... 97 C5
Merton Court Sch
DA14 .... 31 C4
Merton Ct DA16 .... 13 B5
Merton Gdns BR5 ... 53 B4
Merton La CT4 ..... 174 F4
Merton Rd ME15 ... 162 F2
Mervyn Ave SE9 .... 30 C6
Mervyn Stockwood House
SE9 .... 30 C6
Meryl Gdns CT14 ... 215 C1
Mesne Way TN14 ... 121 F7
Messent Rd SE9 ..... 11 D2
Messeter Pl SE9 .... 12 A1
Metcalfe Mews 1
CT1 .... 143 B2
Meteor Ct CT5 ..... 108 B7
Meteor Cl ME10 .... 101 E8
Meteor Rd ME19 ... 158 F3
Methuen Rd Bexley DA6 . 13 F3
Erith DA17 .... 4 A3
Metro Ctr The BR5 ...54 B3
Metropole Cl 2 CT20 . 335 B3
Metropole Rd E CT20 . 335 B3
Metropole Rd W CT20 . 335 B3
Metropole The 3
CT20 .... 335 B3
Meverall Ave CT12 .. 116 C5
Mewsend TN16 .... 118 D1
Mews The
Headcorn TN27 .... 262 C5
Longfield DA3 .... 58 E6
1 Maidstone ME16 . 161 E5
Pembury TN2 .... 287 C6
Rochester ME2 ......62 F7
5 Royal Tunbridge Wells
TN1 .... 286 B3
Sevenoaks TN13 ... 154 A3
7 Sidcup DA14 .... 31 A4
Sittingbourne ME10 . 101 F2
Meyer Rd DA8 ...... 14 D8
Meyrick Rd ME12 ... 28 C2
Micawber Cl ME5 ... 97 A1
Michael Ave CT11 .. 117 G8
Michael Gdns DA12 . 37 E3
Michael Marshall House
SE9 .... 30 C6
Michaels La DA3,TN15 . 91 C8
Michele Cotts ME3 .. 39 C6
Michelle Gdns CT9 .. 82 A8
Micketts Gdns ME10 . 101 B4
Mickleburgh Ave CT6 . 77 B4
Mickleburgh Hill CT6 . 77 B4
Mickleham Cl BR5 ... 54 A7
Mickleham Rd BR5 .. 54 A7
Mid Comp Cotts TN15 . 157 E6
Middelburg Ho CT19 . 334 D6
Middelburg Sq CT20 . 335 D4
Middle Cl TN25 ..... 267 C1
Middle Deal Rd CT14 . 215 B5
Middle Field TN2 ... 287 E8
Middlefields ME8 .... 99 A8
Middle Garth TN17 . 320 D4
Middleham Ct 26 DA2 . 16 B7
Middle La TN15 .... 154 F6
Middle Mead CT19 . 335 B7
Middle Mill N ME19 . 159 F7
Middle Park Ave SE9 . 29 E8
Middle Park Prim Sch
SE9 .... 29 D8
Middle Rd TN3 ..... 315 A5
Middle Row
Ashford TN23 ...... 268 C2
2 Faversham ME13 . 138 D7
6 Maidstone ME14 . 161 F4
Middlesex Rd ME15 . 195 D7
Middle St
Ashford TN23 ...... 268 B2
4 Chatham ME7 ... 64 A6
Deal CT14 .... 215 D6
Middleton Ave DA14 . 31 C3
Middleton Cl ME8 ... 98 E6
Middleton Cotts TN25 . 236 E3
Middleton Ct
13 Bromley BR1 ... 29 B1

Middleton Ct continued
9 Sittingbourne ME10 . 101 E4
Middletune Ave ME10 . 101 E7
Middle Wall CT5 ..... 74 D2
Middle Way ME10 .. 102 B3
Middle Wlk TN2 .... 286 E8
Middlings Rise TN13 . 153 F1
Middlings The TN13 . 153 F2
Middlings Wood
TN13 .... 154 A2
Midfield Ave
Bexley DA7 .... 14 C4
Hextable BR8 .... 33 B2
Midfield Prim Sch BR5 . 31 A1
Midfield Way BR5 ... 54 B8
Midhurst Ct ME15 .. 162 A3
Midhurst Hill DA6 ... 14 A2
Mid Kent Bsns Pk
ME6 .... 128 B7
Mid Kent Coll (City Way
Ctr) ME1 .... 63 D4
Mid Kent Coll of H & F Ed
ME16 .... 161 C3
Mid Kent Coll of Higher & F
Ed ME5 ....96 E6
Mid Kent Sh Ctr The
ME16 .... 161 C7
Midley Cl ME16 .... 161 C7
Midsummer Ct SE12 . 11 A3
Midsummer Hill TN24 . 268 D6
Midsummer Rd ME6 . 127 E8
Midway The TN4 ... 285 D2
Midwinter Cl 3 DA16 . 13 A4
Mierscourt Cl ME8 .. 99 A8
Miers Court Prim Sch
ME8 ....98 F7
Mierscourt Rd ME8 . 98 E6
Mike Spring Ct DA12 . 37 D4
Mikyle Cl CT1 ..... 175 A6
Milbourne Gr ME10 . 101 E7
Milburn Rd ME7 .... 64 C7
Mildmay Pl TN14 ... 121 F8
Mildred Cl DA1 ..... 16 A1
Mildred Cotts CT19 . 334 F7
Mildred Rd DA8 ...... 4 E1
Milebush La TN12 .. 227 E1
Mile End Green Cotts
DA3 .... 58 D7
Mile La TN17 ...... 319 B8
Mile Oak Rd TN12 .. 257 C3
Mile Rd CT12 ...... 113 F6
Miles Ct CT3 ...... 178 A8
Miles Dr SE28 .... 2 E5
Miles Pl ME1 .... 63 D3
Milestone Bldgs TN12 . 260 F3
Mile Stone Rd DA2 .. 16 B1
Milestone Rd CT14 . 215 B5
Miles Way CT7 ......80 F7
Milford Cl Bexley SE2 . 13 E8
Maidstone ME16 ... 161 D5
Military Rd
Canterbury CT1 .... 143 A1
Chatham ME4 .... 63 F5
2 Dover CT17 .... 310 D7
Folkestone CT20 ... 334 E4
Houghton Green TN31 . 368 E3
Hythe CT21 .... 333 B2
Ramsgate CT11 .... 117 E6
Stone in Oxney TN26,
TN30 .... 361 B4
Milk House Cotts
TN17 .... 321 A8
Milking La
Biggin Hill,Downe BR6 . 118 E7
Biggin Hill,Leaves Green
BR2 .... 118 D8
Milk St Bromley BR1 . 29 B2
Newham E16 .... 2 B5
Millais Pl RM18 ..... 19 A7
Millais Rd CT16 .... 278 C5
Millars Mdw SE12 .. 11 A3
Mill Bank Cotts TN13 . 180 A2
Mill Bank TN21 .... 262 C6
Millbank La TN29 .. 371 E7
Mill Bank TN9 ..... 376 B6
Millbank Rd TN23 .. 299 F5
Mill Bank TN9 ..... 222 C2
Millbank Way SE12 . 11 A2
Mill Bay CT20 ..... 335 E5
Millbrook Ave DA16 . 12 D3
Millbrook Cl ME15 . 161 F1
Millbrook Hythe CT21 . 333 D2
Leybourne ME19 ... 127 D1
Millbrook Mdw TN23 . 267 E1
Mill Brook Rd BR5 .. 54 C5
Millbro BR8 .... 56 A8
Mill Cl Crabble CT17 . 277 F2
Lenham ME17 ..... 199 C4
Rochester ME2 ......40 B1
Sandwich CT13 .... 148 E2
Wickhambreaux CT3 . 145 C2
Mill Cotts
Queenborough ME11 . 46 A5
Ramsgate CT11 .... 117 D6
West Farleigh ME15 . 193 B6
Worth CT14 .... 181 A4
Mill Court CT6 ......77 B2
Mill Cres TN9 ..... 222 C2
Millcroft Rd ME3 .... 22 B4
Mill Ct Ashford TN24 . 268 D2
Sittingbourne ME10 . 102 A3
Sutton at H DA4 .... 57 C7
14 Woolwich SE28 .. 3 B6
Milldale Cl CT14 ... 215 B4
Millen Cl DA4 .... 57 C5
Millennium Terr CT1 . 174 C6
Millennium Cl E16 ... 1 B7
Millennium Way
Broadstairs CT10 ....83 C4

Millennium Way continued
Sheerness ME12 ....28 B2
Millen Rd ME10 ....101 E5
Millen's Row ME13 ....170 B3
Miller Ave CT12 ....174 D8
Miller CI Ashford TN24 .. 268 D2
Bromley BR1 ....29 B3
Deal CT14 ....215 C8
Sittingbourne ME10 .....102 A8
Miller Cotts TN24 ....268 C2
Miller Ct Bexley DA7 ...22 A8
Minster (Sheppey) ME12 . 47 A5
Miller Rd DA12 ....38 A6
Millers Cotts TN11 .....255 C6
Millers Ct
Ramsgate CT12 ....83 B1
Whitstable CT5 ....108 D7
Millers La CT12 ....114 C7
Millersthumb TN17 ....292 C4
Millers Wharf 1
ME15 ....161 E2
Millers Wlk DA13 ....93 A7
Millers Yd CT1 ....174 E7
Miller Way ME2 ....40 D2
Mill Field CT3 ....147 E1
Mill Field CT10 ....83 F5
Millfield CI CT18 ......307 B5
Millfield Dr DA11 ....36 E6
Millfield
Folkestone CT20 ....335 D5
Hawkinge CT18 ....307 C6
High Halden TN26 ......324 D7
Millfield La DA3 ....91 E8
Millfield Manor CT5 ....74 E1
Millfield DA3 ....91 E8
Millfield Rd
Faversham ME13 ....138 E7
Ramsgate CT12 ....83 B3
West Kingsdown TN15 ...90 D4
Millfield CT15 ....279 F7
Millfields ME5 ....97 D2
Millfields CI BR5 ....54 B5
Millfields Cotts BR5 ....54 B5
Millfield ME10 ....102 A3
Mill Fields Rd CT21 ...332 F2
Millfields CT15 ....244 E4
Millfordhope Rd ME2 ..62 C7
Mill Gn CT13 ....180 A2
Millhall ME20 ....128 E2
Mill Hall Bsns Est The
ME20 ....128 C2
Mill Hall Rd ME20 .....128 C3
Mill Hamlet CT3 ....145 C2
Mill Hill Deal CT14 ....215 A3
Edenbridge TN8 ....249 D7
Mill Hill La DA12 ....38 D3
Mill Ho CT17 ....277 F3
Millhouse La ME19 ....126 D3
Mill House CI DA4 ......56 E1
Mill La Ashford TN24 ..269 A1
Benover ME18 ....226 A7
Birchington CT7 ....80 F6
Bonnington TN25 ......329 E5
Bridge CT4 ....175 F1
Canterbury CT1 ....142 F1
Canterbury,Harbledown
CT2 ....174 C8
Chatham,Bluebell Hill
ME5 ....96 D1
Chatham,Luton ME5 ....64 C1
Chilham CT4 ....205 D7
Coxheath ME17 ....194 D4
10 Dover CT16 ....310 E7
Eastry CT13 ....180 B2
Eynsford DA4 ....56 E1
Farthing Street BR6 ....36 A1
Frittenden TN17 ......293 D8
Hartlip ME9 ....99 E6
Hawkinge CT18 ....307 B5
Herne Bay CT6 ....77 B2
Hildenborough TN11,
TN15 ....188 C2
Horsmonden TN12 .....258 B1
Ightham TN15 ....156 E5
Lydd TN29 ....376 D7
Lynsted ME9 ....136 C5
Maidstone ME14 ......161 F6
Margate CT9 ....50 I2
Mill Lane Cotts CT14 ..214 A4
Mill La Newchurch TN29 .350 F3
Nonington CT15 ....211 F4
Northbourne CT14 .....213 F4
Oxted RH8 ....183 A1
Preston CT3 ....146 D6
Sevenoaks TN14 ......154 D6
Shepherdswell CT15 ...244 F5
Shoreham TN14 ....88 F1
Sissinghurst TN17 .....320 F8
Smarden TN27 ....264 A2
Snodland ME6 ....128 B8
Stelling Minnis CT4 ...240 F2
Tenterden TN30 ....324 B1
The Chart RH8 ....183 F4
Tonbridge TN9 ....222 C2
Wateringbury ME18 ...192 D2
Westerham TN16 .....184 C8
West Thurrock RM20 ...17 D8
Whitfield CT16 ....278 A8
Woolwich SE18 ....2 A1
Worth CT14 ....181 A4
Millman Ct SE3 ....11 B7
Millmead Rd CT9 ....51 D1
Millmead Gdns CT9 ....51 D1
Millmead Rd CT9 ....51 D1
Mill Mews CT14 ....215 B4
Mill Pl Chislehurst BR7 .52 A4
Crayford DA1 ....15 A3
Faversham ME13 ......138 D8
Millpond CI ME2 ....63 B8

Mill Pond CI TN14 .....154 D6
Millpond La TN30 .....323 D2
Mill Pond Rd DA1 .....15 E1
Mill Race CT17 ....277 F3
Mill Rd
Bethersden TN26 .....297 E5
Bramling CT3 ....177 E6
Deal CT14 ....215 C4
Dymchurch TN29 .....366 B7
Erith DA8 ....14 C7
Gillingham ME7 ....64 C6
Hawley DA2 ....33 F4
Hoath CT3 ....111 F5
Hythe CT21 ....333 D2
Lydd TN29 ....376 D7
Newham E16 ....1 B5
Northfleet DA11 ....36 E8
Rochester ME2 ....63 B8
Sevenoaks TN13 .....153 E6
Staple CT3 ....179 B5
Sturry CT2 ....143 F5
Mill Row Birchington CT7 .80 F6
Sidcup DA5 ....32 B8
Mills CI ME12 ....46 F6
Mills Cres TN15 ....90 D4
Millside Ind Est DA1 ...15 D3
Mills Rd ME20 ....160 E7
Mill St ME19 ....159 F7
Mills Terr ME4 ....64 A3
Mill St
Iden Green TN17,TN18 . 342 C3
Maidstone,Loose ME15 . 194 F5
Maidstone ME15 .....161 F4
Millstock Terr 2
ME15 ....161 E2
Mill Stone CI DA4 ......57 C7
Millstone Mews DA4 ...57 C8
Millstream CI
Ashurst TN3 ....283 D2
Faversham ME13 .....138 C7
Whitstable CT5 ....74 E1
Millstream Cotts CT5 .108 E8
Millstream La TN24 ...300 F7
Mill St
ME19 ....159 F7
Mill Stream Pl TN9 ...222 D3
Millstrood Rd CT5 ....108 E8
Mill St
Sittingbourne ME10 ..161 E5
Snodland ME6 ....128 B8
Temple Ewell CT16 ...277 D5
Westerham TN16 ....184 D8
Mill Terr Bridge CT4 ..175 F1
Chartham CT4 ....173 D3
Mill Vale BR2 ....52 A7
Mill View Ashford TN24 . 300 F8
Hadlow TN11 ....190 D1
Mill View CT6 ....77 A1
Mill View TN26 ....326 A3
Mill Wall Pl CT13 .....181 A8
Mill Way ME10 ....101 F6
Mill Wlk ME16 ....161 A3
Millwood CI 4 ME4 ....63 F4
Millwood Ho 1 SE28 ...2 D3
Millwood Rd BR5 .....54 C6
Millyard Way CT15 ...212 D1
Milne Gdns SE9 ....11 C2
Milne Ho 1 SE18 ......1 F2
Milner CI CT15 ....212 B1
Milner Cres CT3 .....210 E5
Milne Rd TN24 ....300 F8
Milner La CT7 ....143 F5
Milner Rd
Elvington CT15 ....212 B1
Gillingham ME7 ....64 D7
Whitstable CT5 ....108 A6
Milners ME17 ....196 F6
Milner Wlk SE9 ....30 D7
Milroy Ave DA11 ....36 E6
Milstead CI
Maidstone ME14 .....162 C5
West Minst ME12 ......46 B7
Milstead & Frinstead CE
Prim Sch ME9 ....134 E1
Milsted Rd ME8 ....65 C3
Milton Ave
Badgers Mount TN14 ..88 B1
Cliffe Woods ME3 .....40 B8
Gravesend DA12 ....37 C7
Margate CT9 ....50 J1
Milton CI
Canterbury CT1 .....175 C6
Dover CT16 ....278 B4
Milton Court Prim Sch
ME10 ....101 E6
Milton Ct
Gravesend DA12 .....37 C6
Kings Hill ME18 ......159 A3
Sidcup DA15 ....30 F5
Milton Gdns
Tilbury RM18 ....19 B6
Tonbridge TN9 ....253 F7
Milton Hall Rd DA12 ..37 D7
Milton Ho DA1 ....14 E2
Milton La TN15 ....159 B3
Milton Lodge 9 DA14 . 31 A4
Milton Pl DA12 ....19 C1
Milton Rd
Ashford TN23 ....268 B2
Bexley DA16 ....12 F6
Milton Rd Bsns Pk 4
DA12 ....37 C8
Milton Rd
Canterbury CT1 .....175 A6
Dover CT16 ....278 B4
Erith DA17 ....4 A2
Gillingham ME7 ....64 C3
Gravesend DA12 ......37 D8
Sevenoaks TN13 .....153 E6
Sittingbourne ME10 ..17 E1
Milton Regis Halt
ME10 ....102 A6

Milton Sq 4 CT9 ....50 J1
Milton St
Maidstone ME16 .....161 C2
Swanscombe DA10 ...17 D1
Milverton Way SE9 ....30 A4
Milward Wlk 14 SE18 ..12 A8
Mimosa CI BR6 ....87 C8
Mincers CI ME5 ....97 C2
Mineral St SE18 ....2 E2
Miners Way CT3 ......211 A5
Whitstable CT5,CT6 ..109 E8
Minerva Ave CT16 ....278 C2
Minerva CI DA14 ......31 A5
Minerva Ho 4 CT11 ..117 D7
Minerva Rd ME2 ....63 A8
Ministry Way SE9 ......29 F6
Minnis Field CT14 ....240 E2
Minnis Gn CT4 ....240 E2
Minnis La CT15,CT17 .277 C2
Minnis Rd CT7 ....80 E7
Minnis Terr CT17 .....278 A2
Minnis Way CT14 .....240 E2
Minshaw CI DA14 ......30 F4
Minster Abbey ★ ME12 . 47 D6
Minster Abbey ★
CT12 ....115 C5
Minster Agriculture & Rural
Life Mus ★ CT12 ....115 C5
Minster CE Prim Sch
CT12 ....115 B5
Minster CI CT10 ....84 A2
Minster Coll ME12 .....46 F6
Minster Dr
Herne Bay CT6 ....76 D4
Minster (Sheppey) ME12 .47 B8
Minster Gatehouse Mus ★
ME12 ....47 D6
Minster-in-Sheppey Prim
Sch ME12 ....47 C7
Minster Lodge 4
CT11 ....117 C6
Minster Rd
Acol CT12,CT7 ....81 C2
Bromley BR1 ....29 B1
Faversham ME13 .....138 E7
Gillingham ME8 ....65 C3
Minster (Sheppey) ME12 .47 B6
Ramsgate CT11 ....117 B5
Westgate-on-S CT8 ....81 F7
Minster Sta CT12 ....115 C5
Mint Bsns Pk E16 ......1 A8
Mintching Wood La
ME9 ....134 F2
Minter Ave CT18 .....306 F7
Minter CI CT18 ....306 F7
Minterne Ave ME10 ..101 D2
Minterne Com Jun Sch
ME10 ....101 D2
Minters Ind Est CT14 .215 B6
Minters Orch TN15 ...157 B7
Mint The CT2 ....142 C1
Miranda Ct ME12 ......28 B1
Miranda Ho 6 DA17 ....4 A1
Mirfield St SE7 ....1 D8
Miriam Ct DA14 ....31 B4
Miriam Rd SE18 ....2 E1
Mirror Path SE9 ....29 C5
Miskin Cotts ME3 ....30 A3
Miskin Rd Dartford DA1 . 33 D8
Hoo St Werburgh ME3 ..41 E5
Misling La CT4 ....272 C7
Missenden Ct 8 CT20 . 335 D5
Mitcham Rd TN29 ....366 C8
Mitchell Ave
Chatham ME4 ....63 F2
Hawkinge CT18 ......307 B5
Northfleet DA11 ....36 D6
Mitchell CI Dartford DA1 .33 E6
Erith DA17 ....4 C3
Lenham ME17 ....199 C5
Woolwich SE2 ....3 C1
Mitchell Rd
Kings Hill ME19 ......158 F2
Orpington BR6 ....86 F6
Mitchell St CT19 ......334 D6
Mitchell Way 5 BR1 ..52 A8
Mitchell Wlk Newham E6 ..1 F8
Swanscombe DA10 ...35 E8
Mitchem CI TN15 ....90 E3
Mitre Ct 5 Erith DA17 ...4 A2
Tonbridge TN9 ....222 C2
Mitre Rd ME1 ....63 B4
Mittell St TN29 ....376 B6
Moat CI Orpington BR6 ..86 F4
Sevenoaks TN13 .....153 D5
Moat Croft DA16 ......13 C4
Moat Ct Eltham SE9 ...11 F1
Sidcup DA15 ....30 F5
Moat Farm Ct CT19 ..335 C7
Moat Farm Rd
Folkestone CT19 .....335 C7
St Mary Hoo ME3 ......24 D6
Moat Farm TN2 ....314 A7
Moatfield Mdw TN23 . 300 B4
Moat Ho
Canterbury CT1 .....174 F7
Charing TN27 ....234 C7
Moat La Ash CT3 .....147 E1
Cowden TN8 ....282 E7
Erith DA8 ....15 A6
Fordwich CT2 ....144 A3
Rough Common CT2 ..142 B4
Moat Pk TN27 ....234 C6
Moat Rd TN27 ....262 B5
Moat Sole CT13 ......148 F1
Moat The TN27 ......234 C7
Moat Way ME11 ....46 A5
Mockbeggar La TN17,
TN27 ....322 C4
Mockett Ct 4 ME10 ..101 E4
Mockett Dr CT10 ......83 F7
Mock La TN23 ....299 B6

Model Farm CI SE9 ....29 E5
Modest Cnr TN4 ......253 E1
Moira Rd SE9 ....11 F3
Molash Rd BR5 ....54 D5
Molehill Cnr CT5 ......109 D8
Molehill Copse Prim Sch
ME15 ....195 D7
Molehill Rd
Herne Bay CT6 ....76 A1
Whitstable CT5,CT6 ..109 E8
Molescroft SE9 ....30 C5
Molescroft Way TN9 ..253 F7
Moles Mead TN8 .....217 C2
Molineux Rd CT12 ....115 B6
Molland CI CT3 ....147 C2
Molland La
Ash,Guilton CT3 .....147 C2
Ash,Paramour Street
CT3 ....147 D6
Molland Lea CT3 .....147 C2
Mollison Rise DA12 ....37 E3
Molloy Rd TN26 ......299 B1
Molyneux Almshouses
TN4 ....285 F4
Molyneux Ct TN4 .....285 F4
Molyneux Park Gdns
TN4 ....285 F4
Molyneux Park Rd
TN4 ....285 F4
Monarch CI
Chatham ME5 ....97 A6
Tilbury RM18 ....19 B5
Monarch Dr E16 ....1 D8
Monarch Rd 8 DA17 ...4 A3
Monarch Terr ME18 ..159 C3
Monastery Ave CT16 ..278 E1
Monastery St CT1 ....175 A8
Monckton's Ave CT14 . 161 F7
Monckton's Dr ME14 .161 E7
Monckton's La ME14 .161 F7
Moncrieff CI 5 E6 ......1 E7
Moncrif CI ME14 ......163 B4
Monds Cotts TN14 ...152 E3
Mongeham Church CI
CT14 ....214 D3
Mongeham Prim Sch
CT14 ....214 E4
Mongeham Rd CT14 ..214 E3
Mongeham View
CT14 ....214 E4
Monica CI ME13 ......171 E6
Monica James Ho 12
DA14 ....31 A5
Monins Rd Dover CT17 . 310 B7
Iwade ME9 ....68 D3
Monkdown ME15 .....163 A1
Monk Dr E16 ....1 A4
Monkery La TN25,
TN27 ....202 C3
Monkreed Villas DA3 ..59 D4
Monks CI
Canterbury CT2 .....143 A2
Erith SE2 ....3 D2
Faversham ME13 .....138 B8
Monks Hill Cotts
TN26 ....348 A5
Monkshill Rd ME13 ..107 B2
Monks La
Limpsfield TN8 ....216 E6
Newbury's TN5 ......337 B8
Monks Orch DA1 ......33 D6
Monk St SE18 ....2 A2
Monks Way
Dover CT16 ....278 A3
Orpington BR5 ....53 D1
Monk's Well DA9 ......17 C3
Monks Wlk
Charing TN27 ....234 C7
Northfleet DA13 ....36 A2
6 Tonbridge TN9 ....254 B8
Monkton CE Prim Sch
CT12 ....114 D7
Monkton Court La
CT15 ....245 D7
Monkton Gdns CT9 ....51 E3
Monkton Manor CT12 .114 C7
Monkton Pl CT11 .....117 D7
Monkton Rd
Bexley DA16 ....12 F5
Borough Green TN15 .156 F7
Monkton Rdbt CT12 ..114 D8
Monkton Rd CT12 ....115 A6
Monkton St CT12 .....114 D7
Monkwood CI ME1 .....96 B8
Monmouth CI
Bexley DA16 ....13 A3
Gillingham ME8 ....65 D2
Mons Ct ME10 ....68 F1
Monson Rd TN1 ......286 B4
Monson Way 5 TN1 ..286 B4
Mons Way BR2 ....52 E3
Montacue Ct CT20 ...335 B4
Montacute Gdns TN2 . 285 F2
Montacute Rd TN2 ...286 A1
Montague Ct
Sheerness ME12 ......28 B1
16 Sidcup DA15 ......31 A5
Montague Pl BR8 ......55 F5
Montague Rd CT11 ...117 E8
Montague St CT6 ......76 D5
Montague Terr 1 BR2 . 52 A5
Montbelle Prim Sch
SE9 ....30 B5
Montbelle Rd SE9 .....30 B5
Montbretia CI BR5 .....54 C5
Montcalm CI BR2 ......52 A3
Montcalm Rd SE7 .....11 D7
Montefiore Ave
Broadstairs CT10 ......84 A1
Ramsgate CT11 ....83 F1
Montefiore Cotts
CT11 ....117 F8
Monteith CI TN3 .....285 A3

Monterey CI DA5 ......32 C6
Montfort CI
Ashford TN23 ....299 F7
Canterbury CT2 .....143 A4
Montfort Dr ME19 ....159 A2
Montfort Rd
Chatham ME5 ....96 F2
Kemsing TN15 ....122 C2
Rochester ME2 ....63 A8
Montgomery Ave ME5 .97 A7
Montgomery Cl DA15 ..12 F1
Montgomery Rd
Gillingham ME7 ....64 C3
Royal Tunbridge Wells
TN4 ....286 B2
Sutton at H DA4 ......57 B2
Montgomery Sch CT2 .144 C8
Montgomery Way
CT19 ....335 E6
Montpelier Ave
Sidcup DA5 ....31 D8
Whitstable CT5 ......108 D6
Montpelier Bsns Pk
TN23 ....267 F1
Montpelier Gate
ME16 ....161 D6
Montreal CI 8 CT16 ..278 B3
Montreal Rd
Sevenoaks TN13 .....153 E4
Tilbury RM18 ....19 A5
Montrose Ave
Bexley DA16 ....12 E4
Gillingham ME5 ....64 E2
Sidcup DA15 ....31 A8
Montrose CI DA16 ....12 E4
Mont St Aignan Way
TN8 ....249 C8
Monument Way TN24 . 300 F5
Monypenny CI TN11 ..223 D8
Monypenny TN17 ....343 F3
Moon Ct SE12 ....11 A3
Moonfleet CI ME10 ....69 A1
Moon Hill CT15 ......244 E4
Moon's La RH7 ....249 A1
Moonstone Dr ME5 ....97 B2
Moonstone Sq ME10 .101 D6
Moorcroft Gdns BR2 ..52 E4
Moorden La TN11 ....220 A1
Moordown SE18 ....11 C3
Moore Ave Grays RM20 .17 B8
Tilbury RM18 ....19 B5
Moore CI
Brenzett TN29 ....363 A3
Dartford DA10 ....17 E1
Moore Rd DA10 ....17 E1
Moore St ME2 ....63 A8
Moorfield CT2 ....142 F4
Moorfield Rd BR6 ......54 A2
Moorhead Way SE3 ...11 B4
Moorhen CI DA8 ....15 B7
Moor Hill CT18 ....354 F8
Moorhouse Cotts
TN16 ....184 A7
Moorhouse Rd RH8,
TN16 ....184 A6
Mooring Rd ME1 ......63 D1
Moorings The
Conyer ME9 ....103 E6
Newnham E16 ....1 C8
Moor La
Edenbridge TN8 .....249 A4
Ivychurch TN29 ......363 C4
Moorland Rd CT15 ...244 E4
Moorlands BR7 ....30 B1
Moor La TN26 ....346 E6
Moor Park Cl ME8 .....99 A8
Moor Rd The TN14 ...154 C7
Moorside Rd BR1 ......29 A4
Moor St ME8 ....99 B8
Moorstock La TN25 ..303 C2
Moor The TN18 ......354 F8
Moorwell Dr CT15 ...244 D5
Morants Court Cross
TN14 ....121 C1
Morants Court Rd
TN13 ....153 C8
Moray Ave CT7 ....80 F8
Mordaunt Ave CT8 ....81 E8
Morden Rd SE3 ....11 A5
Morden Road Mews
SE3 ....11 A5
Morden St ME1 ....63 C4
Morebreddis Cotts
TN17 ....291 A1
Morehall Ave CT19 ...334 F6
Morehall Prim Sch
CT19 ....334 F6
Morel Ct TN13 ....154 B5
Morella Wlk ME17 ...199 C5
Morello Cl Swanley BR8 . 55 D5
Teynham ME9 ....103 C2
Morement Rd ME3 ....41 D6
More Park RC Prim Sch
ME19 ....159 D8
Moreton Almhouses 3
TN13 ....151 D1
Moreton Ct
Crayford DA1 ....14 E4
Deal CT14 ....215 C2
Moreton Ind Est BR8 ..56 A4
Moreton DA14 ....31 A3
Moreton Terr TN26 ..299 A1
Morewood CI TN13 ..153 F4
Morgan Dr DA9 ....34 D8
Morgan Kirby's Gdn
ME13 ....170 D5
Morgan Rd Bromley BR1 . 29 A1
Rochester ME2 ....63 A8
Morgan St E16 ....1 B8
Morhen CI ME6 ......127 C7
Morland Ave DA1 ......15 C2

Morland Dr
Lamberhurst TN3 .....317 B5
Rochester ME2 ....40 A1
Morland Ho 4 BR7 ....53 A8
Morley Bsns Ctr TN9 .222 D1
Morley CI BR6 ....86 B8
Morley Dr TN12 ......290 A6
Morley Rd
Chislehurst BR7 ....53 C8
Tonbridge TN9 ....222 D1
Morley's Rd TN14 ....187 D2
Morne Cotts TN14 ...121 F8
Morning Cross Cotts
ME3 ....22 B4
Mornington Ave BR1 ..52 C6
Mornington CI TN16 .118 C2
Mornington Ct DA5 ...32 D7
Morris Ave CT6 ....75 C4
Morris CI
Maidstone ME17 ....195 D5
Orpington BR6 ....86 E7
West Malling ME19 ..127 F1
Morris Court CI ME9 .102 D2
Morris Gdns DA1 ......16 A2
Morrison Rd CT20 ...335 E6
Morry La
Chartway Street ME17 .197 D1
Ulcombe ME17 ....230 D7
Morston Gdns SE9 ....29 F4
Mortgramit Sq SE18 ...2 A3
Mortimer CI TN23 ...300 B7
Mortimer Rd
Biggin Hill TN16 .....118 C7
Dover CT16 ....310 F8
Erith DA8 ....14 D8
Orpington BR6 ....54 A1
Mortimers Ave ME3 ...40 A8
Mortimer St CT6 ....76 F5
Mortlake Rd E16 ....1 B7
Mortley CI TN9 ......222 C2
Morton CI
Maidstone ME15 ....195 D6
Swanley BR8 ....55 E7
Morvale CI DA17 ....3 F2
Moselle Rd TN16 .....118 F1
Mosquito Rd ME19 ..158 F3
Mossbank ME5 ....97 A3
Mossdown CI DA17 ....4 A2
Moss End Mews CT11 ..83 D2
Mosslea Rd
Bromley BR2 ....52 D4
Orpington BR6 ....86 C7
Moss Way DA2 ....34 D4
Mossy Glade ME8 .....98 E6
Mostyn Rd ME14 .....162 C4
Mosul Way BR2 ....52 E3
Mosyer Dr BR5 ....87 D8
Mote Ave ME15 ......162 B3
Mote Cotts TN15 .....189 A7
Mote Hall Villas ME14 .163 A4
Mote Pk ME15 ....162 D2
Mote Rd
Maidstone ME15 ....162 A3
Shipbourne TN15,TN11 .189 A7
Mote The DA3 ....91 F8
Motherwell Way RM20 .17 A8
Motney Hill Rd ME8 ...66 A4
Mottingham Gdns SE9 .29 F7
Mottingham La
Bromley SE12,SE9 ....29 C7
Eltham SE12 ....29 C8
Mottingham Prim Sch
SE9 ....29 F5
Mottingham Rd SE9 ..29 F5
Mottingham Sta SE9 ..29 F7
Mottisfont Rd SE2 ......3 B2
Mouat St ME5 ....97 A3
Mouchotte CI TN16 ..118 C7
Moultain Hill BR8 ......56 A5
Mound The SE9 ....30 A5
Mountain CI TN15 ...124 F3
Mountain St CT4 .....205 B6
Mount Ave ME18 .....193 A1
Mountbatten Ave
Chatham ME5 ....97 A7
Higham ME3 ....39 C4
Mountbatten CI SE18 ..12 E8
Mountbatten Ho CT14 .215 D3
Mountbatten Way
TN25 ....302 E6
Mount Castle La ME17 .199 F1
Mount Charles Wlk
CT4 ....175 F1
Mount CI Bromley BR1 ..52 E8
Sevenoaks TN13 .....153 F4
Mount Culver Ave
DA14 ....31 D2
Mount Dr Bexley DA6 ..13 E2
Maidstone ME14 .....163 B4
Mount Edgcumbe Rd
TN4 ....286 A3
Mount Ephraim ★
ME13 ....140 A4
Mount Ephraim Ct
TN4 ....285 F4
Mount Ephraim Rd
TN1 ....286 A4
Mount Ephraim TN4 ..286 A4
Mountfield CI CT13 ...93 F2
Mountfield Ct 4 TN1 .286 B3
Mount Field ME13 ...138 B6
Mountfield Gdns TN1 .286 B3
Mountfield Pk TN9 ...254 C8
Mount Field ME11 .....46 A5
Mountfield Rd
New Romney TN28 ..373 C6
Royal Tunbridge Wells
TN1 ....286 B3
Mountfield Way
1 Orpington BR5 ....54 C5
Westgate-on-S CT8 ...81 D6

Mount Green Ave
CT12 . . . . 116 D5
Mount Harry Rd TN13 . 154 B4
Mounthurst Rd BR2 . . 52 A2
Mountjoy CI SE2 . . . . 3 B4
Mount La Hartlip ME9 . . 99 A4
Maidstone ME14 . . . . . . 163 B4
Mount Lodge ME1 . . . . . . 63 B2
Mount Pleasant TN25 . 330 A6
Mount Pleasant Ave 2
TN1 . . . . 286 B3
Mount Pleasant
Aylesford ME20 . . . . . . 129 A3
Biggin Hill TN16 . . . . . . 118 D2
Blean CT2 . . . . 142 A6
Chatham ME5 . . . . 64 B3
Mount Pleasant CI
CT18 . . . . 305 C7
Mount Pleasant Ct
TN11 . . . . 221 D6
Mount Pleasant Dr
ME14 . . . . 163 A5
Mount Pleasant
Durgates TN5 . . . . 336 C6
Faversham ME13 . . . . . 105 B2
Ide Hill TN14 . . . . 185 F4
Kingsdown CT14 . . . . . . 248 D5
Mount Pleasant La
TN3 . . . . 317 A6
Mount Pleasant
Lamberhurst TN3 . . . . . 316 E6
Minster (Thanet) CT12 . 115 C8
Paddock Wood TN12 . . . 256 F7
Mount Pleasant PI SE18 . .2 D2
Mount Pleasant Rd
Dartford DA1 . . . . 15 F1
4 Folkestone CT20 . . . 335 D5
Royal Tunbridge Wells
TN1 . . . . 286 A3
Sevenoaks Weald TN14 . 187 B2
Mount Pleasant TN30 . 345 C8
Mount Pleasant Terr
ME17 . . . . 198 E2
Mount Pleasant
The Moor TN18 . . . . 354 F8
Tonbridge TN11 . . . . . . 221 D6
Mount Pleasant Wlk
DA5 . . . . 14 C2
Mount Rd Bexley DA6 . . .13 E2
Canterbury CT1 . . . . . . 175 C6
Chatham ME4 . . . . 63 F3
Crayford DA1 . . . . 14 F1
Dover CT17 . . . . 310 A6
Rochester ME1 . . . . 63 B2
Mounts CI CT14 . . . . . . 215 A5
Mountsfield CI ME16 . 161 D5
Mounts Hill TN17 . . . . 342 B7
Mount Sion TN1 . . . . . . 286 A2
Mounts La TN17 . . . . . . 344 A3
Mounts Rd DA9 . . . . 17 B1
Mount St CT21 . . . . 333 C2
Mounts View TN23 . . . . 267 F4
Mount The Bexley DA6 . . 14 B2
3 Chislehurst BR7 . . . . . 53 A8
Mountview ME9 . . . . . . 101 B2
Mount View Ct 3 ME4 . .63 F3
Mount View ME13 . . . . 138 A5
Mount View Rd CT6 . . . . 77 A2
Mountview Rd BR6 . . . . 54 A2
Moyes CI CT12 . . . . 116 D5
Moyle CI ME8 . . . . 98 D4
Mozart Ct ME4 . . . . 63 A3
Muddy Bush Cnr CT3 . . 177 F2
Muddy La ME10 . . . . . . 102 B2
Muir Rd
Maidstone ME15 . . . . . 162 A2
Ramsgate CT11 . . . . . . 117 F8
Muir St E16 . . . . 1 E5
Mulbarton Ct BR7 . . . . . . 30 D2
Mulberry CI
Gillingham ME7 . . . . 98 A4
Greenwich SE7 . . . . 11 D8
Meopham Station DA13 . .60 B3
Ramsgate CT11 . . . . . . 117 F8
Royal Tunbridge Wells
TN4 . . . . 254 D1
Mulberry Ct
Bexley DA16 . . . . 12 F5
Canterbury CT1 . . . . . . 174 F8
Hythe CT21 . . . . 333 D3
Littlestone-on-Sea TN28 . 373 E5
Maidstone ME14 . . . . . 162 B5
Mulberry Field CT13 . 148 F1
Mulberry Hill CT4 . . . . 172 D1
Mulberry Rd
Ashford TN23 . . . . 267 D3
Northfleet DA11 . . . . . . .36 E4
Mulberry Way DA17 . . . .4 C4
Mulgrave Ho 13 SE18 . . . .1 F2
Mulgrave Prim Sch SE18 . .2 B3
Mulgrave Rd SE18 . . . . . . 2 A2
Mullein Ct 7 RM17 . . . . .18 D8
Mullender Ct DA12 . . . . . 38 A7
Muller Ho SE18 . . . . .2 A1
Multon Rd TN15 . . . . 90 E4
Mummery Ct ME13 . . . 137 E2
Munday Bois Cotts
TN27 . . . . 264 E8
Munday Bois Rd TN27 . 232 E1
Munday Rd E16 . . . . 1 A7
Munday Works Est
TN9 . . . . 222 C1
Mundella Prim Sch
CT19 . . . . 335 D6
Munford Dr DA10 . . . . . . 35 E8
Mungeam Ho ME1 . . . . . .63 A3
Mungo Park Rd DA12 . . 37 D3
Mungo Park Way BR5 . . 54 D2
Munnery Way BR6 . . . . . .86 B8
Munnings Ho E16 . . . . 1 E8
Munn's La ME9 . . . . 99 E6
Munsgore La ME9 . . . . . 100 E3
Murchison Ave DA5 . . . .31 E7

Murrain Dr ME15 . . . . . 163 A1
Murray Ave BR1 . . . . 52 B7
Murray Bsns Ctr BR5 . . 54 B6
Murray Ho 15 SE18 . . . . . 1 F2
Murray Lodge TN2 . . . . 286 D2
Murray Rd
Orpington BR5 . . . . 54 B6
Rochester ME1 . . . . 63 C8
Murray Sq E16 . . . . 1 B6
Murston Inf Sch ME10 . 102 B4
Murston Jun Sch
ME10 . . . . 102 B5
Murston Rd ME10 . . . . 102 B4
Murthwaite Ct ME12 . . . 47 A5
Murton-Neale CI 3
TN18 . . . . 341 A2
Murton PI ME13 . . . . . . 106 E1
Muscovy Ho DA18 . . . . . . .3 E4
Muscovy Rd TN25 . . . . . 268 C7
Muscovy Way CT6 . . . . . . 76 E3
Museum of Canterbury ★
CT1 . . . . 174 F8
Museum of Kent Rural
Life ★ ME14 . . . . 129 D1
Musgrave CI CT12 . . . . . .81 F2
Musgrave Rd ME10 . . . 101 F6
Musgrove TN23 . . . . . . 300 A8
Muskerry Ct TN4 . . . . . 285 B4
Musket La
Eyhorne Street ME17 . . 164 C2
Leeds ME17 . . . . 164 A2
Mus of Artillery in the
Rotunda ★ SE18 . . . . . . 1 F1
Mussenden La DA3,DA4 . .57 E3
Mustang Rd ME19 . . . . 158 F3
Mustards Rd ME4 . . . . . . 49 D2
Mutrix Gdns CT9 . . . . . . 50 E1
Mutrix Rd CT9 . . . . 82 B8
Mutton La ME13 . . . . . . 138 A6
Mycenae Rd SE3 . . . . 11 A8
Mymms CI CT5 . . . . 109 C8
Mynn Cres ME14 . . . . . 163 A4
Myra St SE2 . . . . 3 A2
Myrtle Alley SE18 . . . . . . .2 A3
Myrtle CI DA8 . . . . 14 E6
Myrtle Cres ME5 . . . . . . .96 F5
Myrtledene Rd SE2 . . . . . 3 A1
Myrtle Gn TN23 . . . . . . 267 D4
Myrtle PI DA2 . . . . 34 D8
Myrtle Rd
Dartford DA1 . . . . 33 D6
5 Folkestone CT19 . . . 335 E6
Mystole Ho CT4 . . . . . . 206 B8
Mystole La CT4 . . . . . . 206 C8

N

Nacholt CI CT5 . . . . 75 A2
Nackington Ct CT1 . . . . 175 B6
Nackington Pk CT4 . . . . 175 A4
Nackington Rd CT1,
CT4 . . . . 175 A3
Nadine St SE7 . . . . 1 C1
Nagpur Ho 4 ME15 . . . 195 E5
Nag's Head La
Bexley DA16 . . . . 13 B4
Rochester ME1 . . . . 63 B4
Nailbourne CI CT4 . . . . 209 D3
Nailbourne Ct CT18 . . . 305 C7
Naildown CI CT21 . . . . . 334 A3
Naildown Rd CT21 . . . . 334 A3
Nairn Ct RM18 . . . . 18 F5
Nairne Ct TN26 . . . . 327 A8
Naldera CT10 . . . . 84 C7
Namur PI CT15 . . . . 278 F3
Nansen Rd DA12 . . . . 37 D4
Napchester Rd CT16 . . 278 A8
Napier CI ME10 . . . . . . 101 C4
Napier Com Sch ME7 . . 64 D4
Napier Ct
2 Lewisham SE12 . . . . . 29 B5
Maidstone ME14 . . . . . 161 F7
Napier Gdns CT21 . . . . 333 C1
Napier Rd
Broadstairs CT10 . . . . . .83 E6
Bromley BR2 . . . . 52 B5
Dover CT16 . . . . 278 B2
Erith DA17 . . . . .3 F2
Gillingham ME7 . . . . 64 D4
Northfleet DA11 . . . . . . .36 F7
Royal Tunbridge Wells
TN2 . . . . 286 D2
Napleton Ct 7 CT11 . . 117 C6
Napleton Rd
Faversham ME13 . . . . . 138 C7
Ramsgate CT11 . . . . . . 117 C6
Napoleon Dr TN12 . . . . 259 D5
Napoleon Wlk ME17 . . 199 C5
Napwood CI ME8 . . . . . . 98 D6
Nares Rd ME8 . . . . 98 D4
Nargate CI CT3 . . . . 177 A8
Nargate St CT3 . . . . 177 A8
Narrabeen Rd CT19 . . . 334 E6
Narrow Boat CI SE28 . . . .2 D4
Narrowbush La TN29 . . 371 B7
Narrow Way BR2 . . . . 52 E3
Naseby Ave CT20 . . . . . 334 D5
Naseby Ct DA14 . . . . 30 F4
Nash Bank DA13 . . . . 59 F7
Nash CI ME5 . . . . 62 C6
Nash Cotts 10 DA14 . . . 31 A5
Nash Court Farming
World ★ ME13 . . . . . . 139 D4
Nash Court Gdns CT9 . . .82 F8
Nash Court Rd CT9 . . . . . 82 F8
Nash Croft DA11 . . . . . . .36 E4
Nashenden Farm La
ME1 . . . . 96 A8
Nashenden La ME1 . . . . .62 F1
Nash Gdns CT10 . . . . . . .84 B4
Nash Gn BR1 . . . . 29 A2
Nash Hill CT18 . . . . 305 D6

Nash La Margate CT9 . . . .82 F7
Nash BR2 . . . . 85 A4
Nash Rd
Margate CT9,CT10 . . . . .82 F7
Wingham CT3 . . . . 146 D2
Nash St DA13 . . . . 60 A7
Nasmyth Rd CT7 . . . . . . .81 A8
Nassau Path 6 SE28 . . . . 3 C5
Natal Rd Chatham ME4 . . 64 A3
Dover CT16 . . . . 278 C4
Nathan Way SE28,SE18 . . .2 E3
Nativity CI ME10 . . . . . . 101 E4
Nat's La TN25 . . . . 270 A5
Nautilus CI ME12 . . . . . . 47 A6
Nautilus Dr ME12 . . . . . . 47 A6
Naval Terr ME12 . . . . 28 A3
Naylands CT9 . . . . 50 H1
Naylor's Cotts ME7 . . . . 98 B1
Neale St ME4 . . . . .63 F2
Neal Rd TN15 . . . . 90 E5
Neal's Place Rd CT2 . . 142 C3
Neame Ct CT7 . . . . 81 A7
Neames Forstal ME13 . 171 E7
Neason Ct CT19 . . . . . . 335 F6
Neason Way CT19 . . . . . 335 F6
Neath Rd TN29 . . . . 375 A2
Neatscourt Cotts ME12 . 46 C4
Neatscourt Rd ME6 . . . . .1 D8
Neills Rd TN3 . . . . 316 D2
Nellington Ct TN4 . . . . 285 B4
Nellington Rd TN3,
TN4 . . . . 285 B4
Nelson Ave
Minster (Sheppey) ME12 . 47 D5
Tonbridge TN9 . . . . 222 A1
Nelson CI
Ashford TN24 . . . . 301 B8
Biggin Hill TN16 . . . . . . 118 E2
West Minot ME12 . . . . . . 46 A8
Nelson Cres CT11 . . . . . 117 E6
Nelson Ct
Birchington CT7 . . . . 80 E8
Chatham ME5 . . . . 64 C1
Nelson Gdns ME13 . . . 138 C6
Nelson Ho
8 Maidstone ME15 . . . 195 F5
Swanscombe DA9 . . . . . . 17 D2
Nelson Mandela Rd
SE3 . . . . 11 C4
Nelson Mews TN28 . . . 373 E5
Nelson Park Rd CT15 . . 279 E8
Nelson PI CT10 . . . . .84 B5
Nelson Rd Bromley BR2 . 52 C5
Dartford DA1 . . . . 15 C1
Erith DA17 . . . . 3 F1
Northfleet DA11 . . . . . . .36 F6
Royal Tunbridge Wells
TN2 . . . . 286 D2
Sidcup DA14 . . . . 31 A4
Whitstable CT5 . . . . 74 D1
Wouldham ME1 . . . . 95 C5
Nelson St Deal CT14 . . 215 D7
Faversham ME13 . . . . . 138 C6
Nelson Terr ME5 . . . . . . .64 C1
Nelson Wlk ME10 . . . . . 101 B5
Nepicar Farm ★ TN15 . 125 D3
Nepicar La CT15 . . . . . . 125 D3
Neptune Bsns Pk ME2 . .63 E7
Neptune CI ME2 . . . . 63 E7
Neptune Terr ME12 . . . . 28 D2
Neptune Way ME2 . . . . . .63 E6
Neptune Wlk DA8 . . . . . . 4 D2
Nesbit Rd Eltham SE9 . . 11 D3
St Mary's Bay TN29 . . . 365 F4
Nesbitt Ho DA6 . . . . 14 A8
Ness Rd Erith DA8 . . . . . 15 D8
Lydd TN29 . . . . 376 C6
Ness The CT1 . . . . 175 B5
Nestor Ct ME18 . . . . . . 193 A8
Nether Ave TN28 . . . . . 373 D6
Nethercombe Ho 4
SE3 . . . . 11 A8
Nethercourt Cir CT12 . 117 A6
Nethercourt Farm Rd
CT11 . . . . 117 B7
Nethercourt Gdns
CT11 . . . . 117 B6
Nethercourt Hill CT11 . 117 B6
Nethergong Hill CT3 . . 112 D3
Netherhale Farm Rd
CT7 . . . . 80 B3
Nethersole CI CT2 . . . . 143 A4
Nethersole Rd CT4 . . . . 210 F1
Nethewode Ct DA17 . . . .4 B3
Netley CI ME14 . . . . 162 D6
Nettlefield TN24 . . . . . . 268 E5
Nettlepole La TN27 . . . 233 D1
Nettlestead Cotts
TN12 . . . . 257 A7
Nettlestead St ME18 . . 192 C5
Nettlestead La ME19 . . 192 A6
Nevill Ct ME14 . . . . 127 C1
Neville CI
Maidstone ME14 . . . . . 162 B8
Sidcup DA15 . . . . 30 F4
Neville Ho CT14 . . . . . . 215 D6
Neville Rd ME4 . . . . 63 E2
Nevill Gate TN2 . . . . . . 286 B1
Nevill Gdns CT14 . . . . . 215 B1
Nevill Lodge TN2 . . . . . 286 C4
Nevill Pk TN4 . . . . 285 E5
Nevill PI ME6 . . . . 128 A7
Nevill Rd ME6 . . . . 128 A7
Nevill Ridge TN4 . . . . . 285 D3
Nevill St TN2 . . . . 286 A2
Nevill Terr TN2 . . . . 285 F2
New Acres Rd SE28 . . . . 2 E4
Newark Ct 1 ME4 . . . . . .63 B7
Newark Knok E6 . . . . 2 A7
Newark Yd CT7 . . . . .63 F7
New Ash Green Prim Sch
DA3 . . . . 91 F8

Newbarn La TN14,
TN16 . . . . 119 C2
New Barn Pk BR8 . . . . . . 55 E8
New Barn Rd
Northfleet DA11 . . . . 36 C3
Sutton Valence ME17,
TN12 . . . . 229 E2
Swanley BR8 . . . . 55 F8
New Barns Rd ME14 . . 162 A8
New Barn St E13 . . . . 1 B8
New Bassetts Cotts
TN12 . . . . 290 B5
New Beach Holiday Centre
TN29 . . . . 353 A4
New Beacon Sch
TN14 . . . . 186 F8
Newbery Rd DA8 . . . . . . .14 F6
New Beverley Ho CT2 . 142 F2
Newborough St TN10 . 222 C6
Newbridge Ave ME10 . 101 B5
New Bridge 12 CT16 . . 310 E7
Newbridge Pk TN12 . . 225 A1
New Bridge Way
TN29 . . . . 365 E3
Newbury Ave ME16 . . . 161 C6
Newbury CI
Birchington CT7 . . . . 81 B6
Cliffe Woods ME3 . . . . . 40 B8
Dartford DA1 . . . . 34 B8
Dover CT17 . . . . 309 F7
Folkestone CT20 . . . . . 334 D5
Newbury Cotts TN5 . . . 337 B8
Newbury Ct DA14 . . . . . .30 F4
Newbury La TN5 . . . . . . 337 C8
Newbury Rd BR2 . . . . . . 52 A6
Newcastle Hill 8
CT11 . . . . 117 E7
Newchurch La TN26 . . 364 A7
Newchurch Rd ME15 . . 162 A1
New College of Cobham
DA12 . . . . 61 A5
Newcomen Rd
Royal Tunbridge Wells
TN4 . . . . 286 A5
Sheerness ME12 . . . . . . 28 C2
New Cotts Bean DA2 . . . .35 B5
Guston CT15 . . . . 278 E6
Harbledown CT2 . . . . . 141 E1
Shipbourne TN11 . . . . . 189 D5
Teynham ME9 . . . . 103 A4
The Moor TN18 . . . . 354 B7
Tilbury RM18 . . . . .19 B8
New Covenant PI 4
ME1 . . . . 63 D4
New Cross St CT9 . . . . . .50 I2
New Ct 3 TN9 . . . . 222 C2
New Cut Chatham ME4 . . 63 F4
East Farleigh ME15 . . . 194 D7
New Cut Rd
Chilham CT4,ME13 . . . 172 A3
Harbledown ME13 . . . . 141 A1
Maidstone ME14 . . . . . 162 D5
New Delhi Ho 5
ME15 . . . . 195 E5
New Dover Rd
Canterbury CT1,CT4 . . 175 C6
Capel-le-F CT18 . . . . . 308 C2
Newenden CI
Ashford TN23 . . . . 299 F6
Maidstone ME14 . . . . . 162 D6
Newenden Rd ME4 . . . . .40 C2
New England Rd TN4 . . 286 A7
New Farm Ave BR2 . . . . 52 A5
New Ferry App SE18 . . . . 2 A3
New Forest La CT4 . . . . 172 B3
New Gardens Rd ME9 . 103 C2
Newgate Gap CT9 . . . . . 51 A3
Newgate Lower Prom
CT9 . . . . 51 A3
Newgate Prom CT9 . . . . 51 A3
New Haine Rd CT12 . . . .83 A3
New Hall CI TN29 . . . . . 366 C8
New Hall Farm La ME3 . .25 B6
New House CI CT1 . . . . 174 E4
New House La
Canterbury CT4 . . . . . . 174 C2
Gravesend DA11 . . . . . . 37 A6
Newhouse La ME13 . . . 170 D7
Newhouse Terr TN8 . . . 217 C3
New Hythe La ME20 . . 128 B3
New Hythe Sta ME20 . . 128 C4
Newick CI DA5 . . . . 14 B1
Newing CI CT3 . . . . 176 E8
Newing Gn BR1 . . . . 29 D1
Newington CE Prim Sch
ME9 . . . . 100 B7
Newington Ct
Ramsgate CT12 . . . . 83 B1
Ticehurst TN5 . . . . 338 E1
Newington Ent Ctr
ME9 . . . . 100 C8
Newington Ho 9 BR5 . . 54 D1
Newington Ind Est ME9 . .99 F6
Newington Inf Sch
CT12 . . . . 117 B8
Newington Jun Foundation
Sch CT12 . . . . 117 A8
Newington Rd
Peene CT18 . . . . 334 A8
Ramsgate CT12,CT11 . . .83 B1
Newington Sta ME9 . . . 100 B6
Newington Wlk ME14 . 162 C6
New Inn Cotts ME15 . . 194 C7
Newitt Rd ME3 . . . . .41 E5

New Kempes Ho ME25 . 237 E2
New La TN29 . . . . 376 B1
Newland Green La
TN27 . . . . 264 D8
Newland Rd ME12 . . . . . 45 F7
Newlands TN23 . . . . . . 299 D6
Newlands Ave ME10 . . 101 B5
Newlands Ct 8 SE9 . . . 12 A1
Newlands Dr CT14 . . . . 248 B8
Newlands Farm Cotts
ME13 . . . . 202 C4
Newlands Farm Rd
ME3 . . . . .24 B4
Newlands Ho ME11 . . . . 83 E2
Newlands La DA13 . . . . .92 F1
Newlands TN3 . . . . 285 A3
Newlands La CT12 . . . . . 83 D2
Newlands Lodge DA8 . . 14 D8
Newlands Prim Sch
CT11 . . . . 83 E1
Newlands Rd
Charing TN27 . . . . 233 F5
Ramsgate CT12 . . . . 83 D1
Royal Tunbridge Wells
TN4 . . . . 286 B7
Newlands Rise TN4 . . . 286 A6
Newlands TN29 . . . . 365 F3
Newland St E16 . . . . 1 F5
Newlands Way TN4 . . . 286 B7
Newlands CT16 . . . . . . 278 B6
New Lincoln Ho CT19 . 335 D8
Newling CI E6 . . . . 1 F7
New Lydenburg
Commercial Est SE7 . . . 1 C3
New Lydenburg St SE7 . . 1 C3
Newlyn CI BR6 . . . . 87 A6
Newlyn Ct 1 ME4 . . . . . 162 A4
Newlyn Dr TN12 . . . . . . 260 F5
Newlyn Rd ME16 . . . . . . 12 F5
Newlyn's Mdw CT15 . . 276 D1
Newman Ct
11 Bromley BR1 . . . . . . 52 A8
Hythe CT21 . . . . 333 B1
Newman Dr ME10 . . . . 102 A8
Newman Ho SE18 . . . . . 12 A7
Newman Rd
Aylesham CT3 . . . . 210 G5
Bromley BR1 . . . . 52 A8
Newmans CI CT10 . . . . . 84 A6
Newman's Rd DA11 . . . .36 F6
Newmarket Gn SE9 . . . . 29 D8
Newmarsh Rd SE28 . . . . 2 F5
New Mill Rd BR5 . . . . . . 54 C8
Newnham CI BR7 . . . . . . 65 C2
Newnham La ME9,
ME13 . . . . 168 D7
Newnham Lodge DA17 . . 4 A1
Newnhams CI BR1 . . . . . 52 F6
Newnham St ME4 . . . . . .64 B3
New Pond Rd TN17 . . . 342 D6
Newport Ct CT1 . . . . . . 175 B6
Newports BR8 . . . . 55 D2
New Pound La ME18 . . 158 C1
New Rd Bexley DA16 . . . .13 B5
Burham ME1 . . . . 95 F1
Chatham ME4 . . . . 63 F4
Cliffe ME3 . . . . 22 A4
Cranbrook TN17 . . . . . . 320 B4
Ditton ME20 . . . . 128 C1
East Malling ME19 . . . . 160 A8
Egerton TN27 . . . . 233 A2
Elham CT4 . . . . 273 F4
Erith SE2 . . . . 3 D1
Eythorne CT15 . . . . 245 C7
Fordcombe TN11 . . . . . 252 A1
Gravesend DA11 . . . . . . 19 B1
Grays RM17 . . . . 18 D4
Harbledown CT2 . . . . . 141 D3
Headcorn TN27 . . . . . . 262 D5
Herne CT2,CT6 . . . . . . 110 C4
Hextable BR8 . . . . 32 F1
Hythe CT21 . . . . 333 B1
Hythe, Saltwood CT21 . . 333 B4
Langley ME17 . . . . 196 C5
Limpsfield RH8 . . . . 183 B5
Meopham Station DA13 . .59 F4
Minster (Sheppey) ME12 . 47 C6
Orpington BR6 . . . . 54 A2
Paddock Wood TN12 . . . 257 A6
Rochester ME1 . . . . 63 D4
Rough Common CT2 . . 142 B3
Sheerness ME12 . . . . . . 28 A1
Sundridge TN14 . . . . . 152 E2
Sutton at H DA4 . . . . . . .57 D7
Swanley BR8 . . . . 55 F6
New Rectory La TN3 . . 300 B4
New Rents 5 TN23 . . . . 268 B2
New Road Ave ME4 . . . . 48 A2
New Road Cotts CT6 . . 110 C5
New Road Hill
Bonnington TN25 . . . . . 329 F4
Farthing Street BR2,BR4 . .85 F7
New Road Ind Est
ME12 . . . . 28 A1
New Road Sch ME4 . . . . 64 A3
New Romney PI CT13 . 180 F8
New Romney Sta
TN28 . . . . 373 C6
New Ruttington La
CT1 . . . . 143 A1
New Sch at West Heath The
TN13 . . . . 187 B6
New Stairs ME4 . . . . .63 F6
New St Ash CT3 . . . . . . 147 E1
Ashford TN24 . . . . 268 A2
Canterbury CT1 . . . . . . 174 E7
Canterbury,St Dunstan's
CT2 . . . . 142 E1
Chatham ME4 . . . . 63 E4
Deal CT14 . . . . 215 D7
12 Dover CT16,CT17 . . 310 C8
Newstead Ave BR6 . . . . .86 E8

Newstead Wood Sch for
Girls BR6 . . . . 86 D7
New St
Folkestone CT20 . . . . . 335 D5
Herne Bay CT6 . . . . .76 F5
Lydd TN29 . . . . 376 C6
Margate CT9 . . . . 50 I2
New Street TN15 . . . . . . 92 D4
New Street Hill BR1 . . . 29 C3
New Street Rd DA13,
TN15 . . . . 92 C3
New St Sandwich CT13 . 181 A8
Sheerness ME11 . . . . . . 28 B1
Westerham TN16 . . . . . 184 C8
2 Whitstable CT5 . . . . . 74 D2
New Swan Yd 8 DA12 . .19 B1
New Tavern Fort ★
DA12 . . . . 19 C1
Newton Abbot Rd DA11 . 36 F6
Newton Ave TN10 . . . . . 222 E7
Newton CI Chatham ME5 . 97 C2
1 Maidstone ME16 . . . 161 E3
Newton Ct 4 BR1 . . . . . .52 E6
Newton Gdns TN12 . . . 256 F7
Newton Ho
Swanscombe DA9 . . . . . 17 D2
Woolwich SE2 . . . . 3 C1
Newton Rd Bexley DA16 . 13 A4
Faversham ME13 . . . . . 138 D7
Royal Tunbridge Wells
TN1 . . . . 286 B4
Tilbury RM18 . . . . 19 A5
Whitstable CT5 . . . . 75 B2
Newton's Ct DA9 . . . . . . 16 D3
Newton Terr BR2 . . . . . . 52 D3
Newton Willows TN3 . . 312 C7
Newton Ho
Swanscombe DA9 . . . . . 17 D2
Newtown Cotts
TN11 . . . . 220 A3
Newtown Cotts TN12 . 260 E6
New Town Gn TN24 . . . 300 D8
Newtown Rd TN23,
TN24 . . . . 300 D7
New Town St
Canterbury CT1 . . . . . . 143 B2
Chartham CT4 . . . . 173 C5
New Villas ME15 . . . . . 194 C7
New Wharf Rd TN9 . . . 222 B1
New Wlk TN15 . . . . 124 F3
New Years La BR6,
TN14 . . . . 120 A5
Niagara CI ME18 . . . . . 159 B3
Nicholas CI ME16 . . . . 161 A3
Nicholas Ct SE12 . . . . . . 29 A7
Nicholas Dr CT12 . . . . . 116 D7
Nicholas Rd BR5 . . . . . . 54 D2
Nicholas Stacey Ho 4
SE7 . . . . 1 B1
Nichol La BR1 . . . . 29 A1
Nicholls Ave CT10 . . . . . .83 F2
Nicholson Ho SE18 . . . . 11 E7
Nickelby CI SE28 . . . . 3 C7
Nicklaus Dr ME5 . . . . . . .96 F3
Nickleby Ct ME1 . . . . . . 63 C2
Nickleby Rd DA12 . . . . . 38 A7
Nickle Cotts CT4 . . . . . 173 A4
Nickley Wood Rd
TN26 . . . . 327 C6
Nicola Terr DA7 . . . . .13 E6
Nicolson Rd BR5 . . . . . . 54 D2
Nicolson Way TN13 . . . 154 D5
Nigeria Rd SE7 . . . . 11 D7
Nightingale Ave
Hythe CT21 . . . . 353 D6
Whitstable CT5 . . . . . . 108 B6
Nightingale CI
Ashford TN24 . . . . 301 B7
Biggin Hill TN16 . . . . . . 118 C4
Chartham CT4 . . . . 173 C6
Gillingham ME8 . . . . . . .98 E6
Larkfield ME20 . . . . 127 F2
Northfleet DA11 . . . . . . .36 E4
Nightingale Cnr BR5 . . . 54 D5
Nightingale CI ME2 . . . . 62 C6
Nightingale Gr 3 DA1 . . 16 A3
Nightingale Ho SE18 . . . .2 A1
Nightingale La
Bromley BR1 . . . . 52 D7
Goathurst Common
TN14 . . . . 186 B5
Nonington CT15 . . . . . . 211 C2
Nightingale PI
Margate CT9 . . . . 51 A2
Woolwich SE18 . . . . . . .12 B8
Nightingale Prim Sch
SE18 . . . . 2 B1
Nightingale Rd
Dover CT16 . . . . 278 C2
Faversham ME13 . . . . . 138 C7
Herne CT6 . . . . 110 F7
Kemsing TN15 . . . . 122 F2
Orpington BR5 . . . . 53 C3
Nightingales The
Royal Tunbridge Wells
TN4 . . . . 286 A5
Sissinghurst TN27 . . . . 321 F8
Nightingale Vale SE18 . 12 A8
Nightingale Way
ME16 . . . . 1 E8
Swanley BR8 . . . . 55 E6
Nile Path 6 SE18 . . . . . 12 A8
Nile Rd ME7 . . . . 64 C4
Nimrod Ho E16 . . . . 1 B8
Nine Acres CI ME4 . . . . 268 C5
Nine Acres Rd ME2 . . . . .62 B3
Nine Ash La ME13 . . . . 139 D3
Nine Elms Gr DA11 . . . . 37 A8
Nine Hams Rd CT9 . . . . 286 B7
Nineveh La TN17,TN18 . 341 E6
Ninhams Wood BR6 . . . 86 A6
Ninn La TN23 . . . . 267 B2

Nita Ct SE12 . . . . **29** A7
Nithdale Rd SE18 . . . . . . **12** C7
Niven Cl ME3 . . . . **40** C3
Nixon Ave CT12 . . . . . . **83** C1
Nizels La TN11 . . . . . . **220** F8
No 1 St SE18 . . . . **2** B3
Noah's Ark TN15 . . . . . **123** B1
Noah's Ark Rd CT17 . . **310** A8
Noah's Ark Terr CT17 . **310** B8
Noakes Mdw TN23 . . . . **300** A8
Nobel Cl ME9 . . . . **103** C2
Nobel Ct ME13 . . . . . . **138** C7
Noble Ct CT9 . . . . **82** A8
Noble Gdns CT9 . . . . . . **82** A8
Noble Tree Cross
  TN11 . . . . **221** B6
Noble Tree Rd TN11 . . **221** B6
Noel Terr **15** DA14 . . . **31** B4
No Name St **3** CT13 . . **149** A1
Nonington CE Prim Sch
  CT15 . . . . **211** C5
Nonington Ct CT15 . . . **211** E5
Nonsuch Cl CT1 . . . . . **175** C8
Nook The ME18 . . . . . . **192** F2
Norah La ME3 . . . . **39** B3
Nordenfeldt Rd DA8 . . . . .**4** D1
Nore Cl Gillingham ME7 . **64** E1
  Sheerness ME12 . . . . **28** C1
Noreen Ave ME12 . . . . . **47** A6
Norfield Rd DA2 . . . . . . **32** D3
Norfolk Cl Chatham ME5 . **97** C3
  Dartford DA1 . . . . **16** A2
  Gillingham ME8 . . . . . **65** D2
Norfolk Cres DA15 . . . . . **30** E8
Norfolk Dr TN23 . . . . . **268** A2
Norfolk Gdns DA7 . . . . **13** F6
Norfolk Pl DA16 . . . . . . **13** A5
Norfolk Rd
  Canterbury CT1 . . . . **174** E6
  Gravesend DA12 . . . . . **37** D8
  Maidstone ME15 . . . **195** C8
  Margate CT9 . . . . **82** B5
  Margate,Lydden CT9 . . **82** D5
  Royal Tunbridge Wells
    TN1 . . . . **286** B2
  Tonbridge TN9 . . . . . **222** A1
Norfolk Sq CT1 . . . . . . **83** B2
Norfolk St CT5 . . . . . . **108** D8
Norham Ct **25** DA2 . . . **16** B1
Norheads La TN16 . . . . **118** B2
Norlands Cres BR7 . . . . **53** B8
Norman Castle★ CT1 . **174** F7
Norman Cl
  Gillingham ME8 . . . . . **98** B5
  Kemsing TN15 . . . . . **122** D2
  Maidstone ME14 . . . **162** B6
  Orpington BR6 . . . . . . **86** C7
  Rochester ME2 . . . . . . **62** F4
Norman Ct TN8 . . . . . . **217** B2
Normandy Prim Sch
  DA7 . . . . **14** D6
Normandy Terr DA7 . . . **14** E7
Normandy Way DA8 . . . **14** E6
Normanhurst Ave DA7,
  DA16 . . . . **13** D6
Normanhurst Rd
  Borough Green TN15 . **157** A7
  Orpington BR5 . . . . . . **54** B7
Norman Par DA14 . . . . . **31** D6
Norman Rd
  Ashford TN23,TN24 . . **300** B7
  Broadstairs CT10 . . . . **83** F6
  Canterbury CT1 . . . . **175** A7
  Dartford DA1 . . . . **33** E7
  Erith DA17 . . . .**4** B5
  Erith DA17 . . . .**4** B5
  Faversham ME13 . . . . **138** C7
  Ramsgate CT11 . . . . . **117** B6
  Royal Tunbridge Wells
    TN1 . . . . **286** B2
  St Margaret's at Cliffe
    CT15 . . . . **280** B6
  Snodland ME6 . . . . . **128** A6
  Warden ME12 . . . . . . **49** A6
  Westgate-on-S CT8 . . **50** D1
  West Malling ME19 . . **159** B8
  Whitstable CT5 . . . . . **108** E8
Norman Rise TN17 . . . . **320** D4
Normans Cl DA11 . . . . . **37** A8
Norman St
  8 Dover CT17 . . . . **310** D8
  Ide Hill TN14 . . . . . . **185** F5
Norman Tailyour Ho
  CT14 . . . . **215** D5
Norman Villas **4**
  TN18 . . . . **340** F2
Norreys Rd ME8 . . . . . . **98** E2
Norrie Rd CT7 . . . . **81** A6
Norrington Mead **3**
  CT19 . . . . **335** A7
Norrington Rd ME15 . . **195** B6
Norris Ho **14** SE7 . . . **11** C8
Norris Way DA1 . . . . . . **14** F4
Norstead Gdns TN4 . . . **286** B8
Norsted La BR6 . . . . . . **120** B8
Northall Rd DA7 . . . . . **14** C5
North Ash Rd DA3 . . . . **91** F7
North Ave CT11 . . . . . . **117** D6
North Bank Cl ME2 . . . . **62** F5
North Barrack Rd
  CT14 . . . . **215** D4
North Beckton Prim Sch
  E6 . . . .**1** B8
North Borough Jun Sch
  ME14 . . . . **162** A6
Northbourne Ave
  CT17 . . . . **310** D7
Northbourne CE Prim Sch
  CT14 . . . . **213** F5

Northbourne Court Gdns★
  CT14 . . . . **214** B5
Northbourne Rd BR2 . . **52** A2
Northbourne Park Sch
  (Annexe) CT14 . . . . **213** D6
Northbourne Park Sch
  CT14 . . . . **213** C6
Northbourne Rd
  East Studdal CT15 . . **213** E1
  Gillingham ME8 . . . . . **65** B4
  Great Mongeham CT14 **214** C4
Northbourne Way CT9 . . **51** E2
Northbrooke TN24 . . . . **268** C3
Northbrooke La TN24 . . **268** C3
North Camber Way
  CT16 . . . . **279** B1
North Cl Bexley DA6 . . . **13** F7
  Folkestone CT20 . . . . **334** D4
Northcliffe Gdns CT10 . . **84** A7
North Close Bsns Ctr
  CT20 . . . . **334** D4
Northcote Rd
  Deal CT14 . . . . **215** D5
  Kingsdown CT14 . . . . **248** A6
  Northfleet DA11 . . . . . **36** F7
  Rochester ME2 . . . . . . **63** A7
  Sidcup DA14 . . . . **30** E4
  2 Tonbridge TN9 . . **222** B1
North Court Cl CT3 . . . **178** A8
North Court La CT14 . . **213** A4
Northcourt Prim Sch
  DA12 . . . . **37** E7
North Court Rd CT3 . . **178** A8
North Cray Rd DA14 . . . **31** E4
North Cres ME17 . . . . . **194** D4
North Ct **4** Bromley BR1 **52** B8
  Deal CT14 . . . . **215** C7
  2 Maidstone ME15 . **162** A1
  Ramsgate CT12 . . . . . **117** B7
North Dane Way ME5 . . **97** C4
Northdown TN24 . . . . . **268** D6
Northdown Ave CT9 . . . **51** B2
Northdown Bsns Pk
  ME17 . . . . **199** F6
Northdown Cl
  Lenham ME17 . . . . . **199** F6
  Maidstone ME14 . . . **162** B7
  Paddock Wood TN12 . **256** F6
Northdown ME9 . . . . . . **167** F7
Northdown Hill CT10,
  CT9 . . . . **83** D7
Northdown Park Rd
  CT9 . . . . **51** C1
Northdown Prim Sch
  CT9 . . . . **51** C1
Northdown Rd
  Bexley DA16 . . . . **13** C5
  Broadstairs CT10 . . . . **83** E6
  Kemsing TN15 . . . . . **122** E2
  Longfield DA3 . . . . . . **58** E7
  Margate CT9 . . . . **51** B2
North Downs Bsns Pk
  TN13 . . . . **121** C3
Northdowns Cl CT15 . . **246** B6
North Downs Cl CT4 . . **172** C2
North Down TN12 . . . . **260** E4
North Downs Terr
  ME19 . . . . **126** A5
Northdown ME9 . . . . . . **132** D8
North Down View
  ME17 . . . . **198** F6
Northdown Way CT9 . . . **51** C1
North Dr BR6 . . . . **86** E6
North Eastling Rd
  ME13 . . . . **168** F8
North End Farm DA13 . . **59** F7
North End La BR6 . . . . . **86** B2
Northend Prim Sch
  DA8 . . . . **14** F6
Northend Rd DA8 . . . . . **14** F6
North End Trad Est
  DA8 . . . . **14** E6
Northern By-Pass
  TN27 . . . . **234** C8
North Exit Rd CT15 . . **310** H8
North Farm La TN2 . . . **254** E2
North Farm Rd TN2 . . **286** C8
Northfield Ave BR5 . . . . **54** C3
Northfield Cl BR1 . . . . . **52** B8
Northfield DA3 . . . . **58** F6
Northfields
  Maidstone ME16 . . . **160** F2
  Speldhurst TN3 . . . . . **285** A8
Northfleet CE ME14 . . **162** C5
Northfleet Ind Est
  DA11 . . . .**17** F3
Northfleet Sch for Girls
  DA11 . . . . **36** D6
Northfleet Sta DA11 . . . **18** B1
Northfleet Tech Coll
  DA11 . . . . **36** D7
North Folly Rd ME15 . . **193** F3
North Foreland Ave
  CT10 . . . .**84** B7
North Foreland Hill
  CT10 . . . .**84** B8
North Foreland Rd
  CT10 . . . .**84** B7
North Frith Pk TN11 . . **189** F1
Northgate
  Canterbury CT1 . . . . **143** A1
  Rochester ME1 . . . . . . **63** C6
North Glade The DA5 . . .**31** F7
Northgrove Rd **9**
  TN18 . . . . **340** F2
North Hill Rd TN18 . . . **340** F2
North Holmes Rd CT1 . **175** B8
Northiam Sta★ TN31 . **357** C2
North Kent Ave DA11 . . **18** C1
North La
  Canterbury CT2 . . . . **142** F1
  Faversham ME13 . . . **138** C8
  7 Folkestone CT20 . **334** E3

North West Kent Coll
  DA12 . . . . **37** F7
Northwood Ave ME23 . . **23** E4
Northwood Dr ME10 . . **101** F1
Northwood Pl DA18 . . . . .**3** F3
Northwood Prim Sch
  DA18 . . . .**3** F3
Northwood Rd
  Broadstairs, Ramsgate
    CT10,CT12 . . . . . . **83** C3
  Tonbridge TN10 . . . . **222** C6
  Whitstable CT5 . . . . . .**74** F2
North Woolwich Old Sta
  Mus★ E16 . . . .**2** A4
North Woolwich Rdbt
  E16 . . . .**1** D5
North Woolwich Rd E16 . .**1** A5
North Woolwich Sta E16 . .**2** A4
Norton Ave CT6 . . . . . **111** A8
Norton Cres TN10 . . . . **222** B7
Norton Dr CT12 . . . . . **115** B6
Norton Gr ME5 . . . .**96** E3
Norton Knatchbull Sch The
  TN24 . . . . **268** C2
Norton La TN26 . . . . . **297** D5
Norton Rd
  Five Wents ME17 . . . **196** D1
  Lewson Street ME13,
    ME9 . . . . **136** E5
  Royal Tunbridge Wells
    TN4 . . . . **254** A1
Nortons La TN30 . . . . . **323** E5
Nortons Way TN12 . . . . **256** B7
Norvic Ho DA8 . . . .**14** F7
Norview Rd CT5 . . . . . **108** B7
Norway Dro CT15 . . . . **280** A8
Norway Terr **4** ME14 . **162** A7
Norwich Ave TN10 . . . . **222** D5
Norwich Cl ME2 . . . . . . **62** D6
Norwich Pl **7** DA6 . . . **14** A3
Norwood Cl ME3 . . . . . .**22** B4
Norwood Ct **5** DA1 . . . **16** A3
Norwood Gdns TN23 . . **268** B2
Norwood La
  Meopham Station DA13 .**60** B3
  St Mary in the Marsh
    TN29 . . . . **364** E8
Norwood Rise ME2 . . . . **47** C7
Norwood St TN23 . . . . **268** B2
Norwood Wlk E ME10 . **101** C5
Norwood Wlk W
  ME10 . . . . **101** B5
Notley St CT1 . . . . **143** A1
Notley Terr **3** CT1 . . **143** A1
Notre Dame RC Prim Sch
  SE18 . . . . **12** B8
Nottidge Rd TN4 . . . . . **285** D1
Nottingham Ave
  Maidstone ME15 . . . **195** D7
  Newham E16 . . . .**1** C7
Nottingham Rd CT7 . . . . **80** F5
Nottingham Wlk ME2 . . **62** D6
Nouds La ME9 . . . . **136** D6
Nouds Rd ME9 . . . . . . **136** D7
Novar Cl BR6 . . . . **53** F2
Novar Rd SE9 . . . . **30** C7
Nower The TN14,TN16 . **151** F8
Nuffield Hospl TN2 . . **286** C3
Nuffield Rd BR8 . . . . . . **33** A2
Nugent Ind Pk BR5 . . . . **54** C5
Nunappleton Way
  RH8 . . . . **183** A3
Nunnery Fields CT1 . . **175** A7
Nunnery Fields Hospl
  CT1 . . . . **174** F6
Nunnery La TN11 . . . . **283** F8
Nunnery Rd CT1 . . . . . **174** F7
Nunnington Cl SE9 . . . . **29** E5
Nursery Ave Bexley DA7 . **13** C7
  Maidstone,Bearsted
    ME14 . . . . **163** B3
  Maidstone ME16 . . . **161** B6
Nursery Cl Dartford DA2 . **34** C8
  Densole CT18 . . . . . **307** A7
  Flimwell TN5 . . . . . . **339** B3
  Orpington BR6 . . . . . . **54** A2
  Ramsgate CT11 . . . . . **117** C7
  Sevenoaks TN13 . . . . **154** C5
  Sheerness ME12 . . . . . **28** D1
  Swanley BR8 . . . . **55** C7
  Tonbridge TN10 . . . . **222** E4
  Whitstable CT5 . . . . . **55** E7
Nursery Fields Acol CT7 . **81** B3
  Hythe CT21 . . . . **333** A2
Nursery Gdns
  Broadstairs CT10 . . . . **51** E1
  Chislehurst BR7 . . . . . **30** B2
  Hoo St Werburgh ME3 . **41** E5
Nursery Ho DA4 . . . . . . **57** C5
Nursery La CT18 . . . . . **307** A7
Nurserylands CT6 . . . . . **76** F3
Nursery La
  Sheldwich ME13 . . . . **170** D5
  Whitfield CT16 . . . . . **277** F7
Nursery Pl TN13 . . . . . **153** D4
Nursery Rd
  Ditton ME20 . . . . . . **128** C1
  Gillingham ME8 . . . . . **98** D8
  Meopham Station DA13 . **60** A4
  Paddock Wood TN12 . **256** F8
  Royal Tunbridge Wells
    TN4 . . . . **286** B8
Nursery The DA8 . . . . . .**14** F7
Nursery Wlk CT2 . . . . . **142** E2
Nurstead Ave DA3 . . . . . **59** D6
Nurstead Church La
  DA13 . . . . **60** A5
Nurstead La DA3,DA13 . **59** D5
Nurstead Rd DA8 . . . . . **14** A7
Nutberry La ME9 . . . . . **103** D2
Nutfield Cl ME5 . . . . . . **97** B8
Nutfield Ct **7** BR1 . . . **52** A6

Nutfields
  Ightham TN15 . . . . . **156** B4
  Sittingbourne ME10 . . **102** B3
Nutfield Way BR6 . . . . . **86** B8
Nuthatch Gdns SE28 . . . .**2** D4
Nuthatch Cl DA5 . . . . . . **32** C7
Nuttall Ct BR5 . . . . **54** B6
Nutmead Cl DA5 . . . . . . **32** C7
Nut Tree Ct BR6 . . . . . . **87** D7
Nutts Ave ME12 . . . . . . **49** G2
Nutts Cvn Site ME12 . . . **49** H1
Nutwood Cl ME14 . . . . **162** C4
Nuxley Rd DA17 . . . .**4** A1
Nyanza St SE18 . . . . . . **12** D8

O

Oak Apple Ct SE12 . . . . **29** A7
Oakapple Ho **10** ME16 . **161** A3
Oakapple La ME16 . . . . **161** A3
Oak Ave
  Biddenden TN27 . . . . **323** D7
  Eythorne CT15 . . . . . **245** D5
  Gillingham ME7 . . . . . .**64** E6
  Minster (Sheppey) ME12 . .**47** F6
  Sevenoaks TN13 . . . . **187** B7
Oak Bglws TN29 . . . . . **376** C6
Oakbrook Cl BR1 . . . . . .**29** B4
Oak Caer TN25 . . . . . . **329** F4
Oak Cl Crayford DA1 . . . .**14** C3
  Hoo St Werburgh ME3 . **41** E3
Oak Cotts
  Barrowhill TN25 . . . . **331** D7
  East Studdal CT15 . . **246** E8
  Four Elms TN8 . . . . . **218** B6
  Selling ME13 . . . . . . **171** D4
Oakcroft **3** SE12 . . . . **29** B5
Oak Ct BR1 . . . . **52** F7
Oakdale La TN8 . . . . . . **184** C2
Oakdale Rd
  Herne Bay CT6 . . . . . .**77** A4
  Royal Tunbridge Wells
    TN4 . . . . **285** F4
Oakdene Ave
  Chislehurst BR7 . . . . . **30** A3
  Erith DA8 . . . . **14** C8
Oakdene Rd
  Orpington BR5 . . . . . . **54** A3
  Ramsgate CT12 . . . . . **83** C1
  Sevenoaks TN13 . . . . **154** A5
Oak Dr
  Boughton Street ME13 . **140** A3
  Hawkinge CT18 . . . . **307** B5
  Higham ME3 . . . . **39** B4
  Larkfield ME20 . . . . . **128** B2
  St Mary's Bay TN29 . . **365** F3
  Newham E16 . . . .**1** C7
Oak End Cl TN4 . . . . . . **254** A2
Oakenden La TN26 . . . . **251** C2
Oakenden Rd DA13 . . . . **60** E1
Oakenholt Ho **1** SE2 . . .**3** A4
Oakenpole TN23 . . . . . **267** E1
Oakes Cl E6 . . . .**1** F7
Oak Farm Gdns TN27 . **262** D6
Oak Farm La TN15 . . . . **92** E1
Oakfield Cotts TN17 . . **342** A4
Oakfield Court Rd
  TN2 . . . . **286** C3
Oakfield Ct CT12 . . . . . **117** B8
Oakfield TN18 . . . . **340** F2
Oakfield Inf Sch DA1 . . . **33** D6
Oakfield Jun Sch DA1 . . **33** D6
Oakfield La
  Dartford DA1,DA2 . . . . **33** B6
  Orpington BR2 . . . . . . **85** D6
Oakfield Park Rd DA1 . . **33** D6
Oakfield Pl DA1 . . . . . . **33** D6
Oakfield Rd
  Ashford TN24 . . . . . . **268** D5
  Marlpit Hill TN8 . . . . **217** B5
  Matfield TN12 . . . . . . **288** D8
Oakfield TN17 . . . . **344** A1
Oakfields
  Sevenoaks TN13 . . . . **154** B1
  Sittingbourne ME10 . . **101** C3
Oak Gr CT15 . . . . **212** B2
Oak Hall Pass CT21 . . . **333** C2
Oakham Dr Bromley BR2 . **52** A5
  Lydd TN29 . . . . **376** D7
Oakhill House BR5 . . . . . **54** A8
Oakhill Rd BR6 . . . . **86** F8
Oak Hill Rd TN13 . . . . **154** A2
Oak Hill CT13 . . . . **180** B6
Oak Ho **6** Chatham ME5 . . **96** F4
  3 Royal Tunbridge Wells
    TN2 . . . . **286** C7
  18 Sidcup DA15 . . . **31** A5
Oakhouse Rd DA6 . . . . . **14** A2
Oakhurst Ave DA7 . . . . . **13** C7
Oakhurst Cl
  Bromley BR7 . . . . **52** F8
  Chatham ME5 . . . . **96** F5
Oakhurst Gdns DA7 . . . . **14** A1
Oak La Gillingham ME8 . . **99** D8
  Headcorn TN27 . . . . . **262** D5
  Lydd TN29 . . . . **376** B6
  Minster (Sheppey) ME12 . **47** F7
Oakland Cl ME5 . . . . **96** F3
Oakland Ct
  Cliffs End CT12 . . . . . **116** C5
  Herne Bay CT6 . . . . . . **76** E5
Oaklands TN23 . . . . . . **267** F1
Oaklands Ave
  Broadstairs CT10 . . . . **83** E5
  Sidcup DA15 . . . . **30** F8
Oaklands Cl Bexley DA6 . .**13** F6
  Orpington BR5 . . . . . . **53** E3
  West Kingsdown TN15 . . **90** E4
Oaklands TN17 . . . . . . **320** D4
Oaklands Cl BR6 . . . . . . **86** C8

Oaklands Inf & Jun Sch
  ME5 . . . . **96** F4
Oaklands Inf Sch
  TN16 . . . . **118** C3
Oaklands Jun Sch
  TN16 . . . . **118** C3
Oaklands La TN16 . . . . **118** C5
  TN25 . . . . **301** E4
Oaklands Rd Bexley DA6 . .**13** F2
  Dartford DA2 . . . . **34** C7
  Groombridge TN3 . . . **312** B6
  Hawkhurst TN18 . . . . **341** A1
  Northfleet DA11 . . . . . .**36** F4
Oaklands CT2 . . . . **144** B7
Oaklands Way
  Sturry CT2 . . . . **144** B7
  Tonbridge TN11 . . . . **221** F4
Oakland Villas TN3 . . . **312** B7
Oak La Sevenoaks TN13 . **187** A8
  Upchurch ME9 . . . . . . **66** D2
Oaklea Rd TN12 . . . . . **256** F6
Oakleigh Cl
  Chatham ME5 . . . . **96** E2
  Swanley BR8 . . . . **55** E6
Oakleigh Ct TN12 . . . . **289** F6
Oakleigh Gdns BR6 . . . . **86** E6
Oakleigh Ho TN23 . . . . **299** E8
Oakleigh La CT4 . . . . . **176** B5
Oakleigh Park Ave BR7 . **53** A8
Oakley Cl **8** Newham E6 . .**1** E7
  West Thurrock RM20 . . **17** C8
Oakley Ct DA1 . . . . **34** B2
Oakley Dr Orpington BR2 . **85** E7
  Sidcup SE9 . . . . **30** D7
Oakley Lodge SE12 . . . . **29** A8
Oakley Pk DA5 . . . . **31** C8
Oakley Rd BR2 . . . . **85** E8
Oakleys The CT15 . . . . **244** D5
Oak Lodge La TN16 . . . **151** D2
Oak Lodge Rd TN28 . . **373** B7
Oak Lodge
  Royal Tunbridge Wells
    TN2 . . . . **286** D2
  Sevenoaks TN13 . . . . **154** A3
Oakmead Ave BR2 . . . . . **52** A3
Oakmead
  Meopham DA13 . . . . . **93** A8
  Tonbridge TN10 . . . . **222** C6
Oakmere Rd SE2 . . . . . . **13** A4
Oakmont Pl **6** BR1 . . . **53** D1
Oak Rd Erith DA8 . . . . . **15** A5
  Erith,Northumberland Heath
    DA8 . . . . **14** C7
  Five Oak Green TN12 . **256** B7
  Gravesend DA12 . . . . . **37** C4
  Grays RM17 . . . . **18** C8
  Hoo St Werburgh ME3 . . **41** E3
  Orpington BR6 . . . . . . **87** A3
  Rochester ME2 . . . . . . **62** E6
  Royal Tunbridge Wells
    TN2 . . . . **286** D7
  Sittingbourne ME10 . . **102** C5
  Stone DA9 . . . . **16** E1
  Westerham TN16 . . . . **151** D2
Oakridge CT10 . . . . **51** G1
Oak Ridge TN26 . . . . . **349** F6
Oaks Ave CT6 . . . . **76** D2
Oaks Bsns Village The
  ME5 . . . . **97** C1
Oaks Com Inf Sch The
  ME10 . . . . **101** D2
Oaks Dene ME5 . . . . **96** F1
Oaks Forstal TN18 . . . . **356** C7
Oakside Rd CT3 . . . . . . **210** E5
Oaks Pk CT2 . . . . **142** B3
Oaks Rd
  Folkestone CT20 . . . . **334** D6
  Tenterden TN30 . . . . **345** B8
Oak St CT14 . . . . **215** D6
Oaks The
  Aylesford ME20 . . . . **128** E1
  Broadstairs CT10 . . . . .**83** F7
  Dartford DA2 . . . . **16** B1
  Hawkinge CT18 . . . . **307** B3
  Hersden CT3 . . . . **111** F1
  St Nicholas at Wade CT7 . **79** F2
  Smarden TN27 . . . . . **263** F2
  Swanley BR8 . . . . **55** E7
  Whitstable CT5 . . . . . **108** B6
  Woolwich SE18 . . . .**2** C1
Oaks View CT21 . . . . . **353** C8
Oak Terr **3** TN18 . . . . **340** F2
Oak Tree Ave
  Maidstone ME15 . . . **195** C4
  Stone DA9 . . . . **34** F8
Oak Tree Cl
  Marden TN12 . . . . . . **259** D5
  Royal Tunbridge Wells
    TN2 . . . . **286** A1
Oak Tree Gdns BR1 . . . . **29** B3
Oak Tree Gr CT9 . . . . . . **82** A8
Oaktree Ho ME10 . . . . **102** B3
Oak Tree Prim Sch
  TN23 . . . . **299** F8
Oak Tree Rd TN23 . . . . **299** F8
Oak Trees Com Sch
  ME15 . . . . **195** C2
Oakum Ct ME4 . . . . **64** B2
Oakvale Cl CT17 . . . . . **310** B7
Oak View TN8 . . . . **217** B2
Oak Warren TN13 . . . . **187** A6
Oakway SE9 . . . . **13** E1
Oakways SE9 . . . . **12** B1
Oak Wlk CT21 . . . . **333** C2
Oakwood Ave BR2 . . . . . **52** B6
Oakwood Cl
  Chislehurst BR7 . . . . . **30** A2
  Dartford DA1 . . . . **34** B7
Oakwood Ct
  Maidstone ME16 . . . **161** D3
  Swanley BR8 . . . . **55** C7
Oakwood Dr Bexley DA7 . **14** C3
  Sevenoaks TN13 . . . . **154** B4

Oakwood Dr continued
Whitstable CT5 ....75 A1
Oakwood Gdns BR6 ...86 C8
Oakwood Ind Est
Broadstairs CT10 ....83 E6
Northfleet DA11 ...18 A2
Oakwood CT9 ....83 C8
Oakwood Park Gram Sch
ME16 ....161 C3
Oakwood Rd
Maidstone ME16 ....161 D3
Orpington BR6 ....86 C8
Sturry CT2 ....144 A7
Oakwood Rise
Longfield DA3 ....58 E6
Royal Tunbridge Wells
TN2 ....286 E7
Oakwood Sch DA7 ...14 D3
Oakwood Terr ME10 ...102 C4
Oakwood Villas CT11 ..83 E1
Oare Marshes Nature
Reserve★ ME13 ....105 B6
Oare Marshes Nr & Watch
Tower Info Ctr★
ME13 ....105 C6
Oare Rd ME13 ....105 C1
Oasis The 7 BR1 ....52 C7
Oast Cl CT1 ....286 D7
Oast Cotts
Dargate ME13 ....140 D8
Sheldwich ME13 ....170 C8
Wormshill ME9 ....166 C5
Oast Ct Margate CT9 ...82 F8
Sittingbourne ME10 ...101 E2
Yalding ME18 ....192 F1
Oast Ho The
Canterbury CT3 ....175 F8
3 Gillingham ME8 ....98 F8
Oasthouse Field TN29 ..363 F4
Oast House Way BR5 ..54 B5
Oast La
Throwley Forstal ME13 ...202 E6
Tonbridge TN10 ....222 A4
Oast Mdw TN24 ....268 F1
Oast Paddock The
CT3 ....179 A6
Oasts The ME14 ....163 C4
Oast The
Canterbury CT1 ....175 B6
Staple CT3 ....179 A6
Oastview ME8 ....99 A8
Oast View TN12 ....290 A6
Oast Way DA3 ....58 E3
Oaten Hill CT1 ....175 A7
Oaten Hill Pl CT1 ....175 A7
Oatfield Cl TN17 ....320 C5
Oatfield Dr TN17 ....320 C5
Oatfield Rd BR6 ....53 F1
Oaze The CT5 ....108 C6
Occupation La SE18 ...12 B6
Occupation Rd TN25 ...237 F2
Ocean Cl CT7 ....81 B8
Ocean View
Broadstairs CT10 ....84 A1
Herne Bay CT6 ....77 F6
Ocelot Ct 6 ME4 ....64 B3
Ockham Dr BR5 ....31 A1
Ockley Ct DA14 ....30 E5
Ockley La TN18 ....341 A3
Ockley Rd TN18 ....341 A2
Octavia Ct ME5 ....97 B3
Octavian Dr CT21 ....332 A3
Octavian Way TN23 ...299 E5
Octavia Way 12 SE28 ...3 B6
Odeon Ct 1 E16 ....1 A8
Odeon Par SE9 ....11 B3
Odiham Dr ME16 ....161 C7
Odo Rd CT17 ....310 C8
Offenham Rd SE9 ....29 F4
Offen's Dr TN12 ....260 E3
Offham Prim Sch
ME19 ....158 D8
Offham Rd ME19 ....159 A7
Officers' Rd ME4 ....64 B8
Officers Terr ME4 ....63 F7
Offley Cl CT9 ....51 C1
Ogilby St SE18 ....1 F2
Ogilvy Ct CT10 ....83 E7
Okehampton Cl TN24 ..268 F7
Okehampton Cres
DA16 ....13 C6
Okemore Gdns BR5 ...54 C5
Olantigh Ct CT7 ....81 A7
Olantigh Rd TN25 ....237 F3
Olave Rd CT9 ....51 B1
Old Ash Cl TN24 ....268 C5
Old Ashford Rd
Charing TN27 ....234 C4
Lenham ME17 ....199 E5
Old Badgins Rd ME13 ..170 B6
Old Bailey The ME17 ..198 E6
Old Bakery Cl TN29 ...365 F4
Old Bakery Mews
ME13 ....139 F4
Old Bakery The ME12 ..46 F5
Old Barn Cl
Gillingham ME7 ....97 A2
Kemsing TN15 ....123 A2
Tonbridge TN9 ....253 F8
Old Barn Rd ME19 ....127 E2
Old Barn Way DA7 ....14 D4
Old Bexley Bsns Pk
DA5 ....32 B8
Old Bexley CE Prim Sch
DA5 ....31 F7
Old Bexley La DA5 ....32 E6
Old Billet La ME17 ....216 E3
Oldborough Manor Com
Sch ME15 ....195 B6
Old Boundary Rd CT8 ..50 D1
Old Bridge Rd CT5 ....74 E1

Oldbury Cl
Oldbury TN15 ....156 B5
Orpington BR5 ....54 D5
Oldbury Cotts TN15 ...156 B6
Oldbury La TN15 ....156 B6
Old Carriageway The
Gillingham ME7 ....97 F4
Sevenoaks TN13 ....153 C5
Old Castle Wlk ME8 ...98 D4
Old Chapel Rd BR8 ...55 C2
Old Charlton Rd CT16 ..278 D2
Old Chatham Rd
Kit's Coty ME20 ....129 D6
Sandling ME14 ....129 C1
Oldchurch Ct 3 ME16 ..161 E3
Old Church La TN12 ...191 E4
Old Church Rd
Burham ME1 ....95 C1
Chartham CT4 ....173 E1
Mereworth ME18,TN12 ..191 D5
Pembury TN2 ....255 D2
Old Clem Sq SE18 .....12 A8
Old Coach Rd TN15 ...124 E5
Old Coachworks The 10
CT13 ....148 F1
Old Coal Yd The 7
CT5 ....74 D1
Old Coastguard Cotts
TN29 ....380 D3
Old Corn Stores The
ME14 ....163 C4
Old Court Hill CT15,
CT3 ....211 C6
Old Court Ho The
TN13 ....154 C3
Old Crossing Rd 1
CT9 ....82 B8
Old Dairy Cl 4 CT11 ...117 F7
Old Dairy The TN12 ...224 E6
Old Dairy Yd CT12 ...117 C7
Old Dartford Rd DA4 ..56 F6
Old Dover Rd
Barham CT4 ....210 B1
Canterbury CT1 ....175 B6
Capel-le-F CT18 ....308 C1
Greenwich SE3 ....11 B7
Old Downs DA3 ....58 E4
Old Downs The DA3 ...58 E4
Old Dr ME15 ....194 F6
Old Dungeness
Lighthouse★ TN29 ...380 D2
Old Farm Ave DA15 ...30 A6
Old Farm Cl CT5 ....108 C6
Old Farm Gdns DA15 ..55 F6
Old Farmhouse The
BR8 ....32 E1
Old Farm Rd CT7 ....80 D1
Old Farm Rd E DA15 ..31 A6
Old Farm Rd W DA15 ..30 F6
Old Ferry Rd ME9 ....66 A2
Oldfield Cl Bromley BR1 ..52 F5
Gillingham ME8 ....98 D8
Maidstone ME15 ....162 E1
Oldfield Dr ME1 ....95 C5
Oldfield Rd Bexley DA7 ..13 F5
Bromley BR1 ....52 F5
Old Fire Sta The SE18 ..12 B7
Old Flour Mill The
CT17 ....278 B2
Old Fold CT5 ....109 C8
Old Folkestone Rd
CT17 ....310 A4
Old Forge La ME9 ....132 F3
Old Forge Way DA14 ...31 B4
Old Garden Ct CT4 ...173 E1
Old Gardens Cl TN2 ...314 A8
Old Gate Rd ME13 ....138 B8
Old Gdn The TN13 ....153 D4
Old George Ct ME3 ...40 F4
Old Green Rd
Broadstairs CT10 ....83 F7
Margate CT9 ....51 C1
Old Hadlow Rd TN10 ..222 F4
Old Hall Dr CT12 ....116 C5
Old Halls The 8 CT5 ...74 D2
Old Ham La ME17 ....199 A4
Oldhawe Hill CT3,CT6 ..111 D7
Old High St The CT20 ..335 E5
Old Hill Chislehurst BR7 ..53 A8
Orpington BR6 ....86 E4
Old Hockley Rd ME13 ..169 C2
Old Homestead Rd BR2 ..52 C5
Old Hook Rd ME12 ....47 F2
Old Hop Gdn The
TN31 ....367 C2
Old Ho The BR7 ....53 D8
Oldhouse La TN29 ....362 E1
Old House La
Hartlip ME9 ....99 E4
Langton Green TN3 .....284 D4
Old Kent Rd TN12 ....257 A6
Old Kingsdown Cl TN10 ..83 E3
Old La TN15 ....156 C4
Old Lain ME17 ....198 F6
Old La TN16 ....150 D6
Old Lenham Rd ME9 ...167 C4
Old London Rd
Badgers Mount TN14 ...88 A1
Halstead TN14 ....120 E4
Hythe CT21 ....332 F2
Tonbridge TN10 ....222 C3
Wrotham TN15 ....124 F4
Old Loose Cl ME15 ...194 F5
Old Loose Hill ME15 ..194 F4
Old Maidstone Rd
Keycol ME9 ....100 F5
Sidcup DA14 ....31 F1
Oldman Ct SE12 ....29 B6
Old Manor Dr DA12 ...37 C7
Old Manor Way
Bexley DA7 ....14 D5
Bromley BR7 ....29 F3

Old Mead CT19 ....335 A7
Old Mill Cl DA4 ....56 E1
Old Mill La ME20 ....129 C3
Old Mill Mews CT19 ...334 F7
Old Mill Rd
Maidstone ME17 ....163 F1
Woolwich SE18 ....12 D8
Old Oast Bsns Ctr The
ME20 ....129 A1
Old Orchard La ME19 ..127 D1
Old Orch Ashford TN23 ..299 D8
Charcott TN11 ....220 A3
Old Orch The ME8 ....99 A8
Old Otford Rd ME15 ...193 E7
Old Palace Rd CT4 ...176 C3
Old Park Ave
Canterbury CT1 ....143 C2
Dover CT16 ....278 A3
Old Park Cl CT16 ....278 A4
Old Park Hill CT16 .....278 B4
Old Park Rd
Dover CT16 ....278 B2
Woolwich SE2 ....3 A1
Old Parsonage Ct
ME19 ....159 C7
Old Pattens La ME4 ...63 D2
Old Perry St
Chislehurst BR7 ....30 E1
Northfleet DA11 ....36 E6
Old Polhill TN14 ....121 D4
Old Police Sta The 4
CT5 ....74 D2
Old Pond Rd TN3 ....299 F8
Old Post Office La SE3 ..11 B7
Old Print Ho E16 ....310 E7
Old Priory Sch The
CT11 ....117 D6
Old Railway Works (Ind
Est) TN24 ....300 D8
Old Rd Chatham ME4 ..63 F4
Crayford DA1,DA7 ....14 D3
East Peckham TN12 ...225 A6
Old Rd E DA12 ....37 D7
Old Rd Elham CT4 ....273 F4
Sarre CT7 ....113 C6
Wateringbury ME18 ...192 C7
Old Rd W DA11 ....37 A7
Old Rectory Cl
Hawkinge CT18 ....307 B4
Mersham TN25 ....301 E5
Old Rectory The TN26 ..236 E2
Old Regent Dr TN17 ...343 E3
Old Riding School The
TN3 ....312 B2
Old Roman Rd CT15 ..247 C1
Old Ruttington La
CT1 ....143 A1
Old Saltwood La CT21 ..333 B4
Old Saw Mill The
Bethersden TN26 ....297 E6
Platt TN15 ....157 D5
Old School Cl
Lenham ME17 ....199 D4
Sturry CT2 ....143 F6
Old School Ct
Chattenden ME3 ....40 F4
Egerton TN27 ....232 F3
Folkestone CT20 ....335 B4
Swanley BR8 ....55 E7
Old School Gdns CT5 ..51 A1
Old School Ho The 3
TN8 ....217 C1
Old School La ME19 ...126 F4
Old School Mews CT4 ..173 E1
Old School Pl ME14 ...162 A5
Old School The
Ashford TN24 ....300 D8
Goudhurst TN17 ....318 F4
Maidstone ME16 ....160 E1
Old School Yd
2 Broadstairs CT10 ...83 E5
Gravesend DA12 ....37 E8
Old Sch The BR6 ....86 B5
Old Soar Manor★
TN15 ....157 B1
Old Soar Rd TN15 ....157 C1
Old Stables The CT11 ..117 C5
Oldstairs Rd CT14 ....248 D4
Old Station Rd TN5 ...336 E6
Old Surrenden Manor
TN26 ....298 C5
Old Surrenden Manor Rd
TN26 ....298 C5
Old Tannery Cl TN30 ..344 F7
Old Terry's Lodge Rd
TN15 ....124 A4
Old Timber Top Cotts The
TN15 ....154 C4
Old Timber Yard Ind Est
CT17 ....117 A7
Old Tovil Rd ME15 ....162 A2
Old Town Gaol Mus★
CT17 ....310 D8
Old Town Hall Mus★
CT9 ....50 I3
Old Trafford Ct 6 ME16 ..161 B6
Old Tramyard SE18 ...2 E2
Old Tree La ME17 ....195 D3
Old Tree Rd CT3 ....112 B7
Old Tye Ave TN16 ....118 E2
Old Valley Rd CT4 ....242 F7
Old Vicarage Gdn CT2 ..143 F6
Old Vicarage Gdns
TN25 ....237 E2
Old Vicarage The
Meopham DA13 ....60 A1
Woodnesborough CT13 ..180 C7
Old Wardsdown TN5 ..339 B3
Old Watling St
Gravesend DA11 ....37 A3
Rochester ME2 ....62 B8

Old Way TN26 ....361 D7
Old Weavers Cotts
TN17 ....342 D5
Old Whetsted Rd
TN12 ....225 A2
Old White Hart Cotts
TN16 ....152 C3
Old Wlk The TN14 ....122 C2
Old Yard The TN14 ....152 C3
Old Yews The DA3 ....59 B6
Oleander Cl BR6 ....86 D5
Olive Gr 2 CT11 ....117 F7
Oliver Cl Chatham ME4 ..64 B2
West Thurrock RM20 ...16 C1
Oliver Cres DA4 ....56 F2
Oliver Ct SE18 ....2 C1
Olive Rd DA1 ....33 D7
Oliver Gdns E6 ....1 E8
Oliver North Ho ME15 ..193 E7
Oliver Rd
Staplehurst TN12 ....260 E4
Swanley BR8 ....55 D6
West Thurrock RM20 ...16 C1
West Thurrock RM20 ...17 A7
Olivers Mill DA3 ....91 E8
Olivers Row ME14 .....163 C4
Oliver Twist Cl ME1 ...63 D4
Olivier Dr ME2 ....40 B2
Olivine Cl
Chatham ME5 ....130 A8
Sittingbourne ME10 ...101 C7
Olliffe Cl ME5 ....96 F2
Olron Cres DA6 ....13 C2
Olven Rd SE18 ....12 C8
Olyffe Ave DA16 ....13 A5
Omer Ave CT9 ....51 C2
O'Neill Path 11 SE18 ..12 A8
Onslow Cres BR7 ....53 B8
Onslow Dr DA14 ....31 D6
Onslow Rd ME1 ....63 D3
Ontario Way CT16 .....278 B3
Opal Cl DA1 ....1 D7
Opal Gn ME5 ....97 B2
Openshaw Rd SE2 ....3 B2
Opie Wlk CT18 ....306 F3
Orache Dr ME4 ....162 E5
Orange Court La BR6 ..86 A2
Orangery La SE9 ....11 F2
Orange St CT1 ....174 F8
Orange Terr ME1 ....63 D5
Orbital One DA1 ....34 B6
Orbital Pk TN24 ....300 F6
Orbit Cl ME5 ....130 A8
Orchard Ave
Aylesford ME20 ....128 C1
Bexley DA17 ....13 F8
Dartford DA1 ....33 B7
Deal CT14 ....215 B5
Gravesend DA11 ....37 B3
Rochester ME2 ....39 F1
Orchard Bank ME7 ...196 B1
Orchard Bsns Ctr
Maidstone ME16 ....161 C8
Paddock Wood TN12 ...257 A8
Royal Tunbridge Wells
TN2 ....286 D8
Tonbridge TN9 ....222 E1
Orchard Cl Bexley DA7 ..13 E6
Canterbury CT1 ....142 F4
Coxheath ME17 ....194 C3
Edenbridge TN8 ....217 B2
Horsmonden TN12 .....289 F6
Langley Heath ME17 ..196 E4
Littlebourne CT3 ....176 F7
Mersham TN25 ....301 E3
Minster (Thanet) CT12 ..115 B7
New Barn DA3 ....59 B7
Ramsgate CT12 ....83 B3
Royal Tunbridge Wells
TN2 ....286 D6
Sevenoaks TN14 ....154 C7
Whitfield CT16 ....277 F8
Whitstable CT5 ....74 F3
Wingham CT3 ....178 A7
Orchard Cotts
Chislehurst BR7 ....30 E2
East Farleigh ME16 ...194 A8
Nettlestead Green
ME18 ....192 C1
Orchard Cres
Horsmonden TN12 .....290 A6
Wateringbury ME18 ...192 D6
Orchard Ct
Benenden TN17 ....342 D6
Chillenden CT3 ....211 F8
Herne Bay CT6 ....76 F1
Sidcup DA15 ....12 F2
Orchard Dr
Crabble CT17 ....277 E3
Edenbridge TN8 ....217 B2
Hythe CT21 ....333 B1
Littlestone-on-Sea TN28 ..373 E6
Maidstone ME14 ....162 E4
Meopham Station DA13 ..59 F4
Newington ME9 ....100 A5
Tonbridge TN10 ....222 E5
Wye TN25 ....237 F1
Orchard End CT11 ....117 A5
Orchard Field TN26 ...297 D4
Orchard Fields CT21 ..304 E2
Orchard Flats CT1 ....175 D7
Orchard Gdns CT9 .....82 A8
Orchard Glade TN27 ..262 C5
Orchard Gn
Bromley BR1 ....52 C8
Orpington BR6 ....86 E8
Orchard Gr
Larkfield ME20 ....128 B2
Minster (Sheppey) ME12 ..47 C6
Orpington BR6 ....86 E8
Royal Tunbridge Wells
TN1 ....286 B5

Orchard Hill DA1 ....14 E7
Orchard Ho Erith DA8 ..14 A7
9 Faversham ME13 ...138 C7
Orchard Hts TN23 .....267 F5
Orchard Ind Est ME15 ..195 B6
Orchard La
Ashford TN24 ....268 C5
Challock TN25 ....203 B2
Monkton CT7,CT12 ...114 A8
St Nicholas at Wade CT7 ..79 F1
Orchardlea DA13 ....35 F3
Orchard Lea TN11 ....221 F5
Orchard Mews CT14 ..215 D5
Orchard Pk CT6 ....77 D4
Orchard Pl
Faversham ME13 ....138 C7
Keston BR2 ....85 D2
2 Maidstone ME16 ...161 E3
Orpington BR5 ....54 C6
Sittingbourne ME10 ...102 A3
Sundridge TN14 ....152 D3
Orchard Prim Sch
DA14 ....31 B3
Orchard Rd Bexley DA16 ..13 A4
Bromley BR1 ....52 C8
East Peckham TN12 ...225 A6
Eastry CT13 ....180 B3
Erith DA17 ....4 A2
Herne Bay CT6 ....76 F3
Margate CT9 ....82 A8
Northfleet DA11 ....36 C6
Orpington BR6 ....86 B5
Otford TN14 ....121 F3
Pratt's Bottom BR6 ...87 C1
St Mary's Bay TN29 ...366 A5
Sevenoaks TN13 ....153 C5
Sidcup DA14 ....30 E4
Swanscombe DA10 ...17 C3
Tenterden TN30 ....324 A3
Orchard Residences The
CT1 ....175 A5
Orchard Rise E DA15 ..12 F2
Orchard Rise TN3 ....312 B7
Orchard Rise W DA15 ..12 F2
Orchard Row CT6 ....77 A1
Orchard Sch The CT1 ..174 F6
Orchards Sh Ctr The
DA1 ....15 E1
Orchard St
Canterbury CT2 ....142 E1
Dartford DA1 ....15 E1
Gillingham ME8 ....98 E8
Orchards The CT4 ....273 F4
Orchard St ME15 ....162 A3
Orchard Terr DA9 ....16 E2
Orchard The
Maidstone ME14 ....163 B4
Monkton CT12 ....114 C6
Sevenoaks TN13 ....153 E6
Swanley BR8 ....55 D7
Orchard Valley CT1 ...333 A2
Orchard View Ash CT3 ..147 F1
Detling ME14 ....163 A8
Tenterden TN30 ....345 C8
Teynham ME9 ....103 C3
Orchard Villas
Chainhurst TN12 ....227 A4
1 Chatham ME4 ....63 F3
Chislehurst BR7 ....30 E2
Kearsney CT17 ....277 E4
Sidcup DA14 ....31 C2
Orchard Way
Cranbrook TN17 ....320 B6
Dartford DA2 ....33 D5
Eastchurch ME12 ....48 D1
Horsmonden TN12 .....290 A6
Kemsing TN15 ....123 A2
Oxted RH8 ....183 A2
Peasmarsh TN31 ....367 C1
Snodland ME6 ....127 F7
Orchid Cl
Minster (Sheppey) ME12 ..47 A4
1 Newham E6 ....1 E8
Rochester ME2 ....62 C6
Orchidhurst TN2 ....286 D7
Orchids The
Etchinghill CT18 ....305 D4
Mersham TN25 ....301 E4
Ordnance Rd
Gravesend DA12 ....19 C1
Woolwich SE18 ....12 A8
Ordnance St ME4 ....63 E4
Ordnance Terr 9 ME4 ..63 E4
Oregon Sq BR6 ....53 D1
Orford Ct 7 DA2 ....16 B1
Orford Rd SE18 ....12 A2
Orgarswick Ave TN29 ..366 C7
Orgarswick Way TN29 ..366 C7
Oriental Rd E16 ....1 D5
Orient Pl CT2 ....142 F1
Oriole Way
Larkfield ME20 ....127 F2
Woolwich SE28 ....3 B6
Orion Rd ME1 ....96 C7
Orion Way TN24 ....300 E8
Orissa Rd SE18 ....2 E1
Orlestone Gdns BR6 ..87 E5
Orlestone Villas TN26 ..349 A8
Orlick Rd DA12 ....38 B7
Ormesby Cl SE28 ....3 C6
Ormiston Rd SE10 ....1 A1
Ormonde Ave BR6 ....86 C8
Ormonde Ct CT21 ....333 C1
Ormonde Rd
11 Folkestone CT20 ..335 E6
Hythe CT21 ....333 C1
Ormsby Gn ME8 ....98 E3
Ormsby Point 8 SE18 ..2 A2
Orpines The ME18 ....192 C7
Orpington By-Pass
TN14 ....88 A2
Orpington Coll of Further
Education BR6 ....54 A1
Orpington Hospl BR6 ..86 F6

Orpington Rd BR7 ....53 E6
Orpington Sta BR6 .....86 E8
Orpington Trad Est 10
BR5 ....54 C5
Orpins Cl TN25 ....302 D6
Orr Cl CT18 ....306 F4
Orwell Cl
Lunsford ME20 ....127 F3
Rainham RM13 ....4 D8
Orwell Spike ME19 ...159 A5
Osberton Rd SE12 ....11 A2
Osborne Gdns CT6 ...77 D4
Osborne Rd
Ashford TN24 ....300 F8
Bexley DA17 ....13 F8
Gillingham ME7 ....64 C5
Kingsdown CT14 ....248 C6
Osborne Terr CT9 ....50 J1
Osbourn Ave CT8 ....81 E8
Osbourne Rd
Broadstairs CT10 ....83 F4
Dartford DA2 ....16 B1
Oscar Rd CT10 ....84 B4
Osgood Ave BR6 ....86 F5
Osgood Gdns 1 BR6 ..86 F5
Osier Field TN24 ....268 E7
Osier Rd ME9 ....103 E3
Oslin Wlk ME18 ....159 C2
Osmers Hill TN5 ....336 F7
Osmunda Ct TN2 ....286 C4
Osney Ho 4 SE2 ....3 D4
Osney Way DA12 ....37 F6
Osprey Ave ME5 ....64 E2
Osprey 1 Newham E6 ...1 E8
Whitstable CT5 ....108 C7
Osprey Ct
2 Dover CT16 ....278 B2
Hawkinge CT18 ....306 F3
Sittingbourne ME10 ...102 A3
Osprey Wlk ME20 ....127 F1
Ospringe CE Prim Sch
ME13 ....138 A6
Ospringe Ct SE9 ....12 C1
Ospringe Pl
Faversham ME13 ....138 B6
Royal Tunbridge Wells
TN2 ....286 F6
Ospringe Rd ME13 .....138 B7
Ospringe St ME13 .....138 A6
Ostend Ct ME10 ....68 F1
Osterberg Rd DA1 ....15 F3
Osterley Cl BR5 ....54 A8
Ostlers Ct 2 ME6 ....128 A8
Ostlers La CT17 ....113 D6
Oswald Pl CT17 ....278 B2
Oswald Rd CT17 ....278 B2
Otford Cl Bromley BR1 ..53 A6
Sidcup DA5 ....14 B1
Otford Court (St Michael's
Sch) TN14 ....122 E4
Otford La TN14 ....122 B3
Otford Prim Sch TN14 ..122 B3
Otford Rd TN14 ....154 B7
Otford Sta TN14 ....122 C3
Otham Cl CT2 ....143 A4
Otham La ME15 ....163 C2
Otham St
Maidstone ME15 ....163 C2
Otham ME15 ....196 B2
Otley Rd E16 ....1 C7
Otlinge Rd BR5 ....54 D5
Ottawa Cres CT16 .....278 C3
Ottawa Rd RM18 ....19 A5
Ottawa Way TN16 .....278 B3
Otterbourne Pl ME15 ..162 E1
Otterden Cl
Ashford TN23 ....299 D8
Orpington BR6 ....86 E6
Otterden Rd ME13 .....168 D3
Ottersham Quay La
Gillingham ME8 ....66 B2
Gillingham ME8 ....99 B8
Otteridge Rd ME14 ...163 A3
Otterpool La CT21,
TN25 ....331 D4
Otters Cl BR5 ....54 D5
Ottershaw Ho BR5 .....54 B8
Otway St Chatham ME4 ..64 A3
Gillingham ME7 ....64 D6
Otway Terr 1 ME4 ....64 A3
Oulton Cl SE28 ....3 C7
Our Lady of Grace RC Prim
Sch SE7 ....11 B8
Our Lady of Hartley RC
Prim Sch DA3 ....58 F4
Our Lady of the Rosary RC
Prim Sch DA15 ....12 E1
Our Lady's RC Prim Sch
DA1 ....15 D1
Out Elmstead La CT4 ..209 F2
Outfall Ave TN29 ....380 C4
Oval The
Dymchurch TN29 ....352 D1
New Barn DA3 ....59 C6
Ovenden Rd
Sevenoaks TN14 ....152 F6
Sundridge TN14 ....152 D6
Overcliffe DA11 ....19 A1
Overcourt Cl DA15 .....13 B1
Overdale TN14 ....187 B2
Overland La CT3 ....147 A3
Overmead Eltham DA15 ..30 D8
Swanley BR8 ....55 C4
Over Minnis DA3 ....91 F7
Overton Ho ME12 ....28 C2
Overton Rd SE2 ....3 D3
Overy Liberty DA1 ....33 E8
Overy St DA1 ....15 E1

Owen Cl
East Malling ME19 ..... 159 F8
Woolwich SE28 ....3 C5
Owenite St SE2 ....3 B2
Owen's Cl CT21 .... 334 B3
Owens Court Cotts
ME13 .... 170 F8
Owen Sq CT14 .... 215 B2
Owens Way ME7 .... 65 A6
Owletts Cl ME15 ...... 195 D8
Owletts★ DA12 ....60 F6
Owl House Gdns★
TN3 .... 316 E7
Owl's Hatch Rd CT6 .... 76 C1
Oxenden Cnr CT3 ....77 F1
Oxenden Cres CT3 .... 178 A8
Oxenden Park Dr CT6 ...76 E4
Oxenden Rd CT20 ..... 334 E4
Oxenden St CT6 ....76 E5
Oxenden Way CT4 ..... 242 F8
Oxenden Wood Rd BR6 . 87 C4
Oxenhill Rd TN15 ..... 122 E2
Oxenhoath Rd TN11 ... 190 D4
Oxen Lease TN23 ...... 299 E8
Oxenturn Rd TN25 .... 269 E8
Oxfield TN8 .... 217 D3
Oxford Cl
Gravesend DA12 ....37 F6
5 Whitstable CT5 ...... 74 D1
Oxford Ct
Canterbury CT1 .... 174 F7
Sidcup DA14 ....30 F4
Oxford Mans 6 CT5 .... 74 D1
Oxford Mews DA5 ...... 32 A8
Oxford Rd
Canterbury CT1 .... 174 F7
Gillingham ME7 .... 64 D3
Maidstone ME15 .... 195 D8
Sidcup DA14 ....31 B3
Oxford St
6 Margate CT9 ....50 J1
Snodland ME6 .... 128 A8
Whitstable CT5 .... 74 D1
Oxford Terr CT20 ..... 335 D4
Oxhawth Cres BR2 ......53 B3
Ox La TN30 .... 324 B2
Ox Lea TN3 .... 285 A3
Oxleas Cl DA16 .... 12 D5
Oxleas E6 ....2 B7
Oxleas Wood Nature
Reserve★ SE18 .... 12 C4
Oxley Shaw La ME19 .. 127 E2
Oxney Cl CT7 ....80 F7
Oxney Cotts TN30 ..... 361 A4
Oyster Catchers Cl E16 ...1 B7
Oyster Cl Herne Bay CT6 ..76 B3
Sittingbourne ME10 .... 101 E6
Oyster Mews 4 CT5 .... 74 D1
Ozolins Way E16 ....1 A7

P

Pacific Cl DA10 ....17 E2
Pacific Rd E16 ....1 A7
Packer Pl ME5 .... 97 A8
Packer's La 5 CT11 ... 117 E7
Packham Cl BR6 .... 87 C7
Packham Rd DA11 ....36 F5
Packhorse Rd TN13 ... 153 C4
Packmores Rd SE9 ....12 E2
Padbrook Cl RH8 ...... 183 B6
Padbrook La CT3 ...... 146 D6
Padbrook RH8 .... 183 A6
Paddlesworth Rd ME6 .. 94 D1
Paddock Cl Deal CT14 .. 214 F5
Folkestone CT20 .... 334 F5
Fordcombe TN3 .... 284 B5
Greenwich SE3 .... 11 A5
Limpsfield RH8 .... 183 A4
Lydd TN29 .... 376 B6
Orpington BR6 ....86 B6
Platt TN15 .... 157 C6
Sutton at H DA4 .... 57 C8
Paddock Rd
Ashford TN23 .... 299 E7
Bexley DA6 ....13 E3
2 Birchington CT7 ...... 81 A7
Paddocks Cl BR5 .... 87 D8
Paddocks The
Ashford TN23 .... 267 C1
Broadstairs CT10 ....83 F7
Cowden TN8 .... 282 B7
Densole CT18 .... 307 A8
Gillingham ME7 .... 98 A5
Herne Bay CT6 ....77 F5
Margate CT9 .... 51 C1
Sevenoaks TN13 .... 154 D3
Paddock The
Ashurst TN3 .... 283 F5
Canterbury CT1 .... 175 B8
Chatham ME4 ....63 F4
Dartford DA2 ....34 E6
Dover CT16 .... 310 D8
Farthing Street BR2 ......85 E2
Hadlow TN11 .... 190 E1
Old Wives Lees CT4 .... 172 C2
Pembury TN2 .... 287 C6
Vigo Village DA13 ...... 125 F7
Westerham TN16 ...... 151 C1
Woodchurch TN26 ..... 326 A1
Paddock View CT5 ..... 108 E7
Paddock Way BR7 ...... 30 D1
Paddock Wood Bsns Ctr
TN12 .... 257 A7
Paddock Wood Prim Sch
TN12 .... 257 A6
Paddock Wood Sta
TN12 .... 257 A7
Pad's Hill ME15 .... 162 A4
Padsole La ME15 ...... 162 A4
Padstow Cl 3 BR6 ......86 F6
Padstow Manor 1
ME7 .... 64 C6
Padwell La TN23 ...... 299 C8
Paffard Cl CT2 .... 143 F6
Paffard Ct CT2 .... 143 F6
Pageant Cl RM18 .... 19 C6
Page Cl DA2 .... 35 C5
Page Cres DA8 ....14 F7
Page Heath La BR1 .... 52 D6
Page Heath Villas BR1 .. 52 D6
Pagehurst Rd TN12 .... 260 B3
Page Pl CT19 .... 335 D8
Page Rd CT18 .... 306 F3
Paget Gdns BR7 ....53 B8
Paget Rise SE18 .... 12 A7
Paget Row ME7 .... 64 C5
Paget St ME7 .... 64 C5
Paget Terr SE18 ....12 B8
Pagitt St ME4 ....63 E3
Paiges Farm Cl TN14 .. 187 C2
Paine Ave TN29 .... 376 C6
Painesfield Cl TN29 ... 352 C4
Pains Hill RH8 .... 183 C4
Painters Ash La DA11 .. 36 D5
Painters Ash Prim Sch
DA11 .... 36 D5
Painters Farm Camping &
Cvn Site ME13 .... 137 E3
Painter's Forstal Rd
ME13 .... 137 E3
Palace Ave ME15 ...... 162 A4
Palace Cl CT5 ....75 B2
Palace Cotts ME9 ..... 167 F8
Palace Ct
5 Bromley BR1 ....52 B8
Eltham SE9 ....11 F1
Gillingham ME5 .... 64 D2
Hythe CT21 .... 333 C2
Palace Gr BR1 ....52 B8
Palace Ind Est ME15 ... 195 F4
Palace Rd Bromley BR1 ...52 B8
Hill Park TN16 .... 151 A6
Palace St 17 CT1 ...... 143 A1
Palace View
Bromley BR1 ....52 B6
Lewisham SE12 .... 29 A6
Palace Wood Inf Sch
ME16 .... 161 C6
Palace Wood Jun Sch
ME16 .... 161 C6
Palewell Cl BR5 ....54 B7
Pallant Way BR6 .... 86 A7
Pallet Way SE18 ....11 E6
Palmar Cres DA7 .... 14 A5
Palmar Rd Bexley DA7 ... 14 A5
Maidstone ME16 .... 161 D6
Palmars Cross Hill
CT2 .... 142 A1
Palmarsh Ave CT21 .... 353 D7
Palmarsh Cres CT21 ... 353 D7
Palmarsh Prim Sch
CT21 .... 353 D8
Palmarsh Rd BR5 ...... 54 D5
Palm Ave DA14 .... 31 D2
Palm Bay Ave CT9 ...... 51 D3
Palm Bay Gdns CT9 .... 51 C3
Palm Bay Prim Sch
CT9 .... 51 D3
Palmbeach Ave CT21 .. 353 D8
Palm Ct CT8 .... 50 C1
Palmeira Rd DA7 .... 13 D4
Palmer Ave DA12 .... 37 D4
Palmer Cl CT6 .... 111 B8
Palmer Cres CT9 .... 83 C8
Palmer Rd CT3 .... 178 A8
Palmers Brook TN11 .. 190 F2
Palmers Green La
TN12 .... 257 D1
Palmers Orch TN14 ... 121 F8
Palmerston Ave
Broadstairs CT10 ....84 B3
Deal CT14 .... 215 C2
Palmerston Cres SE18 .. 12 C8
Palmerston Ct CT14 .. 215 D2
Palmerston Rd
Chatham ME4 ....63 F1
Dover CT16 .... 277 F4
Grays RM20 .... 17 D8
Orpington BR6 .... 86 C5
Palmerston St 4
CT19 .... 335 D6
Palmerston Wlk ME10 . 102 C4
Palmers Yd TN27 ...... 262 E5
Palm Tree Cl CT15 .... 245 D7
Palm Tree Way CT18 ... 305 B7
Palting Way CT20 ..... 335 B4
Pamela Ct ME7 .... 64 D5
Panbro Ho SE18 ....11 F6
Panfield Rd SE2 ....3 A3
Pankhurst Ave E16 ....1 B5
Pankhurst Ho SE18 ...... 12 A7
Pankhurst Rd ME3 ..... 41 D6
Pannell Dr CT18 ...... 306 F4
Pannell Rd ME3 .... 27 A6
Panteny La ME9 ...... 102 E2
Panter's BR8 ....32 F1
Pantheon Gdns TN23 .. 299 F5
Pantiles The Bexley DA7 ..13 F7
Bromley BR1 ....52 E6
20 Royal Tunbridge Wells
TN2 .... 286 A2
Panton Cl ME5 .... 97 C4
Pantyles The TN14 .... 186 B5
Paper La TN24 .... 300 F6
Papillons Wlk SE3 ...... 11 A4
Papion Gr ME5 ....96 E2
Papworth Cl 1 CT19 .. 335 A7
Parade CT1 .... 174 F8
Parade Rd CT20 ...... 334 F3
Parade The
Ashford TN24 .... 300 F5
Parade The *continued*
Birchington CT7 .... 80 D8
Crayford DA1 ....14 F2
Eastry CT13 .... 180 B2
Folkestone CT20 .... 335 E5
Gravesend DA12 .... 37 D6
Greatstone-on-S TN28,
TN29 .... 377 E7
Kemsing TN15 .... 122 E2
Margate CT9 ....50 I3
Meopham Station DA13 .. 60 A2
Rochester ME2 ....62 E8
Sittingbourne ME10 .... 101 F2
Staplehurst TN12 ...... 260 F3
Swanscombe DA10 ....17 F2
Paradise Cotts ME9 .....99 E5
Paradise Path SE28 ......3 A5
Paradise Pl 14 SE18 ......1 E2
Paradise CT11 .... 117 D7
Paradise Row CT13 .... 148 F1
Paragon Cl E16 ....1 A7
Paragon CT11 .... 117 E5
Paragon St CT11 ...... 117 D5
Paragon The SE3 .... 11 A5
Paraker Way CT21 ..... 334 B4
Parbrook Rd ME3 ....24 B2
Pardoner Cl CT2 ...... 174 C7
Pardoners Way CT16 .. 278 A3
Parfitt Way CT16 ..... 278 B2
Parham Cl CT1 .... 143 B2
Parham Ct CT1 .... 143 B2
Parham Rd
Canterbury CT1 .... 143 B2
Chatham ME4 ....63 F2
Paris Cnr TN26 .... 297 F6
Parish CE Prim Sch
BR1 .... 29 A1
Parish Gate Dr DA15 ....12 E1
Parish Rd
Chartham CT4 .... 173 C3
Minster (Sheppey) ME12 . 47 A6
Parish Wharf 5 SE18 .....1 E2
Park App DA16 ....13 B3
Park Ave
Birchington CT7 .... 81 A6
Broadstairs CT10 ....83 E2
Bromley BR1 .... 29 A2
Deal CT14 .... 215 C5
Dover CT16 .... 278 D1
Edenbridge TN8 .... 217 B2
Gillingham ME7 .... 64 D3
Gravesend DA12 .... 37 C7
Leysdown-on-S ME12 ... 49 G1
Maidstone ME17 .... 194 E2
Maidstone, Penenden Heath
ME14 .... 162 B6
Northfleet DA11 ....36 E7
Park Avenue Holiday
Village ME12 .... 49 G1
Park Ave Orpington BR6 .. 86 A8
Orpington BR6 ....87 B7
Queenborough ME11 .....46 B4
Sittingbourne ME10 .... 101 E1
Tonbridge TN11 .... 221 F5
West Thurrock RM20 .....17 B8
Whitstable CT5 ....74 F3
Park Barn Rd ME17 ... 197 C5
Park Chase CT10 ....83 E2
Park Cl CT18 .... 307 A4
Park Cliff Rd DA9 ...... 17 C3
Park Cl CT9 .... 51 D1
Park Corner Rd DA13 ...35 F4
Park Cotts
8 Hawkhurst TN18 ..... 341 A2
Preston CT3 .... 146 B6
Ramsgate CT11 ....83 E2
Sevenoaks TN13 .... 154 C2
Park Crescent Rd
Erith DA8 .... 14 D8
Margate CT9 .... 51 A1
Park Cres Chatham ME4 ...96 F8
Erith DA8 .... 14 D8
Park Ct ME13 .... 138 E7
Parkdale Rd SE18 ....2 E1
Park Dr Hothfield TN26 .. 267 A6
Longfield DA3 ....58 E6
Sittingbourne ME10 .... 101 D1
Woolwich SE7 ....11 E8
Parker Ave RM18 .... 19 C6
Parker Cl
Gillingham ME8 ....98 E5
Hamstreet TN26 .... 349 A7
Newham E16 ....1 E5
Parker Ho 4 SE18 ....2 B1
Parker Ind Ctr DA1 ..... 34 C7
Parker Pl CT18 .... 307 C5
Parker Rd RM17 ....17 F8
Parker's Cnr ME3 ....9 C2
Parker St E16 ....1 E5
Park Farm Cl
Folkestone CT19 .... 335 C8
Shadoxhurst TN26 ..... 299 A1
Tyler Hill CT2 .... 142 E6
Park Farm Houses
ME20 .... 160 B8
Park Farm Prim Sch
CT19 .... 335 C6
Park Farm Rd
Bromley BR1 .... 52 D8
Folkestone CT19 .... 335 C7
Ryarsh ME19 .... 126 F6
Parkfield DA3 ....58 E5
Parkfield Rd
Folkestone CT19 .... 335 C6
Rainham ME8 ....65 F1
Parkfield TN15 .... 154 F4
Parkfields ME2 .... 62 C7
Parkfield Way BR2 ......52 F4
Park Gate CT10 ....83 F2
Parkgate Cotts BR6 .... 88 C6
Parkgate Rd BR6 ...... 88 C6
Park Gdns DA8 ....4 D2
Park Gr Bexley DA7 ..... 14 C3
Park Gr *continued*
Bromley BR1 ....52 B8
Park Hill Bromley BR1 ....52 F5
Meopham Station DA13 ...59 F5
Park Hill Rd TN14 ..... 122 E2
Parkhill Rd Sidcup DA15 ..30 E5
Sidcup, Old Bexley DA5 ....31 F8
Park Ho Dover CT16 .... 278 D1
Maidstone ME14 .... 162 B6
Sevenoaks TN13 .... 154 C5
Sidcup DA14 .... 31 A3
Park House Cotts DA4 ...89 F5
Park House Gdns TN4 . 254 A2
Parkhurst Gdns 2 DA5 . 32 A8
Parkhurst Rd DA5 ...... 32 A8
Park La
Bethersden TN26 ...... 298 C8
Birchington CT7 .... 81 A6
Bishopsbourne CT4 ..... 209 C5
Elham CT4 .... 273 F5
Gill's Green TN17,TN18 .. 340 D7
Godden Green TN15 .... 155 A4
Kemsing TN15 .... 123 A1
Maidstone, Cock Stone
ME17 .... 195 D2
Maidstone, Ringlestone
ME14 .... 161 F7
Margate CT9 .... 51 A2
Parkland Cl TN13 ..... 187 D6
Parkland Ct CT10 ....83 F6
Parklands TN4 .... 285 E8
Park La
Sevenoaks TN13 .... 154 C3
Swanley Village BR8 ..... 56 C7
Park Lea CT14 .... 215 C5
Park Mall 2 TN24 ..... 268 B2
Park Manor ME7 ....64 B5
Park Mead DA15 ....13 B1
Park Mews
Chislehurst BR7 ....30 B2
6 Dover CT16 .... 310 D8
Parkmore BR7 ....30 B1
Park Par TN29 .... 366 C7
Park Place 8 BR1 ....52 B8
Park Pl
Ashford,Beaver TN23 ... 300 B7
Ashford,Willesborough
TN24 .... 300 F8
Dover CT16 .... 310 D8
Gravesend DA12 .... 37 C8
Herne CT6 .... 111 A8
Hever TN8 .... 250 D4
Margate CT9 ....50 I1
Sevenoaks TN13 .... 153 D4
Park Rd
Addington ME19 .... 126 C3
Ashford TN24 .... 268 D6
Broadstairs CT10 ....84 B6
Bromley BR1 ....52 B8
Chislehurst BR7 ....30 B2
Dartford DA1 .... 34 A8
Dover CT16 .... 278 B2
Dunk's Green TN11 .... 190 C5
Faversham ME13 ...... 138 D7
Folkestone CT19 .... 334 E6
Gravesend DA11 ....37 B7
Herne Bay CT6 ....76 F4
Hythe CT21 .... 333 B1
Leybourne ME19 ...... 127 D3
Limpsfield RH8 .... 183 A8
Littlestone-on-Sea TN28 . 373 E5
Marden Thorn TN12 .... 260 A4
Margate CT9 .... 51 A2
Mereworth TN12 .... 191 F5
Park Rd N TN24 ...... 268 B3
Park Rd Orpington BR5 .. 54 C4
Preston CT3 .... 146 D7
Queenborough ME11 .....45 F5
Ramsgate CT11 .... 117 C7
Royal Tunbridge
Wells,Southborough
TN4 .... 254 A2
Royal Tunbridge Wells
TN4 .... 286 B5
Sheerness ME12 .... 28 D1
Sittingbourne ME10 .... 101 E3
Swanley BR8 ....55 F5
Swanscombe DA10 ....17 E1
Temple Ewell CT16 .... 277 D5
Westgate-on-S CT7 ...... 81 D6
Park Road Ind Est BR8 ..55 F6
Parkside Ave
Bexley DA1,DA7 ....14 E5
Bromley BR1 ....52 E5
Tilbury RM18 ....19 B5
Parkside ME3 ....40 B7
Parkside Com Prim Sch
CT1 .... 143 D2
Parkside Cotts TN16 .. 150 E6
Parkside Cross DA7 .....14 E5
Parkside Ct
Herne Bay CT6 ....76 F5
Ramsgate CT11 .... 117 D7
Tenterden TN30 .... 344 F7
Park Side CT14 .... 215 C5
Parkside TN14 .... 120 F6
Parkside Lodge DA17 .....4 C1
Parkside Par DA1 ....14 F5
Parkside Pl CT1 .... 143 D3
Parkside Rd DA17 ....4 C2
Parkside DA14 ....31 B6
Park St Ashford TN24 ... 268 C2
Deal CT14 .... 215 D6
Dover CT16 .... 310 D8
Lydd TN29 .... 376 C6
Royal Tunbridge Wells
TN2 .... 286 C3
Park Terr
Sundridge TN14 .... 152 D3
Swanscombe DA9 ....17 B2
Throwley ME13 .... 169 D1
Woodnesborough CT13 .. 180 D7
Park The DA14 .... 31 A3
Park Vale TN24 .... 268 D6
Park View Cl
Edenbridge TN8 .... 217 B2
Goodnestone CT3 ...... 178 D2
Parkview Ct DA11 ...... 37 A6
Park View Ct
2 Lewisham SE12 ...... 29 C5
Maidstone ME15 .... 162 E1
Park View
Folkestone CT19 .... 335 E7
Hodsoll Street TN15 .... 92 C2
Margate CT9 .... 51 A2
Peasmarsh TN31 .... 367 B2
Park View Rd DA16 ..... 13 C4
Parkview Rd SE9 ....30 B6
Park View Rise CT15 ... 211 D4
Parkview TN2 .... 286 D4
Park View
Sevenoaks TN13 .... 154 C3
Sturry CT2 .... 143 F6
Park View Terr 2
TN30 .... 345 A7
Park Villas ME14 ...... 162 E4
Park Way ME17 .... 194 D3
Parkway DA18 ....3 E3
Park Way
Joyden's Wood DA5 ......32 E5
Maidstone ME15 .... 162 B1
Parkway Prim Sch DA18 ..3 E3
Park Way Prim Sch
ME15 .... 162 B1
Parkway The CT7 ....81 B7
Parkway TN10 .... 222 D5
Parkwood Cl CT10 ....83 F2
Park Wood Cl TN23 .... 300 B5
Parkwood Cl TN2 ..... 286 C6
Park Wood Forest Wlks★
TN26 .... 347 C4
Park Wood Gn ME8 .... 98 D5
Parkwood Hall Sch
BR8 ....56 B6
Parkwood TN31 .... 368 B4
Parkwood Inf Sch ME8 ..98 E5
Parkwood Jun Sch
ME8 ....98 E5
Park Wood La TN12 ... 261 C1
Park Wood Par ME15 .. 195 F5
Parkwood Rd TN16 .... 150 F6
Park Wood Rd CT2 .... 142 C4
Parkwood Rd DA5 ....31 F8
Park Wood Trad Est
Maidstone ME15 .... 195 F4
Otham ME15 .... 196 A4
Paroma Rd DA17 ....4 A3
Parr Ave ME7 .... 64 D6
Parr Ct DA10 ....35 E8
Parrock Ave DA12 ...... 37 C7
Parrock Rd DA12 .... 37 C7
Parrock St DA12 ....37 B8
Parrock The DA12 ..... 37 C7
Parrs Head Mews ME1 . 63 C6
Parry Ave E6 ....1 F7
Parry Pl SE18 ....2 B2
Parsonage Chase ME12 ..46 F5
Parsonage Cl TN4 ..... 285 B5
Parsonage Cotts ME9 . 134 A5
Parsonage Farm (Rural
Heritage Ctr)★ CT4 . 274 A6
Parsonage Farm
ME13 .... 169 F4
Parsonage Fields
CT12 .... 114 C7
Parsonage La
Cold Harbour ME9 ..... 100 F8
Lamberhurst TN3 ...... 317 B6
Rochester ME2 .... 63 C8
Sidcup DA14 ....31 F4
Sittingbourne ME9 ..... 101 A8
Sutton at H DA4 ....34 B2
Parsonage Manorway
DA17 .... 14 A8
Parsonage Oast CT12 .. 114 C7
Parsonage Rd
Herne Bay CT6 .... 77 A3
Rusthall TN4 .... 285 B5
West Thurrock RM20 .... 17 C8
Parsonage Stocks Rd
ME13 .... 169 F5
Parsonage Villas
CT15 .... 309 C5
Parson's Croft TN8 .... 250 C5
Parsons La Dartford DA2 .33 B5
Stansted TN15 ....91 E1
Partridge Ave ME20 ... 127 F3
Partridge Cl
Herne Bay CT6 .... 77 C3
1 Newham E16 ....1 D8
Partridge Dr
Orpington BR6 .... 86 C7
St Mary's Island ME4 .....41 B1
Partridge Gn SE9 ...... 30 A5
Partridge La ME13 .... 138 D7
Partridge Rd DA14 ......30 E4
Partridge Sq 3 E6 ....1 E8
Pasadena Cvn Pk TN15 ..90 B1
Pasley Rd ME4,ME7 ..... 64 A7
Pasley Rd E ME7 ....64 B7
Pasley Rd N ME4 ....64 B7
Pasley Rd W ME7 ...... 64 A7
Passey Pl SE9 ....11 F1
Passfield Ho SE18 ....2 D2
Passfield Path 13 SE28 ...3 B6
Pastens Rd RH8 .... 183 C4
Pastime Cl ME10 ...... 101 E8
Paston Cres SE12 ....29 B8
Pasture The
Ashford TN24 .... 268 D6
Hawkinge CT18 .... 307 B4
Patagonia Ho TN2 .... 286 C3
Pat Bassant Row DA10 ..35 E8
Patch The TN13 .... 153 E5
Patchways TN29 ...... 350 E3
Pat Drew Ho BR1 ...... 52 C8
Path Field Cotts CT15 . 308 E5
Patience Cotts TN14 .. 187 B2
Patricia Ct Bexley SE2 ....13 B7
Chislehurst BR7 .... 53 D8
Patricia Way CT10 ...... 83 D3
Patrixbourne Ave ME8 .. 65 C2
Patrixbourne Rd CT4 .. 176 B2
Pattenden Gdns TN12 . 225 A7
Pattenden La TN12 .... 259 C7
Pattens Gdns ME1 ......63 E2
Pattens La ME1,ME4 .....63 E1
Pattens Pl ME1 .... 63 D2
Patterdale Rd DA2 ..... 34 D7
Patterson Cl CT14 .... 215 A4
Patterson Ct DA1 ...... 16 A2
Pattinson Point 14 E16 ...1 A8
Pattison Farm Cl
TN25 .... 329 F4
Pattison Wlk SE18 ....2 C1
Paulinus Cl BR5 .... 54 C6
Paul's Pl 8 CT16 ...... 278 C1
Pavement The TN30 ... 324 B3
Pavilion Cl CT14 ...... 215 C8
Pavilion Ct CT20 ...... 335 E4
Pavilion Dr ME10 ....68 F1
Pavilion Gdns TN13 ... 154 C3
Pavilion La ME18 ...... 192 A8
Pavilion Mdw CT17 .... 277 E4
Pavilion Rd CT19 ...... 335 D6
Pavilion The 5 TN9 ... 222 B1
Pavings The ME17 ..... 164 C2
Paxton Ave CT18 ...... 306 F3
Paxton Ct 5 SE12 ...... 29 C5
Paxton Rd BR1 .... 29 A1
Payden St ME17 .... 200 D8
Payers Pk CT20 .... 335 D5
Paynes Cotts TN13 .... 121 D1
Paynesfield Rd
Tatsfield TN16 .... 150 D7
Tatsfield TN16 .... 150 D8
Payne's La ME15 ...... 195 B7
Pays La TN25 .... 202 D1
Pay St CT18 .... 306 F7
Payton Cl CT9 .... 83 A7
Payton Mews 4 CT1 .. 143 B1
Peace Cotts ME15 ..... 226 D7
Peace St SE18 .... 12 A8
Peach Croft DA11 ....36 E4
Peach Hall TN10 ...... 222 C6
Peacock Mews 7
ME16 .... 161 E4
Peacock Pl ME13 ...... 171 A6
Peacock Rise ME5 ...... 97 A4
Peacock St DA12 .... 37 C8
Peacock Wlk E16 ....1 B7
Peafield Wood Rd
CT4 .... 241 E4
Peak Dr CT13 .... 180 B3
Peal Cl ME3 ....41 E5
Pean Court Rd CT5 .... 108 D3
Pean Hill CT5 .... 108 D2
Peareswood Rd DA8 ....14 F6
Pearl Cl E6 ....2 A7
Pearl Way ME18 .... 159 C3
Pearmain Wlk CT1 .... 175 C7
Pearman Cl ME8 .... 66 A1
Pearse Pl TN3 .... 317 B5
Pearson's Green Rd
Paddock Wood,Mile Oak
TN12 .... 257 D5
Paddock Wood,Pearson's Green
TN12 .... 257 F3
Pearson's Way CT10 .....83 E7
Pearson Way DA1 ....33 F6
Pear Tree Alley 2
ME10 .... 101 E5
Pear Tree Ave ME20 ... 128 C1
Peartree Cl DA8 .... 14 D6
Pear Tree Cl
Broadstairs CT10 .... 83 C4
Cranbrook TN17 .... 320 D3
Swanley BR8 .... 55 D7
Peartree Cotts ME8 .....99 B8
Pear Tree La
Dymchurch TN29 ...... 352 D1
Gillingham ME7 ....97 E7
Peartree La DA12 ...... 39 A2
Pear Tree La ME15 .... 195 B6
Pear Tree Pl ME3 ....39 B3
Peartree Rd CT6 .... 77 C3
Pear Tree Row ME17 .. 196 B5
Peartree Way SE10 ....1 A2
Pear Tree Wlk ME9 .... 100 A5
Pease Hill TN15 ....91 F4
Peasley La TN17 ...... 318 D6
Peasmarsh CE Prim Sch
TN31 .... 367 B1
Peatfield Cl DA15 ....30 E5
Peat Way ME3 .... 10 D1
Pebble Hill Cotts RH8 . 183 B6
Peckham Cl ME2 .... 63 C8
Peckham Ct TN12 ..... 224 F6
Peckham Ho 6 BR5 .... 54 D1
Peckham Hurst Rd
TN11 .... 190 E7
Pedding Hill CT3 ...... 147 A1
Pedding La CT3 .... 179 A8
Pedham Place Est BR8 . 56 A4
Peel Dr ME10 .... 102 C4
Peelers Ct CT2 .... 142 F1
Peel Rd BR6 .... 86 C5
Peel St ME14 .... 162 A6
Peel Yates Ho 12 SE18 ...1 E2
Peene Cotts CT18 ..... 306 B1
Peens La ME17 .... 228 C7
Pegasus Ct DA12 .... 37 C5
Peggoty Cl ME3 ....39 B3
Pegley Gdns SE12 ..... 29 A6
Pegwell Ave CT11 .... 117 A5
Pegwell Bay Ctry Pk★
CT12 .... 116 C2
Pegwell Bay Nature
Reserve★ CT12 ...... 116 C3

Pegwell Cl CT11 117 A5
Pegwell Ct CT11 117 B5
Pegwell Rd CT11 117 B5
Pegwell St SE18 12 E7
Pelham Cotts DA5 32 B7
Pelham Ct 19 DA14 31 A5
Pelham Gdns CT20 335 A4
Pelham Prim Sch DA7 14 A4
Pelham Rd Bexley DA7 14 A4
Gravesend DA11 37 A8
Pelham Rd S DA11 36 F7
Pelham Terr 4 DA11 36 F8
Pelican Cl ME2 62 C6
Pelican Ct ME18 192 E7
Pell Cl TN5 337 A6
Pellipar Gdns SE18 1 F1
Pellipar Rd SE18 1 F1
Pells La TN15 124 A7
Pelwood Rd TN31 374 A2
Pemberton Ct CT21 334 B3
Pemberton Gdns BR8 55 E7
Pemberton Rd TN24 268 D2
Pemberton Sq 4 ME2 63 C8
Pemble Cl TN12 256 A7
Pembroke Ave CT9 50 F1
Pembroke ME4 64 B8
Pembroke Cl DA8 4 D2
Pembroke Ct
Chatham ME4 64 A4
Folkestone CT19 335 E6
1 Ramsgate CT11 117 E7
Pembroke Gdns ME8 98 E4
Pembroke Ho TN28 373 E5
Pembroke Lodge Mus & Art Gall CT7 80 F7
Pembroke Mews
TN28 373 C8
Pembroke Par DA8 4 C1
Pembroke Pl DA4 57 B8
Pembroke Rd
Bromley BR1 52 D7
Coxheath ME17 194 C3
Erith DA8 4 D2
Newham E6 1 F8
Sevenoaks TN13 154 B2
Tonbridge TN9 222 A1
Pembroke Rise ME4 64 A7
Pembury Cl TN2 287 D7
Pembury Cres DA14 31 E6
Pembury Ct 6 ME10 101 E4
Pembury Gdns ME16 161 D3
Pembury Grange TN2 287 A6
Pembury Gr TN9 254 C8
Pembury Hall Rd
TN11,TN2 255 C3
Pembury Hospl TN2 287 B7
Pembury Pl TN25 267 F4
Pembury Rd Bexley DA7 13 E8
Pembury TN11 255 A2
Royal Tunbridge Wells
TN2 286 E4
Tonbridge TN11,TN9 254 D7
Pembury Sch TN2 287 D8
Pembury St ME10 101 E4
Pembury Vineyard★
TN2 255 F1
Pembury Way ME8 65 E2
Pembury Wlks TN11,
TN2 255 C2
Penbury CT14 215 C1
Pencester Ct 8 CT16 310 E8
Pencester Rd CT16 310 D8
Pencroft Dr DA1 33 C8
Pendant Ct BR6 87 A5
Penda Rd DA8 14 B7
Pendennis Rd
Orpington BR6 87 C8
Sevenoaks TN13 154 B4
Penderel Mews TN30 345 B8
Pendlebury Gn SE18 11 E6
Pendragon Rd BR1,
SE12 29 A5
Pendragon Sch BR1 29 A5
Pendrell St SE18 12 D8
Pendrill Pl TN5 336 F5
Penenden Ct ME14 162 B7
Penenden Heath Rd
ME14 162 C7
Penenden DA3 91 F8
Penenden St ME14 162 A6
Penfield La ME9 135 A4
Penfold Cl Chatham ME5 97 B7
Maidstone ME15 195 E5
Penfold Gdns CT15 244 E5
Penfold Hill ME17 197 B8
Penfold Ho 14 SE18 12 B8
Penfold La DA5 31 D7
Penfold Rd CT19 335 F6
Penfolds Cl TN10 222 C5
Penfold Way ME15 194 F6
Penford Gdns SE9 11 D4
Pengarth Rd DA5 13 D1
Pengelly Pl CT2 142 F2
Penguin Cl ME2 62 D6
Penhale Cl BR6 87 A6
Penhall Rd SE7 1 D2
Penhill Rd DA5 31 C8
Penhurst Cl ME14 162 F5
Peninsular Park Rd SE7 1 A2
Penlee Cl TN8 217 C2
Penlee Point TN24 268 D5
Penmon Rd SE2 3 A3
Pennant Rd ME1 96 C7
Penn Cl ME10 102 B2
Penney Cl DA1 33 D8
Penn Gdns BR7 53 B7
Penn Hill TN23 299 E6
Pennine Way
Ashford TN24 268 B4
Bexley DA7 14 E6
Maidstone ME15 163 A1
Northfleet DA11 36 E5
Pennine Wlk TN2 286 D5
Pennington Cl CT2 144 C7
Pennington Manor 1
TN4 253 F2
Pennington Pl TN4 254 B1
Pennington Rd TN4 254 A2
Pennington Way SE12 29 B6
Penn La Bexley DA5 13 D1
Ide Hill TN14 185 E8
Penns Yd TN2 287 C6
Penny Cress Gdns
ME16 161 C3
Penny Cress Rd ME12 47 A4
Penn Yd TN2 287 C6
Pennyfields TN17 320 D4
Pennypot Ind Est
CT21 332 F1
Penny Pot La CT4 206 B4
Pennyroyal Ave E6 2 A7
Penny Spring Farm (Cvn Pk) ME14 131 B2
Penpool La DA16 13 B4
Penrith Ct ME7 65 A5
Penrose Ct CT21 333 C1
Penryn Manor 4 ME7 64 C6
Pensand Ho CT21 333 D1
Penshurst Ave DA15 13 A1
Penshurst CE Prim Sch
TN11 252 A4
Penshurst Cl
Canterbury CT2 143 A3
Gillingham ME8 65 E2
New Barn DA3 59 D7
West Kingsdown TN15 90 E4
Penshurst Enterprise Ctr
TN11 252 C4
Penshurst Gdns CT9 51 F2
Penshurst Place★
TN11 252 B4
Penshurst Rd
Bexley DA7 13 F6
Penshurst TN3,TN11 252 A5
Poundsbridge TN11,TN3 284 E8
Ramsgate CT11 117 F7
Penshurst Rise ME13 138 B8
Penshurst Sta TN11 219 F1
Penshurst Vineyard★
TN11 251 F2
Penshurst Way BR5 54 C5
Penstocks The ME15 161 D2
Pentagon Sh Ctr ME4 63 F4
Penton Ho 3 SE2 3 D4
Pentstemon Dr DA10 17 E2
Pent Vale Cl CT19 335 A6
Pent Valley Sch CT19 334 F7
Penventon Ct 3 RM18 19 A5
Pen Way TN10 222 E5
Pepingstraw Cl ME19 158 D7
Pepper Cl E6 1 F8
Pepperhill La DA11 36 C5
Pepper Hill DA11 36 C5
Pepys Ave ME12 28 B2
Pepys Cl
4 Dartford DA1 16 A3
Northfleet DA11 36 D5
Tilbury RM18 19 C6
Pepys Cres E16 1 A5
Pepys Rise BR6 53 F1
Pepy's Way ME2 62 F8
Perch La TN3 288 D1
Percival Rd BR6 86 B8
Percival Terr CT17 310 B7
Percy Ave CT10 51 F2
Percy Rd Bexley DA7 13 E5
Broadstairs CT10 83 F5
Margate CT9 51 A3
Ramsgate CT11 117 D8
Percy St 13 RM17 18 C8
Percy Terr TN4 286 A6
Peregrine Cl CT21 353 D8
Peregrine Ct DA16 12 F6
Peregrine Dr ME10 102 A2
Peregrine Rd ME19 159 A2
Peri Ct CT1 174 E6
Peridot Ct ME15 195 E5
Peridot St E6 1 E8
Perie Row 9 ME7 64 A6
Perimeter Rd
Dover CT16 310 G8
New Hythe ME20 128 C3
Periton Rd SE9 11 D3
Periwinkle Cl ME10 101 E5
Periwinkle Ct 3
ME10 101 E5
Perkins Ave CT9 82 F8
Perkins Cl DA9 16 F2
Perpins Rd SE9 12 E1
Perran Cl DA3 58 F5
Perries Mead CT19 335 B7
Perrot Way CT18 307 B5
Perry Court Rudolf Steiner Sch CT4 206 E7
Perryfield St ME14 161 F6
Perry Gr DA1 16 A3
Perry Hall Cl BR6 54 A2
Perry Hall Prim Sch
BR6 53 F3
Perry Hall Rd BR6 54 A2
Perry Hill ME3 22 C1
Perry Ho DA14 31 A3
Perry La CT3 146 C3
Perrys La BR6,TN14 120 C6
Perry St Chatham ME4 63 E3
Chislehurst BR7 30 E2
Crayford DA1 14 E4
Maidstone ME14 161 F6
Northfleet DA11 36 F7
Perry Street Gdns BR7 30 E2
Perry Wood Local Nature Reserve★ ME13 171 D4
Perth Gdns ME10 101 C4
Perth Ho 4 RM18 19 A5
Perth Way CT16 278 C3
Pescot Ave DA3 59 B6
Pested Bars Rd ME17 195 D5
Pested La TN25 203 C4
Petchart Cl ME2 62 C3
Petchell Mews 11 CT1 143 B2
Peterborough Gdns
ME2 62 C6
Peter Candler Way
TN24 268 E4
Peters Cl DA16 12 E5
Petersfield Dr DA13 92 F1
Petersfield TN2 287 E7
Petersham Dr BR5 54 A6
Petersham Gdns BR5 53 F7
Peter St Deal CT14 215 D7
Dover CT16 310 C8
Folkestone CT20 335 E5
5 Gravesend DA12 37 B8
Peterstone Rd SE2 3 B4
Petfield Cl ME12 47 C6
Petham Court Cotts
BR8 55 F4
Petham Gn ME8 65 C2
Petham Prim Sch CT4 207 C3
Petlands ME17 195 D5
Petrel Cl CT6 77 F4
Petrel Way CT18 307 A3
Petrie Ho 3 SE18 12 A8
Pett Bottom Rd CT4 208 C5
Petten Cl BR5 54 D1
Petten Gr BR5 54 D1
Petteridge La TN12 288 F7
Pettfield Hill Rd ME13 169 B1
Pett Hill CT4 175 F1
Pettits Row TN12 258 D8
Pett La TN27 234 D7
Pett Lane ME9 133 B7
Pettman Cl CT6 76 F3
Pettman Cres SE28,SE18 2 D3
Pettman Ct 5 CT10 83 E5
Pettmans Mews CT5 74 C2
Pett's Cres CT12 115 B5
Petts La CT3 178 A8
Pett St SE18 1 E2
Petts Wood Rd BR5 53 D4
Petts Wood Sta BR5 53 C4
Petworth Rd DA6 14 A2
Peverel Dr ME14 163 A5
Peverel Gn ME8 98 D4
Peverell Rd CT16 278 B4
Peverel E6 2 A7
Peveril Ct 15 DA2 16 B1
Pewter Ct CT1 174 F7
Phalarope Way ME4 41 C2
Pharos Dr CT16 278 E1
Pheasant Cl E16 1 B7
Pheasant La ME15 195 B8
Pheasant Rd ME4 64 C2
Pheasants' Hall Rd
CT4 208 F2
Phelps Cl TN15 90 E4
Philimore Cl SE18 2 E1
Philip Ave BR8 55 D5
Philip Corby Cl CT9 51 B2
Philipine Craft Ctr★
TN29 370 A6
Philipot Almshouse
SE9 11 F1
Philipot Path SE9 11 F1
Philippa Gdns SE9 11 D2
Phillippa Ho CT19 335 F6
Phillippa Ct ME10 101 E8
Phillip Rd CT19 334 E6
Phillips Cl DA1 15 B1
Phillips Ct ME8 65 B2
Phillips Rd CT7 81 A6
Philpots La TN11 220 E6
Philpott's Cross TN18 340 E2
Phineas Pett Rd SE9 11 E4
Phipps Ho 1 SE7 1 B1
Phoenix Com Prim Sch
TN24 268 D5
Phoenix Cotts ME18 192 D6
Phoenix Ct 11 ME7 64 C6
Phoenix Dr
Orpington BR2 85 D7
Wateringbury ME18 192 E7
Phoenix Ind Est ME2 63 D7
Phoenix Pk ME15 195 F4
Phoenix Pl DA1 33 D8
Phoenix Rd ME5 97 B2
Phoenix Yard Cotts
ME18 159 F1
Picardy Manorway DA17 4 B3
Picardy Rd DA17 4 A2
Picardy St DA17 4 A3
Piccadilly Apartments 4
ME5 64 B3
Pickelden La CT4 205 F8
Pickering Ct 20 DA2 16 B1
Pickering Ho 4 SE18 2 A2
Pickering St ME15 195 B6
Pickford Cl DA7 13 E5
Pickforde La TN5 338 D1
Pickford La DA7 13 E5
Pickford Rd DA7 13 E4
Pickhill Oast TN30 345 B4
Pickhurst La BR2 52 A1
Pickle's Way ME3 22 A6
Pickmoss La TN14 122 A3
Pickneybush La TN29 365 A7
Pickwick Cres ME1 63 C3
Pickwick Ct SE9 29 F7
Pickwick Gdns DA11 36 D5
Pickwick House DA11 36 D5
Pickwick Way BR7 30 C2
Picton Rd CT11 117 C7
Piedmont Rd SE18 2 D1
Pie Factory Rd CT15 211 E2
Pier Approach Rd ME7 64 D7
Pier Ave Herne Bay CT6 76 E4
Whitstable CT5 75 A2
Pierce Mill La TN11 224 C6
Piermont Pl BR1 52 E7
Pier Par 8 E16 2 A5
Pier Pl ME2 41 A3
Pierpoint Rd CT5 108 D7
Pier Rd Erith DA8 14 F8
Gillingham ME7 64 E7
Pier Rd Ind Est ME7 64 D7
Pier Rd Newham E16 2 A4
Northfleet DA11 18 F1
Swanscombe DA9 17 B3
Pierremont Ave CT10 84 A5
Pier The CT16 277 F8
Pier Way SE28 2 D3
Pigdown La TN8 250 D4
Pigeon La CT6 77 A2
Piggott's Cross TN8 218 D7
Pigsdean Rd DA13 61 B2
Pigtail Cnr ME12 47 E6
Pike Cl Bromley BR1 29 B3
Folkestone CT19 335 A7
New Hythe ME20 128 A4
Pikefields ME8 65 C2
Pikefish La TN12,ME18 225 F2
Pike Rd CT14,CT15 212 E4
Pikey La ME19 159 E5
Pilar Ct CT8 50 D1
Pilckem Cl CT1 143 D1
Pile La TN12 261 A5
Pilgrims Ct
Charing TN27 234 C7
Dartford DA1 16 A2
Greenwich SE3 11 A6
Pilgrims La CT4 172 E1
Pilgrims Lakes ME17 198 E6
Pilgrims La Titsey RH8 150 D3
Whitstable CT5 108 B4
Pilgrim Spring CT19 335 D8
Pilgrims Rd CT1 175 C7
Pilgrims' Rd DA10 17 E3
Pilgrims Rd
Upper Halling ME2 94 F6
Wouldham ME1 95 E5
Pilgrims View
Sandling ME14 129 E3
Swanscombe DA9 17 C1
Pilgrims Way
Boughton Aluph TN25 237 A4
Boxley ME14 130 E3
Pilgrims' Way TN25 303 E8
Pilgrims Way
Broad Street ME14,
ME17 164 C6
Canterbury CT1 175 C7
Charing TN27 234 E8
Pilgrim's Way Cotts
TN15 123 A2
Pilgrims Way
Cuxton ME2 62 C3
Dartford DA1 34 B8
Detling ME14 131 B1
Dover CT16 278 A3
Eccles ME20 129 B6
Pilgrims Way E TN14 122 D3
Pilgrims' Way TN16 151 B4
Pilgrims Way ME17 164 F3
Pilgrims' Way TN14,
TN15 123 C3
Pilgrims Way ME17 199 B7
Pilgrims Way Prim Sch
CT1 175 C7
Pilgrims Way
Thurnham ME14 163 E8
Upper Halling ME2,ME6,
ME19 94 D3
Vigo Village ME19 126 B7
Westwell TN25 235 D5
Pilgrims Way W TN14 121 E3
Pilgrims Way
Wrotham TN15 125 A3
Wrotham TN15 125 C4
Pilkington Rd BR6 86 C8
Pillar Box La
Crouch TN11 190 D5
Oldbury TN15 155 E5
Pilot Rd ME1 96 C8
Pilots Ave CT14 215 A4
Pilot's Farm Rd CT4 208 A4
Pilots Pl DA12 19 C1
Pimpernel Cl ME14 163 B4
Pimpernel Way ME5 96 E4
Pimp's Court Cotts
ME15 194 E6
Pimp's Court Farm Ctr
ME15 194 E6
Pinchbeck Rd BR6 86 F4
Pincott Rd DA6 14 A3
Pincroft Wood DA3 59 C6
Pincus Ho ME10 101 D5
Pine Ave DA12 37 D7
Pine Cl Larkfield ME20 128 A2
Swanley BR8 55 F5
Pine Cotts ME14 161 E8
Pinecrest Gdns BR6 86 B6
Pinecroft DA16 13 A7
Pine Glade BR6 85 F6
Pine Gr Edenbridge TN8 217 B2
Gillingham ME7 98 A5
Maidstone ME14 162 B6
Pineham Rd CT15 278 D6
Pine Ho
3 Chatham ME5 96 F5
5 Maidstone ME14 162 B4
Pinehurst
Chislehurst BR7 30 B2
Sevenoaks TN14 154 E6
Pinehurst Wlk 4 BR6 53 D1
Pine Lodge Ct CT14 215 B5
Pine Lodge ME16 161 C3
Pine Lodge Touring Pk
ME17 163 F2
Pineneedle La TN13 154 B4
Pine Pl ME15 161 E1
Pine Rd ME2 62 F6
Pine Ridge TN10 222 B6
Pine Rise DA13 60 A3
Pinesfield La ME19 126 B6
Pines Gardens The★
CT15 280 B5
Pineside Rd CT3 176 E8
Pines Rd BR1 52 E7
Pines The
Broadstairs CT10 83 D4
Canterbury CT1 175 A6
Pine Tree Ave CT2 142 E2
Pine Tree Cl CT7 81 B7
Pinetree Cl CT5 74 F3
Pine Tree La TN15 156 A2
Pine View TN15 157 C7
Pine Way CT19 334 D7
Pine Wlk CT6 77 E5
Pinewood Ave
Sevenoaks TN13 154 D6
Sidcup DA15 30 E7
Pinewood BR7 30 A2
Pinewood Cl
Orpington BR6 53 D1
Paddock Wood TN12 256 F6
Ramsgate CT12 83 C1
Pinewood Ct TN4 254 A1
Pinewood Dr
Chatham ME5 130 D8
Orpington BR6 86 E5
Pinewood Gdns TN4 254 A1
Pinewood Pl DA2 32 E6
Pinewood Rd
Bexley SE2 13 D8
Bromley BR2 52 A5
Royal Tunbridge Wells
TN2 286 D5
Pin Hill CT1 174 F7
Pinkham TN12 225 A5
Pinkham Gdns TN12 225 A6
Pinks Cnr CT12 115 D6
Pinks Hill BR8 55 E4
Pinnacle Hill DA7 14 B3
Pinnacle Hill N DA7 14 B3
Pinnacles The ME4 41 C1
Pinnell Rd SE9 11 D3
Pinners Hill CT15,CT3 211 C6
Pinners La CT15 211 C5
Pinnock La TN12 260 E1
Pinnock's Ave DA11 37 B7
Pintail Cl Grain ME3 27 B6
Newham E6 1 E8
Pintail Dr ME9 68 E3
Pintails The ME4 41 B1
Pintail Way CT6 77 C2
Pinton Hill TN5 338 B3
Pinto Way SE3 11 B3
Pioneer Bsns Pk CT11 117 C8
Pioneer Cotts TN11 252 A1
Pioneer Ct 5 DA11 19 A1
Pioneer Rd CT16 278 A3
Pioneer Way BR8 55 E6
Pipers Cl TN5 337 A4
Piper's Green Rd
TN16 185 B7
Pipers La TN16 185 A8
Pippenhall SE9 12 B1
Pippin Ave CT4 209 B8
Pippin Cl
Coxheath ME17 194 B2
Sittingbourne ME10 101 D6
Pippin Croft ME7 98 A6
Pippin Rd TN12 224 F6
Pippins The DA13 60 A3
Pippin Way ME19 159 A2
Pip's View ME3 22 F5
Pirbright Cl ME5 97 D2
Pirie St E16 1 B5
Pirrip Cl DA12 37 F6
Pitchfont La RH8 183 B8
Pitfield Cres SE28 3 A5
Pitfield Dr DA13 92 F7
Pitfield DA3 58 F5
Pitfold Cl SE12 11 B1
Pitfold Rd SE12 11 A1
Pit La TN8 217 C4
Pitstock Rd ME9 135 B5
Pittlesden Pl 1 TN30 345 A7
Pittlesden TN30 345 A7
Pittock Ho CT14 215 B3
Pitt Rd
Chartway Street ME17 197 A2
Maidstone ME16 161 B1
Orpington BR6 86 C6
Pittsmead Ave BR2 52 A2
Pittswood Cotts TN11 223 A8
Pivington La TN27 233 C2
Pivington Mill Ind Est
TN27 233 C2
Pixot Hill TN12 257 B2
Pix's La TN17 344 A3
Pixwell La CT14 214 D3
Pizien Well Rd ME18 192 B7
Place Farm Ave BR6 53 D1
Place La Hartlip ME9 99 D4
Woodchurch TN26 326 B3
Place The CT4 210 F1
Plain Cotts CT20 335 A4
Plain Rd
Brabourne Lees TN25 302 F5
Folkestone CT20 335 B4
Marden TN12 259 C4
Plains Ave ME15 162 C1
Plains of Waterloo
CT11 117 F7
Plain The TN17 318 E8
Plaistow Gr BR1 29 B1
Plaistow La BR1 52 C8
Plaistow Sq ME14 162 C6
Plane Ave DA11 36 D8
Plane Tree Ho SE7 1 D1
Plane Wlk TN10 222 C7
Plantagenet Ho SE18 1 F3
Plantation Cl
Hothfield TN26 267 A7
Plantation Cl *continued*
Stone DA9 16 F1
Plantation Dr BR5 54 D1
Plantation La ME14 163 A4
Plantation Rd Erith DA8 15 A6
Faversham ME13 138 C7
Gillingham ME7 65 A6
Hextable BR8 33 A2
Whitstable CT5 75 D2
Plantation The SE3 11 A5
Platt CE Prim Sch
TN15 157 C7
Platt Comm TN15 157 C7
Platters The ME8 98 C7
Plat The TN8 217 D1
Platt House La TN15 125 C6
Platt Ind Est TN15 157 C8
Platt Mill Cl TN15 157 B7
Platt Mill Terr TN15 157 B7
Platt's Heath Prim Sch
ME17 198 F2
Platt The Frant TN3 314 B1
Sutton Valence ME17 229 E7
Plaxdale Green Rd
TN15 124 D7
Plaxtol Cl BR1 52 C8
Plaxtol La TN15,TN11 189 D8
Plaxtol Prim Sch
TN15 189 E7
Plaxtol Rd DA8 14 A7
Playdell Ct 12 CT20 335 D4
Playden La TN31 368 C3
Playing Fields CT13 180 E7
Playstool Cl ME9 100 B6
Playstool Rd ME9 100 A6
Plaza Ct 7 ME10 102 A4
Pleasance Rd N TN29 377 E5
Pleasance Rd BR5 54 B6
Pleasance Road Central
TN29 380 D7
Pleasant Row 10 ME7 64 A6
Pleasant Valley La
ME15 194 B4
Pleasant View
15 Erith DA8 4 E1
Orpington BR6 86 C5
Pleasaunce Ct SE9 11 F3
Pleasent Pl ME12 46 E6
Pleasure House La
ME17 230 A8
Plenty Brook Dr CT6 76 F3
Plewis Ho ME7 64 E7
Pleydell Cres CT2 143 F7
Pleydell Gdns CT20 335 D4
Plimsoll Ave CT19 335 E8
Plomley Cl ME8 98 D4
Plough Cotts ME17 196 D2
Plough Ct CT6 77 D2
Plough Hill
Basted TN15 156 F4
Church Hougham CT15 309 C4
Plough La CT5 75 D3
Ploughmans Way
Ashford TN23 299 D5
Chatham ME5 97 A1
Gillingham ME8 98 E6
Plough Rd ME12 48 C5
Plough Wents Rd
ME17 196 B2
Plough Wlk TN8 217 C3
Plover Cl Chatham ME5 97 D1
Herne Bay CT6 77 F5
Marlpit Hill TN8 217 C3
Plover Rd
Hawkinge CT18 306 F3
Larkfield ME20 127 F2
Minster (Sheppey) ME12 47 A5
Plowenders Cl ME19 126 D2
Pluckley CE Prim Sch
TN27 265 D7
Pluckley Cl ME8 65 C3
Pluckley Gdns CT9 51 E2
Pluckley Rd
Bethersden TN26 297 D7
Charing TN27 234 B5
Hothfield TN26,TN27 266 B4
Smarden TN27 264 D2
Pluckley Sta TN27 265 C3
Plug La DA13 93 D5
Plumcroft Prim Sch
SE18 12 C8
Plumey Feather Cotts
TN6 311 E3
Plumford Rd ME13 138 A2
Plum La SE18 12 C7
Plummer La TN30 344 F6
Plummers Croft TN13 153 E6
Plumpton Wlk
5 Canterbury CT1 143 B1
9 Maidstone ME15 195 F6
Plumpudding La
ME13 107 E1
Plumstead Common Rd
SE18 12 C8
Plumstead High St SE18,
SE2 2 E2
Plumstead Manor Sch
SE18 12 D8
Plumstead Rd SE18 2 C2
Plumstead Sta SE18 2 D2
Plumstone Rd CT7 80 F1
Plum Tree Cotts TN18 354 E8
Plum Tree Gdns TN26 326 B1
Plumtree Gr ME7 98 A4
Plum Tree La ME9 132 B8
Plumtree Rd TN27 261 F7
Plumtrees ME16 161 A2
Plurenden Manor Farm Cotts TN26 325 D7
Plurenden Rd TN26 325 E7

Plymouth Dr TN13 .... 154 C3
Plymouth Pk TN13 .... 154 C3
Plymouth Rd
Bromley BR1 .... 52 B8
Newham E16 .... 1 A8
Plympton Cl 8 DA17 ..... 3 E3
Plymstock Rd DA16 .... 13 C7
Poachers Cl ME5 .... 97 C5
Pochard Cl ME4 .... 41 B1
Pochard Cres CT6 ...... 76 E3
Pocket Hill TN13 ...... 187 A7
Pococks Bank TN8 .... 218 C3
Podkin Wood ME5 .... 129 F8
Poets Cnr CT9 .... 50 J1
Poets Wlk CT14 ...... 215 C1
Pointer Cl SE28 .... 3 D7
Pointer Sch The SE3 .... 11 A7
Poison Cross CT13 .... 180 B4
Poldark Ct 22 CT11 .... 117 F7
Polebrook Rd SE3 ...... 11 C4
Polegate Cotts RM17 .... 17 E8
Polesden Rd TN2 ..... 286 D2
Polesteeple Hill TN16 . 118 D2
Poles The ME9 .... 66 E4
Polhill TN13,TN14 ...... 121 C4
Polhill Dr ME5 .... 96 F2
Police Station Rd
ME19 .... 159 C8
Pollard Cl
Ashford TN23 .... 299 F8
Newham E16 .... 1 A6
Pollard Ct ME7 .... 64 C5
Pollard Pl CT5 .... 108 C6
Pollards Oak Cres
RH8 .... 183 A3
Pollards Oak Rd RH8 .. 183 A3
Pollards Wood Hill
RH8 .... 183 B5
Pollards Wood Rd
RH8 .... 183 B4
Pollard Wlk DA14 ...... 31 C2
Polley Cl TN2 .... 287 D7
Pollyhaugh DA4 .... 89 E7
Polo Way CT5 .... 75 D1
Polperro Cl BR6 .... 53 F3
Polthorne Gr SE18 .... 2 D2
Polytechnic St 14 SE18 ... 2 A2
Pomfret Ho CT4 .... 173 D1
Pomfret Rd CT4 .... 173 D1
Pommeus La CT14 .... 247 D7
Poncia Rd TN23 ...... 300 A7
Pond Cl SE3 .... 11 A5
Pond Cotts
Herne Bay CT6 .... 77 D2
Sittingbourne ME10 .... 134 D8
Pond Dr ME10 .... 102 A2
Pond Farm Rd
Hucking ME17 .... 132 D1
Oad Street ME9 .... 100 F1
Pondfield La DA12 ...... 38 E1
Pondfield Rd BR6 ...... 86 B7
Pond Hill Adisham CT3 . 177 D1
Cliffe ME3 .... 22 B6
Pond Hill Rd CT20 .... 334 C5
Pond La
St Margaret's at Cliffe
CT15 .... 279 D7
Stone Street TN15 ...... 155 E2
Womenswold CT4,CT3 .. 210 D3
Pondmore Way TN25 .. 267 F4
Pond Path BR7 .... 30 B2
Pondwood Rise BR6 .... 53 E2
Pontefract Rd BR1 ..... 29 A3
Pontoise Cl TN13 ..... 153 F5
Ponycart La CT4 ...... 240 E3
Pook La TN27 .... 295 D3
Poona Rd TN1 .... 286 B2
Poorhole La CT10 ...... 83 B5
Pootings Rd TN8 ..... 217 E7
Poot La ME9 .... 66 E5
Pope Dr TN12 .... 260 E4
Pope House La TN30 .. 324 B4
Pope Rd BR2 .... 52 D4
Popes La
Limpsfield RH8 .... 216 A8
Sturry CT2 .... 143 F7
Popes Row Cotts
TN17 .... 317 F2
Pope St
Godmersham CT4 ...... 205 E4
Maidstone ME16 ...... 161 C2
Pope Street Ct SE9 ...... 29 F7
Popes Wood ME14 .... 162 F6
Poplar Ave
Gravesend DA12 .... 37 C4
Orpington BR6 .... 86 B8
Poplar Cl Ashford TN23 . 267 F3
Hoo St Werburgh ME3 .... 41 E3
Rochester ME2 .... 62 F5
Poplar Dr
Elvington CT15 .... 212 B2
Herne Bay CT6 .... 76 D2
Poplar Field TN30 .... 359 D4
Poplar Gr ME16 .... 161 C5
Poplar La TN29 .... 376 D7
Poplar Mount DA17 ...... 4 C2
Poplar Pl SE28 .... 3 C6
Poplar Rd
Broadstairs CT10 .... 83 E6
Ramsgate CT11 .... 117 D7
Rochester ME2 .... 62 E5
Wittersham TN30 ...... 359 D4
Poplars Cl DA3 .... 59 C6
Poplars TN26 .... 348 A7
Poplars The
Ashford TN23 .... 300 A7
Bethersden TN26 ...... 297 E5
Gravesend DA12 .... 37 E8
Hersden CT3 .... 111 F1
Poplar View ME13 ..... 139 E3
Poplar Wlk DA13 .... 60 B3
Poplicans Rd ME2 .... 62 B3
Poppy Cl Erith DA17 ...... 4 B4
Gillingham ME7 .... 64 E5
Maidstone ME16 ...... 161 D3
Poppyfield TN31 ...... 368 C1
Popsal La CT3 .... 178 B6
Porchester Cl
Hartley DA3 .... 58 F5
Loose ME15 .... 195 A6
Porchfield Cl DA12 ..... 37 C6
Porcupine Cl SE9 ...... 29 E6
Porrington Cl BR7 ..... 53 A8
Portal House Sch
CT15 .... 280 A6
Port Ave DA9 .... 17 B1
Port Cl Chatham ME5 ..... 97 B3
Maidstone ME14 ...... 163 A5
Portebello Ct CT14 ... 215 D7
Porter Cl
Minster (Sheppey) ME12 . 47 A6
West Thurrock RM20 .... 17 C8
Porter Rd E6 .... 1 F7
Porters Cl TN12 ...... 288 F6
Porter's La ME13 ..... 138 B2
Porters Wlk ME17 ..... 196 E4
Porters Wood TN12 ... 288 E6
Portery The CT14 ..... 215 D6
Porteus Ct DA1 .... 33 D6
Port Hill BR6 .... 120 B7
Porthkerry Ave DA16 ... 13 A3
Portland Ave
Gravesend DA12 .... 37 B6
Sidcup DA15 .... 13 A1
Sittingbourne ME10 ... 102 C4
Portland Cl
Ashford TN24 .... 268 C7
Hythe CT21 .... 333 B2
Tonbridge TN10 ...... 222 D7
Portland Cres SE9 ...... 29 E6
Portland Ct
3 Hythe CT21 .... 333 B2
Ramsgate CT11 ...... 117 E7
Portland Pl 1 ME6 .... 128 A8
Portland Rd
Bromley,Mottingham SE9 .. 29 E6
Bromley,Sundridge BR1 .. 29 C3
Gillingham ME7 .... 64 E6
Gravesend DA12 .... 37 B7
Hythe CT21 .... 333 B2
Northfleet DA11 .... 18 D1
Wouldham ME1 .... 95 C4
Portland St 1 ME4 ...... 64 B2
Portland Terr
Ripple CT14 .... 247 D8
Sheerness ME12 .... 28 C2
Portland Villas DA12 ..... 37 B7
Portlight Pl CT5 ...... 108 A6
Port Lympne Wild Animal
Pk★ CT21 .... 331 D2
Portman Cl Bexley DA7 ... 13 E4
Maypole DA5 .... 32 E7
Portman Pk TN9 ...... 222 C3
Portmeadow Wlk SE2 ..... 3 D4
Portobello Par TN15 .... 91 A2
Portree Mews ME7 ...... 64 E3
Port Rise ME4 .... 63 F3
Portsdown Cl ME16 ... 161 B2
Portsea Rd RM18 .... 19 C6
Portsmouth Cl ME2 ..... 62 D6
Portsmouth Mews E16 ... 1 B5
Port Victoria Rd ME3 .... 27 C4
Portway Gdns SE18 .... 11 D7
Portway Rd ME3 .... 40 B7
Portway CT5 .... 108 C8
Post Barn Rd ME4 ...... 63 F2
Postern La TN9,TN11 ... 222 E1
Postley Commercial Ctr
ME15 .... 162 A2
Postley Rd ME15 ..... 162 A1
Postling TN23 .... 267 E1
Postling Rd CT19 ..... 334 E7
Postling Wents CT21 .. 332 F8
Postmill Dr ME15 ..... 161 F1
Post Office Rd 12
TN18 .... 340 F2
Post Office Row CT4 .. 171 D1
Post Office Sq TN1 .... 286 A3
Potash La TN15 ...... 157 C6
Pot Kiln La TN26 ..... 296 E4
Potten Street Rd CT7 .... 79 E3
Potteries The ME9 ...... 66 E3
Potters Cl TN24 ...... 267 E6
Potters Cnr TN24 ..... 267 E6
Potter's La TN18 ..... 341 A6
Potter St CT13 .... 149 A1
Pottery Cotts TN25 ... 269 E5
Pottery Rd
Coldblow DA5 .... 32 C6
Hoo St Werburgh ME3 ... 41 D5
Potyn Ho ME1 .... 63 C4
Pouces Cotts CT12 ...... 81 F1
Poulders Gdns CT13 ... 180 E8
Poulders Rd CT13 .... 180 E8
Poulsen Ct 8 ME10 ... 102 B4
Poulters Wood BR2 .... 85 D5
Poulton Cl CT17 ...... 309 F8
Poulton Close Bsns Pk
CT17 .... 277 E1
Poulton La CT3 .... 179 C8
Pound Bank Cl TN15 .... 90 F2
Pound Cl BR6 .... 86 D8
Pound Court Dr BR6 .... 86 D8
Pound Ct TN23 .... 300 A3
Pound Farm Cotts
CT18 .... 334 A7
Poundfield Rd TN18 ... 356 B5
Pound Green Ct 4
DA5 .... 32 A8
Pound Ho
Ashford TN23 .... 300 B8
Hadlow TN11 .... 223 E8
Poundhurst Rd TN26 .. 328 C3
Pound La Ashford TN23 . 299 F4
Brabourne Lees TN25 ... 302 F5
Canterbury CT1 .... 142 F1
Elham CT4 .... 273 F4
Halstead TN14 .... 120 D4
Molash CT4 .... 203 F4
Sevenoaks TN13 ...... 154 C3
Pound Park Rd SE7 ...... 1 D2
Pound Pl SE9 .... 12 A1
Pound Rd TN12 .... 224 F6
Poundsbridge Hill
TN11,TN3 .... 284 D7
Poundsbridge La
TN11 .... 252 D2
Pounsley Rd TN13 .... 153 E6
Pout Rd ME6 .... 127 F7
Poverest Prim Sch BR5 . 54 A4
Poverest Rd BR5 .... 54 A4
Povey Ave ME2 .... 40 C2
Powdermill Cl TN4 .... 286 C8
Powder Mill La
Dartford DA1 .... 33 F6
Leigh TN11 .... 221 B1
Royal Tunbridge Wells
TN4 .... 286 B8
Tonbridge TN11 ...... 221 E2
Powell Ave DA2 .... 34 E6
Powell Cl ME20 .... 129 A3
Powell Cotton Dr CT7 ... 81 B6
Powell-cotton Mus★
CT7 .... 81 B5
Powell Sch The CT16 .. 278 B4
Power Ind Est DA8 ..... 15 A6
Powerscroft Rd DA14 ... 31 C2
Power Station Rd
Grain ME3 .... 27 B4
Halfway Houses ME12 .... 46 E7
Powis St SE18 .... 2 A3
Powlett Rd ME2 .... 40 C1
Powster Rd BR1 .... 29 B3
Powys Cl DA7 .... 13 D8
Poynder Rd RM18 .... 19 B6
Poynings Cl BR6 .... 87 C8
Poyntell Cres BR7 ..... 53 D8
Poyntell Rd TN12 ..... 260 F4
Pragnell Rd SE12 .... 29 B6
Prall's La TN12 ...... 256 E2
Pratling St ME20 ..... 129 C4
Pratts Bottom Prim Sch
TN14 .... 120 C8
Precincts The CT1 .... 175 A8
Premier Bsns Ctr ME4 .. 64 C1
Premier Par ME20 .... 128 E1
Prentis Cl ME10 ...... 101 C5
Prentis Quay ME10 ... 101 F5
Prentiss Ct SE7 .... 1 D2
Prescott Ave BR5 .... 53 B3
Prescott Cl CT15 ..... 278 E6
Prescott Ho TN28 .... 373 A7
Presentation Ho 9
DA12 .... 37 B8
Prestbury Sq SE9 ...... 29 F4
Prestedge Ave CT11 ..... 83 E2
Preston Ave
Faversham ME13 ..... 138 E6
Gillingham ME7 .... 64 E1
Preston Ct
Faversham ME13 ..... 138 D6
Sidcup DA14 .... 30 F4
Preston Dr DA7 .... 13 D6
Preston Gr ME13 ..... 138 D6
Preston Hall Gdns
ME12 .... 49 E4
Preston Hall Hospl
ME20 .... 128 F1
Preston Hill CT3 ..... 146 B1
Preston Ho
Sutton at H DA4 .... 57 D7
1 Woolwich SE18 .... 2 A2
Preston La
Faversham ME13 ..... 138 D6
Preston CT3 .... 146 B5
Preston Malt Ho
ME13 .... 138 D6
Preston Par CT5 ..... 107 F7
Preston Pk ME13 ..... 138 D6
Preston Prim Sch
CT3 .... 146 C6
Preston Rd
Manston CT12 .... 82 E2
Northfleet DA11 .... 36 E7
Stourmouth CT3 ...... 113 D1
Tonbridge TN9 .... 222 A1
Wingham CT3 .... 146 B3
Prestons Rd BR2 ...... 85 A8
Preston St ME13 ..... 138 D7
Preston Way ME8 .... 65 B2
Prestwood Cl SE18 ..... 13 A8
Pretoria Ho
4 Erith DA8 .... 14 E7
8 Maidstone ME15 .... 195 E5
Pretoria Rd
Canterbury CT1 .... 175 B8
Chatham ME4 .... 63 F2
Gillingham ME7 .... 64 D3
Prettymans La TN8 ... 217 F4
Price's Ave Margate CT9 .. 51 B2
Ramsgate CT11 ...... 117 C6
Prices Ct 5 ME10 .... 102 B4
Pridmore Rd ME6 .... 127 F8
Priest Ave CT2 .... 174 C7
Priestdale Ct ME4 ...... 63 E3
Priestfield Rd ME7 ..... 64 E5
Priest Fields CT6 .... 77 F5
Priestfields ME1 .... 63 B3
Priestfield Stad
(Gillingham FC) ME7 ... 64 E5
Priest Hill RH8 .... 183 B6
Priestlands Park Rd
DA15 .... 30 F5
Priestley Dr
Lunsford ME20 .... 127 F4
Tonbridge TN10 ...... 222 E7
Priest & Sow Cnr CT5 ... 75 B3
Priest's Wlk DA12 ...... 38 A6
Priest Wlk CT5 .... 75 C3
Priestwood Rd DA13 ... 93 C5
Primmett Cl TN15 ...... 90 E4
Primrose Ave ME8 ...... 98 B5
Primrose Cl ME4 .... 96 E7
Primrose Dr
Aylesford ME20 ...... 128 D1
Kingsnorth TN23 ..... 300 B4
Primrose Gr ME9 .... 134 A6
Primrose Hill CT4 .... 173 B7
Primrose Ho 10 ME15 . 195 E7
Primrose La ME9 .... 134 A6
Primrose Pl CT17 .... 278 B1
Primrose Rd
Dover CT17 .... 278 A1
Upper Halling ME2 ...... 94 E5
Primrose Terr DA12 .... 37 C7
Primrose Way
Cliffs End CT12 .... 116 C5
Whitstable CT5 .... 75 C1
Primrose Wlk TN12 ... 257 A5
Prince Andrew Rd
CT10 .... 83 E7
Prince Arthur Rd ME7 ... 64 B6
Prince Charles Ave
Chatham ME5 .... 97 B4
Minster (Sheppey) ME12 . 47 C6
Sittingbourne ME10 ... 102 C3
Sutton at H DA4 .... 57 D7
Prince Charles Rd
CT10 .... 83 E7
Prince Consort Dr BR7 . 53 D8
Prince Henry Rd SE7 ... 11 D7
Prince Imperial Rd
Chislehurst BR7 .... 30 B1
Woolwich SE18 .... 11 F6
Prince John Rd SE9 .... 11 E2
Prince Michael of Kent Ct
DA1 .... 15 A5
Prince of Wales Rdbt
CT17 .... 310 D6
Prince Of Wales Rd
SE3 .... 11 A6
Prince Of Wales
Residential Pk CT21 .. 353 E8
Prince Of Wales Terr
CT14 .... 215 D5
Prince Phillip Lodge The
ME20 .... 128 F1
Prince Regent La E16 .... 1 C7
Prince Regent Sta E16 ... 1 C6
Prince Rupert Rd SE9 ... 11 F3
Princes Ave
Chatham ME5 .... 97 B5
Dartford DA2 .... 34 B7
Minster (Sheppey) ME12 . 47 D7
Orpington BR5 .... 53 E4
Prince's Ave CT12 .... 83 B1
Princes Cl
Birchington CT7 .... 80 D7
Sidcup DA14 .... 31 D5
Princes Cres 10 CT9 .... 50 J2
Princes Dr CT13 ..... 182 A8
Princes Gate 18 CT20 . 335 E5
Prince's Gdns CT9 ..... 51 C2
Princes Par CT21 .... 333 E2
Prince's Plain BR2 ..... 52 E1
Princes Plain Prim Sch
BR2 .... 52 E2
Princes Rd Dartford DA1 . 33 D7
Dartford,Fleet-Downs
DA1 .... 34 C7
Gravesend DA12 .... 37 C5
Hextable BR8 .... 33 A2
Prince's Rd CT11 ..... 117 D8
Princess Alice Way
SE28 .... 2 D4
Princess Anne Rd CT10 .. 83 E7
Princess Cl Erith SE28 .... 3 D7
Whitstable CT5 .... 75 C3
Princess Margaret Ave
Margate CT9 .... 51 E2
Ramsgate CT12 .... 83 A1
Princess Margaret Rd
RM18 .... 20 D7
Princess Mary Ave
ME4 .... 64 B7
Princess Par BR6 ...... 86 A7
Princess Rd CT5 .... 75 C3
Princess Royal University
Hospl BR6 .... 86 A6
Princess St Bexley DA7 ... 13 F4
Folkestone CT19 ...... 335 E6
Princes St Deal CT14 ... 215 D7
11 Dover CT16 .... 310 D7
Gravesend DA11 .... 19 B1
Maidstone ME14 ...... 162 A5
Prince's St Margate CT9 .. 50 J2
9 Ramsgate CT11 .... 117 E6
Rochester ME1 .... 63 C4
Royal Tunbridge Wells
TN2 .... 286 C3
Princes Terr CT21 ..... 332 F1
Princes View DA1 ...... 34 A7
Princes Way
Canterbury CT2 .... 142 E1
Detling ME14 .... 131 A1
Prince's Wlk CT9 .... 51 D3
Prince William Ct
CT14 .... 215 D7
Prinys Dr ME8 .... 98 C4
Priolo Rd SE7 .... 1 C1
Prioress Cres DA9 ...... 17 C3
Prioress Rd CT2 ..... 174 D8
Prioress Wlk CT16 .... 278 A3
Prior Rd TN28 .... 377 E8
Priorsdean Cl ME16 .. 160 E1
Priorsford Ave BR5 ..... 54 B5
Priors Heath TN17 .... 318 C2
Prior's Lees 8 CT20 .. 335 D4
Prior's Way TN8 ..... 282 A6
Priory Ave BR5 .... 53 D3
Priory Cl
Broadstairs CT10 .... 83 F3
Bromley BR7 .... 52 F8
Dartford DA1 .... 15 D2
East Farleigh ME15 .... 194 B8
New Romney TN28 .... 372 F6
Priory Ct
5 Dartford DA1 .... 15 D1
Gillingham ME8 .... 65 A2
Leysdown-on-S ME12 .... 49 G1
Rochester ME1 .... 63 D5
Priory Ctr The DA1 ..... 33 E8
Priory Dr SE2 .... 3 D1
Priory Fields DA4 ...... 89 F8
Priory Fields Sch
CT17 .... 310 B8
Priory Gate 4 ME14 .. 162 A5
Priory Gate Rd CT17 .. 310 C8
Priory Gdns
Canterbury CT1 ...... 175 A6
Dartford DA1 .... 15 D2
Folkestone CT20 ..... 335 D4
Priory Gdns★ BR6 ..... 54 B2
Priory Gr
Aylesford ME20 ...... 128 D1
Dover CT17 .... 310 C8
Tonbridge TN9 .... 254 B8
Priory Hill Camp ME12 .. 49 H1
Priory Hill Dartford DA1 . 15 D1
Dover CT17 .... 310 C8
Priory Ho Dover CT17 .. 310 C7
4 Greenwich SE7 ...... 11 C8
Priory Hospl Hayes Grove
The BR2 .... 85 A8
Priory Inf Sch CT11 ... 117 D7
Priory La Eynsford DA4 ... 56 F1
Herne Bay CT6 .... 77 A3
Sellindge TN25 .... 303 D4
Priory Leas SE9 .... 29 E7
Priory Mews DA2 ...... 34 C8
Priory of St Jacob
CT1 .... 174 E6
Priory Pl Dartford DA1 ... 15 D1
Faversham ME13 ..... 105 C1
Priory Rd
Aldington Frith TN25 .... 329 C4
Dartford DA1 .... 15 D1
Dartford DA1 .... 15 D2
Dover CT16,CT17 ..... 310 D8
Faversham ME13 ..... 138 C8
Gillingham ME8 .... 65 A2
Maidstone ME15 ...... 162 A3
Ramsgate CT11 ...... 117 D6
Rochester ME2 .... 63 A6
Tonbridge TN9 .... 254 C8
Priory Retail Pk DA1 ... 15 D2
Priory Row ME13 ..... 138 C8
Priory Sch The BR5 .... 54 C1
Priory Station Approach Rd
CT17 .... 310 C7
Priory St
10 Dover CT16 .... 310 D8
Tonbridge TN9 .... 254 B8
Priory The TN29 ..... 376 C6
Priory Way TN30 ..... 345 C7
Priory Wlk TN9 ...... 254 B8
Pristling La TN12 .... 292 B8
Pritchard Ct ME7 ...... 64 C3
Pritchard Dr CT18 .... 307 A4
Probyn Mews CT18 ... 306 F3
Proctor Wlk CT18 .... 306 F4
Progress Est The
ME15 .... 196 A4
Promenade
Birchington CT7 .... 80 F8
Deal CT14 .... 215 D3
Promenade The ME12 .. 49 G2
Prospect Ave ME2 ...... 63 B8
Prospect Cl Erith DA17 ... 4 A2
Westgate-on-S CT8 ...... 81 E7
Prospect Cotts
Boughton Lees TN25 ... 236 E3
Harbledown CT2 ...... 141 E1
Lamberhurst TN3 ..... 317 A3
Pratt's Bottom BR6 ..... 87 C2
Shepherdswell CT15 ... 244 D4
Prospect Ct 20 CT11 .. 117 E6
Prospect Gdns CT12 .. 115 B7
Prospect Gr DA12 ...... 37 D8
Prospect Hill CT6 ...... 77 A5
Prospect Mews CT21 .. 333 C2
Prospect Pk TN4 ..... 253 F1
Prospect Pl
7 Broadstairs CT10 ..... 84 B4
Bromley BR2 .... 52 B6
Canterbury CT1 ...... 175 A7
Collier Street TN12 ... 226 C2
Dartford DA1 .... 15 F1
Dover CT17 .... 278 B1
Eastling ME13 .... 168 E6
Gravesend DA12 .... 37 D8
Grays RM17 .... 18 B8
Hamstreet TN26 ...... 348 F7
Maidstone ME16 ...... 161 E3
St Nicholas at Wade CT7 .. 79 E1
Prospect Rd
Birchington CT7 .... 80 F7
Broadstairs CT10 .... 84 B4
Folkestone CT20 ..... 334 D3
Hythe CT21 .... 333 C2
Minster (Thanet) CT12 .. 115 B6
Royal Tunbridge
Wells,Camden Park TN2 286 C3
Royal Tunbridge Wells
TN4 .... 285 F8
Sevenoaks TN13 ...... 154 C4
Prospect Row
Chatham ME4 .... 64 A3
Chatham ME7 .... 64 A6
Prospect Terr
Elham CT4 .... 273 F4
21 Ramsgate CT11 .... 117 E6
Prospect Vale SE18 ...... 1 E2
Prospect Way TN25 ... 302 E5
Prospero Ho 7 DA17 ..... 4 A1
Provender La ME13,
ME9 .... 137 A6
Provender Way ME14 .. 162 E5
Providence Chapel
TN12 .... 259 C6
Providence Cotts
Groombridge TN3 ..... 312 C7
Higham ME3 .... 39 B2
Providence Pl TN27 ... 262 A7
Providence St
Ashford TN23 .... 300 C8
Stone DA9 .... 17 A2
Prudhoe Ct 27 DA2 ..... 16 B1
Puckle La CT1 .... 175 A6
Pucknells Cl BR8 ...... 55 C8
Puddingcake La TN17 . 344 C5
Pudding La Ash CT3 ... 147 D1
Maidstone ME14 ...... 161 F4
Seal TN15 .... 154 F6
Pudding Rd ME8 .... 98 F8
Puddledock La
Hextable BR8,DA2 .... 32 F2
Toy's Hill TN16 .... 185 A3
Puffin Ct CT18 .... 307 A3
Puffin Rd Grain ME3 ..... 27 B5
Herne Bay CT6 .... 77 F4
Pullington Cotts TN17 . 342 E6
Pullman Cl CT12 ..... 117 C8
Pullman Mews SE12 .... 29 B5
Pullman Pl SE9 .... 11 E2
Pump Cl ME19 .... 127 D1
Pump La Chelsfield BR6 .. 88 B5
Gillingham ME7,ME8 .... 65 D3
1 Margate CT9 .... 50 J2
Pump Terr TN1 .... 286 B4
Punch Croft DA3 .... 91 E7
Purbeck Rd ME4 .... 63 E3
Purcell Ave TN10 .... 222 F6
Purchas Ct CT2 ...... 142 C4
Purchase La TN26 .... 298 E8
Purfleet By-Pass RM19 . 16 D8
Purland Rd SE28 .... 2 F4
Purneys Rd SE9 .... 11 D3
Purrett Rd SE18 .... 2 F1
Purr Wood CT4 ...... 205 B2
Purser Way ME7 ...... 64 C7
Pursey Cl TN15 .... 90 E4
Puttenden Rd TN11 ... 189 F3
Puttney Dr ME10 .... 102 A8
Pye Alley La CT5 ..... 108 C3
Pym Ho TN27 .... 234 D7
Pym Orch TN16 ...... 152 C3
Pynham Cl SE2 .... 3 B3
Pynson's Ind Est CT10 .. 83 D4
Pyott Mews 3 CT1 .... 143 B1
Pyrus Cl ME5 .... 130 A8
Pyson's Rd CT10,CT12 ... 83 D3
Pyson's Road Ind Est
CT10 .... 83 D3

Q

Quadrant The DA7 ...... 13 D7
Quaggy Wlk SE3 .... 11 A3
Quain Ct CT20 .... 335 C4
Quaker Cl TN13 ...... 154 D4
Quaker Dr TN17 ...... 320 D6
Quaker La TN17 ...... 320 D6
Quakers Cl DA3 .... 58 E6
Quaker's Hall La
TN13 .... 154 C5
Quantock Cl TN2 ..... 286 D5
Quantock Dr TN24 .... 268 B4
Quantock Gdns CT12 ... 83 B3
Quantock Rd DA1 ...... 14 E5
Quarries The ME17 .... 195 C4
Quarrington La TN25 .. 302 B8
Quarry Bank TN9 ..... 254 A7
Quarry Cotts
Rockrobin TN5 .... 336 D7
Sevenoaks TN13 ...... 154 A4
Stone in Oxney TN30 .... 360 C3
Quarry Hill Par 3
TN9 .... 254 B8
Quarry Hill Rd
Borough Green TN15 ... 156 F6
Tonbridge TN9 .... 254 B8
Quarry Hill TN15 ..... 154 D4
Quarry Rd Hythe CT21 .. 333 B3
Maidstone ME15 ...... 162 A2
Royal Tunbridge Wells
TN1 .... 286 B5
Quarry Rise TN9 ..... 254 A7
Quarry Sq ME14 ..... 162 A5
Quarry View TN23 .... 299 D7
Quarry Wlk CT21 ..... 334 A3
Quarry Wood TN25 .... 330 A6
Quarry Wood Ind Est
ME20 .... 160 E8
Quay Cotts ME9 ...... 103 E6
Quay Ct CT5 .... 74 E2
Quay La
Faversham ME13 ..... 138 D8
Sandwich CT13 ...... 149 A1
Swanscombe DA9 .... 17 B3
Quayside ME4 .... 64 B8
Quay The ME9 .... 103 E6
Quebec Ave TN16 .... 151 D1
Quebec Cotts 9
TN16 .... 151 D1
Quebec Ho★ TN16 ... 151 D1
Quebec Rd RM18 .... 19 A5
Quebec Sq 10 TN16 ... 151 D1
Queen Anne Ave BR2 ... 52 A6
Queen Anne Gate DA7 .. 13 D4
Queen Anne Rd ME14 . 162 B4
Queen Bertha Rd
CT11 .... 117 C6

Queen Bertha's Ave
CT7 .... 81 C8
Queenborough Dr
ME12 ....47 B7
Queenborough Fst Sch
ME11 ....46 B5
Queen Borough Gdns
BR7 .... 30 D2
Queenborough Rd
Halfway Houses ME12 .. 46 C6
Queenborough ME12 .. 46 C4
Queenborough Sta
ME11 .... 46 A5
Queenbridge Ind Pk
RM20 .... 17 A8
Queendown Ave ME8 .98 D5
Queendown Rd CT7 .. 82 A3
Queen Elizabeth Ave
CT9 .... 51 D1
Queen Elizabeth Military
Hospl The SE18 .....11 E7
Queen Elizabeth Rd
CT16 .... 310 F8
Queen Elizabeth's Gram
Sch ME13 .... 138 D8
Queen Elizabeth Sq
ME15 .... 195 D6
Queen Elizabeth the Queen
Mother Hospl CT9 ..82 F8
Queen Mary's Hospl
DA14 .... 31 A2
Queen Mother Ct
CT14 .... 215 D2
Queen Mother Ct The
ME1 ....63 B4
Queen's Ct CT6 .... 77 A4
Queen's Lea CT15 .. 308 E5
Queen's Ave
Birchington CT7 ...... 80 D7
Broadstairs CT10 ....84 B6
Queens Ave
Canterbury CT2 .... 142 E1
Dover CT17 .... 310 A7
Folkestone CT20 ... 334 B6
Herne Bay CT6 ..... 77 D5
Queen's Ave
Maidstone ME16 .... 161 D5
Margate CT9 ....50 I1
Ramsgate CT12 .... 83 B1
Snodland ME6 ..... 128 A8
Queensbridge Dr CT6 . 76 C4
Queens Cotts TN5 .. 336 E6
Queenscroft Rd SE9 .. 11 D1
Queens Ct
Ashford TN24 ...... 268 C3
Edenbridge TN8 .... 217 D1
Gillingham ME8 ...... 99 A8
[11] Hawkhurst TN18 .. 341 A2
Hythe CT21 .... 333 B1
Margate CT9 .... 51 A3
[1] Sidcup DA14 ..... 31 A4
Queensdown Rd CT14 .248 D4
Queen's Dr TN14 ... 154 C7
Queen's Farm Rd DA12 .38 E7
Queens Gate Gdns BR7 . 53 D8
Queen's Gate Rd
CT11 .... 117 C8
Queens Gdns
Broadstairs CT10 ....84 B3
Dartford DA2 ....34 B7
Queen's Gdns CT16,
CT17 .... 310 D8
Queens Gdns CT6 ...76 F5
Queens Gdns TN4 ... 286 B6
Queens Ho ME16 .. 161 B3
Queensland Ct RM18 ..18 F5
Queensland Ho [2] E16 ..2 A5
Queens Lodge CT15 .. 279 E4
Queens Mews CT14 .. 215 D6
Queen's Mews [12]
TN18 .... 341 A2
Queens Par
[12] Faversham ME13 .. 138 D7
Margate CT9 .... 51 A3
Queen's Pas BR7 .....30 B2
Queen's Prom CT9 ...51 B3
Queen's Rd Ash CT3 .. 147 D2
Ashford TN24 ...... 269 A1
Queens Rd CT3 .... 210 F5
Queen's Rd Bexley DA16 .13 B5
Broadstairs CT10 ....84 B4
Bromley BR1 .... 52 A7
Chatham ME5 .... 64 D1
Chislehurst BR7 ......30 B2
Queens Rd DA8 .....14 E8
Queen's Rd
Faversham ME13 .... 138 B7
Gillingham ME7 ..... 64 C4
Queens Rd DA12 ... 37 C5
Queen's Rd
Hawkhurst TN18 .... 341 A1
Littlestone-on-Sea TN28 . 373 D6
Lydd TN29 .... 376 C6
Maidstone ME16 ... 161 C4
Queens Rd ME12 ... 47 D7
Queen's Rd
Ramsgate CT11 .... 117 F7
Royal Tunbridge Wells
TN4 .... 286 B6
Snodland ME6 ..... 128 A8
Westgate-on-S CT8 ....81 F8
Queens Rd CT5 .... 75 A2
Queen's Rise CT14 .. 247 F5
Queen St Ashford TN23 . 268 B2
Bexley DA7 ....13 F4
Chatham ME4 .... 64 A4
Deal CT14 .... 215 D6
Dover CT16,CT17 ... 310 D7
Erith DA8 ....14 E8
Folkestone CT20 ... 335 E5
Gravesend DA12 .....19 B1
Queens The CT14 ... 215 D5
Queen St Herne Bay CT6 .76 F5

Queen St *continued*
Kings Hill ME18 ... 159 B3
Margate CT9 ....50 I2
Paddock Wood TN12 . 257 D7
Ramsgate CT11 .... 117 E6
Rochester ME1 ..... 63 C4
Sandhurst TN18 ... 356 B5
Queensway ME3 ......9 D3
Queens Way ME14 . 131 A1
Queensway
Dymchurch TN29 ... 352 E2
Hayes BR2,BR4 ..... 85 A6
Lydd TN29 .... 376 C6
Orpington BR5 ...... 53 C3
Queen's Way ME12 .. 46 A8
Queenswood Rd
Kit's Coty ME20 .... 129 D7
Sidcup DA15 ....12 F1
Queen Victoria Meml Hospl
CT6 ....77 B4
Quentins Rd TN16 . 119 B3
Quernmore Cl BR1 .. 29 A2
Quernmore Rd BR1 .. 29 A2
Quern Rd CT14 .... 215 A2
Querns Pl CT1 .... 175 B8
Querns Rd CT1 .... 175 C8
Quern The ME15 .. 161 E1
Quested Rd CT19 .. 334 E6
Quested Way ME17 . 198 C6
Questor DA1 ....33 F6
Quetta Rd CT12 .....82 F1
Quex Ct CT7 ....81 B6
Quex Rd CT8 ....81 F8
Quex View Rd CT7 .. 81 A5
Quickrells Ave ME3 .. 22 B5
Quickstep Cl ME3 . 101 F8
Quickthorn Cres ME5 ..96 E5
Quiet Nook BR2 ..... 85 D7
Quilter Rd BR5 ..... 54 D1
Quilter St SE18 ...... 2 F1
Quince Orch TN26 .. 349 A7
Quincewood Gdns
TN10 .... 222 B7
Quinion Cl ME5 ... 130 A8
Quinnell St ME8 .....65 E1
Quinton Rd ME10 .. 101 C7
Quixote Cres ME2 ...40 B1

R

Rabbit Hole CT4 ... 243 A7
Rabbits Rd DA4 ......57 E7
Rablus Pl DA4 ......56 F3
Racecourse Cvn Site
CT21 .... 332 B7
Racefield Cl DA12 ...38 E1
Rackham Cl DA16 ...13 B5
Radburn Pl DA10 ....17 E2
Radcliffe Ct CT21 .. 333 B2
Radfall Cnr CT5 .... 109 C6
Radfall Gate CT5 ... 109 C6
Radfall Hill CT5 .... 109 D5
Radfall Rd CT5 .... 109 D4
Radfall Ride CT5 ... 109 C5
Radfield Way DA15 ...30 D8
Radland Rd E16 ...... 1 A7
Radleigh Gdns ME1 ...63 E1
Radley Cl CT10 ..... 84 A6
Radley Ho [5] SE2 ..... 3 D4
Radnor Ave DA16 ....13 B2
Radnor Bridge Rd
CT19,CT20 .... 335 E5
Radnor Chambers [13]
CT20 .... 335 D4
Radnor Cl
Chislehurst BR7 .....30 E2
Herne Bay CT6 ..... 77 B1
Radnor Cliff Cres
CT20 .... 335 A3
Radnor Cliff CT20 .. 335 A3
Radnor Ct ME14 ... 161 E7
Radnor Cres SE18 .. 13 A7
Radnor Park Ave
CT19 .... 335 C6
Radnor Park Cres
CT19 .... 335 C5
Radnor Park Gdns
CT19 .... 335 C6
Radnor Park Ho CT19 . 335 C6
Radnor Park Rd CT19 . 335 C6
Radnor Pk W CT19 . 335 B6
Radnor St [20] CT19 . 335 E5
Radzan Cl DA2 ......32 E6
Raeburn Ave DA1 ...15 B2
Raeburn Cl TN10 .. 222 E6
Raeburn Rd DA15 ...12 E1
Rafford Way BR1 ....52 B6
Raggatt Pl ME15 .. 162 B2
Ragge Way TN15 .. 154 F7
Ragglesworth BR7 .. 53 A8
Rag Hill Cl TN16 ... 150 E6
Rag Hill Rd TN16 .. 150 E6
Rag Hill TN16 .... 150 E6
Raglan Ct [11] 2 C1
Raglan Pl [10] CT10 ..84 B4
Raglan Prim Sch BR2 . 52 C5
Raglan Rd Bromley BR2 . 52 C5
Erith DA17 ....3 F2
Woolwich SE18 ......2 C1
Ragstone Ct ME20 . 160 C8
Ragstone Hollow
TN25 .... 330 A6
Ragstone Rd ME15 . 163 A2
Railway Ave CT5 .....74 E1
Railway Cotts
Cowden TN8 ...... 282 D8
Marden TN12 ..... 259 D6
Teynham ME9 .... 103 D3
Railway Hill CT4 .. 242 E8
Railway Pl Erith DA17 ...4 A3

Railway Pl *continued*
[21] Gravesend DA12 ...19 B1
Railway Rd DA12 .....19 B1
Railway St Ind Pk ME7 . 64 D6
Railway St Chatham ME4 .63 F4
Gillingham ME7 ..... 64 D6
Northfleet DA11 .... 18 A2
Railway Terr
Margate CT9 ....50 H1
Queenborough ME11 .. 46 A5
Westerham TN16 .... 151 D1
Rainham Cl
Maidstone ME15 ... 162 A1
Sidcup SE9 ....12 E1
Rainham Mark Gram Sch
ME8 .... 65 D2
Rainham Rd ME5 ... 64 C3
Rainham Sch for Girls
ME8 .... 98 C8
Rainham Sh Ctr [2] ME8 .65 F1
Rainham Sta ME8 ...65 F1
Rainton Rd SE7 ...... 1 A1
Raleigh Cl
Ashford TN24 ...... 301 A8
Chatham ME5 .... 97 A6
Erith DA8 ....14 F8
Raleigh Ct [1] CT11 .. 117 F8
Raleigh Mews [6] BR6 ..86 F5
Raleigh Way ME12 ...46 E6
Ramac Ind Est SE7 .....1 B1
Ramac Way SE7 ...... 1 B1
Ramillies Cl ME5 .... 97 A6
Ramillies Rd DA15 ...13 B1
Ram La TN25,TN27 . 266 C8
Rammell Mews TN17 . 320 D4
Ramp A CT16 ...... 310 H8
Rampart Rd CT21 .. 333 B2
Ramparts The CT13 . 181 A8
Ramp B CT16 ...... 310 H8
Ramp C CT16 ...... 310 G8
Ramp D CT16 ...... 310 G8
Rampion Cl ME14 .. 162 E5
Ramsden Cl BR5 ... 38 C5
Ramsden La TN17 .. 342 F4
Ramsden Rd Erith DA8 . 14 D7
Orpington BR5 ...... 54 B1
Ramsey Cl CT12 ... 142 E1
Ramsey Ho
[8] Canterbury CT1 .. 174 F7
Deal CT14 .... 215 C3
Ramsgate Cl E16 .....1 B5
Ramsgate Maritime Mus ★
CT12 .... 117 E6
Ramsgate Model Village ★
CT11 .... 117 D5
Ramsgate Motor Mus ★
CT11 .... 117 D5
Ramsgate Rd
Broadstairs CT10 ....84 B4
Broadstairs,Dumpton
CT10,CT11 ....83 F2
Margate CT10,CT9 ... 83 A6
Sandwich CT13 .... 149 A7
Ramsgate Sch The
CT12 .... 83 A2
Ramsgate Sta CT12 . 117 C8
Ramslye Rd TN4 ... 313 E8
Ramstone Ct TN25 . 302 E5
Ramus Wood Ave BR6 ..86 E5
Rance Ho [11] SE18 ..... 1 C7
Rancliffe Gdns SE9 ..11 E3
Rancorn Rd CT9 .... 50 G1
Randall Cl DA8 ..... 14 C8
Randall Hill Rd TN15 . 124 F3
Randall Rd ME4 .....63 E1
Randalls Row ME15 . 194 F5
Randall St ME14 ... 161 F6
Randle's La TN14 .. 120 D5
Randle Way ME9 .. 102 E2
Randolph App E16 ....1 A7
Randolph Cl Bexley DA7 . 14 C4
Canterbury CT1 .... 175 A7
Randolph Cotts ME2 ...40 B1
Randolph Ct CT8 ...50 C1
Randolph Gdns TN24 . 268 E5
Randolph Ho
[15] Folkestone CT20 . 335 E5
Gillingham ME7 ..... 64 C5
Randolph La TN31 . 368 B3
Randolph Rd
Dover CT17 .... 278 B1
Gillingham ME7 ..... 64 C5
Orpington BR2 ......52 F1
Randolph Sq CT9 ....50 J3
Ranelagh Gdns
[1] Broadstairs CT10 ...83 E5
Northfleet DA11 .... 18 F8
Ranelagh Gr CT10 ...83 E5
Ranelagh Rd
Deal CT14 .... 215 D6
Sheerness ME12 .... 28 C2
Rangefield Rd BR1 .. 29 A3
Range Rd
Eastchurch ME12 ... 48 D1
Gravesend DA12 .... 37 E8
Hythe CT21 .... 333 B1
Range Road Ind Est
CT21 .... 333 B1
Rangeworth Pl DA15 ...30 F5
Rankine Rd TN2 ... 286 D7
Ranleigh Gdns DA7 ...13 F7
Ranmore Path BR5 .. 54 A5
Ranscombe Cl ME2 . 62 D5
Ranscombe Farm Cotts
ME2 .... 62 C4
Ransley Gn TN26 .. 349 F8
Ransome Way CT7 ..80 F6
Ransom Rd [1] SE7 .....1 C7
Ranters La TN17 ... 318 C7
Ranworth Cl DA7,DA8 ...14 E5
Raphael Ave RM18 ...19 B7

Raphael Ct TN11 ... 221 E7
Raphael Rd DA12 ... 37 D8
Rashleigh Ave DA4 . 57 C5
Raspberry Hill La ME9 . 68 D6
Ratcliffe Ct SE12 ... 29 A8
Ratcliffe Highway
High Halstow ME3 .. 24 D5
Hoo St Werburgh ME3 .. 41 C6
Rathmore Rd
Gravesend DA11 .....37 B8
Greenwich SE7 ......1 B1
Ratling Rd CT3 .... 210 F7
Rattington St CT4 .. 173 E2
Ravelin Ho ME12 ... 28 C2
Raven Cl ME20 .... 128 A1
Ravenlea Rd CT20 . 335 A5
Ravensbourne Ave CT6 .77 B3
Ravensbourne Coll of
Design & Communication
BR7 .... 29 F3
Ravensbourne Ct [28]
BR5 .... 54 D1
Ravensbourne Rd
Bromley BR1 .... 52 A6
Crayford DA1 ...... 15 A4
Ravensbourne Sch The
BR2 .... 52 B5
Ravenscourt Rd
Deal CT14 .... 215 C5
Orpington BR5 ..... 54 B7
Rough Common CT2 . 142 B3
Ravenscroft Cl [5] E16 .. 1 A8
Ravenscroft Cres SE9 ..29 F5
Ravenscroft Rd E16 ....1 A8
Ravens Dane Cl ME15 . 163 A1
Ravenshill BR7 ..... 53 B8
Raven's Hoe DA14 .. 31 A3
Ravens Knowle ME1 ..95 D4
Ravensleigh Gdns BR1 .29 B3
Ravensquay Bsns Ctr
BR5 .... 54 B4
Ravens Way SE12 ... 11 A2
Ravenswood Ave
Rochester ME2 ..... 40 B1
Royal Tunbridge Wells
TN2 .... 286 D6
Ravenswood DA5 .. 31 E7
Ravensworth Rd SE9 ..29 F4
Ravine Gr SE18 ..... 12 E8
Rawdon Rd
Maidstone ME15 ... 162 A3
Ramsgate CT11 .... 117 C6
Rawlings Cl [3] BR6 .. 86 F5
Rawling St ME9 ... 134 F3
Rawsthorne Ct E16 .....1 F5
Rayfield Cl BR2 .... 52 E3
Rayfield Ct ME6 .....95 B1
Rayford Cl DA1 .... 15 C2
Rayham Rd CT5 ... 109 A8
Ray Lamb Way DA8 ...15 B7
Rayleas Cl SE18 .....12 B6
Rayleigh Cl ME16 .. 161 D7
Rayleigh Ho [2] ME15 . 195 D8
Rayleigh Rd E16 ...... 1 B5
Raymere Gdns SE18 ..12 E7
Raymer Rd ME14 .. 162 B8
Raymond Ave CT1 . 175 A6
Raymond Fuller Way
TN24 .... 268 E4
Raymond Postgate Ct [5]
SE28 .... 3 B6
Raymoor Ave TN29 . 366 A4
Raynehurst Jun & Inf Sch
DA12 .... 37 F5
Rayner Hill Cotts
ME17 .... 200 C5
Rayners Ct DA11 .....18 B1
Rayners Hill ME17 . 200 C5
Raynham Villas TN12 . 227 A4
Rays Hill CT4 ...... 57 C4
Raywood Office Complex
TN27 .... 234 B4
Reach Cl CT15 .... 279 F5
Reachfields CT21 .. 333 A1
Reach Mdw CT15 .. 280 A6
Reach Rd Lympne CT21 . 331 D2
St Margaret's at Cliffe
CT15 .... 279 F5
Reader's Bridge Rd
TN30 .... 323 E4
Readers Ct ME18 .. 193 A4
Readers La TN31 ... 367 F5
Reading Cl CT14 .. 215 B1
Reading Ho [4] ME15 . 195 F5
Reading Rd CT17 .. 309 F7
Reading St CT10 ....83 F8
Reading Street Rd
CT10,CT9 ....83 E8
Reading St TN30 .. 346 C2
Readscroft Rd ME8 . 98 D5
Read Way DA12 .....37 E3
Rebecca Ct
[6] Margate CT9 .....51 B2
Sidcup DA14 ....31 B4
Recca La CT15,CT18 . 275 C4
Recreation Ave ME6 . 128 A8
Recreation Cl ME14 . 162 B6
Recreation Ground Rd
TN30 .... 345 B7
Recreation Way ME10 . 69 A1
Rectory Bglws TN26 . 326 F8
Rectory Bsns Ctr [2]
DA14 .... 31 B4
Rectory Cl Crayford DA1 . 14 E3
Sidcup DA14 ....31 B4
Snodland ME6 ..... 128 A8
Woodchurch TN26 .. 326 A2
Wouldham ME1 ..... 95 C5
Rectory Ct [3] RM17 ...18 D8
Rectory Dr TN3 ... 253 D3

Rectory Field Cres SE7 . 11 C7
Rectory Fields TN17 . 320 D5
Rectory Gdns CT5 .. 75 D2
Rectory Grange ME1 . 63 C2
Rectory La
Barham CT4 .... 210 A2
Brasted TN16 ..... 152 C3
Harrietsham ME17 . 198 E5
Hythe CT21 .... 333 B1
Ightham TN15 ..... 156 C5
Lyminge CT18 .... 305 C6
Maidstone ME16 ... 161 A1
Rectory La N ME19 . 127 C2
Rectory La
Sevenoaks TN13 ... 154 C1
Sutton Valence ME17 . 229 C6
Sutton Valence ME17 . 229 F7
Titsey TN16 ...... 150 E4
Rectory La S ME19 . 127 C1
Rectory Mdw DA13 . 36 A2
Rectory Paddock Sch
BR5 .... 54 C7
Rectory Park Rd TN12 . 290 A2
Rectory Pl SE18 ...... 2 A2
Rectory Rd
Broadstairs CT10 ....84 B5
Cliffe ME3 .... 22 A3
Deal CT14 .... 214 F4
[4] Grays RM17 ..... 18 D8
New Ash Green TN15 . 92 C5
Orpington BR2 ..... 85 D3
St Mary in the Marsh
TN29 .... 365 B4
Sittingbourne ME10 . 102 B3
Swanscombe DA10 ...35 E8
West Tilbury RM18 .. 19 D8
Rectory Way TN24 . 268 C5
Rectory Wlk TN26 . 349 A7
Rectory Yd CT6 .....80 E8
Reculver CE Prim Sch
CT6 .... 78 A4
Reculver Cl CT6 .....77 F5
Reculver Ctry Pk ★
CT6 ....78 B6
Reculver Dr CT6 ....77 E5
Reculver La CT6 ....78 B6
Reculver Rd CT6 ....77 D5
Reculvers Rd CT8 ...81 F7
Reculver Wlk ME15 . 195 F7
Redan Pl ME12 .... 28 C2
Redbank ME19 .... 127 C2
Red Barracks Rd [4]
SE18 ....1 F2
Redberry Rd TN23 . 300 B5
Redbourne Dr SE28 .. 3 D7
Red Brick Cotts ME13 . 172 A6
Redbridge Cl ME5 .. 97 C4
Redbrook St TN26 . 325 D5
Red Cedars Rd BR6 . 53 E2
Redcliffe La ME14 . 162 B7
Redcot La CT2 .... 144 B7
Redding Cl DA2 .... 34 E6
Redding Ho SE18 .....1 E3
Reddy Rd DA8 ...... 14 F8
Redfern Ave ME7 .. 64 C5
Redfern Ho ME2 .... 94 F5
Redgate Dr BR2 .... 85 B8
Red Hill BR7 .... 30 B3
Redhill Rd
New Ash Green DA3 . 91 F6
Westgate-on-S CT8 ..81 E8
Red Hill ME18 .... 159 F1
Redhill Wood DA3 .. 92 A7
Red Ho The
Limpsfield RH8 .... 183 C5
Littlestone-on-Sea TN28 . 373 E6
Red House ★ DA6 . 13 E3
Redhouse Farm CT14 . 182 B1
Red House Gdns
ME18 .... 192 C7
Red House La DA6 .. 13 E3
Redhouse La CT4 .. 207 D6
Redhouse Rd TN16 . 150 C6
Redhouse Wall CT14 . 182 B1
Redington TN24 ... 268 C3
Redlands Cl CT17 .. 277 E4
Redland Shaw ME4 ...63 E1
Redlands Rd TN13 . 153 F3
Redlane Cotts RH8 . 183 B2
Red La RH8 .... 183 B2
Redleaf Cl Erith DA17 . 14 A8
Royal Tunbridge Wells
TN2 .... 286 D6
Red Lion Cl BR5 ... 54 C3
Red Lion Ct [6] CT21 . 333 B2
Red Lion La
[11] Whitstable CT5 .. 74 D2
Woolwich SE18 .... 12 A6
Red Lion Pl SE18 .. 12 A6
Red Lion Sq
[7] Hythe CT21 .... 333 B2
Plaxtol TN15 ..... 189 E8
Red Lodge Cres DA5 . 32 C5
Red Lodge Rd DA5 . 32 C5
Redmans Ind Est RM18 . 20 A8
Redmans La BR6,TN14 . 88 E4
Redmill Cl CT20 ... 334 C5
Red Oak Cl BR6 .....86 B8
Red Oak TN18 .... 354 E8
Red Oast Cotts TN5 . 339 C4
Redoubt Way TN29 . 353 B4
Redpoll Way DA18 ...3 D2
Redruth Manor [3] ME7 . 64 C6

Redsells Cl ME15 .. 163 A1
Redshank Rd ME4 ...41 B1
Redstart Cl E6 ...... 1 E8
Red St DA13 ....36 B2
Redsull Ave CT14 .. 215 A3
Red Tree Orch TN23 . 299 E7
Redvers Cotts CT16 . 277 E5
Redvers Rd ME4 .... 64 C2
Redwall La ME15,ME17 . 227 C6
Redwell La TN15 .. 156 B4
Redwing Cl ME20 .. 128 A2
Redwing Path SE28 ...2 D4
Redwing Rd ME5 ...97 B3
Redwings La TN2 .. 255 E2
Redwood Cl
Canterbury CT2 .... 142 E2
Chartham CT4 .... 173 E1
Chatham ME5 ....97 B2
Sidcup DA15 ...... 31 A7
Redwood Ct DA1 ... 16 A1
Redwood Pk TN26 . 256 A5
Redyear Cotts TN24 . 269 A1
Redyear Ct TN24 .. 269 A1
Reece Adams Ho
CT18 .... 308 B1
Reed Ave
Canterbury CT1 .... 143 D3
Orpington BR6 ......86 F2
Reed Cl Eltham SE12 . 11 A2
Newham E16 ....1 A8
New Hythe ME20 .. 128 A5
Reed Court Cotts
TN12 .... 227 A5
Reed Court Farm Trail ★
TN12 .... 227 A5
Reed Cres TN23 ... 300 C3
Reedham Cres ME3 . 40 C7
Reedland Cres ME13 . 138 C8
Reedmace Cl TN23 . 299 D8
Reeds Cl CT6 ...... 77 C4
Reeds La TN11 .... 189 E5
Reed St ME3 .... 22 B6
Reeves Alley [1] CT5 . 74 D1
Reeves Cl TN12 ... 260 E4
Reeves Cres BR8 ... 55 D6
Reeves Ct Ditton ME19 . 128 A1
Fordcombe TN3 ... 284 B5
Reeves Pas [7] ME13 . 138 C7
Reeves Rd SE18 .... 12 B8
Reeves Terr TN5 ... 338 E1
Reeves Way CT5 ... 75 C2
Reeves Yd CT5 .....74 D2
Reflection The E16 ...2 B4
Reform Rd ME4 .....64 B2
Regency Cl
Gillingham ME8 .... 98 C3
Sheerness ME12 ... 28 A3
West Kingsdown TN15 ..90 E4
Whitstable CT5 .... 108 F7
Regency Ct ME10 .. 101 D4
Regency Hall [1] TN2 . 286 A2
Regency Ho TN2 ... 286 B2
Regency Pl CT1 ... 143 B2
Regency Villas CT4 . 243 C5
Regency Way ME4 .. 13 C4
Regent Dr ME15 .. 195 A8
Regent Pl TN2 .... 286 D3
Regent Rd ME7 .... 64 C4
Regents Ct
[14] Ashford TN23 .. 268 B2
[3] Gravesend DA11 ...19 B1
Regents Dr BR2 .... 85 D5
Regents Pl TN23 .. 268 B2
Regent's Pl SE3 ... 11 A5
Regent Sq DA17 .....4 B2
Regent St
Rolvenden TN17 ... 343 E4
Whitstable CT5 .... 74 D2
Regents Wlk CT6 .. 77 D5
Regent Way ME18 . 159 C3
Regina Ct TN4 .... 285 F4
Reginald Ave ME2 .. 62 C3
Reginald Rd ME16 . 161 E3
Regis Bsns Pk ME12 . 28 A1
Regis Cres ME10 .. 101 E7
Regis Manor Com Prim Sch
ME10 .... 101 E7
Regvlbivm Roman Fort &
Reculver Twrs ★ CT6 . 78 D7
Reidhaven Rd SE18 ...2 A2
Reigate Rd BR1,SE12 .. 29 A5
Reinckendorf Ave SE9 . 12 D1
Reinden Gr ME15 .. 162 F1
Rembrandt Cl TN10 . 222 E6
Rembrandt Dr DA11 ...36 E5
Remington Rd E6 .....1 E7
Remston Mews [12]
CT1 .... 143 B2
Remus Cl TN23 ... 299 F4
Renault Cl CT6 .... 76 A4
Rendezvous St CT20 . 335 D5
Rendezvous The CT9 . 50 I3
Rendlebury Ho [12] SE18 . 1 F2
Renfrew Cl E6 ....2 A6
Rennets Cl SE3 .... 11 F6
Rennets Wood Ho SE9 . 12 D2
Rennets Wood Rd SE9 . 12 D2
Renovation The E16 ...2 B4
Renown Rd ME5 ....97 C2
Renshaw Cl [7] DA17 . 13 F8
Rentain Rd CT4 ... 173 D2
Renton Dr BR5 .... 54 D2
Repository Rd SE18 ...1 F1
Repton Ct CT10 .....83 F6
Repton Manor Rd
TN23 .... 268 A3
Repton Rd BR6 .... 87 A6
Repton Way ME5 ...96 F4
Reservoir Ave TN29 . 380 D2

Reservoir Cl DA9 ...... 17 C1
Reservoir Rd CT5 ......74 E2
Resolution Cl ME5 ..... 97 A6
Resolution Wlk SE18 ....1 F3
Restavon Cvn Pk
TN16 .... 119 B3
Restharrow Rd ME14 .. 162 E4
Rest Harrow ME13 .. 170 C5
Restharrow Way ME4 .. 41 C1
Restmore Cl ME3 ..... 22 A4
Restons Cres SE9 ......12 E1
Retreat Cvn Pk The
ME18 .... 192 D6
Retreat The
Birchington CT7 ....81 B8
Doddington ME9 .... 167 D7
Grays RM17 ....18 B8
Orpington BR6 ....87 B4
Platt TN15 .... 157 D8
Ramsgate CT12 ..... 117 B8
Rettendon Dr ME10 .. 101 F8
Revell Rise SE18 ....12 F8
Revenge Rd ME5 .... 130 C8
Reventlow Rd SE9 ..... 30 C7
Reynard Cl BR1 ...... 53 A6
Reynolah Gdns 3 SE7 ...1 B1
Reynolds Cl
Herne Bay CT6 ....77 B4
Tonbridge TN10 .... 222 E6
Reynolds Fields ME3 .. 39 C6
Reynolds La
Herne Bay CT3 ...... 78 D3
Royal Tunbridge Wells
TN4 .... 285 F7
Reynolds Pl SE3 ....11 B7
Rhee Wall TN26 .... 361 D7
Rheims Ct CT2 .... 142 D1
Rheims Way CT1,CT2 .. 174 E8
Rhodaus Cl CT1 ..... 174 F7
Rhodaus Ho CT1 ..... 174 F7
Rhodaus Town CT1 .. 174 F7
Rhodes Gdns CT10 .... 84 A6
Rhode St ME4 .... 64 C2
Rhodewood Cl ME15 .. 163 A1
Rhododendron Ave
DA13 .... 93 A2
Ribblesdale Rd DA2 .. 34 C7
Ribston Cl BR2 ....52 F1
Ribston Gdns TN12 .. 256 F7
Ricardo Path 5 SE28 ...3 D5
Rice Par BR5 .... 53 D4
Richard Beau Nash
Apartments 4 TN1 .. 286 B4
Richard Cl SE18 ....1 E2
Richard Ct 7 CT9 .....51 B2
Richard House Dr E16 ...1 E7
Richard Neve Ho SE18 ...2 E2
Richard's Cl TN11 ... 219 F2
Richardson Cl 7 DA9 .. 17 A2
Richardson Rd TN4 .. 286 A5
Richardson Way CT12 .116 D5
Richard St Chatham ME4 ..63 F4
Rochester ME1 .... 63 C3
Richborough Castle &
Mus★ CT13 .... 108 E7
Richborough Cl BR5 .. 54 D5
Richborough Drive
ME2 .... 40 A1
Richborough Rd CT8 ...81 F7
Richborough Way
TN23 .... 299 C5
Richburgh Rd CT13 .. 148 E3
Richdore Rd CT4 .... 239 C6
Richings House BR5 .. 54 A8
Richmer Rd DA8 ..... 15 A7
Richmond Ave CT9 .....51 B1
Richmond Cl
Biggin Hill TN16 .... 150 B8
Chatham ME5 ....97 B4
Rochester ME2 ....40 F1
Richmond Ct
Bromley BR1 ....29 B1
Dover CT16 .... 278 D1
Sevenoaks TN13 .... 154 B4
Richmond Dr
Gravesend DA12 .....37 E4
Herne Bay CT6 ....77 E5
New Romney TN28 .. 373 C8
Sittingbourne ME10 .. 101 E7
Richmond First Sch
ME12 .... 28 D2
Richmond Gdns CT2 .. 142 C2
Richmond Ho 26 CT20 . 335 E5
Richmond Inf Sch ME7 .. 64 C6
Richmond Meech Dr
TN24 .... 268 E4
Richmond Pl
Royal Tunbridge Wells
TN2 .... 286 B1
Woolwich SE18 ....2 C2
Richmond Rd
Gillingham ME7 ..... 64 C7
1 Grays RM17 ....18 C8
Ramsgate CT11 .... 117 D6
Whitstable CT5 ....75 B1
Richmond St
Folkestone CT19 .... 334 D6
Herne Bay CT6 ....76 F5
Sheerness ME12 .... 28 D2
Richmond Way ME15 .. 195 A8
Richmount Gdns SE3 .. 11 A4
Ricketts Hill Rd TN16 .. 150 F7
Rickyard Path SE9 .....11 E3
Riddlesdale Ave TN4 .. 286 A6
Riddles Rd ME10,ME9 .. 101 C3
Riddons Rd SE12 ..... 29 C4
Rideout St SE18 ....1 F2
Rider Cl DA15 ....12 E1
Ridge Ave DA1 ....14 F1

Ridgebrook Rd SE3 .... 11 D4
Ridge Cl SE28 ....2 D4
Ridgecroft Cl DA5 .... 32 C7
Ridgelands TN3 .... 253 C4
Ridge Meadow Prim Sch
ME5 ....96 F6
Ridge The
Ashford TN24 .... 268 E6
Groombridge TN3 .. 312 A6
Orpington BR6 ...... 86 D8
Sidcup DA5 ....31 F8
Ridge View Sch TN10 .. 222 D5
Ridgeway Ave DA12 .....37 B5
Ridgeway Bglws DA12 ..38 F1
Ridgeway Cliff CT6 .. 76 C5
Ridge Way DA1 ....14 F1
St Margaret's at Cliffe
CT15 .... 280 B6
Ridgeway Crescent Gdns
BR6 ....86 E7
Ridgeway Cres
Orpington BR6 ....86 E7
Tonbridge TN10 .... 222 D4
Ridgeway Dr BR1 .....29 B4
Ridgeway E DA15 ......12 F2
Ridgewaye The TN4 .. 254 B1
Ridgeway Hayes BR2 .. 85 A8
Hurst Green TN19 ... 354 A3
Lympne CT21 ...... 332 A3
Ridge Way TN8 .... 217 D4
Ridgeway TN2 ...... 287 D7
Ridgeway Terr TN25 .. 302 C5
Ridgeway The
Boughton Street ME13 .. 140 A3
Broadstairs CT10 .....83 F3
Chatham ME4 ....96 E7
Crabble CT17 ...... 277 E2
Gillingham ME7 ..... 64 C7
Margate CT9 ....51 B1
Ridgeway TN18 .... 354 E8
Ridgeway The
Shorne DA12 ....38 E1
Smeeth TN25 ...... 302 B5
Tonbridge TN10 .... 222 D4
Ridgeway CT5 .... 75 C1
Ridgeway Wlk CT6 .. 111 A7
Ridgeway W DA15 ......12 E2
Ridgewood DA3 .... 59 C7
Ridgway ME6 ...... 161 B2
Ridgwell Rd E16 ....1 C8
Ridgy Field Cl TN15 .. 125 A2
Ridham Ave ME10 .... 69 A1
Ridham Dock ME9 ..... 69 B6
Riding Hill TN24 .... 268 C6
Riding La TN11 ..... 188 D2
Riding Pk TN11 .... 221 D7
Ridings The
Biggin Hill TN16 .... 118 E2
7 Canterbury CT1 .. 143 B1
Margate CT9 ....51 F3
Paddock Wood TN12 .. 257 A7
Royal Tunbridge Wells
TN2 .... 286 F6
Whitstable CT5 ...... 75 D1
Ridlands Cl CT1 .... 175 A5
Ridlands Gr RH8 .. 183 E5
Ridlands La RH8 .. 183 E5
Ridlands Rise RH8 .. 183 E4
Ridley Cl CT16 ..... 111 A8
Ridley Ct BR6 ...... 86 C6
Ridley Rd Bexley DA16 ..13 B6
Bromley BR2 .... 52 A6
Rochester ME1 ....63 B4
Riefield Rd SE9 ..... 12 C2
Rigden Rd TN23 .... 300 B7
Rigden's Ct 6 ME10 .. 101 E5
Riggall Ct ME2 ...... 62 A3
Riggs Way TN15 .... 124 F3
Rigshill Rd ME13 .... 201 B6
Riley Ave CT6 ....75 F4
Rimpton Ct CT10 .....83 F7
Ring Cl BR1 ....29 B1
Ringden Ave TN12 .. 256 F6
Ringer's Ct 5 BR1 .. 52 A6
Ringer's Rd BR1 .... 52 A6
Ringle Gn TN18 .... 356 C5
Ringlestone Cres
ME14 .... 161 F8
Ringlestone Rd ME17 ..165 D4
Ringlet Cl E16 ....1 B8
Ringlet Rd ME4 ....41 B2
Ringold Ave CT12 .. 117 A8
Ringshall Rd BR5 .... 54 A6
Rings Hill TN11 .... 221 B4
Ringside TN8 ...... 217 C2
Ringsloe Ct CT7 ..... 80 D8
Ring Wall CT14 .... 181 E2
Ringwood Ave BR6 .. 87 C1
Ringwood Cl
Canterbury CT2 .... 142 E3
Gillingham ME8 .....98 D8
Ringwood Rd ME15 .. 195 C8
Ringwould Rd
Kingsdown CT14 .... 248 B5
Ringwould CT14,CT15 .. 247 D4
Ripley Cl BR1 ....52 F4
Ripley Rd
Ashford TN24 .... 301 A8
Erith DA17 ....4 A2
Newham E16 ....1 C7
Ripleys Market DA1 .. 33 E8
Ripper's Cross TN26 .. 266 D4
Rippersley Rd DA16 .. 13 A6
Ripple Cross CT14 .. 247 F6
Ripple Rd CT14 .... 247 F5
Ripple Sch The CT14 .. 247 E8
Ripplevale Sch CT14 .. 247 E8
Rippolson Rd SE18 .....2 F1

Risborough La CT19,
CT20 .... 334 D5
Risborough Way CT20 . 334 A4
Risden La TN18 .... 355 D7
Risdon Cl CT2 ..... 143 F6
Risedale Rd DA7 ..... 14 C4
Rise The Ashford TN23 .. 299 E7
Borden ME9 ...... 101 B2
Chatham ME4 ....64 A7
Crayford DA1 ....14 F7
Gillingham ME7 ..... 98 A3
Gravesend DA12 .....37 E4
Halfway Houses ME12 .. 46 C5
Kingsdown CT14 .... 248 D5
Rochester ME1 ....63 D3
Sevenoaks TN13 .. 187 C7
Sidcup DA5 .... 31 C8
Rising Rd TN23 .... 268 A1
Ritch Rd ME6 ...... 127 E8
Ritter St SE18 .... 12 A8
Ritz Blgs TN1 ...... 286 A3
Rivendell Cl ME3 .....27 B5
River Bank Cl 8
ME15 .... 162 B4
Riverbank Rd BR1 .... 29 A5
Riverbank Way TN24 .. 300 D6
Riverbourne Ct 6
ME10 .... 101 F4
River Cl ME15 ...... 194 A7
River Cotts BR5 ..... 54 C7
River Ct Chartham CT4 .. 173 D3
Crabble CT17 ...... 277 F2
Sevenoaks TN13 .. 153 E5
River Dale CT17 .... 277 F3
Riverdale Est TN9 .. 254 D8
Riverdale Rd
Canterbury CT1 .... 143 B2
Erith DA8 ....4 C1
Sidcup DA5 ....13 F1
Woolwich SE18 ....2 F1
River Dr Crabble CT17 .. 277 F2
Rochester ME2 ....62 E7
Riverhead Cl
Maidstone ME16 .... 161 D6
Margate CT9 ....51 B1
Sittingbourne ME10 .. 101 D7
Riverhead Inf Sch
TN13 .... 153 E5
Riverhead Mews
TN13 .... 153 E4
Riverhill Cotts TN15 .. 187 E5
Riverhill House Gdns★
TN15 .... 187 E5
Riverhill TN15 ...... 187 E5
Riverhope Mans SE18 ....1 E3
River Lawn Rd TN9 .. 222 B1
River Mdw CT17 .... 277 F3
Rivermead ME4 ..... 41 C2
River Park View BR6 ..54 B2
River Prim Sch CT17 .. 277 E3
River Rd Barking IG11 ...3 A8
Sandwich CT13 .... 149 B4
Rivers Cl SE18 ..... 192 E4
Riversdale DA11 .....36 E5
Riversdale Rd
Ashford TN23 .... 300 C8
Ramsgate CT12 .....83 B1
Riverside Bsns Pk
TN24 .... 268 D2
Riverside CT4 ..... 173 C3
Riverside Cl
Bridge CT4 .... 176 A1
Kingsnorth TN23 .. 300 A4
Orpington BR5 ...... 54 C7
Riverside Cotts TN14 ..88 F1
Riverside CT17 .... 277 F3
Riverside Ct
11 Canterbury CT2 .. 142 F1
2 Orpington BR5 .. 54 C4
Riverside Ctry Pk & Visitor
Ctr★ ME7 .... 65 D5
Riverside East Rd ME4 . 41 C1
Riverside
Edenbridge TN8 .... 217 C1
Eynsford DA4 ...... 89 D8
Greenwich SE7 ....1 B3
Riverside Ind Est
Dartford DA1 ....15 E2
West Hythe CT21 ... 332 B1
Riverside Mews CT4 .. 176 A1
Riverside Pk ME16 .. 194 A8
Riverside Prim Sch
ME8 ....66 A1
Riverside Rd
Cliffs End CT13 .... 116 A1
Sidcup DA14 ....31 E4
Riverside Ret Pk
Canterbury CT1 .... 174 D6
Sevenoaks TN14 .. 154 C8
Riverside Sch TN23 .. 267 F1
Riverside CT16 .... 277 F1
Riverside Way DA1 ...15 E2
Rivers St CT17 .... 277 E3
Riverton Sch SE12 .. 11 A2
River St CT17 ...... 277 E3
Rivers Wlk CT17 .. 199 C5
Riverview TN23 .... 267 E1
River View Cl 6 ME4 ..63 F3
Riverview
16 Erith DA17 ....4 A1
Stone DA9 ....1 E1
Riverview 6 DA1 .. 16 A3
River View
Gillingham ME8 ..... 65 D3
Greenwich SE7 ....1 C3
Rushenden ME11 .....45 F3
Sturry CT2 .... 143 F7

Riverview Inf Sch DA12 .37 E4
Riverview Jun Sch
DA12 .... 37 F8
Riverview Rd DA9 ... 17 A2
River View
Rushenden ME11 .....45 F3
Sturry CT2 .... 143 F7
River Way ME20 ... 128 B4
River Wlk TN9 ..... 222 B1
Riverwood La BR7 ... 53 D8
Riviera Ct 6 CT20 .. 334 E3
Riviera Rd CT20 ... 335 A3
Riviera The CT20 ... 334 F3
Rixon Ho SE18 ....12 B8
Roach St ME1 .... 61 F8
Road of Remembrance
CT20 .... 335 D4
Roan Ct ME2 ....62 F8
Robert Brundett Cl
TN24 .... 268 E5
Robert Napier Sch The
ME7 ....64 E3
Roberton Dr BR1 .... 52 C8
Roberts Cl Eltham SE9 .. 30 D7
8 Orpington BR5 .. 54 C4
Sittingbourne ME10 .. 101 D7
Roberts Ho SE18 .....11 E6
Roberts Mews BR6 .. 54 A1
Robertson Ho SE18 .....11 F6
Roberts Orchard Rd
ME16 .... 160 F3
Roberts Rd Erith DA17 ...4 A1
Gillingham ME8 .....98 E8
Greatstone-on-Sea
TN28 .... 373 E1
Snodland ME6 ..... 127 F8
Whitstable CT5 .... 107 F6
Robert St Deal CT14 .. 215 D7
Newham E16 ....2 B5
Woolwich SE18 ....2 D2
Robeshaw ME9 .... 134 C2
Robina Cl DA6 ...... 13 D3
Robina Ct Margate CT9 .. 51 D3
Swanley BR8 .... 56 A5
Robin Cres E6 ....1 D8
Robin Ct
6 Rochester ME1 .. 63 D4
Whitstable CT5 ......75 A3
Robin Hill Dr BR7 ....29 E2
Robin Ho 5 ME16 .. 161 E4
Robin Hood Gn BR5 .. 54 A4
Robin Hood La
Bexley DA6 ....13 E2
Chatham ME5 ....96 D1
Lydd TN29 .... 376 C5
Robin Hood Lane (Lower)
ME5 ....96 F2
Robin Hood Lane (Upper)
ME5 ....96 F2
Robinia Ave DA11 .... 36 D8
Robin La TN29 .... 376 C6
Robins Ave ME17 .. 199 C5
Robin's Cl CT21 ... 353 C8
Robins Cl ME17 ... 199 C4
Robins Ct
Lewisham SE12 ..... 29 C5
Maidstone ME14 .. 162 B7
Robins Gr BR4 ..... 85 A7
Robin Way BR5 .....54 B6
Robinwood Dr TN15 .. 154 F8
Robson Cl E6 ....1 D7
Robson Dr
Aylesford ME20 .... 128 D2
Hoo St Werburgh ME3 .. 41 D6
Robson Ho SE18 .... 12 A7
Robson's Yd CT17 .. 310 C8
Robus Cl CT18 .... 305 C7
Robus Terr CT18 .. 305 C7
Robyn Cotts TN26 .. 324 E8
Robyns Croft 6 DA11 ..36 E5
Robyns Way
Edenbridge TN8 .... 249 D8
Sevenoaks TN13 .. 153 F5
Rocfort Rd ME6 .... 128 A8
Rochdale Ho TN1 .. 286 C5
Rochdale Rd
Royal Tunbridge Wells
TN1 .... 286 C6
Woolwich SE2 ....3 B2
Rochester Airport Ind Est
ME1 .... 96 C5
Rochester Airport ME1,
ME5 .... 96 C6
Rochester Ave
Bromley BR1 ....52 B7
Canterbury CT1 ... 175 B7
Rochester ME1 .... 63 C4
Rochester Castle★
ME1 .... 63 C6
Rochester Cath★ ME1 . 63 C6
Rochester Cl Dartford DA15 .13 B1
Rochester Cres ME3 . 41 D6
Rochester Ct
Canterbury CT1 ... 175 B6
Rochester ME2 ....63 E8
Rochester Dr DA5 .. 14 A1
Rochester Gate ME1 .. 63 D5
Rochester Gram Sch for
Girls The ME1 ..... 63 C2
Rochester Ho 1
ME15 .... 195 D7
Rochester Ind Coll
ME1 .... 63 D4
Rochester Rd
Burham ME1 ....95 C2
Chalk DA12 ....38 B6
Chatham ME1,ME5 .. 96 C4
Dartford DA1 ..... 34 A8
Pratling Street ME20 .. 129 B4
Rochester ME2 ....62 D4
Tonbridge TN10 .... 222 D4
Rochester Sta ME1 .. 63 D5

Rochester St ME4 ....63 E3
Rochester Way
Dartford DA1 ....32 F8
Eltham,Kidbrooke SE3,
SE9 .... 11 D4
Eltham SE9 ....12 B4
Rock Ave ME7 ..... 64 C3
Rock Cotts TN3 .... 314 B1
Rockdale Rd TN13 .. 154 C2
Rockdale TN13 .... 154 B2
Rock Farm Oasthouse
ME18 .... 192 C6
Rock Hill BR6 ......88 B4
Rock Hill Rd TN27 .. 232 E2
Rockingham Pl CT6 ....77 B2
Rockliffe Manor Prim Sch
SE18 .... 12 B8
Rockmount Rd SE18 .....2 F1
Rock Rd
Borough Green TN15 .. 156 F7
Maidstone ME14 .. 162 A6
Sittingbourne ME10 .. 101 E4
Rocks Cl ME19 .... 160 A6
Rocks Hill TN17 .. 293 A4
Rocks Rd The ME19 .. 160 B6
Rockstone Way CT12 .. 83 A1
Rock Villa Rd TN1 .. 286 A4
Rocky Bourne Rd
TN25 .... 329 D5
Rocky Hill ME16 .. 161 E4
Rocky Hill Terr 2
ME16 .... 161 E4
Rodeo Cl DA8 ....15 B6
Roding Rd E6 ....2 B8
Rodmell Rd TN2 .. 286 A2
Rodmer Cl ME10 .... 47 C8
Rodmersham Gn ME9 . 135 B7
Rodmersham Sch
ME9 .... 135 B7
Rodney Ave TN10 .. 222 E4
Rodney Gdns BR4 .. 85 A6
Rodney St ST11 ... 117 D6
Rodway Rd BR1 .....52 B8
Roebourne Way E16 .....2 A5
Roebuck Ho ME1 ......63 E5
Roebuck Rd
Faversham ME13 ... 138 A7
Rochester ME1 .... 63 C5
Roedean Cl BR6 ....87 B6
Roedean Rd TN2 .. 286 A1
Roehampton Cl DA12 .. 37 E8
Roehampton Dr BR7 .. 30 C2
Roentgen Ho ME10 .. 101 D5
Roethorne Gdns TN30 . 345 B8
Roffen Rd ME1 .... 63 C2
Rogers Ct BR8 ..... 56 A5
Rogersmead TN30 .. 345 A7
Rogers Rough Rd
TN17 .... 318 B2
Rogers Wood La DA3 .. 91 B6
Rogley Hill TN27 .. 322 B6
Rokesby Cl DA16 .. 12 D5
Rokesley Rd CT16 .. 278 B5
Rolfe La TN28 .... 373 B7
Rolinsden Way BR2 .. 85 D6
Rollesby Way SE28 .....3 C7
Rolleston Ave BR5 .. 53 B3
Rolleston Cl BR5 ... 53 B2
Rollo Rd BR8 ....32 F1
Roll's Ave ME12 .... 48 C1
Rolvenden Ave ME8 .. 65 C3
Rolvenden Dr ME10 .. 101 B5
Rolvenden Gdns BR1 .. 29 D1
Rolvenden Hill TN17 .. 344 C5
Rolvenden Prim Sch
TN17 .... 343 E3
Rolvenden Rd
Rochester ME2 .... 40 C2
Tenterden TN30 .. 344 E7
Rolvenden Sta★
TN17 .... 344 D6
Roly Eckhoff Ho CT16 . 278 B3
Roman Amphitheatre★
CT13 .... 148 E4
Roman Cl Chatham ME5 . 96 D1
Deal CT14 .... 215 B6
Roman Hts ME14 .. 162 C6
Roman Rd
East Studdal CT15 .. 246 C5
Edenbridge TN8 .... 249 D5
Faversham ME13 .. 138 C7
Northfleet DA11 ... 36 C5
Ramsgate CT12 ..... 83 C2
Snodland ME6 ..... 127 F8
Whitfield CT15 .... 278 D8
Roman Sq
Sittingbourne ME10 .. 101 F3
Woolwich SE28 ....3 A5
Roman Villa Rd DA2,
DA4 .... 34 C2
Roman Way
Crayford DA1 ....14 E2
Elvington CT15 .... 212 B2
Folkestone CT19 .. 334 C6
Kingsnorth TN23 .. 300 C4
Rochester ME2 ....62 F4
St Margaret's at Cliffe
CT15 .... 279 F5
Romany Ct ME5 .... 64 D1
Romany Rd ME8 ... 65 C2
Romany Rise BR5 .. 53 C1
Romden Rd TN27 .. 296 B8
Rome House Cnr
TN28 .... 373 A6
Rome Rd TN28 .... 373 A6
Romero Sq SE3 .. 11 C3
Rome Terr ME4 .....63 F4
Romford Rd TN2 .. 287 F7
Romilly Gdns CT12 .. 83 C2
Romney Ave CT20 .. 334 C5
Romney Cl
4 Birchington CT7 .. 81 A7

Romney Cl continued
Maidstone ME14 .. 163 A3
Romney Ct ME10 .. 101 E5
Romney Dr BR1 .... 29 D1
Romney Gdns DA7 .....13 F6
Romney, Hythe &
Dymchurch Rly★
CT21 .... 333 A2
Romney Marsh Ho
TN29 .... 366 C7
Romney Marsh Rd
TN23,TN24 .... 300 B6
Romney Pl ME15 .. 162 A4
Romney Rd
Ashford TN24 .... 268 E1
Chatham ME5 ....97 B5
Hamstreet TN26 .. 349 A7
New Romney TN29 .. 372 E3
Northfleet DA11 .....36 E5
Woolwich SE18 ....2 C3
Romney Sands Holiday
Village CT21 ..... 377 D8
Romney Sands Sta
TN28 .... 377 E8
Romney St TN15 .. 123 A7
Romney Street Cvn Pk
TN15 .... 123 A7
Romney Warren Ctry Pk★
TN28 .... 365 D1
Romney Way
Hythe CT21 .... 332 F1
Tonbridge TN10 .. 222 E5
Romsey Cl
Ashford TN24 .... 269 A2
Orpington BR6 ..... 86 C6
Rochester ME2 ....62 E8
Romulus Gdns TN23 .. 299 F4
Ronald Ho SE3 ..... 11 C3
Ronalds Ct 6 ME10 .. 102 A4
Ronalds Rd BR1 ..... 52 A8
Ronaldstone Rd DA15 .. 12 F8
Ronfearn Ave BR5 .. 54 D4
Ron Green Ct DA8 .. 14 D8
Ronver Rd SE12 ..... 29 A7
Roodlands La TN8 .. 218 D6
Rookdean TN13 .. 153 C5
Rookery Cl
Ashford TN24 .... 268 D7
Bredgar ME9 ...... 134 A6
Rookery Cres ME3 .....22 B6
Rookery Ct RM20 .. 17 A8
Rookery Dr BR7 .... 53 A8
Rookery Gdns BR5 .. 54 C4
Rookery Hill ME6 .. 127 F8
Rookery La 2 BR2 .. 52 D3
Rookery Lodge ME3 .. 22 C5
Rookery Rd BR6 ..... 86 A1
Rookery The RM20 .. 17 A8
Rookery View RM17 .. 18 D8
Rookesley Rd BR5 .. 54 D2
Rook La ME9 ...... 100 F6
Rookley Cl TN2 .. 286 D2
Rooks Hill TN15 .. 188 D6
Rookston Cnr CT3 .. 113 D1
Rook Wlk 2 E6 ....1 E7
Roonagh Ct ME10 .. 101 E2
Roopers TN3 ...... 285 A7
Roosevelt Ave ME5 .. 97 A8
Roosevelt Rd CT16 .. 278 B3
Ropemakers Ct ME4 .. 64 A1
Roper Cl
Canterbury CT2 .... 142 E1
Gillingham ME8 .....98 C3
Roper Rd
Canterbury CT2 .... 142 E1
Teynham ME9 ..... 103 D3
Roper's Gate TN2 .. 285 E1
Roper's Green La ME3 .. 24 B2
Roper's La TN11 ....41 F8
Roper St 1 SE9 ..... 12 A1
Ropery Bsns Pk SE7 . 1 C2
Rope Walk Mews
CT13 .... 180 F8
Rope Wlk Chatham ME4 ..63 F5
Cranbrook TN17 .. 320 C5
Rope Wlk The TN18 .. 356 B5
Rope Yard Rails SE18 ...2 B3
Rosamund Ct CT19 .. 335 C6
Roseacre Ct CT2 .. 142 E1
Roseacre Gdns ME14 . 163 A3
Roseacre Jun Sch
ME14 .... 163 A4
Roseacre La ME14 .. 163 A4
Roseacre RH8 .. 183 A1
Roseacre Rd DA16 .. 13 B4
Rose Acre Rd CT3 .. 176 F7
Rose Ave DA12 ....37 E4
Rosebank Gdns DA11 ..36 E7
Rosebank Wlk 13 SE18 ..1 C2
Roseberry Gdns
Dartford DA1 ...... 33 C8
Orpington BR6 ....86 E7
Rosebery Ave
Herne Bay CT6 ....77 E5
Ramsgate CT11 .....83 F1
Sidcup DA15 ....30 E8
Rosebery Gdns ME10 . 102 A4
Rosebery Ho DA11 .....36 F7
Rosebery Rd
Chatham ME4 ....63 E2
Gillingham ME7 .... 64 D7
Grays RM17 ....17 E8
Rose Bruford Coll
DA15 ....31 B7
Rose Cotts Hythe CT21 . 333 B4
Lamberhurst TN3 .. 317 A5
Lenham Heath ME17 .. 233 B8
Ramsgate CT12 .....82 F2
Rochester ME2 ....62 B8
St Mary Hoo ME3 .....24 E6
Rosecroft Cl
Biggin Hill TN16 .... 118 F1

Rosecroft Cl continued
Orpington BR5 .... 54 C3
Rose Ct ME17 .... 194 D1
Rosedale Cl
Dartford DA2 .... 34 B8
Woolwich SE2 ....3 B3
Rosedale Cnr BR7 .... 52 F8
Rose Dale BR6 .... 86 B8
Rosedale Rd CT9 .... 51 A1
Rosedene Cl DA1 .... 33 C8
Rose Farm La TN27 . 265 A5
Rosefield
Sevenoaks TN13 ..... 154 A3
15 Sidcup DA14 .... 31 A4
Rosegarth DA13 .... 59 E8
Rose Gdns
Birchington CT7 ....80 F6
Eythorne CT15 ...... 245 D7
Herne Bay CT6 ....79 C7
Minster (Thanet) CT12 . 115 B6
Rose Hill 11 CT11 ... 117 E6
Rosehill Rd TN16 .... 118 C2
Rose Hill Sch TN4 ... 285 E5
Rose Hill TN30 .... 360 B5
Rosehill Wlk TN1 .... 286 A3
Roseholme ME16 .... 161 D2
Rose La
Bishopsbourne CT4 ... 209 C6
Canterbury CT1 .... 174 F8
Lenham Heath ME17 .. 233 B8
Roselands CT14 ...... 215 C1
Roselands Gdns CT2 . 142 D2
Roselare Cl TN16 .... 151 D1
Roselawn Gdns 3 CT9 .82 B8
Roselea Ave CT6 ......76 F3
Roseleigh Ave ME16 . 161 C5
Roseleigh Rd ME10 .. 101 D2
Rosemary Ave
Broadstairs CT10 ...... 84 A3
Halfway Houses ME12 . 46 D6
Rosemary Cl
4 Chatham ME5 ....96 F4
Oxted RH8 .... 183 A2
Rosemary Cnr TN29 . 370 D8
Rosemary Ct 1 ME1 . 63 D4
Rosemary Gdns
Broadstairs CT10 ......83 F2
Whitstable CT5 .... 109 A8
Rosemary La
16 Canterbury CT1 .. 174 F8
Flimwell TN5 .... 339 A5
Hodsoll Street TN15 ... 92 D3
Swift's Green TN27 ... 263 F5
Rosemary Rd
Bexley DA16 ....12 F6
Maidstone ME15 ..... 163 A3
West Malling ME19 ... 127 F1
Rosemead Gdns TN27 . 262 B7
Rosemount Cl ME15 . 194 F4
Rosemount Ct ME2 ... 40 A1
Rosemount Dr BR1 ... 52 F5
Roseneath Cl BR6 .... 87 C3
Rose St DA11 .... 18 B1
Rose Street Prim Sch
ME12 ....28 B2
Rose St Rochester ME1 . 63 D3
Sheerness ME12 ......28 B2
Tonbridge TN9 .... 254 C8
Rose Terr
Faversham ME13 ..... 138 D5
Offham ME19 .... 158 D7
Rosetower Ct CT10 ...83 F8
Rosetta Prim Sch E16 .1 B8
Roseveare Rd SE12 .. 29 C4
Rose Way SE12 .... 11 A2
Rose Wlk CT18 .... 307 A4
Rosewood Cl DA14 ... 31 C5
Rosewood Ct BR1 .... 52 D8
Rosewood Dr TN25 .. 267 F4
Rosewood DA2 ....32 E4
Rosewood Way CT7 ..81 B7
Rose Yd ME14 .... 162 A4
Rosher Ho DA11 ......18 B1
Rosherville CE Prim Sch
DA11 ....18 E1
Rosherville Way DA11 .18 E1
Rosiers Ct 1 CT2 ... 142 E1
Roslin Way BR1 ..... 29 A3
Ross Ct BR7 ....29 F1
Rossdale TN2 .... 286 D5
Rosse Mews SE3 .....11 B6
Rossendale Ct 10
CT20 .... 335 E6
Rossendale Gdns 8
CT20 .... 335 E6
Rossendale Rd CT20 . 335 E6
Rossetti Ct CT7 ....80 F7
Rossetti Rd CT7 ......80 F8
Ross Gdns CT7 ...... 142 B3
Ross House SE18 .....11 E6
Rossland Cl DA6 ......14 B2
Rossland Rd CT12 ... 117 A8
Rosslyn Gn ME16 .... 161 B5
Rossmore DA14 ...... 31 A3
Ross Rd DA1 .... 15 A1
Ross St ME1 .... 63 D4
Ross Way Eltham SE9 .11 A4
Folkestone CT20 ..... 334 E5
Rothbrook Dr TN24 .. 268 C7
Rother Ct 24 BR5 ... 38 A5
Rothermere Cl TN17 . 342 E6
Rother Rd TN10 ..... 222 C5
Rother Vale ME5 .... 97 C3
Rothesay Ct 6 SE12 .29 B5
Rothley Cl TN30 .... 345 B8
Rothsay Ct CT11 ......83 F1
Rouge La DA12 ....37 E2
Rougemont St ME18 . 159 C2
Rough Common Rd
CT2 .... 142 B3
Roughetts Rd ME19 . 126 F3
Roughway La TN11 .. 190 C7
Round Ash Way DA3 ..58 E3

Roundel Cl ME9 ...... 103 D2
Roundel The ME10 .. 101 F2
Roundel Way TN12 .. 259 D5
Round Green Cotts
TN17 .... 291 F4
Roundhay ME19 ..... 127 E1
Roundhill Rd TN2 ... 286 D1
Roundlyn Gdns BR5 . 54 B5
Round St DA12,DA13 . 60 D5
Roundtable Rd BR1 .. 26 A5
Roundway TN16 ..... 118 D4
Roundwell ME14 .... 163 D3
Roundwood BR7 .....53 B7
Round Wood Cl ME5 . 97 A1
Routh St E6 ....1 F8
Rover Rd ME5 ....97 B2
Rowan Cl Ashford TN23 . 267 E2
Aylesford ME20 ..... 128 E1
Meopham Station DA13 ..60 B3
Paddock Wood TN12 . 256 F5
Staple CT3 .... 179 A6
Sturry CT2 .... 143 F6
Rowan Cres DA1 ..... 33 C7
Rowan Ct
4 Chatham ME5 .....96 F5
Broadstairs CT10 ... 103 F4
2 Lewisham SE12 .. 29 A8
Rowan Ho
4 Chatham ME5 .....96 F5
7 Maidstone ME16 . 161 A3
Royal Tunbridge Wells
TN4 .... 285 E4
Rowan House DA14 ..30 F5
Rowan Lea ME5 ....64 B1
Rowan Rd Bexley DA7 . 13 C4
Swanley BR8 .... 55 D6
Rowans Cl DA3 ....58 D7
Rowan Shaw TN10 .. 222 D6
Rowans The ME12 ...47 B7
Rowan Tree Pk CT5 . 108 B6
Rowan Tree Rd TN2 . 285 C1
Rowan Wlk
Chatham ME4 ....63 E3
Orpington BR2 ....85 F7
Rowanwood Ave DA15 . 31 A7
Rowbrocke Cl ME4 .. 98 D3
Rowdow La TN14,TN15 . 122 E5
Rowe Cl CT9 ....82 F7
Rowena Rd CT8 ...... 50 C1
Rowenden Vineyard ★
TN17 .... 343 B2
Rowe Pl ME20 .... 128 F6
Rowetts Way ME12 .. 48 D3
Rowfield 6 TN8 .... 217 D3
Rowhill Cotts DA2 ....32 E2
Rowhill Rd DA2 ...... 33 A3
Rowhill Sch DA2 ..... 33 C4
Rowland Ave ME7 ....64 E2
Rowland Cl
Gillingham ME7 ....64 E1
Maidstone ME16 .... 161 E2
Rowland Cotts CT21 . 331 F3
Rowland Cres CT6 ....77 E5
Rowland Dr CT6 ...... 76 C2
Rowlands Manor BR5 . 54 C3
Rowlatt Cl DA2 ...... 33 C4
Rowlatt Rd DA2 ..... 33 C5
Rowley Ave DA15 .....31 B8
Rowley Hill TN2 ..... 255 D1
Rowmarsh Cl DA11 .. 36 B4
Rowntree Path 1 SE28 ..3 B5
Row The Ash CT3 ... 147 E5
Chillenden CT3 ...... 211 F8
Elham CT4 .... 273 F5
New Ash Green DA3 ...91 F8
Ruckinge TN26 ...... 349 F8
Rowton Rd SE18 ..... 12 C7
Rowzill Rd BR8 ....32 F2
Roxburgh Rd CT8 .... 50 D1
Royal Albert Sta E16 ..1 E6
Royal Albert Way
Newham,Cyprus E16 ....2 A6
Newham E16 ....1 E6
Royal Ave
Tonbridge TN9 ...... 254 D8
Whitstable CT5 ...... 108 C5
Royal Chase TN4 .... 285 F4
Royal Cl
Broadstairs CT10 .....83 F4
Orpington BR6 ....86 B6
Royal Connaught
Apartments ME1 .....1 C5
Royal Cres Margate CT9 . 50 H2
Ramsgate CT11 ...... 117 D6
Royal Ct Eltham SE9 . 29 F7
Whitstable CT5 ...... 75 A3
Royal Docks Com Sch The
E16 ....1 C7
Royal Docks Rd E6 ...2 B7
Royal Eagle Cl ME2 . 63 E7
Royal Engineers Mus ★
ME7 ....64 B6
Royal Engineers' Rd
ME14 .... 161 F7
Royal Espl Margate CT9 . 50 F1
Ramsgate CT11 ...... 117 C5
Royal Fountain Mews
ME12 .... 28 A2
Royal Harbour App
CT11 .... 117 C5
Royal Mews 16 CT11 . 117 F7
Royal Military Ave
CT20 .... 334 D5
Royal Military Rd
Aldington TN25 ...... 330 D1
Hythe CT21 .... 332 D1
Royal Mus & art Gallery
with Buffs Regimental
Mus ★ CT1 .... 174 F8
Royal Oak Cotts TN8 . 184 C2
Royal Oak Rd DA6 ...13 F3
Royal Oak Terr DA12 . 37 C7

Royal Parade Mews
BR7 ....30 C1
Royal Par BR7 .... 30 C1
Royal Park Prim Sch
DA14 ....31 E5
Royal Par CT11 ...... 117 E6
Royal Pier Rd DA12 . 19 C1
Royal Rd Newham E16 ..1 F7
Ramsgate CT11 ...... 117 D6
Sheerness ME12 ..... 28 C2
Sidcup DA14 .... 31 D5
Sutton at H DA2 ..... 34 A3
Royal Rise TN9 ...... 254 C8
Royal St George's Golf
Links ★ CT13 .... 149 E2
Royal Sch of Military
Engineering ME3 .... 40 C4
Royal School for Deaf
Children CT9 ....50 J2
Royal Sovereign Ave
ME4 ....64 B7
Royal Star Arc 5
ME14 .... 161 F4
Royal Tunbridge Wells
Bsns Pk TN2 .... 254 D1
Royal Victoria Hospl
CT19 .... 335 C6
Royal Victoria Pl
5 Dover CT16 ...... 310 D8
Newham E16 ....1 B5
Royal Tunbridge Wells
TN1 .... 286 B4
Royal Victoria Sq E16 .1 B6
Royal Victoria Sta E16 .1 A6
Royal West Kent Ave
TN10 .... 222 D4
Roydene SE18 ....2 E1
Roydon Hall ★ TN12 . 191 F4
Roydon Hall Rd TN12 . 191 F4
Royds Rd TN24 ...... 300 D6
Royston Gdns CT15 . 279 F6
Royston Rd
Crayford DA1 ....14 F1
Maidstone ME15 .... 163 A3
Roystons Cl ME8 .....65 F2
Royton Ave ME17 ... 199 D5
RSPB Dungeness Nature
Reserve ★ TN29 ... 379 F5
Rubery Dro CT3 ..... 148 C2
Rubin Pl ME19 ...... 159 B3
Ruckinge Cnr TN26 . 349 F8
Ruckinge Rd TN26 .. 349 A7
Ruckinge Way ME8 .. 65 C3
Ruck La TN12 .... 289 E3
Ruddstreet Cl SE18 ...2 C1
Rudge Cl ME5 .... 97 D2
Rudland Rd DA7 .....14 B4
Ruegg Ho 5 SE18 .. 12 A8
Ruffet Ct TN2 .... 285 E1
Ruffets Wood
Gravesend DA12 ..... 37 C2
Kingsnorth TN23 .... 300 C3
Rugby Cl
Broadstairs CT10 .....83 F5
Chatham ME5 ....96 F4
Rugby Gdns TN23 ... 300 C8
Rugby Rd CT17 ...... 310 A6
Ruggles St ME13 .... 23 E3
Ruins Barn Rd ME10,
ME9 .... 134 D6
Rule Ct ME12 .... 46 B8
Rumania Wlk DA12 .. 37 F5
Rumfields Rd CT10 .. 83 D4
Rumstead La ME17,
ME9 .... 132 D4
Rumstead Rd ME9 .. 132 E4
Rumwood Ct ME17 .. 196 B5
Runcie Ho 6 CT1 .. 174 F7
Runcie Pl CT2 .... 142 D1
Runciman Ct BR6 .... 87 C1
Runham La ME17 ... 198 E3
Running Horse Rdbt The
ME14 .... 129 E1
Runnymede Ct DA2 . 34 C7
Runnymede Gdns
ME15 .... 195 A8
Runnymede Mews
ME13 .... 138 C7
Rural Vale DA11 ......36 E8
Ruscombe Cl TN4 ... 253 F2
Rusham Rd CT3 ..... 146 C1
Rushbrook Rd SE9 .. 30 C6
Rush Cl Chatham ME5 . 97 A3
Rushdean Rd ME2 .. 62 D5
Rushdene SE2 ....3 D3
Rushdene Wlk TN16 . 118 D2
Rushenden Rd ME11 . 45 F3
Rushenden Rd ME11 . 46 A4
Rushes The ME20 ... 128 B4
Rushet Rd BR5 ...... 54 A7
Rushetts TN3 .... 284 F4
Rushetts Rd TN15 ....90 E3
Rusheymead Ho 5 SE18 .2 F1
Rushford Cl TN27 ... 262 D5
Rushgrove St SE18 ...1 F2
Rushley Cl BR2 ......85 E6
Rushlye Cl TN3 ..... 314 F5
Rushmead Cl CT2 ... 142 D2
Rushmead Dr ME15 . 195 A7
Rushmere Ct TN15 .. 156 D7
Rushmore Cl BR1 ....52 E6
Rushmore Hill BR6,
TN14 .... 120 D6
Rushymead TN15 ... 123 A1
Ruskin Ave DA16 .... 13 A4
Ruskin Cl ME19 .... 159 F8
Ruskin Ct SE5 .... 11 F1
Ruskin Dr Bexley DA16 . 13 A4
Orpington BR6 ....86 E7
Ruskin Gr Bexley DA16 . 13 A5
Dartford DA1 .... 16 A2
Ruskin Rd DA17 ....4 A2

Ruskins View CT6 ... 77 A1
Ruskin Wlk BR2 .....52 F3
Rusland Ave BR6 .... 86 D7
Russell Cl Bexley DA7 . 14 A3
Crayford DA1 .... 15 A3
Greenwich SE7 ...... 11 C7
Sittingbourne ME10 . 101 C3
Russell Ct ME4 ...... 64 B3
Russell Dr CT5 ...... 75 D3
Russell House Sch
TN14 .... 122 C3
Russell Pl
Faversham ME13 .... 105 B3
Sutton at H DA4 .... 57 A8
Russell Quay 2 DA11 . 19 A1
Russell Rd
1 Folkestone CT19 . 335 D6
Gravesend DA12 ..... 19 D1
Kit's Coty ME20 ..... 129 D7
Newham E16 ....1 B1
Tilbury RM18 .... 18 F5
Tilbury RM18 .... 18 F5
Russells Ave ME8 ... 99 A8
Russell Sq DA3 ...... 58 D6
Russell St Dover CT16 . 310 E1
Sheerness ME12 ..... 28 B2
Russells Yd TN17 ... 320 D4
Russell Terr CT5 ..... 57 C5
Russet Ave ME13 ... 138 C5
Russet Cl ME2 ....62 E8
Russet Ct
Coxheath ME17 ..... 194 C3
17 Erith DA17 ....4 A1
Russets The
Maidstone ME16 .... 161 B5
Meopham Station DA13 . 60 A3
Whitstable CT5 ...... 75 D1
Russett Cl Ditton ME20 . 160 E8
Orpington BR6 ....87 B5
Russett Rd
Canterbury CT1 ..... 175 C8
East Peckham TN12 . 224 F6
Russett Way BR8 .... 55 D8
Russet Way ME19 .. 158 F2
Rusthall Grange TN4 . 285 D4
Rusthall Pk TN4 .... 285 D4
Rusthall Rd TN4 .... 285 D4
Rustic Wlk E16 ....1 B7
Ruston Ct SE18 ....1 E3
Rustwick TN4 .... 285 D4
Rutherford Coll CT2 . 142 E4
Rutherford Rd TN24 . 268 C2
Rutherford Way TN10 . 222 D7
Rutherglen Rd SE2 . 13 A8
Ruth Ho 2 ME16 .. 161 E5
Ruthin Rd SE3 .... 11 A8
Ruth St ME4 .... 64 A2
Rutland Ave
Margate CT9 .... 51 C2
Sidcup DA15 .... 31 A8
Rutland Cl
Canterbury CT1 ..... 175 D7
Dartford DA1 .... 33 D8
Sidcup DA5 .... 31 D7
Rutland Ct
Chislehurst BR7 ..... 53 A8
Sidcup SE9 .... 30 C6
Rutland Gate DA17 .. 4 B1
Rutland Gdns
Birchington CT7 ......80 F7
Margate CT9 .... 51 C2
Rutland Ho
3 Margate CT9 ......51 B2
10 Woolwich SE18 ...1 F2
Rutland Pl ME8 ...... 98 C3
Rutland Rd CT16 .... 278 B3
Rutland Way
Maidstone ME15 .... 195 E8
Orpington BR5 ...... 54 C3
Ruxley Cl DA14 ...... 31 E2
Ruxley Cnr DA14 ....31 E2
Ruxley Corner Ind Est
DA14 ....31 D2
Ruxley Ct 1 BR1 ... 52 C7
Ruxton Ct BR8 ...... 55 E6
Ruxton St BR8 ...... 55 E6
Ryan Cl SE3 .... 11 C3
Ryan Dr ME15 ...... 163 A2
Ryarsh Cres BR6 ....86 E6
Ryarsh La ME19 ... 127 B5
Ryarsh Pk ME19 ... 126 F4
Ryarsh Prim Sch
ME19 .... 127 A4
Ryarsh Rd ME19 ... 127 B5
Rycault Cl 4 ME16 . 161 E3
Rycaut Rd ME8 ..... 98 D3
Rycroft La TN14 ... 186 E5
Rydal Ave CT11 .... 117 B7
Rydal Cl TN4 .... 285 E5
Rydal Dr Bexley DA7 . 14 A6
Royal Tunbridge Wells
TN4 .... 285 E5
Rydal Ho ME15 ..... 195 E7
Ryde Cl ME5 ....97 B8
Rydens Ho SE9 ..... 29 C5
Ryder Cl BR1 .... 29 B3
Ryder's Ave CT8 .... 81 D8
Ryders TN3 .... 285 A3
Ryde St CT2 .... 142 E1
Rydons Cl SE9 ..... 11 E4
Rye Cl DA5 ....14 B1
Rye Cres BR5 ...... 54 D1
Ryecroft Rd
Orpington BR5 ...... 53 D3
Otford TN14 .... 122 A2
Rydale Ct TN13 .... 153 E6
Ryedale TN30 ..... 360 B5
Rye Field 25 BR5 .. 54 D1
Ryegrass Cl ME5 ... 97 C6

Ryelands Cres SE12 . 11 C1
Rye La Otford TN14 . 122 A2
Sevenoaks TN13,TN14 . 153 F7
Rye Rd Brookland TN29 . 370 D8
Four Throws TN18 .. 355 D8
Hawkhurst TN18 .... 341 B1
Peasmarsh TN31 .... 367 C2
Wittersham TN30 ... 360 A2
Rye Wlk CT6 .... 77 C2
Rye Wood Cotts TN14 . 153 F7
Ryland St 5 CT20 .. 335 E5
Ryland Pl 6 CT20 .. 335 E5
Rylands Rd TN24 ... 268 D5
Rymers Cl TN2 ...... 286 D7
Rymill St E16 ....2 A5
Rype Cl TN29 .... 376 C5
Rysted La CT14 ..... 151 D1
Ryswick Mews TN28 . 373 C8

S

Sabre Rd ME7 .... 65 A1
Sackett's Gap CT9 ... 51 C3
Sacketts Hill CT10 .. 83 C6
Sackville Ave BR2 ... 52 A1
Sackville Cl
Hothfield TN26 ..... 267 A7
Sevenoaks TN13 .... 154 B5
Sackville Cres TN23 . 268 A2
Sackville Rd DA2 .....33 E6
Sackville Sch TN11 . 221 C6
Sacred Heart Sch
TN5 .... 336 D5
Saddington St DA12 . 37 E8
Saddlebrook Pk ME12 . 49 E2
Saddlers Cl ME14 .. 162 E5
Saddlers Hill CT3 .. 178 D2
Saddlers Mews CT5 . 75 D1
Saddler's Pk DA4 ... 89 D7
Saddler's Wall La
TN29 .... 362 B1
Saddlers Way TN23 . 300 B5
Saddleton Gr CT5 .. 108 D3
Saddleton Rd CT5 .. 108 D3
Sadlers Cl ME5 ..... 96 D2
Saffron Cl ME16 .... 161 B3
Saffron's Pl 14 CT20 . 335 E5
Saffron Way
1 Chatham ME5 ....96 F5
Sittingbourne ME10 . 101 F7
Sage Cl 7 E6 ....1 F8
Sage Rd ME1 ....63 B3
Saigasso Cl ME16 ....1 D7
Sailfield Dr ME4 .....63 F7
Sailmakers Ct 5 ME4 . 64 B2
St Agnes Gdns ME12 . 28 C1
St Aidan's Way DA2 . 37 E5
St Albans Cl ME7 ... 64 E7
St Alban's Cl DA12 . 37 D5
St Alban's Gdns DA12 . 37 D5
St Alban's Rd
Dartford DA1 .... 15 F1
Hersden CT3 .... 111 E1
St Alban's Rd Inf Sch
DA1 ....15 F1
St Albans Rd ME2 .. 62 D6
St Alfege Rd SE7 .... 11 D8
St Alphege CE Prim Sch
CT5 .... 74 D1
St Alphege Cl CT5 .. 108 B7
St Alphege La 17 CT1 . 142 F1
St Alphege Rd 4
CT16 .... 278 C8
St Ambrose Gn TN25 . 237 E2
St Andrews Cl
Canterbury CT1 ..... 174 C1
Erith SE28 ....3 D7
Folkestone CT19 .... 335 B7
Herne Bay CT6 ...... 77 A4
St Andrew's Cl ME16 . 161 A2
St Andrews Cl
Margate CT9 ....82 F7
Paddock Wood TN12 . 257 A6
St Andrew's Cl CT5 . 108 E7
St Andrews Ct
26 Gravesend DA12 . 19 B1
Royal Tunbridge Wells
TN4 .... 254 A1
St Andrew's Dr BR5 . 54 B2
St Andrews Ct TN19 . 335 E5
St Andrews Gdns
CT17 .... 278 B2
St Andrew's Gdns
CT15 .... 244 E5
St Andrews Ho BR1 . 29 B2
St Andrew's Lees
CT13 .... 181 A8
St Andrews Mews SE3 . 11 A7
St Andrews Park Rd
TN4 .... 254 A1
St Andrews Pk ME16 . 161 A3
St Andrew's Rd CT14 . 215 C6
St Andrews Rd ME7 . 64 D7
St Andrew's Rd RM18 . 18 E5
St Andrews Sch ME1 . 63 C2
St Andrews Way
The Chart RH8 ...... 183 F4
Tilmanstone CT14 ... 213 A3
St Andrew's Wlk ME3 . 9 D2
St Andrew Terr CT17 . 278 A2
St Angela's Sch CT8 . 81 D7
St Anne's Ct
1 Dover CT16 ..... 278 B2
Herne Bay CT6 ...... 76 C5

St Annes Ct ME16 .. 161 E4
St Anne's Dr CT6 ... 76 D4
St Anne's Gdns CT9 . 82 F8
St Anne's Rd
Ashford TN23 .... 299 F7
Whitstable CT5 ....74 F2
St Ann's Green La
TN12 .... 259 E5
St Ann's Rd
Dymchurch TN29 ... 366 B7
Faversham ME13 ... 138 B7
St Anns Way TN16 . 119 B3
St Anselm's RC Prim Sch
DA1 ....16 A2
St Anselm's RC Sch
CT1 .... 175 C5
St Anthony's Ct BR6 . 86 B8
St Anthony's Sch CT9 . 51 C1
St Anthony's Way CT9 . 51 C1
St Aubyns Cl BR6 ...86 F7
St Aubyns Gdns BR6 . 86 F8
St Audrey Ave DA7 . 14 A5
St Augustine Ho 1
TN9 .... 254 B8
St Augustine of Canterbury
RC Prim Sch ME8 .. 98 D3
St Augustine's Abbey
CT11 .... 117 D5
St Augustine's Abbey (rems
of) ★ CT1 .... 175 A8
St Augustine's Ave
Bromley BR2 .... 52 E4
Margate CT9 ....82 F8
St Augustines Bsns Pk
CT5 .... 75 E3
St Augustine's Cres
CT5 .... 75 D3
St Augustine's Ct 3
CT1 .... 175 B8
St Augustines Ct CT6 . 76 F2
St Augustine's of
Canterbury CE Prim Sch
St Augustine's Pk
CT11 .... 117 C6
St Augustine's RC Prim Sch
Hythe CT21 .... 333 C2
Royal Tunbridge Wells
TN4 .... 286 A7
St Augustine's Rd
Canterbury CT1 ..... 175 B7
Deal CT14 .... 214 F4
Erith DA17 ....3 F2
Ramsgate CT11 ..... 117 D5
St Barnabas CE Prim Sch
TN1 .... 286 B5
St Barnabas Cl
Ashford TN23 .... 299 F7
Gillingham ME7 ..... 64 D3
Maidstone ME16 ... 161 E4
St Barnabas' Cl TN1 . 286 B5
St Bartholomews Cl 4
CT17 .... 310 C8
St Bartholomew's Hospl
Rochester ME1 ...... 63 C4
Sandwich CT13 ..... 181 A7
St Bartholomew's La 4
ME1 .... 63 E4
St Bartholomews RC Prim
Sch BR8 .... 55 E6
St Bartholomew's Terr 2
ME1 .... 63 E4
St Bart's Cl 5 CT7 . 310 C8
St Bart's Rd CT13 .. 180 F8
St Benedict Rd ME6 . 127 E8
St Benedict's Ave DA12 . 37 E6
St Benedict's Lawn
CT11 .... 117 D5
St Benedicts RC Prim Sch
ME5 .... 97 C2
St Benets Ct TN30 .. 345 B8
St Benet's Rd CT8 ...81 E7
St Benets Way TN30 . 345 B8
St Benjamins Dr BR6 . 87 C2
St Bernards Rd TN10 . 222 C6
St Blaise Ave BR1 ...52 B7
St Boltophs Ct TN13 . 154 B3
St Botolph Rd DA11 . 36 D5
St Botolph's Ave
TN13 .... 154 B3
St Botolph's CE Prim Sch
DA11 .... 36 D8
St Botolph's Rd TN13 . 154 B3
St Brelade's Ct TN8 . 217 A3
St Brides Cl DA18 ....3 D4
St Catherines Ct
Ramsgate CT11 ......83 F1
Rochester ME1 ..... 63 D5
St Catherine's Dr
ME13 .... 138 D6
St Catherine's Gr CT12 . 82 D1
St Catherine's Hospl
ME1 .... 63 D4
St Catherines CT13 . 83 D8
St Catherine's RC Sch for
Girls DA6 ....14 B2
St Cecelia CT14 .... 215 B1
St Chad's Dr DA12 .. 37 E5
St Chad's Rd RM18 . 19 A6
St Chad's Sch RM18 . 19 A6
St Christopher CT7 .. 83 D8
St Christophers Gn
CT10 .... 83 F5
St Christopher's Sch
CT11 .... 175 B6
St Clare Rd CT14 ... 215 C1
St Clement's Ave RM20 . 17 B8
St Clements Cl
Leysdown-on-S ME12 . 49 D2
Northfleet DA11 .....36 F5

St Clements Ct
Broadstairs CT10 ....83 E6
Folkestone CT20 ......335 F5
Grays RM17 ....17 F8
St Clement's Ct CT17 .. 77 A3
St Clement's Ct CT11 .. 117 D7
St Clement's Ho ME1 .. 63 D5
St Clements Rd ME12 .... 49 E3
St Clement's Rd
Westgate-on-S CT8 .... 50 C1
West Thurrock RM20 .... 17 C7
St Clements 8 CT13 .. 149 A1
St Clement's Way
RM20 ....16 F8
St Clere Hill Rd TN15 .. 123 F7
St Columba's Cl CT12 ...37 E5
St Columba's RC Boys Sch
DA6 ....14 B2
St Cosmus Cl TN25 .... 203 B1
St Crispin's Com Prim Inf
Sch CT8 ....81 E7
St Crispin's Rd CT8 .....81 E7
St Cuby CT10 ....84 C7
St Davids Ave CT17 .. 310 A5
St David's Bridge
TN17 ....320 D4
St David's Cl
Birchington CT7 ....81 B8
Whitstable CT5 .... 108 E8
St David's Cres DA12 ...37 D4
St Davids Gate ME16 .. 161 A2
St David's Rd
Allhallows ME3 ....9 D2
Deal CT14 .... 215 C6
Hextable BR8 ....32 F1
Ramsgate CT11 ....83 F1
Royal Tunbridge Wells
TN4 ....286 B6
St Denys Rd CT18 ..... 307 B5
St Domingo Ho SE18 .....1 F3
St Dunstans Cl CT2 .. 142 E1
St Dunstans Ct 4 CT2 .. 142 E1
St Dunstan's Dr DA12 ...37 E5
St Dunstan's Rd CT9 ... 51 A2
St Dunstan's St CT2 .. 142 E1
St Dunstan's Terr CT2 .. 142 E1
St Dunstans Wlk
TN17 ....320 D4
St Eanswythe's CE Prim
Sch CT20 .... 335 D4
St Eanswythe Way 19
CT20 ....335 D5
St Edith's Rd TN15 .. 123 A2
St Edmund Ho SE2 .... 13 D8
St Edmund's Cl DA18 ....3 C4
St Edmund's Cotts
TN15 ....91 A2
St Edmund's Ct TN15 .. 91 A2
St Edmund's RC Sch
CT16 ....278 D2
St Edmunds Rd
Canterbury CT1 .... 174 F8
Dartford DA1 ....16 A3
St Edmund's Rd CT14 .. 214 E4
St Edmund's Sch CT2 .. 142 C3
St Edmunds Way ME8 ...66 B1
St Edward's RC Prim Sch
ME12 ....28 B2
St Elisabeth Ho CT1 .. 143 A1
St Ethelbert's RC Prim Sch
CT11 ....117 C8
St Faith's at Ash Sch
CT3 ....147 C1
St Faith's La ME14 .. 163 B4
St Faith's St ME14 .. 161 F4
St Fidelis RC Prim Sch
DA8 ....14 C8
St Fidelis' Rd DA8 ......4 D1
St Francis Ave DA12 ....37 E4
St Francis Cl
Deal CT14 .... 214 F4
Maidstone ME14 ...... 162 B7
Margate CT9 ....83 D8
Orpington BR6 ....53 E3
Rochester ME2 ....62 E6
St Francis RC Prim Sch
ME15 ....142 E1
St Francis' Rd DA8 ......4 D2
St Francis Rd
Folkestone CT19 ...... 334 F6
Harvel DA13 ....93 B3
St Gabriel's Ct 12
CT20 ....335 E6
St Georges Ave ME12 .. 48 D2
St George's Ave
Herne Bay CT6 ....76 D4
Sheerness ME12 ....28 B1
St George's Bickley CE
Prim Sch BR1 .... 52 D7
St George's Bsns Ctr
TN23 ....267 F2
St Georges Bsns Pk
ME10 ....102 B4
St George's CE Foundation
Sch CT10 ....83 C5
St George's CE Mid Sch
ME12 ....47 E6
St George's CE Prim Sch
TN15 ....124 F3
St George's CE Sch
DA11 ....19 A1
St Georges Cl SE28 ......3 D7
St George's Cl CT15 .. 108 E7
St Georges Cres CT17 .. 310 B5
St George's Cres DA12 .. 37 D4
St Georges Ct CT17 ....37 E2
St George's Ctr DA11 ....19 B1
St Georges Ct TN4 .. 286 A5
St George's Ct
West Minst ME12 ....46 B8

St George's Ct continued
Wrotham TN15 .... 124 F3
St Georges La CT1 .. 175 A8
St George's Lees
CT13 ....181 A8
St George's Mews 11
TN9 ....254 B8
St George's Pas CT14 .. 215 D6
St George's Pk TN2 .. 313 F8
St George's Pl
Canterbury CT1 .... 175 A8
Hythe CT21 .... 353 D8
St George's Pl
St Margaret's at Cliffe
CT15 ....279 F6
Sandwich CT13 .... 181 B8
St George's Rd CT10 .. 84 A4
St Georges Rd BR1 .....52 F6
St George's Rd
Deal CT14 .... 215 D6
Folkestone CT19 ...... 334 F6
Gillingham ME7 ....64 C6
St Georges Rd BR5 .. 53 D3
St George's Rd
Ramsgate CT11 .... 117 F8
Sandwich CT13 .... 181 A8
Sevenoaks TN13 ...... 154 B5
Sidcup DA14 ....31 D2
St Georges Rd BR8 .....55 F5
St Georges Rd W BR1 .. 52 E7
St George's Sq 3
TN24 ....268 B2
St Georges Sq DA3 .....58 E6
St George's Sq ME16 .. 161 E3
St Georges St CT1 .. 175 A8
St George's Terr CT6 ...76 E5
St George's Wlk ME3 ....9 D2
St German's Pl SE3 .. 11 A6
St Giles Cl Dover CT17 .. 310 B5
Orpington BR6 ....86 D5
St Giles Rd CT17 .... 310 B5
St Giles Wlk CT17 .... 310 B5
St Gregory's Ct CT1 .. 143 B1
St Gregory's 9 CT1 .. 143 B1
St Gregory's Ct CT14 .. 214 F4
St Gregory's Cres DA12 .. 37 E6
St Gregory's Ct DA12 ...37 E6
St Gregory's RC Comp Sch
TN4 ....286 A7
St Gregory's RC Prim Sch
CT9 ....82 E8
St Gregory's Rd CT1 .. 143 B1
St Helens CE Prim Sch
ME3 ....22 B5
St Helens Cotts ME15 .. 193 E8
St Helens La ME15 .. 193 E8
St Helens Rd Cliffe ME3 .. 22 B5
7 Erith DA18 ....3 D4
St Helen's Rd ME12 .... 28 D1
St Helens DA14 ....31 B5
St Helier's Cl ME16 .. 161 B2
St Hilda Rd CT19 .... 334 E6
St Hildas TN15 ...... 189 F8
St Hilda's Rd CT21 .. 333 B1
St Hilda's Way DA12 ...37 E5
St Jacob's Pl CT1 .. 174 D6
St James' Ave
Broadstairs CT10 ....83 E6
Ramsgate CT12 ....83 B1
St James' CE Inf Sch
TN2 ....286 C4
St James' CE Jun Sch
TN2 ....286 C4
St James' CE Prim Sch
ME3 ....27 B6
St James Cl
East Malling ME19 .... 159 F8
Grain ME3 ....27 B6
Tonbridge TN10 ...... 222 D7
Warden ME12 ....49 E4
St James Ct
3 Bromley BR2 ....52 A7
Greenwich SE3 ....11 B6
Stone DA9 ....16 F1
St James' Gdns CT5 .. 108 D8
St James' Inf Sch
ME19 ....159 F8
St James La 7 CT16 .. 310 E7
St James' La DA9 ......34 E8
St James Oaks DA11 .. 37 A8
St James' Park Rd CT9 .. 82 A8
St James' Pk TN1 .. 286 C5
St James Pl DA11 .. 15 D1
St James RC Prim Sch
BR5 ....53 B4
St James Rd Grain ME3 .. 27 B5
Kingsdown CT14 ...... 248 D5
St James' Rd TN15 .. 124 F3
St James's Ave DA11 ....37 A8
St James's Cl SE18 ......2 C1
St James's Ct TN1 .. 286 B4
St James Sq DA3 ......58 E6
St James's Rd
Gravesend DA11 ....19 A1
Sevenoaks TN13 ...... 154 B5
St James's St DA11 .. 19 A1
St James St CT16 .... 310 E7
St James's Terr CT7 ...81 B8
St James Way DA14 .. 31 E3
St Jean's Rd CT8 ......81 E7
St Joachim's RC Prim Sch
E16 ....1 C7
St John Bsns Ctr The 10
CT9 ....50 J1
St John Fisher RC Comp
(Lower) Sch ME4 ......63 D7
St John Fisher RC Comp
Sch ME4 ....63 D7
St John Fisher RC Prim Sch
DA18 ....3 D3
St John's Cotts
Bethersden TN26 ...... 297 D5

St John's Cotts continued
12 Sandwich CT13 .... 148 F1
St John's Ave
Ramsgate CT12 ....83 A1
Sittingbourne ME10 .. 102 B3
St John's CE Inf Sch
ME4 ....63 E3
St John's CE Prim Sch
Maidstone ME14 ...... 162 E4
Royal Tunbridge Wells
TN4 ....286 B7
Sevenoaks TN13 ...... 154 D4
St John's Church Rd
CT19 ....335 C6
St John's Cl
Densole CT18 .... 307 A7
Higham ME3 ....39 C4
St John's Commandery
(rems of) ★ CT15 .... 275 E4
St Johns Cres CT12 .. 142 D6
St John's Ct TN24 .... 301 A6
St Johns Ct DA8 ....4 D1
St John's Ct TN13 .. 154 C5
St John's Hill TN13,
TN14 ....154 C5
St John's Hospl 6
CT1 ....143 A1
St John's Jerusalem ★
DA4 ....34 B1
St John's La
Ashford TN23,TN24 .. 268 C2
Canterbury CT1 .... 174 F8
Hartley DA3 ....58 F3
St John's Par 4 DA14 .. 31 B4
St John's Pk
Greenwich SE3 .... 11 A7
Royal Tunbridge Wells
TN4 ....286 A8
St John's Pl CT1 .. 143 A1
St John's RC Comp Sch
DA12 ....37 D7
St John's RC Prim Sch
DA12 ....37 E7
St John's Rd
Bexley DA16 ....13 B4
Dartford DA2 ....34 C8
Dover CT17 .... 310 C7
St Johns Rd CT12 .. 212 B2
St John's Rd Erith DA8 ....4 D1
Faversham ME13 ...... 138 D7
Gillingham ME7 ....64 C3
Gravesend DA12 ....37 D8
Higham ME3 ....39 C4
St Johns Rd
Hoo St Werburgh ME3 .. 41 E6
Hythe CT21 .... 333 A3
St John's Rd
Margate CT9 ....50 J2
Newham E16 ....1 A7
New Romney TN28 .. 373 A6
Orpington BR5 ....53 E3
Royal Tunbridge Wells
TN4 ....286 A6
Sevenoaks TN13 ...... 154 C5
Sidcup DA14 ....31 B4
Whitstable CT5 ....75 D3
St John's St
Folkestone CT20 ...... 335 D5
7 Margate CT9 ....50 J2
St John's Terr SE18 .. 12 D8
St John's Way CT18 .. 307 A7
St Johns Way
Edenbridge TN8 ...... 217 C3
Rochester ME1 ....63 A2
St Josephs Cl BR6 .....86 F6
St Josephs Ct 4 SE12 ..29 B5
St Josephs Prep Sch
DA12 ....37 C6
St Joseph's RC Prim Sch
Aylesham CT3 .... 211 A5
Broadstairs CT10 ....83 F5
Bromley BR1 ....29 B1
Crayford DA1 ....14 E3
Northfleet DA11 ....36 D8
St Julien Ave CT1 .. 143 D1
St Justin Cl BR5 ....54 D6
St Katharine's Knockholt
CE Prim Sch TN14 .... 120 B2
St Katherine Rd ME12 ..46 E7
St Katherines Cotts
DA12 ....38 E4
St Katherine's La ME14 .. 127 F7
St Katherines Rd DA18 ..3 D4
St Katherine's Sch
ME6 ....127 F7
St Keverne Rd SE9 .....29 E4
St Kilda Rd BR6 ....53 F1
St Laurence Ave
ME16 ....161 C8
St Laurence Cl
Orpington BR5 ....54 D6
Sittingbourne ME9 .. 102 D2
St Laurence Ct CT11 .. 117 C7
St Laurence In Thanet CE
Jun Sch CT11 .... 117 B8
St Lawrence Ave
Bidborough TN4 ...... 253 D3
Ramsgate CT11 .... 117 B5
St Lawrence CE Prim Sch
TN15 ....155 E3
St Lawrence Cl CT1 .. 175 B6
St Lawrence Coll Jun Sch
CT11 ....117 C6
St Lawrence Coll
CT11 ....117 D8
St Lawrence Ct TN28 .. 373 A6
St Lawrence Forstal
CT1 ....175 B6
St Lawrence Gd (Kent Cty
Cricket Club)** CT1 .. 175 B6
St Lawrence Ind Est
CT11 ....117 B7
St Lawrence Rd CT1 .. 175 B6

St Lenard's Tower ★
ME19 ....159 A7
St Leonards Ave ME4 ....63 F2
St Leonards Cl
4 Bexley DA16 ...... 13 A4
Grays RM17 ....17 F8
St Leonards Ct CT21 .. 333 B1
St Leonards Mews
CT21 ....333 B1
St Leonard's Rd CT14 .. 215 B4
St Leonards Rd
Hythe CT21 .... 333 B1
Maidstone ME16 ...... 161 C8
St Leonards Rise BR6 ..86 E6
St Leonard's St ME19 .. 159 B7
St Louis Gr CT6 ....76 C4
St Luke's Wlk CT18 .. 306 F4
St Luke's Ave
Maidstone ME14 ...... 162 B5
Ramsgate CT11 .... 117 E8
St Luke's CE Inf Sch
TN4 ....286 C7
St Lukes Cl
Dartford DA2 ....34 E3
Swanley BR8 ....55 D7
St Luke's Cl CT8 ......81 E8
St Lukes Cl CT5 .... 108 E7
St Lukes Cotts BR8 ....55 D7
St Lukes Ct
Ashford TN23 .... 299 F7
Maidstone ME14 ...... 162 A6
St Luke's Rd
Maidstone ME14 ...... 162 B5
Ramsgate CT11 .... 117 E8
Royal Tunbridge Wells
TN4 ....286 B6
St Luke's Way ME3 ......9 D2
St Magnus Cl CT7 ......81 A8
St Magnus Ct CT7 ......81 A8
St Malo Ct 2 CT20 .. 335 C4
St Margaret Clitherow RC
Prim Sch
Tonbridge TN10 ...... 222 B6
Woolwich SE28 ....3 B5
St Margaret's-at-Cliffe
Prim Sch CT15 ...... 280 A6
St Margaret's at Troy Town
CE Prim Sch ME1 ..... 63 A4
St Margarets Ave DA15 .. 30 D5
St Margaret's Banks
ME1 ....63 D5
St Margaret's CE Jun Sch
ME8 ....98 E8
St Margarets CE Prim Sch
TN12 ....226 D1
St Margaret's CE Prim Sch
SE18 ....2 C1
St Margaret's Cl DA2 .. 34 D6
St Margarets Cl
Maidstone ME16 ...... 161 B2
Orpington BR6 ....87 B6
St Margaret's Cl CT5 .. 108 A6
St Margaret's Cres
DA12 ....37 E5
St Margarets Ct 1
CT20 ....335 B5
St Margaret's Ct
6 Gillingham ME8 .. 98 F8
High Halstow ME23 ....23 E3
St Margarets Dr
Deal CT14 .... 248 B8
Gillingham ME8 ....98 C5
St Margaret's Gr SE18 .. 12 C8
St Margaret's Inf Sch
ME8 ....98 E8
St Margaret's Mews
ME1 ....63 C5
St Margaret's Rd
Dartford DA2,DA4 ......34 E2
Northfleet DA11 ....36 E7
St Margarets Rd CT15 .. 248 A1
St Margaret's Rd
CT15 ....280 A5
St Margaret's Rd CT7 ...81 F3
St Margaret's Rd CT8 ...81 E7
St Margaret's St
Canterbury CT1 .... 174 F8
Rochester ME1 ....63 C5
St Margaret's Terr SE18 ..2 C1
St Margarets Villas
TN12 ....258 D8
St Mark's Ave DA11 ....36 F8
St Mark's CE Prim Sch
BR2 ....52 A6
St Marks CE Prim Sch
TN4 ....285 D1
St Mark's Cl CT20 .. 334 D5
St Marks Cl CT5 .... 108 E8
St Marks Ct ME20 .. 128 F6
St Marks Ho ME7 .....64 C5
St Marks Ind Est E16 ....1 D5
St Mark's Rd
Bromley BR2 ....52 B6
Royal Tunbridge Wells
TN2 ....313 F7
St Martins Ave CT1 .. 175 B8
St Martins Cl CT1 .. 175 B8
St Martin's Cl
Detling ME14 .... 131 A1
Dover CT17 .... 310 D5
St Martins Cl Erith DA18 ..3 D4
Newington ME9 .... 100 C7
St Martins Ct 4 CT1 .. 175 B8
St Martins Cvn Site
CT3 ....175 E8
St Martin's Dr DA4 ....89 D7
St Martin's Hill CT1 .. 175 B8
St Martins Ho CT17 .. 310 D5
St Martins Hospl CT1 .. 175 D8
St Martins Mdw TN16 .. 152 C4
St Martin's Pl CT1 .. 175 B8

St Martin's Rd
Canterbury CT1 .... 143 B1
Dartford DA1 ....15 F1
Deal CT14 .... 214 F4
Dover CT15 .... 278 E4
St Martins Rd
Folkestone CT20 ...... 334 D6
New Romney TN28 .. 373 B6
St Martin's Sch CT17 .. 310 A7
St Martin's Terr CT1 .. 175 B8
St Martin's View CT1 .. 175 A8
St Mary Cray Prim Sch
BR5 ....54 C3
St Mary Cray Sta BR5 .. 54 B5
St Mary Ct 13 ME13 .. 138 D7
Saint Mary Magdalene CE
Prim Sch SE18 ....2 A2
St Mary of Charity CE Prim
Sch ME13 .... 138 D7
St Mary's Abbey
ME19 ....159 C8
St Mary's Ave
Margate CT9 ....51 D1
Margate CT9 ....83 D8
St Mary's Bay Sta
TN29 ....365 F4
St Mary's CE Prim Sch
Ashford TN23 .... 268 A3
Chilham CT4 .... 205 B8
Dover CT15 .... 310 E8
Swanley BR8 ....55 E5
St Mary's Church Rd
TN14 ....152 F2
St Mary's Church ★
CT6 ....78 C7
St Mary's Cl CT13 .. 180 C2
St Marys Cl CT18 .. 305 D3
St Mary's Cl
Gravesend DA12 ....37 C6
Grays RM17 ....18 D8
Hamstreet TN26 ...... 349 A8
Laddingford ME18 .... 225 E4
Nonington CT15 ...... 211 C5
Orpington BR5 ....54 C7
Platt TN15 .... 157 C7
Ticehurst TN5 .... 338 D1
Woodnesborough CT13 .. 180 B6
St Mary's Ct
Biggin Hill TN16 .... 118 C1
Tilmanstone CT14 .... 213 A4
Whitstable CT5 .... 107 F7
St Mary's Island CE Prim
Sch ME4 ....41 B2
St Mary's La
Speldhurst TN3 ...... 285 A8
Ticehurst TN5 .... 338 D1
St Mary's Mdw CT3 .. 178 A8
St Marys Mews TN24 .. 300 F8
St Mary's Pl Eltham SE9 .. 12 A1
Newington ME9 .... 100 C7
St Mary's Prim Sch
ME2 ....63 B7
St Mary's RC Prim Sch
Deal CT14 .... 214 F4
Eltham SE9 ....12 A2
Gillingham ME7 ....64 D6
Tilbury RM18 ....18 F5
Whitstable CT5 ....74 F2
St Mary's Rd
5 Broadstairs CT10 .. 84 B4
Coldblow DA5 ....32 C7
Deal CT14 .... 215 C1
Elham CT4 .... 273 F4
Faversham ME13 ...... 138 D7
Gillingham ME7 ....64 C6
Minster (Thanet) CT12 .. 115 B6
Patrixbourne CT4 .... 176 B3
Rochester ME2 ....63 B7
St Mary in the Marsh
TN28,TN29 .... 365 C5
Stone DA9 ....16 C2
Swanley BR8 ....55 E5
Tonbridge TN9 .... 254 B7
West Hythe CT21 .... 332 B1
Wrotham TN15 .... 125 A2
St Mary's Row ME12 .. 47 A6
St Mary's St CT1 .. 174 F8
St Mary's Terr 2
CT20 ....335 B5
St Mary St SE18 ....2 A2
St Mary's View ME9 .. 100 C7
St Marys Way DA3 ......58 C6
St Mary's Westbrook
CT20 ....335 A5
St Mary's Wlk ME1 ....95 F1
St Matthew's CE Inf Sch
ME1 ....63 B7
St Matthew's Cl ME9 .. 100 C7
St Matthews Dr
Bromley BR1 ....52 F6
Rochester ME1 ....63 A2
St Matthew's High Brooms
CE Prim Sch TN4 .... 286 B8
St Matthew's Way ME3 ..9 D2
St Mawes CT8 ....50 C1
St Mellion Cl SE28 ......3 D7

St Merryn Cl SE18 .... 12 D7
St Michael & All Angels
Church CT14 .... 215 C4
St Michael's CE Prim Sch
TN31 ....368 C2
CT18 ....306 F4
St Michael's Alley 14
CT11 ....117 E6
St Michaels Ave CT9 .. 83 D8
St Michael's CE Inf Sch
ME16 ....161 E3
St Michael's CE Prim Sch
TN30 ....324 A3
St Michaels Cl
Bromley BR1 ....52 E6
Canterbury CT2 ...... 142 A1
St Michael's Cl
Chatham ME4 ....63 F3
Erith DA18 ....3 D4
St Michaels Cl
4 Newham E16 ......1 D8
Pratling Street ME20 .. 129 C3
St Michael's Cl 5
ME10 ....101 F4
St Michael's Ct
8 Folkestone CT20 .. 335 E5
6 Rochester ME2 ....63 B8
St Michaels Ct TN11 .. 221 E7
St Michaels Dr TN14 .. 122 E3
St Michael's East Wickham
CE Prim Sch DA16 .... 13 C6
St Michaels RH8 ...... 183 A5
St Michael's Pl CT2 .. 142 E2
St Michael's Prim Sch
TN7 ....311 B6
St Michael's RC Prim Sch
ME4 ....63 F3
St Michael's Rd
Bexley DA16 ....13 B4
Canterbury CT2 ...... 142 E2
Maidstone ME16 ...... 161 D3
Royal Tunbridge Wells
TN4 ....286 B7
Sittingbourne ME10 .. 101 F4
St Michael's Rise DA16 .. 13 B6
St Michael's St CT20 .. 335 E5
St Michael's Terr
TN30 ....324 A3
St Mildred's Ave
Birchington CT7 ....80 E8
Broadstairs CT10 ......84 A4
Ramsgate CT11 .... 117 B5
St Mildred's Cl 4
TN30 ....345 A7
St Mildreds Ct
Canterbury CT1 .... 174 E8
Deal CT14 .... 215 C1
Westgate-on-S CT8 .... 50 D1
St Mildred's Gdns CT8 .. 50 D1
St Mildreds Pl CT1 .. 174 E7
St Mildred's Prim Inf Sch
CT10 ....84 A4
St Mildreds Rd 5 SE12 .. 29 A8
St Mildred's Rd
Margate CT9 ....51 A2
Minster (Thanet) CT12 .. 115 B5
Ramsgate CT11 .... 117 C6
Westgate-on-S CT8 .... 50 C1
St Monicas Deal CT14 .. 248 D6
St Monicas Rd CT14 .. 248 D6
St Nicholas at Wade CE
Prim Sch CT7 .... 79 E2
St Nicholas CE Inf Sch
ME2 ....63 A7
St Nicholas CE Prim Sch
TN28 ....373 B7
St Nicholas Cl
Deal CT14 .... 214 F4
Sturry CT2 .... 143 F7
St Nicholas Cnr CT7 ...79 F1
St Nicholas Ct TN13 .. 154 B2
St Nicholas Dr TN13 .. 154 C1
St Nicholas Gdns ME2 .. 62 F7
St Nicholas Ho CT3 .. 147 D2
St Nicholas Hospl
CT2 ....142 C1
St Nicholas Rdbt CT7 ...80 B2
St Nicholas Rd
Canterbury CT1 .... 174 D6
Faversham ME13 ...... 138 A7
Hythe CT21 .... 333 A2
Littlestone-on-Sea TN28 .. 373 E6
Woolwich SE18 ....2 F2
St Nicholas Sch CT1 .. 174 F6
St Nicholas Terr 1
CT21 ....333 B2
St Nicolas La BR7 .....52 E8
St Olaves Prep Sch
SE9 ....30 B6
St Olave's & St Saviour's
Gram Sch BR6 ....87 B7
St Patrick's Cl
Deal CT14 .... 215 C6
Whitstable CT5 .... 108 E7
St Patrick's Gdns DA12 .. 37 D5
St Patrick's RC Prim Sch
SE18 ....2 D2
St Patrick's Rd CT14 .. 215 C6
St Patricks Rd CT17 .. 310 A4
St Patrick's Rd CT11 .. 117 F8
St Paulinus' CE Prim Sch
DA1 ....14 E3
St Paulinus Ct DA1 .. 14 E3
St Paul's Ave ME13 .. 138 A7
St Pauls CE Inf Sch
TN4 ....285 B4
St Pauls CE Jun Sch
TN4 ....285 B4
St Paul's CE Prim Sch
BR8 ....56 B8

St Paul's CI
　Greenwich SE7 ....1 D1
　Rochester ME2 .... 62 D5
　Swanscombe DA10 .... 35 E8
St Pauls CI TN10 .... 222 D5
St Paul's Cray CE Prim Sch
　BR5 .... 54 D6
St Paul's Cray Rd BR5,
　BR7 .... 53 D8
St Pauls Cres ME13 .. 140 A3
St Paul's Ct
　Folkestone CT20 .... 334 E4
　Rusthall TN4 .... 285 C4
St Pauls Inf Sch ME14 .. 162 A7
St Paul's RC Sch SE2 .... 13 A8
St Pauls Rd ME13 .... 140 A3
St Paul's Rd Erith DA8 .. 14 C7
　Margate CT9 .... 51 A3
St Paul's Sq BR2 ...... 52 A7
St Paul's St
　Rusthall TN4 .... 285 C4
St Pauls Terr CT1 .... 175 A8
St Paul's Way CT20 .... 334 F4
St Paul's Wood Hill
　BR5 .... 53 F7
St Peter Ave TN16 ..... 119 B3
St Peter Chanel RC Prim
　Sch DA14 .... 31 C3
St Peter-in-Thanet CE Jun
　Sch CT10 .... 83 F7
St Peter's Row TN26 .. 297 D5
St Peter's Way TN26 .. 327 A8
St Peter & St Paul RC Prim
　Sch BR5 .... 53 E7
St Peter's Bridge
　ME14 .... 161 F4
St Peter's CE Prim Sch
　Aylesford ME20 ...... 129 A3
　Royal Tunbridge Wells
　TN2 .... 286 C3
St Peters CI
　Chislehurst BR7 ...... 30 D1
　Ditton ME20 .... 128 B1
St Peter's CI
　Halfway Houses ME12 .. 46 D6
　Swanscombe DA10 .... 35 F8
St Peters Cotts ⑤ CT5 .. 74 D2
St Peter's Ct
　Broadstairs CT10 .... 83 F5
　Ditton ME20 .... 128 C1
　Faversham ME13 .... 138 A7
St Peter's Footpath
　Margate CT9 .... 50 J1
　Margate,Drapers Mill
　CT9 .... 83 A8
St Peter's Gr CT1 ..... 174 F8
St Peter's Inf Sch ME1 .. 63 C3
St Peters La CT1 ..... 142 F1
St Peter's Meth Prim Sch
　CT1 .... 174 F8
St Peter's Park Rd
　CT10 .... 83 F5
St Peter's Path ME1 .... 63 D5
St Peters Pl CT1,CT2 .. 174 F8
St Peters Pl
　Eccles ME20 .... 128 F6
　Lynsted ME9 .... 136 A6
St Peter's RC Prim Sch
　Sittingbourne ME10 .. 101 D2
　Woolwich SE18 .... 2 B1
St Peter's Rd
　Boughton Street ME13 .. 140 A3
　Broadstairs CT10 .... 83 F5
St Peters Rd ME20 .... 128 B1
St Peter's Rd
　Margate CT10,CT9 .... 83 A7
　Whitstable CT5 ...... 74 D2
St Peters Row TN3 .... 284 B5
St Peter's St CT1,CT2 .. 174 F8
St Peters St ME16 .... 161 F4
St Peter's St
　Royal Tunbridge Wells
　TN2 .... 286 C3
　Sandwich CT13 ...... 149 A1
St Peter St ME1 ...... 63 D4
St Philip Howard RC Prim
　Sch CT6 .... 76 E5
St Philip's Ave ME15 .. 162 B2
St Philips Ct TN2 .... 286 D6
St Philomena's RC Prim
　Sch BR5 .... 54 C2
St Pierre Ct CT14 .... 215 D5
St Quentin Rd DA16 .... 12 F1
St Radigund's Ct
　CT17 .... 278 A1
St Radigund's Com Prim
　Sch CT17 .... 278 A1
St Radigund's Pl CT1 .. 143 A1
St Radigund's Rd
　CT17 .... 278 A1
St Radigunds St CT1 .. 142 F1
St Richard's RC Prim Sch
　CT16 .... 278 D1
St Richard's Rd CT14 .. 214 F3
St Richard's Wlk
　CT17 .... 310 A4
St Ronan's CI ME15 .. 195 C7
St Ronan's Sch TN18 .. 341 D2
St Saviours CE Jun Sch
　CT8 .... 81 E8
St Saviour's CI ME13 .. 138 E7
St Saviours Ct CT17 .. 335 D7
St Saviours Ct CT8 .... 81 E8
St Saviour's Hospl
　CT21 .... 333 F2
St Saviours Rd ME15 .. 195 D6
Saints Hill TN11 ...... 284 A8
St Simon of England RC
　Prim Sch TN23 ...... 300 A8
St Simon Stock Sch
　ME16 .... 161 C4

St Stephen's Manor
　CT10 .... 84 B7
St Stephen's Mews
　TN23 .... 300 A6
St Stephen's CI
　Canterbury CT2 ...... 142 F2
　Newington ME9 ...... 100 C7
St Stephen's Cotts
　TN1 .... 286 B5
St Stephen's Ct
　Canterbury CT2 ...... 142 F2
　Royal Tunbridge Wells
　TN1 .... 286 B5
St Stephens Fields ⑤
　CT2 .... 142 F1
St Stephen's Gn CT2 .. 142 F1
St Stephen's Hill CT2 .. 142 E4
St Stephens Ho ❶
　CT2 .... 142 F1
St Stephen's Inf Sch
　CT2 .... 142 F1
St Stephen's Jun Sch
　CT2 .... 142 F1
St Stephen's Lodge
　CT2 .... 142 F1
St Stephens Mews ME1 .96 E8
St Stephens Pathway ❹
　CT2 .... 142 F1
St Stephen's Prim Sch
　TN9 .... 254 D8
St Stephen's RC Prim Sch
　DA16 .... 13 A5
St Stephen's Rd CT2 .. 142 F2
St Stephen's Sq ME15 .. 161 E2
St Stephen's St TN9 .. 254 B8
St Stephen's Way
　CT20 .... 334 F4
St Stephen's Wlk
　TN23 .... 299 F7
St Swithin's Rd CT5 .... 75 B3
St Teresa's RC Prim Sch
　TN24 .... 268 B4
St Theresa's CI TN24 .. 268 B1
St Thomas-a-Becket RC
　Prim Sch SE2 .... 3 A3
St Thomas' Cross
　TN26 .... 327 C4
St Thomas' CI DA5 .... 32 A8
St Thomas' Dr BR5 .... 53 C1
St Thomas Hill CT2 .. 142 D3
St Thomas More RC Prim
　Sch
　Bexley DA7 .... 13 F5
　Eltham SE9 .... 11 E4
St Thomas More RC Sec
　Sch SE9 .... 12 A1
St Thomas More Roman
　Catholic Prim Sch
　ME5 .... 97 A5
St Thomas of Canterbury
　RC Prim Sch ME8 .... 65 B2
St Thomas' RC Prim Sch
　Canterbury CT1 ...... 143 A1
　Grays RM17 .... 18 C8
St Thomas RC Prim Sch
　TN13 .... 154 B2
St Thomas Rd Erith DA17 .. 4 C4
　Newham E16 .... 1 A7
　Northfleet DA11 ...... 36 E6
St Thomas's Almshouses
　DA11 .... 37 B7
St Thomas's Ave DA11 .. 37 B7
St Thomas's Hospl
　CT13 .... 148 F1
St Thomas's Pl ⑮
　RM17 .... 18 C8
St Timothy's Mews ❸
　BR1 .... 52 B8
St Vincent Rd CT15 .. 279 F7
St Vincents Ave CT14 .. 16 A2
St Vincent's CI
　Littlebourne CT3 .... 144 F1
　Whitstable CT5 ...... 108 E7
St Vincents La ME19 .. 126 A2
St Vincent's Pl
　SE9 .... 29 C4
St Vincents Rd DA1 .... 16 A1
St Welcume's Way
　ME17 .... 198 E6
St Werburgh Cres ME3 .. 41 D5
St Werburgh Rd ME3 .... 41 D5
St William of Perth RC
　Prim Sch ME1 .... 63 B2
St William's Way ME1 .. 63 D2
St Winifred Rd CT19 .. 334 F6
St Winifred's Rd TN16 .. 118 F1
Sala Ho SE3 .... 11 B3
Salamons Way RM13 .... 4 E7
Salbris CI TN29 ...... 366 D8
Salem Pl DA11 .... 36 D8
Salem St ME15 .... 162 A3
Salhouse CI SE28 ...... 3 C7
Salisbury Ave
　Broadstairs CT10 .... 83 F2
　Gillingham ME8 ...... 98 D8
　Ramsgate CT11 ...... 117 F8
　Swanley BR8 .... 56 A5
Salisbury CI
　Sittingbourne ME10 .. 102 C4
　Tonbridge TN10 ...... 222 D5
Salisbury Ho
　Canterbury CT2 ...... 142 D2
　④ Maidstone ME15 .. 195 D7
Salisbury Mews ME2 .. 52 E4
Salisbury Rd
　Bromley BR2 .... 52 E4
　Canterbury CT2 ...... 142 E2
　Chatham ME4 .... 64 A3
　Dartford DA2 .... 34 C7
　Deal CT14 .... 215 B2
　Dover CT16 .... 278 D1
　Folkestone CT19 .... 334 E7

Salisbury Rd continued
　❷ Grays RM11 .... 18 C8
　Herne Bay CT6 ...... 77 C5
　Kit's Coty ME20 ...... 129 D7
　Langton Green TN3 .. 284 F3
　Maidstone ME14 .... 162 A6
　Northfleet DA11 ...... 36 F7
　Royal Tunbridge Wells
　TN4 .... 286 C8
　St Margaret's at Cliffe
　CT15 .... 280 B6
　Sidcup DA5 .... 32 A7
　Tonbridge TN10 ...... 222 D4
　Whitstable CT5 ...... 108 D8
Salix Rd RM17 .... 18 D8
Sallow CI ME4 .... 41 C1
Sallows Shaw DA13 .... 60 C4
Sally Port ME7 .... 64 A6
Sally Port Gdns ME7 ..64 B6
Salmestone Grange ★
　CT9 .... 82 E8
Salmestone Prim Sch
　CT9 .... 82 E8
Salmestone Rd CT9 ..82 F8
Salmestone Rise CT9 ..82 E8
Salmon Cres ME12 .... 46 F6
Salmon La CT9 .... 82 E8
Salmond Rd Dartford DA1 ..15 F4
　Erith DA17 .... 4 A1
Salomons Rd
　Newham E13 .... 1 C8
　Rusthall TN4 .... 285 C4
Saltash Rd DA16 ...... 13 C6
Saltbox Hill TN16 .... 118 B6
Saltcote CI DA1 ...... 14 E1
Salter's Cross ME18 .. 193 A1
Salters La TN29 ...... 370 C8
Salters La ME13 .... 138 C4
Saltford CI ❷ DA8 .... 4 E1
Salthouse CI TN29 .. 370 D8
Saltings Rd ME6 ...... 128 A7
Saltings The
　Littlestone-on-Sea TN28 .. 373 E5
　❿ Whitstable CT5 .... 74 D2
Salt La ME3 .... 21 F4
Saltley CI E6 .... 1 E7
Salt Marsh La ❷❶ CT5 .. 74 D2
Salt's Ave ME15 ...... 194 F3
Salts CI CT5 .... 74 D1
Salt's Dr CT10 .... 83 E5
Salts La ME15 .... 195 A4
Saltwood CE Prim Sch
　CT21 .... 333 B4
Saltwood CI BR6 ...... 87 C6
Saltwood Gdns CT9 .. 51 E2
Saltwood Rd ME15 .. 161 F1
Salvadori Ct TN2 .... 287 D6
Samara CI ME5 .... 97 A1
Samian Cres CT19 .. 334 B3
Samphire CI ME14 .. 162 E4
Samphire Ct
　Dover CT16 .... 310 E8
　Grays RM17 .... 18 E8
Samphire Hoe Ctry Pk★
　CT15 .... 309 C2
Samphire Way ME4 .... 41 A2
Sampson CI DA17 ...... 3 D3
Samson Ho SE18 ...... 2 C2
Samuel CI SE18 .... 1 E2
Samuel Ct CT9 .... 51 A3
Samuel Mews TN29 .. 376 D7
Samuel Palmer Ct BR6 .. 54 A2
Samuel St SE18 .... 1 F2
Sancroft Ave CT2 .... 142 C1
Sanctuary CI
　Broadstairs CT10 .... 83 F2
　Dartford DA1 .... 15 D1
　Kearsney CT17 ...... 277 D4
Sanctuary Rd ME8 .... 65 A3
Sanctuary The
　Sandwich CT13 ...... 182 A7
　Sidcup DA5 .... 13 D1
Sandalwood Dr CT7 ..79 F1
Sandalwood House
　DA15 .... 30 F5
Sandbach Ho CT9 ....51 B3
Sandbach Rd ME13 .... 51 B3
Sandbanks Hill DA2 .. 35 B2
Sandbanks Rd ME13 .. 106 C2
Sandbourne Dr ME14 .. 129 F1
Sandby Gn SE9 .... 11 B4
Sandcliff Rd DA8 ...... 4 D1
Sandcroft TN28 ...... 373 F7
Sand Ct ME12 .... 49 G2
Sand End CT5 .... 108 C6
Sanderling Ct SE28 .... 3 D5
Sanderling Rd CT6 .... 77 F5
Sanderling Way
　Iwade ME9 .... 68 D5
　Swanscombe DA9 .... 17 A1
Sanders Ct ME12 ...... 47 A5
Sandersons Ave TN14 .. 88 B1
Sanderson Way TN9 .. 222 E1
Sanderstead Rd BR5 ..54 B3
Sandfield Rd TN11 .. 284 A4
Sandford Rd
　Bexley DA7,DA6 ...... 13 C4
　Bromley BR2 .... 52 A5
　Sittingbourne ME10 .. 101 B5
Sandgate Espl CT20,
　CT21 .... 334 D2
Sandgate High St
　CT20 .... 334 E3
Sandgate Hill CT20 .. 335 A4
Sandgate Prim Sch
　CT20 .... 334 F4
Sandgate Rd
　Bexley DA16 .... 13 C7
　Folkestone CT20 .... 335 C4
Sandham Point SE18 ..2 B2
Sandhill La ME3 ...... 39 D6

Sandhills Cvn Pk
　CT14 .... 182 B1
Sandhole Cotts TN12 .. 288 C3
Sandhurst Ave TN2 .. 287 E5
Sandhurst CI
　Canterbury CT2 ...... 143 A4
　Gillingham ME8 ...... 65 C3
　Royal Tunbridge Wells
　TN2 .... 286 C6
　Sandhurst Cross TN18 .. 356 A4
Sandhurst Cross TN12 .. 261 F1
Sandhurst Ho TN2 .. 286 D5
Sandhurst La TN7 .... 343 B2
Sandhurst Pk TN2 .. 286 C6
Sandhurst Prim Sch
　TN18 .... 356 C5
Sandhurst Rd
　Bexley DA5 .... 13 D2
　Margate CT9 .... 51 F2
　Orpington BR6 .... 87 A6
　Royal Tunbridge Wells
　TN2 .... 286 D6
　Sidcup DA15 .... 31 A5
　Tilbury RM18 .... 19 C5
Sandilands
　Ashford TN24 .... 268 C2
　Sevenoaks TN13 .... 153 D5
Sand La TN17 .... 293 F4
Sandle's Rd CT7 ......80 F7
Sandling CI TN23 .... 299 F6
Sandling Ct ME14 .. 162 B7
Sandling La ME14 .... 162 A8
Sandling Prim Sch
　ME14 .... 162 B8
Sandling Rd
　Hythe CT21 .... 332 F6
　Maidstone ME14 .... 161 F6
　Maidstone,Ringlestone
　ME14 .... 161 F7
Sandling Rise SE9 .... 30 A5
Sandling Sta CT21 .. 332 F6
Sandling Way ME4 .... 41 B1
Sandown CI Deal CT14 .. 182 C1
　Royal Tunbridge Wells
　TN2 .... 286 F6
Sandown Cotts
　Margate CT9 .... 51 A3
　Teynham ME9 .... 103 E1
Sandown Ct CT14 .. 215 C7
Sandown Dr
　Gillingham ME8 ...... 98 D7
　Herne Bay CT6 ...... 76 D4
Sandown Gr TN2 .... 286 F6
Sandown Lees CT13 .. 181 D8
Sandown Pk TN2 .... 286 F6
Sandown Pl TN2 .... 215 C7
Sandown Rd
　Deal CT14 .... 215 D8
　Gravesend DA12 .... 37 C2
　Sandwich CT13 ...... 181 B8
　West Malling ME19 .. 159 B8
Sandown Sch CT14 .. 215 C7
Sandpiper CI DA9 .... 17 A1
Sandpiper Ct
　❸ Birchington CT7 ..80 F8
　Margate CT9 .... 50 J3
Sandpiper Dr DA8 .... 15 B7
Sandpiper Rd
　Chatham ME5 .... 97 D2
　Hawkinge CT18 ...... 307 A3
　Whitstable CT5 ...... 108 B7
Sandpipers The DA12 .. 37 D6
Sandpiper Way BR5 .. 54 D6
Sandpit Hill CT3 .... 112 C4
Sandpit Pl SE7 .... 1 E1
Sandpit Rd DA1 ...... 15 C3
Sandra Ct ⑤ ME2 ....63 B8
Sand Rd TN3 .... 317 A4
Sandringham Ct
　ME19 .... 159 A1
Sandringham Dr
　Bexley DA16 .... 12 E5
　Maypole DA2 .... 32 E6
Sandringham Ho ME1 ..63 B4
Sandringham Mews
　TN4 .... 286 A5
Sandringham Rd
　Bromley BR1 .... 29 A3
　Gillingham ME8 ...... 98 E3
Sandrock Ho TN2 .... 286 D4
Sandrock Rd ME14 .. 286 C4
Sandrock Villas TN18 .. 340 F3
Sandshaw Ct CT3 .... 58 E4
Sandstone Ct CT20 .. 335 A3
Sandstone Dr ME10 .. 101 E8
Sandstone La E16 ...... 1 B6
Sandstone Rd SE12 .. 29 B6
Sandstone Rise ME5 .. 130 C8
Sandtoft Rd SE7 ...... 11 B8
Sandway Path ❻ BR5 .. 54 C5
Sandway Rd
　Harrietsham ME17 .. 198 F4
　Orpington BR5 .... 54 C5
Sandwich Bay Bird Obsy★
　CT13 .... 181 E7
Sandwich CI CT20 .. 334 F5
Sandwich Ind Est
　CT13 .... 149 B1
Sandwich Inf Sch
　CT13 .... 148 F1
Sandwich Jun Sch
　CT13 .... 148 F1
Sandwich Rd Ash CT3 .. 147 F1
　Cliffs End CT12 ...... 116 D4
　Eastry CT13 .... 180 C3
　Eythorne CT15 ...... 245 C8
　Nonington CT15,CT3 .. 211 F6
　Sandwich CT13,CT14 .. 180 D5
　Whitfield CT15,CT16 .. 261 A6
　Woodnesborough CT13 .. 180 D7
　Sandwich Sta CT13 .. 181 A8

Sandwich Tech Sch
　CT13 .... 180 F6
Sandwich Town Mus ★
　CT13 .... 148 F1
Sandwood Rd
　Ramsgate CT10 ......83 F1
　Sandwich CT13 ...... 180 F8
Sandy Bank Rd DA12 .. 37 B7
Sandy Bury BR5 ...... 86 D7
Sandy Cnr TN26 ...... 298 F5
Sandycroft Rd ME9 .... 39 F1
Sandycroft SE2 .... 13 A8
Sandy Dell ME7 .... 98 A3
Sandy Hill Ave SE18 .... 2 B1
Sandy Hill La SE18 .... 2 B2
Sandy Hill Rd SE18 .... 2 B1
Sandyhurst La TN25 .. 268 B8
Sandy La Ashford TN24 .. 269 B1
　Bean DA13,DA2 ...... 35 D5
　Daniel's Water TN26 .. 298 C6
　Hythe CT20,CT21 .... 334 B3
　Ightham TN15 .... 156 B3
　Limpsfield RH8 ...... 183 B7
　Maidstone,Harbourland
　ME14 .... 162 C8
　Maidstone,Penenden Heath
　ME14 .... 162 C7
　Maidstone,Ware Street
　ME14 .... 163 B5
　New Town ME19 .... 127 A1
　Orpington BR6 .... 54 A2
　Ruxley BR5 .... 54 D8
　Sevenoaks TN13 .... 154 C4
　Snodland ME6,ME19 .. 127 C6
　Tenterden TN30 .... 345 B7
　Tilbury RM16 .... 19 B8
　Westerham TN16 .... 151 D2
　West Thurrock RM20 .. 17 B8
　ME19 .... 125 F1
Sandy Mount ME14 .. 163 B5
Sandy Pl TN25 ...... 302 C5
Sandy Ridge
　Borough Green TN15 .. 157 A7
　Chislehurst BR7 ...... 30 A2
Sanger Ct CT9 .... 50 J1
Sangro Pl CT1 .... 143 D1
San Remo CT5 .... 50 C1
Sanspareil Ave ME12 .. 47 A6
Santana Ho SE18 ...... 12 B7
Santer Ho TN18 ...... 354 E8
Santon La CT3 .... 146 E8
Sapho Pk DA12 .... 37 F6
Saphora CI BR6 ...... 86 D5
Sappers Wlk ME7 .... 64 C5
Sapphire CI Newham E6 .. 2 B7
　Sittingbourne ME10 .. 101 C7
Saracen CI ME7 ...... 65 A1
Saracen Fields ME5 .. 130 C8
Sara Cres DA9 .... 17 B3
Sarafand Ho ME1 ......63 B4
Sarah Ct ❼ DA6 ...... 13 E3
Sarah Gdns CT9 ...... 83 D8
Sara Ho ❶ DA8 ...... 14 E7
Sara Pk DA12 .... 37 E4
Sara Turnbull Ho ❸
　SE18 .... 1 F2
Sark Ct TN29 .... 366 C8
Sark Wlk E16 .... 1 B7
Sarre Ct CT7 .... 113 D6
Sarre Mill ★ CT7 .... 113 D7
Sarre Pl CT13 .... 180 F8
Sarsen Hts ME5 ......96 F1
Sarsens CI DA12 ...... 60 F6
Sassoon CI
　Hawkinge CT18 .... 307 A4
　New Hythe ME20 .... 128 A4
Saunders CI DA11 .... 36 E6
Saunder's Cross TN14 .. 88 B2
Saunders La CT3 .... 147 F1
Saunders Rd
　Royal Tunbridge Wells
　TN4 .... 285 E1
　Woolwich SE18 .... 2 F1
Saunders St
　❼ Chatham ME4 ......63 F3
　Gillingham ME7 ...... 64 C6
Saunders Way
　Camber TN31 .... 374 A2
　Dartford DA1 .... 33 F6
　Woolwich SE28 .... 3 B6
Savage Gdns E6 .... 1 F7
Savage Rd ME5 .... 97 B3
Savernake Dr CT6 ....77 B2
Saville CI TN10 ...... 222 D7
Saville Ho E16 .... 2 B5
Saville Rd E16 .... 1 E5
Savoy Rd DA1 .... 15 D2
Savoy The ❽ CT11 .. 117 C6
Saw Lodge Field
　TN23 .... 300 C4
Sawpit Rd ME9 .... 135 B2
Sawyers Ct ME4 ...... 64 B2
Saxbys Rd TN15 ...... 155 D5
Saxby Wood TN11 .. 220 F1
Saxon Ave ME13 ...... 47 B6
Saxon CI Hythe CT21 .. 333 E2
　Kings Hill ME19 .... 158 F2
　Northfleet DA11 ...... 36 C5
　Otford TN14 .... 121 F2
　Rochester ME2 ...... 39 F1
Saxon Pl
　Horton Kirby DA4 .... 57 C4
　Rochester ME2 ......62 F5
Saxon Rd Bridge CT4 .. 176 A1
　Bromley BR1 .... 29 A1
　Faversham ME13 .... 138 C2
　Hawley DA2 .... 33 E4
　Ramsgate CT11 ...... 117 B6

St P-Sco 427

Saxon Rd continued
　Westgate-on-S CT8 .. 50 D1
Saxons CI CT14 ...... 215 C8
Saxons Dr ME14 ...... 162 B7
Saxon Shore
　Sittingbourne ME10 .. 69 A1
　Whitstable CT5 ...... 108 C8
Saxon St ⑨ CT17 .... 310 D8
Saxon Way Prim Sch
　ME7 .... 64 E6
Saxon Wlk Iwade ME9 .. 68 D4
　Sidcup DA14 .... 31 C2
Saxton Rd TN29 ...... 377 E5
Saxton St ME7 .... 64 C5
Saxville Rd BR5 ...... 54 B6
Sayer CI DA9 .... 17 A2
Sayer Rd TN27 ...... 234 C8
Sayers La ❻ TN30 .. 345 A7
Sayes Court Rd BR5 .. 54 B5
Scabharbour Rd TN14 .. 187 C1
Scadbury Gdns BR5 .. 54 A7
Scadbury Park Nature
　Reserve ★ BR7 .... 30 F2
Scads Hill CI BR6 ...... 53 F3
Scanlons Bridge Rd
　CT21 .... 333 A2
Scarborough CI TN16 .. 118 C1
Scarborough Dr ME12 .. 47 C8
Scarborough La ME1 .. 95 D2
Scarlet CI ME5 .... 97 C5
Scarlett CI ME5 ...... 97 C5
Scarsbrook Rd SE3 .... 11 D4
Sceales Dr CT12 .... 116 D6
Sceptre Way CT5 .... 108 B7
Schofield Wlk SE3 .... 11 A7
Scholars Rise ME2 .... 62 D7
Scholey CI ME2 ......95 B4
School App TN15 .... 156 F7
School Ave ME7 ...... 64 C6
School CI DA13 ...... 60 A2
School CI The CT8 .... 50 C1
School Cotts
　Bromley BR1 .... 29 A1
　Crockenhill BR8 ...... 55 D2
　Seal TN15 .... 154 F6
　Sidcup DA14 .... 31 C3
School Cres DA1 ...... 14 F3
School Field TN8 .... 217 C2
Schoolfield Rd RM20 .. 17 A8
School Hill
　Chilham CT4 .... 205 B8
　Lamberhurst TN3 .... 317 B6
School Ho ME10 ...... 101 E3
School House La
　TN12 .... 290 E7
School La Bean DA2 .. 35 C5
　Bekesbourne CT4 .... 176 C4
　Bexley DA16 .... 13 B4
　Blean CT2 .... 142 A6
　Boughton Street ME13 .. 139 F3
　Chestnut Street ME9 .. 100 F4
　Culverstone Green DA13 .. 93 A2
　Fordwich CT2 .... 144 A4
　Goodnestone CT3 .... 178 D2
　Hadlow TN11 .... 223 E8
　Herne Bay CT6 ......77 B1
　Hextable BR8 .... 33 B1
　Higham ME3 .... 39 C5
　Hoath CT3 .... 111 E6
　Horton Kirby DA3,DA4 .. 57 C4
　Ickham CT3 .... 177 C8
　Iwade ME9 .... 68 C4
　Knockmill TN15 ...... 123 F8
　Lower Halstow ME9 ..67 B2
　Lower Hardres CT4 .. 208 B6
　Maidstone ME15 .... 162 E1
　Newington ME9 ...... 100 B7
　Peasmarsh TN31 .... 367 B2
　Platt's Heath ME17 .. 198 F2
　Plaxtol TN11,TN15 .. 189 E6
　Ramsgate CT11 ...... 117 E7
　Seal TN15 .... 154 F6
　Sittingbourne ME9 .. 102 D2
　Stalisfield Green ME13 .. 201 D6
　Staple CT3 .... 179 A6
　Stourmouth CT3 .... 113 C2
　Sutton Valence ME17 .. 229 E7
　Trottiscliffe TN15 .... 126 A5
　Wingham CT3 .... 178 A7
　Wouldham ME1 ...... 95 D5
School Path CT3 .... 176 F7
School Rd
　Appledore Heath TN26 .. 347 C1
　Ash CT3 .... 147 C2
　Bethersden TN26 .... 297 D4
　Charing TN27 .... 234 C8
　Chislehurst BR7 ...... 30 C1
　Densole CT18 .... 306 E7
　Faversham ME13 .... 138 C6
　Gravesend DA12 .... 37 C5
　Hothfield TN26 ...... 267 A7
　Hythe CT21 .... 333 B4
　Sandwich CT13 ...... 148 F1
　Sittingbourne ME10 .. 102 B3
　Tilmanstone CT14 .. 212 F4
School Rise TN2 ...... 285 F1
School Terr ❽ TN18 .. 340 F2
School View ME9 .... 134 C8
School Villas ME13 .. 192 D5
Schooner Ct DA2 ...... 16 C3
Schooner Ho ❶❶ DA8 ....4 E1
Schooner Wlk ❼ ME3 ..40 F3
Schreiber Mews ME7 .. 64 D5
Scilla Ct ❶❶ RM17 .... 18 D8
Scimitar CI ME7 ...... 65 A1
Scocles Cotts ME12 .. 47 C5
Scocles Rd ME12 ...... 47 C5
Scoggers Hill ME13 .. 172 A7
Scoones CI ME9 ...... 102 E2
Scords La TN16 ...... 185 C4

Scotby Ave ME5 . . . . .97 B4
Scotchmen Cl ME12 . . .46 E7
Scotland La DA12 . . . . . .60 F6
Scotney Castle Gdns ★
TN3 . . . . .317 D3
Scotney Castle ★ TN3 . 317 D3
Scotney Cl BR6 . . . . .86 A6
Scotney Ho ME2 . . . . . . 40 C1
Scotsdale Rd BR5 . . . . . .53 E5
Scotsdale Rd SE12 . . . . . .11 B2
Scot's La TN25 . . . . . . .303 F8
Scott Ave
Canterbury CT1 . . . . . . 174 E6
Gillingham ME7 . . . . .66 A1
Gillingham ME8 . . . . .99 A8
Scott Cl ME20 . . . . 160 C8
Scott Cres DA8 . . . . .14 F6
Scotteswood Ave ME4 . .63 F2
Scott Ho 4 DA17 . . . . . . .3 F1
Scotton St TN25 . . . . . 237 F2
Scott Rd
Gravesend DA12 . . . . . . 37 D3
Tonbridge TN9 . . . . . . .253 F7
Scotts Ho DA16 . . . . . . 13 C6
Scotts Park Prim Sch
BR1 . . . . .52 C8
Scotts Passage 11 SE18 . . .2 B3
Scotts Rd BR1 . . . . 29 A1
Scotts Terr SE9 . . . . . . .29 E6
Scott's Terr ME4 . . . . . . .63 F3
Scott St ME14 . . . . 161 F6
Scotts Way
Royal Tunbridge Wells
TN2 . . . . 313 D8
Sevenoaks TN13 . . . . . 153 E5
Scott Wilkie Prim Sch
E16 . . . . .1 C7
Scoulding Rd E16 . . . . . . .1 A7
Scragged Oak Cvn Pk
ME14 . . . . 131 B2
Scragged Oak Rd
Detling ME14 . . . . 131 C5
Hucking ME14 . . . . 132 C1
Scrapsgate Rd ME12 . . 47 A7
Scraps Hill ME9 . . . . . . 102 F4
Scratchers La 90 E7
Scratton Fields DA12 . . 60 D4
Scrubbs La ME16 . . . . . 161 D4
Scudders Hill DA3 . . . . . 58 C3
Sea App ME12 . . . . .49 E4
Seabourne La TN29 . . . 366 B6
Seabourne Way TN29 . 366 B6
Seabrook CE Prim Sch
CT21 . . . . 334 B2
Seabrook Ct CT21 . . . . 334 B3
Seabrooke Rise RM17 . .18 B8
Seabrook Gdns CT21 . . 334 B2
Seabrook Gr CT21 . . . . 334 A2
Seabrook Rd
Hythe CT21 . . . . 333 E2
Tonbridge TN10 . . . . . . 222 A3
Seabrook Vale CT21 . . .334 B4
Seacourt Rd SE2 . . . . . . .3 D4
Seacroft Rd CT10 . . . . . .84 A1
Seadown Ct CT21 . . . . . 334 A4
Seafield Rd
Broadstairs CT10 . . . . . .84 A4
Ramsgate CT11 . . . . . . 117 C6
Whitstable CT5 . . . . .75 B3
Seaford Ct ME1 . . . . .63 B5
Seagar Rd ME13 . . . . . . 105 B1
Seager Rd ME12 . . . . . . .28 E2
Seagrave Cres CT19 . . .335 F6
Seagull La E16 . . . . .1 A6
Seagull Rd ME2 . . . . . . .62 D6
Sealand Ct ME1 . . . . .63 B5
Seal CE Prim Sch
TN15 . . . . 154 F7
Sealcroft Cotts TN15 . . 154 F8
Seal Dr TN15 . . . . 154 F6
Seal Hollow Rd TN13 . . 154 D4
Seal Ho TN15 . . . . 154 F6
Seal Rd TN13,TN14,
TN15 . . . . 154 D6
Seamark Cl CT12 . . . . . 114 D7
Seamark Rd CT12,CT7 . .80 E2
Seamew Ct ME2 . . . . . . 62 C7
Seapoint Rd CT10 . . . . . .84 B3
Sea Rd Deal CT14 . . . . 248 D6
Hythe CT21 . . . . 334 A2
Westgate-on-S CT8 . . . 50 C1
Searles Dr E6 . . . . .2 B8
Seasalter Beach CT5 . . 108 A7
Seasalter CI ME12 . . . . . .49 E4
Seasalter Cross CT5 . . 108 A6
Seasalter La CT5 . . . . . 108 A5
Seasalter Rd ME13 . . . 106 E3
Seascape CT20 . . . . . . .334 E3
Seaside Ave ME12 . . . . . 47 C8
Sea St Herne Bay CT6 . . 76 C3
St Margaret's at Cliffe
CT15 . . . . 280 A6
Whitstable CT5 . . . . .74 C3
Seathorpe Ave ME12 . . 47 C8
Seaths Cnr CT3 . . . . 178 A7
Seaton Ave CT21 . . . . . 333 B3
Seaton Cotts TN25 . . . .236 E3
Seaton Rd Bexley DA16 . . 13 C7
Dartford DA1 . . . . 33 A8
Gillingham ME7 . . . . .64 E3
Wickhambreaux CT3 . . .145 D2
Sea View Ave CT7 . . . . . .80 E8
Seaview Ave ME12 . . . . 49 F1
Sea View CI CT18 . . . . . 308 B1
Seaview Cotts 6 CT8 . .84 B4
Sea View Cotts ME9 . . . .67 B3
Seaview Ct CT10 . . . . . . .84 B3
Seaview Cvn & Chalet Pk
CT5 . . . . .75 E4
Sea View Gdns ME12 . . .49 E3

Seaview ME3 . . . . .27 B5
Seaview Ho CT19 . . . . . 335 D8
Seaview Holiday Camp
ME12 . . . . .49 E3
Sea View Hts CT7 . . . . . 80 D8
Seaview Hts TN29 . . . . 366 C7
Sea View Rd
Birchington CT7 . . . . . . .80 E8
Broadstairs CT10 . . . . . .84 A6
Cliffs End CT12 . . . . . . 116 D6
Seaview Rd
Gillingham ME7 . . . . . . 64 C4
Greatstone-on-Sea
TN28 . . . . .373 E1
Sea View Rd
Herne Bay CT6 . . . . 77 C5
St Margaret's at Cliffe
CT15 . . . . 279 F4
Sea View Sq CT6 . . . . .76 F5
Sea View Terr
Folkestone CT20 . . . . . 334 D3
Margate CT9 . . . . 50 G2
Minster (Sheppey) ME12 . 48 A5
Seaville Dr CT4 . . . . .77 E5
Sea Wall
Dymchurch TN29 . . . . . 366 D8
Whitstable CT5 . . . . .74 D2
Seaway Cotts CT5 . . . . 74 C1
Seaway Cres TN29 . . . .365 F4
Seaway Gdns TN29 . . . 365 F4
Seaway Rd TN29 . . . . . 366 A4
Second Ave
Broadstairs CT10 . . . . . .51 G2
Chatham ME4 . . . . .64 C1
Eastchurch ME12 . . . . .48 F5
Gillingham ME7 . . . . . . .64 E3
Margate CT9 . . . . .51 B3
Rushenden ME11 . . . . . .45 F3
Sheerness ME12 . . . . . . .27 F5
West Thurrock RM20 . . . 17 A8
Secretan Rd ME1 . . . . . 161 C6
Sedcombe Cl DA14 . . . . 31 C4
Sedgebrook Rd SE3 . . . 11 D4
Sedge Cres ME5 . . . . . . .96 E4
Sedge Ct RM17 . . . . . . .18 E7
Sedgemere Rd SE2 . . . . .3 C3
Sedgemoor Ho ME1 . . . .63 E5
Sedley Cl
Aylesford ME20 . . . . . . 128 F2
Cliffe Woods ME3 . . . . . 40 C7
Gillingham ME8 . . . . . . .98 C3
Sedley Sch13 . . . . 36 A2
Sedley's CE Prim Sch
DA13 . . . . 36 A3
Seeshill Cl CT5 . . . . 108 E8
Sefton Cl BR5 . . . . .53 F5
Sefton Rd BR5 . . . . .53 F5
Segrave Rd CT19 . . . . . 335 F5
Sejant Ho 4 RM17 . . . .18 B8
Selah Dr BR8 . . . . 55 C8
Selbey Cl CT6 . . . . .74 A1
Selborne Ave DA5 . . . . . 31 E7
Selborne Ho CT17 . . . . 310 C7
Selborne Rd
Margate CT9 . . . . .83 B8
Sidcup DA14 . . . . .31 B4
Selbourne Cl DA3 . . . . . .59 D6
Selbourne Rd ME7 . . . . .64 D7
Selbourne Terr CT17 . . .310 C7
Selbourne Wlk ME5 . . .195 F6
Selby Cl Chislehurst BR7 . . 30 A2
14 Newham E6 . . . . .1 E8
Select Bsns Ctr TN12 . . 260 E5
Selkirk Dr DA8 . . . . .14 E6
Selkirk Rd CT16 . . . . . . 278 B3
Sellbourne Pk TN3 . . . . 314 C4
Sellindge Prim Sch
TN25 . . . . 303 C1
Selling CE Prim Sch
ME13 . . . . 171 B6
Selling Ct ME13 . . . . . . 171 C5
Sellinge Gn ME8 . . . . . . 65 C3
Selling Rd Chilham CT4 . 172 B3
Faversham ME13 . . . . . 138 F3
Selling ME13 . . . . 171 E6
Selling Sta ME13 . . . . . 171 E7
Selling St ME13 . . . . . . 171 B6
Sellwood Ct DA1 . . . . . . .34 B7
Selsea Ave CT6 . . . . 76 D4
Selsey Cres DA16 . . . . . 13 D6
Selstead Ct ME8 . . . . . . 65 C2
Selsted CE Prim Sch
CT15 . . . . 275 C6
Selway Ct CT14 . . . . . . 215 B3
Selwood Cl ME12 . . . . . .46 E6
Selwood Ho BR7 . . . . . . 30 C2
Selwyn Cres DA16 . . . . .13 B3
Selwyn Ct CT10 . . . . . . .83 F5
Selwyn Dr CT10 . . . . . . .83 F5
Selwyn Pl 1 BR5 . . . . 54 B6
Selwyn Rd RM18 . . . . . . 18 F5
Semaphore Rd CT7 . . . .80 F8
Semple Ct CT12 . . . . . . 115 C7
Semple Gdns ME4 . . . . .63 E3
Senacre La ME15 . . . . . 196 E6
Senacre Sq ME15 . . . . .195 F7
Senacre Tech Coll
ME15 . . . . 195 D6
Senacre Wood Prim Sch
ME15 . . . . 195 F7
Senator Wlk 4 SE28 . . .2 D3
Sencler Ho Bexley SE2 . 3 D8
Erith SE2 . . . . .3 D1
Sene Pk CT21 . . . . .333 D3
Senlac Cl CT11 . . . . 117 B6
Senlac Pl TN3 . . . . .312 C7
Senlac Rd SE12 . . . . . . .29 B7
Sennen Wlk SE9 . . . . . . .29 E5

Sennocke Ct TN13 . . . . 154 B2
Sequoia Gdns BR6 . . . . .53 F2
Serene Ct 12 CT10 . . . . .84 B4
Serene Pl 9 CT10 . . . . . .84 B4
Sermon Dr BR8 . . . . 55 C6
Serpentine Ct TN13 . . . 154 D5
Serpentine Rd TN13 . . . 154 D4
Serviden Dr BR1 . . . . . . 52 D8
Sessions House Sq
ME14 . . . . 161 F5
Setford Rd ME5 . . . . 97 C6
Setterfield Ho CT21 . . . 333 D2
Setterfield Rd CT9 . . . . .50 J1
Settington Ave ME5 . . . 64 C1
Sevastopol Pl CT1 . . . . 143 D1
Sevenacre Rd ME13 . . . 138 C8
Seven Acres
Crockenhill BR8 . . . . 55 D3
New Ash Green DA3 . . . .91 E7
Seven Mile La
Kings Hill TN15,ME18 . . 158 A3
Mereworth TN11,TN12 . . 191 C5
Wrotham Heath TN15 . . 157 F7
Sevenoaks Bsns Ctr
TN14 . . . . 154 C6
Sevenoaks By-Pass
TN13,TN14 . . . . 186 F7
Sevenoaks Cl ME7 . . . . .14 B3
Sevenoaks Hospl
TN13 . . . . 154 C2
Sevenoaks Mus & Gallery ★
TN13 . . . . 154 C2
Sevenoaks Prep Sch
TN15 . . . . 155 A1
Sevenoaks Prim Sch
TN13 . . . . 154 B5
Sevenoaks Rd
Borough Green TN15 . . 156 F7
Ightham TN15 . . . . 156 A4
Orpington BR6 . . . . .86 F6
Otford TN14 . . . . 122 B3
Pratt's Bottom BR6,TN14 . 87 C2
Sevenoaks Sch Int Ctr
TN13 . . . . 154 B1
Sevenoaks Sch TN13 . . 154 C1
Sevenoaks Sta TN13 . . 154 A3
Sevenoaks Way Ind Est 1
BR5 . . . . 54 C6
Sevenoaks Way BR5 . . . 54 C7
Sevenscore CT12 . . . . . 116 A5
Sevenscore Farm Cotts
CT12 . . . . 116 A5
Seven Stones Dr CT10 . .84 A1
Seven Wents TN15 . . . 156 A4
Severn Cl TN10 . . . . . . .222 C5
Severn Rd ME5 . . . . .97 C5
Sevington La TN24 . . . .301 A7
Sevington Pk ME15 . . . 194 F6
Sewell Cl CT7 . . . . .81 A6
Sewell Rd SE2 . . . . .3 B4
Sexburga Dr ME12 . . . . .47 B8
Sextant Pk ME2 . . . . . . .63 E6
Sexton Rd RM18 . . . . . . .18 F6
Seymour Ave
Westgate-on-S CT9 . . . . 50 D1
Whitstable CT5 . . . . .74 E1
Seymour Cl CT6 . . . . . . .77 B1
Seymour Dr BR2 . . . . . . .52 F1
Seymour Pl CT1 . . . . . . 174 E7
Seymour Rd
1 Chatham ME5 . . . . . .64 B3
Gillingham ME8 . . . . . . .66 C1
Gillingham ME8 . . . . . . .99 C8
Northfleet DA11 . . . . . . .36 F6
St Margaret's at Cliffe
CT15 . . . . 279 F8
Seymour St SE18 . . . . . . .2 C3
Seymour Villas 10
CT20 . . . . 334 F3
Seymour Wlk DA10 . . . . .15 E8
Shacklands Rd TN14 . . .88 D1
Shackleton Cl ME5 . . . . .97 B6
Shades The ME2 . . . . . . 62 C7
Shadoxhurst Rd TN26 . 326 C7
Shaftesbury Ave CT19 . 334 F7
Shaftesbury Cl ME19 . . 127 F1
Shaftesbury Ct
Deal CT14 . . . . 215 D2
Erith DA8 . . . . .14 F6
3 Woolwich SE28 . . . . .3 C5
Shaftesbury Dr ME16 . . 161 C4
Shaftesbury La DA1 . . . .16 B3
Shaftesbury Rd
Canterbury CT2 . . . . . . 142 F3
Hersden CT3 . . . . 111 E1
Royal Tunbridge Wells
TN4 . . . . 286 A5
Whitstable CT5 . . . . .74 D1
Shaftsbury Ct E6 . . . . . . .2 A7
Shaftsbury St CT11 . . . 117 F7
Shah Pl CT11 . . . . 117 D7
Shakespeare Ave ME18 . .19 B6
Shakespeare Ct CT17 . . 310 B7
Shakespeare Farm Rd
ME3 . . . . .24 F7
Shakespeare Ho 1
DA17 . . . . .3 F1
Shakespeare Pas CT9 . . 50 H2
Shakespeare Rd
Bexley DA7 . . . . .13 E6
Birchington CT7 . . . . . . .81 A8
Dartford DA1 . . . . 16 A3
Dover CT17 . . . . 310 B6
Gillingham ME7 . . . . 64 C3
Margate CT9 . . . . .50 J1
Sittingbourne ME10 . . . 102 A4
Tonbridge TN9 . . . . . . .253 F8
Shakespeare Terr 12
CT20 . . . . 335 C4
Shalder Ho ME7 . . . . . . 64 D7

Shalfleet Cl 1 ME5 . . . . 97 A7
Shalford Cl BR6 . . . . . . .86 C6
Shalloak Rd CT2 . . . . . . 143 D6
Shallons Rd SE9 . . . . . . .30 B4
Shallows Rd CT10 . . . . . 83 D6
Shalmsford Ct CT4 . . . . 173 C2
Shalmsford Rd CT4 . . . 172 E2
Shalmsford St CT4 . . . . 173 B2
Shambles The TN13 . . . 154 C2
Shamel Bsns Ctr ME2 . .63 C7
Shamley Rd ME4 . . . . . . 97 D2
Shamrock Ave CT5 . . . 108 B7
Shamrock Rd DA12 . . . .37 F8
Shandon Cl TN2 . . . . . . 286 C4
Shanklin Cl ME5 . . . . . . .97 C8
Shannon Ct BR6 . . . . . . 54 A2
Shapland Cl CT6 . . . . . . .77 C3
Share & Coulter Rd
CT5 . . . . 75 D1
Sharfleet Cres ME9 . . . . 68 D4
Sharfleet Dr ME2 . . . . . .62 B7
Sharland Rd DA12 . . . . . 37 C6
Sharman Ct DA4 . . . . . . 31 A4
Sharnal La ME6 . . . . . . 128 A2
Sharnal St ME3 . . . . 24 A2
Sharnbrooke Cl DA16 . . 13 C4
Sharon Cres ME5 . . . . . .96 F4
Sharon Ct 10 DA14 . . . . 31 B4
Sharp's Field TN27 . . . 262 E5
Sharps Gn ME8 . . . . 65 D5
Sharp Way DA1 . . . . .15 F4
Sharsted Hill ME9 . . . . 168 C8
Sharsted Way
Gillingham ME7 . . . . 98 A3
Maidstone ME14 . . . . . 163 B5
Shawbrooke Rd SE9 . . . 11 D3
Shaw Cl
Cliffe Woods ME3 . . . . . .40 B8
Maidstone ME14 . . . . . 162 C7
Woolwich SE28 . . . . .3 B5
Shaw Cres TN18 . . . . . . 19 B6
Shaw Cross TN24 . . . . 268 D5
Shawdon Ave CT13 . . . 182 A7
Shawfield Pk BR1 . . . . . 52 D7
Shawhill Ho ME19 . . . . 126 B1
Shaw Ho 6 Erith DA17 . . .3 F1
5 Newham E16 . . . . .2 A5
Shaw Rd TN16 . . . . 109 C8
Shawstead Rd ME7,ME7 . 97 D5
Shaws Way ME1 . . . . . . .63 C3
Shaw The TN2 . . . . 286 C2
Sheafe Dr TN17 . . . . . . 320 C5
Sheal's Cres ME15 . . . . 162 A2
Sheals Ct ME15 . . . . . . 162 A2
Shearers Cl ME14 . . . . 162 C5
Shears Cl DA2 . . . . 33 C6
Shears Green Ct DA11 . . 37 A6
Shears Green Inf Sch
DA11 . . . . .36 F5
Shears Green Jun Sch
DA11 . . . . .36 F5
Shearwater Ave CT5 . . 108 C7
Shearwater Cl ME2 . . . . 62 C7
Shearwater Cl ME12 . . .46 B8
Shearwater Ho TN29 . . 366 A3
Shearwater
Maidstone ME16 . . . . . 161 B5
New Barn DA3 . . . . .59 B6
Shear Way TN29 . . . . . 352 C5
Shearway Rd CT19 . . . .334 F7
Sherwood Cres DA1 . . . 15 A4
Sheen Ct CT9 . . . . .50 L2
Sheen Rd BR5 . . . . .53 F5
Sheepbarn La ME17 . . . .63 B3
Sheepcote La BR5,BR8 . .54 F4
Sheepfold La TN23 . . . 300 C4
Sheephurst La TN12 . . 258 E5
Sheerness Harbour Est
ME12 . . . . .27 F3
Sheerness ME12 . . . . . . 28 A3
Sheerness Heritage Ctr
(Mus) ★ ME12 . . . . . . .28 C2
Sheerness Mews E16 . . . .2 B4
Sheerness-on-Sea Sta
ME12 . . . . .28 B2
Sheerstone ME9 . . . . . . 68 D4
Sheerwater Rd
Newham E16 . . . . .1 D7
Preston CT3 . . . . 146 F5
Sheerways ME3 . . . . . . 138 A6
Sheet Glass Rd ME11 . . 46 A3
Sheet Hill TN15 . . . . . . 156 D2
Sheffield Gdns CT14 . . 215 C4
Sheffield Rd 4 TN4 . . . 253 F2
Sheilings The TN15 . . . 154 F7
Shelbury Cl DA14 . . . . . .31 A5
Shelden Dr ME8 . . . . . . .98 F8
Sheldon Bsns Ctr ME2 . 63 D8
Sheldon Cl
Aylesham CT3 . . . . 211 A6
Eltham SE12 . . . . .11 B2
Swanley BR8 . . . . .55 F6
Sheldon Ct
Dartford DA1 . . . . 16 A3
Rochester ME1 . . . . .63 A6
Sheldon Lodge 1
BR2 . . . . 52 C5
Sheldon Rd Bexley DA7 . .13 E4
Dover CT16 . . . . 278 B3
Erith DA17 . . . . .4 C2
Sheriff Dr ME5 . . . . 97 A2
Sheringham ME14 . . . . 161 D7
Sheridale Bsns Ctr
ME2 . . . . 63 A6
Sheridan Cl
Chatham ME5 . . . . .97 C7
Maidstone ME14 . . . . . 161 E8
Swanley BR8 . . . . .55 F6
Sheridan Cres BR7 . . . . .53 B7
Sheridan Ct
Dartford DA1 . . . . 16 A3
Rochester ME1 . . . . .4 A2
Sheridan Lodge 1
BR2 . . . . 52 C5
Sheridan Rd Bexley DA7 . .13 E4
Dover CT16 . . . . 278 B3
Erith DA17 . . . . .4 C2
Sheriff Dr ME5 . . . . 97 A2
Sheringham ME14 . . . . 161 D7
Sheringham Ho 5
ME15 . . . . 195 D8
Sherington Prim Sch
SE7 . . . . .11 B8
Sherington Rd SE7 . . . . .11 B8
Sherlies Ave BR6 . . . . . .86 E8
Sherman Cl ME7 . . . . . . .65 B1
Sherman Rd BR1 . . . . . . 52 A8
Shernden La TN8 . . . . . 249 C4
Shernold Sch ME16 . . . 161 D5
Shernolds ME15 . . . . . . 195 B7

Sheron Cl CT14 . . . . . . 215 A5
Sherriffs Court La
CT12 . . . . 114 E6
Sherway Cl TN27 . . . . . 262 E5
Sherway Rd TN27 . . . . .263 D6
Sherwin Knight Inf Sch
ME2 . . . . .62 E5
Sherwin Knight Jun Sch
ME2 . . . . .62 E5
Sherwood Ave ME5 . . . . 97 A2
Sherwood Cl
Ashford TN24 . . . . 268 C7
Faversham ME13 . . . . . 105 B1
Herne Bay CT6 . . . . 77 C2
Sidcup DA5 . . . . 13 C1
Whitstable CT5 . . . . . . 108 C6
Sherwood Ct CT8 . . . . . 50 C1
Sherwood Dr CT5 . . . . . 108 C6
Sherwood Gdns CT11 . . .83 E1
Sherwood Ho
Chatham ME5 . . . . .97 A3
Erith DA8 . . . . .14 E8
Sherwood Park Ave
DA15 . . . . .13 B1
Sherwood Park Com Prim
Sch TN2 . . . . 286 D6
Sherwood Park Prim Sch
DA15 . . . . .13 B1
Sherwood Pl TN3 . . . . . 284 E3
Sherwood Rd
Bexley DA16 . . . . .12 E4
Birchington CT7 . . . . . . .80 F5
Royal Tunbridge Wells
TN2 . . . . 286 C5
Sherwood Way TN2 . . . 286 D6
Shieldhall St SE2 . . . . . . .3 C2
Shillingheld Cl TN4 . . . 162 F5
Shinecroft TN14 . . . . . . 122 A3
Shingle Barn La ME15 . 193 C3
Shinglewell Rd DA8 . . . 14 A7
Shipbourne Rd
Shipbourne TN11 . . . . . 189 D2
Tonbridge TN10 . . . . . .222 C5
Shipbourne Sch TN11 . 189 C4
Ship Cl TN29 . . . . 366 C8
Ship Field Cl TN16 . . . .150 C6
Ship Hill TN16 . . . . 150 D6
Shipland Ho TN27 . . . . 265 D8
Ship La Rochester ME1 . .63 E4
Sutton at H BR8,DA4 . . .56 E8
Shipley Ct ME14 . . . . . 162 A4
Shipley Hills Rd DA13 . . 59 E1
Shipley Mill Cl TN23 . . 300 C4
Shipman Ave CT2 . . . . 174 C8
Shipman Rd E16 . . . . .1 C7
Shipmans Way CT16 . . 278 A3
Ship St CT19 . . . . .335 D6
Shipway Ho CT21 . . . . .333 D1
Shipwrights Ave ME4 . . .64 B2
Shipwrights Lee CT5 . . . 74 C2
Shipyard Area ME13 . . 105 D1
Shirebrook Rd SE3 . . . . 11 D4
Shire Ct DA18 . . . . .3 D3
Shirehall Rd DA2 . . . . . . .33 E4
Shire La
Farthing Street BR6 . . . . 86 C3
Orpington BR6 . . . . .86 E5
Stalisfield Green ME13 . 201 C6
Shires The TN12 . . . . . .257 A7
Shireway Cl CT19 . . . . .335 A7
Shirkoak Pk TN26 . . . . 326 A5
Shirley Ave
Chatham ME5 . . . . .96 D5
Ramsgate CT11 . . . . . . .83 E1
Sidcup DA5 . . . . 31 D7
Shirley Cl Chalk DA12 . .38 B6
Dartford DA1 . . . . 15 C3
Shirley Ct ME15 . . . . . . 195 E5
Shirley Gdns TN4 . . . . .285 C5
Shirley Gr TN4 . . . . 285 C5
Shirley House Dr SE7 . . 11 C7
Shirley Hts 5 DA6 . . . . .13 E3
Shirley Rd DA15 . . . . 30 E5
Shirley Way ME15 . . . . 163 A3
Shoebury Terr ME12 . . . 48 A3
Sholden Bank CT14 . . . 214 E4
Sholden CE Prim Sch
CT14 . . . . 214 F5
Sholden Gdns BR5 . . . . 54 C4
Sholden New Rd CT14 . 214 F6
Sholden Rd ME2 . . . . . . 40 C1
Shooter's Hill 8
CT17 . . . . 278 C1
Shooters Hill CT15 . . . . 245 C8
Shooters Hill Rd SE18,
SE3 . . . . 11 D6
Shore Cl Birchington CT7 . 80 D8
Herne Bay CT6 . . . . .76 B3
Shorefields ME8 . . . . . . .66 B2
Shoregate La ME9 . . . . .66 F6
Shoreham Aircraft Mus ★
TN14 . . . . 121 F8
Shoreham Cl DA5 . . . . . 31 D7
Shoreham Ho TN14 . . . 122 B8
Shoreham La
Badgers Mount TN14 . . 121 A7
Chelsfield BR6 . . . . 88 A3
Sevenoaks TN13 . . . . . 153 F4
Tenterden TN30 . . . . . . 324 A3
Shoreham Pl TN14 . . . . 122 A7
Shoreham Rd
Orpington BR5 . . . . .54 B7
Otford TN14 . . . . 122 B5
Shoreham Sta TN14 . . . 122 B8
Shoreham Village Sch
TN14 . . . . 121 F8
Shoreham Way BR2 . . . . 52 A3
Shoreham Wlk ME15 . . 195 F7
Shorehill CT15 . . . . 122 F2
Shorehill La TN15 . . . . .122 F4
Shore The
Northfleet DA11 . . . . 18 C2

Shore The continued
Northfleet,Rosherville
DA11 . . . . .18 F1
Shorland Ct ME1 . . . . .63 B5
Shorncliffe Cres CT20 .**334** E5
Shorncliffe Ind Est
CT20 . . . .**334** D4
Shorncliffe Rd CT20 . .**334** F5
Shorne CE Prim Sch
DA12 . . . . .38 E3
Shorne Cl
Orpington BR5 . . . . .54 D5
3 Sidcup DA15 . . . . .13 B1
Shornefield Cl BR1 . . . . .53 A6
Shorne Ifield Rd DA12 . .38 C2
Shornells Way SE2 . . . . . . .3 C1
Shorne Wood Ctry Pk ★
DA12 . . . . .38 C1
Short La Alkham CT15 . .276 D1
Limpsfield RH8 . . . . . . .183 B3
Shortlands Cl DA17 . . . . . .3 E3
Shortlands Gn ME15 . . .195 F5
Shortlands Rd ME10 . . .102 B4
Short La TN29 . . . . .362 D6
Short Path SE18 . . . . .12 B8
Short's Prospect ME12 . .71 C8
Short St
3 Chatham ME4 . . . . . . .64 B3
Chillenden CT3 . . . . . . .212 A8
5 Sandwich CT13 . . . . .149 A1
Sheerness ME12 . . . . . . .28 B2
Shorts Way ME1 . . . . .63 A3
Shortway SE9 . . . . .11 E4
Shotfield Cl CT3 . . . . . . .146 C6
Shottendane Rd CT9,
CT8 . . . . .82 C7
Shottenden La CT4 . . . .204 A7
Shottenden Rd
Gillingham ME7 . . . . .64 D7
Shottenden CT4,ME13 . .203 D8
Shottery Cl SE9 . . . . .29 E5
Showfields Rd TN2 . . . .285 F1
Shrapnel Cl SE18 . . . . . . .11 E7
Shrapnel Rd SE9 . . . . . . .11 F4
Shrewsbury La SE18 . . . .12 B6
Shrimpton Cl CT4 . . . . .172 B3
Shroffold Rd BR1 . . . . . . .29 A5
Shropshire Terr 1
ME15 . . . . .195 E7
Shrubbery Rd
Gravesend DA12 . . . . . . .37 C2
Sutton at H DA4 . . . . . . .57 D8
Shrubbery The CT14 . . .215 C1
Shrubcote TN30 . . . . . . .345 C2
Shrub Hill Rd CT5 . . . . .109 D7
Shrublands Ct
Royal Tunbridge Wells
TN2 . . . . .286 C4
1 Tonbridge TN9 . . . . .222 C1
Shrubsall Cl SE9 . . . . . . .29 E7
Shrubshall Mdw TN15 .190 A8
Shrubsole Ave ME12 . . . .28 C1
Shrubsole Dr ME14 . . . .129 F3
Shuart La CT7 . . . . .79 F4
Shurland Ave
Leysdown-on-S ME12 . . . .49 H1
Minster (Sheppey) ME12 . .47 B6
Sittingbourne ME10 . . . .101 F1
Shurland Pk ME12 . . . . . .48 E5
Shurlock Ave BR8 . . . . . .55 D7
Shurlock Dr BR6 . . . . . . .86 C6
Shuttle Cl
Biddenden TN27 . . . . . .295 A2
Sidcup DA15 . . . . .30 F8
Shuttlemead DA5 . . . . . . .31 F8
Shuttle Rd
Broadstairs CT10 . . . . . . .84 B5
Crayford DA1 . . . . .15 A4
Shuttlesfield La CT4 . . .273 D1
Sibert's Cl CT15 . . . . . . .244 F5
Sibertswold CE Prim Sch
CT15 . . . . .244 E4
Sibley Cl DA6 . . . . .13 E2
Sibthorpe Rd SE12 . . . . .29 C8
Sidcup By Pass Rd
Orpington BR5,BR7,DA14 . .31 B1
Sidcup DA14 . . . . .30 D8
Sidcup Hill DA14 . . . . . . .31 B3
Sidcup Hill Gdns DA14 . .31 C3
Sidcup Hill DA14 . . . . . . .31 B3
Sidcup Pl DA14 . . . . .31 A3
Sidcup Rd SE12,SE9 . . . .29 D7
Sidcup Sta DA15 . . . . . . .31 A6
Sidcup Tech Ctr DA14 . .31 D2
Sidewood Rd SE9 . . . . . . .30 D7
Sidings The
Dymchurch TN29 . . . . . .366 B7
Lyminge CT18 . . . . .305 C2
Whitstable CT5 . . . . .74 E2
Sidmouth Ct DA1 . . . . . . .34 B7
Sidmouth Rd
Bexley DA16 . . . . .13 C7
Orpington BR5 . . . . .54 B5
Sidney Cl TN2 . . . . .313 F8
Sidney Gdns TN14 . . . . .122 C2
Sidney Ho SE18 . . . . .11 F6
Sidney Rd
Gillingham ME7 . . . . .64 C7
Rochester ME1 . . . . .63 A2
Sidney St
Folkestone CT19 . . . . . .335 C7
Maidstone ME16 . . . . . .161 C2
Siebert Rd SE3 . . . . .11 A8
Siedle Ho 9 SE18 . . . . . .12 A8
Siemens Rd SE18 . . . . .1 D3
Signal Ct 6 ME8 . . . . . . .65 F1
Silchester Ct ME4 . . . . .162 C7
Silecroft Ct TN23 . . . . . .267 E1
Silecroft Rd DA7 . . . . . . .14 A6
Silk Cl SE12 . . . . .11 A1
Silk Mills Cl TN13 . . . . .154 C6
Silvanus Ho 5 CT11 . . . .117 D7
Silver Ave CT7 . . . . .81 B6
Silver Bank ME5 . . . . . . .97 A6

Silver Birch Ave DA13 . .92 F1
Silver Birch Cl
Joyden's Wood DA2 . . . . .32 E4
Woolwich SE28 . . . . .3 A5
Silver Birch Cl TN26 . . .299 A1
Silver Birches ME5 . . . . . .97 A3
Silver Birches Mobile
Homes Pk TN26 . . . . . .328 A4
Silver Birches ME12 . . . .28 G1
Silver Birch Gr TN23 . . .300 B4
Silver Birch Wlk
ME18 . . . . .192 D6
Silver Cl TN9 . . . . .254 B6
Silverdale Ave ME12 . . . .47 A6
Silverdale Dr
Bromley SE9 . . . . .29 E6
Gillingham ME8 . . . . .98 F7
Herne Bay CT6 . . . . .77 D2
Silverdale Gr ME10 . . . .101 D3
Silverdale Gr DA3 . . . . . .58 F5
Silverdale La
Royal Tunbridge Wells
TN4 . . . . .286 B6
Sandhurst Cross TN18 . .355 F5
Silverdale Rd
Bexley DA7 . . . . .14 B5
Orpington,Petts Wood
BR5 . . . . .53 C5
Orpington,St Paul's Cray
BR5 . . . . .54 A6
Ramsgate CT11 . . . . . . .117 A5
Royal Tunbridge Wells
TN4 . . . . .286 B6
Silverden Cotts TN18 . . .355 F4
Silver Hill ME4 . . . . .63 F3
Silver Hill Gdns
Ashford TN24 . . . . .269 A1
4 Chatham ME4 . . . . . .63 F3
Silver Hill TN19 . . . . . . .354 B1
Silver Hill Rd TN24 . . . .269 A1
Silver Hill
Rochester ME1 . . . . .62 F2
Tenterden TN30 . . . . . . .324 B1
Silverhurst Dr TN10 . . . .222 C7
Silverlands Rd CT18 . . . .305 C7
Silverland St TN16 . . . . .151 D6
Silverlocke Rd RM17 . . . .18 D8
Silver Rd DA12 . . . . .37 E6
Silverspot Cl ME8 . . . . . . .98 F7
Silver Spring Cl DA8 . . . .14 B8
Silver St CT14 . . . . .215 D7
Silversted La TN16 . . . . .151 D6
Silvers The CT10 . . . . . . .83 C4
Silverstone Ct 10 BR1 . . .52 C7
Silver St ME9 . . . . .133 F5
Silvertown Sta E16 . . . . . . .1 E5
Silvertown Way E16 . . . . . .1 A5
Silver Tree ME5 . . . . .97 B1
Silverweed Rd ME5 . . . . . .96 F4
Silwood CT12 . . . . .286 E7
Simmonds Ct TN4 . . . . . .285 B4
Simmonds Dr DA3 . . . . . .59 A4
Simmonds La ME15 . . . .196 B6
Simmonds Rd CT1 . . . . .174 E7
Simmons Rd SE18 . . . . . . .2 B1
Simnel Rd SE12 . . . . .29 B8
Simon Ave CT9 . . . . .51 D2
Simon Cl 5 SE28 . . . . . . .3 B5
Simone Cl BR1 . . . . .52 D8
Simone Weil Ave
TN24 . . . . .268 B4
Simon Langton Girls Gram
Sch CT1 . . . . .175 C5
Simon Langton Gram Sch
for Boys CT1 . . . . .175 A4
Simon's Ave TN23 . . . . . .299 F7
Simpson Rd
Sittingbourne ME10 . . . .101 C5
Snodland ME6 . . . . .128 A6
Simpson's Cotts BR2 . . . .85 C7
Simpsons Pl 6 BR1 . . . . .52 A6
Simpson's Rd BR1,BR2 . . .52 A6
Sinclair Cl ME8 . . . . .98 E5
Sinclair Way DA2 . . . . . . .34 B7
Sindal Shaw Ho ME5 . . . .96 E4
Singapore Dr ME7 . . . . . .64 B5
Singer Ave CT6 . . . . .76 B4
Singledge Ave CT16 . . . .277 F6
Singledge La CT15 . . . . .245 C2
Single's Cross TN14 . . . .120 D4
Single's Cross La
TN14 . . . . .120 C5
Single St TN16 . . . . .119 B4
Singleton Cl CT12 . . . . . .115 B6
Singleton Ctr The
TN23 . . . . .299 D8
Singleton Hill TN23 . . . .299 C8
Singleton Rd TN23 . . . . .267 C1
Singlewell Prim Sch
DA12 . . . . .37 D2
Singlewell Rd DA11 . . . . .37 B4
Sinkertweazel TN17 . . . .320 E2
Sion Hill CT11 . . . . .117 E6
Sion Pass 12 CT11 . . . . .117 E6
Sion Wlk 8 TN1 . . . . . . .286 A2
Sirdar Strand DA12 . . . . .37 F6
Sir David's Pk TN4 . . . . .253 E1
Sir Evelyn Rd ME1 . . . . . .63 B1
Sir John Hawkins Hospl
ME4 . . . . .63 F4
Sir John Hawkins Way
ME4 . . . . .63 F4
Sir John Moore Ave
CT21 . . . . .333 B2
Sir John Moore Ct 5
CT20 . . . . .334 E3
Sir Joseph Williamson's
Mathematical Sch
ME1 . . . . .63 C1
Sir Martin Bowes Ho 11
SE18 . . . . .2 A2

Sir Roger Manwood's Sch
CT13 . . . . .181 B8
Sir Thomas Longley Rd
ME2 . . . . .63 E6
Siscup Cl SE9 . . . . .30 B6
Siskin Cl Ashford TN25 . .268 B7
Hawkinge CT18 . . . . . . .306 F4
Siskin Gdns TN12 . . . . . .135 F7
Siskin Wlk ME20 . . . . . . .127 F2
Sissinghurst Castle Gdns ★
TN17 . . . . .293 D1
Sissinghurst CE Prim Sch
TN17 . . . . .321 B8
Sissinghurst Dr ME16 . . .161 B4
Sissinghurst Rd
Biddenden TN27 . . . . . .294 C2
Sissinghurst TN17,TN27 . .321 D8
Sittingbourne Com Coll
ME10 . . . . .102 C2
Sittingbourne Ind Pk
ME10 . . . . .101 F5
Sittingbourne & Kemsley
Light Rly ★ ME10 . . . .102 A7
Sittingbourne Rd
Maidstone,Detling ME14 . .162 E8
Maidstone,Penenden Heath
ME14 . . . . .162 B6
Sittingbourne Retail Pk
ME10 . . . . .101 F5
Sittingbourne Sta
ME10 . . . . .101 F4
Siward Rd ME2 . . . . .52 C6
Six Bells La TN13 . . . . . .154 C1
Six Bells Pk TN26 . . . . . .326 A3
Six Fields Path TN30 . . .345 A7
Six Penny Cl TN8 . . . . . .249 C8
Sixth Ave ME12 . . . . .49 A5
Skeete Rd CT18 . . . . .304 E7
Skeet Hill La BR5,BR6 . . . .87 E8
Skeffington St SE18 . . . . . .2 C3
Skene Cl ME8 . . . . .66 A1
Skeynes Rd TN8 . . . . . . .217 B1
Skibbs La BR5,BR6 . . . . . . .87 E7
Skinner Gdns SN17 . . . . .321 A8
Skinner Rd TN9 . . . . .376 C6
Skinner's Alley 3 CT5 . . .74 D1
Skinners Cl ME20 . . . . . .129 A6
Skinners La TN8 . . . . . . .217 D2
Skinners' Sch The
TN4 . . . . .286 A6
Skinner St ME4 . . . . .63 F3
Skinner's Terr 15 TN9 . .254 B8
Skinner St ME7 . . . . .64 C5
Skinner Street Prim Sch
ME7 . . . . .64 C6
Skinner's Way ME17 . . .196 E4
Skinney La DA4 . . . . .57 D6
Skippers Cl DA9 . . . . .17 B2
Skua Ct ME2 . . . . .62 C7
Skye Cl ME15 . . . . .195 A7
Skylark Way TN23 . . . . . .300 D3
Sky Studios E16 . . . . .2 A4
Slade Cl ME5 . . . . .97 B2
Sladebrook Rd SE3 . . . . . .11 D4
Sladedale Rd SE18 . . . . . . .2 E1
Slade Gdns DA8 . . . . .14 F6
Slade Green Inf Sch
DA8 . . . . .15 A7
Slade Green Jun Sch
DA8 . . . . .15 A7
Slade Green Rd DA8 . . . . .15 B7
Slade Green Sta DA8 . . . .15 A6
Slade Prim Sch TN9 . . . .222 B2
Slade Rd ME17 . . . . .200 D8
Slades Cl CT5 . . . . .109 C8
Slades Dr BR7 . . . . .30 C4
Slade The
Lamberhurst TN3 . . . . . .317 A3
Tonbridge TN9 . . . . .222 B2
Woolwich SE18 . . . . .12 F4
Slaney Rd TN12 . . . . .260 F4
Slater Cl 9 SE18 . . . . .2 A2
Slaters TN5 . . . . .218 F2
Slatin Rd ME2 . . . . .63 B8
Sleeches Cross TN3 . . . .314 B2
Sleepers Stile Rd TN5 . . .316 B1
Sleigh Rd CT2 . . . . .143 F6
Slicketts Hill ME4 . . . . . . .64 A4
Slip La CT15 . . . . .276 C2
Slip Mill Rd TN18 . . . . . .340 E4
Slip The TN16 . . . . .151 C1
Slipway Rd ME12 . . . . . . .27 F3
Sloane Gdns BR6 . . . . . . .86 C7
Sloane Sq DA3 . . . . .58 E6
Slocum Cl SE28 . . . . .3 C6
Sloe La CT10,CT9 . . . . . . .40 B8
Slough Rd ME9 . . . . .135 A3
Small Bridge Cotts
TN17 . . . . .290 B2
Small Bridge Rd TN12,
TN17 . . . . .290 B2
Small Grains DA3 . . . . . . .91 B7
Small Hythe Cl ME15 . . .163 B2
Smallhythe Place (Mus) ★
TN30 . . . . .359 C8
Smallhythe Place ★
TN30 . . . . .345 C1
Small Hythe Rd TN30 . . .345 B4
Small Profits ME15,
ME18 . . . . .193 A4
Smarden Bsns Est
TN27 . . . . .295 D7
Smarden Cl 3 DA17 . . . . .4 A1
Smarden Gr SE9 . . . . .29 F4
Smarden Prim Sch
TN27 . . . . .264 A1
Smarden Rd
Pluckley TN27 . . . . .265 B6
Standen TN27 . . . . .295 B6
Swift's Green TN27 . . . . .263 B4
Smarden Wlk ME8 . . . . . . .66 B1
Smarts Cotts ME14 . . . .163 C4
Smarts Hill TN11 . . . . . .252 A1

Smarts Rd DA12 . . . . .37 C6
Smeed Cl 4 ME10 . . . . . .102 B4
Smeed-Dean Ctr The
ME10 . . . . .102 A4
Smeeth Com Prim Sch
TN25 . . . . .302 D5
Smetham Gdns ME2 . . . . .40 B1
Smithers Cl TN11 . . . . . .190 E1
Smithers Ct TN12 . . . . . .225 A7
Smithers La TN12 . . . . . .225 A7
Smithfield Rd ME3 . . . . . .27 C5
Smithies Rd SE2 . . . . .3 B2
Smith Rd ME5 . . . . .97 B3
Smith's Hill ME15 . . . . . .193 C5
Smiths Orch ME9 . . . . . .133 F5
Smith St ME2 . . . . .63 A6
Smithy Dr TN23 . . . . .300 C4
Smithy Field 7 TN8 . . . .217 D3
Smithy The TN5 . . . . .336 A3
Smugglers TN18 . . . . . . .341 A1
Smugglers Leap Cvn Pk
CT12 . . . . .115 C8
Smuggler's Way CT7 . . . .81 A8
Smugglers Wlk DA9 . . . . .17 B2
Smythe Cl TN4 . . . . .253 E3
Smythe Rd DA4 . . . . .57 A8
Snag La TN14 . . . . .119 D7
Snakes Hill CT15 . . . . . . .178 A5
Snape La TN5 . . . . .336 D1
Snape View TN5 . . . . . . .336 F4
Snargate La TN29 . . . . . .362 C5
Snargate St CT17 . . . . . . .310 D7
Snelgrove Ho 12 CT16 . .310 D8
Snell Gdns CT6 . . . . .76 B2
Snelling Ave CT1 . . . . . . .136 F6
Snipe Cl Ashford TN25 . .268 B7
Erith DA8 . . . . .15 B7
Snipe Ct ME2 . . . . .62 C7
Snoad La TN12 . . . . .292 A8
Snodhurst Ave ME5 . . . . .96 E5
Snodhurst Ho 6 ME5 . . . .97 A7
Snodland CE Prim Sch
ME6 . . . . .127 F8
Snodland Rd ME19 . . . . .127 D7
Snodlands Cl BR6 . . . . . . .86 A1
Snodland Sta ME6 . . . . . .128 B8
Snoll Hatch Rd TN12 . . .224 F5
Snowball Rd TN23 . . . . . .300 B4
Snowdon Ave ME14 . . . .162 B5
Snowdon Cl ME5 . . . . .97 B7
Snowdon Par ME14 . . . . .162 C5
Snowdown Caravan Site
CT15 . . . . .211 A4
Snowdown Ct CT3 . . . . . .210 F5
Snowdown Sta CT15 . . . .211 B3
Snowdrop Cl CT19 . . . . . .335 C8
Snow Ho ME7 . . . . .64 C7
Snughorne La TN27 . . . .295 D8
Sobraon Villas TN15 . . . .157 C7
Sobraon Way CT1 . . . . . .143 D1
Solar Ct CT12 . . . . .117 C7
Solefield Prep Sch
TN13 . . . . .187 C8
Solefields Rd TN13 . . . . .187 C8
Sole Fields TN13 . . . . . . .187 C8
Solent Gdns ME5 . . . . . . .97 B8
Soleoak Dr TN13 . . . . . . .187 B8
Soleshill Rd CT4 . . . . . . .171 C5
Sole Street Cotts CT4 . . .239 B7
Sole Street Farm ME3 . . . .40 B3
Sole Street Sta DA13 . . . .60 D4
Sole St DA12,DA13 . . . . . .60 D4
Solomon Ho CT14 . . . . . .215 B3
Solomon Rd
Gillingham ME8 . . . . .66 A1
Gillingham ME8 . . . . .99 A8
Rainham ME8 . . . . .65 F1
Solomons La ME13 . . . . .138 D7
Solomons Rd ME4 . . . . . . .63 F4
Somerden Rd BR5 . . . . . . .54 D2
Somerfield Barn Ct
TN25 . . . . .331 C8
Somerfield Cl ME16 . . . .161 D5
Somerfield Hospl The
ME16 . . . . .161 E5
Somerfield La ME16 . . . .161 D4
Somerfield Rd ME16 . . . .161 D4
Somerhill Ave DA15 . . . . .31 B8
Somerhill Rd
Bexley DA16 . . . . .13 B5
Tonbridge TN9 . . . . .254 D8
Somerset Ave DA16 . . . . .12 F3
Somerset Cl
Chatham ME5 . . . . .97 C8
Sittingbourne ME10 . . . .101 C4
Whitstable CT5 . . . . .108 B7
Somerset Ct
2 Broadstairs CT10 . . . .84 A4
Deal CT14 . . . . .215 B3
Ramsgate CT12 . . . . .83 B2
Somerset Rd
Ashford TN24 . . . . .268 B3
Canterbury CT1 . . . . . . .175 D8
Dartford DA1 . . . . .33 B8
Deal CT14 . . . . .215 C3
Folkestone CT19 . . . . . .334 E6
Maidstone ME15 . . . . . .195 C8
Orpington BR6 . . . . .54 A2
Royal Tunbridge Wells
TN4 . . . . .286 A6
Somerset Villas TN3 . . . .312 C7
Somersham Rd DA7 . . . . .13 E5
Somertrees Ave SE12 . . . .29 B6
Somerville Gdns TN4 . . .285 F4
Somerville Rd DA1 . . . . . .15 F1
Somme Ct CT1 . . . . .143 D1
Sommerville Cl ME13 . . .138 E7
Somner Cl CT2 . . . . .142 D1
Somner Wlk ME15 . . . . . .195 F4
Sondes Cl CT6 . . . . .77 A2
Sondes Rd CT14 . . . . .215 D5

Sonnet Wlk TN16 . . . . . .118 C1
Sonora Way ME10 . . . . . .101 C7
Soper's La TN18 . . . . .340 D4
Sophia Rd E16 . . . . .1 C1
Sophurst La TN12 . . . . . .288 C5
Sopurst Wood TN12 . . . .288 D5
Sopwith Cl TN16 . . . . . . .118 D3
Sorrel Cl SE28 . . . . .3 A5
Sorrel Ct 8 RM17 . . . . . . .18 C8
Sorrel Gdns CT6 . . . . .1 E8
Sorrell Cl 4 TN8 . . . . . . .217 D3
Sorrell Rd ME5 . . . . .96 F4
Sorrell Way DA11 . . . . . . .36 A5
Sortmill Rd ME6 . . . . . . .128 B7
Sotherton TN24 . . . . .300 E7
Souberg Cl CT14 . . . . . . .215 C8
Sounds Lodge BR8 . . . . . .55 C3
Southall Cl CT12 . . . . . . .115 C7
Southampton Mews E16 . .1 B5
South Ash Rd TN15 . . . . . .91 E4
South Ave
Aylesham CT15 . . . . .211 A3
Gillingham ME8 . . . . .65 B2
South Avenue Jun & Inf
Schs ME10 . . . . .102 A3
South Ave ME10 . . . . .102 A3
South Aylesford Ret Pk
ME20 . . . . .160 E8
South Bank Cliffe ME3 . . .22 B2
Staplehurst TN12 . . . . . .260 E2
Sutton Valence ME17 . . .229 E7
Westerham TN16 . . . . . .151 D1
South Barham Rd CT4 . . .242 E6
Southborough CE Prim Sch
& Tunbridge Wells
Language Unit TN4 . . .285 F8
Southborough Ct TN4 . . .254 A2
Southborough La BR2 . . .52 F4
Southborough Prim Sch
BR2 . . . . .53 A4
South Borough Prim Sch
ME15 . . . . .162 A2
Southborough Rd BR1 . . .52 E5
Southbourne TN23 . . . . . .299 E5
Southbourne Gdns
SE12 . . . . .11 B2
Southbourne Gr ME5 . . . .97 A4
Southbourne BR2 . . . . . . .52 A2
Southbourne Rd CT19 . . .335 E5
South Brook La TN8 . . . .218 C7
South Brooks Rd
TN29 . . . . .378 H6
South Bush La ME8 . . . . .99 B6
South Camber Way
CT16 . . . . .279 B1
South Canterbury Rd
CT1 . . . . .175 A6
South Cl Bexley DA6 . . . . .13 D3
Canterbury CT1 . . . . . . .175 A6
South Court Dr CT3 . . . . .178 A7
South Cres ME17 . . . . . . .194 C4
Southcroft Ave DA16 . . . .12 E4
South Ct Deal CT14 . . . . .215 D6
Ramsgate CT12 . . . . .83 B2
Royal Tunbridge Wells
TN4 . . . . .286 A6
South Deal Prim Sch
CT14 . . . . .215 B4
Southdene TN14 . . . . . . .120 F6
Southdown Rd ME12 . . . .46 E6
South Dr BR6 . . . . .86 E5
South Eastern Rd
Ramsgate CT11 . . . . . . .117 D7
Rochester ME2 . . . . .63 C7
Southenay La TN25 . . . . .303 C4
Southend Cl SE9 . . . . .12 B1
Southend Cres SE9 . . . . . .12 B1
Southernden Rd TN27 . . .231 E1
Southern Pl BR8 . . . . .55 D5
Southern Way CT19 . . . . .335 D4
Southernwood Rise
CT20 . . . . .334 F4
South Exit Rd CT16 . . . . .310 G8
Southey Mews E16 . . . . . . .1 C1
Southey Way 1 ME7 . . . .127 F4
Southey Wlk RM18 . . . . . .19 B6
Southfield Cl DA1 . . . . . . .15 F4
Southfield Rd
Orpington BR7 . . . . .54 A6
Royal Tunbridge Wells
TN4 . . . . .286 A6
Southfield Shaw DA13 . . .93 B1
Southfields BR8 . . . . .32 F1
Southfields Way TN4 . . .286 B8
Southfleet Ave DA3 . . . . .59 B7
Southfleet Rd Bean DA2 . .35 C4
8 Northfleet DA11 . . . . .36 F7
Orpington BR6 . . . . .86 C6
Swanscombe DA10 . . . . .36 A7
South Frith TN4 . . . . .254 A6
Southgate Rd TN30 . . . . .345 C7
Southgate TN4 . . . . .285 F3
South Gipsy Rd DA16 . . . .13 D4
South Glade The DA5 . . . .31 F7
South Goodwin Ct
CT14 . . . . .215 D8
South Green La ME9 . . . .132 F6
South Gr TN1 . . . . .286 A2
South Hall Dr DA4 . . . . . .56 F2
South Hill BR7 . . . . .29 F2
South Hill Rd DA12 . . . . . .37 C6
Southill Rd Bromley BR7 . .29 F1
Chatham ME4 . . . . .63 F3
South Kent Ave DA11 . . . .18 C1

Sho–Sou 429

South Kent Coll
Dover CT16 . . . . .310 D8
Folkestone CT19 . . . . . .335 B5
South Kent Coll Jemmett
Campus TN23 . . . . . . .300 A8
South Kent Coll of Tech
TN23 . . . . .268 C1
South Kent Coll South
Ashford Campus
TN23 . . . . .299 F6
Southland's Com Comp Sch
TN28 . . . . .373 B7
Southland Rd SE18 . . . . . .12 F7
Southlands BR6 . . . . .86 E5
Southlands Ct BR2 . . . . . .52 D5
Southlands Gr BR1 . . . . . .52 E6
Southlands Rd BR1,BR2 . .52 E5
South La ME17 . . . . .229 E6
South Lea TN23 . . . . .300 A3
Southlees La ME9 . . . . . .132 F3
South Lodge Cl CT5 . . . . .74 E3
South Lodge CT5 . . . . .74 E3
Southmead Cl CT19 . . . . .335 A6
South Military Rd
CT17 . . . . .310 C5
South Molton Rd E16 . . . . .1 A7
South Motto TN23 . . . . . .300 B5
Southold Rise SE9 . . . . . . .29 F5
Southover BR1 . . . . .29 A3
Southover Ct 2 CT20 . . .334 E3
South Park Bsns Village
ME15 . . . . .162 A1
South Park Rd ME15 . . . .162 C1
South Pk TN13 . . . . .154 F3
South Pondside Rd
ME4 . . . . .64 A8
Southport Rd SE18 . . . . . . .2 D2
South Quay ME13 . . . . . .105 D1
South Rd Chatham ME4 . . .64 B7
Chatham ME4,ME7 . . . . .64 A7
Dover CT17 . . . . .310 B8
Erith DA8 . . . . .14 F7
Faversham ME13 . . . . . .138 C7
Herne Bay CT6 . . . . .77 A5
Hythe CT21 . . . . .333 D1
Kingsdown CT14 . . . . . .248 D5
Marden TN12 . . . . .259 E5
Sandwich CT13 . . . . . . .149 A8
South Ridge BR2 . . . . .52 C5
South Rise Prim Sch
SE18 . . . . .2 D1
South Rise Way SE18 . . . .2 D2
South Row
Greenwich SE3 . . . . .11 A5
Penshurst TN8 . . . . .251 D5
Southsea Ave ME10 . . . . .47 C8
Southsea Dr CT6 . . . . .76 D4
South Side Three Rd
ME4 . . . . .64 C8
Southspring DA15 . . . . . . .30 D8
South St Bromley BR1 . . . .52 A7
Canterbury CT1 . . . . . . .143 C2
Deal CT14 . . . . .215 D6
Folkestone CT20 . . . . . .335 E4
Gravesend DA12 . . . . . . .37 B8
Lydd TN29 . . . . .376 C6
Maidstone ME16 . . . . . .160 E1
Southstone Ct CT21 . . . . .333 C1
South Stour Ave TN23 . . .300 B8
South St ME11 . . . . .45 F5
Southstreet Crossing
CT5 . . . . .109 A7
South Street Rd ME9 . . . .132 F7
South St Selling ME13 . . .171 F8
Whitstable CT5 . . . . . . .109 A7
South Swale Nature
Reserve ★ ME13 . . . . .106 A6
South Terr
Chattenden ME3 . . . . . . .40 F6
Farningham DA4 . . . . . . .56 F2
South Turbine Hall Rd
TN29 . . . . .380 C2
Southview Ave RM18 . . . .19 A6
South View BR1 . . . . .52 C7
South View Cl DA5 . . . . . .13 F1
South View Ct 11 BR1 . . .52 C7
South View Gdns ME12 . .28 C1
South View Ct3 . . . . .111 F1
Southview Hts RM20 . . . .17 C8
South View RH8 . . . . . . .183 A2
South View Rd
Dartford DA2 . . . . .33 D5
Royal Tunbridge Wells
TN4 . . . . .286 B6
Turner's Green TN5 . . . .336 F6
West Thurrock RM20 . . . .17 C8
Whitstable CT5 . . . . . . .108 D6
South View Terr TN17 . . .318 E8
Southwall Ind Est
CT14 . . . . .215 B7
Southwall Rd CT14 . . . . .215 B6
Southwark Pl BR1 . . . . . . .52 F6
Southwark Rd ME2 . . . . . .62 D6
Southway BR2 . . . . .52 A2
Southways ME17 . . . . . . .229 E7
Southwell Rd ME2 . . . . . . .62 E6
Southwold Pl CT8 . . . . . . .81 E7
Southwold Rd DA5 . . . . . .14 B1
Southwood Ave TN4 . . . .286 A6
Southwood Bldgs
TN4 . . . . .285 B4
Southwood Cl BR1 . . . . . .52 F5
Southwood Gdns
CT11 . . . . .117 B6
Southwood Ho SE9 . . . . . .30 B6
Southwood Hts CT11 . . . .117 C6

Southwood ME16 ...... 160 F2
Southwood Rd
　Eltham SE9 .... 30 B6
　Ramsgate CT11 .... 117 C6
　Rusthall TN4 .... 285 B5
　Whitstable CT5 .... 75 B2
　Woolwich SE28 .... 3 B5
Sovereign Bvd ME7,
　ME8 .... 65 A2
Sovereign Ct
　Bromley BR2 .... 52 F3
　Sutton at H DA4 .... 57 B8
Sovereign Ho SE18 ...... 1 F3
Sovereigns The ME16 ... 161 D4
Sovereigns Way TN12 . 259 C6
Sovereign Way TN9 .... 222 C1
Soverign Ho BR7 .... 30 D1
Sowell St CT10 .... 83 F5
Sowerby Cl SE9 .... 11 F2
Spade La ME9 .... 99 C6
Spa Ind Pk TN2 .... 286 E8
Spanton Cres CT21 ..... 333 A3
Spar Cl TN11 .... 190 F1
Sparepenny La DA4 ...... 56 E1
Sparkes Cl BR2 .... 52 B5
Sparkeswood Ave
　TN17 .... 343 F3
Sparkeswood Cl TN17 .. 343 F3
Sparrow Castle 3 CT9 .. 50 J1
Sparrow Dr BR5 .... 53 D1
Sparrow's Farm L Ctr
　SE9 .... 30 C8
Sparrows Green Rd
　TN5 .... 336 F5
Sparrows La SE9 .... 30 C7
Spa Valley Rly ★ TN4 .. 312 D7
Speakman Ct 5 CT11 .. 117 C6
Spearhead Rd ME14 .... 161 F7
Spearman St 8 SE18 .... 12 A4
Spearpoint Cnr TN24 ... 268 F5
Spectrum Bsns Ctr
　ME2 .... 63 E8
Spectrum Bsns Est
　ME15 .... 195 F4
Speedgate Farm DA3 .... 90 F8
Speedgate Hill DA3 ..... 91 A8
Speedwell Ave ME5 ..... 96 F4
Speedwell Cl
　Gillingham ME7 .... 64 E5
　Maidstone ME14 ...... 162 E5
　5 Marlpit Hill TN8 .... 217 D3
Speedwell Ct RM17 ...... 18 E7
Speedwell Rd CT5 ...... 108 B6
Spekehill SE9 .... 29 F5
Speke Rd CT10 .... 83 E6
Spekes Rd ME7 .... 98 B6
Spelders Hill TN25 ..... 270 A5
Speldhurst CE Prim Sch
　TN3 .... 285 A7
Speldhurst Cl TN23 ... 299 E5
Speldhurst Ct ME16 ... 161 D4
Speldhurst Gdns CT9 ... 51 F3
Speldhurst Hill TN3 ... 285 B8
Speldhurst Rd
　Langton Green TN3 ... 284 F5
　Royal Tunbridge Wells
　TN3,TN4 .... 285 E8
Spelmonden Rd TN12 .. 289 F2
Spembley Cl ME4 .... 63 E4
Spence Cl CT18 .... 307 A4
Spencer Cl
　Chatham ME5 .... 97 A1
　Orpington BR6 .... 86 F8
Spencer Ct 5 BR6 ...... 86 C5
Spencer Flats ME5 ...... 97 B8
Spencer Gdns SE9 .... 11 F2
Spencer Ho 3 CT20 ... 334 F5
Spencer Mews
　6 Royal Tunbridge
　Wells,Mount Sion TN1 . 286 A2
　10 Royal Tunbridge Wells
　TN1 .... 286 B4
Spencer Rd CT7 .... 81 A8
Spencer Sq CT11 ...... 117 D6
Spencer St
　Gravesend DA11 .... 37 A8
　9 Ramsgate CT11 .... 117 D6
Spencer Way ME15 ..... 195 E7
Spencer Wlk RM18 ...... 19 B5
Spenlow Dr ME5 .... 130 A8
Spenny La TN12 .... 258 B7
Spenser Rd CT6 .... 76 F4
Speranza St SE18 .... 2 F1
Speyside TN10 .... 222 B5
Spicer Homes ME10 .... 101 F2
Spicers Ct CT21 .... 333 C1
Spicers Field CT6 ...... 77 D2
Spicer's Pl CT3 .... 145 C2
Spielman Rd DA1 .... 15 F3
Spiers The ME7 .... 65 C5
Spillett Cl ME13 .... 138 B6
Spillway The ME15 .... 161 D2
Spindle SE18 .... 1 E3
Spindle Glade ME14 ... 162 C5
Spindle Ho 8 DA15 .... 31 A5
Spindles RM18 .... 19 A7
Spindlewood Cl ME5 ... 97 B3
Spindlewood End
　TN23 .... 267 D4
Spinel Cl SE18 .... 2 F1
Spinnaker Ct 4 ME4 ... 63 C1
Spinnens Acre Com Jun
　Sch ME5 .... 97 C1
Spinners Cl TN27 ...... 295 A2
Spinners Wents TN11 . 190 D8
Spinney La CT3 .... 210 E4
Spinney Oak BR1 .... 52 E7
Spinneys The BR1 ...... 52 F7
Spinney The
　Ashford TN23 .... 267 E3

Spinney The continued
　Chatham ME5 .... 97 B1
　Crabble CT17 .... 277 E2
　Maidstone ME16 ...... 162 B2
　Margate CT9 .... 51 E1
　Swanley BR8 .... 55 E7
　Tonbridge TN9 .... 254 A7
Spinney Way TN14 .... 119 D8
Spire Ave CT5 .... 109 A8
Spire Cl DA12 .... 37 B7
Spires The
　Canterbury CT2 ...... 142 F2
　Dartford DA1 .... 33 D6
　Maidstone ME16 ...... 161 D4
　Rochester ME2 .... 62 D5
Spitalfield La TN28 .... 372 F6
Spitalfield Terr TN28 .. 372 F6
Spital St DA1 .... 15 D1
Spitfire Cl ME5 .... 97 B6
Spitfire & Hurricane Meml
　Mus ★ TN28 .... 82 A2
Spitfire Rd ME19 ...... 158 F3
Spitfire Way TN28 .... 307 B3
Split Ho CT17 .... 278 A1
Split La CT4 .... 241 A5
Spode La TN8 .... 282 A7
Sponden La TN18 ..... 356 A7
Spongs La TN17 ...... 293 A1
Sportsfield ME14 ..... 162 B5
Sportsmans Cotts
　ME19 .... 159 B5
Spot La ME15 .... 163 A2
Spout La
　Brenchley TN12 ...... 289 C5
　Crockham Hill TN8 ... 184 C1
Spratling La CT12 ..... 82 F1
Spratling St CT12 ...... 82 E1
Spray Hill TN3 .... 317 B4
Spray St SE18 .... 2 B2
Sprig The ME14 ...... 163 A4
Spring Cott DA1 .... 33 D8
Springcroft DA3 .... 59 A4
Spring Cross DA3 .... 92 A7
Spring Ct 17 DA15 ..... 31 A5
Springdale Cotts ME3 .. 40 A3
Springett Almshouses
　TN18 .... 354 E8
Springett Cl ME20 .... 128 F6
Springett Way ME17 .. 194 D3
Spring Farm TN29 .... 363 D5
Springfarm Rd TN29 .. 363 C5
Springfield Ave
　Maidstone ME14 ...... 161 F7
　Swanley BR8 .... 55 F5
　Tenterden TN30 ...... 324 C2
Springfield Cl CT11 .... 83 E2
Springfield Cotts
　TN12 .... 289 F5
Springfield Gdns BR1 .. 52 F5
Springfield Gr SE7 .... 11 C8
Springfield Ind Est
　TN18 .... 340 F3
Springfield Pass CT21 . 333 B2
Springfield Rd
　Bexley,Bexleyheath DA7 14 B3
　Bexley,Welling DA16 ... 13 A3
　Bromley BR1 .... 52 F5
　Dover CT16 .... 278 B2
　Edenbridge TN8 ...... 217 B1
　Gillingham ME7 .... 64 E6
　Groombridge TN3 .... 312 C7
　Lunsford ME20 .... 127 F4
　Margate CT9 .... 51 E3
　Royal Tunbridge Wells
　TN4 .... 253 F1
　Sittingbourne ME10 .. 101 D5
Springfields TN5 .... 338 E1
Springfield Terr 7
　ME4 .... 63 F4
Springfield Way CT21 . 334 B3
Springfield Wlk 3 BR6 . 53 D1
Spring Gdns
　Biggin Hill TN16 ..... 118 C1
　Orpington BR6 .... 87 B4
　Rusthall TN4 .... 285 B4
Spring Gr DA12 .... 37 B7
Spring Grove Sch
　TN25 .... 237 C2
Springhead Ent Pk
　DA11 .... 36 C7
Springhead Rd
　Erith DA8 .... 14 F8
　Faversham ME13 ...... 105 D1
Spring Head Rd TN15 . 122 F2
Springhead Rd DA11 ... 36 C7
Springhead TN2 ...... 286 D5
Spring Hill TN11,TN3 . 284 A7
Spring Ho CT21 .... 333 C2
Spring Hollow TN29 .. 366 A4
Springholm TN16 ..... 118 C1
Spring La
　Bidborough TN3 ...... 253 D3
　Canterbury CT1 ...... 175 C7
　Fordwich CT2 .... 144 A4
　Hythe CT21 .... 334 A4
　Oldbury TN15 .... 156 B5
Spring Lodge 3 BR5 ... 54 C4
Springrove Cotts
　TN12 .... 259 B5
Springshaw Cl TN13 .. 153 D4
Spring Shaw Rd BR5 ... 54 A8
Springside Terr CT18 . 305 C6
Spring Terr 18 CT20 .. 335 C5
Spring Vale DA7 .... 14 B3
Spring Vale Cl BR8 ..... 55 F8
Springvale Ct
　Eltham SE12 .... 11 A3
　Northfleet DA11 .... 36 C3
Spring Vale DA1 .... 33 D8
Springvale
　Gillingham ME8 .... 98 C6
　Iwade ME9 .... 68 D4

Spring Vale ME16 ..... 161 E4
Spring Vale N DA1 ...... 33 D8
Springvale Ret Pk 2
　BR5 .... 54 C6
Spring Vale S DA1 ...... 33 D8
Spring Vale DA9 .... 17 C1
Springvale Way BR5 ... 54 C6
Springview Apartments
　TN2 .... 286 D6
Springwater Cl SE18 ... 12 A6
Springwell Rd TN9 .... 254 B8
Spring Wlk CT5 .... 108 C7
Springwood Cl
　Ashford TN23 .... 267 E3
　1 Maidstone ME16 .. 161 A3
Springwood Dr TN28 . 373 B6
Springwood Dr TN23 . 267 E3
Springwood Hall
　TN11 .... 189 D1
Springwood Rd ME16 . 161 A3
Sprivers Gdns ★ TN12 289 E4
Sprotlands Ave TN24 . 268 F5
Sprotshill Cl ME10 .... 101 E6
Spruce Cl ME20 ...... 128 B2
Sprucedale Cl BR8 ...... 55 E7
Spruce Ho TN4 .... 285 E4
Spruce Rd TN16 ...... 118 D3
Spurgeon Cl RM17 ..... 18 C8
Spurgeons Cotts
　ME17 .... 194 E2
Spur Rd BR6 .... 87 A8
Spurrell Ave DA5 .... 32 D4
Spurway ME14 .... 163 A4
Square Hill ME15 ..... 162 B4
Square Hill Rd ME15 .. 162 B4
Square The
　Birchington CT7 .... 81 A7
　Chilham CT4 .... 205 B8
　Cowden TN8 .... 282 B6
　Elham CT4 .... 273 F4
　Hadlow TN11 .... 223 E8
　Hunton ME15 .... 226 D7
　Leigh TN11 .... 220 F1
　Lenham ME17 .... 199 D5
　Selling ME13 .... 171 A6
　Sevenoaks TN13 ..... 153 E5
　Sittingbourne ME10 ... 68 F1
　Swanley BR8 .... 55 D6
　Tatsfield TN16 ...... 150 C7
　Wadhurst TN5 .... 337 A4
Squeeze Gut Alley 14
　CT5 .... 74 D2
Squerryes Court ★
Squerryes Mede TN16 . 184 C8
Squire Ave CT2 .... 174 C8
Squires Cl ME2 .... 62 B7
Squires Ct ME12 .... 48 E3
Squires Field BR8 .... 55 F8
Squires Ho 3 SE18 .... 12 B8
Squires Way
　Dover CT16 .... 278 A3
　Joyden's Wood DA2 ... 32 D8
Squires Wood Dr BR7 ... 29 F1
Squirrel La TN25 ...... 267 F5
Squirrel Way TN2 ..... 286 E5
Stable Cl ME5 .... 97 C5
Stable Ct Chilham CT4 . 205 B7
　Faversham ME13 ...... 137 B8
Stabledene Way TN2 .. 287 D6
Stablemead CT19 ..... 335 A7
Stables End BR6 .... 86 C7
Stables The TN18 ..... 354 E8
Stace Cl TN30 .... 345 C8
Stacey Cl DA12 .... 37 E3
Stacey Rd TN10 ...... 222 A4
Staceys St ME14 ...... 161 F5
Stackfield 1 TN8 ..... 217 D3
Stack La DA3 .... 58 F4
Stacklands Cl TN15 ..... 90 E4
Stack Rd DA4 .... 57 D5
Stade St CT21 .... 333 C1
Stade The CT19 ...... 335 E5
Stadium Rd SE18 .... 11 F8
Stadium Way
　Crayford DA1 .... 14 E2
　Sittingbourne ME10 .. 102 C6
Stadler Cl ME16 ...... 161 D7
Staffa Rd ME15 .... 195 A7
Staffhurst Wood Rd
　TN8,RH8 .... 216 C6
Stafford Cl
　Ashford TN23 .... 267 F2
　Stone DA9 .... 16 F2
Stafford Rd
　Royal Tunbridge Wells
　TN2 .... 286 E4
　Sidcup DA14 .... 30 E4
　Tonbridge TN9 .... 222 B2
Staffordshire St 11
　CT11 .... 117 E7
Stafford St ME7 .... 64 C5
Stafford Way TN13 ... 187 C8
Stag Rd Chatham ME5 .. 97 B5
　Royal Tunbridge Wells
　TN2 .... 286 D8
Stagshaw Cl ME15 .... 162 A2
Stainer House SE3 ..... 11 C3
Stainer Rd TN10 ...... 222 F6
Staines Hill CT2 ...... 144 B7
Staines Pl CT10 .... 84 B5
Staines Wlk DA14 ...... 31 C2
Stainmore Cl BR7 ...... 53 D8
Stairfoot La TN13 ..... 153 C5
Stair Rd TN10 .... 222 F4
Stake La ME2 .... 95 A6
Staleys Rd TN15 ...... 156 F7
Stalham Ct ME7 .... 98 A4
Stalin Ave ME5 .... 97 B8
Stalisfield Pl BR6 .... 86 A1
Stalisfield Rd
　Charing TN27 .... 201 E3

Stalisfield Rd continued
　Stalisfield Green ME13,
　TN27 .... 201 C5
Throwley ME13 .... 169 C6
Stamford Villas ME12 .. 48 C2
Stampers The ME15 ... 161 D2
Stanam Rd TN2 ...... 287 E6
Stanbridge Rd TN8 ... 217 B2
Stanbrook Rd
　Northfleet DA11 .... 36 F8
　Woolwich SE2 .... 3 B4
Stanbury Cres CT19 .. 335 F7
Stancomb Ave CT11 .. 117 C5
Standard Ave CT6 ...... 76 A4
Standard Ind Est E16 ... 1 F4
Standard Rd Bexley DA6 13 E3
　Erith DA17 .... 4 A1
　Farthing Street BR6 ... 86 A1
Standen Cl ME8 .... 98 E4
Standen La CT18 ...... 307 E5
Standen St
　Benenden TN17,TN18 . 342 D2
　Royal Tunbridge Wells
　TN4 .... 286 A5
　Standen Street TN17 .. 356 E8
Standings Cross TN12 . 256 E1
Standish Ho SE3 .... 11 B3
Staner Ct CT12 .... 117 A8
Staner Hill CT12 ...... 116 F8
Stane Way SE18 .... 11 E7
Stanford Dr ME16 .... 161 C3
Stanford La TN11 ..... 191 C2
Stanford Way ME2 ..... 62 C2
Stangate Dr ME9 .... 68 D4
Stangate Rd
　Birling ME19 .... 127 B8
　Rochester ME2 .... 62 C7
Stangrove Rd TN8 .... 217 C1
Stanham Pl DA1 .... 15 A3
Stanham Rd DA1 .... 15 C2
Stanhill Cotts DA2 ..... 32 D2
Stanhope Ave
　Hayes BR2 .... 52 A1
　Sittingbourne ME10 .. 102 A3
Stanhope Cl ME14 .... 161 E7
Stanhope Rd
　Ashford TN23 .... 299 C6
　Bexley DA7 .... 13 E5
　Deal CT14 .... 215 D6
　Dover CT16 .... 278 C2
　Rochester ME2 .... 63 A7
　Royal Tunbridge Wells
　TN1 .... 286 C5
　Sidcup DA15 .... 31 A4
　Swanscombe DA10 ..... 17 F1
Stanhopes RH8 .... 183 B7
Stanhope Sq TN23 ... 299 F6
Stanhope Way TN13 .. 153 D5
Stan La ME18 .... 191 A7
Stanley Ave
　Minster (Sheppey) ME12 . 47 D7
　Queenborough ME11 .. 46 A4
Stanley Cl
　Dymchurch TN29 .... 353 B4
　Staplehurst TN12 .... 260 E4
　Stone DA9 .... 16 E2
Stanley Cotts DA2 ...... 34 E3
Stanley Cres DA12 ..... 37 D3
Stanley Gdns CT6 ...... 76 F3
Stanley Glyn Ct BR7 ... 30 A3
Stanley Holloway Ct E16 .1 A7
Stanley Pl
　Broadstairs CT10 ...... 84 A4
　Ramsgate CT11 ...... 117 E7
Stanley Rd
　Broadstairs CT10 ...... 84 A6
　Bromley BR2 .... 52 C5
　Chatham ME5 .... 97 C6
　Deal CT14 .... 215 D5
　Folkestone CT19 ..... 334 E6
　Gillingham ME7 .... 64 C6
　Grays RM17 .... 18 B8
　Herne Bay CT6 .... 76 F4
　Marden TN12 .... 259 D5
　Margate CT9 .... 51 A3
　Northfleet DA11 .... 36 E7
　Orpington BR6 .... 53 F1
　Ramsgate CT11 ...... 117 D8
　Royal Tunbridge Wells
　TN1 .... 286 B5
　Sidcup DA14 .... 31 A5
　Swanscombe DA10 ..... 17 F1
　Whitstable CT5 ...... 108 D7
Stanley Way BR5 .... 54 B4
Stanmore Ct CT1 ..... 175 B7
Stanmore Ho SE12 ..... 29 B7
Stanmore Rd DA17 ...... 4 C2
Stansfeld Ave CT18 ... 307 A4
Stansfeld Rd E16 .... 1 D7
Stansted CE Prim Sch
　TN15 .... 91 F1
Stansted Cl ME16 .... 161 D7
Stansted Cres DA5 ..... 31 D7
Stansted Hill TN15 ..... 92 A1
Stansted La TN15 ...... 91 C1
Stanton Cl BR5 .... 54 C2
Stanton Ct
　9 Bromley BR1 .... 52 C7
　5 Sidcup DA15 .... 31 A5
Staple Cl
　Joyden's Wood DA5 ... 32 D5
　Sittingbourne ME10 .. 101 E5
Staple Dr TN12 .... 260 F4
Stapleford Ct TN13 ... 153 F4
Staplehurst Ave CT10 .. 84 A2
Staplehurst Gdns CT9 .. 51 E2
Staplehurst Ho BR5 ..... 54 C4
Staplehurst Lodge Ind Est
　ME10 .... 101 D5
Staplehurst Rd
　Bogden TN12 .... 228 C2
　Frittenden TN12,TN17 . 261 D1
　Gillingham ME8 .... 65 B3

Staplehurst Rd continued
　Sittingbourne ME10 .. 101 D5
Staplehurst Sch TN12 . 260 E3
Staplehurst Sta TN12 . 260 E5
Staple Rd CT3 .... 178 C6
Staplers Ct ME14 ..... 162 B8
Staples Ho E6 .... 2 A7
Staple St ME13 .... 139 F5
Staples The BR8 .... 56 B8
Staplestreet Rd ME13 . 140 A4
Stapleton Rd
　Bexley DA7 .... 13 F8
　Orpington BR6 .... 86 F7
Staple Vineyard ★
　CT3 .... 178 E5
Stapley Rd DA17 .... 4 A1
Starboard Ave DA9 ..... 17 B1
Star Bsns Ctr RM13 ..... 4 D8
Star Hill DA1 .... 14 E2
Star Hill Rd TN14 .... 121 A2
Star Hill ME1 .... 63 D5
Star Ho TN3 .... 317 B5
Star La
　Folkestone CT19 .... 334 D7
　Gillingham ME7 .... 98 A7
　Margate CT9 .... 83 A5
　Orpington BR5,BR8 .... 54 E5
Starle Cl CT1 .... 143 B1
Starling Cl DA3 .... 59 B6
Star Mill Ct ME5 .... 64 D2
Star Mill La ME5 .... 64 D2
Starnes Ct 5 ME14 ... 162 A5
Starr Cotts TN12 ..... 226 C2
Star Rd TN24 .... 268 D2
Starts Cl BR6 .... 86 A7
Starts Hill Ave BR6 ..... 86 B6
Starts Hill Rd BR6 ...... 86 B6
Starvation Cnr 1 CT5 .. 74 D2
Starveacre La ME9 .... 101 B1
Starve Goose La TN17 . 319 E4
State Farm Ave BR6 .... 86 C6
Stately Pk ME18 ...... 192 C1
Station App
　Adisham CT3 .... 210 E8
　Bexley,Barnehurst DA7 . 7 B4
　Bexley,Bexleyheath DA7 .13 B4
　Bexley,Welling DA16 .. 13 A5
　Birchington CT7 .... 80 F7
　Borough Green TN15 . 156 F7
　Bromley BR7 .... 29 C2
　Chelsfield BR6 .... 87 B5
　Chislehurst BR7 .... 53 A7
　Dartford DA1 .... 15 C1
　Edenbridge TN8 ..... 217 C2
　Grays RM17 .... 18 A8
　Greenwich SE3 .... 11 B4
　Halling ME2 .... 95 A5
　Hayes BR2 .... 52 A1
　Maidstone ME16 ...... 161 D3
　Martin Mill CT15 .... 247 C2
　Minster (Thanet) CT12 115 C5
　New Romney TN28 .. 373 C6
　Orpington BR6 .... 86 F8
　Orpington,St Mary Cray
　BR5 .... 54 B5
　Otford TN14 .... 122 C3
　Paddock Wood TN12 . 257 A7
Station Approach Rd
　CT11 .... 117 D8
Station App
　Staplehurst TN12 .... 260 E5
　Swanley BR8 .... 55 E5
Station Cotts
　Gill's Green TN18 .... 340 F5
　Hartley TN17 .... 319 C2
　Horsmonden TN12 ... 290 B5
　Selling ME13 .... 171 E7
Station Cres SE3 .... 1 A1
Station Ct TN15 ...... 156 F7
Station Dr CT14 ...... 215 A1
Station Hill TN11 .... 252 H8
Station Hill Cotts
　ME15 .... 194 A7
Station Hill BR2 .... 85 A8
Station Mews
　Elham CT4 .... 273 F4
　3 Tenterden TN30 .. 345 A7
Station Par
　Sevenoaks TN13 ..... 154 A3
　Sidcup DA15 .... 31 A6
Station Rd
　Adisham CT3 .... 177 E1
　Ashford TN23 .... 268 C2
　Aylesford ME20 ..... 128 E2
　Bekesbourne CT4 ... 176 C4
　Betsham DA13 .... 36 A4
　Bexley DA7 .... 13 E4
　Birchington CT7 .... 81 A7
　Borough Green TN15 . 156 F7
　Brasted TN16 .... 152 B4
　Bridge CT4 .... 175 F2
　Bromley BR1 .... 52 A8
　Charing TN27 .... 234 C2
　Chartham CT4 .... 173 D3
　Cliffe ME3 .... 22 B3
　Crayford DA1 .... 14 F1
　Cuxton ME2 .... 62 C2
　Deal CT14 .... 215 B1
　Dymchurch TN29 .... 366 B7
　East Farleigh ME15 . 194 A7
　East Tilbury RM18 .... 20 B7
Station Rd E CT1 ..... 174 F7
Station Rd
　Edenbridge TN8 ..... 217 C2
　Erith DA17 .... 4 A3
　Eynsford DA4 .... 89 D7
　Faversham ME13 .... 138 D6
　Folkestone CT19 .... 334 F5
　Gillingham ME8 .... 66 A2
　Goudhurst TN17 .... 318 C2
　Groombridge TN3 ... 312 C6
　Halstead TN14 ...... 120 F8
　Harrietsham ME17 .. 198 D6

Station Rd continued
　Headcorn TN27 ...... 262 D5
　Herne Bay CT6 .... 76 E4
　Hurst Green TN19 ... 354 A3
　Hythe CT21 .... 333 D3
　Longfield DA3 .... 58 E6
　Lydd TN29 .... 376 D7
　Lyminge CT18 .... 305 C6
　Maidstone ME14 ...... 161 F5
　Margate CT9 .... 50 H2
　Martin Mill CT15 .... 247 D1
　Meopham Station DA13 . 60 A4
　Minster (Thanet) CT12 115 C5
Station Rd N DA17 ...... 4 B3
Station Rd
　Nettlestead Green
　ME18 .... 192 C1
　Newington ME9 ...... 100 B6
　New Romney TN28 .. 373 C6
　Northfleet DA11 .... 18 B1
　Northiam TN31 ...... 357 C1
　Orpington BR6 .... 86 F8
　Orpington,St Mary Cray
　BR5 .... 54 C5
　Otford TN14 .... 122 C3
　Paddock Wood TN12 . 256 F7
　Pluckley TN27 ...... 265 C5
　Rainham ME8 .... 65 F1
　Rochester ME2 .... 63 C7
　Rockrobin TN5 ...... 336 C6
　St Margaret's at Cliffe
　CT15 .... 279 E8
　Sevenoaks TN13 ..... 153 E7
　Shepherdswell CT15 . 244 D5
　Shoreham TN14 ..... 122 A7
　Sidcup DA14,DA15 .... 31 A5
　Smeeth TN25 .... 302 B3
　Staplehurst TN12 .... 260 F5
　Stone DA9 .... 17 A2
　Sutton at H DA4 .... 57 B7
　Swanley BR8 .... 55 E5
　Tenterden TN30 ..... 345 A4
　Teynham ME9 .... 103 D2
Station Rd W CT2 .... 142 F1
Station Rd
　Westgate-on-S CT8 .... 50 D1
　Whitstable CT5 .... 74 E2
　Withyham TN7 .... 311 B5
Station Row ME9 ..... 103 D3
Station Sq BR5 .... 53 C4
Station St Newham E16 .. 2 B5
　Sittingbourne ME10 .. 101 F4
Station Terr TN28 .... 373 C6
Steadman Cl ME3 ...... 39 C6
Stede Hill ME17 ...... 165 F3
Stedley 17 DA14 .... 31 A4
Steed Cl CT6 .... 111 B8
Steeds Cl TN23 ...... 300 A1
Steeds La TN23,TN26 . 300 B1
Steele Ave DA9 .... 17 A2
Steele's La DA13 .... 93 A6
Steele St ME2 .... 63 A8
Steele Wlk DA8 .... 14 B7
Steellands Rise TN5 ... 338 F1
Steep Cl BR6 .... 86 F4
Steephill Sch DA3 ...... 58 D5
Steeple Heights Dr
　TN16 .... 118 D2
Steerforth Cl ME1 ...... 63 C2
Steers Pl TN11 .... 190 E2
Stella CT19 .... 329 D5
Stella Maris RC Prim Sch
　CT19 .... 335 C6
Stelling Minnis CE Prim
　Sch CT4 .... 240 F6
Stelling Rd DA8 .... 14 D7
Stembrook Ct 4
　CT16 .... 310 D7
Stembrook CT16 ..... 310 D8
Stempe Cl CT18 ...... 307 B3
Stenning Ct TN10 .... 222 C4
Stephen Cl
　Broadstairs CT10 ...... 84 A4
　Orpington BR6 .... 86 F7
Stephen Ct 2 CT20 .. 335 D5
Stephen Rd DA7 .... 14 C4
Stephens Cl ME13 .... 138 B8
Stephen's Cl CT9 ...... 82 B7
Stephens Cl CT11 .... 117 C8
Stephenson Ave RM18 . 19 A6
Stephenson Ho SE2 ..... 3 D1
Stephenson Rd CT2 .. 142 F3
Stephen's Rd TN4 .... 286 B6
Stepneyford La TN17 . 343 C7
Steps Hill Rd ME9 .... 132 D6
Step Style ME10 ...... 102 B2
Sterling Ave ME16 .... 161 C5
Sterling Cl CT10 .... 83 E5
Sterling Ct 12 CT1 ... 142 F1
Sterling Ho SE3 .... 11 B3
Sterling Rd
　Queenborough ME11 .. 46 A5
　Sittingbourne ME10 .. 101 D1
Sterndale Rd DA1 ...... 33 F8
Sterry Gdns ME15 .... 195 E7
Stevanne Ct 1 DA17 .... 4 A1
Stevedale Rd DA16 ..... 13 C5
Steven Cl ME4 .... 64 A3
Stevens Ct Dartford DA2 . 34 E3
　Egerton TN27 .... 232 F3
　Joyden's Wood DA5 ... 32 D4
　Snodland ME6 .... 128 A8
Stevens Cotts TN30 .. 345 A7
Stevens Ho CT17 ..... 310 C8
Stevenson Cl Erith DA8 ..15 B7
　Maidstone ME15 ..... 161 F3
Stevenson Way ME20 . 127 F4
Stevens Rd ME20 ..... 129 C6
Stewart Ct BR7 .... 30 B4
Stewart Ho ME3 .... 40 F6
Stewart Rd TN4 ...... 286 C7
Steyning Gr SE9 .... 29 F4

Steynton Ave DA5 . . . . . . 31 D6
Stickens La ME19 . . . . . 159 E7
Stickfast La
Sittingbourne ME9 . . . . . . 68 A1
Ulcombe ME17 . . . . 230 D3
Stickland Rd 2 DA17 . . . . 4 A2
Stilebridge La
Underling Green ME17 . . 228 A5
Underling Green TN12 . . 227 E3
Stiles Cl Bromley BR2 . . . . . 52 F3
Erith DA8 . . . . 4 B1
Folkestone CT19 . . . . 335 A7
Minster (Sheppey) ME12 . 47 A6
Still La TN4 . . . . 253 F2
Stillwater Mews ME4 . . . . 41 B2
Stirling Cl
Gillingham ME8 . . . . 98 E4
Rochester ME1 . . . . 63 A3
Sidcup DA14 . . . . 30 F4
Stirling Dr BR6 . . . . 87 B5
Stirling Ho 5 SE18 . . . . 2 B1
Stirling Rd ME19 . . . . . . 158 F3
Stirling Way CT12 . . . . . . 83 A2
Stirling Rd TN24 . . . . 300 D7
Stisted Way TN27 . . . . . 232 F3
Stockbury Dr ME16 . . . . 161 D7
Stockbury Gdns CT9 . . . . 51 E2
Stockbury Ho 7 BR5 . . . 54 D1
Stockdale Gdns CT14 . . 215 C4
Stockenbury TN12 . . . . . 224 F6
Stockers Brow ME9 . . . . 135 A7
Stocker's Hill ME13 . . . . 139 E4
Stockers Hill ME9 . . . . . 135 A7
Stockett La ME15 . . . . . 194 D6
Stockham Ct CT19 . . . . 334 E7
Stock Hill TN16 . . . . 118 D2
Stock La DA2 . . . . 33 C4
Stockland Green Rd
TN3 . . . . 285 B8
Stock La TN25 . . . . 302 A4
Stocks Green Prim Sch
TN11 . . . . 221 E5
Stocks Green Rd
TN11 . . . . 221 C5
Stocks Rd TN30 . . . . 359 F3
Stocks The ME13 . . . . . . 170 C6
Stockton Cl ME14 . . . . . 162 B8
Stockwell Cl BR1 . . . . 52 B7
Stockwood Chase
CT2 . . . . 142 A2
Stoddart Rd CT19 . . . . . 334 E6
Stodmarsh National Nature
Reserve★ CT3 . . . . 145 D8
Stodmarsh Rd CT3 . . . . 144 C3
Stofield Gdns SE9 . . . . . . 29 D5
Stoke Com Sch ME3 . . . . 25 C5
Stoke Rd Allhallows ME3 . . . 9 C1
Hoo St Werburgh ME3 . . . 41 F6
Kingsnorth ME3 . . . . 42 C8
Lower Stoke ME3 . . . . 24 E1
Stokesay Ct 14 DA2 . . . . 16 B1
Stombers La CT18 . . . . . 307 C6
Stonar Cl
Ramsgate CT11 . . . . 83 E1
Sandwich CT13 . . . . 149 A1
Stonar Gdns CT13 . . . . . 149 A2
Stoneacre Cl ME8 . . . . . . 98 D5
Stoneacre Ct 7 ME15 . 162 A1
Stoneacre La ME15 . . . . 196 B7
Stoneacre★ ME15 . . . . . 196 B7
Stone Barn Ave CT7 . . . . 81 A6
Stone Bay Sch CT10 . . . . 84 B6
Stonebridge TN25 . . . . . 270 A5
Stonebridge Cotts
TN23 . . . . 300 B8
Stonebridge Green Rd
TN27 . . . . 233 A4
Stonebridge Rd DA11 . . . 18 B2
Stonebridge Way
ME13 . . . . 138 B7
Stonechat Sq 6 E6 . . . . . . 1 E8
Stone Cnr TN30 . . . . 360 A6
Stone Cotts TN3 . . . . . . 316 F4
Stone Court La TN2 . . . 287 E8
Stonecroft Rd DA8 . . . . . 14 C7
Stonecroft DA13 . . . . . . 126 A8
Stonecrop Cl ME4 . . . . . 41 C1
Stone Crossing Halt
DA9 . . . . 16 E2
Stonecross Lea ME5 . . . . 64 C1
Stone Cross Lees
CT13 . . . . 180 F7
Stone Cross Rd TN5 . . . 337 A4
Stone Ct DA8 . . . . 4 F1
Stonedane Ct ME13 . . . 138 C8
Stonefield Cl DA7 . . . . . . 14 A4
Stonefield Way SE7 . . . . 11 D7
Stonegate Cl BR5 . . . . . . 54 C6
Stonegate Rd TN5 . . . . 337 C1
Stonegate TN25 . . . . . . 237 E2
Stone Gdns CT10 . . . . . . 84 B5
Stone Gn TN30 . . . . 360 F4
Stonehall Rd CT15 . . . . 276 F8
Stoneheap Rd CT14,
CT15 . . . . 213 E1
Stone Hill Rd TN27 . . . . 232 F2
Stone Hill TN25 . . . . 303 A2
Stonehill Woods Pk
DA14 . . . . 32 B2
Stone Ho CT10 . . . . 84 B7
Stonehorse Ct ME3 . . . . 40 A3
Stonehorse La ME2 . . . . 40 A2
Stonehouse Cnr RM19 . . 16 E8
Stone House Hospl
DA2 . . . . 16 C1
Stonehouse La
Halstead TN14 . . . . 120 E8
Pratt's Bottom TN14 . . . . 87 E1
Purfleet RM19 . . . . 16 E8
Stone House Mews
CT10 . . . . 84 B7
Stonehouse Rd BR6,
TN14 . . . . 87 D1
Stoneings La TN14 . . . . 151 F8
Stone Lake Ind Pk SE7 . . . 1 C2
Stone Lake Ret Pk SE7 . . . 1 C2
Stoneleigh Rd RH8 . . . . 183 E5
Stone Lodge Farm Park★
DA2 . . . . 16 D1
Stoneness Rd RM20 . . . . 17 C7
Stone Pit La TN18 . . . . . 356 E5
Stone Place Rd DA9 . . . . 16 E2
Stone Rd
Broadstairs CT10 . . . . 84 B5
Bromley BR2 . . . . 52 A5
Stone Row Cotts TN3 . 284 D1
Stone Row TN3 . . . . 284 B5
Stone, St Mary's CE Prim
Sch DA9 . . . . 34 E8
Stones Cross Rd BR8 . . . 55 C4
Stones Rdbt ME4 . . . . 41 B1
Stone St
Cranbrook TN17 . . . . 320 D5
Faversham ME13 . . . . 138 C7
Gravesend DA11 . . . . 19 B1
Stonestile Bsns Pk
TN27 . . . . 262 A7
Stonestile Farm Rd
TN27 . . . . 201 A3
Stone Stile La CT4 . . . . 171 D1
Stonestile Rd TN27 . . . 262 A7
Stone St CT21 . . . . 332 A4
Stone Street Rd TN15 . 155 E2
Stone St
Royal Tunbridge Wells
TN1 . . . . 286 B4
Stanford TN25 . . . . 304 C3
Stelling Minnis CT4 . . . . . 240 D4
Westenhanger TN25,
CT21 . . . . 332 B6
Stoneswood Rd RH8 . . 183 B5
Stonewall E6 . . . . 2 A8
Stonewall Park Rd
TN3 . . . . 284 F3
Stoneway Pk CT4 . . . . . 240 D7
Stone Wood DA2 . . . . 35 C5
Stonewood Cl TN4 . . . . 286 A8
Stonewood Rd DA8 . . . . . . 4 A2
Stoney Alley SE18 . . . . . . 12 A5
Stoney Bank ME7 . . . . . . 64 F1
Stoney Rd ME13 . . . . . . 140 B3
Stony Cnr DA13 . . . . 59 E6
Stonyfield TN8 . . . . 217 D3
Stony La ME1 . . . . 96 C5
Stonyway La CT15 . . . . 309 C5
Stopford Rd ME7 . . . . . . 64 D4
Storehouse Wharf
ME12 . . . . 27 F3
Store Rd E16 . . . . 2 A4
Storey St E16 . . . . 2 A4
Stornaway Strand
DA12 . . . . 37 F4
Stotfold BR1 . . . . 52 E8
Stour Cl Ashford TN23 . . 267 E1
Chartham CT4 . . . . 173 D2
Orpington BR2 . . . . 85 C6
Rochester ME2 . . . . 62 F7
Tonbridge TN10 . . . . 222 B5
Stour Cres CT1 . . . . 143 D3
Stour Ct
7 Canterbury CT1 . . . . . 174 F8
22 Orpington BR5 . . . . . . 54 D1
8 Sandwich CT13 . . . . . 148 F1
Stourfields TN24 . . . . . . 268 D4
Stourmouth Rd CT3 . . . 146 C8
Stour Rd Chartham CT4 . 173 D2
Crayford DA1 . . . . 15 A4
Stourside Studios 13
CT1 . . . . 142 F1
Stour St CT1 . . . . 174 F8
Stour Valley Cl CT3 . . . 112 D3
Stour Valley Ind Est
CT4 . . . . 173 E4
Stourville 9 CT1 . . . . . . 174 F8
Stow Ct DA2 . . . . 34 C8
Stowell Cl TN23 . . . . . . 299 C8
Stowe Rd BR6 . . . . 87 B6
Stowting CE Prim Sch
TN25 . . . . 304 B8
Stowting Hill TN25 . . . . 272 A1
Stowting Rd BR6 . . . . . . 86 E6
Straight La TN29 . . . . . . 362 F1
Strait Rd E6 . . . . 1 F6
Strakers Hill CT15 . . . . . 246 D8
Strand Approach Rd
ME7 . . . . 64 E7
Strand Cl DA13 . . . . 60 A3
Strand Ct SE18 . . . . 2 E1
Strandfield Cl SE18 . . . . . 2 E1
Strand Rdbt The ME7 . . . 64 E7
Strand St CT13 . . . . 148 F1
Strand The CT14 . . . . . . 215 D4
Stranger's Cl CT1 . . . . . 174 C6
Stranger's La CT1 . . . . . 174 C6
Strangford Pl CT6 . . . . . . 77 B2
Strangford Rd CT5 . . . . . 74 F2
Strasbourg St CT9 . . . . . 83 A6
Stratfield Ho SE12 . . . . . 29 A6
Stratford Ave ME8 . . . . . 98 D8
Stratford Dr ME15 . . . . 195 D6
Stratford House Ave
BR1 . . . . 52 E6
Stratford La 2 ME8 . . . . 98 F8
Stratford Rd ME19 . . . . 159 A8
Stratford St TN1 . . . . . . 286 C5
Strathaven Rd SE12 . . . . 11 B1
Stratheden Par SE3 . . . . 11 A7
Stratheden Rd SE3 . . . . . 11 A7
Stratton Cl DA7 . . . . 13 E4
Stratton Rd DA7 . . . . 13 E4
Stratton Terr TN16 . . . . 184 C8
Strawberry Cl TN2 . . . . 313 E7
Strawberry Fields BR8 . . 55 E7
Strawberry Vale TN9 . . 222 C1
Straw Mill Hill ME15 . . 161 E1
Streamdale SE2 . . . . 13 B8
Stream La TN18 . . . . 355 A7
Stream Pit La TN18 . . . 356 B5
Streamside Cl BR2 . . . . . 52 A5
Streamside ME20 . . . . . 128 B1
Stream Side TN10 . . . . . 222 D6
Stream The ME20 . . . . . 128 C1
Stream Way DA17 . . . . . . 14 A8
Stream Wlk CT5 . . . . 74 D2
Streatfield TN8 . . . . 217 D1
Streatfield Ho TN16 . . . 151 C1
Streete Court Rd CT8 . . . 81 F8
Streete Ct CT8 . . . . 81 F8
Street End CT3 . . . . 147 E1
Street End Rd ME5 . . . . . 64 B1
Street Farm Cotts ME3 . . 41 F6
Streetfield CT6 . . . . 111 B8
Streetfield Mews SE3 . . 11 A4
Streetfield Rd ME8 . . . . . 65 F1
Streetfield ME17 . . . . . 230 F7
Street The Acol CT7 . . . . 81 B3
Adisham CT3 . . . . 210 C8
Appledore TN26 . . . . 361 D8
Ash CT3 . . . . 147 D1
Ashford,Great Chart
TN23 . . . . 267 C1
Ashford,Kennington
TN24 . . . . 268 E6
Ashford,Willesborough Lees
TN24 . . . . 301 B8
Ash TN15 . . . . 91 E5
Barham CT4 . . . . 209 F1
Benenden TN17 . . . . 342 D6
Bethersden TN26 . . . . . . 297 D5
Bishopsbourne CT4 . . . . . 209 C6
Borden ME9 . . . . 101 B2
Bossingham CT4 . . . . 241 A7
Boughton Street ME13 . . . 140 A3
Boxley ME14 . . . . 130 C3
Brabourne TN25 . . . . 303 C8
Bredgar ME9 . . . . 134 A5
Bredhurst ME7 . . . . 98 B1
Brook TN25 . . . . 270 B6
Chilham CT4 . . . . 205 B8
Cobham DA12 . . . . 60 F6
Deal CT14 . . . . 214 F6
Denton CT4 . . . . 243 B3
Detling ME14 . . . . 131 A1
Doddington ME9 . . . . 167 E7
East Langdon CT15 . . . . . 247 A1
Eastling ME13 . . . . 168 E6
Egerton TN27 . . . . 232 F3
Eythorne CT15 . . . . 245 D7
Faversham ME13 . . . . 105 B2
Finglesham CT14 . . . . 214 B8
Frittenden TN17 . . . . 293 E7
Godmersham CT4 . . . . . . 205 B2
Godnestone CT3 . . . . 178 D2
Guston CT15 . . . . 278 E6
Hamstreet TN26 . . . . 349 A7
Hartlip ME9 . . . . 99 D5
Hastingleigh TN25 . . . . . . 271 B6
Hawkinge CT18 . . . . 307 B5
High Halstow ME23 . . . . . . 23 E3
Horton Kirby DA4 . . . . 57 C5
Hothfield TN26 . . . . 267 A6
Ickham CT3 . . . . 145 C1
Ightham TN15 . . . . 156 D6
Iwade ME9 . . . . 68 E4
Kingston CT4 . . . . 209 D3
Lower Halstow ME9 . . . . . . 67 B3
Lympne CT21 . . . . 331 F2
Lynsted ME9 . . . . 136 A6
Maidstone ME14 . . . . 163 C4
Martin Mill CT15 . . . . 247 B3
Meopham DA13 . . . . 60 A1
Mereworth ME18 . . . . 191 D8
Mersham TN25 . . . . 301 E4
Molash CT4 . . . . 203 F4
Newnham ME9 . . . . 168 C8
Nonington CT15 . . . . 211 D1
Northbourne CT14 . . . . . . 214 A5
Patrixbourne CT4 . . . . . . 176 B3
Peene CT18 . . . . 334 A7
Petham CT4 . . . . 207 B3
Plaxtol TN15 . . . . 189 F7
Pluckley TN27 . . . . 265 D7
Postling CT21 . . . . 304 F2
Preston CT3 . . . . 146 C6
Ryarsh ME19 . . . . 126 F4
St Nicholas at Wade CT7 . . 79 F2
Selling ME13 . . . . 171 B6
Shadoxhurst TN26 . . . . . . 327 A8
Shorne DA12 . . . . 38 E3
Silver Street ME9 . . . . 133 F5
Sissinghurst TN17 . . . . . . 321 B8
Sittingbourne ME9 . . . . . . 102 E3
Smarden TN27 . . . . 264 A1
Staple CT3 . . . . 178 F6
Stockbury ME9 . . . . 132 E8
Stone in Oxney TN30 . . . . 361 A5
Stourmouth CT3 . . . . 113 E1
Teston ME18 . . . . 193 A7
Trottiscliffe ME19 . . . . . . 126 A5
Ulcombe ME17 . . . . 230 F7
Upchurch ME9 . . . . 66 F4
Upper Halling ME2 . . . . 94 E5
West Hougham CT15 . . . . 308 F5
Wickhambreaux CT3 . . . . 145 C2
Wittersham TN30 . . . . . . 359 D3
Womenswold CT4 . . . . . . 210 D2
Woodnesborough CT13 . . 180 C7
Wormshill ME9 . . . . 166 A7
Worth CT14 . . . . 181 B5
Strettitt Gdns TN12 . . . . 224 F5
Stretton Ct CT14 . . . . . . 215 D5
Strickland Ave DA1 . . . . . 15 F4
Strickland Way 5 BR6 . . 86 F6
Stringer Dr CT7 . . . . 81 A6
Strode Cres ME12 . . . . . . 28 C2
Strode Park Rd CT6 . . . . 77 A2
Strond St CT17 . . . . 310 D6
Strongbow Cres SE9 . . . . 11 F2
Strongbow Rd SE9 . . . . . 11 F2
Strood Ret Pk ME2 . . . . . . 63 B7
Strood Sta ME2 . . . . 63 C7
Strouts Rd TN23 . . . . . . 299 D7
Strover St ME7 . . . . 64 C7
Struttons Ave DA11 . . . . . 36 F6
Stuart Ave BR2 . . . . 52 A1
Stuart Cl Hextable BR8 . . . 33 A1
Maidstone ME14 . . . . 162 C6
Royal Tunbridge Wells
TN2 . . . . 313 F8
Stuart Ct
Canterbury CT1 . . . . 175 A6
Dover CT17 . . . . 310 C8
Stuart Evans Cl DA16 . . . 13 C4
Stuart Ho CT14 . . . . 215 A5
Stuart Mantle Way DA8 . . 14 E7
Stuart Rd Bexley DA16 . . . 13 B6
Folkestone CT19 . . . . 335 E6
Gillingham ME7 . . . . 64 D3
Gravesend DA11 . . . . 19 A1
Stubbs Hill BR6,TN14 . . 120 C6
Studds Cotts CT6 . . . . . . 76 A3
Studfall Cl CT21 . . . . . . 353 D8
Studio Cl TN24 . . . . 268 E6
Studios The DA3 . . . . 91 F8
Studland Cl DA15 . . . . . . 30 F5
Studley Cres DA3 . . . . . . 59 C7
Studley Ct DA14 . . . . 31 B3
Stumble Hill TN11 . . . . . 189 C5
Stumble La TN23 . . . . . . 300 B1
Stuppington Court Farm
CT1 . . . . 174 E4
Stuppington La CT1 . . . . 174 F5
Sturdee Ave ME7 . . . . . . 64 E4
Sturdee Cotts ME3 . . . . . 42 A6
Sturdy Cl CT21 . . . . 333 D2
Sturges Field BR7 . . . . . . 30 D2
Sturges Rd TN24 . . . . . . 268 B3
Sturla Rd ME4 . . . . 64 A3
Sturmer Cl CT1 . . . . 175 C7
Sturmer Ct ME19 . . . . . . 159 A2
Sturry CE Prim Sch
CT2 . . . . 144 A7
Sturry Court Mews
CT2 . . . . 143 F5
Sturry Hill CT2 . . . . 143 F6
Sturry Rd CT1,CT2 . . . . . 143 C3
Sturry Sta CT2 . . . . 143 F5
Sturry Way ME8 . . . . 65 C2
Styants Bottom Rd
TN15 . . . . 155 F5
Style Cl ME8 . . . . 98 E4
Styles Cl TN8 . . . . 218 B5
Styles Cotts TN8 . . . . . . 218 B5
Styles Ct TN12 . . . . 256 F7
Styles La ME14 . . . . 130 C3
Subdown Cotts TN25 . . 303 C8
Sudbury Cres BR1 . . . . . . 29 A3
Sudbury E6 . . . . 2 A7
Sudbury Pl CT8 . . . . 81 E7
Suffolk Ave
Rainham ME8 . . . . 65 F1
Westgate-on-S CT8 . . . . . . 81 D7
Suffolk Ct 7 ME8 . . . . . . 65 F1
Suffolk Dr TN23 . . . . . . 268 A2
Suffolk Gdns CT17 . . . . 309 F7
Suffolk Mews 1 TN1 . . 286 A4
Suffolk Rd
Canterbury CT1 . . . . 175 D8
Dartford DA1 . . . . 15 E1
Gravesend DA12 . . . . 19 D1
Maidstone ME15 . . . . 195 D8
Sidcup DA14 . . . . 31 C2
Suffolk St CT5 . . . . 108 D8
Suffolk Way TN13 . . . . . 154 C2
Sugarloaf Wlk CT19 . . . 335 D8
Sullivan Ave E16 . . . . 1 D8
Sullivan Cl DA1 . . . . 33 C8
Sullivan Rd
Tilbury RM18 . . . . 19 A6
Tonbridge TN10 . . . . 222 E5
Sultan Mews ME5 . . . . . . 97 C2
Sultan Rd ME5 . . . . 97 C2
Summer Cl Hythe CT21 . 332 F2
Tenterden TN30 . . . . 324 C1
Summer Ct
Canterbury CT2 . . . . 142 C1
Whitstable CT5 . . . . 75 C2
Summerfield Ave CT5 . . . 74 F1
Summerfield
6 Bromley BR1 . . . . 52 B7
Marden TN17 . . . . 291 B6
Summerfield Rd CT9 . . . . 51 E2
Summerfield St 9
SE12 . . . . 29 A8
Summerhill TN23 . . . . . . 299 E6
Summerhill Ave TN4 . . . 253 F1
Summer Hill
Canterbury CT2 . . . . 142 C1
Chislehurst BR7 . . . . 53 A7
Summerhill Cl BR6 . . . . . 86 E7
Summerhill TN27 . . . . . 262 A6
Summer Hill Pk TN24 . . 301 C7
Summerhill Rd
Bogden TN12 . . . . 228 C1
Dartford DA1 . . . . 33 D8
Summerhill Villas BR7 . . . 53 B8
Summerhouse Dr DA2,
DA5 . . . . 32 D4
Summerlands Lodge
BR6 . . . . 86 A6
Summer La CT2 . . . . 142 E6
Summer Leeze TN24 . . . 300 E8
Summer Leeze Gdns
TN24 . . . . 300 E8
Summer Rd CT7 . . . . 79 E1
Summerton Way SE28 . . . 3 D7
Summervale Rd TN4 . . . 285 E1
Summerville Ave ME12 . . 47 A5
Sumner Cl
Orpington BR6 . . . . 86 C6
Rolvenden TN17 . . . . 343 F3
Sumpter Way ME13 . . . . 137 F7
Sunbeam Ave CT6 . . . . . . 75 F4
Sunburst Cl TN12 . . . . . 259 D5
Sunbury St SE18 . . . . 1 F3
Sun Ct DA8 . . . . 14 F5
Sunderland Cl ME1 . . . . . 63 A3
Sunderland Dr ME8 . . . . 99 A8
Sunderland Ho 3 ME7 . . 64 C7
Sunderland Point E16 . . . 2 C5
Sundew Ct 9 RM17 . . . . 18 D8
Sundew Gr CT11 . . . . . . 117 E8
Sundorne Rd SE7 . . . . 1 C1
Sundridge Ave
Bexley DA16 . . . . 12 D4
Bromley BR1 . . . . 52 D8
Sundridge & Brasted CE
Prim Sch TN14 . . . . . . 152 E2
Sundridge Cl
Canterbury CT2 . . . . 143 A4
Dartford DA1 . . . . 16 A1
Sundridge Ct 10 BR1 . . . . 29 B1
Sundridge Dr ME5 . . . . . 97 A4
Sundridge Hill
Cuxton ME2 . . . . 62 C3
Halstead TN14 . . . . 120 C1
Sundridge Ho BR1 . . . . . 29 B3
Sundridge La TN14 . . . . 120 C2
Sundridge Park Sta
BR1 . . . . 29 B1
Sundridge Rd TN14 . . . . 153 B8
Sunfields Pl SE3 . . . . 11 B7
Sunhill Ct TN2 . . . . 287 C6
Sun Hill DA3 . . . . 91 A8
Sun La Gravesend DA12 . . 37 C6
Greenwich SE3 . . . . 11 B7
Hythe CT21 . . . . 333 C2
Sunland Ave DA6 . . . . 13 E3
Sun La CT7 . . . . 79 F2
Sunningdale Ave 4
CT19 . . . . 335 A7
Sunningdale Cl
Erith SE28 . . . . 3 E7
Gillingham ME8 . . . . 98 D6
Sunningdale Ct ME15 . . 162 B4
Sunningdale Dr ME8 . . . 98 D6
Sunningdale Rd BR1 . . . . 52 E4
Sunningdale Wlk CT6 . . 76 D1
Sunninghill DA11 . . . . . . 36 E6
Sunningvale Ave
TN16 . . . . 118 D3
Sunningvale Cl TN16 . . 118 D3
Sunny Bank CT15 . . . . . 245 B8
Sunnybank TN5 . . . . 339 E3
Sunny Bank
Hythe CT21 . . . . 332 F2
Sittingbourne ME10 . . . . 102 B5
Sunny Cnr CT17 . . . . . . 310 B5
Sunnydale BR6 . . . . 86 A8
Sunnydale Rd SE12 . . . . . 11 B2
Sunnyfield Rd BR7 . . . . . 54 A6
Sunnyfields Cl ME8 . . . . . 98 E8
Sunnyfields Dr ME12 . . . 46 C6
Sunnyhill Rd CT6 . . . . . . 76 C4
Sunnymead Ave ME7 . . . 64 E5
Sunnymead Camp
ME12 . . . . 48 E5
Sunnymead Cvn Pk
ME12 . . . . 48 F5
Sunnymead CT2 . . . . . . 142 D7
Sunnyside Ave ME12 . . . 47 A6
Sunnyside Chalet Pk
ME12 . . . . 48 E5
Sunnyside Cl CT14 . . . . 214 D1
Sunnyside Cotts CT14 . 215 C6
Sunnyside Cvn Pk
ME12 . . . . 48 E5
Sunnyside ME9 . . . . 167 E7
Sunnyside Gdns CT13 . 180 E8
Sunnyside
Littlestone-on-Sea TN28 . 373 D6
Lydd TN29 . . . . 376 B6
Marlpit Hill TN8 . . . . 217 B3
Sunnyside Rd
Folkestone CT20 . . . . 334 D3
Rusthall TN4 . . . . 285 C4
Sunray Ave Bromley BR2 . . 52 F3
Whitstable CT5 . . . . 108 B7
Sun Rd DA10 . . . . 17 F1
Sun Rise TN25 . . . . 267 F5
Sunset Cl
Eastchurch ME12 . . . . 48 F6
Erith DA8 . . . . 15 B7
Whitstable CT5 . . . . 108 C6
Sunset Rd SE28 . . . . 3 A5
Sunshine Ct 1 ME8 . . . . 98 F8
Sun St CT1 . . . . 174 F8
Sunstone Dr ME10 . . . . 101 C7
Sun Terr ME5 . . . . 97 B4
Sun Valley Way CT15 . . 245 C8
Superabbey Est ME20 . . 129 B2
Superior Dr 4 BR6 . . . . . 86 F4
Surf Cres ME12 . . . . 48 F6
Surlingham Cl SE28 . . . . . 3 D6
Surrenden Rd
Folkestone CT19 . . . . 334 F6
Staplehurst TN12 . . . . 260 E3
Surrey Cl
Ramsgate CT12 . . . . 83 B1
Royal Tunbridge Wells
TN2 . . . . 313 F8
Surrey Gdns CT7 . . . . . . 80 F7
Surrey Rd
Canterbury CT1 . . . . 175 D7
Maidstone ME15 . . . . 195 D8
Margate CT9 . . . . 51 B3
Surtees Cl TN24 . . . . . . 300 E6
Susan Rd SE3 . . . . 11 B5
Susan's Hill TN26 . . . . . 325 E3
Susan Wood BR7 . . . . . . 53 A8
Sussex Ave
Ashford TN24 . . . . 268 B3
Canterbury CT1 . . . . 175 D7
Margate CT9 . . . . 50 J1
Sussex Cl Herne Bay CT6 . . 76 B4
Sussex Cl continued
Royal Tunbridge Wells
TN2 . . . . 286 C1
Sussex Dr ME5 . . . . 97 A4
Sussex Gdns
Birchington CT7 . . . . 80 F7
Herne Bay CT6 . . . . 76 B4
Westgate-on-S CT8 . . . . . . 50 D1
Sussex Mans CT8 . . . . . . 50 D1
Sussex Mews 19 TN2 . . 286 A2
Sussex Rd Dartford DA1 . . 34 A8
Erith DA8 . . . . 14 B7
5 Folkestone CT19 . . . . 335 D6
Maidstone ME15 . . . . 195 D8
New Romney TN28 . . . . . 373 A6
Orpington BR5 . . . . 54 C3
Sidcup DA14 . . . . 31 B3
Tonbridge TN9 . . . . 254 A8
Sussex Road Prim Sch
TN9 . . . . 254 A8
Sussex St CT11 . . . . 117 E7
Sussex Wlk CT1 . . . . 175 D7
Sutcliffe Rd
Bexley DA16 . . . . 13 C5
Woolwich SE18 . . . . 12 E8
Sutherland Ave
Bexley DA16 . . . . 12 E3
Biggin Hill TN16 . . . . 118 E1
Orpington BR5 . . . . 53 F4
Sutherland Cl
Chalk DA12 . . . . 38 B6
Hythe CT21 . . . . 333 A2
Stone DA9 . . . . 16 F2
Sutherland Dr CT7 . . . . . 81 B6
Sutherland Gdns ME8 . . . 98 E6
Sutherland Ho
Hythe CT21 . . . . 333 C1
Woolwich SE18 . . . . 11 F6
Sutherland Rd
Deal CT14 . . . . 215 C6
Erith DA17 . . . . 4 A3
Royal Tunbridge Wells
TN1 . . . . 286 B3
Sutlej Rd SE7 . . . . 11 C7
Sutton at Hone CE Prim
Sch DA4 . . . . 34 A1
Sutton Baron Rd ME9 . 134 A8
Sutton Cl
Folkestone CT19 . . . . 335 A7
Gillingham ME8 . . . . 99 A8
Sutton Cotts ME13 . . . . 171 C3
Sutton Ct TN12 . . . . 259 C5
Sutton Forge TN12 . . . . 259 D5
Sutton La CT14 . . . . 247 F5
Sutton Rd Hersden CT3 . 111 E1
Langley ME17 . . . . 196 C5
Maidstone ME15 . . . . 195 D6
Ripple CT14 . . . . 247 C8
Sutton Row CT14 . . . . . 215 B5
Suttons The TN31 . . . . . 374 A1
Sutton St ME14 . . . . 163 D4
Sutton Valence Castle★
ME17 . . . . 229 F7
Sutton Valence Prep Sch
ME17 . . . . 229 C7
Sutton Valence Prim Sch
ME17 . . . . 229 E7
Sutton Valence Sch
ME17 . . . . 229 E7
Swadelands Cl ME17 . . 199 C5
Swadelands Sch
ME17 . . . . 199 C5
Swaffield Rd TN13 . . . . 154 C5
Swain Cl ME2 . . . . 62 F8
Swain Rd
Gillingham ME8 . . . . 98 B6
Tenterden TN30 . . . . 324 D3
Swaisland Rd DA1 . . . . . 15 B1
Swaislands Dr DA1 . . . . . 14 F2
Swakeley Wlk CT5 . . . . . 75 D3
Swale Ave
Rushenden ME11 . . . . 45 F3
Sheerness ME12 . . . . 28 B1
Swale Cl CT6 . . . . 77 A3
Swalecliffe Ave CT6 . . . . 76 B4
Swalecliffe Com Prim Sch
CT5 . . . . 75 B2
Swalecliffe Court Dr
CT5 . . . . 75 D3
Swalecliffe Rd CT5 . . . . . 75 B2
Swaledale Rd DA2 . . . . . 34 C7
Swale Ho ME11 . . . . 45 F5
Swale Rd Crayford DA1 . . 15 A3
Rochester ME2 . . . . 62 C7
Swale Sta ME9 . . . . 69 A7
Swale View ME13 . . . . . 140 B6
Swallow Ave CT5 . . . . . 108 B6
Swallow Cl Bexley DA8 . . 14 E6
Margate CT9 . . . . 82 C8
Stone DA9 . . . . 16 F2
Swallow Ct Herne CT6 . . 110 F7
3 Lewisham SE12 . . . . . . 29 A8
Swallow Dr TN2 . . . . 286 F6
Swallowfield TN24 . . . . 300 E7
Swallowfield Rd SE7 . . . . 1 B1
Swallowfields 2 DA11 . . 36 E5
Swallow Ho
Dover CT17 . . . . 310 A6
4 Maidstone ME16 . . . . . 161 E4
Swallow Rd ME20 . . . . . 127 F2
Swallow Rise ME5 . . . . . 97 A5
Swallows The CT13 . . . . 181 A8
Swallow St E6 . . . . 1 E8
Swallowtail Cl BR5 . . . . 54 D5
Swamp Rd TN29 . . . . . . 372 B4
Swan Apartments 12
ME15 . . . . 195 E5
Swan App E6 . . . . 1 E8
Swanbridge Rd DA7 . . . . 14 B6
Swan Bsns Pk DA1 . . . . . 15 C3

Swan Cl Orpington BR5 .... 54 A6
Sittingbourne ME10 .... 102 B4
Swan Cotts TN30 ...... 359 D3
Swanfield Rd CT5 .... 108 D8
Swan Gn TN25 .... 303 D1
Swan La
Brandfold TN17 .... 290 F3
Dartford DA1 ....32 F8
Marlpit Hill TN8 ..... 217 C4
Swanland Dr TN9 ..... 253 F7
Swan La TN25 ...... 303 E2
Swanley Ctr BR8 ....55 E6
Swanley La BR8 ....55 F6
Swanley New Barn
Railway ★ BR8 ....55 E8
Swanley Rd DA16 .... 13 C6
Swanley Sch BR8 ....55 E6
Swanley Sta BR8 ..... 55 D5
Swanley Village Rd
BR8 ....56 B8
Swanmead Way TN9 .. 222 D2
Swann Way TN18 .... 307 A4
Swan Rd SE18 ....1 D3
Swan Ridge TN8 ..... 217 D4
Swanscombe Bsns Ctr
DA10 ....17 E2
Swanscombe Ho 1
BR5 ....54 B7
Swanscombe Inf Sch
DA10 ....35 F8
Swanscombe Sta DA10 ..17 F2
Swanscombe St DA10 ..17 F1
Swansea Ct E16 ....2 B4
Swanstree Ave ME10 .. 102 B2
Swan St
West Malling ME19 .. 159 C8
Wittersham TN30 ...... 359 C3
Swanton La
Littlebourne CT3 ...... 144 D2
Lydden CT15 .... 276 C6
Swanton Mill ★ TN25 .. 301 B2
Swanton Rd Erith DA8 ... 14 B7
Mereworth ME18 ..... 191 A8
Swan Valley Com Sch
DA10 ....35 F8
Swanzy Rd TN14 .... 154 C7
Sward Rd BR5 .... 54 A3
Swarling Hill Rd CT4 .. 207 C7
Swattenden La TN17 .. 320 B1
Swaylands DA17 .... 14 A8
Swaynesland Rd RH8 .. 183 F1
Swaynes Way CT13 ... 180 B2
Sweechbridge Rd CT6 ... 77 F3
Sweechgate CT2 ...... 143 F2
Sweeps Hill Cl TN2 .... 287 F3
Sweeps La BR5 .... 54 D5
Sweet Bay Cres TN24 .. 157 A1
Sweet Briar Ct ME16 .. 161 D5
Sweetbriar La CT15 ... 212 B2
Sweetings La TN3,TN5 .. 316 D1
Sweetlands La TN12 ... 261 A5
Sweetlove Pl CT3 .... 178 A8
Sweets La ME19 ...... 160 A4
Swetenham Wlk SE18 ....2 C1
Sweyne Jun Sch The
DA10 ....35 F8
Sweyn Rd DA10 ......17 E1
Sweyn Pl SE3 .... 11 A5
Sweyn Rd CT9 ...... 51 A3
Swievelands Rd TN16 .. 118 C1
Swift Cl Larkfield ME20 .. 128 A2
Woolwich SE28 ....3 B6
Swift Cres ME5 ...... 97 C6
Swift Ho 6 ME16 .... 161 E4
Swifts View TN17 .... 320 D6
Swiller's La DA12 ....38 E3
Swinburne Ave CT10 .... 84 A3
Swinburne Gdns RM18 .. 19 B5
Swinford Gdns CT9 .... 83 C8
Swinford Manor Sch
TN23 .... 267 B4
Swingate Ave ME3 ...... 22 B6
Swingate Cl ME5 ....97 B2
Swingate Inf Sch ME5 .. 97 C1
Swingate La SE18 ..... 12 E7
Swingfield Ct BR2 .... 52 D4
Swinton Ave ME3 .... 40 F5
Swires Shaw BR2 ...... 85 D6
Swiss Way CT19 ..... 335 F7
Switch House Ave
TN29 .... 380 C2
Swithland Gdns SE9 .... 30 A4
Syamore Mews DA8 .....4 D1
Sycamore Ave
Aylesham CT3 .... 210 E5
Sidcup DA15 .... 12 F1
Sycamore Cl
Broadstairs CT10 ...... 83 C4
Chartham CT4 .... 173 F1
Dymchurch TN29 .... 366 C8
Eltham SE9 ....29 E6
Gravesend DA12 ..... 37 D8
Herne Bay CT6 ...... 77 C5
Hythe CT21 .... 332 E1
Lydd TN29 .... 376 D7
Margate CT9 ....82 E7
Tilbury RM18 ...... 19 A5
Sycamore Cotts
Bidborough TN3 .... 253 D3
Pembury TN2 ...... 287 C6
Sycamore Cres ME16 .. 161 C5
Sycamore Ct Erith DA8 ...4 D1
Stone DA9 ....34 E8
Sycamore Dr
Aylesford ME20 .... 128 E1
Deal CT14 .... 215 B4
Swanley BR8 .... 55 E7
Sycamore Gdns
Dymchurch TN29 .. 366 C8
Paddock Wood TN12 .. 256 F5

Sycamore Grange CT11 ..83 F1
Sycamore La TN23 ... 267 E4
Sycamore Lodge BR6 ...86 F8
Sycamore Rd
Dartford DA1 .... 33 D7
Rochester ME2 ....62 E5
Sycamores The CT3 .... 144 E8
Sychem La TN12 ..... 256 A6
Sychem Pl TN12 ..... 256 A7
Sydcot Dr CT14 ..... 215 D8
Sydenham Cotts SE12 .. 29 C6
Sydenham Rd CT14 .. 215 D7
Sydenham St CT5 ...... 74 D2
Sydney Ave ME10 .... 101 C4
Sydney Cooper Cl
CT2 .... 142 B2
Sydney Cotts 11 BR5 .. 54 C6
Sydney Rd Bexley DA6 ... 13 D3
Chatham ME4 ....64 A3
Deal CT14 .... 215 A1
Erith DA17 ....3 D8
Ramsgate CT11 ...... 117 F8
Sidcup DA14 ....30 E4
Tilbury RM18 ...... 19 A5
Whitstable CT5 ..... 108 E8
Sydney St TN23 ..... 300 C8
Sydney Terr TN18 .... 340 F3
Sylewood Cl ME1 .....96 B8
Sylvan Cl RH8 ..... 183 B6
Sylvan Glade ME5 .... 130 A8
Sylvan Mews DA9 .....17 B3
Sylvan Rd ME8 .... 98 C8
Sylvan Wlk BR1 ..... 52 F6
Sylvester Ave BR7 ...... 29 F2
Sylvestre Cl ME2 ...... 95 A4
Sylvestres TN13 ..... 153 E6
Symmonds Dr ME10 .. 102 A6
Symonds Cl TN15 ....90 E5
Symonds La ME18 .... 225 F6
Symonds Rd ME3 ...... 22 A4
Symons Ave ME4 .... 64 A2
Syndale Pl 5 CT11 .. 117 F7
Syndale Valley Vineyard ★
ME9 .... 168 C7
Syon Lodge 9 SE12 .... 29 A8
Syringa Ct 10 RM17 ... 18 D8

T

Tabor Ct TN12 ...... 290 A6
Tabret Cl TN24 ..... 268 D6
Tadburn Gn ME5 ......97 B4
Taddington Wood La
ME5 ....96 E2
Taddy Gdns CT9 ...... 83 C8
Tadley Ct
Gillingham ME7 ......64 F6
Rochester ME1 .... 96 C8
Tadworth Rd TN24 .. 268 D5
Taillour Cl ME10 ..... 101 F7
Tail Race The ME15 .. 161 E2
Tainter Rd TN11 ..... 190 E1
Talavera Rd CT1 ..... 175 D8
Talbot Ave CT6 ....76 B3
Talbot Pk TN2 ...... 286 D5
Talbot Rd
Maidstone ME16 ...... 161 C6
Margate CT9 .... 51 B2
The Moor TN18 .... 354 F8
Tallents Cl DA4 .... 34 B1
Tallis Cl E16 ....1 B7
Tallis Gr SE7 ....11 B8
Tall Trees Cl ME17 .... 197 D2
Tally Ho Rd TN26 .... 299 C2
Tally Rd RH8 .... 183 E4
Tamar Dr ME2 ....62 F7
Tamarind Cl ME7 ...... 98 A4
Tamarisk ME12 ....73 E5
Tamar Rd TN10 .... 222 B5
Tamar St SE7 ....1 E2
Tame La CT21,TN29 .. 351 F6
Tamesis Strand DA12 .. 37 E3
Tamley La TN25 ..... 271 B6
Tams Gdns ME12 ...... 47 D6
Tandridge Dr BR6 ..... 53 D1
Tandridge Pl 2 BR6 .. 53 D1
Tangier Cl CT5 ...... 278 E3
Tangier La TN3 .... 314 B6
Tangleberry Cl BR1 .... 52 F5
Tanglewood Cl ME8 .. 98 C6
Tanglewood Ct BR5 .... 54 C6
Tangmere Cl ME7 ......64 F5
Tanhouse La TN31 .... 367 A2
Tanhurst Wlk SE2 ....3 D3
Tanker Hill ME8 .... 98 D6
Tankerton Cir CT5 .....74 F3
Tankerton Ct CT5 ......75 B3
Tankerton Hts CT5 .....74 E3
Tankerton Mews CT5 ..74 E3
Tankerton Rd CT5 .....74 F3
Tanner's Hill Gdns
CT21 .... 333 C3
Tanner's Hill CT21 ... 333 C3
Tanners Mead TN8 ... 217 C1
Tanners St ME13 ..... 138 C7
Tannery Ct 5 ME10 .. 101 E5
Tannery La
Ashford TN23 .... 268 C2
11 Sandwich CT13 .. 148 F1
Tannery Rd TN9 ..... 222 C1
Tansy Cl E6 ....2 A7
Tanyard Cotts DA12 .. 38 E1
Tanyard Hill DA12 .... 38 E2
Tanyard La TN4 ..... 253 F1
Tan Yard La DA5 ..... 32 A8
Tanyard
Rolvenden TN17 ..... 343 E4
Sandhurst TN18 .... 356 B5
Tanyard The TN17 .... 320 D4
Tapleys Hill CT4 .... 208 B5
Taplin Ct 5 CT7 ...... 81 A7
Tappan Dr ME4 ....41 B2

Tapsell's La TN5 ..... 336 D5
Tarbutts TN17 ...... 320 D4
Target Bsns Ctr ME15 .. 195 F4
Target Firs CT16 ..... 277 D5
Tariff Reform Cotts
ME13 .... 138 D5
Tarland Ho TN2 ..... 286 D3
Tarling Cl DA14 .... 31 B5
Tarnwood Pk SE9 ....29 F7
Tarragon Rd ME16 .. 161 B3
Tartane La TN29 .... 366 C8
Taryes Ho 2 CT11 .... 117 C6
Tasker Cl ME3 ...... 163 B3
Tasmania Ho RM18 .... 19 A6
Tasman Wlk E16 ....1 D7
Tassell Cl ME9 ...... 128 A1
Tassell's Wlk CT5 ...... 75 D3
Taswell Ct CT16 .... 310 E8
Taswell Rd ME8 ...... 66 A1
Taswell St CT16 .... 310 E8
Tatchell Dr TN27 ... 234 C7
Tate Rd E16 ....1 F5
Tates TN18 .... 341 A1
Tates Orch DA3 ....58 F3
Tatler Cl ME5 .... 97 D2
Tatsfield Cl ME8 ...... 65 A2
Tatsfield La
Biggin Hill TN16 .... 150 F6
Hill Park TN16 ..... 151 A6
Tatsfield Prim Sch
TN16 .... 150 D6
Tattersall Cl SE9 ...... 11 E2
Tattershall Ct 22 DA2 ..16 B1
Tattershall Rd ME15 .. 162 A1
Tattlebury La TN17 .. 290 F1
Tattlebury Rd TN27 .. 262 C8
Taunton Cl Bexley DA2 .. 14 D5
Maidstone ME15 .... 195 F6
Taunton Rd DA11 ...... 18 A2
Taunton Vale DA12 .... 37 D5
Tavern Cl ME3 ......27 A8
Tavern Cotts TN15 ... 155 A3
Taverners Rd ME8 ......98 E7
Tavistock Cl
Chatham ME5 ....96 F1
Gillingham ME8 ......98 E2
Sittingbourne ME10 .. 101 D4
Tavistock Rd
Bexley DA16 .... 13 C6
2 Bromley BR2 ..... 52 A5
Ramsgate CT11 ....83 E1
Tavy Bridge SE2 ....3 C4
Tawney Rd SE28 ....3 B6
Tay Cl ME5 .... 97 B5
Tayfields TN12 ..... 261 C6
Taylers Yd TN25 .... 237 E2
Taylor Cl
Harrietsham ME17 ... 198 D6
4 Orpington BR6 ......86 F6
Taylor Ct 1 TN2 .. 286 C7
Taylor Rd
Folkestone CT19 .... 334 E6
Lydd-on-S TN29 .... 377 E6
Minster (Thanet) CT12 .. 115 B6
Snodland ME6 .... 127 F8
Taylor Row DA2 ...... 33 C5
Taylor's Bldgs SE18 .....2 B2
Taylors Cl
St Mary's Bay TN29 .. 365 F3
Sidcup DA14 ....30 F4
Taylors Hill CT4 ..... 205 B8
Taylor's La Higham ME3 .. 39 B5
Rochester ME2 .... 63 B7
Taylors La
St Mary's Bay TN29 .. 365 F3
Vigo Village ME19 .. 125 F6
Taylors Pl ME19 .... 125 E5
Taylor St TN4 .... 286 A8
Taymouth Ho 1 CT16 .. 310 E8
Taywood Cl TN24 .... 268 F1
Tea Garden La ME3 .. 285 C2
Teakcroft Ctr RM13 ....4 D7
Teal Ave BR5 .... 54 D5
Teal Cl Grain ME3 .....27 B5
Hawkinge CT18 ..... 306 F3
Newham E16 ....1 D8
Teal Dr CT6 ...... 76 C2
Teal Way ME9 ....68 E3
Teapot La ME20 .... 128 E1
Teardrop Ctr BR8 .... 56 C4
Teasaucer Hill ME15 .. 194 F8
Teasel Cl ME14 ..... 162 F4
Teasel Cres SE28 ....2 E5
Teasel Rd ME5 ....96 F1
Teasels TN27 ...... 295 A1
Teasley Mead TN3 .. 283 C4
Tebbs Way TN15 .... 156 C3
Teddars Leas Rd CT18 .. 305 E4
Tedder Ave ME5 ...... 97 A7
Tedder Rd TN4 ..... 286 B7
Teddington Cl CT1 .. 143 B2
Teelin Cl TN29 ..... 366 A4
Teesdale Rd DA2 ..... 34 C7
Teeswater Ct DA18 .....3 D3
Teign Mews SE9 ....29 E6
Teignmouth Rd DA16 .. 13 C5
Teise Cl TN2 .... 286 D2
Telegraph Hill ME3 .. 39 C3
Telegraph Hill Ind Pk
CT12 .... 115 D7
Telegraph Rd CT14 .. 215 B3
Telemann Sq SE3 ....11 B6
Telescope Alley ME12 .. 28 D2
Telford Cl
Folkestone CT19 .... 335 E6
Herne Bay CT6 ...... 76 C2
Telford Ho 2 Erith DA17 ...4 A3
11 Maidstone ME14 .. 162 A6
Telford Rd SE9 .... 30 D6
Telford St CT6 ....76 E5
Telham Ave CT12 .... 117 B8
Tellson Ave SE18 .....11 B3
Telscombe Cl BR6 ....86 E8

Telston La TN14 .... 121 F2
Temeraire Hts CT20 .. 334 C3
Temeraire Manor 2
ME7 .... 64 A6
Tempest Rd ME19 ... 158 F3
Templar Ct
9 Canterbury CT2 .. 142 F1
11 Dover CT17 .... 278 C1
Templar Dr Erith SE28 ....3 D7
Gravesend DA11 ...... 37 A3
Templar Rd CT16 ... 277 D5
Templars Ct 11 TN8 .. 217 D3
Templar St CT17 .... 310 C8
Temple Cl
Ashford TN23 ...... 299 F5
Temple Ewell CT16 ... 277 D6
Woolwich SE28 ....2 C3
Temple Ct CT2 ..... 142 D1
Temple Ewell CE Prim Sch
CT16 .... 277 D5
Temple Gdns
Rochester ME2 ...... 63 A6
Sittingbourne ME10 .. 102 B3
Temple Hill Com Prim Sch
DA1 .... 16 A2
Temple Hill DA1 ......15 F7
Temple Hill Sq DA1 .. 15 F7
Templeman Liby CT2 .. 142 E4
Temple Manor ★ ME2 .. 63 A6
Temple Mews 10 CT1 .. 174 F8
Temple Mill Prim Sch
ME2 ....40 B1
Templemore DA14 .... 31 B3
Temple Rd
Biggin Hill TN16 .... 118 C2
Canterbury CT2 ..... 142 D1
Temple Sch ME2 .....40 B2
Temple Side CT16 ... 277 D6
Temple Way
West Malling ME19 .. 127 F1
Worth CT14 .... 181 A4
Ten Acre Way ME8 .....66 B1
Tenby Rd DA16 .... 13 D6
Tenchley's La
Limpsfield RH8 ..... 183 D4
The Chart RH8 ..... 183 E2
Tenney Ho RM17 ......18 B7
Tennyson Ave
Canterbury CT1 ..... 143 D3
Cliffe Woods ME3 ....40 B7
Tennyson Cl DA16 .... 12 F6
Tennyson Gdns CT3 .. 210 F6
Tennyson Ho
Canterbury CT1 ..... 143 D3
2 Erith DA17 ....3 F1
Tennyson Pl
Canterbury CT1 ..... 143 D3
Folkestone CT19 .... 335 E7
Tennyson Rd
Ashford TN23 ...... 300 A6
Dartford DA1 ...... 16 A2
Gillingham ME7 ...... 64 C3
Tennyson Wlk
Northfleet DA11 ...... 36 D5
Tilbury RM18 .... 19 B5
Ten Perch Rd CT1 ... 174 D6
Tensing Ave DA11 .... 36 E5
Tenterden CE Jun Sch
TN30 .... 345 B7
Tenterden Cl SE9 ...... 29 F4
Tenterden & District Mus ★
TN30 .... 345 A7
Tenterden Dr CT2 .... 143 A4
Tenterden Inf Sch
TN30 .... 345 B7
Tenterden Rd
Appledore Heath TN26 .. 347 B1
Biddenden TN27 .... 323 B7
Chatham ME5 ....97 B5
Fosten Green TN27 .. 322 F4
Rolvenden TN17 .... 344 A5
Tenterden Station Est
TN30 .... 345 A8
Tenterden Town Sta ★
TN30 .... 345 A8
Tenterden Vineyard ★
TN30 .... 345 C1
Tenterden Way CT9 .... 51 C1
Tent Peg La BR5 .... 53 C4
Tenzing Ct SE9 ....29 E6
Terance Butler Ave
ME2 ....63 E8
Terence Cl
Chatham ME4 ....64 A2
Gravesend DA12 ..... 37 F6
Terence Ct 6 DA17 .. 13 F8
Terlingham La CT18 .. 307 A2
Terminus Dr CT6 ......77 D5
Terminus Rd ME16 .. 161 A2
Terminus Wlk 3
CT20 .... 335 E5
Tern Cres ME2 .... 62 C6
Terrace Apartments The
TN21 .... 333 C1
Terrace Cotts CT4 .. 241 A6
Terrace Rd
Elvington CT15 ..... 212 B1
Maidstone ME16 .... 161 E3
Sittingbourne ME10 .. 102 B3
Terrace St DA12 ......19 B1
Terraces The DA2 .... 34 C8
Terrace The
Canterbury CT2 ..... 142 F3
Faversham ME13 .... 138 A7
26 Gravesend DA12 .. 19 B1
Pluckley TN26 ...... 234 A1
Rochester ME1 ...... 63 C5
Sevenoaks TN13 .... 153 D5
Shepherdswell CT15 .. 244 D5
Terry's La CT5 ...... 74 D2
Terry's Lodge Rd
TN15 .... 124 C6
Terry Wlk ME7 .... 127 C2

Testers CT RH8 ..... 183 B3
Teston Ho ME18 .... 193 A7
Teston La ME15,ME18 .. 193 C7
Teston Rd
Kings Hill ME19 ..... 159 B5
Offham ME19 ...... 158 C7
Red Hill ME18 ..... 159 E2
West Malling ME19 .. 159 A6
Tetty Way BR1,BR2 .... 52 A7
Teviot Cl DA16 ......13 B6
Tewson Rd SE18 ....2 E1
Teynham Cl CT9 ......51 F2
Teynham Dr CT5 ......74 F2
Teynham Gn
Gillingham ME8 ...... 65 A4
Hayes BR2 .... 52 A4
Teynham Ho SE9 .... 12 D1
Teynham Parochial CE
Prim Sch ME9 ..... 103 C2
Teynham Rd
Dartford DA2 ...... 34 C8
Whitstable CT5 ....74 F2
Teynham Sta ME9 ... 103 D3
Teynham St ME9 ... 103 F4
Thackeray Ave RM18 .. 19 B6
Thackeray Rd ME20 .. 127 F3
Thames Ave
Gillingham ME8 ......98 E8
High Halstow ME23 .. 23 E4
Sheerness ME12 ...... 28 B1
Thamesbank Pl SE28 ....3 C7
Thames Barrier Visitor
Ctr ★ SE18 ....1 D3
Thames Ct 9 ME10 .. 49 G2
Thames Gate DA1 .... 16 A3
Thamesgate Sh Ctr 20
DA11 ....19 B1
Thameside Ind Est E16 ...1 A4
Thameside Inf & Jun Schs
RM17 .... 18 C8
Thamesmead Sh Ctr
SE28 ....3 A6
Thamesmere Dr SE28 ...3 A6
Thames Rd
Crayford DA1 ...... 15 A4
Grays RM17 ....18 B7
Newham E16 ....1 D5
Tonbridge TN10 ... 222 C5
Thames Road Ind Est
E16 ....1 D4
Thames Terr ME3 ......22 B6
Thames View ME3 .... 40 C7
Thames View Cotts
ME3 .... 39 D3
Thames View Inf Sch
ME8 .... 65 D2
Thames View Jun Sch
ME8 .... 65 D2
Thamesview Sch DA12 ..37 F5
Thameswater Dr DA9 .. 17 C2
Thames Way
Gravesend DA11 ..... 19 A1
Northfleet DA11 ...... 36 E7
Thanet Cl CT10 ....84 B5
Thanet Coll
Broadstairs CT10 .... 84 A3
Margate CT9 .... 50 J2
Thanet Dr BR2 ..... 85 D7
Thanet Ent Ctr CT10 .. 83 D7
Thanet Gdns CT19 ... 335 F6
Thanet Ho
7 Maidstone ME15 .. 195 F5
7 Northfleet DA11 ....36 F7
Thanet Place Gdns
CT10 .... 84 B6
Thanet Rd
Broadstairs CT10 .....84 B4
Erith DA8 .... 14 E7
Margate CT9 .... 50 J2
Ramsgate CT11 ..... 117 F7
Sidcup DA5 .... 32 A8
Westgate-on-S CT8 .. 81 D8
Thanet View
Eythorne CT15 ..... 245 B8
St Nicholas at Wade CT7 ..79 F2
Thanet Way
Boughton Street ME13 .. 139 D6
Herne Bay CT6 ...... 77 C3
Whitstable CT5 ...... 75 C2
Yorkletts CT5,ME13 .. 107 E2
Thanington Ct Farm
CT1 .... 174 C6
Thanington Cl SE9 .... 12 E1
Thanington Rd CT1 .. 174 C6
Thatch Barn Rd TN27 .. 262 D6
Thatcher Ct DA1 ...... 33 D8
Thatcher Rd TN12 .. 260 E4
Thatchers La ME3 ......22 B5
Thatchers The ME16 .. 161 A5
Thaxted Rd SE9 ...... 30 C6
Theaker Ho DA4 ..... 57 D7
Theatre Sq 7 TN30 .. 345 A7
Theatre St CT21 ..... 333 C2
Thelma Cl DA2 ...... 37 F3
Thelma Gdns SE3 ......11 E6
Theobalds Cl TN15 .. 123 A1
Theobalds Rd TN18 .. 340 F2
Theodore Cl TN2 .... 286 E7
Theodore Pl ME7 ...... 64 C5
Theresa Rd CT21 .... 333 B1
Thicketts TN13 ..... 154 C4
Third Ave Chatham ME5 .. 64 C1
Eastchurch ME12 .....48 F6
Gillingham ME7 ......64 F4
Margate CT9 ....51 B3
West Thurrock RM20 .. 17 A8
Third St TN3 ...... 284 F3
Thirlemere Cl ME16 .. 161 D8
Thirlmere TN24 .... 268 D6
Thirlmere Ave CT11 .. 117 A7

Thirlmere Cl
Gillingham ME7 ..... 65 A5
Rochester ME2 ...... 40 C1
Thirlmere Gdns CT3 .. 210 F6
Thirlmere Rd
Bexley DA7 .... 14 C6
Royal Tunbridge Wells
TN4 .... 285 E5
Thirsk Ho 6 ME15 .. 195 F6
Thirza Rd ME15 ...... 15 F1
Thistlebank ME5 ...... 97 A3
Thistlebrook Ind Est
SE2 ....3 C4
Thistlebrook SE2 ......3 C4
Thistle Ct DA1 ....34 B7
Thistledown Cl ME7 ... 98 A4
Thistledown
Gravesend DA12 .... 37 D2
Maidstone ME14 .... 162 F4
Thistle Dr CT5 ..... 108 B6
Thistlefield Cl DA5 .... 31 D7
Thistle Hill Way
Minster (Sheppey) ME12 .. 47 A4
Minster (Sheppey) ME12 .. 47 C5
Thistlemead BR7 ......53 B7
Thistle Rd DA12 ...... 37 E8
Thistle Wlk ME10 .. 102 B5
Thomas Aveling Sch The
ME1 .... 96 C8
Thomas Cotts DA13 ...36 B1
Thomas Cribb Mews E6 ..2 A7
Thomas Ct 9 ME10 .. 102 B4
Thomas Dinwiddy Rd
SE12 ....29 B6
Thomas Dr DA12 .... 37 D6
Thomas Dunk Almshouses
13 TN18 .... 341 A1
Thomas Rd
Faversham ME13 .... 138 D7
Sittingbourne ME10 .. 102 B4
Thomas Seth Bsns Pk
ME11 .... 46 A3
Thomas Shearley Ct
DA5 ....32 B8
Thomas St
Rochester ME1 ...... 63 C3
Royal Tunbridge Wells
TN4 .... 286 A5
Woolwich SE18 ....2 B2
Thomas Tallis Sch SE3 ..11 B4
Thomas Wyatt Way
TN15 .... 124 F3
Thompson Cl
Deal CT14 .... 248 B8
Folkestone CT19 .... 335 B7
Gillingham ME8 ......99 A8
Thomson Cl ME6 ...... 95 A1
Thomson Rd TN25 .. 268 B5
Thong La Basted TN15 .. 156 F5
Gravesend DA12 ..... 38 A2
Thornbridge Rd CT14 .. 215 B2
Thorn Cl Bromley BR2 .. 53 A3
Chatham ME5 .... 96 D1
Thorndale BR7 ....29 F1
Thorndale ME5 .... 96 D4
Thornden Cl CT6 ......76 B2
Thornden Ct
Canterbury CT2 .... 142 C4
Rolvenden Layne TN17 .. 358 A8
Thornden La
Rolvenden Layne TN17 .. 358 A8
Rolvenden TN17 .... 344 A1
Thornden Wood Rd
Herne Bay CT6 ......76 B1
Whitstable CT6 ..... 109 E4
Thorndike Cl ME4 .....96 F8
Thorndike Ho ME4 ....96 F8
Thorndike Rd TN29 .. 352 C4
Thorndon Cl BR5 ...... 53 F7
Thorndon Rd BR5 .... 53 F7
Thorndyke Way TN15 .. 124 F3
Thorne Cl Erith DA8 .. 14 B8
Newham E16 ....1 A7
Thorne Hill CT12 ..... 116 A6
Thorne Rd CT12 ..... 115 B6
Thorn Est The TN27 .. 265 B6
Thornet Wood Rd BR1 .. 53 A6
Thorney Croft Cl
ME17 .... 197 D2
Thorneycroft Rd
ME13 .... 201 D5
Thornfield Gdns TN2 .. 286 F5
Thorn Gdns CT11 ......83 E1
Thornhill Ave SE18 .... 12 E7
Thornhill Pl ME14 .... 162 A6
Thorn Hill Rd ME12 .. 49 D4
Thornhurst CT6 ....77 D4
Thorn La CT4 ...... 240 C2
Thornlea TN23 ..... 267 E2
Thorn Rd TN12 .... 259 E4
Thorn's Mdw TN12 .. 152 C4
Thornton Cl TN24 .. 269 A4
Thornton Dene DA14 .. 31 A3
Thornton La CT13,
CT14 .... 212 E7
Thornton Rd
Bromley BR1 .... 29 A3
Erith DA17 ....4 B2
Thornton's La 9
CT16 .... 310 E7
Thorntree Prim Sch SE7 ..1 D1
Thorntree Rd SE7 ....1 D1
Thorn Wlk ME10 .. 102 C5
Thorold Rd ME5 ......64 B3
Thorpe Ave TN10 .. 222 C5
Thorpe Cl BR6 ......86 E8
Thorpe Wlk ME8 ..... 98 D3
Thrale Way ME8 ......98 E4
Thread La ME13 .... 140 B4
Three Acres Site
CT19 .... 335 B8
Three Corners DA7 .....14 B5

Three Elm La TN11 .... **223** D5	Titsey Place ★ .... RH8 ... **150** B3	Tovil Hill ME15 .... **161** E2	Treewall Gdns BR1 .... **29** B4
Three Gates Rd DA3 .... **78** A3	Titsey Rd	Tovil Rd ME15 .... **161** E2	Trefoil Ho Erith DA18 ...... **3** E4
Three King's Yd CT13 .. **149** A1	Limpsfield RH8 .... **183** B8	Tovil, St Stephen's CE Inf	Grays RM17 .... **18** B7
Three Leg Cross Rd	Titsey RH8 .... **150** B1	Sch ME15 .... **161** E2	Trefoil The ME9,ME13 .. **136** E6
TN5 .... **338** D3	Tivoli Brooks CT9 .... **50** I1	Tower Bglws CT7 .... **81** A8	Trefor Gdns Ct CT16 ... **278** B2
Three Oaks La TN5 ...... **336** D7	Tivoli Gdns	Tower Cl	Tregony Rd BR6 .... **86** F6
Thresher Field TN8 .... **251** A6	Gravesend DA12 .... **37** B7	Gravesend DA12 .... **37** E3	Trelawn Cres ME5 .... **97** B2
Threshers Dr ME14 .... **162** E5	Woolwich SE18 .... **1** E2	Orpington BR6 .... **86** F7	Trellyn Cl ME16 .... **160** F2
Thrift The DA2 .... **35** C5	Tivoli Park Ave CT9 ...... **50** H1	Tower Croft CT20 .... **334** E3	Trench Rd TN10 .... **222** C6
Throckmorten Rd E16 ....**1** B7	Tivoli Rd CT9 .... **82** E8	Tower St **4** CT20 ..... **334** E3	Trenear Cl BR6 .... **87** A6
Throwley Cl SE2 .... **3** C3	Tobruk Way ME5 .... **96** F6	Tower St TN9 .... **222** C2	Trenley Dr CT3 .... **143** F1
Throwley Dr CT6 .... **76** C4	Toby Gdns TN11 .... **223** E8	Towerfields BR2 .... **85** E6	Trentham Dr BR5 .... **54** A5
Throwley Rd ME13 ..... **169** D5	Toby Rd TN29 .... **377** E6	Tower Gdns	Trenton Cl ME16 .... **161** B7
Thrupp Paddock CT10 ... **51** G1	Tockwith Ct TN13 ...... **154** D4	Hythe CT21 .... **333** C1	Trent Rd ME5 .... **97** B5
Thrush Cl ME5 .... **97** B7	Todd Cres ME10 .... **102** A8	Maidstone ME14 .... **163** B4	Trevale Rd ME1 .... **63** B1
Thruxted La CT4 .... **173** B1	Toddington Cres ME5 ... **96** D1	Tower Hamlets Rd	Trevelyan Cl DA1 .... **15** F3
Thunderer Rd RM9 .... **3** F7	Toke Cl TN23 .... **267** C1	CT17 .... **310** C8	Trevereux Hill RH8 ..... **183** F4
Thundersland Rd CT6 ... **77** B4	Toke Pl ME17 .... **227** E8	Tower Hamlets St **1**	Trevino Dr ME5 .... **96** F2
Thurlow Ave CT6 .... **77** C5	Tolcairn Ct **2** DA17 .....**4** A1	CT17 .... **310** C8	Trevithick Dr DA1 .... **15** F3
Thurnham CE Inf Sch	Tolgate La ME2 .... **63** B7	Tower Hill Ho Dover CT17 . **310** C8	Trevor Cl BR2 .... **52** C6
ME14 .... **163** A4	Tolgate Way ME14 ...... **129** E4	Offham ME19 .... **158** D7	Trevor Dr ME16 .... **161** C5
Thurnham Ho **5** BR5 ... **54** D1	Tolhurst Rd TN12 .... **256** A7	Whitstable CT5 .... **75** A3	Trewin Cl ME16 .... **128** D2
Thurnham La ME14 .... **163** C7	Tollemache Ct CT12 ...... **81** F2	Tower Ind Est TN15 .... **124** D5	Trewsbury Ho **2** SE2 .....**3** D4
Thurrock Bssns Ctr	Tollgate Cl CT5 .... **108** C8	Tower La ME14 .... **163** B4	Triangle Ct E16 ....**1** C8
RM20 .... **16** F8	Tollgate Mews TN15 ... **157** A8	Tower Park Rd DA1 ...... **14** F2	Triangle The DA15 .... **31** A8
Thurrock Ent Ctr RM18 .. **18** A8	Tollgate Pl TN27 .... **262** E5	Tower Par CT5 .... **74** E3	Tribune Ct ME12 .... **46** B8
Thurrock Park Way	Tollgate Rd	Tower Rd Bexley DA7 ...... **14** A3	Tribune Dr ME10 .... **101** F6
RM17 .... **18** D7	Dartford DA2 .... **34** D8	Dartford DA1 .... **15** C1	Tricorn Ho SE28 ....**2** D5
Thursland Rd DA14 ...... **31** E3	Newham E6 ....**1** E8	Erith DA17 ....**4** C2	Trident Cl ME2 .... **63** E7
Thursley Rd SE9 .... **29** F5	Toll La TN27 .... **234** E7	Orpington BR6 .... **86** F7	Triggs Cotts ME9 .... **103** D2
Thurston Dr ME2 .... **62** D7	Tolputt Ct CT19 .... **335** E6	Whitstable CT5 .... **74** F2	Trigg's Row ME9 .... **103** D2
Thurstone Ct ME14 .... **161** F6	Tolsey Mead TN15 ...... **157** A8	Tower Ret Pk DA1 .... **14** F2	Trilby Way CT5 .... **108** B6
Thurston Pk CT5 .... **74** E1	Tolsford Cl	Towers Point ME1 .... **63** B4	Trimworth Rd CT19 ..... **334** F6
Thwaite Cl DA8 .... **14** C8	Etchinghill CT18 .... **305** D3	Towers Sch The TN24 ... **268** D8	Trinity Cl Orpington BR2 .. **52** E1
Thyer Rd BR6 .... **86** C6	Folkestone CT19 .... **334** D6	Towers The TN27 .... **201** E1	Royal Tunbridge Wells
Thyme Cl SE3 .... **11** C4	Tomar Owl Sanctuary ★	Towers View TN24 ...... **268** C7	TN2 .... **286** D4
Thyme Wlk ME16 .... **161** B3	TN25 .... **300** F2	Tower Way ME4 .... **57** D8	Trinity Cres CT20 .... **335** B4
Tibbs Court La TN12 .... **289** A6	Tomay Cotts CT6 .... **78** A3	Tower View	Trinity Ct
Tiber Ct CT19 .... **334** C6	Tom Coombs Cl SE9 ......**11** E3	Chartham CT4 .... **173** F1	Aylesford ME20 .... **129** A3
Ticehurst Cl BR5 .... **31** A1	Tom Cribb Rd SE28 ....**2** D3	Kings Hill ME19 .... **159** B3	Dartford DA1 .... **34** B7
Tichborne Cl ME16 ..... **161** C6	Tom Jenkinson Rd E16 ....**1** A5	Tower Way **1** CT1 ..... **174** F8	Deal CT14 .... **215** A4
Tickford Cl SE2 ....**3** C4	Tom Joyce Cl ME6 .... **127** F7	Towncourt Cres BR5 ...... **53** D5	Eltham SE9 ....**12** B1
Tickham La ME9 .... **136** C5	Tomlin Cl	Towncourt La BR5 .... **53** C5	Margate CT9 .... **50** J3
Tickner's La TN29 ...... **363** B1	Snodland ME6 .... **128** A8	Townfield Cnr DA12 ...... **37** D7	Trinity Gdns
Tidal Basin Rd E16 ....**1** A6	Staplehurst TN12 .... **260** E4	Towngate Wood Pk Mobile	Dartford DA1 .... **15** D1
Tidebrook Ct **4** BR5 ... **54** C5	Tomlin Dr CT9 .... **83** C8	Home Pk TN10 .... **222** A4	Folkestone CT20 .... **335** C4
Tidelock Ho SE28 ....**2** D4	Tonbridge By-Pass	Town Hill CT4 .... **175** F2	Trinity Ho CT9 .... **50** J3
Tideside Ct SE18 ....**1** E3	Tonbridge,Stocks Green	Town Hill CT4 ME19 .... **127** C1	Trinity Homes CT14 .... **215** C1
Tideway The ME1 .... **96** C8	TN11,TN9,TN4,TN14,	Town Hill	Trinity Mews SE9 .... **12** D1
Tidford Rd DA16 .... **12** F5	TN15 .... **221** B5	Lamberhurst TN3 .... **317** A4	Trinity Pl Bexley DA6 ..... **13** F3
Tiger La BR2 .... **52** B5	Tonbridge TN4,TN9,	West Malling ME19 ..... **127** C1	Deal CT14 .... **215** A4
Tilbrook Rd SE3 .... **11** D4	TN11 .... **254** C6	Town La CT4 .... **173** C6	Ramsgate CT11 .... **117** F7
Tilbury Cl BR5 .... **54** B7	Tonbridge Castle ★	Townland Ct TN27 ...... **295** A2	Trinity Rd
Tilbury Fort ★ RM18 ..... **19** C3	TN9 .... **222** B2	Townlands Rd TN5 ...... **336** F4	Ashford TN24 .... **268** B7
Tilbury Manor Inf Sch	Tonbridge Chambers **10**	Townley Gram Sch for Girls	Folkestone CT20 .... **335** B4
RM18 .... **19** B7	TN9 .... **254** B8	DA6 ....**13** F2	Gillingham ME7 .... **64** C6
Tilbury Manor Jun Sch	Tonbridge Cottage Hospl	Townley Rd DA6 ....**13** F2	Gravesend DA12 .... **37** C8
RM18 .... **19** B7	TN11 .... **254** C6	Townley St CT1 .... **117** D6	Sheerness ME12 .... **28** C2
Tilbury PRU RM18 ...... **18** F6	Tonbridge Ct ME16 ..... **161** D3	Town Lock Ho **4** TN9 . **222** C2	Sittingbourne ME10 ..... **101** F7
Tilbury Rd ME8 .... **66** A2	Tonbridge Gram Sch for	Town Mdw TN17 .... **320** D4	Trinity Sch, Belvedere
Tilbury Town Sta RM18 ..**18** F5	Girls TN9 .... **254** C7	Town Pier Sq **5** DA11 ...**19** B1	DA17 ....**4** C2
Tilden Ct TN26 .... **324** D7	Tonbridge Ho ME2 .... **40** C1	Town Rd	Trinity Sch ME1 .... **63** D4
Tilden Ct TN26 .... **324** E1	Tonbridge Rd	Cliffe Woods ME3 .... **40** A6	Trinity Sq
Tilden Gill Rd TN30 .... **345** C7	Hadlow TN11 .... **223** C7	Petham CT4 .... **207** C5	Broadstairs CT10 .... **83** F7
Tilden La TN12 .... **227** C3	Ightham TN15 .... **156** C3	Townsend Farm Rd	Margate CT9 .... **50** J3
Tilden Rd ME17,TN27 ... **230** E2	Little Mill TN11,TN12 ... **224** D4	CT15 .... **279** F6	Trinity Trad Est CT19 ... **101** F6
Tilebarn Cnr TN10 ...... **222** E4	Maidstone,East Barming	Townsend Rd ME14 .... **127** F8	Tristan Gdns TN4 .... **285** D4
Tile Farm Rd BR6 .... **86** D7	ME16 .... **160** E1	Townsend Sq ME19 .... **159** A2	Triton Lodge **9** DA8 .....**4** E1
Tile Fields ME17 .... **164** D2	Maidstone,Upper Fant	Townsend Terr CT17 .... **310** B5	Tritton Ct CT14 .... **268** F7
Tile Ho The CT21 .... **333** C4	ME16 .... **161** C3	Townshend Cl DA14 ...... **31** C2	Tritton Fields TN24 .... **268** F7
Tilehurst Point **2** SE2 .....**3** A4	Pembury TN2 .... **287** A7	Townshend Ho **14** SE18 ....**1** F7	Tritton Gdns TN29 ..... **352** D1
Tile Kiln Hill CT2 .... **142** B5	Sevenoaks TN13,TN15 .. **187** D7	Townshend Rd BR7 .... **30** B3	Tritton La TN28 .... **373** B6
Tile Kiln La	Tonbridge TN11 .... **221** E5	Town Sq DA8 .... **14** E8	Triumph Rd E6 ....**1** F7
Coldblow DA5 .... **32** C6	Wateringbury ME18 ..... **192** C8	Town Square Cres DA9 ... **34** F8	Trivett Cl CT4 .... **174** B8
Dartford DA2,DA5 .... **32** F5	Tonbridge Sch TN10 .... **222** C3	Town Station Cotts	Trolling Down Hill DA2 .. **34** C6
Folkestone CT19 .... **334** F4	Tonbridge Sta TN9 ..... **222** B1	TN8 .... **217** D1	Troodos Hill ME14 ...... **161** F8
Tile Kiln Rd TN24 ...... **268** C7	Tonford La	Townwall St CT16 ...... **310** E7	Troon Cl SE28 ....**3** D7
Tile Lodge Cotts TN23 .. **233** E8	Canterbury CT1 .... **174** B6	Town Wlk CT20 .... **335** D4	Trosley Ave DA11 .... **37** B6
Tile Lodge Rd TN27 .... **233** E8	Harbledown CT2 .... **174** A7	Toynbec Cl BR7 .... **30** B4	Trosley Ctry Pk ★
Tilghman Way ME6 ...... **95** B1	Tonge Rd ME10 .... **102** C4	Toy's Hill TN16,TN8 .... **185** A8	ME19,DA13 .... **126** A7
Tillard Cl CT4 .... **207** B3	Tong La TN12 .... **289** B2	Tracies The ME9 .... **100** C6	Trosley Ctry Pk Visitor
Till Ave DA4 .... **56** F2	Tong Rd TN12,TN3 ...... **289** A4	Trader Rd E6 ....**2** B7	Ctr ★ DA13 .... **125** E7
Tillery La TN29 .... **371** A8	Tongswood Dr TN18 .... **341** C1	Tradescant Dr DA13 ..... **60** B3	Trosley Rd DA17 .... **14** A8
Tilley Cl ME3 .... **41** D5	Tontine St CT20 .... **335** E5	Tradewinds CT5 .... **108** B6	Trottiscliffe CE Prim Sch
Tillingbourne Gn BR5 ... **54** A5	Tony Law Ho SE12 ....**11** A2	Trafalgar Par ME12 ...... **47** B6	ME19 .... **126** D3
Tillmans TN15 .... **157** A7	Tookey Rd TN28 .... **373** B6	Trafalgar Rd	Trottiscliffe Rd ME19 .. **126** D3
Tilmans Mead DA4 ...... **57** A2	Tooley St DA11 .... **36** D8	Dartford DA1 .... **33** E6	Trotts Hall Gdns ME10 . **101** E3
Tilsden La TN17 .... **320** E3	Topaz Dr ME10 .... **101** C6	Gravesend DA11 .... **37** A8	Trotts La TN16 .... **184** C8
Tilton Rd TN15 .... **156** F7	Topcliffe Dr BR6 .... **86** D6	Westgate-on-S CT7 ...... **81** F3	Trotwood Cl ME5 .... **130** A8
Tilt Yard App SE9 .... **11** F1	Top Dartford Rd BR8,	Wouldham ME1 .... **95** C5	Trotwood Pl **14** CT10 .. **84** B4
Timberbank ME5 .... **97** A6	DA2 ....**33** A2	Trafalgar St ME7 .... **64** C5	Troubridge Cl TN24 .... **301** B7
Timber Bank DA13 ..... **125** F8	Topley Dr ME23 .... **23** E3	Tram Rd The CT20 ...... **335** E5	Troughton Mews CT9 .... **50** H1
Timber Cl BR7 .... **53** A7	Topley St SE9 ....**11** D3	Tramways ME5 .... **64** C2	Troughton Rd SE7 ....**1** B1
Timbercroft La SE18 ..... **12** E7	Top Rd TN30 .... **360** E3	Tranquil Rise DA8 ....**4** E1	Troutbeck Ho ME20 .... **128** C1
Timbercroft Prim Sch	Torbay Rd TN12 .... **225** B5	Transfesa Rd TN12 ..... **257** A7	Trove Ct **7** CT11 ..... **117** F7
SE18 ....**12** E7	Torbrook Cl DA5 ....**13** E1	Transformer Ave	Troy Ct **5** SE18 ....**2** B2
Timber Ct RM17 .... **18** A8	Tor Gr SE28 ....**2** E5	TN29 .... **380** C2	Troy La TN8 .... **216** F4
Timbertop Rd TN16 .... **118** C1	Tormore Mews CT14 ... **215** A4	Transmere Cl BR5 .... **53** C3	Troy Mews ME1 .... **63** C4
Timber Tops ME5 .... **130** D8	Tormore Pk CT14 .... **215** A4	Transmere Rd BR5 .... **53** C3	Troys Mead ME17 ...... **164** D2
Timeball Tower Mus ★	Tormount Rd SE18 .... **12** E8	Transom Ho **3** ME1 .... **63** C1	Troy Town La TN25 ..... **270** B5
CT14 .... **215** D5	Toronto Cl **6** CT16 ... **278** B3	Trapfield Cl ME14 ...... **163** C4	Trubridge Rd ME3 .... **41** E5
Timothy Cl DA6 ....**13** E3	Toronto Rd	Trapfield La ME14 ...... **163** C4	Trueman Cl CT2 .... **142** A7
Timothy Ho DA18 ....**3** E4	Gillingham ME7 ....**64** E4	Trapham Rd ME16 ...... **161** D5	Trumpet Ho TN23 ...... **300** B8
Timperley Ct CT14 ..... **215** B6	Tilbury RM18 .... **19** A5	Trasa Ct **10** RM17 ...... **18** C8	Truro Cl ME8 .... **65** D3
Tina Gdns CT10 .... **84** A6	Tor Rd DA16 .... **13** C6	Travers Gdns ME9 ...... **133** F5	Truro Rd
Tinbridge Pk CT5 .... **139** A5	Torrens Wlk DA12 .... **37** E3	Travers Rd CT14 .... **215** A5	Gravesend DA12 .... **37** D5
Tinker Pot La TN15 .... **123** D6	Torrington Ho ME18 ... **191** D8	Travertine Rd ME5 ...... **97** B1	Ramsgate CT11 .... **117** F7
Tinkerpot Rise TN15 ... **123** C5	Torrington Cotts	Treasury View CT3 ..... **177** C8	Truro Wlk TN10 .... **222** D5
Tinker's Alley ME4 ....**63** F7	CT12 .... **115** D7	Trebble Rd DA10 ....**17** E1	Trusedale Rd E6 ....**1** F7
Tinkers La TN5 .... **338** E3	Torrington Rd TN23 .... **300** C8	Trebilco Ct TN2 .... **286** D7	Trycewell La TN15 ...... **156** D6
Tintagel Gdns ME2 ....**62** F7	Torver Way BR6 .... **86** D7	Tredegar Rd DA2 .... **33** A5	Tuam Rd SE18 .... **12** D8
Tintagel Manor **6** ME7 . **64** C6	Tothill St CT12 .... **115** C7	Tredwell Cl BR1 .... **52** E5	Tubbenden Cl BR6 .... **86** D6
Tintagel Rd BR5 .... **54** C1	Totnes Rd DA16 ....**13** C7	Treebourne Rd TN16 ... **118** C1	Tubbenden Dr BR6 ...... **86** D6
Tintern Rd ME16 .... **161** D7	Tourmaline Dr ME10 .... **101** C6	Tree La TN15 .... **189** E8	Tubbenden La BR6 .... **86** E7
Tippens Ct TN17 .... **320** D4	Tournay Cl TN23 .... **299** F8	Tree Rd E16 ....**1** C7	Tubbenden La S BR6 ..... **86** D5
Titan Rd RM17 .... **18** B8	Tourney Cl CT21 .... **331** F3	Treetops CT5 .... **108** B6	Tubs Hall Cl TN13 ...... **154** A3
Titchfield Cl **5** ME15 . **195** F6	Tourney Rd TN29 .... **376** C5	Treetops Cl SE2 ....**3** E1	Tubs Hill TN13 .... **154** B3
Titchfield Rd ME15 .... **195** F6	Tourtel Rd CT1 .... **143** A1	Tudeley La	Tudeley La continued
Tithe Barn La TN23 .... **299** D8	Tovil Gn ME15 .... **161** E2	Tonbridge TN9 .... **254** D7	Tonbridge,Tudeley
Tithe Yd ME17 .... **199** D5	Tovil Green Bsns Pk		TN11,TN9 .... **255** B8
Titmuss Ave SE28 ....**3** B6	ME15 .... **161** E1		
Titsey Cnr RH8 .... **183** B7			Tudor Ave
Titsey Hill CR6,RH8 .... **150** B4			Dymchurch TN29 .... **352** D1
			Maidstone ME14 .... **162** B6

Tudor Byway TN24 ..... **268** D6	Turner St Cliffe ME3 ...... **22** B5
Tudor Cl Birchington CT7 ..**81** B8	Ramsgate CT11 .... **117** E7
Bromley BR7 .... **52** F8	Turnpike Cl CT21 .... **333** A2
Dartford DA1 .... **15** B1	Turnpike Dr BR6 .... **87** D2
Northfleet DA11 .... **36** E7	Turnpike Hill CT21 ..... **333** A3
Tudor Cres TN14 .... **122** D3	Turnpike La RM18 .... **19** D8
Tudor Ct	Turnstone Cl ME5 .... **68** E4
Biggin Hill TN16 .... **118** E2	Turnstone Ct TN29 ..... **365** F3
Canterbury CT2 .... **142** C4	Turnstone DA3 .... **59** A7
Crockenhill BR8 .... **55** C2	Turnstones The DA12 .... **37** D6
Royal Tunbridge Wells	Turpington Cl BR2 .... **52** E2
TN2 .... **285** E1	Turpington La BR2 .... **52** E3
Sidcup DA14 .... **31** A3	Turpin La DA8 .... **14** F1
Whitstable CT5 .... **75** A3	Turrets The Deal CT14 .. **215** C1
Tudor Dr TN14 .... **122** C3	**9** Sittingbourne ME10 .. **102** A4
Tudor End TN24 .... **268** D5	Turton Ho **5** SE18 ...... **12** B8
Tudor Farm Cl TN23 .... **300** A3	Tuscan Dr ME5 .... **97** C1
Tudor Gr	Tuscan Rd SE18 ....**2** D1
Chattenden ME3 .... **40** F4	Tutsham Way TN12 .... **256** F6
Gillingham ME8 .... **98** F8	Tuxford Rd ME4 .... **285** B5
Tudor Ho Deal CT14 .... **215** A5	Tweed Rd TN10 .... **222** C5
Tudor Mews ME14 ..... **215** B4	Tweedy Rd BR1 .... **52** A8
Tudor Par SE9 ....**11** E3	Twelve Acres TN24 ..... **300** F8
Tudor Rd Ashford TN24 . **268** D5	Twigg Cl DA8 .... **14** E7
Canterbury CT1 .... **174** E7	Twin Tumps Way SE28 ....**3** A6
Folkestone CT19 .... **334** D6	Twisden Rd ME19 ...... **159** F8
Tudor Way BR5 .... **53** D3	Twiss Ave CT21 .... **333** D2
Tudor Wlk DA5 ....**13** E1	Twiss Gr CT21 .... **333** D2
Tudway Rd SE3 .... **11** C3	Twiss Ho **6** SE18 ....**2** B1
Tufa Cl ME5 .... **97** B1	Twiss Rd CT21 .... **333** D2
Tuffs Cotts ME3 .... **25** C3	Twistleton Ct DA1 .... **15** D1
Tufnail Rd DA1 .... **15** F1	Twitton La TN14 .... **121** E3
Tufton Rd	Twitton Mdws TN14 ... **121** E3
Ashford TN24 .... **268** D2	Two Gates Hill ME3 ...... **39** F5
Hothfield TN26 .... **267** A7	Twydall Ent Ctr ME8 ..... **65** C4
Rainham ME8 .... **65** F1	Twydall Gn ME8 .... **65** B3
Tufton St Ashford TN23 . **268** B2	Twydall Inf Sch ME8 ..... **65** B2
Maidstone ME14 .... **162** A4	Twydall Jun Sch ME8 .... **65** B2
Tufton Wlk **9** TN23 .. **268** B2	Twydall La ME8 .... **65** B2
Tugboat St SE28 ....**2** E4	Twyford Cl ME8 .... **66** A2
Tugmutton Cl BR6 .... **86** B6	Twyford Ct ME14 ...... **162** D6
Tulip Cl E6 ....**1** F8	Twyford Rd TN11 ...... **190** E1
Tulip Tree Cl TN9 ...... **254** B8	Twyman Cl ME14 .... **159** E1
Tumblefield Est TN15 .. **124** F8	Twymans Mill ME13 ... **138** C7
Tumblefield Rd TN15 .. **124** E7	Twyne Cl CT2 .... **144** A6
Tumblers Hill ME17 .... **229** F7	Twysden Cotts TN18 ... **356** A4
Tunbridge Way TN23 ... **299** C8	Twysden Ct TN25 ...... **237** E2
Tunbridge Wells Girls'	Tydeman Rd ME15 ...... **162** F2
Gram Sch TN4 .... **286** A6	Tydeman's Ave CT5 ...... **75** C1
Tunbridge Wells Gram Sch	Tye La BR6 .... **86** C5
for Boys TN4 .... **286** A7	Tyeshurst Cl SE2 ....**3** E1
Tunbridge Wells High Sch	Tyland Barn Wildlife
TN2 .... **286** B4	Conservation Ctr ★
Tunbridge Wells Ind Hospl	ME14 .... **129** E3
The TN3 .... **284** B3	Tyland La ME14 .... **129** F3
Tunbridge Wells Mus &	East Malling ME19 ..... **159** F8
Gall ★ TN1 .... **286** B4	Erith DA8 .... **14** B7
Tunbridge Wells Sta	Tyler Dr ME8 .... **98** E4
TN1 .... **286** A3	Tyler Gr DA1 ....**15** F3
Tunbridge Wells Trad Pk	Tyler Hill Rd CT2 .... **142** C6
TN2 .... **286** D8	Tylers Green BR8 .... **55** C2
Tunbridge Wells West	Tyler Way CT5 .... **75** E3
Sta ★ TN2 .... **285** F1	Tylney Rd BR1 .... **52** D7
Tunbury Ave ME5 .... **96** F1	Tyndale Pk CT6 .... **77** B5
Tunbury Ave S ME5 ...... **96** F1	Tyndall Rd DA16 ....**12** F4
Tunbury Prim Sch ME5 .. **96** F1	Tyne Cl ME5 .... **97** C5
Tunis Cl CT1 .... **143** D1	Tynedale Cl DA2 .... **34** D7
Tunis Row CT10 .... **84** B5	Tyne Rd TN10 .... **222** B5
Tunnan Leys E6 ....**2** A7	Typhoon Rd ME19 ...... **158** F3
Tunnel Ave **1** SE10 .....**1** A1	Tyron Way DA14 .... **30** F2
Tunnel Cotts RM20 ...... **17** A8	Tyrrell Ave DA16 ....**13** B2
Tunnel Est RM20 .... **16** F8	Tyrrells Hall Cl **5**
Tunnel Rd TN1 .... **286** B4	RM17 .... **18** D8
Tunstall CE Prim Sch	Tyrwhitt-Drake Mus of
ME9 .... **134** C8	Carriages ★ ME15 .... **162** A3
Tunstall Cl BR6 .... **86** E6	Tysoe Ct ME12 .... **47** A5
Tunstall Rd	Tyson Ave CT9 .... **50** E1
Canterbury CT2 .... **143** A4	Tyson Rd CT19 .... **335** E7

U
Uckfield La TN8 .... **250** D4
Udall Cotts DA15 .... **30** E5
Uden Rd TN29 .... **353** B4
Uffington Ct CT3 .... **178** A2
Ufton Cl ME15 .... **162** E1
Ufton La ME10 .... **101** E3
Ulcombe CE Prim Sch
ME17 .... **230** F6
Ulcombe Gdns CT2 ..... **143** A3
Ulcombe Hill ME17 .... **197** F1
Ulcombe Rd
Headcorn TN27 .... **262** C6
Langley Heath ME17 ... **196** F3
Ulley Rd TN24 .... **268** D7
Ullswater Gdns CT3 .... **210** F6
Ullswater Ho **5** ME15 . **195** E7
Ulster Rd CT19 .... **82** F8
Undercliffe Rd CT14 ... **248** D5
Undercliff CT20 .... **334** E3
Underdown Ave ME4 .....**63** F1
Underdown La CT6 .... **76** F2
Underdown Rd
Dover CT17 .... **310** B7
Herne Bay ME3 .... **76** F5
Underhill Cotts CT18 ... **334** B8
Underhill Rd CT18 ..... **334** B5
Underlyn Ind Est
TN12 .... **227** F2
Underlyn La TN12 ...... **227** D1
Underriver House Rd
TN15 .... **188** D5
Underwood Cl
Ashford TN24 .... **268** D6

Underwood Cl continued
Canterbury CT4 . . . . **175** B5
Maidstone ME15 . . . . **161** F2
Underwood Ct CT1 . . . . . **175** B6
Underwood
Hawkinge CT18 . . . . **307** C6
Offham ME19 . . . . **158** D7
Underwood The SE9 . . . . . **29** F6
Unicorn Cotts CT4 . . . . . **176** B5
Unicorn Wlk DA9 . . . . **16** F2
Unicumes La ME16 . . . . . **161** C2
Union Cres CT9 . . . . **50** J2
Union Pk ME15 . . . . **195** F4
Union Pl
4 Canterbury CT1 . . . . . **143** A1
Chatham ME4 . . . . **64** A4
Union Rd Bridge CT4 . . . **175** F1
Bromley BR2 . . . . **52** D4
Deal CT14 . . . . **215** D6
Minster (Sheppey) ME12 . . **47** C7
Ramsgate CT11 . . . . **117** F8
Union Row CT9 . . . . **50** J2
Union Sq
3 Broadstairs CT10 . . . . **84** B4
22 Royal Tunbridge Wells
TN2 . . . . **286** A2
Union St
Canterbury CT1 . . . . **143** A1
Chatham ME4 . . . . **64** A3
Dover CT17 . . . . **310** D6
Faversham ME13 . . . . . . **138** C7
Flimwell TN5 . . . . **339** B3
Maidstone ME14 . . . . . . **162** A5
12 Ramsgate CT11 . . . . . **117** E7
Rochester ME1 . . . . **63** C5
Sheerness ME12 . . . . **28** A2
Unity Pl 3 CT11 . . . . . . **117** E7
Unity St Sheerness ME12 . **28** D2
Sittingbourne ME10 . . . . **101** E3
Unity Way SE18 . . . . **1** D3
University Gdns DA5 . . . . **31** F8
University Pl DA8 . . . . **14** C7
University Rd CT2 . . . . . . **142** D3
University Way
Dartford DA1 . . . . **15** E4
Woolwich SE18 . . . . **2** B6
Univ of East London E16 . **2** A6
Univ of Greenwich Avery
Hill Campus (Mansion
Site) SE9 . . . . **12** C1
Univ of Greenwich Avery
Hill Campus (Southwood
Site) SE9 . . . . **12** D1
Univ of Greenwich Avery
Hill Campus Southwood
Site SE9 . . . . **30** D8
Univ of Greenwich
ME4 . . . . **64** B8
Univ of Kent at Canterbury
CT2 . . . . **142** D4
Unwin Cl ME20 . . . . **129** A3
Upbury Arts Coll ME7 . . . **64** B4
Upbury Way ME4 . . . . **64** A4
Upchat Rd ME2,ME3 . . . . **40** F3
Upchurch Wlk CT9 . . . . . . **51** E2
Updale Rd DA14 . . . . **30** F4
Updown Way CT4 . . . . . . **173** F1
Uphill CT18 . . . . **307** B4
Upland Prim Sch DA7 . . . **13** F4
Upland Rd DA7 . . . . **13** F4
Uplands CT2 . . . . **142** F4
Uplands Cl
Rochester ME2 . . . . **62** D6
Sevenoaks TN13 . . . . . . **153** F4
Uplands Com Tech Coll
TN5 . . . . **337** A4
Uplands Rd BR6 . . . . **54** B1
Uplands Way
Halfway Houses ME12 . . . **46** C5
Sevenoaks TN13 . . . . . . **153** F4
Uplands SE18 . . . . **3** B1
Uplees Cotts ME13 . . . . . **104** F5
Uplees Rd ME13 . . . . **105** A3
Upnor Castle ★ ME2 . . . . **40** F2
Upnor Ho ME15 . . . . **195** E8
Upnor Rd ME2 . . . . **40** E2
Upper Abbey Rd DA17 . . . **4** A2
Upper Approach Rd
CT10 . . . . **84** A3
Upper Austin Lodge Farm
Cotts **89** D4
Upper Austin Lodge Rd
DA4 . . . . **89** D4
Upper Ave DA13 . . . . **189** E3
Upper Barn Hill ME15 . . **193** E3
Upper Brents ME13 . . . . **138** D8
Upper Bridge St
Canterbury CT1 . . . . **175** A8
Wye TN25 . . . . **237** F2
Upper Britton Pl ME7 . . . **64** B5
Upper Bush Rd ME2 . . . . . **61** F2
Upper Chantry La
CT1 . . . . **175** A7
Upper Church Hill DA9 . . **16** D2
Upper Corniche CT20 . . **334** C3
Upper Cumberland Wlk
TN1 . . . . **286** B1
Upper Dane Ct TN9 . . . . . **51** B1
Upper Dane Rd CT9 . . . . . **51** B1
Upper Denmark Rd
TN23 . . . . **300** B8
Upper Dr TN16 . . . . **118** C1
Upper Dumpton Park Rd
CT11 . . . . **117** D8
Upper Dunstan Rd
TN4 . . . . **286** B6
Upper East Rd ME4 . . . . . **64** B8
Upper Fans La ME9 . . . . . **68** C4
Upper Fant Rd ME16 . . . **161** D2
Upper Field Rd ME10 . . . **102** B5

Upper Free Down CT6 . . . **77** B2
Upper Gore La CT13 . . . **180** A2
Upper Green La TN11 . . . **189** D5
Upper Green Rd TN11 . . **189** D5
Upper Gr CT7 . . . . **50** J2
Upper Grosvenor Rd
TN1,TN4 . . . . **286** B6
Upper Grove Rd DA17 . . . **13** F8
Upper Haysden La
TN11,TN9 . . . . **253** E6
Upper Holly Hill Rd
DA17 . . . . **4** B1
Upper Hunton Hill
ME15 . . . . **194** A3
Upper Luton Rd ME5 . . . . **64** C2
Upper Malthouse Hill
CT21 . . . . **333** B2
Upper Maltings Pl CT7 . . **80** F7
Upper Mill ME18 . . . . . . **192** D8
Upper Nellington TN3 . . **285** B4
Upper Park Rd
Bromley BR1 . . . . **52** C8
Erith DA17 . . . . **4** B2
Upper Platts TN5 . . . . . . **338** F1
Upper Profit TN3 . . . . . . **285** A3
Upper Queens Rd
TN24 . . . . **268** B3
Upper Rd
Dover CT15,CT16 . . . . . **279** C2
Dover,Eastern Docks
CT16 . . . . **310** G8
Maidstone ME15 . . . . . . **162** B2
Upper Ruxley Cotts
DA14 . . . . **32** A1
Upper St Ann's Rd
ME13 . . . . **138** B6
Upper Sheridan Rd
DA17 . . . . **4** A2
Upper Spring La TN15 . . **156** B5
Upper Stephens TN3 . . . **285** A3
Upper St
Hollingbourne ME17 . . . **164** E3
Kingsdown CT14 . . . . . . **248** D5
Leeds ME17 . . . . **196** F5
Upper Stone St ME15 . . **162** A3
Upper Strand St CT13 . . **149** A1
Upper Street N DA3 . . . . . **91** F8
Upper Street S DA3 . . . . . **91** F8
Upper St Rusthall TN4 . . **285** D4
Tilmanstone CT14 . . . . . **213** A3
Upper Tickham Cotts
ME9 . . . . **136** D6
Upperton Rd DA14 . . . . . . **30** F3
Upper Vicarage Rd
TN24 . . . . **268** D7
Upper Wickham La
DA16 . . . . **13** B6
Upstreet CT18 . . . . **305** D3
Upton Cl Bexley DA5 . . . . **13** F1
Folkestone CT19 . . . . . . **335** A7
Upton Day Hospl DA6 . . . **13** E3
Upton Jun Sch CT10 . . . . **83** F4
Upton Prim Sch DA6 . . . . **13** F2
Upton Quarry TN3 . . . . . **284** F3
Upton Rd
Bexley DA5,DA6 . . . . **13** E2
Broadstairs CT10 . . . . . . **83** F5
Upton Rd S DA5 . . . . **13** F1
Upton Rd SE SE18 . . . . . . **12** C8
Uptons TN27 . . . . **262** C6
Upton Villas DA6 . . . . . . **13** E1
Upwood Rd SE12 . . . . **11** A1
Uridge Cres TN10 . . . . . **222** C4
Uridge Rd TN10 . . . . **222** C4
Urquhart Cl ME5 . . . . **97** A5
Ursula Lodges DA14 . . . . **31** B3
Ursuline Dr CT8 . . . . **81** D7
Usborne Cl TN12 . . . . . . **260** E3

V

Vaizeys Wharf SE7 . . . . . . **1** B3
Vale Ave
Royal Tunbridge
Wells,Mount Sion TN1 . **286** A3
Royal Tunbridge
Wells,Southborough
TN4 . . . . **253** F1
Valebrook Cl CT20 . . . . **334** C5
Vale Cl BR6 . . . . **86** A6
Vale Cotts ME9 . . . . **133** A8
Vale Ct
10 Ramsgate CT11 . . . . **117** D6
Royal Tunbridge Wells
TN4 . . . . **254** A2
Vale Dr ME5 . . . . **96** E6
Valence Ho ME15 . . . . . **195** C7
Valence Rd DA8 . . . . **14** D7
Valence Sch TN16 . . . . . **151** F1
Valence View TN17 . . . . **293** E7
Valenciennes Ho ME4 . . . **64** A4
Valenciennes Rd
ME10 . . . . **101** E3
Valentine Ave DA5 . . . . . . **31** E7
Valentine Cl ME7 . . . . **65** A1
Valentine Dr ME23 . . . . . **23** E4
Valentine Rd ME15 . . . . **195** E7
Vale Pl CT11 . . . . **117** D6
Vale Rd Broadstairs CT10 . **83** F4
Bromley BR1 . . . . **52** C8
Dartford DA1 . . . . **33** B7
Hawkhurst TN18 . . . . . . **340** F3
Maidstone ME15 . . . . . . **194** E4
Northfleet DA11 . . . . **36** E7
Ramsgate CT11 . . . . **117** D6
Ripple CT14,CT15 . . . . . **247** B8
Royal Tunbridge
Wells,Mount Sion TN1 . **286** A3
Royal Tunbridge
Wells,Southborough
TN4 . . . . **253** F1
Tonbridge TN9 . . . . **222** C1

Vale Rd continued
Whitstable CT5 . . . . **108** D8
Valerian Cl ME5 . . . . **96** E4
Vale Rise TN9 . . . . **254** E8
Vale Sq CT11 . . . . **117** D6
Vale The CT10 . . . . **84** A4
Valetta Way ME1 . . . . **63** B4
Vale View Com Sch
CT17 . . . . **310** B7
Vale View Rd
Aylesham CT3 . . . . **210** E5
Dover CT17 . . . . **310** B7
Valiant Ho 5 SE7 . . . . **1** C1
Valiant Rd ME5 . . . . **97** C2
Valkyrie Ave CT5 . . . . . . **108** C7
Vallance The ME9 . . . . . **136** A6
Valley (Charlton Athletic
FC) The SE7 . . . . **1** C1
Valley Cl DA1 . . . . **14** F1
Valley Cotts
Alkham CT15 . . . . **276** C5
Stalisfield Green ME13 . . **201** D8
Valley Dr
Gravesend,Riverview Park
DA12 . . . . **37** D4
Gravesend,Singlewell
DA12 . . . . **37** E1
Maidstone ME15 . . . . . . **194** F6
Sevenoaks TN13 . . . . . . **154** B1
Valley Forge Cl TN10 . . . **222** F4
Valley Gdns DA9 . . . . **17** B1
Valley Gr SE7 . . . . **1** C1
Valley Hts DA1 . . . . **15** F3
Valley Industries
TN11 . . . . **223** B7
Valley La DA13 . . . . **93** B2
Valley L Ctr SE9 . . . . **30** C8
Valley Mushroom Farm
TN16 . . . . **118** D1
Valley Park Com Sch
ME14 . . . . **162** C4
Valley Rd Barham CT4 . . **209** E2
Canterbury CT1 . . . . **174** E6
Crabble CT17 . . . . **277** E3
Crayford DA1 . . . . **14** F1
Erith DA8 . . . . **4** D2
Fawkham Green DA3 . . . . **58** C2
Folkestone CT20 . . . . . . **334** E4
Gillingham ME7 . . . . **64** E4
Margate CT9 . . . . **82** E4
Orpington BR5 . . . . **54** B8
Rusthall TN4 . . . . **285** D4
Valley Rise ME5 . . . . **96** F1
Valley The ME17 . . . . **194** D3
Valleyside SE7 . . . . **1** D1
Valley View
Biggin Hill TN16 . . . . . . **118** D1
Eythorne CT15 . . . . **245** C8
Valley View Rd ME1 . . . . . **63** B1
Valley View
Royal Tunbridge Wells
TN4 . . . . **254** A2
Swanscombe DA9 . . . . . . **17** B1
Valley View Terr DA4 . . . . **56** F1
Valley Wlk CT21 . . . . **334** B3
Valliers Wood Rd DA15 . . **30** E7
Vambery Rd SE18 . . . . **2** C8
Vanbrugh Cl 2 E16 . . . . . **1** D8
Vanbrugh Pk SE3 . . . . **11** A7
Vanburgh Cl BR6 . . . . **53** E1
Vancouver Cl BR6 . . . . . . **87** A6
Vancouver Dr ME8 . . . . . . **65** C1
Vancouver Rd CT16 . . . . **278** C3
Vandome Cl E16 . . . . **1** B7
Vandyke Cross SE9 . . . . . **11** E2
Vanessa Cl DA17 . . . . **4** A1
Vanessa Way DA5 . . . . **32** D5
Vanessa Wlk DA12 . . . . . . **37** F3
Vange Cottage Mews
ME1 . . . . **63** B4
Vanguard Cl E16 . . . . **1** A8
Vanguard Way ME7 . . . . . **63** B8
Vanity Holiday Village
ME12 . . . . **49** G2
Vanity La ME17 . . . . **194** D1
Vanity Rd ME12 . . . . **49** F2
Vanoc Gdns BR1 . . . . **29** A4
Vanquisher Wlk DA12 . . . **37** F5
Varley Rd E16 . . . . **1** B7
Varne Cl 6 CT20 . . . . . . **334** F3
Varne Lodge 5 CT20 . . . **334** F3
Varne Mews TN28 . . . . . **373** E4
Varne Pl CT19 . . . . **335** F5
Varne Rd CT19 . . . . **335** F5
Varnes St ME20 . . . . **128** F6
Vaughan Ave TN10 . . . . . **222** E6
Vaughan Dr ME10 . . . . . **101** F8
Vaughan Rd DA16 . . . . . . **12** F5
Vauxhall Ave
Canterbury CT1 . . . . **143** C3
Herne Bay CT6 . . . . **76** A3
Vauxhall Cl DA11 . . . . **36** F8
Vauxhall Cres
Canterbury CT1 . . . . **143** C3
Snodland ME6 . . . . **128** A6
Vauxhall Gdns TN9 . . . . **254** C7
Vauxhall Industrial Rd
CT1 . . . . **143** D4
Vauxhall La
Bidborough TN11,TN4 . . **254** B4
Tonbridge TN11 . . . . . . **254** D6
Vauxhall Pl DA1 . . . . **33** E8
Vauxhall Rd CT1,CT2 . . . **143** C4
Vectis Dr ME10 . . . . **101** F8
Veitchii Barn BR8 . . . . **55** F8
Veles Rd ME6 . . . . **127** F8
Venmead Ct 4 DA17 . . . . . **4** A2
Venners Ct **14** E5
Ventnor Cl ME5 . . . . **97** C8
Ventnor La 12 CT9 . . . . . **50** J2

Venture Cl
Dymchurch TN29 . . . . . **352** D1
Sidcup DA5 . . . . **31** E8
Venture Ct SE12 . . . . **29** A8
Venus Rd SE18 . . . . **1** F7
Verdun Rd SE18,SE2 . . . . **13** A8
Vere Rd CT10 . . . . **84** A4
Vereth Rd 2 CT11 . . . . . **117** D6
Verity Farm Holiday Camp
ME12 . . . . **49** F1
Vermont Rd TN4 . . . . . . **285** C4
Vernham Rd SE18 . . . . . . **12** C8
Vernon Cl Orpington BR5 . **54** B6
West Kingsdown TN15 . . . **90** F2
Vernon Pl
Canterbury CT1 . . . . **175** A7
Deal CT14 . . . . **215** D8
Vernon Rd
Royal Tunbridge Wells
TN1 . . . . **286** C6
Swanscombe DA10 . . . . . **17** C1
Veroan Rd DA7 . . . . **13** E5
Verona Ho DA8 . . . . **14** F7
Verona Rd DA8 . . . . **14** F7
Vert Ho RM17 . . . . **18** C7
Verwood Cl CT2 . . . . **142** E2
Veryan Cl BR5 . . . . **54** C5
Vespasian Way TN23 . . . **299** F4
Vesper Ct TN27 . . . . **264** A1
Vestey Ct CT8 . . . . **50** C1
Vestry Cotts
New Barn DA3 . . . . **59** C5
Sevenoaks TN14 . . . . . . **154** C8
Vestry Rd TN14 . . . . **154** C8
Viaduct Cl CT12 . . . . **117** C8
Viaduct Terr
Hamstreet TN26 . . . . . . **348** F7
Sutton at H DA4 . . . . **57** C7
Viaduct The CT17 . . . . . **310** D5
Via Romana DA2 . . . . **38** B7
Viburnum Cl TN23 . . . . . **267** E2
Vicarage Ave SE3 . . . . **11** A7
Vicarage Cl
Aylesford ME20 . . . . **128** F3
Erith DA8 . . . . **14** C8
Halling ME2 . . . . **95** A5
Stoke ME3 . . . . **25** A3
Vicarage Cotts ME9 . . . . **67** C3
Vicarage Cres 8 DA12 . . . **37** J1
Vicarage Ct Chalk DA12 . . **38** A7
Newington ME9 . . . . **100** B7
Vicarage Dr DA11 . . . . . . **18** C1
Vicarage Gdn CT12 . . . . **114** C7
Vicarage Gdns CT3 . . . . **178** A7
Vicarage Hill
Petham CT4 . . . . **207** B4
Westerham TN16 . . . . . **151** D1
Vicarage La
Ashford TN23 . . . . **268** C2
Blean CT2 . . . . **142** A6
Chalk DA12 . . . . **38** A6
Charing Heath TN27 . . . **233** C7
Deal CT14 . . . . **214** F5
East Farleigh ME15 . . . . **194** B6
Elham CT4 . . . . **273** F4
Faversham ME13 . . . . . **138** A4
Hoo St Werburgh ME3 . . . **41** E4
Lower Halstow ME9 . . . . **67** C3
Nonington CT15 . . . . . . **211** C5
St Margaret's at Cliffe
CT15 . . . . **279** F6
4 Sandwich CT13 . . . . **148** F1
Selling ME13 . . . . **171** C6
Sevenoaks TN13 . . . . . . **153** D8
Tilmanstone CT14 . . . . . **213** A3
Vicarage Pk SE18 . . . . **2** C1
Vicarage Pl CT9 . . . . **50** J1
Vicarage Rd
Coldblow DA5 . . . . **32** B7
Folkestone CT20 . . . . . . **334** F3
Gillingham ME7 . . . . **64** C5
Halling ME2 . . . . **94** F5
Minster (Sheppey) ME12 . **47** D2
Rochester ME2 . . . . **63** B8
Royal Tunbridge Wells
TN4 . . . . **253** F2
Sittingbourne ME10 . . . **101** E6
Woolwich SE18 . . . . **2** C1
Yalding ME18 . . . . **193** A1
Vicarage Row ME3 . . . . . **39** C4
Vicarage Sq RM17 . . . . . . **18** A8
Vicarage St
Broadstairs CT10 . . . . . . **83** E5
Faversham ME13 . . . . . **138** D6
Vicarage Way TN19 . . . . **354** A3
Vicary Way ME16 . . . . . . **161** D5
Vickers Cl CT18 . . . . **307** A4
Vickers Rd DA8 . . . . **4** D1
Victor Ave CT9 . . . . **51** D2
Victoria Ave
Broadstairs CT10 . . . . . . **83** E8
3 Gravesend DA12 . . . . **37** B8
Hythe CT21 . . . . **333** D1
Margate CT9 . . . . **51** B1
St Margaret's at Cliffe
CT15 . . . . **280** B6
Westgate-on-S CT8 . . . . **81** F8
Victoria Bglws DA16 . . . . **13** B5
Victoria Bsns Ctr DA16 . . **13** B5
Victoria Cl
Chatham ME5 . . . . **96** D2
Edenbridge TN8 . . . . . . **249** C8
Victoria Cotts
Cranbrook TN17 . . . . . . **320** D5
Edenbridge TN8 . . . . . . **249** C8
Victoria Cres
Ashford TN23 . . . . **268** B1
Dover CT16 . . . . **310** D8
Victoria Ct Hythe CT21 . . **333** C1
6 Maidstone ME16 . . . . **161** B2
Victoria Dock Rd E16 . . . . **1** B6
Victoria Dr TN16 . . . . . . **76** C5
Victoria Dr ME19 . . . . . . **158** F1

Victoria Dr DA4 . . . . **57** D7
Victoria Gdns TN16 . . . . **118** C4
Victoria Gr
12 Folkestone CT20 . . . **335** D5
Hythe CT21 . . . . **334** B2
Victoria Hill Rd BR8 . . . . **56** A8
Victoria Hospl SE14 . . . . **215** B5
Victoria Ho 7 CT5 . . . . . **74** D2
Victoria Ind Pk DA1 . . . . . **15** E2
Victoria Mews
Deal CT14 . . . . **215** C6
Westgate-on-S CT8 . . . . **50** D1
Victoria Orch ME16 . . . . **161** B3
Victoria Par CT10 . . . . . . **84** B4
Victoria Park Mews 2
CT16 . . . . **310** E8
Victoria Par CT11 . . . . . **117** F7
Victoria Pk Dover CT16 . . **310** E8
Herne Bay CT6 . . . . **77** A5
Victoria Pl
Faversham ME13 . . . . . **138** C7
Hythe CT21 . . . . **333** B4
Victoria Rd
Ashford TN23 . . . . **268** B1
Bexley DA6 . . . . **14** A3
Broadstairs CT10 . . . . . . **83** E6
Bromley BR2 . . . . **52** D4
Canterbury CT1 . . . . **174** E7
Capel-le-F CT18 . . . . . . **308** B2
Chatham,Luton ME4 . . . . **64** B2
Chatham,Walderslade
ME5 . . . . **96** E3
Chislehurst BR7 . . . . **30** A3
Dartford DA1 . . . . **15** E2
Deal CT14 . . . . **215** D5
Edenbridge TN8 . . . . . . **249** C8
Erith DA8 . . . . **14** E8
Folkestone CT19 . . . . . . **335** C5
Golden Green TN11 . . . . **223** F6
Hythe CT21 . . . . **333** C1
Kingsdown CT14 . . . . . . **248** C4
Littlestone-on-Sea TN28 . **373** E5
Margate CT9 . . . . **50** J2
Margate,Lydden CT9 . . . . **82** D4
Northfleet DA11 . . . . **36** F7
Ramsgate CT11 . . . . **117** F7
Royal Tunbridge
Wells,Southborough
TN4 . . . . **253** E1
Royal Tunbridge Wells
TN1 . . . . **286** B4
Sevenoaks TN13 . . . . . . **154** B2
Sidcup DA15 . . . . **31** A5
Sittingbourne ME10 . . . **101** D4
Victoria Rd W TN28 . . . . **373** E5
Victoria Road Prim Sch
TN23 . . . . **268** B1
Victoria Row
Canterbury CT1 . . . . **143** A1
Ramsgate CT11 . . . . **117** F7
Victoria Scott Ct DA1 . . . **14** F4
Victoria St Dover CT17 . . **278** B1
Eccles ME20 . . . . **128** F6
Erith DA17 . . . . **3** F1
Gillingham ME7 . . . . **64** D6
Maidstone ME16 . . . . . . **161** E3
New Romney TN28 . . . . **373** A6
Rochester ME1 . . . . **63** D5
Rochester,Strood ME2 . . . **63** B7
Sheerness ME12 . . . . . . **28** C1
Whitstable CT5 . . . . **74** D2
Victoria Terr
Hythe CT21 . . . . **334** B2
Minster (Sheppey) ME12 . **48** A5
Rochester ME1 . . . . **63** A2
Sittingbourne ME10 . . . **101** D4
Victoria Way SE7 . . . . **1** B1
Victoria Wharf DA1 . . . . . **15** E2
Victoria Yd 22 CT1 . . . . . **143** A1
Victor Mills Cotts DA14 . . **32** A1
Victory Cotts TN14 . . . . **187** C2
Victory Lodge ME8 . . . . . **63** F8
Victory Manor 1 ME7 . . . **64** A6
Victory Pk ME2 . . . . **63** E7
Victory Rd CT15 . . . . **247** F5
Victory St ME12 . . . . **28** B2
Victory Way DA2 . . . . **16** C3
Vidal Manor ME7 . . . . . . **64** C5
Vidgeon Ave ME3 . . . . **41** D6
View Cl TN16 . . . . **118** C3
Viewfield Rd DA5 . . . . **31** C7
Viewland Rd SE18 . . . . **2** F1
Viewlands Ave TN16 . . . **151** F7
Viewlands ME5 . . . . **64** C3
Viewpoint Ct DA3 . . . . . . **58** F5
Viewpoint ME14 . . . . **162** C8
View Rd ME3 . . . . **40** B7
View The SE2 . . . . **3** E1
Vigilant Way DA12 . . . . . . **37** F3
Vigo Hill ME19,TN15 . . . **125** E6
Vigo Rd TN15 . . . . **125** C7
Vigo Terr ME9 . . . . **103** C1
Vigo Village Sch
DA13 . . . . **126** A8
Viking Cl
Birchington CT7 . . . . **80** D8
Rochester ME2 . . . . **62** F4
Viking Ct
Broadstairs CT10 . . . . . . **84** B3
Canterbury CT2 . . . . **142** F2
Margate CT9 . . . . **51** B2
Viking Ho 3 SE18 . . . . **1** F7
Viking Rd DA11 . . . . **36** C5
Viking Ship ★ CT12 . . . **116** E5
Viking Way Erith DA8 . . . . **4** F3
West Kingsdown TN15 . . . **90** F8
Villa Cl DA12 . . . . **38** B6
Villacourt Rd SE18,SE2 . . **13** A8
Villa Cl DA12 . . . . **33** E6
Village Green Ave
TN16 . . . . **118** C4
Village Green Rd DA1 . . . **15** A3

Village Green Way
TN16 . . . . **118** E2
Village The SE7 . . . . **11** D8
Village View ME5 . . . . **64** C2
Village Way TN26 . . . . . . **349** A7
Villa Rd ME3 . . . . **39** B3
Villas Ct CT17 . . . . **310** C7
Villas The CT3 . . . . **112** A1
Villiers Ct CT17 . . . . **310** C7
Villiers Ho CT10 . . . . **84** B7
Villiers Rd CT1 . . . . **143** D1
Vincent Cl
Broadstairs CT10 . . . . . . **83** C3
Bromley BR2 . . . . **52** B5
Folkestone CT20 . . . . . . **334** E5
Sidcup DA15 . . . . **30** E7
Vincent Ct ME12 . . . . **28** C1
Vincent Gdns ME12 . . . . . **28** C1
Vincent Pl TN24 . . . . **268** F4
Vincent Rd
Kit's Coty ME20 . . . . **129** C7
Margate CT9 . . . . **82** C4
Sittingbourne ME10 . . . **102** C3
Woolwich SE18 . . . . **2** B2
Vincent Sq TN16 . . . . . . **118** C6
Vincent St 13 E16 . . . . . . **1** A8
Vine Ave TN13 . . . . **154** B3
Vine Cl CT11 . . . . **83** E2
Vine Court Rd TN13 . . . . **154** C4
Vine Ct
16 Gravesend DA11 . . . . **19** B1
Staplehurst TN12 . . . . . **260** F3
Wateringbury ME18 . . . . **192** D8
Vine End CT11 . . . . **83** E2
Vine Lands TN29 . . . . . . **376** B6
Vine Lodge TN13 . . . . . . **154** C3
Vine Lo CT11 . . . . **83** E2
Vine Rd BR6 . . . . **86** F4
Vineries The ME7 . . . . . . **64** E5
Viners Cl ME10 . . . . **101** F1
Vines La
Hildenborough TN11 . . . **188** C1
Rochester ME1 . . . . **63** C5
Vine The TN13 . . . . **154** C3
Vine Wlk TN12 . . . . **260** E3
Vineyard Cres ME4 . . . . . **66** B1
Vineyard La TN5 . . . . **338** C2
Viney's Gdns TN30 . . . . **324** C1
Vinson Cl
Culmers ME13 . . . . **106** D1
Orpington BR6 . . . . **54** A1
Vinson Ct DA15 . . . . **31** A6
Vinten Cl CT6 . . . . **111** B8
Vinters Ct ME14 . . . . **162** B4
Vinters Way ME14 . . . . . **162** E4
Viola Ave SE2 . . . . **3** B1
Violet Ave CT12 . . . . **83** C2
Violet Cl ME5 . . . . **130** A8
Violets The TN12 . . . . . . **257** A5
VIP Trad Est SE7 . . . . **1** C2
Virginia Rd
Gillingham ME7 . . . . **64** C7
Whitstable CT5 . . . . **109** A8
Virginia Wlk DA12 . . . . . . **37** E2
Viscount Dr E6 . . . . **1** F8
Vista The Eltham SE9 . . . . **29** E8
Sidcup DA14 . . . . **30** F3
Vixen Cl ME5 . . . . **97** C6
Vlissingen Dr CT14 . . . . **215** C8
Voce Rd SE18 . . . . **12** D7
Vogue Ct 11 BR1 . . . . **52** B8
Volante Dr ME10 . . . . . . **101** E7
Voyagers Cl SE28 . . . . **3** C7
Vulcan Cl Chatham ME5 . . **97** B7
Newham E6 . . . . **2** A7
Whitstable CT5 . . . . **108** C7
Vyne The DA7 . . . . **14** B4
Vyvyan Cotts TN17 . . . . **342** C3
Vyvyan Ho SE18 . . . . **12** A6

W

Wacher Cl CT2 . . . . **142** F2
Wadard Terr BR8 . . . . **56** C4
Waddenhall Barns
CT4 . . . . **240** B5
Waddington Dr CT18 . . . **307** A4
Waddle Cnr TN30 . . . . . **360** D3
Wade Ave BR5 . . . . **54** D2
Wades Cl TN29 . . . . **365** B4
Wadeville Cl DA17 . . . . . . **4** A1
Wadham Pl ME10 . . . . . . **102** B2
Wadhurst Bsns Pk
TN5 . . . . **336** B7
Wadhurst CE Prim Sch
TN5 . . . . **336** F5
Wadhurst Rd TN3 . . . . . . **314** D1
Wadhurst Sta TN5 . . . . . **336** C6
Wadlands Rd ME3 . . . . . . **22** B5
Waghorn Rd ME6 . . . . . . **128** A8
Waghorn St ME14 . . . . . **162** E4
Wagoners Cl ME14 . . . . . **162** E4
Wagon La TN12 . . . . **225** C1
Wagtail Way BR5 . . . . **54** D5
Waid Cl DA1 . . . . **15** F1
Wain Ct ME12 . . . . **47** A5
Wainhouse Cl TN8 . . . . . **217** D3
Wainscott Prim Sch
ME2 . . . . **40** D2
Wainscott Rd ME2 . . . . . . **40** D2
Wainscott Wlk ME2 . . . . . **40** D3
Wainwright Cl ME3 . . . . . . **34** B6
Wainwright Pl TN24 . . . . **300** D8
Waite Davies Rd 6
SE12 . . . . **29** A8
Wakefield Cl ME2 . . . . . . **62** D6
Wakefield Rd DA9 . . . . . . **17** C2
Wakefield Way CT21 . . . **333** D1
Wakefield Wlk CT21 . . . **333** D1
Wakehurst Cl ME17 . . . . **194** B3
Wakeley Rd ME8 . . . . **66** A1
Wakeleys Cotts ME8 . . . . **99** B8

Wakely Cl TN16 . . . . .118 C1
Wake Rd ME1 . . . . .96 C8
Wakerley Cl 6 E6 . . . . . . .7 A6
Walcheren Cl CT14 . . . .215 C8
Walcot Pl CT6 . . . . .77 B3
Waldair Ct E16 . . . . .2 B4
Waldeck Rd DA1 . . . . . . .16 A1
Waldegrave Rd BR1 . . . .52 F5
Walden Ave BR7 . . . . . . .29 F4
Walden Cl DA17 . . . . .3 F1
Waldenhurst Rd BR5 . . .54 D2
Walden Par BR7 . . . . . . .29 F2
Walden Rd BR7 . . . . .29 F2
Waldens Cl BR5 . . . . . . .54 D2
Waldens Rd BR5 . . . . . . .54 E3
Waldens The ME17 . . . .197 E2
Waldershare Ave
  CT13 . . . . .182 A1
Waldershare Ho CT15 .245 D5
Waldershare La CT15 . .246 E2
Waldershare Rd CT15 . .246 A5
Waldeslade Ctr ME5 . . .97 A3
Waldeslade Girls Sch
  ME5 . . . . .97 A3
Waldeslade Prim Sch
  ME5 . . . . .96 F6
Waldeslade Rd ME5 . . . .96 F6
Waldeslade Woods
  ME5 . . . . .96 E2
Waldo Ind Est BR1 . . . . .52 D6
Waldo Rd BR1 . . . . .52 D6
Waldrist Way DA18 . . . . . .3 F4
Waldron Dr ME15 . . . . .194 F6
Waldron Rd CT10 . . . . . .84 B2
Waldstock Rd SE28 . . . . . .3 A6
Walkden Rd BR7 . . . . . . .30 A3
Walker Cl Crayford DA1 .14 F4
  Woolwich SE18 . . . . .2 C1
Walker La CT7 . . . . .80 D8
Walker Pl TN15 . . . . . . .156 D6
Walkhurst Cotts TN17 .342 F7
Walkhurst Rd TN17 . . . .342 F7
Walkley Rd DA1 . . . . . . .15 B2
Walks The TN3 . . . . . . .312 C8
Walk The ME17 . . . . . . .197 E2
Wallace Cl Erith SE28 . . . .3 D6
  Royal Tunbridge Wells
  TN2 . . . . .314 A8
Wallace Gdns DA10 . . . .17 E1
Wallace Mews CT19 . . .335 D7
Wallace Rd ME1 . . . . . . .96 E8
Wallace Terr TN15 . . . . .91 E4
Wallace Way CT10 . . . . .83 E4
Wallbridge La ME8 . . . . .66 D3
Wall Cl ME3 . . . . .41 D7
Waller Hill TN17 . . . . . .293 B5
Waller Rd TN28 . . . . . . .377 E2
Wallers Rd ME13 . . . . . .138 A2
Wallers TN3 . . . . .285 A8
Wallhouse Rd DA8 . . . . .15 C7
Wallis Ave ME15 . . . . . .195 E5
Wallis Cl DA2 . . . . .32 F5
Wallis Field TN3 . . . . . .312 B6
Wallis Pk DA11 . . . . .18 B2
Wallis Rd TN24 . . . . . . .268 D2
Wall Rd TN24 . . . . .268 B3
Wall The ME10 . . . . .101 E5
Wallwood Rd CT11 . . . .117 F8
Walmer Castle ★
  CT14 . . . . .215 D1
Walmer Castle Rd
  CT14 . . . . .215 C1
Walmer Cl BR6 . . . . .86 D6
Walmer Cl 3 ME14 . . . .162 A5
Walmer Gdns
  Cliffs End CT12 . . . . . .116 D5
  Deal CT14 . . . . .215 A2
  Sittingbourne ME10 . . .101 D5
Walmer Ho ME2 . . . . . . .40 C1
Walmer Rd CT5 . . . . . . .108 E8
Walmers Ave ME3 . . . . .39 A4
Walmer Sch CT14 . . . . .215 B2
Walmer Sta CT14 . . . . .215 A1
Walmer Terr SE18 . . . . . .2 D2
Walmer Way
  Deal CT14 . . . . .215 A2
  1 Folkestone CT20 . . .334 F5
Walmsley Ho 4 CT19 . .335 E6
Walmsley Rd CT10 . . . . .83 F5
Walner Gdns TN28 . . . .373 B7
Walner La TN28 . . . . . . .373 B7
Walnut Cl
  Ashford TN24 . . . . . . .268 D6
  Broadstairs CT10 . . . . .83 F2
  Chatham ME5 . . . . .97 B8
  Eynsford DA4 . . . . .89 D7
  Paddock Wood TN12 . . .257 A6
  Yalding ME18 . . . . .192 F1
Walnut Hill Rd DA3 . . . .59 E6
Walnut Ridge TN25 . . . .330 A6
Walnuts Rd BR6 . . . . . . .54 B1
Walnuts The BR6 . . . . . .54 A1
Walnut Tree Ave
  Dartford DA1 . . . . .33 E6
  Loose ME15 . . . . .195 A5
Walnut Tree Cl
  6 Birchington CT7 . . . .81 A7
  Chislehurst BR7 . . . . . .53 C8
  Westerham TN16 . . . . .151 D1
Walnut Tree Cotts
  ME13 . . . . .171 E8
Walnut Tree Ct ME20 . .128 B1
Walnut Tree Dr ME10 . .101 D4
Walnut Tree La
  Loose ME15 . . . . .195 A5
  Westbere CT2 . . . . .144 D7
Walnut Tree Rd DA8 . . . .4 E1
Walnut Tree Way DA13 .60 B3
Walnut Way
  Royal Tunbridge Wells
  TN4 . . . . .286 D8
  Swanley BR8 . . . . .55 D7
Walpole Cl ME19 . . . . . .127 F1

Walpole Ho 4 BR7 . . . . .53 D8
Walpole Pl SE18 . . . . .2 B2
Walpole Rd
  Bromley BR2 . . . . .52 D4
  Margate CT9 . . . . .50 J3
Walsby Dr ME10 . . . . . .102 A8
Walsham Cl SE28 . . . . . . .3 D6
Walsham Rd ME5 . . . . . .96 F1
Walshaw Ho 2 ME14 . .162 A6
Walsingham Cl ME8 . . . .98 D3
Walsingham Ho 3
  ME14 . . . . .162 A6
Walsingham Pk BR7 . . . .52 F5
Walsingham Rd BR5 . . . .54 B8
Walter Burke Ave ME1 . .95 C5
Walter's Farm Rd
  TN9 . . . . .222 C1
Walters Green Rd
  TN11 . . . . .283 F6
Walters Ho SE18 . . . . . .12 A7
Walters Rd ME3 . . . . . . .41 E6
Walterstown Ct DA1 . . .33 D8
Walters Yd BR1 . . . . . . .52 A7
Waltham Cl
  Ashford TN24 . . . . . . .269 A2
  Dartford DA1 . . . . .15 A1
  Margate CT9 . . . . .51 E2
  27 Orpington BR5 . . . .54 D1
Waltham Rd
  Gillingham ME8 . . . . . .65 C3
  Waltham CT4 . . . . .206 F1
Walthamstow Hall (Nursery
  Unit) TN13 . . . . .154 B5
Walthamstow Hall
  TN13 . . . . .154 C4
Walton Gdns CT19 . . . .335 D7
Walton Manor Cl
  CT19 . . . . .335 D7
Walton Rd
  Folkestone CT19 . . . . .335 D6
  Sidcup DA14 . . . . .31 C5
  Tonbridge TN10 . . . . . .222 F6
Waltons The CT19 . . . . .335 C8
Walwyn Ave BR1 . . . . . .52 D6
Wanden La TN27 . . . . . .264 C8
Wansbury Way BR8 . . . .56 A5
Wanstall Ct CT7 . . . . . . .81 A7
Wanstead Br BR1 . . . . . .52 C7
Wanstead Rd BR1 . . . . .52 C7
Wansunt Rd DA5 . . . . . .32 C7
Wantsum Cl CT6 . . . . . . .77 F5
Wantsume Lees CT13 . .148 E2
Wantsum Mews 7
  CT13 . . . . .148 F1
Wantsum Way CT7 . . . . .79 E3
Warberry Park Gdns
  TN4 . . . . .285 E6
Warblers Cl 3 ME2 . . . .63 A7
Ward Cl Durgates TN5 . .336 E5
  Erith DA8 . . . . .14 D8
Warden Bay Pk ME12 . .49 E3
Warden Bay Rd ME12 . .49 E3
Warden Cl ME16 . . . . . .161 C4
Warden Ct 10 CT17 . . . .278 C1
Warden House Mews
  CT14 . . . . .215 A4
Warden House Prim Sch
  CT14 . . . . .215 A5
Warden Mill Cl ME18 . .192 F2
Warden Point Way
  CT5 . . . . .108 C6
Warden Rd
  Rochester ME1 . . . . . . .63 C2
  Warden ME12 . . . . .49 B3
Wardens Field Cl 2
  BR6 . . . . .86 F4
Warden Spring Cvn Pk
  ME12 . . . . .49 D5
Warden Terr ME12 . . . . .48 A6
Warden View Gdns
  ME12 . . . . .49 D1
Wardona Ct DA10 . . . . .17 F1
Wardour Cl CT10 . . . . . .84 B4
Wardour Ct 11 DA2 . . . .16 B1
Wards Hill Rd ME12 . . . .47 C8
Ward's La TN5 . . . . .337 C4
Wards Wharf App E16 . . .1 D4
Wardwell La
  Lower Halstow ME9 . . . .67 C1
  Newington ME9 . . . . . .100 C8
Warehorne Rd TN26 . . .349 A7
Warepoint Dr SE28 . . . . .2 D4
Ware St ME14 . . . . .163 A5
Warham Rd TN14 . . . . .122 B3
Waring Cl BR6 . . . . .87 A4
Waring Dr BR6 . . . . .87 A4
Waring Rd DA14 . . . . . . .31 C2
Warland Rd
  West Kingsdown TN15 . .90 F2
  Woolwich SE18 . . . . . . .12 E7
Warlingham Cl ME8 . . . .66 A1
Warmlake Bsns Est
  ME17 . . . . .196 E1
Warmlake Rd ME17 . . .196 C1
Warmlake ME17 . . . . . .196 F1
Warne Pl 4 DA15 . . . . . .13 B1
Warner St ME4 . . . . .63 F3
Warnett Ct ME6 . . . . . . .95 A1
Warnford Gdns ME15 . .195 A8
Warnford Rd BR6 . . . . . .86 F5
Warre Ave CT11 . . . . . . .117 C5
Warren Ave BR6 . . . . . . .86 F5
Warren Cl Bexley DA6 . .14 A2
  Folkestone CT19 . . . . .335 F6
  Sittingbourne ME10 . . .102 B2
Warren Cotts TN11 . . . .252 A3
Warren Ct TN15 . . . . . . .154 C3
Warren Dr
  Broadstairs CT10 . . . . .83 E5
  Orpington BR6 . . . . . . .87 B5

Warren Dr The CT8 . . . .81 D7
Warren Farm La TN4 . . .313 B6
Warren Gdns BR6 . . . . .87 A5
Warren Hastings Ct
  DA11 . . . . .18 F1
Warren Hos TN27 . . . . .233 E8
Warren Hts TN25 . . . . .302 E5
Warren La
  Ashford TN24 . . . . . . .268 A4
  Lydden CT15 . . . . .276 D6
  Oxted RH8 . . . . .183 A1
  Yelsted ME9 . . . . .99 C3
Warren Lo CT1 . . . . .174 B6
Warren Rd Bexley DA6 . .14 A2
  Dartford DA1 . . . . .33 E5
  Folkestone CT19 . . . . .335 F6
  Hayes BR2 . . . . .85 A8
  Kit's Coty ME5 . . . . . . .129 D7
  Littlestone-on-Sea TN28 .373 D6
  Luddesdown ME2 . . . . .61 D3
  Northfleet DA11 . . . . . .36 B3
  Orpington BR6 . . . . . . .87 C5
  Sidcup DA14 . . . . .31 F6
  Smarden TN27 . . . . . . .263 F2
  Sturry CT2 . . . . .143 F5
  West Malling ME19 . . . .159 C8
Warren Ret Pk TN24 . . .268 B4
Warren Ridge TN3 . . . . .314 C3
Warren Road Prim Sch
  BR6 . . . . .86 F6
Warrens The DA3 . . . . . .58 F3
Warren St
  Stalisfield Green TN27 . .201 A3
  Warren Street ME17 . . .200 D7
Warren The
  Brabourne Lees TN25 . .302 E5
  Gravesend DA12 . . . . . . .37 E5
  2 Greenwich SE7 . . . . .11 C8
  Penshurst TN11 . . . . . .252 A4
  Selling ME13 . . . . .171 E7
  Ticehurst TN5 . . . . . . .338 E1
  Whitstable CT5 . . . . . . .108 C6
Warren View
  Ashford TN23 . . . . . . .267 F4
  Shorne DA12 . . . . .38 C2
Warren Way CT11 . . . . .259 A5
Warren Wlk 1 SE7 . . . . .11 C8
Warren Wood Rd BR5 . .88 A5
Warren Wood Com Prim
  Sch & Language Unit
  ME1 . . . . .96 C8
Warren Wood Rd ME1 . .96 C7
Warrington Rd TN12 . . . .37 A6
Warrior Ave DA12 . . . . . .37 C4
Warsop Trad Est TN8 . .249 D8
Warspite Rd SE18 . . . . . .1 E3
Warwall E6 . . . . .2 B7
Warwick Ave
  Orpington BR6 . . . . . . .87 A7
  Sidcup DA16 . . . . .31 F8
Warwick Cres
  Rochester ME1 . . . . . . .62 F2
  Sittingbourne ME10 . . .101 C5
Warwick Ct 8 DA8 . . . . .14 C7
Warwick Dr CT11 . . . . .117 B5
Warwick Gdns DA13 . . .93 A8
Warwick Pk TN2 . . . . . .286 B1
Warwick Pl
  Maidstone ME16 . . . . .161 B3
  Northfleet DA11 . . . . . .18 B2
Warwick Rd
  Ashford TN24 . . . . . . .268 E5
  Bexley DA16 . . . . .13 C4
  Canterbury CT1 . . . . . .175 C8
  Deal CT14 . . . . .215 D2
  Margate CT9 . . . . .51 B2
  4 Royal Tunbridge Wells
  TN1 . . . . .286 A2
  Sidcup DA14 . . . . .31 B3
  Whitstable CT5 . . . . . . .74 D2
Warwick Terr SE18 . . . . .12 D8
Warwick Way ME14 . . . .33 E6
Washford Farm Rd
  TN23 . . . . .299 E5
Washington Cl 4
  CT16 . . . . .278 B3
Washington Ho ME15 . .195 E5
Washington La ME29 . . .371 C6
Washneys Rd BR6 . . . . .120 B6
Washwell La TN5 . . . . . .336 F5
Wassall La TN17 . . . . . .357 E7
Wass Dro CT3 . . . . .147 B7
Watchester Ave CT11 . .117 C5
Watchester La CT12 . . .115 B5
Watchgate DA2 . . . . .34 E3
Watchmans Terr 6
  ME5 . . . . .64 C2
Waterbrook Ave TN24 . .301 A4
Watercress Ct TN14 . . .154 C7
Watercress Dr TN14 . . .154 C7
Watercress Ho TN23 . . .267 F1
Watercress La
  Ashford TN23 . . . . . . .299 F4
  Wingham CT3 . . . . . . .177 F6
Watercroft Rd TN14 . . . .87 F1
Waterdale Rd SE2 . . . . .13 A8
Waterdales DA11 . . . . . .36 D7
Waterditch La ME17,
  TN27 . . . . .200 D5
Waterdown Rd TN4 . . . .285 E6
Waterfall Rd TN26 . . . . .267 B6
Water Farm CT4 . . . . . .273 F4
Waterfield Cl Erith DA17 . .4 A3
  Woolwich SE28 . . . . .3 B5
Waterfield TN2 . . . . . . .314 A7
Waterfrets Cotts TN5 . .284 F5
Waterfront Studios Bsns
  Ctr E16 . . . . .1 A5
Watergate Ho 5 SE18 . . .2 A1
Waterglade Ind Pk
  RM20 . . . . .16 F8
Waterham Rd ME13 . . .107 C1
Waterhead CT DA8 . . . . .14 C7
Waterhouse Cl E16 . . . . .1 D8

Wateringbury CE Prim Sch
  ME18 . . . . .192 C6
Wateringbury Cl BR5 . . .54 B7
Wateringbury Rd
  ME19 . . . . .159 F3
Wateringbury Sta
  ME18 . . . . .192 C6
Water La
  Canterbury CT1 . . . . . .174 F8
  6 Faversham ME13 . . .138 C7
  Harrietsham ME17 . . . .198 B5
  Hawkhurst TN18 . . . . .341 B4
  Headcorn TN17,TN27 . .262 A4
  Hunton ME15 . . . . .226 D6
Waterlakes TN8 . . . . . . .249 C8
Water La
  Kingswood ME17 . . . . .197 F3
  Limpsfield RH8 . . . . . . .183 A8
  Maidstone,Bearsted
  ME14 . . . . .163 E6
  6 Maidstone ME15 . . .162 A4
  Painters Forstal ME13 . .137 F4
  Shoreham TN14 . . . . . .121 F6
  Sidcup DA14 . . . . .31 F6
  Smarden TN27 . . . . . . .263 F2
  Sturry CT2 . . . . .143 F5
  West Malling ME19 . . . .159 C8
Waterlock Cotts CT3 . . .178 A7
Waterloo Cres CT16,
  CT17 . . . . .310 E7
Waterloo Ho 11 ME12 . .47 D6
Waterloo Mans 14
  CT16,CT17 . . . . .310 E7
Waterloo Pl
  Cranbrook TN17 . . . . . .320 D5
  10 Ramsgate CT11 . . . .117 F7
  Tonbridge TN9 . . . . . . .254 B8
Waterloo Rd
  Cranbrook TN17 . . . . . .320 D6
  Folkestone CT20 . . . . .334 D5
  Gillingham ME7 . . . . . .64 C4
  Sittingbourne ME10 . . .101 D5
  Tonbridge TN9 . . . . . . .254 B8
Waterloo St
  1 Gravesend DA12 . . . .37 C8
  Maidstone ME15 . . . . .162 A3
Waterloo Terr ME12 . . . .48 A5
Waterlow Rd
  Maidstone ME14 . . . . .162 A6
  Vigo Village DA13 . . . .125 F7
Waterman Ho TN23 . . .300 B8
Waterman's La TN12 . . .257 B3
Watermans Way DA9 . . .17 B3
Water Mdws CT2 . . . . . .143 F4
Watermead TN23 . . . . . .299 F7
Watermeadow Cl
  Erith DA8 . . . . .15 B6
  Gillingham ME7 . . . . . .97 F6
Watermill Cl
  Maidstone ME16 . . . . .161 B5
  Rochester ME2 . . . . . . .63 C8
Water Mill Way DA4 . . . .57 B7
Watermint Cl BR5 . . . . . .54 D5
Waters Cotts TN5 . . . . .337 A4
Waters Edge Ct DA8 . . . .4 F1
Waters Edge ME15 . . . .161 E2
Watersend CT17 . . . . . .277 D5
Waterside TN24 . . . . . . .268 F1
Waterside Cl ME13 . . . .105 D1
Waterside DA1 . . . . .34 A1
Waterside Ct
  5 Hythe CT21 . . . . . . .333 B2
  Leybourne ME19 . . . . .127 E2
  Rochester ME2 . . . . . . .63 D8
Waterside Dr CT8 . . . . . .50 D1
Waterside Gate ME16 . .161 F5
Waterside La ME7 . . . . .64 F7
Waterside Mews ME15 .161 E2
Waterside Mews
  ME18 . . . . .192 D6
Waterside Sch SE18 . . . .2 D1
Waterside Terr TN23 . . .267 C1
Waterside View ME12 . .49 E4
Water Slippe TN11 . . . . .190 D1
Watersmeet Cl ME15 . .162 A1
Watersmeet Way SE28 . .3 D7
Waters Pl ME7 . . . . .98 A6
Water St CT14 . . . . .215 D1
Waterstone Pl ME13 . . .138 A6
Waterton Ave DA12 . . . .37 E8
Waterton BR8 . . . . .55 D5
Waterworks Cotts
  TN14 . . . . .154 B6
Waterworks Hill CT15 . .247 B3
Waterworks La CT15 . . .247 B3
Watery La
  Heaverham TN15 . . . . .155 D7
  Petham CT4 . . . . .207 C5
  Sidcup BR5,DA14 . . . . .31 B2
Watford Rd E16 . . . . .1 A8
Watkin Rd CT19 . . . . . . .335 C6
Watkins Cl TN12 . . . . . .260 E5
Watling Ave ME6 . . . . . .64 D2
Watling Ho 10 SE18 . . . .12 A8
Watling Pl ME10 . . . . . .102 A3
Watling St
  Bexley DA6,DA7 . . . . . .14 C3
  Canterbury CT1 . . . . . .174 F8
  Dartford DA1,DA2 . . . . .34 C8
  Gillingham ME7 . . . . . .64 D2
  Gravesend DA11,DA12 . .37 C2
  Northfleet DA11,DA13 . .36 C5
  Rochester ME2 . . . . . . .62 D7
Watson Ave ME5 . . . . . .96 D5
Watson Cl RM20 . . . . . . .17 A6
Watsons Cl TN25 . . . . . .268 C8
Watsons Hill ME10 . . . .101 E5
Watt Ho 5 SE28 . . . . .3 C1
Wattle Cnr TN30 . . . . . .360 D3
Watts' Ave ME1 . . . . . . .96 C8
Watts Cl 5 Snodland ME6 .128 B8
Wadhurst TN5 . . . . .336 F4

Watts Cotts TN24 . . . . .268 C7
Watt's Cross Rd TN11 . .221 B6
Watt's La BR7 . . . . .53 C8
Watts' St ME4 . . . . .63 E2
Watts Yd 13 CT13 . . . . .148 F1
Wat Tyler Way ME15 . . .162 A4
Wauchope Rd CT5 . . . . .107 F6
Wave Crest CT5 . . . . . . .74 C1
Wavell Dr DA15 . . . . . . .12 C1
Waveney Rd TN10 . . . . .222 B5
Waverley Ave ME12 . . . .47 B7
Waverley Cl
  Bromley BR2 . . . . .52 D4
  Chatham ME5 . . . . .97 D2
  Coxheath ME17 . . . . . .194 C3
Waverley Cres
  Woolwich SE18 . . . . . .12 D8
  Woolwich SE18 . . . . . . .2 D1
Waverley Dr TN2 . . . . . .286 F6
Waverley Gdns E6 . . . . . .1 E8
Waverley Rd
  Margate CT9 . . . . .82 C8
  Woolwich SE18 . . . . . . .2 D1
Wayborough Hill
  CT12 . . . . .115 D7
Way Farm Cotts CT12 . .115 E7
Wayfield Com Prim Sch
  ME5 . . . . .97 A4
Wayfield Link SE9 . . . . .12 C1
Wayfield Rd ME5 . . . . . .97 A4
Way Hill CT15 . . . . .115 E7
Waylands Cl TN14 . . . . .120 E4
Waylands BR8 . . . . .55 F5
Wayne Cl
  Broadstairs CT10 . . . . .83 E5
  Orpington BR6 . . . . . . .86 F7
Wayne Ct ME2 . . . . .40 D2
Wayside Ave TN30 . . . .324 B3
Wayside 3 BR7 . . . . . . .53 D8
Wayside Dr TN8 . . . . . . .217 D3
Wayside Flats TN30 . . .324 B2
Wayside Gr SE9 . . . . . . .29 F4
Wayside TN30 . . . . .324 B2
Wayville Rd DA1 . . . . . . .34 B8
Way Volante DA12 . . . . .37 E4
Weald Cl
  Istead Rise DA13 . . . . .36 E1
  Maidstone ME15 . . . . .195 C6
  Orpington BR2 . . . . . . .87 A3
  Sevenoaks Weald TN14 . .187 C2
Weald Com Prim Sch
  TN14 . . . . .187 B2
Weald Ct Charing TN27 .201 E1
  Sittingbourne ME10 . . .101 D2
  Tonbridge TN11 . . . . . .221 D6
Wealden Ave TN30 . . . .324 B1
Wealden Cl TN11 . . . . . .221 E5
Wealden Ct 5 ME5 . . . .64 B3
Wealden Pl TN13 . . . . . .154 D6
Wealden View TN17 . . .318 E8
Wealden Way ME20 . . .160 E2
Wealdhurst Pk CT10 . . .83 D5
Weald The
  Ashford TN24 . . . . . . .268 C3
  Bromley BR7 . . . . .29 F2
Weald View
  Frittenden TN17 . . . . . .293 E6
  Paddock Wood TN12 . . .257 E1
Weald View Rd TN9 . . .254 B7
Weald View TN5 . . . . . .336 F6
Wear Bay Cres CT19 . . .335 F6
Wear Bay Rd CT19 . . . .335 F6
Weardale Ave DA2 . . . . .34 C7
Weare Rd TN4 . . . . .286 C8
Weatherall Cl ME13 . . .140 B2
Weatherly Cl ME1 . . . . .63 C4
Weatherly Dr CT10 . . . . .83 F2
Weathersfield Ct SE9 . .11 F1
Weaver Cl E6 . . . . .2 B2
Weavering Cl ME2 . . . . .40 B2
Weavering Cotts
  ME14 . . . . .162 E3
Weavering St ME14 . . .162 F4
Weavers Cl
  Gravesend DA11 . . . . . .37 A7
  Staplehurst TN12 . . . . .260 F4
Weavers Cotts TN17 . . .318 E8
Weavers La TN14 . . . . . .154 C6
Weaver's Orch DA13 . . .36 A2
Weavers The
  Biddenden TN27 . . . . . .295 A1
  Maidstone ME16 . . . . .161 B5
Weavers Way
  Ashford TN23 . . . . . . .299 E7
  Dover CT16 . . . . .278 A3
Webb Cl
  Folkestone CT19 . . . . .335 A4
  Hoo St Werburgh ME3 . .41 D6
Webb Ct 6 SE28 . . . . . . .3 B6
Webber Cl DA8 . . . . .15 B7
Webb's Mdw TN15 . . . .154 C2
Webster Rd ME8 . . . . . .65 F1
Webster Way CT18 . . . .307 B4
Weddington La CT3 . . . .147 E2
Wedgewood Cl ME16 . .161 B5
Wedgewood Dr DA5 . . . .31 F8
Wedgwood Dr ME5 . . . .97 A2
Wedgwoods TN16 . . . . .150 C6
Weeds Wood Rd ME5 . .96 F4
Weekes Ct ME11 . . . . . .46 A5
Weekes La TN27 . . . . . .295 A5
Week St ME14 . . . . .162 A4
Weigall Pl CT11 . . . . . . .117 C7
Weigall Rd SE2,SE3 . . . .11 A3
Weighbridge Way
  CT16 . . . . .310 H8
Weir Mill ME19 . . . . . . .159 F7
Weir Rd DA5 . . . . .32 B8

Welbeck Ave
  Bromley BR1 . . . . .29 A4
  Royal Tunbridge Wells
  TN4 . . . . .286 C8
  Sidcup DA15 . . . . .31 A7
Welcombe Ct ME8 . . . . .98 D8
Weld Cl TN12 . . . . .260 F4
Weldstock Ho 2 SE28 . . .2 B3
Wellan Cl DA15 . . . . .13 B2
Welland Rd TN10 . . . . . .222 B4
Wellands Cl BR1 . . . . . .52 F7
Well Cl Leigh TN11 . . . .220 F1
  Sturry CT2 . . . . .144 A6
Wellcome Ave DA1 . . . .15 E3
Weller Ave ME1 . . . . . . .63 D2
Weller Pl BR6 . . . . .119 A8
Weller Rd TN4 . . . . .285 C4
Wellers Cl TN16 . . . . . .184 C8
Wellesley Ave CT14 . . .215 C3
Wellesley Cl
  Broadstairs CT10 . . . . .83 E3
  7 Greenwich SE7 . . . . .1 C1
  Westgate-on-S CT8 . . .81 E7
Wellesley Ho CT14 . . . .215 C1
Wellesley Rd
  Ashford TN23 . . . . . . .268 C2
  Dover CT16 . . . . .310 E7
  Margate CT9 . . . . .51 B1
  Sheerness ME12 . . . . . .28 D2
  Westgate-on-S CT8 . . .81 E7
Wellesley Terr TN13 . . .181 A8
Wellesley Villas TN24 . .268 C3
Well Field DA3 . . . . .58 F5
Wellfield Rd CT20 . . . . .335 A5
Well Hall Par SE9 . . . . . .11 E3
Well Hall Par SE9 . . . . . .11 C1
Well Hall Rd SE18,SE9 . .11 E3
Well Hill BR6 . . . . .88 B5
Well Hill La BR6 . . . . . . .88 B4
Well Hill Nursery BR6 . .88 C4
Wellingfield Ct 1
  DA16 . . . . .13 A4
Welling High St DA16 . .13 B4
Welling Sch DA16 . . . . .13 B6
Welling Sta DA16 . . . . . .13 A5
Wellington Ave
  Sidcup DA15 . . . . .13 A1
  Woolwich SE18 . . . . . . .2 B3
Wellington Cl ME8 . . . . .50 C1
Wellington Cotts
  Gill's Green TN18 . . . . .340 E4
  Meopham DA13 . . . . . .93 A7
Wellington Cres CT11 . .117 F6
Wellington Ct CT14 . . . .215 D3
Wellington Gdns
  2 Dover CT16 . . . . . . .278 B3
  Greenwich SE7 . . . . .1 C1
  Margate CT9 . . . . .50 J3
Wellington Ho
  6 Maidstone ME15 . . .195 E5
  Margate CT9 . . . . .51 C3
Wellingtonia Way
  TN8 . . . . .217 C2
Wellington Mews SE7 . .11 C8
Wellington Par
  Bexley DA15 . . . . .13 A2
  Deal CT14 . . . . .248 D7
  Kingsdown CT14 . . . . .248 E6
Wellington Pl
  Folkestone CT20 . . . . .334 D3
  Maidstone ME14 . . . . .161 F6
  Sparrow's Green TN5 . .336 F5
Wellington Rd
  Bexley DA5 . . . . .13 D2
  Bromley BR2 . . . . .52 C5
  Dartford DA1 . . . . .15 C1
  Deal CT14 . . . . .215 D5
  Erith DA17 . . . . .3 F1
  Folkestone CT20 . . . . .334 D5
  Gillingham ME7 . . . . . .64 C4
  Margate CT9 . . . . .82 D4
  Orpington BR5 . . . . . . .54 C3
  Sittingbourne ME10 . . .101 B6
  Temple Ewell CT16 . . .277 D5
  Tilbury RM18 . . . . .19 A5
  Westgate-on-S CT8 . . .81 E7
Wellington St
  Gravesend DA11 . . . . . .37 C8
  Woolwich SE18 . . . . . . .2 A2
  Yorkletts CT5 . . . . . . .108 D5
Wellington Terr CT20 . .334 D3
Wellington Way ME19 . .158 F3
Welling Way DA16 . . . . .12 C4
Wellis Gdns CT9 . . . . . .50 G1
Well La
  Fordwich CT2,CT3 . . . .144 A3
  Painters Forstal ME13 . .137 B3
  St Margaret's at Cliffe
  CT15 . . . . .279 F6
Wellmeade Dr TN13 . . .187 B8
Well Penn Rd ME3 . . . . .22 C3
Well Rd Lyminge CT18 . .305 C6
  Maidstone ME14 . . . . .162 A6
  Otford TN14 . . . . .122 C3
  Queenborough ME11 . .46 A5
  Rushenden ME11 . . . . .45 F3
Wells Ave CT1 . . . . .175 B7
Wells Cl
  New Romney TN28 . . . .373 C6
  Royal Tunbridge Wells
  TN1 . . . . .286 A3
  Tenterden TN30 . . . . .345 B8
  Tonbridge TN10 . . . . . .222 D4
  Westerham TN16 . . . . .184 C8
Wells Cotts ME18 . . . . .192 C2
Wells Ct ME2 . . . . .62 D5
Wells Ho Bromley BR1 . .29 B3
  Royal Tunbridge Wells
  TN4 . . . . .285 F4

Wells Ho *continued*
Sittingbourne ME10 ... 102 B4
Wellsmoor Gdns BR1 ... 53 A6
Wells Rd Bromley BR1 ... 52 F7
Folkestone CT19 ... 334 F6
Rochester ME2 ... 62 D5
Well St
East Malling ME19 ... 159 E6
Maidstone ME15,ME17 ... 194 E4
Wells Way ME13 ... 105 B1
Well Winch Rd ME10 ... 101 D5
Welsdene Rd CT9 ... 82 B8
Welson Rd CT20 ... 335 A5
Welton Cl TN9 ... 253 F7
Welton Rd SE18 ... 12 E7
Wemmick Cl ME1 ... 96 D7
Wemyss Ct 13 CT1 ... 143 B2
Wemyss Ho 14 CT1 ... 143 B2
Wemyss Way CT1 ... 143 C1
Wenderton La CT3 ... 146 A2
Wendover Cl ME2 ... 95 B5
Wendover Ct BR2 ... 52 B6
Wendover Rd
Bromley BR1,BR2 ... 52 B6
Eltham SE9 ... 11 D4
Wendover Way
Bexley DA16 ... 13 A3
Orpington BR6 ... 54 A3
Wenham's La TN29 ... 363 E2
Wensley Cl SE9 ... 11 F1
Wents Wood ME14 ... 162 F5
Wentworth Ave CT9 ... 50 E1
Wentworth Cl Erith SE28 ... 3 D7
Gravesend DA11 ... 37 A3
Hayes BR2 ... 85 A8
Lyminge CT18 ... 305 C6
Orpington BR6 ... 86 E5
Wentworth Dr
Cliffe Woods ME3 ... 40 B8
Dartford DA1 ... 15 A1
Gillingham ME8 ... 98 E7
Ramsgate CT12 ... 83 A1
Sittingbourne ME10 ... 101 C5
Wentworth Gdns CT6 ... 76 D2
Wentworth Ho
3 Greenwich SE3 ... 11 A7
Sittingbourne ME10 ... 101 C5
Wentworth Prim Sch
DA1 ... 33 A8
Wenvoe Ave DA7 ... 14 B5
Wernbrook St SE18 ... 12 C8
Wesley Ave E16 ... 1 B5
Wesley Cl
Maidstone ME16 ... 160 F3
Orpington BR5 ... 54 C6
Wesley Ho BR1 ... 52 D6
Wesley Terr CT18 ... 305 C7
Wessex Dr DA8 ... 14 E6
Wessex Wlk DA2 ... 32 E6
West App BR5 ... 53 C4
West Beach CT5 ... 74 C1
Westbere Ho BR5 ... 54 C4
Westbere La CT2 ... 144 B7
West Borough Prim Sch
ME16 ... 161 B3
Westbourne TN23 ... 299 D6
Westbourne Gdns
CT20 ... 335 B4
Westbourne Rd DA7 ... 13 E7
Westbourne St ME10 ... 101 E4
Westbrook Ave CT9 ... 50 F1
Westbrook Cotts CT9 ... 50 G1
Westbrook Ct SE3 ... 11 B6
Westbrook Dr BR5 ... 54 D1
Westbrooke Cl ME4 ... 64 A2
Westbrooke Cres DA16 ... 13 C4
Westbrooke Rd
Bexley DA16 ... 13 C4
Sidcup DA15 ... 30 D6
Westbrooke Sch DA16 ... 13 D4
Westbrook Gdns CT9 ... 50 G1
Westbrook La CT6 ... 76 B3
Westbrook Prom CT9 ... 50 G2
Westbrook Rd
Greenwich SE3 ... 11 B6
Margate CT9 ... 50 G2
Westbrook Terr TN2 ... 286 D1
West Brow BR7 ... 30 B3
Westbury Cres CT17 ... 310 B6
Westbury Ct 5 DA14 ... 31 A4
Westbury Hts CT17 ... 310 B6
Westbury Rd
Bromley BR1 ... 52 D8
Dover CT17 ... 310 B6
Westgate-on-S CT8 ... 81 E8
Westbury Terr TN16 ... 184 C8
West Cliff Arc 10
CT11 ... 117 E6
West Cliff Ave CT10 ... 84 B3
West Cliff Ct CT10 ... 84 B3
West Cliff Dr CT6 ... 76 B4
Westcliff Dr ME12 ... 47 D8
West Cliff Gdns
Folkestone CT20 ... 335 D4
Herne Bay CT6 ... 76 B4
Westcliff Gdns CT9 ... 50 F1
Westcliff Ho 4 CT20 ... 335 D4
West Cliff Prom CT11 ... 117 D5
West Cliff Rd CT10 ... 84 B3
Westcliff Rd CT9 ... 50 G1
West Cliff Rd CT11 ... 117 D6
West Cliff Terr CT11 ... 117 B5
West Cliff CT5 ... 74 D1
Westcombe Hill SE3 ... 11 A8
Westcombe Park Rd
SE3 ... 11 A7
Westcombe Park Sta
SE3 ... 1 A1
West Common Rd BR2 ... 85 B7
Westcott Ave DA11 ... 37 A5
Westcott Cl BR1 ... 52 F4
Westcourt La CT15 ... 244 C5
Westcourt Prim Sch
DA12 ... 37 E6
Westcourt Rd ME7 ... 64 A6
West Crescent Rd
DA12 ... 19 C1
West Cross Gdns
TN30 ... 344 F7
West Cross TN30 ... 344 F7
West Ct 3 ME15 ... 162 A1
Westdale Rd SE18 ... 12 B8
Westdean Ave SE12 ... 29 C7
Westdean Cl CT17 ... 277 E2
West Dr Chatham ME5 ... 96 D5
Sutton Valence ME17 ... 230 B7
West Dumpton La CT11 ... 83 E1
Wested Farm Cotts
BR8 ... 55 F2
Wested La BR8 ... 56 A3
West End TN16 ... 152 B2
West End Cotts ME9 ... 167 D7
West End
High Halden TN26 ... 325 F3
Kemsing TN15 ... 123 A2
Marden TN12 ... 259 C6
Westenhanger Sta
TN25 ... 332 B7
Westerdale Rd 5 SE10 ... 1 A1
Westergate Rd
Bexley SE2 ... 13 E8
Rochester ME2 ... 39 F1
Westerham Cl
Canterbury CT2 ... 143 A4
Gillingham ME8 ... 65 B3
Margate CT9 ... 51 F1
Westerham Dr DA15 ... 13 C1
Westerham Hill TN16 ... 151 B5
Westerham Rd
Brasted TN16 ... 152 A2
Limpsfield RH8,TN16 ... 183 C6
Orpington BR2 ... 85 D4
Sevenoaks TN13 ... 153 C4
Sittingbourne ME10 ... 101 C3
Westerham TN16 ... 184 A8
Westerhill Rd ME17 ... 194 C1
Westerhout Cl CT14 ... 215 C8
Westerly Mews 5
CT2 ... 142 E1
Western Ave
Ashford TN23 ... 268 A3
Bridge CT4 ... 176 A1
Chatham ME4 ... 64 A8
Halfway Houses ME12 ... 46 D6
7 Hawkhurst TN18 ... 340 F2
Herne Bay CT6 ... 76 E4
Western Beach Apartments
E16 ... 1 A5
Western Cl CT17 ... 310 C6
Western Cross Cl DA9 ... 17 C1
Western Espl
Broadstairs CT10 ... 84 B2
Herne Bay CT6 ... 76 C5
Western Gateway E16 ... 1 A6
Western Gdns TN24 ... 300 E8
Western Heights Rdbt
CT17 ... 310 C5
Western Ho CT14 ... 215 C7
Western Hts★ CT17 ... 310 C6
Western Link ME13 ... 138 A8
Western Rd
Borough Green TN15 ... 156 F7
Deal CT14 ... 215 C7
Hawkhurst TN18 ... 340 F2
Maidstone ME16 ... 161 C2
Margate CT9 ... 83 C8
Royal Tunbridge
Wells,Southborough
TN4 ... 254 A1
Royal Tunbridge Wells
TN1 ... 286 C5
Turner's Green TN5 ... 336 F6
Western Service Rd
CT16 ... 310 G8
Western Undercliff
CT11 ... 117 C5
Western Way SE28 ... 2 E4
Westfield CT2 ... 142 A6
Westfield Bsns Ctr
ME2 ... 63 C7
Westfield Cl DA12 ... 37 C2
Westfield Cotts
Cudham TN14 ... 119 D3
Lower Halstow ME9 ... 67 A2
West Kingsdown TN15 ... 90 F4
Westfield Gdns ME9 ... 100 C3
Westfield Ho TN30 ... 344 F7
Westfield La CT18 ... 305 C3
Westfield
New Ash Green DA3 ... 91 F6
1 Orpington BR6 ... 86 C5
Westfield Rd
Bexley DA7 ... 14 C4
Birchington CT7 ... 81 A7
Margate CT9 ... 82 C8
Westfield TN13 ... 154 C5
Westfield Sole Rd
ME5,ME14 ... 130 D8
Westfields TN27 ... 265 D8
Westfield St SE18 ... 1 D3
Westfield Terr TN17 ... 319 F1
Westfield Villas TN12 ... 259 B5
Westgate Ave CT7 ... 82 A4
Westgate Bay Ave CT8 ... 50 C1
Westgate Cl CT2 ... 142 C1
Westgate College for Deaf
People CT9 ... 50 J2
Westgate Court Ave
CT2 ... 142 D1
Westgate Ct
8 Canterbury CT2 ... 142 E1
Lewisham SE12 ... 29 A7
Westgate Garden Flats
CT2 ... 174 E8
Westgate Gr CT2 ... 142 F1
Westgate Hall Rd 14
CT1 ... 142 F1
Westgate Ho 6 DA1 ... 15 D1
Westgate-on-Sea Sta
CT8 ... 81 E8
Westgate Prim Sch
DA1 ... 33 D8
Westgate Rd
Dartford DA1 ... 15 D1
Faversham ME13 ... 138 E7
Westgate Terr CT5 ... 74 E2
West Gn ME10 ... 68 F1
West Hallowes SE9 ... 29 E7
Westharold BR8 ... 55 D6
West Heath Cl DA1 ... 14 F1
West Heath La TN13 ... 187 B7
West Heath Rd
Bexley SE2 ... 13 D8
Crayford DA1 ... 14 F1
West Hill BR6 ... 118 F7
Westhill Cl DA12 ... 37 B7
West Hill DA1 ... 15 D1
West Hill Dr DA1 ... 15 C1
West Hill Prim Sch
DA1 ... 15 C1
West Hill Rd CT6 ... 76 C5
West Hill Rise DA1 ... 15 D1
West Holme DA8 ... 14 C6
Westholme BR6 ... 53 F2
Westhorne Ave SE12,
SE9 ... 11 C2
Westhurst Dr BR7 ... 30 B3
West Hythe Rd CT21 ... 353 A8
West Kent Ave DA11 ... 18 C1
West Kent Coll TN9 ... 254 A7
West Kingsdown CE Prim
Sch TN15 ... 91 A2
West Kingsdown Ind Est
TN15 ... 90 F2
West La ME3 ... 26 F6
Westland Ho 1 E16 ... 2 A5
Westland Lodge 2
BR1 ... 52 C7
Westlands Ave ME10 ... 101 B4
Westlands Rd CT6 ... 76 C3
Westlands Sch The
ME10 ... 101 B4
Westland Way CT18 ... 307 B3
West Lane Trad Est
ME10 ... 102 A4
West La Sheerness ME12 ... 28 A2
Sittingbourne ME10 ... 102 A4
West Lawn Gdns
CT20 ... 334 D3
Westlea Ct CT20 ... 335 A3
West Lea CT14 ... 215 C7
Westleigh Dr BR1 ... 52 E8
Westleigh Rd CT8 ... 81 D8
West Lodge Prep Sch
DA14 ... 31 A5
West Malling CE Prim Sch
ME19 ... 159 B8
West Malling Ind Pk
ME19 ... 126 E2
West Malling Sta
ME19 ... 159 D8
Westmarsh Cl ME15 ... 195 F7
Westmarsh Dr CT9 ... 51 E2
Westmarsh Dro CT3 ... 147 A8
Westmead ME20 ... 128 C4
Westmeads Com Inf Sch
CT5 ... 74 E2
Westmeads Rd CT5 ... 74 E2
West Mersea Cl E16 ... 1 B5
West Mill DA11 ... 18 F1
West Mill Rd ME20 ... 128 C4
Westminster Ind Est
SE18 ... 1 D3
West Minster Prim Sch
ME12 ... 46 B8
Westminster Rd CT1 ... 143 C4
Westminster Sq ME16 ... 161 B4
Westminster Wlk CT12 ... 83 C1
Westmoors TN23 ... 299 E6
Westmoor St SE7 ... 1 D3
Westmoreland Ave
DA16 ... 12 E3
Westmoreland Dr ME9 ... 67 C3
Westmoreland Pl 9
BR1 ... 52 A6
Westmoreland Rd BR2 ... 52 A5
Westmore Rd TN16 ... 150 C7
Westmorland Cl ME15 ... 195 E7
Westmorland Gn
ME15 ... 195 E7
Westmorland Rd
ME15 ... 195 E7
West Motney Way
Gillingham ME8 ... 66 A3
Rainham ME8 ... 65 F3
Westmount Ave ME4 ... 63 F3
Westmount Ho 4 CT9 ... 51 B2
Westmount Rd SE9 ... 12 A3
West Norman Rd
CT16 ... 310 E8
Weston Ave RM20 ... 16 F8
Weston Rd ME2 ... 63 A8
Westonville Ave CT9 ... 50 F1
Westover Gdns CT10 ... 83 E7
Westover Rd CT10 ... 83 E6
West Par CT21 ... 333 B1
West Park Ave
Margate CT9 ... 51 D1
Royal Tunbridge Wells
TN4 ... 253 F1
West Park Farm North Ret
Pk CT19 ... 335 B8
West Park Rd ME15 ... 162 B2
West Parkside SE10 ... 1 A2
West Pas ME12 ... 28 A2
West Pk SE9 ... 29 E7
West Pl TN29 ... 370 D8
West Ramp CT16 ... 310 G8
West Rd Chatham ME4 ... 64 A7
Cliffs End CT13 ... 116 A1
Folkestone CT20 ... 334 C4
Goudhurst TN17 ... 318 E8
Kilndown TN17 ... 317 F3
Westree Ct 7 ME16 ... 161 E3
Westree Rd ME16 ... 161 E3
West Ridge ME10 ... 101 D3
Westrise TN9 ... 254 A7
West Shaw DA3 ... 58 D7
Westside Apartments 10
CT2 ... 142 F1
West Side CT15 ... 247 A1
West St Ashford TN23 ... 268 B2
Bexley DA7 ... 13 F4
Bromley BR1 ... 52 A7
Deal CT14 ... 215 D6
Dover CT17 ... 310 C8
Erith DA8 ... 4 E1
Faversham ME13 ... 138 C7
Gillingham ME7 ... 64 D6
Gravesend DA11 ... 19 B1
Grays RM17 ... 18 A8
Harrietsham ME17 ... 198 C6
Hothfield TN26 ... 266 F7
Hunton ME15 ... 226 D7
Lenham ME17 ... 166 E1
New Romney TN28 ... 373 A6
Queenborough ME11 ... 45 F5
West Street Cotts
CT14 ... 181 A1
West St Rochester ME2 ... 40 B1
Sheerness ME12 ... 28 A2
Sittingbourne ME10 ... 101 E4
West Malling ME19 ... 159 B8
Wrotham TN15 ... 124 F3
West Tank Farm Rd
TN29 ... 380 C2
West Terr
Folkestone CT20 ... 335 D4
Sidcup DA15 ... 30 E7
West Thurrock Prim Sch
RM20 ... 17 A8
West Thurrock Way
RM20 ... 17 B8
West View Cl CT6 ... 76 C2
West View CT19 ... 335 D8
West View Hospl
TN30 ... 344 E6
West View Rd
Crockenhill BR8 ... 55 D3
Dartford DA1 ... 15 F1
Swanley BR8 ... 56 A5
Westview ME4 ... 41 B2
Westway ME17 ... 194 C3
West Way BR5 ... 53 D4
Westway TN2 ... 287 D7
Westways
Edenbridge TN8 ... 217 C2
Westerham TN16 ... 151 C1
Westwell Cl BR5 ... 54 D1
Westwell Ct
Tenterden TN30 ... 344 F7
Westwell TN25 ... 235 E3
Westwell Ho TN30 ... 344 F7
Westwell La
Charing TN25,TN27 ... 234 F5
Potters Corner TN24,
TN25 ... 267 E7
Westwell TN25,TN26 ... 235 B4
West Wlk ME16 ... 161 B3
Westwood Cl BR1 ... 52 D6
West Wood Cott BR6 ... 88 B4
Westwood Ct ME13 ... 138 E3
Westwood Farm DA13 ... 35 D2
Westwood Ind Est CT9 ... 83 A6
Westwood La DA16 ... 12 F4
Westwood Pl ME13 ... 138 D5
Westwood Rd
Betsham DA13 ... 35 E2
Broadstairs CT10 ... 83 C4
East Peckham TN12 ... 224 E6
Loose ME15 ... 195 A7
Rusthall TN4 ... 285 C5
West Wood Rd ME9 ... 132 B8
Westwood Ret Pk CT10 ... 83 A5
West Woodside DA5 ... 31 E7
Westwood Tech Coll
DA16 ... 12 E3
Westwood Way TN13 ... 153 F5
Westwood Wlk ME9 ... 100 B7
West Yoke TN15 ... 91 D7
Wetheral Dr ME5 ... 97 B4
Weybridge Cl ME5 ... 97 C4
Weyburn Dr CT12 ... 83 A1
Wey Cl ME5 ... 97 C5
Weyhill Cl ME14 ... 162 C6
Weyman Rd SE3 ... 11 C6
Weymouth Cl
Folkestone CT19 ... 334 D7
Newham E6 ... 2 B7
Weymouth Rd CT19 ... 334 D6
Weymouth Terr CT19 ... 334 D7
Wey St TN26 ... 349 D3
Whalf Rd CT13 ... 149 B4
Wharfedale Rd
Dartford DA2 ... 34 C7
Margate CT9 ... 51 A1
Wharf La ME3 ... 22 B6
Wharf Rd
Gillingham ME7 ... 64 C7
Gravesend DA12 ... 19 E1
Grays RM17 ... 17 F8
Maidstone ME15 ... 161 E2
Wharf Rd S RM17 ... 17 F8
Wharfside Cl DA8 ... 4 F1
Wharnecliffe Ho DA9 ... 17 B1
Wharton Gdns TN24 ... 300 E8
Wharton Rd BR1 ... 52 B8
Whatcote Cotts TN15 ... 157 C7
Whatman Cl ME14 ... 162 C6
Whatman Ho ME13 ... 139 F4
Whatmer Cl CT2 ... 144 A6
Wheatcroft Cl ME10 ... 102 B4
Wheatcroft DA12 ... 37 C7
Wheatcroft Gr ME8 ... 98 F7
Wheatear Way ME5 ... 97 B7
Wheatfield Cl TN17 ... 320 C5
Wheatfield Dr TN17 ... 320 C5
Wheatfield Lea TN17 ... 320 C5
Wheatfield ME19 ... 127 E1
Wheatfields
Chatham ME5 ... 97 D2
Maidstone ME14 ... 162 D4
Newham E6 ... 2 B7
Wheatfield Way TN17 ... 320 C5
Wheatley Cl DA9 ... 17 A2
Wheatley Rd
Ramsgate CT12 ... 83 C1
Whitstable CT5 ... 74 E2
Wheatley Terrace Rd
DA8 ... 14 F8
Wheatsheaf Cl
Boughton Street ME13 ... 140 A3
Loose ME15 ... 195 B8
Wheatsheafe La CT15 ... 247 B2
Wheatsheaf Gdns
ME12 ... 28 B1
Wheatsheaf Hill
Chelsfield TN14 ... 87 F2
Ide Hill TN14 ... 185 F4
Wheatsheaf Way
TN10 ... 222 D6
Wheatstone Rd DA8 ... 4 D1
Wheelbarrow Park Est
TN12 ... 259 B7
Wheeler Pl ME18 ... 159 A2
Wheeler's La ME17 ... 227 E7
Wheeler St TN27 ... 262 E5
Wheelers The ME8 ... 98 B6
Wheeler St ME14 ... 162 A5
Wheelock Cl DA8 ... 14 B7
Wheelwrights The
ME17 ... 198 D6
Wheelwrights Way
CT13 ... 180 B2
Wheelwrites TN15 ... 189 E7
Wheler Ct ME13 ... 138 A7
Wheler Rd TN27 ... 234 C8
Whenman Ave DA5 ... 32 C5
Whernside Cl SE28 ... 3 C6
Whetsted Rd
Five Oak Green TN12 ... 256 C8
Whetsted TN12 ... 224 F1
Whetstone Rd SE3 ... 11 D6
Whewell Terr 1 CT20 ... 335 E5
Whiffen's Ave ME4 ... 63 F5
Whiffen's Ave W ME4 ... 63 F5
Whiffen Wlk ME19 ... 128 B1
Whigham Cl TN23 ... 299 D7
Whimbrel Cl
Sittingbourne ME10 ... 101 F8
Woolwich SE28 ... 3 C6
Whimbrel Gn ME20 ... 127 F2
Whimbrels The ME4 ... 41 B1
Whimbrel Wlk ME5 ... 97 C1
Whinchat Rd SE28 ... 2 D3
Whinfell Ave CT11 ... 116 F7
Whinfell Way DA12 ... 37 F4
Whinless Rd CT17 ... 310 A8
Whinyates Rd SE9 ... 11 E4
Whippendell Cl BR5 ... 54 B8
Whippendell Way BR5 ... 54 B7
Whistler Rd TN10 ... 222 D6
Whiston Ave TN26 ... 297 C4
Whitbourne Ct CT5 ... 108 D8
Whitby Cl
Biggin Hill TN16 ... 118 B1
Stone DA9 ... 17 A2
Whitby Rd
Folkestone CT20 ... 334 D6
Woolwich SE18 ... 1 F2
Whitchurch Cl ME16 ... 161 E4
Whitcombe Cl ME5 ... 97 C3
White Acre Dr CT14 ... 248 B8
Whiteacre La CT4 ... 239 E4
White Ave DA11 ... 36 F5
Whitebeam Ave BR2 ... 53 A3
Whitebeam Cl
Ashford TN23 ... 267 D4
Kemsing TN15 ... 123 A2
Whitebeam Dr ME17 ... 194 B3
White Bear Pas 3
TN1 ... 286 A2
Whitebine Gdns TN12 ... 225 A6
White Cliffs Bsns Ctr
CT16 ... 278 A6
White Cliffs Bsns Pk
CT16 ... 278 B6
White Cliffs 11 CT20 ... 335 D4
Whitecliff Way CT19 ... 335 F6
White Cottage Rd
TN10 ... 222 D6
Whitecroft BR8 ... 55 E7
White Ct 8 CT20 ... 334 E3
Whitefield Cl BR5 ... 54 C6
Whitefield Rd TN4 ... 286 A6
Whitefriars Mdw 15
CT13 ... 148 F1
Whitefriars TN13 ... 187 A8
Whitefriars Way 14
CT13 ... 148 F1
Whitefriars Wharf
TN9 ... 222 C1
Whitegate Cl TN4 ... 286 A8
Whitegate Ct ME8 ... 98 D5
White Gate ME2 ... 62 F8
Whitegates Ave TN15 ... 90 E4
Whitegates La TN5 ... 336 D8
White Gates DA14 ... 31 A3
Whitehall Bridge Rd
CT2 ... 174 E8
Whitehall TN29 ... 370 E8
Whitehall Cl CT2 ... 174 E8
Whitehall Dr ME17 ... 197 D3
Whitehall Gdns CT2 ... 142 E1
Whitehall La Erith DA8 ... 14 F5
6 Grays RM17 ... 18 C8
Whitehall Rd
Broad Street ME14 ... 164 A6
Bromley BR2 ... 52 D5
Canterbury CT2 ... 174 E8
Canterbury,Harbledown
CT2 ... 174 D7
Ramsgate CT12 ... 83 C1
Sittingbourne ME10 ... 101 E2
Whitehall CT13 ... 182 A7
Whitehall Way TN25 ... 303 D1
White Hart Cl TN13 ... 187 C7
White Hart Mans CT9 ... 50 I3
White Hart Par TN13 ... 153 E5
White Hart Rd
Orpington BR6 ... 54 A2
Woolwich SE18 ... 2 E2
White Hart Wood
TN13 ... 187 C6
White Hart Yd 10 DA11 ... 19 B1
Whitehaven Cl BR2 ... 52 A5
Whitehaven Ct 6 DA6 ... 13 E3
Whitehead Cl DA2 ... 33 C5
Whiteheads La ME14 ... 163 B4
White Hill
Boughton Aluph TN25 ... 237 B6
Challock TN25 ... 203 E1
Chilham CT4 ... 172 E1
White Hill Cl CT4 ... 208 A8
Whitehill Inf Sch DA12 ... 37 C5
Whitehill Jun Sch
DA12 ... 37 C5
Whitehill La DA12 ... 37 D5
Whitehill Par DA12 ... 37 C5
Whitehill Rd
Dartford DA1 ... 15 A2
Gravesend DA12 ... 37 C6
Longfield,Whitehill DA13 ... 58 D8
Meopham DA13 ... 93 B7
White Hill Rd ME9,
ME14 ... 98 D1
Whitehill TN15 ... 125 B3
Whitehorse Hill ME5 ... 64 B3
White Horse Hill
Eltham BR7,SE9 ... 30 A4
Hawkinge CT18 ... 307 C3
White Horse La
6 Canterbury CT1 ... 174 F8
Harvel DA13 ... 93 C2
Otham Hole ME15 ... 196 A6
Rhodes Minnis CT4 ... 273 A3
White Horse Rd DA13 ... 93 E1
White House Cl ME3 ... 41 E4
Whitehouse Cres ME1 ... 129 A8
Whitehouse Dro CT13,
CT3 ... 148 D7
White House Farm Ct
CT15 ... 211 E5
White House La TN14 ... 186 F5
White House Rd TN14 ... 186 F5
Whitelake Rd TN10 ... 222 C5
White La RH8,TN16 ... 150 B3
Whiteleaves Rise ME2 ... 62 B3
Whitelimes TN18 ... 340 D8
Whitelocks Cl CT4 ... 209 D3
White Lodge Cl TN13 ... 154 B4
White Lodge TN1 ... 286 C4
White Marsh Ct CT5 ... 74 E2
White Mill & Folk Mus★
CT13 ... 148 E2
Whitenbrook Dell
CT21 ... 334 A3
Whitenbrook CT21 ... 334 A3
Whiteness Gn CT10 ... 51 F1
Whiteness Rd CT10 ... 51 G1
White Oak Cl 13 TN9 ... 254 B8
Whiteoak Ct 1 BR8 ... 55 E6
White Oak Gdns DA15 ... 30 F8
White Oak Prim Sch
BR8 ... 55 E7
White Oak Sq 3 BR8 ... 55 E6
White Post Cnr TN11 ... 189 F5
White Post TN8 ... 218 A6
White Post Gdns CT3 ... 147 E1
White Post Hill DA4 ... 57 A2
White Post ME17 ... 165 B5
White Post La
Culverstone Green DA13 ... 92 F2
Sole Street DA13 ... 60 B5
Whitepost La DA13 ... 126 A8
Whitepost 12 CT5 ... 74 D2
White Rd ME4 ... 64 A2
White Rock Ct ME16 ... 161 E3
White Rock Pl 5
ME16 ... 161 E3
Whites Cl DA9 ... 17 C1
Whites Hill CT14 ... 213 B2
White's La TN18 ... 341 B2
White's Mdw BR1 ... 53 A5
Whitewall Ctr ME2 ... 63 D8
Whitewall Rd ME2 ... 63 D7
Whitewall Way ME2 ... 63 D7
Whiteway Rd ME11,
ME12 ... 45 F6
Whitewebbs Way BR5 ... 53 F8
Whitewell La TN17 ... 320 D7
White Willow Cl TN24 ... 300 D6
Whitewood Cotts
TN16 ... 150 C7
White Wood Rd CT13 ... 180 B1
Whitfeld Rd TN23 ... 300 B8
Whitfield Ave
Broadstairs CT10 ... 83 E7
Dover CT16 ... 278 B2
Whitfield Cotts TN23 ... 300 B8
Whitfield Cres DA2 ... 34 C8
Whitfield Ct CT16 ... 278 A6

Whitfield Hill
Dover CT16 ....277 F4
Temple Ewell CT16 ..277 E4
Whitfield Lodge CT16 .278 A8
Whitfield Rd CT16 ....278 A8
Whitfield Rdbt CT16 ..278 A6
Whitfield Sch & Aspen
Specl Unit CT16 .....278 A7
Whitgift Ct CT2 ......142 D1
Whiting Cres ME13 ...138 A8
Whiting Ho TN29 ....376 C5
Whitings Way E6 ....2 A8
Whitmore St ME16 ...161 D2
Whitney Wlk DA14 ....31 E2
Whitstable Jun Sch
CT5 ....74 D1
Whitstable Mus & Art
Gallery ★ CT5 ....74 D1
Whitstable Rd
Canterbury CT2 .....142 D2
Faversham, Goodnestone
ME13 ....139 B6
Faversham ME13 ....138 E7
Herne Bay CT5,CT6 ...76 B3
Rough Common CT2 ..142 D8
Whitstable & Seasalter CE
Jun Sch CT5 ....74 D1
Whitstable & Tankerton
Hospl CT5 ....75 A2
Whitstable & Tankerton Sta
CT5 ....74 E1
Whittaker St ME4 ....64 A4
Whittington Terr
CT15 ....244 D4
Whitworth Rd SE18 ...12 A7
Whybornes Chase
ME12 ....47 C7
Whybourne Crest
TN2 ....286 D1
Whyman Ave ME4 ....64 A1
Whytecliffs CT10 .....84 A2
Wichling Cl
Canterbury CT2 .....143 A3
Orpington BR5 ....54 D1
Wickenden Cres TN24 .301 A8
Wickenden Rd TN13 ..154 C5
Wicken Ho ME16 ....161 E4
Wicken La TN25,TN27 .234 E6
Wickens Pl ME19 ....159 C8
Wickets The
Ashford TN24 ....300 F7
Sevenoaks Weald TN14 .187 C2
Wickham Ave CT11 ...117 G8
Wickham Cl ME9 ....100 B6
Wickham Common Prim
Sch BR4 ....85 A6
Wickham Court La
CT3 ....145 B3
Wickham Ct DA16 ....12 E5
Wickham Field TN14 ..121 F3
Wickham Gdns TN4 ..285 D5
Wickham La
Ickham CT3 ....145 B1
Woolwich SE2,SE18 ...13 A8
Wickham Mill CT3 ...145 C2
Wickham Pl ME17 ....199 D5
Wickham Rd CT3 ....145 B2
Wickham St
Bexley DA16 ....13 A6
Rochester ME1 ......63 D3
Wickhams Way DA3 ...58 F4
Wickham Terr ME11 ...45 F5
Wickhurst Rd TN14 ..186 F3
Wick La CT4 ....243 E7
Wicks Cl SE9 ....29 D4
Wicksteed Cl DA5 ....32 D5
Widbury TN3 ....284 F3
Widecombe Rd SE9 ...29 E5
Widgeon Cl E16 ....1 B7
Widgeon Path SE28 ....2 D3
Widgeon Rd Erith DA8 .15 B7
Rochester ME2 ....62 D6
Widgeon Wlk CT18 ..307 B3
Widmore Lodge Rd
BR1 ....52 F2
Widmore Rd BR1 .....52 C7
Widred Rd CT17 .....310 C8
Wierton Hill ME17 ...228 D7
Wierton La ME17 ....195 E1
Wierton Rd ME17 ....228 E8
Wife Of Bath Hill CT2 .174 C8
Wigmore La CT15 ....245 C8
Wigmore Rd ME8 .....98 B4
Wigmore Wood CT15 .245 C8
Wigwam Paddocks
CT7 ....81 A8
Wihtred Rd ME9 ....102 D2
Wilberforce Ct 2 SE28 ..3 C5
Wilberforce Rd
Coxheath ME17 .....194 D3
Folkestone CT20 ....334 E3
Wilberforce Way DA12 .37 D3
Wilbrough Rd CT7 ....81 A7
Wilcox Cl CT3 ....210 D5
Wild Air CT7 ....80 F8
Wilde Cl RM18 ....19 C5
Wilden Park Rd TN12 .291 E7
Wilde Rd DA8 ....14 B7
Wildernesse Ave
TN15 ....154 F5
Wildernesse Mount
TN13 ....154 D5
Wilderness Sch The
TN13 ....154 E6
Wilderness Hill CT9 ...51 A2
Wilderness Rd BR7 ....30 B1
Wildfell Cl ME5 .....130 C8
Wildish Rd ME13 ....138 A8
Wildman Cl ME8 ......98 D3

Wildwood Cl
Kingswood ME17 .....197 E2
1 Lewisham SE12 .....29 A8
Wildwood Glade ME7 ..98 B4
Wildwood Rd CT2 ....143 C7
Wildwood Wealden Forest
Pk ★ CT2,CT6 ......110 D4
Wiles Ave TN28 .....373 B6
Wiles Ho TN28 ......373 B6
Wilford Ho 3 SE18 ....2 B1
Wilford Rd CT11 .....117 C8
Wilfred St 2 DA12 ....19 B1
Wilgate Green Rd
ME13 ....169 F6
Wilkes Rd CT10 ....83 E4
Wilkie Rd CT7 ....81 A8
Wilkinson Cl 1 DA1 ..16 A3
Wilkinson Dr CT14 ...215 D3
Wilkinson Pl ME18 ...159 A2
Wilkinson Rd E16 .....1 C7
Wilkins Way TN16 ...152 B3
Wilks Ave DA1 ....33 F6
Wilks Cl ME8 ....66 B2
Will Adams Ct 9 ME7 .64 C6
Will Adams Rdbt ME8 .64 F1
Will Adams Way ME8 ..64 F1
Will Crooks Gdns SE9 .11 D3
Willenhall Rd SE18 ....2 B1
Willersley Ave
Orpington BR6 ....86 D7
Sidcup DA15 ....30 D7
Willersley Cl DA15 ....30 D7
Willesborough Ct
TN24 ....269 A2
Willesborough Ind Pk
TN24 ....269 A1
Willesborough Inf & Jun
Schs TN24 ....301 A8
Willesborough Rd
TN24 ....268 F4
Willesborough Windmill ★
TN24 ....269 A1
Willesley Gdns TN17 .320 D6
Willett Cl BR5 ....53 E3
Willetts Cotts TN3 ...283 C4
Willetts Hill CT12 ....114 D7
Willetts La TN3 .....283 C4
Willett Way BR5,BR6 ..53 E3
William Ave
Folkestone CT19 ....335 B7
Margate CT9 ....83 C8
William Baker Ho
ME20 ....160 F8
William Barefoot Dr
SE9 ....30 A5
William Gibbs Ct 14
ME13 ....138 D7
William Harvey Hospl
TN24 ....269 C1
William Ho 4 DA12 ...37 B8
William Judge Cl
TN30 ....345 D7
William Luck Cl TN12 .224 E6
William Muge Ho 15
CT16 ....310 D4
William Pitt Ave CT14 .215 B6
William Pitt Cl CT21 .333 D2
William Rd
Ashford TN23 ....300 B8
Cuxton ME2 ....62 C2
William Rigby Dr ME12 .46 E7
William Smith Ho 10
DA17 ....4 A3
Williamson Rd TN29 .377 E5
William St
Faversham ME13 ....138 D7
Gillingham ME7 .....66 A1
Gravesend DA12 .....37 B8
Grays RM17 ....18 C8
Herne Bay CT6 ......76 F5
Royal Tunbridge Wells
TN4 ....286 A5
Sittingbourne ME10 ..101 E4
Whitstable CT5 ......74 D1
Williams Way DA2 ....32 D6
Willicombe Ho TN4 ..286 A4
Willicombe Pk TN2 ..286 A4
Willingdon TN23 ....299 E5
Willingdon Pl CT14 ..215 C1
Willingdon Rd CT16 ..278 A5
Willington Gn ME15 ..195 E7
Willington St ME15 ..162 F2
Willis Ct ME12 ....46 F5
Willis Ho ME1 ....63 C4
Willis Rd DA8 ....4 D2
Willop Cl TN29 ......352 F3
Willop Way TN29 ....352 F3
Willoughby Ct 14 CT1 .174 C7
Willoughby Way SE7 ...1 B2
Willow Ave
Broadstairs CT10 .....83 D4
Faversham ME13 ....138 A7
Hoo St Werburgh ME3 .41 E3
Sidcup DA15 ....13 A1
Swanley BR8 ....33 D8
Willowbank Cl TN29 .366 A4
Willowbank Ct 12
ME15 ....162 B4
Willowbank Dr ME23 ..23 E4
Willow Bank Ind Est
ME9 ....68 E6
Willowby Gdns ME8 ...98 E4
Willow Cl Bromley BR2 .52 F4
Canterbury CT2 .....143 A2
Hythe CT21 ....332 E1
Margate CT9 ....51 C2
Orpington BR5 ....54 B2
Sidcup DA15 ....13 F1
Willow Cres
Five Oak Green TN12 .256 B7
Staplehurst TN12 ...260 F5

Willow Ct
Broadstairs CT10 .....84 A5
Dartford DA1 ....33 C7
Folkestone CT20 ....334 E4
Loose ME15 ....195 A6
Willow Dene Sch SE18 .12 E6
Willow Dr
Hamstreet TN26 ....349 A7
St Mary's Bay TN29 ..365 F3
Willow Farm Way CT6 ..77 C2
Willowfields CT18 .....2 E1
Willow Grange DA14 ..31 B5
Willow Gr BR7 ....30 B2
Willowherb Cl ME4 ...41 C1
Willow Ho
Ashford TN23 ....267 F1
2 Chatham ME5 .....96 F5
8 Maidstone ME16 ..161 A3
Sheerness ME12 ......28 B2
Sittingbourne ME10 ..102 B3
Willow La
Paddock Wood TN12 .257 E6
Woolwich SE18 ......2 A2
Willow Lea TN10 ....222 C7
Willow Lodge
Folkestone CT19 ....335 D7
Royal Tunbridge Wells
TN4 ....285 E4
Willowmead ME19 ...127 E2
Willow Pk TN14 .....121 F7
Willow Rd Dartford DA1 .33 C7
Erith DA8 ....15 A6
Great Mongeham CT14 .214 F3
Larkfield ME20 .....127 F3
Rochester ME2 ......62 E6
Whitstable CT5 .....108 C5
Willow Rise ME15 ...162 F1
Willows Ct CT1 .....142 C4
Willowside ME6 ......95 A1
Willows The
Ashford TN24 ....268 D6
Gillingham ME8 ......65 E2
Grays RM17 ....18 D8
Newington ME9 .....100 B6
Sheerness ME12 ......28 H1
Sittingbourne ME10 ..68 F1
Willow Terr DA4 ......89 E8
Willow Tree Cl
Ashford TN24 ....268 F1
Herne Bay CT6 ......77 D5
Willow Tree Ct CT14 ..30 F3
Willow Tree Rd TN2 ..285 F1
Willow Tree Wlk BR1 ..52 B8
Willow Vale BR7 ......30 B2
Willow Way ME27 ...323 D7
Willow Waye CT15 ..245 D7
Willow Way
Maidstone ME15 ....162 B3
Margate CT9 ....82 C8
Whitstable CT5 .....109 C8
Willow Wents ME18 .158 D1
Willow Wlk
Culverstone Green DA13 ..92 F3
Orpington BR6 ....86 B7
Royal Tunbridge Wells
TN2 ....286 E8
Willow Wood Rd DA13 .92 F2
Willrose Cres SE2 .....3 B1
Wills La TN29 ....100 C7
Willson's Rd CT11 ...117 D6
Will Thorne Pav The
E16 ....1 E7
Wilman Rd TN4 .....286 B7
Wilmar Way TN15 ...154 E7
Wilmecote Ct ME8 ...98 D8
Wilmington Ave BR6 ..87 C8
Wilmington Court Rd
DA2 ....33 A6
Wilmington Gram Sch for
Boys DA2 ....33 B5
Wilmington Hall Sch
DA2 ....33 B5
Wilmington Ho DA2 ..33 D6
Wilmington Prim Sch
DA2 ....33 B5
Wilmington Way ME8 ..65 B2
Wilmot Rd DA1 ......15 B2
Wilmott Pl CT13 ....180 B2
Wilmount St SE18 .....2 B2
Wilson Ave Deal CT14 .214 F4
Rochester ME1 ......96 E7
Wilson Cl
Ashford TN23 ....269 A1
Maidstone ME15 ....195 A1
Tonbridge TN11 ....221 E5
Wilson Ct ME18 .....193 A1
Wilson Ho 3 SE7 .....11 C8
Wilson La DA4 ....57 F7
Wilson Rd TN10 ....222 E5
Wilsons La ME15 ....194 A5
Wilsons Way DA13 ....92 F3
Wiltie Ct CT19 ......335 C5
Wiltie Gdns CT19 ...335 C5
Wilton Cl CT14 .....215 C5
Wilton Dr ME20 ....160 B8
Wilton Ho 2 BR7 .....53 D8
Wilton Rd
Folkestone CT19 ....335 B6
Ramsgate CT12 ......82 F1
Woolwich SE2 ....3 C2
Wiltshire Terr ME10 ..101 B5
Wiltshire Rd
Bromley BR6 ....54 A2
Dartford DA2 ....34 D8
Wiltshire Rd BR6 .....54 A2
Wiltshire Way
4 Maidstone ME15 ..195 A8
Royal Tunbridge Wells
TN2 ....286 C3
Wimborne Ave BR7 ...53 F6
Wimborne Ho DA12 ..37 D5
Wimborne Pl CT12 ..117 B8
Wimborne 6 DA14 ...31 B4

Wimbourne Dr ME8 ...98 D6
Wimpole Cl BR2 ......52 C5
Winant Way CT16 ...278 B3
Winch Cl TN17 ......320 D3
Winchcomb Gdns SE9 ..11 D4
Wincheap CT1 ....174 E7
Wincheap Foundation Prim
Sch CT1 ....174 E6
Wincheap Gn 4 CT1 .174 F7
Wincheap Ind Est
CT1 ....174 D7
Winchelsea Ave DA7 ..13 F7
Winchelsea Ct CT17 .310 C7
Winchelsea Rd
Chatham ME5 ....97 B5
Dover CT17 ....310 B7
Winchelsea St CT17 .310 B7
Winchelsea Terr CT17 .310 B7
Winchester Ave ME5 ..96 F5
Winchester Cl 11 ME6 .67 F7
Winchester Cres DA12 .37 D5
Winchester Ct 14 DA17 ..4 A1
Winchester Gdns CT1 .175 A6
Winchester Gr TN13 .154 B4
Winchester Ho
3 Maidstone ME15 ...195 D4
Woolwich SE18 ......11 D7
Winchester Mews
CT14 ....215 B3
Winchester Pl 9
ME14 ....162 A5
Winchester Rd
Bexley DA7 ....13 D5
Hawkhurst TN18 ....341 A2
Orpington BR6 ....87 C6
Tonbridge TN10 ....222 D5
Winchester Way ME8 ..99 A8
Winch's Garth TN12 ..260 F5
Wincliff Rd TN9 .....254 B8
Wincrofts Dr SE9 .....12 D3
Windermere Ave
CT11 ....117 A7
Windermere Cl
Dartford DA1 ....33 B7
Orpington BR6 ....86 B7
Windermere Ct TN24 .268 C4
Windermere Dr ME8 ..98 D7
Windermere Ho ME13 .138 E6
Windermere Gdns
CT3 ....210 F6
Windermere Rd DA7 ..14 C5
Windermere Ho 4
ME15 ....195 E7
Windermere Rd DA7 ..14 C5
Wind Hill ME7 ....233 E7
Wind Hill La TN27 ..233 E7
Windhover Way DA12 ..37 E4
Winding Hill ME13 ..170 F6
Windmill Ave CT12 ...83 B3
Windmill Cl
Ashford TN24 ....269 A1
Bridge CT4 ....176 A1
Canterbury CT1 .....175 C8
Herne Bay CT6 ......77 A2
Rochester ME2 ......40 B1
Windmill Cotts
Cranbrook TN17 ....320 D6
Lower Stoke ME3 ....25 C5
Windmill Ct
Maidstone ME17 ...195 B3
Royal Tunbridge Wells
TN2 ....286 C3
Whitstable CT5 .....108 C7
Windmill Dr BR2 .....85 C6
Windmill Grange TN15 .90 F3
Windmill Hill
Brenchley TN12 ....257 B1
Fairbourne Heath ME17 .198 B1
Platt TN15 ....157 D7
Pye Corner ME4 ....231 B7
Windmill Hts ME14 .163 B4
Windmill La
Cousley Wood TN5 ..337 C8
Durgates TN5 ....336 E4
Windmill La E ME19 .159 C6
Windmill La W ME9 .159 A6
Windmill Manor ME7 ..64 C4
Windmill Par CT11 ..117 C6
Windmill Pk TN15 ..157 E7
Windmill Quay Rd
ME12 ....47 E2
Windmill Rd
Canterbury CT1 .....175 C8
Gillingham ME7 ......64 C4
Herne Bay CT6 ......77 A2
Sevenoaks TN13 ....187 B6
Sevenoaks Weald TN14 .187 B2
Sittingbourne ME10 ..101 D6
Whitstable CT5 .....108 C7
Windmill Rise ME12 ..47 E6
Windmill Row ME17 .196 D2
Windmill St
Gravesend DA12 .....37 B7
Hythe CT21 ....333 B1
Rochester ME2 ......40 B1
Royal Tunbridge Wells
TN2 ....286 C3
Windmill View CT19 ..83 A8
Windmill Wlk CT12 ...83 B1
Windrush Cl 8 DA8 ....4 E1
Windrush Prim Sch
SE28 ....3 B5
Windsor Ave
Chatham ME4 ....63 F2
Margate CT9 ....51 B1
Windsor Cl
Broadstairs CT10 .....83 E5
Chislehurst BR7 ......30 B3
Maidstone ME14 ...162 B6

Windsor Ct
1 Bromley BR1 ......52 E6
Deal CT14 ....215 C2
Gillingham ME7 ......64 D5
Margate CT9 ....51 B1
18 Sidcup DA14 .....31 A5
Windsor Dr
Dartford DA1 ....15 A1
Orpington BR6 ....87 A4
Sittingbourne ME10 ..101 D2
Windsor Gdns
Herne Bay CT6 ......76 B3
Warden ME12 ....49 D4
Windsor Hall E16 .....1 B5
Windsor Ho Deal CT14 .215 A5
6 Dover CT17 ......310 D7
Whitstable CT5 ......74 D1
Windsor Mews
9 Margate CT9 ......50 J2
New Romney TN28 ..373 C8
Windsor Rd Bexley DA6 .13 C3
Cliffs End CT12 .....116 D7
Gillingham ME7 ......64 D5
Gravesend DA12 .....37 B4
Windward Rd ME1 ....63 C1
Windy Ridge BR1 .....52 E8
Windyridge ME7 .....64 E1
Winehouse La CT18 ..308 D3
Wineycock ME9 .....168 C8
Winfield La TN15 ...156 E3
Winford Mews ME1 ...63 C2
Win'freds Ct TN17 ...343 E3
Wingate Ct 7 ME10 .101 E4
Wingate Rd
Folkestone CT19 ....335 D7
Sidcup DA14 ....31 C2
Wingfield Ct CT15 ....30 F7
Wingfield Prim Sch
SE3 ....11 B4
Wingfield Rd DA12 ...37 B8
Wingham Cl
Gillingham ME8 ......65 C3
Maidstone ME15 ....195 F7
Wingham Ind Est CT3 .178 B6
Wingham Prim Sch
CT3 ....178 A7
Wingham Rd CT3 ...177 D8
Wingham Well La CT3 .177 F5
Wingham Wildlife Pk ★
CT3 ....146 C1
Wing Ho ME12 ....49 H1
Wing Rd ME12 ......49 H1
Wingrove Dr
Maidstone ME14 ...162 C5
Rochester ME2 ......63 C7
Wingrove Hill CT17 ..277 C2
Wings Cl CT10 ....84 B5
Winifred Ave CT12 ...83 C2
Winifred Rd
Dartford DA1 ....15 B2
Erith DA8 ....4 E1
Maidstone ME15 ....162 F3
Winifred St E16 ....1 F5
Winkle Cl ME15 ......76 B3
Winn Common Rd
SE18 ....12 E8
Winnipeg Cl CT16 ...278 C3
Winnipeg Dr BR6 .....86 F4
Winn Rd SE12,SE9 ....29 B7
Win Pine Ho CT21 ...333 A1
Winser Rd TN17 ....344 A1
Winsor Prim Sch E6 ...2 A7
Winstanley Cres CT11 .117 D8
Winstanley Rd ME12 ..28 C2
Winston Ave ME18 ..159 B3
Winston Cl
Canterbury CT1 .....175 C7
Stone ME3 ....16 F1
Winston Ct
Birchington CT7 ......81 A8
10 Bromley BR1 .....52 E8
Winston Dr ME2 ......40 D2
Winstone Scott Ave
TN3 ....284 E4
Winston Gdns CT6 ...77 D4
Winston Ho 4 CT20 .334 F5
Winston Rd ME2 .....62 D5
Winterage La CT18 ..306 C2
Winterborne Ave BR6 ..86 D7
Winter Dr CT18 .....307 B5
Winterfield La ME19 .159 E8
Wintergarden Cres
DA9 ....35 A8
Wintergreen Cl
8 Newham E16 ....1 E8
St Mary's Island ME4 .41 C1
Winters Croft DA12 ...37 D2
Winterstoke Cres
CT11 ....117 G8
Winterstoke Way
CT11 ....117 F8
Winterton Ct 8 TN16 .151 D1
Winton Ct 8 BR6 .....55 E5
Winton Rd BR6 ......86 B6
Winton Way TN29 ..366 A5
Wireless Rd TN16 ...118 D4
Wirrals The ME5 ......97 A4
Wirral Wood Cl BR7 ..30 A2
Wiseacre TN30 ......317 A3
Wise Ho SE18 ....12 A7
Wises La ME10,ME9 ..101 A4
Wise's La TN15 ....91 E2
Wishart Rd SE3 ......11 D5
Wish The TN26 .....347 F6
Wisley Bd BR5 ....31 B1
Wissenden La TN26 ..297 B6
Wistaria Ct BR6 ......86 B8
Wisteria Gdns BR8 ...55 D7
Wisteria Ho 11 ME15 .195 E7
Witches La TN13 ....153 D4
Witham Way ME2 ....62 F7

Withens Cl BR5 ....54 C5
Withersdane Cotts
TN25 ....238 A2
Witherston Way SE9 ..30 A8
Withyham Rd TN3 ...312 B7
Witley Sch CT6 ......278 B7
Wittersham CE Prim Sch
TN30 ....359 D2
Wittersham Cl ME5 ...97 B5
Wittersham Ho 2 BR5 .54 D1
Wittersham La TN31 ..368 B7
Wittersham Rd
Iden TN31 ....368 B7
Stone in Oxney TN30 .360 C3
Wittersham,Potman's Heath
TN17,TN30 ....358 D4
Wittersham TN30 ...359 C5
Wittersham Road Sta ★
TN17 ....358 D6
Wivenhoe TN23 ....299 E5
Wivenhoe Cl ME8 ....66 A2
Wixom Ho SE3 ....11 C3
Woburn Cl SE28 ......3 D7
Woburn Ct 1 DA6 ....13 F3
Wodehouse Cl ME20 .127 F4
Wodehouse Rd DA1 ..14 B3
Wold Cvn Pk The ME12 .48 F6
Woldham Pl BR2 .....52 C5
Woldham Rd BR2 ....52 C5
Wolds Dr BR6 ....86 A6
Wolfe Cl BR2 ....52 A3
Wolfe Cres SE7 ....1 D1
Wolfe Ct CT14 ....215 D3
Wolfe Rd ME16 .....161 B2
Wolf Ho ME4 ....64 B8
Wolf's Cnr RH8 ......183 B6
Wolf's Hill RH8 ......183 A4
Wolf's Rd RH8 ......183 B5
Wolf's Row RH8 .....183 B6
Wolfs Wood RH8 ...183 A3
Wollaston Cl ME8 ....98 D3
Wollaston Rd CT14 ..215 D4
Wolseley Ave CT6 ....76 A4
Wolseley Pl 4 TN4 ..268 B3
Wolseley Rd TN4 ...286 C7
Wolseley Terr TN29 ..376 C5
Wolsey Ct SE9 ....11 F1
Wolsey Mews BR6 ....86 F5
Wolsley Cl DA1 ......14 E2
Wolsley Ho DA1 .....14 E2
Wolvercote Rd SE2 ....3 D4
Wombwell Gdns DA11 .36 E6
Women's Land Army Mus
The ★ TN26 ....309 E5
Wood Ave CT19 .....335 E7
Woodberry Dr ME10 .102 C3
Woodberry Flats CT10 .84 A3
Woodberry Gr DA5 ...32 D5
Woodbine Cotts ME2 ..94 E5
Woodbine Rd DA15 ...13 B8
Woodbridge Dr ME15 .161 F1
Woodbrook TN27 ...234 D7
Woodbrook Rd SE2 ..13 B8
Woodbury Cl
Biggin Hill TN16 ....118 F1
Royal Tunbridge Wells
TN4 ....286 A5
Woodbury Gdns SE12 .29 B4
Woodbury La TN30 ..345 A7
Woodbury Park Gdns
TN4 ....286 B6
Woodbury Park Rd
TN4 ....286 B6
Woodbury Rd
Chatham ME5 ....96 F1
Hawkhurst TN18 ....341 A2
Woodchurch CE Prim Sch
TN26 ....326 A2
Woodchurch Cl
Chatham ME5 ....97 B5
Sidcup DA14 ....30 B8
Woodchurch Cotts CT7 .81 F4
Woodchurch Cres ME8 .65 C2
Woodchurch Cl 1 BR5 .54 C4
Woodchurch Dr BR1 ..29 D1
Woodchurch House
ME8 ....65 C2
Woodchurch Rd
Appledore Heath TN26 .347 C4
Margate CT7,CT9 .....82 A5
Shadoxhurst TN26 ..299 A1
Tenterden TN30 ....345 D8
Westgate-on-S CT7 ...81 F3
Woodchurch Windmill
(dis) ★ TN26 ......326 A3
Woodclyffe Dr BR7 ...53 A7
Woodcock Gdns CT18 .307 A4
Woodcock La
Grafty Green ME17 .231 E5
Iden Green TN17 ...342 E3
Woodcocks
Headcorn TN27 .....262 D5
Newham E16 ....1 D8
Woodcote Dr BR6 ....53 D2
Woodcote CT5 ....75 D1
Wood Cottage La
CT19 ....334 D7
Woodcourt CT14 ME10 .101 E2
Woodcroft SE9 ....29 F5
Woodcut ME1 ....162 A8
Wood Dr Bromley BR7 .29 E2
Sevenoaks TN13 ....153 F1
Wood End BR8 ....55 D5
Woodfall Dr DA1 .....14 E7
Woodfalls Ind Est
ME18 ....225 D6
Woodfield Ave
Folkestone CT19 ....334 E7

Woodfield Ave continued
Gravesend DA11 ...,.....37 B6
Tonbridge TN11 ....221 E5
Woodfield Cl CT19 ....334 E7
Woodfield Rd TN9 ....254 B8
Woodfields TN13 ......153 D4
Woodfield Way ME3 ....40 E4
Woodford Ave CT11,
CT12 ....83 D1
Woodford Ct CT7 ....81 A7
Woodford Gr ME18 .....159 A8
Woodford Ho SE18 ...12 B8
Woodford Rd ME16 ....161 B2
Woodgate CT4 ....208 E3
Woodgate Cl ME18 ....138 C8
Woodgate Ct ME13 ....171 E7
Woodgate La ME19 ....100 C2
Woodgate Rd ME19 ...126 D4
Woodgates Cl TN26 ...324 D7
Woodgate Way TN9,
TN11 ....254 E7
Woodgers Gr BR8 ......55 F7
Woodget Cl E6 ....1 E7
Woodhall Terr ME11 ....46 A5
Woodhatch Cl E6 ....1 E7
Woodhayes BR7 ....30 B2
Woodhead Dr BR6 ....86 E8
Woodhill Pk TN2 ......287 C6
Woodhill Prim Sch SE18 ..1 E2
Woodhill SE18 ....1 E2
Woodhurst Ave BR5 ....53 C3
Woodhurst ME5 ....96 D4
Woodhurst Cl ME2 .....62 B2
Woodhurst Rd SE2 ......17 A3
Woodington Cl SE9 ....12 A1
Woodknoll Dr BR7 ......52 F8
Wood La
Dartford DA2 ....34 F4
East End TN17 ....322 C3
Kingsnorth TN23 ....300 D3
Woodland Ave
Aylesham CT3 ....210 E5
Birchington CT7 ....81 B6
Hartley DA3 ....58 F5
Woodland Cl
Crabble CT17 ....277 C2
New Barn DA3 ....59 C6
Royal Tunbridge Wells
TN4 ....286 C7
West Malling ME19 ....159 A8
Woodland Cotts CT18 ..305 B7
Woodland Dr
Marlpit Hill TN8 ....217 D3
Minster (Sheppey) ME12 ..47 B7
Woodland Rd
Herne Bay CT6 ....76 B2
Lyminge CT18 ....304 E8
Royal Tunbridge Wells
TN4 ....286 C7
Woodland Rise TN15 ...154 E4
Woodlands Ave
Sidcup DA15 ....30 E7
Snodland ME6 ....127 F8
Woodlands Bexley DA6 ..14 B2
Blean CT2 ....141 F7
Chatham ME5 ....97 A2
Woodlands Cl
Bromley BR1 ....52 F7
Maidstone ME14 ....162 B7
Peasmarsh TN31 ....367 C2
Swanley BR8 ....55 F7
Teston ME18 ....193 B8
Woodlands
Coxheath ME17 ....194 B3
Cranbrook TN17 ....320 D6
Woodlands Ct ME5 .....96 F3
Woodlands Dr CT21 ...334 A4
Woodlands Farm DA16 ..12 C5
Woodlands ME13 ......140 C7
Woodlands Inf & Jun Schs
TN10 ....222 E6
Woodlands La DA12 ....38 E1
Woodlands TN12 ......256 F7
Woodlands Par ME20 ..160 D8
Woodlands TN2 ....287 F7
Woodlands Pk (Cvn Pk)
TN27 ....323 D7
Woodlands Pk DA5 .....32 D4
Woodlands Prim Sch
ME7 ....64 F4
Woodlands Rd
Adisham CT3 ....210 C8
Ashford TN24 ....268 F2
Bexley DA7 ....13 E4
Bromley BR1 ....52 F7
Ditton ME20 ....160 D8
Gillingham ME7 ....64 F4
Orpington BR6 ....87 A4
Sittingbourne ME10 ...102 B3
Tonbridge TN9 ....254 B7
Woodlands Rise BR8 ....55 F7
Woodlands TN4 ......254 A2

Woodlands Terr
Crockenhill BR8 ....55 B3
Gillingham ME7 ....64 F3
Woodlands The BR6 ....87 B4
Woodlands View TN14 ..88 A1
Woodland Terr SE7 ......1 E2
Woodland Way
Bidborough TN4 ....253 D3
Broadstairs CT10 ....51 G1
Canterbury CT2 ....142 D4
Dymchurch TN29 ....353 A5
Erith SE2 ....3 D2
Maidstone ME14 ....162 B7
Orpington BR5 ....53 C4
Swanscombe DA9 ......17 A3
Woodnesborough CT13 ..180 C6
Woodlark Rd ME4 ......41 B1
Woodlawn St CT5 ......74 D2
Woodlea Ashford TN24 ..268 C3
Leybourne ME19 ......127 F1
New Barn DA3 ....59 C6
Woodleas ME16 ......160 F2
Woodley Rd BR6 ....87 C8
Wood Lodge Gdns BR1 ..29 E1
Wood Lodge Grange
Eltham SE12 ....11 A1
Lewisham SE12 ....11 A1
Woodman Ave CT5 .....75 C3
Woodman Par E16 ......2 A5
Woodman St E16 ....2 A5
Woodmere SE9 ....29 F7
Woodmount BR8 ....55 D2
Woodnesborough La
CT13 ....180 B3
Woodnesborough Rd
CT13 ....180 E7
Woodpecker Cl 2
TN8 ....217 D3
Woodpecker Dr ME9 ...68 E4
Woodpecker Glade
ME8 ....98 D6
Woodpecker Rd
Larkfield ME20 ....127 F1
Woolwich SE28 ....3 C6
Royal Tunbridge Wells
TN4 ....253 F1
Wood Point E16 ....1 A8
Wood Rd
Biggin Hill TN16 ....118 C1
Hythe CT21 ....333 B1
Wood Retreat SE18 ....12 D7
Wood Ride BR5 ....53 E5
Woodrow Chase CT6 ...77 A1
Woodrow SE18 ....1 F2
Woodruff Cl ME8 ....66 D4
Woodrush Pl ME4 ......41 B1
Woods Green Cotts
TN5 ....336 F7
Woods Hill CT4 ....239 C5
Woodshole Cotts ME9 ..68 D1
Woodside TN23 ....299 E6
Woodside Ave
Chartham CT4 ....173 D2
Chislehurst BR7 ....30 C3
Sidcup DA15 ....140 B2
Woodside Cl
Crayford DA7 ....14 D3
Pembury TN2 ....287 E6
Temple Ewell CT16 ...277 E4
Woodside Cotts ME13 ..140 B2
Woodside Cres DA15 ...30 E5
Woodside Dr DA2 ....32 E4
Woodside Gdns ME10 ..101 D2
Woodside Gn ME8 ......98 C6
Woodside Gn ME6 ......40 B7
Woodside TN17 ....317 F2
Woodside La DA5 ....13 D1
Woodside BR6 ....87 B5
Woodside Par DA15 ....30 E5
Woodside Rd
Bromley BR1 ....52 E4
Crayford DA7 ....14 D3
Maidstone ME15 ....195 C7
Pembury TN2 ....287 E6
Rusthall TN4 ....285 D4
Sevenoaks TN13 ......154 B4
Sidcup DA15 ....30 E5
Sturry CT2 ....143 F7
Sundridge TN14 ....152 E3
Tonbridge TN9 ....254 B7
Woodside Sch DA17 .....4 B2
Woods Ley CT3 ....147 D2
Wood's Pl CT17 ....278 B2
Wood St Chatham ME7 ...64 A6
Cuxton ME2 ....62 B2
Dover CT16 ....310 D8
Grays RM17 ....18 C8
Lynsted ME9 ....135 F8
Woodstock Cl DA5 ......31 F7
Woodstock Ct SE12 ....11 A1
Woodstock Rd
Deal CT14 ....215 C4
Rochester ME2 ....63 A7
Sittingbourne ME10 ...101 B1
Woodstock Way TN24 ..268 C6

Wood St
Royal Tunbridge Wells
TN1 ....286 B4
Sheerness ME12 ....28 C2
Swanley Village BR8 ...56 D8
Woodvale Ave CT5 ....109 C8
Woodvale Ct BR1 ....52 B8
Woodview Cl BR6 ....86 C8
Woodview Cres TN11 ...221 F5
Wood View CT3 ....111 E5
Woodview Rd BR8 ......55 D7
Woodview Rise ME2 ....39 F1
Woodville Cl
Canterbury CT1 ....174 D6
Eltham SE12 ....11 A2
Woodville SE3 ....11 B6
Woodville Pl DA12 ......37 B8
Woodville Rd
Maidstone ME15 ....162 A2
Ramsgate CT12 ....83 C1
Woodville St SE18 ....1 E2
Woodward Terr DA9 ....16 E1
Wood Way BR6 ....86 A8
Woodyates Rd
Eltham SE12 ....29 B8
Lewisham SE12 ....11 A1
Woolacombe Rd SE3 ....11 C5
Woolaston Cl ME15 ....161 F1
Woolbrook Cl ME8 ......66 B2
Woolbrook Rd ME9 ....100 B4
Woolcomber St CT16 ..310 E7
Wooldeys Rd ME8 ....65 F2
Woolett Rd ME10 ......101 C5
Woolf Cl SE28 ....3 B5
Woolf Wlk RM18 ....19 C5
Woollets Cl CT6 ....76 C3
Woollett Cl DA1 ....15 A3
Woollett St ME14 ......162 A5
Woolley Cl TN4 ....253 F1
Woolley Rd
Maidstone ME15 ....195 F7
Royal Tunbridge Wells
TN4 ....253 F1
Woolmer Dr TN24 .....301 A7
Woolpack Cnr TN27 ....323 A7
Woolpack Cotts TN27 ..323 A7
Woolpack Hill TN25 ...302 D5
Woolreeds Rd TN23 ...300 A7
Woolwich Arsenal Sta
SE18 ....3 B2
Woolwich Church St
SE18 ....1 E3
Woolwich Cl ME5 ....97 A7
Woolwich Comm SE18 ..12 A8
Woolwich Dockyard Ind Est
SE18 ....1 E3
Woolwich Dockyard Sta
SE18 ....1 F2
Woolwich High St SE18 ..2 A3
Woolwich Manor Way
E6 ....2 A7
Woolwich Manorway
E16 ....2 B4
Woolwich New Rd SE18 ..2 B2
Woolwich Polytechnic Sch
for Boys SE28 ....3 A5
Woolwich Rd
Bexley DA7 ....14 A4
Erith SE2 ....3 E1
Greenwich SE10,SE7 .....1 C2
Wootton Cl CT4 ....207 A4
Wootton Dr CT4 ....207 A4
Wootton Gn ME8 ....65 D3
Wootton Ho SE9 ....12 D1
Wootton La CT15,CT4 ..275 C2
Wopsle Cl ME1 ....96 D7
Worcester Ave ME19 ..159 A2
Worcester Cl
Faversham ME13 ....138 E6
Istead Rise DA13 ....36 F1
Minster (Sheppey) ME12 ..47 C6
Rochester ME2 ....62 E8
Swanscombe DA9 ......17 B3
Worcester Dr ME10 ...101 D6
Worcester Gr CT10 .....83 F6
Worcester La CT3 ......175 E7
Worcester Rd ME15 ...195 D7
Wordsworth Cl
Chatham ME5 ....97 C7
Tilbury RM18 ....19 C5
Wordsworth Gdns
CT3 ....210 F6
Wordsworth Ho SE18 ..12 A8
Wordsworth Rd
Bexley DA16 ....12 E6
Maidstone ME14 ....162 B7
Wordsworth Way
Dartford DA1 ....16 A3
New Hythe ME20 ....128 A4
Workhouse La
Coxheath ME15 ....194 C4
Sutton Valence ME17 ..230 A8

Workhouse Rd
Chartway Street ME17 ..197 A1
Ryarsh ME19 ....126 F4
Throwley ME13 ....169 F1
World of Silk * DA1 ...14 E2
Worlds End La BR6 ......87 B3
World's End ME15 ......45 F3
Wormdale Hill ME9 ....100 B3
Wormdale Rd ME9 ....100 B4
Worsenden TN27 ......294 E1
Worsfold Ct 5 ME15 ..162 A1
Worships Hill TN13 ....153 E4
Worth Cl BR6 ....86 E6
Worthgate Pl 2 CT1 ...174 F7
Worthing Cl RM17 .....17 E8
Worthington St 11
CT16,CT17 ....310 D8
Worth La CT20 ....334 E3
Worth Prim Sch CT14 ..181 B5
Wotton Cl ME15 ....195 E5
Wotton Gn BR5 ....54 D5
Wotton Rd TN23 ....300 B6
Wotton Trad Est TN23 ..300 B6
Wouldham All Saints CE
Prim Sch ME1 ....95 C5
Wouldham Rd
Grays RM17,RM20 ....17 E8
Rochester ME1 ....62 E1
Wouldham Terr 3 BR5 ..54 B6
Wraightsfield Ave
TN29 ....366 D8
Wraik Hill CT5 ....108 C5
Wrangleden Cl ME15 ..195 E5
Wrangleden Rd ME15 ..195 E5
Wrangling La DA13 ....193 F3
Wreight Ct ME13 ......105 B1
Wrekin Rd SE18 ....12 C7
Wren Cl Larkfield ME20 ..127 F1
Orpington BR5 ....54 D6
Wren Ind Est ME15 ....195 F4
Wren Path SE28 ....2 D4
Wren Rd ME4 ....62 E7
Wrens Croft DA11 ......36 E4
Wren's Cross ME15 ....162 A3
Wrens Ct ME9 ....134 A8
Wrens Rd
Silver Street ME9 ......133 F6
Sittingbourne ME9 ....134 A7
Wrentham Ave CT6 .....76 B2
Wren Way ME5 ....97 B6
Wren Wlk RM18 ....19 B7
Wricklemarsh Rd
Greenwich SE3 ....11 B6
Greenwich SE3 ....11 D6
Wright Cl
Gillingham ME8 ....65 C2
Swanscombe DA10 .....17 D1
Wrights Cl TN30 ....345 A8
Wright's Way ME12 ....71 C8
Wrotham Ave 20 CT10 ..84 B4
Wrotham Hill Rd
TN15 ....125 A6
Wrotham Rd
Bexley DA16 ....13 C6
Borough Green TN15 ...157 A8
Broadstairs CT10 ....84 B4
Culverstone Green DA13 ..92 F4
Gravesend DA11,DA13 ...37 A4
Meopham Station DA13 ..60 A3
Wrotham Road Prim Sch
DA11 ....37 B8
Wrotham Sch TN15 ....125 A1
Wrotham Water La
ME19,TN15 ....125 E5
Wrotham Water Rd
TN15,ME19 ....125 E4
Wrottesley Rd SE18 ....12 C8
Wrott & Hill Ct DA4 ....57 B8
Wroxham Rd SE28 ....3 D6
Wulfred Way TN15 ....123 B1
Wyatt Cl TN15 ....156 F7
Wyatt Ho 1 ME2 ....63 A7
Wyatt Pl ME2 ....63 A7
Wyatt Rd DA1 ....14 F4
Wyatt St ME14 ....162 A4
Wyborne Prim Sch SE9 ..30 B7
Wybourne Rise TN2 ...314 B8
Wybournes La ME23 ....23 C3
Wych Elm Way CT21 ...353 E8
Wycherley Cres CT16 ..278 B4
Wycliffe Cl DA16 ....12 F6
Wycliffe Ho 6 DA11 ...36 F7
Wycliffe Row DA11 .....36 F7
Wycombe Cl SE3 ....11 A7
Wydeville Manor Rd
SE12 ....29 B4
Wye Cl BR6 ....53 F2
Wye Coll (Imperial Coll
London) TN25 ....237 F2
Wye Gdns CT9 ....51 F2
Wye National Nature
Reserve * TN25 ......270 D7
Wye Rd
Borough Green TN15 ...157 A8
Boughton Lees TN25 ...236 F3
Gravesend DA12 ....37 D6

Wye Rd continued
Tonbridge TN10 ....222 C5
Wye Sta TN25 ....237 D2
Wyfold Ho 10 SE2 ......3 D4
Wykeham Cl
Gravesend DA12 ....37 E2
Rushenden ME11 ....45 F3
Wykeham Cotts ME17 ..194 F2
Wykeham Ct BR7 ....30 E2
Wykeham Gr ME17 ....197 A7
Wykeham Rd ME10 ....102 B4
Wykeham St ME2 ....63 B8
Wyke Manor Rd ME14 ..162 A4
Wyles Cl ME4 ....63 E2
Wyles St ME7 ....64 C7
Wylie Ho ME3 ....40 F6
Wylie Rd ME3 ....41 D6
Wyllie Ct ME10 ....101 E7
Wyncham Ave DA15 ....30 E7
Wyncroft Cl BR1 ....52 F6
Wyndcliff Rd SE3,SE7 ..11 B8
Wyndham Ave
Leigh TN11 ....220 F1
Margate CT9 ....51 B2
Wyndham Cl
Leigh TN11 ....220 F1
Orpington BR6 ....53 C1
Wyndham Rd
Chatham ME4 ....63 E2
Dover CT17 ....310 B8
Wynd The TN27 ....201 D1
Wyndy La TN25 ....267 F4
Wynford Gr BR5 ....54 B6
Wynford Pl DA17 ....14 A8
Wynford Way SE9 ......29 F5
Wynn Ellis Ho CT5 ......74 E3
Wynn Rd CT5 ....75 A2
Wynn's Ave DA15 ....13 A2
Wytchlings The ME17 ..197 D2
Wythens Wlk SE9 ......12 B1
Wytherling Cl ME14 ...162 F5
Wythes Cl BR1 ....52 F7
Wythes Rd E16 ....1 E5
Wythfield Rd SE9 ....11 F1
Wyvern Cl Dartford DA1 ..33 C8
Orpington BR6 ....87 B7
Sittingbourne ME10 ...101 E2
Snodland ME6 ....128 A7
Wyvern Rd 9 RM17 .....18 B8
Wyvern Sch The TN23 ..267 E1
Wyvern Way TN24 ......268 E3
Wyvill Cl ME8 ....98 E5

Y

Yalding Cl ME2 ....40 B1
Yalding Gr BR5 ....54 D5
Yalding Hill ME18 ......193 A3
Yalding Organic Gdns *
ME18 ....225 F7
Yalding St Peter & St Paul
CE Prim Sch ME18 ....193 A1
Yalding Sta ME18 ......192 D1
Yantlet Dr ME2 ....62 C7
Yardhurst Gdns CT9 ....51 F3
Yardley Cl TN9 ....222 D3
Yardley Court Prep Sch
TN11 ....254 F7
Yardley Ho CT10 ....84 B7
Yardley Park Rd TN9 ...222 D3
Yard The Barham CT4 ..209 F1
Chatham ME5 ....97 B3
Yarnton Way SE2,DA18 ..3 E4
Yarrow Cl CT10 ....84 A3
Yarrow Cres E6 ....1 E8
Yarrow Ct ME14 ....162 F5
Yarrow Rd ME5 ....96 F4
Yateley St SE18 ....1 D3
Yates Cl TN31 ....374 A2
Yaugher La ME9 ....99 C3
Yeates Dr ME10 ....102 A8
Yellow Sands ME12 .....73 E5
Yelsted La
Chatham ME14 ....130 D7
Yelsted ME9 ....99 A1
Yelsted Rd ME9 ....132 A7
Ye Olde Tudor Ct BR7 ...30 B3
Yeoman Cl 2 B6
Yeoman Ct ME14 ......163 B3
Yeoman Dr ME7 ....64 F1
Yeoman Gdns
Ashford TN24 ....301 B8
Paddock Wood TN12 ..256 F6
Yeoman Ho ME1 ....63 D4
Yeoman La ME14 ......163 B4
Yeoman Pk ME15 .....163 A3
Yeoman's Mdws TN13 ..154 A1
Yeomans Sq TN23 .....299 D8
Yeoman Way ME15 ...163 A2
Yeovil Cl BR6 ....86 E8
Yester Dr BR7 ....29 E1
Yester Pk BR7 ....29 E1
Yester Rd BR7 ....29 F1
Yevele Cl ME11 ....46 A5

Yewhedges ME13 ......168 E4
Yew Rd ME3 ....41 E3
Yews The DA12 ....37 D7
Yew Tree Cl
Aylesford ME20 ....128 E1
Bexley DA16 ....13 A6
Broadstairs CT10 ....83 D4
Chatham ME5 ....97 D1
Deal CT14 ....215 A4
New Barn DA3 ....59 D7
Sevenoaks TN13 ......153 D4
Stanford TN25 ....304 B1
Yew Tree Cotts
Groombridge TN3 .....312 F8
Halstead TN14 ....120 F7
Sandling ME14 ....129 F1
Yewtree Cross CT18 ...305 C8
Yew Tree Farm CT3 ....212 A8
Yew Tree Gdns
Birchington CT7 ....81 A7
Fordwich CT2 ....144 A4
Yew Tree Green Rd
TN12 ....258 A1
Yewtree Ho 2 ME1 .....63 D4
Yewtree Ind Est ME20 ..128 D2
Yew Tree Mews
Deal CT14 ....215 A3
Westerham TN16 ......184 D8
Yew Tree Pk ME17 .....200 F1
Yew Tree Pk Cvn &
Camping Site CT4 ....207 D2
Yew Tree Pl ME7 ....98 B1
Yew Tree Rd
Royal Tunbridge Wells
TN4 ....286 B8
St Mary's Bay TN29 ...365 F3
Yoakes La TN29 ....363 F1
Yoakley Sq CT9 ....82 F8
Yoke Cl ME2 ....63 B8
Yokosuka Way ME7,
ME8 ....65 A7
Yolande Gdns SE9 ......11 E2
Yopps Gn TN15 ....156 E1
York & Albany Cl
CT14 ....215 B1
York Ave
15 Broadstairs CT10 ...84 B4
Chatham ME5 ....96 F3
Gillingham ME7 ....64 C4
Sidcup DA15 ....30 F6
York Cl Herne Bay CT6 ..76 D4
Newham E6 ....1 F7
York Hill ME5 ....64 C2
York Ho 10 CT17 ....310 D7
Yorkland Ave DA16 .....12 F3
York Mews CT19 ....334 E7
York Par TN10 ....222 C6
York Pl RM17 ....18 A8
York Rd Ashford TN24 ..268 D5
Biggin Hill TN16 ....150 B8
Canterbury CT1 ....174 E7
Dartford DA1 ....33 F8
Deal CT14 ....215 D4
Gravesend DA12 ....37 C5
Herne Bay CT6 ....76 D5
Maidstone ME15 ....162 C2
Northfleet DA11 ....36 D8
Rochester ME1 ....63 C3
Royal Tunbridge Wells
TN1 ....286 A4
Tonbridge TN10 ......222 D5
York Rise BR6 ....86 E8
York Road Jun Sch
DA1 ....33 F8
York St Broadstairs CT10 ..84 B4
Dover CT16,CT17 .....310 D7
Ramsgate CT11 ....117 E6
York Street Rdbt
CT16,CT17 ....310 D7
York Terr Bexley DA8 ...14 C6
Birchington CT7 ....81 B7
Youens Pl ME3 ....39 B3
Young Cl CT14 ....215 B6
Young Rd E16 ....1 C7
Young's Pl CT15 ....308 F5
Ypres Ct CT1 ....143 D1
Ypres Dr ME10 ....68 F1

Z

Zambra Way TN15 .....154 F7
Zangwill Rd SE18,SE3 ..11 D6
Zarena Ct 8 CT20 .....334 F3
Zealand Ho SE18 ....1 E2
Zealand Rd CT1 ....174 F6
Zelah Rd BR5 ....54 C2
Zetland Ave ME7 ....64 E2
Zillah Gdns ME8 ....98 C6
Zion Pl Gravesend DA12 ..37 B8
Margate CT9 ....50 J3
Zion St TN15 ....154 F6